Index of English Literary Manuscripts

Volume IV
1800—1900

Part 2 *Hardy – Lamb*

Barbara Rosenbaum

MANSELL

LONDON AND NEW YORK

First published 1990 by
Mansell Publishing Limited, *A Cassell Imprint*
Villiers House, 41/47 Strand, London WC2N 5JE
125 East 23rd Street, Suite 300, New York 10010, U.S.A.

British Library Cataloguing in Publication Data
Index of English literary manuscripts.
Vol 4 1800–1900
Pt. 2, Hardy–Lamb
1. English literature. Manuscripts.–Catalogues, indexes
I. Rosenbaum, Barbara
016.8208

ISBN 0-7201-1660-0

Library of Congress Cataloging-in-Publication Data
(Revised for vol. 4, pt. 2)

Index of English literary manuscripts.

Vol. 2, pt. 1, have imprint: London ; New York : Mansell ; v. have imprint : London ; New York : Mansell ; Bronx, N.Y. : Distributed in the U.S. and Canada by Wilson.

Includes bibliographical references.

Contents: v. 1. 1450–1625 / compiled by Peter Beal (2 v.) — v. 2. 1625–1700, pt. 1. Behn–King / compiled by Peter Beal — [etc.] — v. 4. 1800–1900 / compiled by Barbara Rosenbaum and Pamela White 1800–1900, Hardy–Lamb / Barbara Rosenbaum.

1. English literature — Manuscripts — Indexes. I. Beal, Peter. II. Rosenbaum, Barbara
Z6611.L7I5PR83   016.8208'008   79-88658
ISBN 0-7201-1779-8 (Mansell : set)
ISBN 0-7201-1660-0 (volume)

Typeset from author's disk by Saxon Printing Ltd., Derby, England.
Printed and bound in Great Britain by Bookcraft (Bath) Ltd.

Contents

'There is something to me repugnant, at any time, in written hand. The text never seems determinate. Print settles it. I had thought of the Lycidas as of a full grown beauty — as springing up with all its parts absolute — till, in an evil hour, I was shown the original written copy of it...in the Library of Trinity, kept like treasures to be proud of. I wish they had thrown them into the Cam, or sent them, after the latter cantos of Spenser, into the Irish Channel. How it staggered me to see the fine things in their ore! interlined, corrected! as if their words were mortal, alterable, displaceable at pleasure! as if they might have been otherwise, and just as good! as if inspirations were made up of parts, and those fluctuating, successive, indifferent! I will never go into the work-shop of any great artist again.'

— From the first version of Charles Lamb's essay 'Oxford in the Vacation', a passage deleted in revision.

Preface and Acknowledgements

Part 2 of Volume IV (1800–1900) of the *Index of English Literary Manuscripts* attempts to list the extant literary manuscripts of six English authors who flourished during the nineteenth century. The manuscripts described, however, were produced over a period of nearly 150 years — including manuscripts of Charles Lamb's earliest verses written in the 1790s and proofs corrected by Rudyard Kipling in 1936 for the last authorized edition of his works.

The manuscript sources listed include not only those which have been located in public and private collections, but also those unlocated items well described in published scholarship and other sources (sometimes in facsimile reproductions) which are likely to survive. Nonetheless, knowing all too well the impossibility of producing a definitive listing which will stand in every detail the test of time, the following *Index* is offered as a kind of working paper. Scholars, librarians and collectors are eagerly invited to forward additions, corrections and other improvements which can be included in a later volume.

Originally, and perhaps unwisely, the *Index* set out in 1974 to include all the authors listed in the *Concise Cambridge Bibliography of English Literature*. As in Volume IV, Part 1, however, the unexpectedly large numbers of surviving papers of nineteenth century writers necessitated a severe restriction on the number of authors that could practicably be included. The revised list for Part 2 with which I began in 1982 contained the names of nine of the sixteen authors listed in the *Concise Cambridge Bibliography*; excluded, for various reasons, were James Hogg, Thomas Hood, Henry James, Henry Arthur Jones, John Keble, Alexander William Kinglake and Henry Kingsley. The other three authors who do not appear in these pages — A. E. Housman, Leigh Hunt and Charles Kingsley — were dropped following the theft of the working drafts for much of Part 2 in 1986; in the case of those authors, the loss was fatal.

In the General Introduction to Volume I of the *Index*, John Horden explained the history of the project and the overall format and design. This description, as well as the few variations outlined in the Preface to Volume IV Part 1 — allowing for the introduction of a new design of the entries — still applies. Entries in Part 2 differ from those in Part 1 in that information about *texts* has been separated from information about *manuscripts of texts*. The first block of information (the headnote) about a particular text now contains the title in boldface type (and first line if verse) followed by publication details and any other bibliographical or general notes about the text. The headnote is followed by the entries, a numbered list of manuscript sources of that text, including descriptions of the manuscripts, notes about them and their locations. By this means, the possibility of confusion between *text* and *manuscript* will hopefully be decreased.

It is worth repeating that private owners are named only if they have already been named in previous scholarship or if express permission has been obtained. Readers should address queries concerning any of the entries marked 'Privately owned' to the *Index*, in care of the publishers.

Acknowledging all those who have helped in the compilation of this work is impossible. Correspondence with librarians, cataloguers, archivists, researchers and other staff members in hundreds of repositories has gone on for nearly fifteen years. I am still surprised at the grace and goodwill with which such people answer seemingly endless questions and requests. To say nothing of the hospitality which has been extended to me personally in public and private libraries on both sides of the Atlantic. Without the help of all these individuals, too numerous to be named, compilation of the *Index* would be impossible.

Among them are some who deserve special thanks: Cathy Henderson and Heather Moore at the Humanities Research Center of the University of Texas at Austin; David Stam and Mark Weimer at the Syracuse University Library; Karen Smith and Julia M. Landry at the Dalhousie University Library; Mark Farrell (Curator of the Robert H. Taylor Collection) and Jean Preston at the Princeton University Library; Laetitia Yeandle at the Folger Shakespeare Library; Hilton Kelliher in the Department of Manuscripts at the British Library; Dr Judith Priestman at the Bodleian Library; Christina Gee at Keats House, London; E. D. Yeo at the National Library of Scotland; Christopher Sheppard at the Brotherton Library, Leeds University; Lola Szladitz at the Berg Collection of the New York Public Library; Mihai Handrea at the Pforzheimer Collection of the New York Public Library; Sara Hodson and Tom Lange at the Huntington Library; Elizabeth Inglis at the Sussex University Library; Mark N. Brown and Barbara Filipac at the Brown University Library; R. N. R. Peers at the Dorset County Museum; A. de R. Davis, Bursar of Haileybury College; William H. Loos at the Buffalo and Erie County Library; Robert H. Bertholf at the State University of New York at Buffalo; J. J. Wisdom at the Guildhall Library, London; J. Fraser Cocks III at the Colby College Library; Bernard Crystal and Kenneth Lohf at the Columbia University Library; Donald D. Eddy at the Cornell University Library; Herbert Cahoon at the Pierpont Morgan Library; Eileen Cahill at the Rosenbach Museum and Library; Elizabeth Rainey at the Durham University Library; Richard Virr at the McGill University Library; Robert N. Smart at the University of St Andrews Library; Mrs E. M. Coleman at the Pepys Library, Magdalene College, Cambridge; Glenys Matthieson at the John Rylands Library; Michael Cropper at the University of Southern California Library; Philip Endean, S.J., at Campion Hall, Oxford; Fergus O'Donoghue, S.J., at the Irish Jesuit Archive in Dublin; Sergeant-Major O'Neill at the Irish Guards; and, especially, the staff in the North Library of the British Library where most of my research has been conducted.

Among the scholars to whom I am especially indebted are the following: for help with the Thomas Hardy section, Richard L. Purdy, James Gibson, Samuel Hynes, Tim Armstrong and, above all, for his meticulous and unsentimental commentary on the entire final draft, Michael Millgate; Eleanor Gates and Heather Jackson for invaluable contributions to the William Hazlitt section and to Stanley Jones for reading the final draft under difficult circumstances and generously sharing his unrivalled knowledge about Hazlitt; Norman Mackenzie for early advice about Gerard Manley Hopkins; Jack Stillinger for carefully reading the typescript of the Keats Introduction and, indeed, for his Keats scholarship which has made my task largely one of transcription; for useful guidance into the *terra inexplorata* of Kipling manuscripts, Lisa Lewis, Andrew Rutherford, Robert Hampson, Ronald King and, especially, Thomas Pinney who cheerfully responded to lists of queries and prevented numerous errors; and to Lorna Arnold and Edwin L. Marrs, Jr, for invaluable help with the Charles Lamb section.

I am also grateful to Lord Bridges for allowing access to the Bridges Collection of Hopkins papers at the Bodleian Library; to Lord Baldwin for permission to consult the Baldwin Papers at the University of Sussex; to the Trustees of Miss E. A. Dugdale and the English Province of the Society of Jesus for permission to reproduce facsimiles of manuscripts; to the British Academy for a generous travel grant; and to Warwick Gould and John Creaser of Royal Holloway and Bedford New College of the University of London.

Special thanks must go to Pamela White, co-compiler of Volume IV Part 1, and Margaret M. Smith, compiler of Volume III, for their first versions of the Thomas Hardy and William Hazlitt sections and countless other contributions; to Peter Beal, compiler of Volumes I and II; to John Goodridge for research on my behalf at the Durham University Library; to John Duncan and Veronica Higgs of Mansell Publishing for their long and unwavering support of the project; and to Jasmine and Pamela Greenfield for their meticulous keyboarding and infinite patience.

And, finally, to my friends, for all their everyday kindnesses: Keven Bridge, Bella Center, Maud Ellmann, Anne Janowitz, Anne Karpf, Laura Marcus, Nancy Platt, Joanna Savory, Sabina Sharkey, Catherine Sharrock, Sue Wiseman and Stanley Mitchell who even helped me to examine every volume in Thomas Hardy's library on a snowy morning in Dorchester.

Barbara Rosenbaum
London
November 1989

List of Repositories

The institutional repositories cited in Volume IV, Part 2, are listed with their full postal addresses in strict alphabetical order according to the short titles of the repositories used in the entries and Introductions. Thus, 'Library of Congress' may be found under 'L' and 'University of Nottingham' under 'U'. Addresses are in England unless otherwise stated.

American Antiquarian Society
185 Salisbury Street, Worcester, MA, U.S.A. 01609

Archives of John Murray
John Murray (Publishers) Ltd., 50 Albemarle Street, London W1X 4BD

Archives of the Irish Province of the Society of Jesus, Dublin
Irish Province of the Society of Jesus, 35 Lower Leeson Street, Dublin 2, Republic of Ireland

Arizona State University, Tempe
Department of Rare Books and Special Collections, University Library, Arizona State University, Tempe, AZ, U.S.A. 85281

Balliol College, Oxford
The Library, Balliol College, Oxford OX1 3BJ

Bateman's, Burwash, Sussex
Bateman's (The National Trust), Burwash, Sussex TN19 7DS

Bath Reference Library
Bath Reference Library, 18 Queen Square, Bath BA1 2HP

Berg
The Albert A. and Henry W. Berg Collection, The New York Public Library, Fifth Avenue and 42nd Street, New York, NY, U.S.A. 10018

Berkshire Record Office, Reading
Berkshire Record Office, Shire Hall, Reading RG1 3EE

Bibliotheca Bodmeriana, Cologny-Geneva
Bibliotheca Bodmeriana, Fondation Martin Bodmer, CH-1223 Cologny-Genève, Switzerland

Bibliothèque Nationale, Paris
Bibliothèque Nationale, 58 rue de Richelieu, 75084 Paris 2, France

Birmingham City Museum and Art Gallery
Birmingham City Museum and Art Gallery, Birmingham B3 3DH

Bodleian
Bodleian Library, Oxford OX1 3BG

Boston Public Library
Department of Rare Books and Manuscripts, Boston Public Library, Copley Square, Boston, MA, U.S.A. 02117

Boston University
Department of Special Collections, Mugar Memorial Library, Boston University, 771 Commonwealth Avenue, Boston, MA, U.S.A. 02215

Bowdoin College
The Library, Bowdoin College, Brunswick, ME, U.S.A. 04011

Brandeis University
Special Collections, Goldfarb Library, Brandeis University, 415 South Street, Waltham, MA, U.S.A. 02154

Bristol Reference Library
Bristol Reference Library, College Green, Bristol BS1 5TL

British Library
Department of Manuscripts, The British Library, Great Russell Street, London WC1B 3DG

British Library, Department of Printed Books
Department of Printed Books, The British Library, Great Russell Street, London WC1B 3DG

Britten-Pears Library, Aldeburgh
Britten-Pears Library, The Red House, Aldeburgh, Suffolk IP15 5PZ
Brown University
Department of Special Collections, The John Hay Library, Brown University, Providence, RI, U.S.A. 02912
Bryn Mawr College
Bryn Mawr College, Bryn Mawr, PA, U.S.A. 19010
Buffalo and Erie County Public Library
Rare Book Room, Buffalo and Erie County Public Library, Lafayette Square, Buffalo, NY, U.S.A. 14203
Cambridge University Library
Cambridge University Library, West Road, Cambridge CB3 9DR
Campbell College, Belfast
The Library, Campbell College, Belfast, Northern Ireland
Campion Hall, Oxford
Campion Hall, Oxford OX1 1QS
Charles Lamb Society, London
Charles Lamb Society Library, Guildhall Library, Aldermanbury, London EC2P 2EJ
Cheltenham College
Cheltenham Ladies' College, Cheltenham, Gloucestershire GL50 3EP
Claremont Colleges
Special Collections, The Honnold Library for the Claremont Colleges, Claremont, CA, U.S.A. 91711
Clifton College
The Library, Clifton College, Bristol BS8 3JH
Colby College
Miller Library, Colby College, Waterville, ME, U.S.A. 04901
College of the Holy Cross, Worcester
Dinand Library, College of the Holy Cross, College Street, Worcester, MA, U.S.A. 01610–2394
Columbia University
Department of Rare Books and Manuscripts, Butler Library, Columbia University, New York, NY, U.S.A. 10027
Connecticut Historical Society
The Connecticut Historical Society, 1 Elizabeth Street, Hartford, CT, U.S.A. 06105
Cornell University
Department of Rare Books, Cornell University Library, Ithaca, NY, U.S.A. 14853
Dalhousie University
Dalhousie University Library, Halifax, Nova Scotia, Canada B3H 4H8
Dedham (Massachusetts) Historical Society
Dedham Historical Society, 612 High Street, Dedham, MA, U.S.A. 02026
Dr Williams's Library
Dr Williams's Library, 14 Gordon Square, London WC1H 0AG
Dorchester Reference Library
Dorset County Library, Colliton Park, Dorchester DT1 1XJ
Dorset County Museum
Dorset Natural History and Archaeological Society, Dorset County Museum, Dorchester DT1 1XA
Dorset Record Office, Dorchester
Dorset County Record Office, County Hall, Dorchester
Dudley Public Library
Dudley Public Library, 3 St James's Road, Dudley, West Midlands DY1 1HU
Duke University
William R. Perkins Library, Duke University, Durham, NC, U.S.A. 27706
Dumbarton Oaks Research Library, Washington D.C.
Dumbarton Oaks Research Library and Collection (Harvard University), 1703 32nd Street, Washington D.C., U.S.A. 20007
Dunedin Public Library, New Zealand
Dunedin Public Library, P.O. Box 906, Moray Place West, Dunedin, New Zealand
Durham County Library, Darlington Branch
Durham County Library, Darlington Branch, Crown Street, Darlington
English Folk Dance and Song Society, London
English Folk Dance and Song Society, Cecil Sharp House, 2 Regents Park Road, London NW1
Eton College
The School Library, Eton College, Windsor, Berkshire SL4 6DB
Fitzwilliam Museum
The Fitzwilliam Museum, Cambridge CB2 1RB
Florida State University
Special Collections Department, Robert Manning Strozier Library, The Florida State University, Tallahassee, FL, U.S.A. 32306
Folger
The Folger Shakespeare Library, 201 East Capitol Street, Washington, D.C., U.S.A. 20003
Free Library of Philadelphia
Rare Books Department, The Free Library of Philadelphia, Logan Square, Philadelphia, PA, U.S.A. 19103
Georgetown University
The University Library, Georgetown University,

37th and O Streets N.W., Washington, D.C., U.S.A. 20007
Gonzaga University
Crosby Library, Gonzaga University, East 502 Boone Avenue, Spokane, WA, U.S.A. 99202
Grolier Club, New York
The Grolier Club, 47 East 60th Street, New York, NY, U.S.A. 10022
Haileybury
Haileybury, Hertford SG13 7NU
Harvard
The Houghton Library, Harvard University, Cambridge, MA, U.S.A. 02138
Harvard, Widener Collection
Harry Elkins Widener Collection, Widener Library, Harvard University, Cambridge, MA, U.S.A. 02138
Hertfordshire Record Office
Hertfordshire Record Office, County Hall, Hertford SG13 8DE
Heythrop College, London
Heythrop College, 11–13 Cavendish Square, London W1M 0AN
Historical Society of Pennsylvania
The Historical Society of Pennsylvania, 1300 Locust Street, Philadelphia, PA, U.S.A. 19107
House of Lords Record Office
House of Lords Record Office, Westminster, London SW1A 0PW
Huntington
The Huntington Library, 1151 Oxford Road, San Marino, CA, U.S.A. 91108
Imperial War Museum
Imperial War Museum, Department of Documents, Lambeth Road, London SE1 6HZ
India Office Library
India Office Library and Records (The British Library), 197 Blackfriars Road, London SE1 8NG
Indiana University
Department of Rare Books, S. T. Lilly Library, Indiana University, Tenth Street and Jordan Avenue, Bloomington, IN, U.S.A. 47401
Institute of Russian Literature, Leningrad
Institute of Russian Literature, Pushkin House, Na. Makarova 4, 199164 Leningrad, U.S.S.R.
Iowa State Historical Library
State Historical Society of Iowa, The Historical Division of the Department of Cultural Affairs, Capitol Complex, Des Moines, IA, U.S.A. 50319
Irish Guards
Regimental Headquarters of the Irish Guards, Birdcage Walk, London SW1
Isabella Stewart Gardner Museum, Boston
Isabella Stewart Gardner Museum, 2 Palace Road, Boston, MA, U.S.A. 02115
John Murray, London
See 'Archives of John Murray'
John Rylands Library
The John Rylands University Library of Manchester, Oxford Road, Manchester M13 9PP
Keats House, London
Keats House, Keats Grove, Hampstead, London NW3 2RR
Keats-Shelley Memorial House, Rome
Keats-Shelley Memorial House, Piazza di Spagna 26, 00187 Roma, Italy
Kent Archives Office
Kent Archives Office, County Hall, Maidstone, Kent ME14 1XQ
King's College, Cambridge
The Library, King's College, Cambridge CB2 1ST
King's School, Canterbury
The King's School, Canterbury, Kent CT1 2ES
Kipling Society
Kipling Society Library, The Royal Commonwealth Society, 18 Northumberland Street, London WC2N 5BJ
Lancashire Record Office
Lancashire Record Office, Bow Lane, Preston PR1 8ND
Library of Congress, Manuscript Division
Manuscript Division, The Library of Congress, Washington, D.C., U.S.A. 20540
Library of Congress, Rare Book Division
Rare Book Division, The Library of Congress, Washington, D.C., U.S.A. 20540
Liverpool City Libraries
Liverpool City Libraries, Brown, Picton and Hornby Libraries, William Brown Street, Liverpool L3 8EW
Local History Library, Battersea District Library, London
Local History Library, Battersea District Library, Lavender Hill, London SW11 1JB
London Library
The London Library, 14 St James's Square, London SW1Y 4LG
Longleat
Longleat House, Warminster, Wiltshire BA12 7NN
Loyola-Notre Dame Library
Loyola-Notre Dame Library (serving Loyola University and the College of Notre Dame of Maryland), 200 Winston Avenue, Baltimore, MD, U.S.A. 21212
Magdalene College, Cambridge
The Pepys Library, Magdalene College, Cambridge CB3 0AG

Maidstone Museum
Maidstone Museum and Art Gallery, St Faith's Street, Maidstone, Kent
Manchester Central Library
Language and Literature Library, Manchester Central Library, St Peter's Square, Manchester M2 5PD
Marlboro College, Vermont
Howard and Amy Rice Library, Marlboro College, Marlboro, VT, U.S.A. 05344
Massachusetts Historical Society
Massachusetts Historical Society, 1154 Boylston Street, Boston, MA, U.S.A. 02215
McGill University
Department of Rare Books and Special Collections, McGill University Libraries, 3459 McTavish Street, Montreal H3A 1Y1, Canada
Miami University, Ohio
Special Collections, King Library, Miami University, Oxford, OH, U.S.A. 45056
Mount Saint Vincent University
The Library, Mount Saint Vincent University, 166 Bedford Highway, Halifax, Nova Scotia, Canada B3M 2J6
National Army Museum
National Army Museum, Royal Hospital Road, London SW3 4HT
National Library of Australia
National Library of Australia, Canberra, ACT 2600, Australia
National Library of Canada
National Library of Canada, 395 Wellington, Ottawa, Ontario, Canada K1A 0NA
National Library of Scotland
Department of Manuscripts, National Library of Scotland, George IV Bridge, Edinburgh EH1 1EW, Scotland
National Maritime Museum, Greenwich
Printed Books and Manuscripts Department, National Maritime Museum, Greenwich, London SE10 9NF
National Portrait Gallery
National Portrait Gallery, 2 St Martin's Place, London WC2
National Trust
See 'Bateman's', 'Stourhead' and 'Wimpole Hall'
New York Public Library
See 'Berg' and 'NYPL'
New York University
Department of Special Collections, Elmer Holmes Bobst Library, New York University, 70 Washington Square South, New York, NY, U.S.A. 10012
Norfolk Record Office
Norfolk Record Office, Central Library, Norwich NR2 1NJ
Northamptonshire Record Office
Northamptonshire Record Office, Delapre Abbey, Northampton NN4 9AW
NYPL
See also 'Berg'
NYPL, Arents Collection
The Arents Collection, New York Public Library, Fifth Avenue and 42nd Street, New York, NY, U.S.A. 10018
NYPL, Manuscripts Division
Rare Books and Manuscripts Division, New York Public Library, Room 324, Fifth Avenue and 42nd Street, New York, NY, U.S.A. 10018
NYPL, Pforzheimer Collection
The Carl H. Pforzheimer Shelley and His Circle Collection, New York Public Library, Room 319, Fifth Avenue and 42nd Street, New York, NY, U.S.A. 10018
Pembroke College, Cambridge
The Library, Pembroke College, Cambridge CB2 1RF
Pierpont Morgan
The Pierpont Morgan Library, 29 East 36th Street, New York, NY, U.S.A. 10016
Plymouth Free Public Library
Devon Library Services, Central Library, Drake Circus, Plymouth PL4 8AL
Princeton
Princeton University Library, Princeton, NJ, U.S.A. 08540
Princeton, Robert H. Taylor Collection
The Robert H. Taylor Collection, Princeton University Library, Princeton, NJ, U.S.A. 08540
Privately owned
For entries so marked, write to the *Index of English Literary Manuscripts*, c/o Mansell Publishing Limited
Queen's College, Oxford
The Library, The Queen's College, Oxford OX1 4AW
Rhodes House, Oxford
The Library, Rhodes House, South Parks Road, Oxford OX1 3RG
Rosenbach Foundation
The Philip H. and A. S. W. Rosenbach Foundation Museum and Library, 2010 DeLancey Place, Philadelphia, PA, U.S.A. 19103
Royal Academy
Royal Academy of Arts, Burlington House, Piccadilly, London W1

Royal Australasian College of Surgeons, Melbourne
The Royal Australasian College of Surgeons, Spring Street, Melbourne, Victoria 3000, Australia
Royal Library, Windsor
The Royal Library, Windsor Castle, Windsor, Berkshire
Royal Society of Literature
Royal Society of Literature, 1 Hyde Park Gardens, London W2
Rutgers University
Special Collections and Archives, Rutgers University Libraries, New Brunswick, NJ, U.S.A. 08903
Rylands Library
See 'John Rylands Library'
Scottish National Portrait Gallery
Scottish National Portrait Gallery, 1 Queen Street, Edinburgh EH2 1JD, Scotland
Scottish Record Office
Scottish Record Office, HM General Register House, P.O. Box 36, Edinburgh EH1 3YY, Scotland
Signet Library, Edinburgh
Signet Library, Parliament Square, Edinburgh EH1 1RF, Scotland
Somerset County Library, Street
Somerset County Library, 1 Leigh Road, Street BA16 0HA
Somerset House, London
Somerset House, Strand, London WC2
South African Library, Cape Town
South African Library, Queen Victoria Street, Cape Town 8001, South Africa
Stanford University
Division of Special Collections, The Stanford University Libraries, Stanford, CA, U.S.A. 94305
State Archives of Hawaii
Hawaii State Department of Accounting and General Services, Public Archives, Iolani Palace Grounds, Honolulu, HI, U.S.A. 96817
State Library of Victoria, Melbourne
The State Library of Victoria, Swanston Street, Melbourne, Australia
Stonyhurst College, Lancashire
Stonyhurst College, Stonyhurst, near Blackburn, Lancashire
Stourhead
Stourhead (The National Trust), Stourton, Warminster, Wiltshire BA12 6QD
Strange Africana Library, Johannesburg
Strange Africana Library, Johannesburg Public Library, Market Square, Johannesburg 2001, South Africa
SUNY at Buffalo
The Poetry/Rare Books Collection, University Libraries, 420 Capen Hall, Buffalo, NY, U.S.A. 14260
Sussex
University of Sussex Library, Brighton BN1 9QL
Syracuse University
George Arents Research Library for Special Collections, Ernest S. Bird Library, Room 600, Syracuse University, Syracuse, NY, U.S.A. 13210
Texas
Harry Ransom Humanities Research Center, The University of Texas at Austin, P.O. Drawer 7219, Austin, TX, U.S.A. 78713–7219
Texas Christian University
Special Collections Department, Mary Couts Burnett Library, Texas Christian University, Fort Worth, TX, U.S.A. 76129
Thomas Hardy Society
Thomas Hardy Society, Ltd., 18 Tristram Drive, Creech Street Michael, Taunton TA3 5QU
Tulane University
Special Collections, Tulane University Library, New Orleans, LA, U.S.A. 70118
UCLA
Department of Special Collections, A1713 University Research Library, University of California, Los Angeles, CA, U.S.A. 90024
University College Dublin
The Main Library, University College Dublin, Belfield, Dublin 4, Republic of Ireland
University of Aberdeen
Manuscripts and Archives Section, University of Aberdeen Library, King's College, Aberdeen AB9 2UB, Scotland
University of Birmingham
The Main Library, The University of Birmingham, P.O. Box 363, Birmingham B15 2TT
University of Bristol
University Library, University of Bristol, Tyndall Avenue, Bristol BS8 1TJ
University of California at Berkeley
Manuscripts Division, The Bancroft Library, University of California, Berkeley, CA, U.S.A. 94720
University of California at Riverside
Department of Special Collections, University Library, University of California, 4045 Canyon Crest Drive, P.O. Box 5900, Riverside, CA, U.S.A. 92507
University of Cape Town
The Library, University of Cape Town, Private Bag, Rondebosch, Cape 7700, South Africa
University of Delaware
Special Collections, The Library, University of Delaware, Newark, DE, U.S.A. 19716

University of Durham
University Library, University of Durham, Palace Green, Durham DH1 3RN
University of Edinburgh
Department of Manuscripts, Edinburgh University Library, George Square, Edinburgh EH8 9LJ, Scotland
University of Illinois
Rare Book Room, University of Illinois, Urbana, IL, U.S.A. 61801
University of Indiana
See 'Indiana University'
University of Iowa
Special Collections, The University Libraries, University of Iowa, Iowa City, IA, U.S.A. 52242
University of Kentucky
Special Collections and Achives, Margaret I. King Library, University of Kentucky, Lexington, KY, U.S.A. 40506
University of Leeds
The Brotherton Library, University of Leeds, Leeds LS2 9JT
University of London
The Paleography Room, University of London Library, Senate House, Malet Street, London WC1E 7HU
University of New Brunswick
Archives and Special Collections, Harriet Irving Library, University of New Brunswick, Box 7500, Fredericton, New Brunswick, Canada E3B 5H5
University of North Carolina
Wilson Library, University of North Carolina, Chapel Hill, NC, U.S.A. 27514
University of Nottingham
Manuscripts Department, University of Nottingham Library, University Park, Nottingham NG7 2RD
University of Reading
The Library, University of Reading, Whiteknights, Reading RG6 2AE
University of St Andrews
University Library, University of St Andrews, St Andrews KY16 9TR, Scotland
University of Southern California
University Library, University of Southern California, University Park, Los Angeles, CA, U.S.A. 90007
University of Sussex
See 'Sussex'
University of Toronto
Thomas Fisher Rare Book Library, University of Toronto Library, Toronto, Ontario M5S 1A5, Canada
University of Virginia
Alderman Library, The University of Virgina, Charlottesville, VA, U.S.A. 22901
Victoria and Albert Museum
The Library, The Victoria and Albert Museum, London SW7 2RL
Victoria College Library
Victoria College Library, University of Toronto, Toronto 5, Ontario, Canada
Washington University, St Louis
Department of Rare Books and Special Collections, Washington University Libraries, Skinner and Lindell Boulevards, St Louis, MO, U.S.A. 63130
Watt Monument Library, Greenock
Watt Monument Library, Union Street, Greenock PA16 8JH, Scotland
William Andrews Clark Library, Los Angeles
William Andrews Clark Memorial Library, 2520 Cimarron Street at West Adam, Los Angeles, CA, U.S.A. 90018
Dr Williams's Library
See under 'D'
Wiltshire Record Office
Wiltshire County Record Office, County Hall, Trowbridge BA14 8JG
Wimpole Hall
Wimpole Hall (The National Trust), Wimpole, Royston, Cambridgeshire
Wisbech and Fenland Museum
Wisbech and Fenland Museum, Museum Square, Wisbech, Cambridgeshire PE13 1ES
Wordsworth Library, Grasmere
Wordsworth Museum Trust, Dove Cottage and Wordsworth Museum, Town End, Grasmere, Near Ambleside, Cumbria
Yale
The Beinecke Rare Book and Manuscript Library, Yale University, 1603A Yale Station, New Haven, CT, U.S.A. 06520
Yale, Osborn Collection
The James Marshall and Marie-Louise Osborn Collection, The Beinecke Rare Book and Manuscript Library, Yale University, 1603A Yale Station, New Haven, CT, U.S.A. 06520

List of Auction Houses and Booksellers

The list is in alphabetical order by the first letter of the abbreviated form; addresses are in England unless otherwise stated.

Alan G. Thomas
Alan G. Thomas, Bookseller, c/o Westminster Bank, 300 King's Road, London SW3 5UJ

American Art Association
The American Art Association–Anderson Galleries, Inc., New York, NY, U.S.A.
[Last sale in 1939; the firm's nominal successor was Parke Bernet]

Anderson Auction Company
Original name of the auction house 'Anderson Galleries'

Anderson Galleries
See 'American Art Association': Anderson Galleries merged with the American Art Association in 1929

Bangs
Bangs & Co., 93 Fifth Avenue, New York, NY, U.S.A.
[No longer in business]

Bertram Dobell
See 'Percy Dobell'

Bertram Rota
See 'Rota'

Barnet J. Beyer
Barnet J. Beyer, 45 East 50th Street, New York, NY, U.S.A.
[No longer in business]

Blackwell's
Blackwell's, Fyfield Manor, Fyfield, Abingdon OX13 5LR

Bristow
Henry Bristow, 12 Springfield Road, Verwood, Dorset BH21 6HY

Charles Hamilton Galleries
Charles Hamilton Galleries, Inc., 25 East 77th Street, New York, NY, U.S.A. 10021

Christie's
Christie, Manson & Woods Ltd., 8 King Street, St James's, London SW1Y 6QT

Christie's (New York)
Christie, Manson & Woods, 502 Park Avenue, New York, NY, U.S.A. 10021

City Book Auction (New York)
City Book Auction, 313–15 Broadway, New York, NY, U.S.A.
[Last sale, 1957]

Commin
Horace G. Commin, Bookseller, 100 Old Christchurch Road, Bournemouth BH1 1LT

David Holmes
David J. Holmes Autographs, 230 South Broad Street, Philadelphia, PA, U.S.A. 19102

David Magee
David Magee, 2475 Filbert Street, San Francisco, CA, U.S.A. 94123

Edwards
Francis Edwards Ltd., 83 Marylebone High Street, London W1M 4AL

El Dieff
House of El Dieff, Inc., 139 East 63rd Street, New York, NY, U.S.A. 10021

Elkin Mathews
Elkin Mathews Ltd., Scriveners, Blakeney, Norfolk NR25 7NL

Export Book Company
Export Book Company, 63 Havelock Terrace, Garstang Road, Preston, Lancashire
First Edition Bookshop
First Edition Bookshop, Ltd., 56 Maddox Street, London W1
Fleming
John F. Fleming, Inc., 322 East 57th Street, New York, NY, U.S.A. 10022
Fletcher
Ifan Kyrle Fletcher, Bookseller, 22 Buckingham Gate, London SW1
Francis Edwards
See 'Edwards'
Goddard and Smith
Goddard and Smith, Surveyors, Valuers, Auctioneers, Estate Agents, 22 King Street, London SW1
Goodspeed's
Goodspeed's Book Shop, Inc., 18 Beacon Street, Boston, MA, U.S.A. 02108
Hamill & Baker
Hamill & Baker, 400 N. Michigan Avenue, Chicago, IL, U.S.A. 60611
Hanzel Galleries
Hanzel Galleries, 1120 S. Michigan Avenue, Chicago, IL, U.S.A. 60605
Heffer
W. Heffer & Sons Ltd., 20 Trinity Street, Cambridge CB2 3NG
Hodgson
See 'Sotheby's (Hodgson's Rooms)'
Hofmann and Freeman
Hofmann and Freeman (Antiquarian Booksellers), 8 High Street, Otford, Sevenoaks, Kent TN14 5PQ
Hollings
Frank Hollings, 7 Great Turnstile, London WC1
Kenneth W. Rendell
Kenneth W. Rendell, 154 Wells Avenue, Newton, MA, U.S.A. 02159
Maggs
Maggs Brothers Ltd., 50 Berkeley Square, London W1X 6EL
Parke Bernet
Sotheby Parke Bernet, Inc., 980 Madison Avenue, New York, NY, U.S.A. 10021
Paul C. Richards
Paul C. Richards, P.O. Box 62, 49 Meadow Lane, Bridgewater, MA, U.S.A. 02324
[Stock sometimes deposited at Boston University]
Pearson
John Pearson & Co., 5 Pall Mall Place, London
[No longer in business]
Percy Dobell
Percy J. Dobell & Son, 24 Mount Ephraim Road, Tunbridge Wells, Kent
[Successor to Bertram Dobell, London; not in business since 1972; some of the firm's papers are in the Bodleian Library]
Phillips
Phillips, 7 Blenheim Street, New Bond Street, London W1Y 0AS
Phillips, Son & Neale
Phillips, Son & Neale, 406 East 79th Street, New York, NY, U.S.A. 10021
Pickering & Chatto
Pickering & Chatto Ltd. (Antiquarian Booksellers), 16 Pall Mall, London SW1Y 5NB
Puttick & Simpson
Puttick & Simpson, 47 Leicester Square, London
[Not in business since 1949]
Quaritch
Bernard Quaritch Ltd., 5–8 Lower John Street, Golden Square, London W1R 4AU
Riddetts Auction Galleries
Riddetts Auction Galleries, Richmond Hill, Bournemouth
Rosenbach
The Rosenbach Company, Locust Street, Philadelphia, PA, U.S.A.
[Not in business since 1953; some MSS now at the Rosenbach Foundation; the firm's successor was Fleming.]
Rota
Bertram Rota Ltd., 30–31 Long Acre, London WC2E 9LT
Samuel T. Freeman
Samuel T. Freeman & Co., Auctioners, 1808–1810 Chestnut Street, Philadelphia, PA, U.S.A. 19103
Sawyer
Charles J. Sawyer, No.1 Grafton Street, New Bond Street, London W1X 3LB
Scheuer
Alwin J. Scheuer, 26 East 56th Street, New York, NY, U.S.A.
Sotheby's
Sotheby Parke Bernet & Co., 34–35 New Bond Street, London W1A 2AA
Sotheby's (Hodgson's Rooms)
Sotheby Parke Bernet & Co., Hodgson's Rooms, 115 Chancery Lane, London WC2A 1LR
[No longer in business; incorporated into Sotheby's]
Sotheby's (New York)
Sotheby's, 1334 York Avenue (at 72nd Street), New York, NY, U.S.A. 10021

Sotheran
Henry Sotheran Ltd., 2–5 Sackville Street, Piccadilly, London W1X 2DP

Spencer
Walter T. Spencer, 47 Upper Berkeley Street, London W1H 7PN
[No longer in business]

Swann Galleries
Swann Galleries Inc., 104 East 25th Street, New York, NY, U.S.A. 10010

Wreden
William P. Wreden, Books and Manuscripts, 200 Hamilton Avenue, Palo Alto, CA, U.S.A. 94302

Facsimiles

1. Thomas Hardy. An early version of 'The Ballad-Singer' (HrT 111.5), as sent to Smith, Elder & Co. for publication in the *Cornhill Magazine*. National Library of Scotland, MS 23173, f. 197. Reproduced courtesy of the Trustees of Miss E. A. Dugdale.

2. Thomas Hardy. The first page of the draft of 'The Melancholy Hussar of the German Legion' (HrT 1516). Iowa State Historical Library. Reproduced courtesy of the State Historical Society of Iowa, Special Collections, and the Trustees of Miss E. A. Dugdale.

3. William Hazlitt. This fragment is the only extant MS of the four-volume *Life of Napoleon Buonaparte* (HzW 57). It is written on the verso of the paper cover (now loose) of Hazlitt's copy of François Auguste Mignet's *Histoire de la Revolution Française* (1826). SUNY at Buffalo. Reduced by 24 per cent.

4. William Hazlitt. The first page of the essay on 'The Late Mr Horne Tooke' (HzW 105) for *The Spirit of the Age*. SUNY at Buffalo. Reduced by 24 per cent.

5. Gerard Manley Hopkins. A version of the sonnet 'Andromeda' (HpG 16). Princeton, Robert H. Taylor Collection. Reproduced courtesy of the English Province of the Society of Jesus.

6a, b. John Keats. Fourth leaf of the draft of 'I stood tip-toe upon a little hill' (KeJ 159), containing lines 87–106 (recto, plate 6a) and lines 123–50 (verso, plate 6b). British Library, Zweig 163. Reproduced courtesy of the British Library.

7. Rudyard Kipling. First page (cut in two) of an early version of 'The Three-Decker' (KpR 1230). Dalhousie University. Reproduced courtesy of the Kipling Collection, Dalhousie University Library.

8. Rudyard Kipling. Unpublished 'Preface' to *Just So Stories* (kpR 1786). British Library, Add. MS 59840, f. 3. Reproduced courtesy of the British Library.

9a, b. Charles Lamb. One scrap of a leaf containing two early sonnets, 'A timid grace sits trembling in her eye' (LmC 3), wanting the first two words (plate 9a), and 'Methinks how dainty sweet it were reclin'd' (LmC 103) (plate 9b). In the Coleridge Collection at Victoria College Library, S.MS.F4.5.

10. Charles Lamb. First page of the essay by Elia 'Mackery End, in Hertfordshire' (LmC 251). Victoria and Albert Museum, Forster Collection. Reproduced courtesy of the Board of Trustees of the Victoria and Albert Museum.

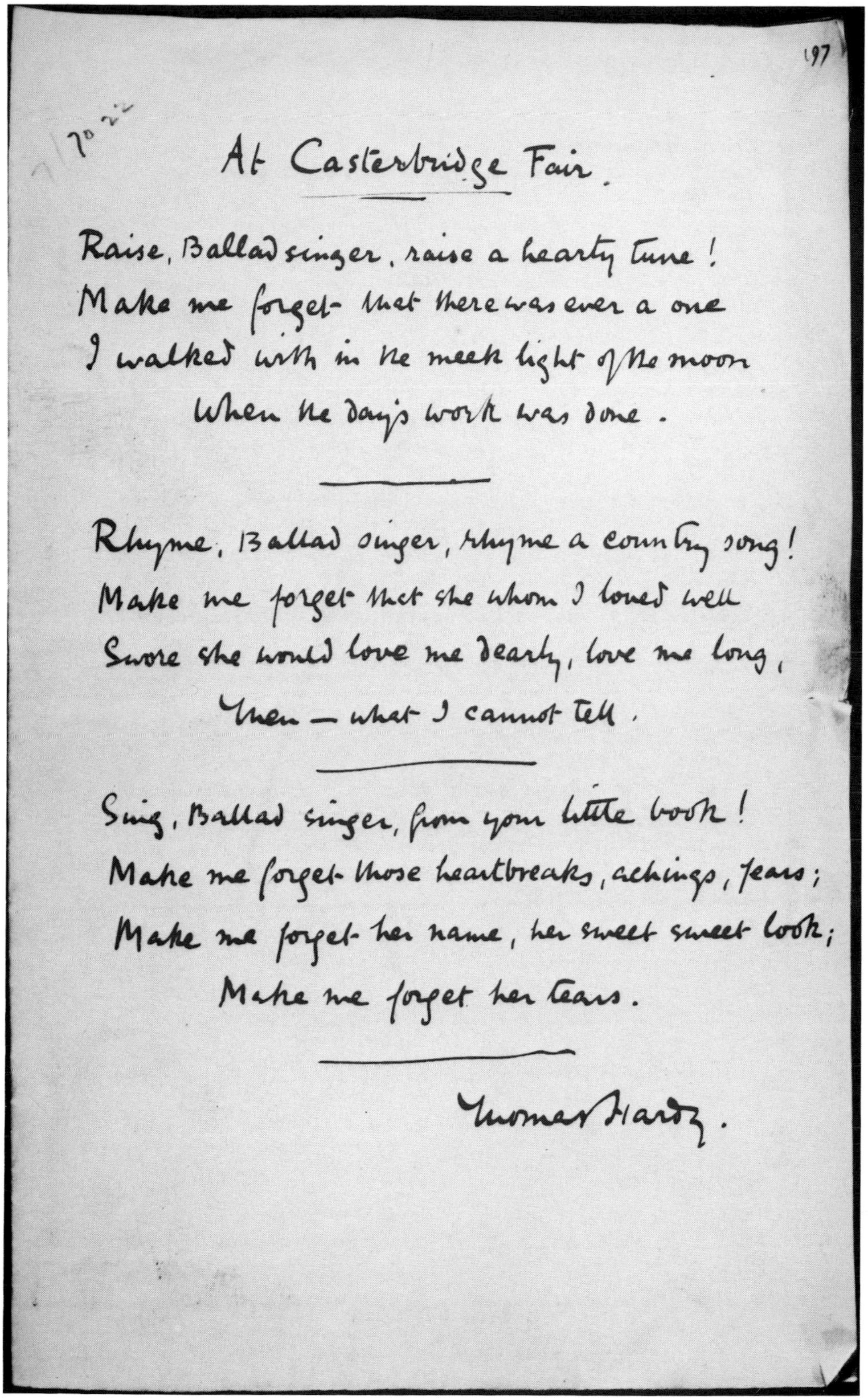

197

At Casterbridge Fair.

Raise, Ballad singer, raise a hearty tune!
Make me forget that there was ever a one
I walked with in the meek light of the moon
When the day's work was done.

Rhyme, Ballad singer, rhyme a country song!
Make me forget that she whom I loved well
Swore she would love me dearly, love me long,
Then – what I cannot tell.

Sing, Ballad singer, from your little book!
Make me forget those heartbreaks, achings, fears;
Make me forget her name, her sweet sweet look;
Make me forget her tears.

Thomas Hardy.

{ ~~The Melancholy Hussar~~
{ The Corporal in the German Legion

By Thomas Hardy.

Oct. 1889

C 1

Here stretch the downs, fresh & breezy & green, absolutely unchanged since those eventful ~~[illegible]~~ days: ~~days of [illegible] military display~~. A plough has never disturbed ~~[illegible]~~ a sod. Here stood the camp; here are distinct traces of the banks thrown up for the horses of the cavalry, & the place of the mixens still is marked. At night when I walk there it is impossible to avoid hearing ~~it can [illegible] I hear~~ amid the brushings of the wind over the grass-bents, the bygone trumpet & bugle calls, the rattle of the halters; ~~to help seeing spectral tents, [illegible]~~ to avoid ~~catching~~ the outlines of spectral tents, ~~&~~ from within which come guttural syllables of foreign tongues [~~from the inside of tents~~], & songs of the fatherland; for they were mostly regiments of the German Legion who slept under canvas hereabout at that ~~day~~ time.

It was nearly ninety years ago. The uniform with its immense epaulettes, queer cocked hat, ~~long coat-tails~~, breeches, gaiters, buckled shoes, & what not, would look strange & barbarous now. Ideas have changed; soldiers were monumental objects then: a divinity still hedged kings, ~~[illegible]~~ & war was ~~[illegible]~~ considered a glorious thing.

Secluded old ~~country~~ manor houses & hamlets lay in the ravines among these hills, where a stranger had hardly ever been seen till the King chose to take the baths yearly at the seaside watering-place a few miles off, & as a consequence soldiers descended ~~in~~ a cloud upon ~~on~~ the district ~~[illegible]~~ around. Is it necessary to add that the echoes of many episodic tales, dating from that picturesque time, still linger here. Some of them I have ~~[illegible]~~ repeated; most of them I have ~~[illegible]~~ forgotten; one I have never repeated, & assuredly can never forget.

this darling weakness of the human heart is pampered by flattery, confirmed by prejudice, sanctified by religion, is seated on a throne, blazes from the altar, has the voice of past & future generations in its favour, & transmitted down from age to age without the consent or intervention of his subjects, raises the possessor to a rank above the ~~insect~~ or to that of a God upon earth.[1] And is it to be supposed that he will part with this rank tamely, or not die in the attempt to recover the smallest iota of that right, the delirious of which he considers as treason, rebellion, sacrilege & worse against the laws of heaven & earth.[2] To tell him of the rights of the people is as if so many wild asses had broke loose & set up a claim of right to freedom. To be told that he ~~exists~~ reigns by & for the people, millions of whom he had been taught to consider as cyphers that were nothing without him at their head, or as worms that he might crush at his pleasure, is altogether as odious as it is incredible to his imagination, & the taint of which ~~can~~ can only be washed out with rivers of blood. To suppose that a man so qualified & brought up will voluntarily relinquish his claim, will give up or share his sovereignty with the people is to expect milk from tygers, honey from scorpions. It is not that I blame him for being what he is, a king; but I blame those who think he can ever forget that he was one. He is what they have made him, for a tyrant is the work of slaves; but let them beware how they attempt to undo their own handywork. Therefore, there can be no compromise, no confidence nor reliance on his good-nature or professions or [illegible] city, the abstract idea but he is a king takes possession of his hum

Printed in N.M

[3]

The Spirit of the Age. — No. ~~5~~ 6

The late Mr. Horne Tooke.

Mr. Horne Tooke was one of those who may be considered as connecting links between a former period & the existing generation. His education & accomplishments, nay his political opinions, were of the last age; his mind & the tone of his feelings were <u>modern</u>. There was a hard, dry materialism in the very texture of his understanding, ~~glossed~~ varnished over by the external refinements of the old school. Mr. Tooke had great scope of attainment & great versatility of pursuit, but the same shrewdness, quickness, cool self-possession, the same <u>literalness</u> of perception & absence of passion & enthusiasm characterised nearly all he did, said, or wrote. He was without a rival (almost) in private conversation, an ~~able~~ expert public speaker, a keen politician, ~~the first grammarian of this or any other age,~~ a first rate grammarian & the finest gentleman (~~at~~ to say the least) of his own party. He had no imagination (or he would not have scorned it!) — no delicacy of taste, no rooted prejudices or

The Catholic Church Andromeda

Now Time's Andromeda, on this rock rude,
With not her either beauty's equal or
Her injury's, looks off by both horns of shore,
Her flower, her piece of being, doomed dragon's food.

Time past, she has been attempted and pursued
With many blows and banes. but now hears roar
A wilder beast from West than all were, more
Rife in her wrongs, more lawless, and more lewd.

Her Perseus linger and leave her to her extremes? —
Pillowy air he treads a time and hangs
His thoughts on her, forsaken that she seems,

All while her patience, morselled into pangs,
Mounts, soon to alight, disarming (no one dreams)
With Gorgongear and barebill thongs and fangs.

Gerard Manley Hopkins

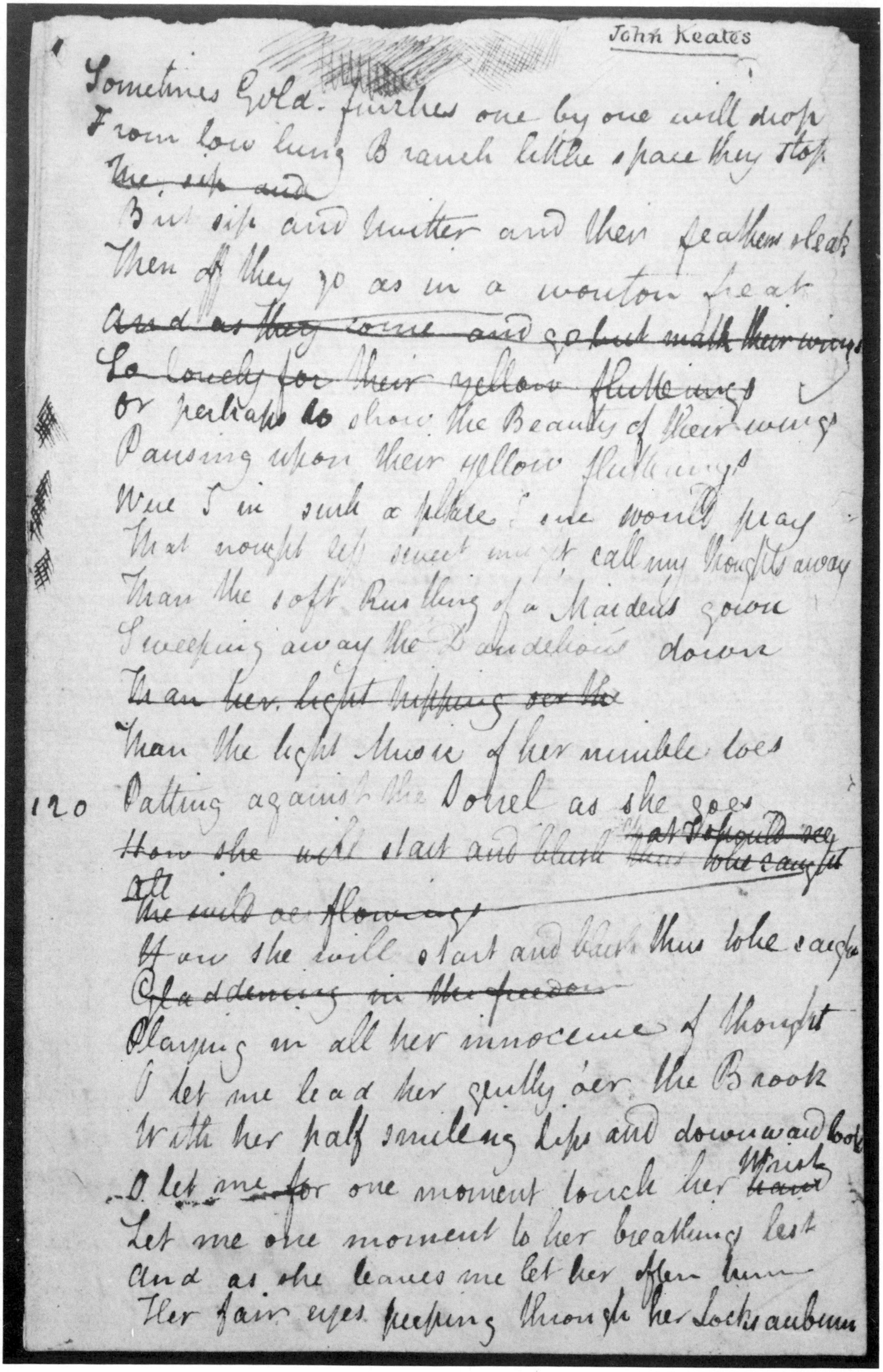
John Keates

Sometimes Gold-finches one by one will drop
From low hung Branch little space they stop
~~But sip and~~
But sip and twitter and their feathers sleek
Then off they go as in a wanton freak
~~And as they come and go but mark their ways~~
~~So lonely for their yellow flutterings~~
Or perhaps ~~to~~ show the Beauty of their wings
Pausing upon their yellow flutterings
Were I in such a place I sure would pray
That nought less sweet might call my thoughts away
Than the soft Rustling of a Maidens gown
Sweeping away the Dandelions down
~~Than her light tripping over the~~
Than the light Music of her nimble toes
Patting against the Sorrel as she goes
~~How she will start and blush~~ ~~thus~~ ~~that I should see~~ ~~to be caught~~
~~All the wild or flowing~~
How she will start and blush thus to be caught
~~Gladdening in the freedom~~
Playing in all her innocence of thought
O let me lead her gently o'er the Brook
Watch her half smiling lips and downward look
O let me for one moment touch her wrist ~~hand~~
Let me one moment to her breathing list
And as she leaves me let her often turn
Her fair eyes peeping through her Locks auburn

6a

Thee must I praise above all other ~~Bustlings~~ Glories
That smile us on to tell delightful Stories
For what has made the Sage or Poet write
But the fair Paradise of Nature's Light
In the calm Grandeur of a sober Line
We see the waving of a Mountain Pine
And when a ~~Page is~~ Tale is beautifully staid
We feel the safety of a Hawthorn glade
~~And so~~
When it is moving on luxurious wings
The soul is lost in pleasant smotherings
Fair dewy roses brush against our faces
~~And we can see them fl~~
And flowering Laurels spring from diamond vases
O'er head we see the Jasmine and sweet Briar
And blooming Grapes laughing from green attire
~~While at our feet the voice of crystal Bubbles~~
~~Charms us at once away from all our trou~~ble
So that we feel uplifted from the world
Walking upon the white clouds wreath'd and curl'd
So felt he who first told how Psyche went
On the soft Wind to Realms of Wonderment
What Psyche felt and Love when their full lips
First Touch'd — what fondling and tender sips
They gave each others cheeks, with all their sighs
And how they kist each others tremulous eyes.
The silver Lamp — the Ravishment — the Wonder
The Darkness, loneliness — the fearful Thunder
Their woes gone by and both to heaven upflown
To bow for gratitude before Jove's Throne —

The Old Three Decker.

And the ~~three~~ volume novel is doomed. Daily paper.

R. Kipling
18 Stanhope Gdns
S.W
or Savile
Wed. noon.

Full thirty foot she towered from waterline to rail—
It cost a watch to steer her and a week to shorten sail;
1 But, spite all modern notions, I've found her first and best—
The only certain packet for the Islands of the Blest.

By ways no gaze could follow, a course unserved of cook,
3 Per Fancy, agent in man, our high-born berths we took,
With maids of matchless beauty and parentage unguessed,
And a Church of England parson, for the Islands of the blest.

Fair held the trade behind us, 'twas warm with lovers' prayers;
2 We'd stolen wills for ballast and a crew of missing heirs.
They shipped as Able Bastards till the Wicked Nurse confessed,
And they worked the old Three-Decker to the Islands of the Blest.

Carambas and ~~cap~~ serapes we waved to every wind,
We smoked good Corpo Bacco when our sweethearts proved unkind;
T'was "ay de mi, Dolores!" Aminta and the rest
As we worked the old Three-Decker to the Islands of the Blest.

We asked no social questions, we pumped no hidden shame;
4 We never talked obstetrics when the Little Stranger came:
We left the Lord in Heaven, we left the friends in Hell;
We weren't exactly Yussufs but—Zuleika didn't tell.

And through the maddest welter and neath the wildest skies,
We'd pipe all hands to listen to the skipper's homilies;
For oft he'd back his topsle or moor in open sea
To draw a just reflection from a pirate on the lee.

No moral doubt assailed us, ~~but~~ so when the port we neared
5 The Villain took his flogging at the gangway and we cheered.
T'was fiddle on the foc'sle—'twas garlands at the mast
For every one got married and I went ashore at last.

I left 'em all in couples a kissing on the decks;
6 I left the lovers loving and the parents signing cheques—
In endless English comfort, by county-folk caressed,
I left the old Three-Decker at the Islands of the Blest.

That route is barred to steamers—you'll never lift again
Our purple pictured headlands or the lordly Keeps o' Spain.
7 They're just below the Sky-line howe'er so far you cruise
In a ram-you-damn-you liner with a brace of kicking screws.

Preface.

After you have read these stories you can play some of them if you like.
Of course you can't play the Whale but you can play the Rhino and the Parsee with a tree for a palm tree and a piece of real cake (pretence is no good) for the cake the Rhino took. You finish with an awful scuffle inside a grown-up's ulster for the skin that got wrinkly but otherwise it is quite a quiet play.
The Camel is a quiet play too. You can play it indoors with a cushion for a hump and three of you for Dog, Horse and Ox. A grown up in a dressing-gown makes a good Djinn and you say the Humphs as loud as you like.

I don't so much care to play Armadillos. It always ends with the Hedgehog and the Tortoise rolling about head over heels like they hit something: and besides it is hard to remember all the things they say to Jaguar. A grown up ought to be Jaguar if he knows how to roar.

You can play Kangaroo in a garden but not across the flower beds. You begin by dancing from one end to the other all down the lawn; ~~[illegible]~~ but you don't hop till Dingo says:- What that cat rabbit. Then you hop till the sing-song is finished. Dingo has to go on all fours. Grown ups won't play Dingo or Kangaroo very long but you can use them for Gods. Indoors, the sing-song goes to music on the piano and you must not stop hopping till it is quite finished.

~~In~~ Indoors, Leopard is best played in the dark. If you can get a grown up to be Giraffe or Zebra and be still while you say:- "What have you at your end of the table Brother" it is very nice but grown ups generally want to be Baviaan and give the advice. If you must have real spots on the Leopard's face use burnt cork. If you play it outdoors a wood or a shrubbery is the very thing: because you ~~[illegible]~~ can come in under the branches and keep talking about the ~~shadows and things~~. Stickly-speckly shadows, then too. You can really see how you ~~will~~ match your background.

We tried the Cat play once but it is long and serious and you can't be trusted with anything like a real baby and ~~it~~ you simply cannot use a real cat. But the Woman and the cave and the mutton bone are rather fun by themselves because you can make up magic as you go on. A tennis bat is just as good as a real mutton bone for magic.

Pau Amma can be played in the nursery with cushions for the canoe and Pau Amma gets under a ~~[illegible]~~ rug to make the sea go up and down. If you can get a grown up for Pau Amma he ought to be all covered over with cushions and come up through them. Any grown up even when they are busy can be Fisherman of the Moon because ~~she~~ they have only to say the answers and go on with their sewing but the best end is to have the canoe dropped back to the mouth of the Perak river on a rug.

The Elephant's Child isn't a good play. Somebody's nose always gets hurt and the spanking parts are too exciting.

It is just the same with the First Letter on account of the mud in the Stranger man's hair and the Neolithic ladies sitting in a long line of six. But if you can get a good grown up for the Stranger man it is a good play.

The Alphabet play is no use. It is too like a lesson for the very small people and ~~it is~~ there isn't any fun in it for the bigger ones, unless they invent a secret Tegumai-talk of their own and write secret messages on walls and posts for the rest of the tribe. Everybody can belong to a Tegumai tribe but Tegumai Bopsulai is the Chief of course and Taffimai Metallumai would be the eldest girl.

~~The Butterfly takes a long time to play and needs a lot of people~~

The Butterfly takes a long time to play and needs a lot of people. The best thing is to build the palace with bricks on a tea-tray and lift it at the proper time. The smallest people ought to be the butterflies if they can remember what to say. If they can't they can be Queens and help make the awful noise in the stairs when the Queens come shouting into ~~the~~ the garden, one hundred abreast. It is very hard to stop the Djinns from upsetting the tea-tray just at the last. The Queens must throw themselves flat on their faces.

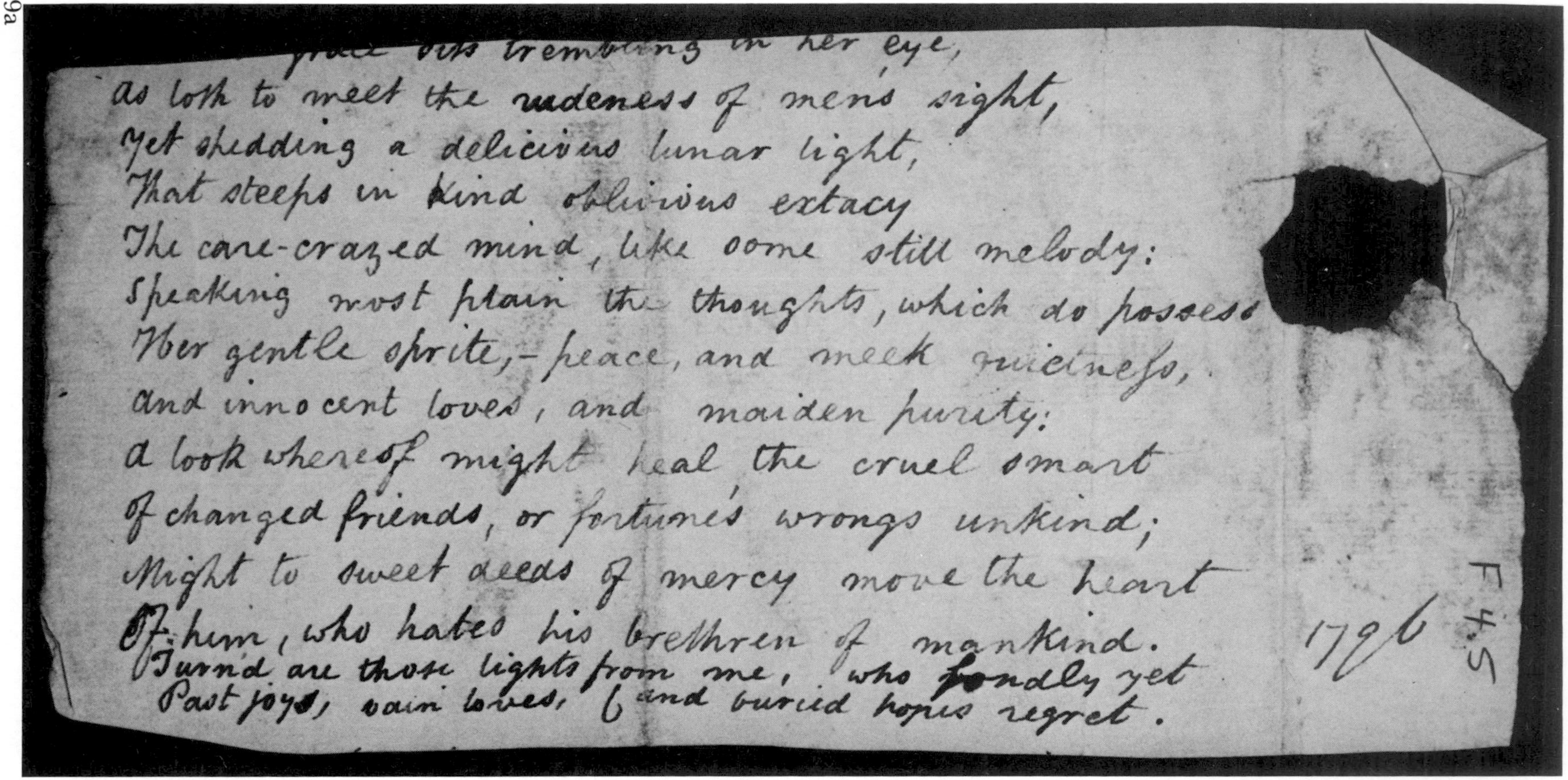
grace sits trembling in her eye,
As loth to meet the rudeness of men's sight,
Yet shedding a delicious lunar light,
That steeps in kind oblivious extacy
The care-crazed mind, like some still melody:
Speaking most plain the thoughts, which do possess
Her gentle sprite, – peace, and meek quietness,
And innocent loves, and maiden purity:
A look whereof might heal the cruel smart
Of changed friends, or fortune's wrongs unkind;
Might to sweet deeds of mercy move the heart
Of him, who hates his brethren of mankind.
Turn'd are those lights from me, who fondly yet
Past joys, vain loves, and buried hopes regret.
F 4.5
1796

9a

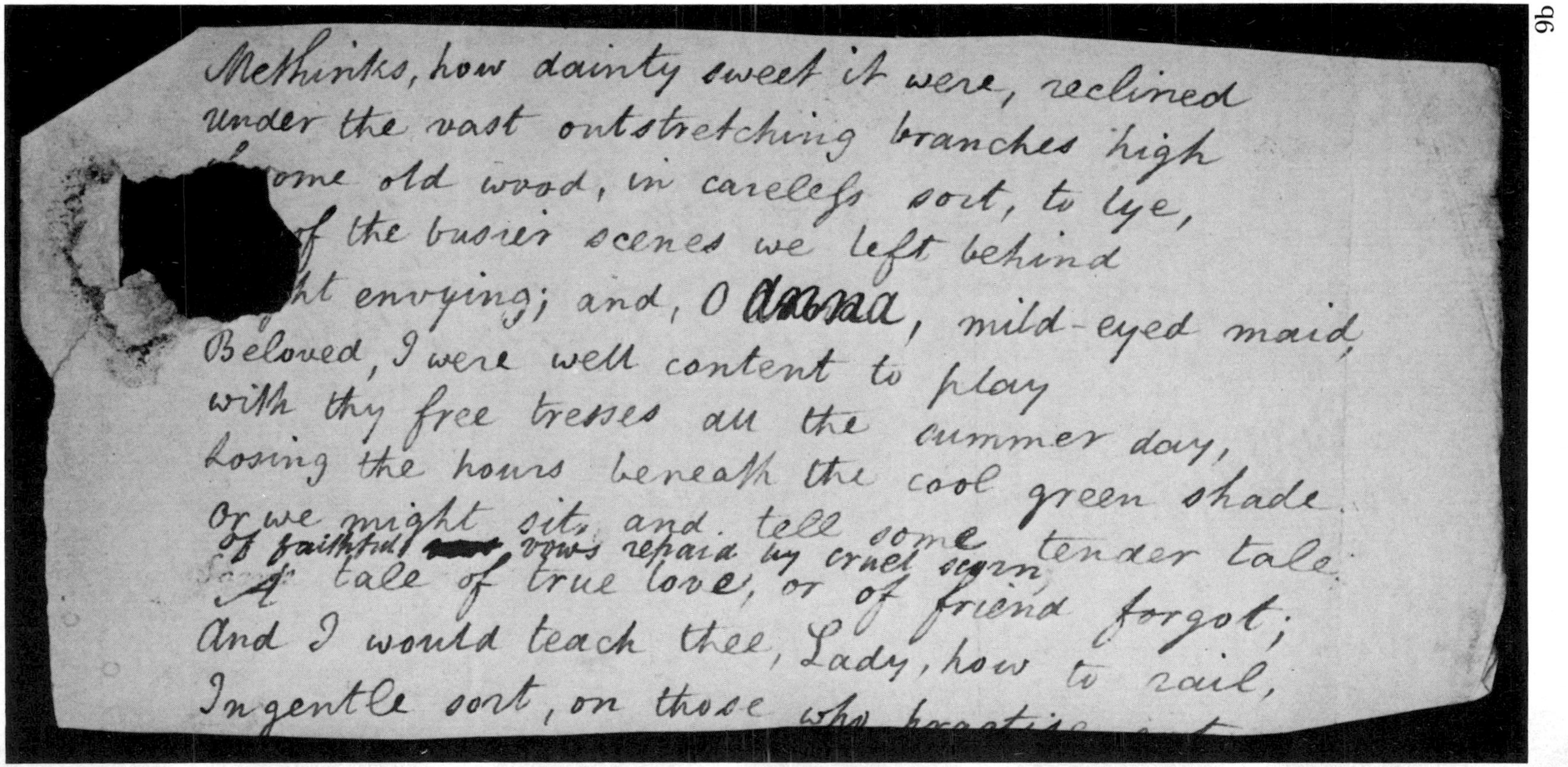
Methinks, how dainty sweet it were, reclined
under the vast outstretching branches high
[illegible] some old wood, in carelefs sort, to lye,
[illegible] of the busier scenes we left behind
[illegible]ht envying; and, O Anna, mild-eyed maid,
Beloved, I were well content to play
with thy free tresses all the summer day,
Losing the hours beneath the cool green shade.
Or we might sit, and tell some tender tale.
Of faithful [redacted] vows repaid by cruel scorn,
A tale of true love, or of friend forgot;
And I would teach thee, Lady, how to rail,
In gentle sort, on those who practise not

9b

B

Mackery End in Hertfordshire.

 (28)

Bridget Elia has been my housekeeper for many a long year. I have obligations to Bridget, extending beyond the period of memory. We house together, old bachelor and maid, in a sort of double singleness; with such tolerable comfort upon the whole, that for one ~~[illegible]~~ find in myself no sort of disposition to go out upon the mountains, with the rash King's offspring, to bewail my celibacy. We agree pretty well in our tastes and habits — yet so, as "with a difference". We are generally in harmony, with occasional bickerings — *as it should be among near relations*. Our sympathies are rather understood, than expressed; and once, upon my dissembling a tone in my voice more *kind* than ordinary, my cousin burst into tears, and complained that I was altered. We are both great readers in different directions. While I am hanging over (for the thousandth time) some passage in old Burton, or one of his strange contemporaries, she is abstracted in some modern tale, or adventure, whereof our common reading-table is daily fed with assiduously fresh supplies. Narrative teazes me. I have little concern in the progress of events. She must have *a story* — well, ill, or indifferently told — so there be life stirring in it, and plenty of good or evil accidents. The fluctuations of fortune in fiction — and almost in real life — have ceased to interest, or operate but dully upon me. Out-of-the-way humours and opinions — heads with some diverting twist in them — the oddities of authorship — please me most. My cousin has a native disrelish of any thing, that sounds odd or bizarre. Nothing goes down with her, that is quaint, irregular, or out of the road of common sympathy. She "holds Nature more clever". I can pardon her blindness to the beautiful obliquities of the Religio Medici; but she must apologize to me for certain disrespectful insinuations, which she has been pleased to throw out latterly, touching the intellectuals of a dear favorite of mine, of the last century but one — the Thrice Noble, chaste, and virtuous, but again somewhat fantastic, and original-brain'd, generous Margaret Newcastle.

It has been the lot of my cousin, oftener perhaps than I could have wished, to have had for her associates and mine, free-thinkers — leaders, and disciples, of novel philosophies and systems; but she neither wrangles with, nor accepts, their opinions. That which was good and venerable to her, when she was a child, retains its authority over her mind still. She never juggles or plays tricks with her understanding.

We are both of us inclined to be a little too positive; and I have observed the result of our disputes to be almost uniformly this — that in

Glossary and Symbols

All MSS in Volume IV are assumed to be autograph unless otherwise stated; therefore the term autograph is suppressed except where clarity demands it, e.g. 'partly autograph and partly in an unidentified hand'. The definitions that follow apply whenever sufficient information about the MS was available. When an entry has been dependent upon second-hand information, its terminology may not always accord with these definitions.

annotation
: Note, distinct from the text, written by an author on a MS of his own work (see 'marginalia').

autograph
: Written in the hand of the author concerned.

cancelled
: Rejected, by the author unless otherwise stated, by some obvious indication such as lines drawn through the text.

commonplace book
: Volume wherein the owner has transcribed from printed or MS sources extracts from other authors.

copy
: In Volume IV, usually a printed book, in contrast to the use of the term 'exemplum' to mean a copy of a printed book in Volume I (see 'fair copy' and 'transcript').

correction
: Alteration made to rectify a mechanical error of transcribing or typesetting (see 'revision').

diary
: Book used for keeping a daily record of events; usually preferred to the term 'journal'.

draft
: MS that represents the first attempt at a work.

fair copy
: Transcript by the author of an earlier version, sometimes containing extensive revisions.

imperfect
: Physically defective MS.

incomplete
: Not containing a portion of the text as published in the reference edition.

journal
: See 'diary'.

marginalia
: Annotations by the author on the margins of other leaves of a text by someone else.

markings
: Underlinings, marginal lines, tics, queries, asterisks, or any non-verbal annotations, usually in the margins of a text by someone else (see 'annotation' and 'marginalia').

MS, MSS
: Manuscript, manuscripts; any handwritten text(s).

printer's copy
: MS or printed copy of a text used by the printer.

quotation
: MS passage written out upon request, frequently for an autograph collector.

reference edition
: Edition of the works of the author in question used as the standard text and from which titles and first lines are quoted.

revision
: Alteration constituting a textual innovation by the author (see 'correction').

transcript
: MS, or typescript, copied out by someone other than the author (a transcript in the author's hand is a 'fair copy').

typescript
Typewritten text or transcript made by typing; assumed to be typed by the author unless otherwise stated.

unfinished
MS obviously abandoned in midst (see 'imperfect', 'incomplete').

version
Text which varies substantially from the reference edition.

[ ]
Indicates a lacuna in the text.

[?]
Indicates an illegible word or phrase.

[word?]
Indicates the compiler's guess at an illegible word.

< >
Indicates a cancelled word or words.

Abbreviations

The following abbreviations are used throughout Volume IV, Part 2; for abbreviations used in individual authors' sections, see the INTRODUCTIONS to each author.

Ashley Library
T. J. Wise, *The Ashley Library: A Catalogue of Printed Books, Manuscripts and Autograph Letters Collected by Thomas James Wise*, 11 vols (privately printed, 1922–36).

BC
The Book Collector

Berg Catalogue
Dictionary Catalog of the Henry W. and Albert A. Berg Collection of English and American Literature, 5 vols (Boston, 1969); *Supplements*, 2 vols (Boston, 1975 and 1983)

BLR
Bodleian Library Record

BMQ
British Museum Quarterly

BNYPL
Bulletin of the New York Public Library

British Literary Manuscripts
British Literary Manuscripts. Series II from 1800 to 1914, catalogue by Verlyn Klinkenborg, checklist by Herbert Cahoon (New York, 1981)

CLQ
Colby Library Quarterly

CLSB
Charles Lamb Society Bulletin

Croft, *Autograph Poetry*
P. J. Croft, *Autograph Poetry in the English Language*, 2 vols (Oxford, 1973)

EA
Études Anglaises

ELH
English Literary History

ELN
English Language Notes

ELT
English Literature in Transition

Healey
G. H. Healey, *The Cornell Wordsworth Collection: A Catalogue of Books and Manuscripts* (Ithaca, NY, 1957)

HLB
Harvard Library Bulletin

HLQ
Huntington Library Quarterly

Houtchens
The English Romantic Poets and Essayists, revised ed, ed. Carolyn Washburn Houtchens and Lawrence Huston Houtchens (New York, 1968)

HQ
Hopkins Quarterly

HRB
Hopkins Research Bulletin

Index
Index of English Literary Manuscripts (London, 1981—)

JEGP
Journal of English and Germanic Philology

KJ
Kipling Journal

KSJ
Keats-Shelley Journal

KSMB
Keats-Shelley Memorial Bulletin

LCUT
Library Chronicle of the University of Texas

Location Register
Location Register of Twentieth Century English Literary Manuscripts and Letters, 2 vols (London, 1988)
MLN
Modern Language Notes
N & Q
Notes and Queries
NCF
Nineteenth-Century Fiction
NUC
National Union Catalogue (1968—)
NUCMC
National Union Catalogue of Manuscript Collections (Washington, D.C., 1957—)
PBSA
Papers of the Bibliographical Society of America
PMLA
Publications of the Modern Language Association of America
PULC
Princeton University Library Chronicle
RES
Review of English Studies
SB
Studies in Bibliography
Sentimental Library
Harry Bache Smith, *A Sentimental Library* (privately printed, 1914)
Shelley and His Circle
The Carl H. Pforzheimer Library: Shelley and His Circle 1773–1822, ed. K. N. Cameron and Don Rieman (Cambridge, MA, 1961—)
SP
Studies in Philology
Tinker Library
Robert F. Metzdorf, *The Tinker Library: A Bibliographical Catalogue of the Books and Manuscripts Collected by Chauncey Brewster Tinker* (New Haven, CT, 1959)
TLS
Times Literary Supplement
Tobacco Catalogue
Tobacco. A Catalogue of the Books, Manuscripts and Engravings acquired since 1942 in the Arents Tobacco Collection at the New York Public Library, from 1507 to the Present, comp. Sarah Augusta Dickson (New York, 1958)
VP
Victorian Poetry
WC
Wordsworth Circle
YULG
Yale University Library Gazette

Volume IV
Part 2

Thomas Hardy
1840–1928

INTRODUCTION

At the age of twenty-seven, Thomas Hardy — a young architect and a private poet — began writing a novel called *The Poor Man and the Lady*; the MS was rejected by at least four publishers. His first novel to be published, *Desperate Remedies*, appeared in print in 1871. At the age of fifty-eight, some thirty years later — after publishing fourteen novels, several of which are among the most famous in English literature — he returned to verse and published *Wessex Poems*, his first collected volume. From that point until his death, Hardy devoted himself almost exclusively to writing poetry; the only significant exception is *Life*, his autobiography.

That Hardy managed to have two rich and virtually distinct literary careers, each one spanning some thirty years, is in itself remarkable. But his achievement in becoming both one of the major novelists *and* one of the major poets of English literature is awesome.

Richard Taylor, an editor of Hardy's 'personal notebooks', writes that 'among [Hardy's] own papers, we have no more than he wanted us to have'. The truth of this statement, however, extends far beyond Hardy's personal papers. As his reputation grew, and in so far as he was able, Hardy sought to control which of his papers and MSS would be preserved and also where they would be lodged. He generally destroyed his working drafts and carefully arranged the fair copies of his works for preservation. He also scrupulously attended to what was written *about* him: he sometimes instructed contemporary critics as to what he would have them write (see, e.g., HrT 1527, 1527.3, 1527.5) and often agreed to receive visitors only after they had undertaken not to publish an account of the meeting.

When he was nearing the age of eighty, Hardy began to sort through all of his own and ELH's, his deceased first wife's, papers. During this process, he destroyed what he didn't want preserved: on 7 May 1919, he wrote to Sir George Douglas 'I have not been doing much — mainly destroying papers of the last 30 or 40 years, & they raise ghosts'. He burnt diaries — his reported destruction of ELH's MS entitled 'What I think of my husband' raising the most doubts as to his motives — and transcribed the extracts from them he wished to save into the two notebooks known as 'Memoranda Books I and II' (HrT 1685–6). Out of this sorting came *Life*, his own version of his life which was published posthumously as the work of FEH, his widow. This process of sifting through a lifetime's worth of papers continued: one of the items Hardy listed as needing to be done in a memo to himself dating from the late 1920s (inserted in 'Memoranda Book II') was 'Continue to examine & destroy useless old MSS, entries in notebooks, & marks in printed books'.

Hardy signed his will on 24 August 1922 and in it he gave careful instructions to his literary executors (FEH and Sydney Cockerell) to use their 'absolute discretion' in deciding on the publication, the dispersal or the destruction of any of Hardy's papers or MSS that did survive; ensuring that no 'prejudice or injury to any person's character or repute or depreciation of my published writings' could occur. The will is printed in 'Thomas Hardy's Will and Other Wills of His Family', *Monographs on the Life, Times and Works of Thomas Hardy*, ed. J. Stevens Cox, no. 36 (Guernsey, CI, 1967). And, indeed, following Hardy's death,

Cockerell is reported to have spent 'a whole morning' burning Hardy's notebooks.

The list of over 2,000 MSS which follows is a testimony to the success of Hardy's intrepid attempt to define the shape of his own literary reputation. The vast majority of verse entries and many prose entries represent those MSS that Hardy himself decided to preserve, located in the repositories that Hardy himself chose. However, it must be said that even a cursory glance at any bibliography of works about Hardy will reveal the extent of his ultimate failure. An enormous number of biographical works, critical studies and editions of his letters — the latter at least containing papers whose destiny he was not able to control — have been published in the sixty years since his death. Many of them contain information, speculations or conclusions of which Hardy would most assuredly have disapproved. And, indeed, dotted throughout the list of literary MSS below are a few which slipped through Hardy's own net: stray drafts of literary works (sometimes preserved by publishers), miscellaneous jottings, notes for unwritten stories or dramatizations, leaves from destroyed diaries, even the occasional item bearing Hardy's instruction that it be 'destroyed'.

The most dramatic scuttling of Hardy's own plans, however, comes ironically from papers he himself preserved but had presumably counted on his widow to destroy — namely, the MSS of *Life*. Through these MSS, scholars and editors have not only been able to study in minute detail Hardy's composition of his own life story but also the degree to which he attempted to mask his authorship through the use of disguised 'calligraphic' handwriting. That this attempt failed resoundingly was made evident as early as 1929, in the first correct speculation as to the true author of *Life* by Lascelles Abercrombie in his essay on Hardy in the 14th edition of the *Encyclopaedia Britannica*. In *Life and Work* (1984), Michael Millgate, by careful scrutiny of the MSS, surgically removed any posthumous intervention by FEH and published Hardy's final version of the *Life*, attributed, for the first time, to its true author, Thomas Hardy.

On 29 September 1911, Sydney Cockerell — director of the Fitzwilliam Museum, Cambridge, and a tireless tracker of literary MSS — visited Max Gate to discuss the future of Hardy's literary MSS. Three items bear that date: Hardy's presentation inscription to Cockerell in his MS of 'The Three Strangers' (HrT 1585); Hardy's pencil list (on a scrap) of the MSS in his possession, annotated by Cockerell '... written by him today at Max Gate, Dorchester/SCC Sept 29 1911'; and Cockerell's list of Hardy's MSS which were handed over to him for distribution (all three items now at the Berg).

In the course of October, Cockerell — in accordance with Hardy's view that 'it would not be becoming for a writer to send his own MSS to a museum on his own judgement' — arranged for the presentation of the following MSS: *Tess of the d'Urbervilles* (HrT 1569) and *The Dynasts* (HrT 1613, 1617, 1620) to the British Library; *Wessex Poems* (see below) to the Birmingham City Museum and Art Gallery; *Poems of the Past and the Present* (see below) to the Bodleian; *Time's Laughingstocks* (see below) and *Jude the Obscure* (HrT 1427) to the Fitzwilliam Museum; *A Group of Noble Dames* (see below) to the Library of Congress; *The Trumpet-Major* (HrT 1591) to the Royal Library, Windsor; the stories 'For Conscience' Sake' (HrT 1415) to the University of Manchester (now the John Rylands Library) and 'A Tragedy of Two Ambitions' (HrT 1589) to the John Rylands Library; 'An Imaginative Woman' (HrT 1426) to the University of Aberdeen; 'On the Western Circuit' (HrT 1531) to the Manchester Central Library. In November, Hardy personally gave the MS of *The Mayor of Casterbridge* (HrT 1514) to the Dorset County Museum.

On 25 October 1911, he wrote to Cockerell that the 'cupboard which contained the MSS is now agreeably empty'. After 1911, Hardy disposed of a few MSS of stories and poems by giving them to friends; see, for example, 'The Duke's Reappearance' (HrT 1403), 'A Few Crusted Characters' (HrT 1410), 'God's Funeral' (HrT 423) and 'When I set out for Lyonnesse' (HrT 1306); by selling them privately (see, for example, 'The Abbey Mason' (HrT 1) and 'The Romantic Adventures of a Milkmaid' (HrT 1557)); or by sending them to charity sales (see, for example, *Far from the Madding Crowd* (HrT 1405), 'The Oxen' (HrT 885) and 'Moments of Vision' (HrT 780)). As for the printer's copies of his subsequent volumes of verse he meanwhile continued to arrange for their eventual bequest to selected institutions.

In 1928, the MSS of *Moments of Vision* and *Winter Words* (see below), were presented to Magdalene College, Cambridge, and Queen's College, Oxford, respectively. In 1939 — on behalf of her sister, FEH, who died in 1937 — Eva Dugdale bequeathed the MS of *Human Shows* (see below) to Yale University.

The great mass of Hardy's miscellaneous papers, letters, books and MSS at Max Gate, however, were not dispersed through the agency of Sydney Cockerell. Even after Hardy's own selective destruction of papers and diaries during the preparation of *Life* (c. 1918–20), a sizeable collection remained; it included a few of the major literary MSS, printer's copies of *Satires of Circumstance*, *Late Lyrics* (see below) and the principal MS of *Under the Greenwood Tree* (HrT 1595) which were all gifts to FEH, as well as the MSS of *Life*.

After FEH's death in 1937 and according to her will, the executor of her estate Irene Cooper Willis arranged for the Max Gate collection to become the cornerstone of the Thomas Hardy Memorial Collection at the Dorset County Museum, the largest and most important Hardy archive in the world; more than a third of all the entries below are in this one collection. All of the MSS and papers (including drawings, music books, documents and much miscellanea) in this collection are available on the first ten reels of the eighteen-reel Microfilm Edition; only letters and printed books are not so included. The other eight reels include Hardy's major literary MSS at other British repositories. References to this microfilm, which is widely available, are provided throughout the entries.

The small but significant collection of Hardy MSS, letters, corrected proofs and printed copies owned by Sydney Cockerell — who served not only as one of Hardy's literary executors but also as proof reader for the later volumes of verse — was sold at Sotheby's on 29–30 October 1956 (Cockerell Sale). The present locations of most of these items have been traced and references to the sale are provided in all of the relevant entries.

While Hardy's MSS, papers and books outside of Dorchester are certainly widely scattered, two large private collections are worth noting: the one amassed by Richard L. Purdy, a distinguished Hardy scholar, which is destined for Yale University; and another owned by Frederick B. Adams.

Prose Works

Not surprisingly, the MSS of Hardy's novels and stories are less tidy than those of his volumes of verse. Fiction writing was his first literary career; since the care that Hardy took with his papers increased as his reputation grew, the MSS of his earliest novels and stories tend to be lost — or destroyed — while those for the later works have usually been preserved.

The reference edition for the novels and short stories is the Wessex Edition. Purdy says emphatically that 'the Wessex Edition is in every sense the definitive edition of Hardy's work and the last authority in questions of text' (p. 286); while this statement needs some qualification in light of more recent scholarship, it remains true that this Edition represents the fullest and certainly the most comprehensive expression of Hardy's 'final' intentions. References to the Wessex Edition are provided throughout the Prose section. In a few cases, modern critical editions of individual novels have subsequently been published which provide collations of manuscript sources and successive editions; these are also cited. For the short stories, additional references are given to Pinion, which includes the few stories which Hardy himself never collected. References to Purdy are also provided throughout the Prose section.

There is no ambiguity about Hardy's prose fiction canon. The only short story which Hardy himself never published is 'Old Mrs Chundle' (HrT 1529–30), published first in 1929 and collected in Pinion.

The MSS of most of the major novels survive as well as a good many of the short stories. In addition, corrected proofs for the original serial publication or first edition of three of the novels are also extant: *The Hand of Ethelberta* (HrT 1422), *A Laodicean* (HrT 1436) and *Jude the Obscure* (HrT 1428). Corrected proofs for subsequent editions are discussed below under 'Collected Editions'.

After the paper sorting that accompanied the preparation of *Life*, Hardy compiled two lists concerning the MSS of his novels and short stories; both date from 1923 and are included in his 'Memoranda Notebook II' (HrT 1686) (printed Taylor, pp. 65–8). The first, of lost items only, is headed 'MSS. *not in existence* — (among others)' and the second, headed '*Depositories of T. H.'s MSS.*' (and subtitled '[Partly copied from a list sent by Mr John Lane...]') attempts to give the whereabouts of all his extant prose MSS. The MSS he lists as 'not in existence' are as follows, in order of date of composition/publication:

1. Architectural Prize Essay (i.e., 'The Application of Coloured Bricks and Terra Cotta to Modern Architecture': This essay won the RIBA prize medal in 1862; see Purdy, p. 293.
2. *The Poor Man and the Lady*: Hardy notes in the first list that this unpublished novel, composed 1867–8, was 'not in existence'; Purdy, pp. 275–6 says that an eighty-page portion of the MS, extant in 1916, was subsequently destroyed by Hardy (see also HrT 1595).
3. *Desperate Remedies*, 3 vols (London, 1871): Purdy, p. 4 says that Hardy himself destroyed the original

and possibly also a transcript by Emma Lavinia Gifford (later ELH); see also HrT 1395.

4. *The Hand of Ethelberta* (see also HrT 1422–4): In 1918, Isabel Smith (widow of Reginald Smith, editor of *Cornhill* where the novel was serialized) found a portion of the original MS of the novel (together with HrT 1100 and 1405); she notified Hardy and, in his reply of 23 January 1918 (*Letters*, V, 243–4), he asked her to return the fragment saying that he would look for the rest of the MS. Hardy, who noted in the first list that the MS of this novel was 'not in existence', apparently destroyed the fragment on its return.
5. *A Laodicean* (see HrT 1436–9): Hardy destroyed the original MS of this novel which he had dictated to ELH from his sick-bed in 1880–1; see Purdy, pp. 39–40.
6. *The Well-Beloved* (see HrT 1597–8): Hardy describes this MS, in the second list, as 'unknown' (rather than 'not in existence') implying that he did not destroy it himself.
7. 'Rejected Scene or two of Dynasts (Sarragossa. St Petersburg)': This item appears on Hardy's first list only; see Purdy, p. 127n and Taylor, p. 65n259.
8. 'A Changed Man' (see HrT 1384): In the second list, Hardy describes the whereabouts of the MS of this story as 'unknown'; the printer's copy is now in the Berg Collection.
9. 'Alicia's Diary', 'A Mere Interlude' and 'A Waiting Supper': these three stories collected in *A Changed Man* (1913) are listed as being 'not in existence'; though not on the list, no MS of a fourth story from this collection, 'Enter a Dragoon', has ever come to light.

Although Hardy did not include them on these lists, MSS of another eight short stories have not been traced (see Purdy, *passim*, for details). Unknown to Purdy, however, manuscripts of 'The Distracted Preacher' (HrT 1396), sold at auction in 1973, and of 'The Melancholy Hussar of the German Legion' (HrT 1516, see FACSIMILES), now at the Iowa State Historical Library, are extant.

One MS volume and one volume of corrected proofs, both containing short stories, are referred to throughout the entries by catch-titles:

MS Group of Noble Dames

The nucleus of this collection of stories was the six stories first pub. (in England in bowdlerized versions) *The Graphic*, Christmas Number, 1 December 1890 and (in the United States, complete) *Harper's Weekly*, 29 November–20 December 1890; collected with four other (previously written) stories London, 1891; Wessex Edition, XIV (1912); Purdy, pp. 61–7.

Volume in which Hardy bound up his MSS of seven stories (including the six first pub. *The Graphic* and 'The Lady Penelope' first pub. *Longman's Magazine*, January 1890), containing also: a title page and table of contents (both for the 1891 collected edition and one page each); a 'Preliminary' (fair copy, revised, on 5 numbered leaves, rectos only) and a concluding note (fair copy, revised, on 2 leaves, rectos only, dated April 1890), both for *The Graphic*; a paper cover bound in, annotated by Hardy 'A Group of Noble Dames (3 missing) Original MS.'; 152 leaves (5 in the hand of ELH) numbered erratically: the 'Preliminary', six *Graphic* stories and concluding note foliated 1–138, wanting ff. 74 and 84 which contained linking passages; the title page and contents foliated separately as ff. 1–2; 'The Lady Penelope' foliated separately as ff. 1–14.

Contents: HrT 1377, 1380, 1433, 1434, 1435, 1512, 1568.

This MS described Purdy, pp. 64–5; it was presented to the Library of Congress through the agency of Sydney Cockerell in October 1911; bound in is a letter from Cockerell to Mrs [Flora?] Livingston of 6 October 1911 with instructions for the presentation.

Library of Congress, Manuscript Division, Thomas Hardy Collection.

Life's Little Ironies Proof

The collection of short stories *Life's Little Ironies* first pub. London, 1894; without 'A Tradition of Eighteen Hundred and Four' and 'The Melancholy Hussar of the German Legion' but including 'An Imaginative Woman' in Wessex Edition, VIII (1912); Purdy, pp. 81–6.

Bound volume of corrected galley proofs of the 9 stories as pub. in first edition; date stamped 1–30 December 1893.

Contents: HrT 1412, 1413, 1416, 1518, 1532, 1564, 1587, 1588, 1590.

This volume described briefly Purdy, p. 84; formerly

owned by Kate Hardy.

Dorset County Museum.

As for MSS of Hardy's uncollected or miscellaneous non-fictional prose writings, most of those which have been included in the entries — including essays, prefaces to his own or other writers' works, contributions to symposia, speeches, letters to the editor, an obituary (HrT 1440), one review (HrT 1542), an edition of the poems of William Barnes (HrT 1560) — are listed in Purdy's indispensable Part III 'Uncollected Contributions to Books, Periodicals, and Newspapers'; it should be noted that, in the absence of any reference edition for such works, these MSS are listed by the titles, authorial or supplied, which are used in Purdy. Some of Hardy's non-fictional writings have been collected in Orel and such references are given when applicable.

However, the entries also include a few miscellaneous MSS which have not been listed in Purdy: Hardy's replies to questionnaires about poetry (HrT 1375.5, 1376); a response to an article in the *Daily News* (HrT 1379.5); a survey of books about Dorset published in the *Daily Chronicle* (HrT 1382); a contribution to a lecture by Alfred Pope (HrT 1398); a contribution to Clement Shorter's literary column (HrT 1416.5); an unpublished letter to the editor (HrT 1442.5); notes on Wessex place-names and the Cerne Giant (HrT 1523.5–1526); notes of suggestions to authors of books about Hardy (HrT 1527–1527.5); notes regarding the restoration of Stinsford Church (HrT 1528); outlines of projected stories (HrT 1533–8); an unpublished preface to the poems of 'Laurence Hope' (HrT 1545); suggestions for a guide to Dorchester (HrT 1568.5); and an addition to the entry about him in *Men & Women of the Time* (HrT 1584.5).

THE LIFE AND WORK OF THOMAS HARDY

This 'biography', as already mentioned, was published and meant to be seen as the work of FEH but was, in fact, virtually written by Hardy himself. Begun in 1917, a complete draft of the narrative (up to May 1918, i.e., Chapters 1–34) was complete by 30 November 1919 though Hardy continued to make revisions as well as accumulate materials for the post-1918 chapters until his death in 1928. The final four chapters (35–8) were put together by FEH; the first two drew almost exclusively on materials left by Hardy, including many completed passages, while the last two were more unequivocally FEH's work.

Hardy's first draft of *Life* was destroyed in June 1918 after FEH had produced three copies (an original and two carbons) of a typescript; to these Hardy made his revisions, often using his so-called 'calligraphic' hand in order to disguise his authorship. Hardy's plan was to revise the third ('working') copy (see HrT 1445) and to have FEH transfer those revisions to the second ('file') copy (see HrT 1444) and ultimately to the top copy (see HrT 1446); in that way, the top copy, destined for the printer, would contain MS revisions only in FEH's hand. In practice, the system broke down and Hardy's hand is, in fact, evident in all three copies. For a full description of Hardy's *modus operandi*, see the Introduction to *Life and Work*, pp. x–xxix.

Throughout the text, Hardy has incorporated many of his own letters and other discrete pieces of work, often in edited versions; Purdy, pp. 263–4, 269–72 lists most of these items, except for personal letters. The edited versions of these items published in *Life* — sometimes originally composed as many as fifty years earlier — are generally included in the extant typescripts prepared for *Life* (see HrT 1444–58). Sometimes, however, MSS of the *original* versions (i.e., not those among the *Life* typescripts) also survive. Such MSS are listed under their individual titles throughout the entries: see HrT 303–4, 1374, 1381, 1391, 1393–4, 1441, 1442, 1511, 1566, 1567, 1599.

Many of the originals of letters which Hardy later included in *Life* (either those sent or drafts kept at Max Gate) are extant. Despite the general exclusion of letters from the scope of the *Index*, these letters have been entered individually — at the end of the other *Life* entries, under the heading 'Originals of Hardy's letters included in *Life*' (HrT 1466–1510) — because of their possible significance as MS sources of *Life*.

VERSE

Even though Hardy published his first poem 'The Bride-Night Fire' in 1875 and his first volume of poems, *Wessex Poems*, did not appear until 1898, he was writing poetry at least as early as the late 1850s and well into the 1860s before he felt forced to abandon it in favour of writing novels and stories. He always maintained, however, that writing poetry was the work which mattered most to him.

The earliest known verse by Hardy is 'Domicilium' — composed between 1857 and 1860 but not printed until 1916 and only as a privately printed pamphlet — but the extant MS sources for these lines (HrT 303–4) were made many years later. This is also true for all other verses — save one — which date from the 1850s and 1860s. The exception is the draft of 'Retty's Phases', not published until 1925 in *Human Shows*, which apparently dates from the time when it was composed in 1868; see HrT 975 however for some debate on the dating of this MS.

Hardy habitually destroyed his poetical drafts, regardless of how recently they had been written, after making fair copies for the printer. Of the nearly 1,400 verse entries below, only a handful are working drafts; as Hardy was an inveterate reviser, however, the vast majority of his fair copies bear his emendations.

Every few years Hardy collected virtually all of the verses he had written up to that date; in all, he published eight such volumes, the last, *Winter Words*, published posthumously in 1928. The bound up fair copies for the printer of these collections have all been carefully preserved in the repositories to which Hardy himself presented or bequeathed them (see discussion above). The contents of these MS volumes (described below) represent about two-thirds of all the poetical MSS listed in the entries.

The rest of the entries are made up of various sorts of items: drafts and fair copies of poems, either preserved among Hardy's personal papers or transcribed by him for friends; materials used for various separate publications of the poems, usually in periodicals, including fair copies or typescripts prepared for the printer, corrected proofs and even corrections or revisions sent in last-minute notes to the printer; the contents of HS Proof (described below), the only extant corrected proof for any of the collected volumes; corrections and revisions which Hardy made in copies of *Selected Poems* (1916), *Selected Poems* (1917) and *Collected Poems* (1923) as well as in his own copy of the Wessex Edition (all described below); typescripts and corrected proofs used for the pamphlets of Hardy's poems privately printed by Clement Shorter or FEH (see Purdy, pp. 349–50 and HrT 9, 41–2, 131, 180, 231, 242–3, 252–3, 304, 334, 338, 446–7, 530, 631–2, 636–7, 741–2, 754, 811–12, 918, 955, 1207–8, 1222, 1267 and the headnote to 1336). A few corrected copies of Hardy's volumes of verse have not been analysed and are listed by their volume title: see *Moments of Vision* (HrT 781, 781.5), *Poems of the Past and the Present* (HrT 927) and *Wessex Poems* (HrT 1297).

The reference edition for Hardy's verse is Hynes, from which titles and first lines are quoted. This edition takes the first editions of Hardy's first seven volumes of verse and MS Winter Words as copy texts and collates any variants from the MS sources as well as Hardy's subsequent revisions, including those adopted in the Wessex Edition. References are also cited throughout the entries to Gibson which occasionally mention MSS, typescripts or proofs (usually without authority) which Hynes omits.

Virtually no ambiguity surrounds Hardy's poetical canon; he published his poems under his signature and, except for a tiny number, collected all of them in his published volumes of verse. Therefore, no 'questionable attributions' punctuate the long list of verse MSS.

Two autograph poems, not of Hardy's composition, are not listed in the entries. One of them — three 12-line stanzas by Charles Swain beginning 'Oh the old old clock of the household stock' — was written in pencil by Hardy on the door of the grandfather's clock in the Hardy Cottage at Upper Bockhampton which was acquired by Dr E. W. Mann from Kate Hardy's estate (see Purdy, p. 325). These lines were twice mistakenly published as Hardy's: once in a privately printed pamphlet by Carl Weber, *Thomas Hardy's First Poem* (Portand, Maine, 1946); and again, with a partial facsimile, in *TLS*, 23 August 1947, p. 432. Another similar item is the pencil MS of lines beginning 'There was a man, he had a clock' which was sold at Sotheby's, 5 December 1967, Lot 577 to Maggs.

The lines in FEH's hand beginning 'The hurricane shrieks an aria round' (MS at Eton College) are listed in the Hardy section of the *Location Register* as being possibly by Hardy; however, in the opinion of Samuel Hynes, there is no evidence of Hardy's authorship of these lines which are more likely to be FEH's own.

A few points regarding the tiny number of poems that Hardy did not collect are worth noting. One item listed below (HrT 556) is the typescript of his rearrangement of words supplied by the Mayor of Dudley that Hardy sent to the Mayor for inscription on that town's War Memorial Clock Tower. As for the twenty-six poems included by Hynes in his section 'Uncollected Poems' — 'The Sound of Her' (HrT 1106), incidentally, was *first* published in this section — twenty of them are represented by manuscripts. Also included in this section are verses printed in *Life* and songs from the dramas *The Dynasts* and *The Famous Tragedy of the Queen of Cornwall*; extant manuscripts of these verses and songs have been included with the materials for *Life* and in the Dramatic Works section.

Quite a few manuscripts, typescripts or corrected proofs have come to light since Hynes was published and they are identified as such throughout the entries. Some of them are significant additions, such as the three fair copies of early versions of poems sent to Smith Elder and Co. for publication in *Cornhill Magazine* and now with other George Smith papers at the National Library of Scotland (see HrT 111.5, 685.5, 912.5 and FACSIMILES); or curious ones, like the fair copy of the closing lines of 'Departure' (now with Benjamin Britten's papers in the Britten-Pears Library in Aldeburgh) which Hardy may have written out to be set to music.

Fair copies of three poems which Hardy presented to the Plymouth Free Public Library in 1923 were destroyed during the Second World War; they were 'The Marble-Streeted Town' (see HrT 736), 'Places' (see HrT 921) and 'The West-of-Wessex Girl' (see HrT 1298).

But, as already stated, the majority of Hardy's extant poetical MSS are included in the eight bound volumes of printer's copies of each of his published collections and the one extant set of corrected proofs for those volumes (HS Proof). They are listed here in the order of their dates of publication.

MS Wessex Poems

This collection first pub. London and New York, 1898; Wessex Edition, Verse Vol. I (London, 1912); Gibson, pp. [5]–81; Hynes, I, [1]–106; Purdy, pp. 96–106.

Revised fair copies of the Preface and 51 poems (as published) and 32 illustrations by Hardy (31 as published), printer's copy for the first edition, including a title page, 107 leaves (rectos only) numbered 1–106 and one unnumbered, annotated (last page) 'Glossary of Local words (to be sent.)'.

Contents: HrT 33, 35, 56, 70, 156, 164, 185, 235, 265, 294, 397, 437, 470, 476, 481, 484, 485, 525, 558, 562, 569, 615, 628, 682, 698, 745, 761, 796, 798, 802, 903, 935, 979, 1003, 1026, 1032, 1042, 1043, 1045, 1046, 1065, 1084, 1121, 1144, 1168, 1178, 1180, 1203, 1234, 1249, 1258, 1296.5.

This MS described Purdy, pp. 104–5 and Hynes, I, 361; Microfilm Edition, Reel 18. The illustrations are discussed in Appendix A, 'A Note on the *Wessex Poems* Drawings' in Hynes, I, [388]–9; facsimiles of two of them printed in J. B. Bullen, *The Expressive Eye* (Oxford, 1986), plates 5–6; for the illustration not included in the first edition, see HrT 185. This MS was presented to the Birmingham City Museum and Art Gallery in October 1911.

Birmingham City Museum and Art Gallery.

MS Poems of the Past and the Present

This collection first pub. London and New York, 1902; Wessex Edition, Verse Vol. I (London, 1912); Gibson, pp. [83]–187; Hynes, I, [107]–228; Purdy, pp. 107–19.

Revised fair copies of the Preface and 99 poems (as published), printer's copy for the first edition, including also title page (f. xi), a table of contents (ff. xiii–xvi, rectos only) which includes the cancelled and unidentified title 'The Complaint of the Common Man'; 157 numbered leaves (rectos only) of texts; as sent to Harper & Bros in August 1901.

Contents: HrT 18, 53, 61, 65, 91, 98, 118, 140, 149, 159, 160, 163, 173, 177, 181, 190, 203, 210, 221, 224, 229, 246, 262, 269, 286, 308, 310, 318, 326, 402, 410, 420, 429, 486, 488, 500, 511, 521, 531, 535, 582, 583, 585, 601, 617, 646, 653, 662, 676, 690, 706, 714, 724, 729, 747, 767, 788, 795, 848, 852, 926, 939, 950, 974, 988, 991, 992, 993, 998, 1004, 1014, 1025, 1053, 1061, 1082, 1092, 1094, 1095, 1101, 1111, 1123, 1136, 1137, 1150, 1151, 1187, 1193, 1194, 1195, 1213, 1226, 1255, 1276, 1293, 1324, 1329, 1334, 1345, 1372, 1373.

This MS described Purdy, pp. 117–18 and Hynes, I, [367]–8; Microfilm Edition, Reel 18. The leaves of preliminary matter in this volume have been refoliated from Hardy's original ff. i–vi to xi–xvi due to the insertion of letters by Sydney Cockerell. The MS was presented to the Bodleian in October 1911.

Bodleian, MS Eng. poet. d. 18.

MS Time's Laughingstocks

This collection first pub. London, 1909; Wessex Edition, Verse Vol. III (London, 1913); Gibson, pp. [189]–299; Hynes, I, [229]–359; Purdy, pp. 138–50.

Revised fair copies of the Preface and 95 poems (the 94 as published and HrT 709 'Looking Back' which was omitted from the collection before publication), printer's copy for the first edition, including a table of contents (ff. ii–vi, rectos only) and 144 leaves (rectos only) of texts numbered 1–141 (wanting f. 104) and 4 unnumbered leaves following ff. 48, 62 (two) and 123; as sent to Macmillan in September 1909.

Contents: HrT 5, 21, 23, 24, 95, 100, 112, 127, 136, 172, 202, 211, 236, 257, 267, 273, 278, 279, 283, 297, 315, 329, 368, 373, 384, 391, 392, 401, 414, 415, 421, 448, 475, 480, 482, 503, 507, 516, 536, 560, 573, 594, 600, 606, 620, 639, 643, 686, 709, 731, 737, 770, 772, 808, 814, 817, 820, 824, 829, 863, 876, 877, 880, 888, 913, 958, 959, 969, 971, 973, 978, 987, 995, 1036, 1059, 1064, 1113, 1129, 1131, 1174.5, 1184, 1185, 1192, 1211, 1219, 1236, 1243, 1252, 1259, 1264, 1269, 1300, 1326, 1330, 1360, 1366.

This MS described Purdy, pp. 148–9 and Hynes, I, [379]; Microfilm Edition, Reel 17. It was presented to the Fitzwilliam Museum in October 1911.

Fitzwilliam Museum.

MS Satires of Circumstance

This collection first pub. London, 1914; Wessex Edition, Verse Vol. IV (London, 1919); Gibson, pp. [301]–423; Hynes, II, [1]–139; Purdy, pp. 160–72.

Revised fair copies of 94 poems (93 as published and HrT 866 'On the Doorstep' which was omitted before publication), printer's copy for the first edition, including a table of contents, revised (ff. i–iii, rectos only) and sectional title pages, 185 leaves of text (rectos only) numbered 1–184 and the last leaf being a later addition; as sent to Macmillan in August 1914, inscribed to FEH on her birthday, 12 January 1923.

Contents: HrT 2, 12, 25, 32, 51, 72, 73, 119, 123, 137, 143, 192, 194, 214, 241, 244, 247, 284, 285, 289, 292, 313, 325, 349, 353, 416, 422, 424, 436, 443, 491, 501, 518, 533, 574, 576, 586, 587, 602, 642, 649, 659, 711, 749, 786, 787, 797, 813, 837, 866, 907, 919, 921, 923, 928, 956, 962, 963, 966, 985, 1000, 1002, 1006, 1007, 1011, 1020, 1023, 1028, 1034, 1073, 1107, 1108, 1117, 1126, 1141, 1143, 1174, 1199, 1214, 1215, 1238, 1246, 1262, 1273, 1290, 1295, 1305, 1311, 1341, 1342, 1350, 1355, 1358, 1368.

This MS described Purdy, p. 171 and Hynes, II, 487; Microfilm Edition, Reel 5. One of the fair copies originally in this volume (HrT 748) was excised and sent by Hardy to a Red Cross sale; it was replaced by HrT 749.

Dorset County Museum.

MS Moments of Vision

This collection first pub. London, 1917; Wessex Edition, Verse Vol. IV (London, 1919); Gibson, pp. [425]–553; Hynes, II, [151]–309; Purdy, pp. 193–208.

Revised fair copies of the 159 poems (as published) and also 'Men Who March Away' (HrT 750) (added to the collection later) and two cancelled drafts of 'The Coming of the End' (HrT 225–6) (i.e., 162 entries in all), printer's copy for the first edition, including a revised title page and typescript table of contents (7 pages), 201 leaves (rectos only) of text, numbered 1–199 and 2 unnumbered leaves (following ff. 21 and 141); as sent to Macmillan in August 1917.

Contents: HrT 28, 29, 31, 43, 45, 48, 49, 58, 69, 75, 76, 77, 87, 92, 93, 106, 107, 114, 126, 128, 151, 152, 174, 176, 178, 191, 198, 200, 218, 219, 225, 226, 227, 237, 245, 255, 276, 302, 320, 322, 332, 333, 348, 355, 376, 379, 383, 387, 395, 419, 433, 456, 463, 466, 467, 469, 487, 496, 498, 499, 504, 509, 528, 529, 532, 534, 544, 547, 557, 566, 567, 568, 578, 590, 603, 608, 614, 625, 627, 629, 640, 641, 650, 668, 669, 693, 699, 704, 707, 708, 718, 733, 734, 739, 746, 750, 758, 764, 778, 779, 792, 799, 801, 810, 838, 839, 840, 842, 850, 851, 861, 862, 867, 883, 884, 898, 899, 900, 904, 905, 912, 915, 916, 954, 980, 982, 983, 997, 1031, 1037, 1067, 1080, 1090, 1091, 1119, 1135, 1156, 1164, 1175, 1202, 1205, 1212, 1225, 1227, 1228, 1253, 1254, 1265, 1283, 1313, 1315, 1319, 1320, 1321, 1331, 1332, 1356, 1362, 1363, 1364, 1365, 1369.

This MS described Purdy, p. 207 and Hynes, II, 496; it was presented to Magdalene College, Cambridge by FEH, 7 February 1928; for a typescript of lines entitled 'The Sound of Her' (a title cancelled in the table of contents in this MS), see HrT 1106.

Magdalene College, Cambridge.

MS Late Lyrics

This collection first pub. London, 1922; Wessex Edition, Verse Vol. V (London, 1926); Gibson, pp. [555]–698; Hynes, II, [311]–485; Purdy, pp. 214–27.

Revised fair copies of the 'Apology' and 151 poems (as published), printer's copy for the first edition, including a typescript table of contents (ff. xiii–xvi, rectos only), 193 leaves (rectos only) of text; as sent to Macmillan on 23 January 1922, the 'Apology' sent 21 February 1922.

Contents: HrT 8, 15, 16, 27, 37, 40, 55, 63, 74, 78, 83, 84, 88, 89, 103, 115, 116, 139, 170, 175, 186, 193, 195, 197, 199, 201, 220, 222, 238, 249, 251, 254, 260, 293, 309, 311, 312, 317, 321, 331, 335, 339, 343, 351, 359, 363, 372, 378, 407, 411, 428, 435, 445, 457, 473, 493, 494, 510, 523, 524, 540, 548, 549, 551, 553, 555, 565, 604, 621, 626, 630, 638, 645, 660, 670, 672, 673, 701, 705, 726, 728, 732, 735, 736, 740, 743, 765, 766, 773, 790, 816, 835, 843, 844, 845, 846, 847, 856, 858, 872, 873, 879, 882, 896, 906, 941, 957, 961, 981, 999, 1001, 1010, 1016, 1022, 1027, 1035, 1039, 1047, 1063, 1078, 1105, 1120, 1125, 1134, 1138, 1158, 1179, 1183, 1232, 1237, 1239, 1240, 1256, 1266, 1274, 1288, 1289, 1291, 1298, 1299, 1302, 1314, 1316, 1318, 1327, 1343, 1346, 1347, 1352, 1353, 1354, 1367.

This MS described Purdy, p. 226 and Hynes, II, 508; Microfilm Edition, Reel 5. It was presented to the Dorset County Museum in 1937.

Dorset County Museum.

MS Human Shows

This collection first pub. London, 1925; Wessex Edition, Verse Vol. VI (London, 1931); Gibson, pp. [699]–831; Hynes, III, [1]–157; Purdy, pp. 234–48.

Revised fair copies of 152 poems (as published) and a draft of 'The Two Wives' (HrT 1241, published *Late Lyrics*), printer's copy for the first edition, including an autograph title page and typescript table of contents (ff. i–iv, rectos only), 196 numbered leaves (rectos only) of text; as sent to Macmillan on 29 July 1925.

Contents: HrT 6, 10, 34, 46, 59, 66, 79, 80, 82, 86, 96, 109, 117, 134, 138, 146, 148, 182, 184, 188, 208, 215, 223, 228, 230, 261, 274, 290, 305, 323, 324, 341, 346, 352, 357, 361, 366, 374, 386, 388, 393, 396, 403, 408, 432, 434, 438, 440, 459, 483, 497, 502, 505, 514, 552, 564, 579, 580, 588, 605, 618, 624, 651, 655, 657, 663, 664, 665, 667, 671, 674, 678, 680, 684, 692, 694, 717, 722, 762, 774, 776, 783, 785, 791, 807, 818, 823, 827, 830, 832, 833, 854, 868, 869, 875, 878, 887, 891, 893, 895, 897, 901, 924, 932, 934, 937, 944, 946, 952, 965, 976, 996, 1013, 1015, 1029, 1038, 1040, 1049, 1051, 1055, 1057, 1069, 1077, 1081, 1085, 1087, 1097, 1109, 1133, 1148, 1155, 1157, 1159, 1163, 1181, 1190, 1216, 1229, 1233, 1241, 1244, 1257, 1270, 1277, 1278, 1286, 1303, 1304, 1309, 1322, 1323, 1336, 1357.

This MS described Purdy, p. 247 and Hynes, III, [310]–11; it was presented to Yale by Eva Dugdale, April 1939, on behalf of her sister FEH.

Yale.

HS Proof

This is the only extant complete set of corrected proofs for any of Hardy's volumes of poems.

Page proof for the first edition of *Human Shows* (1925), containing corrections and revisions by Hardy to 68 poems, those in ink being made for the 1925 first edition (and so incorporated), those in green and those in pencil apparently made later for various editions (some never printed), containing corrections on the title page and in the contents and an explanatory pencil note on front flyleaf, stamped 'Final Proof', annotated 'Press' and (on last page) '[returned for press 26 Sept '25]'; date stamped 8 September 1925 and 11 September 1925.

Contents: HrT 7, 11, 60, 67, 81, 97, 110, 135, 147, 183, 189, 275, 291, 307, 342, 347, 367, 375, 389, 394, 409, 439, 441, 460, 506, 515, 581, 589, 619, 652, 656, 658, 666, 675, 681, 685, 763, 775, 777, 784, 819, 828, 834, 855, 892, 894, 902, 925, 933, 945, 947, 977, 1030, 1041, 1050, 1052, 1056, 1058, 1070, 1086, 1110, 1149, 1217, 1231, 1245, 1272, 1279, 1337.

No indication is given in the entries as to whether the corrections are in ink, pencil or green; this proof described Hynes, III, [310]–11, but not mentioned Gibson; Hardy's note about the contents on the flyleaf is printed in Millgate, p. 561.

Dorset County Museum.

MS Winter Words

This collection first pub. posthumously London, 1928; Wessex Edition, Verse Vol. VI (London, 1931); Gibson, pp. [833]–930; Hynes, III, [159]–274; Purdy, pp. 252–62.

Revised fair copies, left unfinished at Hardy's death, of his last volume of verse, containing an Introductory Note and 104 poems (wanting 'Childhood among the Ferns') of the 105 in the published volume, including a title page, 136 numbered leaves (rectos only) and one inserted leaf at the end (see HrT 464), annotated on title page 'unrevised'.

Contents: HrT 20, 22, 30, 54, 108, 111, 153, 154, 162, 169, 187, 204, 206, 207, 217, 232, 234, 250, 272, 277, 282, 288, 316, 344, 345, 350, 362, 365, 371, 390, 404, 406, 413, 453, 462, 464, 472, 490, 512, 517, 527, 550, 593, 616, 644, 654, 689, 691, 703, 710, 719, 721, 723, 782, 789, 793, 794, 800, 805, 806, 822, 825, 831, 881, 911, 922, 931, 936, 938, 943, 948, 953, 970, 1017, 1019, 1021, 1068, 1079, 1089, 1098, 1099, 1115, 1116, 1140, 1142, 1154, 1162, 1165, 1172, 1173, 1182, 1198, 1247, 1248, 1275, 1280, 1281, 1285, 1301, 1317, 1333, 1339, 1340, 1351, 1371.

This volume not used as printer's copy for the first edition which was probably set from a now-lost typescript prepared by FEH after Hardy's death; this MS described Purdy, pp. 261–2 and Hynes, III, [321]–3; Microfilm Edition, Reel 18. It was presented to Queen's College by FEH in the summer of 1928.

Queen's College, Oxford, MS 420.

In March 1916, Macmillan proposed that Hardy bring out a selection of his poems aimed at a 'general' audience, to be published in the Golden Treasury Series. The resulting volume — *Selected Poems* (1916) — included 105 poems from the four volumes of verse then published, six songs from *The Dynasts* and nine poems from the then-unpublished volume *Moments of Vision*. Twenty-two of the verse entries represent Hardy's revisions in his own copy of this selected edition.

Selected Poems (1916)

Hardy's copy containing his corrections and revisions for various subsequent editions, made on at least two occasions, in black, blue and green ink and in pencil; labelled '[study copy] 1st Ed^{n} (marked to be corrected in reprint)' and on inside front flyleaf '*Corrections*/In black ink—have been sent to publishers for reprint of this edition./blue—Corrected in Wessex Ed^{n}, Mellstock, & Collected ed^{n}; not in this./green—in this ed^{n} only'; inserted (inside back cover) are: 1) 2 pages (one folded leaf) containing two versions of a list of corrections in the volume, in pencil, the first (incomplete) headed 'Golden Treasury Selection—(corrections sent Dec 4. 1918)/[On examining 1925 reprint all these (including 1920 list at bottom) are found to have been made.]'; the second headed 'Selected Poems of Thomas Hardy. Golden Treasury Series.' and annotated 'Sept 26. 1920/copy in duplicate/sent to Macmillan...', complete; 2) typescript of table of contents, 4 leaves (rectos only) numbered ii–v, annotated (pencil) 'Selected Poems of Thomas Hardy' and (in red) 'containing titles of those afterwards omitted', followed by a pencil list of titles headed '*Some at first chosen: afterwards omitted.—*'.

Contents: HrT 13, 120, 270, 299, 354, 380, 399, 417, 425, 451, 519, 538, 571, 597, 612, 755, 759, 1075, 1127, 1146, 1307, 1624.

Only one correction in this volume (HrT 597) did not appear in any subsequent publication; this volume described in Appendix D in Hynes, III, 352, where it is designated *DCM2*.

Dorset County Museum.

Hardy planned an extensively revised edition of *Selected Poems* and its preparation in 1927 was what Purdy called Hardy's 'last literary activity'. The revised edition was not published until 1929 with Hardy's revised title *Chosen Poems*. Eight poems from the first edition were discarded and forty-nine poems were added, including forty-three from the volumes of verse published since 1916 and two songs from *The Famous Tragedy of the Queen of Cornwall*. Hardy used a copy of the 1917 reprint of *Selected Poems* in preparing this edition:

Selected Poems (1917)

Hardy's copy containing his extensive corrections and revisions (in black and red) made in the autumn of 1927, copy text for the projected revised edition of *Selected Poems* (published posthumously as *Chosen Poems*), including, as well as contents listed below, instructions to the printer and revisions to the table of contents (pp. v–ix); annotated on inside front cover 'As enlarged for *Second Edition*', half title and title page revised to 'Chosen Poems'.

Contents: HrT 14, 36, 71, 94, 113, 121, 125, 133, 161, 166, 213, 248, 271, 280, 287, 295, 300, 319, 328, 381, 400, 418, 426, 431, 452, 478, 520, 522, 539, 561, 563, 572, 577, 584, 598, 613, 688, 712, 756, 760, 803, 821, 865, 886, 908, 929, 967, 990, 994, 1009, 1012, 1044, 1060, 1076, 1083, 1103, 1112, 1128, 1147, 1169, 1188, 1196, 1250, 1263, 1296, 1308, 1312, 1615, 1625.

The corrections in black ink correspond to those sent to Macmillan in 1918–20; this copy described in Appendix D in Hynes, III, 353, where it is designated *DCM4*; eight poems printed in *Selected Poems* (1917) were dropped by Hardy during revision and are cancelled in this copy; they are 'Middle-Age Enthusiasms', 'News for Her Mother', 'Without Ceremony', 'A Dream or No', 'The Dear', 'One We Knew', 'The Face at the Casement', 'The Pine Planters'.

Dorset County Museum.

Hardy also collected all of his verse to date in *Collected Poems* (London, 1919) which included the contents of all the verse volumes except *Late Lyrics*, *Human Shows* and *Winter Words*; subsequent editions of *Collected Poems* incorporated the poems from these volumes. Hardy's corrected proof of the preliminary pages of the 1919 edition are extant (see HrT 219.5). His copy of the second edition (1923) was extensively revised by him for later editions:

Collected Poems (1923)

Hardy's copy containing his corrections and revisions, used as a record of revisions made at various stages, in four colours (black pencil, green pencil, two colours of ink), containing the addition of an epigraph from Job on the title page and revisions to the table of contents, including corrections not made in any published edition; annotated on front flyleaf (in green pencil) '26 July '26./The green corrections...have not been sent anywhere...[in black pencil] nor the pencil ones...(Sept 1926).../The inked corrections...have been embodied in the Wessex Edition...'.

Contents: HrT 101, 105, 158, 167, 239, 259, 266, 301, 314, 336, 360, 458, 468, 474, 479, 489, 495, 542, 554, 575, 599, 622, 633, 661, 673.5, 700, 744, 769, 859, 874, 890, 909, 940, 1008, 1033, 1104, 1176, 1189, 1197, 1224, 1292, 1294, 1328, 1349.

This copy described in Hynes, III, 353, where designated *DCM3*; the epigraph from Job is printed on the half title of Hynes, Vol. I; Siegfried Sassoon's copy of this edition, in which the epigraph has been added by Hardy and in which a list of poems by Hardy is inserted (suggestions for an anthology of Hardy poems to be edited by Sassoon), is owned (1989) by Michael Millgate.

Dorset County Museum.

Collected Editions and Lists of Corrections

In 1895–6, Osgood, McIlvaine & Co. published the first collected edition of Hardy's Wessex Novels in 16 volumes. With the exception of *Jude the Obscure* (this being the *first* edition), *The Well-Beloved* and *A Changed Man* (not published until 1897 and 1913 respectively), this edition contains newly and painstakingly revised texts of all of Hardy's novels and most of his short stories. The copies which Hardy used to prepare these revised editions have, with two exceptions, been lost; for the exceptions, see *The Mayor of Casterbridge* (HrT 1515) and *Tess of the d'Urbervilles* (HrT 1579).

The next significant edition of Hardy's works was the 'definitive' Wessex Edition in twenty-four volumes; the first twenty volumes were published in 1912–13, the last four added at intervals until the final posthumous volume of 1931. This edition includes all of Hardy's collected prose fiction (Vols I–XVIII), verse and dramatic works (Verse Vols I–VI).

Only three entries represent items which Hardy used specifically during the preparation of the Wessex Edition: a corrected proof for the 'General Preface to the Novels and Poems' (HrT 1419) which was published in Vol. I; preliminary matter for the volume of *Wessex Tales* (HrT 1546); and the copy of *The Woodlanders* (HrT 1605) which Hardy used for revising the text.

Most of the volumes in Hardy's own set of the Wessex Edition contain his corrections and revisions and are listed in the entries below:

DCM Wessex Edition

Volumes I–XVIII contain Hardy's novels and short stories; those works for which there is no revised copy in this set are *The Mayor of Casterbridge* (Vol. VI), *The Trumpet-Major* (Vol. XI), *Two on a Tower* (Vol. XII), *A Group of Noble Dames* (Vol. XIV) and *Desperate Remedies* (Vol. XV). Verse Vols I (*Wessex Poems, Poems of the Past and the Present*) and III (*The Dynasts, Part Third, Time's Laughingstocks*) are designated *DCM1* in Hynes (and described there in Appendix D, III, 351–2); Verse Vol. II (*The Dynasts, Parts First and Second*) is listed as HrT 1610. Verse Vols IV (*Satires of Circumstance, Moments of Vision*) and V (*Late Lyrics, The Famous Tragedy of the Queen of Cornwall*) from this set were presented to Sydney Cockerell by FEH in 1928 and sold to Maggs in the Cockerell Sale as part of Lot 252; they are now owned by Frederick B. Adams (see Hynes, III, 352 and HrT 433.5, 545, 568.5, 623, 634, 669.5, 860, 964, 1024, 1642). For the poems in *Human Shows* (in Wessex Edition, Verse Vol. VI, not published until 1931), Hardy used HS Proof (described above) as the record of his intended corrections.

Hardy's revised and/or corrected copy of the Wessex Edition, used to record changes meant for later editions and as the source for his lists of corrections for such editions, periodically sent to Macmillan; the corrections are made in different coloured pencils each indicating when they were made (i.e., for which edition), some never having been incorporated into a printed edition; including (on the flyleaves of most volumes) Hardy's lists of which corrections and revisions were sent for which editions.

Contents: HrT 57, 150, 157, 165, 264, 298, 330, 385, 450, 471, 477, 537, 559, 570, 596, 607, 648, 677, 683, 716, 849, 889, 914, 951, 960, 1062, 1093, 1096, 1124, 1145, 1186, 1223, 1260, 1325, 1335, 1385, 1404, 1409, 1420, 1424, 1432, 1439, 1519, 1541, 1546, 1548, 1553, 1559, 1580, 1586, 1596, 1598, 1606, 1610.

Dorset County Museum.

The 37-volume Mellstock Edition (1919–20) includes all of Hardy's poetry and prose except *Late Lyrics*, *Human Shows* and *Winter Words* which were all added in subsequent editions. With the exception of an addition to the Preface to *Wessex Tales* (Vol. XV) and *A Pair of Blue Eyes* (Vols XVI–XVII), which was revised especially for this edition (see HrT 1541), the texts published in the Mellstock Edition were the same as those in the Wessex Edition. A copy of the Mellstock Edition owned by Hardy and containing his annotations in two of the volumes — *A Pair of Blue Eyes* (HrT 1540) and *The Dynasts* (HrT 1612) — is at Colby College.

In preparation for new editions of his works, Hardy often compiled lists of the corrections and revisions he had made to date in various working copies of his texts — usually in DCM Wessex Edition — and sent those lists to the publisher or printer.

Hardy sent Macmillan a list of corrections for the reprint of *Satires of Circumstance* with a postcard dated 5 February 1915; the postcard is extant (*Letters*, V, 79–80 from the original at the British Library, Add. MS 54924, f. 51) but the list has not survived. Similarly lost are three lists of corrections to *Moments of Vision*: the first was sent to Macmillan with a letter of 10 December 1917 (*Letters*, V, 234 from the original at the British Library, Add. MS 54924, f. 88); the two others were sent to Macmillan in 1918: one with a letter of 24 March, the other with a letter of 4 December (*Letters*, V, 259–60 and 286–7 from the originals at the British Library, Add. MS 54924, ff. 94, 104). Though none of these lists has survived, the list of corrections to *Moments of Vision* among the R. & R. Clark papers at the National Library of Scotland (described below) may be a duplicate or composite of any or all of them.

Hardy's own draft of two lists of corrections sent to Macmillan for the Mellstock Edition are extant at the Dorset County Museum (see Hynes, III, 351–4); they are both written in pencil on the versos of printed forms. The first (three numbered pages) is annotated '[sent to publishers for use in the Mellstock Edition—June 18. 1919]' and includes corrections to *Tess of the d'Urbervilles*, *The Return of the Native*, *Under the Greenwood Tree*, the Prefaces of *Life's Little Ironies* and *Wessex Tales*, *A Pair of Blue Eyes*, and *A Laodicean*. The second list (two pages numbered 4–5) is annotated '[sent to publishers June 22. '19]' and includes corrections to a few poems in *Wessex Poems*, *Time's Laughingstocks* and *Satires of Circumstance* (all of which are also made in DCM Wessex Edition) and extensive corrections to *The Dynasts* (a few appended additional corrections to the latter are annotated '[sent...July 2. 1919]').

Among the papers of Macmillan's printers R. & R. Clark, on deposit in the National Library of Scotland (Dep. 229/292) is a typescript list of corrections, revised by Hardy and date stamped 19 June 1919, sent for the Wessex Edition, Verse Vol. IV (*Satires of Circumstance, Moments of Vision*); for corrections unique to this list, see 'An Anniversary' and 'Her Secret'. Together with it are two scraps: the first, in an unidentified hand, is a list of corrections for *Moments of Vision*, possibly related to the three lost lists of such corrections Hardy is known to have sent to Macmillan in 1917–18 (see above); the second is Hardy's autograph list of a few 'corrections [for Verse Vol. IV] omitted in proofs returned for press' (containing a unique correction to 'The Last Signal'), date stamped 12 July 1919. For another similar scrap, see HrT 3.

Another lost leaf of fourteen corrections — printed as the errata slip inserted in unsold copies of *Collected Poems* (1919) — was originally sent to Macmillan with a letter of 22 November 1919 (*Letters*, V, 342 from the original at the British Library, Add. MS 54924, f. 122). Sydney Cockerell's copy of *Collected Poems* (the 1920 reprint) in the Bodleian (Don. c. 426) includes this errata slip annotated by Hardy that 'these corrections are made in the 1923 edition & after'.

On 18 April 1920 Hardy sent a four-page typescript list of corrections for the reprint of the Wessex Edition to Macmillan (the covering letter printed *Letters*, VI, 14 from the original at the British Library, Add. MS 54924, f. 129). This typescript is lost but the carbon copy that Hardy retained is still extant in the Dorset County Museum (see Hynes, III, 351–4). It is annotated '[sent up Ap[l] 18. 1920]' and includes corrections to *Tess of the d'Urbervilles*, *The Return of the Native*, *Under the Greenwood Tree*, the Preface to *Wessex Tales*, *A Pair of Blue Eyes*, *A Laodicean*, *The Dynasts* and to poems in *Wessex Poems* and *Time's Laughingstocks* (virtually all of these corrections are also made in DCM Wessex Edition). Attached to f. 3 of this list are two further lists of corrections to *The Dynasts* and poems in *Time's Laughingstocks*, annotated that they were sent to the printers on 15 and 26 May 1920 respectively.

Other lost lists of corrections were mentioned in (and probably enclosed with) Hardy's letters to Macmillan of 28 October 1922 (for *Late Lyrics*), 8 October 1925 (for Wessex Edition Verse Vol. IV), 20 November 1925 (for *Human Shows*) and 24 June 1926 (for a limited edition of *The Dynasts*); the original letters at the British Library, Add. MS 54925, ff. 13, 93, 97 and 112 respectively are printed in *Letters*, VI, 164, 361, 368–9 and VII, 31.

Dramatic Works

This section of the entries includes MS sources for Hardy's 'closet dramas' — *The Dynasts* and *The Famous Tragedy of the Queen of Cornwall* — and for adaptations for the stage of Hardy's novels and stories. Hardy first attempted to dramatize one of his novels in 1879 when, in collaboration with J. Comyns Carr, he adapted *Far from the Madding Crowd* into a drama entitled *The Mistress of the Farm* (see HrT 1643); it was produced in 1882.

Throughout his life, Hardy experimented with the notion of adapting his own novels to the stage and quite a few of his draft sketches for dramatizations are extant. Most of these schemes, however, were never carried out.

In 1908, the Dorchester Debating and Dramatic Society produced a dramatization of *The Trumpet-Major* written by their director A. H. Evans. This was the first of a series of dramatizations of Hardy's Wessex novels which this group — renamed the Hardy Players in 1916 — would produce. A list of the principal productions of the Hardy Players is given in Purdy, pp. 351–3. While most of their adaptations were either by A. H. Evans or his successor T. H. Tilley, Hardy himself wrote the dramatization of *The Dynasts*, *The Famous Tragedy of the Queen of Cornwall*, *Tess*, *The Three Wayfarers* and *O Jan! O Jan! O Jan!*. That Hardy was actively involved with these productions is evident from the appearance of his hand *passim* in the surviving records.

Numbered entries are provided for all surviving autograph material and for all typescript or printed items which bear Hardy's annotations or revisions. Other materials directly relating to the various dramatizations of Hardy's works are described in the relevant headnotes to the entries.

Two large collections of materials for dramatizations of Hardy's works are extant. The first, in the Dorset County Museum, includes the great many outlines which Hardy himself made for projected dramatizations which were never realized; some of these were gathered together with a cover annotated by Hardy 'Possible schemes of Dramatization—(mostly by request from would-be Dramatizers)' and '*To be destroyed uncopied at my death. T. H.*'. It also includes typescripts of adaptations by others, scriptbooks and miscellaneous materials, many with Hardy's revisions or annotations. This collection contains nearly half of the items listed in the Dramatic Works section.

One interesting note in this collection is not, however, listed in the entries. On a scrap and in Hardy's hand, it is headed '*Dorchester Dramatic Society.*/Conditions of any other performance:—' (Microfilm Edition, Reel 2). Also at Dorset County Museum (and included in Microfilm Edition) are: a large number of programmes for productions by the Hardy Players, many signed by Hardy (Reel 4); a few theatre posters (Reel 4); a few letters to T. H. Tilley from Harley Granville Barker, J. M. Barrie, etc. (Reel 4); the visitors' book to the Old Theatre, Dorchester containing an autograph prefatory note signed by Hardy (Reel 9); birthday greetings to Hardy on his eighty-fifth birthday from the Hardy Players (Reel 9); and a book of autographs of the Hardy Players (Reel 9).

A large collection of the working papers of A. H. Evans and T. H. Tilley was purchased by the University of California at Riverside (Riverside Collection) from J. Stevens Cox in 1972. These papers (including 146 items and dating from 1908–24) have been listed in the sale catalogue of that collection, *Hardy Players Collection*. While only five items in this collection are represented by numbered entries, other papers are described in the headnotes throughout the Dramatic Works section. A great deal of the material, however, is not described anywhere in the entries: correspondence regarding various productions, including letters to Tilley and letters from FEH; prop plans and costume details; photographs and drawings of sets, actors and characters; theatre programmes; and writings about Hardy.

A bound volume of programmes of productions by the Hardy Players, which Hardy inscribed and sent to J. S. Udal, is now owned by F. B. Adams (see *Letters*, V, 204 and 209).

Diaries and Notebooks

Of the twenty-three entries in this section, fifteen represent sixteen of Hardy's notebooks (including school notebooks, personal notebooks, commonplace books and literary notebooks), four represent scrapbooks and four represent loose leaves from notebooks which are apparently otherwise lost.

Scholars generally treat Hardy's well-organized extant notebooks as being in two distinct categories: personal notebooks and commonplace books (or literary notebooks). The first category includes the 'Schools of Painting Notebook' (HrT 1675), the 'Trumpet-Major Notebook' (HrT 1680) and the two pocket notebooks in which Hardy recorded the details of his life and activities which he wished to preserve, the 'Memoranda Books I–II' (HrT 1685–6). These four notebooks have been discussed and published in full in Taylor (1978).

Hardy began the series of the so-called commonplace books — 'Literary Notes I' (HrT 1678), 'Literary Notes II' (HrT 1681), 'Literary Notes III' (HrT 1683) and the '1867 Notebook' (HrT 1677) — early in his career as a novelist. They were used (and re-used) by Hardy as source materials for his novels. They have been published in full, with excellent annotations, in Björk (1985). These eight notebooks are preserved at Dorset County Museum as, indeed, are all but three of the notebooks and all of the scrapbooks.

Of the other eight notebooks, only one, the 'Architectural Notebook' (HrT 1674) has been published in full in 1966 by C. J. P. Beatty. The seven remaining unpublished notebooks include two — the 'Studies, Specimens &c Notebook' (HrT 1676) and the 'Facts from Newspapers, Histories, Biographies, & other chronicles—(mainly Local)' (HrT 1679) — which were known to both Taylor and Björk and are mentioned in their editions of Hardy's notebooks. The former is one of the two notebooks owned by R. L. Purdy (destined for Yale).

A third unpublished notebook, the 'Poetical Matter' notebook (HrT 1684) — a photocopy of which is owned by R. L. Purdy — was not known until Michael Millgate's 1982 biography of Hardy in which it was described and an extract from it was printed.

The four other unpublished notebooks are relatively unimportant. They include the earliest extant notebooks: three school notebooks (HrT 1672–3) which are dated 1854–5 and a fourth, 'Nomenclature of the Wessex novels' (HrT 1682), which is an almost blank exercise book containing a few interesting entries.

Hardy's Library and Marked Books

In Hardy's will, he carefully instructed FEH to give to his brother Henry and sister Kate any books that they 'agree upon for such gift' and to make the presentation of books to friends that he will have named in a list found 'among my papers'. Apparently no such list is now extant and no attempt has been made to determine what presentations (if any) FEH made of Hardy's books after his death.

In any case, apart from these two wishes, Hardy left it to the discretion of his executors to dispose of the bulk of his library — along with the rest of his papers. Except for the notebooks and diaries which FEH and Cockerell destroyed after Hardy's death (and the occasional item which FEH presented to friends or sold), she seems to have preserved Hardy's papers and books virtually intact at Max Gate.

In her will (dated 18 May 1937), she arranged for the establishment of the Thomas Hardy Memorial Collection at Dorset County Museum; she left it to the discretion of her executor Irene Cooper Willis to select books and papers from those at Max Gate to be the cornerstone of that collection. Willis apparently so bequeathed *all* of Hardy's papers found at Max Gate but she did make a selection of the books, the most important among them — including those containing extensive autograph marginalia — being included in the gift to the Dorset County Museum.

Of the hundreds of books not given to Dorset County Museum, many bear evidence of Hardy's use — annotations or markings — as the entries in the Marginalia section will attest. However, many others were probably not used or even read by Hardy; the Max Gate library also included unsolicited books presented to Hardy, uncut books, books published after his death and books owned (or presented to) both ELH and FEH. All the books in the library, despite their status or particular owner, include the

Hardy bookplate: 'From the library of Thomas Hardy, O.M. Max Gate'. A further complication is that, after Hardy's death, Sydney Cockerell made another version of the Max Gate bookplate for books which had not been so labelled and for future use; this bookplate is sometimes called 'fake' despite there being no evidence that it appears in books which were *never* at Max Gate.

The books not preserved at Dorset County Museum (along with a few letters to FEH) were sent to the saleroom and sold at Hodgson's on 26 May 1938 as Lots 1–309, representing some 2,300 volumes (the Max Gate Sale); references to this sale are provided throughout the Marginalia section when possible, given the vagaries of the sale catalogue. Immediately following this sale, many booksellers' catalogues appeared which were either devoted solely to books from the library at Max Gate or included a large number of such books; some of the more important of these catalogues are: Maggs Catalogue 664 (1938): *Thomas Hardy. A Collection of Books from his Library at Max Gate, Dorchester* (222 items); Hollings Catalogue 212 (n.d.): *Modern Times...with a Preliminary Supplement of Books from the Library of Thomas Hardy*; Wreden Catalogue 11 (1938): *A Selection of Books from the Library of Thomas Hardy, O.M.* (467 items); Elkin Mathews Catalogue 77 (1939): *Books from the Library of Thomas Hardy* (items 1–88); Export Book Co. Catalogue 287 (July 1938): *Selections from the Library of...Thomas Hardy, O.M.* (c. 106 items); Heffer Catalogue 532 (1938) (items 1828–2033); First Edition Bookshop Catalogue 33 (November 1938): *A List of Books from the Library of Thomas Hardy, O.M.* (188 items); Rota Catalogue 58 (1938), Items 356–437. Catalogues containing smaller numbers of Max Gate books are: Percy Dobell Catalogue 421 (July 1938), Items 1–13; Commin Catalogue 111 (Winter 1938), Items 371–93; Rota Catalogue 61 (1939), Items 309–32; and David Magee Catalogue 23 (n.d.), Items 160–200.

Hardy's books offered for sale in these catalogues are, undoubtedly, now widely scattered. Locating them is made difficult by the fact that their connection to Hardy has probably often been lost in the cataloguing process. Nonetheless, since there is no reason to assume that any of the books listed in these catalogues would have been destroyed since 1938, those described as being marked or annotated by Hardy are listed in the Marginalia section whether or not they have been located. There is, then, throughout these entries, a greater reliance than is desirable on these sale catalogues which are apt to be misleading or wrong in any number of details: in the bibliographical data, the omission of information about marginalia or the misrepresentation of marginalia by others as being Hardy's own.

It cannot be stressed too strongly that, for these reasons, the Marginalia section is merely a first attempt to list Hardy's annotated books; it is incomplete and probably perpetuates inaccuracies. Neither is it a reconstruction of Hardy's library, though scholars will perhaps be able to use it as a starting point for such a reconstruction.

Collections of books from Hardy's library have been amassed in a few repositories and these have been examined. The British Library's Department of Printed Books preserves a collection of forty-nine of Hardy's volumes, mostly guidebooks and maps, quite a few containing his marginalia. Colby College owns about seventy books from Hardy's library, including Hardy's unannotated copies of works by, *inter alia*, Thackeray, Edna St Vincent Millay, Byron, Matthew Arnold, Tennyson, Milton, Zola and Voltaire; see 'Books from Hardy's Max Gate Library', *CLQ*, 2Ser15 (1950), 246–54.The collections at Texas include about 300 books bearing the Max Gate bookplate; those containing Hardy's marginalia are listed in the entries. The collection of R. L. Purdy (destined for Yale) is inaccessible at present; it includes over 250 of Hardy's books, many more of which contain Hardy's annotations than are listed in the entries.

Miscellaneous Papers, Documents and Hardyana

A great many papers and documents of literary interest survive, in repositories all over the world. Many of Hardy's letters to his various publishers, printers, editors, etc. have been published in *Letters* from originals which are widely scattered. A few publishers' archives — or chunks of them — also survive intact.

Hardy's thirty-year correspondence with his publishers, Macmillan & Co., is bound in three volumes in the Macmillan Archive in the British Library (Add. MS 54923–5). Included in this correspondence are typescript accounts by Hardy of his dealings with the American publisher Harper & Bros; see Add. MS 54924, ff. 136–41, 165 and 167 and letters to Macmillan in *Letters*, VI, 20–1, 87–8 and 88–9.

Some of Harper & Bros's own records regarding their relationship with Hardy, including a few letters, can be found in the Harper & Bros Archive at

Columbia University and the Harper Collection at the Pierpont Morgan Library (MA 1950).

An important early series of letters (1875–87), between George Smith of Smith, Elder & Co. — regarding the publication of *The Hand of Ethelberta*, *The Return of the Native*, *The Trumpet-Major* and *The Mayor of Casterbridge* — was presented to the National Library of Scotland in 1976 by Elizabeth Gordon (née Badger); see also HrT 111.5, 685.5, 912.5. The letters were all printed in *Letters*, Vol. I.

A few other letters from the file of Smith, Elder & Co. (including an unpublished one from Hardy of 29 May 1877) were acquired by the University of North Carolina in 1986. That library also owns a collection of papers from the files of A. P. Watt & Co.— Hardy's literary agent — which includes two unpublished letters from Hardy dated 13 and 27 June 1891.

Some thirty letters and notes to R. R. Bowker — the London representative of Harper & Bros from 1880–2 — which Hardy wrote during the printing of *A Laodicean* are extant in two R. R. Bowker collections, one in the Manuscripts Division of the NYPL and the other in the Library of Congress, Manuscript Division (see HrT 1436–8); they are all printed in *Letters*.

Also in the Manuscripts Division of the NYPL are records of Macmillan & Co. which include a series of thirty-six letters (none by Hardy) to and from Frederick Macmillan regarding, among other things, the posthumous publication of Hardy's last collection of verse *Winter Words*; also included is a letter of 1928 to Macmillan from FEH about an advance on the royalties for *Life*.

Two other publishers' archives which include material relating to Hardy are the Blackwood Papers at the National Library of Scotland (the Hardy letters dating from 1877–92 are all published in *Letters*) and the Tillotson Archive at the John Rylands Library (the three Hardy letters of 1881–9 were printed in *Letters*, two of them from transcripts). The collection of papers of Macmillan's printers, R. & R. Clark, described above, is now on deposit in the National Library of Scotland (Dep. 229/292); see also HrT 3.

Several formal agreements or other documents concerning the publication of Hardy's works have come to light:

1. Account drawn up by Tinsley Bros for the publication of *Desperate Remedies*, submitted to Hardy on 22 February 1872 and annotated by him; formerly owned by Howard Bliss; facsimile in Purdy, p. 5; Princeton.
2. Hardy's signed agreement with Tinsley Bros for the publication of *Under the Greenwood Tree*, dated 22 April 1872; owned F. B. Adams.
3. Hardy's signed agreement with Henry S. King for the re-publication of *A Pair of Blue Eyes*, dated 25 April 1877; sold American Art Association, 26–7 February 1931, Lot 254 (facsimile printed in the catalogue).
4. Two signed agreements with Tillotson & Son (see the 'Note on Tillotson & Son...' in Purdy, Appendix III, pp. 340–1): one (dated 24 September 1885) assigning the newspaper rights to Hardy's story 'A Mere Interlude'; the other (dated 29 June 1887) assigning the first publication serial rights to a then-undetermined novel by Hardy as well as the right to distribute the work in America (this agreement is annotated '...cancelled in accordance with Author's letter Dated Sept. 24th 1889...'); Bodleian, MS. Eng. misc. f. 395/1, ff. 176 and 152–61, respectively.
5. Hardy's signed agreement with Macmillan & Co. for the publication of Macmillan's Colonial Library edition of Hardy's novels, enclosed with a letter (printed *Letters*, II, 59) to Frederick Macmillan of 22 May 1894; British Library, Add. MS 54923, ff. 39 (letter), 40r–v (agreement).
6. Hardy's signed 'Memorandum of Agreement' with Osgood, McIlvaine & Co. for the publication of *Hearts Insurgent* (i.e., *Jude the Obscure*), dated 4 April 1895; Pierpont Morgan, MA 1950 (Harper Collection).
7. Hardy's signed contract with Harrison Grey Fiske (see Purdy, p. 78) for a New York production of a dramatization of *Tess of the d'Urbervilles*, 10 pages, dated 3 July 1896; Columbia University. Receipts and other documents regarding the New York production of *Tess* are in the New York University Library.
8. Hardy's signed 'Memorandum of Agreement' with Osgood, McIlvaine & Co. for the publication of *The Well-Beloved*, dated 14 January 1897; Pierpont Morgan, MA 1950 (Harper Collection).
9. Hardy's signed agreement covering the transfer of fifteen of his titles from Harper & Bros to Macmillan & Co., dated 2 April 1902; British Library, Add. MS 54923, ff. 60–2.
10. Hardy's signed agreement with Macmillan & Co. for the publication of *The Dynasts*, dated 16

October 1903, enclosed with a letter (printed *Letters*, III, 80) to Frederick Macmillan, 21 October 1903; British Library, Add. MS 54923, ff. 81v–2 (letter), 83–4 (agreement).

11. Hardy's signed contract (carbon copy) with Metro Pictures Corp., assigning the motion picture rights to *Tess*, dated 15 September 1922; David Holmes Catalogue 16 [1987], Item 35.

12. Hardy's signed agreement with Macmillan & Co. for *Collected Works*, dated 26 September 1923, enclosed with a letter (printed *Letters*, VI, 214) to Frederick Macmillan of 27 September 1923; British Library, Add. MS 54925, ff. 40–1 (agreement), 42 (letter).

Before his death, Hardy contemplated the publication of a volume of 'Miscellanea' which would collect some of his non-fictional prose writings. A two-page typed list of such items selected for the volume — headed 'Miscellanea: By Thomas Hardy' — is extant (owned by David Holmes; facsimile in British Library, RP 2146). Whether or not the list is a typescript made from Hardy's own autograph list, it almost certainly embodies his own selection of articles. A heading to the list reads, in part: 'A copy of most of these articles is contained in the bundle with which this is enclosed.'; some surviving copies of the listed articles, now also owned by David Holmes, were presumably originally part of 'the bundle' which the list enclosed (see HrT 1383, 1399, 1523, 1542, 1547).

Three MS bibliographical listings of Hardy's work survive. A one-page list of works, in ELH's hand with Hardy's revisions, covers the years 1864–80; it is in the Dorset County Museum (see Purdy, p. 294 and Microfilm Edition, Reel 10). Another curious item, also at the Dorset County Museum, is a notebook entitled by ELH 'A Chronological List of Thomas Hardy's Works in verse & prose—'. Each page is headed by a year (up to 1909) under which titles are meant to be listed; however, the titles have been only sparsely filled in.

The last of these bibliographical items is composed of three corrected proofs of Hardy's bibliography as published in the Authors Club (of New York) Manual: to the first proof, which lists Hardy's works up to 1909, Hardy has added his works up to 1914 and signed it 'from Thos Hardy (corrected)/Dorchester, England'; the second lists Hardy's works to 1914 and is signed 'Max Gate/Dorchester. Eng./Corrected & returned as requested/T. H.'; and the third, listing works to 1914, contains the addition by Hardy of his works up to 1919 and is signed '(with Mr Hardy's compliments.)'. These proofs are in the Manuscripts Division of the NYPL.

The Dorset County Museum owns a great many of Hardy's architectural and other drawings. In the former category are plans for churches; designs and inscriptions for tombstones (including those for himself, ELH, FEH, his parents, his sister and others); designs for a memorial brass to his ancestors, memorial plaques for ELH and himself and a memorial to the staff of the Dorchester G.P.O.; designs for town houses; plans to seclude the Hardy Cottage at Upper Bockhampton; and the original plans for Max Gate. Many more such drawings are contained in Hardy's 'Architectural Notebook' (see HrT 1647).

The collection of other drawings includes mostly pencil sketches of Wessex landscapes and buildings—including the churches at Stinsford and St Juliot, the restoration of which Hardy had planned. The entire collection of drawings — including the albums of sketches by ELH and a few loose sketches by others — is available on Reel 10 of the Microfilm Edition; a few facsimiles are also printed in J. B. Bullen, *The Expressive Eye: Fiction and Perception in the Work of Thomas Hardy* (Oxford, 1986).

Another collection of twenty architectural drawings is at Texas; for reproductions, see *LCUT*, 7 (1962), 12. These sketches, in pencil and ink, and watercolours of St Juliot's Church were made in the late 1860s for John Hicks, the Dorchester architect to whom Hardy was articled.

The Berg Collection at the NYPL now owns a collection of Hardy's photographs and drawings formerly owned by Howard Bliss. It includes pencil sketches of St Juliot's Church (dated 1870), a drawing of a memorial tablet for himself at St Juliot's Church (to match ELH's), a sketch of 'St Neighton's Kieve nr Tintagel, Cornwall' (dated October 1871), four miniature pencil 'Sketches made in the Vallency Valley' (facsimile printed in *Early Life*, facing p. 102) as well as a few sketches by ELH; most of the photographs — of ELH, of St Juliot's Church and of ELH's grave — bear Hardy's captions.

Hardy's own sketch of a scene from *A Pair of Blue Eyes*, for the second instalment of the first serial publication in *Tinsley's Magazine*, is in the Robert H. Taylor Collection at Princeton; it was enclosed in a letter to William Tinsley of 30 August [1872] (printed *Letters*, I, 18).

Among the Hardy materials at the Dorchester Reference Library is a pencil drawing by Hardy captioned 'Dairymaid about 1870'. Hardy gave this drawing to Vivien Gribble, for her use in preparing the wood engravings for the illustrated edition of *Tess of the d'Urbervilles* (London, 1926) (facsimile printed in *A Catalogue of the Works of Thomas Hardy (1840–1928) in the Dorchester Reference Library*, comp. Charles P. C. Pettit (Dorchester, 1984), p. 79). The Lock Collection, deposited in this same library (and described below), includes a book of drawings annotated 'By Thomas Hardy or his sisters' but apparently mostly the work of Mary Hardy. Of the other four folios containing more than eighty drawings and watercolours — probably mostly by Mary Hardy — in the Lock Collection, only one or two are possibly attributable to Hardy. However, the six architectural drawings of 'Talbothays' on linen are almost certainly Hardy's.

Two of Hardy's responses to questionnaires sent to him have been listed in the entries (HrT 1375.5, 1376), while two others have not. One is the MS copy retained by Hardy of the completed questionnaire which he presumably submitted to the Royal Observatory at Greenwich on [27 November 1881?] requesting permission to visit; the copy in ELH's hand (headed by Hardy) is at the Dorset County Museum and was printed *Letters*, I, 96. Hardy's answers to a questionnaire sent by the United Press about the American Copyright Act of 1891 was acquired by David Holmes after it was sold at Sotheby's in 1974.

A few curious autograph scraps survive which resist being described as 'literary manuscripts' but are nonetheless not without interest. A photocopy of a scrap containing Hardy's signed draft of a statement (fragment of a letter?) congratulating 'members' for using the term 'English' rather than 'British' was lodged at the British Library (RP 1381) when the original was granted an export licence.

The Dorset County Museum collection includes a few miscellaneous autograph scraps which are included on Reel 10 of the Microfilm Edition: Hardy's transcript of an extract from Shelley's will; his note on Keats's grave in Rome; an extract from *The Times*; a note on country remedies. On Reel 6 is a card containing his fair copy of the inscription for the bronze plate on the gate of the Dorset County Hospital — signed by Hardy and dated January 1925.

The passage from Corinthians 1, 14:20 ('Be not children in understanding') is transcribed by Hardy (and signed) on one page now at Texas; the quotation was a favourite which Hardy marked in his Bibles and transcribed in his commonplace book 'Literary Notes II' (HrT 1681). Also at Texas are the copies of Hardy's works into which in 1904 he inscribed, on the front flyleaves, rather interesting notes: a copy of *Jude the Obscure* (London, 1903) bearing the signed note beginning 'The criticisms which this story received...' and dated October 1904; a copy of *The Return of the Native* (London, 1895) bearing the signed note beginning '*Note* 1. The "Quiet woman" Inn is now no longer an inn...' and dated November 1904; and a copy of *Two on a Tower* (London, 1895) bearing the note beginning 'The backgrounds in this novel...' and dated December 1904. All of these notes are printed in *LCUT*, 7 (1962), 8.

A similar copy of *Far from the Madding Crowd* (London, 1895) is at Yale; the note, signed and dated July 1904, begins 'In point of form, this is the best edition...'. A copy of *Life's Little Ironies* (London, 1895) — containing a note, signed and dated September 1904, beginning 'It may be mentioned in connection with one of the following tales...' — has not been located; it was listed in the sale catalogue of Carroll A. Wilson's collection, *Thirteen Author Collections of the Nineteenth Century*, ed. Jean C. S. Wilson and David A. Randall, 2 vols (privately printed, New York, 1950).

Hardy's collection of music books, manuscript and printed, is in the Dorset County Museum archive. The collection includes: a printed book of country dance tunes; Hardy's book of transcripts of the lyrics of country songs compiled c. 1926; Hardy's grandfather's MS music book; Hardy's father's MS book of Christmas carols; a MS book of dance music; and another MS book of Christmas carols, used on the rounds on Christmas Eve at Stinsford, 1820. All of these items are reproduced on Reel 10 of the Microfilm Edition. On Reel 9 is the one other album of miscellaneous materials which contains musical MSS, some possibly in Hardy's hand, including songs from plays as well as old country tunes.

The association materials and documents which make up the remainder of the Dorset County Museum collection are all included in the Microfilm Edition: Hardy's address book (Reel 9); receipts, bills and accounts, as well as a copy of the lease for the Hardy Cottage at Upper Bockhampton (Reel 10); catalogues of the auction sales of the contents of Max Gate (16 February 1938) and of Max Gate itself (6 May 1938) issued by H. Y. Duke & Son, Dorchester (Reel 10). In addition, there are materials of biographical importance, including diaries and manuscripts of both ELH and FEH. Of special interest are two of ELH's diaries (Reel 9) kept during her honeymoon (September–

October 1874) and several European journeys (of 1875, 1876 and 1887); these are published (with some facsimile pages) in *Emma Hardy Diaries*, ed. Richard H. Taylor (Mid-Northumberland Arts Group and Carcanet New Press, 1985). Also in the collection are a few MSS or typescripts of poems, stories and memoirs by both ELH and FEH, some of which contain Hardy's annotations; these are listed in the Marginalia section (HrT 1811, 1812, 1813; see also HrT 1810.5 and 1812.5 for similar items, located elsewhere). Other Hardy-related material at Dorset County Museum is described in the Dramatic Works section (above).

A significant collection of material related to the Hardy family is that of H. E. F. Lock — the son of Henry Lock of the Hardy family's firm of solicitors — now deposited (on permanent loan) in the Dorchester Reference Library. Kenneth Carter has described the history and contents of the collection in 'Thomas Hardy in Dorset County Library' (*Thomas Hardy Society Review*, nos. 6–7 (1980–81), pp. 169–71 and 204–7). The collection includes — as well as the two items listed as entries, HrT 1114 and 1673.5, and the drawings mentioned above — Kate Hardy's MS diaries kept from 1915–39, accounts and receipts regarding the domestic affairs of members of the Hardy family, letters between family members and friends, letters *to* Hardy, photographs, press cuttings, playbills, Hardy family memorabilia and a few books from Hardy's library.

Some documents signed by Hardy dating from 1892–1908 — including the deeds to 51 High West Street, Dorchester — are now deposited in the Dorset Record Office in Dorchester.

The Visitor's Book kept at Max Gate from 2 June 1920 to 10 June 1927 is now in the British library (Add. MS 60396). It records visits by Siegfried Sassoon, Edmund Blunden, E. M. Forster, Virginia and Leonard Woolf, T. E. Lawrence, Robert Graves, J. M. Barrie, John Galsworthy, Max Beerbohm, Gustav Holst, Walter de la Mare, H. G. Wells, Rebecca West, Marie Stopes, etc. The book contains thirty-one surviving pages and evidence that excised pages may have contained manuscript verses — possibly in Hardy's hand.

A volume compiled by Siegfried Sassoon for Hardy's seventy-ninth birthday in 1919 was sold in the Cockerell Sale (1956) and is now in the Huntington Library (HM 39033–87). It includes the autograph poems contributed by the leading poets of the day and the related correspondence between them and Sassoon.

Letters

Hardy's personal correspondence file at Max Gate — including letters to him and drafts or retained copies of his replies — were weeded out during the sorting of papers that accompanied the preparation of *Life*. Much was apparently destroyed. However, the files representing the following years (i.e., the 1920s) presumably survive intact, as Hardy originally kept them, in the Dorset County Museum archive. This archive is the principal repository for letters *to* Hardy. It also includes two especially important series of his own letters — seventy-four to ELH (1885–1911) and 153 to Florence Henniker (1893–1922) — as well as twenty-five letters to his sisters and brother and other family members (1862–1916), the sixty-three letters to Hermann Lea (1899–1924) and the twenty-six letters to Hamo Thornycroft (1904–24).

More than 4,000 surviving letters by Hardy have been collected and published in the seven volumes of *Letters*, the last volume of which was published in 1988. The vast majority of these letters date from the second half of Hardy's life; indeed, only about 150 letters have been traced which Hardy wrote before he was forty years old.

Nearly 100 letters have come to light which were not published in *Letters*; these will be included in a supplementary volume now in preparation.

Hardy's letters are widely dispersed. In addition to the Dorset County Museum, some of the major repositories (holding fifty or more letters) are: Texas (including letters to Robert Pearce Edgcumbe (1888–1927), Frederic Harrison (1892–1922), Sir Henry Newbolt (1902–27), St John Ervine (1921–7) and Newman Flower (1897–1927)); Harvard (including letters to William and Alice Rothenstein (1897–1920)); National Library of Scotland (including letters to George Smith (1869–87), William Blackwood (1877–1901) and Sir George Douglas (1887–1924)); Eton College (including letters to Siegfried Sassoon (1917–1925); University of Leeds (including 80 letters to Edmund Gosse (1886–1927), about 50 to Edward Clodd (1895–1923) and 14 to Clement Shorter (1893–1916)); British Library (including letters to Macmillan & Co. (1868–1927, Add. MS 54923–5), 32 letters to Edmund Gosse in the Ashley Collection (1882–1927), 37 to Edward Clodd in the Ashley Collection (1891–1927), 20 to William Archer (1892–1909, Add. MS 45292), correspondence with G. Herbert Thring of the Society of Authors (1909–27, Add. MS 56721) and 16 to Rutland Boughton (1923–6, Add. MS 52364)); Yale (including letters to John Drinkwater (1909–26)); the Berg Collection (including letters to Clement

Shorter (1894–1918), J. H. Morgan (1916–26) and John Middleton Murray (1919–24)); New York University; Bodleian Library (including 23 letters to Oxford University Press, 1907–8 (MS. Eng. lett. e. 1); Princeton; the Robert H. Taylor Collection at Princeton (including letters to William Tinsley (1871–5), Sydney Cockerell (1912–25), J. C. Squire (1919–25)); and Colby College (including letters to Rebekah Owen, 1897–1912).

The two large private collections of R. L. Purdy and F. B. Adams also contain a great many Hardy letters. Among the over 300 letters owned by Adams are some fifty to Edmund Gosse (1883–1927), and series of letters to Clive Holland (1897–1923) and Sydney Cockerell (1911–27). Purdy's collection (destined for Yale) — containing almost 400 letters — includes series of letters to Mary, Lady Jeune (later Lady St Helier) (1886–1923), Agnes, Lady Grove (1895–1922), Dorothy Allhusen (1892–1927) and most of the surviving letters to FEH, written both before and after her marriage to Hardy (1905–24).

ABBREVIATIONS

For general abbreviations, see the list at the front of this volume.

Björk
 The Literary Notebooks of Thomas Hardy, ed. Lennart A. Björk, 2 vols (London, 1985).
A Changed Man
 Thomas Hardy, *A Changed Man. The Waiting Supper. And Other Tales* (London, 1913).
Cockerell Sale
 Sotheby's, 29–30 October 1956.
Collected Poems (1923)
 For Hardy's revised copy of *Collected Poems of Thomas Hardy*, 2nd ed (London, 1923) (also known as *DCM3*), see INTRODUCTION.
DCM1, *DCM2*, *DCM3*, *DCM4*
 See the descriptions of DCM Wessex Edition, *Selected Poems* (1916), *Collected Poems* (1923) and *Selected Poems* (1917), respectively, in the INTRODUCTION.
DCM Wessex Edition
 For Hardy's revised copy of the Wessex Edition (Verse Vols I and III also known as *DCM1*), see INTRODUCTION.
The Dynasts
 Thomas Hardy, *The Dynasts* (London, 1910).
ELH
 Emma Lavinia Hardy (née Gifford).
Early Life
 Florence Emily Hardy, *The Early Life of Thomas Hardy 1840–1891* (London, 1928).
FEH
 Florence Emily Hardy (née Dugdale).
Gibson
 The Variorum Edition of the Complete Poems of Thomas Hardy, ed. James Gibson (London, 1979).
Grolier Catalogue
 A Descriptive Catalogue of the Grolier Club Centenary Exhibition 1940 of the Works of Thomas Hardy, O.M. 1840–1928, Colby College Monograph No. 9 (Waterville, ME, 1940).
Hardy Players Collection
 'A Catalogue of Unique Hardy Items Offered for Sale by Stevens Cox, Toucan Press, Mt Durand, St Peter Port, Guernsey, via Britain' reprinted in *The Thomas Hardy Year Book*, No. 3 (1972–3), pp. 101–9.
Hollings Catalogue
 Modern Times...with a Preliminary Supplement of Books from the Library of Thomas Hardy, Frank Hollings Sale Catalogue (7 Great Turnstile, London WC1), No. 212 (n.d.).
HS Proof
 For corrected proof of *Human Shows*, see INTRODUCTION.
Human Shows
 Thomas Hardy, *Human Shows. Far Phantasies. Songs, and Trifles* (London, 1925).
Hynes
 The Complete Poetical Works of Thomas Hardy, ed. Samuel Hynes (Oxford, 1982–) (Vols I–III published to date).
Late Lyrics
 Thomas Hardy, *Late Lyrics and Earlier with Many Other Verses* (London, 1922).
Later Years
 Florence Emily Hardy, *The Later Years of Thomas Hardy 1892–1928* (London, 1930).
Letters
 The Collected Letters of Thomas Hardy, ed. Richard Little Purdy and Michael Millgate, 7 vols (Oxford, 1978–88).
Life
 Florence Emily Hardy, *The Life of Thomas Hardy 1840–1928* (London, 1962).
Life and Work
 Thomas Hardy, *The Life and Work of Thomas Hardy*, ed. Michael Millgate (London, 1984).

Life's Little Ironies
Thomas Hardy, *Life's Little Ironies. A Set of Tales with Some Colloquial Sketches Entitled A Few Crusted Characters* (London, 1894).
Life's Little Ironies Proof
For corrected proof of *Life's Little Ironies*, see INTRODUCTION.
Microfilm Edition
The Original Manuscripts and Papers of Thomas Hardy, 18 reels (EP Microform, Yorkshire, 1975).
Millgate
Michael Millgate, *Thomas Hardy. A Biography* (New York, 1982; Oxford, 1982).
Millgate, *Career*
Michael Millgate, *Thomas Hardy. His Career as a Novelist* (London, 1971).
Moments of Vision
Thomas Hardy, *Moments of Vision and Miscellaneous Verses* (London, 1917).
MS Group of Noble Dames
For this MS volume, see INTRODUCTION.
MS Human Shows
For this MS volume, see INTRODUCTION.
MS Late Lyrics
For this MS volume, see INTRODUCTION.
MS Moments of Vision
For this MS volume, see INTRODUCTION.
MS Poems of the Past and the Present
For this MS volume, see INTRODUCTION.
MS Satires of Circumstance
For this MS volume, see INTRODUCTION.
MS Time's Laughingstocks
For this MS volume, see INTRODUCTION.
MS Wessex Poems
For this MS volume, see INTRODUCTION.
MS Winter Words
For this MS volume, see INTRODUCTION.
Orel
Thomas Hardy's Personal Writings, ed. Harold Orel (London and Melbourne, 1967).
Pinion
The Stories of Thomas Hardy, ed. F. B. Pinion, New Wessex Edition, 3 vols (London, 1977).
Poems of the Past and the Present
Thomas Hardy, *Poems of the Past and the Present* (London and New York, 1902).
Purdy
Richard Little Purdy, *Thomas Hardy. A Bibliographical Study* (London, 1954; reprinted with corrections 1968, 1978, 1979).
Riverside Collection
Collection of papers of A. H. Evans and T. H. Tilley (directors of the Hardy Players) purchased by University of California at Riverside in 1972; see *Hardy Players Collection*.
Rutland
W. R. Rutland, *Thomas Hardy. A Study of His Writings and Their Background* (Oxford, 1938).
Satires of Circumstance
Thomas Hardy, *Satires of Circumstance; Lyrics and Reveries; with Miscellaneous Pieces* (London, 1914).
Selected Poems (1916)
For Hardy's revised copy of *Selected Poems of Thomas Hardy* (London, 1916) (also known as *DCM2*), see INTRODUCTION.
Selected Poems (1917)
For Hardy's revised copy of *Selected Poems of Thomas Hardy* (London, 1917) (also known as *DCM4*), see INTRODUCTION.
Taylor
The Personal Notebooks of Thomas Hardy, ed. Richard H. Taylor (London, 1978).
Time's Laughingstocks
Thomas Hardy, *Time's Laughingstocks and Other Verses* (London, 1909).
Wessex Edition
The Works of Thomas Hardy in Verse and Prose, 24 vols (London, 1912–31).
Wessex Poems
Thomas Hardy, *Wessex Poems and Other Verses* (London and New York, 1898).
Wessex Tales
Thomas Hardy, *Wessex Tales. Strange, Lively, and Commonplace*, 2 vols (London and New York, 1888).
Winter Words
Thomas Hardy, *Winter Words in Various Moods and Metres* (London, 1928).
Wreden Catalogue
A Selection of Books from the Library of Thomas Hardy, O.M., William Wreden Sale Catalogue No. 11 (Burlingame, CA, 1938).
Wright
Walter F. Wright, *The Shaping of The Dynasts* (Lincoln, Nebraska, 1967).

ARRANGEMENT

Verse	HrT 1–1373
Prose	HrT 1374–1606
Dramatic Works	HrT 1607–71
Diaries and Notebooks	HrT 1672–93
Marginalia in Printed Books and Manuscripts	HrT 1694–1984

Thomas Hardy

VERSE

The Abbey Mason ('The new-vamped Abbey shaped apace')
First pub. *Harper's Monthly Magazine*, December 1912; collected *Satires of Circumstance* (1914); Gibson, pp. 403–11; Hynes, II, 124–33.

HrT 1 Fair copy, signed, 13 numbered leaves (rectos only); dated December 1911, written before March 1912, watermarked 1906.

Facsimile of pp. 12–13 in *British Literary Manuscripts*, plate 96.

Pierpont Morgan, MA 821.

HrT 2 Fair copy, revised, in MS Satires of Circumstance (pp. 168–77).

Dorset County Museum.

HrT 3 Fair copy of title and subtitle, sent as a proof correction, on a scrap headed 'Omitted corrections to Wessex Edition — Verse Vol IV.' (containing also a correction to 'In the Days of Crinoline').

Not mentioned Hynes.

National Library of Scotland, R. & R. Clark Papers, Dep. 229/292 (on deposit).

Aberdeen ('I looked and thought, "All is too gray and cold')
First pub. *Alma Mater* (Aberdeen University Magazine), September 1906; collected *Time's Laughingstocks* (1906); Gibson, p. 297; Hynes, I, 357–8.

HrT 4 Fair copy, here entitled 'Aberdeen, April 1905' and beginning 'I looked, and thought, "She is too gray and cold', as sent for publication in *Alma Mater* with a covering letter to Theodore Watt, Dorchester, 30 July 1906.

Letter printed *Letters*, III, 220.

University of Aberdeen, MS 593.

HrT 5 Fair copy, here beginning 'I looked & thought, "She is too gray and cold', in MS Time's Laughingstocks (f. 139).

Fitzwilliam Museum.

The Absolute Explains ('"O no," said It: "her lifedoings')
First pub. *Nineteenth Century and After*, February 1925; revised and collected *Human Shows* (1925); Gibson, pp. 754–7; Hynes, III, 68–72.

HrT 6 Fair copy, revised, in MS Human Shows (ff. 79–82, rectos only); dated 'New Year's Eve: 1922.'.

Yale.

HrT 7 Correction to line 1 in HS Proof (p. 115).

Dorset County Museum.

'According to the Mighty Working' ('When moiling seems at cease')
First pub. *The Athenaeum*, 4 April 1919; collected *Late Lyrics* (1922); Gibson, p. 571; Hynes, II, 336.

HrT 8 Fair copy, revised, in MS Late Lyrics (f. 13); dated 1917.

Dorset County Museum.

HrT 9 Typescript, here originally entitled '<Transmutation>' and beginning 'When moiling seems to cease', one page, annotated by printer 'To fill page under Contents.', dated 1917; together with 2 copies of a page proof for the first publication, one revised and annotated by Hardy '[*revised proof*]' and '[Press when corrected.]', dated 1917.

Berg.

The Aërolite ('I thought a germ of Consciousness')
First pub. *Human Shows* (1925); Gibson, pp. 769–70; Hynes, III, 86–7.

HrT 10 Fair copy, revised, in MS Human Shows (ff. 101–2, rectos only).

Yale.

HrT 11 Revisions to lines 17, 19–20 in HS Proof (p. 145).

Dorset County Museum.

After a Journey ('Hereto I come to view a voiceless ghost')

First pub. *Satires of Circumstance* (1914), beginning 'Hereto I come to interview a ghost'; Gibson, p. 349; Hynes, II, 59–60.

HrT 12 Fair copy, here beginning 'Hereto I come to interview a ghost', in MS Satires of Circumstance (pp. 87–8), subscribed 'Pentargan Bay'.

Dorset County Museum.

HrT 13 Revised first line in *Selected Poems* (1916), p. 67.

Dorset County Museum.

HrT 14 Revisions to lines 1 and 12 in *Selected Poems* (1917), p. 67.

Dorset County Museum.

After a Romantic Day ('The railway bore him through')
First pub. *Late Lyrics* (1922); Gibson, p. 641; Hynes, II, 417–18.

HrT 15 Fair copy, revised, including a cancelled epigraph, in MS Late Lyrics (f. 111).

Dorset County Museum.

After Reading Psalms XXXIX., XL., etc. ('Simple was I and was young')
First pub. *Late Lyrics* (1922); Gibson, pp. 697–8; Hynes, II, 484–5.

HrT 16 Fair copy, revised, in MS Late Lyrics (f. 192); dated '187–'.

Dorset County Museum.

After Schiller ('Knight, a true sister-love')
First pub. *Poems of the Past and the Present* (1902); Gibson, p. 182; Hynes, I, 223.

HrT 17 Draft, signed (initials), written beside Hardy's transcription of the first stanza of Schiller's original German in 'Literary Notes II' (HrT 1681) (f. 3v); c. 1889.

This MS printed Hynes, I, 377 and Björk, II, 7.

Dorset County Museum.

HrT 17.5 Written between the lines of Schiller's original, in Hardy's copy of Sonnenschein and Stallybrass's *German for the English* (see HrT 1940.5).

Mentioned Purdy, p. 117.

Owned (1989) R. L. Purdy; destined for Yale.

HrT 18 Fair copy, in MS Poems of the Past and the Present.

Bodleian, MS Eng. poet. d. 18, f. 150.

After the Burial ('The family had buried him')
First pub. *Winter Words* (1928); Gibson, p. 876; Hynes, III, 213.

HrT 19 Fair copy, revised, signed, one page.

Microfilm Edition, Reel 5.

Dorset County Museum.

HrT 20 Fair copy, revised, in MS Winter Words.

Queen's College, Oxford, MS 420, f. 61.

After the Club-Dance ('Black'on frowns east on Maidon')
First pub. *Time's Laughingstocks* (1909), as 'At Casterbridge Fair. III.'; Gibson, p. 240; Hynes, I, 292.

HrT 21 Fair copy, headed 'III', in MS Time's Laughingstocks (f. 65).

Fitzwilliam Museum.

After the Death of a Friend ('You died, and made but little of it! —')
First pub. *Daily Telegraph*, 10 July 1928; collected *Winter Words* (1928); Gibson, pp. 861–2; Hynes, III, 196.

HrT 22 Fair copy, revised, in MS Winter Words.

Queen's College, Oxford, MS 420, f. 40.

After the Fair ('The singers are gone from the Cornmarket-place')
First pub. *Time's Laughingstocks* (1909), as 'At Casterbridge Fair. VII.'; Gibson, pp. 242–3; Hynes, I, 294–5.

HrT 23 Fair copy, revised, headed 'VII.', in MS Time's Laughingstocks (f. 68); dated 1902.

Fitzwilliam Museum.

After the Last Breath ('There's no more to be done, or feared, or hoped')
First pub. *Time's Laughingstocks* (1909); Gibson, p. 270; Hynes, I, 326–7.

HrT 24 Fair copy, revised, in MS Time's Laughingstocks (f. 101); dated 190[4].

Fitzwilliam Museum.

After the Visit ('Come again to the place')
First pub. *The Spectator*, 13 August 1910; collected *Satires of Circumstance* (1914); Gibson, pp. 309–10; Hynes, II, 14–15.

HrT 25 Fair copy, revised, in MS Satires of Circumstance (pp. 10–11).

Dorset County Museum.

HrT 26 Fair copy of first publication version, signed, 2 leaves (rectos only), inscribed to Florence Emily Dugdale.

Owned (1984) R. L. Purdy (see Hynes); destined for Yale.

After the War ('Last Post sounded')
First pub. *Late Lyrics* (1922); Gibson, pp. 631–2; Hynes, II, 405.

HrT 27 Fair copy, revised, in MS Late Lyrics (f. 99).

Dorset County Museum.

Afternoon Service at Mellstock ('On afternoons of drowsy calm')
First pub. *Moments of Vision* (1917); Gibson, p. 429; Hynes, II, 161–2.

HrT 28 Fair copy, revised, in MS Moments of Vision (f. 5).

Magdalene College, Cambridge.

Afterwards ('When the Present has latched its postern behind my tremulous stay')
First pub. *Moments of Vision* (1917); Gibson, p. 553; Hynes, II, 308–9.

HrT 29 Fair copy, revised, here beginning 'When night has closed its shutters on my dismantled day', in MS Moments of Vision (f. 199).

Magdalene College, Cambridge.

The Aged Newspaper Soliloquizes ('Yes; yes; I am old. In me appears')
First pub. *The Observer*, 14 March 1926, as 'The Newspaper Soliloquizes'; collected *Winter Words* (1928); Gibson, p. 913; Hynes, III, 256.

HrT 30 Fair copy, revised, signed, in MS Winter Words, annotated '[*Published in Observer 1926.*]' and '*Omit*'.

Facsimile in *New York Times*, 11 April 1926.

Queen's College, Oxford, MS 420, f. 116.

The Ageing House ('When the walls were red')
First pub. *Moments of Vision* (1917); Gibson, p. 491; Hynes, II, 233–4.

HrT 31 Fair copy, in MS Moments of Vision (f. 104).

Magdalene College, Cambridge.

'Ah, are you digging on my grave?' ('"Ah, are you digging on my grave')
First pub. *Saturday Review*, 27 September 1913; collected *Satires of Circumstance* (1914); Gibson, pp. 330–1; Hynes, II, 38–9.

HrT 32 Fair copy, revised, in MS Satires of Circumstance (pp. 43–4).

Dorset County Museum.

The Alarm ('In a ferny byway')
First pub. *Wessex Poems* (1898); Gibson, pp. 35–9; Hynes, I, 46–51.

HrT 33 Fair copy, revised, here subtitled '(1804)/*vide* "The Trumpet Major"', in MS Wessex Poems (ff. 43–7).

Birmingham City Museum and Art Gallery.

Albuera ('They come, beset by riddling hail'), see HrT 1617.

Alike and Unlike ('We watched the selfsame scene on that long drive')
First pub. *Human Shows* (1925); Gibson, pp. 788–9; Hynes, III, 108.

HrT 34 Fair copy, revised, in MS Human Shows (f. 133).

Yale.

Amabel ('I marked her ruined hues')
First pub. *Wessex Poems* (1898); Gibson, pp. 8–9; Hynes, I, 8–9.

HrT 35 Fair copy, revised, in MS Wessex Poems (f. 3); dated 1866.

Birmingham City Museum and Art Gallery.

HrT 36 Revision of date (to 1865) in *Selected Poems* (1917), p. 83.

Dorset County Museum.

An Ancient to Ancients ('Where once we danced, where once we sang')
First pub. *Century Magazine*, May 1922; collected *Late Lyrics* (1922); Gibson, pp. 695–7; Hynes, II, 481–4.

HrT 37 Fair copy, revised, in MS Late Lyrics (ff. 189–91).

Dorset County Museum.

HrT 38 Corrected galley proof for the first publication, one leaf.

Texas.

'And There was a Great Calm' ('There had been years of Passion — scorching, cold')
First pub. *The Times*, 11 November 1920; reprinted separately by FEH in a privately printed pamphlet (1920); collected *Late Lyrics* (1922); Gibson, pp. 588–90; Hynes, II, 355–7.

HrT 39 Fair copy, revised, of the earliest version, here subtitled 'Nov. 11. 1918.', 2 leaves (rectos only), signed; watermarked 1914.

Facsimiles in *Ashley Library*, II, following p. 176, and Sotheby's sale catalogue, 22–3 June 1959 (Bliss Sale), p. 61.

Texas.

HrT 40 Fair copy, revised, in MS Late Lyrics (ff. 40–1).

Dorset County Museum.

HrT 41 Corrected typescript, here beginning 'There had been years of Passion — caustic, cold', signed, 3 leaves (rectos only), printer's copy for FEH's pamphlet.

Cockerell Sale, Lot 281, sold to Alan G. Thomas.

Yale.

HrT 42 Slightly corrected proof for FEH's pamphlet, annotated 'Press'; dated 16 December 1920.

Cockerell Sale, Lot 281, sold to Alan G. Thomas.

Yale.

An Anniversary ('It was at the very date to which we have come')
First pub. *Moments of Vision* (1917); Gibson, pp. 470–1; Hynes, II, 209–10. The proof correction to line 13 for the Wessex Edition printed in Hynes, II, 499 appears on the list of corrections sent to R. & R. Clark (now on deposit in the National Library of Scotland) described in the INTRODUCTION.

HrT 43 Fair copy, revised, in MS Moments of Vision (f. 69).

Magdalene College, Cambridge.

HrT 44 [entry deleted]

The Announcement ('They came, the brothers, and took two chairs')
First pub. *Moments of Vision* (1917); Gibson, p. 467; Hynes, II, 205–6.

HrT 45 Fair copy, revised, subtitled (cancelled) '(January 1879)', in MS Moments of Vision (f. 64).

Magdalene College, Cambridge.

'Any little old song' ('Any little old song')
First pub. *Human Shows* (1925); Gibson, p. 702; Hynes, III, 8.

HrT 46 Fair copy, in MS Human Shows (f. 3).

Yale.

HrT 47 Fair copy, one page numbered 3.

Microfilm Edition, Reel 5.

Dorset County Museum.

Apostrophe to an Old Psalm Tune ('I met you first — ah, when did I first meet you?')
First pub. *Moments of Vision* (1917); Gibson, pp. 431–2; Hynes, II, 163–4.

HrT 48 Fair copy, revised, in MS Moments of Vision (ff. 8–9); dated 13 August 1916.

Magdalene College, Cambridge.

An Appeal to America on Behalf of the Belgian Destitute ('Seven millions stand')
First pub. *New York Times*, 4 January 1915, as 'An Appeal to America'; collected *Moments of Vision* (1917); Gibson, p. 541; Hynes, II, 293.

HrT 49 Fair copy, revised, in MS Moments of Vision (f. 182); dated December 1914.

Magdalene College, Cambridge.

HrT 50 Typescript, one page, together with a typescript of 'Before Marching and After' (HrT 131) meant for use in FEH's pamphlet *A Call to National Service* (privately printed, London, 1917); December 1914.

New York University.

Aquae Sulis ('The chimes called midnight, just at interlune')
First pub. *Satires of Circumstance* (1914); Gibson, pp. 376–7; Hynes, II, 90–2.

HrT 51 Fair copy, in MS Satires of Circumstance (pp. 125–6), subscribed 'Bath'.

Dorset County Museum.

HrT 52 Fair copy of lines 1–12, 29–32, subscribed 'Bath.' and 'Thomas Hardy'.

This MS not mentioned Hynes or Gibson.

Bath Reference Library, MS 1606.

Architectural Masks ('There is a house with ivied walls')
First pub. *Poems of the Past and the Present* (1902); Gibson, pp. 160–1; Hynes, I, 199–200.

HrT 53 Fair copy, revised, in MS Poems of the Past and the Present.

Bodleian, MS Eng. poet. d. 18, f. 117.

Aristodemus the Messenian ('Straightway let it be done!')
First pub. *Winter Words* (1928); Gibson, pp. 848–53; Hynes, III, 181–6.

HrT 54 Fair copy, revised, in MS Winter Words.

Queen's College, Oxford, MS 420, ff. 22–7 (rectos only).

'As 'twere to-night' ('As 'twere to-night, in the brief space')
First pub. *Late Lyrics* (1922); Gibson, p. 582; Hynes, II, 348.

HrT 55 Fair copy, revised, in MS Late Lyrics (f. 31).

Dorset County Museum.

At a Bridal ('When you paced forth, to await maternity')
First pub. *Wessex Poems* (1898); Gibson, p. 10; Hynes, I, 11.

HrT 56 Fair copy, revised, in MS Wessex Poems (f. 6); dated 1866.

Birmingham City Museum and Art Gallery.

HrT 57 Addition in pencil of '8 Adelphi Terrace' to date in DCM Wessex Edition (Verse Vol. I, 8).

Dorset County Museum.

At a Country Fair ('At a bygone Western country fair')
First pub. *Moments of Vision* (1917); Gibson, p. 504; Hynes, II, 249–50.

HrT 58 Fair copy, revised, in MS Moments of Vision (f. 127).

Magdalene College, Cambridge.

At a Fashionable Dinner ('We sat with the banqueting-party')
First pub. *Human Shows* (1925); Gibson, pp. 711–12; Hynes, III, 18–19.

HrT 59 Fair copy, revised, in MS Human Shows (f. 17).

Yale.

HrT 60 Revisions and suggested revisions to line 7 in HS Proof (p. 24).

Dorset County Museum.

At a Hasty Wedding ('If hours be years the twain are blest')
First pub. *The Sphere*, 21 April 1900, in the story 'A Changed Man'; collected separately *Poems of the Past and the Present* (1902); Gibson, p. 142; Hynes, I, 179.

HrT 60.5 Fair copy, revised, on f. 7 of the MS of 'A Changed Man' (HrT 1384).

Berg.

HrT 61 Fair copy, in MS Poems of the Past and the Present.

Bodleian, MS Eng. poet. d. 18, f. 87.

At a House in Hampstead ('O Poet, come you haunting here')
First pub. *The John Keats Memorial Volume*, [ed. Dr G. Williamson] (London and New York, 23 February 1921); collected *Late Lyrics* (1922); Gibson, pp. 574–5; Hynes, II, 340–41.

HrT 62 Fair copy, revised, signed, 2 leaves; dated July 1920.

Facsimile in *Ashley Library*, II, following p. 176 and *Victorian and Later English Poets*, ed. James Stephens, Edwin L. Beck and Royall H. Snow (New York, 1934), p. 921.

British Library, Ashley MS 3351.

HrT 63 Fair copy, revised, in MS Late Lyrics (ff. 19–20); dated July 1920.

Dorset County Museum.

HrT 64 Fair copy, transcribed for the opening of Keats House, London, signed, 2 pages (onc leaf); dated July 1920, transcribed 1925.

Keats House, London, KH 209.

HrT 64.3 Typescript, subtitled by Hardy, 2 leaves (rectos only), enclosed in a letter to Dr G. Williamson (for the first publication), 28 July 1920.

The letter is unpublished.

Princeton, General MSS [Bound], Keats Memorial Volume (oversize).

HrT 64.5 Corrected galley proof for the first publication, in Dr G. Williamson's interleaved copy.

Princeton, General MSS [Bound], Keats Memorial Volume.

At a Lunar Eclipse ('Thy shadow, Earth, from Pole to Central Sea')
First pub. *Poems of the Past and the Present* (1902); Gibson, p. 116; Hynes, I, 149–50.

HrT 65 Fair copy, revised, in MS Poems of the Past and the Present.

Facsimile in Rutland, facing p. 76.

Bodleian, MS Eng. poet. d. 18, f. 48.

At a Pause in a Country Dance ('They stood at the foot of the figure')
First pub. *Human Shows* (1925); Gibson, p. 779; Hynes, III, 97–8.

HrT 66 Fair copy, revised, in MS Human Shows (ff. 117–18, rectos only).

Yale.

HrT 67 Correction to line 13, revisions to lines 16–18 and the addition of line 15 in HS Proof (pp. 167–8).

Dorset County Museum.

HrT 68 Two corrections, sent in a note, headed '"Human Shows"', to R. & R. Clark, Max Gate, 9 December 1925.

This MS printed *Letters*, VI, 371; not mentioned Hynes or Gibson.

Owned (1987) R. L. Purdy (see *Letters*); destined for Yale.

At a Rehearsal of One of J. M. B.'s Plays, see HrT 853.

At a Seaside Town in 1869 ('I went and stood outside myself')

First pub. *Moments of Vision* (1917); Gibson, pp. 499–501; Hynes, II, 244–6.

HrT 69 Fair copy, revised, here entitled 'At a Seaside Town, 1869', in MS Moments of Vision (f. 120).

Magdalene College, Cambridge.

At a Watering-Place ('They sit and smoke on the esplanade'), see HrT 1007.

At an Inn ('When we as strangers sought')
First pub. *Wessex Poems* (1898); Gibson, pp. 68–9; Hynes, I, 89–90.

HrT 70 Fair copy, revised, in MS Wessex Poems (ff. 87–8).

Birmingham City Museum and Art Gallery.

HrT 71 Correction to line 20 in *Selected Poems* (1917), p. 34.

Dorset County Museum.

At Casterbridge Fair, see HrT 21, 23, 112–13, 391, 620, 737–8, 1330.

At Castle Boterel ('As I drive to the junction of lane and highway')
First pub. *Satires of Circumstance* (1914); Gibson, pp. 351–2; Hynes, II, 63–4.

HrT 72 Fair copy, revised, in MS Satires of Circumstance (pp. 91–2); dated March 1913 and 'Boscastle: Cornwall' (deleted).

Dorset County Museum.

At Day-Close in November ('The ten hours' light is abating')
First pub. *Satires of Circumstance* (1914); Gibson, p. 334; Hynes, II, 43–4.

HrT 73 Fair copy, revised, the title altered from 'Autumn Evening', in MS Satires of Circumstance (p. 61).

Dorset County Museum.

At Lulworth Cove a Century Back ('Had I but lived a hundred years ago')
First pub. *Late Lyrics* (1922); Gibson, p. 602; Hynes, II, 371.

HrT 74 Fair copy, revised, in MS Late Lyrics (f. 59); dated September 1920.

Dorset County Museum.

At Madame Tussaud's in Victorian Years ('"That same first fiddler who leads the orchéstra to-night')
First pub. *Moments of Vision* (1917); Gibson, p. 492; Hynes, II, 235.

HrT 75 Fair copy, revised, the title altered from 'At Madame Tussaud's and later' to 'At Madame Tussaud's in Victorian Times', in MS Moments of Vision (f. 106).

Magdalene College, Cambridge.

At Mayfair Lodgings ('How could I be aware')
First pub. *Moments of Vision* (1917); Gibson, pp. 450–1; Hynes, II, 185–6.

HrT 76 Fair copy, revised, the title altered from 'At Lodgings in London', in MS Moments of Vision (f. 36).

Magdalene College, Cambridge.

At Middle-Field Gate in February ('The bars are thick with drops that show')
First pub. *Moments of Vision* (1917); Gibson, p. 480; Hynes, II, 220–1.

HrT 77 Fair copy, revised, the title altered from 'At Middle-Hill Gate in February', in MS Moments of Vision (f. 85).

Magdalene College, Cambridge.

At Moonrise and Onwards ('I thought you a fire')
First pub. *Late Lyrics* (1922); Gibson, pp. 566–7; Hynes, II, 330.

HrT 78 Fair copy, revised, in MS Late Lyrics (f. 6).

Dorset County Museum.

At Rushy-Pond ('On the frigid face of the heath-hemmed pond')

First pub. *Human Shows* (1925); Gibson, pp. 713–14; Hynes, III, 21–2.

HrT 79 Fair copy, revised, in MS Human Shows (f. 20).

Yale.

At Shag's Heath ('I grieve and grieve for what I have done')
First pub. *Human Shows* (1925); Gibson, pp. 750–2; Hynes, III, 64–6.

HrT 80 Fair copy, revised, in MS Human Shows (ff. 74–6, rectos only).

Yale.

HrT 81 Correction in HS Proof (p. 110).

Dorset County Museum.

At Tea ('The kettle descants in a cosy drone'), see HrT 1007.

At the Altar-Rail ('"My bride is not coming, alas!" says the groom'), see HrT 1007.

At the Aquatic Sports ('With their backs to the sea two fiddlers stand')
First pub. *Human Shows* (1925); Gibson, pp. 784–5; Hynes, III, 104.

HrT 82 Fair copy, revised, in MS Human Shows (f. 126).

Yale.

At the Dinner-Table ('I sat at dinner in my prime')
First pub. *Late Lyrics* (1922); Gibson, pp. 654–5; Hynes, II, 432–3.

HrT 83 Fair copy, revised, in MS Late Lyrics (f. 132).

Dorset County Museum.

At the Draper's ('I stood at the back of the shop, my dear'), see HrT 1007.

At the Entering of the New Year ('Our songs went up and out the chimney')
First pub. *The Athenaeum*, 31 December 1920; collected *Late Lyrics* (1922); Gibson, pp. 639–40; Hynes, II, 415–16.

HrT 84 Fair copy, revised, in MS Late Lyrics (ff. 108–9); dated '31 December. During the War' (altered from 'Dec. 1917 or 1918').

Dorset County Museum.

HrT 85 Four successive corrected proofs for the first publication, the first a galley proof (dated 16 December 1920 and annotated 'Proof: The Athenaeum'), the second a first page proof (dated 20 December 1920) and two copies of a revise page proof, the second annotated 'Press' (dated 24 December 1920).

Berg.

At the Mill ('O Miller Knox, whom we knew well')
First pub. *Human Shows* (1925); Gibson, pp. 787–8; Hynes, III, 107–8.

HrT 86 Fair copy, revised, in MS Human Shows (f. 132).

Yale.

At the Piano ('A woman was playing')
First pub. *Moments of Vision* (1917); Gibson, pp. 529–30; Hynes, II, 279.

HrT 87 Fair copy, revised, in MS Moments of Vision (f. 163).

Magdalene College, Cambridge.

At the Pyramid of Cestius Near the Graves of Shelley and Keats, see HrT 988–90.

At the Railway Station, Upway ('"There is not much that I can do')
First pub. *Late Lyrics* (1922); Gibson, p. 607; Hynes, II, 377.

HrT 88 Fair copy, in MS Late Lyrics (f. 67).

Dorset County Museum.

At the Royal Academy ('These summer landscapes — clump, and copse, and croft —')

First pub. *Late Lyrics* (1922); Gibson, pp. 627–8; Hynes, II, 400–401.

HrT 89 Fair copy, revised, in MS Late Lyrics (f. 92).

Dorset County Museum.

At the War Office, London ('Last year I called this world of gaingivings')
First pub. (facsimile) *The Sphere*, 27 January 1900, as 'At the War Office After a Bloody Battle'; collected *Poems of the Past and the Present* (1902); Gibson, pp. 89–90; Hynes, I, 120–1.

HrT 90 Fair copy, signed, here entitled 'At the War Office/ After a Bloody Battle', one page.

For facsimile, see first publication.

Texas.

HrT 91 Fair copy, in MS Poems of the Past and the Present.

Bodleian, MS Eng. poet. d. 18, f. 8.

At the Wicket-Gate ('There floated the sounds of church-chiming')
First pub. *Moments of Vision* (1917); Gibson, p. 430; Hynes, II, 162.

HrT 92 Fair copy, revised, in MS Moments of Vision (f. 6).

Magdalene College, Cambridge.

At the Word 'Farewell' ('She looked like a bird from a cloud')
First pub. *Selected Poems* (1916); collected *Moments of Vision* (1917); Gibson, pp. 432–3; Hynes, II, 164–5.

HrT 93 Fair copy, revised, in MS Moments of Vision (f. 10); dated 1913 (cancelled).

Magdalene College, Cambridge.

HrT 94 Corrections to lines 3, 16, 20, 25 and 27 and revisions to line 16 in *Selected Poems* (1917), pp. 18–19.

Dorset County Museum.

At Waking ('When night was lifting')
First pub. *Time's Laughingstocks* (1909); Gibson, p. 224; Hynes, I, 274.

HrT 95 Fair copy, revised, in MS Time's Laughingstocks (f. 47); dated Weymouth, 1869.

Fitzwilliam Museum.

At Wynyard's Gap ('The hounds pass here?')
First pub. *Human Shows* (1925); Gibson, pp. 745–50; Hynes, III, 58–64.

HrT 96 Fair copy, revised, in MS Human Shows (ff. 68–73, rectos only).

Yale.

HrT 97 Annotations (and a sketch added) in HS Proof (pp. 99–106).

Dorset County Museum.

An August Midnight ('A shaded lamp and a waving blind')
First pub. *Poems of the Past and the Present* (1902); Gibson, pp. 146–7; Hynes, I, 184.

HrT 98 Fair copy, revised, in MS Poems of the Past and the Present; dated Max Gate, 1899.

Bodleian, MS Eng. poet. d. 18, f. 93.

Autumn in King's Hintock Park ('Here by the baring bough')
First pub. *Daily Mail Books' Supplement*, 17 November 1906, as 'Autumn in my Lord's Park'; collected *Time's Laughingstocks* (1909), as 'Autumn in the Park'; Gibson, p. 215; Hynes, I, 264–5.

HrT 99 Fair copy, signed, here entitled 'Autumn in my Lord's Park', one leaf, printer's copy for the first publication; 1901.

University of California at Berkeley.

HrT 100 Fair copy, revised, here entitled 'Autumn in the Park', in MS Time's Laughingstocks (f. 34); dated 1901.

Fitzwilliam Museum.

HrT 101 Addition to title (i.e., 'Autumn in King's Hintock [Melbury] Park') in *Collected Poems* (1923), p. 200.

Dorset County Museum.

HrT 102 Fair copy, as sent to Lady Ilchester with a covering letter of 26 November 1915.

This MS mentioned Purdy, p. 141 as having been presented by Hardy to Lady Ilchester in 1915; Gibson says the MS is untraced and Hynes does not mention it. *Letters*, V, 134 prints the covering letter from a transcript (supplied by Lady Ilchester) owned (1985) R. L. Purdy.

Unlocated.

An Autumn Rain-Scene ('There trudges one to a merrymaking')
First pub. *Fortnightly Review*, 1 December 1921, as 'A December Rain-scene'; collected *Late Lyrics* (1922); Gibson, pp. 612–13; Hynes, II, 382–3.

HrT 103 Fair copy, in MS Late Lyrics (f. 73); dated October 1904.

Dorset County Museum.

HrT 104 Corrected proof for the first publication, enclosed with a letter to Florence Henniker, Max Gate, 19 December 1921.

This letter printed *Letters*, VI, 110–11; proof not mentioned Hynes or Gibson.

Dorset County Museum.

HrT 105 Revision to line 16 in *Collected Poems* (1923), p. 580.

Dorset County Museum.

The Background and the Figure ('I think of the slope where the rabbits fed')
First pub. *Moments of Vision* (1917); Gibson, p. 454; Hynes, II, 190.

HrT 106 Fair copy, in MS Moments of Vision (f. 42).

Magdalene College, Cambridge.

A Backward Spring ('The trees are afraid to put forth buds')
First pub. *Moments of Vision* (1917); Gibson, p. 498; Hynes, II, 243.

HrT 107 Fair copy, in MS Moments of Vision (f. 118); dated April 1917.

Magdalene College, Cambridge.

The Bad Example ('Fie, Aphrodite, shamming you are no mother')
First pub. *Winter Words* (1928); Gibson, p. 839; Hynes, III, 171. For the source epigram from Meleager, see HrT 1804.

HrT 108 Fair copy, revised, in MS Winter Words.

Queen's College, Oxford, MS 420, f. 9.

Bags of Meat ('"Here's a fine bag of meat"')
First pub. *Human Shows* (1925); Gibson, pp. 807–8; Hynes, III, 129–31.

HrT 109 Fair copy, revised, in MS Human Shows (ff. 162–3, rectos only), annotated '<Wimborne.>'.

Yale.

HrT 110 Revisions to lines 16 and 21 in HS Proof (pp. 229–30).

Dorset County Museum.

The Ballad of Love's Skeleton ('"Come, let's to Culliford Hill and Wood')
First pub. *Winter Words* (1928); Gibson, pp. 925–7; Hynes, III, 269–71.

HrT 111 Fair copy, revised, in MS Winter Words.

Queen's College, Oxford, MS 420, ff. 131–2 (rectos only)

The Ballad-Singer ('Sing, Ballad-singer, raise a hearty tune')
First pub. *Cornhill*, April 1902, as 'At Casterbridge Fair'; collected *Time's Laughingstocks* (1909), as 'At Casterbridge Fair. I.'; Gibson, p. 239; Hynes, I, 291.

HrT 111.5 Fair copy of an early version, here entitled 'At Casterbridge Fair.' and beginning 'Raise, Ballad singer, raise a hearty tune!', containing variants, signed, one page, as sent to Smith, Elder & Co. for the first publication.

For a reproduction, see FACSIMILES; this MS not mentioned Gibson or Hynes.

National Library of Scotland, MS 23173, f.197.

HrT 112 Fair copy, revised, headed 'At Casterbridge Fair. I.', in MS Time's Laughingstocks (f. 63); dated 1901 (cancelled).

Fitzwilliam Museum.

HrT 113 Correction to line 11 in *Selected Poems* (1917), p. 27.

Dorset County Museum.

The Ballet ('They crush together — a rustling heap of flesh —')
First pub. *Moments of Vision* (1917); Gibson, pp. 492–3; Hynes, II, 236.

HrT 114 Fair copy, revised, in MS Moments of Vision (f. 107).

Magdalene College, Cambridge.

Barthélémon at Vauxhall ('He said: "Awake my soul, and with the sun,"...')
First pub. *The Times*, 23 July 1921; collected *Late Lyrics* (1922); Gibson, pp. 567–8; Hynes, II, 331–2.

HrT 115 Fair copy, revised, in MS Late Lyrics (f. 8).

Dorset County Museum.

The Beauty ('O do not praise my beauty more')
First pub. *Late Lyrics* (1922); Gibson, pp. 616–17; Hynes, II, 387.

HrT 116 Fair copy, revised, in MS Late Lyrics (f. 77).

Dorset County Museum.

A Beauty's Soliloquy during her Honeymoon ('Too late, too late! I did not know my fairness')
First pub. *Human Shows* (1925); Gibson, pp. 795–6; Hynes, III, 115–16.

HrT 117 Fair copy, revised, in MS Human Shows (ff. 144–5, rectos only); dated 'In a London Hotel: 1892'.

Yale.

The Bedridden Peasant to an Unknowing God ('Much wonder I — here long low-laid —')
Stanzas 4–8 first pub. in a pre-publication review of *Poems of the Past and the Present*, 'Mr Thomas Hardy's New Poems', *The Academy*, 23 November 1901; first pub. in full in *Poems of the Past and the Present* (1902); Gibson, pp. 124–5; Hynes, I, 159–60.

HrT 118 Fair copy, revised, the title altered from 'A Peasant's Philosophy', in MS Poems of the Past and the Present.

Bodleian, MS Eng. poet. d. 18, ff. 62–3 (rectos only).

Beeny Cliff ('O the opal and the sapphire of that wandering western sea')
First pub. *Satires of Circumstance* (1914); Gibson, pp. 350–1; Hynes, II, 62–3.

HrT 119 Fair copy, revised, in MS Satires of Circumstance (p. 90).

Facsimile in Gibson, p. [300].

Dorset County Museum.

HrT 120 Revision to line 15 in *Selected Poems* (1916), p. 70.

Dorset County Museum.

HrT 121 Revision to line 15 in *Selected Poems* (1917), p. 70.

Dorset County Museum.

HrT 122 Revision to line 9 in the hand of Sydney Cockerell, in a copy of *Selected Poems* (1916) (containing also HrT 382, 753) presented to Cockerell by Hardy, October 1916, and annotated by Cockerell on inside front cover 'The corrections...were given me by the author at Max Gate May 25, 1918.'.

Cockerell Sale, Lot 260, sold to Maggs.

Owned (1984) F. B. Adams (see Hynes, II, 491).

Before and after Summer ('Looking forward to the spring')
First pub. *New Weekly*, 4 April 1914; collected *Satires of Circumstance* (1914); Gibson, pp. 333–4; Hynes, II, 43.

HrT 123 Fair copy, revised, in MS Satires of Circumstance (p. 60).

Dorset County Museum.

HrT 124 Typescript, revised by Hardy in line 10, one page numbered 2, dated by Hardy 1910; enclosed (together with HrT 1359) in a letter to R. A. Scott-James (editor of *New Weekly*), 25 January 1914.

This letter printed *Letters*, V, 6 from the original at Texas; typescript not mentioned Hynes or Gibson.

Texas.

HrT 125 Correction to line 3 in *Selected Poems* (1917), p. 14.

Dorset County Museum.

Before Knowledge ('When I walked roseless tracks and wide')
First pub. *Moments of Vision* (1917); Gibson, pp. 445–6; Hynes, II, 180.

HrT 126 Fair copy, revised, in MS Moments of Vision (f. 29).

Magdalene College, Cambridge.

Before Life and After ('A time there was — as one may guess')
First pub. *Time's Laughingstocks* (1909); Gibson, p. 277; Hynes, I, 333.

HrT 127 Fair copy, revised, in MS Time's Laughingstocks (f. 111).

Fitzwilliam Museum.

Before Marching and After ('Orion swung southward aslant')
First pub. *Fortnightly Review*, 1 October 1915; collected *Selected Poems* (1916) and *Moments of Vision* (1917); Gibson, pp. 544–5; Hynes, II, 297–8.

HrT 128 Fair copy, in MS Moments of Vision (f. 187); dated September 1915.

Magdalene College, Cambridge.

HrT 129 Fair copy, revised in lines 2, 6, 7 and 21, one page, signed, annotated '(Original MS.)'; dated 'Sept. 1915', watermarked 1906.

Facsimile in Sotheby's sale catalogue, 20–2 December 1937 (J. M. Barrie sale), p. 16.

Texas.

HrT 130 Fair copy, revised in line 6 only, one page, signed; dated 'Sept: 1915', watermarked 1906.

Texas.

HrT 131 Typescript, one page, together with the typescript of 'An Appeal to America...' (HrT 50), probably meant for use in FEH's pamphlet *A Call to National Service* (privately printed, London, 1917) from which this poem was subsequently omitted, annotated in an unidentified hand 'to come second'; dated September 1915.

Cockerell Sale, Lot 259, sold to Hollings; New York University also owns an uncorrected copy of the second proof of *A Call to National Service* containing this poem and dated by Sydney Cockerell 13 April 1917 (Cockerell Sale, Lot 304, sold to Hollings).

New York University.

HrT 132 [entry deleted]

HrT 133 Corrections and revisions to lines 20–1 in *Selected Poems* (1917), pp. 201–2.

Dorset County Museum.

Before my Friend Arrived ('I sat on the eve-lit weir')
First pub. *Human Shows* (1925); Gibson, pp. 821–2; Hynes, III, 146.

HrT 134 Fair copy, revised, in MS Human Shows (f. 183).

Yale.

HrT 135 Corrections to lines 8 and 16 in HS Proof (p. 260).

Dorset County Museum.

Bereft ('In the black winter morning')
First pub. *Time's Laughingstocks* (1909); Gibson, pp. 206–7; Hynes, I, 263.

HrT 136 Fair copy, in MS Time's Laughingstocks (f. 23); dated 1901.

Fitzwilliam Museum.

Bereft, She Thinks She Dreams ('I dream that the dearest I ever knew')

First pub. *Satires of Circumstance* (1914); Gibson, p. 381; Hynes, II, 97–8.

HrT 137 Fair copy, revised, here entitled 'She thinks she dreams', in MS Satires of Circumstance (p. 133).

Dorset County Museum.

The Best She Could ('Nine leaves a minute')
First pub. *Human Shows* (1925); Gibson, p. 724; Hynes, III, 323.

HrT 138 Fair copy, revised, the title altered from 'The Fall of the Leaf', in MS Human Shows (f. 36); dated 8 November 1923.

Yale.

Best Times ('We went a day's excursion to the stream')
First pub. *Late Lyrics* (1922); Gibson, pp. 683–4; Hynes, II, 467–8.

HrT 139 Fair copy, revised, here entitled 'Best Times. <Not Again.>', annotated 'Rewritten from an old draft.', in MS Late Lyrics (f. 172).

Facsimile in Gibson, p. [554] and Robert Gittings, *The Older Hardy* (London, 1978), facing p. 101.

Dorset County Museum.

'Between us now' ('Between us now and here —')
First pub. *Poems of the Past and the Present* (1902); Gibson, pp. 136–7; Hynes, I, 172–3.

HrT 140 Fair copy, in MS Poems of the Past and the Present.

Bodleian, MS Eng. poet. d. 18, f. 80.

HrT 141 Typescript of stanza one only, sent in a letter (containing also HrT 771) to Rutland Boughton (for use in his opera of 'The Famous Tragedy of the Queen of Cornwall'), Max Gate, 18 June 1924.

This MS printed *Letters*, VI, 257.

British Library, Add. MS 52364, f. 127.

Beyond the Last Lamp ('While rain, with eve in partnership')
First pub. *Harper's Monthly Magazine*, December 1911, as 'Night in a Suburb'; collected *Satires of Circumstance* (1914); Gibson, pp. 314–15; Hynes, II, 20–21.

HrT 142 Fair copy, signed, here entitled 'Night in a Suburb. (Near Tooting Common.)', 2 numbered leaves (rectos only); dated September 1911.

Facsimile of last page in Kern sale catalogue, Anderson Galleries, 7–10 January 1929, p. 221.

Texas.

HrT 143 Fair copy, revised, the title altered from 'Night in a Suburb', in MS Satires of Circumstance (pp. 19–20).

Dorset County Museum.

The Bird-catcher's Boy ('"Father, I fear your trade:')
First pub. *The Sphere*, 4 January 1913; revised and collected *Human Shows* (1925); Gibson, pp. 825–7; Hynes, III, 150–3.

HrT 144 Fair copy, here beginning '"I don't like your trade, father', signed (initials), 4 pages (2 folded leaves), printer's copy for first publication; watermarked 1906.

Texas.

HrT 145 Corrected galley proof for first publication, here beginning '"I don't like your trade, father', annotated 'Press'.

Texas.

HrT 146 Fair copy, including a footnote to line 65, in MS Human Shows (ff. 189–90, rectos only); dated 21 November 1912.

Footnote printed Hynes, III, 320.

Yale.

HrT 147 Revisions to lines 18 and 49 and correction to line 52 in HS Proof (pp. 268–9).

Dorset County Museum.

A Bird-scene at a Rural Dwelling ('When the inmate stirs, the birds retire discreetly')

First pub. *Chambers's Journal*, 1 January 1925; collected *Human Shows* (1925); Gibson, p. [701]; Hynes, III, [7].

HrT 148 Fair copy, revised, in MS Human Shows (f. 2).

Yale.

Birds at Winter Nightfall ('Around the house the flakes fly faster')
First pub. *Poems of the Past and the Present* (1902); Gibson, p. 148; Hynes, I, 185.

HrT 149 Fair copy, in MS Poems of the Past and the Present, subscribed 'Max Gate'.

Bodleian, MS Eng. poet. d. 18, f. 95.

HrT 150 Dated 1900, in DCM Wessex Edition (Verse Vol. I, 211).

Dorset County Museum.

The Blinded Bird ('So zestfully canst thou sing?')
First pub. *Moments of Vision* (1917); Gibson, p. 446; Hynes, II, 181.

HrT 151 Fair copy, revised, in MS Moments of Vision (f. 30)

Magdalene College, Cambridge.

HrT 151.5 Corrections to this poem in a clipping of a review (containing also HrT 176.5) of *Moments of Vision* (1917) in which it is quoted, in Scrapbook III (HrT 1689).

This review was printed in *The New Witness*, 18 October 1918; not mentioned Gibson or Hynes; Microfilm Edition, Reel 6.

Dorset County Museum.

The Blow ('That no man schemed it is my hope —')
First pub. *Moments of Vision* (1917); Gibson, pp. 478–9; Hynes, II, 218–19.

HrT 152 Fair copy, revised, in MS Moments of Vision (f. 81).

Magdalene College, Cambridge.

The Boy's Dream ('Provincial town-boy he, — frail, lame')
First pub. *Daily Telegraph*, 12 July 1928; collected *Winter Words* (1928); Gibson, p. 918; Hynes, III, 261–2.

HrT 153 Fair copy, revised, in MS Winter Words.

Queen's College, Oxford, MS 420, f. 124.

Boys Then and Now ('"More than one cuckoo?"')
First pub. *Winter Words* (1928); Gibson, pp. 887–8; Hynes, III, 226–7.

HrT 154 Fair copy, in MS Winter Words.

Queen's College, Oxford, MS 420, f. 79.

The Bride-Night Fire ('They had long met o' Zundays — her true love and she —')
First pub. *Gentleman's Magazine*, November 1875, as 'The Fire at Tranter Sweatley's'; revised version collected *Wessex Poems* (1898), as 'The Fire at Tranter Sweatley's'; Gibson, pp. 71–4; Hynes, I, 93–81; first pub. version reprinted Hynes, I, Appendix C, pp. [390]–3.

HrT 155 Transcript by ELH, revised by Hardy, here entitled 'The Fire at Tranter Sweatley's', 5 numbered leaves; as sent to John Lane for publication in Lionel Johnson, *The Art of Thomas Hardy* (London, 1894), with a covering letter of [late July 1894].

The covering letter to John Lane printed *Letters*, II, 61.

University of California at Berkeley.

HrT 156 Fair copy, revised, here entitled 'The Fire at Tranter Sweatley's', in MS Wessex Poems (ff. 92–6); annotated 'Written, 1867: printed 1874 [sic]'.

Birmingham City Museum and Art Gallery.

HrT 157 Subtitle added (as in first publication), in pencil, in DCM Wessex Edition (Verse Vol. I, 94).

Dorset County Museum.

HrT 158 Pencil addition to title ('or The Fire at Tranter Sweatley's') in *Collected Poems* (1923), p. 63.

Dorset County Museum.

The Bridge of Lodi ('When of tender mind and body')
First pub. *Poems of the Past and the Present* (1902); Gibson, pp. 107–9; Hynes, I, 139–42.

HrT 159 Fair copy, revised, here subtitled '(Visited 23 April, 1887: Battle fought May 10, 1796)', in MS Poems of the Past and the Present.

Bodleian, MS Eng. poet. d. 18, ff. 33–6 (rectos only).

A Broken Appointment ('You did not come')
First pub. *Poems of the Past and the Present* (1902); Gibson, p. 136; Hynes, I, 172.

HrT 160 Fair copy, revised, in MS Poems of the Past and the Present.

Bodleian, MS Eng. poet. d. 18, f. 79.

HrT 161 Corrections in *Selected Poems* (1917), p. 36.

Dorset County Museum.

HrT 161.5 One revision to this poem on a clipping of a review of *Collected Poems* (1919) in which it is quoted, in Scrapbook III (HrT 1689).

This review printed *The Outlook*, November 1919; not mentioned Gibson or Hynes; Microfilm Edition, Reel 6.

Dorset County Museum.

The Brother ('O know you what I have done')
First pub. *Winter Words* (1928); Gibson, p. 880; Hynes, III, 218.

HrT 162 Fair copy, revised, in MS Winter Words.

Queen's College, Oxford, MS 420, f. 67.

Budmouth Dears ('When we lay where Budmouth Beach is'), see HrT 1620–21, 1625.

Building a New Street in The Ancient Quarter, see HrT 991.

The Bullfinches ('Brother Bulleys, let us sing')
First pub. *Poems of the Past and the Present* (1902); Gibson, pp. 122–3; Hynes, I, 156–7.

HrT 163 Fair copy, revised, in MS Poems of the Past and the Present.

Bodleian, MS Eng. poet. d. 18, ff. 57–8 (rectos only).

The Burghers ('The sun had wheeled from Grey's to Dammer's Crest')
First pub. *Wessex Poems* (1898); Gibson, pp. 24–6; Hynes, I, 31–3.

HrT 164 Fair copy, revised, the title altered from 'The Three Burghers', in MS Wessex Poems (ff. 28–30).

Birmingham City Museum and Art Gallery.

HrT 165 Revision to line 45 in DCM Wessex Edition (Verse Vol. I, 31).

Dorset County Museum.

HrT 166 Corrections to lines 5, 45, 49 in *Selected Poems* (1917), pp. 163–6.

Dorset County Museum.

HrT 167 Revision to line 63 in *Collected Poems* (1923), p. 22.

Dorset County Museum.

Burning the Holly ('O you are sad on Twelfth Night')
First pub. *Daily Telegraph*, 20 August 1928; collected *Winter Words* (1928); Gibson, pp. 889–91; Hynes, III, 228–31.

HrT 168 Draft 3 numbered leaves (rectos only).

Microfilm Edition, Reel 5.

Dorset County Museum.

HrT 169 Fair copy, revised, in MS Winter Words.

Queen's College, Oxford, MS 420, ff. 82–4 (rectos only).

By Henstridge Cross at the Year's End ('Why go the east road now?...')
First pub. *Fortnightly Review*, 1 December 1919, as 'By Mellstock Cross at the Year's End'; collected *Late Lyrics* (1922); Gibson, pp. 629–30; Hynes, II, 402–3.

HrT 170 Fair copy, revised, in MS Late Lyrics (ff. 95–6).

Dorset County Museum.

HrT 171 Typescript, here entitled 'By Mellstock Cross at the Year's End', inscribed by Lady Hoare 'Sent me by Florence Hardy, from the great Poet, when just finished writing, Nov[r]. 10th 1919'.

Both Gibson and Hynes give the location of this typescript as Stourhead but the Wiltshire Record Office (where most of the Hardy papers from Stourhead are deposited) reports that it is not among their collection; it is possibly inserted in one of Lady Hoare's books still kept in the library at Stourhead.

Unlocated.

By Her Aunt's Grave ('"Sixpence a week," says the girl to her lover'), see HrT 1007.

By the Barrows ('Not far from Mellstock — so tradition saith — ')
First pub. *Time's Laughingstocks* (1909); Gibson, p. 262; Hynes, I, 317.

HrT 172 Fair copy, extensively revised, in MS Time's Laughingstocks (f. 91).

Fitzwilliam Museum.

By the Earth's Corpse ('"O Lord, why grievest Thou? —')
First pub. *Poems of the Past and the Present* (1902); Gibson, pp. 126–7; Hynes, I, 161–2.

HrT 173 Fair copy, revised, in MS Poems of the Past and the Present.

Bodleian, MS Eng. poet. d. 18, ff. 64–5 (rectos only).

'By the Runic Stone' ('By the Runic Stone')
First pub. *Moments of Vision* (1917); Gibson, p. 471; Hynes, II, 210.

HrT 174 Fair copy, revised, in MS Moments of Vision (f. 70).

Magdalene College, Cambridge.

A Bygone Occasion ('That night, that night')
First pub. *Late Lyrics* (1922); Gibson, p. 603; Hynes, II, 372.

HrT 175 Fair copy, revised, in MS Late Lyrics (f. 60).

Dorset County Museum.

The Caged Goldfinch ('Within a churchyard, on a recent grave')
First pub. *Moments of Vision* (1917); Gibson, p. 491; Hynes, II, 234.

HrT 176 Fair copy of 3-stanza version in MS Moments of Vision (f. 105).

Magdalene College, Cambridge.

HrT 176.5 Corrections to this poem on a clipping of a review (containing also HrT 151.5) of *Moments of Vision* (1917) in which it is quoted, in Scrapbook III (HrT 1689).

This review printed in *The New Outlook*, 18 October 1918; not mentioned Gibson or Hynes; Microfilm Edition, Reel 6.

Dorset County Museum.

The Caged Thrush Freed and Home Again ('"Men know but little more than we')
First pub. *Poems of the Past and the Present* (1902); Gibson, p. 147; Hynes, I, 184–5.

HrT 177 Fair copy, revised, in MS Poems of the Past and the Present.

Bodleian, MS Eng. poet. d. 18, f. 94.

A Call to National Service ('Up and be doing, all who have a hand')
First pub. *The Times* (without title) and *Morning Post*, as 'For National Service', 12 March 1917; collected *Moments of Vision* (1917); privately printed in FEH's pamphlet *A Call to National Service* (London, 1917); Gibson, p. 546; Hynes, II, 300.

HrT 178 Fair copy, revised, the title altered from 'For National Service', sent for publication in *The Times* and subsequently incorporated in MS Moments of Vision (f. 190), signed; dated March 1917.

Magdalene College, Cambridge.

HrT 179 Typescript of the *Morning Post* version, here entitled 'For National Service', as sent to Frederick Higginbottom with a letter of 7 March 1917.

The letter printed *Letters*, V, 206 from the original owned F. B. Adams.

Owned (1984) F. B. Adams (see Hynes).

HrT 180 Corrected title (from 'For National Service'), probably by Sydney Cockerell, in a copy of the first proof of FEH's *A Call to National Service* (containing also HrT 754); dated by Cockerell 27 March 1917.

Purdy, p. 192 describes these corrections as being by Hardy; the proof is together with an uncorrected second proof (dated by Cockerell 13 April 1917) and 2 copies of the published pamphlet presented by FEH to Cockerell; Cockerell Sale, Lot 304, sold to Hollings.

New York University.

Cardinal Bembo's Epitaph on Raphael ('Here's one in whom Nature feared — faint at such vying —')
First pub. *Poems of the Past and the Present* (1902); Gibson, p. 183; Hynes, I, 224.

HrT 181 Fair copy, in MS Poems of the Past and the Present.

Bodleian, MS Eng. poet. d. 18, f. 151.

The Caricature ('Of the Lady Lu there were stories told')
First pub. *Human Shows* (1925); Gibson, pp. 766–7; Hynes, III, 82–4.

HrT 182 Fair copy, revised, in MS Human Shows (ff. 96–8, rectos only); dated '<About 1890>'.

Yale.

HrT 183 Corrections in HS Proof (p. 141).

Dorset County Museum.

The Carrier ('"There's a seat, I see, still empty?"')
First pub. *Human Shows* (1925); Gibson, p. 706; Hynes, III, 12–13.

HrT 184 Fair copy, revised, in MS Human Shows (f. 9).

Yale.

The Casterbridge Captains ('Three captains went to Indian wars')
First pub. *Wessex Poems* (1898); Gibson, pp. 48–9; Hynes, I, 63–4.

HrT 185 Fair copy, revised, in MS Wessex Poems (ff. 60–1), here subtitled 'In memory of L----, B----, and L----', including an illustration.

The illustration is reproduced in Hynes.

Birmingham City Museum and Art Gallery.

The Casual Acquaintance ('While he was here with breath and bone')
First pub. *Late Lyrics* (1922); Gibson, p. 684; Hynes, II, 468–9.

HrT 186 Fair copy, revised, in MS Late Lyrics (f. 173).

Dorset County Museum.

The Catching Ballet of the Wedding Clothes ('"A gentleman's coming')
First pub. *Winter Words* (1928); Gibson, pp. 921–4; Hynes, III, 264–8.

HrT 187 Fair copy, revised, in MS Winter Words; dated 1919.

Queen's College, Oxford, MS 420, ff. 128–9.

A Cathedral Façade at Midnight ('Along the sculptures of the western wall')
First pub. *Human Shows* (1925); Gibson, p. 703; Hynes, III, 9.

HrT 188 Fair copy, in MS Human Shows (f. 5); dated 1897 (cancelled).

Yale.

HrT 189 Annotated 'Salisbury —' in HS Proof (p. 6).

Dorset County Museum.

Catullus: XXXI ('Sirmio, thou dearest dear of strands')
First pub. *Poems of the Past and the Present* (1902); Gibson, p. [181]; Hynes, I, [222].

HrT 190 Fair copy, revised, in MS Poems of the Past and the Present.

Bodleian, MS Eng. poet. d. 18, f. 149.

The Change ('Out of the past there rises a week —')
First pub. *Moments of Vision* (1917); Gibson, pp. 454–6; Hynes, II, 190–2.

HrT 191 Fair copy, revised, in MS Moments of Vision (f. 43); dated January–February 1913.

Magdalene College, Cambridge.

Channel Firing ('That night your great guns, unawares')
First pub. *Fortnightly Review*, 1 May 1914; collected *Satires of Circumstance* (1914); Gibson, pp. 305–6; Hynes, III, 9–10.

HrT 192 Fair copy, in MS Satires of Circumstance (pp. 4–5); dated April 1914.

Dorset County Museum.

The Chapel-Organist ('I've been thinking it through, as I play here to-night, to play never again')
First pub. *Late Lyrics* (1922); Gibson, pp. 633–6; Hynes, II, 406–12.

HrT 193 Fair copy, revised, here beginning 'I've been thinking and thinking it <over> through, as I play here to-night again', in MS Late Lyrics (ff. 101–3).

Dorset County Museum.

The Cheval-Glass ('Why do you harbour that great cheval-glass')
First pub. *Satires of Circumstance* (1914); Gibson, pp. 360–1; Hynes, II, 72–4.

HrT 194 Fair copy, revised, in MS Satires of Circumstance (pp. 100–1).

Dorset County Museum.

The Child and the Sage ('You say, O Sage, when weather-checked')
First pub. *Late Lyrics* (1922); Gibson, pp. 610–11; Hynes, II, 380–81.

HrT 195 Fair copy, revised, in MS Late Lyrics (f. 71); dated 'Dec. 21. 1908./<(recopied)>'.

Dorset County Museum.

Childhood among the Ferns ('I sat one sprinkling day upon the lea')
First pub. *Daily Telegraph*, 29 March 1928; collected *Winter Words* (1928); Gibson, p. 864; Hynes, III, 199–200.

HrT 196 Fair copy, revised, one leaf.

No MS of this poem is included in MS Winter Words; this MS sold Cockerell Sale, Lot 270, to Maggs.

Owned (1985) F. B. Adams (see Hynes).

The Children and Sir Nameless ('Sir Nameless, once of Athelhall, declared:')
First pub. *Salisbury Times and South Wilts Gazette*, 21 April 1922; reprinted *Nash's and Pall Mall Magazine*, May 1922; collected *Late Lyrics* (1922); Gibson, p. 627; Hynes, II, 399–400.

HrT 197 Fair copy, revised, the title altered from 'The Children versus Sir Nameless', in MS Late Lyrics (f. 91).

Dorset County Museum.

The Chimes ('That morning when I trod the town')
First pub. *Moments of Vision* (1917); Gibson, pp. 475–6; Hynes, II, 215–16.

HrT 198 Fair copy, revised, in MS Moments of Vision (f. 77).

Magdalene College, Cambridge.

The Chimes Play 'Life's a Bumper!' ('"Awake! I'm off to cities far away"')
First pub. *Late Lyrics* (1922); Gibson, p. 606; Hynes, II, 375–6.

HrT 199 Fair copy, revised, in MS Late Lyrics (f. 65); dated 1913.

Dorset County Museum.

The Choirmaster's Burial ('He often would ask us')
First pub. *Moments of Vision* (1917); Gibson, pp. 534–5; Hynes, II, 284–5.

HrT 200 Fair copy, revised, the title altered from 'The Choirmaster's Funeral', in MS Moments of Vision (f. 170).

Magdalene College, Cambridge.

Chorus of the Pities ('To Thee whose eye all Nature owns'), see HrT 1620, 1625.

The Chosen ('"A woman for whom great gods might strive!"')
First pub. *Late Lyrics* (1922); Gibson, pp. 676–8; Hynes, II, 458–60.

HrT 201 Fair copy, revised, in MS Late Lyrics (ff. 163–4).

Dorset County Museum.

The Christening ('Whose child is this they bring')
First pub. *Time's Laughingstocks* (1909); Gibson, pp. 260–1; Hynes, I, 315–16.

HrT 202 Fair copy, in MS Time's Laughingstocks (f. 89); dated 1904.

Fitzwilliam Museum.

A Christmas Ghost-Story ('South of the Line, inland from far Durban')
First pub. *Westminster Gazette*, 23 December 1899; revised version collected *Poems of the Past and the Present* (1902); Gibson, p. 90; Hynes, I, 121. See also HrT 1387.

HrT 203 Fair copy, revised, in MS Poems of the Past and the Present; dated 23 December 1899.

Bodleian, MS Eng. poet. d. 18, f. 8.

Christmas in the Elgin Room ('What is the noise that shakes the night')
First pub. *The Times*, 24 December 1927; privately printed by FEH as a separate pamphlet (London, 1927); collected *Winter Words* (1928); Gibson, pp. 927–8; Hynes, III, 272–3.

HrT 204 Fair copy, revised, in MS Winter Words; dated '1905 and 1926'.

Queen's College, Oxford, MS 420, ff. 134–5 (rectos only).

HrT 205 Fair copy, revised, 2 leaves, framed; c. 1926–7.

Facsimile of lines 1–10 in *The Times*, 1 February 1928, p. 8.

Magdalene College, Cambridge.

Christmas: 1924 ('"Peace upon earth!" was said. We sing it')
First pub. *Daily Telegraph*, 18 June 1928, as '"Peace upon Earth"'; collected *Winter Words* (1928); Gibson, p. 914; Hynes, III, 256.

HrT 206 Fair copy, revised, in MS Winter Words.

Queen's College, Oxford, MS 420, f. 117.

Christmastide ('The rain-shafts splintered on me')
First pub. *Winter Words* (1928); Gibson, p. 846; Hynes, III, 179.

HrT 207 Fair copy, revised, in MS Winter Words.

Queen's College, Oxford, MS 420, f. 19.

The Church and the Wedding ('"I'll restore this old church for our marriage:"')
First pub. *The Chapbook*, March 1923; collected *Human Shows* (1925); Gibson, pp. 780–1; Hynes, III, 99–100.

HrT 208 Fair copy, revised, in MS Human Shows (f. 120).

Yale.

HrT 209 Corrected galley proof for the first publication, enclosed with a card to Harold Monro (editor of *The Chapbook*), Max Gate, 22 February 1923.

The card printed *Letters*, VI, 185.

Colby College.

The Church-Builder ('The church projects a battled shade')

First pub. *Poems of the Past and the Present* (1902) beginning 'The church flings forth a battled shade'; Gibson, pp. 170–2 (beginning as first publication); Hynes, I, 210–13.

HrT 210 Fair copy, revised, the title altered from 'Nisi Dominus Frustra', in MS Poems of the Past and the Present.

Bodleian, MS Eng. poet. d. 18, ff. 132–5 (rectos only).

A Church Romance ('She turned in the high pew, until her sight')
First pub. *Saturday Review*, 8 September 1906; collected *Time's Laughingstocks* (1909); Gibson, p. [252]; Hynes, I, [306].

HrT 211 Fair copy, subtitled 'circa 1835', in MS Time's Laughingstocks (f. 81).

Fitzwilliam Museum.

HrT 212 Fair copy, here beginning 'In the high pew she turned, until her sight' and subtitled 'circa 1835.', one page, together with a covering letter to Harold Hodge, (editor of *Saturday Review*), 28 August 1906.

Facsimile of poem and letter in British Library, RP 1913; letter printed *Letters*, III, 223.

Owned (1982) David Holmes (see Hynes).

HrT 213 Correction to line 9 in *Selected Poems* (1917), p. 128.

Dorset County Museum.

A Circular ('As "legal representative"')
First pub. *Satires of Circumstance* (1914); Gibson, pp. 347–8; Hynes, II, 58.

HrT 214 Fair copy, revised, in MS Satires of Circumstance (p. 84).

Dorset County Museum.

Circus-rider to Ringmaster ('When I am riding round the ring no longer')
First pub. *Harper's Monthly Magazine*, June 1925; collected *Human Shows* (1925); Gibson, pp. 708–9; Hynes, III, 15.

HrT 215 Fair copy, revised, here subtitled '<(Casterbridge Fair: 188—)>', in MS Human Shows (f. 12).

Yale.

The Clasped Skeletons ('O why did we uncover to view')
First pub. *Daily Telegraph*, 2 August 1928; collected *Winter Words* (1928); Gibson, pp. 873–4; Hynes, III, 209–11.

HrT 216 Fair copy, extensively revised, 2 pages (one folded leaf).

Microfilm Edition, Reel 5.

Dorset County Museum.

HrT 217 Fair copy, revised, in MS Winter Words.

Queen's College, Oxford, MS 420, ff. 57–8 (rectos only).

The Clock of the Years ('And the Spirit said')
First pub. *Moments of Vision* (1917); Gibson, pp. 528–9; Hynes, II, 278–9.

HrT 218 Fair copy, revised, the title altered from 'The Clock of Time', in MS Moments of Vision (f. 162); dated 1916.

Magdalene College, Cambridge.

The Clock-Winder ('It is dark as a cave')
First pub. *Moments of Vision* (1917); Gibson, pp. 519–20; Hynes, II, 268–9.

HrT 219 Fair copy of lines 1–28 only, in MS Moments of Vision (f. 151).

Magdalene College, Cambridge.

Collected Poems
First pub. London, 1919. For Hardy's corrected copy of the 1923 second edition, see INTRODUCTION.

HrT 219.5 Corrected page proofs of the half-title, title page and table of contents, for the first edition, annotated by Hardy 'Press'; stamped 'First Proof' and 13 June 1919.

National Library of Scotland, R. & R. Clark Papers, Dep. 229/292 (on deposit).

The Collector Cleans His Picture ('How I remember cleaning that strange picture!...')
First pub. *Late Lyrics* (1922); Gibson, pp. 617–18; Hynes, II, 388–9.

HrT 220 Fair copy, revised, in MS Late Lyrics (ff. 78–9).

Dorset County Museum.

The Colonel's Soliloquy ('"The quay recedes. Hurrah! Ahead we go!...')
First pub. *Poems of the Past and the Present* (1902); Gibson, pp. 87–8; Hynes, I, 117–18.

HrT 221 Fair copy, revised, in MS Poems of the Past and the Present.

Bodleian, MS. Eng. poet. d. 18, ff. 4–5 (rectos only).

The Colour ('"What shall I bring you?')
First pub. *Late Lyrics* (1922); Gibson, pp. 693–4; Hynes, II, 479–80.

HrT 222 Fair copy, in MS Late Lyrics (f. 186).

Dorset County Museum.

Come Not; Yet Come! ('In my sage moments I can say')
First pub. *Human Shows* (1925); Gibson, pp. 709–10; Hynes, III, 16.

HrT 223 Fair copy, revised, in MS Human Shows (f. 14).

Yale.

The Comet at Yell'ham ('It bends far over Yell'ham Plain')
First pub. *Poems of the Past and the Present* (1902), as 'The Comet at Yalbury or Yell'ham'; Gibson, p. 151; Hynes, I, 188–9.

HrT 224 Fair copy, revised, here entitled 'The Comet at Yalbury, or Yell'ham', in MS Poems of the Past and the Present.

Bodleian, MS Eng. poet. d. 18, f. 100.

The Coming of the End ('How it came to an end!')
First pub. *Moments of Vision* (1917); Gibson, p. 552; Hynes, II, [307]–8.

HrT 225 Draft of lines 1–3, 5–8, here entitled 'Afterwards', the whole cancelled, in MS Moments of Vision (f. 139v).

This MS printed Gibson, p. 552n and Hynes, II, 507.

Magdalene College, Cambridge.

HrT 226 Draft of lines 1–4, the whole cancelled, in MS Moments of Vision (f. 9v).

This MS printed Gibson, p. 552n and Hynes, II, 507.

Magdalene College, Cambridge.

HrT 227 Fair copy, in MS Moments of Vision (f. 198).

Magdalene College, Cambridge.

Coming up Oxford Street: Evening ('The sun from the west glares back')
First pub. *The Nation and the Athenaeum*, 13 June 1925; revised and collected *Human Shows* (1925); Gibson, p. 717; Hynes, III, 25.

HrT 228 Fair copy, revised, in MS Human Shows (f. 25); dated '<Oxford Street> As seen July 4: 1872.'.

Yale.

A Commonplace Day ('The day is turning ghost')
First pub. *Poems of the Past and the Present* (1902); Gibson, pp. 115–16; Hynes, I, 148–9.

HrT 229 Fair copy, revised, in MS Poems of the Past and the Present.

Bodleian, MS Eng. poet. d. 18, ff. 46–7 (rectos only).

Compassion/An Ode ('Backward among the dusky years')
First pub. *A Century of Work for Animals*, ed. Edward G. Fairholme and Wellesley Pain (London, 1924) and *The Times*, 16 June 1924; privately printed by FEH as a separate pamphlet (London, 1924); collected *Human Shows* (1925); Gibson, pp. 822–3; Hynes, III, 147–8.

HrT 230 Fair copy, revised, in MS Human Shows (ff. 184–5, rectos only); dated 22 January 1924.

Yale.

HrT 231 Corrected page proof for FEH's pamphlet, annotated on title page 'Please send Revise'.

Microfilm Edition, Reel 5.

Dorset County Museum.

The Complaint of the Common Man, see the description of MS Poems of the Past and the Present in the INTRODUCTION.

Concerning Agnes ('I am stopped from hoping what I have hoped before —')
First pub. *Daily Telegraph*, 21 May 1928; collected *Winter Words* (1928); Gibson, p. 878; Hynes, III, 215.

HrT 232 Fair copy, revised, in MS Winter Words.

Queen's College, Oxford, MS 420, f. 64.

Concerning his Old Home ('I wish to see it never —')
First pub. *Daily Telegraph*, 16 August 1928; collected *Winter Words* (1928); Gibson, pp. 859–60; Hynes, III, 194.

HrT 233 Draft, here entitled '<Moods> Concerning <an> his Old <House> Home', one page.

Microfilm Edition, Reel 5.

Dorset County Museum.

HrT 234 Fair copy in MS Winter Words.

Queen's College, Oxford, MS 420, f. 37.

A Confession to a Friend in Trouble ('Your troubles shrink not, though I feel them less')
First pub. *Wessex Poems* (1898); Gibson, pp. 11–12; Hynes, I, 12–13.

HrT 235 Fair copy, revised, in MS Wessex Poems (f. 8); dated 1866.

Birmingham City Museum and Art Gallery.

The Conformers ('Yes; we'll wed, my little fay')
First pub. *Time's Laughingstocks* (1909); Gibson, pp. 229–30; Hynes, I, 279–80.

HrT 236 Fair copy, revised, including a cancelled version of lines 1–5 on verso, in MS Time's Laughingstocks (f. 53r–v).

Fitzwilliam Museum.

Conjecture ('If there were in my kalendar')
First pub. *Moments of Vision* (1917); Gibson, pp. 477–8; Hynes, II, 218.

HrT 237 Fair copy, revised, in MS Moments of Vision (f. 80).

Magdalene College, Cambridge.

The Contretemps ('A forward rush by the lamp in the gloom')
First pub. *Late Lyrics* (1922); Gibson, pp. 582–4; Hynes, II, 348–50.

HrT 238 Fair copy, revised, in MS Late Lyrics (ff. 32–3).

Dorset County Museum.

HrT 239 Revision to line 20 in *Collected Poems* (1923), p. 552.

Dorset County Museum.

The Convergence of the Twain ('In a solitude of the sea')
First printed in the Souvenir Programme of the 'Dramatic and Operatic matinée in Aid of the "Titanic" disaster Fund', Covent Garden, 14 May 1912; first pub. (revised version) in *Fortnightly Review*, 1 June 1912; limited separate edition (London, 1912); collected *Satires of Circumstance* (1914); Gibson, pp. 306–7; Hynes, II, 11–13.

HrT 240 Fair copy, signed, annotated by Hardy '[Replica of Original MS]', and '(Written to be sold in aid of the "Titanic" disaster fund, and republished in the Fortnightly Review for June 1912.)', 2 leaves, including a title page in an unidentified hand; dated 24 April 1912.

University of California at Berkeley.

HrT 241 Fair copy, revised, in MS Satires of Circumstance (pp. 6–7).

Dorset County Museum.

HrT 242 Corrected first proof for the 1912 limited edition; date stamped 29 July 1912.

Another copy of this proof, corrected in an unidentified hand, is owned (1982) David Holmes.

Yale.

HrT 243 Two copies of second proof, corrected by Hardy, for the 1912 limited edition: (1) annotated by Hardy 'Press.' and 'Correct very carefully & *revise* urgent', date stamped both 8 and 13 August 1912; (2) bound with 3 letters to B. F. Stevens & Brown, one of them (dated July 1912) being a draft of the one printed in the edition, date stamped 8 August 1912.

The letters to B. F. Stevens & Brown printed *Letters*, IV, 222–3, 225–6.

Berg.

A Conversation at Dawn ('He lay awake, with a harassed air')
First pub. *Satires of Circumstance* (1914); Gibson, pp. 366–72; Hynes, II, 80–6.

HrT 244 Fair copy, revised, including an additional cancelled stanza, in MS Satires of Circumstance (pp. 110–18); dated Autumn 1910.

Additional stanza printed Purdy, p. 167 and Hynes, II, 86.

Dorset County Museum.

Copying Architecture in an Old Minster ('How smartly the quarters of the hour march by')
First pub. *Moments of Vision* (1917); Gibson, pp. 438–9; Hynes, II, 171–3.

HrT 245 Fair copy, revised, in MS Moments of Vision (f. 21).

Magdalene College, Cambridge.

The Coquette, and After ('For long the cruel wish I knew')
First pub. *Poems of the Past and the Present* (1902); Gibson, p. 139; Hynes, I, 175.

HrT 246 Fair copy, revised, in MS Poems of the Past and the Present.

Bodleian, MS Eng. poet. d. 18, f. 82.

The Coronation ('At Westminster, hid from the light of day')
First pub. *Satires of Circumstance* (1914); Gibson, pp. 374–6; Hynes, II, 88–90.

HrT 247 Fair copy, revised, in MS Satires of Circumstance (pp. 121–4); dated 1911.

Dorset County Museum.

HrT 248 Corrections in *Selected Poems* (1917), pp. 167–9.

Dorset County Museum.

'Could he but live for me' see HrT 1637–9.

'Could I but will' ('Could I but will')
First pub. *Late Lyrics* (1922); Gibson, pp. 637–8; Hynes, II, 413–14.

HrT 249 Fair copy, revised, in MS Late Lyrics (f. 105).

Dorset County Museum.

A Countenance ('Her laugh was not in the middle of her face quite')
First pub. *Winter Words* (1928); Gibson, pp. 864–5; Hynes, III, 200.

HrT 250 Fair copy, revised, in MS Winter Words; dated 1884.

Queen's College, Oxford, MS 420, f. 44.

The Country Wedding ('Little fogs were gathered in every hollow')
First privately printed by FEH (without stanza 2) as a pamphlet *The Fiddler's Story* (London, October 1917); first pub. in full in *Cassell's Winter Annual 1921–2*, November 1921; collected *Late Lyrics* (1922); Gibson, pp. 650–1; Hynes, II, 427–9.

HrT 251 Fair copy, revised, in MS Late Lyrics (ff. 126–7).

Dorset County Museum.

HrT 252 Typescript, revised, here entitled 'The Fiddler's Story', printer's copy for FEH's pamphlet; dated 1917.

Cockerell Sale, Lot 271, sold to Maggs.

Owned (1984) R. L. Purdy (see Hynes); destined for Yale.

HrT 253 Corrected proof for FEH's pamphlet (including also HrT 637), here entitled 'The Fiddler's Story'; proof dated 25 September 1917.

Cockerell Sale, Lot 271, sold to Maggs.

Owned (1984) R. L. Purdy (see Hynes); destined for Yale.

Cross-Currents ('They parted — a pallid, trembling pair')
First pub. *Late Lyrics* (1922); Gibson, p. 675; Hynes, II, 457–8.

HrT 254 Fair copy, revised, here beginning 'They parted — a <tearful, trembling> <silent, sombre> pensive, trembling pair', in MS Late Lyrics (f. 161).

Dorset County Museum.

Cry of the Homeless ('"Instigator of the ruin —')
First pub. *The Book of the Homeless*, ed. Edith Wharton (New York and London, 1916); collected *Moments of Vision* (1917); privately printed by FEH in pamphlet *A Call to National Service* (London, 1917); Gibson, pp. 543–4; Hynes, II, 296–7.

HrT 255 Fair copy, in MS Moments of Vision (f. 186); dated August 1915.

Magdalene College, Cambridge.

HrT 256 Fair copy of first publication version, signed, one page; dated August 1915, watermarked 1906.

Library of Congress, Rare Book Division, Rosenwald Collection, MS 8.

The Curate's Kindness ('I thought they'd be strangers aroun' me')
First pub. *Time's Laughingstocks* (1909); Gibson, pp. 208–9; Hynes, I, 256–8.

HrT 257 Fair copy, revised, in MS Time's Laughingstocks (ff. 25–6).

Fitzwilliam Museum.

HrT 258 Correction to line 17 on p. 32 of Hardy's copy of *Time's Laughingstocks* (1909) (containing also HrT 449, 595).

Dorset County Museum.

HrT 259 Correction to line 17 in *Collected Poems* (1923), p. 194.

Dorset County Museum.

'The curtains now are drawn' ('The curtains now are drawn')
First pub. *Late Lyrics* (1922); Gibson, pp. 570–1; Hynes, II, 335.

HrT 260 Fair copy, revised, in MS Late Lyrics (f. 12); dated 1913.

Dorset County Museum.

Cynic's Epitaph ('A race with the sun as he downed')
First pub. *London Mercury*, September 1925; collected *Human Shows* (1925); Gibson, p. 795; Hynes, III, 115.

HrT 261 Fair copy, revised, in MS Human Shows (f. 143).

Yale.

The Dame of Athelhall ('"Dear! Shall I see thy face", she said')
First pub. *Poems of the Past and the Present* (1902); Gibson, pp. 154–6; Hynes, I, 192–4.

HrT 262 Fair copy, revised, here beginning '"Soul! Shall I see…', in MS Poems of the Past and the Present.

In the Table of Contents in MS Poems of the Past and the Present, this poem originally entitled (cancelled) 'The Return to Athels-hall'.

Bodleian, MS Eng. poet. d. 18, ff. 106–8 (rectos only).

HrT 263 Alternative version of line 29, written in 'Errata' list in Hardy's copy of *Poems of the Past and the Present* (1902) (see HrT 927).

Owned (1982) F. B. Adams (see Hynes).

HrT 264 Revision to line 29 in DCM Wessex Edition (Verse Vol. I, 224).

Dorset County Museum.

The Dance at the Phœnix ('To Jenny came a gentle youth')
First pub. *Wessex Poems* (1898); Gibson, pp. 43–8; Hynes, I, 57–62.

HrT 265 Fair copy, revised, without stanza 15 (lines 99–105), here reading 'Nelly' for 'Jenny' throughout, in MS Wessex Poems (ff. 54–9).

Birmingham City Museum and Art Gallery.

HrT 266 Revision in lines 49, 79 and 107 in *Collected Poems* (1923), pp. 39–41.

Dorset County Museum.

The Dark-Eyed Gentleman ('I pitched my day's leazings in Crimmercrock Lane')
First pub. *Time's Laughingstocks* (1909); Gibson, p. 243; Hynes, I, 295–6.

HrT 267 Fair copy, here beginning 'I pitched my day's leaze-nitch...', in MS Time's Laughingstocks (f. 69).

Fitzwilliam Museum.

The Darkling Thrush ('I leant upon a coppice gate')
First pub. *The Graphic*, 29 December 1900, as 'By the Century's Deathbed'; collected *Poems of the Past and the Present* (1902); Gibson, p. 150; Hynes, I, 187–8.

HrT 268 Fair copy, revised, here entitled 'By the Century's Deathbed' and beginning 'I leant upon a paddock gate', signed, 2 leaves, printer's copy for first publication; dated December 1900.

Facsimile in Barnet J. Beyer Catalogue No. 10 (1928), pp. 18–19.

Owned (1982) F. B. Adams (see Hynes).

HrT 269 Fair copy, in MS Poems of the Past and the Present; dated 'The Century's End, 1900.'

Bodleian, MS Eng. poet. d. 18, ff. 98–9. (rectos only).

HrT 270 Correction to line 26 in *Selected Poems* (1916), p. 44.

Dorset County Museum.

HrT 271 Revision to line 25 and correction to line 24 in *Selected Poems* (1917), p. 44.

Dorset County Museum.

Daughter Returns ('I like not that dainty-cut raiment, those earrings of pearl')
First pub. *Winter Words* (1928); Gibson, p. 904; Hynes, III, 245–6.

HrT 272 Fair copy, revised, in MS Winter Words; dated 17 December 1901.

Queen's College, Oxford, MS 420, f. 104.

The Dawn after the Dance ('Here is my parents' dwelling with its curtained windows telling')
First pub. *Time's Laughingstocks* (1909); Gibson, p. 230; Hynes, I, 280–1.

HrT 273 Fair copy, revised, in MS Time's Laughingstocks (f. 54); dated Weymouth, 1869.

Fitzwilliam Museum.

Days to Recollect ('Do you recall')
First pub. *Human Shows* (1925); Gibson, p. 811; Hynes, III, 133–4.

HrT 274 Fair copy, revised, in MS Human Shows (f. 168).

Yale.

HrT 275 Revision to line 4 in HS Proof (p. 237).

Dorset County Museum.

The Dead and the Living One ('The dead woman lay in her first night's grave')
First pub. *The Sphere*, 25 December 1915; collected *Moments of Vision* (1917); Gibson, pp. 547–8; Hynes, II, 300–302. A proof of this poem, for the first publication and apparently uncorrected, is at the Berg.

HrT 276 Fair copy, revised, in MS Moments of Vision (f. 191); dated 1915.

Magdalene College, Cambridge.

HrT 276.5 Transcript by Lady Hoare of an early version.

Mentioned in Roger Alma, 'Thomas Hardy and Stourhead' in *National Trust Studies 1979*, ed. Gervase Jackson-Stops (London, 1978), pp. 109–10.

Wiltshire Record Office, Stourhead Papers.

The Dead Bastard ('Many and many a time I thought')
First pub. *Daily Telegraph*, 7 September 1928; collected *Winter Words* (1928); Gibson, pp. 872–3; Hynes, III, 209.

HrT 277 Fair copy, revised, the title altered from 'The Bastard' in MS Winter Words.

Queen's College, Oxford, MS 420, f. 56.

The Dead Man Walking ('They hail me as one living')
First pub. *Time's Laughingstocks* (1909); Gibson, pp. 217–19; Hynes, I, 267–8.

HrT 278 Fair copy, revised, in MS Time's Laughingstocks (ff. 38–9); dated 1896.

Fitzwilliam Museum.

The Dead Quire ('Beside the Mead of Memories')
First pub. *The Graphic*, Christmas Number, [25 November] 1901; revised and collected *Time's Laughingstocks* (1909); Gibson, pp. 255–9; Hynes, I, 310–14.

HrT 279 Fair copy, revised, without stanza 20 (lines 77–80), in MS Time's Laughingstocks (ff. 85–8); dated 1897.

Fitzwilliam Museum.

HrT 280 Corrections in *Selected Poems* (1917), pp. 155, 157.

Dorset County Museum.

Dead 'Wessex' the Dog to the Household ('Do you think of me at all')
First pub. *Daily Telegraph*, 10 May 1928 (2 stanzas only); first pub. in full *Winter Words* (1928); Gibson, pp. 915–16; Hynes, III, 258–9.

HrT 281 Extensively revised, one page, here entitled 'Dead "Wessex"/To the <Wandering ones> Household.'

Microfilm Edition, Rccl 5.

Dorset County Museum.

HrT 282 Fair copy, revised, in MS Winter Words, the title altered from 'Dead "Wessex", To the Household'.

Queen's College, Oxford, MS 420, f. 120.

The Dear ('I plodded to Fairmile Hill-top, where')
First pub. *Monthly Review*, June 1902; revised and collected *Time's Laughingstocks* (1909); Gibson, p. 274; Hynes, I, 330–1. This poem is cancelled in *Selected Poems* (1917); see INTRODUCTION.

HrT 283 Fair copy, in MS Time's Laughingstocks (f. 106); dated 1901.

Fitzwilliam Museum.

The Death of Regret ('I opened my shutter at sunrise')
First pub. *Satires of Circumstance* (1914); Gibson, p. 395; Hynes, II, 114–15.

HrT 284 Fair copy, revised, in MS Satires of Circumstance (p. 155).

Dorset County Museum.

Death-Day Recalled ('Beeny did not quiver')
First pub. *Satires of Circumstance* (1914); Gibson, p. 350; Hynes, II, 61.

HrT 285 Fair copy, revised, in MS Satires of Circumstance (p. 89).

In the Table of Contents in MS Satires of Circumstance, this poem originally listed (later cancelled) as 'A Death-day'.

Dorset County Museum.

HrT 285.5 Corrected page proof wherein the printer has queried the spelling of 'Valency', page numbers altered (in an unidentified hand) from 117–18 to 89–90.

Mentioned Hynes, II, 491 in the notes to 'A Dream or No' (see HrT 314.5).

National Library of Scotland, R. & R. Clark Papers, Dep. 229/292 (on deposit).

Departure ('While the far farewell music thins and fails')
First pub. *Poems of the Past and the Present* (1902); Gibson, pp. [86]–7; Hynes, I, [116]–17.

HrT 286 Fair copy, revised, in MS Poems of the Past and the Present.

Bodleian, MS Eng. poct. d. 18, f. 3.

HrT 286.5 Fair copy of the last 4 lines (beginning 'When shall the saner softer politics'), one page, signed, possibly written out to be set to music.

Britten-Pears Library, Aldeburgh.

HrT 287 Corrections and revisions in *Selected Poems* (1917), p. 188.

Dorset County Museum.

The Destined Pair ('Two beings were drifting')
First pub. *Daily Telegraph*, 7 June 1928; collected *Winter Words* (1928); Gibson, pp. 908–9; Hynes, III, 251.

HrT 288 Fair copy, revised, in MS Winter Words.

Queen's College, Oxford, MS 420, f. 112.

The Difference ('Sinking down by the gate I discern the thin moon')
First pub. *Satires of Circumstance* (1914); Gibson, p. 311; Hynes, II, 16.

HrT 289 Fair copy, in MS Satires of Circumstance (p. 13).

Dorset County Museum.

Discouragement ('To see the Mother, naturing Nature, stand')
First pub. *Human Shows* (1925); Gibson, p. 829; Hynes, III, 155.

HrT 290 Fair copy, in MS Human Shows (f. 193); dated 'Westbourne Park Villas: 1865–7/(From old MS.)'.

Yale.

HrT 291 Corrections and addition of subtitle '(Natura Naturans)' in HS Proof (p. 275).

Dorset County Museum.

The Discovery ('I wandered to a crude coast')
First pub. *Satires of Circumstance* (1914); Gibson, pp. 332–3; Hynes, II, 41–2.

HrT 292 Fair copy, revised, in MS Satires of Circumstance (p. 58).

Dorset County Museum.

The Dissemblers ('"It was not you I came to please')
First pub. *Late Lyrics* (1922); Gibson, pp. 578–9; Hynes II, 344.

HrT 293 Fair copy, revised, here entitled 'The Evaders', in MS Late Lyrics (f. 25).

Dorset County Museum.

Ditty ('Beneath a knap where flown')
First pub. *Wessex Poems* (1898); Gibson, pp. 17–18; Hynes, I, 21–2.

HrT 294 Fair copy, revised, in MS Wessex Poems (ff. 18–19); dated 1870.

Birmingham City Museum and Art Gallery.

HrT 295 Correction in line 39 in *Selected Poems* (1917), p. 21.

Dorset County Museum.

The Division ('Rain on the windows, creaking doors')
First pub. *Time's Laughingstocks* (1909); Gibson, p. 221; Hynes, I, 270.

HrT 296 Draft, containing a variant last stanza, possibly torn from a letter.

Owned (1982) R. L. Purdy (see Hynes); destined for Yale.

HrT 297 Fair copy, revised, in MS Time's Laughingstocks (f. 42).

Fitzwilliam Museum.

HrT 298 Revision to line 7 and added date '189–' in DCM Wessex Edition (Verse Vol. III, 305).

Dorset County Museum.

HrT 299 Date '189–' added in *Selected Poems* (1916), p. 28.

Dorset County Museum.

HrT 300 Date '189–' added in *Selected Poems* (1917), p. 28.

Dorset County Museum.

HrT 301 Date '1893' added in *Collected Poems* (1923), p. 205.

Dorset County Museum.

The Dolls ('"Whenever you dress me dolls, mammy')
First pub. *Moments of Vision* (1917); Gibson, pp. 496–7; Hynes, II, 241.

HrT 302 Fair copy, in MS Moments of Vision (f. 115).

Magdalene College, Cambridge.

Domicilium ('It faces west, and round the back and sides')
First privately printed as a pamphlet by Clement Shorter (London, 1916) and by FEH (London, 1918); first pub. *Early Life* (1928); Gibson, pp. [3]–4; Hynes, III, [279]–80.

HrT 303 Fair copy, revised, signed (initials), one page, annotated '[T. Hardy's <first> earliest known production in verse]' and '(original written between 1857 and 1860/ this being a copy some years later.)'.

Facsimile in Gibson, p. [2]; Microfilm Edition, Reel 5.

Dorset County Museum.

HrT 304 Typescript, together with 3 pages of corrections (dictated by Hardy) in FEH's hand, printer's copy for FEH's pamphlet.

Cockerell sale catalogue says the corrections are in Hardy's hand; Lot 305 included an uncorrected? six-page proof dated 20 June 1918 also for FEH's pamphlet.

Cockerell Sale, Lot 305, sold to Alan G. Thomas.

Donaghadee ('I've never gone to Donaghadee')
First pub. *Human Shows* (1925); Gibson, pp. 796–7; Hynes, III, 117–18.

HrT 305 Fair copy, revised, in MS Human Shows (f. 146).

Yale.

HrT 306 Fair copy, one line cancelled, signed (initials), one page, as sent to St John Ervine with a letter of 13 September 1925.

This letter printed *Letters*, VI, 350–1; this MS is bound with an apparently non-authoritative typescript of the poem.

Texas.

HrT 307 Revisions to lines 3 and 23 in HS Proof (pp. 205–6).

Dorset County Museum.

Doom and She ('There dwells a mighty pair —')
First pub. *Poems of the Past and the Present* (1902); Gibson, pp. 118–20; Hynes, I, 152–4.

HrT 308 Fair copy, revised, in MS Poems of the Past and the Present.

Bodleian, MS Eng. poet. d. 18, ff. 52–3 (rectos only).

Drawing Details in an Old Church ('I hear the bell-rope sawing')
First pub. *Late Lyrics* (1922); Gibson, p. 690; Hynes, II, 475–6.

HrT 309 Fair copy, revised, in MS Late Lyrics (f. 183).

Dorset County Museum.

The Dream-Follower ('A dream of mine flew over the mead')
First pub. *Poems of the Past and the Present* (1902); Gibson, p. 143; Hynes, I, 179–80.

HrT 310 Fair copy, revised, in MS Poems of the Past and the Present.

Bodleian, MS Eng. poet. d. 18, f. 87.

The Dream is — Which? ('I am laughing by the brook with her')

First pub. *Late Lyrics* (1922); Gibson, p. 650; Hynes, II, 427.

HrT 311 Fair copy, revised, the title altered from 'As if not there', in MS Late Lyrics (f. 125); dated March 1913.

Dorset County Museum.

Dream of the City Shopwoman (''Twere sweet to have a comrade here')
First pub. *Late Lyrics* (1922); Gibson, pp. 609–10; Hynes, II, 379–80.

HrT 312 Fair copy, revised, in MS Late Lyrics (f. 69), annotated '<(From old MS.)>'; dated Westbourne Park Villas, 1866.

Dorset County Museum.

A Dream or No ('Why go to Saint-Juliot? What's Juliot to me?')
First pub. *Satires of Circumstance* (1914); Gibson, p. 348; Hynes, II, 58–9. This poem is cancelled in *Selected Poems* (1917); see INTRODUCTION.

HrT 313 Fair copy, revised, here entitled 'A <The> Dream Indeed?' and beginning 'Why journey to Juliot?...', in MS Satires of Circumstance (pp. 85–6); dated 1913.

Dorset County Museum.

HrT 314 Correction to line 8 in *Collected Poems* (1923), p. 327.

Dorset County Museum.

HrT 314.5 Corrected page proof, annotated by Hardy to explain the different spellings of 'Vallency' in this poem and 'A Death-Day Recalled' (see HrT 285.5), signed (initials), page numbers altered (in an unidentified hand) from 113–14 to 85–6.

Annotation printed Hynes, II, 491.

National Library of Scotland, R. & R. Clark Papers, Dep. 229/292 (on deposit).

Dream Question ('I asked the Lord: "Sire, is this true')
First pub. *Time's Laughingstocks* (1909); Gibson, pp. 261–2; Hynes, I, 316–17.

HrT 315 Fair copy, revised, the title altered from 'An Inquiry', in MS Time's Laughingstocks (f. 90).

Fitzwilliam Museum.

Drinking Song ('Once on a time when thought began')
First pub. *Daily Telegraph*, 14 June 1928; collected *Winter Words* (1928); Gibson, pp. 905–8; Hynes, III, 247–50.

HrT 316 Fair copy, revised, the title altered in pencil to 'Drinking Song on Great Thoughts belittled (?)', in MS Winter Words.

Queen's College, Oxford, MS 420, ff. 106–8 (rectos only).

A Drizzling Easter Morning ('And he is risen? Well, be it so....')
First pub. *Late Lyrics* (1922); Gibson, pp. 658–9; Hynes, II, 437.

HrT 317 Fair copy, revised, the title altered from 'A Wet Easter Morning', in MS Late Lyrics (f. 137).

Dorset County Museum.

Drummer Hodge ('They throw in Drummer Hodge, to rest')
First pub. *Literature*, 25 November 1899, as 'The Dead Drummer'; collected as 'The Dead Drummer' in *Poems of the Past and the Present* (1902); Gibson, pp. 90–1; Hynes, I, 122.

HrT 318 Fair copy, here entitled 'The Dead Drummer', in MS Poems of the Past and the Present.

Bodleian, MS Eng. poet. d. 18, f. 9.

HrT 319 Revision to line 16 in *Selected Poems* (1917), p. 191.

Dorset County Museum.

The Duel ('"I am here to time, you see')
First pub. *Moments of Vision* (1917); Gibson, pp. 449–50; Hynes, II, 184–5.

HrT 320 Fair copy, revised, in MS Moments of Vision (f. 34).

Magdalene College, Cambridge.

A Duettist to Her Pianoforte ('Since every sound moves memories')
First pub. *Late Lyrics* (1922); Gibson, pp. 586–7; Hynes, II, 353–4.

HrT 321 Fair copy, revised, the title altered from 'The Duettist...' and subtitled '<A Song of Silence>', in MS Late Lyrics (ff. 37–8).

Dorset County Museum.

During Wind and Rain ('They sing their dearest songs —')
First pub. *Moments of Vision* (1917); Gibson, pp. 495–6; Hynes, II, 239–40.

HrT 322 Fair copy, revised, in MS Moments of Vision (f. 112).

Facsimile in Maurice Douglas Brown, *Thomas Hardy* (London, 1954), facing p. 96.

Magdalene College, Cambridge.

The Dynasts, see HrT 1610–35.

An East-End Curate ('A small blind street off East Commercial Road')
First pub. *London Mercury*, November 1924; collected *Human Shows* (1925); Gibson, p. 713; Hynes, III, 19–20.

HrT 323 Fair copy, in MS Human Shows (f. 19).

Yale.

The Echo-elf Answers ('How much shall I love her?')
First pub. *Human Shows* (1925); Gibson, pp. 794–5; Hynes, III, 114–15.

HrT 324 Fair copy, revised, subtitled '<(Impromptu)>', in MS Human Shows (f. 142).

Yale.

The Elopement ('"A woman never agreed to it!" said my knowing friend to me.')
First pub. *Satires of Circumstance* (1914); Gibson, pp. 377–8; Hynes, II, 93–4.

HrT 325 Fair copy, revised, in MS Satires of Circumstance (p. 128).

Dorset County Museum.

Embarcation ('Here, where Vespasian's legions struck the sands')
First pub. *Daily Chronicle*, 25 October 1899, as 'The Departure'; collected *Poems of the Past and the Present* (1902); Gibson, p. [86]; Hynes, I, [116].

HrT 326 Fair copy, revised, in MS Poems of the Past and the Present.

Bodleian, MS Eng. poet. d. 18, f. 2.

HrT 327 Fair copy, signed, here entitled 'The Departure./Southampton Docks: Oct., 1899', one page (one leaf containing also HrT 430).

Facsimile at Dorset County Museum.

Riddetts Auction Galleries, 4 December 1980, sold to Mr Rushton, Commins.

HrT 328 Corrections and addition of date 'October 1899' to subtitle in *Selected Poems* (1917), p. 187.

Dorset County Museum.

The End of the Episode ('Indulge no more may we')
First pub. *Time's Laughingstocks* (1909); Gibson, pp. 226–7; Hynes, I, 277.

HrT 329 Fair copy, in MS Time's Laughingstocks (f. 50).

Fitzwilliam Museum.

HrT 330 Revision to line 4 in DCM Wessex Edition (Verse Vol. III, 315).

Dorset County Museum.

End of the Year 1912 ('You were here at his young beginning')
First pub. *Late Lyrics* (1922); Gibson, p. 605; Hynes, II, 375.

HrT 331 Fair copy, revised, the title altered from 'End of the Old Year', in MS Late Lyrics (f. 64).

Dorset County Museum.

The Enemy's Portrait ('He saw the portrait of his enemy, offered')
First pub. *Moments of Vision* (1917); Gibson, pp. 523–4; Hynes, II, 272–4.

HrT 332 Fair copy, revised, in MS Moments of Vision (f. 156).

Magdalene College, Cambridge.

England to Germany in 1914 ('"O England, may God punish thee!"')
First printed privately by FEH as a pamphlet (London, February 1917); first pub. *Moments of Vision* (1917); Gibson, p. 540; Hynes, II, 291–2.

HrT 333 Fair copy, revised, in MS Moments of Vision (f. 180); dated Autumn 1914.

Magdalene College, Cambridge.

HrT 334 Proof for FEH's pamphlet, corrected in an unidentified hand, here entitled 'England to Germany' (including also HrT 530, 812); dated 8 February 1917.

Cockerell Sale, Lot 261, sold to Alan G. Thomas; these corrections not mentioned Gibson or Hynes.

Owned (1984) F. B. Adams (see Hynes, II, 304).

Epeisodia ('Past the hills that peep')
First pub. *Late Lyrics* (1922); Gibson, pp. 565–6; Hynes, II, 328–9.

HrT 335 Fair copy, revised, in MS Late Lyrics (f. 4).

Dorset County Museum.

HrT 336 Revision to line 24 in *Collected Poems* (1923), p. 535.

Dorset County Museum.

Epilogue to *The Dynasts* ('We have now set forth, in our imperfect way')
Recited at performances of 'The Dynasts' (Granville Barker production) at the Kingsway Theatre, London (and printed in the accompanying programme), 25 November 1914–January 1915; privately printed by Clement Shorter in pamphlet *The Dynasts. The Prologue and Epilogue* ([c. December 1914]); last six lines first pub. *Fortnightly Review*, February 1915; first pub. in full Gibson (1976), p. 950; Hynes, III, 298–9.

HrT 337 Draft, in pencil, on a leaf (one page) stuck onto p. 523 of Hardy's copy of *The Dynasts* (1910), used for Granville Barker's 1914–15 production (HrT 1630) (including also HrT 942).

Dorset County Museum.

HrT 338 Typescript, containing one correction, signed, as sent for use in Shorter's pamphlet; [1914].

Texas.

HrT 338.5 Typescript, revised by Hardy, on f. 47 of a typescript of 'Wessex Scenes from "The Dynasts"' (HrT 1634); [1916].

Microfilm Edition, Reel 3.

Dorset County Museum.

Epitaph ('I never cared for Life: Life cared for me')
First pub. *Late Lyrics* (1922); Gibson, p. 695; Hynes, II, 481.

HrT 339 Fair copy, revised, in MS Late Lyrics (f. 188).

Dorset County Museum.

Epitaph [for G. K. Chesterton] ('Here lies nipped in this narrow cyst')
First pub. J. O. Bailey, *The Poetry of Thomas Hardy* (Chapel Hill, NC, 1970); Gibson, p. 954; Hynes, III, 308–9.

HrT 340 Transcript by FEH, revised, one page, in an envelope (containing also HrT 857, 1462) annotated by FEH 'Last lines dicated [sic] by T. H. referring to George Moore and G. K. Chesterton. Also a pencilled note, by himself, about my biography.' and 'Two epitaphs...dictated by Hardy on his death-bed.'; dated in an unidentified hand January 1928.

Microfilm Edition, Reel 6.

Dorset County Museum.

Epitaph for George Moore ('"No mortal man beneath the sky'), see HrT 857.

Epitaph on a Pessimist ('I'm Smith of Stoke, aged sixty-odd')

First pub. *London Mercury*, September 1925; collected *Human Shows* (1925); Gibson, p. 803; Hynes, III, 124. For a source epigram in Greek, see HrT 1804.

HrT 341 Fair copy, in MS Human Shows (f. 154), annotated 'From the French.'.

Yale.

HrT 342 Annotation revised to 'From the French and Greek' in HS Proof (p. 219).

Dorset County Museum.

The Eve of Waterloo ('The eyelids of eve fall together at last'), see HrT 1620, 1624–5.

Evelyn G. of Christminster ('I can see the towers')
First pub. *Late Lyrics* (1922); Gibson, pp. 621–3; Hynes, II, 393–4.

HrT 343 Fair copy, revised, the title altered from 'To Evelyn of Christminster', in MS Late Lyrics (f. 84).

Dorset County Museum.

An Evening in Galilee ('She looks far west towards Carmel, shading her eyes with her hand')
First pub. *Winter Words* (1928); Gibson, pp. 879–80; Hynes, III, 216–17.

HrT 344 Fair copy, revised, in MS Winter Words.

Queen's College, Oxford, MS 420, f. 66.

Evening Shadows ('The shadows of my chimneys stretch afar')
First pub. *Daily Telegraph*, 7 May 1928; collected *Winter Words* (1928); Gibson, p. 853; Hynes, III, 186–7.

HrT 345 Fair copy, revised, in MS Winter Words.

Queen's College, Oxford, MS 420, f. 28.

Every Artemisia ('"Your eye-light wanes with an ail of care')
First pub. *Human Shows* (1925); Gibson, pp. 722–3; Hynes, III, 31–2.

HrT 346 Fair copy, revised, in MS Human Shows (ff. 34–5, rectos only).

Yale.

HrT 347 Corrections in HS Proof (pp. 50–1).

Dorset County Museum.

Everything Comes ('"The house is bleak and cold')
First pub. *Moments of Vision* (1917); Gibson, p. 508; Hynes, II, 254.

HrT 348 Fair copy, revised, in MS Moments of Vision (f. 133).

Magdalene College, Cambridge.

Exeunt Omnes ('Everybody else, then, going')
First pub. *Satires of Circumstance* (1914); Gibson, p. 414; Hynes, II, 137–8.

HrT 349 Fair copy, revised, the title altered from 'Epilogue', in MS Satires of Circumstance (p. 183); dated 2 June 1913.

Dorset County Museum.

Expectation and Experience ('"I had a holiday once," said the woman —')
First pub. *Winter Words* (1928); Gibson, p. 847; Hynes, III, 180.

HrT 350 Fair copy, revised, in MS Winter Words.

Queen's College, Oxford, MS 420, f. 21.

An Experience ('Wit, weight, or wealth there was not')
First pub. *Late Lyrics* (1922); Gibson, pp. 615–16; Hynes, II, 386–7.

HrT 351 Fair copy, revised, in MS Late Lyrics (f. 76).

Dorset County Museum.

An Expostulation ('Why want to go afar')
First pub. *Human Shows* (1925); Gibson, p. 793; Hynes, III, 113.

HrT 352 Fair copy, in MS Human Shows (f. 140).

Yale.

The Face at the Casement ('If ever joy leave')
First pub. *Satires of Circumstance* (1914); Gibson, pp. 315–17; Hynes, II, 22–4. This poem is cancelled in *Selected Poems* (1917); see INTRODUCTION.

HrT 353 Fair copy, revised, in MS Satires of Circumstance (pp. 21–3).

Dorset County Museum.

HrT 354 Revisions to lines 3 and 13 in *Selected Poems* (1916), p. 152.

The revision to line 3 is printed Hynes, II, 488.

Dorset County Museum.

The Faded Face ('How was this I did not see')
First pub. *Moments of Vision* (1917); Gibson, pp. 447–8; Hynes, II, 182–3.

HrT 355 Fair copy, revised, in MS Moments of Vision (f. 32).

Magdalene College, Cambridge.

HrT 356 Proof corrections for the Wessex Edition to lines 19 and 21, sent in a postcard to R. & R. Clark, 26 July 1919, date stamped 29 July 1919.

Corrections printed Hynes, II, 498; note not in *Letters*.

National Library of Scotland, R. & R. Clark Papers, Dep. 229/292 (on deposit).

The Fading Rose ('I saw a rose, in bloom, but sad')
First pub. *Human Shows* (1925); Gibson, pp. 771–2; Hynes, III, 89.

HrT 357 Fair copy, revised, in MS Human Shows (f. 105).

Yale.

Faintheart in a Railway Train ('At nine in the morning there passed a church')
First pub. *London Mercury*, January 1920, as 'A Glimpse from the Train'; collected *Late Lyrics* (1922); Gibson, p. 566; Hynes, II, 329.

HrT 358 Fair copy of first publication version, here entitled 'A Glimpse from the Train', pasted on an uncorrected proof of 'Going and Staying' and sent to J. C. Squire (editor of *London Mercury*) with a letter dated 14 October 1919.

Letter only printed *Letters*, V, 330.

Colby College.

HrT 359 Fair copy, in MS Late Lyrics (f. 5).

Dorset County Museum.

HrT 360 Revision to line 7 in *Collected Poems* (1923), p. 536.

Dorset County Museum.

The Faithful Swallow ('When summer shone')
First pub. *Human Shows* (1925); Gibson, p. 759; Hynes, III, 73–4.

HrT 361 Fair copy, revised, in MS Human Shows (f. 85).

Yale.

Faithful Wilson ('"I say she's handsome, by all laws')
First pub. *Daily Telegraph*, 16 April 1928; collected *Winter Words* (1928); Gibson, pp. 892–3; Hynes, III, 233.

HrT 362 Fair copy, in MS Winter Words.

Queen's College, Oxford, MS 420, f. 88.

The Fallow Deer at the Lonely House ('One without looks in to-night')
First pub. *Late Lyrics* (1922); Gibson, p. 598; Hynes, II, 366.

HrT 363 Fair copy, in MS Late Lyrics (f. 53).

Dorset County Museum.

HrT 364 Fair copy, signed, inscribed '(For Cheltenham College Library.)', one page; dated March 1925.

Facsimile in British Library, MS Facs. Suppl. XI (15), f. 61.

Cheltenham College.

Family Portraits ('Three picture-drawn people stepped out of their frames —')
First pub. (7-stanza version) *Nash's and Pall Mall Magazine*, December 1924, as 'The Portraits'; reprinted as Appendix B, Hynes, III, 343–4; first pub. in full *Daily Telegraph*, 6 August 1928; collected in *Winter Words* (1928); Gibson, pp. 919–21; Hynes, III, 262–4.

HrT 365 Fair copy, revised, in MS Winter Words, annotated '*[Sent to Macm — for serial pubn in America]*'.

Queen's College, Oxford, MS 420, ff. 126–7 (rectos only).

The Famous Tragedy of the Queen of Cornwall, see HrT 1637–42.

Farmer Dunman's Funeral ('"Bury me on a Sunday"')
First pub. *Human Shows* (1925); Gibson, pp. 776–7; Hynes, III, 94–5.

HrT 366 Fair copy, revised, in MS Human Shows (f. 113).

Yale.

HrT 367 Revision to line 5 and additional (unpublished) stanza in HS Proof (p. 161).

Additional stanza printed Hynes, III, 315.

Dorset County Museum.

The Farm-Woman's Winter ('If seasons all were summers')
First pub. *Pall Mall Magazine*, January 1905; collected *Time's Laughingstocks* (1909); Gibson, pp. 214–15; Hynes, I, 262.

HrT 368 Fair copy, in MS Time's Laughingstocks (f. 33).

Fitzwilliam Museum.

HrT 369 Fair copy, signed, one leaf.

University of California at Berkeley.

The Felled Elm and She ('When you put on that inmost ring')
First pub. *Winter Words* (1928); Gibson, pp. 868–9; Hynes, III, 204.

HrT 370 Fair copy, revised, of an early version, here entitled 'The Thrown Elm', one page.

Facsimile in David Holmes Catalogue.

David Holmes Catalogue 5 (n.d.), Item 48.

HrT 371 Fair copy, revised, the title altered from 'The Thrown Elm and She', in MS Winter Words.

Queen's College, Oxford, MS 420, f. 50.

Fetching Her ('An hour before the dawn')
First pub. *Late Lyrics* (1922); Gibson, pp. 636–7; Hynes, II, 412–13.

HrT 372 Fair copy, revised, in MS Late Lyrics (f. 104).

Dorset County Museum.

The Fiddler ('The fiddler knows what's brewing')
First pub. *Time's Laughingstocks* (1909); Gibson, p, 248; Hynes, I, 300–301.

HrT 373 Fair copy, in MS Time's Laughingstocks (f. 75).

Fitzwilliam Museum.

The Fiddler's Story, see HrT 251—3.

The Fight on Durnover Moor ('We'd loved, we two, some while')
First pub. *Human Shows* (1925); Gibson, pp. 763–5; Hynes, III, 79–81.

HrT 374 Fair copy, revised, in MS Human Shows (ff. 92–4, rectos only).

Yale.

HrT 375 Revision to line 15 and correction to line 20 in HS Proof (p. 134).

Dorset County Museum.

The Figure in the Scene ('It pleased her to step in front and sit')

First pub. *Moments of Vision* (1917); Gibson, p. 476; Hynes, II, 216–17.

HrT 376 Fair copy, revised, in MS Moments of Vision (f. 78).

Magdalene College, Cambridge.

HrT 377 Quotation of lines 3–5 only, on a pen-and-ink sketch of the scene described in the poem, annotated 'Beeny Cliff (Aug. 22. '70)/ *The Figure in the Scene*.'.

The drawing (and another pencil version of same scene) mentioned Hynes, II, 499–500.

Dorset County Museum.

The Fire at Tranter Sweatley's, see HrT 155–8.

First or Last ('If grief come early')
First pub. *Late Lyrics* (1922); Gibson, p. 652; Hynes, II, 429.

HrT 378 Fair copy, in MS Late Lyrics (f. 128).

Dorset County Museum.

First Sight of Her and After ('A day is drawing to its fall')
First pub. *Selected Poems* (1916), as 'The Return from First Beholding Her'; collected *Moments of Vision* (1917), as 'The Day of First Sight'; Gibson, p. 433; Hynes, II, 165–6.

HrT 379 Fair copy, here entitled 'The Day of First Sight', in MS Moments of Vision (f. 12).

Magdalene College, Cambridge.

HrT 380 Revision of title in *Selected Poems* (1916), p. 15.

Dorset County Museum.

HrT 381 Revision of title and corrections to lines 8 and 10 in *Selected Poems* (1917), p. 15.

Dorset County Museum.

HrT 382 Revision of title to 'The Return from First Meeting Her' in the hand of Sydney Cockerell, in a copy of *Selected Poems* (1916) (containing also HrT 122, 753) presented to Cockerell by Hardy, October 1916, and annotated by Cockerell on the inside front cover 'The corrections...were given mc by the author at Max Gate May 25, 1918.'.

Cockerell Sale, Lot 260, sold to Maggs.

Owned (1984) F. B. Adams (see Hynes, II, 496).

The Five Students ('The sparrow dips in his wheel-rut bath')
First pub. *Moments of Vision* (1917); Gibson, pp. 493–4; Hynes, II, 236–7.

HrT 383 Fair copy, revised, containing 2 additional (unpublished) stanzas, in MS Moments of Vision (f. 108).

The additional stanzas printed Hynes, II, 237.

Magdalene College, Cambridgc.

The Flirt's Tragedy ('Here alone by the logs in my chamber')
First pub. *Time's Laughingstocks* (1909); Gibson, pp. 210–13; Hynes, I, 258–62.

HrT 384 Fair copy, revised, in MS Time's Laughingstocks (ff. 27–31).

Fitzwilliam Museum.

HrT 385 Revisions to lines 31–2 in DCM Wessex Edition (Verse Vol. III, 289).

Dorset County Museum.

The Flower's Tragedy ('In the bedchamber window, near the glass')
First pub. *Human Shows* (1925); Gibson, p. 784; Hynes, III, 103.

HrT 386 Fair copy, revised, in MS Human Shows (f. 125); dated '<About 1910.>'.

Yale.

'For Life I had never cared greatly' ('For Life I had never cared greatly')
First pub. *Moments of Vision* (1917); Gibson, p. 537; Hynes, II, 288.

HrT 387 Fair copy, revised, in MS Moments of Vision (f. 174).

Magdalene College, Cambridge.

The Forbidden Banns ('"O what's the gain, my worthy Sir')
First pub. *Human Shows* (1925); Gibson, pp. 813–14; Hynes, III, 136–7.

HrT 388 Fair copy, revised, in MS Human Shows (f. 171).

Yale.

HrT 389 Revisions to lines 2 and 9 and correction to line 24 in HS Proof (p. 241).

Dorset County Museum.

A Forgotten Miniature ('There you are in the dark')
First pub. *Winter Words* (1928); Gibson, pp. 899–900; Hynes, III, 240–1.

HrT 390 Fair copy, revised, in MS Winter Words.

Queen's College, Oxford, MS 420, f. 97.

Former Beauties ('These market-dames, mid-aged, with lips thin-drawn')
First pub. *Time's Laughingstocks* (1909), as 'At Casterbridge Fair. II.'; Gibson, pp. 239–40; Hynes, I, 291–2.

HrT 391 Fair copy, here headed 'II.', in MS Time's Laughingstocks (f. 64).

Fitzwilliam Museum.

The Forsaking of the Nest ('The hoers quit the mangel-field'), see HrT 1160–2.

Four Footprints ('Here are the tracks upon the sand')
First pub. *Time's Laughingstocks* (1909); Gibson, p. 225; Hynes, I, 275.

HrT 392 Fair copy, revised, in MS Time's Laughingstocks (f. 48).

Fitzwilliam Museum.

Four in the Morning ('At four this day of June I rise:')
First pub. *Human Shows* (1925); Gibson, pp. 714–15; Hynes, III, 22.

HrT 393 Fair copy, revised, in MS Human Shows (f. 21), annotated 'Bockhampton'.

Yale.

HrT 394 Suggested revision to line 6 in HS Proof (p. 31).

Dorset County Museum.

Fragment ('At last I entered a long dark gallery')
First pub. *Moments of Vision* (1917); Gibson, pp. 513–14; Hynes, II, 261.

HrT 395 Fair copy, revised, in MS Moments of Vision (f. 142).

Magdalene College, Cambridge.

'Freed the fret of thinking' ('Freed the fret of thinking')
First pub. *The Adelphi*, May 1925; collected *Human Shows* (1925); Gibson, pp. 753–4; Hynes, III, 67–8.

HrT 396 Fair copy, revised, in MS Human Shows (f. 78).

Yale.

Friends Beyond ('William Dewy, Tranter Reuben, Farmer Ledlow late at plough')
First pub. *Wessex Poems* (1898); Gibson, pp. 59–60; Hynes, I, 78–9.

HrT 397 Fair copy, revised, in MS Wessex Poems (ff. 76–7).

Birmingham City Museum and Art Gallery.

HrT 398 Revision to line 16 in a copy of *The Oxford Book of Victorian Verse*, ed. Arthur Quiller-Couch (Oxford, 1912), p. 632.

Dorset County Museum.

HrT 399 Correction to line 21 in *Selected Poems* (1916), p. 113.

Dorset County Museum.

HrT 400 Corrections in *Selected Poems* (1917), p. 113.

Dorset County Museum.

From Her in the Country ('I thought and thought of thy crass clanging town')
First pub. *Time's Laughingstocks* (1909); Gibson, p. 234; Hynes, I, 284–5.

HrT 401 Fair copy, revised, in MS Time's Laughingstocks (f. 59); dated 16 Westbourne Park Villas, 1866.

Fitzwilliam Museum.

From *The Dynasts*, see HrT 1613–15, 1617, 1620–22, 1624–5, 1635.

From *The Queen of Cornwall*, see HrT 1637.

From Victor Hugo ('Child, were I king, I'd yield my royal rule')
First pub. *Poems of the Past and the Present* (1902); Gibson, pp. 182–3; Hynes, I, 224.

HrT 402 Fair copy, extensively revised, here entitled '<After> From Victor Hugo', in MS Poems of the Past and the Present.

Bodleian, MS Eng. poet. d. 18, f. 151.

The Frozen Greenhouse ('"There was a frost')
First pub. *Human Shows* (1925); Gibson, pp. 736–7; Hynes, III, 47–8.

HrT 403 Fair copy, in MS Human Shows (f. 54).

Yale.

Gallant's Song ('When the maiden leaves off teasing')
First pub. *Winter Words* (1928); Gibson, p. 893; Hynes, III, 234.

HrT 404 Fair copy, in MS Winter Words; dated November 1868.

Queen's College, Oxford, MS 420, f. 89.

HrT 405 Fair copy, the title altered from 'Dandy's Song'.

Owned (1985) F. B. Adams (see Hynes).

The Gap in the White ('Something had cracked in her mouth as she slept')
First pub. *Winter Words* (1928); Gibson, p. 919; Hynes, III, 262.

HrT 406 Fair copy, revised, in MS Winter Words.

Queen's College, Oxford, MS 420, f. 125.

The Garden Seat ('Its former green is blue and thin')
First pub. *Late Lyrics* (1922); Gibson, p. 567; Hynes, II, 331.

HrT 407 Fair copy, revised, in MS Late Lyrics (f. 7).

Dorset County Museum.

General Preface to the Novels and Poems, see HrT 1419–20.

Genitrix Laesa ('Nature, through these generations')
First pub. *Human Shows* (1925); Gibson, pp. 770–1; Hynes, III, 88–9.

HrT 408 Fair copy, revised, here subtitled '(<Metre> Measure of a Sarum Sequence.)', in MS Human Shows (f. 104).

Yale.

HrT 409 Revision to subtitle in HS Proof (p. 148).

Dorset County Museum.

Genoa and the Mediterranean ('O epic-famed, god-haunted Central Sea')
First pub. *Poems of the Past and the Present* (1902); Gibson, p. 100; Hynes, I, 132.

HrT 410 Fair copy, revised, in MS Poems of the Past and the Present.

Bodleian, MS Eng. poet. d. 18, ff. 22–3 (rectos only).

A Gentleman's Epitaph on Himself and a Lady, who were Buried Together ('I dwelt in the shade of a city')

First pub. *Late Lyrics* (1922); Gibson, pp. 584–5; Hynes, II, 350–1.

HrT 411 Fair copy, in MS Late Lyrics (f. 34).

Dorset County Museum.

'A Gentleman's Second-hand Suit' ('Here it is hanging in the sun')
First pub. *Harper's Monthly Magazine*, March 1928; collected *Winter Words* (1928); Gibson, pp. 883–4; Hynes, III, 221–2.

HrT 412 Draft, 2 leaves (rectos only), on the versos of two printed forms, one dated 22 November 1926.

Microfilm Edition, Reel 5.

Dorset County Museum.

HrT 413 Fair copy, revised, annotated in pencil '[Harpers Magazine through Mr Wells Dec. 1927]', in MS Winter Words.

Queen's College, Oxford, MS 420, ff. 72–3 (rectos only).

Geographical Knowledge ('Where Blackmoor was, the road that led')
First pub. *The Outlook*, 1 April 1905 (7-stanza version); collected *Time's Laughingstocks* (1909) (6-stanza version); Gibson, pp. 287–8; Hynes, I, 345–6.

HrT 414 Fair copy, revised, of 6-stanza version, in MS Time's Laughingstocks (f. 126).

Fitzwilliam Museum.

George Meredith ('Forty years back, when much had place')
First pub. *The Times*, 22 May 1909, as 'G. M. 1828–1909'; collected *Time's Laughingstocks* (1909), as 'G. M. 1828–1909'; Gibson, pp. 297–8; Hynes, I, 358.

HrT 415 Fair copy, here entitled 'G. M. 1828–1909' in MS Time's Laughingstocks (f. 140); dated May 1909.

Fitzwilliam Museum.

The Ghost of the Past ('We two kept house, the Past and I')
First pub. *Satires of Circumstance* (1914); Gibson, pp. 308–9; Hynes, II, 13–14.

HrT 416 Fair copy, revised, in MS Satires of Circumstance (pp. 8–9).

Dorset County Museum.

HrT 417 Revision to line 31 in *Selected Poems* (1916), p. 48.

Dorset County Museum.

HrT 418 Corrections and revision to lines 23, 31 and 39 in *Selected Poems* (1917), pp. 47–8.

Dorset County Museum.

The Glimpse ('She sped through the door')
First pub. *Moments of Vision* (1917); Gibson, pp. 501–2; Hynes, II, 246–7.

HrT 419 Fair copy, revised, in MS Moments of Vision (p. 123).

Magdalene College, Cambridge.

God-Forgotten ('I towered far, and lo! I stood within')
First pub. *Poems of the Past and the Present* (1902); Gibson, pp. 123–4; Hynes, I, 157–9.

HrT 420 Fair copy, revised, in MS Poems of the Past and the Present.

Bodleian, MS Eng. poet. d. 18, ff. 59–61 (rectos only).

God's Education ('I saw him steal the light away')
First pub. *Time's Laughingstocks* (1909), as 'His Education'; Gibson, pp. 278–9; Hynes, I, 335.

HrT 421 Fair copy, revised, here entitled 'His Education', in MS Time's Laughingstocks (f. 113).

Fitzwilliam Museum.

God's Funeral ('I saw a slowly-stepping train –')
First pub. *Fortnightly Review*, 1 March 1912; collected *Satires of Circumstance* (1914); Gibson, pp. 326–9; Hynes, II, 34–7.

HrT 422 Fair copy, in MS Satires of Circumstance (pp. 38–41); dated 1908–10.

Dorset County Museum.

HrT 423 Fair copy, revised, 4 numbered leaves, annotated by Hardy '[Original MS.]' and '[First published in the Fortnightly Review from a type-written copy.]'; dated 'Begun 1908: finished 1910', inscribed on separate title page to Edmund Gosse, July 1913.

Facsimile of separate title page in Sotheby's sale catalogue, 30 July 1928 (Gosse Sale), p. 12.

Owned (1984) F. B. Adams (see Hynes).

The Going ('Why did you give no hint that night')
First pub. *Satires of Circumstance*(1914); Gibson, pp. 338–9; Hynes, II, [47]–8.

HrT 424 Fair copy, in MS Satires of Circumstance (pp. 69–70); dated December 1912.

Dorset County Museum.

HrT 425 Revision to line 9 in *Selected Poems* (1916), p. 59.

Dorset County Museum.

HrT 426 Revision to line 9 in *Selected Poems* (1917), p. 59.

Dorset County Museum.

Going and Staying ('The moving sun-shapes on the spray')
First pub. *London Mercury*, November 1919 (stanzas 1–2 only); first pub. in full *Late Lyrics* (1922); Gibson, pp. 573–4; Hynes, II, 338–9. An uncorrected proof of the first publication (as sent to the *London Mercury* with HrT 358 pasted on to it) is at Colby College.

HrT 427 Fair copy of first publication version (i.e., without stanza 3).

Eton College.

HrT 428 Fair copy, in MS Late Lyrics (f. 17).

Dorset County Museum.

The Going of the Battery ('O it was sad enough, weak enough, mad enough —')
First pub. *The Graphic*, 11 November 1899 (without stanza 1); first pub. in full *Poems of the Past and the Present* (1902); Gibson, pp. 88–9; Hynes, I, 118–20.

HrT 429 Fair copy, revised, in MS Poems of the Past and the Present.

Bodleian, MS Eng. poet. d. 18, ff. 6–7 (rectos only).

HrT 430 Fair copy, wanting stanzas 1 and 5, headed '*Wives' Voices*:', signed, including an introductory note, 2 pages (one leaf containing also HrT 327).

Facsimile in Dorset County Museum.

Riddetts Auction Galleries, 4 December 1980, sold to Mr Rushton, Commins.

HrT 431 Addition of stanza 1 and subtitle (including the date 2 November 1899) in *Selected Poems* (1917), pp. 189–90.

Dorset County Museum.

The Graveyard of Dead Creeds ('I lit upon the graveyard of dead creeds')
First pub. *Human Shows* (1925); Gibson, pp. 724–5; Hynes, III, 33–4.

HrT 432 Fair copy, revised, in MS Human Shows (f. 37).

Yale.

Great Things ('Sweet cyder is a great thing')
First pub.*Moments of Vision* (1917); Gibson, pp. 474–5; Hynes, II, 214–15.

HrT 433 Fair copy, revised, in MS Moments of Vision (f. 76).

Magdalene College, Cambridge.

HrT 433.5 Corrections in Hardy's copy of the Wessex Edition (Verse Vol. IV, 275–6), presented to Sydney Cockerell by FEH, 30 March 1928 (see DCM Wessex Edition).

Cockerell Sale, Lot 252, sold to Maggs.

Owned (1985) F. B. Adams (see Hynes, III, 352).

Green Slates ('It happened once, before the duller')
First pub. *Human Shows* (1925); Gibson, p. 712; Hynes, III, 19–20.

HrT 434 Fair copy, revised, in MS Human Shows (f. 18).

Yale.

Growth in May ('I enter a daisy-and-buttercup land')
First pub. *Late Lyrics* (1922); Gibson, p. 626; Hynes, II, 398–9.

HrT 435 Fair copy, revised, in MS Late Lyrics (f. 90).

Dorset County Museum.

Had you Wept ('Had you wept; had you but neared me with a hazed uncertain ray')
First pub. *Satires of Circumstance* (1914); Gibson, p. 380; Hynes, II, 96–7.

HrT 436 Fair copy, revised, here beginning 'Had you wept; had you neared me with a frail uncertain ray', in MS Satires of Circumstance (p. 132).

Dorset County Museum.

The Hangman's Song, see HrT 1121–2, 1665.

Hap ('If but some vengeful god would call to me')
First pub. *Wessex Poems* (1898); Gibson, p. 9; Hynes, I, 10.

HrT 437 Fair copy, here entitled 'Chance', in MS Wessex Poems (f. 4); dated 1866.

Birmingham City Museum and Art Gallery.

The Harbour Bridge ('From here, the quay, one looks above to mark')
First pub. *Human Shows* (1925); Gibson, pp. 774–5; Hynes, III, 92–3.

HrT 438 Fair copy, revised, in MS Human Shows (ff. 110–11, rectos only), annotated 'Weymouth.'.

Yale.

HrT 439 Correction, revision and annotation in HS Proof (p. 157).

Dorset County Museum.

The Harvest-supper ('Nell and the other maids danced their best')
First pub. *New Magazine*, December 1925; revised and collected *Human Shows* (1925); Gibson, pp. 777–8; Hynes, III, 95–7.

HrT 440 Fair copy, revised, in MS Human Shows (ff. 115–16, rectos only).

Yale.

HrT 441 Revision to line 15 in HS Proof (p. 164).

Dorset County Museum.

The Hatband ('She held it out. "But you can't both have it," she said')
First pub. in Evelyn Hardy, 'Some Unpublished Poems by Thomas Hardy', *London Magazine*, 3 (1956), 28–39 (37–8); Gibson, pp. 953–4; Hynes, III, 307–8.

HrT 442 Fair copy, slightly revised, 2 leaves (rectos only), including a footnote.

Microfilm Edition, Reel 5.

Dorset County Museum.

The Haunter ('He does not think that I haunt here nightly:')
First pub. *Satires of Circumstance* (1914); Gibson, pp. 345–6; Hynes, II, 55–6.

HrT 443 Fair copy, revised, in MS Satires of Circumstance (pp. 80–1).

Dorset County Museum.

Haunting Fingers ('"Are you awake')
First pub. *New Republic*, 21 December 1921, as 'The Haunting Fingers'; privately printed by FEH in pamphlet *Haunting Fingers* (London, 1922); collected *Late Lyrics* (1922); Gibson, pp. 590–2; Hynes, II, 357–9.

HrT 444 Fair copy, extensively revised, here entitled '<The Dead> Haunting Fingers.', 2 leaves (rectos only); annotated 'sent to New Republic Nov. 7. 1921.'.

Microfilm Edition, Reel 5.

Dorset County Museum.

HrT 445 Fair copy, revised, in MS Late Lyrics (ff. 42–4).

Dorset County Museum.

HrT 446 Typescript, slightly revised, 2 numbered leaves (rectos only), printer's copy for FEH's pamphlet, together with HrT 1267.

Cockerell Sale, Lot 287, sold to Hollings.

New York University.

HrT 447 Corrected first proof and uncorrected second proof for FEH's pamphlet; first proof dated by Sydney Cockerell 24 January 1922, second proof dated by Cockerell 31 January 1922.

Cockerell Sale, Lot 287, sold to Hollings; this lot also included another copy of first proof, corrected by Cockerell, now also at New York University.

New York University.

He Abjures Love ('At last I put off love')
First pub. *Time's Laughingstocks* (1909); Gibson, pp. 236–7; Hynes, I, 288–9.

HrT 448 Fair copy, in MS Time's Laughingstocks (f. 62A); dated 1883.

Fitzwilliam Museum.

HrT 449 Correction to line 19 on p. 87 of Hardy's copy of *Time's Laughingstocks* (1909) (containing also HrT 258, 595).

Dorset County Museum.

Hrt 450 Correction to line 19 in DCM Wessex Edition (Verse Vol. III, 332).

Dorset County Museum.

HrT 451 Revision to line 19 in *Selected Poems* (1916), p. 90.

Dorset County Museum.

HrT 452 Revision to line 19 in *Selected Poems* (1917), p. 90.

Dorset County Museum.

He Did Not Know Me ('He said: "I do not know you')
First pub. *Daily Telegraph*, 17 May 1928; collected *Winter Words* (1928); Gibson, p. 869; Hynes, III, 205.

HrT 453 Fair copy, revised, in MS Winter Words.

Queen's College, Oxford, MS 420, f. 51.

HrT 454 Fair copy, revised, wanting subtitle, annotated in pencil '[best]', one page, sent by FEH to an unidentified recipient with a covering letter dated 24 September 1928.

Facsimile in Sir Newman Flower and A. N. L. Munby, *English Poetical Autographs* (London, 1938), plate 38.

Texas.

He Fears His Good Fortune ('There was a glorious time')
First pub. *Moments of Vision* (1917); Gibson, pp. 509–10; Hynes, II, 255–6.

HrT 455 Draft, one page, annotated '[First rough draft]'.

Facsimile in Hodgson's sale catalogue, 23 February 1961, p. 5.

Owned (1984) F. B. Adams (see Hynes).

HrT 456 Fair copy, in MS Moments of Vision (f. 135).

Magdalene College, Cambridge.

He Follows Himself ('In a heavy time I dogged myself')
First pub. *Late Lyrics* (1922); Gibson, pp. 645–6; Hynes, II, 422–3.

HrT 457 Fair copy, revised, in MS Late Lyrics (ff. 117–18).

Dorset County Museum.

HrT 458 Suggested alternative lines 21, 26 and 28 in *Collected Poems* (1923), p. 611.

Dorset County Museum.

He inadvertently Cures his Love-pains ('I said: "O let me sing the praise')

First pub. *Human Shows* (1925); Gibson, pp. 797–8; Hynes, III, 118.

HrT 459 Fair copy, revised, in MS Human Shows (f. 147).

Yale.

HrT 460 Revisions to lines 10 and 12 in HS Proof (p. 207).

Dorset County Museum.

He Never Expected Much ('Well, World, you have kept faith with me')
First pub. *Daily Telegraph*, 19 March 1928; collected *Winter Words* (1928); Gibson, p. 886; Hynes, III, 225.

HrT 461 Draft, here entitled 'A Reconsideration/On my eighty-sixth birthday', one page; composed c. 2 June 1926.

British Library, Add. MS 59878.

HrT 462 Fair copy, revised, in MS Winter Words.

Queen's College, Oxford, MS 420, f. 77.

He Prefers Her Earthly ('This after-sunset is a sight for seeing')
First pub. *Moments of Vision* (1917); Gibson, p. 496; Hynes, II, 240–1.

HrT 463 Fair copy, here entitled 'He prefers the earthly', in MS Moments of Vision (f. 114).

Magdalene College, Cambridge.

He Resolves to Say No More ('O my soul, keep the rest unknown!')
First pub. *Daily Telegraph*, 18 September 1928; collected *Winter Words* (1928); Gibson, pp. 929–30; Hynes, III, 274.

HrT 464 Fair copy, revised, inserted in MS Winter Words, here beginning 'O my <heart> soul, keep the rest unknown'.

Facsimile in *Later Years*, facing p. 262 and as frontispiece to *Human Shows*, Wessex Edition, Verse Vol. VI (London, 1931); facsimile at Dorset County Museum is included on Microfilm Edition, Reel 5.

Queen's College, Oxford, MS 420, [f. 137].

HrT 465 Extensively revised, here beginning 'O my heart, keep the rest unknown', one page, annotated in pencil.

This MS discussed in Evelyn Hardy, 'Hardy's Last Poem: Some Revelations', *Thomas Hardy Society Review*, I (1978), 127–8.

Dorset County Museum.

He Revisits His First School ('I should not have shown in the flesh')
First pub. *Moments of Vision* (1917); Gibson, pp. 511–12; Hynes, II, 258–9.

HrT 466 Fair copy, revised, here beginning 'I should not have gone in the flesh', in MS Moments of Vision (f. 139).

Magdalene College, Cambridge.

He Wonders about Himself ('No use hoping, or feeling vext')
First pub. *Moments of Vision* (1917); Gibson, p. 510; Hynes, II, 256–7

HrT 467 Fair copy, revised, in MS Moments of Vision (f. 136); dated November 1893.

Magdalene College, Cambridge.

HrT 468 Revisions to lines 10–11 in *Collected Poems* (1923), p. 480.

Dorset County Museum.

The Head above the Fog ('Something do I see')
First pub. *Moments of Vision* (1917); Gibson, p. 481; Hynes, II, 222.

HrT 469 Fair copy, in MS Moments of Vision (f. 87).

Magdalene College, Cambridge.

Heiress and Architect ('She sought the Studios, beckoning to her side')
First pub. *Wessex Poems* (1898); Gibson, pp. 75–6; Hynes, I, 98–100.

HrT 470 Fair copy, revised, here subtitled 'To A. W. B.', in MS Wessex Poems (ff. 97–9); dated 1867.

Birmingham City Museum and Art Gallery.

HrT 471 Addition of '8 Adelphi Terrace' to date in DCM Wessex Edition (Verse Vol. I, 101).

Dorset County Museum.

Henley Regatta ('She looks from the window: still it pours down direly')
First pub. *Winter Words* (1928); Gibson, pp. 878–9; Hynes, III, 215–16.

HrT 472 Fair copy, revised, in MS Winter Words.

Queen's College, Oxford, MS 420, f. 65.

Her Apotheosis ('There were years vague of measure')
First pub. *Late Lyrics* (1922); Gibson, pp. 670–1; Hynes, II, 451–2.

HrT 473 Fair copy, revised, of a version beginning 'There was a certain summer', here subtitled '(Woman's Song)', in MS Late Lyrics (f. 153).

Dorset County Museum.

HrT 474 Correction to line 1 and suggested alterations to lines 5, 7 and 8 in *Collected Poems* (1923), p. 634.

Dorset County Museum.

Her Confession ('As some bland soul, to whom a debtor says')
First pub. *Time's Laughingstocks* (1909); Gibson, p. 234; Hynes, I, 285–6.

HrT 475 Fair copy, in MS Time's Laughingstocks (ff. 59–60); dated Westbourne Park Villas, 1865–7.

Fitzwilliam Museum.

Her Death and After ('The summons was urgent: and forth I went –')
First pub. *Wessex Poems* (1898); Gibson, pp. 39–43; Hynes, I, 51–6.

HrT 476 Fair copy, revised, here beginning ''Twas a death-bed summons, and forth I went –', in MS Wessex Poems (ff. 48–53).

Facsimile of Hardy's illustration for this poem in J. B. Bullen, *The Expressive Eye* (Oxford, 1986), plate 5.

Birmingham City Museum and Art Gallery.

HrT 477 Revisions to lines 80 and 89 in DCM Wessex Edition (Verse Vol. I, 50).

Dorset County Museum.

HrT 478 Corrections and revisions to lines 37, 41, 70, 72, 75, 80, 81, 89–90 in *Selected Poems* (1917), pp. 172–7.

Dorset County Museum.

HrT 479 Revision to line 82 in *Collected Poems* (1923), p. 36.

Dorset County Museum.

Her Definition ('I lingered through the night to break of day')
First pub. *Time's Laughingstocks* (1909); Gibson, p. [220]; Hynes, I, [269]–70.

HrT 480 Fair copy, in MS Time's Laughingstocks (f. 41); dated Westbourne Park Villas, Summer 1866.

Fitzwilliam Museum.

Her Dilemma ('The two were silent in a sunless church')
First pub. *Wessex Poems* (1898); Gibson, pp. 13–14; Hynes, I, 16–17.

HrT 481 Fair copy, revised, in MS Wessex Poems (f. 12); dated 1866.

Birmingham City Museum and Art Gallery.

Her Father ('I met her, as we had privily planned')
First pub. *Time's Laughingstocks* (1909); Gibson, p. 223; Hynes, I, 273.

HrT 482 Fair copy, in MS Time's Laughingstocks (f. 46), the last 3 lines pasted on; dated Weymouth, 1869 (cancelled).

Fitzwilliam Museum.

Her Haunting-ground ('Can it be so? It must be so')
First pub. *Human Shows* (1925); Gibson, p. 809; Hynes, III, 131–2.

HrT 483 Fair copy, revised, in MS Human Shows (f. 165).

Yale.

Her Immortality ('Upon a noon I pilgrimed through')
First pub. *Wessex Poems* (1898); Gibson, pp. 55–6; Hynes, I, 72–4.

HrT 484 Fair copy, revised, here beginning 'Upon a noon I wayfared through', in MS Wessex Poems (ff. 69–71).

Birmingham City Museum and Art Gallery.

Her Initials ('Upon a poet's page I wrote')
First pub. *Wessex Poems* (1898); Gibson, p. 13; Hynes, I, 15.

HrT 485 Fair copy, revised, in MS Wessex Poems (f. 11); dated 1869.

Birmingham City Museum and Art Gallery.

Her Late Husband ('"No – not where I shall make my own')
First pub. *Poems of the Past and the Present* (1902); Gibson, pp. 165–6; Hynes, I, 205.

HrT 486 Fair copy, revised, in MS Poems of the Past and the Present.

Bodleian, MS Eng. poet. d. 18, ff. 125–6 (rectos only).

Her Love-Birds ('When I looked up at my love-birds')
First pub. *Moments of Vision* (1917); Gibson, pp. 505–6; Hynes, II, 251–2.

HrT 487 Fair copy, revised, the title altered from 'The Love-Birds', in MS Moments of Vision (f. 129).

Magdalene College, Cambridge.

Her Reproach ('Con the dead page as 'twere live love: press on!')
First pub. *Poems of the Past and the Present* (1902); Gibson, p. 135; Hynes, I, 171.

HrT 488 Fair copy, revised, in MS Poems of the Past and the Present; dated Westbourne Park Villas, 1867.

Bodleian, MS Eng. poet. d. 18, f. 77.

HrT 489 Addition of footnote in *Collected Poems* (1923), p. 123.

Dorset County Museum.

Her Second Husband Hears her Story ('"Still, Dear, it is incredible to me')
First pub. *Daily Telegraph*, 23 July 1928; collected in *Winter Words* (1928); Gibson, p. 860; Hynes, III, 194–5.

HrT 490 Fair copy, revised, in MS Winter Words.

Queen's College, Oxford, MS 420, f. 38.

Her Secret ('That love's dull smart distressed my heart')
First pub.*Satires of Circumstance* (1914); Gibson, p. 365; Hynes, II, 78. The proof correction to line 8 for the Wessex Edition printed in Hynes, II, 491–2 appears on the list of corrections sent to R. & R. Clark (now on deposit in National Library of Scotland) described in the INTRODUCTION.

HrT 491 Fair copy, revised, entitled in pencil (erased) 'The jealous husband', in MS Satires of Circumstance (p. 107).

Dorset County Museum.

HrT 492 [entry deleted]

Her Song ('I sang that song on Sunday')
First pub. *Late Lyrics* (1922); Gibson, pp. 577–8; Hynes, II, 343.

HrT 493 Fair copy, revised, in MS Late Lyrics (f. 23).

Dorset County Museum.

Her Temple ('Dear, think not that they will forget you:')
First pub. *Late Lyrics* (1922); Gibson, p. 628; Hynes, II, 401.

HrT 494 Fair copy, revised, in MS Late Lyrics (f. 93).

Dorset County Museum.

HrT 495 Suggested alternative to line 8 in *Collected Poems* (1923), p. 594.

Dorset County Museum.

Heredity ('I am the family face')
First pub. *Moments of Vision* (1917); Gibson, p. 434; Hynes, II, 166–7.

HrT 496 Fair copy, in MS Moments of Vision (f. 14).

Magdalene College, Cambridge.

The High-school Lawn ('Gray prinked with rose')
First pub. *Human Shows* (1925); Gibson, p. 812; Hynes, III, 135.

HrT 497 Fair copy, revised, in MS Human Shows (f. 170).

Yale.

His Country ('I journeyed from my native spot')
First pub. *Moments of Vision* (1917); Gibson, pp. 539–40; Hynes, II, 290–1.

HrT 498 Fair copy, revised, in MS Moments of Vision (f. 176); dated 1913.

Magdalene College, Cambridge.

His Heart ('At midnight, in the room where he lay dead')
First pub. *Moments of Vision* (1917); Gibson, pp. 461–2; Hynes, II, 198–200.

HrT 499 Fair copy, revised, in MS Moments of Vision (f. 53).

Magdalene College, Cambridge.

His Immortality ('I saw a dead man's finer part')
First pub. in a pre-publication review of *Poems of the Past and the Present*, 'Mr Thomas Hardy's New Poems', *The Academy*, 22 November 1901; collected *Poems of the Past and the Present* (1902); Gibson, p. 143; Hynes, I, 180.

HrT 500 Fair copy, revised, in MS Poems of the Past and the Present; dated February 1899.

Bodleian, MS Eng. poet. d. 18, f. 88.

His Visitor ('I come across from Mellstock while the moon wastes weaker')
First pub. *Satires of Circumstance* (1914); Gibson, p. 347; Hynes, II, 57–8.

HrT 501 Fair copy, revised, in MS Satires of Circumstance (p. 83); dated 1913.

Dorset County Museum.

The History of an Hour ('Vain is the wish to try rhyming it, writing it!')
First pub. *Human Shows* (1925); Gibson, p. 786; Hynes, III, 105.

HrT 502 Fair copy, revised, in MS Human Shows (f. 129).

Yale.

The Homecoming ('Gruffly growled the wind on Toller downland broad and bare')
First pub. *The Graphic*, Christmas Number, [23 November] 1903; revised and collected *Time's Laughingstocks* (1909); Gibson, pp. 250–1; Hynes, I, 303–5.

HrT 503 Fair copy, revised, in MS Time's Laughingstocks (ff. 78–80); dated December 1901.

Fitzwilliam Museum.

Honeymoon-time at an Inn ('At the shiver of morning, a little before the false dawn')
First pub. *Moments of Vision* (1917); Gibson, pp. 514–16; Hynes, II, 262–4.

HrT 504 Fair copy, revised, in MS Moments of Vision (f. 144).

Magdalene College, Cambridge.

Horses Aboard ('Horses in horsecloths stand in a row')
First pub. *Human Shows* (1925); Gibson, pp. 785–6; Hynes, III, 105.

HrT 505 Fair copy, revised, in MS Human Shows (f. 128).

Yale.

HrT 506 Revisions to lines 6–7 in HS Proof (p. 182).

Dorset County Museum.

The House of Hospitalities ('Here we broached the Christmas barrel')
First pub. *New Quarterly*, January 1909; revised and collected *Time's Laughingstocks* (1909); Gibson, p. 206; Hynes, I, 255.

HrT 507 Fair copy, in MS Time's Laughingstocks (f. 22).

Fitzwilliam Museum.

The House of Silence ('"That is a quiet place —')
First pub. *Moments of Vision* (1917); Gibson, p. 474; Hynes, II, 213–14.

HrT 508 Fair copy, revised, one page.

Facsimile in *Strand Magazine*, October 1924; Microfilm Edition, Reel 5.

Dorset County Museum.

HrT 509 Fair copy, in MS Moments of Vision (f. 75).

Magdalene College, Cambridge.

A House with a History ('There is a house in a city street')
First pub. *Late Lyrics* (1922); Gibson, p. 643; Hynes, II, 419–20.

HrT 510 Fair copy, revised, in MS Late Lyrics (f. 114).

Dorset County Museum.

'How great my grief' ('How great my grief, my joys how few')
First pub. *Poems of the Past and the Present* (1902); Gibson, p. 137; Hynes, I, 173.

HrT 511 Fair copy, the title altered from 'His Love brings little Pleasure', in MS Poems of the Past and the Present.

Bodleian, MS Eng. poet. d. 18, f. 80.

How She Went to Ireland ('Dora's gone to Ireland')
First pub. *Winter Words* (1928); Gibson, p. 915; Hynes, III, 258.

HrT 512 Fair copy, in MS Winter Words.

Queen's College, Oxford, MS 420, f. 119.

Human Shows
This collection of poems first pub. London, 1925. For a description of the MS printer's copy (MS Human Shows) and corrected page proof (HS Proof) for the first edition, see INTRODUCTION; contents have been listed individually. Hollings Catalogue 212 (n.d.) lists a copy of the New York, 1925 edition containing two pencil corrections by Hardy in the text and his note concerning misprints on the front flyleaf (Item 56); no such copy has been located.

A Hundred Years Since ('When first you fluttered on this scene')
First pub. *North American Review*, February 1915; Gibson, pp. 951–2; Hynes, III, 302–3.

HrT 513 Fair copy, revised, signed, 2 numbered leaves (rectos only), annotated '[Original MS.]'; watermarked 1906.

Texas.

A Hurried Meeting ('It is August moonlight in the tall plantation')
First pub. *Human Shows* (1925); Gibson, pp. 827–9; Hynes, III, 153–4.

HrT 514 Fair copy, revised, in MS Human Shows (ff. 191–2, rectos only).

Yale.

HrT 515 Correction to line 7 in HS Proof (p. 271).

Dorset County Museum.

The Husband's View ('"Can anything avail')
First pub. *Time's Laughingstocks* (1909); Gibson, pp. 248–9; Hynes, I, 301–2.

HrT 516 Fair copy, revised, in MS Time's Laughingstocks (ff. 75–6).

Fitzwilliam Museum.

Hussar's Song/Budmouth Dears ('When we lay where Budmouth Beach is'), see HrT 1620–1, 1625.

'I am the one' ('I am the one whom ringdoves see')
First pub. *Daily Telegraph*, 2 April 1928; collected *Winter Words* (1928); Gibson, p. 837; Hynes, III, 169–70.

HrT 517 Fair copy, revised, in MS Winter Words.

Queen's College, Oxford, MS 420, f. 6.

'I found her out there' ('I found her out there')
First pub. *Satires of Circumstance* (1914); Gibson, pp. 342–3; Hynes, II, 51–2.

HrT 518 Fair copy, revised, in MS Satires of Circumstance (p. 76).

Dorset County Museum.

HrT 519 Revision to line 22 in *Selected Poems* (1916), p. 62.

Dorset County Museum.

HrT 520 Revision to line 22 and date cancelled in *Selected Poems* (1917), p. 62.

Dorset County Museum.

'I have lived with Shades' ('I have lived with Shades so long')
First pub. *Poems of the Past and the Present* (1902); Gibson, pp. [184]–5; Hynes, I, [225]–6.

HrT 521 Fair copy, revised, in MS Poems of the Past and the Present; dated 2 February 1899.

Bodleian, MS Eng. poet. d. 18, ff. 153–4 (rectos only).

HrT 522 Lines 2–4 rewritten in *Selected Poems* (1917), p. 182.

Dorset County Museum.

'I knew a lady' ('I knew a lady when the days')
First pub. *Late Lyrics* (1922); Gibson, pp. 642–3; Hynes, II, 419.

HrT 523 Fair copy, in MS Late Lyrics (f. 113).

Dorset County Museum.

'I look in her face' ('I look in her face and say')
First pub. *Late Lyrics* (1922); Gibson, p. 631; Hynes, II, 404–5.

HrT 524 Fair copy of stanza 1 and an early version of stanza 3, in MS Late Lyrics (f. 98).

Dorset County Museum.

'I look into my glass' ('I look into my glass')
First pub. *Wessex Poems* (1898); Gibson, p. 81; Hynes, I, 106.

HrT 525 Fair copy, in MS Wessex Poems (f. 106).

Birmingham City Museum and Art Gallery.

HrT 526 Fair copy, signed (initials), one page.

University of California at Berkeley.

'I looked back' ('I looked back as I left the house')
First pub. *Daily Telegraph*, 24 May 1928; collected *Winter Words* (1928); Gibson, p. 913; Hynes, III, 255–6.

HrT 527 Fair copy, revised, in MS Winter Words.

Queen's College, Oxford, MS 420, f. 115.

'I looked up from my writing' ('I looked up from my writing')
First pub. *Moments of Vision* (1917); Gibson, p. 551; Hynes, II, 305–6.

HrT 528 Fair copy, revised, in MS Moments of Vision (f. 196).

Magdalene College, Cambridge.

'I met a man' ('I met a man when night was nigh')
First pub. *Fortnightly Review*, 1 February 1917; collected *Moments of Vision* (1917); privately printed by FEH in pamphlet *England to Germany* (London, 1917); Gibson, pp. 549–51; Hynes, II, 304–5.

HrT 529 Fair copy, revised, in MS Moments of Vision (f. 194); dated 1916.

Magdalene College, Cambridge.

HrT 530 Proof of lines 1–21 only, corrected in an unidentified hand, for *England to Germany* (scc also HrT 334, 812); dated 8 February 1917.

Cockerell Sale, Lot 261, sold to Alan G. Thomas.

Owned (1984) F. B. Adams (see Hynes).

'I need not go' ('I need not go')
First pub. *Poems of the Past and the Present* (1902); Gibson, p. 138; Hynes, I, 174.

HrT 531 Fair copy, revised, in MS Poems of the Past and the Present.

Bodleian, MS Eng. poet. d. 18, f. 81.

'I rose and went to Rou'tor Town' ('I rose and went to Rou'tor Town')
First pub. *Moments of Vision* (1917); Gibson, p. 517; Hynes, II, 265–6.

HrT 532 Fair copy, revised, in MS Moments of Vision (f. 147).

Magdalene College, Cambridge.

'I rose up as my custom is' ('I rose up as my custom is')
First pub. *Satires of Circumstance* (1914); Gibson, pp. 378–9; Hynes, II, 94–5.

HrT 533 Fair copy, revised, in MS Satires of Circumstance (pp. 129–30).

Dorset County Museum.

'I said and sang her excellence' ('I said and sang her excellence:')
First pub. *Moments of Vision* (1917); Gibson, pp. 465–6; Hynes, II, 203–4.

HrT 534 Fair copy in MS Moments of Vision (f. 61).

Magdalene College, Cambridge.

'I said to Love' ('I said to Love')
First pub. *Poems of the Past and the Present* (1902); Gibson, p. 114; Hynes, I, 147–8.

HrT 535 Fair copy, revised, in MS Poems of the Past and the Present.

Bodleian, MS Eng. poet. d. 18, ff. 44–5 (rectos only).

'I sat me down in a foreign town', see HrT 1684.

'I say I'll seek her' ('I say, "I'll seek her side')
First pub. *Time's Laughingstocks* (1909); Gibson, pp. 222–3; Hynes, I, 272–3.

HrT 536 Fair copy, revised, in MS Time's Laughingstocks (f. 45).

Fitzwilliam Museum.

HrT 537 Revision to line 6 in DCM Wessex Edition (Verse Vol. III, 308).

Dorset County Museum.

HrT 538 Revision to line 6 in *Selected Poems* (1916), p. 11.

Dorset County Museum.

HrT 539 Revision to line 6 in *Selected Poems* (1917), p. 11.

Dorset County Museum.

'I sometimes think' ('I sometimes think as here I sit')
First pub. *Late Lyrics* (1922); Gibson, p. 568; Hynes, II, 332.

HrT 540 Fair copy, revised, in MS Late Lyrics (f. 9).

Facsimile in *Later Years*, facing p. 225.

Dorset County Museum.

HrT 541 Fair copy, slightly revised, one page.

Microfilm Edition, Reel 5.

Dorset County Museum.

HrT 542 Suggested revision to line 13 in *Collected Poems* (1923), p. 538.

This revision printed Hynes, II, 511.

Dorset County Museum.

'I thought, my Heart' ('I thought, my Heart, that you had healed')
Two-stanza version first pub. *Moments of Vision* (1917); third stanza first pub. in *Pages from the Works of Thomas Hardy*, ed. Ruth Head (London, 1922), p. 171; Gibson, pp. 512–13; Hynes, II, 259–60.

HrT 543 Fair copy, revised, of 2-stanza version, one page.

Microfilm Edition, Reel 5.

Dorset County Museum.

HrT 544 Fair copy of 2-stanza version on recto (annotated 'a third verse, as overleaf, was not printed') and third stanza on verso, in MS Moments of Vision (f. 141r–v).

Magdalene College, Cambridge.

HrT 545 Fair copy of stanza 3 only, tipped into Hardy's copy of the Wessex Edition (Verse Vol. IV), presented to Sydney Cockerell by FEH, 30 March 1928 (see DCM Wessex Edition).

This MS printed Hynes, II, 260; Cockerell Sale, Lot 252, sold to Maggs.

Owned (1985) F. B. Adams (see Hynes, III, 352).

HrT 546 Transcript of stanza 3 only by Sydney Cockerell, in his copy of *Moments of Vision* (1917) (HrT 781), annotated that it was transcribed 'from a copy I took at Max Gate Jan. 11, 1925.'.

Cockerell Sale, Lot 269, sold to Maggs.

Owned (1984) F. B. Adams (see Hynes).

'I travel as a phantom now' ('I travel as a phantom now')
First pub. *Moments of Vision* (1917); Gibson, p. 458; Hynes, II, 194–5.

HrT 547 Fair copy, revised, in MS Moments of Vision (f. 47); dated 1915.

Magdalene College, Cambridge.

'I was not he' ('I was not he — the man')
First pub. *Late Lyrics* (1922); Gibson, pp. 571–2; Hynes, II, 336–7.

HrT 548 Fair copy, revised, in MS Late Lyrics (f. 14).

Dorset County Museum.

'I was the midmost' ('I was the midmost of my world')
First pub. *Late Lyrics* (1922); Gibson, p. 666; Hynes, II, 445–6.

HrT 549 Fair copy, revised, in MS Late Lyrics (f. 147).

Dorset County Museum.

'I watched a blackbird' ('I watched a blackbird on a budding sycamore')
First pub. *Daily Telegraph*, 2 July 1928; collected *Winter Words* (1928); Gibson, p. 866; Hynes, III, 202.

HrT 550 Fair copy, revised, in MS Winter Words.

Queen's College, Oxford, MS 420, f. 47.

'I worked no wile to meet you' ('I worked no wile to meet you')
First pub. *Late Lyrics* (1922); Gibson, pp. 606–7; Hynes, II, 376–7.

HrT 551 Fair copy, revised, in MS Late Lyrics (f. 66).

Dorset County Museum.

Ice on the Highway ('Seven buxom women abreast, and arm in arm')
First pub. *Human Shows* (1925); Gibson, pp. 734–5; Hynes, III, 45–6.

HrT 552 Fair copy, revised, in MS Human Shows (f. 51), annotated 'Yell'ham Hill'.

Yale.

'If it's ever spring again' ('If it's ever spring again')
First pub. *Late Lyrics* (1922); Gibson, pp. 594–5; Hynes, II, 362–3.

HrT 553 Fair copy, revised, in MS Late Lyrics (f. 48).

Dorset County Museum.

HrT 554 Suggested revisions to lines 3 and 9 (in pencil, erased) in *Collected Poems* (1923).

Dorset County Museum.

'If you had known' ('If you had known')
First pub. *Late Lyrics* (1922); Gibson, pp. 632–3; Hynes, II, 406.

HrT 555 Fair copy, revised, the title (and first line) altered from 'If I had known', in MS Late Lyrics (f. 100); dated 1920.

Dorset County Museum.

'If you think, have a kindly thought'
These lines (Hardy's rearrangement of words supplied by the Mayor of Dudley) are inscribed on the War Memorial Clock Tower in Dudley, Worcestershire; they were first pub. in the report of the formal dedication (on 16 October 1928) in *The Times*, 17 October 1928; not included in Gibson or Hynes. See William W. Morgan, 'Verses Fitted for a Monument: Hardy's Contribution to the Dudley War Memorial', *Thomas Hardy Journal*, I (1985), 25–32.

HrT 556 Typescript, in a letter to James Smellie, Mayor of Dudley, dated from Max Gate, 25 September 1925.

This MS printed *Letters*, VI, 357.

Dudley Public Library, Archives and Local History Department.

Imaginings ('She saw herself a lady')
First pub. *Moments of Vision* (1917); Gibson, p. 525; Hynes, II, 274.

HrT 557 Fair copy, revised, in MS Moments of Vision (f. 158).

Magdalene College, Cambridge.

The Impercipient ('That with this bright believing band')
First pub. *Wessex Poems* (1898); Gibson, pp. 67–8; Hynes, I, 87–8.

HrT 558 Fair copy, revised, including an additional stanza, the title altered from 'The Agnostic', here subtitled '(Evensong; — Cathedral.)' and beginning 'That from this bright believing band', in MS Wessex Poems (ff. 85–6).

The additional stanza printed in Purdy, p. 102, Gibson and Hynes.

Birmingham City Museum and Art Gallery.

HrT 559 Revision in line 29 in DCM Wessex Edition (Verse Vol. I, 88).

Dorset County Museum.

In a Cathedral City ('These people have not heard your name')
First pub. *Time's Laughingstocks* (1909); Gibson, p. 222; Hynes, I, 272.

HrT 560 Fair copy, revised, in MS Time's Laughingstocks (f. 44).

Fitzwilliam Museum.

HrT 561 Revision to line 10 in *Selected Poems* (1917), p. 10.

Dorset County Museum.

In a Eweleaze near Weatherbury ('The years have gathered grayly')
First pub. *Wessex Poems* (1898); Gibson, pp. 70–1; Hynes, I, 92.

HrT 562 Fair copy, revised, in MS Wessex Poems (f. 91); dated 1890.

Facsimile of Hardy's illustration for this poem in J. B. Bullen, *The Expressive Eye* (Oxford, 1986), plate 6.

Birmingham City Museum and Art Gallery.

HrT 563 Corrections and revisions to title and line 11 in *Selected Poems* (1917), p. 41.

Dorset County Museum.

In a Former Resort after Many Years ('Do I know these, slack-shaped and wan')

First pub. *Human Shows* (1925); Gibson, p. 702; Hynes, III, 8.

HrT 564 Fair copy, revised, the title altered from 'In an old place of resort after many years', in MS Human Shows (f. 4).

Yale.

In a London Flat ('"You look like a widower," she said')
First pub. *Late Lyrics* (1922); Gibson, pp. 689–90; Hynes, II, 474–5.

HrT 565 Fair copy, revised, the title altered from 'In a London Lodging 1888', in MS Late Lyrics (f. 182).

Dorset County Museum.

In a Museum ('Here's the mould of a musical bird long passed from light')
First pub. *Moments of Vision* (1917); Gibson, p. 430; Hynes, II, 163.

HrT 566 Fair copy, revised, in MS Moments of Vision (f. 7).

Magdalene College, Cambridge.

In a Waiting-Room ('On a morning sick as the day of doom')
First pub. *Moments of Vision* (1917); Gibson, pp. 518–19; Hynes, II, 266–7.

HrT 567 Fair copy, revised, in MS Moments of Vision (f. 149).

Magdalene College, Cambridge.

In a Whispering Gallery ('That whisper takes the voice')
First pub. *Moments of Vision* (1917); Gibson, p. 522; Hynes, II, 271.

HrT 568 Fair copy, here beginning 'That whisper seems the voice', in MS Moments of Vision (f. 154).

Magdalene College, Cambridge.

HrT 568.5 Correction in Hardy's copy of the Wessex Edition (Verse Vol. IV, 353), presented to Sydney Cockerell by FEH, 30 March 1928 (see DCM Wessex Edition).

Cockerell Sale, Lot 252, sold to Maggs.

Owned (1985) F. B. Adams (see Hynes, III, 352).

In a Wood ('Pale beech and pine so blue')
First pub. *Wessex Poems* (1898); Gibson, pp. 64–5; Hynes, I, 83–4.

HrT 569 Fair copy, revised, subtitled '*vide* "The Woodlanders"' and here beginning 'Pale beech and pine-tree blue', in MS Wessex Poems (f. 81); dated '1887:1896'.

Birmingham City Museum and Art Gallery.

HrT 570 Revision to line 30 in DCM Wessex Edition (Verse Vol. I, 82).

Dorset County Museum.

HrT 571 Revision to line 30 in *Selected Poems* (1916), p. 89.

Dorset County Museum.

HrT 572 Revision to line 30 in *Selected Poems* (1917), p. 89.

Dorset County Museum.

In Childbed ('In the middle of the night')
First pub. *Time's Laughingstocks* (1909); Gibson, p. 271; Hynes, I, 327.

HrT 573 Fair copy, revised, in MS Time's Laughingstocks (f. 102).

Fitzwilliam Museum.

In Church ('"And now to God the Father," he ends'), see HrT 1007.

In Death Divided ('I shall rot here, with those whom in their day')
First pub. *Satires of Circumstance* (1914); Gibson, pp. 320–1; Hynes, II, 27–8.

HrT 574 Fair copy, revised, in MS Satires of Circumstance (p. 28).

Dorset County Museum.

HrT 575 Addition of date '189–.' in *Collected Poems* (1923), p. 302.

Dorset County Museum.

In Front of the Landscape ('Plunging and labouring on in a tide of visions')

First pub. *Satires of Circumstance* (1914); Gibson, pp. [303]–5; Hynes, II, [7]–9.

HrT 576 Fair copy, revised, in MS Satires of Circumstance (pp. 1–3).

Dorset County Museum.

HrT 577 Revisions to lines 8, 13 and 56 in *Selected Poems* (1917), pp. 115 and 117.

Dorset County Museum.

In Her Precincts ('Her house looked cold from the foggy lea')
First pub. *Moments of Vision* (1917); Gibson, p. 473; Hynes, II, 212.

HrT 578 Fair copy, in MS Moments of Vision (f. 73).

Magdalene College, Cambridge.

In St Paul's a While Ago ('Summer and winter close commune')
First pub. *Human Shows* (1925); Gibson, pp. 716–17; Hynes, III, 23–4.

HrT 579 Fair copy, revised, the title altered from 'In St Paul's: 1869', in MS Human Shows (ff. 23–4, rectos only).

Yale.

In Sherborne Abbey ('The moon has passed to the panes of the south-aisle wall')
First pub. *Human Shows* (1925); Gibson, pp. 759–60; Hynes, III, 74–5.

HrT 580 Fair copy, revised, in MS Human Shows (ff. 86–7, rectos only), annotated '<From> A family tradition.'.

Yale.

HrT 581 Revision to line 27 in HS Proof (p. 126).

Dorset County Museum.

In Tenebris I ('Wintertime nighs')
First pub. *Poems of the Past and the Present* (1902), as 'De Profundis I'; Gibson, p. 167; Hynes, I, 206–7.

HrT 582 Fair copy, revised, here entitled both 'De Profundis' and 'In Tenebris' (both cancelled, the former stetted) in MS Poems of the Past and the Present.

Bodleian, MS Eng. poet. d. 18, f. 128.

In Tenebris II ('When the clouds' swoln bosoms echo back the shouts of the many and strong')
First pub.*Poems of the Past and the Present* (1902), as 'De Profundis II'; Gibson, p. 168; Hynes, I, 207–8.

HrT 583 Fair copy, revised, here entitled both 'De Profundis' and 'In Tenebris' (both cancelled, the former stetted), including a cancelled epigraph, in MS Poems of the Past and the Present; dated '1895–6'.

Bodleian, MS Eng. poet. d. 18, f. 129.

HrT 584 Revisions to lines 5 and 6 in *Selected Poems* (1917), p. 180.

Dorset County Museum.

In Tenebris III ('There have been times when I well might have passed and the ending have come —')
First pub. *Poems of the Past and the Present* (1902), as 'De Profundis III'; Gibson, p. 169; Hynes, I, 208–10.

HrT 585 Fair copy, revised, here entitled both 'De Profundis' and 'In Tenebris' (both cancelled, the former stetted), in MS Poems of the Past and the Present; dated 1896.

Bodleian, MS Eng. poet. d. 18, ff. 130–1 (rectos only).

In the British Museum ('"What do you see in that time-touched stone')
First pub. *Satires of Circumstance* (1914); Gibson, pp. 381–2; Hynes, II, 98–9.

HrT 586 Fair copy, revised, in MS Satires of Circumstance (pp. 134–5).

Dorset County Museum.

In the Cemetery ('"You see those mothers squabbling there?"'), see HrT 1007.

In the Days of Crinoline ('A plain tilt-bonnet on her head')
First pub. *Satires of Circumstance* (1914); Gibson, pp. 395–6; Hynes, II, 115–16. For a proof correction for the Wessex Edition, see HrT 3.

HrT 587 Fair copy, revised, the title altered from 'The Vicar's Young Wife', in MS Satires of Circumstance (pp. 156–7); dated July 1911 (cancelled).

Dorset County Museum.

In the Evening ('In the evening, when the world knew he was dead')
First pub. *The Times*, 5 January 1924 (early version); revised version first pub. *The Dorset Year-Book* (pub. Society of Dorset Men in London) (London, 1924); collected *Human Shows* (1925); Gibson, p. 820; Hynes, III, 144–5. The last 3 lines of the first version are inscribed on the Sir Frederick Treves Monument in Dorchester Cemetery.

HrT 588 Fair copy, revised, in MS Human Shows (f. 181).

Yale.

HrT 589 Correction to line 7 and revision to line 16 in HS Proof (pp. 256–7).

Dorset County Museum.

In the Garden ('We waited for the sun')
First pub. *Moments of Vision* (1917); Gibson, p. 531; Hynes, II, 281.

HrT 590 Fair copy, revised, in MS Moments of Vision (f. 165); dated 1915.

Magdalene College, Cambridge.

In the Marquee ('It was near last century's ending')
First pub. *Daily Telegraph*, 16 July 1928; collected *Winter Words* (1928); Gibson, pp. 874–6; Hynes, III, 211–12. Purdy, p. 256 mentions Hardy's 'rough notes' for this poem, headed 'The party at W[estbourne] P[ark] V[illas]', which were, according to Hynes, III, 327, in a notebook now lost.

HrT 591 Fair copy, revised, here beginning (in a stanza added later in pencil) 'It was in the century vanished', without lines 5–8 (stanza 2), 2 leaves (rectos only).

Texas.

HrT 592 Fair copy, revised, incomplete (lines 1–24 only), here beginning 'It was <during the> near last century's <vanished> ending', one page.

Microfilm Edition, Reel 5.

Dorset County Museum.

HrT 593 Fair copy, revised, in MS Winter Words.

Queen's College, Oxford, MS 420, ff. 59–60.

In the Mind's Eye ('That was once her casement')
First pub. *Time's Laughingstocks* (1909), as 'The Phantom'; reprinted *Selected Poems* (1916), as 'The Face in the Mind's Eye'; Gibson, p. 226; Hynes, I, 276.

HrT 594 Fair copy, here entitled 'The Phantom', in MS Time's Laughingstocks (f. 49).

Fitzwilliam Museum.

HrT 595 Annotation to title (i.e., '*Ghost=face*') on p. 66 of Hardy's copy of *Time's Laughingstocks* (1909) (containing also HrT 258, 449).

Dorset County Museum.

HrT 596 Annotation to title (i.e., 'Better=In the mind's eye') in DCM Wessex Edition (Verse Vol. III, 314).

Dorset County Museum.

HrT 597 Title cancelled, altered to 'The Phantom', cancelled and annotated '[Better] In the Mind's Eye' in *Selected Poems* (1916), p. 81.

Dorset County Museum.

HrT 598 Corrections and title revised to 'In the Mind's Eye', in *Selected Poems* (1917), p. 81.

Dorset County Museum.

HrT 599 Annotation to title in *Collected Poems* (1923), p. 210.

Annotation printed in Hynes, I, 383.

Dorset County Museum.

In the Moonlight ('"O lonely workman, standing there'), see HrT 1007, 1009.

'In the night she came' ('I told her when I left one day')

First pub. *Time's Laughingstocks* (1909); Gibson, pp. 228–9; Hynes, I, 278–9.

HrT 600 Fair copy, revised, in MS Time's Laughingstocks (f. 52).

Fitzwilliam Museum.

In the Nuptial Chamber ('"O that mastering tune!" And up in the bed'), see HrT 1007.

In the Old Theatre, Fiesole ('I traced the Circus whose gray stones incline')
First pub. (early version) in a pre-publication review of *Poems of the Past and the Present*, 'Mr Thomas Hardy's New Poems', *The Academy*, 23 November 1901; collected *Poems of the Past and the Present* (1902); Gibson, p. 102; Hynes, I, 134.

HrT 601 Fair copy, revised, in MS Poems of the Past and the Present.

Bodleian, MS Eng. poet. d. 18, f. 25.

In the Restaurant ('"But hear. If you stay, and the child be born'), see HrT 1007–8.

In the Room of the Bride-Elect ('"Would it had been the man of our wish!"'), see HrT 1007.

In the Servants' Quarters ('"Man, you too, aren't you, one of these rough followers of the criminal?')
First pub. *Satires of Circumstance* (1914); Gibson, pp. 382–3; Hynes, II, 99–101.

HrT 602 Fair copy, revised, the title altered from 'Humour in the servants' quarters', in MS Satires of Circumstance (pp. 136–7).

Dorset County Museum.

'In the seventies' ('In the seventies I was bearing in my breast')
First pub. *Moments of Vision* (1917); Gibson, p. 459; Hynes, II, 196–7.

HrT 603 Fair copy, revised, in MS Moments of Vision (f. 49).

Magdalene College, Cambridge.

In the Small Hours ('I lay in my bed and fiddled')
First pub. *Late Lyrics* (1922); Gibson, p. 648; Hynes, II, 424–5.

HrT 604 Fair copy, in MS Late Lyrics (f. 122).

Dorset County Museum.

In the Street ('Only acquaintances')
First pub. *Human Shows* (1925); Gibson, pp. 743–4; Hynes, III, 56.

HrT 605 Fair copy, in MS Human Shows (f. 65).

Yale.

In the Study ('He enters, and mute on the edge of a chair'), see HrT 1007.

In the Vaulted Way ('In the vaulted way, where the passage turned')
First pub. *Time's Laughingstocks* (1909), as 'In the Crypted Way'; Gibson, pp. 225–6; Hynes, I, 275–6.

HrT 606 Fair copy, revised, here entitled 'In the Crypted Way' and beginning 'In the crypted way...', in MS Time's Laughingstocks (f. 48A); dated 1870.

Fitzwilliam Museum.

HrT 607 Revision to line 3 in DCM Wessex Edition (Verse Vol. III, 313).

Dorset County Museum.

In Time of 'the Breaking of Nations' ('Only a man harrowing clods')
First pub. *Saturday Review*, 29 January 1916; collected *Selected Poems* (1916) and *Moments of Vision* (1917); Gibson, p. 543; Hynes, II, 295–6.

HrT 608 Fair copy, in MS Moments of Vision (f. 185); dated 1915.

Magdalene College, Cambridge.

HrT 609 Fair copy, here beginning 'Only a hind harrowing clods', subtitled '(Jer. LI. 20.)', signed, two leaves, including a separate title page, annotated 'No copyright Reserved'.

University of California at Berkeley.

HrT 610 Fair copy, signed, one page, annotated 'From "Moments of Vision"'; dated 1915.

Parke Bernet, 4–5 January 1940 (Paul Lemperley Sale), Lot 381.

HrT 611 Fair copy, subtitled '(Jer. LI. 20.)', signed, one page, in the autograph album of Sir Edward Marsh (f. 1); dated 1915 and annotated 'written here Nov: 1918/EM'.

Facsimile in Rota Catalogue 186 (1973), facing p. 2.

Eton College.

HrT 612 Revision to line 11 in *Selected Poems* (1916), p. 203.

Dorset County Museum.

HrT 613 Revision to line 11 and corrections in *Selected Poems* (1917), p. 203.

Dorset County Museum.

In Time of Wars and Tumults (' "Would that I'd not drawn breath here!" some one said')
First pub. *The Sphere*, 24 November 1917, as 'In the Time of War and Tumults'; collected *Moments of Vision* (1917); Gibson, pp. 542–3; Hynes, II, 294–5.

HrT 614 Fair copy, revised, in MS Moments of Vision (f. 184); dated 1915.

Magdalene College, Cambridge.

'In vision I roamed' ('In vision I roamed the flashing Firmament')
First pub. *Wessex Poems* (1898); Gibson, pp. 9–10; Hynes, I, 10–11.

HrT 615 Fair copy, revised, in MS Wessex Poems (f. 5); dated 1866.

Birmingham City Museum and Art Gallery.

In Weatherbury Stocks ('"I sit here in these stocks')
First pub. *Winter Words* (1928); Gibson, pp. 900–1; Hynes, III, 242–3.

HrT 616 Fair copy, revised, in MS Winter Words.

Queen's College, Oxford, MS 420, f. 99.

The Inconsistent ('I say, "She was as good as fair!"')
First pub. *Poems of the Past and the Present* (1902); Gibson, pp. 135–6; Hynes, I, 171–2.

HrT 617 Fair copy, revised, in MS Poems of the Past and the Present.

Bodleian, MS Eng. poet. d. 18, f. 78.

An Inquiry ('I said to It: "We grasp not what you meant"')
First pub. *Human Shows* (1925); Gibson, p. 758; Hynes, III, 73.

HrT 618 Fair copy, revised, in MS Human Shows (f. 84).

Yale.

HrT 619 Revision to line 19 in HS Proof (p. 122).

Dorset County Museum.

The Inquiry ('And are ye one of Hermitage —')
First pub. *Time's Laughingstocks* (1909), as 'At Casterbridge Fair. V.'; Gibson, p. 241; Hynes, I, 293.

HrT 620 Fair copy, headed 'V.', in MS Time's Laughingstocks (f. 66).

Fitzwilliam Museum.

The Inscription ('Sir John was entombed, and the crypt was closed, and she')
First pub. *Late Lyrics* (1922); Gibson, pp. 678–81; Hynes, II, 460–4.

HrT 621 Fair copy, revised, the title altered from 'The Words on the Brass', in MS Late Lyrics (ff. 165–8); dated 30 October 1907.

Dorset County Museum.

HrT 622 Revisions to lines 58–9 in *Collected Poems* (1923), p. 643.

Dorset County Museum.

HrT 623 Revisions to lines 58–9 in Hardy's copy of the Wessex Edition (Verse Vol. V, 184), presented to Sydney Cockerell by FEH, 30 March 1928 (see DCM Wessex Edition).

Cockerell Sale, Lot 252, sold to Maggs.

Owned (1985) F. B. Adams (see Hynes, III, 352).

Inscriptions for a Peal of Eight Bells ('Thomas Tremble new-made me')
First pub. *Human Shows* (1925); Gibson, pp. 800–1; Hynes, III, 122.

HrT 624 Fair copy, revised, in MS Human Shows (f. 152).

Yale.

The Interloper ('There are three folk driving in a quaint old chaise')
First pub. *Moments of Vision* (1917); Gibson, pp. 488–9; Hynes, II, 230–2.

HrT 625 Fair copy, revised, the title altered from 'One who ought not to be there', in MS Moments of Vision (f. 100).

Magdalene College, Cambridge.

Intra Sepulchrum ('What curious things we said')
First pub. *Late Lyrics* (1922); Gibson, pp. 684–5; Hynes, II, 469–70.

HrT 626 Fair copy, revised, in MS Late Lyrics (ff. 174–5).

Dorset County Museum.

'It never looks like summer' ('"It never looks like summer here')
First pub. *Moments of Vision* (1917); Gibson, pp. 507–8; Hynes, II, 253–4.

HrT 627 Fair copy, in MS Moments of Vision (f. 132); dated 'Boscastle <Saturday> 8 March: 1913.'.

Magdalene College, Cambridge.

The Ivy-Wife ('I longed to love a full-boughed beech')
First pub. *Wessex Poems* (1898); Gibson, p. 57; Hynes, I, 75.

HrT 628 Fair copy, slightly revised, in MS Wessex Poems (f. 72).

Birmingham City Museum and Art Gallery.

A January Night ('The rain smites more and more')
First pub. *Moments of Vision* (1917); Gibson, p. 466; Hynes, II, 204–5.

HrT 629 Fair copy, here beginning 'The rain beats more and more', in MS Moments of Vision (f. 62).

Magdalene College, Cambridge.

Jezreel ('Did they catch as it were in a Vision at shut of the day —')
First pub. *The Times*, 27 September 1918; privately printed by FEH in a separate pamphlet (London, 1919); collected *Late Lyrics* (1922); Gibson, p. 569; Hynes, II, 333–4.

HrT 630 Fair copy, without subtitle, in MS Late Lyrics (f. 10); dated 24 September 1918.

Dorset County Museum.

HrT 631 Corrected typescript, one page, printer's copy for FEH's pamphlet; dated 27 September 1918.

Cockerell Sale, Lot 279, sold to Alan G. Thomas.

SUNY at Buffalo.

HrT 632 Corrected proof for FEH's pamphlet (containing also HrT 742), annotated by Hardy '(marked for press)'; dated in an unidentified hand 11 September 1919.

Cockerell Sale, Lot 279, sold to Alan G. Thomas.

SUNY at Buffalo.

HrT 633 Revision to line 9 in *Collected Poems* (1923), p. 539.

Dorset County Museum.

HrT 634 Revision to line 9 in Hardy's copy of the Wessex Edition (Verse Vol. V, 12), presented to Sydney Cockerell by FEH, 30 March 1928 (see DCM Wessex Edition).

Cockerell Sale, Lot 252, sold to Maggs.

Owned (1985) F. B. Adams (see Hynes, III, 352).

A Jingle on the Times ('"I am a painter')

First privately printed in FEH's pamphlet *The Fiddler's Story* (London, October 1917); Gibson, pp. 947–9; Hynes, III, 299–302.

HrT 635 Revised, as sent to Elizabeth Asquith who had solicited a contribution for an Arts Fund album, here subtitled '(In aid of the Arts Fund)'; sent December 1914 for a projected spring 1915 publication.

Owned (1985) R. L. Purdy (see Hynes); destined for Yale.

HrT 636 Typescript, revised, printer's copy for *The Fiddler's Story*.

Cockerell Sale, Lot 271, sold to Maggs.

Owned (1985) R. L. Purdy (see Hynes); destined for Yale.

HrT 637 Corrected first proof for *The Fiddler's Story* (containing also HrT 253); proof dated 25 September 1917.

Cockerell Sale, Lot 271, sold to Maggs.

Owned (1985) R. L. Purdy (see Hynes); destined for Yale.

A Jog-Trot Pair ('Who were the twain that trod this track')
First pub. *Late Lyrics* (1922); Gibson, pp. 569–70; Hynes, II, 334–5.

HrT 638 Fair copy, revised, in MS Late Lyrics (f. 11).

Dorset County Museum.

John and Jane ('He sees the world as a boisterous place')
First pub. *Time's Laughingstocks* (1909); Gibson, pp. 207–8; Hynes, I, 256.

HrT 639 Fair copy, in MS Time's Laughingstocks (f. 24).

Fitzwilliam Museum.

Joys of Memory ('When the spring comes round, and a certain day')
First pub. *Moments of Vision* (1917); Gibson, p. 437; Hynes, II, 170.

HrT 640 Fair copy, revised, in MS Moments of Vision (f. 19).

Magdalene College, Cambridge.

Jubilate ('"The very last time I ever was here," he said')
First pub. *Moments of Vision* (1917); Gibson, pp. 510–11; Hynes, II, 257–8.

HrT 641 Fair copy, revised, in MS Moments of Vision (f. 137).

Magdalene College, Cambridge.

The Jubilee of a Magazine ('Yes; your up-dated modern page —')
First pub. *Cornhill*, January 1910, as 'An Impromptu to the Editor'; collected *Satires of Circumstance* (1914); Gibson, pp. 411–12; Hynes, II, 134–5.

HrT 642 Fair copy, revised, the title altered from '"The Cornhill's" Jubilee', in MS Satires of Circumstance (pp. 178–9).

Dorset County Museum.

Julie-Jane ('Sing; how 'a would sing!')
First pub. *Time's Laughingstocks* (1909); Gibson, pp. 245–6; Hynes, I, 298–9.

HrT 643 Fair copy, in MS Time's Laughingstocks (ff. 72–3).

Fitzwilliam Museum.

June Leaves and Autumn ('Lush summer lit the trees to green')
First pub. *Daily Telegraph*, 28 June 1928; collected Winter Words (1928); Gibson, pp. 910–11; Hynes, III, 252–3.

HrT 644 Fair copy, revised, in MS Winter Words; dated 19 November 1898.

Queen's College, Oxford, MS 420, f. 114.

Just the Same ('I sat. It all was past')
First pub. *Late Lyrics* (1922); Gibson, p. 686; Hynes, II, 471.

HrT 645 Fair copy, revised, in MS Late Lyrics (f. 177).

Dorset County Museum.

The King's Experiment ('It was a wet wan hour in spring')
First pub. *Poems of the Past and the Present* (1902); Gibson, pp. 162–3; Hynes, I, 201–2.

HrT 646 Fair copy, revised, in MS Poems of the Past and the Present.

Bodleian, MS Eng. poet. d. 18, ff. 119–21 (rectos only).

HrT 647 Correction to line 34, written in 'Errata' list of Hardy's copy of *Poems of the Past and the Present* (1902) (see HrT 927).

Owned (1982) F. B. Adams (see Hynes).

HrT 648 Revision to line 34 in DCM Wessex Edition (Verse Vol. I, 236).

Dorset County Museum.

A King's Soliloquy ('From the slow march and muffled drum')
First pub. *Satires of Circumstance* (1914); Gibson, pp. 373–4; Hynes, II, 87–8.

HrT 649 Fair copy, revised, the title altered from 'The King's Soliloquy', in MS Satires of Circumstance (pp. 119–20); dated May 1910.

Dorset County Museum.

A Kiss ('By a wall the stranger now calls his')
First pub. *Moments of Vision* (1917); Gibson, p. 467; Hynes, II, 205.

HrT 650 Fair copy, revised, here beginning 'By the wall where now the stranger is', in MS Moments of Vision (f. 63).

Magdalene College, Cambridge.

'Known had I' ('Known had I what I knew not')
First pub. *Human Shows* (1925); Gibson, p. 806; Hynes, III, 128.

HrT 651 Fair copy, revised, in MS Human Shows (f. 160).

Yale.

HrT 652 Annotation in HS Proof (p. 227).

Dorset County Museum.

The Lacking Sense ('"O Time, whence comes the Mother's moody look amid her labours')
First pub. *Poems of the Past and the Present* (1902); Gibson, pp. 116–18; Hynes, I, 150–2.

HrT 653 Fair copy, revised, in MS Poems of the Past and the Present.

Bodleian, MS Eng. poet. d. 18, ff. 49–50 (rectos only).

The Lady in the Furs ('"I'm a lofty lovely woman"')
First pub. *Saturday Review*, 4 December 1926, as 'The Lady in the Christmas Furs'; collected *Winter Words* (1928); Gibson, pp. 863–4; Hynes, III, 198–9.

HrT 654 Fair copy, revised, annotated in pencil 'Sent to Ed of Saturday Review 22 Nov. 1926.', in MS Winter Words; dated 1925.

Queen's College, Oxford, MS 420, f. 43.

The Lady of Forebodings ('"What do you so regret, my lady')
First pub. *Human Shows* (1925); Gibson, pp. 824–5; Hynes, III, 149–50.

HrT 655 Fair copy, revised, in MS Human Shows (f. 188).

Yale.

HrT 656 Correction to line 8 in HS Proof (p. 266).

Dorset County Museum.

Lady Vi ('There goes the Lady Vi. How well')
First pub. *Human Shows* (1925); Gibson, p. 799; Hynes, III, 119–20.

HrT 657 Fair copy, revised, the title altered from 'Lady Clo', in MS Human Shows (ff. 149–50, rectos only).

Yale.

HrT 658 Extensive revision to last stanza in HS Proof (p. 211).

Dorset County Museum.

Lament ('How she would have loved')

First pub. *Satires of Circumstance* (1914); Gibson, pp. 344–5; Hynes, II, 53–5.

HrT 659 Fair copy, revised, in MS Satires of Circumstance (pp. 78–9).

Dorset County Museum.

The Lament of the Looking-Glass ('Words from the mirror softly pass')
First pub. *Late Lyrics* (1922); Gibson, pp. 674–5; Hynes, II, 456–7.

HrT 660 Fair copy, revised, in MS Late Lyrics (f. 160).

Dorset County Museum.

HrT 661 Suggested revision to line 12 in *Collected Poems* (1923), p. 638.

Dorset County Museum.

Last Chorus ('Last as first the question rings'), see HrT 1620, 1625.

The Last Chrysanthemum ('Why should this flower delay so long')
First pub. *Poems of the Past and the Present* (1902); Gibson, p. 149; Hynes, I, 186–7.

HrT 662 Fair copy, revised, in MS Poems of the Past and the Present.

Bodleian, MS Eng. poet. d. 18, ff. 97–8 (rectos only).

A Last Journey ('"Father, you seem to have been sleeping fair?"')
First pub. *Human Shows* (1925); Gibson, pp. 717–18; Hynes, III, 25–6.

HrT 663 Fair copy, revised, in MS Human Shows (ff. 26–7, rectos only).

Yale.

The Last Leaf ('"The leaves throng thick above: —')
First pub. *Nash's and Pall Mall Magazine*, November 1924; collected *Human Shows* (1925); Gibson, pp. 744–5; Hynes, III, 56–7.

HrT 664 Fair copy, revised, in MS Human Shows (ff. 66–7, rectos only).

Yale.

Last Look round St Martin's Fair ('The sun is like an open furnace door')
First pub. *Human Shows* (1925); Gibson, p. 765; Hynes, III, 82.

HrT 665 Fair copy, revised, in MS Human Shows (f. 95).

Yale.

HrT 666 Revision to line 2 in HS Proof (p. 137).

Dorset County Museum.

Last Love-word ('This is the last; the very, very last!')
First pub. *Human Shows* (1925); Gibson, pp. 742–3; Hynes, III, 55.

HrT 667 Fair copy, in MS Human Shows (f. 63); dated '189–.'.

Yale.

The Last Performance (' "I am playing my oldest tunes," declared she')
First pub. *Moments of Vision* (1917); Gibson, p. 487; Hynes, II, 229.

HrT 668 Fair copy, revised, in MS Moments of Vision (f. 98).

Magdalene College, Cambridge.

The Last Signal ('Silently I footed by an uphill road')
First pub. *Moments of Vision* (1917); Gibson, p. 473; Hynes, II, 212–13. The unique correction to line 7 for the Wessex Edition printed in Hynes, II, 499 appears on the list of corrections in the R. & R. Clark papers (at the National Library of Scotland) described in the INTRODUCTION.

HrT 669 Fair copy, here subtitled 'In Memoriam William Barnes', in MS Moments of Vision (f. 74).

Magdalene College, Cambridge.

HrT 669.5 Correction in Hardy's copy of the Wessex Edition (Verse Vol. IV, 273), presented to Sydney Cockerell by FEH, 30 March 1928 (see DCM Wessex Edition).

Cockerell Sale, Lot 252, sold to Maggs.

Owned (1985) F. B. Adams (see Hynes, III, 352).

The Last Time ('The kiss had been given and taken')
First pub. *Late Lyrics* (1922); Gibson, p. 687; Hynes, II, 472.

HrT 670 Fair copy, revised, in MS Late Lyrics (f. 178).

Dorset County Museum.

Last Week in October ('The trees are undressing, and fling in many places —')
First pub. *Human Shows* (1925); Gibson, p. 709; Hynes, III, 15–16.

HrT 671 Fair copy, revised, in MS Human Shows (f. 13).

Yale.

Last Words to a Dumb Friend ('Pet was never mourned as you')
First pub. *Late Lyrics* (1922); Gibson, pp. 657–8; Hynes, II, 435–6.

HrT 672 Fair copy, revised, in MS Late Lyrics (ff. 135–6); dated 2 October 1904.

Dorset County Museum.

Late Lyrics
This collection of poems first pub. London, 1922. For a description of the MS printer's copy (MS Late Lyrics), see INTRODUCTION; contents have been listed individually. See also HrT 1524.

HrT 673 Fair copy, revised, of the 'Apology.', in MS Late Lyrics (ff. i–xii, rectos only), first page headed 'Late Lyrics & Earlier./with many other verses/By Thomas Hardy.', signed (initials); dated February 1922, sent to Macmillan 21 February 1922.

Hardy's prefatory 'Apology' was first pub. *Late Lyrics* (1922); Gibson, pp. 556–62; Orel, pp. 50–9; Hynes, II, [317]–25.

Dorset County Museum.

HrT 673.5 Revisions to the 'Apology' in *Collected Poems* (1923), pp. 530–1.

Dorset County Museum.

The Later Autumn ('Gone are the lovers, under the bush')
First pub. *Saturday Review*, 28 October 1922; collected *Human Shows* (1925); Gibson, p. 710; Hynes, III, 17.

HrT 674 Fair copy, revised, in MS Human Shows (f. 15); dated 1921.

Yale.

HrT 675 Revision to line 15 in HS Proof (p. 21).

Dorset County Museum.

Lausanne: In Gibbon's Old Garden: 11–12 p.m. ('A spirit seems to pass')
First pub. *Poems of the Past and the Present* (1902); Gibson, pp. 105–6; Hynes, I, 138.

HrT 676 Fair copy, revised, the title altered from 'At Lausanne', in MS Poems of the Past and the Present, line 16 annotated '<Prose Works: "Doctrine & Discipline of Divorce.">'.

Bodleian, MS Eng. poet. d. 18, f. 31.

HrT 677 Annotation to line 16 and revision to line 5 in DCM Wessex Edition (Verse Vol. I, 146).

Dorset County Museum.

A Leader of Fashion ('Never has she known')
First pub. *The Adelphi*, November 1925; collected *Human Shows* (1925); Gibson, pp. 767–8; Hynes, III, 85.

HrT 678 Fair copy, revised, the title altered from 'The Fine Lady', in MS Human Shows (f. 99).

Yale.

A Leaving ('Knowing what it bore')
First pub. *Human Shows* (1925); Gibson, pp. 829–30; Hynes, III, 155–6.

HrT 679 Fair copy, revised, here entitled 'A last Leaving' and beginning '<With> Knowing what it bore', one leaf.

Facsimile in Roger Fry and E. A.Lowe, *English Handwriting*, S.P.E. Tract, No. 23 (Oxford, 1926), plate 22.

Owned (1985) R. L. Purdy (see Hynes); destined for Yale.

HrT 680 Fair copy, revised, the title altered from 'A last Leaving', in MS Human Shows (f. 194).

Yale.

HrT 681 Revision to line 12 in HS Proof (p. 276).

Dorset County Museum.

Leipzig ('"Old Norbert with the flat blue cap —') First pub. *Wessex Poems* (1898); Gibson, pp. 26–30; Hynes, I, 34–9. Some lines from stanzas 6, 11, 16 and the whole of stanzas 26–7 and 30–3 used later in *The Dynasts*, Part Third (III, ii, iv and v); see HrT 1610–12, 1619–28.

HrT 682 Fair copy, revised, here subtitled 'Interior of the Old Ship Inn, Casterbridge. Evening.', in MS Wessex Poems (ff. 31–6).

Birmingham City Museum and Art Gallery.

HrT 683 Revision to line 15 in DCM Wessex Edition (Verse Vol. I, 33).

Dorset County Museum.

'Let me believe' ('Let me believe it, dearest') First pub. *Human Shows* (1925), as 'Let me'; Gibson, p. 711; Hynes, III, 18.

HrT 684 Fair copy, revised, here entitled '"Let me"', in MS Human Shows (f. 16).

Yale.

HrT 685 Title revised from '"Let me"' in HS Proof (p. 23).

Dorset County Museum.

Let Me Enjoy ('Let me enjoy the earth no less') First pub. *Cornhill*, April 1909 and *Putnam's Magazine*, April 1909; collected *Time's Laughingstocks* (1909); Gibson, p. [238]; Hynes, I, [290].

HrT 685.5 Fair copy of an early version, here subtitled '(Song: minor key.)', signed, one page, as sent to Smith, Elder and Co. for the first publication.

This MS not mentioned Gibson or Hynes.

National Library of Scotland, MS 23173, f. 199.

HrT 686 Fair copy, in MS Time's Laughingstocks (f. 62B).

Fitzwilliam Museum.

HrT 687 Corrected page proof for first publication, 2 pages.

Owned (1982) F. B. Adams (see Hynes).

HrT 688 Corrections to line 10 and subtitle in *Selected Poems* (1917), p. 26.

Dorset County Museum.

'Let's meet again to-night, my Fair', see HrT 1637–9.

The Letter's Triumph ('Yes: I perceive it's to your Love') First pub. *Daily Telegraph*, 19 July 1928; collected *Winter Words* (1928); Gibson, pp. 898–9; Hynes, III, 239–40.

HrT 689 Fair copy, revised, in MS Winter Words, annotated '<Based on an incident.>'.

Queen's College, Oxford, MS 420, f. 96.

The Levelled Churchyard ('"O Passenger, pray list and catch') First pub. *Poems of the Past and the Present* (1902); Gibson, pp. 157–8; Hynes, I, 196–7.

HrT 690 Fair copy, revised, in MS Poems of the Past and the Present; dated 'About 1882.'.

Bodleian, MS Eng. poet. d. 18, f. 112.

Liddell and Scott ('"Well, though it seems') First pub. *Winter Words* (1928); Gibson, pp. 844–6; Hynes, III, 176–8.

HrT 691 Fair copy, revised, in MS Winter Words, annotated 'Written after the Death of Liddell in 1898...'.

Queen's College, Oxford, MS 420, ff. 16–18 (rectos only).

Life and Death at Sunrise ('The hills uncap their tops')
First pub. *Human Shows* (1925); Gibson, pp. 730–1; Hynes, III, 40–1.

HrT 692 Fair copy, revised, the title altered from 'A Long-ago Sunrise at Dogbury Gate: 1867.', in MS Human Shows (f. 45).

Yale.

Life Laughs Onward ('Rambling I looked for an old abode')
First pub. *Moments of Vision* (1917); Gibson, pp. 463–4; Hynes, II, 201.

HrT 693 Fair copy, in MS Moments of Vision (f. 57).

Magdalene College, Cambridge.

A Light Snow-fall after Frost ('On the flat road a man at last appears:')
First pub. *Human Shows* (1925); Gibson, p. 733; Hynes, III, 43–4.

HrT 694 Fair copy, revised, in MS Human Shows (f. 49), annotated 'Near Surbiton.'.

Yale.

Lines ('Before we part to alien thoughts and aims')
Spoken by Ada Rehan at the Lyceum Theatre, London, 23 July 1890; first pub. (lines 13–24, 31–4) in *Pall Mall Gazette*, 23 July 1890; first pub. in full *Dorset County Chronicle* (Dorchester), 31 July 1890; collected *Wessex Poems* (1898); Gibson, pp. 79–80; Hynes, I, 104–5.

HrT 695 Draft (Mary Jeune's copy), here entitled 'Lines Spoken by Miss Ada Rehan/On behalf of Mrs Jeune's Holiday Fund/for poor city children', 3 pages; dated 'Savile Club. July 20, 1890'.

Owned (1982) R. L. Purdy (see Hynes); destined for Yale.

HrT 696 Fair copy, revised in pencil and ink, here entitled 'Lines/spoken by Miss Ada Rehan/ on behalf of Mrs Jeune's Holiday Fund/for poor city children:/Written by Thomas Hardy', one page.

Texas.

HrT 697 Three corrections, headed 'Corrections: —', on a leaf of Savile Club notepaper enclosed in a letter to Augustin Daly (manager of theatre where Ada Rehan worked), Savile Club, 21 July 1890.

This MS printed Hynes, I, 366; letter only printed *Letters*, I, 213.

UCLA, 100/bx 36.

HrT 698 Fair copy, revised, in MS Wessex Poems (ff. 104–5).

Birmingham City Museum and Art Gallery.

Lines/To a Movement in Mozart's E-Flat Symphony ('Show me again the time')
First pub. *Moments of Vision* (1917); Gibson, pp. 458–9; Hynes, II, 195–6.

HrT 699 Fair copy, revised, in MS Moments of Vision (f. 48).

Magdalene College, Cambridge.

HrT 700 Revision to line 19 in *Collected Poems* (1923), p. 430.

Dorset County Museum.

The Little Old Table ('Creak, little wood thing, creak')
First pub. *Late Lyrics* (1922); Gibson, pp. 648–9; Hynes, II, 425.

HrT 701 Fair copy, revised, in MS Late Lyrics (f. 123).

Dorset County Museum.

The Lizard ('If on any warm day when you ramble around')
First pub. Florence Emily Dugdale, *The Book of Baby Pets* (London, 1915) as 'About Lizards'; Gibson, p. 952; Hynes, III, 304.

HrT 702 One page, in pencil.

Owned (1985) R. L. Purdy (see Hynes); destined for Yale.

The Lodging-house Fuchsias ('Mrs Masters's fuchsias hung')

First pub. *Daily Telegraph*, 13 August 1928; collected *Winter Words* (1928); Gibson, p. 855; Hynes, III, 188–9.

HrT 703 Fair copy, revised, in MS Winter Words.

Queen's College, Oxford, MS 420, f. 31.

Logs on the Hearth ('The fire advances along the log')
First pub. *Moments of Vision* (1917); Gibson, pp. 489–90; Hynes, II, 232.

HrT 704 Fair copy, revised, in MS Moments of Vision (f. 102); dated December 1915.

Magdalene College, Cambridge.

Lonely Days ('Lonely her fate was')
First pub. *Late Lyrics* (1922); Gibson, pp. 652–3; Hynes, II, 429–31.

HrT 705 Fair copy, revised, annotated 'Versified from a Diary', in MS Late Lyrics (ff. 129–30).

Dorset County Museum.

Long Plighted ('Is it worth while, dear, now')
First pub. *Poems of the Past and the Present* (1902); Gibson, pp. 140–1; Hynes, I, 176–7.

HrT 706 Fair copy, revised, in MS Poems of the Past and the Present.

Bodleian, MS Eng. poet. d. 18, ff. 84–5 (rectos only).

Looking Across ('It is dark in the sky')
First pub. *Moments of Vision* (1917); Gibson, pp. 498–9; Hynes, II, 243–4.

HrT 707 Fair copy, in MS Moments of Vision (f. 119); dated December 1915.

Magdalene College, Cambridge.

Looking at a Picture on an Anniversary ('But don't you know it, my dear')
First pub. *Moments of Vision* (1917); Gibson, p. 533; Hynes, II, 283–4.

HrT 708 Fair copy, revised, the title altered from 'Looking at her Picture on an Anniversary', in MS Moments of Vision (f. 169); dated '<March,> 1913.'.

Magdalene College, Cambridge.

Looking Back ('When formerly we thought, Dear')
First pub. Purdy (1954), p. 149; Gibson, p. 938; Hynes, III, 295.

HrT 709 Fair copy, in MS Time's Laughingstocks (f. 49).

This poem was omitted from *Time's Laughingstocks* as published.

Fitzwilliam Museum.

Lorna the Second ('Lorna! Yes, you are sweet')
First pub. *Winter Words* (1928); Gibson, p. 903; Hynes, III, 245.

HrT 710 Fair copy, revised, in MS Winter Words.

Queen's College, Oxford, MS 420, f. 103.

Lost Love ('I play my sweet old airs —')
First pub. *Satires of Circumstance* (1914); Gibson, p. 318; Hynes, II, 24.

HrT 711 Fair copy, revised, in MS Satires of Circumstance (p. 24).

Dorset County Museum.

HrT 712 Correction to line 13 in *Selected Poems* (1917), p. 56.

Dorset County Museum.

The Lost Pyx/A Mediæval Legend ('Some say the spot is banned; that the pillar Cross-and-Hand')
First pub. *The Sphere*, 22 December 1900; collected *Poems of the Past and the Present* (1902); Gibson, pp. 173–5; Hynes, I, 213–15.

HrT 713 Fair copy, revised, signed, printer's copy for *The Sphere*, 5 numbered leaves (rectos only), originally enclosed with a covering letter to Clement Shorter, 10 December 1900.

Letter printed *Letters*, II, 275 (from original owned F. B. Adams).

Owned (1982) F. B. Adams (see Hynes).

HrT 714 Fair copy, slightly revised, in MS Poems of the Past and the Present.

Bodleian, MS Eng. poet. d. 18, ff. 136–40 (rectos only).

HrT 715 Corrected galley proof for first publication, one leaf.

Texas.

HrT 716 Revision to line 24 in DCM Wessex Edition (Verse Vol. I, 253).

Dorset County Museum.

Louie ('I am forgetting Louie the buoyant')
First pub. *Human Shows* (1925); Gibson, p. 772; Hynes, III, 90.

HrT 717 Fair copy, in MS Human Shows (f. 107); dated July 1913.

Yale.

Love the Monopolist ('The train draws forth from the station-yard')
First pub. *Moments of Vision* (1917); Gibson, pp. 479–80; Hynes, II, 219–20.

HrT 718 Fair copy, revised, in MS Moments of Vision (f. 83); dated 'Begun 1871'.

Magdalene College, Cambridge.

Love Watches a Window ('"Here in the window beaming across')
First pub. *Winter Words* (1928); Gibson, p. 840; Hynes, III, 172–3.

HrT 719 Fair copy, revised, in MS Winter Words.

Queen's College, Oxford, MS 420, f. 11.

The Love-Letters ('I met him quite by accident')
First pub. *Winter Words* (1928); Gibson, p. 841; Hynes, III, 173–4.

HrT 720 Fragment of an early draft, containing the first stanza and title only.

Owned (1985) R. L. Purdy (see Hynes); destined for Yale.

HrT 721 Fair copy, revised, in MS Winter Words.

Queen's College, Oxford, MS 420, f. 12.

Lover to Mistress ('Beckon to me to come')
First pub. *Human Shows* (1925); Gibson, p. 707; Hynes, III, 13–14.

HrT 722 Fair copy, revised, in MS Human Shows (f. 10).

Yale.

Lying Awake ('You, Morningtide Star, now are steady-eyed, over the east')
First pub. *Saturday Review*, 3 December 1927; collected *Winter Words* (1928); Gibson, p. 863; Hynes, III, 198.

HrT 723 Fair copy, revised, annotated in pencil '[Copy sent to Saturday Review 23 Nov. 1927]', in MS Winter Words.

Queen's College, Oxford, MS 420, f. 42.

Mad Judy ('When the hamlet hailed a birth')
First pub. *Poems of the Past and the Present* (1902); Gibson, p. 151; Hynes, I, 189.

HrT 724 Fair copy, revised, in MS Poems of the Past and the Present.

Bodleian, MS Eng. poet. d. 18, f. 101.

The Maid of Keinton Mandeville ('I hear that maiden still')
First pub. *The Athenaeum*, 30 April 1920; collected *Late Lyrics* (1922); Gibson, pp. [563]–4; Hynes, II, 326–7.

HrT 725 Slightly corrected typescript for first publication, signed, 2 numbered leaves (rectos only), annotated '[For Friday, April 30]', enclosed in a letter to John Middleton Murry, Max Gate, 7 April 1920.

The letter printed *Letters*, VI, 12.

Berg.

HrT 726 Fair copy, revised, in MS Late Lyrics (f. 2); dated '1915 or 1916'.

Dorset County Museum.

HrT 727 Two successive corrected page proofs for the first publication; the first annotated 'Proof 19.4.20', the second annotated 'Revise 26.4.20' and 'Press'.

Berg.

A Maiden's Pledge ('I do not wish to win your vow')
First pub. *Late Lyrics* (1922); Gibson, p. 610; Hynes, II, 380.

HrT 728 Fair copy, revised, in MS Late Lyrics (f. 70).

Dorset County Museum.

A Man ('In Casterbridge there stood a noble pile')
First pub. *Poems of the Past and the Present* (1902); Gibson, pp. 153–4; Hynes, I, 191–2.

HrT 729 Fair copy, revised, in MS Poems of the Past and the Present.

Bodleian, MS Eng. poet. d. 18, ff. 104–5 (rectos only).

The Man He Killed ('"Had he and I but met')
First pub. *Harper's Weekly*, 8 November 1902; collected *Time's Laughingstocks* (1909); Gibson, p. 287; Hynes, I, 344–5.

HrT 730 Fair copy, revised, signed, subtitled 'Scene: The settle of "The Fox" Inn...', one page, printer's copy for *The Sphere* (22 November 1902); watermarked 1901.

Facsimile in Sotheby's sale catalogue, 2–4 April 1928 (Shorter Sale), frontispiece.

Berg.

HrT 731 Fair copy, in MS Time's Laughingstocks (f. 125).

Fitzwilliam Museum.

'A man was drawing near to me' ('On that gray night of mournful drone')
First pub. *Late Lyrics* (1922); Gibson, pp. 579–80; Hynes, II, 345–6.

HrT 732 Fair copy, revised, here subtitled '<(Woman's Song)>', in MS Late Lyrics (ff. 27–8).

Dorset County Museum.

The Man Who Forgot ('At a lonely cross where bye-roads met')
First pub. *Moments of Vision* (1917); Gibson, pp. 535–6; Hynes, II, 286.

HrT 733 Fair copy, revised, in MS Moments of Vision (f. 171).

Magdalene College, Cambridge.

The Man with a Past ('There was merry-making')
First pub. *Moments of Vision* (1917); Gibson, pp. 508–9; Hynes, II, 255.

HrT 734 Fair copy, revised, in MS Moments of Vision (f. 134).

Magdalene College, Cambridge.

The Marble Tablet ('There it stands, though alas, what a little of her')
First pub. *Late Lyrics* (1922); Gibson, p. 655; Hynes, II, 433.

HrT 735 Fair copy, here entitled 'The Marble Monument/(At St. Juliot)', in MS Late Lyrics (f. 133); dated September 1916.

Dorset County Museum.

The Marble-Streeted Town ('I reach the marble-streeted town')
First pub. *Late Lyrics* (1922); Gibson, p. 681; Hynes, II, 465. A fair copy of this poem presented by Hardy to Plymouth Free Public Library in 1923 was destroyed in the Second World War; see also INTRODUCTION.

HrT 736 Fair copy, revised, in MS Late Lyrics (f. 169); dated 'Plymouth (1913?).'.

Dorset County Museum.

The Market-Girl ('Nobody took any notice of her as she stood on the causey kerb')
First pub. *The Venture*, ed. Laurence Housman and W. Somerset Maugham (London, 1903), as 'The Market Girl/(Country Song)'; collected *Time's Laughingstocks* (1909) as 'At Casterbridge Fair. IV.'; Gibson, p. 240; Hynes, I, 292–3.

HrT 737 Fair copy, headed 'IV.', in MS Time's Laughingstocks (f. 65).

Fitzwilliam Museum.

HrT 738 Fair copy, here subtitled '*(Country song)*', one page, signed.

Somerset County Library, Street, Laurence Housman Collection.

The Masked Face ('I found me in a great surging space')
First pub. *Moments of Vision* (1917); Gibson, pp. 521–2; Hynes, II, 270.

HrT 739 Fair copy, revised, in MS Moments of Vision (f. 153).

Magdalene College, Cambridge.

The Master and the Leaves ('We are budding, Master, budding')
First pub. *The Owl* (London), May 1919; privately printed by FEH in pamphlet *Jezreel* (London, September 1919); revised and collected *Late Lyrics* (1922); Gibson, p. 656; Hynes, II, 434–5.

HrT 740 Fair copy, revised, in MS Late Lyrics (f. 134); dated 1917.

Facsimile in Croft, *Autograph Poetry*, No. 141.

Dorset County Museum.

HrT 741 Typescript, revised in last line, one page, printer's copy for FEH's pamphlet.

Cockerell Sale, Lot 279, sold to Alan G. Thomas.

SUNY at Buffalo.

HrT 742 Corrected proof for FEH's pamphlet (containing also HrT 632), annotated '(marked for press)'; proof dated in an unidentified hand 11 September 1919.

Cockerell Sale, Lot 279, sold to Alan G. Thomas.

SUNY at Buffalo.

Meditations on a Holiday (''Tis a May morning')
First pub. *Late Lyrics* (1922); Gibson, pp. 613–15; Hynes, II, 383–6.

HrT 743 Fair copy, revised, here subtitled '(A new chime to an old folk-metre)', the title altered from 'A Meditation on a Holiday', in MS Late Lyrics (ff. 74–5); dated May (altered from 21 April) 1921.

Dorset County Museum.

HrT 744 Revision to line 82 in *Collected Poems* (1923), p. 582.

Dorset County Museum.

A Meeting with Despair ('As evening shaped I found me on a moor')
First pub. *Wessex Poems* (1898); Gibson, pp. 57–8; Hynes, I, 75–6.

HrT 745 Fair copy, including the cancelled subtitle '(Egdon Heath)', in MS Wessex Poems (f. 73).

Birmingham City Museum and Art Gallery.

The Memorial Brass: 186- ('"Why do you weep there, O sweet lady')
First pub. *Moments of Vision* (1917); Gibson, p. 505; Hynes, II, 250–1.

HrT 746 Fair copy, revised, in MS Moments of Vision (f. 128).

Magdalene College, Cambridge.

Memory and I ('"O Memory, where is now my Youth')
First pub. *Poems of the Past and the Present* (1902); Gibson, pp. 185–6; Hynes, I, 226–7.

HrT 747 Fair copy, revised, in MS Poems of the Past and the Present.

Bodleian, MS Eng. poet. d. 18, ff. 155–6 (rectos only).

'Men who march away' ('What of the faith and fire within us')
First pub. *The Times*, 9 September 1914, as 'Song of the Soldiers'; collected *Satires of Circumstance* (1914) and *Selected Poems* (1916); subsequently transferred to 'Moments of Vision' but not published with that collection until *Collected Poems* (1919); Gibson, pp. [538]–9; Hynes, II, [289]–90.

HrT 748 Fair copy, revised, signed, 2 pages (one leaf); dated 5 September 1914.

Facsimile in A. P. Webb, *A Bibliography of the Works of Thomas Hardy* (London, 1916), following p. 46. This MS, originally the final poem in MS Satires of Circumstance, was removed from that volume (replaced with HrT 749) and sent to the Red Cross Sale at Christie's, 26 April 1915, sold to Hollings.

Eton College.

HrT 749 Revisions to lines 15, 19, 20, 26 in a printed copy (as published as 'Song of the Soldiers' in *TLS*, 10 September 1914), headed 'Postscript', in MS Satires of Circumstance, f. [185]; dated 5 September 1914.

This copy was substituted in the MS volume for the excised fair copy, HrT 748.

Dorset County Museum.

HrT 750 Fair copy, in MS Moments of Vision (f. 178), annotated 'This poem first appeared (in volume form) as a postscript to "Satires of Circumstance"'; dated 5 September 1914.

Magdalene College, Cambridge.

HrT 751 Fair copy, signed, 2 pages (one folded leaf); dated 5 September 1914; as sent to Sir Henry Newbolt with a letter dated from Max Gate, 30 December 1918.

Letter printed *Letters*, V, 289 from the original at Texas.

Texas.

HrT 752 Two revisions in an unidentified hand, on a separate leaf (recto only) enclosed in a letter from Hardy to [Edgar] Lane, Max Gate, 14 September 1914.

This MS and letter printed *Letters*, V, 48–9; not mentioned Gibson or Hynes.

Texas.

HrT 753 Revisions to lines 5 and 33 in the hand of Sydney Cockerell, in a copy of *Selected Poems* (1916) (containing also HrT 122, 382) presented to Cockerell by Hardy, October 1916 and annotated by Cockerell on inside front cover 'The corrections...were given me by the author at Max Gate May 25, 1918.'.

Cockerell Sale, Lot 260, sold to Maggs.

Owned (1984) F. B. Adams (see Hynes, II, 504).

HrT 754 Corrections, probably by Sydney Cockerell, in a copy of the first proof of FEH's privately printed pamphlet *A Call to National Service* (London, May 1917) (from which this poem was subsequently omitted) (containing also HrT 180); dated by Cockerell 27 March 1917.

Purdy, p. 192 describes these corrections as being by Hardy; this proof is together with an uncorrected copy of the second proof (dated by Cockerell 13 April 1917) also containing this poem; Cockerell Sale, Lot 304, sold to Hollings.

New York University.

HrT 755 Revisions to lines 5 and 33 in *Selected Poems* (1916), pp. 199–200.

Dorset County Museum.

HrT 756 Revisions to line 5 and 33 in *Selected Poems* (1917), pp. 199–200.

Dorset County Museum.

HrT 757 Revised line 5, sent as a postscript to a letter to Sir Henry Newbolt; letter dated 8 April 1924 and postscript dated 9 April 1924.

This MS printed *Letters*, VI, 246; it was sent to Newbolt in preparation for his inclusion of the poem in his anthology *The Tide of Time in English Poetry* (London, 1925).

Texas.

A Merrymaking in Question ('"I will get a new string for my fiddle')
First pub. *The Sphere*, 27 May 1916; collected *Selected Poems* (1916) and *Moments of Vision* (1917); Gibson, p. 465; Hynes, II, 203.

HrT 758 Fair copy, revised, in MS Moments of Vision (f. 60).

Magdalene College, Cambridge.

HrT 759 Revision to line 10 in *Selected Poems* (1916), p. 32.

Dorset County Museum.

HrT 760 Corrections and revision to line 10 in *Selected Poems* (1917), p. 32.

Dorset County Museum.

Middle-Age Enthusiasms ('We passed where flag and flower')
First pub. *Wessex Poems* (1898); Gibson, p. 63; Hynes, I, 82–3. This poem is cancelled in *Selected Poems* (1917); see INTRODUCTION.

HrT 761 Fair copy, revised, in MS Wessex Poems (f. 80).

Birmingham City Museum and Art Gallery.

Midnight on Beechen, 187– ('On Beechen Cliff self-commune I')
First pub. *Human Shows* (1925); Gibson, pp. 768–9; Hynes, III, 86.

HrT 762 Fair copy, revised, in MS Human Shows (f. 100).

Yale.

HrT 763 Correction to line 11 in HS Proof (p. 144).

Dorset County Museum.

Midnight on the Great Western ('In the third-class seat sat the journeying boy')
First pub. *Moments of Vision* (1917); Gibson, p. 514; Hynes, II, 262.

HrT 764 Fair copy, revised, in MS Moments of Vision (f. 143).

Magdalene College, Cambridge.

The Milestone by the Rabbit-Burrow ('In my loamy nook')
First pub. *Late Lyrics* (1922); Gibson, p. 674; Hynes, II, 455–6.

HrT 765 Fair copy, in MS Late Lyrics (f. 159).

Dorset County Museum.

A Military Appointment ('"So back you have come from the town, Nan, dear!')
First pub. *Late Lyrics* (1922); Gibson, p. 673; Hynes, II, 455.

HrT 766 Fair copy, revised, here subtitled '(Scherzo)' and beginning '"So back you have come from the town, <my dear!> Ann dear!', in MS Late Lyrics (f. 158).

Dorset County Museum.

The Milkmaid ('Under a daisied bank')
First pub. *Poems of the Past and the Present* (1902); Gibson, p. 157; Hynes, I, 195–6.

HrT 767 Fair copy, revised, in MS Poems of the Past and the Present.

Bodleian, MS Eng. poet. d. 18, ff. 110–11 (rectos only).

HrT 768 Revision to line 13, written in the 'Errata' list in Hardy's copy of *Poems of the Past and the Present* (1902).

Owned (1982) F. B. Adams (see Hynes).

HrT 769 Revision to line 13 in *Collected Poems* (1923), p. 144.

Dorset County Museum.

The Minute before Meeting ('The grey gaunt days dividing us in twain')
First pub. *Time's Laughingstocks* (1909); Gibson, p. 236; Hynes, I, 287.

HrT 770 Fair copy, revised, in MS Time's Laughingstocks (f. 62); dated 1871.

Fitzwilliam Museum.

HrT 771 Typescript of stanza one only, here untitled, sent in a letter (containing also HrT 141) to Rutland Boughton (for use in his opera of 'The Famous Tragedy of the Queen of Cornwall'), Max Gate, 18 June 1924.

This MS printed Letters, VI, 257.

British Library, Add. MS 52364, f. 127.

Misconception ('I busied myself to find a sure')
First pub. *Time's Laughingstocks* (1909); Gibson, p. 232; Hynes, I, 283.

HrT 772 Fair copy, revised, in MS Time's Laughingstocks (f. 57).

Fitzwilliam Museum.

Mismet ('He was leaning by a face')
First pub. *Late Lyrics* (1922); Gibson, pp. 611–12; Hynes, II, 381–2.

HrT 773 Fair copy, revised, in MS Late Lyrics (f. 72).

Dorset County Museum.

The Missed Train ('How I was caught')
First pub. *The Owl* (London, 1923); revised and collected *Human Shows* (1925); Gibson, pp. 786–7; Hynes, III, 106.

HrT 774 Fair copy, revised, in MS Human Shows (f. 130).

Yale.

HrT 775 Correction to last line in HS Proof (p. 185).

Dorset County Museum.

The Mock Wife ('It's a dark drama, this; and yet I know the house, and date')
First pub. *Human Shows* (1925); Gibson, pp. 762–3; Hynes, III, 77–9.

HrT 776 Fair copy, revised, in MS Human Shows (ff. 90–1, rectos only).

Yale.

HrT 777 Revision to line 4 in HS Proof (p. 130).

Dorset County Museum.

Molly Gone ('No more summer for Molly and me')
First pub. *Moments of Vision* (1917); Gibson, pp. 497–8; Hynes, II, 241–2.

HrT 778 Fair copy, revised, in MS Moments of Vision (f. 116).

Magdalene College, Cambridge.

Moments of Vision ('That mirror')
First pub. *Moments of Vision* (1917); Gibson, p. [427]; Hynes, II, [159].

HrT 779 Fair copy, revised, in MS Moments of Vision (f. 1).

Magdalene College, Cambridge.

HrT 780 Fair copy, revised, signed, one page; watermarked 1913.

Sent by Hardy to the Red Cross Sale, Christie's, 22 April 1918, sold to Maggs.

Texas.

Moments of Vision
This collection of poems first pub. London, 1917. For lists of corrections for subsequent editions, see INTRODUCTION. For a description of the MS printer's copy (MS Moments of Vision), see INTRODUCTION; contents have been listed individually. See also HrT 1524.

HrT 781 Corrections by Sydney Cockerell on eleven pages (including also HrT 546) of a copy of the first edition; inscribed to Cockerell, November 1917.

Cockerell Sale, Lot 269, sold to Maggs.

Owned (1984) F. B. Adams (see Hynes, II, 496).

HrT 781.5 Corrections 'for the second edition' in a presentation copy of the first edition to Harold Child; Hardy's letter of presentaion (sent separately) dated 11 February 1919.

The letter printed *Letters*, V, 294–5 (from the original owned by F. B. Adams).

Owned (1985) R. L. Purdy (see *Letters*); destined for Yale.

The Mongrel ('In Havenpool Harbour the ebb was strong')
First pub. *Daily Telegraph*, 25 June 1928; collected *Winter Words* (1928); Gibson, p. 877; Hynes, III, 214.

HrT 782 Fair copy, revised, in MS Winter Words.

Queen's College, Oxford, MS 420, ff. 62–3 (rectos only).

The Month's Calendar ('Tear off the calendar')
First pub. *Human Shows* (1925); Gibson, pp. 719–20; Hynes, III, 27–8.

HrT 783 Fair copy, revised, in MS Human Shows (f. 29).

Yale.

HrT 784 Correction to line 3 in HS Proof (p. 44).

Dorset County Museum.

The Monument-maker ('I chiselled her monument')

First pub. *Human Shows* (1925); Gibson, pp. 707–8; Hynes, III, 14.

HrT 785 Fair copy, revised, in MS Human Shows (f. 11); dated 1916.

Yale.

The Moon Looks In ('I have risen again')
First pub. *Satires of Circumstance* (1914); Gibson, pp. 390–1; Hynes, II, 109.

HrT 786 Fair copy, in MS Satires of Circumstance (p. 149).

Dorset County Museum.

The Moth-Signal ('"What are you still, still thinking"')
First pub. *Satires of Circumstance* (1914); Gibson, pp. 392–3; Hynes, II, 111–12.

HrT 787 Fair copy, in MS Satires of Circumstance (p. 152).

Dorset County Museum.

The Mother Mourns('When mid-autumn's moan shook the night-time')
First pub. *Poems of the Past and the Present* (1902); Gibson, pp. [111]–13; Hynes, I, 144–7.

HrT 788 Fair copy, revised, in MS Poems of the Past and the Present.

Bodleian, MS Eng. poet. d. 18, ff. 39–43 (rectos only).

Motto for the Wessex Society of Manchester ('While new tongues call, and novel scenes unfold'), see HrT 1444–5.

The Mound ('For a moment pause: —')
First pub. *Winter Words* (1928); Gibson, p. 843; Hynes, III, 176.

HrT 789 Fair copy, revised, in MS Winter Words.

Queen's College, Oxford, MS 420, f. 15.

MS Human Shows, see INTRODUCTION.

MS Late Lyrics, see INTRODUCTION.

MS Moments of Vision, see INTRODUCTION.

MS Poems of the Past and the Present, see INTRODUCTION.

MS Satires of Circumstance, see INTRODUCTION.

MS Time's Laughingstocks, see INTRODUCTION.

MS Wessex Poems, see INTRODUCTION.

MS Winter Words, see INTRODUCTION.

Murmurs in the Gloom ('I wayfared at the nadir of the sun')
First pub. *Late Lyrics* (1922); Gibson, pp. 694–5; Hynes, II, 480–1.

HrT 790 Fair copy, revised, in MS Late Lyrics (f. 187); annotated '(Copied.) Sept. 22. 1899.'.

Dorset County Museum.

Music in a Snowy Street ('The weather is sharp')
First pub. *Human Shows* (1925); Gibson, pp. 735–6; Hynes, III, 46–7.

HrT 791 Fair copy, revised, in MS Human Shows (ff. 52–3, rectos only).

Yale.

The Musical Box ('Lifelong to be')
First pub. *Moments of Vision* (1917); Gibson, pp. 482–3; Hynes, II, 223–5.

HrT 792 Fair copy, revised, in MS Moments of Vision (f. 90).

Magdalene College, Cambridge.

A Musical Incident ('When I see the room it hurts me')

First pub. *Winter Words* (1928); Gibson, pp. 909–10; Hynes, III, 251–2.

HrT 793 Fair copy, revised, in MS Winter Words.

Queen's College, Oxford, MS 420, f. 113.

The Musing Maiden ('"Why so often, silent one')
First pub. *Winter Words* (1928); Gibson, pp. 902–3; Hynes, III, 244–5.

HrT 794 Fair copy, revised, the title altered from 'The Imaginative Maiden', in MS Winter Words; dated October 1866.

Queen's College, Oxford, MS 420, f. 102.

Mute Opinion ('I traversed a dominion')
First pub. in a pre-publication review of *Poems of the Past and the Present*, 'Mr Thomas Hardy's New Poems', *The Academy*, 23 November 1902; collected *Poems of the Past and the Present* (1902); Gibson, p. 127; Hynes, I, 162.

HrT 795 Fair copy, revised, in MS Poems of the Past and the Present.

Bodleian, MS Eng. poet. d. 18, f. 66.

My Cicely ('"Alive?" — And I leapt in my wonder')
First pub. *Wessex Poems* (1898); Gibson, pp. 51–4; Hynes, I, 67–72.

HrT 796 Fair copy, revised, in MS Wessex Poems (ff. 64–8).

Birmingham City Museum and Art Gallery.

'My Love's gone a-fighting', see HrT 1620, 1625.

'My spirit will not haunt the mound' ('My spirit will not haunt the mound')
First pub. *Poetry and Drama*, December 1913; collected *Satires of Circumstance* (1914); Gibson, pp. 318–19; Hynes, II, 25.

HrT 797 Fair copy, in MS Satires of Circumstance (p. 25).

Dorset County Museum.

Nature's Questioning ('When I look forth at dawning, pool')
First pub. *Wessex Poems* (1898); Gibson, pp. 66–7; Hynes, I, 86–7.

HrT 798 Fair copy, revised, in MS Wessex Poems (f. 84).

Birmingham City Museum and Art Gallery.

Near Lanivet, 1872 ('There was a stunted handpost just on the crest')
First pub. *Moments of Vision* (1917); Gibson, p. 436; Hynes, II, 168–70.

HrT 799 Fair copy, revised, in MS Moments of Vision (f. 17), subscribed '<From an old note>'.

Magdalene College, Cambridge.

A Necessitarian's Epitaph ('A world I did not wish to enter')
First pub. *Winter Words* (1928); Gibson, p. 889; Hynes, III, 228.

HrT 800 Fair copy, revised, in MS Winter Words.

Queen's College, Oxford, MS 420, f. 81.

The Nettles ('This, then, is the grave of my son')
First pub. *Moments of Vision* (1917); Gibson, pp. 517–18; Hynes, II, 266.

HrT 801 Fair copy, in MS Moments of Vision (f. 148).

Magdalene College, Cambridge.

Neutral Tones ('We stood by a pond that winter day')
First pub. *Wessex Poems* (1898); Gibson, p. 12; Hynes, I, 13.

HrT 802 Fair copy, revised, in MS Wessex Poems (f. 9); dated 1867.

Birmingham City Museum and Art Gallery.

HrT 803 Corrections and revisions to lines 6–7 in *Selected Poems* (1917), p. 139.

Dorset County Museum.

HrT 804 Revisions to this poem in a clipping of a review of *Collected Poems* (1919) in which it is quoted, in Scrapbook III (HrT 1689).

This review printed *The Nation*, 8 November 1919; not mentioned Gibson or Hynes; Microfilm Edition, Reel 6.

Dorset County Museum.

The New Boots ('"They are his new boots," she pursued')
First pub. *Winter Words* (1928); Gibson, p. 902; Hynes, III, 243–4.

HrT 805 Fair copy, revised, in MS Winter Words.

Queen's College, Oxford, MS 420, f. 101.

The New Dawn's Business ('What are you doing outside my walls')
First pub. *Daily Telegraph*, 20 March 1928; collected *Winter Words* (1928); Gibson, p. [835]; Hynes, III, 167.

HrT 806 Fair copy, revised, in MS Winter Words.

Queen's College, Oxford, MS 420, f. 3.

The New Toy ('She cannot leave it alone')
First pub. *Human Shows* (1925); Gibson, pp. 739–40; Hynes, III, 52.

HrT 807 Fair copy, revised, in MS Human Shows (f. 59).

Yale.

New Year's Eve ('"I have finished another year", said God')
First pub. *Fortnightly Review*, 1 January 1907; collected *Time's Laughingstocks* (1909); Gibson, pp. 277–8; Hynes, I, 334–5.

HrT 808 Fair copy, revised, in MS Time's Laughingstocks (f. 112).

Fitzwilliam Museum.

HrT 809 Fair copy, signed, transcribed for Edward Clodd.

Texas.

A New Year's Eve in War Time ('Phantasmal fears')
First pub. *The Sphere*, 6 January 1917; collected in *Moments of Vision* (1917); privately printed by FEH in pamphlet *England to Germany* (London, 1917); Gibson, pp. 548–9; Hynes, II, 302–3. Cockerell Sale, Lot 270 (sold to Maggs) included an uncorrected? proof of FEH's pamphlet.

HrT 810 Fair copy, revised, in MS Moments of Vision (f. 193); dated 1916.

Magdalene College, Cambridge.

HrT 811 Printed copy of first publication, revised for FEH's pamphlet.

Cockerell Sale, Lot 261, sold to Alan G. Thomas.

Owned (1984) F. B. Adams (see Hynes, II, 304).

HrT 812 Proof, corrected in an unidentified hand, for FEH's pamphlet (containing also HrT 334, 530); dated 8 February 1917.

Cockerell Sale, Lot 261, sold to Alan G. Thomas; these corrections not mentioned Gibson or Hynes.

Owned (1984) F. B. Adams (see Hynes, II, 304).

The Newcomer's Wife ('He paused on the sill of a door ajar')
First pub. *Satires of Circumstance* (1914); Gibson, p. 366; Hynes, II, 79.

HrT 813 Fair copy, revised, in MS Satires of Circumstance (p. 109).

Dorset County Museum.

News for Her Mother ('One mile more is')
First pub. *Time's Laughingstocks* (1909); Gibson, pp. 246–7; Hynes, I, 299–300. This poem is cancelled in *Selected Poems* (1917); see INTRODUCTION.

HrT 814 Fair copy, revised, in MS Time's Laughingstocks (f. 74).

Fitzwilliam Museum.

HrT 815 Proof, corrected by Hardy in line 7, for publication of the poem in *The Dorset Year-Book* (pub. Society of Dorset Men in London) (London, 1922).

This corrected proof is described by Stanley Galpin in his obituary of Thomas Hardy published in *The Dorset Year-Book* (London, 1928); also mentioned Hynes, I, 384.

Unlocated.

The Newspaper Soliloquizes, see HrT 30.

A Night in November ('I marked when the weather changed')

First pub. *Late Lyrics* (1922); Gibson, p. 586; Hynes, II, 352–3.

HrT 816 Fair copy, in MS Late Lyrics (f. 36); dated '(?) 1913'.

Dorset County Museum.

Night in the Old Home ('When the wasting embers redden the chimney-breast')
First pub. *Time's Laughingstocks* (1909); Gibson, pp. 269–70; Hynes, I, 325–6.

HrT 817 Fair copy, the title altered from 'Night in the old house', in MS Time's Laughingstocks (f. 100).

Fitzwilliam Museum.

A Night of Questionings ('On the eve of All-Souls' Day')
First pub. *Human Shows* (1925); Gibson, pp. 726–8; Hynes, III, 35–7.

HrT 818 Fair copy, revised, in MS Human Shows (ff. 39–41, rectos only).

Yale.

HrT 819 Revision to line 80 in HS Proof (p. 60).

Dorset County Museum.

The Night of the Dance ('The cold moon hangs to the sky by its horn')
First pub. *Time's Laughingstocks* (1909); Gibson, pp. 231–2; Hynes, I, 282–3.

HrT 820 Fair copy, in MS Time's Laughingstocks (f. 56).

Fitzwilliam Museum.

HrT 821 Revision to line 7 in *Selected Poems* (1917), p. 22.

Dorset County Museum.

The Night of Trafalgar ('In the wild October night-time, when the wind raved round the land'), see HrT 1613–15, 1635.

A Nightmare, and the Next Thing ('On this decline of Christmas Day')
First pub. *Winter Words* (1928); Gibson, pp. 866–7; Hynes, III, 202–3.

HrT 822 Fair copy, revised, in MS Winter Words.

Queen's College, Oxford, MS 420, f. 48.

Night-time in mid-fall ('It is a storm-strid night, winds footing swift')
First pub. *Human Shows*(1925); Gibson, p. 731; Hynes, III, 41.

HrT 823 Fair copy, revised, the title altered from 'Autumn Night-time', in MS Human Shows (f. 46).

Yale.

1967 ('In five-score summers! All new eyes')
First pub. *Time's Laughingstocks* (1909); Gibson, p. [220]; Hynes, I, [269].

HrT 824 Fair copy, in MS Time's Laughingstocks (f. 40); dated 1867.

Fitzwilliam Museum.

No Bell-ringing ('The little boy legged on through the dark')
First privately printed by FEH in a separate pamphlet (Dorchester, 28 February 1925); first pub. *The Sphere*, 23 November 1925; collected *Winter Words* (1928); Gibson, pp. 911–12; Hynes, III, 253–5.

HrT 825 Fair copy, revised, in MS Winter Words, annotated '[*Copy made for Mr Shorter's Christmas number — Sent Feb 1925 — <to appear> appeared Xmas 1925*]'.

Queen's College, Oxford, MS 420, ff. 110–11 (rectos only).

HrT 826 Corrected proof for publication in *The Sphere*, one page, annotated 'Press T. H.'.

Microfilm Edition, Reel 5.

Dorset County Museum.

No Buyers ('A load of brushes and baskets and cradles and chairs')

First pub. *Human Shows* (1925); Gibson, pp. 737–8; Hynes, III, 48–9.

HrT 827 Fair copy, revised, in MS Human Shows (f. 56).

Yale.

HrT 828 Revisions to lines 22 and 26 in HS Proof (p. 82).

Dorset County Museum.

The Noble Lady's Tale ('"We moved with pensive paces')
First pub. *Harper's Weekly*, 18 February 1905, as 'The Noble Lady's Story'; revised and collected *Time's Laughingstocks* (1909); Gibson, pp. 289–95; Hynes, I, 348–55.

HrT 829 Fair copy, extensively revised, signed (cancelled), printer's copy for *Cornhill* (pub. March 1905), subsequently incorporated in MS Time's Laughingstocks (ff. 129–36).

Fitzwilliam Museum.

Nobody Comes ('Tree-leaves labour up and down')
First pub. *Human Shows* (1925); Gibson, p. 743; Hynes, III, 55–6.

HrT 830 Fair copy, in MS Human Shows (f. 64); dated 9 October 1924.

Yale.

Not Known ('They know the wilings of the world')
First pub. *Winter Words* (1928); Gibson, p. 917; Hynes, III, 260–1.

HrT 831 Fair copy, in MS Winter Words, subscribed '<1914. After reading criticism.>'.

Queen's College, Oxford, MS 420, f. 123.

'Not only I' ('Not only I')
First pub. *Human Shows* (1925); Gibson, pp. 782–3; Hynes, III, 101–2.

HrT 832 Fair copy, revised, in MS Human Shows (f. 122).

Yale.

'Nothing matters much' ('"Nothing matters much," he said')
First pub. *Human Shows* (1925); Gibson, p. 819; Hynes, III, 143–4.

HrT 833 Fair copy, in MS Human Shows (f. 180).

Yale.

HrT 834 Revisions to lines 2 and 5 in HS Proof (p. 254).

Dorset County Museum.

'O I won't lead a homely life' ('"O I won't lead a homely life')
First pub. *Late Lyrics* (1922); Gibson, p. 647; Hynes, II, 424.

HrT 835 Fair copy, revised, in MS Late Lyrics (f. 121).

Dorset County Museum.

HrT 836 Fair copy, including music, in pencil, signed, one page; on the verso of a circular dated 23 August 1922.

Cockerell Sale, Lot 286.

Owned (1984) F. B. Adams (see Hynes).

The Obliterate Tomb ('"More than half my life long')
First pub. *Satires of Circumstance* (1914); Gibson, pp. 383–8; Hynes, II, 101–6.

HrT 837 Fair copy, revised, in MS Satires of Circumstance (pp. 138–44).

Dorset County Museum.

The Occultation ('When the cloud shut down on the morning shine')
First pub. *Moments of Vision* (1917); Gibson, p. 463; Hynes, II, 200–201.

HrT 838 Fair copy, revised, in MS Moments of Vision (f. 56).

Magdalene College, Cambridge.

'Often when warring' ('Often when warring for he wist not what')

First pub. *The Sphere*, 10 November 1917; collected *Moments of Vision* (1917); Gibson, p. 545; Hynes, II, 290.

HrT 839 Fair copy, revised, in MS Moments of Vision (f. 188); dated 1915.

Magdalene College, Cambridge.

'Oh the old old clock of the household stock', see INTRODUCTION.

Old Excursions ('"What's the good of going to Ridgeway')
First pub. *Moments of Vision* (1917); Gibson, pp. 520–1; Hynes, II, 269–70.

HrT 840 Fair copy, in MS Moments of Vision (f. 152); dated April 1913.

Magdalene College, Cambridge.

HrT 841 Fair copy, revised, one page; dated 'April 1913./(copied)'.

Microfilm Edition, Reel 5.

Dorset County Museum.

Old Furniture ('I know not how it may be with others')
First pub. *Moments of Vision* (1917); Gibson, pp. 485–6; Hynes, II, 227–8.

HrT 842 Fair copy, revised, here beginning 'I don't know how it may be with others', including an alternative stanza 6 (added later), in MS Moments of Vision (f. 95).

Magdalene College, Cambridge.

The Old Gown ('I have seen her in gowns the brightest')
First pub. *Late Lyrics* (1922); Gibson, pp. 585–6; Hynes, II, 351–2.

HrT 843 Fair copy, revised, in MS Late Lyrics (f. 35).

Dorset County Museum.

An Old Likeness ('Who would have thought')
First pub. *Late Lyrics* (1922); Gibson, pp. 669–70; Hynes, II, 450–1.

HrT 844 Fair copy, revised, the title altered from 'The Old Portrait', in MS Late Lyrics (f. 152).

Dorset County Museum.

The Old Neighbour and the New (''Twas to greet the new rector I called here')
First pub. *Late Lyrics* (1922); Gibson, p. 676; Hynes, II, 458.

HrT 845 Fair copy, revised, in MS Late Lyrics (f. 162).

Dorset County Museum.

The Old Workman ('"Why are you so bent down before your time')
First pub. *Late Lyrics* (1922); Gibson, p. 663; Hynes, II, 441–2.

HrT 846 Fair copy, revised, the title altered from 'The Old Mason', in MS Late Lyrics (f. 143).

Dorset County Museum.

On a Discovered Curl of Hair ('When your soft welcomings were said')
First pub. *Late Lyrics* (1922); Gibson, p. 669; Hynes, II, 449.

HrT 847 Fair copy, revised, in MS Late Lyrics (f. 151); dated February 1913.

Dorset County Museum.

On a Fine Morning ('Whence comes Solace? — Not from seeing')
First pub. *Poems of the Past and the Present* (1902); Gibson, pp. 129–30; Hynes, I, 165.

HrT 848 Fair copy, revised, in MS Poems of the Past and the Present; dated February 1899.

Bodleian, MS Eng. poet. d. 18, f. 70.

HrT 849 Revision to line 11 in DCM Wessex Edition (Verse Vol. I, 182).

Dorset County Museum.

On a Heath ('I could hear a gown-skirt rustling')
First pub. *Moments of Vision* (1917); Gibson, p. 470; Hynes, II, 208–9.

HrT 850 Fair copy, revised, in MS Moments of Vision (f. 68).

Magdalene College, Cambridge.

On a Midsummer Eve ('I idly cut a parsley stalk')
First pub. *Selected Poems* (1916); collected *Moments of Vision* (1917); Gibson, p. 443; Hynes, II, 177.

HrT 851 Fair copy, revised, in MS Moments of Vision (f. 26).

Magdalene College, Cambridge.

On an Invitation to the United States ('My ardours for emprize nigh lost')
First pub. *New York Times Saturday Review of Books and Art*, 21 September 1901; collected *Poems of the Past and the Present* (1902); Gibson, p. 110; Hynes, I, 142–3.

HrT 852 Fair copy, revised, in MS Poems of the Past and the Present.

Bodleian, MS Eng. poet. d. 18, f. 37.

On J. M. B. ('If any day a promised play')
First pub. *The Plays of J. M. Barrie* (London, 1928); Gibson, pp. 952–3, as 'At a Rehearsal of One of J. M. B.'s Plays'; Hynes, III, 305.

HrT 853 Draft, in pencil, here entitled in J. M. Barrie's hand, on part of a leaf taken from a notebook (see HrT 1693), annotated 'Written (at a rehearsal of one of J. M. B.'s plays) by Thomas Hardy.'; the leaf includes the dates 29 April and 4 May 1921.

Facsimile in Sotheby's sale catalogue, 20 December 1937 (Barrie Sale), facing p. 7.

Harvard, MS Eng 695.1.

On Martock Moor ('My deep-dyed husband trusts me')
First pub. *Human Shows* (1925); Gibson, pp. 816–17; Hynes, III, 140–1.

HrT 854 Fair copy, revised, the title altered from 'On Durnover Moor' and here beginning 'My dark-<souled> dyed husband trusts me', in MS Human Shows (f. 176); dated 1899.

Yale.

HrT 855 Revision to line 1 and suggested revisions to line 21 in HS Proof (p. 248).

Dorset County Museum.

On One Who Lived and Died where He Was Born ('When a night in November')
First pub. *Late Lyrics* (1922); Gibson, pp. 659–60; Hynes, II, 437–8.

HrT 856 Fair copy, revised, here beginning 'When an eve in November', in MS Late Lyrics (f. 138).

Dorset County Museum.

On One who Thought No Other Could Write Such English as Himself ('"No mortal man beneath the sky')
First pub. J. O. Bailey, *The Poetry of Thomas Hardy* (Chapel Hill, NC, 1970); Gibson, p. 954, as 'Epitaph for George Moore'; Hynes, III, 309.

HrT 857 Transcript by FEH, revised, one page, the title altered from 'On a writer who thought...', in an envelope (containing also HrT 340 and 1462) annotated by FEH 'Last lines dicated [sic] by T. H. referring to George Moore and G. K. Chesterton. Also a pencilled note, by himself, about my biography.' and 'Two epitaphs...dictated by Hardy on his death-bed.'; dated, in an unidentified hand, January 1928.

Microfilm Edition, Reel 6.

Dorset County Museum.

On Stinsford Hill at Midnight ('I glimpsed a woman's muslined form')
First pub. *Late Lyrics* (1922); Gibson, p. 597; Hynes, II, 365–6.

HrT 858 Fair copy, revised, including an explanatory note, in MS Late Lyrics (f. 52).

Explanatory note printed Hynes, II, 513.

Dorset County Museum.

HrT 859 Explanatory note added in pencil (later erased) in *Collected Poems* (1923).

Dorset County Museum.

HrT 860 Explanatory note, annotated '[Omit this note in any new edition.]', in Hardy's copy of the Wessex Edition (Verse Vol. V, 55), presented to Sydney Cockerell by FEH, 30 March 1928 (see DCM Wessex Edition).

Cockerell Sale, Lot 252, sold to Maggs.

Owned (1985) F. B. Adams (see Hynes, III, 352).

On Sturminster Foot-Bridge ('Reticulations creep upon the slack stream's face')
First pub. *Moments of Vision* (1917); Gibson, p. 484; Hynes, II, 225.

HrT 861 Fair copy, revised, here entitled 'On Stourcastle Foot-bridge', including the cancelled subtitle '(1877.)', in MS Moments of Vision (f. 92).

Facsimile in Gibson, p. [424].

Magdalene College, Cambridge.

On the Belgian Expatriation ('I dreamt that people from the Land of Chimes')
First pub. *King Albert's Book*, ed. Hall Caine ([London, 1914]), as 'Sonnet on the Belgian Expatriation'; collected *Moments of Vision* (1917); Gibson, pp. 540–1; Hynes, II, 292–3.

HrT 862 Fair copy, revised, in MS Moments of Vision (f. 181); dated 18 October 1914.

Magdalene College, Cambridge.

On the Death-Bed ('"I'll tell — being past all praying for —'), see HrT 1007.

On the Departure Platform ('We kissed at the barrier; and passing through')
First pub. *Time's Laughingstocks* (1909); Gibson, pp. 221–2; Hynes, I, 271.

HrT 863 Fair copy, revised, in MS Time's Laughingstocks (ff. 42–3).

Fitzwilliam Museum.

HrT 864 Fair copy, signed, one page.

Owned (1982) F. B. Adams (see Hynes).

HrT 865 Correction to line 10 in *Selected Poems* (1917), p. 8.

Dorset County Museum.

On the Doorstep ('She sits in her night-dress without the door')
First pub. *Fortnightly Review*, April 1911, as 'Satires of Circumstance in Twelve Scenes. X.'; Gibson, pp. 944–5; Hynes, III, 295. This poem was intended for, but not published in, *Satires of Circumstance*; see headnote to 'Satires of Circumstance in Fifteen Glimpses'.

HrT 866 Fair copy, revised, headed 'X', in MS Satires of Circumstance (p. 51), the whole cancelled.

Dorset County Museum.

On the Doorstep ('The rain imprinted the step's wet shine')
First pub. *Moments of Vision* (1917); Gibson, pp. 525–6; Hynes, II, 275.

HrT 867 Fair copy, revised, the title altered from 'Staying & Going', in MS Moments of Vision (f. 159); dated January 1914.

Magdalene College, Cambridge.

On the Esplanade ('The broad bald moon edged up where the sea was wide')
First pub. *Human Shows* (1925); Gibson, p. 715; Hynes, III, 23.

HrT 868 Fair copy, in MS Human Shows (f. 22).

Yale.

On the Palatine, see HrT 992.

On the Portrait of a Woman about to be Hanged ('Comely and capable one of our race')
First pub. *London Mercury*, February 1923; collected *Human Shows* (1925); Gibson, p. 780; Hynes, III, 98–9.

HrT 869 Fair copy, revised, in MS Human Shows (f. 119); dated 6 January 1923.

Yale.

HrT 870 Corrected proof for the first publication, one page numbered 344.

Microfilm Edition, Reel 5.

Dorset County Museum.

HrT 871 Revisions, in a copy of *Best Poems of 1923*, ed. L. A. G. Strong (Boston, 1924) wherein this poem was published (see HrT 1729).

Not mentioned Gibson or Hynes.

Wreden Catalogue (1938), Item 133.

On the Tune Called the Old-Hundred-and-Fourth ('We never sang together')
First pub. *Late Lyrics* (1922); Gibson, p. 620; Hynes, II, 391–2.

HrT 872 Fair copy, revised, the title altered from 'On a Tune by Dr Gauntlett' and 'On a Tune by Ravenscroft', in MS Late Lyrics (f. 82).

Dorset County Museum.

On the Way ('The trees fret fitfully and twist')
First pub. *Late Lyrics* (1922); Gibson, p. 625; Hynes, II, 397–8.

HrT 873 Fair copy, revised, here beginning 'The trees writhe fitfully and twist', in MS Late Lyrics (f. 88).

Dorset County Museum.

HrT 874 Correction in line 15 in *Collected Poems* (1923), p. 592.

Dorset County Museum.

Once at Swanage ('The spray sprang up across the cusps of the moon')
First pub. *Human Shows* (1925); Gibson, pp. 783–4; Hynes, III, 103.

HrT 875 Fair copy, revised, in MS Human Shows (f. 124).

Yale.

One Ralph Blossom Soliloquizes ('When I am in hell or some such place')
First pub. *Time's Laughingstocks* (1909); Gibson, pp. 288–9; Hynes, I, 347–8.

HrT 876 Fair copy, in MS Time's Laughingstocks (ff. 127–8).

Fitzwilliam Museum.

One We Knew ('She told how they used to form for the country dances—')
First pub. *The Tatler*, 2 December 1903; collected *Time's Laughingstocks* (1909); Gibson, pp. 274–5; Hynes, I, 331–2. This poem is cancelled in *Selected Poems* (1917); see INTRODUCTION.

HrT 877 Fair copy, in MS Time's Laughingstocks (ff. 107–8); dated 20 May 1902.

Fitzwilliam Museum.

One who Married above him ("''Tis you, I think? Back from your week's work, Steve?'")
First pub. *Human Shows* (1925); Gibson, pp. 738–9; Hynes, III, 49–51.

HrT 878 Fair copy, revised, in MS Human Shows (ff. 57–8, rectos only).

Yale.

The Opportunity ('Forty springs back, I recall')
First pub. *Late Lyrics* (1922); Gibson, p. 621; Hynes, II, 392–3.

HrT 879 Fair copy, revised, in MS Late Lyrics (f. 83).

Dorset County Museum.

The Orphaned Old Maid ('I wanted to marry, but father said, "No —')
First pub. *Time's Laughingstocks* (1909); Gibson, p. 244; Hynes, I, 296–7.

HrT 880 Fair copy, in MS Time's Laughingstocks (f. 70).

Fitzwilliam Museum.

Our Old Friend Dualism ('All hail to him, the Protean! A tough old chap is he:')

First pub. *Winter Words* (1928); Gibson, p. 892; Hynes, III, 233.

HrT 881 Fair copy, in MS Winter Words; dated 1920.

Queen's College, Oxford, MS 420, f. 87.

Outside the Casement ('We sat in the room')
First pub. *Late Lyrics* (1922); Gibson, pp. 664–5; Hynes, II, 443–4.

HrT 882 Fair copy, revised, including the alternative title (erased) 'After the Battle', in MS Late Lyrics (f. 145).

Dorset County Museum.

Outside the Window ('"My stick!" he says, and turns in the lane'), see HrT 1007.

Over the Coffin ('They stand confronting, the coffin between'), see HrT 1007.

Overlooking the River Stour ('The swallows flew in the curves of an eight')
First pub. *Moments of Vision* (1917); Gibson, p. 482; Hynes, II, 223.

HrT 883 Fair copy, revised, here beginning 'The swallows flew in the shape of an eight', the title altered from 'Overlooking the Stour', subtitled '<(1877.)>', in MS Moments of Vision (f. 88).

Magdalene College, Cambridge.

The Oxen ('Christmas Eve, and twelve of the clock')
First pub. *The Times*, 24 December 1915; collected *Selected Poems* (1916) and *Moments of Vision* (1917); Gibson, p. 468; Hynes, II, 206.

HrT 884 Fair copy, in MS Moments of Vision (f. 65).

Magdalene College, Cambridge.

HrT 885 Fair copy, here entitled 'The Oxen, verses for Christmas Eve. First published in "The Times". December 24, 1915', signed, 2 pages.

Facsimile in sale catalogue (cited below), p. 39; this MS sent by Hardy to the Red Cross Sale, Christie's, 28 April 1916, sold to Maggs.

American Art Association/Anderson Galleries, 6–7 December 1932 (Ida O. Folsom sale), Lot 175.

HrT 886 Corrections and addition of date 1915 in *Selected Poems* (1917), p. 130.

Dorset County Museum.

The Pair He Saw Pass ('O sad man, now a long dead man')
First pub. *Human Shows* (1925); Gibson, pp. 760–2; Hynes, III, 75–7.

HrT 887 Fair copy, revised, the title altered from 'The Bridegroom', in MS Human Shows (ff. 88–9, rectos only), annotated 'From an old draft.'.

Yale.

Panthera ('Yea, as I sit here, crutched, and cricked, and bent')
First pub. *Time's Laughingstocks* (1909); Gibson, pp. 280–6; Hynes, I, 337–43. For source notes to this poem, see HrT 1679.

HrT 888 Fair copy, revised, in MS Time's Laughingstocks (ff. 115–23A).

Fitzwilliam Museum.

HrT 889 Correction to line 82 in DCM Wessex Edition (Verse Vol. III, 402).

Dorset County Museum.

HrT 890 Revision in line 218 in *Collected Poems* (1923), p. 268.

Dorset County Museum.

The Paphian Ball ('We went our Christmas rounds once more')
First pub. *McCall's Magazine*, December 1924, as 'The Midnight Revel'; collected *Human Shows* (1925); Gibson, pp. 814–16; Hynes, III, 137–40.

HrT 891 Fair copy, revised, including a cancelled footnote, in MS Human Shows (ff. 172–5, rectos only).

This footnote printed Hynes, III, 319.

Yale.

HrT 892 Revisions and corrections in HS Proof (pp. 243–6).

Dorset County Museum.

HrT 892.5 Title for this poem (i.e., 'The Midnight Revel'), sent to [Harold] Macmillan (for use in the first publication) in a telegram dated 12 September 1924.

This telegram not in *Letters*.

University of Reading, Macmillan Archive, Item 90/9.

Paradox ('Though out of sight now, and as 'twere not the least to us')
First pub. *Human Shows* (1925); Gibson, p. 805; Hynes, III, 127.

HrT 893 Fair copy, revised, here beginning 'Though out of sight now, <lost> & gone quite; not the least to us', in MS Human Shows (f. 158).

Yale.

HrT 894 Revisions to line 1 in HS Proof (p. 224).

Dorset County Museum.

A Parting-scene ('The two pale women cried')
First pub. *Human Shows* (1925); Gibson, p. 810; Hynes, III, 132.

HrT 895 Fair copy, in MS Human Shows (f. 166).

Yale.

The Passer-By ('He used to pass, well-trimmed and brushed')
First pub. *Late Lyrics* (1922); Gibson, pp. 665–6; Hynes, II, 444–5.

HrT 896 Fair copy, revised, here subtitled '<(>In Memoriam L— H— .<)> (*She speaks*)', in MS Late Lyrics (f. 146).

Dorset County Museum.

The Pat of Butter ('Once, at the Agricultural Show')
First pub. *Human Shows* (1925); Gibson, pp. 806–7; Hynes, III, 129.

HrT 897 Fair copy, revised, in MS Human Shows (f. 161).

Yale.

Paths of Former Time ('No; no;')
First pub. *Moments of Vision* (1917); Gibson, pp. 527–8; Hynes, II, 277–8.

HrT 898 Fair copy, revised, the title altered from 'The Old Paths', in MS Moments of Vision (f. 161), annotated '<Copied from the notes of 1912–13.>'; dated 1913.

Magdalene College, Cambridge.

Paying Calls ('I went by footpath and by stile')
First pub. *Selected Poems* (1916); collected *Moments of Vision* (1917); Gibson, pp. 506–7; Hynes, II, 252.

HrT 899 Fair copy, in MS Moments of Vision (f. 130).

Magdalene College, Cambridge.

The Peace-Offering ('It was but a little thing')
First pub. *Moments of Vision* (1917); Gibson, p. 464; Hynes, II, 201–2.

HrT 900 Fair copy, in MS Moments of Vision (f. 58).

Magdalene College, Cambridge.

The Peace Peal ('Said a wistful daw in Saint Peter's tower')
First pub. *The Graphic*, 24 November 1919; collected *Human Shows* (1925); Gibson, p. 798; Hynes, III, 119.

HrT 901 Fair copy, revised, in MS Human Shows (f. 148); dated '<1918.> At the end of the War.'.

Yale.

HrT 902 Correction to line 10 in HS Proof (p. 208).

Dorset County Museum.

The Peasant's Confession ('Good Father!...It was eve in middle June')
First pub. *Wessex Poems* (1898); Gibson, pp. 31–5; Hynes, I, 40–5.

HrT 903 Fair copy, revised, without lines 13–16, here beginning 'Good Father!...'Twas an eve in middle June', in MS Wessex Poems (ff. 37–42).

Birmingham City Museum and Art Gallery.

The Pedestrian ('''Sir, will you let me give you a ride?')
First pub. *Moments of Vision* (1917); Gibson, pp. 502–3; Hynes, II, 247–8.

HrT 904 Fair copy, revised, in MS Moments of Vision (f. 124).

Magdalene College, Cambridge.

The Pedigree ('I bent in the deep of night')
First pub. *Moments of Vision* (1917); Gibson, pp. 460–1; Hynes, II, 197–8.

HrT 905 Fair copy, revised, here beginning 'I bent at the deep of night', in MS Moments of Vision (f. 51); dated 1916.

Magdalene College, Cambridge.

Penance ('''Why do you sit, O pale thin man')
First pub. *Late Lyrics* (1922); Gibson, pp. 630–1; Hynes, II, 403–4.

HrT 906 Fair copy, revised, in MS Late Lyrics (f. 97).

Dorset County Museum.

The Phantom Horsewoman ('Queer are the ways of a man I know:')
First pub. *Satires of Circumstance* (1914); Gibson, pp. 353–4; Hynes, II, 65–6.

HrT 907 Fair copy, in MS Satires of Circumstance (pp. 95–6).

Dorset County Museum.

HrT 908 Correction to line 25 in *Selected Poems* (1917), p. 74.

Dorset County Museum.

HrT 909 Revision to line 13 in *Collected Poems* (1923), p. 333.

Dorset County Museum.

A Philosophical Fantasy ('''Well, if thou wilt, then, ask me')
First pub. *Fortnightly Review*, 1 January 1927; this version reprinted in Appendix C in Hynes, III, 348–51; revised and collected *Winter Words* (1928); Gibson, pp. 893–7; Hynes, III, 234–8.

HrT 910 Fair copy, extensively revised, here entitled 'In the Matter of an Intent/A conversational Fantasy.', 4 leaves (rectos only); dated 1925.

This MS printed in Appendix C in Hynes, III, 344–8; Microfilm Edition, Reel 5.

Dorset County Museum.

HrT 911 Fair copy, revised, annotated in pencil '[*Published in Fortnightly Review, slightly abridged, Jan. 1927.*]', in MS Winter Words; dated '<1920 — 1926> 1920 and 1926'.

Queen's College, Oxford, MS 420, ff. 190–4 (rectos only).

The Photograph ('The flame crept up the portrait line by line')
First pub. *Moments of Vision* (1917); Gibson, p. 469; Hynes, II, 207–8.

HrT 912 Fair copy, revised, in MS Moments of Vision (f. 67).

Magdalene College, Cambridge.

The Pine Planters ('We work here together')
First pub. *Cornhill*, June 1903 (Part II lines 33–68 only); revised and collected *Time's Laughingstocks* (1909); Gibson, pp. 271–3; Hynes, I, 328–30. This poem is cancelled in *Selected Poems* (1917); see INTRODUCTION.

HrT 912.5 Fair copy of an early version of lines 33–68, slightly corrected, here beginning 'From the unbound bundle', signed, 2 pages of a folded leaf, as sent to Smith, Elder and Co. for the first publication, annotated in an unidentified hand 'Set up as 2 CHill pages, proof here on Monday 11th'.

This MS not mentioned Gibson or Hynes.

National Library of Scotland, MS 23173, f. 201.

HrT 913 Fair copy, revised, in MS Time's Laughingstocks (ff. 103–5).

Fitzwilliam Museum.

HrT 914 Revision to line 43 in DCM Wessex Edition (Verse Vol. III, 389).

Dorset County Museum.

HrT 914.5 Transcript by Rebekah Owen of lines 33–68, on 3 pages of a folded leaf of 'Croft, Ambleside' notepaper; annotated by Hardy 'T. H./Cornhill Aug. 1903.'.

Colby College.

The Pink Frock ('"O my pretty pink frock')
First pub. *Moments of Vision* (1917); Gibson, p. 472; Hynes, II, 211.

HrT 915 Fair copy, revised, in MS Moments of Vision (f. 71).

Magdalene College, Cambridge.

The Pity of It ('I walked in loamy Wessex lanes, afar')
First pub. *Fortnightly Review*, 1 April 1915; privately printed by FEH in pamphlet *England to Germany* (London, 1917); collected *Moments of Vision* (1917); Gibson, p. 542; Hynes, II, 294.

HrT 916 Fair copy, in MS Moments of Vision (f. 183); dated February 1915.

Magdalene College, Cambridge.

HrT 917 Fair copy, revised, signed, one page; watermarked 1906, dated 1915.

Facsimile in Elkin Mathews Catalogue 100 (1945).

Texas.

HrT 918 Typescript, printer's copy for FEH's pamphlet.

This poem was not included in the corrected proof of this pamphlet (see HrT 334, 530, 812); unlocated by Gibson and not mentioned Hynes.

Cockerell Sale, Lot 261, sold to Alan G. Thomas.

The Place on the Map ('I look upon the map that hangs by me —')
First pub. *English Review*, September 1913; collected *Satires of Circumstance* (1914); Gibson, pp. 321–2; Hynes, II, 29–30.

HrT 919 Fair copy, revised, in MS Satires of Circumstance (pp. 29–30).

Dorset County Museum.

HrT 920 Revision to subtitle for first publication, sent in a postcard to Austin Harrison, 11 August 1913.

This MS printed in *Letters*, IV, 295.

Yale.

Places ('Nobody says: Ah, that is the place')
First pub. *Satires of Circumstance* (1914); Gibson, pp. 352–3; Hynes, II, 64–5. A fair copy of this poem presented by Hardy to Plymouth Free Public Library in 1923 was destroyed in the Second World War; see INTRODUCTION.

HrT 921 Fair copy, in MS Satires of Circumstance (pp. 93–4); dated Plymouth, March 1913.

Dorset County Museum.

A Placid Man's Epitaph ('As for my life, I've led it')
First pub. *Daily Telegraph*, 19 April 1928; collected *Winter Words* (1928); Gibson, p. 901; Hynes, II, 243.

HrT 922 Fair copy, revised, including pencil drafts of the last two lines, in MS Winter Words; dated 1925.

Queen's College, Oxford, MS 420, f. 100.

A Plaint to Man ('When you slowly emerged from the den of Time')
First pub. *Satires of Circumstance* (1914); Gibson, pp. 325–6; Hynes, II, 33–4.

HrT 923 Fair copy, revised, the title altered from 'The Plaint of a Puppet', in MS Satires of Circumstance (pp. 36–7); dated 1909–10.

Dorset County Museum.

Plena Timoris ('The lovers looked over the parapet-stone:')
First pub. *Human Shows* (1925); Gibson, pp. 741–2; Hynes, III, 53–4.

HrT 924 Fair copy, revised, in MS Human Shows (f. 61).

Yale.

HrT 925 Revision to line 14 in HS Proof (p. 90).

Dorset County Museum.

Poems of the Past and the Present
This collection of poems first pub. London and New York, 1902. For a description of the MS printer's copy (MS Poems of the Past and the Present), see INTRODUCTION; contents have been listed individually.

HrT 926 Fair copy, revised, of the Preface, in MS Poems of the Past and the Present, one page numbered ii, signed (initials); dated August 1901.

The Preface was first pub. *Poems of the Past and the Present* (1902); Gibson, p. 84; Orel, pp. 38–9; Hynes, I, [113].

Bodleian, MS Eng. poet. d. 18, f. xii.

HrT 927 Pencil corrections in Hardy's copy of the first edition (including also HrT 263, 647, 768), inscribed 'First edition 1901 (dated 1902)'.

Owned (1982) F. B. Adams (see Hynes, I, 374–5).

A Poet ('Attentive eyes, fantastic heed')
First pub. *Satires of Circumstance* (1914); Gibson, p. 415; Hynes, II, 138–9.

HrT 928 Fair copy, revised, the title altered from 'The Poet', in MS Satires of Circumstance (p. 184).

Dorset County Museum.

HrT 929 Corrections in *Selected Poems* (1917), p. 184.

Dorset County Museum.

A Poet's Thought ('It sprang up out of him in the dark')
First pub. *Winter Words* (1928); Gibson, p. 865; Hynes, III, 200–201.

HrT 930 Fair copy, revised, one page.

Microfilm Edition, Reel 5.

Dorset County Museum.

HrT 931 Fair copy, in MS Winter Words.

Queen's College, Oxford, MS 420, f. 45.

A Poor Man and a Lady ('We knew it was not a valid thing')
First pub. *Human Shows* (1925); Gibson, pp. 791–3; Hynes, III, 111–13.

HrT 932 Fair copy, revised, including a footnote, in MS Human Shows (ff. 138–9, rectos only).

Yale.

HrT 933 Revision to line 6 in HS Proof (p. 195).

Dorset County Museum.

A Popular Personage at Home ('"I live here: 'Wessex' is my name:')
First pub. *The Flying Carpet*, ed. Cynthia Asquith (London, 1925); revised and collected *Human Shows* (1925); Gibson, p. 800; Hynes, III, 121.

HrT 934 Fair copy, revised, in MS Human Shows (f. 151); dated 1924.

Yale.

Postponement ('Snow-bound in woodland, a mournful word')
First pub. *Wessex Poems* (1898); Gibson, p. 11; Hynes, I, 12.

HrT 935 Fair copy, revised, in MS Wessex Poems (f. 7); dated 1866.

Birmingham City Museum and Art Gallery.

A Practical Woman ('"O who'll get me a healthy child: —')
First pub. *Winter Words* (1928); Gibson, pp. 881–2; Hynes, III, 219–20.

HrT 936 Fair copy, revised, in MS Winter Words.

Queen's College, Oxford, MS 420, f. 69

Premonitions ('"The bell went heavy to-day')
First pub. *Human Shows* (1925); Gibson, p. 818; Hynes, III, 142.

HrT 937 Fair copy, revised, the title altered from 'Forebodings', in MS Human Shows (f. 178).

Yale.

A Private Man on Public Men ('When my contemporaries were driving')
First pub. *Daily Telegraph*, 26 March 1928; collected *Winter Words* (1928); Gibson, p. 927; Hynes, III, 271.

HrT 938 Fair copy, revised, in MS Winter Words.

Queen's College, Oxford, MS 420, f. 133.

The Problem ('Shall we conceal the Case, or tell it —')
First pub. *Poems of the Past and the Present* (1902); Gibson, p. 120; Hynes, I, 154.

HrT 939 Fair copy, revised, in MS Poems of the Past and the Present.

Bodleian, MS Eng. poet. d. 18, f. 54.

HrT 940 Suggested revision to line 8 in *Collected Poems* (1923), p. 109.

Dorset County Museum.

A Procession of Dead Days ('I see the ghost of a perished day')
First pub. *Late Lyrics* (1922); Gibson, pp. 644–5; Hynes, II, 420–1.

HrT 941 Fair copy, revised, in MS Late Lyrics (ff. 115–16).

Dorset County Museum.

Prologue to *The Dynasts* ('In these stern times of ours, when crimson strife')
First recited at performances of Harley Granville Barker's production of *The Dynasts* at the Kingsway Theatre, London, 25 November 1914–January 1915 (and printed in the accompanying programme); first pub. *The Sphere*, 5 December 1914, as 'A Poem on the War'; privately printed by Clement Shorter in *The Dynasts: The Prologue and Epilogue* (London, [1914]); Gibson, pp. 949–50; Hynes, III, 297–8.

HrT 942 Draft, headed 'Fore Scene', on 2 leaves (rectos only) inserted between pp. 4 and 5 of Hardy's copy of *The Dynasts* (1910) used for Granville Barker's production (HrT 1630) (including also HrT 337); one page is the verso of a printed letter dated 3 October 1914.

Dorset County Museum.

HrT 942.5 Typescript, containing one correction by Hardy, on f. 1 of a typescript of 'Wessex Scenes from "The Dynasts"' (HrT 1634); [1916].

Microfilm Edition, Reel 3.

Dorset County Museum.

The Prophetess ('"Now shall I sing')
First pub. *Winter Words* (1928); Gibson, pp. 837–8; Hynes, III, 170.

HrT 943 Fair copy, revised, in MS Winter Words.

Queen's College, Oxford, MS 420, f. 7.

The Prospect ('The twigs of the birch imprint the December sky')
First pub. *Human Shows* (1925); Gibson, p. 770; Hynes, III, 87–8.

HrT 944 Fair copy, revised, in MS Human Shows (f. 103); dated December 1912.

Yale.

HrT 945 Suggested revision to line 1 (i.e., 'twigs' to 'boughs') in HS Proof (p. 147).

Dorset County Museum.

The Protean Maiden ('This single girl is two girls:')
First pub. *Human Shows*(1925); Gibson, p. 803; Hynes, III, 125.

HrT 946 Fair copy, revised, the title altered from 'The Protean Lady', in MS Human Shows (f. 155).

Yale.

HrT 947 Revision to line 3 in HS Proof (p. 220).

Dorset County Museum.

Proud Songsters ('The thrushes sing as the sun is going')
First pub. *Daily Telegraph*, 9 April 1928; collected *Winter Words* (1928); Gibson, pp. [835]–6; Hynes, III, [167]–8.

HrT 948 Fair copy, in MS Winter Words.

Queen's College, Oxford, MS 420, f. 4.

HrT 949 Revised, one leaf.

Cockerell Sale, Lot 270, sold to Maggs.

Owned (1985) F. B. Adams (see Hynes).

The Puzzled Game-Birds ('They are not those who used to feed us')
First pub. *Poems of the Past and the Present* (1902); Gibson, p. 148; Hynes, I, 185–6.

HrT 950 Fair copy, revised, in MS Poems of the Past and the Present.

Bodleian, MS Eng. poet. d. 18, f. 95.

HrT 951 Annotation in pencil (cancelled) in DCM Wessex Edition (Verse Vol. I, 212), where poem entitled 'The Battue'.

Annotation printed Hynes, I, 373.

Dorset County Museum.

Queen Caroline to her Guests ('Dear friends, stay!')
First pub. *Human Shows* (1925); Gibson, pp. 740–1; Hynes, III, 52 3.

HrT 952 Fair copy, in MS Human Shows (f. 60).

Yale.

A Question of Marriage ('"I yield you my whole heart, Countess," said he')
First pub. *Daily Telegraph*, 26 September 1928; collected *Winter Words* (1928); Gibson, pp. 897–8; Hynes, III, 238–9.

HrT 953 Fair copy, revised, in MS Winter Words.

Queen's College, Oxford, MS 420, f. 95.

Quid Hic Agis? ('When I weekly knew')
First pub. *The Spectator*, 19 August 1916, as 'In Time of Slaughter'; privately printed by FEH as a separate pamphlet *'When I weekly knew'* (London, 1916); collected *Moments of Vision* (1917); Gibson, pp. 440–2; Hynes, II, 175–7.

HrT 954 Fair copy, here entitled '"When I weekly knew"', in MS Moments of Vision (f. 24).

Magdalene College, Cambridge.

HrT 955 Typescript, here entitled '"When I weekly knew"', 4 pages, printer's copy for FEH's pamphlet.

Cockerell Sale, Lot 262, sold to Maggs (this lot also included an uncorrected? first proof of this pamphlet dated 5 October 1916).

Owned (1978) R. L. Purdy; destined for Yale.

Rain on a Grave ('Clouds spout upon her')
First pub. *Satires of Circumstance* (1914); Gibson, pp. 341–2; Hynes, II, 50–1.

HrT 956 Fair copy, revised, the title altered from 'Rain on her Grave', in MS Satires of Circumstance (pp. 74–5); dated 31 January 1913.

Dorset County Museum.

Rake-Hell Muses ('Yes; since she knows not need')
First pub. *Late Lyrics* (1922); Gibson, pp. 690–2; Hynes, II, 476–8.

HrT 957 Fair copy, revised, the title altered from 'The Seducer Muses', in MS Late Lyrics (ff. 184–5); dated '189-'.

Dorset County Museum.

The Rambler ('I do not see the hills around')
First pub. *Time's Laughingstocks* (1909); Gibson, p. 269; Hynes, I, 325.

HrT 958 Fair copy, revised, in MS Time's Laughingstocks (ff. 99–100).

Fitzwilliam Museum.

The Rash Bride ('We Christmas-carolled down the Vale, and up the Vale, and round the Vale')
First pub. *The Graphic*, Christmas Number, [24 November] 1902; revised and collected *Time's Laughingstocks* (1909); Gibson, pp. [252]–5; Hynes, I, [306]–10.

HrT 959 Fair copy, revised, in MS Time's Laughingstocks (ff. 82–4).

Fitzwilliam Museum.

HrT 960 Corrections to lines 21, 23 and 60 in DCM Wessex Edition (Verse Vol. III, 363 and 365).

Dorset County Museum.

Read by Moonlight ('I paused to read a letter of hers')
First pub. *Late Lyrics* (1922); Gibson, p. 574; Hynes, II, 339.

HrT 961 Fair copy, revised, in MS Late Lyrics (f. 18).

Dorset County Museum.

The Recalcitrants ('Let us off and search, and find a place')
First pub. *Satires of Circumstance* (1914); Gibson, p. 389; Hynes, II, 107–8.

HrT 962 Fair copy, revised, in MS Satires of Circumstance (p. 147).

Dorset County Museum.

The Re-Enactment ('Between the folding sea-downs')
First pub. *Satires of Circumstance* (1914); Gibson, pp. 361–4; Hynes, II, 74–7. Gibson collates a correction in line 40 from Hardy's copy of the first edition; Hynes mentions no such correction nor has any such copy been located.

HrT 963 Fair copy, revised, in MS Satires of Circumstance (pp. 102–6).

Dorset County Museum.

HrT 964 Correction in Hardy's copy of the Wessex Edition (Verse Vol. IV, 102), presented to Sydney Cockerell by FEH, 30 March 1928 (see DCM Wessex Edition).

Cockerell Sale, Lot 252, sold to Maggs.

Owned (1985) F. B. Adams (see Hynes, III, 352).

A Refusal ('Said the grave Dean of Westminster:')
First pub. *Human Shows* (1925); Gibson, pp. 801–3; Hynes, III, 123–4.

HrT 965 Fair copy, revised, in MS Human Shows (f. 153); dated August 1924.

Yale.

'Regret not me' ('Regret not me')
First pub. *Satires of Circumstance* (1914); Gibson, pp. 388–9; Hynes, II, 106–7.

HrT 966 Fair copy, revised, in MS Satires of Circumstance (pp. 145–6).

Dorset County Museum.

HrT 967 Corrections in *Selected Poems* (1917), p. 80.

Dorset County Museum.

The Rejected Member's Wife ('We shall see her no more')
First pub. *The Spectator*, 27 January 1906, as 'The Ejected Member's Wife'; collected *Time's Laughingstocks* (1909); Gibson, pp. 213–14; Hynes, I, 346–7.

HrT 968 Fair copy, slightly revised, here entitled 'The Rejected One's Wife', signed, one page, printer's copy for *The Spectator*.

Texas.

HrT 969 Fair copy, in MS Time's Laughingstocks (f. 32); dated January 1906.

Fitzwilliam Museum.

Reluctant Confession ('"What did you do? Cannot you let me know?"')
First pub. *Winter Words* (1928); Gibson, pp. 846–7; Hynes, III, 179–80.

HrT 970 Fair copy, revised, in MS Winter Words.

Queen's College, Oxford, MS 420, f. 20.

The Reminder ('While I watch the Christmas blaze')
First pub. *Time's Laughingstocks* (1909); Gibson, pp. 268–9; Hynes, I, 324.

HrT 971 Fair copy, revised, in MS Time's Laughingstocks (f. 99).

Fitzwilliam Museum.

Reminiscences of a Dancing Man ('Who now remembers Almack's balls —')
First pub. *Collier's* (New York), 27 March 1909; reprinted *English Review*, April 1909, as 'London Nights by Thomas Hardy. II. Reminiscences of a Dancing Man'; collected *Time's Laughingstocks* (1909); Gibson, pp. 216–17; Hynes, I, 266–7.

HrT 972 Fair copy, signed, 2 pages (one leaf), sent for publication in the *English Review*; dated 1895.

Yale.

HrT 973 Fair copy, in MS Time's Laughingstocks (ff. 36–7).

Facsimile of f. 36 in Gibson, p. [188].

Fitzwilliam Museum.

The Respectable Burgher on 'the Higher Criticism' ('Since Reverend Doctors now declare')
First pub. *Poems of the Past and the Present* (1902); Gibson, pp. 159–60; Hynes, I, 198–9.

HrT 974 Fair copy, revised, in MS Poems of the Past and the Present.

Bodleian, MS Eng. poet. d. 18, ff. 115–16 (rectos only).

Retty's Phases ('Retty used to shake her head')
First pub. *Human Shows* (1925); Gibson, pp. 790–1; Hynes, III, 110–11.

HrT 975 Draft, the earliest extant poetic MS, here entitled 'Song' and beginning '<Hetty> Retty used to gaily sing', 2 pages (one leaf torn from a notebook); headed 22 June 1868.

This MS printed Gibson, pp. 790–1 and Hynes, III, 316–17; facsimile in Purdy, facing p. 242 and in Gibson. This MS discussed (and said to be a 'second draft') by Nicholas Hillyard in 'The Draft of "Retty's Phases"', *Thomas Hardy Society Review*, I (1982), 257–62.

Dorset County Museum.

HrT 976 Fair copy, revised, including a footnote, subscribed 'From an old <note-book> draft of 1868./<June 22. 1868.>', in MS Human Shows (ff. 136–7, rectos only).

Yale.

HrT 977 Revision to line 3 in HS Proof.

Dorset County Museum.

The Revisitation ('As I lay awake at night-time')
First pub. *Fortnightly Review*, 1 August 1904, as 'Time's Laughingstocks/A Summer Romance'; collected *Time's Laughingstocks* (1909); Gibson, pp. [191]–5; Hynes, I, [237]–43.

HrT 978 Fair copy, revised, signed (cancelled), printer's copy for the first publication and subsequently incorporated into MS Time's Laughingstocks (ff. 1–6).

Fitzwilliam Museum.

HrT 978.5 Revised copy of the first publication.

Texas.

Revulsion ('Though I waste watches framing words to fetter')
First pub. *Wessex Poems* (1898); Gibson, p. 14; Hynes, I, 17.

HrT 979 Fair copy, in MS Wessex Poems (f. 13); dated 1866.

Birmingham City Museum and Art Gallery.

The Riddle ('Stretching eyes west')
First pub. *Moments of Vision* (1917); Gibson, p. 448; Hynes, II, 183.

HrT 980 Fair copy, revised, in MS Moments of Vision (f. 33).

Magdalene College, Cambridge.

The Rift (''Twas just at gnat and cobweb-time')
First pub. *Late Lyrics* (1922); Gibson, p. 623; Hynes, II, 395.

HrT 981 Fair copy, revised, in MS Late Lyrics (f. 85).

Dorset County Museum.

The Rival ('I determined to find out whose it was —')

First pub. *Moments of Vision* (1917); Gibson, pp. 433–4; Hynes, II, 166.

HrT 982 Fair copy, in MS Moments of Vision (f. 13).

Magdalene College, Cambridge.

The Robin ('When up aloft')
First pub. *Moments of Vision* (1917); Gibson, p. 516; Hynes, II, 264–5.

HrT 983 Fair copy, revised, in MS Moments of Vision (f. 146).

Magdalene College, Cambridge.

The Roman Gravemounds ('By Rome's dim relics there walks a man')
First pub. *English Review*, December 1911, as 'Among the Roman Gravemounds'; collected *Satires of Circumstance* (1914); Gibson, pp. 396–7; Hynes, II, 116–17.

HrT 984 Fair copy, revised, printer's copy for the first publication, here entitled 'By the Roman Earthworks', signed, one page; dated 8 November 1910.

New York University.

HrT 985 Fair copy, revised, in MS Satires of Circumstance (p. 158); dated November 1910.

Dorset County Museum.

HrT 986 Two successive corrected galley proofs for the first publication; the first entitled '<By> Among the Roman Earth<works>mounds', the second entitled 'Among the Roman <Earth>Gravemounds'; the first stamped 'Rough Proof', the second annotated '*Press*', stamped 'Revised Proof' and dated 13 November 1911; together with a third page proof (uncorrected) stamped 'Revised Proof' and dated 18 November 1911.

New York University.

The Roman Road ('The Roman Road runs straight and bare')
First pub. *Time's Laughingstocks* (1909); Gibson, pp. 264–5; Hynes, I, 320.

HrT 987 Fair copy, in MS Time's Laughingstocks (f. 95).

Fitzwilliam Museum.

Rome: At the Pyramid of Cestius Near the Graves of Shelley and Keats ('Who, then, was Cestius')
First pub. *Poems of the Past and the Present* (1902); Gibson, pp. 104–5; Hynes, I, 137.

HrT 988 Fair copy, revised, the title altered from 'In Rome. At the Pyramid of Cestius./Near the Graves of Shelley and Keats.', here subtitled '(April, 1887)', in MS Poems of the Past and the Present.

Bodleian, MS Eng. poet. d. 18, ff. 29–30 (rectos only).

HrT 989 Fair copy, signed, 3 leaves (rectos only), transcribed for T.J. Wise; watermarked 1913.

Facsimile of the first page in *Ashley Library*, V, facing p. 135.

British Library, Ashley MS 4165.

HrT 990 Revision to line 16 and correction in *Selected Poems* (1917), pp. 143–4.

Dorset County Museum.

Rome: Building a New Street in the Ancient Quarter ('These umbered cliffs and gnarls of masonry')
First pub. *Poems of the Past and the Present* (1902); Gibson, p. 103; Hynes, I, 135.

HrT 991 Fair copy, revised, in MS Poems of the Past and the Present.

Bodleian, MS Eng. poet. d. 18, f. 27.

Rome: On the Palatine ('We walked where Victor Jove was shrined awhile')
First pub. *Poems of the Past and the Present* (1902); Gibson, pp. 102–3; Hynes, I, 134–5.

HrT 992 Fair copy, revised, in MS Poems of the Past and the Present.

Bodleian, MS Eng. poet. d. 18, f. 26.

Rome: The Vatican: Sala delle Muse ('I sat in the Muses' Hall at the mid of the day')

First pub. *Poems of the Past and the Present* (1902); Gibson, pp. 103–4; Hynes, I, 136.

HrT 993 Fair copy, revised, the title altered from 'In Rome. The Vatican. Sala delle Muse.', in MS Poems of the Past and the Present.

Bodleian, MS Eng. poet. d. 18, ff. 28–9 (rectos only).

HrT 994 Correction and revision to line 20 in *Selected Poems* (1917), pp. 141–2.

Dorset County Museum.

Rose-Ann ('Why didn't you say you was promised, Rose-Ann?')
First pub. *Time's Laughingstocks* (1909); Gibson, pp. 249–50; Hynes, I, 302–3.

HrT 995 Fair copy, in MS Time's Laughingstocks (f. 77).

Fitzwilliam Museum.

The Rover Come Home ('He's journeyed through America')
First pub. *Human Shows* (1925); Gibson, pp. 805–6; Hynes, III, 127–8.

HrT 996 Fair copy, revised, in MS Human Shows (f. 159).

Yale.

Royal Sponsors ('"The king and the queen will stand to the child')
First pub. *Moments of Vision* (1917); Gibson, pp. 484–5; Hynes, II, 225–7.

HrT 997 Fair copy, revised, in MS Moments of Vision (f. 93).

Magdalene College, Cambridge.

The Ruined Maid ('O 'Melia, my dear, this does everything crown!')
First pub. *Poems of the Past and the Present* (1902); Gibson, pp. 158–9; Hynes, I, 197–8.

HrT 998 Fair copy, revised, in MS Poems of the Past and the Present; dated 'Westbourne Park Villas, <1867.> 1866.'.

Bodleian, MS Eng. poet. d. 18, ff. 113–14 (rectos only).

'Sacred to the Memory' ('That "Sacred to the Memory"')
First pub. *Late Lyrics* (1922); Gibson, p. 671; Hynes, II, 452–3.

HrT 999 Fair copy, revised, here subtitled '(M. H.)', in MS Late Lyrics (f. 154).

Dorset County Museum.

The Sacrilege ('"I have a Love I love too well')
First pub. *Fortnightly Review*, 1 November 1911; collected *Satires of Circumstance* (1914); Gibson, pp. 399–403; Hynes, II, 119–24.

HrT 1000 Fair copy, revised, in MS Satires of Circumstance (pp. 161–7).

Dorset County Museum.

The Sailor's Mother ('"O whence do you come')
First pub. *Anglo-Italian Review*, September 1918; collected *Late Lyrics* (1922); Gibson, p. 664; Hynes, II, 442–3.

HrT 1001 Fair copy, revised, annotated 'From "To Please his Wife"', in MS Late Lyrics (f. 144).

Dorset County Museum.

St Launce's Revisited ('Slip back, Time!')
First pub. *Satires of Circumstance* (1914); Gibson, pp. 356–7; Hynes, II, 68–9.

HrT 1002 Fair copy, revised, the title altered from 'At St Launce's', in MS Satires of Circumstance (p. 68); dated 1913 (cancelled).

Dorset County Museum.

San Sebastian ('"Why, Sergeant, stray on the Ivel Way')
First pub. *Wessex Poems* (1898); Gibson, pp. 21–3; Hynes, I, 27–30.

HrT 1003 Fair copy, revised, here subtitled 'In memory of Sergeant M—. Died 184–.', in MS Wessex Poems (ff. 24–6).

Birmingham City Museum and Art Gallery.

Sapphic Fragment ('Dead shalt thou lie; and nought')
First pub. *Poems of the Past and the Present* (1902); Gibson, p. [181]; Hynes, I, [222].

HrT 1004 Fair copy, revised, including a cancelled epigraph from Ecclesiastes, in MS Poems of the Past and the Present.

Bodleian, MS Eng. poet. d. 18, f. 148.

HrT 1005 Written at bottom of p. 113 of Hardy's copy of Henry Thornton Wharton, *Sappho: Memoir, Text, Selected Renderings, and a Literal Translation*, 3rd ed (London, 1895).

Mentioned Björk, I, 304 (522) (without location); this MS not mentioned Gibson or Hynes.

Dorset County Museum.

The Satin Shoes ('"If ever I walk to church to wed')
First pub. *Harper's Monthly Magazine*, January 1910; collected *Satires of Circumstance* (1914); Gibson, pp. 412–14; Hynes, II, 135–7.

HrT 1006 Fair copy, revised, in MS Satires of Circumstance (pp. 180–2).

Dorset County Museum.

Satires of Circumstance
This collection of poems first pub. London, 1914. For lists of corrections for subsequent editions of these poems, see INTRODUCTION. For a description of the MS printer's copy (MS Satires of Circumstance), see INTRODUCTION; contents have been listed individually. See also HrT 1524.

Satires of Circumstance in Fifteen Glimpses
First pub. as a series of 12 poems in *Fortnightly Review*, 1 April 1911, as 'Satires of Circumstance in Twelve Scenes' (including 'I. At Tea', 'II. In Church', 'III. By Her Aunt's Grave', 'IV. In the Room of the Bride-Elect', 'V. At a Watering Place', 'VI. In the Cemetery', 'VII. Outside the Window', 'VIII. At the Altar-rail', 'IX. In the Nuptial Chamber', 'X. On the Doorstep', 'XI. In the Restaurant', 'XII. Over the Coffin'); the series augmented to 15 and collected (with the exception of 'On the Doorstep' (see HrT 866) which was dropped from the series) *Satires of Circumstance* (1914) (including I–VII as in first publication, 'VIII. In the Study', 'IX. At the Altar-rail', 'X. In the Nuptial Chamber', 'XI. In the Restaurant', 'XII. At the Draper's' (first pub. *Saturday Review*, 16 May 1914, as 'How he looked in at the draper's'), 'XIII. On the Death-Bed', 'XIV. Over the Coffin', 'XV. In the Moonlight'); Gibson, pp. [416]–23; Hynes, II, [140]–9.

HrT 1007 Fair copy, revised, of the series, the title altered from 'Satires of Circumstance in Sixteen Glimpses', in MS Satires of Circumstance, including: 'I. At Tea' (p. 45), 'II. In Church' (pp. 45–6), 'III. By her Aunt's Grave' (p. 46), 'IV. In the Room of the Bride-Elect' (pp. 46–7), 'V. At a Watering-Place' (p. 47), 'VI. In the Cemetery' (pp. 47–8), 'VII. Outside the Window' (p. 48), 'VIII. In the Study' (p. 49), 'IX. At the Altar-rail' (p. 50), 'X. In the Nuptial Chamber' (p. 50), 'XI. In the Restaurant' (p. 51), 'XII. At the Draper's' (p. 52), 'XIII. On the Death-Bed' (p. 53), 'XIV. Over the Coffin' (p. 54), 'XV. In the Moonlight' (p. 55); dated at the end 1910.

For changes in the order of the poems in this MS and pencil corrections and revisions, see Hynes, II, 493–4.

Dorset County Museum.

HrT 1008 Correction to line 12 of No. XI ('In the Restaurant') in *Collected Poems* (1923), p. 396.

Dorset County Museum.

HrT 1009 Revision to line 4 of No. XIV ('In the Moonlight') in *Selected Poems* (1917), p. 127.

Dorset County Museum.

Saying Good-bye ('We are always saying')
First pub. *Late Lyrics* (1922); Gibson, pp. 619–20; Hynes, II, 390–1.

HrT 1010 Fair copy, revised, in MS Late Lyrics (f. 81).

Dorset County Museum.

The Schreckhorn ('Aloof, as if a thing of mood and whim')
First pub. F. W. Maitland, *The Life and Letters of Leslie Stephen* (London, 1906); collected *Satires of Circumstance* (1914); Gibson, p. 322; Hynes, II, 30.

HrT 1011 Fair copy, revised, in MS Satires of Circumstance (p. 32).

Dorset County Museum.

HrT 1012 Correction to subtitle in *Selected Poems* (1917), p. 122.

Dorset County Museum.

The Sea Fight ('Down went the grand "Queen Mary"')
First pub. *Human Shows* (1925); Gibson, pp. 804–5; Hynes, III, 126–7.

HrT 1013 Fair copy, revised, in MS Human Shows (f. 157); dated 1916.

Yale.

The Seasons of Her Year ('Winter is white on turf and tree')
First pub. *Poems of the Past and the Present* (1902); Gibson, p. 156; Hynes, I, 195.

HrT 1014 Fair copy, revised, the title altered from 'The Pathetic Fallacy', in MS Poems of the Past and the Present.

Bodleian, MS Eng. poet. d. 18, f. 109.

A Second Attempt ('Thirty years after')
First pub. *Human Shows* (1925); Gibson, pp. 752–3; Hynes, III, 66–7.

HrT 1015 Fair copy, revised, in MS Human Shows (f. 77); dated 'About 1900.' (cancelled).

Yale.

The Second Night ('I missed one night, but the next I went')
First pub. *Late Lyrics* (1922); Gibson, pp. 660–2; Hynes, II, 439–40.

HrT 1016 Fair copy, revised, in MS Late Lyrics (ff. 139–41).

Dorset County Museum.

The Second Visit ('Clack, clack, clack, went the mill-wheel as I came')
First pub. *Daily Telegraph*, 31 May 1928; collected *Winter Words* (1928); Gibson, p. 892; Hynes, III, 232–3.

HrT 1017 Fair copy, revised, in MS Winter Words.

Queen's College, Oxford, MS 420, f. 86.

Seeing the Moon Rise ('We used to go to Froom-hill Barrow')
First pub. *Winter Words* (1928); Gibson, p. 885; Hynes, III, 223–4.

HrT 1018 Draft, here entitled 'At Moonrise, or "We used to go."', one page; on the verso of a memorandum to Hardy dated 28 November 1925.

Microfilm Edition, Reel 5.

Dorset County Museum.

HrT 1019 Fair copy, revised, in MS Winter Words; dated August 1927.

Queen's College, Oxford, MS 420, f. 75.

Seen by the Waits ('Through snowy woods and shady')
First pub. *Satires of Circumstance* (1914); Gibson, pp. 393–4; Hynes, II, 113.

HrT 1020 Fair copy, in MS Satires of Circumstance (p. 153).

Dorset County Museum.

Selected Poems
For Hardy's corrected copies of the 1916 and 1917 editions, see INTRODUCTION. For Sydney Cockerell's copy of the 1916 edition, see HrT 122, 382, 753.

A Self-glamourer ('My little happiness')
First pub. *Winter Words* (1928); Gibson, p. 872; Hynes, III, 208.

HrT 1021 Fair copy, revised, in MS Winter Words.

Queen's College, Oxford, MS 420, f. 55.

The Selfsame Song ('A bird sings the selfsame song')
First pub. *Late Lyrics* (1922); Gibson, p. 598; Hynes, II, 367.

HrT 1022 Fair copy, revised, here beginning 'A bird bills the selfsame song', in MS Late Lyrics (f. 54).

Dorset County Museum.

Self-Unconscious ('Along the way')
First pub. *Satires of Circumstance* (1914); Gibson, pp. 331–2; Hynes, II, 40–1.

HrT 1023 Fair copy, revised, in MS Satires of Circumstance (pp. 56–7).

Dorset County Museum.

HrT 1024 Correction in Hardy's copy of the Wessex Edition (Verse Vol. IV, 48), presented to Sydney Cockerell by FEH, 30 March 1928 (see DCM Wessex Edition).

Cockerell Sale, Lot 252, sold to Maggs.

Owned (1985) F. B. Adams (see Hynes, III, 352).

The Self-Unseeing ('Here is the ancient floor')
First pub. *Poems of the Past and the Present* (1902); Gibson, pp. 166–7; Hynes, I, 206.

HrT 1025 Fair copy, the title pasted over earlier title 'Unregarding', in MS Poems of the Past and the Present.

Bodleian, MS Eng. poet. d. 18, f. 127.

The Sergeant's Song ('When Lawyers strive to heal a breach')
First pub. in the serial publication of *The Trumpet-Major* in *Good Words*, February 1880 (stanzas 1 and 4); reprinted *The Trumpet-Major* (London, 1880); first pub. in full *The Trumpet-Major* (London, 1881); collected separately *Wessex Poems* (1898); Gibson, pp. 18–19; Hynes, I, 23–4. See also HrT 1591.

HrT 1026 Fair copy, in MS Wessex Poems (f. 20); dated 1878, annotated 'Published in "The Trumpet-Major" 1880'.

Birmingham City Museum and Art Gallery.

The Seven Times ('The dark was thick. A boy he seemed at that time')
First pub. *Late Lyrics* (1922); Gibson, pp. 687–8; Hynes, II, 472–4.

HrT 1027 Fair copy, revised, in MS Late Lyrics (ff. 179–80).

Dorset County Museum.

Seventy-Four and Twenty ('Here goes a man of seventy-four')
First pub. *Satires of Circumstance* (1914); Gibson, p. 377; Hynes, II, 92.

HrT 1028 Fair copy of 3-stanza version, in MS Satires of Circumstance (p. 127).

Dorset County Museum.

The Sexton at Longpuddle ('He passes down the churchyard track')
First pub. *Human Shows* (1925); Gibson, p. 777; Hynes, III, 95.

HrT 1029 Fair copy, in MS Human Shows (f. 114).

Yale.

HrT 1030 Draft of additional lines (not used), in pencil, in HS Proof (p. 163).

These lines printed Hynes, III, 315.

Dorset County Museum.

The Shadow on the Stone ('I went by the Druid stone')
First pub. *Moments of Vision* (1917); Gibson, p. 530; Hynes, II, 280.

HrT 1031 Fair copy, revised, in MS Moments of Vision (f. 164); annotated '<From old notes, 1913.>' and '<From an old note, 1913.>' and dated 'Begun 1913: finished 1916'.

Magdalene College, Cambridge.

She at His Funeral ('They bear him to his resting-place —')
First pub. *Wessex Poems* (1898); Gibson, pp. 12–13; Hynes, I, 14.

HrT 1032 Fair copy, in MS Wessex Poems (f. 10); dated '187–'.

Birmingham City Museum and Art Gallery.

HrT 1033 Correction to title in *Collected Poems* (1923), p. 10.

Dorset County Museum.

'She charged me' ('She charged me with having said this and that')
First pub. *Satires of Circumstance* (1914); Gibson, p. 365; Hynes, II, 78–9.

HrT 1034 Fair copy, revised, in MS Satires of Circumstance (p. 108).

Dorset County Museum.

'She did not turn' ('She did not turn')
First pub. *Late Lyrics* (1922); Gibson, p. 626; Hynes, II, 398–9.

HrT 1035 Fair copy, revised, in MS Late Lyrics (f. 89).

Dorset County Museum.

She Hears the Storm ('There was a time in former years —')
First pub. *Time's Laughingstocks* (1909); Gibson, pp. 275–6; Hynes, I, 263–4.

HrT 1036 Fair copy, revised, here entitled 'The Widow's Thought', in MS Time's Laughingstocks (f. 109).

Fitzwilliam Museum.

She, I, and They ('I was sitting')
First pub. *Moments of Vision* (1917); Gibson, p. 435; Hynes, II, 168.

HrT 1037 Fair copy, revised, in MS Moments of Vision (f. 16); dated 1 August 1916.

Magdalene College, Cambridge.

'She opened the door' ('She opened the door of the West to me')
First pub. *Human Shows* (1925); Gibson, p. 773; Hynes, III, 90–1.

HrT 1038 Fair copy, revised, in MS Human Shows (f. 108); dated 1913.

Yale.

She Revisits Alone the Church of Her Marriage ('I have come to the church and chancel')
First pub. *Late Lyrics* (1922); Gibson, pp. 638–9; Hynes, II, 414–15.

HrT 1039 Fair copy, revised, the title altered from 'A Lady revisits alone the church of her marriage', in MS Late Lyrics (ff. 106–7).

Dorset County Museum.

She Saw him, She Said ('"Why, I saw you with the sexton, outside the church-door')
First pub. *Human Shows* (1925); Gibson, p. 783; Hynes, III, 102.

HrT 1040 Fair copy, revised, in MS Human Shows (f. 123).

Yale.

HrT 1041 Suggested revision to line 5 in HS Proof (p. 177).

Dorset County Museum.

She, To Him I ('When you shall see me in the toils of Time')
First pub. *Wessex Poems* (1898); Gibson, pp. 14–15; Hynes, I, 18.

HrT 1042 Fair copy, revised, here beginning 'When you shall see me lined by tool of Time', in MS Wessex Poems (f. 14); dated 1866.

Facsimile of Hardy's illustration for this poem in Millgate, between pp. 144 and 145.

Birmingham City Museum and Art Gallery.

She, To Him II ('Perhaps, long hence, when I have passed away')
First pub. *Wessex Poems* (1898); collected *Selected Poems* (1916), as 'To Him'; Gibson, p. 15; Hynes, I, 19.

HrT 1043 Fair copy, revised, in MS Wessex Poems (f. 15); dated 1866.

Birmingham City Museum and Art Gallery.

HrT 1044 Revision to line 14 and to date in *Selected Poems* (1917), p. 140.

Dorset County Museum.

She, To Him III ('I will be faithful to thee; aye, I will!')
First pub. *Wessex Poems* (1898); Gibson, pp. 15–16; Hynes, I, 19–20.

HrT 1045 Fair copy, in MS Wessex Poems (f. 16); dated 1866.

Birmingham City Museum and Art Gallery.

She, To Him IV ('This love puts all humanity from me')
First pub. *Wessex Poems* (1898); Gibson, p. 16; Hynes, I, 20–1.

HrT 1046 Fair copy, in MS Wessex Poems (f. 17); dated 1866.

Birmingham City Museum and Art Gallery.

She Who Saw Not ('"Did you see something within the house')
First pub. *Late Lyrics* (1922); Gibson, p. 662; Hynes, II, 440–1.

HrT 1047 Fair copy, revised, in MS Late Lyrics (f. 142).

Dorset County Museum.

She Would Welcome Old Tribulations ('I see a fresh-cheeked figure')
First pub. Evelyn Hardy, 'Some Unpublished Poems by Thomas Hardy', *London Magazine*, 3 (1956), 28–39 (38–9); Gibson, pp. 937–8; Hynes, III, 284–5.

HrT 1048 Fair copy, one page, annotated in pencil '[not used]'; dated 'About 1900.'.

Microfilm Edition, Reel 5.

Dorset County Museum.

The Sheep-boy ('A yawning, sunned concave')
First pub. *Human Shows* (1925); Gibson, pp. 789–90; Hynes, III, 109–10.

HrT 1049 Fair copy, revised, in MS Human Shows (f. 135), annotated 'On Rainbarrows'.

Yale.

HrT 1050 Correction to line 5 and revisions to lines 3 and 24 in HS Proof (pp. 191–2).

Dorset County Museum.

A Sheep Fair ('The day arrives of the autumn fair')
First pub. *Human Shows* (1925); Gibson, pp. 731–2; Hynes, III, 41–2.

HrT 1051 Fair copy, revised, in MS Human Shows (f. 47).

Yale.

HrT 1052 Revision to line 27 in HS Proof (p. 68).

Dorset County Museum.

Shelley's Skylark ('Somewhere afield here something lies')
First pub. *Poems of the Past and the Present* (1902); Gibson, p. 101; Hynes, I, 133.

HrT 1053 Fair copy, revised, in MS Poems of the Past and the Present.

Bodleian, MS Eng. poet. d. 18, ff. 23–4 (rectos only).

HrT 1054 Fair copy, signed, 3 leaves (rectos only), transcribed for T. J. Wise; watermarked 1913.

Facsimile in *Victorian and Late English Poets*, ed. James Stephens, Edwin L. Beck and Royall H. Snow (New York, 1934), p. 915 and (first page only) in *Ashley Library*, V, facing p. 134.

British Library, Ashley MS 4164.

The Shiver ('Five lone clangs from the house-clock nigh')
First pub. *Human Shows* (1925); Gibson, pp. 781–2; Hynes, III, 100–1.

HrT 1055 Fair copy, revised, in MS Human Shows (f. 121).

Yale.

HrT 1056 Revision to line 19 in HS Proof (p. 174).

Dorset County Museum.

Shortening Days at the Homestead ('The first fire since the summer is lit, and is smoking into the room:')
First pub. *Human Shows* (1925); Gibson, p. 810; Hynes, III, 133.

HrT 1057 Fair copy, revised, the title altered from 'Autumn at the Homestead' and 'October at the Homestead', in MS Human Shows (f. 167).

Yale.

HrT 1058 Revisions to lines 2, 3, 11–12 in HS Proof (pp. 235–6).

Dorset County Museum.

Shut out that Moon ('Close up the casement, draw the blind')
First pub. *Time's Laughingstocks* (1909); Gibson, p. 216; Hynes, I, 265–6.

HrT 1059 Fair copy, revised, in MS Time's Laughingstocks (f. 35); dated 1904.

Fitzwilliam Museum.

HrT 1060 Revision to line 3 and corrections in *Selected Poems* (1917), p. 78.

Dorset County Museum.

The Sick Battle-God ('In days when men found joy in war')
First pub. *Poems of the Past and the Present* (1902), as 'The Sick God'; Gibson, pp. 97–9; Hynes, I, 129–31.

HrT 1061 Fair copy, revised, here entitled 'The Sick God' and beginning 'In days when men had joy of war', in MS Poems of the Past and the Present.

Bodleian, MS Eng. poet. d. 18, ff. 18–20 (rectos only).

HrT 1062 Revisions to lines 29 and 31 (erased) in DCM Wessex Edition (Verse Vol. I).

These revisions noted Hynes, I, 371.

Dorset County Museum.

Side by Side ('So there sat they')
First pub. *Late Lyrics* (1922); Gibson, pp. 608–9; Hynes, II, 377–8.

HrT 1063 Fair copy, revised, in MS Late Lyrics (f. 68).

Dorset County Museum.

The Sigh ('Little head against my shoulder')
First pub. *Time's Laughingstocks* (1909); Gibson, pp. 227–8; Hynes, I, 277–8.

HrT 1064 Fair copy, in MS Time's Laughingstocks (f. 51).

Fitzwilliam Museum.

A Sign-Seeker ('I mark the months in liveries dank and dry')
First pub. *Wessex Poems* (1898); Gibson, pp. 49–50; Hynes, I, 65–7.

HrT 1065 Fair copy, revised, in MS Wessex Poems (ff. 62–3).

Birmingham City Museum and Art Gallery.

HrT 1066 Quotation of lines 25–8 and 33–6 (stanzas 7 and 9), here untitled, in the autograph album of Dora Sigerson (Mrs Clement) Shorter, signed.

Rosenbach Foundation.

Signs and Tokens ('Said the red-cloaked crone')
First pub. *Moments of Vision* (1917); Gibson, pp. 526–7; Hynes, II, 275–7.

HrT 1067 Fair copy, revised, in MS Moments of Vision (f. 160).

Magdalene College, Cambridge.

Silences ('There is the silence of a copse or croft')
First pub. *Winter Words* (1928); Gibson, pp. 865–6; Hynes, III, 201.

HrT 1068 Fair copy, revised, in MS Winter Words.

Queen's College, Oxford, MS 420, f. 46.

Sine Prole ('Forth from ages thick in mystery')
First pub. *Human Shows* (1925); Gibson, pp. 721–2; Hynes, III, 30.

HrT 1069 Fair copy, revised, here subtitled '(Mediaeval <Latin> sequence-Metre)', in MS Human Shows (f. 32).

Yale.

HrT 1070 Revised subtitle in HS Proof (p. 48).

Dorset County Museum.

A Singer Asleep ('In this fair niche above the unslumbering sea')
First pub. *English Review*, April 1910; collected *Satires of Circumstance* (1914); Gibson, pp. 323–5; Hynes, II, 31–3.

HrT 1071 Fair copy, revised, 2 leaves, here originally entitled '<A South-Coast Nocturn>', here subtitled '(A.C.S. 1837–1909)'.

Facsimile first page in Millgate, facing p. 401; some pencil variants noted in Hynes, II, 489; this MS is the one given to C. H. St John Hornby by FEH in August 1937 (see Purdy, p. 163).

Owned (1989) F. B. Adams.

HrT 1072 Fair copy, revised, printer's copy for the first publication, 3 leaves, here originally entitled '<A South-Coast Nocturne>', here subtitled 'A. C. S. 1837–1909'.

Local History Library, Battersea District Library, London.

HrT 1073 Fair copy, in MS Satires of Circumstance (pp. 33–5); dated Bonchurch, 1910.

Dorset County Museum.

HrT 1074 Fair copy, signed, 7 leaves (rectos only) and separate title page, transcribed for T. J. Wise, annotated 'Written at Max Gate, Dorchester 1909'; watermarked 1920, dated Bonchurch, 1910.

This MS described *Ashley Library*, VIII, 77.

British Library, Ashley MS 4467.

HrT 1075 Correction to line 42 in *Selected Poems* (1916), p. 126.

Dorset County Museum.

HrT 1076 Correction to line 42 in *Selected Poems* (1917), p. 126.

Dorset County Museum.

Singing Lovers ('I rowed: the dimpled tide was at the turn')
First pub. *Human Shows* (1925); Gibson, pp. 718–19; Hynes, III, 27.

HrT 1077 Fair copy, revised, originally subtitled '<(in 1869.)>', in MS Human Shows (f. 28), annotated 'Weymouth.'.

Yale.

The Singing Woman ('There was a singing woman')
First pub. *Late Lyrics* (1922); Gibson, p. 646; Hynes, II, 423.

HrT 1078 Fair copy, in MS Late Lyrics (f. 119).

Dorset County Museum.

The Single Witness ('"Did no one else, then, see them, man')
First pub. *Winter Words* (1928); Gibson, p. 914; Hynes, III, 257.

HrT 1079 Fair copy, revised, in MS Winter Words.

Queen' College, Oxford, MS 420, f. 118.

Sitting on the Bridge ('Sitting on the bridge')
First pub. *Moments of Vision* (1917); Gibson, pp. 456–7; Hynes, II, 192–3.

HrT 1080 Fair copy, revised, here subtitled '*(An old air echoed)*', in MS Moments of Vision (f. 45).

Magdalene College, Cambridge.

The Six Boards ('Six boards belong to me:')
First pub. *Human Shows* (1925); Gibson, pp. 820–1; Hynes, III, 145–6.

HrT 1081 Fair copy, revised, in MS Human Shows (f. 182).

Yale.

The Sleep-Worker ('When wilt thou wake, O Mother, wake and see —')
First pub. *Poems of the Past and the Present* (1902); Gibson, pp. 121–2; Hynes, I, 156.

HrT 1082 Fair copy, revised, in MS Poems of the Past and the Present.

Bodleian, MS Eng. poet. d. 18, f. 56.

HrT 1083 Revision to line 9 in *Selected Poems* (1917), p. 149.

Dorset County Museum.

The Slow Nature ('"Thy husband — poor, poor Heart! — is dead —')
First pub. *Wessex Poems* (1898); Gibson, pp. 69–70; Hynes, I, 90–91.

HrT 1084 Fair copy, revised, in MS Wessex Poems (ff. 89–90); dated 1894.

Birmingham City Museum and Art Gallery.

Snow in the Suburbs ('Every branch big with it')
First pub. *Human Shows* (1925); Gibson, pp. 732–3; Hynes, III, 42–3.

HrT 1085 Fair copy, revised, including the erased alternative title 'Snow at Upper Tooting', in MS Human Shows (f. 48).

Yale.

HrT 1086 Revision to line 16 in HS Proof (p. 70).

Dorset County Museum.

'So, Time' ('So, Time')
First pub. *Human Shows* (1925); Gibson, pp. 757–8; Hynes, III, 72.

HrT 1087 Fair copy, revised, in MS Human Shows (f. 83).

Yale.

So Various ('You may have met a man — quite young —')
First pub. *Daily Telegraph*, 22 March 1928; collected *Winter Words* (1928); Gibson, pp. 870–1; Hynes, III, 206–8.

HrT 1088 Pencil draft of lines 51–65 only, revised in ink, together with an uncorrected proof, inserted in Sydney Cockerell's copy of the Wessex Edition, Verse Vol. VI (London, 1931) (including also HrT 1338).

Cockerell Sale, Lot 252, sold to Maggs.

Owned (1985) F. B. Adams (see Hynes).

Hrt 1089 Fair copy, revised, in MS Winter Words.

Queen's College, Oxford, MS 420, ff. 52–4 (rectos only).

'Something tapped' ('Something tapped on the pane of my room')
First pub. *Moments of Vision* (1917); Gibson, p. 464; Hynes, II, 202.

HrT 1090 Fair copy, in MS Moments of Vision (f. 59); dated 1913.

Magdalene College, Cambridge.

The Something that Saved Him ('It was when')
First pub. *Moments of Vision* (1917); Gibson, pp. 522–3; Hynes, II, 271–2.

HrT 1091 Fair copy, revised, in MS Moments of Vision (f. 155).

Magdalene College, Cambridge.

Song from Heine ('I scanned her picture, dreaming')
First pub. *Poems of the Past and the Present* (1902); Gibson, p. 182; Hynes, I, 223. Hardy marked this lyric in 2 copies of Heine's poems, see HrT 1821–2.

HrT 1092 Fair copy, the title altered from 'Song. After Heine.' and originally subtitled '<Die Heimkehr...>', in MS Poems of the Past and the Present.

Bodleian, MS Eng. poet. d. 18. f. 150.

HrT 1093 Correction in line 1 in DCM Wessex Edition (Verse Vol. I, 266).

Dorset County Museum.

Song of Hope ('O sweet To-morrow! —')
First pub. *Poems of the Past and the Present* (1902); Gibson, p. 132; Hynes, I, 147–8.

HrT 1094 Fair copy, revised, the title altered from 'Young Hope/(Song.)', in MS Poems of the Past and the Present.

Bodleian, MS Eng. poet. d. 18, f. 72.

Song of the Soldiers' Wives and Sweethearts ('At last! In sight of home again')
First pub. *Morning Post*, 30 November 1900, as 'Song of the Soldiers' Wives'; collected *Poems of the Past and the Present* (1902); Gibson, pp. 96–7; Hynes, I, 128–9. Yale owns an uncorrected proof of the first publication.

HrT 1095 Fair copy, revised, here entitled 'Song of the Soldiers' Wives' and beginning 'At last? In sight of home again', in MS Poems of the Past and the Present.

Bodleian, MS Eng. poet. d. 18, ff. 16–17 (rectos only).

HrT 1096 Revision in pencil (later erased) of the title to 'Hope Song' in DCM Wessex Edition (Verse Vol. I).

This revision noted in Hynes, I, 370.

Dorset County Museum.

Song to an Old Burden ('The feet have left the wormholed flooring')
First pub. *Human Shows* (1925); Gibson, p. 830; Hynes, III, 156.

HrT 1097 Fair copy, revised, in MS Human Shows (f. 195).

Yale.

Song to Aurore ('We'll not begin again to love')
First pub. *Daily Telegraph*, 3 May 1928; collected *Winter Words* (1928); Gibson, pp. 885–6; Hynes, III, 224.

HrT 1098 Fair copy, revised, in MS Winter Words.

Queen's College, Oxford, MS 420, f. 76.

Songs from *The Dynasts*, see HrT 1613–15, 1617, 1620–2, 1624–5, 1635.

Songs from *The Queen of Cornwall*, see HrT 1637–8.

The Son's Portrait ('I walked the streets of a market town')
First pub. *Winter Words* (1928); Gibson, p. 862; Hynes, III, 197.

HrT 1099 Fair copy, revised, in MS Winter Words, annotated '[Sent to Macmillan 23.3.24 for American periodl]'.

Queen's College, Oxford, MS 420, f. 41.

The Souls of the Slain ('The thick lids of Night closed upon me')
First pub. *Cornhill*, April 1900; collected *Poems of the Past and the Present* (1902); Gibson, pp. 92–6; Hynes, I, 124–7.

HrT 1100 Fair copy, revised, 6 numbered leaves, printer's copy for first publication, dated December 1899; as sent to Reginald Smith (editor of *Cornhill*) with a letter of 2 March 1900.

Covering letter printed *Letters*, II, 249; this MS 'found' by Isabel Smith (Reginald's widow) in 1918 together with HrT 1405 and a lost fragment of *The Hand of Ethelberta*; she returned the MS to Hardy (see *Letters*, V, 243–4).

Owned (1982) F. B. Adams (see Hynes).

HrT 1101 Fair copy, revised, in MS Poems of the Past and the Present; dated December 1899.

Bodleian, MS Eng. poet. d. 18, ff. 11–15 (rectos only).

HrT 1102 Two corrected page proofs for first publication, one sent to Reginald Smith with a card postmarked 11 March 1900.

Card printed *Letters*, II, 251.

Owned (1982) F. B. Adams (see Hynes).

HrT 1103 Revision to line 53 and minor corrections in *Selected Poems* (1917), pp. 196, 198.

Dorset County Museum.

HrT 1104 Correction to line 54 in *Collected Poems* (1923), p. 86.

Dorset County Museum.

A Sound in the Night ('"What do I catch upon the night-wind, husband?—')
First pub. *Late Lyrics* (1922); Gibson, pp. 667–8; Hynes, II, 446–9.

HrT 1105 Fair copy, revised, in MS Late Lyrics (ff. 148–50).

Dorset County Museum.

The Sound of Her ('I entered her home in the tenderest mood')
First pub. Hynes, III (1985), 304. This title was originally listed in the table of contents in MS Moments of Vision but later cancelled and replaced by 'The Tree and the Lady'; see Millgate, p. 489.

HrT 1106 Revised typescript.

Owned (1985) R. L. Purdy (see Hynes); destined for Yale.

Spectres that Grieve ('"It is not death that harrows us," they lipped')
First pub. *Saturday Review*, 3 January 1914, as 'The Plaint of Certain Spectres'; collected *Satires of Circumstance* (1914); Gibson, p. 329; Hynes, II, 37–8.

HrT 1107 Fair copy, revised, in MS Satires of Circumstance (p. 42).

Dorset County Museum.

The Spell of the Rose ('"I mean to build a hall anon')
First pub. *Satires of Circumstance* (1914); Gibson, pp. 355–6; Hynes, II, 66–8.

Hrt 1108 Fair copy, revised, in MS Satires of Circumstance (pp. 66–7); dated '<1913>'.

Dorset County Museum.

A Spellbound Palace ('On this kindly yellow day of mild low-travelling winter sun')
First pub. *Human Shows* (1925); Gibson, p. 720; Hynes, III, 28–9.

HrT 1109 Fair copy, revised, the title altered from 'A Sleeping Palace', in MS Human Shows (f. 30).

Yale.

HrT 1110 Suggested revisions to lines 5 and 17 in HS Proof (pp. 45–6).

Dorset County Museum.

A Spot ('In years defaced and lost')
First pub. *Poems of the Past and the Present* (1902); Gibson, pp. 139–40; Hynes, I, 175–6.

HrT 1111 Fair copy, revised, in MS Poems of the Past and the Present.

Bodleian, MS Eng. poet. d. 18, f. 83.

HrT 1112 Correction to line 12 in *Selected Poems* (1917), p. 42.

Dorset County Museum.

The Spring Call ('Down Wessex way, when spring's a-shine')
First pub. *Cornhill*, May 1906; collected *Time's Laughingstocks* (1909); reprinted as 'Down Wessex Way' in *Dorset Year Book* (pub. Society of Dorset Men in London) (London, 1914); Gibson, pp. 244–5; Hynes, I 297–8.

HrT 1113 Fair copy, revised, in MS Time's Laughingstocks (f. 71).

Fitzwilliam Museum.

HrT 1114 Proof for the *Dorset Year Book*, containing a correction to line 9.

Not mentioned Purdy, Gibson or Hynes; the correction was incorporated into the final published version.

Dorchester Reference Library, Lock Collection, Box N, Item 2.

Squire Hooper ('Hooper was ninety. One September dawn.')
First pub. *Daily Telegraph*, 12 April 1928; collected *Winter Words* (1928); Gibson, pp. 882–3; Hynes, III, 220–1.

HrT 1115 Fair copy, revised, in MS Winter Words.

Queen's College, Oxford, MS 420, ff. 70–1 (rectos only).

Standing by the Mantelpiece ('This candle-wax is shaping to a shroud')
First pub. *Winter Words* (1928); Gibson, p. 887; Hynes, III, 226.

HrT 1116 Fair copy, in MS Winter Words.

Queen's College, Oxford, MS 420, f. 78.

Starlings on the Roof ('"No smoke spreads out of this chimney-pot')
First pub. *The Nation*, 18 October 1913; collected *Satires of Circumstance* (1914); Gibson, p. 390; Hynes, II, 108–9.

HrT 1117 Fair copy, in MS Satires of Circumstance (p. 148).

Dorset County Museum.

HrT 1118 Corrected galley proof for the first publication, one page, annotated 'Returned — corrected/T. H.'.

Yale.

The Statue of Liberty ('This statue of Liberty, busy man')
First pub. *Moments of Vision* (1917); Gibson, pp. 452–4; Hynes, II, 187–90.

HrT 1119 Fair copy, revised, with cancelled additional stanza, in MS Moments of Vision (f. 39).

Magdalene College, Cambridge.

The Strange House ('"I hear the piano playing —')
First pub. *Late Lyrics* (1922); Gibson, pp. 580–1; Hynes, II, 346–7.

HrT 1120 Fair copy, revised, in MS Late Lyrics (ff. 29–30).

Dorset County Museum.

The Stranger's Song ('O my trade it is the rarest one')
First pub. in the story 'The Three Strangers' in *Longman's Magazine*, March 1883 (see HrT 1585–6 for subsequent publication of the story); revised version included in the dramatization of the story in *The Three Wayfarers* (New York, 1893), as 'The Hangman's Song' (see HrT 1665); collected separately *Wessex Poems* (1898); Gibson, p. 23; Hynes, I, 30.

HrT 1120.5 Fair copy, revised, on ff. 19–22 of the MS of 'The Three Strangers' (HrT 1585), printer's copy for first publication.

Berg.

HrT 1121 Fair copy, in MS Wessex Poems (f. 27); annotated 'Printed in "The Three Strangers", 1883'.

Birmingham City Museum and Art Gallery.

HrT 1122 Fair copy, revised, of the first publication version.

Berg.

The Subalterns ('"Poor wanderer," said the leaden sky')
First pub. in a pre-publication review of *Poems of the Past and the Present*, 'Mr Thomas Hardy's New Poems', *The Academy*, 23 November 1901; collected *Poems of the Past and the Present* (1902); Gibson, pp. 120–1; Hynes, I, 155.

HrT 1123 Fair copy, revised, in MS Poems of the Past and the Present.

Bodleian, MS Eng. poet. d. 18, f. 55.

HrT 1124 Revision to line 3 in DCM Wessex Edition (Verse Vol. I, 168).

Dorset County Museum.

Summer Schemes ('When friendly summer calls again')
First pub. *Late Lyrics* (1922); Gibson, pp. 564–5; Hynes, II, 327–8.

HrT 1125 Fair copy, in MS Late Lyrics (f. 3).

Dorset County Museum.

The Sun on the Bookcase ('Once more the cauldron of the sun')
First pub. *Satires of Circumstance* (1914); Gibson, p. 311; Hynes, II, 17.

HrT 1126 Fair copy, in MS Satires of Circumstance (p. 14); subtitle originally dated 1872 (cancelled).

Dorset County Museum.

HrT 1127 Revision to line 7 and addition of date 1879 to subtitle in *Selected Poems* (1916), p. 16.

Dorset County Museum.

HrT 1128 Revisions and corrections to subtitle and lines 7, 8 and 13 in *Selected Poems* (1917), p. 16.

Dorset County Museum.

The Sun on the Letters ('I drew the letter out, while gleamed')
First pub. *Time's Laughingstocks* (1909); Gibson, p. 231; Hynes, I, 281–2.

HrT 1129 Fair copy, revised, the title altered from 'A Discord', in MS Time's Laughingstocks (f. 55).

Fitzwilliam Museum.

A Sunday Morning Tragedy ('I bore a daughter flower-fair')
First pub. *English Review*, December 1908; collected *Time's Laughingstocks* (1909); Gibson, pp. 201–5; Hynes, I, 250–5. For an abandoned dramatization of this ballad, see HrT 1657.

HrT 1130 Fair copy, signed, 7 numbered leaves (rectos only), subtitled '(186–)', printer's copy for the *English Review*; dated January 1904.

Stanzas 1–4 of this MS printed in Anderson Galleries sale catalogue, 9–11 February 1920, Lot 485.

Huntington, HM 5.

HrT 1131 Fair copy, slightly revised, here subtitled '(*circa* 1860)', in MS Time's Laughingstocks (ff. 16–21); dated January 1904.

Fitzwilliam Museum.

HrT 1132 Corrected proof for the *English Review*, 4 pages; date stamped 'First Proof', 19 September 1908.

Facsimile of the first page in American Art Association sale catalogue; not mentioned Gibson or Hynes.

American Art Association, 20–1 April 1925 (McCutcheon Sale), Lot 77.

The Sundial on a Wet Day ('I drip, drip here')
First pub. *Human Shows* (1925); Gibson, pp. 808–9; Hynes, III, 131.

HrT 1133 Fair copy, in MS Human Shows (f. 164), annotated 'St Juliot.'.

Yale.

The Sun's Last Look on the Country Girl ('The sun threw down a radiant spot')
First pub. *Late Lyrics* (1922); Gibson, p. 689; Hynes, II, 474.

HrT 1134 Fair copy, here beginning 'The sun threw in a radiant spot', in MS Late Lyrics (f. 181); dated December 1915.

Dorset County Museum.

The Sunshade ('Ah — it's the skeleton of a lady's sunshade')
First pub. *Moments of Vision* (1917); Gibson, p. 490; Hynes, II, 233.

HrT 1135 Fair copy, revised, in MS Moments of Vision (f. 103); subscribed 'Swanage'.

Magdalene College, Cambridge.

The Superseded ('As newer comers crowd the fore')
First pub. *The May Book*, compiled by Mrs Aria in aid of Charing Cross Hospital (London, 1901); collected *Poems of the Past and the Present* (1902); Gibson, p. 146; Hynes, I, 183.

HrT 1136 Fair copy, in MS Poems of the Past and the Present.

Bodleian, MS Eng. poet. d. 18, f. 92.

The Supplanter ('He bends his travel-tarnished feet')
First pub. *Poems of the Past and the Present* (1902); Gibson, pp. 177–80; Hynes, I, 217–21.

HrT 1137 Fair copy, revised, the title altered from 'At the Cemetery Lodge', in MS Poems of the Past and the Present.

Bodleian, MS Eng. poet. d. 18, ff. 143–7 (rectos only).

Surview ('A cry from the green-grained sticks of the fire')
First pub. *Late Lyrics* (1922); Gibson, p. 698; Hynes, II, 485.

HrT 1138 Fair copy, revised, in MS Late Lyrics (f. 193).

Dorset County Museum.

Suspense ('A clamminess hangs over all like a clout')
First pub. *Winter Words* (1928); Gibson, p. 891; Hynes, III, 232.

HrT 1139 Draft, one page, on the verso of a circular letter dated 29 August 1927.

Microfilm Edition, Reel 5.

Dorset County Museum.

HrT 1140 Fair copy, in MS Winter Words.

Queen's College, Oxford, MS 420, f. 85.

The Sweet Hussy ('In his early days he was quite surprised')
First pub. *Satires of Circumstance* (1914); Gibson, p. 391; Hynes, II, 109–10.

HrT 1141 Fair copy, revised, in MS Satires of Circumstance (p. 149).

Dorset County Museum.

The Tarrying Bridegroom ('Wildly bound the bells this morning')
First pub. *Winter Words* (1928); Gibson, p. 908; Hynes, III, 250.

HrT 1142 Fair copy, revised, in MS Winter Words.

Queen's College, Oxford, MS 420, f. 109.

The Telegram ('"O he's suffering — maybe dying — and I not there to aid')
First pub. *Harper's Monthly Magazine*, December 1913; collected *Satires of Circumstance* (1914); Gibson, pp. 391–2; Hynes, II, 110–11.

HrT 1143 Fair copy, revised, in MS Satires of Circumstance (pp. 150–1); annotated '(Published 1913.)'.

Dorset County Museum.

The Temporary the All ('Change and chancefulness in my flowering youthtime')
First pub. *Wessex Poems* (1898); Gibson, p. [7]; Hynes, I, 7–8.

HrT 1144 Fair copy, revised, here beginning 'Change and chancefulness in my bloothing youthtime', in MS Wessex Poems (f. 2), annotated in pencil '(To be thrown out)'.

Birmingham City Museum and Art Gallery.

HrT 1145 Revision to line 23 and addition of subtitle '(Sapphics)' in DCM Wessex Edition (Verse Vol. I, 3).

Dorset County Museum.

HrT 1146 Revision to line 23 in *Selected Poems* (1916).

Dorset County Museum.

HrT 1147 Corrections to lines 9, 17, 20 and revision to line 23 in *Selected Poems* (1917), pp. 45–6.

Dorset County Museum.

Ten Years Since (''Tis ten years since')
First pub. *Human Shows* (1925); Gibson, p. 722; Hynes, III, 31.

HrT 1148 Fair copy, in MS Humans Shows (f. 33); dated November 1922.

Yale.

HrT 1149 Correction to line 2 in HS Proof (p. 49).

Dorset County Museum.

The Tenant-for-Life ('The sun said, watching my watering-pot:')
First pub. *Poems of the Past and the Present* (1902); Gibson, pp. 161–2; Hynes, I, 200–1.

HrT 1150 Fair copy, in MS Poems of the Past and the Present.

Bodleian, MS Eng. poet. d. 18, f. 118.

Tess's Lament ('I would that folk forgot me quite')
First pub. *Poems of the Past and the Present* (1902); Gibson, pp. 175–7; Hynes, I, 216–17.

HrT 1151 Fair copy, revised, the title altered from '[A?] Lament' (altered from 'A Lament' in the table of contents as well), here beginning 'O would that folk forgot me quite', in MS Poems of the Past and the Present.

Gibson gives cancelled title as '[Her?] Lament'.

Bodleian, MS Eng. poet. d. 18, ff. 141–2 (rectos only).

That Kiss in the Dark ('Recall it you? —')
First pub. *Daily Telegraph*, 13 September 1928; collected *Winter Words* (1928); Gibson, p. 888; Hynes, III, 227–8.

HrT 1152 Fair copy, revised in ink and pencil, the 20-line (earliest) version, the title altered from 'A Kiss in the Dark' and the first line altered from 'Say that you', one page.

This MS (before revisions) printed Hynes, III, 328–9.

Texas.

HrT 1153 Fair copy, revised in ink and pencil, one page.

Texas.

HrT 1154 Fair copy, revised, in MS Winter Words.

Queen's College, Oxford, MS 420, f. 80.

That Moment ('The tragedy of that moment')
First pub. *Human Shows* (1925); Gibson, pp. 817–18; Hynes, III, 141–2.

HrT 1155 Fair copy, revised, the title (and the first line) altered from 'The Misery of that Moment', in MS Human Shows (f. 177).

Yale.

'The hurricane shrieks an aria round', for lines probably by FEH, see INTRODUCTION.

Then and Now ('When battles were fought')
First pub. *The Times*, 11 July 1917; collected *Moments of Vision* (1917); Gibson, pp. 545–6; Hynes, II, 299.

HrT 1156 Fair copy, revised, in MS Moments of Vision (f. 189); annotated 'Written 1915: published 1917'.

Magdalene College, Cambridge.

'There seemed a strangeness' ('There seemed a strangeness in the air')
First pub. *Human Shows* (1925); Gibson, p. 725; Hynes, III, 34.

HrT 1157 Fair copy, revised, the title altered from 'The Great Adjustment', in MS Human Shows (f. 38).

Yale.

'There was a man, he had a clock', see INTRODUCTION.

They Would Not Come ('I travelled to where in her lifetime')
First pub. *Late Lyrics* (1922); Gibson, pp. 640–1; Hynes, II, 416–17.

HrT 1158 Fair copy, revised, in MS Late Lyrics (f. 110).

Dorset County Museum.

The Thing Unplanned ('The white winter sun struck its stroke on the bridge')
First pub. *Human Shows* (1925); Gibson, p. 789; Hynes, III, 109.

HrT 1159 Fair copy, revised, in MS Human Shows (f. 134).

Yale.

The Third Kissing-gate ('She foots it forward down the town')
First pub. *Nash's Magazine*, February 1912, as 'The Forsaking of the Nest' (nine 4-line stanzas, a version not reprinted by Hardy); reprinted in Appendix A in Hynes, III, 340–1; revised version (five 4-line stanzas) first pub. *Daily Telegraph*, 30 July 1928; collected *Winter Words* (1928); Gibson, pp. 904–5; Hynes, III, 246–7.

HrT 1160 Fair copy of the first publication version, entitled 'The forsaking of the Nest.' and beginning '"The hoers quit the mangel-field', nine 4-line stanzas, signed, 2 pages (one leaf).

This MS printed Gibson, p. 904 and collated Hynes, III, 340–1.

Library of Congress, Manuscript Division, Halsted B. VanderPoel Collection.

HrT 1161 Fair copy of the first version, extensively revised into the second version, here entitled (after revision) 'The Three Kissing-gates', one leaf, annotated '[Sent by request for publication in Nash's Magazine 23 July 1911.]'.

This MS printed in Appendix A in Hynes, III, 341–2.

Owned (1985) F. B. Adams (see Hynes).

HrT 1162 Fair copy, revised, in MS Winter Words.

Queen's College, Oxford, MS 420, f. 105.

This Summer and Last ('Unhappy summer you')
First pub. *Human Shows* (1925); Gibson, pp. 818–19; Hynes, III, 142–3.

HrT 1163 Fair copy, revised, in MS Human Shows (f. 179); dated '?1913.'.

Yale.

A Thought in Two Moods ('I saw it — pink and white — revealed')
First pub. *Moments of Vision* (1917); Gibson, pp. 486–7; Hynes, II, 228–9.

HrT 1164 Fair copy, revised, the title altered from 'One Thought in Two Moods', in MS Moments of Vision (f. 97).

Magdalene College, Cambridge.

Thoughts at Midnight ('Mankind, you dismay me')
First pub. *Winter Words* (1928); Gibson, p. 836; Hynes, III, 168–9.

HrT 1165 Fair copy, in MS Winter Words; annotated 'Part written 25th May, 1906'.

Queen's College, Oxford, MS 420, f. 5.

HrT 1166 Fair copy, revised, one page; annotated 'Part written 25th May, 1906'.

King's College, Cambridge, E. M. Forster Papers.

Thoughts from Sophocles ('Who would here sojourn for an outstretched spell')
First pub. in Evelyn Hardy, 'Some Unpublished Poems by Thomas Hardy', *London Magazine*, 3 (1956), 28–39 (39); Gibson, p. 936; Hynes, III, 307.

HrT 1167 Fair copy, revised, one page.

Facsimile in Evelyn Hardy article cited above; Microfilm Edition, Reel 5.

Dorset County Museum.

Thoughts of Phena ('Not a line of her writing have I')
First pub. *Wessex Poems* (1898); reprinted *Selected Poems* (1916), as 'At News of a Woman's Death'; Gibson, p. 62; Hynes, I, 81–2.

HrT 1168 Fair copy, revised, here entitled 'T—a/At news of her death <(Died 1890.)>', in MS Wessex Poems (f. 79); dated March 1890.

Birmingham City Museum and Art Gallery.

HrT 1169 Revision of title to the above (in an unidentified hand) in *Selected Poems* (1917), pp. 37–8.

Dorset County Museum.

The Three Tall Men ('"What's that tapping at night: tack, tack')
First pub. *Daily Telegraph*, 9 August 1928; collected *Winter Words* (1928); Gibson, pp. 853–4; Hynes, III, 187–8.

HrT 1170 Draft, 2 leaves (rectos only), annotated '[Best]', one verso being a printed form including the date 28 September 1926.

Microfilm Edition, Reel 5.

Dorset County Museum.

HrT 1171 Revised, variant version, here entitled 'The Two Tall Men' and annotated 'Alternative to "The Three Tall Men."', one page, on verso of printed announcement of sale of Wembley Stadium and Greyhound Racecourse shares, dated 24 August 1927.

This MS printed Gibson, p. 854 (facsimile, p. [832]) and in Hynes, III, 324–5.

Colby College.

HrT 1172 Fair copy, one revision, in MS Winter Words.

Queen's College, Oxford, MS 420, ff. 29–30 (rectos only).

Throwing a Tree ('The two executioners stalk along over the knolls')
First pub. *Le commerce* (Paris), Winter 1927 [1928], as 'Felling a Tree'; collected *Winter Words* (1928); Gibson, p. 857; Hynes, III, 191–2.

HrT 1173 Fair copy, revised, in MS Winter Words.

Queen's College, Oxford, MS 420, f. 34.

A Thunderstorm in Town ('She wore a new "terra-cotta" dress')
First pub. *Satires of Circumstance* (1914); Gibson, pp. 312–13; Hynes, II, 18.

HrT 1174 Fair copy, in MS Satires of Circumstance (p. 16).

Dorset County Museum.

Time's Laughingstocks
This collection of poems first pub. London, 1909. For lists of corrections for subsequent editions, see INTRODUCTION. For a description of the MS printer's copy (MS Time's Laughingstocks), see INTRODUCTION; contents have been listed individually. For Hardy's copy of the first edition, see HrT 258, 449, 595. See also HrT 1524.

HrT 1174.5 Fair copy, revised, of the Preface, in MS Time's Laughingstocks (f. i), one page, signed (initials); dated September 1909.

The Preface first pub. *Time's Laughingstocks* (1909); Gibson, p. [190]; Orel, pp. 43–4; Hynes, I, [235].

Fitzwilliam Museum.

Timing Her ('Lalage's coming:')
First pub. *Moments of Vision* (1917); Gibson, pp. 443–5; Hynes, II, 178–80.

HrT 1175 Fair copy, revised, in MS Moments of Vision (f. 27).

Magdalene College, Cambridge.

HrT 1176 Correction to line 59 in *Collected Poems* (1923), p. 417.

Dorset County Museum.

To a Bridegroom ('Swear to love and cherish her?')
First pub. in Evelyn Hardy, 'Some Unpublished Poems by Thomas Hardy', *London Magazine*, 3 (1956), 28–39 (36–7); Gibson, pp. 934–5; Hynes, III, 281–2.

HrT 1177 Fair copy, revised, one page; annotated '1866 (abridged).'.

Microfilm Edition, Reel 5.

Dorset County Museum.

To a Lady ('Now that my page is exiled, — doomed, maybe')
First pub. *Wessex Poems* (1898); Gibson, p. 65; Hynes, I, 85.

HrT 1178 Fair copy, revised, here entitled 'To Lady —./Offended by something the Author had written' and beginning 'Now that my page upcloses, doomed, maybe', in MS Wessex Poems (f. 82).

Birmingham City Museum and Art Gallery.

To a Lady Playing and Singing in the Morning ('Joyful lady, sing!')
First pub. *Late Lyrics* (1922); Gibson, p. 579; Hynes, II, 344–5.

HrT 1179 Fair copy, revised, in MS Late Lyrics (f. 26).

Dorset County Museum.

To a Motherless Child ('Ah, child, thou art but half thy darling mother's')
First pub. *Wessex Poems* (1898), as 'To an Orphan Child'; Gibson, pp. 65–6; Hynes, I, 85–6.

HrT 1180 Fair copy, here entitled 'To an Orphan Child', in MS Wessex Poems (f. 83).

Birmingham City Museum and Art Gallery.

To a Sea-cliff ('Lend me an ear')
First pub. *Human Shows* (1925); Gibson, pp. 793–4; Hynes, III, 113–14.

HrT 1181 Fair copy, revised, in MS Human Shows (f. 141).

Yale.

To a Tree in London ('Here you stay')
First pub. *Winter Words* (1928); Gibson, pp. 867–8; Hynes, III, 203–4.

HrT 1182 Fair copy, revised, in MS Winter Words; dated '192–'.

Queen's College, Oxford, MS 420, f. 49.

To a Well-Named Dwelling ('Glad old house of lichened stonework')
First pub. *Late Lyrics* (1922); Gibson, pp. 671–2; Hynes, II, 453.

HrT 1183 Fair copy, revised, the title altered from 'To a Well-Called Dwelling', in MS Late Lyrics (f. 155).

Dorset County Museum.

To an Actress ('I read your name when you were strange to me")
First pub. *Time's Laughingstocks* (1909); Gibson, p. 235; Hynes, I, 286–7.

HrT 1184 Fair copy, revised, in MS Time's Laughingstocks (f. 61); dated '<Westbourne Park Villas:> 1867.'.

Fitzwilliam Museum.

To an Impersonator of Rosalind ('Did he who drew her in the years ago —')
First pub. *Time's Laughingstocks* (1909); Gibson, p. 235; Hynes, I, 286.

HrT 1185 Fair copy, revised, in MS Time's Laughingstocks (f. 60); dated '<W[estbourne] P[ark] V[illas]>, 8 Adelphi Terrace, 21st April 1867.'.

Fitzwilliam Museum.

HrT 1186 Addition of address '8 Adelphi Terrace' to date in DCM Wessex Edition (Verse Vol. III, 329).

Dorset County Museum.

To an Unborn Pauper Child ('Breathe not, hid Heart: cease silently')
First pub. (stanzas 3–5 only) in a pre-publication review of *Poems of the Past and the Present*, 'Mr Thomas Hardy's New Poems', *The Academy*, 23 November 1901; in full in *Poems of the Past and the Present* (1902); Gibson, pp. 127–8; Hynes, I, 163–4.

HrT 1187 Fair copy, revised, including an unpublished epigraph, the title altered from 'To an Unborn Child', in MS Poems of the Past and the Present.

Facsimile of first page in Gibson, p. [82].

Bodleian, MS Eng. poet. d. 18, ff. 67–8 (rectos only).

HrT 1188 Correction to line 35 in *Selected Poems* (1917), p. 103.

Dorset County Museum.

HrT 1189 Correction to line 35 in *Collected Poems* (1923), p. 117.

Dorset County Museum.

To C. F. H. ('Fair Caroline, I wonder what')
First pub. *Human Shows* (1925); Gibson, pp. 811–12; Hynes, III, 134–5.

HrT 1190 Fair copy, in MS Human Shows (f. 169).

Yale.

HrT 1191 Fair copy of a version, written on vellum and put in a silver box as a christening present for Caroline Fox Hanbury, here entitled 'To Caroline Fox Hanbury/(on her christening day)'.

Owned (1985) F. B. Adams (see Hynes, III, 134).

To Carrey Clavel ('You turn your back, you turn your back')
First pub. *Time's Laughingstocks* (1909); Gibson, p. 244; Hynes, I, 296.

HrT 1192 Fair copy, in MS Time's Laughingstocks (f. 70).

Fitzwilliam Museum.

To Flowers from Italy in Winter ('Sunned in the South, and here to-day')
First pub. *Poems of the Past and the Present* (1902); Gibson, p. 129; Hynes, I, 164–5.

HrT 1193 Fair copy, revised, in MS Poems of the Past and the Present.

Bodleian, MS Eng. poet. d. 18, f. 69.

To Life ('O Life with the sad seared face')
First pub. *Poems of the Past and the Present* (1902); Gibson, p. 118; Hynes, I, 152.

HrT 1194 Fair copy, revised, in MS Poems of the Past and the Present.

Bodleian, MS Eng. poet. d. 18, f. 51.

To Lizbie Browne ('Dear Lizbie Browne')
First pub. *Poems of the Past and the Present* (1902); Gibson, pp. 130–2; Hynes, I, 165–7.

HrT 1195 Fair copy, revised, in MS Poems of the Past and the Present.

Bodleian, MS Eng. poet. d. 18, f. 71.

HrT 1196 Correction to line 34 in *Selected Poems* (1917), p. 24.

Dorset County Museum.

HrT 1197 Suggested revision to line 10 in *Collected Poems* (1923), p. 118.

Dorset County Museum.

To Louisa in the Lane ('Meet me again as at that time')
First pub. *Daily Telegraph*, 26 April 1928; collected *Winter Words* (1928); Gibson, pp. 839–40; Hynes, III, 171–2.

HrT 1198 Fair copy, revised, in MS Winter Words.

Queen's College, Oxford, MS 420, f. 10.

To Meet, or Otherwise ('Whether to sally and see thee, girl of my dreams')
First pub. *The Sphere*, 20 December 1913; collected *Satires of Circumstance* (1914); Gibson, p. 310; Hynes, II, 15–16.

HrT 1199 Fair copy, revised, the title altered from 'To Meet, or Not', in MS Satires of Circumstance (pp. 11–12).

Dorset County Museum.

HrT 1200 Fair copy, signed, here entitled 'To Meet or Otherwise', 2 leaves (rectos only).

Microfilm Edition, Reel 5.

Dorset County Museum.

HrT 1201 Fair copy, signed, 2 leaves (rectos only).

Yale.

To My Father's Violin ('Does he want you down there')
First pub. *Moments of Vision* (1917); Gibson, pp. 451–2; Hynes, II, 186–7.

HrT 1202 Fair copy, revised, wanting lines 19–27, the title altered from 'To My Father's Fiddle', in MS Moments of Vision (f. 37); dated 1916.

Magdalene College, Cambridge.

To Outer Nature ('Show thee as I thought thee')
First pub. *Wessex Poems* (1898); Gibson, p. 61; Hynes, I, 80–1.

HrT 1203 Fair copy, revised, here entitled 'To External Nature', in MS Wessex Poems (f. 78).

Birmingham City Museum and Art Gallery.

To Shakespeare ('Bright baffling Soul, least capturable of themes')
First pub. *Fortnightly Review*, 1 June 1916 and *A Book of Homage to Shakespeare*, ed. Israel Gollancz (Oxford, 1916); privately printed separately by FEH (London, 1916); collected *Moments of Vision* (1917); Gibson, pp. 439–40; Hynes, II, 173–4.

HrT 1204 Fair copy, signed, 7 leaves (rectos only) and separate title page; dated 14 February 1916.

Facsimile of the first page in *Ashley Library*, II, facing p. 172; Purdy, p. 178 says this MS was written out for T. J. Wise but Hynes, II, 497 says that in a letter to Wise (British Library, Ashley MS 5755), FEH describes this MS as the 'original', the one enclosed in Hardy's letter to Israel Gollancz of 17 February 1916 (printed *Letters*, V, 145 from original at the Rosenbach Foundation).

British Library, Ashley MS 3343.

HrT 1205 Fair copy, revised, in MS Moments of Vision (f. 22); dated 14 February 1916.

Facsimile in Carl J. Weber, *Hardy of Wessex*, rev. ed. (New York and London, 1965), pp. 267–8.

Magdalene College, Cambridge.

HrT 1206 Fair copy, signed, on the flyleaf of Sydney Cockerell's copy of the facsimile edition of Shakespeare's First Folio (London, 1910), transcribed for Cockerell; dated 1916.

Facsimile in the Cockerell Sale catalogue.

Cockerell Sale, Lot 256, sold to Alan G. Thomas.

HrT 1207 Typescript, printer's copy for FEH's pamphlet, together with a corrected first proof of same dated 26 July 1916 and uncorrected? second and third proofs.

Cockerell Sale, Lot 266, sold to Alan G. Thomas.

HrT 1208 First and second proofs for FEH's pamphlet, corrected by Sydney Cockerell.

Cockerell Sale, Lot 266A, sold to Maggs.

HrT 1209 Typescript, without unique variants, sent by FEH to Lady Hoare.

This typescript mentioned Gibson but not Hynes.

Wiltshire Record Office, Stourhead Papers.

HrT 1210 Fair copy of stanzas 1, 2 and 6 only, slightly revised, signed, one page, written on behalf of the Shakespeare Memorial Theatre Fund, as sent to Malcolm Watson with a covering note of 12 October 1926; dated 1916 and watermarked 1913.

Facsimile in the programme of the 'Grand Matinée in Aid of the Shakespeare Memorial Theatre Fund' held at Theatre Royal, Drury Lane, on 9 November 1926 (see Purdy, p. 178n1); covering note printed *Letters*, VII, 44.

Folger, Y.d.585(3).

To Sincerity ('O sweet sincerity! —')
First pub. *Review of the Week*, 14 July 1900; collected *Time's Laughingstocks* (1909); Gibson, p. 279; Hynes, I, 336.

HrT 1211 Fair copy, revised, in MS Time's Laughingstocks (f. 114); dated February 1899.

Fitzwilliam Museum.

To the Moon ('"What have you looked at, Moon')
First pub. *Moments of Vision* (1917); Gibson, pp. 437–8; Hynes, II, 170–1.

HrT 1212 Fair copy, revised, the title altered from 'Questions to the Moon', in MS Moments of Vision (f. 20).

Magdalene College, Cambridge.

To the Unknown God, see HrT 1373.

The To-Be-Forgotten ('I heard a small sad sound')
First pub. *Poems of the Past and the Present* (1902); Gibson, pp. 144–5; Hynes, I, 181–2.

HrT 1213 Fair copy, revised, in MS Poems of the Past and the Present, including cancelled subtitle '(In Stourcastle Churchyard.)' and cancelled epigraph from Ecclesiastes; dated 'Feb. 9. <?1889?> 1899?' (the whole then cancelled).

Bodleian, MS Eng. poet. d. 18, ff. 89–90 (rectos only).

Tolerance ('"It is a foolish thing," said I')
First pub. *Satires of Circumstance* (1914); Gibson, p. 333; Hynes, II, 42.

HrT 1214 Fair copy, in MS Satires of Circumstance (p. 59).

Dorset County Muscum.

The Torn Letter ('I tore your letter into strips')
First pub. *English Review*, December 1910; collected *Satires of Circumstance* (1914); Gibson, pp. 313–14; Hynes, II, 19–20.

HrT 1215 Fair copy, revised, in MS Satires of Circumstance (pp. 17–18).

Dorset County Museum.

HrT 1215.5 Proof correction to line 7, in a postcard (headed '*misprint—collected edition. Poems.*') to the printers R. & R. Clark, 17 July 1919, postmarked 19 July.

This postcard not mentioned in Hynes or *Letters*.

National Library of Scotland, R. & R. Clark Papers, Dep. 229/292 (on deposit).

Tragedian to Tragedienne ('Shall I leave you behind me')
First pub. *Human Shows* (1925); Gibson, pp. 823–4; Hynes, III, 148–9.

HrT 1216 Fair copy, in MS Human Shows (f. 187).

Yale.

HrT 1217 Revisions to line 6 in HS Proof (p. 264).

Dorset County Museum.

A Trampwoman's Tragedy ('From Wynyard's Gap the livelong day')
First pub. *North American Review*, November 1903; collected *Time's Laughingstocks* (1909); privately printed separately by FEH (London, 1917); Gibson, pp. 195–9; Hynes, I, 243–7.

HrT 1218 Fair copy, revised, here entitled 'The Tramp's Tragedy', signed, 5 leaves (rectos only), printer's copy for the first publication, the last page containing footnotes.

Facsimile of the last page in Anderson Galleries sale catalogue, 7–10 January 1929 (Kern Sale), p. 219.

Owned (1982) F. B. Adams (see Hynes).

HrT 1219 Fair copy, revised, here subtitled '(1827)', in MS Time's Laughingstocks (ff. 7–12); dated April 1902.

Fitzwilliam Museum.

HrT 1220 First galley proof for first publication, here entitled 'The Tramp's Tragedy'.

Owned (1982) F. B. Adams (see Hynes).

HrT 1221 Corrected revise galley proof for the first publication, here entitled '<The Tramp's> A Trampwoman's Tragedy'.

Berg.

HrT 1222 Corrected first proof (without Hardy's footnote) for FEH's pamphlet; dated 21 February 1917.

This proof is together with another copy containing the same corrections transcribed by Sydney Cockerell and a copy of a second proof including the footnotes, corrected by Cockerell and dated 3 March 1917; all were sold Cockerell Sale, Lot 275 (to Alan G. Thomas) which also included the letter to Cockerell of 23 February 1917 (printed *Letters*, V, 203 from the original at SUNY at Buffalo) originally enclosing HrT 1222 and Hardy's autograph map of the route from Dorchester to Glastonbury travelled in the poem, annotated by Cockerell '...written out by Thomas Hardy Aug 21 1924 for our motoring trip to Glastonbury...'.

SUNY at Buffalo.

HrT 1223 Suggested revisions for line 30 (cancelled) in DCM Wessex Edition (Verse Vol. III).

These revisions noted Hynes, I, 381.

Dorset County Museum.

HrT 1224 Additional footnote to line 27 in *Collected Poems* (1923), p. 185.

This note is printed Hynes, I, 381.

Dorset County Museum.

Transformations ('Portion of this yew')
First pub. *Moments of Vision* (1917); Gibson, p. 472; Hynes, II, 211–12.

HrT 1225 Fair copy, revised, the title altered from 'In a Churchyard', in MS Moments of Vision (f. 72).

Magdalene College, Cambridge.

Translation from Baudelaire, see HrT 1722.

Translation from Hugo, see HrT 1868.

The Tree/An Old Man's Story ('Its roots are bristling in the air')
First pub. *Poems of the Past and the Present* (1902); Gibson, pp. 163–5; Hynes, I, 202–4.

HrT 1226 Fair copy, revised, in MS Poems of the Past and the Present.

Bodleian, MS Eng. poet. d. 18, ff. 122–4 (rectos only).

The Tree and the Lady ('I have done all I could')
First pub. *Moments of Vision* (1917); Gibson, pp. 531–2; Hynes, II, 281–2.

HrT 1227 Fair copy, revised, in MS Moments of Vision (f. 166).

Magdalene College, Cambridge.

The Tresses ('"When the air was damp')
First pub. *Moments of Vision* (1917); Gibson, pp. 468–9; Hynes, II, 207.

HrT 1228 Fair copy, revised, in MS Moments of Vision (f. 66).

Magdalene College, Cambridge.

The Turnip-hoer ('Of tides that toss the souls of men')
First pub. *Cassell's Magazine*, August 1925; collected *Human Shows* (1925); Gibson, pp. 703–6; Hynes, III, 9–12.

HrT 1229 Fair copy, revised, in MS Human Shows (ff. 6–8, rectos only).

Yale.

HrT 1230 Revised page proof for first publication, signed (initials), stanzas 1 and 6 added by Hardy (stanza 1 replacing a cancelled printed stanza beginning 'Of haps engendering gloom, regret').

Facsimile of first page in Sotheby's sale catalogue, 13–14 March 1979, p. 313; facsimile in British Library, RP 1740 (iii).

Eton College.

HrT 1231 Revision to line 2 and correction to line 12 in HS Proof (p. 7).

Dorset County Museum.

The Two Houses ('In the heart of night')
First pub. *The Dial* (New York), August 1921; collected *Late Lyrics* (1922); Gibson, pp. 595–6; Hynes, II, 363–5.

HrT 1232 Fair copy, revised, in MS Late Lyrics (ff. 49–51).

Dorset County Museum.

Two Lips ('I kissed them in fancy as I came')
First pub. *Human Shows* (1925); Gibson, p. 737; Hynes, III, 48.

HrT 1233 Fair copy, here entitled 'Two <red> lips', in MS Human Shows (f. 55).

Yale.

The Two Men ('There were two youths of equal age')
First pub. *Wessex Poems* (1898); Gibson, pp. 77–9; Hynes, I, 100–103.

HrT 1234 Fair copy, revised, here entitled 'The World's Verdict/A Morality-rime.', in MS Wessex Poems (ff. 100–3); dated 1866.

Birmingham City Museum and Art Gallery.

The Two Rosalinds ('The dubious daylight ended')
First pub. *Collier's* (New York), 20 March 1909; first pub. (England) in *English Review*, April 1909, as 'London Nights by Thomas Hardy. I. The Two Rosalinds'; collected *Time's Laughingstocks* (1909); Gibson, pp. 199–201; Hynes, I, 247–50.

HrT 1235 Fair copy, the first publication version, 3 numbered leaves.

Facsimile of the first page in Maggs Catalogue 312 (1913).

Owned (1982) F. B. Adams (see Hynes).

HrT 1236 Fair copy, revised, in MS Time's Laughingstocks (ff. 13–15).

Fitzwilliam Museum.

HrT 1236.5 Corrected typescript, 3 leaves (rectos only).

This typescript not mentioned Gibson or Hynes.

Folger, Y.d.585(1).

Two Serenades ('Late on Christmas Eve, in the street alone')
First pub. *Late Lyrics* (1922); Gibson, pp. 603–4; Hynes, II, 372–4.

HrT 1237 Fair copy, revised, in MS Late Lyrics (ff. 61–2), annotated 'From an old copy'.

Dorset County Museum.

The Two Soldiers ('Just at the corner of the wall')
First pub. *Satires of Circumstance* (1914); Gibson, p. 394; Hynes, II, 113–14.

HrT 1238 Fair copy, revised, the title altered from 'A Rencounter', in MS Satires of Circumstance (p. 154).

Dorset County Museum.

The Two Wives ('I waited at home all the while they were boating together —')
First pub. *Late Lyrics* (1922); Gibson, p. 692; Hynes, II, 418.

HrT 1239 Fair copy, revised, in MS Late Lyrics (f. 112).

Dorset County Museum.

A Two-Years' Idyll ('Yes; such it was')
First pub. *Late Lyrics* (1922); Gibson, pp. 628–9; Hynes, II, 401–2.

HrT 1240 Fair copy, in MS Late Lyrics (f. 94).

Dorset County Museum.

HrT 1241 Draft of title and lines 1–4 in MS Human Shows (f. 158v), the whole cancelled.

This MS printed Hynes, II, 515.

Yale.

The Unborn ('I rose at night, and visited')
First pub. *Wayfarer's Love*, ed. Duchess of Sunderland (London, 1904), as 'Life's Opportunity'; revised and collected *Time's Laughingstocks* (1909); Gibson, pp. 286–7; Hynes, I, 343–4.

HrT 1242 Fair copy, here entitled 'Life's Opportunity', signed, inscribed '(For the Potteries' Crippled Children's Guild.)', one page, as sent to the Duchess of Sunderland for the first publication in August 1903; watermarked 1901.

Berg.

HrT 1243 Fair copy, in MS Time's Laughingstocks (f. 124).

Fitzwilliam Museum.

Under High-Stoy Hill ('Four climbed High-Stoy from Ivel-wards')
First pub. *Human Shows* (1925); Gibson, p. 787; Hynes, III, 106–7.

HrT 1244 Fair copy, revised, in MS Human Shows (f. 131).

Yale.

HrT 1245 Revision to line 13 in HS Proof (p. 186).

Dorset County Museum.

Under the Waterfall ('"Whenever I plunge my arm, like this')
First pub. *Satires of Circumstance* (1914); Gibson, pp. 335–7; Hynes, II, 45–6.

HrT 1246 Fair copy, revised, entitled in pencil (now erased) 'The Lost Glass', in MS Satires of Circumstance (pp. 63–5).

In the table of contents to this MS, this poem is originally listed (cancelled) as 'The glass in the stream'.

Dorset County Museum.

Unkept Good Fridays ('There are many more Good Fridays')
First pub. *Daily Telegraph*, 5 April 1928; collected *Winter Words* (1928); Gibson, pp. 842–3; Hynes, III, 175.

HrT 1247 Fair copy, revised, in MS Winter Words; dated Good Friday, 1927.

Queen's College, Oxford, MS 420, f. 14.

An Unkindly May ('A shepherd stands by a gate in a white smock-frock:')
First pub. *Daily Telegraph*, 23 April 1928; collected *Winter Words* (1928); Gibson, pp. 841–2; Hynes, III, 174.

HrT 1248 Fair copy, revised, including the cancelled subtitle '(1877)', in MS Winter Words.

Queen's College, Oxford, MS 420, f. 13.

Unknowing ('When, soul in soul reflected')
First pub. *Wessex Poems* (1898); Gibson, pp. 58–9; Hynes, I, 76–7.

HrT 1249 Fair copy, in MS Wessex Poems (ff. 74–5).

Birmingham City Museum and Art Gallery.

HrT 1250 Revision to line 13 and corrections in *Selected Poems* (1917), pp. 51–2.

Dorset County Museum.

The Unplanted Primrose ('"A pink primrose from the plant he knows')
First pub. in Evelyn Hardy, 'Some Unpublished Poems by Thomas Hardy', *London Magazine*, 3 (1956), 28–39 (35–6); Gibson, pp. [933]–4; Hynes, III, 280–1.

HrT 1251 Fair copy, revised, one page, annotated '1865–67. Westbourne Park Villas./(From old MS.)'.

Microfilm Edition, Reel 5.

Dorset County Museum.

Unrealized ('Down comes the winter rain —')
First pub. *The Queen's [Christmas] Carol* (London, Manchester and Paris, 1905), as 'Orphaned/A Point of View'; revised and collected *Time's Laughingstocks* (1909); Gibson, p. 296; Hynes, I, 355–6.

HrT 1252 Fair copy, slightly revised, in MS Time's Laughingstocks (f. 137).

Fitzwilliam Museum.

An Upbraiding ('Now I am dead you sing to me')
First pub. *Moments of Vision* (1917); Gibson, p. 532; Hynes, II, 282.

HrT 1253 Fair copy, revised, in MS Moments of Vision (f. 167).

Magdalene College, Cambridge.

The Upper Birch-Leaves ('Warm yellowy-green')
First pub. *Moments of Vision* (1917); Gibson, p. 507; Hynes, II, 253.

HrT 1254 Fair copy, revised, here entitled 'The Upper Leaves', in MS Moments of Vision (f. 131).

Magdalene College, Cambridge.

V. R. 1819–1901 ('The mightiest moments pass uncalendared')
First pub. *The Times*, 29 January 1901; collected *Poems of the Past and the Present* (1902); Gibson, p. [85]; Hynes, I, [115].

HrT 1255 Fair copy, revised, here beginning 'Moments the mightiest pass uncalendared', in MS Poems of the Past and the Present; dated 'Sunday night, 27 January 1901'.

Bodleian, MS Eng. poet. d. 18, f. 1.

Vagg Hollow ('"What do you see in Vagg Hollow')
First pub. *Late Lyrics* (1922); Gibson, pp. 649–50; Hynes, II, 426.

HrT 1256 Fair copy, revised, in MS Late Lyrics (f. 124).

Dorset County Museum.

Vagrant's Song ('When a dark-eyed dawn')
First pub. *Nash's and Pall Mall Magazine*, January 1925; revised and collected *Human Shows* (1925); Gibson, pp. 775–6; Hynes, III, 93–4.

HrT 1257 Fair copy, including a footnote to line 12, in MS Human Shows (f. 112).

Yale.

Valenciennes ('We trenched, we trumpeted and drummed')
First pub. *Wessex Poems* (1898); Gibson, pp. 19–21; Hynes, I, 24–6.

HrT 1258 Fair copy, revised, here beginning 'We bugled, trumpeted, & drummed', in MS Wessex Poems (ff. 21–3); dated '1878–1897'.

Birmingham City Museum and Art Gallery.

The Vampirine Fair ('Gilbert had sailed to India's shore')
First pub. *Time's Laughingstocks* (1909); Gibson, pp. 265–8; Hynes, I, 321–4.

HrT 1259 Fair copy, here entitled 'The Fair Vampire', in MS Time's Laughingstocks (ff. 96–8).

Fitzwilliam Museum.

HrT 1260 Revision to line 92 in DCM Wessex Edition (Verse Vol. III, 382).

Dorset County Museum.

The Vatican: Sala delle Muse, see HrT 993–4.

A Victorian Rehearsal ('A single shine broods gloomily')
First pub. (facsimile) in 'An Unpublished Poem by Thomas Hardy', *TLS*, 2 June 1966, p. 504; Gibson, pp. 935–6; Hynes, III, 283–4.

HrT 1261 Fair copy, revised in ink and pencil, the title altered from 'The Rehearsal', one page, annotated '[not used]'.

Facsimile as first publication and in Gibson, p. [932]; Microfilm Edition, Reel 5.

Dorset County Museum.

The Voice ('Woman much missed, how you call to me, call to me')
First pub. *Satires of Circumstance* (1914); Gibson, p. 346; Hynes, II, 56–7.

HrT 1262 Fair copy, revised, here beginning 'O woman weird, how you call to me, call to me', in MS Satires of Circumstance (p. 82).

Dorset County Museum.

HrT 1263 Correction and revisions to line 11 in *Selected Poems* (1917), p. 64.

Dorset County Museum.

The Voice of the Thorn ('When the thorn on the down')
First pub. *Time's Laughingstocks* (1909); Gibson, p. 233; Hynes, I, 284.

HrT 1264 Fair copy, revised, in MS Time's Laughingstocks (f. 58).

Fitzwilliam Museum.

The Voice of Things ('Forty Augusts — aye, and several more — ago')
First pub. *Moments of Vision* (1917); Gibson, pp. [427]–8; Hynes, II, [159]–60.

HrT 1265 Fair copy, in MS Moments of Vision (f. 2), here beginning 'Forty years — aye, and several more — ago'.

Magdalene College, Cambridge.

Voices from Things Growing in a Churchyard ('These flowers are I, poor Fanny Hurd')
First pub. *London Mercury*, December 1921, as 'Voices from Things Growing'; privately printed by FEH in pamphlet *Haunting Fingers* (London, 1922); collected *Late Lyrics* (1922); Gibson, pp. 623–5; Hynes, II, 395–7.

HrT 1266 Fair copy, revised, in MS Late Lyrics (ff. 86–7).

Dorset County Museum.

HrT 1267 Typescript, revised, here entitled 'Voices from Things Growing', 2 leaves (rectos only) numbered 3–4, printer's copy for FEH's pamphlet, together with HrT 446.

Cockerell Sale, Lot 287, sold to Hollings.

New York University.

HrT 1268 [entry deleted]

Wagtail and Baby ('A baby watched a ford, whereto')
First pub. *Albany Review*, April 1907; collected *Time's Laughingstocks* (1909); Gibson, pp. 296–7; Hynes, I, 357.

HrT 1269 Fair copy, revised, in MS Time's Laughingstocks (f. 138).

Fitzwilliam Museum.

Waiting Both ('A star looks down at me')
First pub. *London Mercury*, November 1924; collected *Human Shows* (1925); Gibson, p. [701]; Hynes, III, [7].

HrT 1270 Fair copy, revised, in MS Human Shows (f. 1).

Yale.

HrT 1271 Fair copy, one page, meant for projected postcard reproduction (apparently never made).

Facsimile in Shun Katayama, *Thomas Hardy* (Tokyo, 1934), p. 129.

Colby College.

HrT 1272 Revision to line 3 in HS Proof (p. 1).

Dorset County Museum.

The Walk ('You did not walk with me')
First pub. *Satires of Circumstance* (1914); Gibson, p. 340; Hynes, II, 49–50.

HrT 1273 Fair copy, in MS Satires of Circumstance (p. 73).

Dorset County Museum.

The Wanderer ('There is nobody on the road')
First pub. *Late Lyrics* (1922); Gibson, pp. 599–600; Hynes, II, 367–8.

HrT 1274 Fair copy, revised, including an alternative title (erased) 'The Beknighted Traveller', in MS Late Lyrics (f. 55).

Dorset County Museum.

The War-wife of Catknoll ('"What crowd is this in Catknoll Street')
First pub. *Daily Telegraph*, 21 June 1928; collected *Winter Words* (1928); Gibson, pp. 858–9; Hynes, III, 192–3.

HrT 1275 Fair copy, revised, including a footnote to line 27, in MS Winter Words.

Queen's College, Oxford, MS 420, ff. 35–6 (rectos only).

A Wasted Illness ('Through vaults of pain')
First pub. *Poems of the Past and the Present* (1902); Gibson, p. 152; Hynes, I, 189–90.

HrT 1276 Fair copy, revised, in MS Poems of the Past and the Present.

Bodleian, MS Eng. poet. d. 18, ff. 102–3 (rectos only).

A Watcher's Regret ('I slept across the front of the clock')
First pub. *Human Shows* (1925); Gibson, p. 785; Hynes, III, 104–5.

HrT 1277 Fair copy, revised, in MS Human Shows (f. 127).

Yale.

A Watering-place Lady Inventoried ('A sweetness of temper unsurpassed and unforgettable')
First pub. *Human Shows* (1925); Gibson, p. 804; Hynes, III, 125–6.

HrT 1278 Fair copy, revised, in MS Human Shows (f. 156).

Yale.

HrT 1279 Revision to line 9 in HS Proof (p. 221).

Dorset County Museum.

'We are getting to the end' ('We are getting to the end of visioning')
First pub. *Daily Telegraph*, 28 May 1928; collected *Winter Words* (1928); Gibson, p. 929; Hynes, III, 273–4.

HrT 1280 Fair copy, revised, in MS Winter Words.

Queen's College, Oxford, MS 420, f. 136.

We Field-women ('How it rained')
First pub. *Winter Words* (1928); Gibson, p. 881; Hynes, III, 218–19.

HrT 1281 Fair copy, in MS Winter Words.

Queen's College, Oxford, MS 420, f. 68.

HrT 1282 Revised, one leaf, framed.

This MS was presented by Howard Bliss to Gerald Finzi in March 1956 (see Purdy, p. 257).

University of Reading.

'We sat at the window' ('We sat at the window looking out')
First pub. *Moments of Vision* (1917); Gibson, pp. 428–9; Hynes, II, 161.

HrT 1283 Fair copy, revised, in MS Moments of Vision (f. 4).

Magdalene College, Cambridge.

'We say we shall not meet' ('We say we shall not meet')
First pub. *Daily Telegraph*, 11 September 1928; collected *Winter Words* (1928); Gibson, p. 884; Hynes, III, 223.

HrT 1284 Draft, here untitled, one page.

Facsimile in *Modern Literary Manuscripts from King's College, Cambridge* [catalogue of an exhibition at the Fitzwilliam Museum, 1976], No. 26.

King's College, Cambridge, E. M. Forster Papers.

HrT 1285 Fair copy, revised, in MS Winter Words.

Queen's College, Oxford, MS 420, f. 74.

The Weary Walker ('A plain in front of me')
First pub. *The Bermondsey Book*, December 1925; collected *Human Shows* (1925); Gibson, p. 742; Hynes, III, 54–5.

HrT 1286 Fair copy, revised, in MS Human Shows (f. 62).

Yale.

HrT 1287 Typescript.

Owned (1979) James Gibson (see Gibson, p. 742).

Weathers ('This is the weather the cuckoo likes')
First pub. *Good Housekeeping* (London), May 1922; collected *Late Lyrics* (1922); Gibson, p. [563]; Hynes, II, 326.

HrT 1288 Fair copy, revised, in MS Late Lyrics (f. 1).

Dorset County Museum.

The Wedding Morning ('Tabitha dressed for her wedding: —')
First pub. *Late Lyrics* (1922); Gibson, p. 605; Hynes, II, 374.

HrT 1289 Fair copy, in MS Late Lyrics (f. 63).

Dorset County Museum.

A Week ('On Monday night I closed my door')
First pub. *Satires of Circumstance* (1914); Gibson, pp. 379–80; Hynes, II, 95–6.

HrT 1290 Fair copy, revised, in MS Satires of Circumstance (p. 131).

Dorset County Museum.

Welcome Home ('Back to my native place')
First pub. *Late Lyrics* (1922); Gibson, p. 573; Hynes, II, 338.

HrT 1291 Fair copy, revised, here beginning 'To my native place', in MS Late Lyrics (f. 16).

Dorset County Museum.

HrT 1292 Revisions to lines 1, 5 and 14 in *Collected Poems* (1923), pp. 542–3.

Dorset County Museum.

The Well-Beloved ('I went by star and planet shine')
First pub. *Poems of the Past and the Present* (1902); Gibson, pp. 133–5; Hynes, I, 168–70.

HrT 1293 Fair copy, revised, here beginning 'I wayed by star and planet shine', in MS Poems of the Past and the Present.

Bodleian, MS Eng. poet. d. 18, ff. 73–6 (rectos only).

HrT 1294 Revisions to lines 2–4 in *Collected Poems* (1923), p. 121.

Dorset County Museum.

Wessex Heights ('There are some heights in Wessex, shaped as if by a kindly hand')
First pub. *Satires of Circumstance* (1914); Gibson, pp. 319–20; Hynes, II, 25–7.

HrT 1295 Fair copy, revised, in MS Satires of Circumstance (pp. 26–7); dated December 1896 (cancelled).

Dorset County Museum.

HrT 1296 Revision to line 12 in *Selected Poems* (1917), p. 94.

Dorset County Museum.

Wessex Poems
This collection of poems first pub. London and New York, 1898. For lists of corrections for subsequent editions, see INTRODUCTION. For a description of the MS printer's copy (MS Wessex Poems), see INTRODUCTION; contents have been listed individually.

HrT 1296.5 Fair copy, revised, of the Preface, in MS Wessex Poems (f. 1a), one page, signed (initials); dated September 1898.

The Preface first pub. *Wessex Poems* (1898); Gibson, p. [6]; Orel, p. 38; Hynes, I, [5].

Birmingham City Museum and Art Gallery.

HrT 1297 Pencil corrections in Hardy's copy of the first edition, incorporated into later editions.

Poems corrected in this copy (not mentioned in Hynes) are not listed individually.

Owned (1978) F. B. Adams.

The West-of-Wessex Girl ('A very West-of-Wessex girl')
First pub. *Late Lyrics* (1922); Gibson, p. 572; Hynes, II, 337. A fair copy of this poem presented by Hardy to Plymouth Free Public Library in 1923 was destroyed in the Second World War; see INTRODUCTION.

HrT 1298 Fair copy, revised, in MS Late Lyrics (f. 15); dated 'Begun in Plymouth, March 1913'.

Dorset County Museum.

A Wet August ('Nine drops of water bead the jessamine')
First pub. *Late Lyrics* (1922); Gibson, p. 578; Hynes, II, 343–4.

HrT 1299 Fair copy, revised, in MS Late Lyrics (f. 24); dated 1920.

Dorset County Museum.

A Wet Night ('I pace along, the rain-shafts riddling me')
First pub. *Time's Laughingstocks* (1909); Gibson, p. 276; Hynes, I, 332–3.

HrT 1300 Fair copy, revised, in MS Time's Laughingstocks (f. 110).

Fitzwilliam Museum.

The Whaler's Wife ('I never pass that inn "The Ring of Bells"')
First pub. *Winter Words* (1928); Gibson, pp. 855–7; Hynes, III, 189–91.

HrT 1301 Fair copy, revised, in MS Winter Words.

Queen's College, Oxford, MS 420, ff. 32–3 (rectos only).

'What did it mean?' ('What did it mean that noontide, when')
First pub. *Late Lyrics* (1922); Gibson, p. 654; Hynes, II, 431–2.

HrT 1302 Fair copy, revised, in MS Late Lyrics (f. 131).

Dorset County Museum.

'What's there to tell?' ('What's there to tell of the world')
First pub. *Human Shows* (1925); Gibson, pp. 773–4; Hynes, III, 91–2.

HrT 1303 Fair copy, in MS Human Shows (f. 109); dated '190–.'.

Yale.

When Dead ('It will be much better when')
First pub. *Human Shows* (1925); Gibson, p. 721; Hynes, III, 29–30.

HrT 1304 Fair copy, revised, in MS Human Shows (f. 31).

Yale.

'When I set out for Lyonnesse' ('When I set out for Lyonnesse')
First pub. *Satires of Circumstance* (1914); Gibson, p. 312; Hynes, II, 17–18.

HrT 1305 Fair copy, in MS Satires of Circumstance (p. 15).

Dorset County Museum.

HrT 1306 Fair copy, revised, signed, inscribed to Sydney Cockerell, one page.

Cockerell Sale, Lot 270, sold to Maggs (facsimile in sale catalogue).

Owned (1984) F. B. Adams (see Hynes).

HrT 1307 Addition of subtitle '(1870)' in *Selected Poems* (1916), p. 17.

Dorset County Museum.

HrT 1308 Addition of subtitle '(1870)' in *Selected Poems* (1917), p. 17.

Dorset County Museum.

When Oats Were Reaped ('That day when oats were reaped, and wheat was ripe, and barley ripening')
First pub. *Human Shows* (1925); Gibson, p. 772; Hynes, III, 90.

HrT 1309 Fair copy, in MS Human Shows (f. 106); dated August 1913.

Yale.

'When shall the saner softer politics', see HrT 286.5.

'When wearily we shrink away' ('When wearily we shrink away')
First pub. J. O. Bailey, *The Poetry of Thomas Hardy* (Chapel Hill, NC, 1970); Gibson, p. [933]; Hynes, III, 283.

HrT 1310 Draft, here untitled, annotated 'Suggested by M. H.', 2 pages (one leaf).

Dorset County Museum.

Where the Picnic Was ('Where we made the fire')
First pub. *Satires of Circumstance* (1914); Gibson, pp. 357–8; Hynes, II, 69–70.

HrT 1311 Fair copy, in MS Satires of Circumstance (p. 31).

Dorset County Museum.

HrT 1312 Corrections and annotated 'Remove to follow "The Phantom Horsewoman"', in *Selected Poems* (1917).

Dorset County Museum.

Where They Lived ('Dishevelled leaves creep down')
First pub. *Moments of Vision* (1917); Gibson, pp. 462–3; Hynes, II, 200.

HrT 1313 Fair copy, revised, here beginning 'Dishevelled leaves come down', in MS Moments of Vision (f. 55); dated first March 1913 and then October 1913 (both cancelled).

Magdalene College, Cambridge.

'Where three roads joined' ('Where three roads joined it was green and fair')
First pub. *Late Lyrics* (1922); Gibson, pp. 587–8; Hynes, II, 354–5.

HrT 1314 Fair copy, revised, the title (and first line) altered from '"Where three roads met"', subtitled '<(Near Tresparret Posts, Cornwall)>', in MS Late Lyrics (f. 39).

Dorset County Museum.

While drawing in a Churchyard ('"It is sad that so many of worth')
First pub. *Moments of Vision* (1917); Gibson, p. 536; Hynes, II, 287.

HrT 1315 Fair copy, revised, the title altered from 'While Drawing Architecture in a Churchyard', in MS Moments of Vision (f. 173).

Magdalene College, Cambridge.

The Whipper-In ('"My father was the whipper-in, —')
First pub. *Late Lyrics* (1922); Gibson, pp. 672–3; Hynes, II, 453–4.

HrT 1316 Fair copy, revised, in MS Late Lyrics (ff. 156–7).

Dorset County Museum.

Whispered at the Church-opening ('In the bran-new pulpit the bishop stands')
First pub. *Daily Telegraph*, 4 June 1928; collected *Winter Words* (1928); Gibson, p. 900; Hynes, III, 241–2.

HrT 1317 Fair copy, revised, in MS Winter Words.

Queen's College, Oxford, MS 420, f. 98.

The Whitewashed Wall ('Why does she turn in that shy soft way')
First pub. *Reveille*, November 1918; revised and collected *Late Lyrics* (1922); Gibson, pp. 685–6; Hynes, II, 470–1.

HrT 1318 Fair copy, revised, in MS Late Lyrics (f. 176).

Dorset County Museum.

'Who's in the next room?' ('"Who's in the next room? — who?')
First pub. *Moments of Vision* (1917); Gibson, pp. 503–4; Hynes, II, 249.

HrT 1319 Fair copy, in MS Moments of Vision (f. 126).

Magdalene College, Cambridge.

'Why be at pains?' ('Why be at pains that I should know')
First pub. *Moments of Vision* (1917); Gibson, p. 428; Hynes, II, 160.

HrT 1320 Fair copy, revised, in MS Moments of Vision (f. 3).

Magdalene College, Cambridge.

'Why did I sketch' ('Why did I sketch an upland green')
First pub. *Moments of Vision* (1917); Gibson, p. 477; Hynes, II, 217.

HrT 1321 Fair copy, revised, in MS Moments of Vision (f. 79).

Magdalene College, Cambridge.

'Why do I?' ('Why do I go on doing these things?')
First pub. *Human Shows* (1925); Gibson, p. 831; Hynes, III, 157.

HrT 1322 Fair copy, revised, in MS Human Shows (f. 196).

Yale.

'Why she moved house' ('Why she moved house, without a word')
First pub. *Human Shows* (1925); Gibson, p. 823; Hynes, III, 148.

HrT 1323 Fair copy, in MS Human Shows (f. 186).

Yale.

The Widow Betrothed ('I passed the lodge and avenue')
First pub. *Poems of the Past and the Present* (1902), as 'The Widow'; Gibson, pp. 141–2; Hynes, I, 177–9.

HrT 1324 Fair copy, revised, here entitled 'The Widow' and beginning 'By Mellstock Lodge and Avenue', in MS Poems of the Past and the Present.

Bodleian, MS Eng. poet. d. 18, ff. 85–6 (rectos only).

HrT 1325 Variant lines 1–2 (erased) in DCM Wessex Edition (Verse Vol. I).

Dorset County Museum.

A Wife and Another ('"War ends, and he's returning')
First pub. *Time's Laughingstocks* (1909); Gibson, pp. 262–4; Hynes, I, 318–20.

HrT 1326 Fair copy, revised, in MS Time's Laughingstocks (ff. 92–4).

Fitzwilliam Museum.

A Wife Comes Back ('This is the story a man told me')
First pub. *Late Lyrics* (1922); Gibson, pp. 600–1; Hynes, II, 368–70.

HrT 1327 Fair copy, revised, in MS Late Lyrics (ff. 56–7).

Dorset County Museum.

HrT 1328 Revision to line 23 in *Collected Poems* (1923), p. 568.

Dorset County Museum.

A Wife in London ('She sits in the tawny vapour')
First pub. *Poems of the Past and the Present* (1902); Gibson, pp. 91–2; Hynes, I, 123.

HrT 1329 Fair copy, revised, in MS Poems of the Past and the Present.

Bodleian, MS Eng. poet. d. 18, f. 10.

A Wife Waits ('Will's at the dance in the Club-room below')
First pub. *Time's Laughingstocks* (1909), as 'At Casterbridge Fair. VI.'; Gibson, pp. 241–2; Hynes, I, 294.

HrT 1330 Fair copy, here entitled 'Waiting' and headed 'VI.', Hardy's footnote to line 3 pasted to the bottom of the page, in MS Time's Laughingstocks (f. 67).

Fitzwilliam Museum.

'The wind blew words' ('The wind blew words along the skies')
First pub. *Moments of Vision* (1917); Gibson, pp. 446–7; Hynes, II, 181–2.

HrT 1331 Fair copy, revised, in MS Moments of Vision (f. 31).

Magdalene College, Cambridge.

The Wind's Prophecy ('I travel on by barren farms')
First pub. *Moments of Vision* (1917); Gibson, pp. 494–5; Hynes, II, 238–9.

HrT 1332 Fair copy, revised, in MS Moments of Vision (f. 110).

Magdalene College, Cambridge.

A Winsome Woman ('There's no winsome woman as winsome as she')
First pub. *Winter Words* (1928); Gibson, pp. 924–5; Hynes, III, 268–9.

HrT 1333 Fair copy, revised, in MS Winter Words.

Queen's College, Oxford, MS 420, f. 130.

Winter in Durnover Field ('Throughout the field I find no grain')
First pub. *Poems of the Past and the Present* (1902); Gibson, pp. 148–9; Hynes, I, 186.

HrT 1334 Fair copy, in MS Poems of the Past and the Present.

Bodleian, MS Eng. poet. d. 18, f. 96.

HrT 1335 One correction and one (erased) revision in DCM Wessex Edition (Verse Vol. I).

Dorset County Museum.

Winter Night in Woodland ('The bark of a fox rings, sonorous and long: —')
First pub. *Country Life*, 6 December 1924; privately printed separately by FEH (London, 1925); collected *Human Shows* (1925); Gibson, p. 734; Hynes, III, 44–5. An uncorrected? proof (dated 22 December 1924) for FEH's pamphlet was sold in the Cockerell Sale, Lot 290, to Charles.

HrT 1336 Fair copy, revised, including the erased title 'Christmas Eve', in MS Human Shows (f. 50).

Yale.

HrT 1337 Revision to line 22 in HS Proof (p. 74).

Dorset County Museum.

Winter Words
This collection of poems first pub. posthumously London, 1928. For a description of the MS volume (MS Winter Words), see INTRODUCTION; contents have been listed individually. Uncorrected galleys for first American edition (91 leaves), which shows some variation from the first English edition, are owned by David Holmes.

HrT 1338 Draft of the title page for the first edition, showing variant titles, and a pencil draft of the last 2 paragraphs of the 'Introductory Note', signed (initials), both inserted in Sydney Cockerell's copy of Wessex Edition, Verse Vol. VI (London, 1931) (including also HrT 1088) ; c. 1927–8.

Cockerell Sale, Lot 252, sold to Maggs; described Hynes, III, 322–3. The 'Introductory Note' first pub. *Winter Words* (1928); Gibson, p. [834]; Orel, pp. 60–1; Hynes, III, [165]–6.

Owned (1985) F. B. Adams (see Hynes).

HrT 1339 Fair copy, revised, of the 'Introductory Note', in MS Winter Words, one page.

Queen's College, Oxford, MS 420, f. 2.

A Wish for Unconsciousness ('If I could but abide')
First pub. *Daily Telegraph*, 5 July 1928; collected *Winter Words* (1928); Gibson, p. 838; Hynes, III, 171.

HrT 1340 Fair copy, in MS Winter Words.

Queen's College, Oxford, MS 420, f. 8.

The Wistful Lady ('"Love, while you were away there came to me —')
First pub. *Satires of Circumstance* (1914); Gibson, p. [359]; Hynes, II, [71]–2.

HrT 1341 Fair copy, revised, in MS Satires of Circumstance (pp. 97–8).

Dorset County Museum.

Without Ceremony ('It was your way, my dear')
First pub. *Satires of Circumstance* (1914); Gibson, p. 343; Hynes, II, 53. This poem is cancelled in *Selected Poems* (1917); see INTRODUCTION.

HrT 1342 Fair copy, revised, in MS Satires of Circumstance (p. 77).

Dorset County Museum.

Without, not within Her ('It was what you bore with you, Woman')
First pub. *Late Lyrics* (1922); Gibson, p. 647; Hynes, II, 423–4.

HrT 1343 Fair copy, revised, in MS Late Lyrics (f. 120).

Dorset County Museum.

Wives in the Sere ('Never a careworn wife but shows')
First pub. *The Tatler*, 31 July 1901; collected *Poems of the Past and the Present* (1902); Gibson, p. 145; Hynes, I, 182–3.

HrT 1344 Fair copy, signed, one leaf, printer's copy for the first publication.

University of California at Berkeley.

HrT 1345 Fair copy, slightly revised, in MS Poems of the Past and the Present.

Bodleian, MS Eng. poet. d. 18, f. 91.

A Woman Driving ('How she held up the horses' heads')
First pub. *Late Lyrics* (1922); Gibson, p. 682; Hynes, II, 465–6.

HrT 1346 Fair copy, in MS Late Lyrics (f. 170).

Dorset County Museum.

The Woman I Met ('A stranger, I threaded sunken-hearted')
First pub. *London Mercury*, April 1921; collected *Late Lyrics* (1922); Gibson, pp. 592–4; Hynes, II, 360–2.

HrT 1347 Fair copy, revised, in MS Late Lyrics (ff. 45–7); dated 'London: <about> 1918.'.

Dorset County Museum.

HrT 1348 Corrected typescript for the first publication, 4 numbered leaves (rectos only); dated London, 1918.

Texas.

HrT 1349 Revision to line 76 in *Collected Poems* (1923), p. 562.

Dorset County Museum.

The Woman in the Rye ('"Why do you stand in the dripping rye')
First pub. *Satires of Circumstance* (1914); Gibson, p. 360; Hynes, II, 72.

HrT 1350 Fair copy, in MS Satires of Circumstance (p. 99).

Dorset County Museum.

The Woman who Went East ('"Where is that woman of the west')
First pub. *Daily Telegraph*, 14 May 1928; collected *Winter Words* (1928); Gibson, pp. 916–17; Hynes, III, 259–60.

HrT 1351 Fair copy, revised, the title altered from 'The Woman of the West', in MS Winter Words.

Queen's College, Oxford, MS 420, ff. 121–2 (rectos only).

A Woman's Fancy ('"Ah, Madam; you've indeed come back here?')
First pub. *Late Lyrics* (1922); Gibson, pp. 576–7; Hynes, II, 341–2.

HrT 1352 Fair copy, revised, in MS Late Lyrics (ff. 21–2).

Dorset County Museum.

A Woman's Trust ('If he should live a thousand years')
First pub. *Late Lyrics* (1922); Gibson, pp. 682–3; Hynes, II, 466–7.

HrT 1353 Fair copy, revised, in MS Late Lyrics (f. 171).

Dorset County Museum.

The Wood Fire ('"This is a brightsome blaze you've lit, good friend, to-night!"')
First pub. *Late Lyrics* (1922); Gibson, pp. 618–19; Hynes, II, 389–90.

HrT 1354 Fair copy, revised, in MS Late Lyrics (f. 80).

Dorset County Museum.

The Workbox ('See, here's the workbox, little wife')
First pub. *Satires of Circumstance* (1914); Gibson, pp. 397–8; Hynes, II, 117–19.

HrT 1355 Fair copy, revised, in MS Satires of Circumstance (pp. 159–60).

Dorset County Museum.

The Wound ('I climbed to the crest')
First pub. *The Sphere*, 27 May 1916; collected *Selected Poems* (1916) and *Moments of Vision* (1917); Gibson, p. 465; Hynes, II, 202–3.

HrT 1356 Fair copy, in MS Moments of Vision (f. 60).

Magdalene College, Cambridge.

Xenophanes, the Monist of Colophon ('"Are You groping Your way?')
First pub. *Nineteenth Century and After*, March 1924; collected *Human Shows* (1925); Gibson, pp. 728–30; Hynes, III, 37–9.

HrT 1357 Fair copy, revised, in MS Human Shows (ff. 42–4, rectos only); dated 1921.

Yale.

The Year's Awakening ('How do you know that the pilgrim track')
First pub. *New Weekly*, 21 March 1914; collected *Satires of Circumstance* (1914); Gibson, p. 335; Hynes, II, 44.

HrT 1358 Fair copy, in MS Satires of Circumstance (p. 62); dated February 1910.

Dorset County Museum.

HrT 1359 Typescript, one numbered page, dated in Hardy's hand 1910, enclosed (together with HrT 124) in a letter to R. A. Scott-James (editor of *New Weekly*), 25 January 1914.

Letter printed *Letters*, V, 6 from the original at Texas; typescript not mentioned Gibson or Hynes.

Texas.

Yell'ham-Wood's Story ('Coomb-Firtrees say that Life is a moan')
First pub. *Time's Laughingstocks* (1909); Gibson, p. 298; Hynes, I, 359.

HrT 1360 Fair copy, revised, in MS Time's Laughingstocks (f. 141); dated 1902.

Fitzwilliam Museum.

The Yellow-hammer ('When, towards the summer's closc')
First pub. Florence Emily Dugdale, *The Book of Baby Birds* (London, 1912); Gibson, p. 946; Hynes, III, 297.

HrT 1361 Revised, in pencil, on verso of Macmillan presentation slip, including an annotation.

Owned (1985) R. L. Purdy (see Hynes); destined for Yale.

'You on the tower' ('"You on the tower of my factory —')
First pub. *Moments of Vision* (1917); Gibson, pp. 487–8; Hynes, II, 230.

HrT 1362 Fair copy, in MS Moments of Vision (f. 99).

Magdalene College, Cambridge.

'You were the sort that men forget' ('You were the sort that men forget')
First pub. *Moments of Vision* (1917); Gibson, pp. 434–5; Hynes, II, 167–8.

HrT 1363 Fair copy, in MS Moments of Vision (f. 15).

Magdalene College, Cambridge.

The Young Churchwarden ('When he lit the candles there')
First pub. *Moments of Vision* (1917); Gibson, p. 457; Hynes, II, 193–4.

HrT 1364 Fair copy, revised, here entitled '<At an Evening Service/Sunday> August 14. 1870', in MS Moments of Vision (f. 46).

Magdalene College, Cambridge.

The Young Glass-Stainer ('"These Gothic windows, how they wear me out')
First pub. *Moments of Vision* (1917); Gibson, p. 532; Hynes, II, 282–3.

HrT 1365 Fair copy, revised, in MS Moments of Vision (f. 168); dated November 1893.

Magdalene College, Cambridge.

A Young Man's Epigram on Existence ('A senseless school, where we must give')
First pub. *Time's Laughingstocks* (1909); Gibson, p. 299; Hynes, I, 359.

HrT 1366 Fair copy, here entitled 'Epigram on Existence', in MS Time's Laughingstocks (f. 139); dated 16 Westbourne Park Villas, 1866.

Fitzwilliam Museum.

A Young Man's Exhortation ('Call off your eyes from care')
First pub. *Late Lyrics* (1922); Gibson, pp. 601–2; Hynes, II, 370–1.

HrT 1367 Fair copy, revised, the title altered from 'An Exhortation', in MS Late Lyrics (f. 58), annotated '<(recopied)>'; dated 1867.

Dorset County Museum.

Your Last Drive ('Here by the moorway you returned')
First pub. *Satires of Circumstance* (1914); Gibson, pp. 339–40; Hynes, II, 48–9.

HrT 1368 Fair copy, revised, in MS Satires of Circumstance (pp. 71–2); dated December 1912.

Dorset County Museum.

The Youth Who Carried a Light ('I saw him pass as the new day dawned')
First pub. *Aberdeen University Review*, February 1916; collected *Moments of Vision* (1917); Gibson, pp. 480–1; Hynes, II, 221–2.

HrT 1369 Fair copy, revised, in MS Moments of Vision (f. 86).

Magdalene College, Cambridge.

HrT 1370 Pencil revision to line 8 in a copy of first publication.

Not mentioned Gibson or Hynes.

Dorset County Museum.

Yuletide in a Younger World ('We believed in highdays then')
First pub. *Ariel Poems*, No. 1 (London, 1927); collected *Winter Words* (1928); Gibson, p. 861; Hynes, III, 195–6.

HrT 1371 Fair copy, revised, in MS Winter Words, annotated in pencil '[For Mr de la Mare] published by Faber & Gwyer as Xmas Card Aug. '27.'.

Queen's College, Oxford, MS 420, f. 39.

Zermatt/To the Matterhorn ('Thirty-two years since, up against the sun')
First pub. *Poems of the Past and the Present* (1902); Gibson, p. 106; Hynes, I, 138–9.

HrT 1372 Fair copy, revised, in MS Poems of the Past and the Present.

Bodleian, MS Eng. poet. d. 18, f. 32.

'ΑΓΝΩΣΤΩι ΘΕΩι ['To the Unknown God'] ('Long have I framed weak phantasies of Thee')
First pub, *Poems of the Past and the Present* (1902); Gibson, pp. 186–7; Hynes, I, 228.

HrT 1373 Fair copy, revised, in MS Poems of the Past and the Present.

Bodleian, MS Eng. poet. d. 18, f. 157.

PROSE

Alicia's Diary, for a lost MS, see INTRODUCTION.

The American National Red Cross Society
First pub. *Biblio* (Pompton Lakes, New Jersey), November–December 1925; reprinted *Later Years*, p. 86; Purdy, p. 270.

HrT 1374 Fair copy, signed (initials), on page 4 of a letter to Frank Higbee, 3 October 1900.

Letter and MS printed in Carl J. Weber, 'Forty Years in an Author's Life', *CLQ*, 4 (1955), 110–11; letter only in *Letters*, II, 267.

Colby College.

The Ancient Cottages of England
First pub. *The Preservation of Ancient Cottages* (printed by the Royal Society of Arts, [London, March 1927]), pp. 13–[16]; Orel, pp. 233–5; Purdy, p. 323.

HrT 1375 Fair copy, here untitled, signed, 2 leaves (rectos only), headed '[Written for the Society of Arts]'.

Microfilm Edition, Reel 5.

Dorset County Museum.

[Answer to a questionnaire]
Extract pub. E. W. Scripture, *Grundzüge der Englischen Verwissenschaft* (Marburg, 1929); not in Purdy; mentioned *Letters*, VII, 36n.

HrT 1375.5 Hardy's typescript, signed, a letter replying to Professor Scripture's questionnaire of 13 questions concerning poetic method, 11 October 1927.

British Library, Add. MS 45186, f. 30.

[Answers to a questionnaire]
No publication traced; not mentioned Purdy.

HrT 1376 Answers, mostly in Hardy's hand, on a questionnaire about poetry, sent to Hardy by Harold Monro in 1922.

Hardy's letter to Monro, 16 June 1922, about being 'spared from' answering the questionnaire, is printed *Letters*, VI, 137–8 (from the original at King's College, Cambridge.

King's College, Cambridge.

Anna, Lady Baxby
First pub. *The Graphic*, Christmas Number, 1 December 1890, as 'A Group of Noble Dames: III. Anna, Lady Baxby'; collected *A Group of Noble Dames* (London, 1891), as 'Dame the Seventh'; Wessex Edition, XIV (1912), 165–74; Purdy, p. 63.

HrT 1377 Fair copy, revised, in MS Group of Noble Dames, 9 leaves (rectos only) numbered 75–83.

Library of Congress, Manuscript Division, Thomas Hardy Collection.

Apology to *Late Lyrics*, see HrT 673–673.5.

[Appeal for Dorothy Allhusen's Canteens]
First printed privately (300 copies) in facsimile by Dorothy Allhusen, [October–November 1918]. Of this piece, Purdy, p. 209 noted that 'there is some reason to believe it was in part the work of Mrs Hardy' and that his own copy of the facsimile (originally Dorothy Allhusen's copy) was the only one he had traced; Dorset County Museum, however, owns a copy of the facsimile, see Microfilm Edition, Reel 6.

HrT 1378 Fair copy, on Max Gate notepaper, 2 pages, beginning 'The sun as it shines on England...', signed; dated October 1918.

Owned (1954) R. L. Purdy (see Purdy); destined for Yale.

An Appeal from Dorset
Hardy's brief letter of endorsement of an appeal by the Rev. H. G. B. Cowley for the restoration of the Stinsford Church bells was pub. with the appeal in *New York Herald*, European Edition, 25 April 1926; Purdy, p. 322.

HrT 1378.5 Pencil draft of Hardy's original version of the appeal, included as a postscript to his draft letter to the Rev. H. G. B. Cowley, 27 February 1926.

This MS and letter printed *Letters*, VII, 9; the published version of Hardy's endorsement was originally sent to the Rev. Cowley with a letter of 13 April 1926 (letter printed *Letters*, VII, 15–16 from the original owned by Canon Cowley).

Dorset County Museum.

The Application of Coloured Bricks and Terra Cotta in Modern Architecture, for a lost MS, see INTRODUCTION.

An Appreciation of Anatole France, see HrT 1441.

Architectural Prize Essay, for a lost MS, see INTRODUCTION.

The Art of Authorship
Hardy's contribution to a symposium first pub. *The Art of Authorship*, comp. and ed. George Bainton (London, 1890); Purdy, p. 299; mentioned Orel, pp. 242–3.

HrT 1379 In a letter to George Bainton, 11 October 1887.

This MS printed *Letters*, I, 168–9.

Owned (1978) R. L. Purdy (see *Letters*); destined for Yale.

Authors and Their Victims
This article of responses (including Hardy's) to James Douglas's article 'The Grave-Worm' (pub. *Daily News*, 5 November 1912) was pub. *Daily News*, 15 November 1912; not mentioned Purdy.

HrT 1379.5 Pencil draft of Hardy's original letter to James Douglas (partially printed as cited above), 10 November 1912.

This MS printed *Letters*, IV, 234–5; a version of an extract from this letter was included in *Later Years*, p. 153.

Dorset County Museum.

Barbara of the House of Grebe
First pub. *The Graphic*, Christmas Number, 1 December 1890, as 'A Group of Noble Dames: I. Barbara (Daughter of Sir John Grebe)'; collected *A Group of Noble Dames* (London, 1891), as 'Dame the Second'; Wessex Edition, XIV (1912), 53–92; Purdy, p. 63.

HrT 1380 Fair copy, revised, here entitled 'Barbara/ Daughter of Sir John Grebe', in MS Group of Noble Dames, 48 leaves (rectos only) numbered 6–53).

Library of Congress, Manuscript Division, Thomas Hardy Collection.

The Beauty of Wessex
Hardy's statement first pub. in Clement Shorter's 'Literary Letter' in *The Sphere*, 7 September 1901; Purdy, p. 307.

HrT 1380.5 Clipping of first publication, revised by Hardy, in Scrapbook I (HrT 1687).

Microfilm Edition, Reel 6. Hardy originally enclosed his statement in a letter to Shorter of [29 August 1901?], printed *Letters*, II, 297 from the original at the Berg.

Dorset County Museum.

The Best Scenery I Know
Hardy's contribution to a symposium first pub. *Saturday Review*, 7 August 1897; reprinted *Later Years*, pp. 70–1; Purdy, p. 270.

HrT 1381 Draft, headed 'To the Editor of the Saturday Review', 2 pages (one leaf), signed; dated 9 July 1897.

Dorset County Museum.

Books of the Day
First pub. anonymously in 'Books of the Day' section in *Daily Chronicle*, 6 July 1906; not mentioned Purdy.

HrT 1382 Variant version of one paragraph regarding books on Dorset and Wessex, in an unidentified hand, enclosed in a letter from Hardy to James Milne (literary editor of *Daily Chronicle*), 4 July 1906.

Letter printed *Letters*, III, 216; this MS printed (and the handwriting discussed) in Dale Kramer, 'Revisions and Visions: Thomas Hardy's *The Woodlanders*', *BNYPL*, 75 (1971), 267n27.

Dorset County Museum.

Candour in English Fiction
Hardy's contribution to a symposium first pub. *New Review*, January 1890, pp. [15]–21; Orel, pp. 125–33; Purdy, p. 299.

HrT 1383 Corrected copy of the first publication.

This is presumably the copy Hardy prepared for a projected collected volume of 'Miscellanea'; see INTRODUCTION.

Owned (1982) David Holmes.

A Changed Man
First pub. *The Sphere*, 21 and 28 April 1900; collected *A Changed Man* (1913); Wessex Edition, XVIII (1914), 1–23; Pinion, II, [197]–213; Purdy, p. 152. For verses included in this story, see HrT 61.

HrT 1384 Fair copy, revised, containing HrT 60.5, 27 numbered leaves (rectos only).

This MS described Purdy, p. 154; facsimile of first page in *The Sphere*, 15 November 1913, p. 180.

Berg.

HrT 1385 Annotation to this story in DCM Wessex Edition (XVIII, 23).

Dorset County Museum.

A Changed Man
This collection of 12 stories first pub. London, 1913; Wessex Edition, XVIII (1914); Purdy, pp. 151–7. For MSS of individual stories, see HrT 1384–5, 1389–90, 1403–4, 1421, 1513, 1557–9, 1593, 1602. For lost MSS, see INTRODUCTION.

HrT 1386 Three draft contents lists, 2 giving first publications of the stories, 3 leaves (rectos only).

Microfilm Edition, Reel 5.

Dorset County Museum.

A Christmas Ghost-Story
First pub. as a letter to the editor in *Daily Chronicle*, 28 December 1899; Orel, pp. 201–2; Hynes, I, 369 (in the notes to the poem 'A Christmas Ghost-Story' (see HrT 203), a response to the publication of which occasioned this letter); Purdy, pp. 306–7.

HrT 1387 Fair copy; dated 25 December 1899.

Princeton, Robert H. Taylor Collection.

HrT 1388 Draft, headed '*To the Editor of the Daily Chronicle*', annotated '[Original Draft.]', signed, 2 pages (one leaf); dated 25 December [1899].

Dorset County Museum.

A Committee-Man of 'The Terror'
First pub. *Illustrated London News*, Christmas Number, 22 November 1896; collected *A Changed Man* (1913); Wessex Edition, XVIII (1914), 211–28; Pinion, II, [347]–59; Purdy, p. 153.

HrT 1389 Fair copy, revised, signed, 19 numbered leaves (rectos only), printer's copy for the first publication, with cancelled annotation 'Roy[l]. Fam. at W[eymou][th]. Sept. 1801, 2, 4, 5 &c. Peace of Amiens March 27, '02 Rupture between Fr. & Eng. & arrest of Bsh. travellers: May 12 '03'.

This MS described Purdy, p. 154.

Berg.

HrT 1390 Corrected galley proof, 5 galleys cut into 13 pages, annotated 'Revise'.

Huntington, HM 6.

Contrainte et liberté
Hardy's contribution to a symposium (translated into French) first pub. *L'Ermitage* (Paris), November 1893; Purdy, p. 269.

HrT 1391 Draft in English, here beginning 'In answer to your question dated July 1st...', addressed to the editors of *L'Ermitage*, one page; dated 14 August 1893.

This MS printed in *Later Years*, p. 23.

Dorset County Museum.

HrT 1391.5 Fair copy (the copy sent), 2 pages (one leaf), headed 'To the Editors of *L'Ermitage*.' and beginning as above; dated 14 August 1893.

Pierpont Morgan, Gordon Ray Collection.

A Correction of Misstatements
First pub. as letter to the editor in *The Athenaeum*, 28 October 1911 (in response to 'Mr Hardy's MSS.' published *Daily News*, 23 October 1911); Purdy, p. 314; mentioned Orel, p. 246.

HrT 1392 Draft, one page, in one of Hardy's scrapbooks (HrT 1687), annotated '[sent to Athenaeum–Oct 24: 1911]'.

Microfilm Edition, Reel 6.

Dorset County Museum.

Country-dances and 'The Collage Hornpipe' (as formerly danced in Wessex)
A letter from Hardy pub. *English Folk Dance Society News*, September 1926; Hardy's later reply to comments elicited by the first letter was pub. as 'English Country dances' in *The Journal of the English Folk Dance Society* (1927); Purdy, p. 323.

HrT 1392.5 Proof of the original letter and Hardy's letter to N. O. M. Cameron which included an additional paragraph for insertion in the proof; letter dated 7 September 1926.

Hardy's own draft of the additional paragraph is at Dorset County Museum; the letter to Cameron printed *Letters*, VII, 41.

English Folk Dance and Song Society, London.

HrT 1393 Hardy's later reply (see headnote), dated 26 October 1926.

This was published with its opening paragraph.

English Folk Dance and Song Society, London.

Dedication of the New Dorchester Grammar School
Address delivered at the Dorchester Grammar School, 21 July 1927. First pub. *The Times*, 22 July 1927; privately printed separately by FEH as *Address Delivered by Thomas Hardy On Laying the Commemoration Stone of the New Dorchester Grammar School...* (Cambridge, 1927); reprinted *Later Years*, pp. 254–6; Orel, pp. 235–7; Purdy, pp. 248–9. For a typescript among the materials for *Life*, see HrT 1456.

HrT 1394 Typescript, revised, 5 pages; together with a corrected proof for FEH's pamphlet, including one typed page of additional corrections, some in Hardy's hand; dated 26 July [1927].

The typescript described Purdy, pp. 248–9; Cockerell Sale, Lot 295, sold to Maggs; this lot also included two uncorrected proofs for this pamphlet.

Owned (1978) F. B. Adams.

Desperate Remedies

First pub. in 3 vols (London, 1871); Wessex Edition, XV (1912); Purdy, pp. 3–5. For a lost MS, see INTRODUCTION. For papers relating to the dramatization, see DRAMATIC WORKS.

HrT 1395 Presentation copy of the first edition to Emma Lavinia Gifford (later ELH) containing an autograph correction of the quotation from Scott on title page of Vol. I.

Dorset County Museum.

The Distracted Preacher

First pub. *New Quarterly Magazine*, April 1879, as 'The Distracted Young Preacher'; collected *Wessex Tales* (1888); Wessex Edition, IX (1912), 215–[287]; Pinion, I, 155–205; Purdy, p. 59. For papers relating to the dramatization, see DRAMATIC WORKS.

HrT 1396 Here entitled 'The Distracted Young Preacher', in ink, 57 leaves (rectos only).

This MS not mentioned Purdy.

Hanzel Galleries, 23–4 September 1973 (David Gage Joyce Sale), Lot 106, sold to Hamill and Barker.

The Doctor's Legend

First pub. *The Independent* (New York), 26 March 1891; uncollected by Hardy; Pinion, III, 41–9; Purdy, pp. 299–300.

HrT 1397 Transcript by ELH, entitled by Hardy, 16 numbered leaves (rectos only), signed, annotated by Hardy '[Written expressly for *The Independent*.]' and containing printer's marks.

Facsimile of first page in Anderson Galleries sale catalogue, 7–10 January 1929 (Kern Sale), p. 220 and of opening lines in American Art Association sale catalogue, 22–4 April 1924, Lot 397.

Berg.

Dorset Dewpond

This lecture by Alfred Pope delivered at the Dorset Natural History and Antiquarian Field Club, 13 February 1912; first pub. *Dorset County Chronicle*, 15 February 1912; not mentioned Purdy.

HrT 1398 Hardy's contribution to Pope's lecture (used verbatim), concerning Green-Hill Pond; [after 24 October 1911].

Hardy offered to write out this anecdote in a letter to Pope of 24 October 1911 (printed *Letters*, IV, 183–4 from the original at the Thomas Hardy Society).

Thomas Hardy Society.

Dorset in London

Hardy's speech (not delivered) for the annual dinner of the Society of Dorset Men in London in May 1908 was first pub. *The Dorset Year-Book* (pub. Society of Dorset Men in London) (London, 1908); Orel, pp. 218–25; Purdy, pp. 312–13.

HrT 1399 Typescript, revised, including a title page and 10 leaves (rectos only) of text.

Facsimile in British library, RP 2146; this is presumably the copy that Hardy prepared for his projected collected volume of 'Miscellanea' (see INTRODUCTION).

Owned (1982) David Holmes.

HrT 1400 Fair copy, revised, of a variant version of the second paragraph, beginning 'No more curious change...', one page, signed.

Facsimile used as frontispiece to first publication.

Unlocated.

The Dorsetshire Labourer

First pub. *Longman's Magazine*, July 1883; Orel, pp. 168–91; Purdy, pp. 50–1 (where the questionable authenticity of the 5 known copies of a separate edition entitled *The Dorset Farm Labourer* (Dorchester, 1834) is discussed). This essay used as quarry for passages in *Tess of the d'Urbervilles*.

HrT 1401 Draft, 31 numbered leaves (mostly rectos only), signed.

This MS mentioned Purdy, p. 50 as having been lost; Microfilm Edition, Reel 5.

Dorset County Museum.

The Duchess of Hamptonshire
First pub. (early version) *Light: A Journal of Criticism and Belles Lettres* (London), 6 and 13 April 1878, as 'The Impulsive Lady of Croome Castle'; second version pub. *The Independent*, 7 February 1884, as 'Emmeline; or Passion versus Principle'; revised and collected *A Group of Noble Dames* (London, 1891), as 'Dame the Ninth'; Wessex Edition, XIV (1912), 189–206; Purdy, pp. 63–4. For a dramatization, see HrT 1609.

HrT 1402 Fair copy, revised, here entitled 'Emmeline; or Passion versus Principle.', 25 numbered leaves (rectos only), printer's copy for *The Independent*.

This MS described Purdy, p. 65.

Pierpont Morgan, MA 182.

The Duke's Reappearance
First pub. *Saturday Review*, Christmas Supplement, 14 December 1896; collected *A Changed Man*(1913); Wessex Edition, XVIII (1914), 245–56; Pinion, II, [372]–8; Purdy, p. 153.

HrT 1403 Fair copy, revised, 11 leaves numbered 1, 1a, 2–10 (rectos only), signed (initials), printer's copy for first publication, inscribed to Edward Clodd, March 1912; together with covering letter to Clodd, 24 March 1912.

This MS described Purdy, p. 155; letter printed *Letters*, IV, 207–8.

Texas.

HrT 1404 Date (1896) added at end of story in DCM Wessex Edition (XVIII, 256).

Dorset County Museum.

The Early Life of Thomas Hardy, see entries for *Life* and HrT 303–4, 1441.5, 1511.

Emmeline, see HrT 1402.

English Country-dances, see HrT 1392.5–1393.

Enter a Dragoon, for a lost MS, see INTRODUCTION; for Hardy's dramatization, see HrT 1636.

Far from the Madding Crowd
First pub. serially in *Cornhill*, January–December 1874; first pub. separately in 2 vols (London, 1874); Wessex Edition, II (1912); Purdy, pp. 13–20. For Hardy's dramatization, see HrT 1643.

HrT 1405 Partly draft, partly fair copy, revised, printer's copy for first publication, without Chapter 16 (which was added in proof), 605 leaves numbered in 3 series: 1–208 (with 6 additional leaves); 2–1 to 2–263 (with two additional leaves); 3–1 to 3–126.

This MS (wanting f. 107 and together with a fragment of *The Hand of Ethelberta* and HrT 1100) was 'found' in 1918 by Isabel Smith (widow of Reginald Smith, former editor of *Cornhill*); Hardy wrote to her on 23 January 1918 (letter is with this MS) enclosing his rewritten copy of the missing f. 107 and endorsing her plan to send the MS to the Red Cross Sale at Christie's, 22 April 1918. Some variants in this MS printed in Parke Bernet sale catalogue, 14–16 May 1941 (A. E. Newton Sale), p. 67 where the letter to Isabel Smith is printed. The MS is discussed (including one facsimile page) in Robert C. Schweik, 'The Early Development of Hardy's *Far from the Madding Crowd*', *Texas Studies in Literature and Language*, 9 (1967), 415–28; also discussed in Simon Gatrell, 'Hardy the Creator: *Far from the Madding Crowd*' in *Critical Approaches to the Fiction of Thomas Hardy*, ed. Dale Kramer (London, 1979), pp. 74–98. The letter to Isabel Smith printed *Letters*, V, 243–4. Facsimile pages in A. E. Newton, *The Amenities of Book-Collecting* (Boston, 1918), p. [14] (f. 3); A. E. Newton, *Thomas Hardy, Novelist or Poet?* (privately printed, Philadelphia, 1929), pp. [7–9] (f. 2–257 and letter to Isabel Smith); *Grolier Catalogue*, facing p. 15 (f. 2–108); A. E. Newton sale catalogue (cited above), p. [69] (f. 1).

Yale.

HrT 1406 Fragment of first draft, 9 leaves (11 pages of text numbered 106a–106k and 3 unnumbered pages), headed 'Chapter.', annotated 'Some pages of 1st draft/(Details of Sheep-rot — omitted from MS when revised./T. H.)'.

This MS discussed in Robert C. Schweik, 'A First Draft Chapter of Hardy's *Far from the Madding Crowd*', *English Studies*, 53 (1972), 344–9; described Purdy, p. 16. Microfilm Edition, Reel 2.

Dorset County Museum.

HrT 1407 Fair copy, revised, 7 pages numbered 2–18 to 2–24, headed 'Chapter XXIII./The shearing-supper.', signed (initials), annotated 'Some pages of the first Draft — afterwards revised.', inscribed to FEH; dated in pencil at end 1873.

This MS described Purdy, pp. 15–16. Microfilm Edition, Reel 2.

Dorset County Museum.

HrT 1408 Two corrected proof copies for editions published by Harper & Bros., London: 1) unbound copy of Harper & Bros., 1900 edition, revised by Hardy, probably used as printer's copy for another edition; 2) corrected page proofs for Harper & Bros., 1901 edition, annotated by Hardy 'press (after correction)', dated stamped by Ballantyne, 16 April–30 April 1901.

These proofs not mentioned Purdy.

Signet Library, Edinburgh.

HrT 1409 Revisions in Chapters 5 and 46 and corrections *passim* in DCM Wessex Edition (II).

These revisions printed in Simon Gatrell, 'Hardy the Creator: *Far from the Madding Crowd*' in *Critical Approaches to the Fiction of Thomas Hardy*, ed. Dale Kramer (London, 1979), p. 91.

Dorset County Museum.

A Few Crusted Characters

First pub. *Harper's New Monthly Magazine*, March–June 1891, as 'Wessex Folk'; collected *Life's Little Ironies* (1894); Wessex Edition, VIII (1912), 187–259; Pinion, II, [139]–93; Purdy, pp. 82–3. For a dramatization of the section entitled 'The History of the Hardcomes', see HrT 1607.

HrT 1410 Draft, incomplete, here entitled 'Wessex Folk', 30 leaves (mostly rectos only), misannotated by Hardy 'First Rough Draft of some of the tales afterwards called "A Group of Noble Dames".'; together with a letter of presentation to Edmund Gosse, 18 July 1913, correcting the mistake.

This MS described Purdy, p. 84; letter printed *Letters*, IV, 287–8.

Berg.

HrT 1411 Fair copy.

Facsimile page (beginning of 'Incident in the Life of Mr George Crookhill') in *Harper's Monthly Magazine*, July 1925, p. 241; this MS mentioned Purdy, p. 84n where it is called a later draft.

Unlocated.

HrT 1412 Corrected galley proof in Life's Little Ironies Proof; date stamped 23–30 December 1893.

Dorset County Museum.

The Fiddler of the Reels

First pub. *Scribner's Magazine* (New York), May 1893; collected *Life's Little Ironies* (1894); Wessex Edition, VIII (1912), pp. 163–85; Pinion, II, [123]–38; Purdy, p. 82.

HrT 1413 Corrected galley proof in Life's Little Ironics Proof; date stamped 20–3 December 1893.

Dorset County Museum.

The First Countess of Wessex

First pub. *Harper's New Monthly Magazine*, December 1889; collected *A Group of Noble Dames* (London, 1891); Wessex Edition, XIV (1912), 1–51; Purdy, pp. 62–3.

HrT 1414 Signed, 50 leaves.

This MS mentioned Purdy, p. 65.

Anderson Auction Company, 29 May 1906, Lot 319.

For Conscience' Sake

First pub. *Fortnightly Review*, March 1891, as 'For Conscience Sake'; collected *Life's Little Ironies* (1894); Wessex Edition, VIII (1912), 53–74; Pinion, II, [47]–61; Purdy, p. 81.

HrT 1415 Fair copy, revised, 24 numbered leaves (rectos only), printer's copy for first publication, annotated at top '[*Life's Little Ironies*]'.

This MS described Purdy, p. 83.

John Rylands Library.

HrT 1416 Corrected galley proof in Life's Little Ironies Proof; date stamped [4]–5 December 1893.

Dorset County Museum.

For Want of a Word, see HrT 1537.

[For *The Sphere*]

Hardy's comments about the role of Frederick Greenwood in the publication of *Far from the Madding Crowd* were used by Clement Shorter in his column 'A Literary Letter' pub. *The Sphere*, 13 May 1905; not in Purdy.

HrT 1416.5 Typed transcript of a paragraph sent for insertion in Shorter's column, enclosed in a letter to Shorter, 1 May 1905.

The letter (without the enclosure) printed *Letters*, VII, 139; Shorter used the paragraph but did not quote it verbatim.

University of Leeds.

G. M.: A Reminiscence

First printed privately by FEH as a pamphlet (Cambridge, 21 November 1927); first pub. *Nineteenth Century and After*, February 1928; Orel, pp. 151–5; Purdy, pp. 250–1.

HrT 1417 Extensively revised, 5 numbered leaves (rectos only), signed; dated 'October: 1927:/(for Feb: 1928.)'.

This MS mentioned Purdy, p. 251; Microfilm Edition, Reel 5.

Dorset County Museum.

HrT 1418 Corrected proof for *Nineteenth Century and After*, used as printer's copy for FEH's pamphlet, dated 31 October 1927; together with corrected first and second proofs for FEH's pamphlet, dated 9 and 14 November 1927 respectively.

Cockerell Sale, Lot 298, sold to Maggs.

Owned (1978) R. L. Purdy; destined for Yale.

General Preface to the Novels and Poems

First pub. Wessex Edition, I (*Tess of the d'Urbervilles*) (1912), vii–xiii; reprinted in each prose volume of the New Wessex Edition; Orel, pp. 44–50; Hynes, II, [520]–5; Purdy, p. 286.

HrT 1419 Corrected revise proof for the Wessex Edition (containing also HrT 1576.5), here entitled (before revision) 'General Preface', together with an uncorrected second proof (date stamped 4 March 1912) incorporating the corrections; preface dated October 1911; date stamped 19 February 1912.

This proof mentioned Purdy, p. 286; facsimiles of corrected pages in *The Thomas Hardy Archive: 1. Tess of the d'Urbervilles*, ed. Simon Gatrell, 2 vols (New York and London, 1986), II, 275–8.

University of California at Berkeley, 71/141z.

HrT 1420 Corrections in DCM Wessex Edition (I).

Facsimiles of corrected pages in *The Thomas Hardy Archive: 1. Tess of the d'Urbervilles* (as above), II, 296–9.

Dorset County Museum.

The Grave by the Handpost

First pub. *St James's Budget*, Christmas Number, 30 November 1897; collected *A Changed Man* (1913); Wessex Edition, XVIII (1914), 127–41; Pinion, II, [288]–98; Purdy, pp. 152–3.

HrT 1421 Fair copy, revised, 16 numbered leaves (rectos only), signed, printer's copy for first publication.

This MS described Purdy, p. 154; facsimile of first page in Parke Bernet sale catalogue, 1 February 1944 (Sachs Sale), p. 13.

Owned (1954) Halsted B. VanderPoel (see Purdy; Pinion, II, 499 says this MS 'when last traced, was the property of Halsted B. VanderPoel, Rome').

A Group of Noble Dames

This collection of ten stories first pub. London, 1891; Wessex Edition, XIV (1912); Purdy, pp. 61–7. For a description of the MS volume (MS Group of Noble Dames), see INTRODUCTION; contents have been listed individually. For other MSS, see HrT 1402, 1414.

The Hand of Ethelberta
First pub. *Cornhill*, July 1875–May 1876; first pub. separately in 2 vols (London, 1876); Wessex Edition, XVI (1912); Purdy, pp. 20–3. For a lost MS, see INTRODUCTION; for a dramatization, see DRAMATIC WORKS.

HrT 1422 Corrected page proof for first publication, wanting Chapters 35–46.

Facsimile page in Parke Bernet sale catalogue, 1 February 1944 (Sachs Sale), p. [17] and in Purdy, facing p. 22.

Owned (1978) R. L. Purdy; destined for Yale.

HrT 1423 'Copy' for title page of the New York, 1876 edition, originally enclosed in a letter to the publisher Henry Holt, 18 March 1876.

Mentioned Purdy, p. 23 as now being inserted in 'Holt's "office sample" of the novel'; letter to Holt printed *Letters*, I, 44 from the original at Colby College.

Unlocated.

HrT 1424 Corrections in DCM Wessex Edition (XVI, 54–6).

Dorset County Museum.

The History of the Hardcomes, for a dramatization of this section of the story 'A Few Crusted Characters', see HrT 1607.

The Hon. Mrs Henniker
First pub. anonymously *Illustrated London News*, 18 August 1894; reprinted in *One Rare Fair Woman*, ed. Evelyn Hardy and F. B. Pinion (London, 1972), Appendix II, pp. 209–10; Purdy, p. 304; mentioned Orel, p. 244.

HrT 1425 One page, as sent for the first publication.

This MS described Purdy, p. 304.

Owned (1978) F. B. Adams.

Hopkins's 'Thomas Hardy and His Folk'
P. Thurston Hopkins's article (pub. *Westminster Gazette* and (extracts only) *Dorset Daily Echo*, 2 June 1926) elicited this letter from Hardy (protesting misstatements) pub. *Westminster Gazette*, 4 June 1926; Purdy, p. 322.

HrT 1425.5 Hardy's draft of an apology to himself, apparently dictated by FEH to the *Dorset Daily Echo* over the telephone.

This editorial apology appeared in the *Dorset Daily Echo* on 3 June 1926.

Dorset County Museum.

How I Won at Monte-Carlo, see HrT 1535.

An Imaginative Woman
First pub. *Pall Mall Magazine*, April 1894; collected Wessex Tales (London, 1896); transferred to *Life's Little Ironies* in Wessex Edition, VIII (1912), 1–31; Pinion, II, [11]–32; Purdy, p. 60.

HrT 1426 Revised, the title altered from 'A Woman of Imagination', 31 numbered leaves (rectos only), signed.

This MS described Purdy, p. 60; Microfilm Edition, Reel 18.

University of Aberdeen, King's College, MS 617.

Introductory Note to *Winter Words*, see HrT 1338–9.

Jude the Obscure
First pub. serially *Harper's Monthly Magazine*, December 1894–November 1895, first as 'The Simpletons' and in later instalments as 'Hearts Insurgent'; first pub. separately London, 1896; Wessex Edition, III (1912); Purdy, pp. 86–91. Textual variants from first edition to Wessex Edition discussed in Robert C. Slack, 'The Text of Hardy's *Jude the Obscure*', *NCF*, 11 (1957), 261–75; for a recent edition, see *Jude the Obscure*, ed. Patricia Ingham (Oxford, 1985). For Hardy's dramatization, see HrT 1644–5.

HrT 1427 Fair copy, revised, the title altered from 'The Simpletons', 377 leaves numbered 1–436 (incomplete, wanting 59 leaves); dated March 1895.

This MS discussed with facsimile of f. 114 in John Paterson, 'The Genesis of *Jude the Obscure*', *SP*, 57 (1960), 87–98 and in Patricia Ingham, 'The Evolution of *Jude the Obscure*', *RES*, 27 (1976), 27–37 and 159–69; described Purdy, pp. 88–9; Microfilm Edition, Reel 16.

Fitzwilliam Museum.

HrT 1428 Corrected page proof for first separate edition, annotated by Hardy 'press.'; date stamped by Ballantyne 2 September–30 September 1895.

This proof described Purdy, p. 90 as being in the possession of George Stewart, a reader for Ballantyne, the printer; discussed in Simon Gatrell, *Hardy the Creator: a textual biography* (Oxford, 1988), pp. 157–64, 254–5.

Signet Library, Edinburgh.

HrT 1429 Postscript to Preface for the Wessex Edition, 8 leaves, as sent to Florence Emily Dugdale (later FEH) for typing; dated October 1911.

Preface and Postscript printed Orel, pp. 32–6; this MS mentioned Purdy, p. 91.

Owned (1954) R. L. Purdy (see Purdy); destined for Yale.

HrT 1430 Key to some allusions in the novel (first edition, pp. 95–7), in a letter to Florence Henniker, Dorchester, 10 November 1895.

This MS printed *Letters*, II, 94–5.

Dorset County Museum.

HrT 1431 List of fictional place-names in the novel with real places written alongside, one page.

Facsimile in Clive Holland, *Thomas Hardy, O. M.* (London, 1933), facing p. 144.

Owned (1933) 'Clive Holland' (i.e., Charles James Hankinson).

HrT 1432 Corrections in DCM Wessex Edition (III), annotated on flyleaf 'Corrections (not sent anywhere Sept 1926)'.

Dorset County Museum.

The Lady Icenway

First pub. *The Graphic*, Christmas Number, 1 December 1890, as 'A Group of Noble Dames: IV. The Lady Icenway'; collected *A Group of Noble Dames* (London, 1891), as 'Dame the Fifth'; Wessex Edition, XIV (1912), 135–49; Purdy, p. 63.

HrT 1433 Fair copy, revised, in MS Group of Noble Dames, 17 leaves (rectos only) numbered 85–101).

Library of Congress, Manuscript Division, Thomas Hardy Collection.

The Lady Mottisfont

First pub. *The Graphic*, Christmas Number, 1 December 1890, as 'A Group of Noble Dames: VI. Lady Mottisfont'; collected *A Group of Noble Dames* (London, 1891), as 'Dame the Fourth'; Wessex Edition, XIV (1912), 113–33; Purdy, p. 63.

HrT 1434 Fair copy, revised, here entitled 'Lady Mottisfont', in MS Group of Noble Dames, 22 leaves (rectos only) numbered 115–36).

Library of Congress, Manuscript Division, Thomas Hardy Collection.

The Lady Penelope

First pub. *Longman's Magazine*, January 1890; collected *A Group of Noble Dames* (London, 1891), as 'Dame the Eighth'; Wessex Edition, XIV (1912), 175–88; Purdy, p. 63.

HrT 1435 Fair copy, revised, in MS Group of Noble Dames, 14 numbered leaves (rectos only) foliated separately from the rest of the volume.

Library of Congress, Manuscript Division, Thomas Hardy Collection.

A Laodicean

First pub. serially in *Harper's New Monthly Magazine* (European Edition), December 1880–December 1881; first pub. separately New York, 1881; first English edition in 3 vols (London, 1881); Wessex Edition, XVII (1912); Purdy, pp. 35–40. For a lost MS and for lists of corrections for the Mellstock Edition, see INTRODUCTION. The corrected proof for the first publication (HrT 1436) is accompanied by 15 related notes and postcards from Hardy to R. R. Bowker of Harper & Bros.; another R. R. Bowker collection at the NYPL, Manuscripts Division, contains in addition 15 similar notes; any of these notes containing specific proof corrections are listed below.

HrT 1436 Corrected proof for the first publication, a combination of galley (Parts 1–4) and page proofs (Parts 5–12), wanting Book III, Chapters 4–7; galleys date stamped 3–6 September 1880, page proofs date stamped 19 January–5 August 1881.

Described Purdy, pp. 3–9.

Library of Congress, Manuscript Division, R. R. Bowker Collection, Volume 10.

HrT 1437 Five slight proof corrections to the opening chapters (for first instalment of first publication), on verso of a letter to R. R. Bowker, Weymouth, 10 September 1880.

Letter only printed in *Letters*, I, 79.

Library of Congress, Manuscript Division, R. R. Bowker Collection, Volume 6.

HrT 1438 Proof corrections for first publication (all to Book I), in three notes to R. R. Bowker: in a postcard dated Tooting, 25 October [1880]; in a postcard postmarked 17 November 1880; and in a letter dated Upper Tooting, 1 February [1881].

These MSS printed *Letters*, I, 81, 83 and 87.

NYPL, Manuscripts Division, R. R. Bowker Collection.

HrT 1439 Corrections in DCM Wessex Edition (XVII, 11, 235, 238, 249, 257, 268, 330).

Dorset County Museum.

The Later Years of Thomas Hardy, see entries for *Life* and HrT 1374, 1379.5, 1381, 1391–1391.5, 1441, 1442, 1511.5, 1566–7, 1599.

Laurence Hope
First pub. *The Athenaeum*, 29 October 1904; no further publication traced; Purdy, p. 309; mentioned Orel, p. 256.

HrT 1440 Draft obituary for 'Laurence Hope' (i.e., Adela Florence (called 'Violet') Nicolson), 3 pages.

Described Purdy, p. 309 as being together with Laurence Hope's presentation copies to Hardy of her two books, *The Garden of Kama* (1901?) and *Stars of the Desert* (1903) (sold in the Max Gate Sale (1938), Lot 214, and the latter listed in David Holmes Catalogue 5 (n.d.), Item 54). Listed in the sale catalogue of Carroll A. Wilson's collection, *Thirteen Author Collections of the Nineteenth Century* ed. Jean C. S. Wilson and David A. Randall, 2 vols (privately printed, New York, 1950) where it was listed together with a letter from Hardy to Arthur Symons, printed *Letters*, III, 142 from the original owned David Holmes.

Unlocated.

A Legend of Thinkers
Hardy's contribution to the symposium pub. *New World*, July 1921; Purdy, p. 321.

HrT 1440.5 Draft.

Dorset County Museum.

HrT 1440.7 Typescript, as sent to Hamilton Fyfe with a letter of 11 June 1921.

The letter only printed *Letters*, VII, 162 (where this typescript is mistakenly said to be lost).

Eton College.

Letter on Anatole France
This letter sent by Hardy was read out by Lord Redesdale at a banquet honouring Anatole France at the Savoy Hotel, 10 December 1913; first pub. *The Times*, 11 December 1913; privately printed in pamphlet *Dinner Given in Honour of M. Anatole France...* (London, December 1913); reprinted in John Lane's 'Thomas Hardy. A Bibliography of First Editions' published in Lionel Johnson, *The Art of Thomas Hardy* (London, 1923), as 'An Appreciation of Anatole France'; extract (closing passage) pub. *Later Years*, p. 159; Purdy, p. 272.

HrT 1441 Typescript, signed, of Hardy's letter of regret that he cannot attend the banquet, beginning 'I particularly regret that, though one of the Committee...', addressed 'To the Chairman' (i.e., Sir Thomas Barclay, Chairman of the reception committee), enclosed in a letter to John Lane of 7 December 1913 for forwarding; on Max Gate notepaper and dated 7 December 1913.

Letter to John Lane printed *Letters*, IV, 326 from the original at Texas. A note in John Lane's 'Bibliography' (cited above) says that 'the MS. was given by Mr Lane to M. Anatole France as a souvenir.'.

Texas.

Letter to A. A. Reade
Hardy's contribution to a symposium first pub. *Study and Stimulants*, ed. A. Arthur Reade (Manchester and London, 1883); variant version reprinted *Early Life*, pp. 204–5; Purdy, p. 264.

HrT 1441.3 Part of the text included in a letter to A. Arthur Reade, 27 February 1882.

Not in *Letters*.

Owned (1989) David Holmes.

HrT 1441.5 Fair copy of the *Early Life* version, 2 pages, addressed 'Dear Sir', including the postscript 'Proof returned'; dated from Wimborne, 5 December 1882.

Not in *Letters*.

Washington University, St Louis.

Letter to H. Rider Haggard
First pub. H. Rider Haggard, *Rural England*, 2 vols (London, 1902), I, 282–5; variant version pub. *Later Years*, pp. 93–6; Purdy, p. 270.

HrT 1442 Draft of a version (differing from that in the first publication and that in *Later Years*).

Dorset County Museum.

Letters on the War, see HrT 1549, 1553.

Letters to the editor, see HrT 1381, 1387–8, 1391, 1392, 1442.5, 1511.5, 1548.5, 1549, 1553, 1599, 1600.

Letter to the editor of *T. P.'s Weekly*
This letter not published in *T. P.'s Weekly*; first pub. in *Letters*, IV (1984), p. 71; not in Purdy.

HrT 1442.5 Draft, inserted (with the article from *T. P.'s Weekly* of 14 January 1910 which occasioned it) in Scrapbook I (HrT 1687), here beginning 'Mr Hardy finds that there has been an article...', annotated '[Letter sent to the Editor]'; dated 17 January 1910.

This MS printed *Letters* (as above); Microfilm Edition, Reel 6.

Dorset County Museum.

The Life of Thomas Hardy
First pub. in 2 separate vols: Chapters 1–19 as *Early Life* (1928), extracts of which first pub. *The Times*, 22–7 October 1928; Chapters 20–38 (but numbered 1–19) as *Later Years* (1930), extracts of which first pub. *The Times*, 8–9 April 1930; first pub. (in one volume) *Life* (1962); Taylor, pp. [189]–294 ('*Appendix*. Typescript Passages omitted from *The Life of Thomas Hardy*') prints some of the cancelled passages from the extant typescripts listed below and some additional materials, as well as listing all the extant MS sources for *Life* at Dorset County Museum; in *Life and Work* (1984), Michael Millgate reconstructs as nearly as possible Hardy's version as it stood at the time of his death, with FEH's later changes and additions given in an Appendix of 'Selected Post-Hardyan Revisions'; Purdy, pp. 262–73. The entries below treat the work as one entity (and not two, as in the first editions *Early Life* and *Later Years*) containing 38 consecutively numbered chapters. For MS sources of discrete works included in the text of *Life*, see HrT 303–4, 1374, 1379.5, 1381, 1391–1391.5, 1441, 1441.5, 1442, 1511, 1511.5, 1566, 1567, 1599. Originals of Hardy's letters included in the text of *Life* are listed below (HrT 1466–1510). For a further discussion, see INTRODUCTION.

HrT 1443 Carbon copy typescript of the first notes for the opening chapters (covering the years 1840–1862), headed 'Notes of Thomas Hardy's Life./by Florence Hardy./(taken down in conversations, etc.)', 19 leaves (rectos only); [completed by 9 September 1917].

Mentioned Taylor, p. [203]; see also *Life and Work*, p. xiii; Microfilm Edition, Reel 7.

Dorset County Museum.

HrT 1444 Carbon copy typescript (the 'file' or second copy), revised by Hardy in his calligraphic hand and by FEH and Sydney Cockerell as well, bound in 2 vols; Vol. I: entitled 'The Life and Work of Thomas Hardy, Vol. I', annotated on cover by Hardy 'Mrs Hardy./(Personal Copy)' and '[2nd. Copy]', containing the Prefatory Note and Chapters 1–19, c. 370 pages (mostly rectos only) numbered 1–332 with some irregularities, including the label of A. P. Watt & Son on the cover, containing (f. 11a) a tracing of Hardy's plan of Stinsford Church; Vol. II: entitled (in a MS title page) 'The Life and Work of Thomas Hardy./Vol. II', annotated on the front cover by Hardy 'Mrs Hardy./(Personal Copy.)' and '[2nd. Copy]', annotated at head of text 'Mem:/ Vol II. might begin here…', containing Chapters 20–34, c. 240 pages (mostly rectos only) numbered 333–545 with some irregularities, including the 'Motto for the Wessex Society of Manchester' (f. 479) and the 'Speech on Receiving the Freedom of the Borough' (ff. 496–500, revised); followed by typescript outline of Chapters 35–8, headed 'Synopsis of Remainder of Book./(probably about 100 more pages of typoscript [sic].' and annotated '(From hereabout the writing is mostly in the form of Memoranda only. F. E. H.)' (see HrT 1686), 3 leaves (rectos only); [virtually complete by 30 November 1919 though revisions to this copy by Hardy continued until his death and thereafer by FEH].

FEH prepared 3 typescripts (original and 2 carbons) of Chapters 1–34; this typescript (now divided into 2 vols) was the first carbon and was designated the 'file' copy, i.e., the copy in which all approved emendations were to be transferred; it is the only typescript of the 3 to have survived intact; described Taylor, pp. [203], 205–6; used as copy text for *Life and Work*; Microfilm Edition, Reels 7 (Vol. II) and 8 (Vol. I). Hardy's drawing of the plan of Stinsford Church is printed in facsimile in *Life*, p. 11; 'Motto for the Wessex Society of Manchester' printed in *Life*, p. 336 and Hynes, III, 294; for the 'Speech on Receiving the Freedom of the Borough', see HrT 1567.

Dorset County Museum.

HrT 1445 Carbon copy typescript (the 'working' or third copy), revised by Hardy in his calligraphic hand and entitled by him (on a MS title page) 'The Life and Work of Thomas Hardy', containing Chapters 20–32 only, c. 214 pages (mostly rectos only) numbered roughly 333–521, annotated by Hardy on the title page '3rd. — [(Rough) Copy.]' and, on the first page of text, 'Mem:/Vol. II. might begin here — if 2 vols.'; including 'Motto for the Wessex Society of Manchester' (f. 479) and the 'Speech on Receiving the Freedom of the Borough' (ff. 496–500) (see HrT 1444).

This copy is the one designated for use by Hardy in revising the typescript, its revisions to be thereafter transferred to the 'file' copy; in practice, the use of the typescripts was less systematic. Facsimile first page in Purdy, p. 273; described Taylor, pp. [203], 205–6; see *Life and Work*, pp. 493–544 *passim* for variants (this typescript designated 'TS3'); Microfilm Edition, Reel 7.

Dorset County Museum.

HrT 1446 Fragments of the original typescript ('top' copy), as sent to the printer, containing revisions by Hardy (in his calligraphic hand), FEH and Sydney Cockerell, including portions of Chapters 3–9, 12, 18–19, 32–3, c. 95 pages on 80 leaves (mostly rectos only) numbered 58–61, 74, 80, 82, 92–3, 96–7, 105, 105a, 106, 128–31, 140–2, 149–52, 162–3, 191, 198–9, 212, 266, 307–12, 314–27, 512–39 (512–14 being retyped pages).

Mentioned Taylor, p. [203]; see *Life and Work*, pp. 493–544 *passim* for variants (this typescript designated 'TS1'); Microfilm Edition, Reel 8.

Dorset County Museum.

HrT 1446.5 Draft of a passage, cancelled, on verso of a leaf apparently torn from a notebook containing (on the recto) Hardy's sketch of the view from his window at 16 Westbourne Park Villas dated 22 June 1866.

This MS mentioned *Life and Work*, p. xvi; facsimile of the sketch in Millgate, plate 19.

Dorset County Museum.

HrT 1447 Typescript of a loose framework of materials, compiled by Hardy for FEH's use in preparing Chapters 35–6, revised by both Hardy and FEH, here entitled by Hardy on a MS title page 'T. H./ Memoranda & Notes towards completing/ the remainder of Vol. II (to end of book)' and annotated '[original]', including summaries of events, transcriptions of letters and Hardy's 'Speech at the Opening of the Mellstock Club' (ff. 562–4, revised) covering the period May 1918 to the end of 1920, 41 leaves (rectos only) numbered 546–86; annotated by Hardy on an inserted slip at the beginning 'From this point...to the end, the compilation is mostly in the form of undigested Memoranda requiring critical consideration as to what biographical particulars should be retained, differently expressed or omitted.' and, on the last page, '<[Refer to Note-Book of Memoranda beginning 1921, for continuation.]>' (see HrT 1686).

Described Taylor, pp. [203], 206–7; see *Life and Work*, pp. 493–544 *passim* (especially 542–3) for variants (this typescript designated 'MN1'); Microfilm Edition, Reel 7; for Hardy's 'Speech at the Opening of the Mellstock Club', see HrT 1566.

Dorset County Museum.

HrT 1448 Typescript (carbon copy of HrT 1447), here entitled by Hardy 'T. H./Memoranda & Notes towards completing/the remainder of Vol. II, (which will/be the end of book.)' and '[3rd. (Rough) Copy.]', revised by Hardy and FEH, including the 'Speech at the Opening of the Mellstock Club' (ff. 562–4, revised), 41 leaves (rectos only) numbered 546–86, annotated (at the end) '[The rest is in small Note books of Memoranda beginning 1921.]' (see HrT 1686).

Described Taylor, pp. [203], 206–7; see *Life and Work*, pp. 493–544 *passim* (especially 542–3) for variants (this typescript designated 'MN3'); Microfilm Edition, Reel 7; for Hardy's 'Speech at the Opening of the Mellstock Club', see HrT 1566.

Dorset County Museum.

HrT 1449 Fragment of typescript of Chapters 35–6, some leaves top copy, some carbon copy, being a retyping made by FEH after Hardy's death, 36 leaves (rectos only) numbered 4, 6–12, 15, 13–39, including the final version of Hardy's 'Speech at the Opening of the Mellstock Club' (ff. 15–17).

Described Taylor, pp. [203], 207; see *Life and Work*, pp. 493–544 *passim* (especially 542–3) for variants (this typescript designated 'MNR'); Microfilm Edition, Reel 7; for Hardy's 'Speech at the Opening of the Mellstock Club', see HrT 1566.

Dorset County Museum.

HrT 1450 Typescript of Chapter 37, revised by FEH, 34 numbered leaves (rectos only), together with 9 leaves (rectos only) of additional material, including: (1) typescript of letter from Margaret Carter to R. L. Purdy, 19 July 1926, one page; (2) fair copy by FEH of the end of Chapter 37, 2 pages; (3) typescript of one unnumbered page, probably discarded; (4) typescript of letter from Hardy to Roy McKay, marked '*COPY*', of 27 April 1926, one page; (5) typescript, revised by Hardy, of letter from Hardy to St John

Ervine, 9 September 1926, one page; (6) typescript of letter from Hardy to Mr and Mrs Harley Granville Barker, 29 December 1926, one page.

All the letters by Hardy mentioned above were printed in Chapter 38; the letter to the Granville Barkers printed *Letters*, VII, 54 (from this typescript); for the letters to Roy McKay and St John Ervine, see also HrT 1508.5 and1509; mentioned Taylor, pp. [203], 207; Microfilm Edition, Reel 7.

Dorset County Museum.

HrT 1451 Two typescripts (top copy and carbon copy) of Chapter 37 (a different typing from HrT 1450), revised by FEH, 30 numbered leaves (rectos only).

Top copy only mentioned Taylor, pp. [203], 207; one typescript only in Microfilm Edition, Reel 8.

Dorset County Museum.

HrT 1452 Fair copy, revised, of Chapter 38, mostly in the hand of FEH, partly in an unidentified hand, 52 leaves (rectos only) numbered erratically, including two inserted typescript pages, one being a letter from Hardy to J. B. Priestley of 8 August 1926.

Mentioned Taylor, pp. [203], 207; the letter to Priestley is printed in *Life*, p. 439 where misdated 1927 (see also HrT 1510); Microfilm Edition, Reel 7.

Dorset County Museum.

HrT 1453 Two typescripts of Chapter 38 (different typings, one top copy, the other mostly carbon copy), both slightly revised by FEH, both 28 numbered leaves (rectos only).

Mentioned Taylor, pp. [203], 207; both typescripts in Microfilm Edition, Reel 8.

Dorset County Museum.

HrT 1454 Typescript, headed 'Extract from Mrs (Emma Lavinia) Hardy's papers,/entitled "Some Recollections".', revised by Hardy, 10 numbered leaves (rectos only).

This extract forms the opening of Chapter 5; mentioned Taylor, pp. [203]–4; Microfilm Edition, Reel 7; see also HrT 1812.

Dorset County Museum.

HrT 1455 MS by Godfrey Elton of a passage describing Hardy's visit to Oxford in 1923, quoted in Chapter 37, 3 leaves (rectos only).

This passge printed, with a few minor variants, in *Life*, pp. 420–2; mentioned Taylor, pp. [203]–4; Microfilm Edition, Reel 7.

Dorset County Museum.

HrT 1456 Typescript of Hardy's 'Dedication of the New Dorchester Grammar School' (see HrT 1393–4), headed 'Appendix I. Address/Delivered by/Thomas Hardy...', 4 numbered leaves (rectos only).

This typescript misdescribed in Taylor, p. [203] as being 'Appendix I' of *Life* (i.e., a note on Hardy's funeral); this address printed *Life*, pp. 437–9; Microfilm Edition, Reel 7.

Dorset County Museum.

HrT 1457 Transcript by FEH of the 3 letters to Dr Caleb Saleeby (included as Appendix II), 21 December 1914, 2 February 1915 and 16 March 1915.

The originals of the letters to Saleeby are listed as HrT 1493; the letter of 2 February was printed twice in *Life*, once in the body of the text (in a version much revised by Hardy) and once in Appendix II (apparently from a transcript of the original supplied by Dr Saleeby); mentioned Taylor, pp. [203], 207–8; Microfilm Edition, Reel 7.

Dorset County Museum.

HrT 1458 Typescript (carbon copy) of Appendix II (the 3 letters to Dr Caleb Saleeby as in HrT 1457), incomplete, wanting the first leaf, 5 leaves numbered 2–6 (rectos only).

Mentioned Taylor, pp. [203]–4, 207–8; Microfilm Edition, Reel 7.

Dorset County Museum.

HrT 1459 Partly autograph (first leaf) and the rest (ff. 2–5) typescript (carbon copy), revised by Hardy, headed 'Private Memorandum.' and beginning '*Information for Mrs Hardy in the preparation of a biography.*', 5 numbered leaves (rectos only).

This MS printed Taylor, pp. [288]–9; Microfilm Edition, Reel 7. An uncorrected typescript of the 'Memorandum' (3 leaves, rectos only) is owned by David Holmes; facsimile in British Library, RP 2146.

Dorset County Museum.

HrT 1460 Pencil notes by Hardy on the versos of 3 leaves (being subscription forms for the Royal Society of the Arts and an invitation to a show at Olympia of 22–30 October 1926) pasted together to form one single sheet, headed '*Insert in Materials.*'.

This MS printed Taylor, pp. 290–1; Microfilm Edition, Reel 7.

Dorset County Museum.

HrT 1461 Pencil note, headed '*H's altruism*'; on the verso of an envelope addressed to Hardy postmarked Philadelphia, 14 November 1927.

This MS printed Taylor, pp. 291–2; Microfilm Edition, Reel 7.

Dorset County Museum.

HrT 1462 Note, possibly autograph, possibly in the hand of FEH as dictated by Hardy, headed '(*Materials for Life of T. H.*)', suggesting a final chapter of 'Anecdotes & Reminiscences' left out of the body of the text; in an envelope (containing also HrT 340, 857) annotated by FEH 'Last lines dicated [sic] by T. H.…a pencilled note, by himself, about my biography'; [January 1928].

Mentioned *Life and Work*, pp. xvii–xviii; Microfilm Edition, Reel 6.

Dorset County Museum.

HrT 1463 Two notes in pencil, for insertion in the 'biography': one on Hardy's attitudes compared to Browning's, annotated 'For insertion in Life of T. H. if necessary'; the other being two passages included in *Later Years*.

The two *Later Years* passages also appear as typescript (carbon copy) strips pasted into 'Memoranda Notebook II' (HrT 1686); the note on Browning quoted in Millgate, p. [409].

Owned (1984) F. B. Adams (see *Life and Work*).

HrT 1464 FEH's personal diary, used for Chapters 37–8, 18 leaves (rectos only) in an exercise book; kept from 6 September–26 December 1927.

Passages from this diary not included in *Life* are printed in Taylor, pp. 292–4; Microfilm Edition, Reel 7.

Dorset County Museum.

HrT 1465 Two letters from J. M. Barrie to FEH containing suggested additions and revisions for *Life*; being Barrie's original of the first, dated 26 March 1928 (sent after reading the complete typescript), and a typed transcript of the second, dated 24 June 1928 (sent after reading the proofs of *Early Life*).

For a further discussion of Barrie's suggestions, see *Life and Work*, pp. xxi–xxii.

Dorset County Museum.

Originals of Hardy letters included in *Life*, autograph letters written from Max Gate unless stated otherwise:

HrT 1466 To Mary Hardy, Kilburn, 17 August [1862].

Printed *Life*, p. 38; this MS printed *Letters*, I, 1–2.

Dorset County Museum.

HrT 1467 To Mary Hardy, Kilburn, 19 February [1863], now divided into two parts.

Printed *Life*, pp. 39–40; this MS printed *Letters*, I, 3–4.

One part at Dorset County Museum, the

other owned (1978) Mrs H. O. Lock (see *Letters*).

HrT 1468 To Mary Hardy, 8 Adelphi Terrace, 19 December 1863.

Printed *Life*, pp. 40–1; this MS printed *Letters*, I, 5.

Campbell College, Belfast.

HrT 1469 To Mary Hardy, [no place], 28 October [1865].

Printed *Life*, pp. 51–2; facsimile in *Early Life*, between pp. 68 and 69; this MS printed *Letters*, I, 5–7.

Owned (1978) Mrs H. O. Lock (see *Letters*).

HrT 1470 To William Tinsley, Bockhampton, 20 December 1870.

Printed *Life*, p. 83; facsimile in A. E. Newton, *The Amenities of Book-Collecting* (Boston, 1918), p. [12]; this MS printed *Letters*, I, 10.

Owned (1978) F. B. Adams (see *Letters*).

HrT 1471 To Smith, Elder & Co., Upper Tooting, 1 October 1878.

Variant version of an extract printed *Life*, p. 122; this MS printed *Letters*, I, 61 (as owned by Mrs E. M. Gordon).

National Library of Scotland, MS 23173, f. 118r–v.

HrT 1472 To Frederick Locker, Upper Tooting, 2 February 1880.

Printed *Life*, pp. 133–4; this MS printed *Letters*, I, [69].

Texas.

HrT 1473 To the Rev. Handley Moule, Savile Club, 11 February 1880.

Printed *Life*, pp. 134–5; this MS printed *Letters*, I, 70.

Owned (1978) R. L. Purdy (see *Letters*); destined for Yale.

HrT 1474 To Mary Christie, Wimborne, 11 April 1883.

Variant version printed *Life*, p. 159; this MS printed *Letters*, I, 116–17.

Owned (1978) R. L. Purdy (see *Letters*); destined for Yale.

HrT 1475 Three letters to Edmund Gosse, 10 and 20 November 1895 and 4 January 1896.

Printed *Life*, pp. 271–3; these MSS printed *Letters*, II, 93–4, 99, 104–5.

British Library, Ashley MS A3357.

HrT 1476 Draft of the letter to [James Nimmo], Brighton, 16 May 1896.

Printed *Life*, pp. 276–7; this MS printed *Letters*, II, 119.

Dorset County Museum.

HrT 1477 To Jeannette Gilder, 16 July 1896.

Printed *Life*, pp. 279–80; facsimile in A. E Newton, *Thomas Hardy, Novelist or Poet?* (privately printed, Philadelphia, 1929); this MS printed *Letters*, II, 126–7.

Owned (1980) F. B. Adams (see *Letters*).

HrT 1478 To [Lewis Hind], 27 March 1897.

Extract printed *Life*, p. 286; this MS printed *Letters*, II, 155–6.

Berg.

HrT 1479 To A. C. Swinburne, 1 April 1897.

Printed *Life*, p. 287; facsimile in *Ashley Library*, II, following p. 68; this MS printed *Letters*, II, 158–9.

British Library, Ashley MS 847.

HrT 1480 Pencil draft of the letter to [Charles Hooper], 2 July 1899.

Extract printed *Life*, p. 304; this MS printed *Letters*, II, 223.

Dorset County Museum.

HrT 1481 To Frederic Chapman, 10 June 1900, postmarked 19 June.

Printed *Life*, pp. 309–10; this MS printed *Letters*, II, 290.

Mount Saint Vincent University.

HrT 1482 Pencil draft of the letter to the Rev. J. Alexander Smith, [early November 1900].

Printed *Life*, p. 307; this MS printed *Letters*, II, 272.

Dorset County Museum.

HrT 1483 To Dr Arnold Cervesato, 20 June 1901.

Printed *Life*, p. 310; not in *Letters*.

Yale.

HrT 1484 To the Rev. S. Whittell Key, 2 March 1904.

Variant version printed *Life*, pp. 321–2 (possibly from the revised draft of the letter owned (1982) R. L. Purdy, destined for Yale); this MS printed *Letters*, III, 110.

Princeton, Robert H. Taylor Collection.

HrT 1485 To Edward Clodd, 22 March 1904.

Printed *Life*, pp. 320–1; this MS printed *Letters*, III, 116–17.

British Library, Ashley MS A3359.

HrT 1486 To ['Clive Holland', i.e., Charles James Hankinson], 5 November 1905.

Variant version printed *Life*, p. 327; this MS printed *Letters*, III, 186.

Owned (1982) F. B. Adams (see *Letters*).

HrT 1487 To Clement Shorter, 24 January 1906.

Extract printed *Life*, p. 37; this MS printed *Letters*, III, 194.

Princeton, Robert H. Taylor Collection.

HrT 1488 Draft of the letter to Edward Wright, 2 June 1907.

Variant version printed *Life*, pp. 334–5; this MS printed *Letters*, III, 255–6.

Dorset County Museum.

HrT 1489 Three letters to Edward Clodd, New Year's Eve 1907, 20 February 1908 and 28 August 1914.

Printed *Life*, Appendix III, pp. 453–4; these MSS printed *Letters*, III, 287, 298 and V, 44.

British Library, Ashley MS A3359.

HrT 1490 To Robert Donald, 10 May 1908.

Printed *Life*, pp. 341–2; this MS printed *Letters*, III, 313.

Owned (1982) Shirley Hazzard (see *Letters*).

HrT 1491 Draft of the letter to Maurice Hewlett, 9 June 1909.

Variant version printed *Life*, p. 346; this MS printed *Letters*, IV, 27–8.

Dorset County Museum.

HrT 1492 Typed draft of the letter to Henry Stainsby, 6 July 1913.

Extract printed *Life*, p. 362; this MS printed *Letters*, IV, 284–5.

Dorset County Museum.

HrT 1493 Three letters to Dr Caleb Saleeby, 21 December 1914, 2 February 1915 and 16 March 1915.

Variant version (possibly from the draft at Dorset County Museum) of 2 February letter printed *Life*, pp. 369–70; all three letters printed (apparently from transcripts of the originals supplied by Dr Saleeby) in *Life*, Appendix II, pp. 449–52; these MSS printed *Letters*, V, 69–70, 78–9, 84–5; see also HrT 1457–8.

Owned (1985) F. B. Adams (see *Letters*).

HrT 1494 Typescript letter to Secretary of the Royal Society of Literature (i.e., Percy Ames), 8 February 1917.

Variant version printed *Life*, pp. 374–5; this MS printed *Letters*, V, 202.

Royal Society of Literature.

HrT 1495 Pencil draft of the letter to Dr Leon Litwinski, 7 March 1917.

Printed *Life*, p. 375; this MS printed *Letters*, V, 206–7.

Dorset County Museum.

HrT 1496 To J. M. Barrie, 23 June 1917.

Printed *Life*, p. 377; this MS printed

Letters, V, 220–1.

Colby College.

HrT 1497 To David Robertson, 7 February 1918.

Variant version (possibly from Hardy's pencil draft at Dorset County Museum) printed *Life*, p. 385; a transcript of this letter (owned R. L. Purdy, destined for Yale) printed *Letters*, V, 250–1.

Owned (1985) D. A. Robertson, Jr.

HrT 1498 Pencil draft of the letter to Arnold Bennett, 8 September 1918.

Variant version of extract printed *Life*, p. 387; this MS printed *Letters*, V, 278.

Dorset County Museum.

HrT 1499 To Florence Henniker, 5 June 1919.

Printed *Life*, p. 389; this MS printed *Letters*, V, 309–10.

Dorset County Museum.

HrT 1500 To Bishop Handley Moule, 29 June 1919.

Printed *Life*, pp. 390–1; this MS printed *Letters*, V, 315–16.

Dorset County Museum.

HrT 1500.5 Pencil draft in the hand of FEH of a letter to Archie Whitfield, [early November 1919].

Extract (misdated by Whitfield's letter of 30 October 1919) printed *Life*, p. 392; this MS printed *Letters*, VII, 161.

Dorset County Museum.

HrT 1501 Typescript letter to Maurice Colbourne, 11 December 1919.

Extract (misdated 11 November as is Hardy's pencil draft at Dorset County Museum) printed *Life*, pp. 392–3; this MS printed *Letters*, V, 347–8.

Owned (1985) R. L. Purdy (see *Letters*); destined for Yale.

HrT 1502 Pencil draft of the letter to [Anita Dudley], 30 December 1919.

Extract printed *Life*, pp. 395–6; this MS printed *Letters*, V, 352–3.

Dorset County Museum.

HrT 1503 Draft of the letter to G. Herbert Thring, 23 August 1920.

Printed *Life*, pp. 406–7; this MS printed *Letters*, VI, 37.

Dorset County Museum.

HrT 1504 Typescript letter to Alfred Noyes, 13 December 1920.

Printed *Life*, pp. 407–8; this MS printed *Letters*, VI, 52.

Princeton, Robert H. Taylor Collection.

HrT 1505 Typescript letter to Alfred Noyes, 20 December 1920.

Variant version (dated 19 December) printed *Life*, pp. 408–9; this MS printed *Letters*, VI, 53–5.

Princeton, Robert H. Taylor Collection.

HrT 1506 To J. H. Morgan, 12 October 1922.

Printed *Life*, pp. 417–18; this MS printed *Letters*, VI, 161–2.

Berg.

HrT 1507 To John Galsworthy, 20 April 1923.

Extract printed *Life*, p. 419; this MS printed *Letters*, VI, 192.

Deposited (1987) University of Birmingham.

HrT 1508 Typescript letter to Harold Child, 11 November 1923.

Extract printed *Life*, pp. 422–3; this MS printed *Letters*, VI, 221–2; Hardy's pencil draft of this letter was presented to Child by FEH after Hardy's death and a carbon copy typescript of it is inserted in 'Memoranda Notebook II' (HrT 1686).

Owned (1987) F. B. Adams (see *Letters*).

HrT 1508.5 Pencil draft of letter to Roy McKay, 27 April 1926.

Printed *Life*, p. 431; for a transcript, see

HrT 1450; this MS printed *Letters*, VII, 21.

Dorset County Museum.

HrT 1508.7 Typescript letter to Arthur M. Hind, 22 May 1926.

Extract printed *Life*, p. 432; this MS printed *Letters*, VII, 24.

Owned (1988) Dennis O'Malley (see *Letters*).

HrT 1509 To St John Ervine, 9 September 1926.

Printed *Life*, p. 433; for a typed transcript, see HrT 1450; Hardy's pencil draft of this letter is at Dorset County Museum; this MS printed *Letters*, VII, 41–2.

Texas.

HrT 1510 To J. B. Priestley, 8 August 1926.

Extract printed *Life*, p. 439 (where misdated 1927); for a transcript, see HrT 1452; this MS printed *Letters*, VII, 38–9.

Texas.

The Life and Death of the Mayor of Casterbridge, see HrT 1514–15.

Life's Little Ironies
This collection of stories first pub. London 1894. For a description of corrected proof for first edition (Life's Little Ironies Proof), see INTRODUCTION; contents have been listed individually. For MSS of stories, see HrT 1410–11, 1415, 1516–17, 1531, 1563, 1589. For the Prefatory Note, see HrT 1548.

Louis Napoleon, and the Poet Barnes
First pub. as a 'Postscript' (on an unpaginated leaf inserted at the last moment) in F. H. Cheetham, *Louis Napoleon and the Genesis of the Second Empire* (London, 1909); Purdy, p. 312; mentioned Orel, p. 251. A brief version was printed in *Early Life*, pp. 229–30 from an entry of 17 October 1885 in a diary presumably now destroyed.

HrT 1511 Fair copy, signed (initials), beginning 'When the Rev[d] William Barnes...', 3 pages (one leaf), enclosed in a letter to John Lane, 4 September 1908.

Letter printed *Letters*, III, 330 from the original at Texas.

Texas.

M. Maeterlinck's Apology for Nature
First pub. as letter to the editor in *Academy and Literature*, 17 May 1902, reprinted in *Later Years* (1930), pp. 97–8; Purdy, p. 271.

HrT 1511.5 Clipping of the first publication, revised by Hardy, in Scrapbook I (HrT 1687).

Microfilm Edition, Reel 6.

Dorset County Museum.

The Marchioness of Stonehenge
First pub. *The Graphic*, Christmas Number 1890, as 'A Group of Noble Dames: II. Lady Caroline (Afterwards Marchioness of Stonehenge)'; collected *A Group of Noble Dames* (London, 1891), as 'Dame the Third'; Wessex Edition, XIV (1912), 93–111; Purdy, p. 63.

HrT 1512 Fair copy, revised, here entitled 'The Lady Caroline/afterwards Marchioness of Stonehenge.', in MS Group of Noble Dames, 20 leaves (rectos only) numbered 54–73).

Library of Congress, Manuscript Division, Thomas Hardy Collection.

Master John Horseleigh, Knight
First pub. *Illustrated London News*, 12 June 1893; collected *A Changed Man* (1913); Wessex Edition, XVIII (1914), 229–44; Pinion, II, [360]–71; Purdy, p. 153.

HrT 1513 Fair copy, revised, here entitled 'Sir John Horseleigh, Knight', 15 numbered leaves (rectos only), printer's copy for first publication.

This MS described Purdy, p. 155.

Texas.

The Mayor of Casterbridge
First pub. serially *The Graphic*, 2 January–15 May

1886; first pub. separate edition, 2 vols, London, 1886; Wessex Edition, V (1912); Purdy, pp. 50–4. For a recent edition, see *The Mayor of Casterbridge*, ed. Dale Kramer (Oxford, 1987). For Hardy's dramatization, see HrT 1646; for source material, see HrT 1679.

HrT 1514 Partly fair copy, revised, partly draft, a few lines only in the hand of ELH, signed, incomplete, c. 407 pages of text on 374 leaves (mostly rectos only) numbered originally 1–479 (but wanting 108 numbered leaves and including 3 leaves numbered 116a–b, 133a), printer's copy for first serial publication, annotated on last page '(Written 1884–1885.)'.

For discussions and facsimile pages, see Dieter Riesner, 'Kunstprosa in der Werkstatt' in *Festschrift für Walter Hübner*, ed. Dieter Riesner and Helmut Gneuss (Berlin, 1964), pp. 267–326 (facsimiles of ff. 17, 111, 130, 174, 193, 220, 428); Christine Winfield, 'The Manuscript of Hardy's *Mayor of Casterbridge*', *PBSA*, 67 (1973), 33–58 (two facsimile pages); see also Purdy, pp. 52–3; Microfilm Edition, Reel 2. This MS presented to Dorset County Museum in 1911.

Dorset County Museum.

HrT 1515 Revisions (including corrections to the Scots language in another hand, probably that of Sir George Douglas), in a copy of Sampson, Low's Half-Crown Edition [n.d.] used for preparing the revised Osgood, McIlvaine edition of the Wessex Novels (London, 1895).

This volume described Purdy, p. 54n.

Owned (1987) R. L. Purdy (see Kramer's edition, p. [337]); destined for Yale.

The Melancholy Hussar of the German Legion
First pub. *Bristol Times and Mirror*, 4 and 11 January 1890, as 'The Melancholy Hussar'; collected *Life's Little Ironies* (1894); transferred to *Wessex Tales* in Wessex Edition, IX (1912), 43–66; Pinion, I, [40]–55; Purdy, p. 82.

HrT 1516 Draft of first 3 pages (numbered 1–3), containing variants from the published version, here entitled 'The Melancholy Hussar/The Corporal in the German Legion', signed, dated October 1889; accompanied by a letter to Charles Aldrich, Max Gate, 31 December 1889.

For a reproduction, see FACSIMILES; letter to Aldrich printed *Letters*, VII, 112; this MS not mentioned Purdy.

Iowa State Historical Library.

HrT 1517 Fair copy, here entitled 'The Melancholy Hussar', 27 leaves (rectos only), printer's copy for first publication.

This MS mentioned Purdy, p. 84.

Huntington, HM 7.

HrT 1518 Corrected galley proof in Life's Little Ironies Proof; date stamped 14–16 December 1893.

Dorset County Museum.

HrT 1519 Pencil footnote (including a clipping from *The Times* of 6 July 1801) added to this story in DCM Wessex Edition (IX, 66), annotated '[The note need not be inserted, unless wanted for any special edition.]'

Dorset County Museum.

HrT 1520 Fair copy of a note regarding this story, beginning '"The Melancholy Hussar" is largely founded on fact...', on a card (recto only); dated 16 August 1907.

Grolier Catalogue, Item 108.

Texas.

The Mellstock Quire, for this dramatization of *Under the Greenwood Tree*, see DRAMATIC WORKS.

Memories of Church Restoration
This paper was read at the General Meeting of the Society for the Protection of Ancient Buildings by Colonel Eustace Balfour, 20 June 1906. First pub. *The Society for the Protection of Ancient Buildings.... Twenty-Ninth Annual Report...and Paper Read by Thomas Hardy, Esq. June, 1906* (London, 1906); reprinted *Cornhill*, August 1906; Orel, pp. 203–18; Purdy, p. 311.

HrT 1521 Fair copy, revised, signed, 20 numbered leaves (rectos only); dated April 1906.

Texas.

HrT 1522 Corrected galley proof for *Cornhill*, 5 numbered galleys.

This proof not mentioned Purdy.

Texas.

HrT 1523 Corrected copy of the first publication, 22 printed pages numbered 59–80.

This is presumably the copy that Hardy prepared for the projected collected volume of 'Miscellanea'; see INTRODUCTION.

Owned (1982) David Holmes.

A Mere Interlude, for a lost MS, see INTRODUCTION.

Miscellanea, for a projected volume of collected non-fictional prose writings, see INTRODUCTION.

The Mistress of the Farm, for Hardy's dramatization of *Far from the Madding Crowd*, see HrT 1643.

[Notes for Hermann Lea]
Hermann Lea published two books about Hardy's Wessex: *A Handbook to the Wessex Country of Thomas Hardy* (London and Bournemouth, [1906]) and *Thomas Hardy's Wessex* (London, 1913) (for Hardy's annotated copy of the latter, see HrT 1847.5); see also Hardy's letters to Lea (at Dorset County Museum) printed in *Letters*, *passim* and Hynes, II, Appendix B 'Hardy's Notes for Hermann Lea', pp. 525–8.

HrT 1523.5 List, identifying Wessex locations in *Wessex Poems*, *Poems of the Past and the Present* and *The Dynasts*, in a letter to Hermann Lea, 6 October 1904.

This MS printed *Letters*, III, 137–8.

Dorset County Museum.

HrT 1523.7 Corrections to a MS submitted by Hermann Lea to Hardy, in a letter to Lea, 1 June 1905.

This MS printed *Letters*, III, 171–2.

Dorset County Museum.

HrT 1524 Two lists identifying Wessex locations in *Satires of Circumstance*, *Moments of Vision*, *Time's Laughingstocks, and Late Lyrics*, one headed 'A Supplementary Chapter to Mr Lea's book may contain some of the following additional illustrations', the other 'Places (of Poem-scenes)'.

These lists printed in Hynes, II, Appendix B.

Owned (1984) R. L. Purdy (see Hynes); destined for Yale.

[Notes identifying Wessex place-names]
First printed (facsimile) A. E. Newton, *Thomas Hardy, Novelist or Poet?* (privately printed, Philadelphia, 1929), following p. 32; see also HrT 1895.

HrT 1525 Five numbered pages in ELH's hand, revised by Hardy and headed by him '(*The Wessex Novels.*)', including an additional leaf (2 pages) of Hardy's rough notes; as sent to Bertram Windle for his use in preparing a new edition of Murray's *Handbook for Residents and Travellers in Wilts and Dorset*, enclosed in a letter dated from Brussels, 28 September 1896 (the additional leaf possibly sent at another time).

Facsimile printed as above; MS and letter printed *Letters*, II, 131–4 (without additional leaf).

Owned (1980) R. L. Purdy (see *Letters*); destined for Yale.

[Notes on Cerne Giant]
First pub. *Letters*, VI (1987), 355; not in Purdy.

HrT 1526 Note confirming that the Cerne Giant had always been drawn in outline, beginning 'The Cerne Giant's figure...', signed (initials), among papers of Sir Henry and Lady Hoare (from Stourhead); [21

September 1925].

Letters describes this as having been sent to Lady Hoare with a covering note by FEH (at Dorset County Museum) in which she says she is enclosing the requested 'few lines'.

Wiltshire Record Office, Stourhead Papers, 383/954.

[Notes on Harold Child's Book]
First pub. *Letters*, VI (1987), 292–4. The first edition of Child's *Thomas Hardy* was published London, 1916; the revised edition in 1925.

HrT 1527 Typescript of notes and suggested revisions to the first edition of Child's book (all adopted in the 1925 edition), headed '"*T. H. by Harold Child.*"/ *ERRATA, & MEMORANDA.*', 2 leaves; sent to Child enclosed in a letter of 9 December 1924.

This MS and letter printed *Letters* (cited above); Hardy's pencil draft of these notes, one leaf, is inserted in his copy of the first edition of Child's book at Dorset County Museum.

Owned (1987) F. B. Adams (see *Letters*).

[Notes on J. H. Fowler's Introduction to Hardy's Novels]
Fowler's Introduction appeared in Macmillan's 'Indian' editions of Hardy's *Far from the Madding Crowd*, *The Mayor of Casterbridge*, *The Return of the Native* and *The Trumpet-Major*.

HrT 1527.3 List of suggested revisions, one leaf, enclosed in a letter to J. H. Fowler, 19 January 1925.

The letter printed *Letters*, VII, 163–4.

Clifton College.

Notes on Professor Chew's Book
First pub. *Letters*, VI (1987) 153–7. The first edition of Samuel Chew's *Thomas Hardy, Poet and Novelist* was published Bryn Mawr, 1921; the revised edition in 1928.

HrT 1527.5 Typescript of notes and suggestions for the first edition of Chew's book (incorporated into the 1928 edition), headed 'Notes on Professor Chew's Book', signed by FEH, sent to Chew with a letter of 17 September 1927.

These notes were based on Hardy's annotations in a copy of Chew's first edition (HrT 1754); this MS and letter printed *Letters* (cited above); Hardy's pencil draft of the letter and the carbon copy of the 'Notes' are in Dorset County Museum.

Owned (1987) F. B. Adams (see *Letters*).

Notes on Stinsford Church
First pub. *Letters*, IV (1984), 18–20. Hardy sent 'copies' of this 'letter' to all members of the Stinsford Church Restoration Committee.

HrT 1528 Original typescript, containing sketch, corrections, valediction and signature in Hardy's hand, 4 pages, headed 'Notes on Stinsford Church' and including letter to the Stinsford Church Restoration Committee, dated Athenaeum Club, Pall Mall, [25*] April 1909.

*An extant envelope (addressed to the Rev. Cyril P. Wix), at Princeton, Robert H. Taylor Collection, is postmarked 25 April 1909. *Letters*, IV, 20n says other 'copies' are owned by F. B. Adams and Dorset County Museum (the latter being a carbon copy of HrT 1528) also containing Hardy's autograph sketch, corrections, valediction and signature.

Owned (1984) C. J. P. Beatty (see *Letters*).

Old Mrs Chundle
First pub. *Ladies' Home Journal* (Philadelphia), February 1929; reprinted Pinion, III, [11]–18; Purdy, pp. 267–8.

HrT 1529 Revised, 13 numbered leaves (rectos only), annotated at end '[Copied from the original rough draft]' and '(Written about 1888–1890. Probably at one time intended to be included in the volume entitled "Life's Little Ironies", or "Wessex Tales".)'.

This MS described Purdy, p. 267; Microfilm Edition, Reel 5.

Dorset County Museum.

HrT 1530 Typescript, 15 pages.

Owned (1982) David Holmes.

On the Western Circuit
First pub. *Harper's Weekly* (USA), 28 November 1891 and *English Illustrated Magazine*, December 1891; collected *Life's Little Ironies* (1894); Wessex Edition, VIII (1912), 107–37; Pinion, II, [85]–106; Purdy, pp. 81–2.

HrT 1531 Fair copy, revised in ink and pencil, containing two cancelled titles ('The Amanuensis' and 'The Writer of the Letters'), 33 numbered leaves (rectos only), printer's copy for first publication, annotated at top '[Life's Little Ironies]'.

This MS described Purdy, pp. 83–4.

Manchester Central Library, MS.Q.823.892.U3.4.

HrT 1531.5 Typescript, revised, originally entitled '<The Writer of the Letters>', 43 pages (one entirely in Hardy's hand).

Facsimile of a portion of a page in Sotheby's sale catalogue, 15 December 1988, p. 55; facsimile in British Library, RP 4044.

Owned (1988) David Holmes.

HrT 1532 Corrected galley proof in Life's Little Ironies Proof; date stamped 8–12 December 1893.

Dorset County Museum.

Outlines for Stories: A–F
First pub. Evelyn Hardy, 'Plots for Five Unpublished Short Stories', *London Magazine*, 5 (1958), 35–45; reprinted Pinion, III, [117]–28; not in Purdy.

HrT 1533 Outline A: notes for a projected story, 4 pages (one leaf); dated (later, by Hardy) [31 October] 1871.

Microfilm Edition, Reel 5.

Dorset County Museum.

HrT 1534 Outline B: notes for a projected story, headed 'Scheme of short story', in pencil, one page; c. 1909–19.

Microfilm Edition, Reel 5.

Dorset County Museum.

HrT 1535 Outline C: notes for a projected story, entitled 'How I Won at Monte-Carlo', in pencil, on an envelope addressed to Hardy postmarked 21 March 1916.

Microfilm Edition, Reel 5.

Dorset County Museum.

HrT 1536 Outline D: notes for a projected story, entitled 'The Vauxhall Fiddler', 4 pages (3 leaves stuck together), containing a list of alternative titles including 'The Morning Hymn', 'An incident in the Life of Barthélémon' and 'The Bandmaster at the Dancing Rooms', in pencil; dated 1909.

Microfilm Edition, Reel 5.

Dorset County Museum.

HrT 1537 Outline E: two draft versions of a projected story, in pencil: (1) draft, headed 'Sparrow story' and annotated 'Form I', 4 pages (one leaf), including alternative titles 'The mistaken symbol' and 'For want of a word'; (2) draft, headed 'For want of a word', annotated 'Form II', 2 pages (one leaf).

Microfilm Edition, Reel 5.

Dorset County Museum.

HrT 1538 Outline F: draft notes for a projected story, headed 'The Sparrow', 3 pages (one leaf).

Microfilm Edition, Reel 5.

Dorset County Museum.

A Pair of Blue Eyes
First pub. serially *Tinsleys' Magazine*, September 1872–June 1873; first separate edition in 3 vols (London, 1873); Wessex Edition, X (1912); revised in Mellstock Edition, XVI–XVII (1920); Purdy, pp. 8–13. For a recent edition, see *A Pair of Blue Eyes*, ed. Alan Manford (Oxford, 1985). For Hardy's

dramatization, see HrT 1648. For lists of corrections for the Mellstock Edition, see INTRODUCTION. Hardy's original sketch for the second instalment of the first publication is at Princeton, Robert H. Taylor Collection, with a letter to William Tinsley of 30 August [1872] (printed *Letters*, I, 18).

HrT 1539 Fair copy, revised, of Chapters 1–8 and 15–18, including [p. 1] title page and (p. 2) 'Names of the persons', containing insertions and a few passages in the hand of Emma Lavinia Gifford (later ELH), 163 leaves (mostly rectos only) numbered [1]–112 (plus 36a, 44a, 65a, 106a), 212–58 (plus 212a and a second 238) and wanting pp. 63 and 243, printer's copy for first publication (representing instalments for September, October and January).

This MS discussed in Purdy, pp. 10–11 and Suleiman M. Ahmad, 'Emma Hardy and the MS of "A Pair of Blue Eyes"', *N&Q*, 224 (1979), 320–2. Facsimile pages in Hodgson's sale catalogue, 16 April 1926 (Mrs John Lane Sale) (one page from Chapter 1) and Anderson Galleries sale catalogue, 7–10 January 1929 (Kern Sale), p. 206 (p. 64). This MS apparently included a fourth instalment when it was owned by John Lane in 1923 (see Taylor, p. 66).

Berg.

HrT 1540 Revisions on pp. 24, 71 and 102 (others erased), in pencil and red pencil, in a copy of the Mellstock Edition (a set also including HrT 1612); annotated on front flyleaf '[The proofs were not read further than p. 48 of this vol.]' and 'Errata–/pp. 24/71/102'.

Colby College.

HrT 1541 Corrections, clippings from a copy of the second edition pasted over passages, and a page headed '*Notes* —' on front flyleaf (dated 1924) explaining the corrections, in DCM Wessex Edition (X).

This copy discussed in Suleiman M. Ahmad, 'Thomas Hardy's Last Revision of *A Pair of Blue Eyes*', *PBSA*, 72 (1978), 109–12.

Dorset County Museum.

***Poems of Rural Life in the Dorset Dialect* by William Barnes**

First pub. anonymously *New Quarterly Magazine*, October 1879; some parts re-used in Hardy's obituary of Barnes in *The Athenaeum*, 16 October 1886, as 'The Rev. William Barnes, B.D.' and one paragraph in *Tess of the d'Urbervilles*, Chapter 2; Orel, pp. 94–100; Purdy, p. 295.

HrT 1542 Corrected galley proof, 7 pages numbered 11–17.

This is possibly the copy sent with materials for the projected collected volume of 'Miscellanea'; see INTRODUCTION.

Owned (1982) David Holmes.

The Poor Man and the Lady, for a lost MS, see INTRODUCTION and HrT 1595.

Preface to *A Book of Remembrance*

First pub. *A Book of Remembrance, Being a short Summary of the Service and Sacrifice Rendered to the Empire during the Great War by one of the many Patriotic Families of Wessex, the Popes of Wrackleford, Co. Dorset* (privately printed, London, 1919); Orel, pp. 85–6; Purdy, p. 320.

HrT 1543 Fair copy; c. September 1918.

Owned (1989) Christopher Pope.

Preface to *Dorchester (Dorset), and its Surroundings*

First pub. F. R. and Sidney Heath, *Dorchester (Dorset), and its Surroundings* (Dorchester and London, 1905–6); Orel, pp. 65–6; Purdy, p. 310. For Hardy's corrections in a copy of the first publication, see HrT 1818.

HrT 1544 Fair copy, revised, headed 'Foreword.', signed, one page.

Texas.

Preface to *Late Lyrics*, see HrT 673–673.5.

Preface to *Poems of the Past and the Present*, see HrT 926.

Preface to *Select Poems of William Barnes*, see HrT 1560.

Preface to the Poems of 'Laurence Hope'
No publication traced; not in Purdy. For Hardy's obituary of 'Laurence Hope', see HrT 1440.

HrT 1545 Typescript of Preface written for Laurence Hope's *Indian Love* (London, 1905) but not published there, here entitled 'Preface [to the posthumous poems of Laurence Hope. Written by request]' and beginning 'The pages which follow contain the last productions in verse of...', signed, 3 pages and title page (4 leaves), annotated 'The only copy supplied by Mrs Crackanthorpe' and, in an unidentified hand, 'Proof to, Thomas Hardy...(never published)'; c. spring 1905.

Microfilm Edition, Reel 5; Hardy's letter to William Heinemann of 16 July 1905, enquiring why the Preface had not been published, was printed *Letters*, VII, 140 (from the original at Eton College).

Dorset County Museum.

Preface to the Wessex Edition, see HrT 1419–20.

Preface to *Time's Laughingstocks*, see HrT 1174.5.

Preface to *Wessex Poems*, see HrT 1296.5.

Preface to *Wessex Tales*
First pub. *Wessex Tales* (London: Osgood, McIlvaine, 1896); Wessex Edition, IX (1912). For lists of corrections for the Mellstock Edition, see INTRODUCTION.

HrT 1546 Revision and pencil addition (slightly erased, signed (initials) and dated June 1919) in DCM Wessex Edition (IX, vii and x), also containing (inserted) the preliminary 8 pages of the Uniform Edition, Vol. XIII (London, 1911) including half-title, title page, Preface and Table of Contents, extensively corrected and revised by Hardy for the Wessex Edition.

Dorset County Museum.

Preface to 'William Barnes'
First pub. in the William Barnes section of *The English Poets*, ed. T. H. Ward, Vol. V (London, 1918), pp. [174]–6; Orel, pp. 82–5; Purdy, pp. 319–20. This essay drew on Hardy's earlier Preface to his edition of *Select Poems of William Barnes* (London, 1908), see HrT 1560.

HrT 1547 Typescript, revised, 5 pages, annotated in an unidentified hand.

Facsimile in British Library, RP 2146; this is presumably the copy that Hardy prepared for the projected collected volume of 'Miscellanea' (see INTRODUCTION).

Owned (1982) David Holmes.

Preface to *Winter Words*, see HrT 1338.

Prefatory Note to *Life's Little Ironies*
First pub. Wessex Edition, VIII (1912). For lists of corrections to the Mellstock Edition, see INTRODUCTION.

HrT 1548 Revisions in DCM Wessex Edition (VIII, vii).

Dorset County Museum.

Recollections of 'Leader Scott'
First pub. as a letter to the editor in *Dorset County Chronicle* and *The Times*, 27 November 1902; Purdy, p. 308.

HrT 1549 Clipping of the first publication (*Dorset County Chronicle*), revised and annotated by Hardy, in Scrapbook I (HrT 1687).

Microfilm Edition, Reel 6.

Dorset County Museum.

A Reply to Critics
First pub. *Manchester Guardian*, 13 October 1914, as a letter to the editor; reprinted *Letters on the War*

(privately printed by Clement Shorter, 1914) and *The Life and Art of Thomas Hardy*, ed. Ernest Brennecke (New York, 1925); Purdy, pp. 159–60; mentioned Orel, p. 253.

HrT 1550 Draft, one page, in Scrapbook I (HrT 1687), headed '[To the Editor of the Manchester Guardian]'.

Microfilm Edition, Reel 6.

Dorset County Museum.

The Return of the Native

First pub. serially *Belgravia*, January–December 1878; first pub. separate edition in 3 vols (London, 1878); Wessex Edition, IV (1912); Purdy, pp. 24–7. For a discussion of the textual changes between the first serial publication and the Wessex Edition, see Otis B. Wheeler, 'Four Versions of *The Return of the Native*', *NCF*, 14 (1959–60), 27–44. For Hardy's extensive use of his commonplace book 'Literary Notes I' (HrT 1678), see Björk, I, xxiii (especially n17). Hardy's surviving letters to the illustrator Arthur Hopkins (one containing sketches by Hardy) are now at University of California at Berkeley and printed *Letters*, I, 52–5, 59; facsimile of the sketches in Purdy, facing p. 25. For lists of corrections for Mellstock Edition, see INTRODUCTION. For a dramatization, see HrT 1653–5. For the epigraph from Keats's *Endymion*, see HrT 1839.

HrT 1551 Fair copy, revised, including 7 pages in the hand of ELH, 439 leaves (rectos only) numbered 1–429 and some unnumbered, printer's copy for the first serial publication.

For a complete facsimile (and discussion), see *The Thomas Hardy Archive: 2. The Return of the Native*, ed. Simon Gatrell (New York and London, 1986); Microfilm Edition, Reel 15. For discussion and facsimile pages, see John Paterson, *The Making of The Return of the Native* (Berkeley and Los Angeles, 1960), Dieter Riesner, 'Über die Genesis von Thomas Hardy's *The Return of the Native*', *Archiv für das Studium der Neueren Sprachen und Litteraturen*, 200 (1963), 398–404 and Simon Gatrell, *Hardy the Creator: a textual biography* (Oxford, 1988), pp. 29–51. This MS described in Purdy, pp. 26–7; given by Hardy in 1908 to Clement Shorter who bequeathed it to University College Dublin.

University College Dublin, MS 11.

HrT 1552 'Sketch Map of the Scene of the Story.', probably the map used by Hardy while writing the novel.

Facsimile printed *The Return of the Native*, ed. James Gindin (New York, 1969), in David Daiches and John Flower, *Literary Landscapes of the British Isles* (New York and London, 1979), in Millgate, plate 25 and in *The Thomas Hardy Archive: 2. The Return of the Native*, ed. Simon Gatrell (New York and London, 1986), p. 487. Another copy of this map enclosed in a letter of 1 October 1878 from Hardy to Smith, Elder & Co. (letter now at National Library of Scotland, MS 23173, f. 118r–v, printed *Letters*, I, 61 as owned Mrs E. M. Gordon) was used as copy for frontispiece for the first three-volume and the 1880 editions of the novel.

Dorset County Museum.

HrT 1553 Corrections in DCM Wessex Edition (IV, viii and 319).

Facsimile in *The Thomas Hardy Archive: 2. Return of the Native*, ed. Simon Gatrell (New York and London, 1986), pp. 491–3.

Dorset County Museum.

The Rev. William Barnes, B.D., see HrT 1542.

Rheims Cathedral

First pub. simultaneously *Manchester Guardian* and *Daily News*, 7 October 1914, as a letter to the editor; reprinted *Letters on the War* (privately printed by Clement Shorter, 1914) and *The Life and Art of Thomas Hardy*, ed. Ernest Brennecke (New York, 1925); Purdy, pp. 159–60; mentioned Orel, pp. 252–3.

HrT 1554 Draft (originally begun as personal letter to Sydney Cockerell), 2 pages, together with a typescript made later (according to Purdy, at Cockerell's request and annotated by him).

This MS described Purdy, p. 159 as owned by Sydney Cockerell.

Princeton, Robert H. Taylor Collection.

HrT 1555 Printed clipping of first publication in *Daily News*, revised by Hardy for use in *Letters on the War*.

This item mentioned Purdy, p. 159.

Dorset County Museum.

Robert Louis Stevenson
First pub. as Hardy's contribution to *I Can Remember Robert Louis Stevenson*, ed. Rosalind Masson (Edinburgh and London, 1922); brief version in *Early Life*, pp. 229, 235, 237; Orel, pp. 149–51; Purdy, p. 321.

HrT 1555.5 Draft.

This MS mentioned Purdy, p. 321.

Dorset County Museum (in an envelope containing Robert Louis Stevenson letters).

HrT 1556 Typescript, revised, beginning 'The memories I have of Louis Stevenson...', 2 numbered leaves (rectos only), enclosed in a letter to John Purves (f. 28) giving him and 'the Committee' permission to publish, 21 May 1922.

The letter printed *Letters*, VII, 163.

National Library of Scotland, MS 15561, ff. 29–30.

The Romantic Adventures of a Milkmaid
First pub. *The Graphic*, 25 June 1883; collected *A Changed Man* (1913); Wessex Edition, XVIII (1914), 297–[399]; Pinion, II, [409]–87; Purdy, pp. 47–8. For a dramatization, see HrT 1656.

HrT 1557 Fair copy, revised, including 3 pages (and two additions on blank versos) in the hand of ELH, signed, 116 leaves (mostly rectos only) numbered 1–14, 14a, 15–115, printer's copy for the first publication.

Facsimile of f. 23 in *British Literary Manuscripts*, plate 95; this MS described Purdy, p. 48 and discussed in Simon Gatrell, *Hardy the Creator: a textual biography* (Oxford, 1988), pp. 71–3. Hardy sold this MS to Pierpont Morgan in March 1912.

Pierpont Morgan, MA 820.

HrT 1558 Revision on p. 87 of a copy of the Seaside Library Pocket Edition (New York, 1884), annotated inside front cover 'First edition — (pirated.)'.

Dorset County Museum.

HrT 1559 Note, in pencil, dated September 1927, added to end of story in DCM Wessex Edition (XVIII, 399).

This note printed Millgate, *Career*, p. 283.

Dorset County Museum.

Saturday Night in Arcady, see HrT 1570–3.

Select Poems of William Barnes
Hardy's edition (including his Preface and glossary) first pub. London, 1908; Preface printed separately Orel, pp. 76–82; Purdy, pp. 135–7. Extracts of the Preface used by Hardy for his later essay on Barnes in *The English Poets* (see HrT 1547); see also HrT 1719–21. For a discussion, see W. J. Keith, 'Thomas Hardy's Edition of William Barnes', *VP*, Summer 1977.

HrT 1560 Hardy's copy of first publication, annotated on front flyleaf '(Study copy)', containing a revision to the Preface (p. iv), pencil translation of 'Woone Smile Mwore' (inserted at end), annotations on pp. 77, 80–1, 102 ('Heedless o' my Love' marked '(Mary's favourite)' and 177, including an inserted proof of 'The Geäte A-Vallèn To' annotated 'This poem, said to be the last written by Barnes, would have been included in the volume; but...copyright was claimed by the owner, and permission refused.'.

Dorset County Museum.

Shall Stonehenge Go?
First pub. *Daily Chronicle*, 24 August 1899, as an interview with Hardy by James Milne; Orel, pp. 196–201; Purdy, p. 306.

HrT 1561 Draft, here untitled and beginning 'I am not entitled to the expression...', 5 numbered leaves (rectos only).

This MS mentioned Purdy, p. 306

Texas.

Some Old-Fashioned Psalm-tunes associated with the County of Dorset
First pub. (facsimile) *Dorset Year-book* (pub. Society of Dorset Men in London) (London, 1910); Purdy, pp. 313–14; mentioned Orel, pp. 251–2.

HrT 1562 Hardy's transcription of ten tunes, headed as above and subtitled 'For the Society of Dorset Men in London'.

Facsimile as above.

Unlocated.

The Son's Veto
First pub. *Illustrated London News*, Christmas Number, 1 December 1891; collected *Life's Little Ironies* (1894); Wessex Edition, VIII (1912), 33–52; Pinion, II, [33]–46; Purdy, p. 81.

HrT 1563 Fair copy, revised, signed, 16 numbered leaves, printer's copy for the first publication.

Facsimile first page in *English and American Autographs in the Bodmeriana*, comp. Margaret Crum (Cologny-Geneva, 1977), p. [38]; this MS described Purdy, p. 83.

Bibliotheca Bodmeriana, Cologny-Geneva.

HrT 1564 Corrected galley proof in Life's Little Ironies Proof; date stamped 1–4 December 1893.

Dorset County Museum.

The Sparrow, see HrT 1537–8.

The Spectre of the Real
This story was a collaboration between Hardy and Florence Henniker; first pub. *To-Day*, 17 November 1894; collected Florence Henniker, *In Scarlet and Grey* (London and Boston, 1896); Purdy, pp. 304–5, 346–8.

HrT 1565 Two typescripts, revised, 37 and 32 leaves; and corrected galley proof, 8 sheets.

Owned (1978) F. B. Adams.

Speech at the Opening of the Mellstock Club
Delivered at Bockhampton, 2 December 1919; first pub. (extracts) *Later Years* (1930), pp. 198–200. For other typescripts among the materials for *Life*, see HrT 1447–9.

HrT 1566 Typescript, headed '2nd. December 1919.', 2 leaves (rectos only).

Dorset County Museum.

Speech on Receiving the Freedom of the Borough
First pub. *The Times*, 17 November 1910, as 'Dorchester and Mr Thomas Hardy'; reprinted *Later Years*, pp. 143–7. For typescripts of this speech among materials for *Life*, see HrT 1444–5.

HrT 1567 Clipping of first publication mounted on a leaf in Scrapbook I (HrT 1687), containing additions in Hardy's hand.

Microfilm Edition, Reel 6.

Dorset County Museum.

Squire Petrick's Lady
First pub. *The Graphic*, Christmas Number 1890, as 'A Group of Noble Dames: V. Square Petrick's Lady'; collected *A Group of Noble Dames* (London, 1891), as 'Dame the Sixth'; Wessex Edition, XIV (1912), 151–64; Purdy, p. 63.

HrT 1568 Fair copy, extensively revised, in MS Group of Noble Dames, 13 leaves (mostly rectos only) numbered 85–101.

Library of Congress, Manuscript Division, Thomas Hardy Collection.

Sudermann's *The Song of Songs*
A revised version of Hardy's letter to John Lane of 15 December 1910 was incorporated in Lane's Introduction to Hermann Sudermann's *The Song of Songs*, trans. Beatrice Marshall (London, 1913); Purdy, p. 316.

HrT 1568.3 Hardy's original letter (not written for publication), together with a corrected proof of the revised version for the 1913 publication and a covering letter to Lane of 5 September 1912.

The original and the covering letters printed *Letters*, IV, 131 and 228.

Eton College.

[Suggestions for a Guide to Dorchester]
Hardy's suggestions pub. *Letters*, III (1982), 19–20.

HrT 1568.5 Suggestions for a proposed guide to Dorchester, included in a letter to the Town Clerk of Dorchester, 28 April 1902.

Hardy's heavily revised draft of the 'suggestions' is also at the Dorset County Museum.

Dorset County Museum.

Tess of the d'Urbervilles
First pub. (early version of Chapter 14 entitled 'The Midnight Baptism') *Fortnightly Review*, August 1891; first pub. in full serially in *The Graphic*, 4 July–26 December 1891; first separate edition, 3 vols (London, 1891); first fully unexpurgated edition, Wessex Edition, I (1912) (reprinted serially *John O'London's Weekly*, 24 October 1925–10 July 1926); for a recent edition, see *Tess of the d'Urbervilles*, ed. Juliet Grindle and Simon Gatrell (Oxford, 1983); Purdy, pp. 67–78. For an earlier essay plundered for use in *Tess*, see HrT 1401. For Hardy's dramatization, see HrT 1658–63. For lists of corrections for the Mellstock Edition, see INTRODUCTION.

HrT 1569 Fair copy, extensively revised, the title altered from 'A Daughter of the D'Urbervilles', foliated 3 times by Hardy as it was revised, final version 525 leaves (mostly rectos only) numbered 1–565 (wanting ff. 8–9, 15–17, 21, 23, 31–3, 40–1, 48, 55–8, 63, 66, 71, 100–1, 109, 114–16, 120–2, 124–6, 134, 138–9, 144–6, 179 and ff. 77/78, 157/8 and 320/1 being single leaves), printer's copy for first serial publication.

For a complete facsimile and discussion, see *The Thomas Hardy Archive: 1. Tess of the d'Urbervilles*, ed. Simon Gatrell, 2 vols (New York and London, 1986); for a discussion of this MS, see also J. T. Laird, *The Shaping of 'Tess of the d'Urbervilles'* (London, 1975) (facsimiles of ff. 1 and 280 as frontispiece and facing p. 15); facsimile of portion of last page in *Early Life*, facing p. 312; facsimile of f. 83 in T. J. Brown, 'English Literary Autographs XIX', *BC*, 5 (1956), facing p. 249; Microfilm Edition, Reel 12. This MS described in Purdy, pp. 70–1 and in Grindle and Gatrell's edition, pp. [55]–60.

British Library, Add. MS 38182.

HrT 1570 Fair copy, slightly revised, of a passage from Chapter 10, headed '*An omitted passage from Tess of the d'Urbervilles*/ Chapter X. p. 78 (1 vol. ed^{n}) — After, "The/pilgrims from Trantridge sought double delights at the/inns on that account" —', 8 numbered leaves (rectos only).

Chapters 10 and 11 of *Tess*, not included in the first serial publication, first pub. separately in a Special Literary Supplement of the *National Observer* (Edinburgh), 14 November 1891, as 'Saturday Night in Arcady'; with the exception of this fragment containing the hay-trusser's dance, they were restored to the text of the novel in the first separate edition; this fragment first included in the Wessex Edition, I, 76–9. This MS not mentioned in Purdy or in Grindle and Gatrell's edition; Microfilm Edition, Reel 2; facsimile in *The Thomas Hardy Archive: 1. Tess of the d'Urbervilles*, ed. Simon Gatrell, 2 vols (New York and London, 1986), II, 265–72. Hardy's letter to W. E. Henley (editor of the *National Observer*) of 21 October 1891 offering 'Saturday Night in Arcady' was sold at Sotheby's, 18 December 1985 as Lot 67.

Dorset County Museum.

HrT 1571 Fair copy, revised, of beginning of Chapters 10–11 (i.e., 'Saturday Night in Arcady'), 8 numbered leaves (rectos only), first 4 pages in Hardy's hand, other 4 in ELH's hand, revised by Hardy, printer's copy for the *National Observer*.

This MS described in Grindle and Gatrell's edition, pp. 60–1 and printed Appendix I, pp. [543]–52; not mentioned Purdy.

Texas.

HrT 1571.5 Fragment of Chapters 10–11 (i.e., 'Saturday Night in Arcady'), in the hand of ELH, revised by Hardy, one page numbered 9, printer's copy for the *National Observer*.

This MS mentioned and facsimile printed in Keith Wilson, 'A Note on the Provenance of folio 9 of "Saturday Night in Arcady"', in *Thomas Hardy Annual No. 5*, ed. Norman Page (London, 1987), pp. 182–4.

University of Leeds, Glenesk-Bathurst MSS (on deposit by Lord Bathurst).

HrT 1572 Fragment of Chapters 10–11 (i.e., 'Saturday Night in Arcady'), one page numbered 10, printer's copy for the *National Observer*.

This MS described Purdy, p. 71 and in Grindle and Gatrell's edition, pp. 60–1 (printed Appendix I, pp. [543]–52).

Berg.

HrT 1573 Fair copy, revised, of the conclusion to Chapters 10–11 (i.e., 'Saturday Night in Arcady'), 3 leaves (rectos only) numbered 11–13, printer's copy for the *National Observer*.

This MS described in Grindle and Gatrell's edition, pp. 60–1 and printed Appendix I, pp. [543]–52; facsimile of f. 12 in Hofmann Catalogue 11 (May–June 1966); not mentioned Purdy.

Princeton, Robert H. Taylor Collection.

HrT 1574 Early title ('The Body and Soul of Sue'), in a letter to Tillotson & Son, London, 11 July 1889.

This MS printed *Letters*, I, 194.

UCLA, 100/bx 36.

HrT 1574.5 Early title ('Too late, Beloved!'), in a letter to James R. Osgood, 4 August 1889.

This MS printed *Letters*, I, 196.

Pierpont Morgan, MA 1950 (Harper Collection).

HrT 1575 Revised title page for the first separate edition, annotated '*Title page. To supersede copy previously sent.*', one page.

Described in Grindle and Gatrell's edition, p. 60; facsimile in Purdy, p. 71; facsimile in *The Thomas Hardy Archive: 1. Tess of the d'Urbervilles*, ed. Simon Gatrell, 2 vols (New York and London, 1986), II, 187.

Dorset County Museum.

HrT 1576 Draft of the 'Explanatory Note' to first separate edition, here headed 'Prefatory Note', one page, signed (initials).

This 'Explanatory Note' published Orel, pp. 25–6; this MS mentioned Purdy, p. 71 and described Grindle and Gatrell's edition, p. 60 (as unlocated); facsimile in American Art Association sale catalogue, 20–1 April 1925 (G. B. McCutcheon Sale), Lot 42; facsimile in *The Thomas Hardy Archive: 1. Tess of the d'Urbervilles*, ed. Simon Gatrell, 2 vols (New York and London, 1986), II, 183.

Dorset County Museum.

HrT 1576.5 Corrected revise proof of the Preface for the Wessex Edition (containing also HrT 1419); the last date revised to 'March 1912'.

Facsimile in *The Thomas Hardy Archive: 1. Tess of the d'Urbervilles*, ed. Simon Gatrell, 2 vols (New York and London, 1986), II, 286–91.

University of California at Berkeley, 71/141.

HrT 1577 Copy of first separate edition, with misprint on III, 198 corrected by Hardy and annotated on flyleaf of Vol. III 'erratum Vide p. 198 T. Hardy'.

Sotheby's, 2–4 April 1928 (Clement Shorter Sale), Lot 212, sold to Heffer.

HrT 1578 Copy of first separate edition, with misprint on III, 198 corrected by Hardy in pencil, annotated '(This misprint is the mark of the first edition)'.

Dorset County Museum.

HrT 1579 Corrections and additions in a copy of the fifth edition (London, 1892), used for preparing the Osgood, McIlvaine edition of Wessex Novels (London, 1895), annotated on the cover 'Corrected for new Edition'; including additional autograph passages in the Preface, signed (initials) and dated January 1895.

Revised Preface published Orel, pp. 26–9; this copy mentioned Purdy, p. 77n1; facsimile of corrected pages in *The Thomas Hardy Archive: 1. Tess of the d'Urbervilles*, ed. Simon Gatrell, 2 vols (New York and London, 1986), II, 191–261.

Berg.

HrT 1580 Corrections and revisions in DCM Wessex Edition (I, 24, 27, 102, 133, 135, 152, 170, 476, 484, 491, 499), annotated on front flyleaf that corrections were sent variously for the reprint of Wessex Edition, for Mellstock Edition and some 'not sent anywhere (Sept. 1926).'.

This copy discussed in Grindle and Gatrell's edition, pp. 23–4, 70–72, 74; facsimiles of corrected pages in *The Thomas Hardy Archive: 1. Tess of the d'Urbervilles*, ed. Simon Gatrell, 2 vols (New York and London, 1986), II, 295, 300–310.

Dorset County Museum.

HrT 1581 Sketch map of the scene of the novel, headed 'Tess's Country', drawn for Lorin and Margaret Deland, enclosed with a letter to Margaret Deland, 21 June 1892.

Facsimile in *Harper's Monthly Magazine*, July 1925, p. 239; letter only printed *Letters*, I, 273.

Owned (1978) R. L. Purdy (see *Letters*); destined for Yale.

HrT 1582 Sketch of the route of Tess's wanderings, on a printed map (*Crutchley's Railway and Telegraphic County Map of Dorset*), used for the Wessex Edition, annotated 'Note. Tess's wanderings are shown in red lines'.

Facsimile in *The Countryman*, 13 (1936), 489–90 and on endpaper of *Concerning Thomas Hardy*, ed. D. F. Barber (London, [1968]); Microfilm Edition, Reel 6.

Dorset County Museum.

HrT 1582.5 Fair copy of Hardy's prefatory Note to the first unexpurgated serial publication in *John O'London's Weekly*, addressed 'Gentle Reader', one page, signed; dated October 1925.

Facsimile printed in the first instalment in *John O'London's Weekly*, 24 October 1925; see Purdy, p. 322.

Unlocated.

HrT 1582.7 Hardy's answers on a list of queries regarding allusions and references, as sent to Hardy by Vera Spasskaia (translator of *Tess* into Russian), enclosed in a letter to Spasskaia, 26 August 1892.

This letter and MS printed *Letters*, I, 281–3.

Institute of Russian Literature, Leningrad.

HrT 1583 Typed list of queries regarding the meanings of words, as sent to Hardy by Madeleine Rolland (translator of *Tess* into French) and containing Hardy's answers and comments; returned to Rolland by Hardy with a letter of 14 March 1921.

This MS and letter printed *Letters*, VI, 74–7; Rolland's French translation first pub. 1901, these queries for her revised translation of 1925.

Owned (1987) Mme Rolland (see *Letters*).

HrT 1583.5 Transcript by Harold Hoffman of a quotation from the opening of Chapter 50, the original (in ELH's hand) enclosed in a letter from Hardy to Frederick Whitehead (also transcribed by Hoffman) for his use as an epigraph to a painting; letter dated 6 February

1894.

Hoffman's transcript of the letter printed *Letters*, VII, 125–6.

Miami University, Ohio.

Thomas Hardy
This sketch first pub. anonymously in the 'World Biographies' series in *Literary World* (Boston), 1 August 1878; ascribed to Hardy in Purdy, p. 295 and *Letters*, I, 56n; described as being 'of doubtful attribution' in Orel, p. 241.

HrT 1584 Version of the sketch in the hand of ELH, 2 pages, enclosed in a letter from Hardy to Edward Abbott (editor of *Literary World*), 9 May 1878.

Letter only printed *Letters*, I, 56.

Bowdoin College.

Thomas Hardy
An entry about Hardy was included in most editions of the biographical dictionary *Men of the Times* (entitled *Men and Women of the Times* from 1891); not mentioned Purdy.

HrT 1584.5 Hardy's addition to his entry, on a card enclosed in a letter to 'Sir', 4 April 1894.

This addition is presumably for the 1895 edition of *Men and Women of the Times*; the letter not in *Letters*.

National Library of Scotland, Purves Autograph Collection, Acc 7175/2.

The Three Strangers
First pub. *Longman's Magazine*, March 1883; collected *Wessex Tales* (1888); Wessex Edition, IX (1912), 1–29; Pinion, I, [13]–32; Purdy, p. 58. For Hardy's dramatization, see HrT 1664–8; for verses published in this story, see HrT 1121–2.

HrT 1585 Fair copy, revised, 33 numbered leaves (mostly rectos only), printer's copy for the first publication; inscribed to Sydney Cockerell, 29 September 1911.

Described Purdy, p. 59. Cockerell Sale, Lot 253 (facsimile first page in sale catalogue), sold to Maggs. A copy of the first publication with the variants in this MS written in by Cockerell (sent to Howard Bliss, 10 November 1925) is at the Berg.

Berg.

HrT 1586 Revision to this story in DCM Wessex Edition (IX, 3).

Dorset County Museum.

To Please his Wife
First pub. *Black and White*, 27 June 1891; collected *Life's Little Ironies* (1894); Wessex Edition, VIII (1912), 139–61; Pinion, II, [107]–22; Purdy, p. 82.

HrT 1587 Corrected galley proof in Life's Little Ironies Proof; date stamped 12–14 December 1893.

Dorset County Museum.

A Tradition of Eighteen Hundred and Four
First pub. *Harper's Christmas* (New York, [1882]), as 'A Legend of the Year Eighteen Hundred and Four'; collected *Life's Little Ironies* (1894); transferred to *Wessex Tales* in the Wessex Edition, IX (1912), 31–41; Pinion, I, [33]–9; Purdy, p. 82.

HrT 1588 Corrected galley proof in Life's Little Ironies Proof; date stamped 23 December 1893.

Dorset County Museum.

A Tragedy of Two Ambitions
First pub. *Universal Review*, December 1888; collected *Life's Little Ironies* (1894); Wessex Edition, VIII (1912), 75–105; Pinion, II, [62]–84; Purdy, p. 81.

HrT 1589 Fair copy, revised, extensively in places, originally entitled '<The Shame of the Halboroughs>', 36 leaves (rectos only), annotated at top '[*Life's Little Ironies*]'.

This MS described Purdy, p. 83.

John Rylands Library, English MS 124.

HrT 1590 Corrected galley proof in Life's Little Ironies Proof; date stamped 6–8

December 1893.

Dorset County Museum.

The Trumpet-Major
First pub. *Good Words*, January–December 1880; first separate edition, 3 vols (London, 1880); Wessex Edition, XI (1912); Purdy, pp. 31–5. For verses published in this novel, see HrT 1026. For Hardy's dramatization, see HrT 1669–70. For a source notebook, see HrT 1680.

HrT 1591 Fair copy, revised, signed, 309 leaves (rectos only) numbered 1–306 (wanting ff. 238–51 from Chapters 33–4 and including 17 unnumbered leaves), one page (f. 209) in the hand of ELH, printer's copy for first publication.

For a discussion and facsimile pages, see W. G. Bebbington, *The Original Manuscript of Thomas Hardy's 'The Trumpet-Major'* (Windsor, [1948]); Microfilm Edition, Reel 11; this MS described Purdy, pp. 33–4. Hardy presented the MS to King George V in October 1911.

Royal Library, Windsor.

HrT 1592 Quotation of second paragraph (beginning 'Anne was fair...'), in a letter to Sir George Forrest, 21 March 1925.

This MS printed *Letters*, VI, 315.

Owned (1987) R. L. Purdy (see *Letters*); destined for Yale.

A Tryst at an Ancient Earthwork
First pub. *Detroit Post*, 15 March 1885, as 'Ancient Earthworks and What Two Enthusiastic Scientists Found Therein'; collected *A Changed Man* (1913); Wessex Edition, XVIII (1914), 169–83; Pinion, II, [317]–26; Purdy, p. 153.

HrT 1593 Fair copy, revised, here entitled 'An Ancient Earthwork', 15 numbered leaves (rectos only), printer's copy for the publication in *English Illustrated Magazine* of December 1893 (where pub. as 'Ancient Earthworks at Casterbridge').

Facsimile of last page in Sotheby's sale catalogue, 2–4 April 1928 (Shorter Sale), facing p. 37; this MS described Purdy, p. 154.

Texas.

Two on a Tower
First pub. *Atlantic Monthly*, May–December 1882; first separate edition, 3 vols (London, 1882); Wessex Edition, XII (1912); Purdy, pp. 41–7. For Hardy's dramatization, see HrT 1671. In *The Thomas Hardy Archive: 1. Tess of the d'Urbervilles*, ed. Simon Gatrell, 2 vols (New York and London, 1986), II, 293, Gatrell mentions an 1895 edition (unlocated) of *Two on a Tower* as being the earliest printed copy Hardy used as a record of his revisions to the text.

HrT 1594 Fair copy, revised, 358 leaves (382 pages) numbered 1–357 and one unnumbered, including 28 pages in ELH's hand, signed, printer's copy for first serial publication.

This MS may be a combination of the original and duplicate MSS of the novel; for a discussion and four facsimile pages, one in ELH's hand (ff. 1, 199, 251, 314), see Carl J. Weber, 'The Manuscript of Hardy's *Two on a Tower*', *PBSA*, 40 (1946), 1–21; see also Robert C. Schweik's comment and correction in *PBSA*, 60 (1966), 219–21 and Simon Gatrell, *Hardy the Creator* (Oxford, 1988), pp. 60–70; this MS described in Purdy, p. 47.

Harvard, MS Eng 695.

Under the Greenwood Tree
First pub. 2 vols (London, 1872); Wessex Edition, VII (1912); Purdy, pp. 6–8. For a recent edition, see *Under the Greenwood Tree*, ed. Simon Gatrell (Oxford, 1985). For A. H. Evans's dramatization entitled *The Mellstock Quire*, see the note in DRAMATIC WORKS.

HrT 1595 Fair copy, revised, the title altered from 'The Mellstock Quire, or Under the Greenwood Tree', c. 212 pages of text on 194 leaves (mostly rectos only) numbered 1–203 (wanting 9 leaves), printer's copy for first edition, inscribed to FEH, annotated on page opposite the last page (f. 202v) '[last page missing.]/(*Rewritten later.*)/T. H.'.

This MS apparently incorporates material from the MS of Hardy's first (and discarded) novel *The Poor Man and the Lady* composed probably 1867–8; facsimile first page in *Early Life*, facing p. 116; this MS described Purdy, pp. 6–7; Microfilm Edition, Reel 2.

Dorset County Museum.

HrT 1596 Corrections and revisions in DCM Wessex Edition (VII).

Dorset County Museum.

The Vauxhall Fiddler, see HrT 1536.

The Waiting Supper, for a lost MS, see INTRODUCTION.

The Well-Beloved
First pub. *Illustrated London News*, 1 October–17 December 1892, as 'The Pursuit of the Well-Beloved'; first separate edition London, 1897; Wessex Edition, XIII (1912); Purdy, pp. 92–6. For a recent edition, see *The Well-Beloved*, ed. Tom Hetherington (Oxford, 1986). For a lost MS, see INTRODUCTION.

HrT 1597 Prospectus of the novel, in ELH's hand, revised by Hardy, headed '*Title: "The Pursuit of the Well-Beloved.*"' and beginning 'The novel is entirely modern in date & subject...', one page, as sent to W. F. Tillotson, probably late 1891.

This MS printed Purdy, p. 95.

John Rylands Library, Tillotson Archive Letter Album, Item 17.

HrT 1598 Corrections in DCM Wessex Edition (XIII, vii and 6).

Dorset County Museum.

The Well-Beloved
First pub. as a letter to the editor *The Academy*, 3 April 1897; partly reprinted *Later Years*, pp. 59–60; Purdy, p. 270.

HrT 1599 Revised, 2 leaves (rectos only), headed '"The Well-Beloved."/To the Editor of The Academy.'; dated Dorchester, 29 March 1897 in an unidentified hand and 'March 29' by Hardy.

Facsimile of first page in Ann Bowden, 'The Thomas Hardy Collection', *LCUT*, 7 (1962), 6; a typed transcript of this MS is in Dorset County Museum.

Texas.

The Wessex of Thomas Hardy
First pub. *Manchester Guardian*, 16 April 1902, as a letter to the editor dated 11 April 1902; Purdy, pp. 307–8; mentioned Orel, pp. 250–1.

HrT 1600 Typescript of letter to editor of *Manchester Guardian*, beginning 'Some unusually distinct misstatements are made by your critic of "The Wessex of Thomas Hardy", by Professor Windle...', 2 leaves (rectos only), in Scrapbook I (HrT 1687), annotated 'Q[uer]y 1902?'.

Dorset County Museum.

Wessex Tales
This collection of 5 stories first pub. in 2 vols (London and New York, 1888); reprinted with a Preface and a sixth story (London, 1896); Wessex Edition, IX (1912) (7 stories). For MSS of individual stories, see HrT 1396, 1426, 1516–20, 1585–6, 1588. For the Preface, see HrT 1546.

HrT 1601 List of stories with their dates of publication, on a scrap (recto).

Microfilm Edition, Reel 5.

Dorset County Museum.

Weymouth
First pub. *The Times*, 6 July 1926; Purdy, p. 13.

HrT 1601.5 Final version of Hardy's message to the citizens of Weymouth, Massachusetts; [March–July 1926].

See *Letters*, VII, 11.

Dorset County Museum.

What the Shepherd Saw
First pub. *Illustrated London News*, Christmas Number, 5 December 1881; collected *A Changed Man* (1913); Wessex Edition, XVIII (1914), 185–210; Pinion, II, [327]–46; Purdy, p. 153.

HrT 1602 Draft, incomplete, including first 3 numbered leaves only, annotated by Hardy at head '[First rough Draught] (1881)' and at end '(Caetera desunt)' and on paper cover '"What the Shepherd Saw" a tale written in 1881 and published in English and American Periodicals. Recently included in Collected Works in the volume entitled "A Changed Man". Original MS. being First Rough Draft (3 pages only — the remainder lost.) Thomas Hardy.'; dated 1881.

This MS described Purdy, pp. 154–5 (as having been sent by FEH to Red Cross Sale at Christie's, 28 April 1916, where sold as Lot 2560 to Hollings).

Yale.

Why I Don't Write Plays
First pub. as Hardy's contribution to a symposium in *Pall Mall Gazette*, 31 August 1892; Orel, p. 139; Purdy, p. 301.

HrT 1603 Draft, here untitled, one page, signed (initials).

Facsimile in *Pall Mall Budget*, 1 September 1892 (a clipping of this facsimile in Scrapbook I (HrT 1687)) and as the frontispiece to *The Life and Art of Thomas Hardy*, ed. Ernest Brennecke (New York, 1925).

Unlocated.

The Woodlanders
First pub. serially *Macmillan's Magazine*, May 1886–April 1887; first separate edition, 3 vols (London, 1887); Wessex Edition, VI (1912); Purdy, pp. 54–7. For a recent edition, see *The Woodlanders*, ed. Dale Kramer (Oxford, 1981). For a dramatization, see the note in DRAMATIC WORKS. See also HrT 1752.

HrT 1604 Fair copy, revised, the title altered from 'Fitzpiers at Hintock', c. 546 pages of text on 498 leaves (mostly rectos only) numbered 1–88, 88a, 89–91, 91a, 92–133, 133a, 134–352, 352a, 353–416, 416a–b, 417–438, 438a, 439–91, including leaves and parts of leaves in the hand of ELH, printer's copy for first serial publication, annotated (f. 1) 'Set up in type for Macmillan's Magazine (for May no)'.

For a discussion and two facsimile pages (ff. 202 and 437), see Dale Kramer, 'Revisions and Visions: Thomas Hardy's *The Woodlanders*', *BNYPL*, 75 (1971), 194–230, 248–82; see also Kramer's edition for a discussion of the MS (pp. 26–30), a description (pp. [59]–61) and a list of variants (pp. [375]–430); MS also described Purdy, p. 56; Microfilm Edition, Reel 1. Hardy lists owner of this MS as Howard Bliss in his 'Memoranda Notebook II' list (see HrT 1686, list printed Taylor, p. 67); it was sold to Bliss in 1924 and resold later to FEH.

Dorset County Museum.

HrT 1605 Revised copy of the London 1906 (Macmillan) edition, printer's copy for the Wessex Edition, annotated by Hardy on title page 'Proofs showing the corrections made for the Wessex Edition. They should be made in this the uniform edition & the thin paper edition', the extensively revised Preface is signed (initials) and the additions are dated April 1912; together with a few corrected page proofs for Wessex Edition (including the title page, copyright page, Preface (pp. vii–[x]), pp. 241–2 (date stamped 18 May 1912) and pp. 371–2).

This copy discussed in Kramer's edition, pp. 49–51, 67; Microfilm Edition, Reel 1.

Dorset County Museum.

HrT 1606 A few corrections in DCM Wessex Edition (VI).

Dorset County Museum.

DRAMATIC WORKS

The Changed Sweethearts
This dramatization of 'The History of the Hardcomes' (one part of the story 'A Few Crusted Characters') was never written. For Hardy's original story, see HrT 1410–12.

HrT 1607 Draft outline for a dramatization in two acts, headed 'Hardcomes.', on a scrap, mounted on the verso of a printed form dated November 1924.

Microfilm Edition, Reel 2.

Dorset County Museum.

A Desperate Remedy
T. H. Tilley's dramatization first produced in Dorchester, 15–17 November 1922. Riverside Collection includes: MS of Tilley's dramatization (1 vol.) (*Hardy Players Collection*, H9); MS carbon copy of stage plans (H18); MS details of costumes (H19); MS synopsis of scenes (H20); MS of band programme (H21). For Hardy's original novel, see HrT 1395.

HrT 1607.5 Scriptbook for the part of 'Gad Weedy', partly in Hardy's hand.

Microfilm Edition, Reel 4.

Dorset County Museum.

The Distracted Preacher
A. H. Evans's dramatization first produced in Dorchester, 15–16 November 1911. A revised typescript of it (3 vols) is in the Riverside Collection (*Hardy Players Collection*, H5). For Hardy's original story, see HrT 1396.

HrT 1608 Copy of theatre programme for the first production, containing one revision by Hardy to 'Mr Hardy's Note on the Story'.

Microfilm Edition, Reel 4.

Dorset County Museum.

The Duchess of Hamptonshire
This dramatization was never written. For Hardy's original story, see HrT 1402.

HrT 1609 Two outlines for a dramatization in five acts: the first, a draft, one page, on the verso of a letter to Hardy dated 17 July 1905; the second, a fair copy, revised, 2 leaves (rectos only), annotated '(Private)' and '(rough idea)'.

Microfilm Edition, Reel 2.

Dorset County Museum.

The Dynasts
Part First first pub. London and New York, 1903; Part Second first pub. London and New York, 1905; Part Third first pub. London, 1908; entire work first pub. in one volume London, 1910; Wessex Edition, Verse Vols II–III (London, 1913); Purdy, pp. 119–35. For a discussion of many of the MSS of *The Dynasts*, see Wright, especially Chapter 5, pp. 287–310. For productions of *The Dynasts*, see below. For lists of corrections for the Mellstock Edition, see INTRODUCTION.

HrT 1610 Corrections in the text, lists of corrections on inside front cover and an inserted leaf in DCM Wessex Edition (Verse Vols II–III).

Dorset County Museum.

HrT 1611 Corrections and revisions (43) in Hardy's copy of the London, 1910 edition, including a list of corrections on inside front cover and typescript list of 16 corrections headed 'The Dynasts. Corrections for 1 volume edition./(being Vol. 2 of complete Poetical Works' and annotated by Hardy '[copy sent to Mess[rs] Macmillan Sept. 5. 1919]'.

This copy discussed and revisions printed in Simon Gatrell, 'An Examination of some Revisions to Printed Versions of *The Dynasts*', *The Library*, 6th Series 1 (1979), [265]–81.

Owned (1979) Julia Shum, Durban, South Africa (see Gatrell).

HrT 1612 Corrections and revisions to Parts First and Third in a copy of the Mellstock Edition (London, 1920) (a set also including HrT 1540).

Colby College.

The Dynasts. Part First
First pub. London and New York, 1903; the song (from V, vii) 'The Night of Trafalgar' ('In the wild October night-time, when the wind raved round the land') collected separately *Selected Poems* (1916); Hynes, III, 285–6; for a typescript of this song, see also HrT 1635.

HrT 1613 Fair copy, revised, 248 leaves (rectos only) numbered by Hardy i–x, 1–87, 87a, 88–236, including title pages, Preface dated September 1903, table of contents and a fair copy of 'The Night of Trafalgar', printer's copy for the first edition.

This MS described Purdy, pp. 120–1; some variants printed in Rutland, p. 284; facsimile of 2 pages (ff. 168–9) in *Printer's Pie* (London, 1904), pp. 59–60; Microfilm Edition, Reel 13.

British Library, Add. MS 38183.

HrT 1614 Fair copy of the song 'The Night of Trafalgar', here entitled 'Song: The Night of Trafalgár', one page, signed.

Facsimile in A. P. Webb, *A Bibliography of the Works of Thomas Hardy* (London, 1916), facing p. 36; this MS written out by Hardy for the Red Cross Sale at Christie's, 26 April 1915, where sold as Lot 1537 to Hollings.

University of California at Berkeley.

HrT 1615 Corrections and annotation to the song 'The Night of Trafalgar' in *Selected Poems* (1917), pp. 204–5.

Dorset County Museum.

HrT 1616 Corrections on pp. 5, 18 and 155 in a copy of second impression of first edition (1903) (incorporated in the first reprint of 1904), presented to Edmund Gosse, January 1904.

This copy mentioned Purdy, p. 123; *Grolier Catalogue*, Item 174.

Princeton, Robert H. Taylor Collection.

The Dynasts. Part Second
First pub. London and New York, 1905; the song (from VI, iv) 'Albuera' ('They come, beset by riddling hail') collected separately in *Chosen Poems* (London, 1929); Hynes, III, 287.

HrT 1617 Fair copy, revised, 293 leaves (rectos only) numbered by Hardy i–vii, 1–131, 131a–b, 132–284, including title pages, table of contents, dramatis personae and a fair copy, revised, of 'Albuera', printer's copy for first edition; dated at end 28 September 1905.

This MS described Purdy, p. 126; Microfilm Edition, Reel 13.

British Library, Add. MS 38184.

HrT 1618 Alterations on 19 pages of Hardy's copy of the first edition, labelled 'marked'.

This copy mentioned Purdy, p. 129; Max Gate Sale, Lot 83.

Owned (1978) F. B. Adams.

The Dynasts. Part Third
First pub. London, 1908; lines from Leipzig scenes (III, ii, iv, v) first pub. in the poem 'Leipzig' in *Wessex Poems* (1898) (for MSS, see HrT 682–3); the song (from II, i) 'Hussar's Song/Budmouth Dears' ('When we lay where Budmouth Beach is') collected separately *Selected Poems* (1916) and Hynes, III, 288–9; the song (from V, vi) '"My Love's gone a-fighting"' collected separately *Selected Poems* (1916) and Hynes, III, 289; the song (from VI, viii) 'The Eve of Waterloo' ('The eyelids of eve fall together at last') collected separately *Selected Poems* (1916) and Hynes, III, 290–1; the song (in 'After-scene') 'Chorus of the Pities' ('To Thee whose eye all Nature owns') collected separately *Selected Poems* (1916) and Hynes, III, 291–3; the song (in 'After-scene') 'Last Chorus' ('Last as first the question rings') first pub. as 'A Latter-Day Chorus' in *The Nation*, 2 March 1907 and collected separately *Selected Poems* (1916) and Hynes, III, 293–4.

HrT 1619 Draft of Acts I–IV, annotated (f. 1) '[Rough Draft]', 117 leaves (rectos only) numbered 1–116 and one unnumbered leaf (f. 90a), dated on first page (cancelled) 15 October 1906; together with a transcript by Mary Hardy, revised by Hardy, of Acts

V (39 leaves, rectos only), VI (50 leaves, rectos only), VII (59 leaves, rectos only) and the 'After-scene' (6 leaves numbered 60–5, rectos only), annotated last page '[Draft finished Good Friday night. March 29. 1907]'.

This MS misdescribed Purdy, pp. 130–1 as draft of Acts I–IV together with a transcript by an amanuensis of Act VI (50 leaves); facsimile pages: f. 90 in Purdy, facing p. 131 and in Evelyn Hardy, *Thomas Hardy* (London, 1954), facing p. 290; ff. 3, 71, 109 in Wright, between pp. 146 and 147.

Dorset County Museum.

HrT 1620 Fair copy, revised, including all 5 songs listed above, 329 leaves (rectos only) numbered by Hardy i–x, 1–318, including title pages, table of contents and dramatis personae, printer's copy for the first edition; dated at end 25 September 1907.

This MS described Purdy, p. 130; Microfilm Edition, Reel 14.

British Library, Add. MS 38185.

HrT 1621 Fair copy of the song 'Hussar's Song/ Budmouth Dears', here entitled 'Song./ Budmouth Dears.', 2 pages (one folded leaf), signed, originally enclosed in a letter to Austin Dobson, 8 June 1908.

This MS incorporates a revision made in proof but not taken up by the printer; letter only printed *Letters*, III, 320; this MS described Purdy, p. 131.

Texas.

HrT 1622 Fair copy, revised, of 'Last Chorus', one page, signed.

Probably transcribed by Hardy for the Red Cross Sale at Christie's, 22 April 1918 where it was sold to Maggs.

Owned (1985) F. B. Adams (see Hynes).

HrT 1623 Alterations on 24 pages in Hardy's copy of the first edition, marked '1st Edition'.

This copy mentioned Purdy, p. 134; Max Gate Sale, Lot 83.

Owned (1978) F. B. Adams.

HrT 1624 Revision to 'The Eve of Waterloo' in *Selected Poems* (1916), p. 210.

Dorset County Museum.

HrT 1625 Corrections and revisions to songs 'From "The Dynasts"' in *Selected Poems* (1917): corrections to 'Hussar's Song/Budmouth Dears' (pp. 206–7); correction to '"My Love's gone a-fighting"' (p. 208); revisions and corrections to 'The Eve of Waterloo' (pp. 209–10); correction to 'Chorus of the Pities' (pp. 211–12); revision to 'Last Chorus' (p. 213).

Dorset County Museum.

HrT 1626 Two paragraph statement about Part Third, in pencil, one page, sent for use in advertising the work with a letter to James Milne, 15 January 1908.

Letter only printed *Letters*, VII, 144; the statement was printed without attribution in Milne's *Book Monthly*, February 1908.

Eton College.

HrT 1627 Extract used as source for VI, vii, 3 pages (one folded leaf), headed 'Bruxelles à travers les ages', transcribed from the book (pub. c. 1884–5) of same title by Louis Hymans.

Microfilm Edition, Reel 5.

Dorset County Museum.

HrT 1628 List of three editions in which a misprint occurred (in the line of the speech of the Spirit of the Pities in the 'After-scene': 'So would we how, despite thy forthshadowing'), in the pencil draft of a letter to Harold Macmillan, 7 May 1921.

Letter printed *Letters*, VI, 85–6.

Dorset County Museum.

The Dynasts. Dramatizations

Hardy's own dramatization (produced by Harley Granville Barker) was first performed at the Kingsway Theatre, London, 25 November 1914; Hardy also composed a Prologue and an Epilogue for this production (see HrT 337–338.5 and HrT 942–942.5). Two copies of the one-volume edition of

The Dynasts (London, 1910), containing alterations and annotations by Harley Granville Barker, are extant: one at Dorset County Museum, the other at the British Library, Department of Printed Books, Cup.504.b.12; a typescript of the dramatization belonging to Lillah McCarthy is in the Dorset County Museum; a prompt copy annotated by Harley Granville Barker is at Harvard in the Theater Collection, MS Thr 159.2.

HrT 1629 Revised outline for a dramatization in three acts (never written), here entitled 'The Fall of Prussia & Austria/(Selected from "The Dynasts" for acting', 2 numbered leaves (rectos only) together with HrT 1630.3.

Microfilm Edition, Reel 2.

Dorset County Museum.

HrT 1630 Alterations (including additional stage directions) by Hardy and Harley Granville Barker, in pencil, in Hardy's copy of the first one-volume edition (London, 1910), used for preparing the 1914 London production, including drafts of Hardy's Prologue and Epilogue (see HrT 337 and 942), annotated on front flyleaf 'This abridgement of "The Dynasts", with temporary Prologue, Epilogue, and other lines inserted (solely for the stage performance) is not to be published or reproduced at any time.'.

This copy mentioned Purdy, p. 135.

Dorset County Museum.

The Dynasts. Dramatization of 'Wessex Scenes from "The Dynasts"'

First performed by the Dorchester Debating and Dramatic Society at The Pavilion, Weymouth, April 1908 and 22 June 1916 and at the Corn Exchange, Dorchester, 6–7 December 1916. The speech by Lady Ilchester (written for the matinée performance of 6–7 December 1916) was published in 'Wessex Scenes from the Dynasts', *Dorset County Chronicle*, 14 December 1916. Three scriptbooks for the 1916 production are at Dorset County Museum (2 of them available on Microfilm Edition, Reel 3); a MS of three scenes from *The Dynasts* used in Rev. Roland Hill's production of *Ye Merrie May Faire* (1908) is in the Riverside Collection (*Hardy Players Collection*, H15).

HrT 1630.3 Draft outline of an early version, headed '(Possible scenes for acting.)', 2 pages (on a scrap), together with HrT 1629.

Microfilm Edition, Reel 2.

Dorset County Museum.

HrT 1630.5 Outline for an early version (fair copy of HrT 1630.3), headed 'The Dynasts. Possible scenes for acting.', one page, annotated in an unidentified hand 'MS notes by Thomas Hardy/Robert B. Gooden'.

Eton College.

HrT 1631 Notes for the 1916 productions, headed 'Explanation of the Rural Scenes from *The Dynasts*', 2 pages.

Microfilm Edition, Reel 2.

Dorset County Museum.

HrT 1632 Speech, in pencil, headed 'Speech written for Mrs Hanbury.', one page, written for the evening performances of 6–7 December 1916 production.

This speech mentioned Purdy, p. 319; Microfilm Edition, Reel 2.

Dorset County Museum.

HrT 1633 Speech, in pencil, headed 'Town Hall Performances of "The Dynasts"/Speech written for Lady Ilchester', one page, written for matinée performance of 6–7 December 1916 production.

This speech mentioned Purdy, p. 319; Microfilm Edition, Reel 2.

Dorset County Museum.

HrT 1634 Revised typescript (containing also HrT 338.5 and 942.5), annotated '[As acted in Dorchester]', 52 leaves (rectos only) numbered i–iii, 1–11, 11a, 12–23, 23a–c, 24–47 (with ff. 28/9 and 32/3 being each one leaf).

Microfilm Edition, Reel 3.

Dorset County Museum.

HrT 1635 Typescript, revised by Hardy, including the song 'The Night of Trafalgar' mostly in

Hardy's hand, 5 volumes (one scene per volume); [1916].

Hardy Players Collection, H7.

University of California at Riverside.

Enter a Dragoon
This dramatization was never written.

HrT 1636 Draft outline for a dramatization of Hardy's story in four acts, one page; on the verso of a letter to Hardy dated 26 October 1908.

Microfilm Edition, Reel 2.

Dorset County Museum.

The Famous Tragedy of the Queen of Cornwall At Tintagel in Lyonnesse
First performed by the Hardy Players at the Corn Exchange, Dorchester, 28–30 November 1923. First pub. London, 1923; Wessex Edition, Verse Vol. IV (London, 1926); Pinion, III, [183]–226; Purdy, pp. 227–31. The two songs in this drama, '"Could he but live for me"' and '"Let's meet again to-night, my Fair', are published separately in Hynes, III, 305, 306. The Riverside Collection includes: pencil drawing of stage setting (either by Hardy or an accurate copy of his drawing) (*Hardy Players Collection*, H28); another similar sketch of stage setting (H29); miscellaneous correspondence about the production (H30); MS carbon copy of production details, 21 February 1924 (H31); MS carbon copy of costume details (H32). For verses Hardy sent to Rutland Boughton for his use in writing an opera based on this drama, see HrT 141, 771.

HrT 1637 Fair copy, revised, wanting Iseult's song in Scene 7 but including (f. 26) '"Let's meet again to-night, my Fair' (here headed 'Tristram (singing)'), 47 numbered leaves (rectos only), including dedication (f.1), title page (f. 2), 2 illustrations by Hardy captioned 'Imaginary View of Tintagel Castle at the Time of the Tragedy' (dated May 1923) and 'Imaginary Aspect of the Great Hall at the Time of the Tragedy', both signed (initials) (on 2 unnumbered leaves between ff. 1 and 2), and 'Characters' (f. 3), printer's copy for first edition; dated at the end (f. 47) 'Begun 1916: resumed & finished 1923.'.

This MS described Purdy, pp. 228–9; facsimile of title page used as the wrapper of first edition (London, 1923); Microfilm Edition, Reel 2.

Dorset County Museum.

HrT 1638 Typescript, revised, containing a fair copy of the song '"Could he but live for me"' on an inserted slip for p. 14 and a revised typescript of stanzas 1–3 of the song here beginning '"Let's meet again to-night, my Dear"' on p. 19 with a fair copy of the fourth stanza written out on an inserted slip, 34 numbered leaves (rectos only) including title page, a 'View of the Stage' (blank) and 'Characters'; as submitted to the Lord Chamberlain for licensing, stamped 6 November 1923 and licensed 14 November 1923.

Not mentioned Purdy.

British Library, LCP 1923/29, no. 5142.

HrT 1639 Typescript, revised by Hardy, containing a fair copy of '"Could he but live for me"' on an inserted page (for p. 14) and a fair copy of the fourth stanza of the song '"Let's meet again to-night...', one volume, for the Hardy Players production.

Described in *Hardy Players Collection*, H10 (facsimile page as frontispiece); not mentioned Purdy.

University of California at Riverside.

HrT 1640 Fair copy quotation, one page: '"A tragedy of dire duresse/That vexed the Land of Lyonnesse."/(From the Prologue to "The Queen/of Cornwall".)/Thomas Hardy'.

Texas.

HrT 1641 Corrected proof for first edition.

Mentioned Purdy, p. 228 as having been owned by George A. Macmillan.

Unlocated.

HrT 1642 Corrections in Hardy's copy of the Wessex Edition (Verse Vol. IV, pp. 217, 276), including an inserted pencil list of extra songs in Rutland Boughton's opera 'Queen of Cornwall', one page; presented to Sydney Cockerell by FEH, 30 March 1928 (see DCM Wessex Edition).

Cockerell Sale, Lot 252, sold to Maggs.

Owned (1985) F. B. Adams (see Hynes, III, 352).

Far from the Madding Crowd

Hardy's first attempt at a dramatization (entitled 'The Mistress of the Farm') was written in 1879; a version produced in collaboration with J. Comyns Carr first performed at Prince of Wales Theatre, Liverpool, 27 February 1882; A. H. Evans's dramatization performed by Dorchester Debating and Dramatic Society at Dorchester, 17–18 November 1909. One typescript, revised, of Evans's 1909 version is in the Riverside Collection (*Hardy Players Collection*, H2); another typescript, revised in an unidentified hand, 144 pages, was owned (1982) by David Holmes. For the original novel, see HrT 1405–9.

HrT 1643 Printed and MS version of 'The Mistress of the Farm' (probably Carr's version of Hardy's first version), as submitted to the Lord Chamberlain for licensing (License No. 29 issued 25 February 1882), including: printed copy of Acts I and II of an early version (pp. numbered 20–58), containing MS revisions, list of characters, and 6 pages of additional text, in more than one unidentified hand, some comments in Hardy's hand; together with a notebook containing Act III in 3 unidentified hands, revised, and including 3 more printed pages (pp. 64–6) of 'The Mistress of the Farm'.

This copy described and discussed in Purdy, pp. 28–30.

British Library, Add. MS 53267.

The Hand of Ethelberta

The typescript of a 3-act dramatization by an American called Kamakis is at Dorset County Museum; Microfilm Edition, Reel 4. For the original novel, see HrT 1422–4.

Jude as a Play

This dramatization never written. For the original novel, see HrT 1427–32.

HrT 1644 Four outlines for a dramatization: (1) draft, in three acts, headed 'Jude as a play' and annotated '(1st Scheme)' and '[By request]', one page, dated 24 October 1895; (2) fair copy, in four acts, headed 'Jude as a Play', including a list of possible titles, annotated '(2^{d} Scheme)', one page, dated 1897; (3) draft, in four acts, headed '"Jude <the Obscure>" as a play' and annotated '(3^{d} Scheme) [without Arabella]', 4 pages, on the versos of scraps of printed forms; (4) draft, in five acts, headed '(4th Scheme) [with Arabella]', one page, on the verso of a printed form dated 8 July 1926.

Microfilm Edition, Reel 2.

Dorset County Museum.

HrT 1645 Four very slightly revised typescripts of the four outlines (HrT 1644): (1) headed '(Ist Scheme)', one page, dated 24 October 1895; (2) headed '(2nd Schema — without Arabella)', 2 numbered leaves (rectos only), dated 1897; (3) headed '(3rd schema)', 3 numbered leaves (rectos only); (4) headed '4th SCHEME', one page; sent by FEH to St John Ervine in 1926.

These typescripts discussed and printed in Joseph Dobrinsky, 'Un Inédit de Thomas Hardy: quatre schémas pour une adaptation dramatique de *Jude the Obscure*', *EA*, 32 (1979), 198–205.

Texas.

The Mayor of Casterbridge

This dramatization was never written. For the original novel, see HrT 1514–15.

HrT 1646 Four outlines for a dramatization in four acts: (1) draft, 2 pages, headed '(Scheme for dramatizing)', including the cancelled annotation '[A Copy sent to Mr Chas. Cartwright — April 27, 1908]', dated at end April 1908; (2) corrected typescript of (1), headed '(Scheme for dramatizing)', 2 pages, annotated in Hardy's hand '(*By request, as an experiment.*)', dated by Hardy at the end April 1908; (3) 4 numbered pages, revised; (4) rough sketch on verso of an envelope addressed to Hardy.

Microfilm Edition, Reel 2.

Dorset County Museum.

The Mellstock Quire
This dramatization of *Under the Greenwood Tree* by A. H. Evans was first performed by the Hardy Players at Dorchester, 16–17 November 1910. The Riverside Collection includes a typescript, revised, of the dramatization (*Hardy Players Collection*, H3) and a MS of a one-act piece entitled 'The Wedding Scene from "The Mellstock Quire"' (produced by T. H. Tilley at London, 21 February 1924, as 'An old-time Rustic Wedding') (*Hardy Players Collection*, H12); five scriptbooks are at Dorset County Museum (Microfilm Edition, Reel 4). For the original novel, see HrT 1595–6.

The Mistress of the Farm, for Hardy's dramatization of *Far from the Madding Crowd*, see HrT 1643.

O Jan! O Jan! O Jan!
This piece (first performed at Dorchester, 28–30 November 1923) was described as 'A Recension of a Wessex Folk-Piece by Thomas Hardy From memories of the Piece as played in his childhood, at his father's house, about 1844'. A MS carbon copy in the hand of T. H. Tilley is in Riverside Collection (*Hardy Players Collection*, H13).

HrT 1647 Typescript, revised by Hardy, 6 numbered leaves (rectos only), including 5 leaves of text and 6 leaves of music.

Microfilm Edition, Reel 10.

Dorset County Museum.

A Pair of Blue Eyes
This dramatization was never written. For the original novel, see HrT 1539–41.

HrT 1648 Two draft outlines for a dramatization in five acts, the second headed 'Better arrangement.', one page each (versos of scraps).

Microfilm Edition, Reel 2.

Dorset County Museum.

The Play of 'Saint George'
Hardy's adaptation of the traditional play of 'Saint George' first performed by the Hardy Players in Act II of T. H. Tilley's dramatization of *The Return of the Native* at the Corn Exchange, Dorchester, 17–18 November 1920; it was performed privately by itself at Max Gate, Christmas 1920. First privately printed by FEH as a pamphlet, Cambridge, April 1921; Purdy, pp. 212–13.

HrT 1649 Two typescripts, revised, 9 numbered leaves (rectos only) each, one annotated 'Spare Copy'.

Microfilm Edition, Reel 3.

Dorset County Museum.

HrT 1650 Typescript, revised by Hardy, 9 leaves (rectos only) numbered 8–16, inserted in Act II of a typescript of T. H. Tilley's dramatization of *The Return of the Native* (HrT 1655).

Microfilm Edition, Reel 3.

Dorset County Museum.

HrT 1651 Typescript, revised by Hardy, 9 leaves (rectos only), here entitled 'The Masque of "St George"...', inserted in Act II of a MS of T. H. Tilley's dramatization of *The Return of the Native*.

Hardy Players Collection, H8; not mentioned Purdy.

University of California at Riverside.

HrT 1652 Corrected first proof for FEH's pamphlet; dated 31 March 1921.

This proof mentioned Purdy, p. 212; Cockerell Sale, Lot 306, sold to Maggs.

Owned (1978) R. L. Purdy; destined for Yale.

The Return of the Native
T. H. Tilley's dramatization performed by the Hardy Players at the Corn Exchange, Dorchester, 17–18 November 1920; see also 'The Play of "Saint George"' (HrT 1649–52) which was introduced into Act II for the performances. The Dorset County Museum owns 3 scriptbooks for the parts of Humphrey and the Turkish Knight, used for the 1920 performances; Microfilm Edition, Reel 3. The Riverside Collection includes a MS of Tilley's dramatization (including HrT 1651) (*Hardy Players Collection*, H8) and a MS scenario (H16). For the original novel, see HrT 1551–3.

HrT 1653 Draft outline for a dramatization in four acts, subtitled '(for Dorchester Society)', one page.

This version by Hardy was never written; Microfilm Edition, Reel 2.

Dorset County Museum.

HrT 1654 Notes on country dances, including a draft (one page) and a typescript (one page), for Tilley's production.

Dorset County Museum.

HrT 1655 Typescript of T. H. Tilley's dramatization, annotated by Hardy (containing HrT 1650).

Microfilm Edition, Reel 3.

Dorset County Museum.

The Romantic Adventures of a Milkmaid
This dramatization was never written. For the original story, see HrT 1557–9.

HrT 1656 Draft outline for a dramatization in four acts, 4 numbered pages and a 5th (unnumbered) containing a second beginning, headed 'Suggestions to Mr Tilley for his writing a Play based on the Story called "The Romantic Adventures of a Milkmaid"...', together with a revised typescript of same, 3 numbered leaves (rectos only).

The outline was sent to T. H. Tilley, the prospective adapter; Microfilm Edition, Reel 2.

Dorset County Museum.

A Sunday Morning Tragedy
This dramatization was never written; for a discussion, see Hynes, I, 382. For the original ballad, see HrT 1130–2.

HrT 1657 Two draft outlines: (1) in two acts, here entitled 'Birthwort.', 3 pages, dated 21 April 1893; (2) in three acts, on the versos of 2 scraps of printed forms, one including the date 24 April 1907.

Microfilm Edition, Reel 2.

Dorset County Museum.

Tess of the d'Urbervilles
Lorimer Stoddard's dramatization first performed Fifth Avenue Theater, New York, 2 March 1897. Hardy's dramatization (written 1894–5) first performed at the Corn Exchange, Dorchester, 26–9 November 1924. For a discussion of the theatrical history of the play and the texts of the three versions (i.e. Hardy's original 1894–5 version, Stoddard's version of 1897 and Hardy's version as produced in 1924), see Marguerite Roberts, *Tess in the Theatre* (Toronto, 1950). For the original novel, see HrT 1569–83. The Riverside Collection includes: MS stage plans (*Hardy Players Collection*, H24); 2 leaves of extracts of dialogue (H25); a drawing of Stonehenge used as a model for scenery (H26). Dorset County Museum owns a typescript promptbook for the part of Jonathan Kail for the 1924 production, 7 leaves (rectos only); Microfilm Edition, Reel 3.

HrT 1658 Five typescripts: (1) slightly revised, in five acts and an after-scene, annotated on wrapper 'Superseded Version. (One of the two prepared in 1894–5 — the other being the one acted in Dorchester Nov. 1924.)' and on title page '*Experimental: Not for Publication.*', 94 numbered leaves (rectos only) including title page and Dramatis Personae, [1894–5]; (2) revised, in five acts and an after-scene, reworked from the 1895 version for the 1924 production, 85 leaves (rectos only) numbered 1–67, 67a–c, 68–85; (3) extensively revised, in four acts, a fore-scene and an after-scene, annotated on front cover '(Rough Study copy)' and 'As performed in London — Sept–Dec. 1925. (with similar pagination.)' and 'The green alterations &

deletions were not in the London performance.' and on title page '(study copy)', c. 80 leaves (rectos only), [1924]; (4) in four acts, a fore-scene and an after-scene, 72 numbered leaves (rectos only), [1924]; (5) Lorimer Stoddard's version, annotated by Hardy, 87 leaves (rectos only).

Microfilm Edition, Reel 3.

Dorset County Museum.

HrT 1659 Typescript, revised, entitled 'Tess of the d'Urbervilles, A Tragedy in Five Acts. In the Old English manner', 93 leaves (rectos only), signed.

This typescript described Purdy, p. 78; the Harper Collection (MA 1950) also includes an uncorrected typescript of the Lorimer Stoddard version.

Pierpont Morgan, MA 1950 (Harper Collection).

HrT 1660 Typescript, revised and annotated by Hardy and by unidentified hands, 83 numbered leaves (rectos only) including title page and dramatis personae, bound, stamped 'This is the property of Philip Ridgeway, Barnes Theatre, S.W.13.'.

Texas.

HrT 1661 Corrected typescript; [1924].

Mentioned Purdy, p. 78.

Owned (1978) F. B. Adams.

HrT 1662 Typescript, revised by Hardy for the 1924 production, one volume.

Described in *Hardy Players Collection*, H11.

University of California at Riverside.

HrT 1663 A few bars of music in Hardy's hand, headed '*Langdon in F.* (Tess's favourite chant.) from T. H. to G. B.', one leaf, enclosed in a letter to Gertrude Bugler ('Tess' in the 1924 production), 2 December 1924.

This letter printed *Letters*, VI, 290.

Owned (1987) Mrs G. Bugler (see *Letters*).

The Three Wayfarers

Hardy's dramatization first performed at Terry's Theatre, 3 June 1893; first pub. New York, 1893 (in an edition of about 6 copies for copyright purposes); these copies were each annotated by Hardy with a note on the production and publication and have been located at Dorset County Museum (2 presentation copies to FEH, 1918), Harvard (see HrT 1667), Library of Congress and one in the collection of F. B. Adams); revised version pub. New York and London, 1930 and in a pamphlet privately printed by FEH, 1935. A. H. Evans's version of the dramatization (including a musical setting of 'The Hangman's Song' provided by Hardy; see 'The Stranger's Song', HrT 1121–2) first performed by the Hardy Players, 15–16 November 1911 at Dorchester; Purdy, pp. 78–80. For the original story 'The Three Strangers', see HrT 1585–6. A typescript of the revised 1930 version (prepared in April 1930) is at Colby College. The Dorset County Museum owns a typescript promptbook for the part of Elijah, the Guest, 4 pages; Microfilm Edition, Reel 4.

HrT 1664 Transcript by ELH, revised and corrected by Hardy, 21 leaves (20 numbered leaves, rectos only, and title page in Hardy's hand), annotated by Hardy '[Correct copy]' and '(To be returned to M[r] Hardy.)'.

Microfilm Edition, Reel 2.

Dorset County Museum.

HrT 1665 Four typescripts: (1) revised, including a fair copy of words and music of 'The Hangman's Song' inserted between pp. 8 and 9, ii + 18 numbered leaves (rectos only), annotated on cover '[correct private copy]'; (2) slightly revised, including a fair copy of words and music of 'The Hangman's Song' inserted between pp. 8 and 9, ii + 19 numbered leaves (rectos only), annotated on cover '(correct copy)'; (3) extensively revised, ii + 18 numbered leaves (rectos only); (4) uncorrected, ii + 20 numbered leaves (rectos only).

Facsimile of the fair copy of 'The Hangman's Song' (in (1) above) printed in the programme for the 1911 Dorchester production, in FEH's pamphlet and in Hynes, Appendix B, p. 389; Microfilm Edition, Reel 4.

Dorset County Museum.

HrT 1666 Corrected typescript, 14 leaves (ff. 1 and 14 in MS), as submitted to the Lord Chamberlain for licensing (Licence No. 152 issued 1 June 1893).

British Library, Add. MS 53528E.

HrT 1667 Fair copy of title page, bound with the presentation copy of first edition to Sydney Cockerell (including also two letters to Cockerell); annotated by Cockerell, 2 March 1918.

Mentioned Purdy, pp. 78–9 (without location); Cockerell Sale, Lot 255, sold to Rota (facsimile in sale catalogue).

Harvard, *EC85.H2224.893t.

HrT 1668 Typescript, revised and annotated in an unidentified hand, of Evans's 1911 version, one volume.

Hardy Players Collection, H4.

University of California at Riverside.

The Trumpet-Major

A. H. Evans's dramatization performed by the Hardy Players at the Corn Exchange, Dorchester, 18–19 November 1908. A typescript promptbook for the part of Bob is in the Dorset County Museum; Microfilm Edition, Reel 4. Two revised typescripts of Evans's dramatization (one used in 1908, the other in 1912) are at the University of California at Riverside; *Hardy Players Collection*, H1(a) and H1(b). For the original novel, see HrT 1591–2.

HrT 1669 Fair copy, revised, of an outline for dramatization in four acts, 2 pages, headed 'The Trumpet Major/A Play in four Acts' and annotated '[Outline of play sent to Mr Evans at his request. Returned by him when he had finished with it.]'; [1908].

Microfilm Edition, Reel 2.

Dorset County Museum.

HrT 1670 Carbon copy of typescript of Evans's dramatization, revised by Hardy, marked 'Prompt Copy', 109 pages.

Owned (1982) David Holmes.

Two on a Tower

This dramatization was never written. For the original novel, see HrT 1594.

HrT 1671 Two draft outlines for a dramatization: (1) in three acts, annotated 'Possible Dramatization.', one page (on verso of an envelope addressed to Hardy), [1895?]; (2) in four acts, annotated '[another arrangem^t^]', one page, [after 1912].

Microfilm Edition, Reel 2.

Dorset County Museum.

Under the Greenwood Tree, for a dramatization, see 'The Mellstock Quire'.

Wessex Scenes from 'The Dynasts', see HrT 1631–5.

The Woodlanders

A. H. Evans's dramatization first produced at Dorchester, 19–20 November 1913. The Riverside Collection includes an extensively revised typescript (3 vols) marked 'Prompt Copy' on cover (*Hardy Players Collection*, H6) and a MS of costume details (H22). For the original novel, see HrT 1604–6.

WORKS EDITED BY HARDY

Select Poems of William Barnes, see HrT 1560.

DIARIES AND NOTEBOOKS

Hardy probably destroyed most of his diaries after using them in the writing of *Early Life* and *Later Years*. At that time, he preserved some extracts by transcribing them into 'Memoranda Books I and II' (HrT 1685–6) and others by including them in *Life*; Sydney Cockerell destroyed almost all of the still surviving notebooks immediately following Hardy's death; for a fuller discussion, see INTRODUCTION. The notebooks below are listed roughly in chronological order of their dates of first usage; they are followed by the scrapbooks and extant fragments; for another leaf, apparently from a notebook, see HrT 1446.5.

[School Notebooks]
No publication traced.

HrT 1672 Two notebooks, one of architectural and mathematical problems, headed 'Miscellaneous Questions', signed and dated on title page 25 March 1854, the other headed 'Conic Sections and Their Solids', signed and dated on title page 4 December 1854.

An extract from the second notebook printed Millgate, p. 52.

Dorset County Museum.

[School Notebook]
No publication traced.

HrT 1673 Exercise book, kept by Hardy while a student at Isaac Last's school, containing sample commercial letters, receipts, etc., signed and dated variously from April to September 1855.

Mentioned Millgate, p. 53.

Dorchester Reference Library, Lock Collection.

The Architectural Notebook
This notebook discussed and printed (in facsimile) in *The Architectural Notebook of Thomas Hardy*, ed. C. J. P. Beatty (Dorchester, 1966).

HrT 1674 Containing architectural notes, sketches and records of daily work, in pencil (drawings mostly) and ink (notes), 156 pages (2 blank), erratically paginated; used in the 1860s, later entries of c. 1920.

Dorset County Museum.

Schools of Painting Notebook
First pub. Taylor (1978), pp. [103]–14.

HrT 1675 Pocket notebook containing notes on European schools of painting, headed '12 May. 1863/Schools of Painting', in ink, 17 pages, roughly half of original leaves have been excised.

This notebook discussed and described in Taylor, pp. xviii–xx, [xxvii]–xxviii; Microfilm Edition, Reel 9.

Dorset County Museum.

Studies, Specimens &c Notebook
No publication traced.

HrT 1676 Notebook used to collect words and phrases, entitled 'Studies, Specimens &c'; dated 1865, used certainly in 1868–9.

Some entries in this notebook mentioned Björk, I, *passim* and Millgate, pp. 87–9.

Owned (1985) R. L. Purdy (see Björk); destined for Yale.

The 1867 Notebook
First pub. *The Literary Notes of Thomas Hardy*, ed. Lennart A. Björk, Gothenburg Studies in English 29 (Gothenburg, 1974); reprinted Björk, II (1985), pp. [453]–79.

HrT 1677 Commonplace book containing mostly notes of reading, marked 'IV' on cover, 45 pages of text on 23 leaves, followed by blank leaves and unnumbered leaves containing an Index in pencil; dated '1867' on verso of front flyleaf, used c. late 1860s–1880s.

Described Björk, II, xxxiv–xxxv; Microfilm Edition, Reel 9.

Dorset County Museum.

Literary Notes I
First partially pub. *The Literary Notes of Thomas Hardy*, ed. Lennart A. Björk, Gothenburg Studies in English 29 (Gothenburg, 1974); first pub. in full Björk, I (1985), pp. 3–228. Many of the earlier notes in this notebook were used for *The Return of the Native*.

HrT 1678 Commonplace book, partly in the hand of ELH, entitled in pencil 'Literary Notes I' and labelled 'Commonplace Book I', containing mostly extracts from readings copied by Hardy or transcribed from earlier notebooks by Hardy or ELH, 143 leaves of text (paginated erratically) and a few inserted leaves (4 of them (8 pages) numbered 518–25, pasted onto a front flyleaf and taken from a destroyed notebook of 1863); used mid-1870s–1888.

Described Björk, I, xxxii–xxxiii; facsimile page Björk, I, 4; Microfilm Edition, Reel 9.

Dorset County Museum.

Facts from Newspapers, Histories, Biographies, & other chronicles — (mainly Local)
No publication traced.

HrT 1679 Commonplace book, partly in the hands of ELH and FEH, including mostly historical notes and some newspaper cuttings, entitled as above and marked 'III' on the cover, c. 220 pages and several inserted leaves; c. 1875–1913.

Mentioned Björk, I, 396 (1454) and 396–7 (1464); Microfilm Edition, Reel 9. This notebook contains source notes for the poem 'Panthera' (HrT 888–90); see Hynes, I, 386; source material for *The Mayor of Casterbridge* is discussed in Millgate, *Career*, pp. 237–43 and William Greenslade, 'Hardy's "Facts" Notebook: A Further Source for *The Mayor of Casterbridge*', *Thomas Hardy Journal*, Vol. II, no. 1 (January 1986), pp. 33–5.

Dorset County Museum.

The Trumpet-Major Notebook
Extracts first pub. Emma Clifford, '"The Trumpet-Major Notebook" and *The Dynasts*', *RES*, NS8 (1957), 146–91; further extracts in Wright (1967), *passim*; first pub. in full in 'Thomas Hardy's "Trumpet-Major" Notebook', ed. J. Stevens Cox, *The Thomas Hardy Year Book*, Nos 2–4 (1971–4); also pub. in full in Taylor (1978), pp. [115]–86.

HrT 1680 Notebook, used primarily for research notes for *The Trumpet-Major* and *The Dynasts*, a few notes in ELH's hand, labelled 'B^{sh}. Museum./Notes/taken for "Trumpet Major"/& other books of time/ of Geo III./in (1878–1879 —)', mostly in ink, erratically paginated, composed of 3 gatherings sewn together (possibly 3 notebooks originally), the first entitled '1803–5 <George III> notes — (i) B.M. &c', the third entitled 'B.M. III'; 122 pages of text, some leaves excised; compiled 1878–9.

This notebook discussed and described in Taylor, pp. xx–xxv, xxviii, xxxi–xxxii; also discussed in Michael Edwards, 'The Making of Hardy's *The Trumpet-Major*', unpublished M.A. thesis, Univerity of Birmingham, pp. 139–42; Microfilm Edition, Reel 9. Hardy sent A. M. Broadley a few notes taken from this notebook in a letter of 7 January 1908 (printed *Letters*, III, [289] from the original at University of California at Berkeley).

Dorset County Museum.

Literary Notes II
First pub. Björk, II (1985), pp. [1]–249.

HrT 1681 Commonplace book, a continuation of HrT 1678, some entries in the hand of ELH, including mostly literary and philosophical notes and some newspaper cuttings, entitled in pencil 'Literary Notes II', c. 280 pages on 128 leaves of text and several inserted leaves, annotated by Hardy '[188–, onwards.]' and '*Not to be printed or promulgated.*'; used 1888–1927.

Described Björk, II, xxxiii, dating discussed pp. xxxviii–xxxix; Microfilm Edition, Reel 9.

Contents: HrT 17.

Dorset County Museum.

Nomenclature of The Wessex Novels
No publication traced.

HrT 1682 Exercise book, labelled by Hardy as above, almost entirely blank; containing pencil list of 'Principal scenes in each of the Wessex novels...' [ff. 8v–9], 'Uniform Edition (changes & corrections of proper names — & new titles' [f. 11v], 'List of Published Works' in ELH's hand, revised by Hardy, including the years 1865–94 [ff. 12v–13], list by ELH of Wessex places and walking tours [ff. 14v–inside back cover]; [1890s].

Dorset County Museum.

Literary Notes III
First pub. Björk, II (1985), pp. [251]–451.

HrT 1683 Scrapbook, entitled (in pencil on inside front cover) 'Literary Notes III', containing commonplace book entries in Hardy's hand, newspaper and periodical cuttings and typescript pages (ff. 43–63), annotated '*To be destroyed uncopied*' on front flyleaf; containing material dated 1906–1910.

Described Björk, II, xxxiii–xxxiv, dating discussed pp. xxxix–xl.

Dorset County Museum.

Poetical Matter Notebook
Extracts printed Millgate (1982), *passim* (especially pp. 89, 112–13, 170–1 and 204).

HrT 1684 Notebook, headed 'Poetical Matter', in which Hardy jotted notes or outlines for potential use in writing poems, etc., including a note containing a rough sketch of a ballad beginning 'I sat me down in a foreign town'.

Photocopy only owned (1985) R. L. Purdy (see Björk, I, xxxi); destined for Yale.

Memoranda Book I
During Hardy's sifting of his papers in preparation for the writing of *Life*, he transcribed extracts of earlier diaries and notebooks into 2 new notebooks; this one (the first) contains entries dating from 1867–1920; he thereafter destroyed the originals (see INTRODUCTION). Selections first pub. (inaccurately) in *Thomas Hardy's Notebooks*, ed. Evelyn Hardy (London, 1955), pp. [25]–88, as 'The First Notebook'; in full in Taylor (1978), pp. [3]–40.

HrT 1685 Pocket notebook, entitled [p. 1] '*Memoranda*/of Customs, Dates, &c — /(*viz: Prose Matter*)/*I*.', entries dated 1867–7 June 1920, 71 pages of text on 65 leaves (mostly rectos only), mostly in pencil and unpaginated, annotated [p. 1] that the notebook should be destroyed; compiled probably 1919–20.

For a continuation, see HrT 1686; Microfilm Edition, Reel 9.

Dorset County Museum.

Memoranda Book II
This notebook is a continuation of HrT 1685 and the book to which Hardy directed FEH for her completion of *Life*, (i.e., Chapters 37–8), see especially HrT 1444, 1447–8. Selections first pub. (inaccurately) in *Thomas Hardy's Notebooks*, ed. Evelyn Hardy (London, 1955), pp. [89]–120, as 'The Second Notebook'; first pub. in full in Taylor (1978), pp. [41]–102.

HrT 1686 Pocket notebook, entitled on [p. 1] '*Memoranda* — (*viz: Prose Matter*)/II.', including some newspaper cuttings, annotated 'This book is to be destroyed when my executors have done with it...', mostly in pencil, 75 pages of text (pp. 1–70 only paginated) and 25 blank pages; dated '*Feb. 1923*' on inside front cover, entries dated 1 January 1921–19 September 1927.

This notebook discussed and described in Taylor, pp. xii–xviii, [xxvii], xxxi; Microfilm Edition, Reel 9. This notebook contains the lists 'MSS. *not in existence* — (among others)' (p. 29) and '*Depositories of T. H.'s MSS.*' (pp. 31–3) discussed in the INTRODUCTION (see also HrT 1604). For two passages of *Later Years*, see HrT 1463.

Dorset County Museum.

Scrapbook I
No publication traced.

HrT 1687 Containing clippings regarding Hardy ('Personal Reviews'), annotated by Hardy *passim*, c. 76 leaves.

Microfilm Edition, Reel 6.

Contents: HrT 1380.5, 1392, 1442.5, 1511.5, 1548.5, 1550, 1567, 1600 (see also 1603).

Dorset County Museum.

Scrapbook II
No publication traced.

HrT 1688 Containing clippings of 'Reviews of Thomas Hardy's Prose Works' (so headed on first page), annotated by Hardy *passim*, c. 96 leaves.

Microfilm Edition, Reel 6.

Dorset County Museum.

Scrapbook III
No publication traced.

HrT 1689 Containing clippings of 'Reviews of Thomas Hardy's Poetical Works' (so entitled), annotated by Hardy *passim*, c. 171 leaves.

Microfilm Edition, Reel 6; this scrapbook discussed briefly in Lloyd Siemens, 'Hardy Among the Critics: The Annotated Scrap Books' in *Thomas Hardy Annual No. 2*, ed. Norman Page (London, 1984), pp. 187–90.

Contents: HrT 151.5, 161.5, 176.5, 804.

Dorset County Museum.

Scrapbook IV
No publication traced.

HrT 1690 Containing clippings of reviews of Hardy's dramatic works, annotated by Hardy *passim*, c. 73 leaves.

Microfilm Edition, Reel 6.

Dorset County Museum.

Fragments from Notebooks
See also HrT 1446.5.

HrT 1690.5 One page from a diary, including a sketch of a painting by Mangiarelli; dated 23 November 1878.

Facsimile in J. B. Bullen, *The Expressive Eye: Fiction and Perception in the Works of Thomas Hardy* (Oxford, 1986), Figure 1.

Dorset County Museum.

HrT 1691 Fragment, beginning 'next day I meet with a keeper...', a description of a pheasant shoot at Wimborne, one page, mounted on a leaf which is annotated in an undentified hand 'From a notebook by T. H.' and 'January 1882./at Wimborne.'.

This MS printed Millgate, p. 235; Microfilm Edition, Reel 10.

Dorset County Museum.

HrT 1692 Extracts from Chatterton, Carlyle, Blackmore and G. H. Lewes, headed 'Thought', one page.

The extract from Lewes printed Björk, I, 353 (1079); the extract from Chatterton marked in Hardy's copy of Chatterton's poems (see HrT 1752), see Björk, I, 263 (123); Microfilm Edition, Reel 10.

Dorset County Museum.

HrT 1693 One page of diary entries, in pencil, on the verso of a leaf taken from a notebook (containing also HrT 853); including the dates 29 April and 4 May 1921.

The notebook was destroyed by FEH and the leaf given to J. M. Barrie; see Purdy, p. 324.

Harvard, MS Eng 695.1.

MARGINALIA IN PRINTED BOOKS AND MANUSCRIPTS

Abercrombie, Lascelles. *The Epic* (London, [192?]).

HrT 1694 Marked and annotated.

Texas.

Aeschylus. *The Tragedies of Aeschylus*, trans. T. A. Buckley, 10 vols (London, 1849).

HrT 1695 Annotated and marked, wanting title page.

Grolier Catalogue, Item 8; mentioned Rutland, p. 35 and Björk, I, 280 (307).

Unlocated.

Aeschylus. *The Tragedies of Aeschylus*, ed. F. A. Paley (London, 1855).

HrT 1696 Annotated.

Mentioned Rutland, pp. 34, 37–9 (when it was in the library at Max Gate).

Owned (1989) R. L. Purdy; destined for Yale.

Alden, Edward C. *Alden's Oxford Guide*.

HrT 1697 Annotated.

Mentioned Millgate, pp. 328–9.

British Library, Department of Printed Books.

Alison, Archibald. *History of Europe from the Commencement of the French Revolution in M.DCC.LXXXIX. to the Restoration of the Bourbons in M.DCCC.XV.*, 7th ed, 20 vols (Edinburgh and London, 1847–8) and *Epitome of Alison's History of Europe*, 3rd ed (Edinburgh and London, 1849).

HrT 1698 Annotated and marked, possibly Hardy's second copy.

Mentioned Rutland, p. 296 and Wright, p. 164.

Dorset County Museum.

American Poetry 1922. A Miscellany (New York, 1922).

HrT 1699 Annotated in pencil on inside back cover; presentation copy from Amy Lowell, November 1922.

Max Gate Sale, Lot 218; this copy mentioned *Letters*, VI, 186n.

Cornell University.

Andersen, Hans Christian. *Fairy Tales — A New Translation* (London and New York, 1892).

HrT 1700 Marked on p. 7.

Wreden Catalogue (1938), Item 96.

Aristotle. *Aristotle's Treatise on Rhetoric...Also the Poetic of Aristotle*, trans. T. A. Buckley (London, 1850).

HrT 1701 Annotated and marked.

Max Gate Sale, Lot 22.

Colby College.

Arnold, Matthew. *Poetical Works* (London and New York, 1890).

HrT 1702 Annotated and marked.

Mentioned Wright, p. 22 and Millgate, p. 378.

Dorset County Museum.

Arnold, Matthew. *Selected Poems* (London and New York, 1893).

HrT 1703 Marked.

Mentioned Wright, p. 22.

Dorset County Museum.

[Arthur, King of Britain], see HrT 1863.

Aurelius Antoninus, Marcus. *The Thoughts of the Emperor*, trans. George Lang (London, 1862).

HrT 1704 Annotated and marked, presentation copy from Henry Moule, New Year's Day 1865.

Mentioned Björk, I, 314 (632).

Owned (1982) R. L. Purdy (see Millgate, p. 587–45); destined for Yale.

Bacon, G. W. and Co. [Map of Devonshire].

HrT 1704.3 With autograph extension by Hardy.

First Edition Bookshop Catalogue 33 (November 1938), Item 1.

Bacon, G. W. and Co. [Map of Central London, c. 1880].

HrT 1704.5 Marked.

First Edition Bookshop Catalogue 33 (November 1938), Item 5.

Baedecker, Carl. *Belgium and Holland*, 4th ed revised (Leipzig and London, 1875).

HrT 1705 Annotated, inscribed June 1876.

Mentioned Millgate, p. 183.

British Library, Department of Printed Books, C.134.bb.1/14.

Baedecker, Carl. *Belgium and Holland including the Grand-Duchy of Luxembourg*, 11th ed revised (Leipzig and London, 1894).

HrT 1706 Inscribed 1896.

British Library, Department of Printed Books, C.134.bb.1/17.

Baedecker, Carl. *Great Britain*, 3rd ed revised (Leipzig and London, 1894).

HrT 1707 Marked.

British Library, Department of Printed Books, C.134.bb.1/35.

Baedecker, Carl. *Index of Streets and Plans of Paris* (Leipzig, 1882).

HrT 1708 Annotated.

Yale.

Baedecker, Carl. *Italy [Handbook for Travellers]...Central Italy and Rome*, 9th ed revised (Leipzig and London, 1886).

HrT 1709 Annotated and marked, inscribed Florence, March 1887.

Mentioned Björk, I, 288 (382) and 372 (1217).

British Library, Department of Printed Books, C.134.bb.1/13.

Baedecker, Carl. *Italy. [Handbook for Travellers]...Northern Italy*, 7th ed revised (Leipzig and London, 1886).

HrT 1710 Annotated, inscribed 1887.

British Library, Department of Printed Books, C.134.bb.1/24.

Baedecker, Carl. *Northern Germany as far as the Bavarian and Austrian Frontiers*, 10th ed revised (Leipzig and London, 1890).

HrT 1711 Annotated on p. 381.

British Library, Department of Printed Books, C.134.bb.1/28.

Baedecker, Carl. *Paris and Its Environs*, 7th ed (Leipzig and London, 1881).

HrT 1712 Annotated and marked.

Mentioned Millgate, p. 306.

British Library, Department of Printed Books, C.134.bb.1/34.

Baedecker, Carl. *The Rhine From Rotterdam to Constance*, 5th ed revised (Coblenz and Leipzig, 1873).

HrT 1713 Inscribed 1876.

British Library, Department of Printed Books, C.134.bb.1/25.

Baedecker, Carl. *Switzerland and the Adjacent Portions of Italy, Savoy, and Tyrol*, 16th ed (Leipzig and London, 1895).

HrT 1714 Marked.

British Library, Department of Printed Books, C.134.b.11.1/3.

Baedecker, Carl. *The Traveller's Manual of Conversation in Four Languages*, 21st ed (Coblenz and Leipzig, 1873).

HrT 1715 Including (pasted to front) a 16-page phrase-book in which Hardy has written words and phrases and German equivalents.

Grolier Catalogue, Item 53; Max Gate Salc, Lot 286.

Owned (1989) R. L. Purdy; destined for Yale.

The Ballad Minstrelsy of Scotland, 2nd ed (Glasgow, n.d.).

HrT 1716 Annotated and marked.

Dorset County Museum.

Balzac, Honoré de. *Le Maison du Chat-Qui-Pelotte* (Paris, 1876).

HrT 1717 Annotated and marked.

Hollings Catalogue 212 (n.d.), Item 4.

Bampfylde, John, see HrT 1963.

Barnes, William. *A Grammar and Glossary of the Dorset Dialect* (Berlin, 1863).

HrT 1718 Annotated.

Annotations printed in Patricia Ingham, 'Thomas Hardy and the Dorset Dialect' in *Five Hundred Years of Words and Sounds*, ed. E. G. Stanley and Douglas Gray (Cambridge, 1983); mentioned in Hynes, III, 364 (in Appendix F 'Glossary of Dialect, Archaic, and Obsolete Words'); Max Gate Sale, Lot 281.

Owned (1985) R. L. Purdy (see Hynes); destined for Yale.

Barnes, William. *Poems in the Dorset Dialect* (Dorchester: 'Dorset County Chronicle' Printing Works, 1906).

HrT 1719 Annotated and marked.

Dorset County Museum.

Barnes, William. *Poems of Rural Life in Common English* (London, 1868).

HrT 1720 Annotated and marked, presentation copy from Barnes to Hardy, 1876.

Dorset County Museum.

Barnes, William. *Poems of Rural Life in the Dorset Dialect*, First Collection, 3rd ed (London, 1862).

HrT 1720.5 Annotated.

King's College, Cambridge.

Barnes, William. *Poems of Rural Life in the Dorset Dialect* (London, 1879).

HrT 1721 Annotated and marked.

Mentioned Wright, p. 73.

Dorset County Museum.

Baudelaire, Charles. *Les Fleurs du mal* (Paris, 1884).

HrT 1722 Pencil translation of last 4 lines of poem 'Spleen' on p. 203.

Hollings Catalogue 212 (n.d.), Item 8.

Baxter, Lucy. *The Life of William Barnes* (London, 1887).

HrT 1723 Annotated.

Dorset County Museum.

Beattie, James, see HrT 1963.

Beaumont, C. W. & Co. *A Catalogue of Rare and Choice Books Autographs and Manuscripts*, no. 32 (Christmas 1917).

HrT 1724 Hardy items annotated (Lots 1 and 4).

Dorset County Museum.

Beaumont, Francis and John Fletcher. *The Works*, introduction by George Darley, 2 vols (London, 1872).

HrT 1725 Annotated and marked.

Mentioned Wright, p. 88.

Dorset County Museum.

Beckmann, Johann. *A History of Inventions and Discoveries*, 4th ed, 2 vols (London, 1846).

HrT 1726 Annotated on II, 524.

Wreden Catalogue (1938), Item 101.

B[erg], E[mil] P. *God the Beautiful* (London, 1901).

HrT 1727 Annotated on pp. 143 and 145 in pencil.

Texas.

Berliner, Emile. *Conclusions* (Philadelphia, 1899).

HrT 1728 Marked.

Texas.

Best Poems of 1923, ed. Leonard Alfred George Strong (Boston, 1924).

HrT 1729 Corrections to a poem by Richard Aldington and markings (also including HrT 871).

Wreden Catalogue (1938), Item 133.

[The Bible]. *The Holy Bible containing the Old and New Testaments* (London, 1859).

HrT 1730 Annotated and marked, inscribed 1861.

This Bible discussed in Kenneth Phelps, 'Annotations by Thomas Hardy in his Bibles and Prayer-Book', *Monographs on the Life, Times and Works of Thomas Hardy*, ed. J. Stevens Cox, No. 32 (Guernsey, 1966).

Dorset County Museum.

[The Bible]. *The Holy Bible, containing the Old and New Testaments* (Oxford, 1898).

HrT 1731 Annotated, a gift from ELH, inscribed 2 June 1899.

Mentioned in Kenneth Phelps, 'Annotations by Thomas Hardy in his Bibles and Prayer-Book', *Monographs on the Life, Times and Works of Thomas Hardy*, ed. J. Stevens Cox, No. 32 (Guernsey, 1966), p. 12.

Dorset County Museum.

[The Bible]. 'Η Καινὴ Διαθήκη. *Griesbach's text, with the various readings of Mill and Scholz...*, 3rd ed (London, 1859).

HrT 1732 Annotated, inscribed 7 February 1860.

Max Gate Sale, Lot 22; mentioned Rutland, pp. 28–9 and Millgate p. 64.

Owned (1982) R. L. Purdy (see Millgate, p. 586n48); destined for Yale.

[The Bible]. 'Η Καινὴ Διαθήκη. *The Greek Testament*, [ed.] S. T. Bloomfield, 10th ed ([187?]).

HrT 1733 Wanting title page, annotated on pp. 124 and 442, marked on pp. 442–5.

Wreden Catalogue (1938), Item 103.

[Black, Adam and Charles Black]. *Black's Picturesque Tourist of Scotland*, 23rd ed (Edinburgh, 1881).

HrT 1734 Annotated.

British Library, Department of Printed Books, C.134.bb.1/8.

Blanchard, Samuel Laman. *Lyric Offerings* (London, 1828).

HrT 1735 Annotated in pencil by Hardy?, inscribed to 'My dear friend —'.

Texas.

The Book of Common Prayer (Cambridge, 1858).

HrT 1736 Annotated, marked and including a list of addresses.

These annotations and markings are discussed in Kenneth Phelps, 'Annotations by Thomas Hardy in his Bibles and Prayer-Book', *Monographs on the Life, Times and Works of Thomas Hardy*, ed. J. Stevens Cox, No. 32 (Guernsey, 1966).

Dorset County Museum.

Boswell, James. *The Life of Samuel Johnson...New Edition...by the Right Hon. John Wilson Croker...To which are added, two supplementary volumes of Johnsoniana*, 10 vols (London, 1859).

HrT 1737 Annotated and marked in Vol. IX.

This copy mentioned in Björk, I, 245 (20).

Dorset County Museum.

Brachet, Auguste. *The Public School Elementary French Grammar*, 2 vols, revised by Elphège Janau (London and Paris, 1894).

HrT 1738 Annotations by Hardy and FEH?, Vol. II inscribed 'Ethel M. Dugdale. 1897.'

Texas.

Brennecke, Ernest. *The Life and Art of Thomas Hardy* (New York, 1925).

HrT 1739 Annotated.

Mentioned Björk, I, 298 (464).

Dorset County Museum.

Broadley, Alexander Meyrick. *Boyhood of a Great King 1841–1858: An Account of the Early Years of the Life of His Majesty Edward VII* (London, 1901).

HrT 1739.5 Correction on p. 16.

David Holmes List [1989], Item 4.

Broadley, Alexander Meyrick and Bartlett (afterwards Bartelot), Richard Grosvenor. *The Three Dorset Captains at Trafalgar* (London, 1906).

HrT 1740 One annotation.

Dorset County Museum.

Browning, Robert. *The Poetical Works*, 2 vols (London, 1897).

HrT 1741 Annotated on the back cover of Vol. II.

Dorset County Museum.

Browning, Robert. *Poetical Works*, 8 vols (London, 1902).

HrT 1742 Annotated on flyleaf of Vol. V.

Wreden Catalogue (1938), Item 105.

Browning, Robert. *Selections from the Poetical Works* (London, 1893).

HrT 1743 Annotated and marked, presentation copy from Florence Henniker, July 1894.

Mentioned Millgate, p. 356 and Björk, I, 372 (1217).

Dorset County Museum.

Burke, *Right Hon.* Edmund. *The Works*, 5 vols (London, 1876–7), Vol. I.

HrT 1744 Marked by Hardy in pencil, Vols II–III uncut..

Colby College.

Byron, George Gordon Noel, Baron Byron. *Poems* (London, 1864).

HrT 1745 'Childe Harold's Pilgrimage', Canto III, lincs 85–7) annotated '14.5.66'.

Mentioned Purdy, p. 297.

Owned (1989) R. L. Purdy; destined for Yale.

Byron, George Gordon Noel, Baron Byron. *Poetry of Byron*, ed. Matthew Arnold (London, 1881).

HrT 1745.5 Annotated and marked in the Preface.

David Holmes List [1989], Item 6.

Campbell, George. *The Philosophy of Rhetoric*, ed. A. Jamieson, 11th ed (London, 1841).

HrT 1746 Extensively annotated.

Mentioned Björk, I, 269 (175).

Wreden Catalogue (1938), Item 12.

Campbell, Thomas. *Poems*, ed. Lewis Campbell (London and New York, 1904).

HrT 1747 Annotated and marked.

Mentioned Wright, pp. 86–7.

Dorset County Museum.

Capefigue, Jean Baptiste Honoré Raymond. *L'Europe pendant le Consulat et l'Empire de Napoléon*, 10 vols (Paris, 1840).

HrT 1748 Marked.

Mentioned Rutland, p. 296 and Wright, pp. 131 and 161.

Dorset County Museum.

Caro, Elme Marie. *Le Pessimisme au XIXe siècle*, 2nd ed (Paris, 1880).

HrT 1749 Annotated and marked.

Mentioned Millgate, p. 246.

Owned (1982) R. L. Purdy (see Millgate); destined for Yale.

Cassels, Walter Richard. *Supernatural Religion* (London, 1902).

HrT 1750 Annotated on title page.

Wreden Catalogue (1938), Item 106.

Catullus and Tibullus. *Erotica. The Poems of Catullus and Tibullus, and The Vigil of Venus*, trans. W. T. Kelly (London, 1887).

HrT 1751 Annotated on 3 pages and marked.

Colby College.

Chatterton, Thomas. *The Poetical Works*, 2 vols (London, 1875).

HrT 1752 Annotated and marked in Vol. II.

One marked stanza (II, 38) was quoted in *The Woodlanders*; this stanza also partly transcribed on a loose leaf from a notebook (HrT 1692); mentioned Björk, I, 263 (123).

Dorset County Museum.

Chaucer, Geoffrey. *The Poetical Works*, ed. Richard Morris, 6 vols (London, 1880–2).

HrT 1753 Annotated and marked.

Dorset County Museum.

Chew, Samuel. *Thomas Hardy, Poet and Novelist*, Bryn Mawr Notes and Monographs No. 3 (Bryn Mawr, 1921).

HrT 1754 Annotated and marked.

For notes, based on these annotations, sent to Samuel Chew, see HrT 1527.5; mentioned Björk, I, 372–3 (1217).

Dorset County Museum.

Child, Harold. *Thomas Hardy* (London, 1916), see HrT 1527.

[Clarke, William]. *The Boy's Own Book: A Complete Encyclopaedia of all the Diversions, Athletic, Scientific and Recreative, of Boyhood and Youth* (London, n.d.).

HrT 1755 Marked.

Mentioned Millgate, *Career*, p. 366 and Millgate, p. 51.

Owned (1982) F. B. Adams (see Millgate).

Coleridge, Mary. *Poems*, 6th ed (London, 1910).

HrT 1756 Marked.

Mentioned Björk, II, 534 (2339).

Dorset County Museum.

Coleridge, Samuel Taylor. *Biographia Literaria and Two Lay Sermons* (London, 1898).

HrT 1757 Annotated and marked.

Mentioned Björk, II, 533 (2320).

Dorset County Museum.

Coleridge, Samuel Taylor. *The Poems*, ed. Derwent and Sara Coleridge (London, 1859).

HrT 1758 Marked, inscribed 1865.

Mentioned Wright, p. 85.

Dorset County Museum.

Collier, William Frederick. *Tales and Sayings of William Robert Hicks*, 3rd ed (London and Plymouth, 1893).

HrT 1759 Annotated and marked.

Dorset County Museum.

Comte, Isidore Auguste. *A General View of Positivism*, trans. J. H. Bridges (London, 1865).

HrT 1760 Annotated and marked by Hardy and Horace Moule.

Mentioned Björk, I, 311–12 (618).

Owned (1985) R. L. Purdy (see Björk); destined for Yale.

Copinger, Walter Arthur. *The Law of Copyright, in Works of Literature and Art* (London, 1870).

HrT 1761 Marked, inscribed 1873.

Mentioned Millgate, *Career*, p. 370 and Millgate, p. 142n.

Dorset County Museum.

Copleston, Reginald Stephen. *Buddhism, Primitive and Present, in Magahda and Ceylon* (London, 1892).

HrT 1762 Marked.

Max Gate Sale (1938), Lot 29; Hollings Catalogue 212 (n.d.), Item 20.

The Cost of Production, 2nd ed ([London], 1891).

HrT 1763 Annotated in pencil, inscribed on the front cover (by Hardy?) 'T. Hardy from W. B.' (Walter Besant?).

Annotation printed Wreden Catalogue, Item 6.

Texas.

Coutts, Francis Burdett Thomas Money. *The Romance of King Arthur* (London, 1907).

HrT 1763.5 Markings on pp. 3, 4, 8.

David Holmes List [1989], Item 10.

Crabbe, George. *The Life and Poetical Works*, ed. by his son [George Crabbe] (London, 1860).

HrT 1764 Annotated.

Mentioned Rutland, p. 12 and Wright, p. 84.

Dorset County Museum.

Cruchley's Railway and Station Map of the County of Wiltshire (London, n.d.).

HrT 1765 Annotated on map only.

British Library, Department of Printed Books, C.134.bb.1/43.

Cruchley's Railway and Telegraphic County Map of Berkshire ([London, n.d.]).

HrT 1766 Annotated on map; inscribed and annotated '(2.)' on front cover.

British Library, Department of Printed Books, C.134.bb.1/40.

Cruchley's Railway and Telegraphic County Map of Dorset, see HrT 1582.

Cruchley's Railway and Telegraphic County Map of Hampshire ([London, n.d.]).

HrT 1767 Inscribed on front cover 'M. Hardy' and annotated on front cover '(5).', annotations on map by Hardy?.

British Library, Department of Printed Books, C.134.bb.1/42.

Cruchley's Railway and Telegraphic County Map of Somerset ([London, n.d.]).

HrT 1768 Inscribed and annotated '(4.)' on front cover, annotated on map.

British Library, Department of Printed Books, C.134.bb.1/44.

Danielson, Henry. *The First Editions of the Writings of Thomas Hardy and their Values* (London, 1916).

HrT 1769 Two copies (one a limited edition on handmade paper, the other a presentation copy to FEH from Clement Shorter, 9 June 1916), both annotated, the second by Hardy and FEH.

Dorset County Museum.

Dante Alighieri. *Dante's Divine Comedy: The Inferno*, trans. John A. Carlyle, 2nd ed (London, 1882).

HrT 1770 Annotated and marked.

Mentioned Wright, pp. 12–13, 77, 89–90 and Björk, I, 287–8 (367) and II, 566 (A118).

Dorset County Museum.

Dante Alighieri. *The Vision; or, Hell, Purgatory, and Paradise*, trans. H. F. Cary (London, 1870).

HrT 1771 Annotated and marked, inscribed by ELH, 1870.

Texas.

Darley, George. *Poetical Works* (London and New York, [1908?]).

HrT 1772 Marked on p. 498.

Texas.

Davies, W. H. *Nature Poems and Others* (London, 1908).
See HrT 1937.

HrT 1772.5 Marked.

David Holmes List [1989], Item 11.

Davyl, Louis. *La Maîtresse légitime* (Paris, 1882).

HrT 1773 Minor annotations on pp. 1 and 12.

David Holmes List [1989], Item 12.

De Casseres, Benjamin. *Forty Immortals* (New York, 1926).

HrT 1774 Presentation copy to Hardy, 1926.

Dorset County Museum.

De la Mare, Walter. *The Listeners and other poems* (London, 1912).

HrT 1775 Marked.

A presentation copy to Hardy, inscribed June 1921 [sic] sold Max Gate Sale, Lot 205.

Cockerell Sale (1956), Lot 325, sold to B. F. Stevens.

Dickinson, F. Lowes. *The Magic Flute* (London, n.d.).

HrT 1775.5 Annotated on p. 7.

David Magee Catalogue 23 (n.d.), Item 166.

Dilworth, Thomas. *A New Guide to the English Tongue...and Select Fables* (London, n.d.).

HrT 1776 Marked, inscribed 'Master Hardy'.

Mentioned Millgate, p. 40.

Dorset County Museum.

Dindorf, Karl Wilhelm. *Poetae scenici graeci* (Leipzig and London, 1841).

HrT 1777 Annotated.

Mentioned Rutland, p. 34 (when it was in the library at Max Gate).

Commin Catalogue 111 (Winter 1938), Item 384.

Donne, John. *Poems*, ed. E. K. Chambers, 2 vols (London and New York, 1896).

HrT 1778 Annotated.

Dorset County Museum.

Dowden, Edward. *The Life of Percy Bysshe Shelley*.

HrT 1779 Annotated and marked.

Mentioned Phyllis Bartlett, 'Hardy's Shelley', *KSJ*, 4 (1955), 25.

Owned (1955) F. B. Adams (see Bartlett).

Drayton, Michael. *The Complete Works*, ed. Rev. Richard Hooper, 3 vols (London, 1876).

HrT 1780 Annotated and marked.

Dorset County Museum.

Dryden, John. *The Poetical Works* (Halifax, 1865).

HrT 1781 Annotated and marked, inscribed 1866.

Mentioned Wright, p. 15.

Dorset County Museum.

Dryden, John. *The Poetical Works*, 5 vols (London, 1852).

HrT 1782 Marked.

Dorset County Museum.

Dugdale, Florence Emily, see Hrt 1813.

Dumas, Alexandre, the Elder. *Memoirs of a Physician*, 2 vols (London and New York, [187?]), Vol. II only.

HrT 1783 Marked.

A copy of Vol. I only was offered for sale by First Editions Bookshop in their Catalogue 33 (November 1938) as Item 110; its date of publication was given as '[c.1885]' and it was described as bearing a 'note in Hardy's hand'.

Texas.

Egerton, George, *pseud.* [i.e. Mary Chavelita Clairmonte, afterwards Bright]. *Keynotes* (London, 1893).

HrT 1784 Florence Henniker's copy, annotated by her and by Hardy.

Mentioned *Letters*, II, 102n, Björk, II, 507 (1918–19) and Millgate, pp. 356–7.

Owned (1985) R. L. Purdy (see Björk); destined for Yale.

Einstein, Albert. *Relativity*, trans. Robert W. Lawson, 3rd ed (London, 1920).

HrT 1785 Marked in Chapters 9 and 31.

Mentioned Björk, II, 544 (2449).

Dorset County Museum.

English Lyrics, Chaucer to Poe, ed. William Ernest Henley (London, 1897).

HrT 1786 Annotated.

Dorset County Museum.

The English Poets, ed. T. H. Ward, 5 vols (London and New York, 1895–1918).

HrT 1786.5 Marked.

Mentioned Björk, II, 528 (2251).

Dorset County Museum.

Euripides. *The Tragedies*, trans. T. A. Buckley, 2 vols (London, 1850, 1867).

HrT 1787 Annotated and marked.

Mentioned Rutland, pp. 35, 43 4 (when it was in the library at Max Gate); Björk, I, 302 (502); *Grolier Catalogue*, Item 7.

Owned (1989) F. B. Adams.

Euripides. *The Hippolytus*, trans. Gilbert Murray (London, 1904).

HrT 1788 Annotated and marked.

Mentioned Wright, p. 10.

Dorset County Museum.

Eutropius. *Breviarum Historiae Romanae* (Eton, 1846).

HrT 1788.5 Annotated on p. [1], inscribed 'T. Hardy: 1854'.

Colby College.

Every Man's Own Lawyer...by a Barrister, 9th ed (London, 1872).

HrT 1789 Marked.

Texas.

Everybody's Book of Epitaphs, comp. W. H. Howe (London, [1891]).

HrT 1789.5 Annotated and marked.

Colby College.

Fielding, Henry. *The Adventures of Joseph Andrews* (London and New York, 1861).

HrT 1790 Marked.

Described in 'Other Recent Accessions', *CLQ*, January 1944, pp. 82–3.

Colby College.

FitzGerald, Edward. *The Rubáiyát of Omar Khayyám* (London, 1897).

HrT 1790.5 Annotated and marked in pencil.

Princeton, Robert H. Taylor Collection.

Flaubert, Gustave. *Madame Bovary* (Paris, 1882).

HrT 1791 Annotated and marked.

Owned (1989) R. L. Purdy; destined for Yale.

Fletcher, John, see HrT 1725.

France, Anatole. *Histoire comique* (Paris, n.d.).

HrT 1792 Annotated on first page of text, containing also printed clipping of interview with Anatole France, annotated by Hardy 'The Observer. Aug. 22, 1920'.

Hollings Catalogue 212 (n.d.), Item 41.

France, Anatole. *The Red Lily* (London, 1908).

HrT 1793 Marked on p. 243.

Wreden Catalogue (1938), Item 111.

Garwood, Helen. *Thomas Hardy* (Philadelphia, 1911).

HrT 1794 Marked.

Mentioned Wright, pp. 38–9.

Dorset County Museum.

Gibbon, Edward. *The History of the Decline and Fall of the Roman Empire*, 7 vols (London, 1853–5).

HrT 1795 Marked.

Mentioned Wright, pp. 5–6 and Björk, I, 253 (84) and 349–50 (1045).

Dorset County Museum.

Gibbon, Edward. *Miscellaneous Works*, with notes by John Lord Sheffield, 7 vols (Basle, 1796–7).

HrT 1796 Annotated and marked.

Dorset County Museum.

Goethe, Johann Wolfgang von. *Faust*, trans. A[braham] Hayward, 7th ed (London, 1860).

HrT 1797 Marked, a gift from Horace Moule.

Mentioned Wright, p. 19 and Millgate, *Career*, p. 168.

Dorset County Museum.

Goethe, Johann Wolfgang von. *Novels and Tales* (London, 1875).

HrT 1798 Marked and inscribed.

Hollings Catalogue 212 (n.d.), Item 50.

Goldsmith, Oliver. *The Poetical Works of Oliver Goldsmith, M.B. and The Vicar of Wakefield* (London and Halifax, 1867).

HrT 1799 Marked.

Dorset County Museum.

Gover, William. *A Guide to the Ancient Church of St Mary, Puddletown* (Dorchester, 1908).

HrT 1800 Annotated.

Elkin Mathews Catalogue 77 (February 1939), Item 26.

Graham, Thomas John. *Modern Domestic Medicine*, 13th ed (London, 1864).

HrT 1801 Annotated.

Wreden Catalogue (1938), Item 19.

Grant, James. *The Scottish Cavalier* (London and New York, [c. 1850]).

HrT 1802 Marked.

Dorset County Museum.

Gray, Thomas. *The Poetical Works* (London, 1885).

HrT 1803 Annotated and marked.

Mentioned Björk, II, 527 (2239).

Dorset County Museum.

[Greek Anthology]. *Select Epigrams from the Greek Anthology*, ed. and trans. J. W. Mackail, 3rd ed (London, 1911).

HrT 1804 Marked (p. 172) at the source epigrams for 'Epitaph on a Pessimist' (see HrT 341–2) and for 'The Bad Example' (from Meleager) (see HrT 108).

Mentioned Purdy, pp. 244, 253 and Hynes, III, 318.

Owned (1989) R. L. Purdy; destined for Yale.

Green, John Richard. *A Short History of the English People* (London and New York, 1905).

HrT 1805 Annotated on inside back cover.

Texas.

Grove, Agnes Geraldine. *The Social Fetich*.

HrT 1806 Proof sheets, annotated by Hardy.

Mentioned Millgate, p. 456.

Owned (1982) R. L. Purdy (see Millgate); destined for Yale.

A Guide to the British Museum (London, 1888).

HrT 1806.5 Annotated.

First Edition Bookshop Catalogue 33 (November 1938), Item 12.

Guillemin, Amédée. *The Heavens*, ed. J. Norman Lockyer, revised Richard A. Proctor, 7th ed (London, 1878).

HrT 1807 Marked and annotated.

Texas.

Guizot, François Pierre Guillaume. *The History of Civilization*, trans. William Hazlitt, 3 vols (London, 1873–8).

HrT 1808 Annotations in Vol. III, markings in Vols I and III.

Wreden Catalogue (1938), Item 113.

Haemmerlein, Thomas, *à Kempis*, see HrT 1835.

Halpérine (afterwards Halpérine-Kaminsky), Ely. *Le Rôle de l'art, d'après Tolstoi* (Paris, 1898).

HrT 1809 One annotation and markings.

Hollings Catalogue 212 (n.d.), Item 55.

Harding, William. *Universal Stenography*, ed. John R. Robinson (London, [c. 1860]).

HrT 1810 Annotated, inscribed 1 October 1863.

Dorset County Museum.

Hardy, Emma Lavinia (née Gifford). *The Maid on the Shore*.

HrT 1811 Typescript, with title page and revisions in Hardy's hand, 87 numbered leaves.

This novel was never published; Microfilm Edition, Reel 5.

Dorset County Museum.

Hardy, Emma Lavinia (née Gifford). 'Some Recollections'.

HrT 1812 ELH's MS, revised, containing Hardy's annotations, cancellations and revisions throughout, 74 pages; dated at end 'E. L. Hardy/Max Gate Jan: 4/1911'.

This MS printed (facsimile of p. 27) in Emma Hardy, *Some Recollections*, ed. Robert Gittings and Evelyn Hardy (London, 1961); an extract was quoted by Hardy as the opening of Chapter 5 of *Life*; for a typescript among materials for *Life*, see HrT 1454.

Dorset County Museum.

Hardy, Florence Emily (née Dugdale). 'Blue Jimmy: the Horse-Stealer'.

HrT 1812.5 Proof for *Cornhill* (where published February 1911), containing additions by Hardy.

Owned (1979) F. B. Adams (see Purdy, p. 314).

Hardy, Florence Emily (née Dugdale). 'The Unconquerable'.

HrT 1813 Typescript, revised by Hardy, 20 numbered leaves (rectos only).

This story was never published; described briefly in *Life and Work*, p. xxixn33; Microfilm Edition, Reel 5.

Dorset County Museum.

Hardy, Thomas. *Memoir of Thomas Hardy, Founder of, and Secretary to, the London Corresponding Society* (London, 1832).

HrT 1814 Presentation copy from Sydney Cockerell, 18 November 1913 (containing inserts and clippings).

Dorset County Museum.

Harper, Charles George. *The Hardy Country* (London, 1904).

HrT 1815 Including inserted carbon typescript list of errors in the book and annotations *passim*, some probably not by Hardy.

Dorset County Museum.

Harrison, Frederic. *The Choice of Books and Other Literary Pieces* (London and New York, 1887).

HrT 1816 Marked.

Mentioned Björk, I, xxivn20 and 256 (94).

Dorset County Museum.

Hart, Henry George. *The New Annual Army List, Militia List, and Indian Civil Service List for 1876* (London, 1876).

HrT 1817 Marked.

Wreden Catalogue (1938), Item 115.

Hawthorne, Nathaniel. *The House of the Seven Gables* (London, 1869).

HrT 1817.5 Annotated in Preface and marked.

David Magee Catalogue 23 (n.d.), Item 172.

Heath, Frank R. and Sidney H. *Dorchester (Dorset), and its Surroundings* (Dorchester and London, 1905–6).

HrT 1818 Proof copy containing Hardy's revisions on pp. 63, 71, 74–5, 113–14.

For Hardy's Preface to this book, see HrT 1544.

Texas.

Heaton, W. J. *The Bible of The Reformation* (London, 1910).

HrT 1819 Marked.

Texas.

Hedgcock, Frank Austin. *Thomas Hardy, penseur et artiste* (Paris, 1911).

HrT 1820 Extensively annotated.

Facsimile page in Robert Gittings, *Thomas Hardy's Later Years* (Boston and Toronto, 1978), facing p. 149; mentioned Purdy, p. 265n5, Millgate, *Career*, p. 38 and *Letters*, IV, 157n and VI, 142n.

Dorset County Museum.

Heine, Heinrich. *The Poems of Heine*, trans. E. A. Bowring (London, 1878).

HrT 1821 Marked.

For one marking, see the headnote to 'Song from Heine'; mentioned Purdy, p. 117 and Björk, I, 346 (1017).

Owned (1989) R. L. Purdy; destined for Yale.

Heine, Heinrich. *Heine's Book of Songs*, trans. C. G. Leland (London, 1881).

HrT 1822 Marked.

For one marking, see the headnote to 'Song from Heine'; mentioned Purdy, p. 117 and Björk, I, 346 (1017).

Owned (1989) R. L. Purdy; destined for Yale.

Henley, William Ernest, see HrT 1786.

Henley, William Ernest. *The Songs of the Sword and Other Verses* (London, 1892).

HrT 1822.5 Annotated on p. 41 and marked.

Princeton, Ex.C.3779.5.386.

Hodgson, William Ballantyne. *Errors in the Use of English*, [ed. Mrs E. Hodgson] (Edinburgh, 1881).

HrT 1823 Annotated on p. 28.

Texas.

Hodgson, William Earl. 'A Prig in the Elysian Fields', *National Review*, April 1892.

HrT 1823.5 Marked.

Fletcher Catalogue 229 (n.d.), Item 431.

Homer. *Homeri Ilias*, ed. Samuel Clarke, 2 vols (London, 1818).

HrT 1824 Inscribed 1858, including Hardy's list of passages on the inside cover.

Mentioned Rutland, pp. 21–2, Millgate, p. 63 and Björk, I, 277 (263–8).

Owned (1982) R. L. Purdy (see Millgate); destined for Yale.

Hone, William. *The Apocryphal New Testament* (London, [188?]).

HrT 1825 Annotated, wanting title page.

Wreden Catalogue (1938), Item 3.

Horatius Flaccus, Quintus. *Part I. Odes* (London, 1855).

HrT 1826 Annotated.

Mentioned Millgate, p. 326.

Owned (1982) R. L. Purdy (see Millgate); destined for Yale.

Horatius Flaccus, Quintus. *The Works*, trans. C. Smart, ed. T. A. Buckley (London, 1859).

HrT 1827 Annotations (many being the addition of the original Latin) and markings.

Mentioned Rutland, p. 26, Wright, p. 10 and Björk, I, 270 (175).

Colby College.

Housman, A. E. *Last Poems* (London, 1922).

HrT 1828 Marked, presentation copy to Hardy.

A copy sold Max Gate Sale, Lot 219.

Unlocated.

Howard, Henry, Earl of Surrey. *Poetical Works of Henry Howard, Earl of Surrey, Minor Contemporaneous Poets and Thomas Sackville, Lord Buckhurst*, ed. Robert Bell (London, [1866]).

HrT 1829 Marked.

Mentioned Wright, p. 15.

Dorset County Museum.

Howe, W. H., see HrT 1789.5.

Hullah, John. *The Song Book* (London, 1866).

HrT 1830 Annotated.

Mentioned Millgate, pp. 19, 191.

Dorset County Museum.

Hughes, William. *A Manual of Geography* (1864).

HrT 1831 One annotation.

Hollings Catalogue 212 (n.d.), Item 47.

Hutchins, John. *The History and Antiquities of the County of Dorset*, 3rd ed, 4 vols (Westminster, 1861–73).

HrT 1832 Annotated and marked.

Mentioned Björk, I, 308–9 (584) and *Letters*, VI, 71n and 172n..

Dorset County Museum.

The Hymnal Companion to the Book of Common Prayer, 3rd ed (London, [1890?]).

HrT 1832.5 Annotated on p. 18, inscribed by ELH in 1905 and by Hardy '(*In Use at St Peter's Ch. Dorchester, & Charles Ch. Plymouth*)'.

Colby College.

[Hymns, Ancient and Modern] [c. 1889].

HrT 1833 Annotated, wanting title page, prefaces dated 1875 and 1889.

Dorset County Museum.

Hymns, Ancient and Modern, Complete Edition (London, n.d.).

HrT 1833.5 Annotated and marked, inscribed 'E. L. Hardy. 1894'.

Colby College.

The Imperial Speaker (London, [c. 1880]).

HrT 1833.7 Sixteen identifications of the authors of anonymous contributions in Hardy's hand.

First Edition Bookshop Catalogue 33 (November 1938), Item 11.

Inge, William Ralph. *Outspoken Essays (Second Series)* (London, [c. 1922]).

HrT 1834 Marked.

Dorset County Museum.

Jesus Christ. *Of the Imitation of Christ...By Thomas à Kempis*, trans. W. T. B. (London: Griffith, Farran & Co., n.d.).

HrT 1835 Marked.

Dorset County Museum.

Johnson, Capt. Charles, ***pseud.*** *The Lives and Actions of the Most Noted Highwaymen...* (London and Glasgow, n.d.).

HrT 1836 Marked.

Dorset County Museum.

Johnson, Lionel Pigot. *The Art of Thomas Hardy* (London and New York, 1894).

HrT 1837 Annotated and marked.

Dorset County Museum.

The Junior Atlas for Schools [186?].

HrT 1838 Including 2 autograph pencil maps pasted on end flyleaf.

Wreden Catalogue (1938), Item 7.

Keats, John. *The Poetical Works*, ed. William Michael Rossetti (London, [1872?]).

HrT 1839 Marked (including the passage in *Endymion* used as the epigraph for *The Return of the Native*).

Mentioned Björk, I, 292 (416) and Wright, pp. 80–1.

Dorset County Museum.

Keats, John. *The Poetical Works*, ed. F. T. Palgrave (London and New York, 1886).

HrT 1840 Annotated on p. 41 and marked.

Cockerell Sale, Lot 312, sold to Maggs.

Owned (1989) F. B. Adams.

[Keble, John]. *The Christian Year: Thoughts in Verse for the Sundays and Holydays Throughout the Year*, 65th ed (Oxford and London, 1860).

HrT 1841 Annotated, inscribed 24 September 1861.

Mentioned Millgate, pp. 65 and 72–3.

Dorset County Museum.

Kelly's Directory of Dorsetshire (London, 1907).

HrT 1842 Annotated on map.

Wreden Catalogue (1938), Item 118.

***King Edward VIth Latin Grammar*.**

HrT 1843 Annotated.

Mentioned Millgate, p. 52.

Owned (1982) R. L. Purdy (see Millgate); destined for Yale.

[Kingdom, William]. *The Secretary's Assistant and Correspondent's Guide*, 13th ed (London, [188?]).

HrT 1843.5 Annotated on p. 9.

Wreden Catalogue (1938), Item 98.

Kingsley, Henry. *Ravenshoe* (London, n.d.).

HrT 1844 Marked.

Dorset County Museum.

Kipling, Rudyard. *Barrack-Room Ballads and Other Verses*, 2nd ed (London, 1892).

HrT 1845 Annotated and marked.

Mentioned Wright, p. 78 and Björk, II, 493 (1675) and 514 (2016).

Dorset County Museum.

Lackmann, C. *Specimens of German Prose... with a literal and interlineal translation.*

HrT 1846 Annotated.

Mentioned Millgate, p. 129.

Owned (1982) R. L. Purdy (see Millgate); destined for Yale.

Lanfrey, Pierre. *Histoire de Napoléon Ier*, 9th ed, 5 vols (Paris, 1876).

HrT 1847 Marked.

Mentioned Rutland, p. 297 and Wright, pp. 161–2.

Dorset County Museum.

Lea, Hermann. *A Handbook to the Wessex Country of Thomas Hardy* (London and Bournemouth, [1906]), see HrT 1523.5–1524.

Lea, Hermann. *Thomas Hardy's Wessex* (London, 1913).
See also HrT 1523.5–1524.

HrT 1847.5 Hardy's corrected copy.

Owned (1989) R. L. Purdy; destined for Yale.

Lemaître, Jules. *Les Contemporains* (Paris, 1890).

HrT 1848 Two annotations and markings.

Owned (1989) R. L. Purdy; destined for Yale.

Lempriere, John. *A Classical Dictionary*, 12th ed (London, 1823).

HrT 1849 Annotated.

Hollings Catalogue 212 (n.d.), Item 66.

Le Sage, Alain René. *Histoire de Gil Blas de Santillane* (Paris, 1861).

HrT 1850 Marked.

Hollings Catalogue 212 (n.d.), Item 67.

Lessing, Gotthold Ephraim. *Selected Prose Works*, trans. E. C. Beasley and Helen Zimmern, ed. Edward Bell (London, 1890).

HrT 1851 Marked.

Hollings Catalogue 212 (n.d.), Item 68.

Lévy, Arthur. *Napoléon intime* (Paris, 1893).

HrT 1852 Marked.

Dorset County Museum.

[Liturgies], see HrT 1736, 1832.5, 1833, 1833.5, 1883, 1912.5, 1925, 1931.5.

Lodge, Edmund. *Portraits of Illustrious Personages of Great Britain*, 8 vols (London, 1849–50).

HrT 1853 Marked in Vols I, IV, VIII.

Wreden Catalogue (1938), Item 119.

Lolme, Jean Louis de. *Cassell's Manual of the French Language* (London, 1853).

HrT 1854 Annotated, inscribed by Hardy, 6 May 1854.

Eton College.

Loth, Dr J. T. *The Tourist's Conversational Guide in English, French, German, & Italian* (London, Edinburgh and Glasgow, n.d.).

HrT 1854.3 A few pencil annotations.

Eton College.

The Lounger, 3 vols (Edinburgh, 1787).

HrT 1854.5 Annotated on flyleaf by Hardy and an unidentified hand.

David Magee Catalogue 23 (n.d.), Item 200.

Lucas, E. V., comp. *The Open Road* (London, 1899).

HrT 1855 Marked.

Owned (1989) R. L. Purdy; destined for Yale.

HrT 1855.5 Marked on 19 pages.

Texas.

Lucretius Carus, Titus. *On the Nature of Things*, trans. Rev. J. S. Watson (London, 1851).

HrT 1856 Annotated and marked.

Mentioned Björk, I, 361–2 (1146).

Colby College.

Ludovici, Anthony Mario. *Who Is to be Master of the World?* (Edinburgh and London, 1909).

HrT 1857 Marked on p. 75 and on inside back cover.

Wreden Catalogue (1938), Item 121.

McCarthy, Justin Huntly. *An Outline of Irish History*, 2nd ed (London, 1892).

HrT 1858 Marked on p. 127.

Wreden Catalogue (1938), Item 123.

MacCulloch, John Ramsay. *The Principles of Political Economy*.

HrT 1859 Annotated.

Mentioned Millgate, pp. 86, 91.

Owned (1982) R. L. Purdy (see Millgate); destined for Yale.

Macdonnell, Annie. *Thomas Hardy* (London, 1894).

HrT 1860 Annotated.

Dorset County Museum.

Mackail, John William. *The Pilgrim's Progress* (London, 1924).

HrT 1861 Annotated.

Texas.

Mackail, John William, see also HrT 1804.

Macpherson, James, see HrT 1902.

Maeterlinck, Maurice Polydore Marie Bérnard. *Joyzelle* (Paris, 1903).

HrT 1862 Annotated.

Hollings Catalogue 212 (n.d.), Item 72.

Malory, Sir Thomas. *The Noble and Joyous History of King Arthur*, ed. Ernest Rhys, 2 vols (London: The Scott Library, n.d.).

HrT 1863 Marked.

Mentioned Purdy, p. 220n2.

Owned (1989) R. L. Purdy; destined for Yale.

Mantell, Gideon Algernon. *The Wonders of Geology*, 6th ed, 2 vols (London, 1848).

HrT 1864 Corrected in II, 559, gift to Hardy from Horace Moule in April 1858.

Mentioned Millgate, p. 68.

Owned (1982) R. L. Purdy (see Millgate); destined for Yale.

Margaret [D'Angoulême], Queen Consort of Henry II, King of Navarre. *The Heptameron: Tales of Marguerite, Queen of Navarre*, [trans. W. H. Thomson] (London, [1896?]).

HrT 1865 Annotated on p. 340, title page annotated '(188–)' in an unidentified hand.

Texas.

Mariette, Alphonse. *Half-hours of French Translation*, 3rd ed (London and Edinburgh, 1863).

HrT 1866 Annotated and marked, inscription dated 1865.

Hardy's use of this French textbook discussed C. J. Weber, 'Thomas Hardy as College Student', *CLQ*, 2 (1948), 113–15.

Colby College.

Marlowe, Christopher. *The Dramatic Works*, ed. Percy E. Pinkerton (London, New York and Toronto, 1889).

HrT 1867 Annotated and marked.

Colby College.

Masson, Gustave. *A Class-Book of French Literature*.

HrT 1868 Annotated, including Hardy's translation into English of a few words from a Victor Hugo poem.

Hollings Catalogue 212 (n.d.), Item 44.

Masson, Gustave. *La Lyre française* (London, 1867).

HrT 1869 Annotated and marked, inscribed 1872.

Mentioned Wright, pp. 223–4.

Dorset County Museum.

Maunder, Samuel. *The Biographical Treasury*, 4th ed (London, 1842).

HrT 1870 Annotated.

Dorset County Museum.

Maunder, Samuel. *The Biographical Treasury*, 13th ed (London, 1878).

HrT 1871 Annotated on p. 138, used for *The Dynasts*.

Wreden Catalogue (1938), Item 124.

Maupassant, Henri René Albert Guy de. *Bel-Ami* (Paris, 1893).

HrT 1872 Marked.

Hollings Catalogue 212 (n.d.), Item 78.

Maupassant, Henri René Albert Guy de. *Une Vie* (Paris, 1886).

HrT 1873 Annotated.

Hollings Catalogue 212 (n.d.), Item 76.

The Men of the Time. A Dictionary of Contemporaries, 12th ed (London and New York, 1887).

HrT 1874 Including a genealogy of Bourbons in Hardy's hand on back end paper.

Hollings Catalogue 212 (n.d.), Item 81.

Meredith, George. *Modern Love* (London, 1892).

HrT 1875 Marked.

Mentioned Wright, p. 78.

Dorset County Museum.

Merivale, Charles. *A General History of Rome* (London, 1883).

HrT 1876 Annotated.

Wreden Catalogue (1938), Item 125.

Merlet, Pierre François. *Le Traducteur, or Selections from the best French Writers* (1847).

HrT 1877 Annotated, marked and inscribed.

Hollings Catalogue 212 (n.d.), Item 43.

Méry, François Joseph Pierre André. *Trafalgar* (Paris, 1865).

HrT 1878 Annotated.

Grolier Catalogue, Item 181; mentioned in Rutland, pp. 300–1 and listed in Wright's bibliography.

Owned (1989) R. L. Purdy; destined for Yale.

Metcalfe, Rev. A. *A popular and illustrated Guide to St Peter's Church, Dorchester* (Dorchester, 1907).

HrT 1878.5 Annotated on pp. 19, 22, 26.

Colby College.

Mill, John Stuart. *On Liberty* (London, 1867).

HrT 1879 Marked.

Mentioned Wright, p. 31 and Björk, I, 368 (1190).

Dorset County Museum.

Milnes, Richard Monckton, *Baron Houghton. The Poetical Works*, 2 vols (London, 1876).

HrT 1880 Marked, a gift from Florence Henniker, September 1893.

Dorset County Museum.

Milton, John. *The Poetical Works*, ed. T. A. Buckley (London and New York, 1864).

HrT 1881 Annotated and marked; inscribed 1865.

Mentioned Wright, pp. 15–16, 73 and Björk, I, 330 (837).

Dorset County Museum.

Milton, John. *Poetical Works* (Halifax, 1865).

HrT 1882 Annotated and marked; inscribed 1866.

Mentioned Wright, pp. 15–16, 72.

Dorset County Museum.

The Missal for the Use of the Laity, [before 1896].

HrT 1883 Annotated and marked.

Mentioned Millgate, p. 411.

Owned (1982) R. L. Purdy (see Millgate); destined for Yale.

Mixing in Society. A complete manual of manners. By the Right Hon. the Countess of *******. (London and New York, 1872).

HrT 1884 Annotated on p. 145.

Texas.

Modern British Poetry, ed. Louis Untermeyer (New York, 1920).

HrT 1885 Annotated and containing Hardy's revision to one of his poems, presentation copy to Hardy, July 1920.

For Hardy's acknowledgement of this copy (23 September 1922), see *Letters*, VI, 158.

Quaritch Catalogue 960 (1976), Item 351.

Modern British Poetry, ed. Louis Untermeyer, 2nd ed (New York, 1925).

HrT 1886 Corrections by Hardy to one of his poems.

Elkin Mathews Catalogue 77 (February 1939), Item 83.

Monro, Harold. *Real Property* (London, 1922).

HrT 1887 Marked (pp. 11 and 22) and annotated (p. 25), presentation copy to Hardy from Monro, April 1922.

David Holmes List [1989], Item 32 (see *Letters*, VI, 126n).

Montaigne, Michel de. *All the Essays of Michael seigneur de Montaigne*, trans. Charles Cotton (London, 1869).

HrT 1888 Marked, possibly by ELH only.

Texas.

Montgomery, James. *The Poetical Works*, 'Chandos Poets', ed. Sir John Gilbert, Birket Foster, etc. (London: Warne & Co, n.d.).

HrT 1889 Marked.

Mentioned Wright, p. 76.

Dorset County Museum.

Moody, Clement. *The New Eton Greek Grammar* (London, 1852).

HrT 1890 Annotated and marked, inscribed by Hardy (in Greek).

Dorset County Museum.

Moore, George. *Memoirs of my Dead Life* (London, 1906).

HrT 1890.5 Annotation on half title.

Rota Catalogue 58 (1938), Item 400.

Moore, George Edward. *Principia Ethica* (Cambridge, 1903).

HrT 1891 Annotated on p. 17, inscribed to Hardy from Raymond Abbott, September 1906.

Colby College.

Morley, George. *A Bunch of Blue Ribbons* (London, 1907).

HrT 1892 Annotated, presentation copy to Hardy, 10 April 1907.

Dorset County Museum.

Morley, John. *Diderot and the Encyclopædists*, 2 vols (London and New York, 1891).

HrT 1893 Marked.

Mentioned Wright, pp. 35–6 and Björk, I, 252 (76–8), 292 (418) and 351–2 (1064).

Dorset County Museum.

Morley, John. *Rousseau*, 2 vols (London and New York, 1895).

HrT 1894 Marked.

Mentioned Wright, p. 35 and Björk, I, 308 (582).

Dorset County Museum.

Murray, Sir James Augustus Herbert, see HrT 1898.5.

[Murray, John, Publishing Firm]. *A Handbook for Residents and Travellers in Wilts and Dorset*, 5th ed (London, 1899).

HrT 1895 Annotated.

See HrT 1525.

British Library, Department of Printed Books, C.134.bb.1/33.

[Murray, John, Publishing Firm]. *A Handbook for Travellers in Switzerland*, 16th ed revised, 2 parts (London and Paris, 1879).

HrT 1896 Annotated and marked.

British Library, Department of Printed Books, C.134.bb.1/15 and C.134.bb.1/32.

[Murray, John, Publishing Firm]. *Handbook for Travellers in Wiltshire, Dorsetshire, and Somersetshire*, 4th ed (London, 1882).

HrT 1897 Annotations to map at end.

British Library, Department of Printed Books, C.134.bb.1/26.

[Murray, John, Publishing Firm]. *A Handbook for Visitors to Paris*, 6th ed revised (London and Paris, 1874).

HrT 1898 Marked.

British Library, Department of Printed Books, C.134.bb.1/12.

A New English Dictionary on Historical Principles Founded Mainly on the Materials Collected by the Philological Society, ed. Sir James Augustus Herbert Murray, Henry Bradley, *et. al.*, 11 vols (Oxford, 1888–1933), wanting Vol. X, Part II.

HrT 1898.5 Including pencil lists of 'words omitted' in most volumes.

David Holmes List [1989], Item 33.

Newman, John Henry. *An Essay in Aid of a Grammar of Assent* (London, 1879).

HrT 1899 Marked.

Mentioned Wright, p. 21 and Björk, I, 241 (2).

Dorset County Museum.

Noel, Hon. Roden Berkeley Wriothesley. *Poems* (London, [1892?]).

HrT 1900 Marked, presentation copy to Hardy.

Texas.

Nouveau guide de conversations modernes…en quart langues (Paris, [c. 1890]).

HrT 1900.3 Front and back end papers containing words and phrases and their German equivalents, as well as other annotations and markings *passim*.

Princeton, Robert H. Taylor Collection.

Nuttall, Peter Austin. *The Standard Pronouncing Dictionary of the English Language* (London, 1864).

HrT 1900.5 Marked.

Dorset County Museum.

Ollendorff, Heinrich Godefroy. *A New Method of Learning to Read, Write and Speak a Language in Six Months, adapted to the French* (London, 1848).

HrT 1901 Annotated and inscribed.

Texas.

Ordnance Survey. Boscastle & Padstow. Sheet 139, 3rd ed (Southampton, 1910).

HrT 1902 Annotated.

Colby College.

Ordnance Survey. Glastonbury and District, [c.1899].

HrT 1902.3 Annotated.

First Edition Bookshop Catalogue 33 (November 1938), Item 3.

Ordnance Survey. Yeovil and District, [c.1899].

HrT 1902.5 Annotated.

First Edition Bookshop Catalogue 33 (November 1938), Item 2.

O'Shaughnessy, Arthur William Edgar. *Music and Moonlight* (London, 1874).

HrT 1903 Marked.

Mentioned Wright, p. 77.

Dorset County Museum.

Ossian. *The Poems of Ossian…translated by James Macpherson*, 2 vols (London, 1803).

HrT 1904 Marked.

Mentioned Wright, pp. 76–7 and Björk, II, 564–5 (A102–A106); see also Evelyn Hardy, *Thomas Hardy* (London, 1954), p. 39.

Dorset County Museum.

Otto, Dr E. *German Conversation — Grammar* (1876).

HrT 1905 Annotated, inscribed 'Carlsruhe, 1876'.

Hollings Catalogue 212 (n.d.), Item 49.

The Oxford Book of Victorian Verse, ed. Arthur Quiller-Couch (Oxford, 1912), see HrT 398.

Oxford English Dictionary, ed. Sir J. A. H. Murray, Henry Bradley, *et. al.*, 10 vols in 12 (Oxford, 1888–1928).

HrT 1905.5 Annotated in pencil, mostly on the end flyleaves of each volume.

Annotations printed and provenance discussed in an anonymous 4-page booklet *Thomas Hardy's Oxford English Dictionary* [1980?]; see also Hynes, III, 364. Max Gate Sale, Lot 288, sold to J. G. Wilson.

Owned (1988) David Holmes.

Palgrave, Francis Turner. *The Golden Treasury* (Cambridge and London, 1861).

HrT 1906 Annotated and marked, given to Hardy by Horace Moule.

Mentioned Millgate, pp. 81 and 155.

Dorset County Museum.

Palgrave, Francis Turner. *The Golden Treasury* (London and New York, 1904).

HrT 1907 Inscribed by Florence E. Dugdale (later Hardy), annotated and marked.

Texas.

Penley, Aaron. *A System of Water-Colour Painting*, 16th ed (London, 1857).

HrT 1908 Marked.

Mentioned Millgate, p. 31n.

Owned (1982) R. L. Purdy (see Millgate); destined for Yale.

Percy, Thomas. *Reliques of Ancient English Poetry*, ed. Robert Avis Willmott (London and New York, [1857]).

HrT 1909 Annotated.

Mentioned Björk, I, 291 (414).

Dorset County Museum.

Petrunkevich, Alexander. *The Freedom of the Will* (Newark, NJ, 1907).

HrT 1909.5 One correction in the text.

First Edition Bookshop Catalogue 33 (November 1938), Item 17.

Pindar. *The Extant Odes of Pindar*, trans. Ernest Myer (London and New York, 1895).

HrT 1910 Marked.

Mentioned Wright, p. 9 and Björk, I, 303 (506).

Dorset County Museum.

Pope, Alexander. *The Works*, 9 vols (London, 1822), wanting Vols V–VI.

HrT 1911 Marked and annotated in Vols IV, VII and IX.

Texas.

Primrose, Archibald Philip, Lord Roseberry. *Pitt* (London and New York, 1892).

HrT 1912 Annotated and marked.

Mentioned Wright, pp. 137, 162.

Dorset County Museum.

The Psalter, or Psalms of David (1843).

HrT 1912.5 Annotated.

Mentioned Millgate, p. 40n.

Dorchester Reference Library, Lock Collection.

Raleigh, Walter. *Wordsworth* (London, 1903).

HrT 1913 Marked.

Dorset County Museum.

Ramage, Craufurd Tait. *Beautiful Thoughts from German and Spanish Authors* (London and New York, 1884).

HrT 1914 Marked and annotated (p. 317).

Texas.

Ramage, Craufurd Tait. *Beautiful Thoughts from Greek Authors* (1859).

HrT 1915 Marked.

Hollings Catalogue 212 (n.d.), Item 53.

Ramage, Craufurd Tait. *Thoughts from Latin Authors*, 3 vols (Liverpool, 1864), Vols II–III only.

HrT 1916 Annotated and marked, inscribed in Vol. III, 1864.

Mentioned Wright, pp. 10–12 and Björk, I, 270 (175) and II, 568 (A136).

Dorset County Museum.

Reed, Henry Hope. *Introduction to English Literature* (London, 1865).

HrT 1917 Annotated and marked, inscribed 1865.

Mentioned Millgate, p. 90.

Dorset County Museum.

Regnier, Henri de. 'Poètes d'aujourd'hui et poésie de demain', *Mercure de France*, August 1900, pp. 321–50.

HrT 1918 Marked.

Mentioned Wright, p. 92.

Dorset County Museum.

Renan, Joseph Ernest. *Saint Paul* (London, [1880]).

HrT 1919 Annotated and marked.

Texas.

Rich, Anthony. *A Dictionary of Roman and Greek Antiquities* (London, 1894).

HrT 1920 Includes an inserted autograph plan of a Roman house, inscribed by ELH.

Hollings Catalogue 212 (n.d.), Item 90.

[Richardson, Samuel]. *Clarissa*, 8 vols (London, 1792).

HrT 1921 Marked.

Dorset County Museum.

Riley, Henry Thomas. *Dictionary of Latin Quotations, Proverbs, Maxims, and Mottos*, 2nd ed (London, 1860).

HrT 1922 Annotated and marked, including 3 additional quotations written on last page of Index.

Mentioned Rutland, p. 26.

Hollings Catalogue 212 (n.d.), Item 16.

Rogers, H. G. *A Brief Survey of the World's History* (London, 1909).

HrT 1923 Marked, presentation copy from author.

Wreden Catalogue (1938), Item 71.

Rousseau, Jean Jacques. *The Social Contract* (New York, 1893).

HrT 1924 Annotated.

Wreden Catalogue (1938), Item 130.

***[Salisbury Cathedral Psalter]*.**

HrT 1925 Annotated.

Mentioned Millgate, p. 388n.

Owned (1982) R. L. Purdy (see Millgate); destined for Yale.

Sand, George *pseud.* (i.e., Baroness Amandine Aurore Lucie Dudevant). *Les Maîtres sonneurs* (Paris, 1869).

HrT 1926 Annotated and containing Hardy's sketch on front flyleaf.

Eton College.

Sappho. *Memoir, Text, Selected Renderings and a Literal Translation*, ed. Henry Thornton Wharton, 3rd ed (London, 1895), see HrT 1005.

Sardou, Victorien. *Nos intimes! Comedie en quatre actes* (Paris, 1872).

HrT 1926.5 Annotated on pp. 58 and 62, inscribed by Hardy Rouen, 1874.

David Holmes List [1989], Item 46.

Saxelby, F. Outwin. *A Thomas Hardy Dictionary* (London, 1911).

HrT 1927 First proof, as submitted by Saxelby to Hardy and containing Hardy's pencil corrections; returned to Saxelby with a covering letter of 9 September 1911.

Letter printed *Letters*, IV, 172–3 from the original at University of California at Berkeley.

Sotheby's, 11 November 1929, Lot 544, sold to Bickers.

Saxelby, F. Outwin. *A Thomas Hardy Dictionary* (London, 1911).

HrT 1928 Annotated.

Dorset County Museum.

Schiller, Johann Christoph Friedrich von. *The Poems and Ballads*, trans. Sir Edward Bulwer-Lytton (London and New York, 1857).

HrT 1929 Annotated and marked.

Mentioned Björk, I, 359 (1133).

Dorset County Museum.

Schopenhauer, Arthur. *Two Essays*, trans. Mme Karl Hillebrand (London, 1889).

HrT 1930 Annotated and marked.

This volume described C. J. Weber, 'Hardy's Copy of Schopenhauer', *CLQ*, 4 (1957), 217–24; mentioned Björk, I, 374 (1232).

Colby College.

Schott, Walter Edgar. *The Immaculate Deception, or Sex Without Dogma* [apparently privately printed, 1924].

HrT 1930.5 One marginal correction, possibly by Hardy.

David Holmes List [1989], Item 47.

Ségur, Philippe Paul de. *Histoire de Napoléon et de la Grande Armée pendant l'année 1812*, 2 vols (Paris, 1839).

HrT 1931 Marked.

Dorset County Museum.

A Selection of Psalms and Hymns, from Various Authors, Intended Chiefly for Public Worship (London, 1858).

HrT 1931.5 Annotated on p. 184, inscribed by Hardy.

Colby College.

Sequences from the Sarum Missal, trans. C. B. Pearson (London, 1871).

HrT 1931.7 Including (inserted) transcripts by Hardy of Latin hymns, dated 'B.M. 28 Ap[l] [1900]'.

Mentioned Purdy, p. 237.

Owned (1989) R. L. Purdy; destined for Yale.

Shafer, Robert. *Christianity and Naturalism* (New Haven, 1926).

HrT 1932 Annotated.

Elkin Mathews Catalogue 77 (February 1939), Item 74.

Shakespeare, William. *The Dramatic Works*, ed. Samuel Weller Singer, 10 vols (London, 1856).

HrT 1933 Annotated and marked.

Mentioned Wright, pp. 13–14, 72 and Björk, I, 275 (253–56) without any mention of markings. See also *Early Life*, pp. 109, 112–13, *Later Years*, p. 10 and Purdy, pp. 322–3.

Dorset County Museum.

Shakespeare, William. *The Poems* (London, 1857).

HrT 1934 Annotated and marked.

Mentioned Björk, I, 334 (875).

Dorset County Museum.

Shakespeare, William. *The Tempest: with...Notes...by Rev. John Hunter...New Edition* (London: Longman, Green, n.d.).

HrT 1935 Marked.

Mentioned Wright, p. 72.

Dorset County Museum.

Shelley, Percy Bysshe. *Queen Mab and Other Poems* (Halifax, 1865).

HrT 1936 Marked, inscribed by Hardy, 1866.

Described Phyllis Bartlett, 'Hardy's Shelley', *KSJ*, 4 (1955), 15–29.

Owned (1982) F. B. Adams (see Millgate, p. 603n20).

Shorter Lyrics of the Twentieth Century 1900–1922, ed. W. H. Davies (London, 1922).

HrT 1937 Marked.

Texas.

Siborne, Capt. William. *The Waterloo Campaign. 1815*, 4th ed (Westminster, 1895).

HrT 1938 Annotated.

Mentioned Rutland, p. 302 and Wright, pp. 260–1.

Dorset County Museum.

Sidney, Sir Philip. *The Complete Poems*, ed. Alexander B. Grosart, 3 vols (London, 1877).

HrT 1939 Annotated and marked, mostly in Vol. I.

Mentioned Wright, pp. 74–5.

Dorset County Museum.

Smith, Sir William. *A Smaller Classical Dictionary of Biography, Mythology, and Geography*, 7th ed (London, 1862).

HrT 1940 Inscribed by W. E. and E. L. Gifford (later ELH), marked by Hardy.

Mentioned Björk, I, 253 (84).

Wreden Catalogue (1938), Item 187.

Sonnenschein, Adolf and James Steven Stallybrass. *German for the English*, 4th ed (London, 1878).

HrT 1940.5 Annotated, containing also HrT 17.5.

Mentioned Purdy, p. 117.

Owned (1989) R. L. Purdy; destined for Yale.

Sophocles. *The Tragedies*, The Oxford Translation, [revised by T. A. Buckley] (London, 1849).

HrT 1941 Annotated and marked.

Mentioned Rutland, pp. 20, 39–42 and Millgate, *Career*, p. 324. Described *Grolier Catalogue*, Item 5.

Owned (1971) F. B. Adams (see Millgate, *Career*).

Sophocles. *The Plays and Fragments. Part I. The Oedipus Tyrannus*, trans. R. C. Jebb, 3rd ed (Cambridge, 1893).

HrT 1942 Marked.

Mentioned Rutland, p. 35.

Owned (1989) R. L. Purdy; destined for Yale.

Spence, James. *Lectures on Surgery*, 3rd ed (Edinburgh, 1882).

HrT 1943 Marked.

Wreden Catalogue (1938), Item 131.

Spencer, Herbert. *An Autobiography*, 2 vols (London, 1904).

HrT 1944 Addition to Index and markings.

Max Gate Sale (1938), Lot 28; Hollings Catalogue 212 (n.d.), Item 101.

Spencer, Herbert. *Essays; Scientific, Political, and Speculative*, 3 vols (London, 1868–74).

HrT 1945 Annotated and marked.

Mentioned Björk, I, 336 (882) where misdescribed as an 1865 edition.

Max Gate Sale (1938), Lot 28; Hollings Catalogue 212 (n.d.), Item 100.

Spenser, Edmund. *The Fairie Queene* (London and New York, 1865).

HrT 1946 Annotated and marked.

Mentioned Wright, p. 74 and Millgate, p. 548.

Dorset County Museum.

Squire, J. C. *Poems in One Volume* (London, 1926).

HrT 1946.5 Marked on pp. 2, 16, 24, 35, 47, 64, 113, 120; presentation copy to Hardy.

David Holmes List [1989], Item 51.

Staunton, Howard. *The Chess-Player's Handbook* (London, 1870).

HrT 1947 Marked.

Wreden Catalogue (1938), Item 132.

Stebbing, William. *Greek and Latin Anthology Thought into English Verse*, 3 vols (London, 1923), Vol. III.

HrT 1948 Marked on p. 140 (i.e., the source epigram for 'Epitaph on a Pessimist').

Mentioned Purdy, p. 244.

Owned (1989) R. L. Purdy; destined for Yale.

Stevenson, Burton Egbert. *The Home Book of Verse, American and English, 1580–1918* (New York, [1912–18]).

HrT 1948.5 Annotated.

David Magee Catalogue 23 (n.d.), Item 183.

Stièvenard, Léonce. *Lectures françaises*.

HrT 1949 Annotated.

Mentioned Millgate, p. 90.

Owned (1982) F. B. Adams (see Millgate).

Swinburne, Algernon Charles. *Atalanta in Calydon* (London, 1885).

HrT 1950 Marked.

Mentioned Wright, pp. 22–4 and Björk, II, 556–7 (A1–A3), 561 (A79–A80).

Dorset County Museum.

Swinburne, Algernon Charles. *Atalanta in Calydon* (Leipzig, 1901).

HrT 1951 Annotated and marked.

Mentioned Wright, pp. 22–4.

Dorset County Museum.

Swinburne, Algernon Charles. *Bothwell* (London, 1874).

HrT 1952 Marked.

Mentioned Wright, pp. 22–4.

Dorset County Museum.

Swinburne, Algernon Charles. *Poems and Ballads*, 5th ed (London, 1873).

HrT 1953 Annotated and marked.

Mentioned Wright, p. 79 and Björk, II, 561 (A82), 563 (A99).

Dorset County Museum.

Swinburne, Algernon Charles. *Poems and Ballads*, Second Series (London, 1887).

HrT 1954 Annotated and marked.

Mentioned Björk, II, 561 (A82).

Dorset County Museum.

Swinburne, Algernon Charles. *Selections from the Poetical Works*, 15th ed (London, 1910).

HrT 1955 Annotated on p. 29 and on last page.

Texas.

Swinburne, Algernon Charles. *Songs Before Sunrise* (London, 1888).

HrT 1956 Marked.

Mentioned Wright, pp. 22–4 and Björk, II, 561 (A82).

Dorset County Museum.

Tate, Thomas. *Principles of Geometry, Mensuration, Trigonometry, Land-Surveying, and Levelling*, 4th ed (London, 1849).

HrT 1957 Annotated and marked on inserted scrap.

Dorset County Museum.

Taylor, Samuel. *Taylor's System of Stenography*, ed. John Henry Cooke (London, 1856).

HrT 1958 Annotated.

Dorset County Museum.

Tennyson, Alfred, Lord. *In Memoriam* (London, 1875).

HrT 1959 Annotated and marked.

Mentioned Evelyn Hardy, *Thomas Hardy* (London, 1954), p. 52, Wright, pp. 20–1, 72 and Björk, I, 284–5 (350).

Dorset County Museum.

Thiers, Louis Adolphe. *History of the Consulate and the Empire of France under Napoleon*, trans. D. Forbes Campbell *et. al.*, 20 vols in 10 (London, 1845–62).

HrT 1960 Marked (including the passage on p. 144 used as the epigraph to 'The Peasant's Confession').

Mentioned Rutland, p. 296 (when in the library at Max Gate), Purdy, p. 100 and Hynes, I, 363.

Owned (1988) R. L. Purdy (see *Letters*, VII, 20n); destined for Yale.

Thiers, Louis Adolphe. *Histoire du Consulat et de l'Empire*, 20 vols (Paris, 1845–84).

HrT 1961 Marked.

Mentioned Rutland, p. 296 and Wright, *passim*.

Dorset County Museum.

Thompson, Francis. *New Poems* (Westminster, 1897).

HrT 1962 Marked.

Dorset County Museum.

Thomson, James. *The Poetical Works of James Thomson, James Beattie, Gilbert West, and John Bampfylde* (London, 1863).

HrT 1963 Annotated and marked, inscribed 1865.

Mentioned Wright, pp. 75–6.

Dorset County Museum.

Through and Round Bath (Bath, [c. 1870]).

HrT 1963.5 Annotated.

First Edition Bookshop Catalogue 33 (November 1938), Item 9.

Tibullus, see HrT 1751.

Tolstoi, Lev Nikolaevich. *War and Peace*, trans. Nathan H. Dole, 4 vols (London: Scott, n.d.).

HrT 1964 Marked.

Mentioned Wright, pp. 222–3 and *passim*.

Dorset County Museum.

Tolstoi, Lev Nikolaevich. *What is Art?*, trans. Aylmer Maude (London, 1899).

HrT 1965 Annotated and marked.

Mentioned *Letters*, II, 225 and Björk, II, 495 (1706).

Owned (1985) R. L. Purdy (see Björk); destined for Yale.

Tomson, afterward Marriott Watson, [Rosamund]. *The Bird-Bride* (London, 1889).

HrT 1966 Marked.

Mentioned Millgate, p. 297.

Maggs Catalogue 664 (1938), Item 197.

Tomson, afterward Marriott Watson, [Rosamund]. *The Poems of Rosamund Marriott Watson* (London and New York, 1912).

HrT 1967 Annotated.

Mentioned Millgate, p. 364n.

Dorset County Museum.

Tyrrell, R. Y. "'Jude the Obscure'", *Fortnightly Review*, June 1896.

HrT 1968 Annotated in pencil.

Fletcher Catalogue 229 (n.d.), Item 425.

Untermeyer, Louis, see HrT 1885–6.

Vaughan, Henry. *Sacred Poems and Pious Ejaculations* (London, 1897).

HrT 1969 Annotated and marked.

Mentioned Wright, pp. 15 and 78.

Dorset County Museum.

Virgilius Maro, Publius. *Opera omnia*, ed. Johann Christian Jahn (London, 1838).

HrT 1970 Annotated, inscribed October 1859.

Sotheby's, 20 July 1981, Lot 502, sold to Sotheran.

Virgilius Maro, Publius. *The Works*, trans. John Dryden (London, n.d.).

HrT 1971 Annotated and marked, inscribed to Hardy, 'the gift of his Mother'.

Mentioned Björk, I, 276 (263–8) and II, 562–3 (A88a–h, A91).

Dorset County Museum.

Walker, John. *A Rhyming Dictionary* (London, 1865).

HrT 1972 Annotated and marked, inscribed 1865.

Mentioned Wright, pp. 83–4.

Dorset County Museum.

Walkingame, Francis. *The Tutor's Assistant*, ed. Rev. T. Smith (London, 1849).

HrT 1973 Annotated, inscribed 1849.

Dorset County Museum.

Ward, Thomas Humphry see HrT 1786.5.

Webb, A. P. *A Bibliography of the Works of Thomas Hardy 1865–1915* (London, 1916).

HrT 1974 Interleaved copy, with corrections and annotations.

Owned (1989) R. L. Purdy; destined for Yale.

Webb, A. P. *A Bibliography of the Works of Thomas Hardy 1865–1915* (London, 1916).

HrT 1975 Annotated.

Dorset County Museum.

Webster, John. *The Dramatic Works*, ed. William Hazlitt, 4 vols (London, 1857).

HrT 1976 Annotated and marked.

Mentioned Björk, I, 301 (496).

Dorset County Museum.

West, Gilbert, see HrT 1963.

Whately, Richard. *Elements of Logic* (London, 1831).

HrT 1977 Annotated.

One annotation printed in Wreden Catalogue; reprinted Björk, I, 350 (1045).

Wreden Catalogue (1938), Item 31.

Whitman, Walt. *Leaves of Grass* (New York and London, 1912).

HrT 1978 Marked.

Dorset County Museum.

Who's Who in 1907 (London, 1907).

HrT 1979 Hardy's revised note about his entry, pasted in at p. 780.

Wreden Catalogue (1938), Item 135.

Who's Who: 1926 (London, 1926).

HrT 1980 Extensive revisions by Hardy to his entry (pp. 1274–7).

Wreden Catalogue (1938), Item 136.

Wordsworth, William. *The Poetical Works* (London and New York, 1864).

HrT 1981 Marked and inscribed.

Mentioned Rutland, pp. 15–16 and Wright, p. 18.

Dorset County Museum.

Wordsworth, William. *The Poetical Works and Prose Works*, ed. William Knight, 10 vols (London, 1896).

HrT 1982 Annotated and marked.

Mentioned Wright, pp. 18, 85–6.

Dorset County Museum.

The World. By Adam Fitz-Adam [i.e., Edward Moore, *et. al.*], 3 vols (Edinburgh, 1774).

HrT 1983 Annotated on flyleaf.

David Magee Catalogue 23 (n.d.), Item 192.

Zola, Émile Édouard Charles Antoine. *His Masterpiece?* (London, 1886).

HrT 1984 Marked.

Texas.

William Hazlitt
1778–1830

INTRODUCTION

William Hazlitt's grandson and editor, William Carew Hazlitt, has described his grandfather's sometimes distressing practice of 'writing out heads of contemplated essays...over the mantelpiece in lead-pencil. Every scrap of paper that came to hand was turned to a similar purpose, and backs of letters, too, if any happened to have been lately received — and kept' (*Memoirs*, II, 263). Despite this description, no such manuscript scraps have come to light and none are listed in the following entries. Extant manuscripts by Hazlitt are almost without exception those written in what Leigh Hunt called his 'majestic hand' — relatively free of revision and apparently written at one sitting on foolscap sheets, each numbered at the top and filled up in a flowing continuous hand. The very look of these manuscripts speaks volumes about their producer and the nature of their production.

Hazlitt accorded great value in literary creation to the qualities of spontaneity and rapid execution. 'What is struck off at a blow is in many respects better than what is produced on reflection, and at several heats,' he says in his essay 'The Periodical Press'. And, again, in 'On Application to Study': 'I do not conceive rapidity of execution necessarily implies slovenliness or crudeness. On the contrary, I believe it is often productive both of sharpness and freedom'. P. G. Patmore remarked that Hazlitt 'stood alone among professional authors' in that he 'never had a book or paper of any kind about him while he wrote'. The qualities in writing that Hazlitt praised were most certainly his own; see Wilcox, pp. 67–87 for a full discussion of Hazlitt's methods of composition.

Whether his *modus laborandi* was influenced by these aesthetic judgments or vice-versa is a matter of conjecture, but that it was shaped by the pressures of earning a living as reviewer and journalist — having sometimes only hours in which to compose a piece — is undeniable. 'With the necessity, the fluency came,' he himself remarked. In fact, Charles Cowden Clarke — after a social visit throughout which Hazlitt managed to keep writing an imminently-due article — pronounced Hazlitt's 'facility in composition...extreme'.

Furthermore, while the pressures of deadlines were spurs to creativity, they never prodded Hazlitt to create more than was required. Having reckoned the amount of manuscript needed for a page of print, Hazlitt numbered his pages and wrote the required length, no more, no less. As P. G. Patmore put it, 'he always knew exactly what progress he had made, at any given time, towards the desired goal to which he was travelling — namely, the end of his task'.

For Hazlitt's manuscripts, therefore, the usual distinction between 'draft' and 'fair copy' is inappropriate. These manuscripts appear to have been written at one sitting in a large clear hand meant to be read by others. Except for a few fleeting glimpses in the entries of Hazlitt drafting and cancelling passages (see HzW 90), it seems likely that, for his essays, Hazlitt wrote only one manuscript.

The extant manuscripts of Hazlitt's several lecture series on English philosophy and literature are, however, a different matter. These manuscripts — presumably written by Hazlitt to be read out by himself to an audience — are full of drafted passages and cancellations, implying a less fluent and more private labour over their composition than that for the essays. The manuscript lectures also tend to vary continually from the versions eventually published —

as the manuscript essays do not. It is possible that extensively corrected proofs representing an intermediate stage between the manuscript and the published lectures have been lost; two leaves of just such a page proof (bound in the Folger Volume) tend to support this possibility.

The only work of Hazlitt's for which *two* autograph manuscripts survive is the last lecture in the series 'On the English Poets' (HzW 48–9), though exactly why Hazlitt wrote this lecture out twice is mysterious. Several of the manuscripts of lectures in this same series were apparently submitted to Charles Lamb, as interpolations in his hand appear throughout.

Hazlitt's writings are not only remarkable for their fluency, however, but also for the range of subjects on which he had something to say. Having started his journalistic career in 1812 as Parliamentary reporter, he served at various times as dramatic critic (for the *Morning Chronicle* in 1813–14, the *Examiner* in 1815–17 and *The Times* in 1817), art critic (for the *Morning Chronicle* in 1814 and *The Champion* in 1814–15), as well as the contributor to a great many of the London papers (and the *Edinburgh Review*), of essays, reviews and articles on every manner of cultural topic: his own list, in 'On the Causes of Popular Opinion', included 'painting, poetry, prose, plays, politics, parliamentary speakers, metaphysical lore, books, men and things'.

In the last seven or eight years of his life, after the peak of his journalistic career, he published several of his most significant works: *Liber Amoris* (1823), the remarkable romantic 'autobiography' which so damaged his reputation; *The Spirit of the Age* (1825), the work generally regarded as his finest and most mature; and the 4-volume *Life of Napoleon Buonaparte* (1828–30), the project he himself regarded as his *magnum opus* and probably the only work he wrote out of passionate commitment rather than financial necessity.

Relatively few of Hazlitt's manuscripts survive; and of the 132 items listed below, only four are not prose manuscripts. None have been located for many of Hazlitt's book-length works — only one fragment of his *Life of Napoleon* has come to light (see FACSIMILES) — nor indeed for the great majority of his essays. And many of those that survive are only fragmentary. It is worth noting that a great many of the 132 items are recorded or identified here for the first time.

One exception to the sparseness of available Hazlitt manuscripts is the cluster of material surrounding the *Liber Amoris*. As Herschel Baker, Hazlitt's biographer says, 'the Episode with Sarah Walker...is, ironically, the most fully documented in his life'. 'Ironically', because *Liber Amoris*, the published version of that episode, has been so much regretted by Hazlitt commentators — Richard Le Gallienne called it a 'document in madness' — that it is the one they would most like to forget. The abundance of documentation bearing on *Liber Amoris* is due, certainly in part, to the fact of its being based on real events, published and manuscript accounts of which, by participants, witnesses and Hazlitt himself, are available. Nonetheless, it is still true that *Liber Amoris*, the fictional version, is the only work (discounting individual essays and some of the lectures) that is so substantially represented by extant primary manuscript sources that some glimpse into the construction of the final text is possible. In addition to the transcript of Part I, probably by P. G. Patmore (HzW 51), Hazlitt's original letters to Patmore which form the basis of Part II (HzW 52–4) and all the association materials, including Sarah Stoddart Hazlitt's journal — all of which have been known to and used by editors over the years — the list below includes the recently-unearthed autograph manuscript of Part I (HzW 50) and a cancelled fragment in the manuscript of 'The Fight' used in Part II (HzW 55). Neither of these manuscripts were available to the various editors of *Liber Amoris*, from William Carew Hazlitt and Richard Le Gallienne to P. P. Howe and Gerald Lahey.

Reference Edition and Canon

The standard 21-volume Centenary Edition of Hazlitt's works (Howe) has been cited as reference edition in the entries; titles of essays are taken from Howe and the portions of texts represented by manuscript fragments have been identified by reference to Howe's texts.

Howe also represents the most definitive statement to date on Hazlitt's canon, superseding its pioneering predecessor Waller & Glover (1902–6) and Jules Douady's ambitious *Liste chronologique des oeuvres de William Hazlitt* (Paris, 1906). A few articles disputing or adding to the canon established by Howe have appeared since 1934; they are listed in Elisabeth W. Schneider's essay on Hazlitt in Houtchens (1966), pp. 78–9 and 88–9 and in *Evidence for Authorship*, ed. David V. Erdman and Ephim G. Fogel (Ithaca, NY, 1966), pp. 508–9.

Of these, by far the most long-lived and energetic debate concerns the authorship of the notorious review of Coleridge's *Christabel* published anonymously in the *Edinburgh Review*, under the editorship of Francis Jeffrey. One of the complications besetting attempts to identify authors of *Edinburgh Review* articles is that Jeffrey's editorial interventions frequently bordered on virtual rewriting. Howe (XVI, 420–1) lists and discusses all the contributions to the *Edinburgh Review* which have been attributed to Hazlitt at some time and which Howe has rejected (including the *Christabel* review); see also P. L. Carver, 'Hazlitt's Contributions to the *Edinburgh Review*, *RES*, 4 (1928), 385–93.

While many of the manuscripts listed below have *not* been used by or even known to Hazlitt editors, only two certainly augment the established canon. One, the complete essay 'On the Punishment of Death' (HzW 85) has never been printed, though an extract was published in 1831.

The other (HzW 113.5) is an unpublished extended letter that Hazlitt wrote in 1803–4 to the *Monthly Review* in reply to a review of Malthus which they published but which, presumably, he never sent. Though Hazlitt included two passages from the letter in his *Reply to the Essay on Population* (London, 1807), this 'reply' has never been published. It is, curiously, among the Coleridge Collection in the Victoria College Library, Toronto and has only recently been identified as Hazlitt's work by Heather Jackson, a Coleridge scholar.

Five other manuscripts (mostly fragments) are listed (see HzW 5, 18, 25, 27, 111) which have not been identified among Hazlitt's published writings. One of them (HzW 27), listed below as 'Imagination', has been available since a facsimile of it was published by William Carew Hazlitt, without comment, in *The Hazlitts* in 1911. In a signed note to 'Sir' at the bottom of the manuscript (which is headed 'Imagination/from Hazlitt's Lectures'), Hazlitt says that he has 'written out' the foregoing, the 'most popular passage I could find'; but neither the exact passage nor the source of the transcript has been identified among Hazlitt's collected works. The attribution to Hazlitt therefore must be questionable; however, the passage expresses the same metaphysical notions that appear in several of Hazlitt's works: in the early *Essay on the Principles of Human Action* or the 'Lectures on English Philosophy' (the most obvious source), to name but two. The other four unidentified manuscripts (all at SUNY at Buffalo) also express ideas and opinions which appear time and time again throughout Hazlitt's works.

While the entries include no other manuscripts of texts which were not published in Howe — except for the 'non-literary' HzW 112 — there are several which were not published in Hazlitt's lifetime but, posthumously, either in *Literary Remains* (1836), edited by his son, or even later by eventual owners of the manuscripts.

Provenance and Hazlitt Collections

A great many of the items listed in the entries were at one time in the possession of Hazlitt's descendants — that is, his son, William Hazlitt the younger, and his grandson, William Carew Hazlitt — both of whom served as editors of and commentators on the works of Hazlitt and his circle. At least a few manuscripts were given away by William Hazlitt the younger after he published them; see, for example, HzW 6, 65 and the editorial note to HzW 16. Despite the vagueness of early editorial documentation, it is clear from William Carew Hazlitt's writings about his grandfather that many manuscripts, certainly more than are entered below, were in his possession at one time or another.

On 23–4 November 1893, he sent 'a portion of my Printed Books and all the Hazlitt, Lamb, and other MSS. which I have hitherto jealously possessed' to Sotheby's saleroom. The sale catalogue is entitled *Catalogue of an Important Selected Portion of Books, Manuscripts, & Letters, collected by William Hazlitt...his son, the late Mr Registrar Hazlitt and His Grandson Mr W. C. Hazlitt...among which will be found The Hazlitt Papers...the original MSS. of the Liber Amoris...original MSS. of Hazlitt's Essays; His own set of his works...and many first editions* and lists much material relating to Hazlitt; a marked copy is printed in facsimile in Munby, *Sale Catalogues*, I, 99–151. Whenever possible, the lot numbers are quoted in the entries for manuscripts definitely sold in the 1893 sale; unfortunately, due to the imprecision of the sale catalogue, many of the items sold cannot be certainly identified. The description of the most important item, Lot 250 — being a bound volume of sixteen autograph essays sold to Pearson — is particularly frustrating in that it names only three of the essays included. This same volume was resold at Sotheby's on 17 December 1898 (Lot 492) to a J. Jones and that catalogue is equally vague. A. C Goodyear bought the sixteen manuscript essays at the Adrian Joline Sale, Anderson Galleries, 22 March 1915; in a letter to P. P. Howe (quoted in the *London Mercury* of February 1926, p. 374) he names another four of the essays — all then unpublished. Goodyear's collection is now at SUNY at Buffalo where the seven named essays are preserved (HzW 60, 64, 76, 84, 91, 92, 93) but no longer bound up together.

In his prefatory notice to the sale catalogue of 1893, William Carew Hazlitt claims that Hazlitt manuscripts are extremely uncommon and that 'there is scarcely any holder of them, to an appreciable extent, save myself'. While there are certainly manuscripts listed below which *never* passed through the hands of Hazlitt's descendants — for example, manuscripts or letters which Hazlitt himself sent to friends or editors, including, presumably, the autograph manuscript of *Liber Amoris* (HzW 50) — it is probably reasonable to assume that, of those whose provenance is unknown, many were indeed among the family's papers and perhaps even sold in the 1893 sale.

The important Hazlitt manuscripts in the Alexander Ireland Collection at Manchester Central Library were themselves originally in the possession of William Carew Hazlitt. He gave them to Ireland, Hazlitt's first bibliographer, and they now form part of Ireland's large collection of Hazlitt, Lamb, Leigh Hunt, etc. which he bequeathed to the Manchester Central Library in the 1880s. The following bound volume in that collection deserves special mention:

Manchester (Ireland) Volume

Bound volume of Hazlitt's prose manuscripts, sometimes misbound (i.e., with rectos and versos reversed), 21 leaves, some watermarked.

This volume described in Stanley Jones, 'Hazlitt's Missing Essay "On Individuality"', *RES*, NS 28 (1977), 430n2 where most of the contents were identified and the rest were labelled 'largely unidentifiable'; all the manuscripts have now been identified and listed in the entries.

Contents: HzW 32, 35–6, 61, 70, 78, 80, 107.

Manchester Central Library, Alexander Ireland Collection, F.824.76.G4.

Many of the Hazlitt manuscripts sold in 1893 were eventually acquired by the late Colonel A. Conger Goodyear, a collector of Hazlitt and his circle, whose collection was given to the Lockwood Memorial Library at SUNY at Buffalo in 1948. Approximately one-third of the 132 items listed are now part of this collection — far more than are held in any other single repository. It is probable that at least several of the unidentified essays in Lot 250 of the Hazlitt Sale are among these manuscripts.

Two other important items included in the 1893 sale are Hazlitt's own complete copy of the weekly journal *Yellow Dwarf*, edited by John Hunt, to which he contributed, and an interleaved copy of the third edition of *The Spirit of the Age*:

Yellow Dwarf

Bound volume of the complete run of *Yellow Dwarf* (i.e., nos. 1–21, 3 January–23 May 1818) belonging to Hazlitt and containing manuscript revisions and annotations, some by Hazlitt and some in an unidentified hand or hands; some marginalia have been lost in the careless trimming of pages; annotated on front flyleaf by William Carew Hazlitt 'W. C. Haslitt [sic]/1862/Ex Dono Patris.'; the volume was mentioned by William Carew Hazlitt in *Memoirs*, I, 241 and sold in the Hazlitt Sale, Lot 563, to Quaritch from whom the British Museum acquired it on 5 December 1893; in addition to the contents listed below, the volume contains the following manuscript emendations:

1. 'Case of Mr Hone': two revisions (pp. [1]–2) in ink to this leading article in the first number (3 January 1818); the hand seems to be Hazlitt's though the article has never been attributed to him and seems unlikely to be his; William Carew Hazlitt raised the possibility (based on these revisions) in *Memoirs*, I, 241.
2. 'On the Clerical Character': this article (in 3 parts, nos 4–6, 24 January–7 February 1818, signed 'X') is annotated in pencil, probably by Hazlitt 'Political Essa[ys]' in no. 4, p. 27; it was collected in *Political Essays* (1819); Howe, VII, 242–59.
3. 'Miscellaneous': this section in no. 4 (24 January 1818), p. 32 contains markings throughout and the change of the title of one of the notes in an unidentified hand, probably not Hazlitt's.
4. 'An Examination of Mr Malthus's Doctrines': this article (first pub. *Morning Chronicle*, 2 September 1817 and reprinted here in no. 14 of 14 April 1818) is annotated (p. 106) 'In Polit Ess [sic]' probably in Hazlitt's hand; the essay was collected in *Political Essays* (1819); Howe, VII, 332–7.
5. 'Letter to Mr Canning': this 'letter' signed 'Your Countryman' in no. 16 (18 April 1818) is annotated in ink at the end 'Hobhouse' in an unidentified hand, possibly Hazlitt's.

Contents: HzW 82, 86, 115, see also the headnote to 'On Court Influence'.

British Library, Department of Printed Books, P.P.3612.aca.

Harvard *Spirit of the Age*

A copy of the third edition of *The Spirit of the Age* (London, 1858), interleaved with 43 leaves (69 pages of text) of autograph MSS, primarily of the essays published in *The Spirit of the Age*, annotated on front flyleaf by William Carew Hazlitt 'This copy is interleaved with crumbs of the autograph MS. as exists among the Papers in the hands of the family. WCH'.

Hazlitt Sale, Lot 231 (interleaved at that time), sold to Sotheran.

Contents: HzW 68.5, 77.5, 105.5, 106, 108.2, 108.4, 108.6, 108.8, 109.5.

Harvard, fMS Eng 716.

The other relatively significant collection of Hazlitt, including autograph manuscripts and, incidentally, the only corrected proofs that have come to light (HzW 8, 42), is that at the Folger. The provenance of the manuscripts and when they were bound into the volume described below are unknown:

Folger Volume

One volume containing autograph manuscripts of essays and lectures, some fragmentary, some varying extensively from the published versions, individual manuscripts paginated by Hazlitt, volume foliated by Folger, 147 leaves and 16 unfoliated pages of proof.

Contents: HzW 8–9, 17, 23, 39–40, 42, 45–6, 68, 85.

Folger, MS.T.b.18.

Unlocated or Lost Manuscripts

The present whereabouts of many Hazlitt manuscripts is not known. In the case of manuscripts which were, at some point, known to exist and which seem likely to exist still, numbered entries are provided giving their last known appearance in a sale catalogue or their last known owner as location. Other unlocated Hazlitt manuscripts which may very well not be extant — those known only through references which are imprecise or out-of-date, i.e., before c. 1900 — are not given numbered entries but are described here against the possibility of their coming to light:

1. 'The Damned Author's Address to his Reviewers': see the headnote to HzW 1–1.5.
2. 'Emancipation of the Jews': Basil Montagu claims to own the manuscript of this essay in a letter to William Hazlitt the younger of 1 September 1838 (at the University of London). The essay was published in *The Tatler*, March 1831.
3. *An Essay on the Principles of Human Action* (London, 1805): Howe, I, 367 notes that William Hazlitt the younger claimed to have used 'marginal corrections in the Author's copy' for his second edition of the *Essay* published London, [1836]. And in *Memoirs* (II, 272) William Carew Hazlitt bemoans the loss of this copy 'enriched, as he left it, with his own notes in his own hand'.
4. *Lectures on the English Comic Writers*: Hazlitt Sale, Lot 248 (sold to Pearson) was described as 118 autograph manuscript pages of these lectures (and at Sotheby's, 14 April 1898 and 23 March 1905, as 64 and 120 pages, respectively); only 18 leaves have been located, at the Folger (HzW 40).
5. *A Letter to William Gifford, Esq* (London, 1819): William Carew Hazlitt in *Memoirs* (I, 246) mentions Hazlitt's own copy 'corrected for a second edition'; no such copy has been traced.
6. 'On Criminal Law': Basil Montagu writes that he owns the manuscript of this essay in a letter to William Hazlitt the younger of 1 September 1838 (at the University of London); Stanley Jones writes that this essay is 'apparently distinct' from the 'Project for a New Theory of Civil and Criminal Legislation'(HzW 97).
7. 'Outlines of Grammar': see headnote to 'Outlines' in the entries and HzW 5.
8. 'Reporting Notes': Lot 258 of the Hazlitt Sale (sold to Dobell) was described as Hazlitt's autograph reporting notes from the period when he was on the staff of the *Morning Chronicle* (1812–14); no such notes have come to light, except those in Sarah Stoddart Hazlitt's commonplace book (see HzW 100.5).
9. *Select British Poets* (London, 1824): Hazlitt's annotated copy of the rare first edition was owned by Edward FitzGerald in 1876 when he presented it to Charles Eliot Norton with a covering letter quoted in *Life*, pp. 334–5n; beyond surmising that the volume was in America, Howe was unable to trace it further.

10. *Table-Talk*: Hazlitt apparently sent a copy of the two-volume second edition (London, 1824), together with a proof copy of the third (never published) volume (eventually Vol. I of *The Plain Speaker*) to the French publisher Galignani with a covering letter of 27 October [1824] (discussed, and the letter published, in Robinson, pp. 22–3). Hazlitt had marked the essays in these three volumes that he thought suitable for inclusion in Galignani's edition of *Table-Talk* and perhaps revised the texts as well.
11. Marginalia in Printed Books: see discussion below for lost books.

A manuscript which invites further investigation is a letter from William Hazlitt the younger to Leigh Hunt (British Library, Add. MS 38523, ff. 126–7) which probably dates from the 1830s when Hazlitt's son was editing his father's remains. The letter contains two pages of notes on Hazlitt's life and works including, at the end, what is apparently a list of Hazlitt's manuscripts (see Stanley Jones's note about this letter in *Etudes Anglaises*, 33 (1980), 189n7). Manuscripts for the following titles on the list have not been traced; three items on the list have not been identified, i.e. 'Fragment on Napoleon', 'On an English Saturday' and 'On Covent Garden' (the last possibly one of the articles published in the *Morning Chronicle* of 1813–14).

1. 'An article on the Report & Committee on Elgin Marbles 8 [pages]': this is presumably 'The Elgin Marbles', first pub. *The Examiner*, 16 June 1816 and not reprinted until Waller & Glover; Howe, XVIII, 100–3.
2. 'On Beggars Opera': this is probably one of the articles entitled 'The Beggars Opera', published in the *Morning Chronicle*, 23 and 30 October 1813.
3. 'On Cant and Hypocrisy 8 [pages]': first pub. *London Weekly Review*, 6–13 December 1828; reprinted *Sketches and Essays by William Hazlitt*, ed. William Hazlitt the younger (London, 1839); Howe, XVII, 345–54.
4. 'On Classical Education': first pub. *Morning Chronicle*, 25 September 1813; reprinted *The Examiner*, 12 February 1815; collected *The Round Table* (1817); Howe, IV, 4–6.
5. 'On Comedy': presumably 'On Modern Comedy', first pub. as 'The Stage' in the *Morning Chronicle*, 25 September 1813; reprinted *The Examiner*, 20 August 1815; collected *The Round Table* (1817); Howe, IV, 10–14.
6. 'On the Feeling of Immortality in Youth': first pub. *Monthly Magazine*, March 1827; reprinted (from manuscript) *Literary Remains* (1836); Howe, XVII, 189–99.
7. 'On the Literary character': first pub. *Morning Chronicle*, 28 October 1813; collected *The Round Table* (1817); Howe, IV, 131–6.
8. 'On the Love of Life': first pub. *Morning Chronicle*, 4 September 1813; reprinted with additions in *The Examiner*, 15 January 1815; collected *The Round Table* (1817); Howe, IV, 1–4.

A few other unlocated manuscripts which *are* entered were last known to be in the hands of private owners now deceased: the Marquess of Crewe (d. 1945) (HzW 37, 54) and P. P. Howe (d. 1944) (HzW 1.5, 22, 96, 104). Two other unlocated manuscripts are listed (HzW 16, 69) because facsimiles are readily available.

Hazlitt's Books and Marginalia

William Carew Hazlitt compiled a list of over 40 books which would, at one point or another, have 'belonged to William Hazlitt or passed through his hands' (*The Hazlitts*, pp. xvi–xvii); of the two annotated books and one annotated playbill listed in the Marginalia section (HzW 116–18), only the work by Francis Bacon was included in this list. Earlier, in *Memoirs* (II, 272), he had discussed three of his grandfather's books and said that 'with these, and two or three other exceptions, the few books which belonged to him have completely disappeared'.

Of those three books, all apparently containing Hazlitt's marginalia — John Flaxman's *Lectures on Sculpture*, Henry Hart Milman's *Fazio* and Thomas Holcroft's *The Road to Ruin* — only the first has been traced and entered below (HzW 117). The annotations in Holcroft's play have, according to William Carew Hazlitt, been printed in an edition of it 'which I have met with' (*Memoirs*, II, 272) but no such edition has been identified.

Also untraced is the copy of the *Historical Atlas* of Count Las Cases used by Hazlitt in writing his *Life of Napoleon Buonaparte*; see the headnote to that work.

Letters

That Hazlitt disliked writing letters is well-known. *Letters* — the first attempt at a complete collection of them — includes only 168, sixty of which are reprinted from published sources, the other 108 from original manuscripts. As well as his personal correspondence, *Letters* includes Hazlitt's public letters to the editors of various newspapers and journals (reprinted from their published versions), his published essay 'On the Conduct of Life' (apparently originally written as a letter, now lost, to his son) and the 'fictional' letters to

'C. P'., 'S. L'. and 'J. S. K.' which make up much of *Liber Amoris*. The publishing history of Hazlitt's letters is outlined in Gerald Lahey's introduction (pp. 20–4); all but three of the 168 letters had been previously published, though a great many only partially so and many in scattered publications.

While this first collected *Letters* is undeniably useful, it is in some respects unreliable and users will ignore Stanley Jones's review in *The Library* (1980), which includes a great many detailed corrections, at their own risk. Twenty-seven new letters or new texts of letters (as well as much useful annotation) have been published in Robinson (1987). A revised edition of Hazlitt's collected letters, incorporating both corrections and the additional letters that have surfaced (see the list below), would indeed be welcome.

The repositories (excluding private collections) holding four or more of Hazlitt's letters are: British Library (including fifteen letters to Macvey Napier, 1816–30: Add. MSS 34611, 34612, 34614); SUNY at Buffalo (including letters to Hazlitt's family, one each to Sarah Stoddart and Sarah Walker, the series of eleven to P. G. Patmore (HzW 52) used for *Liber Amoris*); Duke University (four letters to William Godwin in the Abinger Collection); National Library of Scotland (including eight letters to Archibald Constable, see HzW 101); Dr Williams's Library (four letters to Henry Crabb Robinson and Thomas Robinson); Yale (including seventeen letters to Francis Jeffrey, see HzW 103, 110).

The original manuscripts (or transcripts thereof) of a few letters published in *Letters* from printed sources (or, in one case, from a transcript) have been located:

1. *Letters*, no. 8 to the Rev. William Hazlitt, London, 6 October 1793, Charnwood Collection on deposit at the British Library, Loan 60, II/31(3).
2. *Letters*, no. 46 to Charles Ollier, postmarked 13 May 1815, Yale, Osborn Collection (pub. Robinson).
3. *Letters*, no. 71 to B. W. Procter, [April 1817?] (published from a transcript), privately owned.
4. *Letters*, no. 79 to Archibald Constable, [September] 1818, transcript at National Library of Scotland, MS 674, f. 74r–v.
5. *Letters*, no. 100 to P. G. Patmore, this is actually the closing of the letter printed separately as no. 102 (see next item).
6. *Letters*, no. 102 to P. G. Patmore, postmarked 9 March 1822, Princeton, Robert H. Taylor Collection (see HzW 53).
7. *Letters*, no. 129 to Jane Reynolds, [January 1823], National Library of Scotland.
8. *Letters*, no. 132 to Thomas Cadell, 19 April 1823, Folger, Art Vol. b8 (pub. Robinson).
9. *Letters*, no. 135, a transcript by William Carew Hazlitt of this letter to Messrs Taylor and Hessey, postmarked Melrose, 16 April 1824 (see HzW 104), British Library, Department of Printed Books, C.133.g.10 (Vol. I, between pp. 476 and 477).
10. *Letters*, no. 141 to Henry Colburn, dated '[January 1826]', Folger, Art Vol. b8 (pub. Robinson, dated '[December 1825]').
11. *Letters*, no. 147 to David Constable, Winterslow, 10 January 1826 (mislocated at National Library of Scotland), Univerity of Delaware (pub. Robinson).
12. *Letters*, no. 149 to Charles Cowden Clarke, [January 1828], Dunedin Public Library, New Zealand (without salutation, apparently a fragment).
13. *Letters*, no. 150 to Charles Cowden Clarke, postmarked 1 February 1828, SUNY at Buffalo (pub. *Four Generations*, I, 189–90).
14. *Letters*, no. 163 to George Bartley, 14 June [1830], Folger, Art Vol. b8 (pub. Robinson).
15. *Letters*, no. 165 to [Martin Archer Shee, August 1830], inscribed on the inside back cover of HzW 13, Huntington, RB 26244.

In addition to the above, it should be noted that *Letters* gives the location for nos 72–4 (three letters to Archibald Constable, dated [January or February 1818]) as the National Library of Scotland; but they have not been found in that library. The five Hazlitt letters formerly owned by Sir Geoffrey Keynes (*Letters*, nos 65, 84, 113, 136 and 166) are now at the Cambridge University Library, ADD 8533/1–5.

Two more 'lost' letters have recently passed through the salerooms: *Letters*, no. 37 (to Thomas Hardy, [May or June 1811]) was sold at Sotheby's, 29 October 1976, Lot 194, to Geoffrey; *Letters*, no. 151 (to Charles Cowden Clarke, [February 1828]) was sold at Sotheby's, 20 June 1979, Lot 681 to Dr Schram. Another letter (*Letters*, no. 143 to P. G. Patmore, early August [1826]) was printed in Howe, XIII, 354 from the original then owned by the Marquess of Crewe and now untraced.

Several letters have come to light which were not included in *Letters*; they are listed below in alphabetical order of repository, followed by privately-owned and unlocated items in alphabetical order of recipient (see also the headnote to HzW 1–1.5):

1. Boston Public Library: to Hepworth Dixon, possibly a fragment, one page.

2. British Library, Department of Printed Books, C.44.e.g. (Vol. 42, p. 420): to 'Sir', n.d. (pub. 'New Letters').
3. Brown University, Ms. 52.116: to Owen Rees, 15 February [1830] (pub. Robinson; William Carew Hazlitt's transcript of the original, inserted in his interleaved copy of *The Hazlitts* (1911) at the British Library, Department of Printed Books, C.133.g.10).
4. Bryn Mawr College: to Mr Pearson, 4 April [1830] (facsimile in *Autographic Mirror*, 19 May 1866 and printed 'New Letters'); to 'Gentlemen' (unidentified creditors), [February 1823?]; to [Charles Cowden Clarke or Henry Leigh Hunt?], 28 October 1828 (all three pub. Robinson).
5. Charles Lamb Society Library, p CLS 1211: photocopy of a letter to Leigh Hunt, Thursday, 2 April n.y.
6. Connecticut Historical Society, A. L. Butler Collection, Vol. I, no. 2: to P. G. Patmore, 20 January 1818, one page.
7. Durham County Library, Darlington Branch: to William Bewick, postmarked 25 August 1823 (pub. 'New Letters').
8. Harvard, fMS Eng 1331(11), ff. 97v, 163: two letters to B. R. Haydon, n.d. and 11 August 1820, both in Haydon's Journal, Vol. IX.
9. NYPL, Pforzheimer Collection: to [Leigh Hunt or Henry Leigh Hunt?], 28 October [1814–28?] (pub. by Donald Reiman in *WC*, 10 (1979), 300 and in Robinson); 10 letters to Jean-Antoine Galignani, 27 October [1824]–25 December 1827 (including HzW 1, 64.5 and 110.5) (all pub. Robinson); to W. Underwood, 3 May 1828 (pub. Robinson).
10. Princeton, Robert H. Taylor Collection: to Archibald Constable, 3 January 1816 (pub. Robinson).
11. SUNY at Buffalo: to Thomas Ireland, Addlestone, 9 August 1814; to Miss Reynell, 22 August [n.y.].
12. University of Kentucky, W. Hugh Peal Collection: to George Dyer, [1806–8?] (pub. Robinson).
13. Washington University, St Louis: to unidentified recipient, one page, n.d.
14. Watt Monument Library, Greenock: to Francis Jeffrey, 14 February [1822] (pub. 'New Letters').
15. Yale, Osborn Collection: to [John] Black, [c. mid-August 1823] (facsimile in British Library, RP 329); to Thomas Allsop, postmarked 11 September 1826 (facsimile in British Library, RP 72(2)); both partly pub. 'New Letters' and in full in Robinson.
16. Privately owned by Eleanor Gates (publication forthcoming, see Robinson, p. 5n8): six Hazlitt letters.
17. Archive of John Murray, London: to John Murray, [3 September–26 November 1808?] (pub. Robinson).
18. Maggs Catalogue 411 (1921), Item 1871: to Galignani, 12 June 1825 (sale catalogue quoted 'New Letters').
19. Maggs Catalogue 785 (1949), Item 691: to the Rev. William Hazlitt, Liverpool, [before 31 July] 1790, 4 pages.
20. John Waller (London) Catalogue 80 (1870), Item 159: signed note to [Marianne Hunt or her servant], 2 March 1829, one page (sale catalogue quoted 'New Letters').
21. Sotheby's, 13 June 1913, Lot 79: to Francis Jeffrey, postmarked 4 May 1818, 2 pages (William Carew Hazlitt's transcript of the original, inserted in his interleaved copy of *The Hazlitts* (1911), British Library, Department of Printed Books, C.133.g.10, Vol. I, facing p. 442).
22. American Art Association, 12–13 January 1938 (Alfred Meyer Sale), Lot 127: to J. H. Payne, 8 February 1819 (sale catalogue quoted 'New Letters').
23. Sotheby's, 28 November 1913, Lot 247: to James Perry, [23 February 1818] (sale catalogue quoted 'New Letters').
24. Sotheby's, 3 August 1922, sold to Maggs: to J. A. St John, 14 February [1829] (sale catalogue quoted 'New Letters').

Miscellanea and Association Items

Several items of literary and biographical interest are not listed individually in the entries. A rich manuscript source of information concerning the history of the Hazlitts (focusing particularly on Hazlitt's father, the Rev. William Hazlitt) and the only manuscript source of material on Hazlitt's early life (including the years spent in America) is Margaret Hazlitt's journal, written expressly for the instruction of her nephew, William Hazlitt the younger. The first version of this journal (incomplete, 79 leaves rectos only, in a volume of 88 leaves, watermarked 1828), apparently begun in 1833, was acquired (with HzW 41) in 1908 by the State Library of Victoria, Melbourne, from Lydia Reynell Johns (with whose family Margaret Hazlitt had lived); it is discussed in detail (including its variations from the later version) in Harold Love, 'An Early Version of Margaret Hazlitt's Journal', *Journal of the Australasian Universities Language and Literature Association*, 43 (1975),

24–32. The later version is also incomplete; it fills 186 pages of a bound volume now at the University of Delaware. Long extracts of it were published in *Four Generations* (I, 3–64) and *The Hazlitts*; it has been edited and published in full by Ernest J. Moyne in *The Journal of Margaret Hazlitt* (Lawrence, KS, 1967).

Various listings of Hazlitt's paintings — including the copies he made of Old Masters in the Louvre (1802–3) and portraits for which he was commissioned — are given in *Memoirs* (I, xvi: 16 paintings dating from c. 1800–1825), in *The Hazlitts* (p. xiii: 26 paintings, 1802–1820), and in *Life* (Appendix II, p. 395: 21 paintings, 1800–1812). A number of these paintings have been preserved: his portrait of Charles Lamb as a Venetian senator (c. 1804) hangs in the National Portrait Gallery, London; another is preserved in the Royal Academy, London; all the other extant paintings are among the collection (which also includes works by John Hazlitt) bequeathed to the Maidstone Museum by William Carew Hazlitt in 1909. This latter collection also contains Hazlitt's death mask.

The large Hazlitt collection of A. Conger Goodyear at SUNY at Buffalo, mentioned above, is rich not only in Hazlitt's own papers but also in those of his circle and other Hazlittiana. Some notable items are: Hazlitt's autograph agreement with William Hone for the publication of *Political Essays* (1819), signed by both parties and dated 25 January 1819; the marriage license of William Hazlitt and Sarah Stoddart dated 26 April 1808 (they were married at St Andrew's, Holborn, on 1 May); Mary Lamb's memorable letters to Sarah Stoddart; letters *to* Hazlitt and others by Hazlitt's mother, sister and son, Charles Lamb, Fanny Kelly, Leigh Hunt, John Hunt, T. N. Talfourd, Henry Colburn, J. A. Hessey and John Taylor; Sarah Stoddart Hazlitt's note of Hazlitt's death (pub. *Memoirs*, II, 218). In addition, this collection contains a large number of letters addressed to Hazlitt's son and grandson as well as the latter William Carew Hazlitt's interleaved copy of *Four Generations* into which he inserted many originals of the letters there printed.

Two autograph scraps found among Hazlitt's papers at SUNY at Buffalo have yet to be identified. One contains four lines beginning 'In all about 300 pages…' which could be a fragment of a letter. The other is a rough list of six titles of articles or series of articles, all of which were published in the *Morning Chronicle* of 1813–14; it begins 'Series of critiques of Mr Kean's acting…'.

Also at SUNY at Buffalo is the manuscript material relating to *Liber Amoris* which formed the 'additional matter' included by William Carew Hazlitt and Richard Le Gallienne in their privately printed 1894 edition. The most important of these items is the journal which Sarah Stoddart Hazlitt kept from 14 April–18 July 1822 (sold Hazlitt Sale, Lot 246) when she was residing in Scotland for the purpose of obtaining a divorce; extracts had been included in *Memoirs* before the journal was printed in full (albeit inaccurately) in 1894. A text, re-edited from the original, was published in Bonner (1959), which also included Hazlitt's own journal (HzW 56), a letter from Sarah Walker to Hazlitt (17 January [1821]) and 5 letters of Sarah Stoddart Hazlitt to her son and her sister-in-law Margaret Hazlitt, all of which are also preserved at SUNY at Buffalo.

Other documents concerning the Hazlitts' divorce — including summonses, trial testimony and the decree itself dated 2 August 1822 — are preserved in the Scottish Record Office; they have been partially published in J. A. Houch, 'Hazlitt Divorce: the Court Records', *WC*, 6 (1975), 115–20.

Another large collection of association material is in the British Library, composed of sixteen volumes bequeathed by William Carew Hazlitt in 1913. These volumes contain primarily letters (1814–1913) to William Hazlitt the younger (d. 1893) and William Carew Hazlitt (d. 1913), including the correspondence between them and letters from, *inter alia*, J. P. Collier, W. W. Skeat, F. J. Furnival, Henry Huth, J. O. Halliwell-Phillipps. Some of these letters have been printed in *Four Generations* and *The Hazlitts*. Worth mentioning specifically are Sarah Stoddart Hazlitt's notes (Add. MS 38898, ff. 3–4) chronicling the events of her life, including a sad catalogue of miscarriages and a paragraph on the death and funeral of Hazlitt. Also bequeathed by William Carew Hazlitt to the British Library (and now preserved in the Department of Printed Books, C.133.g.10) is his own interleaved copy of *The Hazlitts* containing his corrections, additions and annotations as well as inserted manuscripts, letters, clippings, portraits and a lock of Hazlitt's hair enclosed with a note by Sarah Stoddart Hazlitt. A facsimile of this last is printed in the published book and, indeed, the originals of other facsimiles so printed (as well as of many letters printed in the text) are also inserted in this copy (e.g., an autograph admission ticket to Hazlitt's lectures and, especially, HzW 27).

A few other miscellaneous items in the British Library are in other collections: another autograph admission ticket to Hazlitt's lectures (Add. MS 20081, f. 144 among letters to Thomas Hill); the manuscript agreement, between Hazlitt (acting as agent for James Northcote) and Colburn & Bentley, for the publication of Northcote's *Life of Titian*, amended in Hazlitt's hand and signed by all three, dated 22 February 1830 (Add. MS 46611, f. 102); Hazlitt's autograph declaration to the trustees of his marriage settlement stating that Sarah Stoddart Hazlitt's trust fund should go to their son in the event of her death, signed and dated 23 April 1822 (Add. MS 62943K).

The one other noteworthy collection of Hazlittiana is that amassed by Alexander Ireland, now in the Manchester Central Library (described above). Preserved there are three boxes of 116 items (Q.824.76.G7) pertaining to Hazlitt, including printed reviews and reminiscences of Hazlitt, printed clippings of works by him, articles about him, scattered manuscript transcripts by Ireland and others of extracts by Hazlitt, as well as HzW 33. Elsewhere in this collection is a transcript of *Free Thoughts on Public Affairs* (London, 1806) (824.76.V.11), Ireland's own annotated copy of his *List of Writings of William Hazlitt and Leigh Hunt* (London, 1868) (824.76.A.2) and Charles Cowden Clarke's annotated copies of *The Plain Speaker*, 2 vols (London, 1826) (824.76.X.1) and *The Life of Napoleon Buonaparte* (HzW 58).

For Hazlitt's agreement with Constable for the publication of *The Round Table*, now at the National Library of Scotland, see HzW 101.

ABBREVIATIONS

For general abbreviations, see the list at the front of this volume.

Baker
Herschel Baker, *William Hazlitt* (Cambridge, MA & London, 1962).

Bonner
The Journals of Sarah and William Hazlitt, ed. W. H. Bonner, *University of Buffalo Studies*, Vol. 24, February 1959.

Folger Volume
For a description of this MS volume, see INTRODUCTION.

Harvard *Spirit of the Age*
For a description of this volume, see INTRODUCTION.

Hazlitt Sale
A Selection from the Books, Manuscripts and Letters collected by William Hazlitt the Essayist, His Son, and Grandson, Sotheby's, 23–4 November 1893.

Four Generations
William Carew Hazlitt, *Four Generations of a Literary Family*, 2 vols (London, 1897).

The Hazlitts
William Carew Hazlitt, *The Hazlitts: An Account of their Origin and Descent* (Edinburgh, 1911).

Howe
The Complete Works of William Hazlitt, ed. P. P. Howe, Centenary Edition, 21 vols (London & Toronto, 1930–4).

Jones
Review of *Letters* by Stanley Jones in *The Library*, 6 Ser 2 (1980), 356–62.

Keynes
Sir Geoffrey Keynes, *Bibliography of William Hazlitt*, 2nd ed (Godalming, Surrey, 1981).

Lamb and Hazlitt
Lamb and Hazlitt, ed. William Carew Hazlitt (London, 1900).

Letters
The Letters of William Hazlitt, ed. Herschel Moreland Sikes, assisted by W. H. Bonner and Gerald Lahey (London, 1979) (first pub. New York University Press, 1978).

Life
P. P. Howe, *The Life of William Hazlitt* (London, 1947).

Literary Remains
Literary Remains of the late William Hazlitt, ed. William Hazlitt the younger, 2 vols (London, 1836).

Manchester (Ireland) Volume
For a description of this MS volume, see INTRODUCTION.

Memoirs
William Carew Hazlitt, *Memoirs of William Hazlitt*, 2 vols (London, 1867).

'New Letters'
Stanley Jones, 'Some New Letters', *N&Q*, 222 (1977), 336–42.

Political Essays
William Hazlitt, *Political Essays* (London, 1819).

Robinson
'William Hazlitt to His Publisher, Friends and Creditors: Twenty-seven New Holograph Letters', ed. Charles E. Robinson, *Keats-Shelley Review*, No. 2 (1987), 1–47.

The Round Table
William Hazlitt, *The Round Table*, 2 vols (Edinburgh, 1817).
Table-Talk
William Hazlitt, *Table-Talk*, 2 vols (London, 1821–2).
Waller & Glover
The Collected Works of William Hazlitt, ed. A. R. Waller and A. Glover, 13 vols (London, 1902–6).
Wilcox
Stewart C. Wilcox, *Hazlitt in the Workshop: the Manuscript of* The Fight (Baltimore, 1943).

ARRANGEMENT

Verse	HzW 1–1.5
Prose	HzW 2–115
Marginalia in Printed Books	HzW 116–18

William Hazlitt

VERSE

The Damned Author's Address to his Reviewers
('The rock I'm told on which I split')
Hazlitt's verses were apparently written in reply to the *Edinburgh Review*'s notice of *The Spirit of the Age* (see Robinson, p. 31n2). First pub. *Lamb and Hazlitt* (1900); Howe, XX, 392–3. Hazlitt apparently sent the verses to several journals for publication; in addition to the two submissions listed below, 'New Letters' notes a letter (not mentioned in *Letters*) from Hazlitt to Thomas Hill (written after August 1825), which included or enclosed these verses and was sold with Hill's estate at Messrs Evans (Pall Mall, London) on 10 March 1841, Lot 1531, to Thorpe.

HzW 1 On one page of a leaf containing a note to Jean-Antoine Galignani, 30 August [1825].

This MS printed Robinson, pp. 29–31.

NYPL, Pforzheimer Collection.

HzW 1.5 On pages 1–2 of a folded leaf containing, on page 3, a note to John Black dated Vevey, 31 August [1825]; addressed to Thomas Hodgskin and apparently sent to him for forwarding, postmarked 8 September 1825.

This MS printed in *The Hazlitts*, pp. 479–80 and Howe, XX, 448; the note to Black reprinted from *The Hazlitts* in *Letters*, no. 140.

Owned (1934) by P. P. Howe (d. 1944) (Howe, XX, 448).

PROSE

Aphorisms on Man
First pub. (70 numbered aphorisms in 6 parts) *Monthly Magazine*, October–December 1830 and April–June 1831; Howe, XX, 330–50.

HzW 2 Nos. XII–XXVII (here headed XLIII–LVIII), 12 pages numbered 33–44 (3 leaves); together with Nos. XLVI–LXI (here headed LXXVII–XCIII, including one cancelled aphorism), 8 pages numbered 53–60 (2 leaves).

SUNY at Buffalo.

HzW 3 Nos. XXXV (here headed LXVI) and XXXVII, 2 pages (one leaf).

Facsimile of no. XXXV in Christie's sale catalogue, p. 37.

Christie's, 4 November 1981, Lot 101, sold to Schram.

HzW 4 Nine unpublished aphorisms, numbered [88]–96 (previously numbered (cancelled) [106]–114), 2 pages (one leaf cut in two) numbered 88–9.

SUNY at Buffalo.

'as to shew the place or [?] word...'
No publication traced.

HzW 5 Fragment on English grammar, one page numbered 5; dated Winterslow, 29 January 1828.

This may be a surviving leaf of the MS (recorded by W. C. Hazlitt in *Memoirs*, I, xxxii) of the 'Outlines of English Grammar' which Hazlitt proposed to David Constable in a letter of 10 January 1828, merely some three weeks before the date of this MS; see the headnote to 'Outlines'.

SUNY at Buffalo.

The Beggars Opera, for a lost MS, see INTRODUCTION.

Belief, whether Voluntary?
First pub. *Literary Remains* (1836); Howe, XX, 363–9.

HzW 6 Four pages, revised, annotated in an unidentified hand 'The handwriting of William Hazlitt, presented to [erased] by his son'.

Two pages of this essay (numbered 7–8) were offered for sale in Kenneth W. Rendell Catalogue 54 [c. 1970] and are possibly two of the four sold in 1938.

American Art Association/Anderson Galleries, 12–13 December 1938 (Edgar W. Dunbar Sale), Lot 216.

Case of Mr. Hone, see description of *Yellow Dwarf* volume in INTRODUCTION.

Characters of Shakespear's Plays
First pub. London, 1817; Howe, IV, [165]–[361]. A few of the essays (or passages therein) had previously been published in the *Morning Chronicle* (1814) and *The Examiner* (1815–16); see the notes to individual essays in Howe for details.

——Preface
First pub. London, 1817; Howe, IV, 171–8.

HzW 7 Opening portion, beginning 'It is observed by Mr Pope...' and ending '...the German critic has executed this part of his design' (i.e. Howe, IV, 171), 2 pages (one leaf).

Boston Public Library, **G.3922.12, no. 9.

——Macbeth
First pub. London, 1817; Howe, IV, 186–94.

HzW 8 Extensively revised page proof, wanting title and opening lines (as published) and with variant first paragraph, 16 pages numbered 17–32, bound in the Folger Volume.

This proof described *Sentimental Library*, p. 114.

Folger, MS T.b.18, last item (unfoliated).

——Much Ado about Nothing
First pub. London, 1817; Howe, IV, 335–8.

HzW 9 Fragment, mostly in Sarah Stoddart Hazlitt's hand (beginning Howe, IV, 335, line 2 but top of f. 146 cut off), 3 pages, bound in the Folger Volume.

Folger, MS T.b.18, ff. 146–7.

Conversations of James Northcote, Esq., R.A.
Conversations I–VI first pub. with an introductory note *New Monthly Magazine*, August–November 1826 and February–March 1827, as 'Boswell Redivivus, Nos. I–VI'; introductory note reprinted Howe, XI, 350; Conversations VII, X, XV, VIII first pub. (in that order) *Court Journal*, 9 and 30 January, 20 February and 3 April 1830, as 'Conversations with an Eminent Living Artist, Nos. I–IV'; Conversations XI, IX, XII first pub. (in that order) *London Weekly Review*, 7 March, 14 March and 11 April, and 18 April 1829, as 'Real Conversations, Nos. I–IV'; Conversations XVI–XXII first pub. as 9 conversations *The Atlas*, 19 and 26 April, 28 June, 9 and 16 August, 13 September, 25 October, 8 and 15 November 1829 (various titles, mostly 'Conversations as Good as Real'; see Howe for details); the greater part revised and collected and Conversations XIII–XIV first pub. in one volume London, 1830; Howe, XI, [185]–320; Conversations uncollected in 1830 pub. Howe, XX, 233–6, 260–1, 272–7, 295–6, 391–2 (see for details of previous publications). A copy of the 1830 edition — apparently bound from advance sheets and inscribed by Northcote himself — was sold at Sotheby's, 13–14 December 1950, Lot 415, to Maggs; at that time, a letter from Hazlitt to Northcote of 29 July 1830 (pub. *Letters*, no. 164 from the original at Cornell University) was inserted.

HzW 10 Twenty-seven leaves (rectos only), including: 1) the introductory note to the first publication of the first six conversations, headed 'Boswell Redivivus — No. I.' and including an epigraph from Armstrong, 2 numbered leaves (rectos only); 2) 'Conversation the First', here entitled '<Conversations of an Artist. — No. I.>', 11 numbered leaves (rectos only); 3) 'Conversation the Second', here entitled '<Second Conversation>' and 'Boswell Redivivus No. II', 9 leaves numbered 12–20 (rectos only); 4) 'Conversation the Third', a variant and incomplete version, here entitled 'Boswell Redivivus No III.' and 'Third Conversation', 5 leaves (rectos only) numbered 21–5.

Hazlitt Sale, Lot 242, sold to Pearson.

SUNY at Buffalo.

HzW 11 Annotations by James Northcote in a copy of the 1830 edition, including the insertion of names left blank in the text and 24 pages (12 interleaved leaves) of alternative text, replacing excised pp. 293–4, 297–8, 303–4,

307–8 and 313–28, annotated in pencil in an unidentified hand on front flyleaf 'Northcote's own copy with Autograph MSS. additions & the blanks (names) filled up by him'.

These annotations given in Notes in Howe, XI, 350–76.

British Library, Department of Printed Books, C.60.k.3.

HzW 12 Revisions and annotations by James Northcote in a copy of the 1830 edition, bound with a few letters to and from Northcote (none from Hazlitt) concerning the publication of the book and the cancellation of controversial passages.

The letters in this copy are printed in Stewart C. Wilcox, 'Hazlitt and Northcote', *ELH*, 7 (1940), 325–32.

Owned (1940) Professor D. Nichol Smith (see Wilcox and Howe, XI, 351).

HzW 13 Proof copy of pp. 313–28 and a paper cover of the 1830 edition, containing a correction on p. 314 by Hazlitt and his presentation inscription to Martin Archer Shee on the inside paper cover; bound by Frederick Locker with the remaining pages of another copy of the 1830 edition.

The proof copy with a paper cover sold Hazlitt Sale, Lot 241 to Pickering; the presentation inscription to Shee reprinted as a letter in *Letters*, no. 165 from *Four Generations*, I, 197.

Huntington, RB 26244.

Covent Garden Theatre, for a lost MS, see INTRODUCTION.

The Dandy School
First pub. *The Examiner*, 18 November 1827; Howe, XX, 143–9.

HzW 14 Variant version, without the ending, 4 leaves (rectos only), the first 3 cut in half making seven pages in all.

SUNY at Buffalo.

Definition of Wit
First pub. *Literary Remains* (1836); Howe, XX, 352–63.

HzW 15 Fragments (i.e., Howe, XX, 353 line 13–355 line 17 and 356 line 21–359 line 1), 9 leaves (rectos only) numbered twice, once by Hazlitt (cancelled) in top right corner 6–9 and 11–15 and once, possibly in another hand, 2–5 and 8–12.

Columbia University, X825H33.P5.

HzW 16 Fragment (i.e., Howe, XX, 361 line 30–362 line 8), one page numbered twice, once '21' by Hazlitt (cancelled) in top right corner, and once '18', possibly in another hand.

A negative photostat of this MS in the Hazlitt Miscellaneous File at NYPL, Manuscripts Division; it is annotated on verso 'Original (1936) owned by Lester F. Lange, Westfield, NJ' and 'Formerly in Authors Club Collection (Stoddard)'. Also in this File is a negative photostat of a letter from William Hazlitt the younger reading in part 'I have much pleasure in forwarding you a page of my father's handwriting...' and also annotated 'Authors Club (Stoddard Collection)' which possibly refers to this MS.

Unlocated.

The Drama: No. II
First pub. *London Magazine*, February 1820; Howe, XVIII, 280–91.

HzW 17 Variant version of the concluding section (i.e., Howe, XVIII, 290 line 9 to the end), headed 'Mr Kean's Coriolanus', 5 numbered pages (4 leaves), annotated at the end 'L—M.' and 'I should like if possible to see a proof of this...'; watermarked 1819, bound in the Folger Volume.

Folger, MS T.b.18, ff. 142–5v.

The Elgin Marbles, for a lost MS, see INTRODUCTION.

Emancipation of the Jews, for a lost MS, see INTRODUCTION.

An Essay on the Principles of Human Action, for a lost annotated copy, see INTRODUCTION.

An Examination of Mr Malthus's Doctrines, see description of *Yellow Dwarf* volume in INTRODUCTION.

'[?] farmer. Corn is the regulator of the price of surplus corn only…'
No publication traced.

HzW 18 Fragment on agricultural economy, one page.

SUNY at Buffalo.

The Fight
First pub. *New Monthly Magazine*, February 1822, signed 'Phantastes'; Howe, XVII, 72–86, as 'Uncollected Essay VIII. The Fight'.

HzW 19 Printer's copy for first publication, incomplete, 25 leaves, the first 15 (rectos only) numbered 9, 11–21, 23, 25–6, the next 10 (rectos and versos) numbered 27–42, 45–8; watermarked 1821, written after 11 December 1821.

For a cancelled passage, see HzW 55; for a discussion, transcript and facsimile page (p. 41) of this MS, see Wilcox; facsimile page (p. 21) in *British Literary Manuscripts*, plate 21.

Pierpont Morgan, MA 190.

Fine Arts
First pub. Supplement to *Encyclopaedia Britannica*, ed. Macvey Napier, 4th and 5th eds (1816–24), Vol. I (1816) (afterwards incorporated into the 7th ed of the *Encyclopaedia* (1842)); Howe, XVIII, 111–24 and 433–6. This essay is composed largely of passages previously published in *Morning Chronicle* and *Champion* articles of 1814; for details, see the Notes in Howe, XVIII, 433–6.

HzW 20 Suggested deletion and revision, in a letter to Macvey Napier, [18 March 1816].

This MS printed *Letters*, no. 56 where misdated [20 March 1816]; date corrected in Jones.

British Library, Add. MS 34611, f. 367r–v.

Flaxman's Lectures on Sculpture, see HzW 117.

Folger Volume, for a description of this volume of MSS, see INTRODUCTION.

Fragment on Napoleon, for an unidentified 'lost' MS, see INTRODUCTION.

[Fragments], see HzW 5, 18, 25, 27, 111.

The Free Admission
First pub. *New Monthly Magazine*, July 1830; Howe, XVII, 365–70, as 'Uncollected Essay XXXVI. The Free Admission'.

HzW 21 Eleven numbered pages (6 leaves), wanting the last few lines, a fair copy of which is included on a separate page (recto and verso) headed 'Conclusion to Free Admission'; addressed to Henry Colburn and dated 21 June [1830] on otherwise blank verso of f. 11.

Hazlitt Sale, Lot 242, sold to Pearson.

SUNY at Buffalo.

Free Thoughts on Public Affairs
First pub. anonymously London, 1806; Howe, I, [93]–[118].

HzW 22 Annotation on p. 27 of a copy of the first edition.

Formerly owned by the late P. P. Howe (d. 1944) (see Keynes, p. 5).

Guy Faux
First pub. in three parts in *The Examiner*, 11, 18 and 25 November 1821, signed 'Z'; Howe, XX, 96–112.

HzW 23 Fragment (i.e., Howe, XX, 99 lines 9–25), one page numbered 7, imperfect, bound in the Folger Volume; written for *London*

Magazine, c. June 1821.

Folger, MS T.b.18, f. 141.

Harvard *Spirit of the Age*, for a description of this volume, see INTRODUCTION.

Hints to Persons in Business and Men of the World
First pub. (10 numbered Hints) Howe, XX (1934), 350–2.

HzW 24 Printer's copy for first publication, here entitled 'Hints to Persons in Business and Men of the World, the Properly Attending to which may save them from losing Hundreds and Thousands', 4 numbered pages (2 leaves).

SUNY at Buffalo.

'I shall proceed to deduce two or three general inferences from the <argument here stated> preceding argument, which it would be difficult to reconcile with the common notion of the formation of our ideas out of physical impressions.'
No publication traced.

HzW 25 Fair copy, revised, of a passage (possibly incomplete) on understanding and reason, 4 pages (one leaf).

SUNY at Buffalo.

The Ideal
First pub. *The Atlas*, 10 January 1830, as 'Specimens of a Dictionary of Definitions, No. II'; reprinted (with additions from a MS) in *Criticisms on Art*, ed. William Hazlitt the younger, second series (London, 1844); Howe, XX, 302–6 (additions on pp. 435–6).

HzW 26 Fragment, being here one passage which, in published version, is scattered with variants throughout the essay (i.e., Howe, XX, 304 lines 4–7, 303 lines 20–31, 436 lines 23–7), one page numbered 5.

SUNY at Buffalo.

Imagination
Questionable attribution; for a discussion, see INTRODUCTION. Facsimile only pub. *The Hazlitts* (1911), between pp. 188 and 189.

HzW 27 Quotation from an unidentified source, beginning 'But it is vain to oppose either facts or arguments to the common prejudice...', headed in an unidentified hand 'Imagination/from Hazlitt's Lectures', 4 pages (one leaf), followed by a signed note (draft) to 'Sir' offering this transcript of 'the most popular passage I could find...'; watermarked 1807.

This MS is inserted in W. C. Hazlitt's interleaved copy of *The Hazlitts* wherein the facsimile of it, without comment, is printed; while the note at the bottom of the MS implies that it was meant to be sent to an unidentified recipient, the provenance implies that it was not.

British Library, Department of Printed Books, C.133.g.10.

The Indian Jugglers
Concluding portion first pub. as 'Death of John Cavanagh' in *The Examiner*, 7 February 1819; first pub. in full *Table-Talk* (1821), as 'Essay IX'; Howe, VIII, 77–89.

HzW 28 Fragment, including variants and footnote (beginning Howe, VIII, 81 line 27), annotated at end 'conclude with article on Cavanagh...', 6 leaves (rectos only) numbered 7–12, some watermarked 1820.

Columbia University, MS X825H33.R7.

Landor's Imaginary Conversations
First pub. *Edinburgh Review*, March 1824; Howe, XVI, 240–64.

HzW 29 Suggestions for cuts, in a letter to Francis Jeffrey, Melrose, 25 April [1824].

This MS printed in Notes in Howe, XVI, 435 and *Letters*, no. 136; facsimile in Keynes, facing p. 90.

Cambridge University Library, ADD 8533.

Lectures, see also HzW 27.

Lectures on English Philosophy
A course of ten lectures delivered at the Russell Institution, London, 14 January–27 April 1812; first

pub. (a defective text of six lectures that may differ from the text as delivered, see Baker, pp. 185–6) in *Literary Remains* (1836) (five lectures) and *Essays on the Principles of Human Action*, ed. William Hazlitt the younger (London, 1836) (one lecture, 'On Abstract Ideas'); reprinted Howe, II, [121]–284.

HzW 30 Outline of the proposed course of ten lectures, in a letter to Henry Crabb Robinson, Winterslow, 29 October 1811, postmarked 2 November 1811.

This MS printed *Life*, pp. 124–5 and *Letters*, no. 39.

Dr Williams's Library, 1809–1817 Volume, f. 57.

HzW 31 Transcript by Edward McDermot (of the Russell Institution) of the minutes of a meeting of the Institution (on 19 December 1811) including a description of Hazlitt's proposed course of ten lectures in English philosophy (this meeting accepted the proposal); written out at the request of W.C. Hazlitt and sent to him with a covering letter dated 20 November 1866.

British Library, Add. MS 38899, ff. 190–1.

——On Liberty and Necessity
First pub. *Literary Remains* (1836); Howe, II, 245–70.

HzW 32 Fragments of this lecture (i.e., Howe, II, 246 line 4–247 line 25 (f. 20v–r) and 266 line 40–267 line 37 (f. 18r–v)), including a rough and cancelled passage and a long quotation from Dr Jonathan Edwards transcribed by Sarah Stoddart Hazlitt, 4 pages on 2 leaves (f. 18r–v numbered 48–9), bound in the Manchester (Ireland) Volume.

Manchester Central Library, Alexander Ireland Collection, F.824.76.G4, ff. 18r–v, 20v–r (misbound).

HzW 33 Fragment of this lecture (i.e., Howe, II, 266 lines 1–40), 2 pages (one leaf) numbered 46–7; watermarked 1807.

Manchester Central Library, Alexander Ireland Collection, Hazlitt Box III (Q.824.76.G7), Item 4.

——On Locke's 'Essay on the Human Understanding'
First pub. *Literary Remains* (1836); Howe, II, 146–91.

HzW 34 Fragment of this lecture (i.e., Howe, II, 146 last line–147 line 14), one page.

Sotheby's, 18 December 1985, Lot 89.

HzW 35 Fragments of this lecture (i.e., Howe, II, 151 lines 12–29 (f. 16); II, 164 line 6–165 line 6 (f. 21v–r); II, 166 line 26–167 line 20 (f. 19v–r); II, 188 lines 2–39 (f. 17r–v)), including some rough and cancelled passages, 7 pages (4 leaves) numbered 43–4 (f. 21v–r), 48–9 (f. 17r–v), 50 (f. 19), bound in the Manchester (Ireland) Volume.

Manchester Central Library, Alexander Ireland Collection, F.824.76.G4, ff. 16, 17r–v, 19v–r (misbound), 21v–r (misbound).

——On Tooke's 'Diversions of Purley'
First pub. *Literary Remains* (1836); Howe, II, 270–84.

HzW 36 Fragments of this lecture (i.e., Howe, II, 273 line 9–274 line 6 (f. 7v–r) and 279 line 13–280 line 4 (f. 13r–v)), 4 pages (2 leaves) numbered 7–8 (f. 7v–r) and 21–2 (f. 13r–v), bound in the Manchester (Ireland) Volume; watermarked 1811.

Most of the passage contained on f. 13r–v also appears in Hazlitt's essay 'Madame de Staël's account of German philosophy' pub. *Morning Chronicle*, 8 April 1814 and Howe, XX, 31–2.

Manchester Central Library, Alexander Ireland Collection, F.824.76.G4, ff. 7v–r (misbound), 13r–v.

Lectures on the Dramatic Literature of the Age of Elizabeth
A course of 8 lectures delivered at the Surrey Institution, London, November–December 1819; first pub. as *Lectures chiefly on the Dramatic Literature of the Age of Elizabeth* (London, 1820); Howe, VI, [169]–364.

HzW 37 Outline of the proposed course of 8 lectures, in a letter to P. G. Patmore,

Westminster, [3 February 1819], postmarked 4 February 1819.

This MS printed Howe, VI, 385–6; reprinted *Letters*, no. 83 where it is misdated [4 February 1819], date corrected in Jones.

Owned (1931) Marquess of Crewe (d. 1945) (see Howe, VI, 385).

HzW 38 Revised list of titles for the lecture series, headed 'Course of Lectures on the Age and Literature of Q. Elizabeth', one page, on verso of address panel addressed to Hazlitt and annotated 'To be returned to me, W. H.'; postmarked 1819.

Bodleian, MS.Dep.b.215/6.

——Lecture I. Introductory. General View of the Subject
First pub. *Lectures chiefly on the Dramatic Literature of the Age of Elizabeth* (London, 1820); Howe, VI, 175–92.

HzW 39 Fragment of this lecture (i.e., Howe, VI, 180 line 39–189 line 32), including a quotation transcribed by Sarah Stoddart Hazlitt, 32 leaves (mostly rectos only) numbered 20–51, bound in the Folger Volume; several leaves watermarked 1818, written c. July–September 1819.

Folger, MS T.b.18, ff. 109–40.

——Lecture VII. Character of Lord Bacon's Works — Compared as to style with Sir Thomas Brown and Jeremy Taylor, see HzW 116.

Lectures on the English Comic Writers
A course of 8 lectures delivered at the Surrey Institution, London, November 1818–January 1819; first pub. London, 1819; Howe, VI, [1]–168. For possibly lost MSS, see INTRODUCTION.

——Lecture I. Introductory. On Wit and Humour
First pub. London, 1819; Howe, VI, 5–30.

HzW 40 Four fragments, bound in the Folger Volume, including rough notes (esp. f. 91v) and early versions of numerous passages, headed 'Lectures on the comic writers, &c. of Great Britain./Lecture I. Introductory./ On Wit & Humour.', including: 1) beginning to Howe, VI, 6 line 7, 2 numbered leaves (ff. 91–2, rectos only), watermarked 1813; 2) from c. top of Howe, VI, 7, 13 pages numbered 6–18 (7 leaves, ff. 93–9v, some watermarked 1815); 3) from Howe, VI, 24 penultimate line, 6 leaves numbered 48–53 (ff. 100–5, mostly rectos only, some jottings on versos), watermarked 1815; 4) Howe, VI, 25 line 26–c. top of 26, one page (f. 108v).

Folger, MS T.b.18, ff. 91–105 (some versos blank), 108v.

——Lecture VI. On the English Novelists, see HzW 110.

Lectures on the English Poets
A course of 8 lectures delivered at the Surrey Institution, London, January–February 1818; repeated at the Crown and Anchor Tavern, London, April–May 1818; first pub. London, 1818; Howe, V, [1]–168.

——Lecture I. On Poetry in General, see HzW 103.

——Lecture II. On Chaucer and Spenser
First pub. London, 1818; Howe, V, 19–44. See also HzW 103.

HzW 41 Ninety-one pages, including transcriptions of quotations by Sarah Stoddart Hazlitt.

State Library of Victoria, Melbourne, La Trobe Collection.

——Lecture III. On Shakspeare and Milton
First pub. London, 1818; Howe, V, 44–68. See also HzW 103.

HzW 42 Here entitled 'Lecture III. On Shakespear & Milton.', including transcriptions of quotations by Sarah Stoddart Hazlitt and revisions probably by Charles Lamb, 53 pages numbered 1–40, 44–7, 47–8, 48–54

(38 leaves); including also (bound between ff. 64 and 65 and unfoliated) two leaves of corrected page proof, probably for the first edition (i.e., Howe, V, 57 line 21–58 line 20 and V, 64 line 25–65 line 23); bound in the Folger Volume.

Folger, MS T.b.18, ff. 37–75.

——Lecture IV. On Dryden and Pope
First pub. London, 1818; Howe, V, 68–85.

HzW 43 Revised, here entitled 'Lecture IV. On Dryden & Pope. —', including transcriptions of quotations by Sarah Stoddart Hazlitt, 36 pages numbered 1–32 (two numbered 22), 35–7 (26 leaves), wanting pp. 33–4 (i.e., Howe, V, 82 line 25–83 line 23).

Photocopy in the British Library.

Buffalo and Erie County Public Library, Gluck Collection.

——Lecture V. On Thomson and Cowper
First pub. London, 1818; Howe, V, 85–104.

HzW 44 Heavily revised in parts, headed 'Lecture V. On Thomson & Cowper. —', 48 pages of text (36 leaves, mostly rectos only) numbered 1–42 and some unnumbered, in ink, 5 pages containing passages, revisions and annotations by Charles Lamb (pp. 22, 33, 35–7); watermarked 1814.

Texas.

——Lecture VI. On Swift, Young, Gray, Collins, &c.
First pub. London, 1818; Howe, V, 104–22.

HzW 45 Fragments, bound in the Folger Volume, including: 1) beginning to Howe, V, 104 penultimate line, headed 'Lecture VI. On Young, Gray, Collins, &c.', 2 leaves (ff. 76–7, rectos only, watermarked 1815); 2) Howe, V, 109 line 43–110 line 13, one page numbered 11 (f. 78), containing revisions by Charles Lamb, watermarked 1815; 3) Howe, V, 114 line 21–116 line 16 (wanting the extracts), 3 pages numbered 25–7 (ff. 79–80, bound out of order).

Folger, MS T.b.18, ff. 76–80.

——Lecture VII. On Burns, and the Old English Ballads
First pub. London, 1818; Howe, V, 123–43.

HzW 46 Fragment (i.e., Howe, V, 128 line 1 more or less to the end, see HzW 47), wanting several extracts and containing variants, 13 pages (8 leaves) erratically numbered [ns], 10–18, one page numbered both 21–2 and 25–6, 27, 30, bound in the Folger Volume; watermarked 1815.

Folger, MS T.b.18, ff. 81–8v.

HzW 47 Two fragments (part of HzW 46, misbound in HzW 49), including: 1) Howe, V, 137 line 25–138 line 36, including transcriptions of quotations by Sarah Stoddart Hazlitt, 2 pages (one leaf), the first numbered 28; 2) Howe, V, 139 line 26–140 line 20, including transcriptions of quotations by Sarah Stoddart Hazlitt, 2 leaves (rectos only) numbered 32–3.

Berg.

——Lecture VIII. On the Living Poets
First pub. London, 1818; Howe, V, 143–68.

HzW 48 Here entitled 'Lecture VIII. & last. — On the living Poets', 33 pages (24 leaves) and a few short interpolations on blank versos.

Described *Tinker Library*, no. 1190.

Yale.

HzW 49 Including the beginning to Howe, V, 145 line 26, 145 last line–152 line 22, 153 line 9–155 line 23, 156 lines 15–33, 161 line 21–164 line 9, 165 line 3–166 line 10, here entitled 'Lecture VIII. — On the Living Poets.', 38 pages (31 leaves) numbered 1–5, 7–24, 27–32, 35–40, 43 and 2 unnumbered (one being a fair copy of the other); some leaves watermarked 1815.

Hazlitt Sale, Lot 247, sold to Withers; HzW 47 is misbound with this MS.

Berg.

Letter to Mr Canning, see description of *Yellow Dwarf* volume in INTRODUCTION.

A Letter to William Gifford, Esq, for a lost annotated copy, see INTRODUCTION.

Liber Amoris; Or, The New Pygmalion
First pub. anonymously London, 1823; reprinted (with additional matter) *Liber Amoris or The New Pygmalion*, [ed. W. C. Hazlitt], introd. Richard Le Gallienne (privately printed, 1894); Howe, IX, [95]–162. Of the letters in the text based on 'real' letters — to 'C. P.' [P. G. Patmore], 'S. L.' [Sarah Walker] and 'J. S. K.' [J. S. Knowles] — only the sent originals of those to Patmore are extant; for a discussion of extant MSS (except HzW 50 and 55 which were not known) and their relationship to this work, see W. H. Bonner's essay in *Letters*, Appendix B, pp. 390–4. For a description of extant related materials — including especially Sarah Stoddart Hazlitt's journal of 14 April–18 July 1822, written during the period of her Scottish residence and the divorce proceedings — see INTRODUCTION.

HzW 50 Revised autograph draft of Part I, in a small octavo notebook, title-page inscribed 'Liber Amoris' and sections entitled 'The Picture', 'The Invitation', 'The Message', 'The Flageolet', 'The Confession', 'The Quarrel', 'The Reconciliation', 'Letters to & from the same', 'Answer' and 'To the same./Encore un coup', the final page marked 'The End' inscribed on inside front cover 'Stamford, Jany 29 [altered from 28], 1822'; title page annotated in an unidentified hand [Patmore's?] '<W. H. to 'P. G. P.>' and 'May 21:1822', 67 numbered leaves (rectos only) of text with some section titles on facing pages, second half of volume blank; [begun 29 January 1822 and finished before 30 March 1822].

This is the MS from which HzW 51 was transcribed and which W. C. Hazlitt presumed was destroyed (see his 1894 edition); 3 facsimile pages (numbered 23, 28, 67) in Sotheby's sale catalogue, 22–3 July 1985, Lot 126; facsimile in British Library, RP 3059.

Pierpont Morgan, MA 4217.

HzW 51 Notebook containing a transcript of HzW 50 in an unidentified hand, probably P. G. Patmore's, printer's copy for the first publication, containing marginal and interlinear annotations by Hazlitt, 63 numbered pages, signed (initials) by Hazlitt; dated (and cancelled) on the inside front cover Stamford, 29 January 1822, probably transcribed after 21 May 1822.

This transcript printed in W. C. Hazlitt's 1894 edition, pp. [175]–205; the transcript herein of one of the letters to Sarah Walker (published version in Howe, IX, 112–13) is printed separately in *Letters*, no. 98 where it is dated [February 1822], Jones dates it more precisely [11–19 February 1822].

SUNY at Buffalo.

HzW 52 Eleven original letters to P. G. Patmore, including nine used as the bases for Part II, Letters III–V, VII–IX, XI–XIII, and two others not used in *Liber Amoris*, 39 pages in all (15 leaves, some folded); Edinburgh, 30 March–8 July 1822.

The letters are printed in *Letters*: (1) no. 105 (dated [30 March 1822] but corrected in Jones to 30 March [1822], the basis for Letter III); (2) no. 106 (postmarked 7 April 1822, the basis for Letter V); (3) no. 109 (postmarked 21 April 1822, the basis for Letter IV); (4) no. 110 (dated [May 1822] but corrected in Jones to [c. 19 June 1822], printed *Memoirs*, II, 45–6); (5) no. 114 (postmarked 31 May 1822, a few lines printed *Memoirs*, II, 45); (6) no. 115 (postmarked 9 June 1822, the basis for Letter VIII); (7) no. 116 (postmarked 18 June 1822, redated in Jones [14 June 1822], the basis for the opening of Letter X, extracts printed *Memoirs*, II, 49–50); (8) no. 117 (postmarked 20 June 1822, the basis for Letter VII); (9) no. 119 (postmarked 28 June 1822, redated [27 June 1822] and faulty readings corrected in Jones, the basis for Letters XI–XII); (10) no. 120 (dated 3 and 5 July [1822], the basis for Letter IX); (11) no. 121 (postmarked 8 July 1822, the basis for Letter XIII). These letters are also printed with one facsimile page (and numerous inaccuracies) in W. C. Hazlitt's 1894 edition of *Liber Amoris*, pp. 210–37.

Hazlitt Sale, Lot 242, sold to Pearson.

SUNY at Buffalo.

HzW 53 Original letter to P. G. Patmore, used as the basis for Part II, Letter II, 4 pages (one leaf); dated Tuesday (Sarah Walker's letter to Hazlitt herein is dated London, 26 February [1822]), postmarked 9 March 1822.

This MS printed Robinson, pp. 16–20; it is not mentioned *Letters* where the variant *Liber Amoris* version is reprinted (no. 102) from the first edition. This letter includes (on the last page) the list of essay titles which Hazlitt was producing at the time for Henry Colburn; this portion was misprinted as a separate (and unlocated) letter in *Letters*, no. 100; see also HzW 77–8.

Princeton, Robert H. Taylor Collection.

HzW 54 Original letter to P. G. Patmore, used as the basis for Part II, Letter the Last; 17 July 1822.

This MS not mentioned *Letters* where the *Liber Amoris* version is reprinted (no. 122) from the first edition.

Owned (1932) Marquess of Crewe (d. 1945) (see Howe, IX, 266).

HzW 55 Cancelled passage on p. 11 of the MS of 'The Fight' (HzW 19), used in Part II, Letter VI (i.e., Howe, IX, 122 lines 17–22) and as second part of 'A Thought' (i.e., Howe, IX, 127 lines 6–10); [late December (after the 11th) 1821].

This MS printed Wilcox, p. 18 (see also pp. 56–8); also printed David Bromwich, *Hazlitt. The Mind of a Critic* (New York and Oxford, 1983), pp. 436–7n10. The previous leaf of HzW 19 (p. 10) is missing and probably contained a passage entirely cancelled that was very likely also later incorporated into *Liber Amoris*.

Pierpont Morgan, MA 190.

HzW 56 Diary, describing the day-by-day experiences of 'Mr F.', a lodger at the Walker's, 11 numbered loose pages (7 leaves); 4–16 March 1823.

This diary first printed in an edited version in *Lamb and Hazlitt* (1900); printed in full in Bonner (1959); reprinted in *Letters*, Appendix A, pp. 379–89 but without taking into account the corrections and revisions to the 1959 text noted in Stanley Jones, 'Hazlitt's Journal of 1823: Some Notes and Emendations', *The Library*, 5 Ser 26 (1971), [325]–36.

SUNY at Buffalo.

The Life of Napoleon Buonaparte

First pub. (Vols I–II only) London, 1828; Vols III–IV first pub. London, 1830 (with reprinted Vols. I–II to make a uniform edition); Howe, XIII–XV. Howe, XV, 381 (in a note to p. 287) mentions that Charles Cowden Clarke's copy of an English edition of A. Le Sage (pseudonym of Marin Joseph Emmanuel Auguste Dieudonné de Las Cases), *Historical Atlas*, 8 vols in 4 (London: Colburn, 1823), marked by Hazlitt and used by him in writing his *Life of Napoleon*, was extant at the time of his writing (1934).

HzW 57 Variant version of fragment (i.e., Howe, XIII, 96, c. line 20–97 line 4), on verso of the (now-loose) cover of Hazlitt's copy of François Auguste Marie Mignet, *Histoire de la Revolution Française*, 3rd ed (Paris, 1826).

This MS unknown to Hazlitt editors, including Howe; for a reproduction, see FACSIMILES. Mignet's *Histoire* was one of Hazlitt's principal sources (see Howe, XIII, 356).

SUNY at Buffalo.

HzW 58 Corrected proof of the original Preface (suppressed) and autograph title-page, both inserted in Vol. I of Charles Cowden Clarke's copy of the first publication (all four volumes) containing Clarke's pencil markings *passim*.

Manchester Central Library, Alexander Ireland Collection, 824.76.X.5.

HzW 59 Two revisions to Chapter XIX and other instructions, in a letter to Henry Leigh Hunt (publisher of Vols I–II), 16 January 1828.

This MS printed *Letters*, no. 148;

mentioned and quoted in Howe, XIII, 358 and XIV, 361.

SUNY at Buffalo.

Madame de Staël's account of German philosophy, see HzW 36.

The Main-Chance
First pub. *New Monthly Magazine*, February 1828; Howe, XVII, 275–90, as 'Uncollected Essay XXVI. The Main-Chance'.

HzW 60 Here entitled 'On Avarice. — <No. 5.>', 20 numbered pages (10 leaves, one imperfect), including the epigraph from Pope, cancelled passages and notes *passim*; dated 23 July 1825.

This MS printed *London Mercury*, February 1926 (as an unpublished essay entitled 'On Avarice'); variants collated in Howe; Hazlitt Sale, Lot 250, sold to Pearson.

SUNY at Buffalo.

Manchester (Ireland) Volume, for a description of this volume of MSS, see INTRODUCTION.

Memoirs of the Late Thomas Holcroft
First pub. in 3 vols (London, 1816); Howe, III. Hazlitt compiled and wrote what Lamb called the 'Life Everlasting' in 1809 from materials put into his hands by Holcroft's widow, including letters and Holcroft's original diary. A copy of the first edition in the London Library has the blanks (names) in the text filled in, evidently from Holcroft's original diary, in an unidentified hand; these are given in the Notes in Howe. In *Memoirs*, I, 179, W. C. Hazlitt says that 'the "Life Everlasting" was finished this year [1810], as far as it was ever finished (for the fourth volume is still in MS.)....'; no such MS has come to light.

HzW 61 Fragment (i.e., Howe, III, 165 line 27–166 line 36), 2 pages (one leaf) numbered 72–3, bound in the Manchester (Ireland) Volume.

Manchester Central Library, Alexander Ireland Collection, F.824.76.G4, f. 1r–v.

HzW 62 Queries regarding details of Holcroft's life, in a letter to William Godwin, [late summer 1809].

This MS printed *Letters*, no. 31.

Owned (1978) Lord Abinger (see *Letters*).

New President of the Royal Academy
First pub. *The Atlas*, 7 February 1830; Howe, XVIII, 184–5.

HzW 63 Here entitled 'Royal Academy', 3 numbered pages (one folded leaf), annotated (signed) by Charles Cowden Clarke 'An Article written for me in the Atlas Newspaper, by William Hazlitt. The autograph is his — I was at his elbow while he wrote it, which occupied him about 10 minutes or a 1/4 of an hour.'

This MS mentioned Howe, XVIII, 442.

SUNY at Buffalo.

Of Persons one would Wish to have Seen
First pub. *New Monthly Magazine*, January 1826; Howe, XVII, 122–34, as 'Uncollected Essay XII. Of Persons...'.

HzW 64 Wanting the two extracts from Donne, 13 pages numbered [1]–3, 5–14 (7 leaves).

This MS collated in Howe; Hazlitt Sale, Lot 250, sold to Pearson.

SUNY at Buffalo.

Old English Theatre
Hazlitt's proposed edition of Elizabethan drama was never published.

HzW 64.5 Outline for a proposed edition, headed 'Old English Theatre: (From the time of Elizabeth to that of Charles II)/Consisting of 30 Comedies & Tragedies...', on 2 pages of a letter to Jean-Antoine Galignani, 14 July [1826?].

This MS printed Robinson, pp. 32–4.

NYPL, Pforzheimer Collection.

On a Sun-Dial
First pub. *New Monthly Magazine*, October 1827;

Howe, XVII, 238–45, as 'Uncollected Essay XXII. On a Sun-Dial'.

HzW 65 Seven numbered pages (7 leaves containing a few jottings on the blank versos), containing HzW 90 on the verso of the last leaf, annotated by Raymond Yates that the MS was presented to him by William Hazlitt the younger on 29 April 1838.

Huntington, HM 12220.

On an English Saturday, for an unidentified 'lost' MS, see INTRODUCTION.

On Avarice, see HzW 60.

On Cant and Hypocrisy, for a lost MS, see INTRODUCTION.

On Classical Education, for a lost MS, see INTRODUCTION.

On Coffee-House Politicians
First pub. *Table-Talk* (1822); Howe, VIII, 189–204.

HzW 66 Wanting the first page (supplied here in typescript), 30 leaves (rectos only) numbered 2–31 and one unnumbered verso containing an insertion; watermarked 1820, [February–March 1822?].

Probably Hazlitt Sale, part of Lot 249, sold to Baddeley.

Princeton, Robert H. Taylor Collection.

On Corporate Bodies
First pub. *Table-Talk* (1822); Howe, VIII, 264–72.

HzW 67 Here entitled 'Essay XII. On Corporate Bodies.', 18 leaves (rectos only) numbered [1]–5, 7–19 (wanting f. 6).

Probably Hazlitt Sale, part of Lot 249, sold to Baddeley.

SUNY at Buffalo.

On Court-Influence
First pub. in two parts *Yellow Dwarf*, 3 and 10 January 1818; collected *Political Essays* (1819); Howe, VII, 230–42. In Hazlitt's copy of the first publication (3 January) in the British Library (see INTRODUCTION), this article is annotated, probably in Hazlitt's hand, 'In Political Essays'.

HzW 68 Variant version, including both parts as one essay, here entitled 'On Political Inconsistency.', 17 numbered pages (16 leaves) and some notes and rough passages on unnumbered versos, bound in the Folger Volume; watermarked 1805.

Folger, MS T.b.18, ff. 1–16v.

On Criminal Law, for a lost MS, see INTRODUCTION.

On Egotism
First pub. *Table-Talk*, 2 vols (Paris, 1825); first pub. in England *The Plain Speaker*, 2 vols (London, 1826); Howe, XII, 157–68.

HzW 68.5 Fragment (i.e., Howe, XII, 160 line 33–162 line 8), in Harvard *Spirit of the Age* (bound in after p. 172, following HzW 106), 4 leaves (mostly rectos only) numbered 11–14.

Harvard, fMS Eng 716.

HzW 69 Fragment (i.e., Howe, XII, 163 lines 24–39), one page numbered 18; [probably 1824].

Facsimile in Howe, XXI, frontispiece.

Unlocated (see facsimile).

HzW 70 Two fragments (i.e., Howe, XII, 165 lines 2–32 (f. 14r–v) and 167 lines 16–43 (f. 15r–v)), four pages (2 leaves) numbered 22–3 (f. 14r–v) and 28–9 (f. 15r–v), bound in the Manchester (Ireland) Volume.

Manchester Central Library, Alexander Ireland Collection, F.824.76.G4, ff. 14–15v.

On Familiar Style
First pub. *Table-Talk* (1822); Howe, VIII, 242–8.

HzW 71 Here entitled 'Essay XV. On familiar style.', incomplete (i.e., beginning to

Howe, VIII, 244 line 37), 6 numbered leaves (rectos only).

Probably Hazlitt Sale, part of Lot 249, sold to Baddeley.

National Library of Scotland, Acc 7175/3.

On Footmen
First pub. *New Monthly Magazine*, September 1830; Howe, XVII, 354–60, as 'Uncollected Essay XXXIV. On Footmen'.

HzW 72 Last paragraph only, revised, beginning 'I remember hearing it said...', 2 pages (one leaf).

This MS not mentioned Howe; described *Tinker Library*, no. 1191.

Yale.

On Going a Journey
First pub. *New Monthly Magazine*, January 1822; collected *Table-Talk* (1822); Howe, VIII, 181–9.

HzW 73 Incomplete (i.e., from the beginning in Howe to VIII, 187 line 2; VIII, 188 line 4189 line 4; VIII, 189 line 20 to the end followed by 8 additional lines beginning '"Bottom! thou are translated" is apt but might be properly addressed....'), here entitled 'Table Talk./Essay IV. On going a journey.', 17 pages (16 leaves, text on rectos only except f. 16) numbered 1–16 and 18, containing annotations on versos of 6 leaves; dated at top 'Tuesday 7th' [August 1821].

Probably Hazlitt Sale, part of Lot 249, sold to Baddeley.

British Library, Add. MS 61732.

On Individuality, see HzW 77–8.

On Means and Ends
First pub. *Monthly Magazine*, September 1827; Howe, XVII, 212–26, as 'Uncollected Essay XX. On Means and Ends'.

HzW 74 Fragment (i.e., beginning to Howe, XVII, 219 line 37), including variants and cancellations, 9 numbered pages (7 leaves), annotated '3d Article'.

SUNY at Buffalo.

On Modern Comedy, for a lost MS, see INTRODUCTION.

On Personal Identity
First pub. *Monthly Magazine*, January 1828; Howe, XVII, 264–75, as 'Uncollected Essay XXV. On Personal Identity'.

HzW 75 Fragment (i.e., Howe, XVII, 268 line 30–269 line 16, with a few omissions), quoted in a letter to [Isabella Jane Towers], 21 November 1827 in response to her request for a contribution to her album; the passage, here untitled, dated Winterslow, 21 November 1827.

This MS mentioned Howe, XVII, 415; printed with letter in *Letters*, no. 144 (two faulty readings corrected in Jones).

Stanford University.

On Reading New Books
First pub. *Monthly Magazine*, July 1827; Howe, XVII, 200–11, as 'Uncollected Essay XIX. On Reading New Books'.

HzW 76 Slightly incomplete (i.e., beginning to Howe, XVII, 211 line 10), including some variants, 10 numbered pages (6 leaves) and an unnumbered page of rough notes on verso of p. [1], containing also HzW 114 on verso of p. 10; [Florence, 1825?].

This MS and particularly its date discussed in Stanley Jones, 'The Dating of a Hazlitt Essay', *EA*, 33 (1980), 18–98.

Hazlitt Sale, Lot 250, sold to Pearson.

SUNY at Buffalo.

On Reason and Imagination
First pub. *The Plain Speaker*, 2 vols (London, 1826); Howe, XII, 44–55.

HzW 77 First third of the essay, here beginning 'I hate those people who have no idea...' and ending '...it was preceded by a burst of partly personal and partly generous feeling.', here entitled 'Essay XI. On <Individuality> Understanding & Imagination', 9 numbered pages of text (8 leaves), containing an extensive annotation on verso of one leaf and jottings on three other versos; watermarked 1815, [5–7 March 1822].

This fragment and HzW 77.5–78 below form one incomplete MS; it was discussed and dated (though the location of HzW 77 and the existence of HzW 77.5 were unknown to him) by Stanley Jones in 'Hazlitt's Missing Essay "On Individuality"', *RES*, NS 28 (1977), 421–30 where Jones demonstrates that this essay is the one referred to in a letter to P. G. Patmore (see HzW 53) as 'On Individuality'.

British Library, Add. MS 61909.

HzW 77.5 Fragment (i.e., Howe, XII, 50 line 32–52 line 30, wanting 51 lines 2–26), in Harvard *Spirit of the Age* (bound in after p. 46), 3 leaves (mostly rectos only) numbered 11–13, the verso of f. 11 (numbered 10) blank except for rough passage (draft of Howe, XII, 49 lines 18–22).

Harvard, fMS Eng 716.

HzW 78 Three fragments of this essay (i.e., Howe, XII, 53 lines 20–34 (f. 16); XII, 54 lines 28–32, 40–55 line 6 (f. 19); XII, 55 lines 21–end (f. 21)), 3 pages (3 leaves) numbered 16 (f. 9), 19 (f. 10), 21 (f. 12), bound in the Manchester (Ireland) Volume; including several annotations, the one reading 'Begun Feb. 11, Monday/ Ended, Thursday March 7, 1822...W. H.' (f. 21) refers to *all* the essays listed in Hazlitt's letter to P. G. Patmore (see HzW 53).

Manchester Central Library, Alexander Ireland Collection, F.824.76.G4, ff. 9, 10, 12.

On the Application to Study, see HzW 110.5.

On the Clerical Character, see the description of *Yellow Dwarf* volume in the INTRODUCTION.

On the Conduct of Life; or Advice to a Schoolboy
First pub. *Table-Talk*, 2 vols (Paris, 1825); reprinted with additions in *Literary Remains* (1836); Howe, XVII, 86–100.

HzW 79 Discarded portion, beginning 'Your pain is her triumph...', 7 leaves (rectos only); watermarked 1816.

This passage, added to the text in 1836, is printed Howe, XVII, 395–7.

SUNY at Buffalo.

On the Fear of Death
First pub. *Table-Talk* (1822); Howe, VIII, 321–30. For a discussion of passages known to have been deleted from now lost MSS, see Stewart C. Wilcox, 'A Manuscript Addition to Hazlitt's Essay "On the Fear of Death"', *MLN*, 55 (1940), 45–7 (see also the Notes to Howe, VIII, 373–4).

HzW 80 Fragments (i.e., somewhat variant versions of Howe, VIII, 326 line 10–328 line 28 and 329 line 10–end of essay), 8 pages (6 leaves) numbered 13–16 (ff. 2–4), 18–20 (ff. 5, 6, 11), one unnumbered, bound in the Manchester (Ireland) Volume; watermarked 1815, dated (f. 11) 1 March [1822].

The variant final paragraph of this MS is unrecorded.

Manchester Central Library, Alexander Ireland Collection, F.824.76.G4, ff. 2–4, 5, 6, 11.

HzW 81 Fragment (i.e., the missing portion in HzW 67, Howe, VIII, 328 line 28–329 line 10), one page numbered 17; watermarked 1815, [1 March 1822].

Quaritch Catalogue 955 (1975), Item 463.

On the Feeling of Immortality in Youth, for a lost MS, see INTRODUCTION.

On the Knowledge of Character, see HzW 110.5.

On the Literary Character, for a lost MS, see INTRODUCTION.

On the Love of Life, for a lost MS, see INTRODUCTION.

On the Opera
First pub. *Yellow Dwarf*, 23 May 1818, as 'The Little Hunch-Back, No. II. — On the Opera.'; Howe, XX, 92–6.

HzW 82 Revisions (some lost due to careless trimming of pages), including the revision of original title to the above title, in Hazlitt's copy of *Yellow Dwarf* (see INTRODUCTION), annotated in pencil, probably by Hazlitt, 'In Polit Essays [sic]'.

These revisions collated in Howe; the essay was *not* collected in *Political Essays*.

British Library, Department of Printed Books, P.P.3612.aca, pp. 165–7.

On the Picturesque and Ideal
First pub. *Table-Talk* (1822); Howe, VIII, 317–21.

HzW 83 Wanting the first 2 pages (i.e., Howe, VIII, 318 line 21–end) and including concluding pages (pp. 11–15) not in the published version, 13 leaves (rectos only) numbered 3–15; annotated at the end 'Finished <Wednesday> Tuesday August 28, 1821/ Begun Thursday August. 2, 1821.'.

For discarded conclusion, see Howe, VIII, 374; probably Hazlitt Sale, part of Lot 249, sold to Baddeley.

SUNY at Buffalo.

On the Prose-Style of Poets
First pub. *The Plain Speaker*, 2 vols (London, 1826); Howe, XII, 5–17.

HzW 84 Fragment (i.e., beginning to Howe, XII, 10 line 10), headed 'Table-talk.' and entitled 'Essay XVI. On the prose-style of poets.', 11 numbered leaves (rectos only); watermarked 1820, probably written c. August 1822.

Hazlitt Sale, Lot 250, sold to Pearson.

SUNY at Buffalo.

On the Punishment of Death
First pub. (extract only) *Fraser's Magazine*, January 1831, in an anonymous article on Capital Punishment; reprinted Howe, XIX, 324–9; complete essay unpublished.

HzW 85 Untitled essay from which the published extract was taken, headed 'mx. 3.' and beginning 'Individual punishment would be a public penance....', incomplete, 22 pages (20 leaves) numbered 89–99, 102–12, bound in the Folger Volume; probably composed c. 1821 for the Society for the Diffusion of Knowledge upon the Punishment of Death.

This MS apparently unknown to Hazlitt editors, including Howe.

Folger, MS T.b.18, ff. 17–36.

On the Regal Character
First pub. *The Champion*, 28 September 1817; reprinted *Yellow Dwarf*, 16 May 1818, as 'The Little Hunchback No. I. — On the Regal Character'; collected *Political Essays* (1819); Howe, VII, 281–7.

HzW 86 Revision of original title to 'Essay XXI — On the Regal Character' and two cancellations in Hazlitt's copy of *Yellow Dwarf* (see INTRODUCTION), annotated in pencil, probably by Hazlitt, 'In the Polit Ess [sic]'.

British Library, Department of Printed Books, P.P.3612.aca, pp. 154, 156.

On the Scotch Character
First pub. *The Liberal*, no. II, January 1823; Howe, XVII, 100–6, as 'Uncollected Essay X. On the Scotch Character'.

HzW 86.5 Fragment (i.e., Howe, XVII, 102 (bottom)–103 (to and including first footnote), one page.

Kenneth W. Rendell Catalogue 54 [c. 1970].

HzW 87 Fragment (i.e., Howe, XVII, 103 line 27–104 line 26), 2 pages, the second numbered 9.

This MS not mentioned Howe.

Iowa State Historical Library.

HzW 88 Fragment (i.e., variant version of Howe, XVII, 105 line 20–106 c. line 7), 3 leaves (rectos only) numbered 13–15.

Facsimile of p. 15 in Baker, p. 377.

Harvard, fMS Eng 1003.

On the Want of Money
First pub. *Monthly Magazine*, January 1827; Howe, XVII, 175–89, as 'Uncollected Essay XVII. On the Want of Money'.

HzW 89 Fragment (i.e., beginning to Howe, XVII, 180 line 40), wanting the footnotes, 4 numbered leaves (rectos only).

This MS not mentioned Howe.

SUNY at Buffalo.

HzW 90 Draft of a fragment of an early version (a version of Howe, XVII, 186–7), here beginning 'Some want to possess a large collection of pictures...', one page, on verso of last leaf of HzW 65.

Huntington, HM 12220, f. 7v *rev.*.

On Understanding & Imagination, see HzW 77–8.

On Vulgarity and Affectation, see HzW 110.5.

Outlines
In a letter to David Constable dated 10 January 1828 (*Letters*, no. 147, pub. Robinson, pp. 38–9 from the original at University of Delaware (mislocated at National Library of Scotland in *Letters*), Hazlitt proposed, for *Constable's Miscellany*, a 'volume of outlines or elements' consisting of (1) Of Law, (2) Of Morals, (3) Of the Human Mind, (4) Of Taste, (5) Of Political Economy, (6) Of English Grammar. The series was never published nor probably ever completed; for a discussion, see Howe, XIX, Notes to 'Outlines of Political Economy'. For (1), see HzW 97; MSS of (2), (3) and (5) are listed below, HzW 91–3. The essay printed by Howe as 'Outlines of Taste' (see HzW 113) apparently does not belong to this series, but is an earlier essay of c. 1815; Stanley Jones, 'Dating Hazlitt's "Essay on Taste"', *EA*, 22 (1969), 68–71, suggests that Hazlitt may never have drafted the outline of taste for this series. A MS of (6) recorded by W. C. Hazlitt (*Memoirs*, I, xxxii) as being in his possession, has not come to light (unless HzW 5 is a surviving leaf); however, the other MSS he mentions at the same time (HzW 60, 91–3) are bound in one volume at SUNY at Buffalo.

Outlines of Morals
First pub. *London Mercury*, June 1926; Howe, XX, 376–86.

HzW 91 Revised, apparently unfinished, annotated throughout by William Hazlitt the younger including his addition of the title 'On the Doctrine of Selfishness' written above Hazlitt's own title '<2> Outlines of Morals.', 14 numbered pages (7 leaves); watermarked 1827, written probably before January 1828.

Hazlitt Sale, Lot 250, sold to Pearson.

SUNY at Buffalo.

Outlines of Political Economy
First pub. *London Mercury*, March 1926, as 'Political Economy'; Howe, XIX, 294–302.

HzW 92 Revised, here entitled '<5.> Political Economy.', annotated throughout by William Hazlitt the younger, including, on the last page, a cancelled unpublished fifth section on the 'Poor-laws', 11 numbered pages (6 leaves); written probably before January 1828.

Hazlitt Sale, Lot 250, sold to Pearson.

SUNY at Buffalo.

Outlines of Taste, see HzW 113.

Outlines of the Human Mind
First pub. Howe, XX (1934), 442–7.

HzW 93 Here entitled '<3.> Outlines of the Human Mind.', 10 numbered pages (5 leaves); written probably before January 1828.

Hazlitt Sale, Lot 250, sold to Pearson.

SUNY at Buffalo.

Personal Politics
First pub. *Literary Remains* (1836); Howe, XIX, 329–34.

HzW 94 Thirteen numbered pages (7 leaves), annotated at top '5th Article'; [August 1830].

SUNY at Buffalo.

The Pictures at Hampton Court
First pub. *London Magazine*, June 1823; collected *Sketches of the Principal Picture-Galleries in England* (London, 1824); Howe, X, 42–9.

HzW 95 Revised, 21 numbered leaves (rectos only), signed (initials), addressed to Messrs Taylor and Hessey (publishers of *London Magazine*).

Yale.

The Plain Speaker, for MSS of essays collected in this volume, see HzW 69–70, 77–8, 84.

Political Essays
First pub. London, 1819; Howe, VII. For MSS of essays collected in this volume, see also description of *Yellow Dwarf* volume in the INTRODUCTION and HzW 68, 82, 86, 98, 115.

HzW 96 A copy of the second edition (London, 1822) containing pencil corrections on pp. 137 and 287 'which are probably in the author's hand' (Keynes).

This copy (the only one of this edition located) described in Keynes, p. 53 without giving present whereabouts.

Owned (1931) P. P. Howe (d. 1944) (see Geoffrey Keynes, *Bibliography of William Hazlitt* (London, 1931), p. 49).

Project for a New Theory of Civil and Criminal Legislation
First pub. *Literary Remains* (1836); Howe, XIX, 302–20. Howe suggests that this essay is probably a recast version of the projected 'Outlines of Law'; see headnote to *Outlines*.

HzW 97 Variant version, 12 pages (6 leaves) numbered [1]–8, 11–14, wanting one leaf (pp. 9–10); watermarked 1826.

SUNY at Buffalo.

Queries Relating to the Essay on Population
First pub. *Political Register*, 24 November 1810, with a letter to the editor headed 'Mr Malthus and the Edinburgh Reviewers'; revised version in *The Examiner*, 29 October 1815, with a letter to the editor headed 'The Round Table, No. 23'; collected *Political Essays* (1819); the latter version reprinted in Howe, VII, 357–[61]. Both letters to the editor are reprinted in Howe, VII, 408–11 and *Letters*, nos. 36 (including the 'Queries…') and 49.

HzW 98 Transcript by Sara Coleridge.

Victoria College Library, LT 18.

A Reply to the Essay on Population, by the Rev. T. R. Malthus
First pub. (Letters I-III) in *Political Register*, 14 March, 16 and 23 May 1807 (signed 'A. O.'); in full anonymously London, 1807; Howe, I, [177]–[364]. For an unpublished 'reply' to Malthus (including two passages used in the 1807 book version of *A Reply*), see HzW 113.5.

HzW 99 Hazlitt's copy of the 1807 edition, containing his signature on the title page and annotations in ink on pp. 361, 366, 371.

This copy, at one time in the possession of Charles and Mary Lamb, is not mentioned Keynes.

Parke Bernet, 14–16 May 1941 (A. E. Newton Sale), Lot 285.

A Reply to 'Z'
First printed privately for the First Edition Club, London, 1923; Howe, IX, [1]–10.

HzW 100 Here untitled, 23 numbered leaves (rectos only), containing HzW 113 on the verso of f. 13 (the page numbered 11), annotated 'The following rough sketch of an answer to the queries/of An Old Friend with a new face (which I wrote with some/intention of publishing it) will convey my defence & my/notions of the state of the question…', annotated by Archibald Constable (f. 23v) 'Blackwoods Magazine/Hazlitt &c/in reply to (?) Lockhart (*unpublished*?).'; watermarked 1815, [August–October 1818].

Facsimile in British Library,

MS.Facs.Vol.I, no. 419.

British Library, Egerton MS 3244.

[Reporting Notes]
No publication traced; for lost reporting notes, see INTRODUCTION.

HzW 100.5 Rough pencil notes, on the last 40 pages (20 leaves) of Sarah Stoddart Hazlitt's commonplace book.

Baker, p. 192 says that these notes of Parliamentary speeches probably date from Hazlitt's tenure as Parliamentary reporter for the *Morning Chronicle* in 1812; see CHARLES LAMB, LmC 338 for a description of the commonplace book.

Berg.

The Round Table
First pub. in 2 vols (Edinburgh, 1817); Howe, IV, 1–[164]. The collection contained 52 essays, 12 written by Leigh Hunt, the other 40 by Hazlitt. Most had been previously published in the *Morning Chronicle*, 1813–14 and *The Examiner*, 1814–17; see Howe for details. No MS sources for the individual essays themselves have come to light.

HzW 101 List of titles of 50 essays by Hazlitt and Leigh Hunt, annotated by Archibald Constable, 'Arrangement with Wm Hazlitt...Series of Essays', enclosed in a letter to Constable proposing publication of this collection, Westminster, 18 December 1815.

This MS printed and discussed in Stanley Jones, 'Nine New Hazlitt Letters and Some Others', *EA*, 19 (1966), 263–77 (264–9); also printed *Letters*, no. 51. Also enclosed with the letter is a 3-page agreement for the publication of *The Round Table* signed by Constable and Messrs Longman (ff. 126–7).

National Library of Scotland, MS 7200, f. 128.

Select British Poets (London, 1824), for a lost annotated copy, see INTRODUCTION.

Self-Love and Benevolence
First pub. in 3 parts *New Monthly Magazine*, October, November and December 1828; Howe, XX, 162–86.

HzW 102 Early version including variants, here entitled 'On the Principle of Self-love' and beginning 'I am not very fond of speaking of my own writings...', 24 pages (12 leaves) numbered [1]–10, 13–26, wanting one leaf (pp. 11–12).

This MS mentioned Howe.

SUNY at Buffalo.

Sismondi's Literature of the South
First pub. *Edinburgh Review*, June 1815; Howe, XVI, 24–57. Portions later incorporated into Lectures I–III of the *Lectures on the English Poets*(first pub. London, 1818); see HzW 41–2.

HzW 103 Two revisions, in a letter to Francis Jeffrey, the editor of the first publication, 18 July 1815.

This MS printed *Letters*, no. 48. The letter was received too late for the revisions to be made in the article and one of them (a correction of fact) remains uncorrected, even by Howe.

Yale.

Sketches of the Principal Picture-Galleries in England
First pub. London, 1824; Howe, X, [1]–81. Most of the essays in this collection had previously been published in *London Magazine*, December 1822–November 1823; see Howe for details. See also HzW 95.

HzW 104 Title page and 'Advertisement', including the alternative title 'The Principal Picture Galleries in England', in a letter to Messrs Taylor and Hessey, postmarked Melrose, 16 April 1824.

'Advertisement' reprinted from previous publication Howe, X, [3]. This MS and letter printed P. P. Howe, 'Hazlitt Letters: An Addition', *London Mercury*, 10 (1924), 73–4; reprinted *Letters*, no. 135. W. C. Hazlitt's transcript of this letter is inserted in his interleaved copy of *The*

Hazlitts (meant as an insertion to the text) and annotated 'The whole of this business-like communication is in Hazlitt's handwriting'; the volume is in the British Library, Department of Printed Books, C.133.g.10.

Owned (1924) P. P. Howe (d. 1944) (see the *London Mercury* article cited above).

The Spirit of the Age

Some essays first pub. *London Magazine*, May 1821 and *New Monthly Magazine*, January–July 1824; some first pub. in first book edition London, 1825; revised editions pub. 1825 in Paris and in London; Howe, XI, [1]–[184]. In W. C. Hazlitt's Preface to his London & New York, 1886 edition, he says he has incorporated changes made by Hazlitt in a copy of the London, 1825 second edition; no such copy has come to light. For a description of Harvard *Spirit of the Age*, see INTRODUCTION.

——The Late Mr Horne Tooke

First pub. *New Monthly Magazine*, March 1824, as 'The Spirit of the Age, No. III'; collected first edition (London, 1825); Howe, XI, 47–57.

HzW 105 Fragment (i.e., beginning to Howe, XI, 50 line 16), headed 'The Spirit of the Age. — No. 6/The late Mr Horne Tooke.', 8 numbered leaves (rectos only).

For a reproduction of the first page, see FACSIMILES.

SUNY at Buffalo.

——Lord Byron

First pub. first edition (London, 1825); Howe, XI, 69–78.

HzW 105.5 Fragment (i.e., Howe, XI, 71 lines 16–29) in Harvard *Spirit of the Age* (bound in after p. 330), one page numbered 6.

Harvard, fMS Eng 716.

——Lord Eldon and Mr Wilberforce

First pub. *New Monthly Magazine*, July 1824, as 'The Spirit of the Age, No. V'; collected first edition (London, 1825); Howe, XI, 141–50.

HzW 106 Two fragments (i.e., Howe, XI, 142 line 23–144 line 19 and 148 line 28–149 line 1), in Harvard *Spirit of the Age*, 5 leaves (mostly rectos only, bound in after p. 172) numbered 3–7 and one page (bound in after p. 184) numbered 20.

Harvard, fMS Eng 716.

HzW 107 Fragment (i.e., Howe, XI, 146 last line–147 line 14), one page numbered 15, bound in the Manchester (Ireland) Volume.

Manchester Central Library, Alexander Ireland Collection, F.824.76.G4, f. 8.

——Mr Brougham and Sir F. Burdett

First pub. first edition (London, 1825); Howe, XI, 134–41.

HzW 108 Fragment (i.e., Howe, XI, 136 last line–137 line 15), one page numbered 8.

Yale.

——Mr Campbell and Mr Crabbe

First pub. (a version of the essay on 'Mr Crabbe' only) *London Magazine*, May 1821, as 'Living Authors, No. V'; first pub. in full first edition (London, 1825); Howe, XI, 159–69.

HzW 108.2 Fragment (i.e., beginning to Howe, XI, 161 line 11), in Harvard *Spirit of the Age* (bound in after p. 356), here entitled 'The Spirit of the Age. — No. VIII./Mr Campbell.' with '& Mr Crabbe.' added later, annotated 'after Lord Byron', 5 leaves (mostly rectos only) numbered [1]–5.

Harvard, fMS Eng 716.

——Mr Gifford

First pub. first edition (London, 1825); Howe, XI, 114–26.

HzW 108.4 Fragment (i.e., Howe, XI, 120 line 7–122 line 37 but without the extracts), in Harvard *Spirit of the Age* (bound in after p. 124), 3 pages (2 leaves).

Harvard, fMS Eng 716.

——Mr Malthus
First pub. first edition (London, 1825); Howe, XI, 103–14.

HzW 108.6 Fragment (i.e., Howe, XI, 106 line 3–108 line 13), in Harvard *Spirit of the Age* (bound in after pp. 94 and 96), 6 leaves (mostly rectos only) numbered 7–12.

Harvard, fMS Eng 716.

——Mr Southey
First pub. first edition (London, 1825); Howe, XI, 78–86.

HzW 108.8 Fragment (i.e., Howe, XI, 80 line 39–83 line 28), in Harvard *Spirit of the Age* (bound in after p. 330), 10 pages (7 leaves) numbered 8–17.

Harvard, fMS Eng 716.

——Mr T. Moore and Mr Leigh Hunt
First pub. first edition (London, 1825); Howe, XI, 169–78.

HzW 109 Fragment (i.e., Howe, XI, 170 line 14–176 line 35), 16 pages (14 leaves) numbered 3–18.

SUNY at Buffalo.

——Sir Walter Scott
First pub. *New Monthly Magazine*, April 1824; first edition (London, 1825); Howe, XI, 57–68.

HzW 109.5 Two fragments (i.e., Howe, XI, 61 line 30–63 line 37 and 64 line 29–65 line 31), in Harvard *Spirit of the Age* (bound in after p. 252), 6 leaves and 3 leaves (mostly rectos only) numbered 13–18 and 22–4.

Harvard, fMS Eng 716.

Standard Novels and Romances
First pub. *Edinburgh Review*, February 1815; Howe, XVI, 5–24. Portions later incorporated into Lecture VI ('On the English Novelists') of the *Lectures on the English Comic Writers* (first pub. London, 1818).

HzW 110 Revisions, in a letter to Francis Jeffrey, editor of the first publication, postmarked 19 February 1815.

This MS printed *Letters*, no. 43.

Yale.

Table-Talk, for MSS of essays in this collection and lost marked copies, see INTRODUCTION and HzW 28, 66–7, 69–71, 73, 79–81, 83, 110.5.

***Table-Talk*, 2 vols (Paris, 1825)**

HzW 110.5 Proof corrections to three essays ('On the Knowledge of Character', 'On the Application to Study' and 'On Vulgarity and Affectation') in a letter to Jean-Antoine Galignani, Florence, 11 March [1825].

This MS printed Robinson, pp. 27–9; not in *Letters*.

NYPL, Pforzheimer Collection.

'the same place, that this principle must be entirely nugatory with respect to the associations of the ideas...'
No publication traced.

HzW 111 Fragment, on the association of ideas, 4 pages (one leaf).

SUNY at Buffalo.

'The humble petition of William Hazlitt...'
First pub. *Lamb and Hazlitt* (1900), pp. 67–76; not in Howe.

HzW 112 Letter to Joseph Hume, without salutation or signature, being 'The humble petition of William Hazlitt...shewing that he is not dead...', part of Lamb and Hazlitt's 'Suicide Joke', 8 pages (2 folded leaves), sent to Hume, dated 10 January 1808, postmarked 11 January 1808.

This MS printed *Letters*, no. 27; described (extracts printed) *Sentimental Library*, pp. 131–2.

SUNY at Buffalo.

Thoughts on Taste
First pub. *Edinburgh Magazine*, October 1818 and

July 1819, signed 'M. N.'; longer version pub. *Sketches and Essays by William Hazlitt*, ed. William Hazlitt the younger (London, 1839), as 'On Taste'; Howe, XVII, 57–66 prints the first publication version as 'Uncollected Essay VI. Thoughts on Taste' and XX, 386–91 prints the additions only, as 'Outlines of Taste' (see headnote to 'Outlines'). Stanley Jones, 'Dating Hazlitt's "Essay on Taste"', *EA*, 22 (1969), 68–71 argues that the original version and the additions are part of the same essay and that neither are related to the 'Outlines of Taste'.

HzW 113 Cancelled fragment, here beginning 'only arise from a proportionable attachment to higher ones, & an impatience of faults...' and ending '...up to that highest point. For example,', one page numbered 11, on f. 13v of HzW 100; [August-October 1818].

This MS printed and discussed in 'Dating Hazlitt's "Essay on Taste"' (cited above).

British Library, Egerton MS 3244, f. 13v.

To the Monthly Reviewers
No publication traced.

HzW 113.5 Revised, headed 'To the Monthly Reviewers' and beginning 'Gentlemen,/ From your account of Mr Malthus's enlarged essay on Population...', 6 pages (3 leaves), signed 'A Lover of Truth'; [1804?].

This extended letter was written in response to a review of Malthus's *Essay on Population*, 2nd ed (London, 1803) which was published in the *Monthly Review* of December 1803 and January 1804; it was possibly never sent and certainly not published there. Two passages were used by Hazlitt in the revised version of his *Reply to the Essay on Population, by T. R. Malthus*, published as a book in 1807 (revised from its first publication as a series of letters in Cobbett's *Political Register* during the summer of 1807). The MS is among the Coleridge Collection at Victoria College Library and was assumed to have been Coleridge's composition until Heather Jackson identified it as Hazlitt's in 1988. It was possibly given to Coleridge by Hazlitt in May 1807. The MS was erroneously listed in the S. T. Coleridge section in the *Index*, Vol. IV, Part 1, CoS 1254.

Victoria College Library, LT 22.

Travelling Abroad
First pub. *New Monthly Magazine*, June 1828; variant version (from a now unlocated MS) pub. *Table-Talk*, ed. William Hazlitt the younger, 3rd ed (London, 1845–6); omitted from the canon in Waller & Glover (1904); first pub. identified and reprinted in *New Writings*, ed. P. P. Howe (London, 1925); Howe, XVII, 332–44, as 'Uncollected Essay XXXII. Travelling Abroad'.

HzW 114 Here entitled 'On Travelling Abroad', including epigraph, 14 numbered pages (13 leaves), p. 14 written on verso of p. 10 (last page) of HzW 76.

SUNY at Buffalo.

[Unidentified fragments], see HzW 5, 18, 25, 27, 111.

What is the People?
First pub. *The Champion*, 12, 19 and 26 October 1817; reprinted in two parts *Yellow Dwarf*, 7–14 March 1818; collected *Political Essays* (1819); Howe, VII, 259–81.

HzW 115 Revision (mostly lost due to careless trimming of pages) in Hazlitt's copy of *Yellow Dwarf* (see INTRODUCTION), annotated in pencil, probably in Hazlitt's hand, 'In Political Essays'.

British Library, Department of Printed Books, P.P. 3612.aca, pp. 74, 76.

Yellow Dwarf, for Hazlitt's corrected copy, see INTRODUCTION and HzW 82, 86, 115.

DIARIES AND NOTEBOOKS

Diary, see HzW 56.

MARGINALIA IN PRINTED BOOKS

Bacon, Sir Francis. *The Two Bookes of Sr Francis Bacon. Of the Proficiency and Advancement of Learning* (London, 1629).

HzW 116 Annotated.

The annotations in this volume were formerly attributed to John Keats; for a discussion and extracts from the marginalia, see Payson G. Gates, 'Bacon, Keats, and Hazlitt', *South Atlantic Quarterly*, 46 (1947), 239–51. The annotations include a passage incorporated into 'Lecture VII. Character of Lord Bacon's Works' of the *Lectures on the Dramatic Literature of the Age of Elizabeth*. Facsimile page in Williamson (see KEATS, Abbreviations), plate II where the annotations are wrongly attributed to Keats. This title is included in W. C. Hazlitt's list of Hazlitt's books in *The Hazlitts*, pp. xvi–xvii.

Keats House, London, Dilke Collection, KH 18.

Flaxman, John. *Lectures on Sculpture* (London, 1829).
Hazlitt's review of this book appeared in the *Edinburgh Review* for October 1829; Howe, XVI, 338–63.

HzW 117 Annotated.

Several of Hazlitt's marginalia in this copy are printed *Memoirs*, II, 269–72; the annotations on pp. 199 and 265 are quoted in David Bromwich, *Hazlitt. The Mind of a Critic* (Oxford and New York, 1983), pp. 6, 336.

Pierpont Morgan, Ray 263.

Holcroft, Thomas. *The Road to Ruin* (unidentified edition), see INTRODUCTION.

Le Sage, A. *pseud* (i.e., Marin Joseph Emmanuel Auguste Dieudonné de Las Cases). *Historical Atlas*, 8 vols in 4 (London: Henry Colburn, 1823). Charles Cowden Clarke's copy of this English edition (no copy listed in British Library Catalogue, NUC or catalogue of the Bibliothèque Nationale, Paris), marked by Hazlitt and used for his *Life of Napoleon Buonaparte*, was extant in 1934, according to Howe, XV, 381.

Mignet, François Auguste Marie. *Histoire de la Revolution Française*, 3rd ed (Paris, 1826), see HzW 57.

Milman, Henry Hart. *Fazio* (unidentified edition), see INTRODUCTION.

Moraes, Francisco de. *Palmerin of England*, [trans. Anthony Munday, corrected by Robert Southey], 4 vols (London, 1807). For more information, see JOHN KEATS, KcJ 569; this volume discussed in Charles Patterson, 'The Keats-Hazlitt-Hunt Copy of *Palmerin of England* in Relation to Keats's Poetry', *JEGP*, 60 (1961), 31–43 which focuses on Keats's marginalia but mentions and prints extracts from Hunt's and Hazlitt's as well (p. 34); the volumes are in the Keats Collection at Harvard.

[Playbill for Theatre Royal Haymarket, London]. (1 or 6?) September 1827.

HzW 118 Annotated.

NYPL, Manuscripts Division, Theatre Collection, *T-Cabinet, Drawer 3.

Yellow Dwarf, for Hazlitt's annotated copy, see INTRODUCTION.

Gerard Manley Hopkins
1844–1889

INTRODUCTION

In 1868, having received a Double First in Greats at Oxford, Gerard Manley Hopkins, whose talents as a poet and a draughtsman were already obvious, decided to enter the Jesuit priesthood. This decision, for him, necessitated another: he burnt his poems as being incompatible with his chosen vocation and 'meant to write no more'. The event is poignantly recorded in a journal entry: 'May 11. Dull; afternoon fine. Slaughter of the innocents.' A seven-year poetic silence followed until, in December 1875, at the suggestion of his superiors, Hopkins set out to commemorate the death in a shipwreck of five Franciscan nuns by writing 'The Wreck of the Deutschland' — a startling piece written in 'the new rhythm'. His attempts to publish the poem in the Jesuit journal *The Month* met with silence; but his *own* silence was broken.

Thereafter, Hopkins neither sought nor received encouragement from the Jesuits for his poetic efforts; he found sustenance for his literary activities outside the community. His rich correspondence with the poets Robert Bridges, Richard Watson Dixon and Coventry Patmore — in which their works were exchanged, analysed and criticized — carried on until his death.

But only a handful of his poems reached a wider audience, a public, through publication during his lifetime. In a letter to Robert Bridges of 1884, Hopkins was able to list, in a few lines, virtually by name, all the people who had read any of his poems. Writing poetry remained, for him, an intimate, private activity. Indeed, one obituary in an Irish newspaper — for the late Father Gerald [sic] Hopkins — referred to him as 'priest and composer'.

Hopkins's poems remained practically unknown until Robert Bridges published the first edition of them in 1918, almost thirty years after the poet's death. Cases for and against Bridges — condemning the lack of understanding or indeed jealousy which caused him to withhold the poems or admiring his prudence in awaiting the right moment to present them — have been put ever since. But, as regards the meticulous care with which he transcribed and preserved the verses Hopkins sent him over the years, there is nothing to feel but gratitude. Without this care, we would very probably have no Gerard Manley Hopkins at all. And, of 'finished' poems, what we do have is what Bridges preserved.

This curious fact — that Hopkins's poems, now thought of as some of the most significant in nineteenth century English literature, were known in his lifetime by only his most intimate colleagues — is perhaps what lends to Hopkins's poetic manuscripts their rather special power. They compel us because they are the only form in which Hopkins *himself* knew and saw his poems. The printed versions, which students and lovers of his verses read, were unknown to him; and we can never know how he would have liked his printed poems to look. By reading his poems in print — as we necessarily almost always do — we are further away from what he wrote than when reading poets who personally accompanied their poems across the threshold from private manuscript to public print. Other poets themselves supersede their manuscripts: Hopkins did not. For him, his poems were realized *only* in manuscript.

The cause of Hopkins's long delayed publication and fame is better located in his own life than in any possible motive of Robert Bridges: he wrote to

Richard Watson Dixon in 1881 that 'there is more peace and it is the holier lot to be unknown than to be known'. For Hopkins's career as a poet was inextricably enmeshed in the career which he unquestionably valued more highly — his career as a Jesuit priest. Though the daily execution of the duties of his vocation did not always suit or satisfy him, Hopkins never doubted or worried over the fundamental rightness of his having chosen it as he did over the rightness of writing poems. Fr Christopher Devlin, who has edited Hopkins's religious papers, has put it vividly:

> Hopkins the Jesuit behaved to Hopkins the poet as a Victorian husband might to a wife of whom he had cause to be ashamed. His muse was a righteous lady, a chaste matron, dedicate to God; but he treated her in public as a slut, and her children as an unwanted and vaguely sinful burden....

though, Devlin goes on, 'it is certain that...in secret he loved them passionately'. (*Sermons*, p. 119)

That Hopkins was torn by this conflict between the impulse to praise God as a priest, anonymously, in humility, and to praise God as a poet, in his own name, vaingloriously, is all too evident in his surviving private papers and letters. As expressed to Richard Watson Dixon in 1881:

> The question then for me is not whether I am willing...to make a sacrifice of hope and fame...but whether I am not to undergo a severe judgment from God for the lothness I have shewn in making it, for the reserves I may have in my heart made, for the backward glances I <may> have given with my hand upon the plough, for the waste of time the very compositions you admire may have caused and their preoccupation of the mind which belonged to more sacred or more binding duties...I have never wavered in my vocation, but I have not lived up to it. (*Correspodence with Dixon*, p. 89)

The Bodleian Collection of Family Papers

Hopkins's own attitude toward the preservation of his verse was revised after his decision to burn all he had written in 1868. 'A very spiritual man,' he wrote to Dixon in 1881, told him that 'the best sacrifice was not to destroy one's work but to leave it entirely to be disposed of by obedience'. In private notes made in 1883 during a retreat, Hopkins expressed — with characteristic anxiety — this same determination to leave the preservation of his poetry in God's hands:

> I earnestly asked our Lord to watch over my compositions, not to preserve them from being lost or coming to nothing, for that I am very willing they should be, but they might not do me harm through the enmity or imprudence of any man or my own; that he should have them as his own and employ or not employ them as he should see fit. (HpG 442)

The haphazard state of Hopkins's papers at his death and the fact that only by the determined efforts of several people over a span of nearly sixty years to find and collect them did they reach their present degree of organization, testify to Hopkins's success in maintaining this attitude of benign neglect toward them.

Humphry House (in his Preface to *Note-Books*) refers to a 'traditional belief' held by members of the Society of Jesus that Hopkins *did* destroy papers. But — apart from a letter to A. W. M. Baillie of 8 May 1885 in which Hopkins describes an abortive attempt to sort through his accumulated 'old letters...destoying all but a very few' — there is no evidence that he ever did so.

After Hopkins died in Dublin on 8 June 1889, Fr Thomas Wheeler (of University College Dublin) replied to a letter from Robert Bridges requesting Hopkins's manuscripts on behalf of Hopkins's family. Despite being aware that, in his will, Hopkins left all his possessions to the English Province of the Society of Jesus, Fr Wheeler wrote that Hopkins had left no instructions of any kind about the disposition of his remains; that he could not 'fancy what he would have wished to be done with them'; that he would forward Bridges's own letters to Hopkins which he had found; that he had destroyed some papers, but on learning of Bridges's interest, would gather others together 'indiscriminately' and send them 'to be used by you or his parents at your discretion'.

On 14 October 1889, Bridges outlined to Kate Hopkins in a letter what of her son's papers he had received, the vast majority of them being poetic manuscripts. The only item he mentioned which does not apparently now survive is a bundle of so-called 'worthless' papers — including old examination papers and 'schemes for discovering the structure of Greek choruses' — which he suggested should be burnt; Graham Storey's opinion (in his Preface to *Journals*) that Bridges did indeed destroy this bundle seems correct. The only 'non-secular' papers received were private retreat notes which Bridges imagined 'ought never to have been sent' and only had been by dint of an 'oversight of the priests'.

After a few weeks organizing the manuscripts, Bridges sent them to Kate Hopkins; the accompanying letter of 28 November describes the package as containing the volumes known now as MS B and MS H, as well as a 'folio case' of loose poems (presumably the loose papers now bound as Bodleian MS Eng. poet. c. 48). All of these manuscripts are part of the collection which the Bodleian purchased from Hopkins's family, through his great-nephew Lionel Handley-Derry, in 1953 (noticed in *BLR*, 4 (1953), 290). That collection also includes manuscripts which the family came to hold by other means: including some juvenilia (school documents, drawings and watercolours (see 'Hopkins as Artist' below), and a commonplace book (HpG 454) kept at Oxford), letters which Hopkins wrote to his family throughout his life and letters and papers accumulated by the family concerning Hopkins's death and the disposition of his remains (including the family's correspondence with Robert Bridges).

The poetical manuscripts (both bound and loose) which Bridges sent to Kate Hopkins in 1889 comprise three of the four principal sources of Hopkins's verse and deserve special mention.

MS B, described by Bridges in his letter to Kate Hopkins as the 'dark 4to MS book which I call B...', was compiled by Bridges in 1883 as a means of introducing Hopkins's poetry to other people. Bridges transcribed into it the manuscript poems which Hopkins had sent him. He then sent it to Hopkins who made revisions to the transcripts, added several poems in his own hand and sent the book to Coventry Patmore (who wasn't impressed) in early March 1884. The volume also contains poems in Hopkins's autograph which Bridges inserted after Hopkins died.

MS B

Bound volume, 79 leaves, containing transcripts by Bridges of 24 poems, revised and annotated by Hopkins (ff. 6–27), 13 autograph poems (marked * in Contents below) (ff. 27v–37v), 6 autograph poems (and Hopkins's 'Preface') inserted after Hopkins's death (marked ** in Contents below) (ff. 1–5, 40–53), a leaf from *Poems* (1918) (ff. 38–9), the rest of the volume blank except for a note by Bridges (f. 77v) about the word 'voel'; including a title page by Bridges: 'Poems by the rev^{d} Gerard Manley Hopkins S.J. copied from the original MS in possession of Robert Bridges.... Note that the MS copied is not in all cases the final draft of the poem: that all the original accents and marks referring to metrical points are omitted: & that the poems are copied in no consistent order. RB. Private Yattendon. 1883.'.

Bridges's own description of the volume in his Preface to *Poems* (1918) is reprinted *Poems 4*, pp. 232–3 and Phillips, p. xl; a fuller description in Bischoff, pp. 560–1.

Contents: HpG 17, 26, 36, 38*, 44, 48, 52, 56, 74, 86**, 87, 112, 121, 122*, 126*, 135, 144, 154**, 159, 169**, 171, 174, 179*, 191**, 192*, 201, 228**, 233*, 236**, 241, 250*, 259*, 260, 266*, 285*, 289, 295, 298*, 301, 341*, 346*, 362, 369, 376**.

Bodleian, MS Eng. poet. d. 149.

The other volume sent on by Bridges to the Hopkins family is that now known as MS H — in which Bridges himself bound up some of 'the more important pieces' among the loose manuscripts he received from Fr Wheeler. Bridges's two accounts of this volume, written thirty years apart on one of its pages (f. 125), relate its history:

> The MS poems of Father Gerard Hopkins S.J. as left at his death — and sent by the Jesuit fathers to his friends. They were arranged & indexed in this book by me, (Robert Bridges) Oct 89. I destroyed of them nothing but one ½ sheet, the verse on which seemed of no account.
>
> What other poetic MS there was was only of poems already in my possession, & these I left with Mr & Mrs Hopkins at Haslemere. From this must be excepted some 'humorous verse'. RB 1889.

> This book was subsequently kept in a safe: and when it was removed in 1917 it was found to be mildewed, & the paper had rotted. I therefore took out the MSS and reinserted them in the volume in which I also insert this old Index, which will serve to identify the contents.
>
> Anything not in this index was not in the original H album: but was inserted at the date of this present record November 1918. RB 1918.

MS H

Bound volume, 130 leaves, including 47 loose poems and 3 prose pieces (mounted), annotations *passim* by RB, an Index by RB (ff. 125v–6) and his accounts of the volume quoted above (f. 125), some leaves blank;

two outsize MSS formerly in this album (at ff. 23 and 29) were removed in 1982 and 1977 respectively and bound in MS Eng. misc. a. 23, ff. 21b (HpG 325, 338) and 21a (HpG 57, 270, 338) respectively; the only other item listed in RB's Index but not in the volume (HpG 155) was given to Sister Mary Roberta Melchner, Malden, Massachusetts, by GMH's nephew Gerard Walter Sturgis Hopkins (see Bischoff, p. 562).

Bridges's own description of this volume in his Preface to *Poems* (1918) is reprinted in *Poems 4*, p. 233 and Phillips, p. xl; a fuller (but somewhat inaccurate) description in Bischoff, p. 562.

Contents: HpG 4, 8, 19, 21, 34, 45, 58, 60, 66, 70, 82, 103, 117, 119, 128, 138, 141, 148, 149, 162, 167, 187, 188, 193, 196, 203, 212, 219, 224, 225, 229, 230, 244, 247, 257, 303, 316, 318, 319, 321, 323, 328, 330, 334, 336, 347, 352, 366, 383, 396, 436.

Bodleian, MS Eng. poet. d. 150.

The 'folio case' which Bridges also sent to Kate Hopkins in 1889 presumably contained the loose manuscripts which he did not select and include in MS H. When the Bodleian acquired the family's collection, all of the loose poetical manuscripts were then bound into one volume:

MS Eng. poet. c. 48

Including MSS of 27 poems, mostly autograph, 62 leaves, a few blank; also including a MS (f. 62r–v) entitled 'A Prayer for the Society' (including an epigraph from St Mark), 38 lines beginning 'Lord is it nothing to Thee that our bark', the last four lines and revisions throughout in GMH's hand, the hand otherwise unidentified.

This volume includes the items listed in Bischoff, pp. 562–3 as III–XI.

Contents: HpG 14, 24, 29, 33, 40, 46, 54, 63, 83, 84, 90, 106, 109, 130, 142, 152, 198, 209, 223, 232, 248, 267, 286, 290, 296, 344, 349.

THE BRIDGES COLLECTION

Bridges kept back for his own collection those papers of Hopkins which he deemed — quite rightly — belonged to him. These included Hopkins's letters to him and all the poems that Hopkins had given to him — from the first 'For a Picture of Saint Dorothea' (HpG 89), written out for Bridges in 1866, to the last, 'To R. B.' (HpG 335) received on 29 April 1889.

Fr Wheeler had found Bridges's letters in Hopkins's room and these he put aside to forward to Bridges along with the other papers. Bridges then apparently destroyed these letters; only three seem to have escaped and only one of them has been published (see below). We therefore have virtually only one side of this extraordinarily rich twenty-four-year correspondence between the two poets.

Bridges inserted Hopkins's manuscript poems, or his transcripts of them, into a volume as he received them. This volume — MS A — is the single richest source for Hopkins's most accomplished verse:

MS A

Rebound in 1967, including a title page (p. 1) ('The poems of Gerard Manley Hopkins S.J.') annotated by RB twice: 'The corrections in this red ink, are from collation with authors later version. Yattendon. Aug 84. [then added in black] & some new versions in fresh copies same date' and 'corrections thus backward inclined from GMH's MS corrections of copy in his possession — among papers — Oct. 89. RB.'; containing 52 autograph poems and 2 prose pieces of 1866–89 (pp. 1–196) and 37 authoritative transcripts, mostly by RB (including his transcript of the lost autograph of 'The Wreck of the Deutschland'), made after Hopkins's death (pp. 200–62); other contents include: 2 photographs (pp. 16, 18); GMH's drawing of Coventry Patmore dated 1 August 1883 (p. 19); RB's pencil transcript of 'Remembrance & Expectation' by Manley Hopkins, signed 'June 14 1868/ M. H.' (pp. 253–4); rough contents list in pencil by RB (p. 276); printed copies of 2 GMH poems (p. 288); drawing by GMH (p. 295); typed description of the volume by Edward, Lord Bridges, in 1967 (p. 298); 303 pages, several blank and wanting pp. 6–13, 198–9, 246–7.

Bridges's own description of this volume in his Preface to *Poems* (1918) is reprinted *Poems 4*, p. 232 and Phillips, p. xl; a fuller (incomplete) description in Bischoff, pp. 558–9. Written permission is required before use of MS A is permitted. Contents lists of MS A by Monica Bridges (f. 31r-v) and RB (f. 32r-v) bound in Dep. Bridges 62 at the Bodleian. A complete facsimile of 'MS A' will soon be published by Oxford University Press, edited by Norman Mackenzie.

Contents (the autograph MSS are marked *): HpG 7*, 15, 20*, 22*, 25, 28*, 31*, 35, 37, 41, 47, 51, 55, 59*, 61*, 62, 73, 77*, 85, 89, 107*, 110, 113, 114, 120, 125, 132, 133*, 134, 143, 150*, 157, 163*, 168, 170, 173, 183*, 189*, 190, 197*, 199, 204*, 208*, 210*, 213*, 215*, 220*, 226, 231*, 234, 238*, 240, 249, 255, 258, 265, 271*, 273, 275, 276, 277, 278, 279, 281, 282, 284, 287, 291*, 292, 297, 300, 302*, 304*, 305, 314, 320*, 324*, 326*, 329*, 331*, 335, 337*, 340, 345, 350*, 353*, 361, 365*, 368*, 435*, 437*.

Bodleian, Dep. Bridges 61.

Manuscripts of and relating to Hopkins comprise only one part of the large Bridges collection which the present Lord Bridges has deposited in the Bodleian; a Royal Commission of Historical Manuscripts report of the entire collection was compiled in 1982 by Elizabeth Turner. The Hopkins papers can be found in the volumes numbered Dep. Bridges 61–4 and 91–3; for a description of the Hopkinsiana in this collection, see 'Miscellaneous Papers' below.

Hopkins's letters to Bridges fill two bound volumes, Dep. Bridges 91–2, containing letters dated 1865–82 and 1883–9 respectively. They have been published in full in *Letters to RB*; for verses contained in these letters, see HpG 53, 153, 180, 181, 222, 253, 268, 274, 354, 355.

Another volume in the collection, Dep. Bridges 93, contains 39 letters that Hopkins wrote to his other 'literary correspondent', Canon Richard Watson Dixon, dating from 1878 and continuing until 1888. These letters were given to Bridges about two years after Dixon's death in January 1900. They have been published in full, together with Dixon's letters to Hopkins, in *Correspondence with Dixon*; for verses contained in the letters, see HpG 42, 43, 251, 293, 294, 339.

The Jesuit Archives

According to Fr Bischoff, who discovered Hopkins's will in 1947, what Fr Wheeler ought to have done with Hopkins's remains after his death was quite different from what was done. Hopkins — unbeknownst to his family or to Bridges — had made a will (dated 11 July 1878) in which all of his possessions and the copyright on his writings were left to the English Province of the Society of Jesus. The will was proved in Dublin, in Fr Wheeler's presence, on 13 July 1889 and, accordingly, Hopkins's room should have been cleared and his remains sent to the English Provincial headquarters in Farm Street, London. But instead, as already described, Fr Wheeler took it upon himself to select out those papers which he sent to Bridges; the bulk of what he selected (apart from Bridges's letters and Hopkins's sketches) was verse. Fr Wheeler, apparently, felt that Hopkins's 'artistic' life was outside and very separate from the sphere of his Jesuit life; and perhaps that the terms of the will somehow did not apply to the poetry — probably a serious misunderstanding of the poet's wishes. Consequently, Hopkins's papers themselves were divided — in much the same way that his two vocations have been — into two discrete groups: the 'artistic' (now mostly at the Bodleian) and the 'spiritual' (now mostly at Campion Hall, Oxford).

How the large collection at Campion Hall was assembled over the years is somewhat difficult to document. There is some evidence, however, that the wishes expressed in Hopkins's will were somewhat belatedly attended to. Claude Colleer Abbott quotes a letter from Fr Aubrey Gwynn (of Dublin, 18 May 1932) written in reply to an inquiry about Hopkins's papers. While he mentions having seen 'a few old note-books in the house...some six years ago...[which] seem to have been mislaid', he also says that 'all that was important...was sent to London at the time of his death, and is now in the keeping of the English Jesuits' (*Letters to RB*, p. vii). But no other mention of such a transfer of Hopkins's papers has been found — and certainly no mention of *which* papers might have been so transferred.

On the other hand, Bischoff describes a rather different state of affairs. He says that the papers left behind after Hopkins's death were apparently left as they were — scattered in the room, in books, in desk drawers — uncatalogued and unprotected. Gradually, these papers were haphazardly lost and dispersed, borrowed and passed from hand to hand.

In any case, the first concerted attempt to redeem the collection was made by Fr Joseph Keating who, in 1909, published a request for information about Hopkins and his poetry in *The Month*, of which he was then assistant editor. Fr Keating planned, 'with the approval of Father Provincial', to publish a selection of Hopkins's verse with a 'suitable memoir'. Thus began an assembly of Hopkins's papers within the Jesuit community — including the diaries, notebooks, letters, sketches, miscellaneous notes as well as a few poems that would finally form the collection housed at Campion Hall, the Jesuit community at Oxford.

Fr Keating also wrote to Bridges seeking access to his and the family's considerable collection of poetical manuscripts; this access was persistently denied. It is as if the conflicting desires which Hopkins struggled all his life to reconcile — to do God's work and to write poetry — became thoroughly estranged after his death in the form of two factions — Bridges and the Hopkins family on the one hand and the Jesuit community on the other — each wishing to be caretaker of his memory, each distrustful of the other and each jealously safeguarding the treasures in their own keeping, one from the other. Fr Keating never succeeded in bringing out an edition of Hopkins's verse; that was accomplished by Bridges in *Poems* (1918).

Nearly forty years later, in 1947, Fr D. Anthony Bischoff, a Hopkins scholar and prospective biographer, once again searched throughout the Jesuit community, as well as outside, for papers and materials by and relating to Hopkins. He discovered a great many. At the headquarters of the English Province in London, for example, he found three more journals (HpG 458–60), a few loose pages from the early diaries (HpG 456–7), as well as Hopkins's will — which retrospectively shows Fr Wheeler's original disposition of the papers to have been inexcusable and Bridges's clear assumption that the Hopkins family retained the copyright on Hopkins's works to have been utterly mistaken.

In any case, the Hopkins material that Fr Bischoff discovered at Farm Street was added to the archive at Campion Hall, Oxford. The summary of that collection first published in 1937 by Humphry House in *Note-Books* was accordingly augmented for the second edition in 1959 in *Journals*. A more detailed listing of the Campion Hall archive is given in Bischoff, pp. 567–78. These catalogues, however, are both somewhat incomplete and inaccurate and a completely revised catalogue of the collection — retaining and augmenting the numbering in *Journals* — has been compiled by Dr Lesley Higgins (hereafter called Higgins) and is awaiting publication in the *Hopkins Quarterly*. In the meantime, it is available on microfilm as an appendix to Dr Higgins's Ph.D. thesis, 'Hidden Harmonies. Walter Pater and Gerard Manley Hopkins' (Queen's University, Kingston, Ontario, 1987). The numbering of notebooks and papers at Campion Hall in the entries is taken from Higgins.

This collection includes two of the most important surviving primary sources: Diaries C.I and C.II (HpG 456–7), two small continuous pencil diaries which Hopkins kept from September 1863 to January 1866 while an undergraduate at Balliol College in Oxford. These books — full of unfinished, rough and fragmentary poems — were spared the decision to destroy all his verse that Hopkins took in 1868 and — because of that 'slaughter of the innocents' — afford the only significant glimpse into Hopkins's early poetry that remains.

All of Hopkins's journals that have come to light are also in this collection (with the exception of Notebook D.II which was presented to Balliol College in 1963), as are the two most important theological manuscripts: the book of sermons — which Hopkins liked to write out in full before he delivered them — known as Fr Humphrey's Book (HpG 467) and his 'Comments on the Spiritual Exercises of St Ignatius Loyola' (HpG 379), the only substantial extant record of his thinking on spiritual matters.

Other Collections

Some other of Hopkins's papers as well as books from his library — which were presumably left in his room in Dublin when he died and never shepherded into the Campion Hall collection — are in various archives scattered throughout the Catholic world. The papers that Fr Bischoff found in the Archives of the English Province were deposited at Campion Hall; but Hopkins manuscripts at the Archives of the Irish Province of the Society of Jesus (35 Lower Leeson Steet, Dublin) remain there. This archive contains two autograph poems (HpG 160, 256) as well as a number of Hopkins's books (see HpG 471).

Stonyhurst College, Lancashire, where Hopkins taught during the years 1882–4, also owns two autograph poems (HpG 115, 177) originally given to Fr Francis Bacon, S.J., probably the only contemporary Jesuit admirer of Hopkins's poems. The journal kept by Hopkins as Porter at Manresa House, Roehampton (HpG 461.5) is still extant and was published in full in 1969. Contemporary transcripts of three of Hopkins's poems (HpG 5, 67, 269) are still in the album prepared for the Episcopal Silver Jubilee of the first Bishop of Shrewsbury, formerly preserved at St Beuno's College in Wales.

In the United States, the College of Notre Dame of Maryland in Baltimore (in the Loyola-Notre Dame Library) contains two Hopkins manuscripts (HpG 155, 411) among a large collection of Hopkinsiana assembled by Sister Mary Roberta Melchner (see *NUCMC*, 62-543); and the College of the Holy Cross in Worcester, Massachusetts, owns another (HpG 237).

On the 'secular' side, while all the manuscripts that Bridges owned seem to have been preserved together and deposited in the Bodleian (there is one stray transcript by Bridges at Harvard, HpG 280), the history of the materials owned by various members of the Hopkins family is somewhat less straightforward. By far the largest portion of the family's collection — and certainly the significant poetical manuscripts (described above) and letters, as well as much miscellaneous material — was sold to the Bodleian after Hopkins's last remaining sibling, his brother Lionel, died in 1952. According to Bischoff's 'catalogue' of 1951 (pp. 560–6), most of this collection (excepting most of Hopkins's letters to his family) had previously been in the custody of the poet's nephew Gerard Walter Sturgis Hopkins (d. 1961) at Amen House, London. It was, incidentally, Gerard Walter Sturgis Hopkins that bequeathed two autograph manuscript poems (HpG 124, 343) to the British Library in 1931 and presented HpG 155 to Sister Mary Roberta Melchner (see description of 'MS H' above).

Bischoff briefly describes two other family collections of Hopkins materials, one (pp. 559–60) at the Hopkins family home, The Garth in Haslemere, Surrey; the other (p. 566) owned by Hopkins's brother Arthur. The collection at The Garth was examined and catalogued, when its last occupant Lionel Hopkins died in 1952, by Humphry and Madeline House; the latter's description of what they found (see *HRB*, 5 (1974), 26–41) includes the family letters and many of the miscellaneous papers which were sold to the Bodleian. What did not go to the Bodleian, however, were the family's accumulated library and collection of paintings, owned by Lionel Handley-Derry, Arthur Hopkins's grandson (see below and HpG 469, 470).

Bischoff describes the Arthur Hopkins collection as including two letters, a musical manuscript and drawings, and as having come into the possession of Arthur's two daughters — Beatrice Handley-Derry and Christabel Marillier (later Lady Pooley) — at his death in 1930. Neither the letters (one being the unlocated HpG 455) nor the musical manuscript has been traced but a great many sketchbooks and drawings were owned, as late as 1975, by Beatrice's son Lionel Handley-Derry. It is possible that he owns other manuscripts and letters and indeed that he has custody of the family's library, paintings and heirlooms from The Garth as well.

Lady Pooley, at the death of Lord Pooley, her second husband, sold some papers at Sotheby's on 13 July 1966, many of which had been collected by Hopkins's sister Grace. Among these are autograph manuscripts of three of Hopkins's poems (HpG 158, 200, 288). Norman Mackenzie (in 'Gerard and Grace Hopkins, Some New Links', *The Month*, June 1965, pp. 347–50) says that, in 1964, Lady Pooley had found these poems in two desks which had belonged to her aunt Grace Hopkins; he speculated that Hopkins probably sent them to her so she might set them to music. Also included in the sale were two letters from Gerard to Grace, 16 lots of drawings by Hopkins and miscellaneous family papers and drawings (including HpG 472). All but two of the drawings were bought by El Dieff and are now at Texas.

The Texas collection also contains other Hopkins manuscripts, eighteen of his letters (see HpG 10, 92, 151, 182, 363) and miscellaneous materials, all acquired from other sources, including some from the collection of Lancelot de Giberne Sieveking. This collection, albeit small, is the only one of any size at all outside Oxford; it is described in Bump (1979).

Apart from an interesting addition to known Hopkins poetical manuscripts in the Robert H. Taylor Collection at Princeton, the only other repository represented in the entries is the Northamptonshire Record Office where the Dolben Family Papers include contemporary transcripts of Hopkins's poems by his friend Digby Mackworth Dolben (HpG 91, 131). The Taylor MS (see HpG 16 and FACSIMILES), not previously recorded, is a fair copy of 'Andromeda' bearing a previously unknown title, 'The Catholic Church Andromeda', which was sent to Hall Caine presumably for publication; beyond Caine's annotation on the verso that the sender was 'Rossetti', the history of this manuscript is still unknown.

Editions, Hopkins's Canon and Unrecorded Manuscripts

That very posthumous first edition of Hopkins's poetry which Bridges brought out in 1918 in 750 copies, contained seventy-four poems and took ten years to sell out. It also contained Hopkins's own Preface (HpG 376) which explains his metrical innovations and which has been printed as an introduction to his mature verse in every subsequent edition. Bridges also included his own Preface to the Notes in which he was less than enthusiastic about the contents of the volume, acknowledging ruefully their 'oddity' and 'obscurity'; he wrote privately that he had included this Preface in order to forestall criticism and that it had done so. Bridges's Preface, too, accompanied Hopkins's poems in all their subsequent editions until *Poems 4* (1967) when it was finally dropped.

Charles Williams added to the canon by including an Appendix of sixteen new poems in his second edition; published in 1930, this edition appeared just as Hopkins was being discovered and recognized as a major poet, especially by such critics at Cambridge as I. A. Richards and F. R. Leavis.

Between this edition and the third edition of 1948 (ed. W. H. Gardner), much new Hopkins material became available. Humphry House published his edition of *Note-Books* in 1937 which included a great many unpublished early poems and fragments; in addition, the discoveries made by Fr Bischoff in 1947 included some more manuscript poetry. The third edition substantially enlarged the canon.

But it was not until *Poems 4* (ed. W. H. Gardner and Norman Mackenzie, 1967) that an attempt was made at completeness; that a re-editing of all the texts from the extant manuscripts was undertaken; and that the poems were re-ordered chronologically *within each generic section*. A few further revisions were incorporated into the second impression of *Poems 4* published in 1970; it is this edition to which reference is made in the entries. Until Norman Mackenzie's forthcoming Oxford English Texts edition — the first to provide a variorum collation of all the manuscripts — is available, the second impression of *Poems 4* will stand as the standard edition of Hopkins's poems.

However, for the purposes of the *Index*, it is Catherine Phillips's 'Oxford Authors' edition which has been taken as the reference edition from which titles and first lines are quoted. Phillips has corrected some inaccuracies in the text of *Poems 4* and has gathered into the canon some scraps which were either not published or previously relegated to the Notes: *Poems 4* contained 183 numbered poems and the contents list in Phillips includes 211 titles. Much of this difference, however, is due to the altered presentation of various fragments; when there is a discrepancy regarding titles of poems, Phillips is followed and a cross-reference is provided at the title used in *Poems 4*. Conversely, Phillips omits altogether seven of the fragments from the diaries and journals that *Poems 4* includes as 'Sundry Fragments and Images' (HpG 307–13).

Only a handful of poems in the Hopkins canon are not represented by surviving manuscripts. These are among the few verses published in Hopkins's lifetime: see 'Ad Mariam' (*Poems 4*, no. 26 and Phillips, p. 98); 'Angelus ad virginem' (*Poems 4*, Appendix D and Phillips, pp. 153–4); 'The Elopement' (see headnote in the entries); 'Milton' (*Poems 4*, no. 181 and Phillips, p. 152); 'A Trio of Triolets' (*Poems 4*, no. 147 and Phillips, pp. 157–8). Only two poems are represented solely by contemporary transcripts, the autographs having been lost: 'Winter with the Gulf Stream' (HpG 364–5), Hopkins's first published poem, and 'The Wreck of the Deutschland' (HpG 368–9).

While the list of poetical manuscripts contains no hitherto unknown poetical texts, it does include a few unrecorded manuscript versions of known texts. As well as the manuscript of 'Andromeda' (HpG 16) at Princeton (mentioned above), there are two manuscripts at Texas not mentioned in either *Poems 4* or Phillips (HpG 182, 200). A manuscript version of 'Penmaen Pool' at the College of the Holy Cross in Massachusetts (HpG 237) was not recorded in *Poems 4* or Phillips, though Norman Mackenzie did print a variant stanza from it in the *Hopkins Quarterly* in 1976.

In both the Prose and Diaries and Notebooks sections, the situation is reversed. While fifty of the eighty-five prose entries listed are of unpublished texts, only five of the manuscripts are not recorded in the standard Hopkins scholarship (particularly Bischoff and the census of Campion Hall manuscripts in *Journals* — only sixteen of the prose entries are in repositories other than Campion Hall). Likewise, fifteen of the twenty-five diaries and notebooks listed are mostly, if not completely, unpublished.

Two of the five unrecorded prose manuscripts are of 'The Prayer En Ego' (HpG 436–7), oddly unmentioned anywhere in the Hopkins scholarship. Two more are short pieces in MS H — one (HpG 383) a religious passage in Latin, the other (HpG 396) a translation of Dryden into Greek, probably for use in an examination — possibly vaguely referred to in Bischoff (p. 562) as 'passage in Latin prose' and 'passage in Greek prose'. The fifth (HpG 411) is the 'notes on death' listed in *NUCMC*, 62-543; no further information on these notes is available.

Three of the fifteen unpublished (or mostly unpublished) diaries and notebooks are not in the Campion Hall collection: HpG 454 is an unpublished undergraduate commonplace book at the Bodleian; HpG 461.5 is the Porter's Journal Hopkins kept at Manresa House, discovered and published in 1969; and Notebook D.II of undergraduate essays was presented by Campion Hall to Balliol College, Oxford, in 1963.

All of the prose manuscripts, diaries and notebooks that have been published (except HpG 376, 377.5,

415, 435, 461.5, 464) are included in either *Journals* (1959) or *Sermons* (1959). These together form the second edition of Humphry House's ground-breaking edition of *Note-Books* in 1937. The materials which have been so far excluded from these editions are, for the most part, undergraduate essays and notes, or miscellaneous notes on metrics, on the classics, etc.

Lost Manuscripts

Given what is known of Hopkins's activities throughout his life, from letters and other sources, his extant manuscripts, taken as a whole, constitute a very incomplete record of his works. The earliest, and probably the most sweeping, loss is, of course, the destruction of all his poems in 1868 by his own hand. The early Diaries C.I and C.II survived the holocaust — though they themselves are missing pages — and they provide clues to what might have been lost. For example, fragments of several ambitious poetical works which do not survive in a more complete state are extant in the early diaries: the verse dramas *Castara Victrix* (HpG 99) and *Floris in Italy* (HpG 100), the two long narrative poems *Richard* (HpG 102) and *Stephen and Barberie* (HpG 93), and the dramatic monologue *Pilate* (HpG 101). In 1947, Fr Bischoff found 2½ pages excised at some point from these diaries which have now been restored to the original volumes; the new text on these pages was included in *Journals* (see also HpG 88, 101, 108, 242). All that remains of an even earlier diary of 1862 is the extract from it quoted by Hopkins in his letter to C. N. Luxmoore of 7 May 1862 (HpG 455).

Another significant poetic loss is that of the autograph manuscript of Hopkins's great ode, 'The Wreck of the Deutschland'. Hopkins showed the manuscript to his friends (both Bridges and Fr Bacon transcribed it) and then submitted it to the Jesuit press for publication — never to be seen again. The story is told at length by Norman Mackenzie in 'The Lost Autograph of "The Wreck of the Deutschland" and its First Readers', *HQ*, 3 (1976), 91–115. When preparing *Poems* (1918), Bridges sent a proof of the poem to Fr Bacon at St Aloysius' College in Glasgow; Fr Geoffrey Bliss collated the proof with Fr Bacon's transcription of the poem and sent Bridges the list of variants. Bridges published some of the variants but Fr Bliss's list has not survived. Neither has Fr Bacon's transcription; Fr Bischoff learned in 1947 that the late Fr Bacon's papers were destroyed at St Aloysius' College during the war. A few leaves containing his transcriptions of Hopkins's work (HpG 116, 178, 450) were reportedly plucked from these flames but, alas, they did not include 'The Wreck of the Deutschland'. Bridges's presentation copy to Fr Bliss of *Poems* (1918) is extant at Stonyhurst College and in it are tipped in two autograph poems by Hopkins originally given to Fr Bacon (HpG 115, 177).

The diaries and journals that are extant are clearly not all that were kept by Hopkins. A gap of three months exists between the end of Diary C.II (HpG 457) and the beginning of Journal A.I (HpG 458); and a gap of an entire year between Journal A.I and A.II (HpG 459). While Journals A.II–A.V (HpG 459, 460, 461, 462) are all continuous, journal-keeping must have carried on afterwards, since the last, Journal A.V, ends mid-sentence.

Also nearly completely lost are the rough notes in the 'little books' from which the fair copy journals were written up, often some time after the events being described. These notes were presumably jotted into pocketbooks which Hopkins carried with him; three pages of just such a book still exist (HpG 459.5) and are now stuck into Journal A.III (HpG 460) alongside the fair copy version of the same material.

These journals contain virtually no entries concerning religious or spiritual matters. According to Humphry House — accepting the statement of G. F. Lahey in his early biography, *Gerard Manley Hopkins* (London, 1930) — Hopkins kept a 'concurrent series of spiritual notes [which] has been lost or destroyed' (*Note-Books*, p. xxvi). Lahey states that Hopkins destroyed his 'spiritual diary' himself. Some commentators have suggested that the diary — labelled '*Please do not open this*' — which Hopkins's two sisters burnt, unread (see *Journals*, p. xiv), was the lost 'spiritual diary' or part of it; but it may just as surely have been one of the missing journals.

Bischoff states (pp. 579–80) that Fr R. McCoy, S.J. told Fr Keating in 1909 that Hopkins had written a full study of the Lake Poets. No trace of this or, indeed, of several other of Hopkins's projects has come to light. Whether they have been lost or destroyed or whether they were never finished or even begun may never be known.

Hopkins's Books

Along with Hopkins's letters to his family and the other papers that Humphry and Madeline House found at The Garth, Haslemere, in 1952, after the death of Lionel Hopkins, were over 200 books belonging to various members of the Hopkins family.

In Madeline House's article — 'Books Belonging to Hopkins and His Family', *HRB*, 5 (1974), 26–41 and 6 (1975), 17–21 — she lists all of those books. Her catalogue includes twenty-two books definitely identified as belonging to Gerard, including two Bibles and his copies of the works of Milton, Southey, Goldsmith, Wordsworth, George Herbert, Browning and Vaughan; six of these volumes were prizes won by Hopkins at Highgate School. The two which are described as containing his marginalia are listed in the entries (HpG 469, 470). Madeline House also lists nineteen 'general family books', forty-one books of Kate Hopkins, sixty-three books of Manley Hopkins and over one hundred other books of unspecified ownership.

While the papers and letters at The Garth were sold to the Bodleian in 1953, the whereabouts of the library is unknown; it is possibly in the possession of Lionel Handley-Derry (see 'Other Collections' above).

In 1947, Fr Bischoff identified 'a number of the school texts in which Hopkins wrote fairly copious marginal comments, textual analyses, and critical observations' (Bischoff, p. 579). These, he said, were left in the Archives of the Irish Province of the Sociey of Jesus, in the care of Fr Aubrey Gwynn, S.J. The archivist now reports that there are thirty-two books at Lower Leeson Street, Dublin, which bear slips saying that Fr Bischoff had examined them. The two which contain Hopkins's annotations are listed in the entries (HpG 468.5 and 473). Others which were definitely owned by Hopkins are: *The Acharnians of Aristophanes*, trans. by Robert Yelverton Tyrrell (Dublin and London, 1883), presented to Hopkins by the translator; two of Robert Bridges's works, *Prometheus the Firegiver* (London, 1884) and *Eros and Psyche* (London, 1885), presumably presented by the author; Hopkins's copies of Richard Watson Dixon's *Lyrical Poems* (Oxford: Daniel Press, 1887), *Odes and Eclogues* (1884) and *The Story of Eudocia and her Brothers* (1888), all bound together; an incomplete edition (breaking off at p. 610) of the Vulgate (Paris, 1865) inscribed by Hopkins, 31 October 1866. Missing from the collection is Hopkins's annotated copy of *Corpus Poetarum Latinorum*, ed. William Walker (1876). Hopkins's annotated copy of Homer (HpG 471), mention of which is made in the scholarship, is not among this collection of books and remains unlocated.

Two stray volumes owned by Hopkins — without any marginalia — have passed through the salerooms. Bridges's presentation copy to Hopkins of one of the twenty-two numbered copies of the Daniel Press first edition of his own *The Growth of Love* (Oxford, 1889) — later presented by Kate Hopkins to her grandniece Christabel Marillier (later Lady Pooley) — was offered for sale by Blackwell's (Catalogue No. 896, 1970). Lady Pooley had previously sent this volume for sale at Sotheby's on 11–12 July 1967 where it was sold as Lot 87 to Blackwell's; in both sale catalogues, it is described as having loosely inserted in it the title page and flyleaf (inscribed by Hopkins) of a copy of the first edition of John Henry Newman's *The Dream of Gerontius* (London, 1866).

In Sotheby's sale of 18 December 1985, Hopkins's copy of Christina Rossetti's *The Prince's Progress* (London, 1866), inscribed by Hopkins and his sister Grace and his brother Everard, was sold as Lot 13.

Hopkins as Artist

The Hopkins family was, in many ways, a typical middle-class Victorian family. Drawing exercises were considered *de rigeur* in the education of young 'gentlemen' and 'gentlewomen'. While the Hopkins children were, altogether, probably more talented than that typical family's — two of his brothers became professional artists — Hopkins himself executed 'Ruskinese' drawings which Norman White has described as 'amateur products of their age, keeping honourable but undistinguished company with numerous leaves from sketch-pads lovingly brought back from thousands of middle-class picnics' (Thornton, p. 58). The significance of his drawings, which are mostly of natural subjects, lies not in their intrinsic qualities but in what they reveal about how this great poet of 'nature and religion' looked at the natural world.

Hopkins seems to have stopped drawing with any regularity in 1868; he did not take it up again until the months before his death. His extant artwork falls into two categories: the rough sketches and the drawings in sketchbooks.

The sketches are hastily made to serve as illustrations to his text; they dot Hopkins's early letters and many are scattered throughout the early diaries and, to a much lesser extent, the later journals. Twenty-nine sketches from the early Diaries C.I and C.II (HpG 456–7) are reproduced in *Journals*, Figures 1–29; seven (including one from Journal A.IV (HpG 461)) are reproduced in Thornton.

Hopkins's extant drawings in the sketchbooks have been well documented. The first summary of them, in Appendix III of *Correspondence with Dixon* (1935), pp. 167–8, included descriptions of the three Sketchbooks (known as A, B and C), owned at that time by Arthur Hopkins's daughters, and mentioned the fourth (D) at Campion Hall, Oxford. These descriptions were probably made when the sketchbooks still contained some inserted drawings which were later removed. The sketch called 'Dandelion, Hemlock and Ivy', for example, is not in Sketchbook A (as stated in 1935) but is one of the loose drawings sold in Lady Pooley's sale (see below).

Two years later, in 1937, Humphry House included facsimiles of sixteen of Hopkins's drawings: ten were taken from the four Sketchbooks and six from loose drawings formerly inserted in them. The fourth Sketchbook D was fully described (with twenty-one drawings listed as the contents) in Bischoff, pp. 573–4.

A much more complete census of Hopkins's surviving artwork was given in *Journals*, Appendix I, pp. [453]–4. This list includes descriptions of the four Sketchbooks A–D; ownership of A, B, and C had in 1954 passed to Arthur Hopkins's grandson, Lionel Handley-Derry and Sketchbook D was at Campion Hall where it remains. Also listed were three lots of loose drawings: those owned by Lady Pooley (formerly Christabel Marillier, one of Arthur Hopkins's daughters); those at the Bodleian; and a drawing on a fragmentary letter (*Journals*, plate 6) owned by Lionel Handley-Derry. The last item described is a family scrapbook, also owned by Handley-Derry, which mainly includes Arthur Hopkins's drawings but has a few by Gerard inserted into it (e.g., *Journals*, plates 4–5).

Journals includes thirty-three facsimile reproductions of drawings by Hopkins, including the sixteen given in *Note-Books*. Of the additional seventeen, ten were taken from Sketchbooks A and D, two from the Bodleian collection, three (as mentioned above) from Lionel Handley-Derry's collection; the other two are illustrated headings to two letters to Arthur Hopkins which *Journals* says 'have not survived'.

Sixteen loose drawings removed from the Sketchbooks and owned by Lady Pooley were sent to the saleroom with her other papers in July 1966 (see 'Other Collections' above) and were sold as Lots 679–94. All but two of these (Lots 688–9) were bought by El Dieff and are now at Texas; these fourteen lots (containing fifteen drawings) are listed in Bump (HA 23–37) and most of them have been reproduced in facsimile in *Journals*, plates 17–18, 22, 28 and in Thornton, pp. 56, 65, 75, 144–6. The one drawing in the sale (Lot 679, sold to El Dieff), but not listed in Bump, is a pencil drawing of 'Mamma' dated 31 December, made by Hopkins as a boy.

The two which did not go to Texas — Lot 688 (sold to Sanders of Oxford), the highly accomplished 'Dandelion, Hemlock and Ivy...Croydon. April–July 1862' (*Journals*, plate 2 and Thornton, p. 56) and Lot 689 (sold to N. Larn), a drawing of an iris captioned 'Manor Farm, Shanklin. 8 July, 1863' (*Journals*, plate 10 and Thornton, p. 65) — are unlocated.

Three of Hopkins's loose drawings and four early watercolours (dating from 1853–8) are part of the collection which the Bodleian purchased from Lionel Handley-Derry in 1953. They are all bound in MS Eng. misc. a. 8, ff. 99–106 and have (with the exception of the earliest watercolour) all been reproduced in Thornton, pp. 68, 114–15; the drawing 'Shanklin, Isle of Wight, 1866' is also reproduced in *Journals*, plate 24 and *Further Letters*, facing p. 189. The Bodleian also owns the fair copy of the poem 'A Vision of the Mermaids' which contains an oft-reproduced elaborate circular drawing on its first page (HpG 349).

With the publication of Thornton (1975), Hopkins's drawings, as well as his 'visual world' in the largest possible sense, receive the careful analysis they deserve, particularly in the essays by Norman White and Jerome Bump. A great many of the surviving drawings are reproduced in facsimile, including the whole of the four Sketchbooks (pp.116–43). Another loose drawing, not previously mentioned, was also published (p. 147); 'Lines in the Dugmores' Garden. Oct 12, 1865' was found inserted in a sketchbook of Arthur Hopkins owned by Lionel Handley-Derry.

Two unpublished drawings are those included in MS A (described above) in the Bridges Collection. One is Hopkins's drawing of Coventry Patmore dated 1883.

Hopkins as Composer

Of equal interest as his drawings to students of Hopkins's poetry are his musical compositions. Opinions differ as to the degree of accomplishment and success his works achieve. They were, nonetheless, produced with a great seriousness and with the benefit of much careful study of harmony and counterpoint.

A short survey of opinions of Hopkins's music is given in *Correspondence with Dixon*, Appendix III, pp. 168–70. A much more serious analysis — as well as the printing of Hopkins's surviving musical compositions and a catalogue of all the extant manuscript sources — is given by John Stevens in *Journals*, Appendix II, pp. [457]–97.

Hopkins rarely set his own poems to music and, of the four of his poems which he did set, no trace of three of the settings survives. The one exception is what must be his only attempt at writing for a popular audience, a patriotic song for soldiers — both lyrics and music — 'What shall I do for the land that bred me'; two autograph manuscripts (HpG 354–5) of the words and music are extant, both in letters to Bridges, as well as Bridges's own transcription (HpG 356).

Stevens describes, discusses and prints (if extant) the twenty-seven settings which Hopkins is known, through his letters, to have attempted. He excludes (in a note) the 'unpublished musical composition "Al Fresco Polka" and possibly other pieces of music' which Bischoff (p. 566) lists as being in the possession of Christabel Marillier (later Lady Pooley); this manuscript remains untraced.

The richest source of Hopkins's music is the bundle that Grace Hopkins is said to have found in 1935 while searching for her brother's transcriptions of poems by Richard Watson Dixon; see *Correspondence with Dixon*, pp.vii, 169. This bundle of manuscripts was among the collection sold to the Bodleian in 1953; they are now bound as MS Mus. c. 97. Included in this volume are twenty-six leaves of musical manuscripts, many in Hopkins's hand; it contains Hopkins's Songs 1, 4, 5, 10, 13, 14, 21 (see HpG 356), 22 (the song numbers refer to Stevens's 'List of Songs', *Journals*, pp. 464–5). Together with his *own* setting of Richard Watson Dixon's 'Wayward Water' (Song 14) are Hopkins's transcripts of his sister Grace's piano accompaniment (ff. 6r–v and 8r–9v). Also bound in are Hopkins's transcripts of two settings by others: a traditional setting of Hood's 'Oft in the stilly night' (f. 10) and the setting of a Christmas carol by John Spencer to words by William Robert Spencer (f. 19). Facsimiles of two of these settings are reproduced in Vol. II of W. H. Gardner's *Gerard Manley Hopkins*, 2 vols (London, 1944–9): two manuscripts, one autograph, of Song 1 (ff. 1–2) and the autograph manuscript of Song 13 (f. 3r–v) (this also reproduced in *Correspondence with Dixon*, facing p. 169).

Hopkins occasionally sent music to Bridges in his letters, now on deposit at the Bodleian in the Bridges Collection. Included are manuscripts of: Song 8 (originally enclosed in a letter of 26 January–8 February 1881, Dep. Bridges 91 and now bound up in Dep. Bridges 62, f. 15; published in facsimile in *Letters to RB*, facing p. 118); Song 21 (HpG 354–5); Song 26a (enclosed in a letter of 28 October 1886, in Dep. Bridges 92); Song 26c (in a letter of 26 January–8 February 1881, Dep. Bridges 91); and a quotation from Song 2 (in a letter of 5–13 September 1880, Dep. Bridges 91). A photostat of a lost transcript by Hopkins of a setting of Bridges's 'Sometimes when my Lady sits by me' to music by Grace Hopkins is bound in Dep. Bridges 62, f. 17r–v.

At Campion Hall are: manuscripts of Song 12 (N.II, on two leaves); draft versions of Song 22 (N.II, on three leaves); manuscripts (one in an unidentified hand) of the two melodies without words, Songs 23–4 (N.IV, on two pages of one leaf); and Hopkins's musical manuscripts, 'Exercises in Counterpoint: Note against Note' (two pages, one leaf) and 'Exercises: firm chant: old English air' (three pages of two leaves, signed), both annotated by Robert P. Stewart (N.III); facsimiles of most of these manuscripts are bound in MS Mus. c. 97 at the Bodleian. Hopkins's notes on music at Campion Hall, '*Fourth Species of Counterpoint*...', are listed in the entries (HpG 393).

The one musical manuscript that has come to light which Stevens does not mention is the two-pages of musical exercises in counterpoint at the Pierpont Morgan. It was sold at Sotheby's, 'for the benefit of "The Tablet"', on 24 July 1979, Lot 238; a facsimile of a portion of the manuscript is reproduced in the sale catalogue, p. 167. A photocopy of the manuscript is lodged at the British Library, RP 1798.

Letters

Apart from letters to members of his family, to Robert Bridges, Richard Watson Dixon, Coventry Patmore or Alexander William Mowbray Baillie — of which quite a few survive — there are less than fifty extant Hopkins letters to other people. And these are widely scattered.

The three published volumes of letters are all edited by Claude Colleer Abbott, originally invited to edit Hopkins's letters to Bridges by Robert Bridges himself. The 'first' of these volumes, *Letters to RB* (1935), contains the 171 letters and postcards to Bridges deposited at the Bodleian with the Bridges Collection (described above). Bridges apparently destroyed two of the last letters but no other gap in the series is known. The letters fill two volumes: Dep. Bridges 91 (1865–82) and Dep. Bridges 92 (1883–9). A facsimile page of one of the letters is printed in *Letters to RB*, facing p. 8. While Bridges's own letters to Hopkins were presumably destroyed by himself, three of them have survived. One, written just before Hopkins's death on 18 May 1889, is among the papers the family sold to the Bodleian (MS Eng. misc. a. 8, ff. 32–3); it has been published in *Further Letters*, p. 433. The other two, both apparently unpublished, are in the Bridges Collection deposited in the Bodleian (Dep. Bridges 62, ff. 2–5); the first is dated 12 September

1867 and the second — an extraordinary note referring to verses sent by Hopkins which Bridges destroyed — was written on 15 June 1881.

In the 'second' of the published editions, *Correspondence with Dixon* (1935), both sides of the long correspondence between Hopkins and Richard Watson Dixon are printed. Thirty-nine (of the forty-one) letters by Hopkins are also in the Bridges Collection deposited in the Bodleian (Dep. Bridges 93). The other two letters (25 October 1884 and 29–30 July 1888) were owned in 1935 by Dixon's sister-in-law, Mrs Barnard; the former was sold at Sotheby's on 6–7 December 1984, Lot 135 (photocopy at British Library, RP 2907). Two different pages of one of Hopkins's letters (30 June 1886) have been printed in facsimile: in *Correspondence with Dixon*, facing p. 132 and in Roger Fry and E. A. Lowe's *English Handwriting*, S. P. E. Tract No. 23 (Oxford, 1926), plate 33. The thirty-six letters from Dixon to Hopkins published in the edition are preserved at Campion Hall, Oxford. Another letter to Dixon has come to light which has not been published: the letter, dated Christmas 1881, passed through the salerooms in 1971 and 1977 and is now at the Pierpont Morgan, MA 3237 (photocopy lodged at the British Library, RP 1410). The two autograph poems at the British Library (HpG 124, 343) may well be the manuscript enclosure originally sent with Hopkins's letter to Dixon of 22 December 1887.

Further Letters, the 'third' volume of letters, contains all the *other* letters of Hopkins that were available at the time of publication. The first edition of 1938 divided the letters into three sections: miscellaneous letters; letter to Alexander William Mowbray Baillie; and correspodence with Coventry Patmore. The second edition of 1956 added a fourth section, family letters (including seventy-eight new letters) and two other new letters; it included, in all, 188 letters by Hopkins.

The acknowledgements in the Preface to the first edition to a few private owners of letters were not revised in the second edition; but the letters in question are unlikely to still be in the hands of their 1938 owners. In most cases, information about new locations of these letters has not come to light. However, the seven letters to E. H. Coleridge (*Further Letters*, nos. 2–5, 7, 24–5) are now at Texas; one of them contains HpG 10, 92, 151, 363. One of the twelve letters to the Rev. E. W. Urquhart (all lent in 1938 by his daughter) is now at Georgetown University (*Further Letters*, no. 6); two facsimile pages of another of them (*Further Letters*, no. 16) were printed in *British Literary Manuscripts*, plate 98 (credited 'anonymous loan').

Claude Colleer Abbott's own collection of twenty-one letters from Hopkins to Coventry Patmore (*Further Letters*, nos. 163–76, 178–9, 181–2, 184, 187–8) has been bequeathed to the University of Durham; a facsimile page of no. 167 is printed in Thornton, p. 111. The Loyola-Notre Dame Library of the College of Notre Dame of Maryland in Baltimore reportedly owns two letters from Hopkins to Patmore (*NUCMC*, 62–543) but further information has not been made available.

The forty-three letters and postcards to A. W. M. Baillie (which form the third section of *Further Letters*) were all owned in 1938 by Miss Hannah, daughter of a former Dean of Chichester.

In the first edition, Abbott included seven letters (two to Kate Hopkins, one to Arthur Hopkins, one to C. N. Luxmoore and three to Edward Bond) which were made available to him by Gerard Walter Sturgis Hopkins on behalf of the family. By the time the second edition was published in 1956, the large collection of family papers sold to the Bodleian had revealed seventy-eight new letters from Hopkins to members of his family: seventy-one to his mother (one being, in fact, not a letter but two sonnets in an envelope, HpG 111, 299), six letters to his father and one to his brother Lionel. Of the seven letters from the first edition, the Bodleian collection contained the two to Kate Hopkins and the three to Edward Bond; the other two, to C. N. Luxmoore (see HpG 455) and Arthur Hopkins (*Further Letters*, no. 112), were listed by Bischoff in 1951 as being in the possession of Arthur Hopkins's daughters and now, possibly, in the possession of Lionel Handley-Derry (see 'Other Collections' above). All the family letters at the Bodleian are bound in two volumes: MS Eng. lett. e. 40–41.

Six additional letters of Hopkins to his father (2), his sister Grace (2) and his brother Everard (2) — not published in *Further Letters* — have been acquired by Texas (Bump, HA 13–18) from various sources: the letters to Manley Hopkins of 23 December 1871 and 5 July 1884 were purchased from Lance Sieveking (in whose book *The Eye of the Beholder* (London, 1957) they were first published); the two letters to Grace of 9 June 1883 and 2 November 1884 were bought at Lady Pooley's sale at Sotheby's, 13 July 1966, Lots 675–6 (they were both published by Jerome Bump, the former in *Renascence*, 31 (1979), 196–7, the latter in the *HQ*, 4 (1978), 181–3); and the two letters to Everard, 5–8 November and 23 December 1885, were published in the *HRB*, 4 (1973), 7–14. Also in the collection at Texas (Bump, HA 5, 19–22) are four letters to Katherine Tynan, 14 November 1886–15 September 1888 (first published in *The Month*, May 1958) and one to Professor Doctor Münke of 8 May [1861] (first published in *The Month*, November 1972).

A few other letters have come to light since the publication of *Further Letters*: a letter to the Archbishop of Liverpool dated Glasgow, 12 August 1881 is at the Lancashire Record Office (first published in *HRB*, 2 (1971), 3–5); a letter to William Butterfield, St Beuno's, 26 April 1877 (first published in full in *HRB*, 5 (1974), 3–5) is among the Starey family's collection of Butterfield's papers; two letters to Dr Michael F. Cox of 26 and 31 March 1887, were presented in the late 1960s to Fr Roland Burke Savage, S. J., then the editor of *Studies* (and first published in *Studies: An Irish Quarterly Review*, 59 (1970), 19–25).

Some confusion surrounds the three (possibly four?) letters of Hopkins to W. A. Comyn Macfarlane which were among the family papers bequeathed to Magdalene College, Cambridge, by G. M. Macfarlane-Grieve, one of the sons of Hopkins's correspondent. *Further Letters* (nos 8, 17–18) includes three other letters to Macfarlane, lent in 1938 by another of his sons, Lt Col Angus Macfarlane-Grieve; but three of the Magdalene College letters (dated 10 July [1866], 15 July 1866 and [November–December 1866]) were not published until they appeared in Graham Storey's article, 'Three New Letters from G. M. Hopkins to W. A. Comyn Macfarlane', *HRB*, 6 (1975), 3–7. These three, together with an additional letter, were sold at Christie's on 23 June 1976, Lot 209; and one of them (the letter of 10 July [1866]) was resold at Sotheby's on 22–3 July 1985 as Lot 127 (photocopy at British Library, RP 3032).

Two completely unpublished letters are in the British Library in a volume of letters (1878–80) to Charles Kent concerning his compilation of *Corona Catholica* (Add. MS 43457); the volume was presented to the British Library in 1900 but not made available until 1933. Hopkins's two letters to Kent are both written on the same day, 27 August 1878 (one misdated 1877), and addressed from 111 Mount Street in London; they concern Hopkins's recommendation to Kent of translators.

Miscellaneous Papers

The Bodleian collection includes a volume (81 leaves) of Hopkins's transcriptions of poems by Richard Watson Dixon (MS Eng. poet. e. 91). With one exception, they were all published, some in *Christ's Company* (1861) or *Historical Odes* (1864); these transcriptions are discussed and the unpublished poem printed in *Correspondence with Dixon*, Appendix IV, pp. 171–2. Campion Hall, Oxford, owns a transcription by Hopkins of lines by Digby Mackworth Dolben beginning 'Methought through many years and lands'; it is annotated 'Found after his death' and 'It seems unfinished/D.A.S. Mackworth Dolben' (Bischoff, p. 575). Also at Campion Hall (H.III(b1)) is Hopkins's transcription of his father's poem 'Remembrance and Expectation'; Bridges's transcript of these lines is bound in MS A (described above).

Another transcription by Hopkins of a poem by Dolben (entitled '"Viva Gesu"') is together with a collection of miscellaneous Hopkins material in the Bridges Collection (Dep. Bridges 62, f. 16r–v). Other miscellanea in Dep. Bridges 62 are: letters to Bridges from Hopkins's family and others (ff. 18–30, 36–89); Bridges's list of thank-you letters from recipients of copies of *Poems* (1918) (f. 35v); printed matter and facsimiles (ff. 90–141). The two other Hopkins-related volumes in the Bridges Collection not so far mentioned are: Dep. Bridges 63, a collection of papers and reviews regarding Hopkins collected by Bridges from 1894–1921, while editing *Poems* (1918) and after; Dep. Bridges 64, a presentation copy of *Poems* (1918) from Bridges to John Sampson, Christmas 1918, containing a few pencil notes by Bridges.

A curious autograph manuscript in the Bodleian collection has not been attributed. Listed in the catalogue as a 'facetious piece' it is entitled 'Elephantiasis or the Homeless Housemaid being a Treatise on backgammon by Alex Mactrump author of the Marquis and the Marionettes, the Regular Dustman and other Epics' (MS Eng. misc. a. 8, f. 14r–v). Other Hopkinsiana bound in this same volume include: school reports and bills, Highgate School, September 1854–April 1862 (ff. 1–10); certificate of degrees (B.A. and M.A.), Royal University Dublin, 27 October 1885 (ff. 11–12); letters concerning Hopkins's death written to and from his family (ff. 34–93); press cuttings (ff. 15–17, 94–7); and a watercolour portrait of Hopkins, 29 June 1859 (f. 107).

The important series of fifty-six letters and postcards that Bridges wrote to Hopkins's mother and his sister Kate after Hopkins's death (1889–1920) are also in the Bodleian (MS Eng. lett. d. 143).

A few miscellaneous leaves containing notes from Hopkins's teaching are at Campion Hall, Oxford (M.VII): a draft for an exam headed 'Royal University/First Examination in Arts: Pass' (two pages); two pages headed 'Changes for 1886 and 1887' about alterations in the syllabus; and notes on examinees' papers (four pages).

According to Tom Dunne's *Gerard Manley Hopkins. A Comprehensive Bibliography* (Oxford, 1976), p. 361, autograph entries by Hopkins can be found among the parish records of St Aloysius' Church, Oxford, and St Francis Xavier's Church, Liverpool.

A curious item was bequeathed to the University of North Carolina in 1949 by J. S. Childers who acquired it in 1947. It is a small notebook whose cover is now loose; on the inside of the cover, Hopkins has written 'Gerard M. Hopkins./Translations.'. Nowhere else in the notebook does his hand appear; it is filled with a rough pencil draft of a sermon by an unidentified author.

A large collection of papers relating to Hopkins's father's appointment as Consul-General of Hawaii (which began in February 1856 and continued for over forty years) is preserved in the State Archives of Hawaii. These papers have been described in Eugene R. August's 'A Checklist of Materials Relating to the Hopkins Family in the State Archives of Hawaii', *HQ*, 6 (1979), 60–83 and in William Foltz's 'Further Correspondence of Manley Hopkins', *HQ*, 9 (1982), 51–77.

Another collection of Hopkinsiana which includes papers relating to the appointment of Manley Hopkins as Hawaiian Consul-General were sold at Sotheby's on 17 July 1973 (Lot 701) to Norman White.

Two large collections of association materials have been amassed in the United States. One, the Sister Mary Roberta Melchner collection at the Loyola-Notre Dame Library of the College of Notre Dame of Maryland in Baltimore (see also HpG 155, 411) includes letters to Sister Mary Roberta from Hopkins's brother Lionel and his sister Grace. The collection is briefly described in *NUCMC*, 62-543. The other is in the Crosby Library at Gonzaga University; the printed materials have been catalogued by Ruth Seelhammer in *Hopkins Collected at Gonzaga* (Chicago, 1970).

ABBREVIATIONS

For general abbreviations, see the list at the front of this volume.

Bischoff
: D. Anthony Bischoff, 'The Manuscripts of Gerard Manley Hopkins', *Thought*, December 1951, pp. 551–7.

Bump
: Jerome Bump, 'Catalogue of the Hopkins Collection in the Humanities Research Center of the University of Texas', *HQ*, 5 (1979), 141–50.

Correspondence with Dixon
: *The Correspondence of Gerard Manley Hopkins and Richard Watson Dixon*, ed. Claude Colleer Abbott (London, 1935).

Diaries C.I–C.II
: See HpG 456–7.

Dublin Notebook
: See HpG 468.

Fr Humphrey's Book
: See HpG 467.

Further Letters
: *Further Letters of Gerard Manley Hopkins*, ed. Claude Colleer Abbott, 2nd ed (London, 1956).

GMH
: Gerard Manley Hopkins.

Higgins
: Lesley Higgins, '"Things counter, original, spare, strange": further explorations of the Hopkins manuscripts at Campion Hall', forthcoming in *HQ*, typescript at Campion Hall.

Journals
: *The Journals and Papers of Gerard Manley Hopkins*, ed. Humphry House, completed by Graham Storey (London, 1959).

Journals A.I–A.V
: See HpG 458, 459, 460–461, 462.

Letters to RB
: *The Letters of Gerard Manley Hopkins to Robert Bridges*, ed. Claude Colleer Abbott (London, 1935).

MSS A, B, H
: See INTRODUCTION.

Notebooks B.I–B.II, D.I–D.XII, G.I–G.II
: See DIARIES AND NOTEBOOKS.

Phillips
: *Gerard Manley Hopkins*, ed. Catherine Phillips, 'The Oxford Authors' (Oxford, 1986).

Poems (1918)
: *The Poems of Gerard Manley Hopkins*, ed. Robert Bridges (London, 1918).

Poems (1930)
The Poems of Gerard Manley Hopkins, ed. Charles Williams (London, 1930).

Poems (1948)
The Poems of Gerard Manley Hopkins, ed. W. H. Gardner, 3rd ed (London, 1948).

Poems (1956)
The Poems of Gerard Manley Hopkins, ed. W. H. Gardner, 3rd ed, 5th impression, revised (London, 1956).

Poems 4
The Poems of Gerard Manley Hopkins, ed. W. H. Gardner and N. H. Mackenzie, 4th ed (London, 1967; 2nd impression, 1970).

RB
Robert Bridges.

Sermons
The Sermons and Devotional Writings of Gerard Manley Hopkins, ed. Christopher Devlin, S. J. (London, 1959).

Thornton
All My Eyes See. The Visual World of Gerard Manley Hopkins, ed. R. K. R. Thornton (Sunderland Arts Centre, Ceolfrith Press, 1975).

ARRANGEMENT

Verse	HpG 1–370
Prose	HpG 371–453.5
Diaries and Notebooks	HpG 454–68
Marginalia in Printed Books and Manuscripts	HpG 468.5–73

Gerard Manley Hopkins

VERSE

'A basket broad of woven white rods'
First pub. *Journals* (1959), p. 58; *Poems 4*, no. 98, as '(Sundry Fragments and Images)', no. xix (p. 137); Phillips, p. 61. These lines are possibly related to HpG 88, 177 and 255.

HpG 1 In Diary C.II (see HpG 457); [2–12 March 1865].

Campion Hall, Oxford.

'A noise of falls I am possessèd by'
First pub. *Journals* (1959), p. 66; *Poems 4*, no. 121; Phillips, p. 70.

HpG 2 In Diary C.II (see HpG 457); [August 1865].

Campion Hall, Oxford.

'A silver scarce-call-silver gloss'
First pub. *Journals* (1959), p. 52; *Poems 4*, no. 98, as '(Sundry Fragments and Images)', no. xvii (p. 137); Phillips, p. 57.

HpG 3 In Diary C.II (see HpG 457); [December 1864–January 1865].

Campion Hall, Oxford.

'Ac tu me madidis noli vexare querellis:', for six unidentified Latin lines, see HpG 80, 245.

Ad Episcopum Salopiensem ('Quòd festas luces juvat instaurare Beatis')
First pub. *Poems* (1948); *Poems 4* no. 173; Phillips, p. 120.

HpG 4 Two fair copies, revised, in MS H: (1) here entitled '*Ad Episcopum Salopiensem annum agentum et sui praesulatus et restituti apud Anglos episcoporum ordinis vicesimum quintum, qui jubilaeus dicitur*', containing 18 opening lines beginning 'Vertitur in gyrum toto pulcherrima gyro', annotated 'They said the beginning was unintelligible and struck out the first nine couplets…', 2 pages (one leaf), dated April 1876 (ff. 53, 54); (2) here entitled as in (1), the unused part here cancelled, 2 pages (one leaf) (ff. 56, 57).

Bodleian, MS Eng. poet. d. 150, ff 53, 54 (mounted on f. 55), 56, 57 (mounted on f. 59).

HpG 5 Transcript in an unidentified hand, on p. [53] of an album (containing also HpG 67 and 269) compiled for presentation to Dr James Brown, first Bishop of Shrewsbury, on his Episcopal Silver Jubilee, July 1876.

This transcript and the album discussed in Alfred Thomas, S.J., 'G. M. Hopkins and the Silver Jubilee Album', *The Library*, 5 Ser 20 (1965), 148–52; not mentioned in *Poems 4* or Phillips.

Unlocated (according to *The Library* in 1965, the album was preserved at St Beuno's College in Wales which was joined to Heythrop College, London, in 1970; however, Heythrop College reports (1988) that the album is not in their collection).

Ad Matrem Virginem ('Mater Jesu mei')
First pub. (with an English translation by Father Ronald Knox) in *The Tablet*, 26 December 1936; reprinted *Note-Books* (1937), p. 255; collected *Poems* (1948); *Poems 4*, no. 178; Phillips, pp. 95–7.

HpG 6 Fair copy, revised, on a long thin strip of paper (recto only), headed 'A.M.D.G./In Festo Nativitatus/Ad Matrem Virginem/ Hymnus Eucharisticus'; [Christmas 1870?].

Campion Hall, Oxford, H.III(a).

HpG 7 Transcript by RB of lines 1–4, written *on* one page in MS A, in pencil.

Bodleian, Dep. Bridges 61, p. 254.

Ad Reverendum Patrem Fratrem Thomam Burke O.P. Collegium S. Beunonis invisentem ('Ignotum spatiari horto, discumbere mensis')
First pub. *Poems* (1948); *Poems 4*, no. 174; Phillips, pp. 129–30.

HpG 8 Fair copy, revised, in MS H, 2 pages (one leaf); dated 23 April 1877.

Bodleian, MS Eng. poet. d. 150, f. 71r–v (mounted on f. 72).

Aeschylus: Promêtheus Desmotês ('Divinity of air, fleet-feather'd gales')
First pub. *Note-Books* (1937), pp. 4–5; collected *Poems* (1948); *Poems 4*, no. 160; Phillips, pp. 6–7.

HpG 9 Fair copy, in Notebook B.II, ff. 39–40, rectos only (see HpG 464), headed 'Promêtheus Desmotês.'.

Campion Hall, Oxford.

HpG 10 Fair copy, revised, of lines 20–36, written on page 2 of a letter to E. H. Coleridge (containing also HpG 92, 151, 363), dated Oak Hill, Hampstead, 3 September 1862.

This MS printed in *Further Letters*, p. 6 (letter on pp. 5–14).

Texas.

The Alchemist in the City ('My window shews the travelling clouds')
First pub. *Note-Books* (1937), pp. 44–5; collected *Poems* (1948); *Poems 4*, no. 15; Phillips, pp. 65–6.

HpG 11 In Diary C.II (see HpG 457); dated 15 May 1865.

This MS mentioned *Journals*, p. 62.

Campion Hall, Oxford.

'Alget honos frondum silvis dependitus, alget'
First pub. Phillips (1986), p. 88.

HpG 12 Draft, on a leaf (containing also HpG 80, 81).

This MS found, according to Higgins, in Journal A.I (HpG 458) in 1947; *Journals* says it was found in Journal A.III.

Campion Hall, Oxford, P.IV(bi).

'All as that moth call'd Underwing, alighted'
First pub. *Journals* (1959), p. 51; *Poems 4*, no. 108, as beginning 'All as the moth...'; Phillips, p. 51.

HpG 13 In Diary C.II (see HpG 457); [November–December 1864].

Campion Hall, Oxford.

Andromeda ('Now Time's Andromeda on this rock rude')
First pub. *Poems* (1918); *Poems 4*, no. 50; Phillips, p. 148.

HpG 14 Fair copy, revised, followed by a few redrafted lines, headed 'A.M.D.G.', one page; dated Oxford, 12 August 1879.

Bodleian, MS Eng. poet. c. 48, f. 40.

HpG 15 Fair copy, revised by GMH and (in red) by RB, title on a scrap (p. 127) and text on one page (p. 128), in MS A; dated Oxford, 12 August 1879.

Bodleian, Dep. Bridges 61, pp. 127–8.

HpG 16 Fair copy, here entitled 'The Catholic Church Andromeda', signed, one page, annotated on verso by Hall Caine 'MS. sonnets apparently sent me by Rossetti'.

For a reproduction, see FACSIMILES. This MS not mentioned *Poems 4* or Phillips; it apparently was sent to Hall Caine for possible inclusion in an anthology (though Caine's annotation may be mistaken).

Princeton, Robert H. Taylor Collection.

HpG 17 Transcript by RB, revised by GMH, in MS B; dated (by GMH) Oxford, 1879, transcribed 1883.

Bodleian, MS Eng. poet. d. 149, f. 14.

'As it fell upon a day'
First pub. *Poems 4* (1967), no. 131; Phillips, p. 78.

HpG 18 In Diary C.II (see HpG 457), headed 'Katie, age 9. (Jan. 8, 1866.)'.

This MS printed *Journals*, p. 71.

Campion Hall, Oxford.

'As kingfishers catch fire, dragonflies draw flame'
First pub. *Poems* (1918); *Poems 4*, no. 57; Phillips, p. 129.

HpG 19 Drafts in MS H, 2 pages (one leaf containing also HpG 316).

Bodleian, MS Eng. poet. d. 150, f. 39r–v.

HpG 20 Transcript by RB, written in MS A.

Bodleian, Dep. Bridges 61, p. 236.

(Ashboughs) ('Not of all my eyes see, wándering on the world')
First pub. *Poems* (1918); *Poems 4*, no. 149; Phillips, pp. 177–8.

HpG 21 Draft, one page (f. 33) and fair copy, revised, one page of a leaf (f. 35) containing also HpG 148, 203, 230, 336, in MS H, both here untitled.

Bodleian, MS Eng. poet. d. 150, ff. 33, 35.

HpG 22 Transcript by RB, herc untitled, written in MS A.

Bodleian, Dep. Bridges 61, p. 224.

HpG 23 [entry deleted]

At the Wedding March ('God with honour hang your head')
First pub. *Poems* (1918); *Poems 4*, no. 52; Phillips, p. 150.

HpG 24 Draft, followed by fair copy, revised, both untitled and cancelled and both beginning 'God with worship hang your head', 2 pages (one leaf); draft dated Leigh, 21 October 1879, fair copy dated Bedford, 21 October 1879.

Bodleian, MS Eng. poet. c. 48, f. 43r–v.

HpG 25 Fair copy, originally entitled 'At a Wedding', revised in red by RB, one page, in MS A; dated Bedford, Lancashire, November 1879.

Bodleian, Dep. Bridges 61, p. 135.

HpG 26 Transcript by RB, here originally entitled 'At a wedding march', in MS B; dated (by GMH) Bedford, Lancashire, 21 October 1879, transcribed 1883.

Bodleian, MS Eng. poet. d. 149, p. 22.

'Atque tribus primum quod flumen fontibus exit', see HpG 103.

Barnfloor and Winepress ('Thou that on sin's wages starvest')
First pub. in *Union Review*, III (1865); reprinted *Lyra Sacra*, ed. H. C. Beeching (London, 1895); collected *Poems* (1930); *Poems 4*, no. 6; Phillips, pp. 25–6.

HpG 27 Draft, in Diary C.I (see HpG 456); [July 1864].

This MS mentioned *Journals*, p. 32.

Campion Hall, Oxford.

HpG 28 Transcript by V. S. S. Coles, in MS A, dated in pencil at the end by RB 'GMH 1865'; on 3 pages of 2 leaves (also containing HpG 133, 208), annotated at the end by RB in pencil 'written at Ball Coll: 1867(?)/copied by V. S. S. Coles'.

Bodleian, Dep. Bridgcs 61, pp. 144–6.

HpG 29 Transcript in an unidentified hand, including the epigraph from *Kings*, 2 pages (one leaf), annotated 'G. M. H. 1865.'.

Bodleian, MS Eng. poet. c. 48, ff. 21, 22.

The Beginning of the End ('My love is lessened and must soon be past')
First pub. 'Early Poems and Extracts from the Notebooks and Papers of Gerard Manley Hopkins', ed. H[umphry] H[ouse], *The Criterion*, October 1935; collected *Poems* (1948); *Poems 4*, no. 14; Phillips, pp. 64–5.

HpG 30 Early draft in Diary C.II (see HpG 457), including 5 lines beginning 'Some men hate their rivals and desire' following the first sonnet; 6–8 May 1865.

This MS printed *Note-Books*, pp. 43–4; the five lines are printed in *Journals*, p. 62 (where this MS is noted), *Poems 4*, p. 250 and Phillips, p. 319.

Campion Hall, Oxford.

HpG 31 Transcript of sonnets i and iii by RB in MS A, here entitled 'Two sonnets./"The beginning of the end."/(a neglected lover's address to his mistress.)'; annotated 'These two sonnets must *never* be printed RB–' and 'GMH. Ball Coll Oxf. [sent to the Corn hill Magazine & refused – RB'.

Bodleian, Dep. Bridges 61, p. 21.

'Bellisle! that is a fabling name, but we'
First pub. *Journals* (1959), p. 60; *Poems 4*, no. 116; Phillips, p. 63. This fragment is possibly a draft for 'To Oxford' (see HpG 332).

HpG 32 In Diary C.II (see HpG 457); [shortly after 24 April 1865].

Campion Hall, Oxford.

Binsey Poplars (‘My aspens dear, whose airy cages quelled’)
First pub. *Poems* (1918); *Poems 4*, no. 43; Phillips, pp. 142–3.

HpG 33 Draft, here beginning ‘My aspens dear whose cages quelled’, one page (verso of a printed notice for needlework classes at St Joseph’s Convent, Oxford); dated Oxford, 13 March 1879.

Bodleian, MS Eng. poet. c. 48, f. 35.

HpG 34 Draft, in MS H, here untitled and beginning variously ‘My aspens dear whose cages quelled’ and ‘The aspens dear that quelled the sun’, one page (on a leaf containing also HpG 70, 128, 318); dated 13 March 1879.

Bodleian, MS Eng. poet. d. 150, f. 51v (mounted on f. 52).

HpG 35 Fair copy, revised by GMH and (in red) by RB, in MS A; dated Oxford, March 1879.

Bodleian, Dep. Bridges 61, pp. 53–4.

HpG 36 Transcript by RB, revised by GMH, in MS B; dated by GMH Oxford, 1879, transcribed 1883.

Bodleian, MS Eng. poet. d. 149, f. 21.

The Blessed Virgin compared to the Air we Breathe (‘Wild air, world-mothering air’)
First pub. as ‘Mary Mother of Divine Grace Compared to the Air we Breathe’ in *A Book of Christmas Verse*, ed. H. C. Beeching (London, 1895); collected *Poems* (1918); *Poems 4*, no. 60; Phillips, pp. 158–61.

HpG 37 Fair copy, revised, in MS A, here entitled ‘Mary Mother of Divine Grace Compared to the Air we Breathe’, annotated by RB, 4 leaves (rectos only) mounted on pp. 157–60 and a scrap mounted on p. 161; dated Stonyhurst, May 1883.

Bodleian, Dep. Bridges 61, pp. 157–61.

HpG 38 Fair copy, in MS B; dated Stonyhurst, May 1883.

Bodleian, MS Eng. poet. d. 149, ff. 31v, 32v.

“‘Boughs being pruned, birds preenèd, show more fair’
First pub. *Note-Books* (1937), pp. 39–40; collected *Poems* (1948); *Poems 4*, no. 96, as ‘Seven Epigrams (vii)’; Phillips, p. 57.

HpG 39 In Diary C.II (see HpG 457); [December 1864–January 1865].

This MS noted *Journals*, p. 52.

Campion Hall, Oxford.

Brothers (‘How lovely the elder brother’s’)
First pub. *Poems* (1918); *Poems 4*, no. 54; Phillips, pp. 151–2.

HpG 40 Draft, here beginning ‘How lovely is <an> the elder brother’s’, one page; dated August 1880.

Bodleian, MS Eng. poet. c. 48, f. 44.

HpG 41 Two fair copies, revised in red by RB, in MS A, the first on scraps mounted on pp. 137–8, the second on 4 scraps mounted on pp. 139–40; both dated Hampstead, August 1880.

Bodleian, Dep. Bridges 61, pp. 137–40.

HpG 42 Fair copy of a variant version, enclosed with a letter to R. W. Dixon, Liverpool, 22 December 1880–16 January 1881 (containing also HpG 293); the poem is dated Hampstead, August 1880.

This MS (letter and verses) printed in *Correspondence with Dixon*, pp. 36–42 (letter), 174–5 (verses).

Bodleian, Dep. Bridges 93, ff. 53–4.

HpG 43 Fair copy of lines 1–4, in a letter (containing also HpG 294) to R. W. Dixon, Liverpool, 6–19 April 1881.

This MS (letter and verses) printed in *Correspondence with Dixon*, p. 49 (letter, 47–9).

Bodleian, Dep. Bridges 93, f. 57.

HpG 44 Transcript by RB, extensively revised by GMH, here originally beginning ‘How lovely is the elder brother’s’, in MS B; dated by GMH Hampstead, 1880, transcribed 1883.

Bodleian, MS Eng. poet. d. 149, ff. 22v–23.

The Bugler's First Communion ('A bugler boy from barrack (it is over the hill')
First pub. *Poems* (1918); *Poems 4*, no. 48; Phillips, pp. 146–8.

HpG 45 Fragmentary draft of stanzas 1–4, here untitled, in MS H, one page (one leaf containing also HpG 60).

Bodleian, MS Eng. poet. d. 150, f. 27v.

HpG 46 Draft, 5 pages (2 leaves, one folded and watermarked 1876, the other recto only); dated 'Oxford July 27(?) 1879'.

Bodleian, MS Eng. poet. c. 48, ff.36–8.

HpG 47 Fair copy, revised by GMH and (in red) by RB, in MS A, on scraps mounted on pp. 129–32; dated 'Oxford <Aug. 8> July 27(?) 1879'.

Bodleian, Dep. Bridges 61, pp. 129–32.

HpG 48 Transcript by RB, revised by GMH, in MS B; dated (by GMH) Oxford, 1879, transcribed 1883.

Bodleian, MS Eng. poet. d. 149, ff. 24–5.

'But if this overlast the day', see HpG 101.

'But what indeed is ask'd of me?'
First pub. *Journals* (1959), p. 62; *Poems 4*, no. 118; Phillips, p. 67. These lines possibly intended for 'The Voice of the World' (HpG 351).

HpG 49 In Diary C.II (see HpG 457); [15 May–24 June 1865].

Campion Hall, Oxford.

By Mrs Hopley ('He's wedded to his theory, they say')
First pub. *Journals* (1959), p. 37; *Poems 4*, no. 97; Phillips, p. 33.

HpG 50 Revised, in Diary C.I (see HpG 456); [August 1864].

Campion Hall, Oxford.

The Caged Skylark ('As a dare-gale skylark scanted in a dull cage')
First pub. *Poems* (1918); *Poems 4*, no. 39; Phillips, p. 133.

HpG 51 Fair copy, revised by GMH and (in red) by RB, in MS A, 2 scraps (one containing the title and a note on the rhythm mounted on p. 97, the other containing the text mounted on p. 98); dated by RB St Beuno's, 1877.

Bodleian, Dep. Bridges 61, pp. 97–8.

HpG 52 Transcript by RB, revised by GMH, in MS B; dated (by GMH) St Beuno's, 1877, transcribed 1883.

Bodleian, MS Eng. poet. d. 149, f. 11.

HpG 53 Lines 12–14, in a letter to RB, Hampstead, 8 August 1877.

This MS printed *Letters to RB*, pp. 42–3.

Bodleian, Dep. Bridges 91, f. 73.

The Candle Indoors ('Some candle clear burns somewhere I come by.')
First pub. *The Poets and the Poetry of the Century*, ed. Alfred H. Miles (London, [1893]); *Poems 4*, no. 46; Phillips, p. 144.

HpG 54 Drafts, cancelled, here beginning 'Some candle clear shines somewhere I come by.', 2 pages (one leaf), annotated '(common rhythm counterpointed)'.

Bodleian, MS Eng. poet. c. 48, f. 41r–v.

HpG 55 Fair copy, revised by GMH and (in red) by RB, in MS A, one page (mounted); Oxford, 1879.

Bodleian, Dep. Bridges 61, p. 122.

HpG 56 Transcript by RB, revised by GMH, annotated by GMH 'Companion to no. 6 ["The Lantern out of doors"]', in MS B; dated (by GMH) Oxford, 1879, transcribed 1883.

Bodleian, MS Eng. poet. d. 149, f. 13.

Caradoc's Soliloquy ('My héart, where have we been? What have we séen, my mind?'), see HpG 105–7.

(Carrion Comfort) ('Not, I'll not, carrion comfort, Despair, not feast on thee')
First pub. *Poems* (1918); *Poems 4*, no. 64; Phillips, p. 168.

HpG 57 Successive drafts, originally f. 29 in MS H (now removed), here untitled and beginning (first draft) 'Out, carrion comfort, despair! not, I'll not feast on thee', 2 pages (one leaf containing also HpG 270, 338); c. August 1885.

Bodleian, MS Eng. misc. a. 23, f. 21ar–v.

HpG 58 Draft of lines 1–12 in MS H, here untitled, one leaf (containing also HpG 212, 347); [probably 1887].

Bodleian, MS Eng. poet. d. 150, f. 31r–v (mounted f. 32).

HpG 59 Transcript by RB in MS A, here entitled as above and annotated '(my title R. B.)'; dated August 1885.

Bodleian, Dep. Bridges 61, p. 218 (annotations on p. 217).

Castara Victrix, for fragments of the unfinished play, see HpG 68, 99.

Cheery Beggar ('Beyond Magdalen and by the Bridge, on a place called there the Plain')
First pub. *Poems* (1918); *Poems 4*, no. 142; Phillips, p. 146.

HpG 60 Draft, here first beginning 'Past Magdalen Bridge, at a place called there the Plain' and then 'Past Magdalen and by that Bridge, on a place called there the Plain', in MS H, one page (on a leaf containing also HpG 45).

Bodleian, MS Eng. poet. d. 150, f. 27.

HpG 61 Transcript by Monica Bridges, one page, written in MS A; annotated by RB 'copied Jan. 1918. M. M. B.'.

Bodleian, Dep. Bridges 61, p. 248.

A Complaint ('I thought that you would have written: my birthday came and went')
First pub. *Poems* (1948); *Poems 4*, no. 128; Phillips, pp. 76–7.

HpG 62 Fair copy, 2 leaves (rectos only) mounted in MS A, on paper embossed 'Oxford Union Society', annotated by RB 'must not be printed RB'; watermarked 1865.

Bodleian, Dep. Bridges 61, pp. 67–8.

HpG 63 Fair copy (the family's copy), 2 pages (one leaf).

Bodleian, MS Eng. poet. c. 48, f. 24r–v.

'Confirmed beauty will not bear a stress; —'
First pub. *Journals* (1959), pp. 60–1; *Poems 4*, no. 117; Phillips, pp. 63–4.

HpG 64 In Diary C.II (see HpG 457); [27–30 April 1865].

Campion Hall, Oxford.

Continuation of R. Garnett's *Nix* ('She mark'd where I and Fabian met')
First pub. *Note-Books* (1937), p. 361; *Poems 4*, no. 120; Phillips, p. 69.

HpG 65 In Diary C.II (see HpG 457); [7–9 July 1865].

This MS printed *Journals*, p. 64.

Campion Hall, Oxford.

Cywydd ('Y mae'n llewyn yma'n llon')
First pub. (with an English translation) W. H. Gardner, 'G. Manley Hopkins as a Cywyddwr', *Transactions of the Honourable Society of Cymmrodorion* (Session 1940–1); collected *Poems* (1948); *Poems 4*, no. 172; Phillips, pp. 120–1.

HpG 66 Fair copy, revised, including the introductory note, in MS H, 2 pages (one leaf); dated 'Brân Maenefa a'i cant Ebrill y pedwerydd ar hugain 1876' ('Brân Maenefa sang this April the twenty-fourth 1876').

Bodleian, MS Eng. poet. d. 150, f. 67v–r.

HpG 67 Transcript in an unidentified hand, on p.[77] of an album (containing also HpG 5, 269), made up for presentation to Dr James Brown, first Bishop of Shrewsbury, on his Episcopal Silver Jubilee, July 1876.

This transcript and album discussed in Alfred Thomas, S.J., 'G. M. Hopkins and the Silver Jubilee Album', *The Library*, 5 Ser 20 (1965), 148–52; not mentioned *Poems 4*.

Unlocated (according to *The Library* in 1965, the album was preserved at St Beuno's College in Wales which was joined to Heythrop College, London, in 1970; however, Heythrop College reports (1988) that the album is not in their collection).

Daphne ('Who loves me here and has my love')
First pub. *Journals* (1959), p. 68; *Poems 4*, no. 124; Phillips, p. 71. These lines intended for the unfinished play 'Castara Victrix' (see HpG 99).

HpG 68 In Diary C.II (see HpG 457); dated 1 September 1865.

Campion Hall, Oxford.

(Dawn) ('In more precision now of light and dark')
First pub. *Journals* (1959), pp. 55–6; *Poems 4*, no. 98, as '(Sundry Fragments and Images)', nos. xxx–xxxi (pp. 139–40); Phillips, p. 58.

HpG 69 In Diary C.II (see HpG 457); [January 1865].

Campion Hall, Oxford.

'Denis,/whose motionable, alert, most vaulting wit'
First pub. *Poems* (1918); *Poems 4*, no. 143; Phillips, p. 140.

HpG 70 Draft, in MS H, one page (on a leaf containing also HpG 34, 128, 318).

Bodleian, MS Eng. poet. d. 150, f. 51 (mounted on f. 52).

'Did Helen steal my love from me?'
First pub. *Journals* (1959), p. 36; *Poems 4*, no. 95; Phillips, p. 31.

HpG 71 In Diary C.I (see HpG 456); [August 1864].

Campion Hall, Oxford.

'Distance/Dappled with diminish'd trees'
First pub. *Journals* (1959), p. 31; *Poems 4*, no. 98, as '(Sundry Fragments and Images)', no. viii (p. 135); Phillips, p. 25.

HpG 72 In Diary C.I (see HpG 456); [22–5 July 1864].

Campion Hall, Oxford.

Duns Scotus's Oxford ('Towery city and branchy between towers')
First pub. *Poems* (1918); *Poems 4*, no. 44; Phillips, p. 142.

HpG 73 Fair copy, revised, in MS A, title on a scrap (mounted on p. 117), text on one page (mounted on p. 118); dated Oxford, March 1879.

Bodleian, Dep. Bridges 61, pp. 117–18.

HpG 74 Transcript by RB in MS B; dated (by GMH) Oxford, 1878, transcribed 1883.

Bodleian, MS Eng. poet. d. 149, f. 12.

'During the eastering of untainted morns'
First pub. *Journals* (1959), p. 30; *Poems 4*, no. 84; Phillips, p. 24.

HpG 75 In Diary C.I (see HpG 456); [18–22 July 1864].

Campion Hall, Oxford.

Easter ('Break the box and shed the nard')
First pub. *Poems* (1930); *Poems 4*, no. 24; Phillips, pp. 83–4.

HpG 76 Fair copy, 2 pages (folded leaf containing also HpG 214); [1866?].

Campion Hall, Oxford, H.II(b).

HpG 77 Transcript by RB, written in MS A, one page.

Bodleian, Dep. Bridges 61, p. 252.

Easter Communion ('Pure fasted faces draw unto this feast:')
First pub. *Note-Books* (1937), p. 47; collected *Poems* (1948); *Poems 4*, no. 11; Phillips, p. 60.

HpG 78 Draft and fair copy, revised, in Diary C.II (see HpG 457); draft of [2–12 March 1865], fair copy dated Lent 1865 [26 June].

The draft is printed *Journals* (1959), p. 57 (fair copy noted p. 63).

Campion Hall, Oxford.

Ecquis binas ('O for a pair like turtles wear')
First pub. *Poems 4* (1967), p. 323; Phillips, p. 88.

HpG 79 Drafts of a translation of the opening of a Latin hymn, one page, following three lines beginning 'How well Thou comfortest!', found (according to Higgins) in Journal A.I (see HpG 458), in 1947; c. 1867–8.

The three lines (a translation from the Latin hymn 'Veni Sanctis Spiritus') printed Phillips, p. 325; according to *Journals*, this MS was found in Journal A.III.

Campion Hall, Oxford, P.IV(g).

Elegiacs: *Tristi tu, memini* ('Tristi tu, memini, virgo cum sorte fuisti')
First pub. *Poems* (1948); *Poems 4*, no. 163; Phillips, p. 88.

HpG 80 MSS found (according to Higgins) in Journal A.I (see HpG 458) in 1947: (1) draft, one page (on a leaf containing also HpG 12, 81) (P.IV(bi)); (2) fair copy, revised, of a 4-line version, one page, written over the beginning of a draft letter to RB (on a leaf containing also HpG 245 and 6 lines beginning 'Ac tu me madidis noli vexare querellis:') (P.IV(biii)).

The 4-line version printed *Poems 4*, p. 320 and Phillips, p. 325; the finished (sent) letter to RB (of 30 August 1867) is printed *Letters to RB*, pp. 16–17; according to *Journals*, these MSS were found in Journal A.III.

Campion Hall, Oxford, P.IV(bi and biii).

Elegiacs: after *The Convent Threshold* ('Fraterno nobis interluit unda cruore')
First pub. *Poems* (1948); *Poems 4*, no. 164: Phillips, pp. 89–90.

HpG 81 MSS found (according to Higgins) in Journal A.I (see HpG 458) in 1947: (1) fair copy, revised, here untitled, 2 pages (one leaf) (P.IV(c)); (2) draft of lines 23–4, on verso of a leaf containing also HpG 12, 80 (P.IV(bi)); (3) drafts (mostly cancelled) of lines 13–18 and other unidentified lines, 2 pages (one leaf) (P.IV(bii)).

According to *Journals*, these MSS were found in Journal A.III.

Campion Hall, Oxford, P.IV(bii and c).

The Elopement ('All slumbered whom our rud red tiles')
These lines were originally contributed to a handwritten weekly journal (each issue in 3 copies) edited by J. Scott Stokes and two pupils of the fifth form of the Oratory School, Birmingham; it was called 'The Early Bird' or 'The Tuesday Tomtit' and only a few issues appeared, the first on 18 February 1866. All copies have disappeared but these verses are included in the essay 'Early Magazines', *The Oratory School Magazine*, November 1895; *Poems 4*, no. 135; Phillips, pp. 94–5. For lines 19–22, see HpG 322.

Epithalamion ('Hark, hearer, hear what I do; lend a thought now, make believe')
First pub. *Poems* (1918); *Poems 4*, no. 159; Phillips, pp. 179–80.

HpG 82 Drafts, in MS H, here untitled and beginning (first) '<Do what I do> <Like me now> Dear hearer, hear what I do [and, neither cancelled] my listener, listen with me, make believe', containing an explanatory note by RB (signed) at top, 5 leaves (4 leaves of Royal University of Ireland examination paper containing text in ink on rectos only of 3 (ff. 7, 9, 11) and recto and verso of fourth (f. 13r–v) and fifth leaf folded containing 3 pages of rough pencil notes (f. 14r–v)), mounted on ff. 8, 10, 12, 15; [1888].

Two additional lines pub. 'Gerard Manley Hopkins', a letter to the editor by Norman White, *TLS*, 22 August 1968.

Bodleian, MS Eng. poet. d. 150, ff. 7, 9, 11, 13–14v.

HpG 83 Draft, here beginning 'Do like me, my listener; make believe', in pencil and ink, 4 pages (one leaf).

Bodleian, MS Eng. poet. c. 48, f. 50r–v.

The Escorial ('There is a massy pile above the waste')
First pub. G. F. Lahey, *Gerard Manley Hopkins* (London, 1930) (extracts only); first pub. in full *Poems* (1930); *Poems 4*, no. 1; Phillips, pp. 1–5.

HpG 84 Transcript by Manley Hopkins, GMH's father, including accompanying notes on the text in GMH's hand, on 9 leaves of a booklet (f. 1 being the title page, ff. 2–9 containing the text on the rectos and notes on the versos), annotated at the top in an unidentified hand '*The Escorial*. Won the prize. Easter 1860'.

The notes are printed *Poems 4*, pp. 245–6 and in Phillips, pp. 1–5.

Bodleian, MS Eng. poet. c. 48, f. 1–9.

Felix Randal ('Félix Rándal the fárrier, O is he déad then? my dúty all énded')
First pub. *Poems* (1918); *Poems 4*, no. 53; Phillips, p. 150.

HpG 85 Fair copy, revised in red by RB, in MS A, on mounted scraps; dated 'Liverpool. April 28 1880'.

Bodleian, Dep. Bridges 61, pp. 133–4.

HpG 86 Fair copy, revised, added to MS B by RB after GMH's death, one page (mounted on f. 51); dated 'April 28 1880, Liverpool.'.

Bodleian, MS Eng. poet. d. 149, f. 50.

HpG 87 Transcript by RB, revised by GMH, in MS B; dated (by GMH) 1880, transcribed 1883.

Bodleian, MS Eng. poet. d. 149, f. 14v.

Floris in Italy, for fragments, see HpG 100, 145.

For a Picture of Saint Dorothea ('I bear a basket lined with grass')
First pub. *Poems* (1918); *Poems 4*, no. 10; Phillips, p. 48. For another version, see HpG 177; for a dramatic version, see HpG 255; for related stanzas, see HpG 1.

HpG 88 Here untitled, in Diary C.II (see HpG 457), on a leaf cut out of the Diary, found by Fr Bischoff in 1947 and now restored to the volume; [November? 1864].

This MS noted in *Journals*, p. 50.

Campion Hall, Oxford.

HpG 89 Fair copy, in MS A, 2 pages (one leaf); annotated by RB.

Bodleian, Dep. Bridges 61, pp. 292–3.

HpG 90 Fair copy, 2 pages (one leaf containing also HpG 130).

Bodleian, MS Eng. poet. c. 48, f. 25r–v.

HpG 91 Transcript by Digby Mackworth Dolben of a version similar to HpG 88, in a notebook containing also HpG 131.

For a brief discussion, see *Journals*, p. 326.

Northamptonshire Record Office, Northampton, Dolben Collection 2.

A fragment of anything you like ('Fair, but of fairness as a vision dream'd')
First pub. J. M. G. Blakiston, 'An Unpublished Hopkins Letter', *TLS*, 25 September 1948; collected *Poems* (1956); *Poems 4*, no. 79; Phillips, p. 11.

HpG 92 Fair copy, on page 6 of a letter to E. H. Coleridge (containing also HpG 10, 151, 363), dated Oak Hill, Hampstead, 3 September 1862.

This MS printed *Further Letters*, p. 13 (letter, 5–14).

Texas.

Fragment of *Stephen and Barberie* ('— She by a sycamore')
First pub. *Journals* (1959), p. 52; *Poems 4*, no. 111; Phillips, pp. 56–7.

HpG 93 In Diary C.II (see HpG 457); [December 1864–January 1865].

Campion Hall, Oxford.

(Fragments) ('How looks the night? There does not miss a star.')
Two of these seven fragments (nos. iv–v) first pub. *Note-Books* (1937), p. 32; no. i first pub. *Poems* (1948); the other four first pub. *Journals* (1959), pp. 43–4, 46–7; *Poems 4*, no. 98, as '(Sundry Fragments and Images)', nos. xxii–xxvi, xii–xiii (pp. 138–9, 136); Phillips, pp. 39–40.

HpG 94 In Diary C.II (see HpG 457); [September 1864].

Fragment no. i noted in *Journals*, p. 44.

Campion Hall, Oxford.

(Fragments) ('The ends of the crisp buds she chips')
These six fragments first pub. *Journals* (1959), pp. 48, 50; *Poems 4*, no. 98, as '(Sundry Fragments and Images)', nos. xiv–xv, xxvii–xxviii, xxxv (pp. 136–7, 139–40) and (no. iv beginning 'Although she be more white') as a fragment possibly connected to 'Io' (p. 303) (see HpG 164); Phillips, p. 47.

HpG 95 In Diary C.II (see HpG 457); [October–November 1864].

Campion Hall, Oxford.

(Fragments) ('The sun just risen')
No. i of these two fragments first pub. *Note-Books* (1937), p. 41; both pub. *Journals* (1959), pp. 58–9; *Poems 4*, no. 98, as '(Sundry Fragments and Images)', nos xxxiv and xxxvii (p. 140); Phillips, pp. 61–2.

HpG 96 In Diary C.II (see HpG 457); [March–April 1865].

Campion Hall, Oxford.

(Fragments) ('The wind, that passes by so fleet')
These four fragments first pub. *Journals* (1959), pp. 9, 18, 20, 22; *Poems 4*, no. 98, as '(Sundry Fragments and Images)', nos i, vii, xxxii and xxxiii (pp. 134–5, 140); Phillips, p. 17.

HpG 97 Four fragments in Diary C.I (see HpG 456): no. i (beginning as above) cancelled in pencil, probably by GMH, [late 1863]; no. ii (beginning 'Whose braggart 'scutcheon, whose complaisant crest') included in a prose synopsis of a (projected?) prose work on the theme of Sophocles's Ajax, [February? 1864]; no. iii (beginning 'The sparky air'), included in a prose note dated 19 March 1864; no. iv (beginning '— on their brittle green quils'), [10–14 April 1864].

Campion Hall, Oxford.

(Fragments) ('Thick-fleeced bushes like a heifer's ear.')
These five fragments first pub. *Journals* (1959), pp. 38–9; *Poems 4*, no. 98, as '(Sundry Fragments and Images)', nos. xi, iv–vi (pp. 135–6) and (no. iv beginning '... in her cheeks that dwell') as a fragment possibly connected to 'Io' (p. 303) (see HpG 164); Phillips, pp. 34–5.

HpG 98 Five fragments in Diary C.I (see HpG 456), the first with two alternative first lines, neither cancelled (as above and 'Out-fleeced bushes like a spaniel's ear.'); [August–September 1864].

Campion Hall, Oxford.

Fragments of *Castara Victrix* ('What was it we should strike the road again?')
First pub. *Journals* (1959), pp. 68–70; *Poems 4*, no. 125; Phillips, pp. 72–3. For other lines intended for this unfinished play, see HpG 68.

HpG 99 In Diary C.II (see HpG 457); dated September 1865.

Campion Hall, Oxford.

Fragments of *Floris in Italy* ('It does amaze me, when the clicking hour')
One of these fragments (iii) first pub. *Note-Books* (1937), pp. 50–1; collected *Poems* (1948); the two other (reconstructed) verse fragments and two prose fragments first pub. *Journals* (1959), pp. 40–3, 44–6; the three verse fragments collected *Poems 4*, no. 102 and, with the prose scenes as well, Phillips, pp. 36–9 and 186–9 (see also pp. 314–15). For another possible fragment, see HpG 145.

HpG 100 In Diaries C.I and C.II (see HpG 456–7); [c. August 1864–September 1865].

Campion Hall, Oxford.

Fragments of *Pilate* ('Unchill'd I handle stinging snow')
First pub. *Note-Books* (1937), pp. 12–15; collected *Poems* (1948); *Poems 4*, no. 80 (where the text begins 'The pang of Tartarus, Christians hold'); Phillips, pp. 18–20.

HpG 101 Drafts in Diary C.I (see HpG 456) and fair copy of last 2½ stanzas in Diary C.II (see HpG 457), the next entry (on a leaf cut out of the Diary, found by Fr Bischoff in 1947 and now restored to the volume) being 4 lines beginning 'But if this overlast the day' possibly for *Pilate*; [June and October 1864].

These MSS noted *Journals*, pp. 25, 49 (the four lines printed p. 49).

Campion Hall, Oxford.

Fragments of *Richard* ('As void as clouds that house and harbour none')
One of the fragments (iv) first pub. *Note-Books* (1937), p. 48; the whole first pub. *Poems* (1948); *Poems 4*, no. 107; Phillips, pp. 49–51. For a first draft, see HpG 252.

HpG 102 Four fragments in Diary C.II (see HpG 457); i and ii dating from [October–November? 1864], iii–iv from [16–24 July 1865].

These MSS noted *Journals*, pp. 51 (i–ii), 65 (iii–iv).

Campion Hall, Oxford.

Fragments on St Winefred ('Iam si rite sequor prisci vestigia facti')
These three fragments first pub. in the Notes to 'In S. Winefridam' in *Poems 4* (1967), p. 334 (without title); Phillips, p. 103.

HpG 103 Drafts of three Latin fragments, the first beginning as above, the second and third beginning 'Quin etiam nostros non aspernata labores' and 'Atque tribus primum quod flumen fontibus exit', in MS H, 3 pages (one leaf), following the opening of a letter in Latin to a fellow Jesuit.

Bodleian, MS Eng. poet. d. 150, ff. 68–9 (mounted on f. 70).

'From any hedgerow, any copse'
First pub. *Journals* (1959), p. 57; *Poems 4*, no. 98, as '(Sundry Fragments and Images)', no. xviii (p. 137); Phillips, p. 61.

HpG 104 In Diary C.II (see HpG 457); [March 1865].

Campion Hall, Oxford.

From *St Winefred's Well* ('What is it, Gwen, my girl? why do you hover and haunt me?')
First pub. *Poems* (1918); *Poems 4*, no. 152, as 'St Winefred's Well'; Phillips, pp. 161–5.

HpG 105 Drafts of Act II, lines 1–30 (or 'Caradoc's Soliloquy'), on ff. [9, 21] of the Dublin Notebook (HpG 468); [late 1884 or early 1885].

Campion Hall, Oxford.

HpG 106 Transcript by Kate Hopkins, GMH's mother, 9 leaves (rectos only), annotated at end 'The above sent to me at my request April 85 as sample of metre....RSB April. 85.' and (also by RB) 'Sample C very imperfect dramatically, I feel; but it may serve as an exercise of versification/G. M. H.'.

Transcribed from MS A; Bischoff, p. 563 gives the hand as Manley Hopkins's.

Bodleian, MS Eng. poet. c. 48, ff. 52–60 (rectos only).

HpG 107 Transcript by Monica Bridges, in MS A, on scraps and leaves (mounted), both annotations in HpG 106 transcribed here as well.

Bodleian, Dep. Bridges 61, pp. 161–7.

(From the Greek) ('Love me as I love thee. O double sweet!'), see HpG 184.

'Glimmer'd along the square-cut steep.'
First pub. *Journals* (1959), p. 35; *Poems 4*, no. 92; Phillips, p. 29.

HpG 108 In Diary C.I (see HpG 456) (the first 9 lines on a half-page torn from the Diary, found by Fr Bischoff in 1947 and restored to the volume); [14 August 1864 or shortly after].

For a discussion, see *Journals*, p. xvii.

Campion Hall, Oxford.

God's Grandeur ('The world is charged with the grandeur of God.')
First pub. *Lyra Sacra*, ed. H. C. Beeching (London, 1895); collected *Poems* (1918); *Poems 4*, no. 31; Phillips, p. 128.

HpG 109 Fair copy, revised, here entitled 'Sonnet', followed by a second beginning (including lines 1–3, 5, 13), one page; dated 23 February 1877.

Bodleian, MS Eng. poet. c. 48, f. 29.

HpG 110 In MS A: (1) fair copy, revised by GMH and (in red) by RB, here untitled, one page (mounted on p. 82), dated 'St Beuno's [in RB's hand] Feb. 23 1877. [in GMH's hand]'; (2) fair copy, revised, title and note concerning the rhythm on a scrap (mounted p. 83), text on one page (mounted p. 84), dated March 1877.

Bodleian, Dep. Bridges 61, pp. 82–4.

HpG 111 Fair copy, revised, here entitled 'Sonnet', one page (containing also HpG 299) as sent to his mother, Kate Hopkins, together with the envelope postmarked St Asaph, 3 March 1877.

This MS printed (with facsimile) in *Further Letters*, pp. 144–5.

Bodleian, MS Eng. lett. e. 41, f. 43.

HpG 112 Transcript by RB, revised by GMH, here originally entitled 'God's Greatness', in MS B; dated (by GMH) St Beuno's, February 1877, transcribed 1883.

Bodleian, MS Eng. poet. d. 149, f. 8.

The Habit of Perfection ('Elected Silence, sing to me')
First pub. *The Poets and the Poetry of the Century*, ed. Alfred H. Miles (London, [1893]); collected *Poems* (1918); *Poems 4*, no. 22; Phillips, pp. 80–1.

HpG 113 Fair copy, slightly revised, subtitled '(The Novice)', in MS A, on scraps mounted; dated 'Jan. 18, 19. 1866.'.

This MS printed Claude Colleer Abbott, 'Gerard Manley Hopkins: A Letter and Drafts of Early Poems', *Durham University Journal*, 32 (1939–40), 71–2.

Bodleian, Dep. Bridges 61, pp. 289–90.

HpG 114 Fair copy, revised, in MS A, 2 leaves (rectos only) mounted; [later than January 1866].

Bodleian, Dep. Bridges 61, pp. 65–6.

HpG 115 Fair copy, here entitled 'The Kind Betrothal', tipped into the copy of *Poems* (1918) (containing also HpG 177) presented by RB to Fr Geoffrey Bliss, the MS originally given to Fr Bacon 'about the year 1870 or 1871' (so annotated).

This MS not mentioned *Poems 4* or Phillips; printed Claude Colleer Abbott, 'Gerard Manley Hopkins: A Letter and Drafts of Early Poems', *Durham University Journal*, 32 (1939–40), 73.

Stonyhurst College, Lancashire, T. 3. 15.

HpG 116 Transcript of a variant version by Fr Francis Bacon, S.J., here entitled 'The Kind Betrothal', one page numbered 1 (together with HpG 178, 450).

Campion Hall, Oxford, H.I(a).

'Haec te jubent salvere, quod possunt, loca'
First pub. (in facsimile) *Poems* (1918) (lines 7–10 only); first pub. in full *Poems 4* (1967), no. 176; Phillips, p. 97.

HpG 117 Revised, in MS H, on 3 scraps, the verso of the first (f. 86v) containing notes on meaning beginning, after false start, 'To mean means to be a mean term between thought and things...'.

Facsimile of lines 7–10 in *Poems* (1918), between pp. 70 and [71].

Bodleian, MS Eng. poet. d. 150, ff. 86, 87, 88r–v.

The Half-way House ('Love I was shewn upon the mountain-side')
First pub. *Note-Books* (1937), p. 52; collected *Poems* (1948); *Poems 4*, no. 20; Phillips, p. 76.

HpG 118 In Diary C.II (see HpG 457); [c. October 1865].

This MS noted *Journals*, p. 71.

Campion Hall, Oxford.

The Handsome Heart: at a gracious answer ('"But tell me child, your choice, your fancy; what to buy')
First pub. *The Spirit of Man*, ed. Robert Bridges (London, New York, Bombay, Calcutta and Madras, 1916); collected *Poems* (1918); *Poems 4*, no. 47; Phillips, pp. 144–5.

HpG 119 Draft, in MS H, here untitled and beginning '"But tell me child, your choice; what shall I buy', one page (on a leaf containing also HpG 352).

Bodleian, MS Eng. poet. d. 150, f. 41 (mounted on f. 43).

HpG 120 Two fair copies, revised, in MS A, both beginning '"But tell me child, your choice; what shall I buy': (1) on 4 scraps (mounted p. 124), dated Oxford, 1879; (2) here untitled, one page (mounted p. 126), dated Oxford, 1879.

Facsimile of title and last 2 stanzas of (1) in *Poems* (1918), between pp. 70 and [71].

Bodleian, Dep. Bridges 61, pp. 124, 126.

HpG 121 Transcript by RB, here beginning '"But tell me child, your choice; What shall I buy', in MS B, cancelled and annotated by GMH 'See later'; transcribed 1883.

This version represents RB's composite version (as printed *Poems 4* and Phillips, pp. 360–1).

Bodleian, MS Eng. poet. d. 149, f. 13v.

HpG 122 Two fair copies written in MS B after the 1883 transcripts: (1) extensively revised, cancelled and annotated 'See later', dated 'Oxford. 18[–]' (f. 28v); (2) dated Oxford, 1879 (f. 35v).

Bodleian, MS Eng. poet. d. 149, ff. 28v, 35v.

HpG 123 Transcripts by RB of three versions, all here untitled, beginning (first) '"But tell me child, your choice; what shall I buy', (second) '"But tell me child, your choice; what shall we buy' and (third) as above, on the verso of a letter from Everard Hopkins to RB, 19 December 1917.

Bodleian, Dep. Bridges 62, f. 33.

Harry Ploughman ('Hard as hurdle arms, with a broth of goldish flue')
First pub. *Poems* (1918); *Poems 4*, no. 71; Phillips, p. 177.

HpG 124 Fair copy, revised, here subtitled '(sonnet, with interpolated burden-lines: sprung rhythm).', one page (on a leaf containing also HpG 343); dated Dromore, September 1887.

This is possibly the MS originally enclosed in the letter to Richard Watson Dixon of 22 December 1887 (see *Correspondence with Dixon*, p. 153).

British Library, Add. MS 42711, f. 154.

HpG 125 Fair copy, revised, in MS A, on scraps (mounted), followed by notes on stress marks; dated Dromore, September 1887, sent to RB, 11 October 1887.

Facsimile in *Letters to RB*, between pp. 62 and 63.

Bodleian, Dep. Bridges 61, pp. 183–4.

HpG 126 Fair copy, revised, written in MS B after the 1883 transcripts; dated Dromore, September 1887.

Bodleian, MS Eng. poet. d. 149, f. 37.

'He hath abolished the old drouth'
First pub. *Note-Books* (1937), p. 26; collected *Poems* (1948); *Poems 4*, no. 8; Phillips, p. 27.

HpG 127 In Diary C.I (see HpG 456), immediately following (and possibly part of) 'New Readings' (HpG 207); [July 1864].

This MS noted *Journals*, p. 32.

Campion Hall, Oxford.

'He mightbe slow and something feckless first'
First pub. 'Gerard Manley Hopkins', a letter to the editor by Norman White, *TLS*, 22 August 1968; Phillips, p. 141.

HpG 128 Draft of 3 lines, in MS H, one page (on a leaf containing also HpG 34, 70, 318).

Bodleian, MS Eng. poet. d. 150, f. 51v (mounted on f. 52).

Heaven-Haven ('I have desired to go')
First pub. *Lyra Sacra*, ed. H. C. Beeching (London, 1895); collected *Poems* (1918); *Poems 4*, no. 9; Phillips, p. 27.

HpG 129 Early version, here entitled 'Rest', in Diary C.I (see HpG 456); [July 1864].

This MS printed *Note-Books*, p. 27 and *Journals*, p. 33.

Campion Hall, Oxford.

HpG 130 Fair copy of an early version, here entitled 'Fair Havens — The Nunnery', one page (on a leaf containing also HpG 90).

This MS printed *Poems 4*, p. 248.

Bodleian, MS Eng. poet. c. 48, f. 25v.

HpG 131 Transcript of an early version by Digby Mackworth Dolben, here entitled 'Fair Havens; or The Convent', in a notebook containing also HpG 91.

See *Journals*, p. 326 for a brief discussion.

Northamptonshire Record Office, Northampton, Dolben Collection 2.

HpG 132 Fair copy, including the subtitle, in MS A, annotated by RB 'This later than autograph in H' and including variants added in pencil by RB.

Bodleian, Dep. Bridges 61, p. 64.

HpG 133 Transcript by V. S. S. Coles, in MS A, here untitled, one page (of 2 leaves containing also HpG 28, 208), annotated by RB in pencil 'written at Ball Coll: 1867 (?)/copied by VSS Coles'.

Bodleian, Dep. Bridges 61, p. 144.

Henry Purcell ('Have fáir fállen, O fáir, fáir have fallen, so déar')
First pub. *Poems* (1918); *Poems 4*, no. 45; Phillips, p. 143.

HpG 134 Fair copy, revised in red by RB, in MS A, title, introductory note and RB's notes on one scrap (p. 119), text on one page (mounted on p. 120); dated Oxford, April 1879.

Bodleian, Dep. Bridges 61, pp. 119–20.

HpG 135 Transcript by RB, revised by GMH, in MS B; dated (by GMH) Oxford, 1879, transcribed 1883.

Bodleian, MS Eng. poet. d. 149, f. 12v.

'Her prime of life — cut down too soon'
First pub. *Journals* (1959), p. 35; not in *Poems 4*; Phillips, p. 31.

HpG 136 In Diary C.I (see HpG 456); [August 1864].

Campion Hall, Oxford.

'— Hill,/Heaven and every field, are still'
First pub. *Journals* (1959), p. 31; *Poems 4*, no. 85; Phillips, p. 24.

HpG 137 In Diary C.I (see HpG 456); [18–22 July 1864].

Campion Hall, Oxford.

'Hope holds to Christ the mind's own mirror out'
First pub. *Poems* (1918); *Poems 4*, no. 151; Phillips, pp. 127–8.

HpG 138 Draft, in MS H, 2 pages (one scrap apparently torn from the Dublin Notebook (HpG 468)); [1884–5].

For two additional lines, see 'Gerard Manley Hopkins', a letter to the editor by Norman White, *TLS*, 22 August 1968; see also *Poems 4*, p. xlix.

Bodleian, MS Eng. poet. d. 150, f. 106r–v (mounted f. 109).

Horace: *Odi profanum volgus et arceo* ('Tread back — and back, the lewd and lay! —')
First pub. *America*, 26 September 1947; collected *Poems* (1948); *Poems 4*, no. 166; Phillips, pp. 92–4.

HpG 139 Draft, 7 pages (4 leaves, the first also containing HpG 216 and the beginning of a letter to Laura [Hodges], written at the Oratory, Edgbaston, [September 1867–Easter 1868] and the second containing a 9-line fragmentary prose note), found, according to Higgins, in Journal A.I (see HpG 458) in 1947.

The letter and the note printed *Journals*, p. 534 (where the MSS are said to have been found in Journal A.III).

Campion Hall, Oxford, P.IV(e).

Horace: *Persicos odi, puer, apparatus* ('Ah child, no Persian-perfect art!')
First pub. *America*, 26 September 1947; collected *Poems* (1948); *Poems 4*, no. 165; Phillips, p. 92.

HpG 140 Draft, here untitled, found (according to Higgins) in Journal A.I (HpG 458) in 1947, one page (the verso containing an imperfect fragment of a draft letter written at the Oratory, Edgbaston, [November 1867–Easter 1868]).

The letter is printed *Journals*, p. 534 (where the MS is said to have been found in Journal A.III).

Campion Hall, Oxford, P.IV(d).

'How all is one way wrought!'
First pub. (facsimile only) *Poems* (1918); *Poems 4*, no. 148, as '(On a Piece of Music)'; Phillips, pp. 145–6.

HpG 141 Drafts, here untitled, in MS H, 3 pages (2 leaves, one (f. 99) containing also HpG 436 and the other (f. 100v) containing a note to GMH from Walter Pater dated 20 May [1879]).

Facsimile in *Poems* (1918), between pp. 92 and [93].

Bodleian, MS Eng. poet. d. 150, ff. 99–100v (mounted on f. 101).

'How well Thou comfortest!', see HpG 79.

Hurrahing in Harvest ('Summer ends now; now, barbarous in beauty, the stooks rise')
First pub. *Poems* (1918); *Poems 4*, no. 38; Phillips, p. 134.

HpG 142 Draft, here originally entitled 'Sonnet in Harvest', revised to 'Heart's Hurrahing in Harvest', here originally beginning 'It is harvest: now, barbarous in beauty...', 2 pages (one leaf); dated Vale of Clwyd, 1 September 1877.

Bodleian, MS Eng. poet. c. 48, f. 32r–v.

HpG 143 Fair copy, revised by GMH and (in red) by RB, in MS A, annotated by RB '"The Hurrahing sonnet was the outcome of ½ an hour of extreme enthusiasm as I walked home alone one day from fishing in the Elwy"/Winter 1878'; dated Vale of Clwyd, 1 September 1877.

Bodleian, Dep. Bridges 61, pp. 45–6.

HpG 144 Transcript by RB, revised by GMH, in MS B; dated (by GMH) Vale of Clwyd, 1 September 1877, transcribed 1883.

Bodleian, MS Eng. poet. d. 149, f. 7v.

'— I am like a slip of comet'
First pub. 'Early Poems and Extracts from the Notebooks and Papers of Gerard Manley Hopkins', ed. Humphry House, *Criterion*, October 1935; collected *Poems* (1948); *Poems 4*, no. 103; Phillips, p. 40. This fragment possibly intended for *Floris in Italy* (see HpG 100).

HpG 145 Draft, in Diary C.II (see HpG 457); [13–14 September 1864].

This MS printed *Note-Books*, p. 30 and noted *Journals*, p. 46.

Campion Hall, Oxford.

'I hear a noise of waters drawn away'
First pub. *Journals* (1959), p. 54; *Poems 4*, no. 112; Phillips, p. 57.

HpG 146 In Diary C.II (see HpG 457); [February 1865].

Campion Hall, Oxford.

'I must hunt down the prize'
First pub. *Note-Books* (1937), p. 27; collected *Poems* (1948); *Poems 4*, no. 88; Phillips, p. 28.

HpG 147 In Diary C.I (see HpG 456); [25 July–1 August 1864].

This MS noted *Journals*, p. 33.

Campion Hall, Oxford.

'I wake and feel the fell of dark, not day.'
First pub. *Poems* (1918); *Poems 4*, no. 67; Phillips, p. 166.

HpG 148 Fair copy, revised, in MS H, one leaf (containing also HpG 21, 203, 230, 336).

Bodleian, MS Eng. poet. d. 150, f. 35r–v.

HpG 149 Version of lines 9–14 only, in MS H, one page (containing also HpG 303).

Bodleian, MS Eng. poet. d. 150, f. 47.

HpG 150 Transcript by RB, one page, in MS A.

Bodleian, Dep. Bridges 61, p. 228.

'Iam si rite sequor prisci vestigia facti', see HpG 103.

Il Mystico ('Hence sensual gross desires')
First pub. J. M. G. Blakiston, 'An Unpublished Hopkins Letter', *TLS*, 25 September 1948; collected *Poems* (1956); *Poems 4*, no. 77; Phillips, pp. 7–10.

HpG 151 Fair copy, on 3 pages of a letter to E. H. Coleridge (containing also HpG 10, 92, 363), dated Oak Hill, Hampstead, 3 September 1862.

This MS printed *Further Letters*, pp. 9–13.

Texas.

'In all things beautiful, I cannot see' ('Nempe ea formosa est: adeo omne quod aut facit aut fit'), see HpG 253.

In honour of St Alphonsus Rodriguez ('Glory is a flame off exploit, so we say')
First pub. *Poems* (1918); *Poems 4*, no. 73, beginning 'Honour is flashed off exploit, so we say'; Phillips, p. 182.

HpG 152 Three versions: (1) two successive pencil drafts, on pp. 2–4 of a folded leaf (ff. 46v–47v, the first page (f. 46) being a letter *to* Hopkins from D. [B.?] Dunne of 28 September 1898), both here untitled, the first beginning 'Honour shd. flower from exploit, so we say' and the second 'Honour should flash from exploit, so we say', the second dated 28 September 1880; (2) fair copy, revised, here entitled '*In honour of St Alphonsus Rodriguez* Lay brother...upon the first falling of his feast after his <glory> canonisation/For the College of Palma in the Island of Majorca, where the saint lived for 40 years as Hall Porter', on pp. 1 and 3 of a folded leaf of Catholic Union of Ireland, Dublin, notepaper; watermarked 1878.

The fair copy serves as copy text in Phillips.

Bodleian, MS Eng. poet. c. 48, ff. 46v–47v, 48, 49.

HpG 153 Here untitled and beginning 'Honour should flash from exploit, so we say', in a letter to RB, Dublin, 3 October 1888.

This MS printed *Letters to RB*, pp. 292–4 (verses, 293).

Bodleian, Dep. Bridges 92, f. 189r–v.

HpG 154 Fair copy, revised, here entitled 'In honour of St Alphonsus Rodriguez lay brother of the Society of Jesus upon the first falling of his feast after his canonisation' and beginning 'Honour is flashed off exploit, so we say', in MS B, one page (a leaf inserted by RB after GMH's death).

This MS serves as copy text in *Poems 4*; it is printed in Phillips, p. 387.

Bodleian, MS Eng. poet. d. 149, f. 45 (mounted on f. 46).

In S. Winefridam ('Temperat aestiva fessis sua balnea membris')
This translation into Latin of 'On St Winefred' (see HpG 224) first pub. *Poems 4* (1967), no. 175; Phillips, p. 103. For related fragments, see HpG 103.

HpG 155 Revised, headed 'A.M.D.G.' and subscribed 'L.D.S.'.

According to Bischoff, p. 562, this MS was removed from MS H by Gerard Hopkins (GMH's nephew) and presented to Sister Mary Roberta Melchner of Malden, Massachussetts.

Loyola-Notre Dame Library (serving the College of Notre Dame of Maryland, Baltimore).

'In the staring darkness'
First pub. *Poems 4* (1967), no. 132; Phillips, p. 78.

HpG 156 In Diary C.II (see HpG 457), following HpG 18, annotated 'Grace (8). (same day.)'; dated 8 January 1866.

This MS printed *Journals*, p. 72.

Campion Hall, Oxford.

In the Valley of the Elwy ('I remember a house where all were good')
First pub. *The Spirit of Man*, ed. Robert Bridges (London, 1918); *Poems 4*, no. 34; Phillips, pp. 131–2.

HpG 157 Fair copy, revised in red by RB, in MS A, one page, together with RB's transcript of GMH's note on the poem, one page (p. 99); dated St Beuno's, 1877.

Bodleian, Dep. Bridges 61, pp. 99–100.

HpG 158 Fair copy, revised, subtitled '(sprung and counterpointed)', one page (on a leaf containing also HpG 288), probably sent to Grace Hopkins to be set to music by her; dated 23 May 1877.

Referred to as 'Lady Pooley's MS' in *Poems 4* and Phillips; sold in Lady Pooley's sale at Sotheby's, 13 July 1966 as Lot 678; Bump, HA2; see Norman Mackenzie, 'Gerard and Grace Hopkins', *The Month*, June 1965, 347–50.

Texas.

HpG 159 Transcript by RB, revised by GMH, in MS B, annotated by GMH 'For the companion to this see no. 26 [i.e., "Ribblesdale"]'; dated (by GMH) 'As above. 1877', transcribed 1883.

Bodleian, MS Eng. poet. d. 149, f. 11v.

In Theclam Virginem ('Longa victa die, cum multo pulvere rerum')
This Latin translation of 'St Thecla' (HpG 256) first pub. *Poems* (1956); *Poems 4*, no. 180; Phillips, p. 123.

HpG 160 Fair copy, these lines facing the English version (HpG 256).

Archives of the Irish Province of the Society of Jesus, Dublin.

Inundatio Oxoniana ('Verna diu saevas senserunt pascua nubes')
First pub. *Poems* (1948); *Poems 4*, no. 162; Phillips, pp. 87–8.

HpG 161 Fair copy, revised, 2 pages (one folded leaf), signed, annotated 'Mr Hopkins' in an unidentified hand, found (according to Higgins) in Journal A.I (HpG 458); probably written 1865.

Journals says this MS was found in Journal A.III.

Campion Hall, Oxford, P.IV(a).

Inversnaid ('This dárksome búrn, hórseback brówn')
First pub. *The Poets and the Poetry of the Century*, ed. Alfred H. Miles (London, [1893]); collected *Poems* (1918); *Poems 4*, no. 56; Phillips, p. 153. For a related fragment, see HpG 222.

HpG 162 Fair copy, revised, here entitled 'Inversnaid Sept. 28 1881', on 3 pages of a little booklet (mounted in MS H on f. 20) the first page of which (f. 16) is the beginning of a musical setting for the hymn '*Adoro te supplex Latens deitas*'.

Bodleian, MS Eng. poet. d. 150, ff. 17–18.

HpG 163 Transcript by RB, here entitled 'Inversnaid Sept. 28 1881', in MS A; annotated 'copied from GMH's MS./Oct 18 '89 by RB'.

Bodleian, Dep. Bridges 61, p. 210.

Io ('Forward she leans, with hollowing back, stock-still')
First pub. *Poems* (1956); *Poems 4*, no. 99; Phillips, p. 34. For possibly related fragments, see HpG 95, 98.

HpG 164 Revised, in Diary C.I (see HpG 456), a fragmentary variant of lines 11–12 being in Diary C.II (see HpG 457); [September 1864 and later].

The fragmentary variant of lines 11–12 printed in *Poems 4*, p. 303, Phillips, p. 313 and *Journals*, p. 48 (see also p. 38).

Campion Hall, Oxford.

'It was a hard thing to undo this knot.'
First pub. *Note-Books* (1937), p. 28; collected *Poems* (1948); *Poems 4*, no. 91; Phillips, p. 29.

HpG 165 In Diary C.I (see HpG 456), subscribed 'Maentwrog'; [early August 1864].

This MS noted *Journals*, p. 34.

Campion Hall, Oxford.

Jesu Dulcis Memoria ('Jesus to cast one thought upon')
First pub. 'Jesu dulcis memoria: an unpublished translation by Gerard Manley Hopkins, S.J.', *Letters and Notices* (private domestic publication of the English Jesuits), September 1947; collected *Poems* (1948); *Poems 4*, no. 167 (7 stanzas); revised version in Phillips, pp. 86–7 (10 stanzas).

HpG 166 Drafts, here untitled, in pencil and ink, 5 pages (2 leaves, one folded, also containing some (unpublished) notes on logic), found (according to Higgins) in Journal A.I (see HpG 458) in 1947.

According to *Journals*, this MS was found in Journal A.III.

Campion Hall, Oxford, P.IV(f).

Justus quidem tu es, Domine ('Thou art indeed just, Lord, if I contend')
First pub. *The Poets and the Poetry of the Century*, ed. Alfred H. Miles (London, [1893]) (partial text); first pub. in full *Poems* (1918); *Poems 4*, no. 74; Phillips, p. 183.

HpG 167 Three successive drafts (the first two cancelled), including the Latin epigraph and beginning (variously) 'Just art thou, O my God, should I contend', 'Just thou art, indeed, my God, should I contend' and 'Thou art indeed just, Lord, would I contend', in MS H; one draft dated 17 March 1889.

Bodleian, MS Eng. poet. d. 150, ff. 110v–11v (mounted f. 112).

HpG 168 Fair copy, revised, including the Latin epigraph, one page, mounted in MS A; dated 17 March 1889.

Bodleian, Dep. Bridges 61, p. 194.

HpG 169 Revised, including the Latin epigraph, one page, mounted (on f. 53) in MS B; dated 17 March 1889.

Facsimile in Croft, *Autograph Poetry*, No. 142.

Bodleian, MS Eng. poet. d. 149, f. 52.

The Lantern out of Doors ('Sometimes a lantern moves along the night.')
First pub. *Poems* (1918); *Poems 4*, no. 40; Phillips, p.134.

HpG 170 Fair copy, revised in red by RB, in MS A, one page.

Bodleian, Dep. Bridges 61, p. 88.

HpG 171 Transcript by RB, revised by GMH, in MS B, annotated by GMH 'For the companion to this see no. 13 [i.e., "The Candle Indoors"]'; dated (by GMH) St Beuno's, 1877, transcribed 1883.

Bodleian, MS Eng. poet. d. 149, f. 9v.

'Late I fell in the ecstasy'
First pub. *Journals* (1959), p. 35; *Poems 4*, no. 93 (together with HpG 327); Phillips, p. 30 (as a separate poem).

HpG 172 In Diary C.I (see HpG 456); [mid-August 1864].

Campion Hall, Oxford.

The Leaden Echo and the Golden Echo ('How to keep — is there ány any, is there none such, nowhere known some, bow or brooch or braid or brace, lace, latch or catch or key to keep')
First pub. *Poems* (1918); *Poems 4*, no. 59; Phillips, pp. 155–6.

HpG 173 Fair copy, extensively revised in red by RB, GMH's first line (before revisions) reads 'How to keep — O is there any any, is there nowhere known...', in MS A, on scraps (mounted); dated Stonyhurst, 13 October 1882.

Bodleian, Dep. Bridges 61, pp. 149–53.

HpG 174 Transcript by RB, revised by GMH, in MS B; dated (by GMH) Hampstead, 1881, transcribed 1883.

Bodleian, MS Eng. poet. d. 149, ff. 25v–27.

'Let me be to Thee as the circling bird'
First pub. *Note-Books* (1937), pp. 52–3; collected *Poems* (1948); *Poems 4*, no. 19; Phillips, p. 75.

HpG 175 In Diary C.II (see HpG 457); 22 October 1865.

This MS noted *Journals*, p. 71.

Campion Hall, Oxford.

'Like shuttles fleet the clouds, and after'
First pub. *Journals* (1959), p. 36; *Poems 4*, no. 98, as '(Sundry Fragments and Images)', no. iii (p. 135); Phillips, p. 32.

HpG 176 In Diary C.I (see HpG 456); [August 1864].

Campion Hall, Oxford.

Lines for a Picture of St Dorothea ('I bear a basket lined with grass.')
First pub. *Poems* (1930); *Poems 4*, no. 25; Phillips, pp. 84–5. For another version, see HpG 88; for a dramatic version, see HpG 255; for related stanzas, see HpG 1.

HpG 177 Fair copy, tipped into a copy of *Poems* (1918) (containing also HpG 115) presented by RB to Fr Geoffrey Bliss; the MS originally given to Fr Bacon 'after the year 1884' (so annotated).

Stonyhurst College, Lancashire, T. 3. 15.

HpG 178 Transcript by Fr Francis Bacon, S.J., 2 leaves numbered 2–3 (rectos only) (together with HpG 116, 450).

Campion Hall, Oxford, H.I(b).

The Loss of the Eurydice ('The Eurydice — it concerned thee, O Lord:')
First pub. *Poems* (1918); *Poems 4*, no. 41; Phillips, pp. 135–8.

HpG 179 Fair copy, written in MS B after 1883; dated 'Mount St Mary's, Derbyshire. April 1878'.

Bodleian, MS Eng. poet. d. 149, ff. 30–3 (rectos only), 34r–v.

HpG 180 Lines 73–84, in a letter to RB, 2 April 1878.

This MS printed *Letters to RB*, pp. 47–9 and Phillips, pp. 229–30.

Bodleian, Dep. Bridges 91, ff. 84v–85.

HpG 181 Lines 1–2, 9–10 and 77–80 (and discussions of other lines), in a letter to RB, Stonyhurst, 30 May 1878.

This MS printed *Letters to RB*, pp. 52–5 and Phillips, pp. 232–4.

Bodleian, Dep. Bridges 91, f. 92r–v.

HpG 182 Fair copy, revised, of lines 113–20, on a scrap; signed 'G. M. H. April 1878/Mount St Mary's, Spink Hall, Derbyshire'.

This MS not mentioned in *Poems 4* or Phillips; listed in Bump, HA3.

Texas.

HpG 183 Transcript by RB (revised in red and annotated by him), in MS A, signed 'GMH. April 1878.'

Bodleian, Dep. Bridges 61, pp. 107–16.

'Love me as I love thee. O double sweet!'
First pub. *Poems* (1948); *Poems 4*, no. 161, as '(From the Greek)'; Phillips, p. 62.

HpG 184 In Diary C.II (see HpG 457); [March 1865].

This MS noted *Journals*, p. 58.

Campion Hall, Oxford.

Love preparing to fly ('He play'd his wings as though for flight')
First pub. *Journals* (1959), p. 31; *Poems 4*, no. 87; Phillips, p. 25.

HpG 185 Draft, in Diary C.I (see HpG 456); [22–5 July 1864].

Campion Hall, Oxford.

The Lover's Stars ('The destined lover, whom his stars')
First pub. *Journals* (1959), pp. 29–30; *Poems 4*, no. 83; Phillips, pp. 23–4.

HpG 186 Drafts, here untitled, in Diary C.I (see HpG 456); including a second version of stanza 2; [16–18 July 1864].

The second version of stanza 2 printed *Journals*, p. 30, *Poems 4*, p. 299 and Phillips, p. 310. Facsimiles of stanza 3 in *Journals*, Figure 19 and Thornton, p. 55.

Campion Hall, Oxford.

(Margaret Clitheroe) ('God's counsel cólumnar-severe')
First pub. *Poems* (1930); *Poems 4*, no. 145; Phillips, pp. 125–7.

HpG 187 Fair copy, revised, of lines 1–21 and cancelled draft of lines 1–5, on a scrap (f. 104), together with drafts of lines 22–61, on 3 pages of a folded leaf (ff. 102–3), here untitled, in MS H.

Bodleian, MS Eng. poet. d. 150, ff. 102–3, 104 (mounted f. 105).

(May Lines) ('O praedestinata bis')
First pub. *Poems* (1948); *Poems 4*, no. 179; Phillips, p. 98.

HpG 188 Fair copy, slightly revised, here untitled but including the Latin epigraph, headed 'A.M.D.G. et B.M.V.' and subscribed 'L.D.S.', in MS H, 2 pages (one folded leaf).

Bodleian, MS Eng. poet. d. 150, ff. 113, 114.

HpG 189 Transcript in an unidentified hand, revised, in pencil, in MS A, here untitled but including the Latin epigraph, headed 'A.M.D.G et B.M.V.' and subscribed 'L.D.S.', annotated by RB, '[?] MS no sign of authorship [externally?] looks as if copied from an original which had dipthongs...'.

This transcript not mentioned *Poems 4* or Phillips.

Bodleian, Dep. Bridges 61, pp. 55–6.

The May Magnificat ('May is Mary's month, and I')
First pub. *Poems* (1918); *Poems 4*, no. 42; Phillips, pp. 139–40.

HpG 190 Fair copy, revised, in MS A; dated Stonyhurst, May 1878.

Bodleian, Dep. Bridges 61, pp. 49–50.

HpG 191 Fair copy, revised, in MS B, on 3 pages of a leaf (mounted f. 49), annotated at the end 'I wrote it at Stonyhurst May 1878 for the statue at the College but it did not pass'.

Bodleian, MS Eng. poet. d. 149, ff. 47–8.

HpG 192 Fair copy, written in MS B after the 1883 transcripts; dated Stonyhurst, May 1878.

Bodleian, MS Eng. poet. d. 149, f. 30v.

'Miror surgentem per puram Oriona noctem'
First pub. *Poems 4* (1967), no. 177; Phillips, p. 104.

HpG 193 Pencil draft, in MS H, 2 pages (one leaf); New Year's Day [1876?].

Bodleian, MS Eng. poet. d. 150, f. 89r–v (mounted f. 90).

'Miss Story's character! too much you ask'
First pub. *Poems* (1956); *Poems 4*, no. 94; Phillips, pp.30–1.

HpG 194 Draft, in Diary C.I (see HpG 456); [August–September 1864].

This MS noted *Journals*, pp. 35, 317.

Campion Hall, Oxford.

'Moonless darkness stands between.'
First pub. *Poems* (1948); *Poems 4*, no. 129; Phillips, p. 77.

HpG 195 In Diary C.II (see HpG 457); [25 December 1865].

This MS noted *Journals*, p. 71.

Campion Hall, Oxford.

Moonrise June 19 1876 ('I awoke in the midsummer not-to-call night,/in the white and the walk of the morning:')
First pub. *Poems* (1918); *Poems 4*, no. 137; Phillips, p. 121.

HpG 196 Fair copy, revised, followed by drafts of line 1, in MS H, one page.

Bodleian, MS Eng. poet. d. 150, f. 21 (mounted f. 22).

HpG 197 Transcript by RB, in MS A; annotated 'copied Oct 89'.

Bodleian, Dep. Bridges 61, p. 214.

Morning, Midday and Evening Sacrifice ('The dappled die-away')
First pub. *The Bible Birthday Book*, comp. Richard Watson Dixon (London, 1887) (first stanza only); first pub. in full *Lyra Sacra*, ed. H. C. Beeching (London, 1895); collected *Poems* (1918); *Poems 4*, no. 49; Phillips, pp. 148–9.

HpG 198 Draft, here untitled, 2 pages (one leaf); dated Oxford, 1879.

Bodleian, MS Eng. poet. c. 48, f. 39r–v.

HpG 199 Fair copy, revised in red by RB, in MS A, 2 leaves (rectos only); dated Oxford, August 1879.

Facsimile of stanza 1 printed *Poems* (1918), between pp. 70 and [71].

Bodleian, Dep. Bridges 61, pp. 105–6.

HpG 200 Fair copy, one minor revision, one page; dated Oxford, summer 1879.

This MS not mentioned *Poems 4* or Phillips; it was sold in the sale of Lady Pooley's papers at Sotheby's, 13 July 1966, Lot 677; listed in Bump, HA4; see Norman Mackenzie, 'Gerard and Grace Hopkins', *The Month*, June 1965, pp. 347–50.

Texas.

HpG 201 Transcript by RB, revised by GMH, in MS B; dated (by GMH) Oxford, 1879, transcribed 1883.

Bodleian, MS Eng. poet. d. 149, f. 21v.

'Mothers are doubtless happier for their babes'
First pub. *Journals* (1959), p. 67; *Poems 4*, no. 123; Phillips, p. 71.

HpG 202 In Diary C.II (see HpG 457); [August 1865].

Campion Hall, Oxford.

'My own heart let me more have pity on; let'
First pub. *Poems* (1918); *Poems 4*, no. 69; Phillips, p. 170.

HpG 203 Fair copy, revised, in MS H, one page (on a leaf containing also HpG 21, 148, 230, 336).

Bodleian, MS Eng. poet. d. 150, f. 35v.

HpG 204 Transcript by RB, revised by him in red, here beginning 'My own heart let me have more pity on; let', in MS A.

Bodleian, Dep. Bridges 61, p. 232.

'My prayers must meet a brazen heaven'
First pub. *Note-Books* (1937), pp. 49–50; collected *Poems* (1948); *Poems 4*, no. 18; Phillips, p. 74.

HpG 205 In Diary C.II (see HpG 457); dated 7 September 1865.

This MS noted *Journals*, p. 70.

Campion Hall, Oxford.

'Myself unholy, from myself unholy'
First pub. *Poems* (1948); *Poems 4*, no. 16; Phillips, p. 67.

HpG 206 Draft, in Diary C.II (see HpG 457); dated 24 June 1865.

This MS noted (and cancelled variants printed) in *Journals*, p. 63.

Campion Hall, Oxford.

New Readings ('Although the letter said')
First pub. 'Early Poems and Extracts from the Notebooks and Papers of Gerard Manley Hopkins', ed. Humphry House, *Criterion*, October 1935; collected *Poems* (1948); *Poems 4*, no. 7; Phillips, pp. 26–7. See HpG 127 for possible continuation.

HpG 207 Early draft, here beginning 'Altho' God's word has said', in Diary C.I (see HpG 456); [July 1864].

This MS printed in *Note-Books*, p. 26 and *Journals*, p. 32.

Campion Hall, Oxford.

HpG 208 Transcript by V. S. S. Coles, in MS A, 2 pages (one of 2 leaves of transcripts containing also HpG 28, 133), annotated in pencil by RB 'written at Ball Coll: 1867(?)/copied by VSS Coles'.

Bodleian, Dep. Bridges 61, pp. 146–7.

The Nightingale ('"From nine o'clock till morning light')
First pub. *Poems* (1930); *Poems 4*, no. 21; Phillips, pp. 79–80.

HpG 209 Fair copy, revised, 2 pages (one leaf); dated 'Jan. 18, 19. 1866.'.

Bodleian, MS Eng. poet. c. 48, f. 23r–v.

HpG 210 Transcript by RB, in pencil, in MS A; dated 'Jan 18. 19. 1866 –'.

Bodleian, Dep. Bridges 61, pp. 257–9.

'No, they are come; their horn is lifted up'
First pub. *Note-Books* (1937), p. 31; collected *Poems* (1948); *Poems 4*, no. 104; Phillips, p. 41.

HpG 211 Draft, in Diary C.II (see HpG 457); [September 1864].

This MS noted (and a few lines printed) in *Journals*, p. 46.

Campion Hall, Oxford.

'No worst, there is none. Pitched past pitch of grief'
First pub. *Poems* (1918); *Poems 4*, no. 65; Phillips, p. 167.

HpG 212 Draft, in MS H, including false starts beginning 'No worst, there is none: grief past pitch of grief' and 'Worst! No worst, o there is none. Grief past grief', one leaf (containing also HpG 58, 347).

Bodleian, MS Eng. poet. d. 150, f. 31r–v (mounted f. 32).

HpG 213 Transcript by RB, in MS A.

Bodleian, Dep. Bridges 61, p. 222.

Nondum ('God, though to Thee our psalm we raise')
First pub. *The Month*, September 1915; collected *Poems* (1930); *Poems 4*, no. 23; Phillips, pp. 81–3. The first publication was based on a MS 'found in a second-hand classical book, lately purchased in Dublin...in the handwriting of Father Gerard Hopkins S.J....'; no such book has come to light.

HpG 214 Fair copy, including the epigraph from *Isaiah*, 3 pages (3 folded leaves containing also HpG 76); dated Lent 1866.

Campion Hall, Oxford, H.II(a).

HpG 215 Transcript by RB, in MS A, headed 'from an autog. of GMH.'; dated in pencil 'Lent 1866' and annotated 'copied May 191[5 or 8]'.

Bodleian, Dep. Bridges 61, pp. 250–1.

'Not kind! to freeze me with forecast'
First pub. *Poems 4* (1967), no. 134; Phillips, p. 92.

HpG 216 One page, containing also HpG 139 and the beginning of a letter to Laura [Hodges] written at the Oratory, Edgbaston, [September 1867–Easter 1868]; found (according to Higgins) in Journal A.I (see HpG 458) in 1947.

The letter printed *Journals*, p. 534 (where the MS is said to have been found in Journal A.III).

Campion Hall, Oxford, P.IV(e).

'Now I am minded to take pipe in hand'
First pub. *Note-Books* (1937), pp. 31–2; collected *Poems* (1948); *Poems 4*, no. 105; Phillips, p. 41.

HpG 217 In Diary C.II (see HpG 457); [after 14 September 1864].

This MS noted *Journals*, p. 46.

Campion Hall, Oxford.

'O Death, Death, He is come.'
First pub. *Journals* (1959), p. 58; *Poems 4*, no. 115; Phillips, p. 61.

HpG 218 In Diary C.II (see HpG 457); [c. 10–11 March 1865].

Campion Hall, Oxford.

O Deus, ego amo te ('O God, I love thee, I love thee —')
First pub. *Poems* (1930); *Poems 4*, no. 170; Phillips, p. 100. For a Welsh version, see HpG 223.

HpG 219 Three MSS in MS H: (1) draft, here entitled '*St Francis Xavier's Hymn*' and beginning 'My God, I love thee, I love thee', 3 pages (one leaf) (ff. 60–1); (2) fair copy, revised, here entitled 'St Francis Xavier's Hymn', one page (on a leaf containing also the original Latin lines) (f. 58r–v, mounted on f. 59); (3) fair copy, slightly revised, one page (on a leaf containing also HpG 257) (f. 74v).

Bodleian, MS Eng. poet. d. 150, ff. 58r–v, 60–1, 74v.

HpG 220 Transcript by RB, headed 'Translation of S. Francis Xavier's hymn/O Deus, ego amo te.', annotated 'no date', in MS A.

Bodleian, Dep. Bridges 61, p. 242.

'O what a silence is this wilderness!'
First pub. *Journals* (1959), pp. 66–7; *Poems 4*, no. 122; Phillips, p. 70.

HpG 221 In Diary C.II (see HpG 457); [August 1865].

Campion Hall, Oxford.

'O where is it, the wilderness'
First pub. *Letters to RB* (1935), pp. 73–4; not in *Poems 4*; Phillips, p. 140. These lines possibly intended for 'Inversnaid' (see HpG 162–3).

HpG 222 In the 25 February section of a letter to RB, Oxford, 22–5 February 1879.

The letter printed *Letters to RB*, pp. 67–74.

Bodleian, Dep. Bridges 91, f. 122v.

Ochenaid Sant Francis Xavier, Apostol yr Indiad
('Nid, am i Ti fy ngwared i')
First pub. *Poems* (1948); *Poems 4*, no. 171, as 'The Same (Welsh Version)' (following 'O Deus, ego amo te'); Phillips, p. 125. For the English version, see HpG 219–20. The Welsh title means 'The Sigh of St Francis Xavier, Apostle of the Indians'.

HpG 223 Transcript by Robert Bridges?, one page.

Bodleian, MS Eng. poet. c. 48, f. 61.

(On a Piece of Music) ('How all's to one thing wrought!'), see HpG 141.

On St Winefred ('As wishing all about us sweet')
First pub. *Poems* (1930); *Poems 4*, no. 139; Phillips, p. 102. For a Latin translation, see HpG 155.

HpG 224 Fair copy, in MS H, headed 'A.M.D.G.' and subscribed 'L.D.S.', one page.

Bodleian, MS Eng. poet. d. 150, f. 63 (mounted f. 64).

On the Portrait of Two Beautiful Young People
('O I admire and sorrow! The heart's eye grieves')
First pub. *Poems* (1918); *Poems 4*, no. 157; Phillips, pp. 176–7.

HpG 225 In MS H: (1) successive drafts and revised fair copies, 4 pages (one leaf), annotated by RB 'I have a *MS* finished to end of IX stanzas Xmas 86 RB' (ff. 93–4v); (2) fair copy of stanzas 1–2, 7 and two discarded stanzas (beginning 'Two men wrestle who shall ride a mare, bestrid'), here untitled, one page (on a leaf of University College Dublin notepaper) (f. 96); (3) draft lines, here untitled, one page (f. 97).

The two discarded stanzas pub. 'Gerard Manley Hopkins', a letter to the editor by Norman White, *TLS*, 22 August 1968; see also Norman Mackenzie's reply in *TLS*, 26 September 1968.

Bodleian, MS Eng. poet. d. 150, ff. 93–4v (mounted f. 95), 96, 97 (mounted f. 98).

HpG 226 Fair copy, revised, in MS A, 4 pages (one folded leaf of University College Dublin notepaper); dated Monasterevan, Co. Kildare, Christmas 1886.

Bodleian, Dep. Bridges 61, p. 180.

'Or else their cooings came from bays of trees'
First pub. *Journals* (1959), p. 34; *Poems 4*, no. 98, as '(Sundry Fragments and Images)', no. ii (p. 134); Phillips, p. 29.

HpG 227 In Diary C.I (see HpG 456), signed 'Maentwrog'; [1–14 August 1864].

Campion Hall, Oxford.

Oratio Patris Condren: O Jesu vivens in Maria ('Jesu that dost in Mary dwell')
First pub. *Poems* (1930); *Poems 4*, no. 169; Phillips, p. 95.

HpG 228 Fair copy, revised, here entitled '*To Jesus living in Mary* a prayer by Fr Condren of the French Congregation of the Oratory of St Philip Neri', in MS B, one page (on a folded leaf mounted on f. 42, p. 3 of which contains the original Latin in GMH's hand).

Bodleian, MS Eng. poet. d. 149, f. 40.

HpG 229 Three fair copies, revised, in MS H: (1) one page (on a leaf containing also HpG 257) (f. 76v); (2) 2 leaves (rectos only) containing the original Latin followed by the translation here entitled '*To Jesus living in Mary* a prayer of Fr Condren of the French Oratory of St Philip Neri' (ff. 80, 81); (3) here untitled, in pencil, on small scrap, dated on verso (in an unidentified hand) 4 June (f. 82v).

Bodleian, MS Eng. poet. d. 150, ff. 76v, 80, 81, 82v.

'Patience, hard thing! the hard thing but to pray'
First pub. *Poems* (1918); *Poems 4*, no. 68; Phillips, p. 170.

HpG 230 Fair copy, revised, in MS H, one page (on a leaf containing also HpG 21, 148, 203, 336).

Bodleian, MS Eng. poet. d. 150, f. 35v.

HpG 231 Transcript by RB, in MS A.

Bodleian, Dep. Bridges 61, p. 230.

Peace ('When will you ever, Peace, wild wooddove, shy wings shut')
First pub. *Poems* (1918); *Poems 4*, no. 51; Phillips, p. 149.

HpG 232 Fair copy, revised, here beginning 'When will you ever, Peace, shy wooddove, wild wings shut', one page; dated Oxford, 2 October 1879.

Bodleian, MS Eng. poet. c. 48, f. 42.

HpG 233 Fair copy, revised, written in MS B after the 1883 transcripts; dated Oxford, 1879.

Bodleian, MS Eng. poet. d. 149, f. 29.

HpG 234 Fair copy, in MS A, one page; dated Oxford, 1879.

Bodleian, Dep. Bridges 61, p. 77.

The peacock's eye ('Mark you how the peacock's eye')
First pub. *Poems* (1956); *Poems 4*, no. 86; Phillips, p. 25.

HpG 235 Two versions, the second annotated 'Overloaded, apparently', in Diary C.I (see HpG 456); [22–5 July 1864].

The first version of this MS printed *Journals*, p. 31, *Poems 4*, p. 300 and Phillips, p. 310.

Campion Hall, Oxford.

Penmaen Pool ('Who long for rest, who look for pleasure')
First pub. *Poems* (1918); *Poems 4*, no. 30; Phillips, pp. 123–5.

HpG 236 Fair copy, revised, including the subtitle and beginning 'Who long for rest, who look for leisure', one page (mounted on f. 44), in MS B; dated 'Barmouth, Merionethshire. Aug. 1876'.

Bodleian, MS Eng. poet. d. 149, f. 43.

HpG 237 Version, including a variant stanza 9.

This MS not mentioned *Poems 4* or Phillips; mentioned (and variant stanza 9 printed) in Norman Mackenzie, 'The Lost Autograph of "The Wreck of the Deutschland" and its First Readers', *HQ*, 3 (1976), 91–115 (note 10).

College of the Holy Cross, Worcester, Massachusetts.

HpG 238 Transcript by RB, here untitled and beginning 'Who longs for rest, who looks for pleasure', written in MS A; dated August 1876.

Bodleian, Dep. Bridges 61, pp. 101–4.

HpG 239 Transcript in an unidentified hand, here untitled and beginning 'Who longs for rest, who looks for pleasure', revisions and one stanza in GMH's hand, 3 pages (one leaf), dated August 1876; followed by a transcript by Fr Francis Bacon, 2 pages (one leaf), dated Barmouth, Merionethshire, August 1876.

The transcript by Fr Bacon is listed Bischoff, p. 575 (discovered in 1947).

Campion Hall, Oxford, H.I(e).

Pied Beauty ('Glory be to God for dappled things —')
First pub. *Poems* (1918); *Poems 4*, no. 37; Phillips, pp.132–3.

HpG 240 Fair copy, in MS A; dated St Beuno's, Tremeirchion, summer 1877.

Bodleian, Dep. Bridges 61, pp. 47–8.

HpG 241 Transcript by RB, in MS B; dated (by GMH) St Beuno's, Vale of Clwyd, 1877, transcribed 1883.

Bodleian, MS Eng. poet. d. 149, f. 6.

***Poems* (1918)**, for GMH's Preface, see HpG 377.

A Prayer for the Society, see the description of MS Eng. poet. c. 48 in the INTRODUCTION.

'Proved Etheredge prudish, selfish, hypocrite, heartless'
First pub. *Journals* (1959), p. 50; *Poems 4*, p. 301; Phillips, p. 48.

HpG 242 In Diary C.II (see HpG 457); the first 5 lines on a leaf torn out of the Diary (found by Fr Bischoff in 1947 and now restored to the volume); [November? 1864].

Campion Hall, Oxford.

The Queen's Crowning ('They were wedded at midnight')
First pub. *Note-Books* (1937), pp. 34–8; collected *Poems* (1948); *Poems 4*, no. 109; Phillips, pp. 51–6.

HpG 243 In Diary C.II (see HpG 457); [December 1864].

This MS noted *Journals*, p. 51.

Campion Hall, Oxford.

'Quique haec membra malis vis esse obnoxia multis'
First pub. in the Notes to 'Miror surgentem' (see HpG 193) in *Poems 4* (1967), p. 336; Phillips, p. 102.

HpG 244 Fragmentary drafts, in pencil, in MS H, one page (on a leaf containing also a fragment of a prose note).

Bodleian, MS Eng. poet. d. 150, f. 85.

'Quin etiam nostros non aspernata labores', see HpG 103.

'Quo rubeant dulcesve rosae vel pomifer aestas?'
First pub. W. H. Gardner, *Gerard Manley Hopkins: a Study of Poetic Idiosyncrasy in Relation to Poetic Tradition*, 2 vols (London, 1944–9); *Poems 4*, p. 320 (in Notes); Phillips, p. 88.

HpG 245 Two versions, written over the beginning of a draft letter to RB, one page (on a leaf containing also HpG 80 and 6 lines beginning 'Ac tu me madidis noli vexare querellis:'), found (according to Higgins) in Journal A.I (see HpG 458) in 1947.

The finished (sent) letter to RB (of 30 August 1867) is printed *Letters to RB*, pp. 16–17; according to *Journals*, this MS was found in Journal A.III.

Campion Hall, Oxford, P.IV(biii).

The rainbow ('See on one hand')
First pub. *Journals* (1959), p. 39; *Poems 4*, no. 100; Phillips, p. 35.

HpG 246 In Diary C.I (see HpG 456); [early September 1864].

Campion Hall, Oxford.

'Repeat that, repeat'
First pub. *Poems* (1918); *Poems 4*, no. 146; Phillips, p. 144.

HpG 247 Draft, in MS H, one page (on a scrap).

Bodleian, MS Eng. poet. d. 150, f. 107 (mounted f. 109).

Ribblesdale ('Earth, sweet Earth, sweet landscape, with leavès throng')
First pub. *Poems* (1918); *Poems 4*, no. 58; Phillips, 156–7.

HpG 248 Fair copy, revised, including an epigraph from *Romans*, followed by an untitled draft of lines 1–8 annotated '[the rest as above]', one page; dated 'Stonyhurst 1882 (begun)'.

Bodleian, MS Eng. poet. c. 48, f. 45.

HpG 249 Fair copy, revised by GMH and (in red and black) by RB, including an epigraph from *Romans*, on scraps mounted in MS A; dated Stonyhurst, 1882.

Bodleian, Dep. Bridges 61, pp. 155–6.

HpG 250 Fair copy, revised, written in MS B after the 1883 transcripts, annotated 'Companion to no. 10 [i.e., "In the Valley of the Elwy"]'; dated Stonyhurst, 1882.

Bodleian, MS Eng. poet. d. 149, f. 29v.

HpG 251 Enclosed with a letter to Richard Watson Dixon, Stonyhurst, 25–9 June 1883.

This MS printed *Correspondence with Dixon*, p. 108n1 (letter, 107–9).

Bodleian, Dep. Bridges 93, f. 106.

Richard ('He was a shepherd of the Arcadian mood')
First pub. *Journals* (1959), p. 27; *Poems 4*, p. 305; Phillips, p. 21. For later fragments of *Richard*, see HpG 102.

HpG 252 In Diary C.I (see HpG 456); [May–June 1864].

Campion Hall, Oxford.

Robert Bridges: *'In all things beautiful, I cannot see'* ('Nempe ea formosa est: adeo omne quod aut facit aut fit')
This Latin translation of lines from Robert Bridges's *The Growth of Love* first pub. *Letters to RB* (1935), p. 242; *Poems 4*, no. 183; Phillips, pp. 174–5.

HpG 253 Headed '(first draught)', together with a letter to RB, dated University College Dublin, 31 October 1886.

Letter printed *Letters to RB*, pp. 242–4.

Bodleian, Dep. Bridges 92, f. 112r–v.

Rosa Mystica ('The rose in a mystery, where is it found?')
First pub. *Weekly Register* (Diocese of Westminster, London), 7 May 1898 and *Irish Monthly*, May 1898; collected *Poems* (1930); *Poems 4*, no. 27; Phillips, pp. 100–2.

HpG 254 Extensively revised fair copy of 8 numbered stanzas, 4 pages (one leaf).

Campion Hall, Oxford, H.II(c).

St Dorothea (lines for a picture) ('I bear a basket lined with grass.')
First pub. Claude Colleer Abbott, 'Gerard Manley Hopkins: A Letter and Drafts of Early Poems', *Durham University Journal*, 32 (1939–40), 70–1; *Poems 4*, Appendix A; Phillips, pp. 90–1. For two other (non-dramatic) versions, see HpG 88 and 177; for related stanzas, see HpG 1.

HpG 255 Fair copy, in MS A, annotated by RB 'Ball[iol] Coll[ege] Oxford'.

Bodleian, Dep. Bridges 61, pp. 58–61.

St Thecla ('That his fast-flowing hours with sandy silt')
First pub. 'St Thecla: an unpublished poem by Gerard Manley Hopkins', *Studies* (Dublin), Summer 1956; collected *Poems* (1956); *Poems 4*, no. 136; Phillips, pp. 59–60. For a Latin translation, see HpG 160.

HpG 256 Fair copy, revised, these lines (on one page of a folded leaf) are facing the Latin translation (HpG 160); [composed 1864–5, this MS probably written mid-1870s].

Archives of the Irish Province of the Society of Jesus, Dublin.

S. Thomae Aquinatis/Rhythmus ad SS. Sacramentum ('Godhead, I adore thee fast in hiding; thou')
First pub. *Poems* (1930); *Poems 4*, no. 168 (as beginning 'Godhead here in hiding, whom I do adore'); Phillips, pp. 104–5.

HpG 257 In MS H: (1) fair copy, revised, of a version of lines 1–14 beginning 'I bow down before thee, Godhead hiding here' (p. 1 of folded leaf) (f. 73); (2) a version of lines 1–2 beginning 'Godhead, I adore thee fast in hiding, thou', headed 'This [?] went to Mr Orby Shipley —' (p. 2 of folded leaf) (f. 73v); (3) fair copy, revised, here untitled (pp. 3–4 of folded leaf, p. 4 also containing HpG 219) (f. 74r–v); (4) revised version of lines 17–28, signed 'Amen', one page (on a leaf containing also HpG 229) (f. 76); (5) fair copy, revised, here untitled and beginning 'Godhead, I adore Thee down on bended knee', one page (f. 78).

Bodleian, MS Eng. poet. d. 150, ff. 73–4v (mounted f. 75), 76 (mounted f. 77), 78 (mounted f. 79).

St Winefred's Well, see HpG 105–7.

The Same (Welsh Version), see HpG 223.

The Sea and the Skylark ('On ear and ear two noises too old to end')
First pub. *Poems* (1918); *Poems 4*, no. 35; Phillips, p. 131.

HpG 258 Fair copy, revised, here entitled 'Walking by the sea', one page mounted in MS A, including variants and notes by RB (p. 89); dated Rhyl, May 1877.

Bodleian, Dep. Bridges 61, p. 90.

HpG 259 Fair copy, revised, written in MS B (after the 1883 transcripts); dated Rhyl, 1877.

Bodleian, MS Eng. poet. d. 149, f. 28.

HpG 260 Transcript by RB, revised by GMH, here entitled 'Walking by the Sea', annotated by GMH 'See later' and line through indicating cancellation, in MS B; transcribed 1883.

Bodleian, MS Eng. poet. d. 149, f. 10.

'See how Spring opens with disabling cold'
First pub. 'Early Poems and Extracts from the Notebooks and Papers of Gerard Manley Hopkins', ed. Humphry House, *Criterion*, October 1935; collected *Poems* (1948); *Poems 4*, no. 17; Phillips, p. 68.

HpG 261 In Diary C.II (see HpG 457); dated 26 June 1865.

This MS printed *Note-Books*, p. 47 and noted *Journals*, p. 63.

Campion Hall, Oxford.

(Seven Epigrams) ('Of virtues I most warmly bless')
First pub. (nos i–ii, iv, vi–vii) *Note-Books* (1937), pp. 28–9; collected *Poems* (1948); *Poems 4*, no. 96 (nos i–ii, iv–vii) and no. iii in Notes to the poem, p. 301 (for the epigram there given as no. vii, see HpG 39); Phillips, pp. 32–3.

HpG 262 In Diary C.I (see HpG 456), no i annotated 'In the van between Ffestiniog and Bala'; [August 1864].

The MSS of nos i–ii, iv, vi–vii noted *Journals*, pp. 35 and 37; the MSS of nos iii and v printed, p. 37.

Campion Hall, Oxford.

Shakspere ('In the lodges of the perishable souls')
First pub. *Poems* (1948); *Poems 4*, no. 126; Phillips, p. 74.

HpG 263 In Diary C.II (see HpG 457); [13 September 1865].

This MS noted *Journals*, p. 70.

Campion Hall, Oxford.

'She schools the flighty pupils of her eyes'
First pub. *Journals* (1959), p. 26; *Poems 4*, no. 82; Phillips, p. 21.

HpG 264 In Diary C.I (see HpG 456); [June 1864].

Campion Hall, Oxford.

The Silver Jubilee ('Though no high-hung bells or din')
First pub. *A Sermon Preached at St Beuno's College, July 30, 1876, On the Occasion of The Silver Jubilee of the Lord Bishop of Shrewsbury by John Morris* (London, 1876); collected *Poems* (1918); *Poems 4*, no. 29; Phillips, p. 119.

HpG 265 Fair copy, revised, subtitled 'in honour of the Most Reverend James first Bishop of Shrewsbury', revised in red by RB, in MS A; dated 'St Beuno's, Vale of Clwyd. 1876, I think' and annotated by RB 'Sent to me from Oxford Jan '79...'.

Bodleian, Dep. Bridges 61, pp. 51–2.

HpG 266 Fair copy, subtitled as above, written in MS B after the 1883 transcripts; dated 'St Beuno's, Vale of Clwyd. Summer 1876'.

Bodleian, MS Eng. poet. d. 149, f. 35.

HpG 267 Fair copy, subtitled as above and cancelled in pencil, 2 pages (one folded leaf).

Bodleian, MS Eng. poet. c. 48, f. 27, 28.

HpG 268 Fair copy of stanza 4, in a letter to RB, Oxford, 15 February 1879.

This MS printed *Letters to RB*, p. 65 (letter, 65–7) and Phillips, p. 234.

Bodleian, Dep. Bridges 91, f. 115.

HpG 269 Transcript in an unidentified hand, here untitled, on p. [69] of an album (containing also HpG 5, 67) made up to be presented to Dr James Brown, First Bishop of Shrewsbury, on his Episcopal Silver Jubilee, July 1876.

The transcript and album discussed (with facsimile of this transcript) in Alfred Thomas, S.J., 'G. M. Hopkins and the Silver Jubilee Album', *The Library*, 5 Ser 20 (1965), 148–52; not mentioned in *Poems 4*.

Unlocated (according to *The Library* in 1965, the album was preserved at St Beuno's College in Wales which was joined to Heythrop College, London, in 1970; however, Heythrop College reports (1988) that the album is not among their collection).

(The Soldier) ('Yes. Whý do we áll, séeing of a soldier, bless him? bléss')
First pub. *Poems* (1918); *Poems 4*, no. 63; Phillips, p. 168.

HpG 270 Draft, here untitled, one page (on a leaf containing also HpG 57, 338), formerly in MS H (removed 1977).

Bodleian, MS Eng. misc. a. 23, f. 21a(verso).

HpG 271 Transcript by RB, in MS A, here untitled; dated Clongowes, August 1885.

Bodleian, Dep. Bridges 61, p. 220.

A Soliloquy of One of the Spies left in the Wilderness ('He feeds me with His manna every day:')
First pub. 'Early Poems and Extracts from the Notebooks and Papers of Gerard Manley Hopkins', ed. Humphry House, *Criterion*, October 1935; collected *Poems* (1948); *Poems 4*, no. 5, as beginning 'Who is this Moses? who made him, we say'; Phillips, pp. 21–3.

HpG 272 Draft, in Diary C.I (see HpG 456), 10 pages; [July 1864].

This MS printed in *Note-Books*, pp. 23–6; variants printed *Journals*, pp. 28–9.

Campion Hall, Oxford.

'Some men may hate their rivals and desire', see HpG 30.

Songs from Shakespeare, in Latin and Greek (i) 'Come unto these yellow sands' ('Ocius O flavas has, ocius O ad arenas')
First pub. *Irish Monthly*, February 1887; collected *Poems* (1948); *Poems 4*, no. 182(i); Phillips, p. 171.

HpG 273 Fair copy of lines 1–8 and transcript by RB of lines 9–12 (from HpG 274), in MS A, here entitled 'Come unto these yellow sands', on two scraps (mounted).

Bodleian, Dep. Bridges 61, p. 168.

HpG 274 Lines 9–12, in a letter to RB, Dublin, 21 October 1886.

This MS printed *Letters to RB*, p. 232 (letter, 232–5).

Bodleian, Dep. Bridges 92, f. 99.

Songs from Shakespeare, in Latin and Greek (ii) 'Full fathom five' ('Occidit, O juvenis, pater et sub syrtibus his est')
First pub. anonymously *Irish Monthly*, November 1886; collected *Poems* (1948); *Poems 4*, no. 182(ii); Phillips, pp. 171–2.

HpG 275 Fair copy, in MS A, here entitled 'Full fathom five (from *The Tempest*)', on two scraps (mounted).

Bodleian, Dep. Bridges 61, p. 171.

Songs from Shakespeare, in Latin and Greek (iii) 'While you here do snoring lie' ('Vos dum stertitis ore sic supino')
First pub. *Poems* (1948); *Poems 4*, no. 182(iii); Phillips, p. 172.

HpG 276 Fair copy, revised, in MS A, here entitled 'While you here do snoring lie (from *The Tempest*)', one scrap (mounted).

Bodleian, Dep. Bridges 61, p. 176.

Songs from Shakespeare, in Latin and Greek (iv) 'Tell me where is Fancy bred' ('Rogo vos Amor unde sit, Camenae.')
First pub. *Poems* (1948); *Poems 4*, no. 182(iv); Phillips, p. 172.

HpG 277 Fair copy, in MS A, here entitled 'Tell me where is Fancy bred (from *The Merchant of Venice*)', on 3 scraps (mounted).

Bodleian, Dep. Bridges 61, p. 172.

Songs from Shakespeare, in Latin and Greek (v) 'Tell me where is Fancy bred' ('τίς ἔρωτος, τίς ποτ' ἄρ' ἁ πατρὶς ἦν')
First pub. *Poems* (1948); *Poems 4*, no. 182(v); Phillips, p. 173.

HpG 278 Two fair copies in MS A: (1) revised, here entitled 'Tell me where is Fancy bred/(Greek: Dorian rhythm...)', on 3 scraps (mounted); (2) here entitled 'Tell me where is Fancy bred/(Dorian measure)', one page.

Bodleian, Dep. Bridges 61, pp. 169–70.

Songs from Shakespeare, in Latin and Greek (vi) 'Orpheus with his lute made trees' ('Orpheus fertur et árbores canendo')
First pub. *Poems* (1948); *Poems 4*, no. 182(vi); Phillips, 173.

HpG 279 Fair copy, in MS A, here entitled 'Orpheus with his lute made trees (from *Henry VIII*)', together with the original English, both on one page (mounted).

Bodleian, Dep. Bridges 61, p. 175.

HpG 280 Transcript by RB, here entitled 'Orpheus with his lute made trees', tipped into a copy of *Poems* (1918).

Harvard, *EC85.B7644.A918h.

Songs from Shakespeare, in Latin and Greek (vii) 'Orpheus with his lute made trees' ('λογος 'Ορφέως λύραν καὶ δένδρεσιν χοραγεῖν')
First pub. *Poems* (1948); *Poems 4*, no. 182(vii); Phillips, p. 174.

HpG 281 Fair copy, in MS A, here entitled 'Orpheus with his lute made trees (Dorian rhythm...)', on scraps (mounted).

Bodleian, Dep. Bridges 61, pp. 173–4.

Songs from Shakespeare, in Latin and Greek (viii) Unfinished rendering of 'When icicles hang by the wall' ('Institit acris hiemps: glacies simul imbrices ad imas')
First pub. *Poems 4* (1967), no. 182(viii); Phillips, p. 174.

HpG 282 Fair copy, revised, in MS A, here entitled 'When icicles hang by the wall (from *Love's Labour's Lost*)', on 2 scraps (mounted).

Bodleian, Dep. Bridges 61, pp. 177–8.

Spelt from Sibyl's Leaves ('Earnest, earthless, equal, attuneable, vaulty, voluminous,...stupendous')
First pub. *Poems* (1918); *Poems 4*, no. 61; Phillips, p. 175.

HpG 283 Early draft (f. [15]) and fair copy, revised (f. [20v]), both here untitled, in the Dublin Notebook (HpG 468); [late 1884 or early 1885].

This MS mentioned *Journals*, p. 531.

Campion Hall, Oxford.

HpG 284 Fair copy, on 3 scraps mounted in MS A.

Bodleian, Dep. Bridges 61, pp. 181–2.

HpG 285 Fair copy, revised, written in MS B after the 1883 transcripts.

Bodleian, MS Eng. poet. d. 149, f. 36.

HpG 286 Fair copy of line 1 and two alternative versions of line 2, here untitled, one page.

Bodleian, MS Eng. poet. c. 48, f. 51.

Spring ('Nothing is so beautiful as Spring —')
First pub. *The Poets and the Poetry of the Century*, ed. Alfred H. Miles (London, [1893]); collected *Poems* (1918); *Poems 4*, no. 33; Phillips, pp. 130–1.

HpG 287 Fair copy, title and note on scrap (mounted p. 85), text on one page (mounted p. 86), in MS A; dated May 1877 and below (in RB's hand) St Beuno's.

Bodleian, Dep. Bridges 61, pp. 85–6.

HpG 288 Fair copy, revised, annotated '(unfolding rhythm, with sprung leadings: no counterpoint)', one page (on a leaf containing also HpG 158), probably sent to Grace Hopkins to be set to music by her; dated May 1877.

Described in *Poems 4* and Phillips as 'Lady Pooley's MS'; sold in Lady Pooley's sale at Sotheby's, 13 July 1966 (Lot 678); listed in Bump, HA1; see Norman Mackenzie, 'Gerard and Grace Hopkins', *The Month*, June 1965, pp. 347–50.

Texas.

HpG 289 Transcript by RB, revised by GMH, in MS B; dated (by GMH) St Beuno's, 1877, transcribed 1883.

Bodleian, MS Eng. poet. d. 149, f. 9.

Spring and Death ('I had a dream. A wondrous thing:')
First pub. *Poems* (1930); *Poems 4*, no. 4; Phillips, pp. 16–17.

HpG 290 Fair copy, 2 pages (one leaf); [1863?].

Bodleian, MS Eng. poet. c. 48, f. 26r–v.

HpG 291 Transcript by RB, in MS A, in pencil.

Bodleian, Dep. Bridges 61, pp. 259–60.

Spring and Fall: to a Young Child ('Margaret, are you grieving')
First pub. *The Poets and the Poetry of the Century*, ed. Alfred H. Miles (London, [1893]); collected *Poems* (1918); *Poems 4*, no. 55; Phillips, p. 152.

HpG 292 Fair copy, revised in red by RB, in MS A, one page, containing notes by RB; dated Lydiate, Lancashire, 7 September 1880.

Bodleian, Dep. Bridges 61, p. 142.

HpG 293 Fair copy, enclosed with a letter (containing also HpG 42) to Richard Watson Dixon, Liverpool, 22 December 1880–16 January 1881; verses dated Lydiate, Lancashire, September 1880.

This MS printed *Correspodence with Dixon*, p. 174 (letter, 36–42).

Bodleian, Dep. Bridges 93, f. 53.

HpG 294 Lines 12–13, in a letter to Richard Watson Dixon (containing also HpG 43), Liverpool, 6–19 April 1881.

This MS printed *Correspondence with Dixon*, p. 49 (letter, 47–9).

Bodleian, Dep. Bridges 93, f. 56v.

HpG 295 Transcript by RB, revised by GMH, in MS B; dated (by GMH) 'near Liverpool. 1881 [sic]', transcribed 1883.

Bodleian, MS Eng. poet. d. 149, f. 23v.

The Starlight Night ('Look at the stars! look, look up at the skies!')
First pub. *The Poets and the Poetry of the Century*, ed. Alfred H. Miles (London, [1893]); collected *Poems* (1918); *Poems 4*, no. 32; Phillips, pp. 128–9.

HpG 296 Two MSS: (1) fair copy, revised, here entitled 'The Starlight Night — Sonnet', followed by alternative versions of lines 4, 13, 3–4, 5, dated 24 February [1877] (f. 30r–v); (2) fair copy, revised, one page, dated 'Feb. 24 1877 — St Beuno's' (f. 31).

Bodleian, MS Eng. poet. c. 48, ff. 30r–v, 31.

HpG 297 Fair copy, revised, 2 leaves (rectos only) mounted in MS A; dated 24 February 1877.

Bodleian, Dep. Bridges 61, pp. 79–80.

HpG 298 Fair copy, written in MS B (after the 1883 transcripts); dated St Beuno's, February 1877.

Bodleian, MS Eng. poet. d. 149, f. 27v.

HpG 299 Fair copy, revised, one page (containing also HpG 111) as sent to Hopkins's mother, Kate Hopkins, together with the envelope postmarked St Asaph, 3 March 1877.

This MS printed (with facsimile) in *Further Letters*, pp. 144–5.

Bodleian, MS Eng. lett. e. 41, f. 43.

HpG 300 Fair copy, revised, annotated by RB on adjacent page (p. 91), one page mounted in MS A; dated March 1877.

Bodleian, Dep. Bridges 61, p. 92.

HpG 301 Transcript by RB, revised by GMH, annotated by GMH 'See later' and line drawn through indicating cancellation, in MS B; transcribed 1883.

Bodleian, MS Eng. poet. d. 149, f. 8v.

HpG 302 Transcript by RB, one page, in MS A, annotated 'copy of August 1884'.

Bodleian, Dep. Bridges 61, p. 78.

'Strike, churl; hurl, cheerless wind, then; heltering hail'
First pub. *Poems* (1918); *Poems 4*, no. 154; Phillips, p. 167.

HpG 303 Two successive drafts, in MS H, one page (containing also HpG 149).

Bodleian, MS Eng. poet. d. 150, f. 47.

HpG 304 Transcript by RB, in MS A, headed 'Another fragment'.

Bodleian, Dep. Bridges 61, p. 240.

Summa ('The best ideal is the true')
First pub. *Poems* (1918) (lines 1–4 only); first pub. in full *Poems 4* (1967), no. 133; Phillips, p. 85.

HpG 305 Fair copy, in MS A, on two scraps (mounted).

Bodleian, Dep. Bridges 61, p. 291.

The Summer Malison ('Maidens shall weep at merry morn')
First pub. *Note-Books* (1937), p. 41; collected *Poems* (1948); *Poems 4*, no. 114; Phillips, p. 59.

HpG 306 In Diary C.II (see HpG 457); [February or March 1865].

This MS noted *Journals*, p. 56.

Campion Hall, Oxford.

Sundry Fragments and Images, for nos i, vii, xxxii–xxxiii, see HpG 97; for no. ii, see HpG 227; for no. iii, see HpG 176; for nos iv–vi, xi, see HpG 98; for no. viii, see HpG 72; for nos ix–x, see HpG 367; for nos xii–xiii, xxii–xxvi, see HpG 94; for nos xiv–xv, xxvii–xxviii, xxxv, see HpG 95; for no. xvii, see HpG 3; for no. xviii, see HpG 104; for no. xix, see HpG 1; for no. xxix, see HpG 322; for nos xxx–xxxi, see HpG 69; for nos xxxiv and xxxvii, see HpG 96.

(Sundry Fragments and Images) (xvi) ('bringing heads of daffodillies')
First pub. *Journals* (1959), p. 49; *Poems 4*, no. 98 (p. 137); not in Phillips.

HpG 307 In Diary C.II (see HpG 457), here untitled; [October 1864].

Campion Hall, Oxford.

(Sundry Fragments and Images) (xx) ('[Stars] float from the borders of the main')
First pub. *Journals* (1959), p. 39; *Poems 4*, no. 98 (p. 138); not in Phillips.

HpG 308 In Diary C.I (see HpG 456), here untitled; [August 1864].

Campion Hall, Oxford.

(Sundry Fragments and Images) (xxi) ('Above')
First pub. *Journals* (1959), p. 43; *Poems 4*, no. 98 (p. 138); not in Phillips.

HpG 309 In Diary C.II (see HpG 457), here untitled; [September 1864].

Campion Hall, Oxford.

(Sundry Fragments and Images) (xxxvi) ('The moonlight-mated glowless glowworms shine.')
First pub. *Journals* (1959), p. 52; *Poems 4*, no. 98 (p. 140); not in Phillips.

HpG 310 In Diary C.II (see HpG 457), here untitled; [December 1864–January 1865].

Campion Hall, Oxford.

(Sundry Fragments and Images) (xxxviii) ('He shook with racing notes the standing air.')
First pub. *Journals* (1959), p. 65; *Poems 4*, no. 98 (p. 141); not in Phillips.

HpG 311 In Diary C.II (see HpG 457), here untitled; [July? 1865].

Campion Hall, Oxford.

(Sundry Fragments and Images) (xxxix) ('Glazed water vaulted o'er a drowsy stone')
First pub. *Journals* (1959), p. 67; *Poems 4*, no. 98 (p. 141); not in Phillips.

HpG 312 In Diary C.II (see HpG 457), here untitled; [July 1865].

Campion Hall, Oxford.

(Sundry Fragments and Images) (xl) ('They are not dead who die, they are but lost who live.')
First pub. *Journals* (1959), p. 141; *Poems 4*, no. 98 (p. 141); not in Phillips.

HpG 313 In Journal A.I (HpG 458), here untitled; in an entry dated 19 June [1866].

Campion Hall, Oxford.

That Nature is a Heraclitean Fire and of the comfort of the Resurrection ('Cloud-puffball, torn tufts, tossed pillows flaunt forth, then chevy on an air —')
First pub. *Poems* (1918); *Poems 4*, no. 72; Phillips, pp. 180–1.

HpG 314 Fair copy, slightly revised, in MS A, on scraps (mounted); dated 'July 26 1888/Co. Dublin'.

Bodleian, Dep. Bridges 61, pp. 191–2.

'The cold whip-adder unespied'
First pub. *Note-Books* (1937), p. 32; collected *Poems* (1948); *Poems 4*, no. 106; Phillips, p. 46.

HpG 315 In Diary C.II (see HpG 457); [October? 1864].

This MS noted *Journals*, p. 48.

Campion Hall, Oxford.

'The dark-out Lucifer detesting this'
First pub. *Poems 4* (1967), p. 281 (in the notes to 'As kingfishers catch fire ...'); Phillips, p. 129 (as a separate poem).

HpG 316 Draft, in MS H, at top of a page (containing also HpG 19), cancelled in pencil.

Bodleian, MS Eng. poet. d. 150, f. 39.

'The earth and heaven, so little known'
First pub. *Poems* (1948); *Poems 4*, no. 130; Phillips, pp. 77–8.

HpG 317 In Diary C.II (see HpG 457); [5 January 1866].

This MS noted *Journals*, p. 71.

Campion Hall, Oxford.

'The furl of fresh-leaved dogrose down'
First pub. *Poems* (1918); *Poems 4*, no. 144; Phillips, p. 141.

HpG 318 Draft, in MS H, one page (on a leaf containing also HpG 34, 70, 128).

Bodleian, MS Eng. poet. d. 150, f. 51 (mounted f. 52).

'The sea took pity: it interposed with doom:'
First pub. *Poems* (1918); *Poems 4*, no. 158; Phillips, p. 180.

HpG 319 Draft, in MS H, in pencil, on a scrap.

Bodleian, MS Eng. poet. d. 150, f. 108 (mounted f. 109).

HpG 320 Transcript by RB, in MS A, annotated 'pencil MS of GMH'.

This transcript not mentioned *Poems 4* or Phillips.

Bodleian, Dep. Bridges 61, p. 179.

'The shepherd's brow, fronting forked lightning, owns'
First pub. *Poems* (1918); *Poems 4*, no. 75; Phillips, p. 183.

HpG 321 Five successive drafts in MS H, on pp. 1–3 of a folded leaf (containing also HpG 334), 2 drafts here beginning 'The shepherd fronting heaven's fork-lightning owns', another beginning 'The shepherd's eye fronting forked lightning owns', one containing lines 5–14 only; annotated in pencil by RB 'I do not think this sonnet worth putting with the rest RB'; two drafts dated 3 April 1889.

Bodleian, MS Eng. poet. d. 150, ff. 44–5.

'The stars were packed so close that night'
First pub. *Note-Books* (1937), p. 53; *Poems 4*, no. 98, as '(Sundry Fragments and Images)', no. xxix (p. 139); Phillips, p. 79. A revised version of these lines appears as lines 19–22 of 'The Elopement' (see note to that title).

HpG 322 In Diary C.II (see HpG 457); [8–23 January 1866].

This MS printed *Journals*, p. 72.

Campion Hall, Oxford.

'The times are nightfall, look, their light grows less'
First pub. *Poems* (1918); *Poems 4*, no. 150; Phillips, p. 161.

HpG 323 Two drafts, on one page in MS H, the first beginning 'The times are nightfall and the light grows less', the second 'The times are nightfall look, their light grows less' or, alternatively (neither cancelled) 'The times are nightfall light of heaven grows less'.

Bodleian, MS Eng. poet. d. 150, f. 37 (mounted f. 38).

HpG 324 Transcript by RB, in MS A, annotated 'no date'.

Bodleian, Dep. Bridges 61, p. 234.

'Thee, God, I come from, to thee go'
First pub. *The Poets and the Poetry of the Century*, ed. Alfred H. Miles (London, [1893]); collected *Poems* (1918); *Poems 4*, no. 155 (24 lines); Phillips, p. 169 (30 lines).

HpG 325 Draft, formerly in MS H (f. 23), containing a discarded opening beginning 'From thee I came, to thee I go', one page (on a leaf containing also HpG 338).

Bodleian, MS Eng. misc. a. 23, f. 21b.

HpG 326 Transcript by RB, in MS A; annotated 'The date of this is Aug. '85.'.

Bodleian, Dep. Bridges 61, pp. 215–16.

'Think of an opening page illuminèd'
First pub. *Journals* (1959), p. 35; *Poems 4*, no. 93 (together with HpG 172); Phillips, p. 30 (as a separate poem).

HpG 327 In Diary C.I (see HpG 456), signed 'Maentwrog'; [mid-August 1864].

Campion Hall, Oxford.

'Thou art indeed just, Lord, if I contend', see HpG 167–9.

'To him who ever thought with love of me'
First pub. *Poems* (1918); *Poems 4*, no. 140; Phillips, p. 133.

HpG 328 Three fair copies, revised, in MS H, the first and third beginning 'The man who ever thought with love of me', one page.

Bodleian, MS Eng. poet. d. 150, f. 25 (mounted f. 26).

HpG 329 Transcript by RB, in MS A, annotated 'collated Jan '18'.

Bodleian, Dep. Bridges 61, p. 244.

To his Watch ('Mortal my mate, bearing my rock-a-heart')
First pub. *Poems* (1918); *Poems 4*, no. 153; Phillips, p. 171. A correction to line 3 ('forge' for 'force') noted first by Norman White in a letter to the *TLS*, 31 October 1968 (see also R. E. Alton and P. J. Croft's following letter, 6 March 1969); the correction not adopted in Phillips.

HpG 330 Revised, in MS H, one page.

Bodleian, MS Eng. poet. d. 150, f. 5 (mounted f. 6).

HpG 331 Transcript by RB, in MS A; annotated 'unfinished' and 'copied by RB Oct 89 collated Jan 1918'.

Bodleian, Dep. Bridges 61, p. 212.

To Oxford ('As Devonshire letters, earlier in the year')
First pub. *Journals* (1959), pp. 63–4; *Poems 4*, no. 119; Phillips, p. 68. For a fragment possibly intended for this poem, see HpG 32.

HpG 332 In Diary C.II (see HpG 457), annotated 'Given to [V. S. S] Coles' and 'The last two lines I have forgotten and must get.'; [24–6 June 1865].

Campion Hall, Oxford.

To Oxford ('New-dated from the terms that reappear')
First pub. *Note-Books* (1937), p. 46; collected *Poems* (1948); *Poems 4*, no. 12; Phillips, pp. 62–3.

HpG 333 Draft, here entitled 'To Oxford. Low Sunday and Monday, 1865', in Diary C.II (see HpG 457), headed 'The two following sonnets [now lost] were sent to Addis, also that on Easter Communion, but I have now only the rough copies of the first two, which are not quite right.'; [24–6 June 1865].

This MS noted *Journals*, p. 63.

Campion Hall, Oxford.

To R. B. ('The fine delight that fathers thought; the strong')
Hopkins's last known poem first pub. *The Poets and the Poetry of the Century*, ed. Alfred H. Miles (London, [1893]); collected *Poems* (1918); *Poems 4*, no. 76; Phillips, p. 184.

HpG 334 Draft, here untitled, in MS H, one page (on a leaf containing also HpG 321), annotated by RB in pencil 'I have a perfectly finished copy of this RB'; dated 22 April 1889.

Bodleian, MS Eng. poet. d. 150, f. 45v.

HpG 335 Fair copy, extensively revised, one page mounted in MS A; dated 22 April 1889.

Bodleian, Dep. Bridges 61, p. 196.

'To seem the stranger lies my lot, my life'
First pub. *The Poets and the Poetry of the Century*, ed. Alfred H. Miles (London, [1893]); collected *Poems* (1918); *Poems 4*, no. 66; Phillips, p. 166.

HpG 336 Fair copy, revised, in MS H, one page (on a leaf containing also HpG 21, 148, 203, 230).

Bodleian, MS Eng. poet. d. 150, f. 35.

HpG 337 Transcript by RB, in MS A.

Bodleian, Dep. Bridges 61, p. 226.

To what serves Mortal Beauty? ('To what serves mortal beauty — dangerous; does set danc-')
First pub. *Poems* (1918); *Poems 4*, no. 62; Phillips, p. 167.

HpG 338 Drafts formerly in MS H (ff. 29 and 23, respectively): (1) successive drafts, here untitled and beginning 'To what serves mortal beauty? dangerous; which lets dance', one page (on a leaf containing also HpG 325), annotated by RB 'I have a finished version of this sonnet in Gerard's own writing RB' (f. 21a); (2) revised, here untitled and beginning 'To what serves mortal beauty; dangerous, which sends or sets danc-' or, alternatively (neither cancelled) 'To what serves mortal beauty; dangerous, which says dance', (neither cancelled), one page (on a leaf containing also HpG 57, 270), dated 23 August 1885 (f. 21b, verso).

Bodleian, MS Eng. misc. a. 23, ff. 21a, 21b (verso).

HpG 339 Fair copy, as sent to Richard Watson Dixon; dated 23 August 1885.

This MS printed *Correspondence with Dixon*, pp. 129–30; *Poems 4* dates this as 'apparently' later than MS A, Phillips as being earlier.

Bodleian, Dep. Bridges 93, f. 156b.

HpG 340 Fair copy, revised, one page mounted in MS A, together with scraps of notes by RB; dated 23 August 1885.

Bodleian, Dep. Bridges 61, p. 187.

HpG 341 Fair copy, revised, written in MS B after the 1883 transcripts; dated 23 August 1885.

Bodleian, MS Eng. poet. d. 149, f. 36v.

'Tomorrow meet you? O not tomorrow.'

First pub. *Note-Books* (1937), p. 39; collected *Poems* (1948); *Poems 4*, no. 110; Phillips, p. 56.

HpG 342 In Diary C.II (see HpG 457); [December 1864].

This MS noted *Journals*, p. 51.

Campion Hall, Oxford.

Tom's Garland: upon the Unemployed ('Tom — garlanded with squat and surly steel')
First pub. *Poems* (1918); *Poems 4*, no. 70; Phillips, p. 178.

HpG 343 Fair copy, revised, here entitled 'Tom's Garland: on the Unemployed (sonnet, with two codas: the rhythm is not sprung)', one page (on a leaf containing also HpG 124); dated Dromore, September 1887.

This is possibly the MS originally enclosed in the letter to Richard Watson Dixon of 22 December 1887 (see *Correspondence with Dixon*, p. 153).

British Library, Add. MS 42711, f. 153.

HpG 344 Fair copy, revised, here untitled, 2 pages (one leaf); dated Dromore, September 1887.

Bodleian, MS Eng. poet. c. 48, f. 33r–v.

HpG 345 Fair copy, on two scraps mounted in MS A; dated Dromore, September 1887, written [12 January 1888].

Bodleian, Dep. Bridges 61, pp. 185–6.

HpG 346 Fair copy, one revision, written in MS B after the 1883 transcripts; dated Dromore, September 1887, written probably [December 1887–January 1888].

Bodleian, MS Eng. poet. d. 149, f. 37v.

HpG 347 Early version of lines 1–10, in MS H, here untitled and beginning 'the garlanded with squat and surly steel', one leaf (containing also HpG 58, 212).

Bodleian, MS Eng. poet. d. 150, f. 31 (mounted f. 32).

'Trees by their yield'
First pub. *Note-Books* (1937), p. 51; collected *Poems* (1948); *Poems 4*, no. 127; Phillips, pp. 74–5.

HpG 348 In Diary C.II (see HpG 457), annotated 'A verse or more has to be prefixed.'; [28 September 1865].

This MS noted *Journals*, p. 71.

Campion Hall, Oxford.

Two Sonnets: To Oxford, see HpG 333.

A Vision of the Mermaids ('Rowing, I reach'd a rock — the sea was low —')
First pub. *The Poets and the Poetry of the Century*, ed. Alfred H. Miles (London, [1893]) (extract only); first pub. in full (facsimile) in a pamphlet (London, 1929); collected *Poems* (1930); *Poems 4*, no. 2; Phillips, pp. 11–15.

HpG 349 Fair copy, headed by an elaborate circular pen-and-ink drawing, 4 pages (one leaf); dated Christmas, 1862.

Facsimile published 1929 (see above); facsimile first page in *Poems 4*, facing p. 8 and Thornton, p. 81; facsimile of drawing in *Journals*, plate 3.

Bodleian, MS Eng. poet. c. 48, ff. 19–20v.

HpG 350 Transcript by RB, here entitled 'A Vision of Mermaids', in MS A; annotated 'written at 18', 'Christmas. 1862' and 'First seen by me & copied some time Oct 1889.'.

Bodleian, Dep. Bridges 61, pp. 200–8.

A Voice from the World ('At last I hear the voice well known')
First pub. 'Early Poems and Extracts from the Notebooks and Papers of Gerard Manley Hopkins', ed. Humphry House, *Criterion*, October 1935; collected *Poems* (1948); *Poems 4*, no. 81; Phillips, pp. 42–6. For lines possibly intended for this poem, see HpG 49.

HpG 351 Drafts, in Diaries C.I and C.II (see HpG 456–7), the last entry followed by a scheme for the poem; [June 1864–January 1865].

These MSS printed *Note-Books*, pp. 16–21 (the scheme printed p. xix) and noted *Journals*, pp. 26 and 52 (the scheme printed p. 52).

Campion Hall, Oxford.

'What being in rank-old nature should earlier have that breath been'
First pub. *Poems* (1918); *Poems 4*, no. 141; Phillips, p. 141.

HpG 352 Three drafts, in MS H: (1) on verso of leaf (containing also HpG 119) (f. 41v); (2) lines 1–2 only, here beginning 'What things should, earlier, in nature have that breath been' (f. 42); (3) without last line, here beginning 'What things in nature shd. have, earlier, that breath been' (f. 42v).

Bodleian, MS Eng. poet. d. 150, ff. 41v, 42r–v (mounted f. 43).

HpG 353 Transcript by RB of a version (6 lines), probably of draft (3) above, headed 'Fragment of Sonnet(?)' and beginning 'What thing in nature sh^{d} have, earlier, that breath been', in MS A.

This transcript not mentioned *Poems 4* or Phillips.

Bodleian, Dep. Bridges 61, p. 238.

'What shall I do for the land that bred me'
First pub. *Poems* (1918); *Poems 4*, no. 156; Phillips, pp. 181–2.

HpG 354 Fair copy of words and music, in a letter to RB, Dublin, 7 September 1888; dated Clongowes, August 1885.

Facsimile in *Letters to RB*, between pp. 284 and 285 (letter printed pp. 283–4); this MS described *Journals*, p. 491.

Bodleian, Dep. Bridges 92, f. 177.

HpG 355 Fair copy of words and music, in a letter to RB, Dublin, 25 September 1888.

This MS printed *Letters to RB*, p. 292 (letter, 290–2); this MS described *Journals*, p. 491.

Bodleian, Dep. Bridges 92, p. 187.

HpG 356 Transcript by RB of musical setting; words by GMH and piano accompaniment by W. S. Rockstro, in a MS volume of music by GMH (for a description, see INTRODUCTION).

Bodleian, MS Mus. c. 97, f. 13.

'When eyes that cast about in heights of heaven'
First pub. *Journals* (1959), p. 56; *Poems 4*, no. 113; Phillips, p. 58.

HpG 357 In Diary C.II (see HpG 457); [February 1865].

Campion Hall, Oxford.

'Where are thou friend, whom I shall never see'
First pub. 'Early Poems and Extracts from the Notebooks and Papers of Gerard Manley Hopkins', ed. Humphry House, *Criterion*, October 1935; collected *Poems* (1948); *Poems 4*, no. 13; Phillips, p. 63.

HpG 358 In Diary C.II (see HpG 457); [25–7 April 1865].

This MS printed *Note-Books*, p. 42 and noted (two variant lines printed) in *Journals*, p. 60.

Campion Hall, Oxford.

'Why if it be so, for the dismal morn'
First pub. *Note-Books* (1937), p. 28; collected *Poems* (1948); *Poems 4*, no. 90; Phillips, p. 28.

HpG 359 In Diary C.I (see HpG 456); [1–14 August 1864].

This MS noted *Journals*, p. 34.

Campion Hall, Oxford.

'Why should their foolish bands, their hopeless hearses'
First pub. *Note-Books* (1937), pp. 27–8; collected *Poems* (1948); *Poems 4*, no. 89; Phillips, p. 28.

HpG 360 In Diary C.I (see HpG 456); [1–14 August 1864].

This MS noted *Journals*, p. 34.

Campion Hall, Oxford.

The Windhover: to Christ our Lord ('I caught this morning morning's minion, king-')
First pub. *Poems* (1918); *Poems 4*, no. 36; Phillips, p. 132.

HpG 361 Two fair copies in MS A: (1) revised, containing a note on rhythm, 2 pages (one leaf), dated by RB 'St Beuno's May 30 1877.' (pp. 94–5); (2) revised in red by RB (including the addition of the title), headed '(Another version)', one page (p. 96).

Bodleian, Dep. Bridges 61, pp. 94–6.

HpG 362 Transcript by RB, revised by GMH (including addition of the subtitle), in MS B; dated (by GMH) St Beuno's, 30 May 1877, transcribed 1883.

Bodleian, MS Eng. poet. d. 149, f. 10v.

A windy day in summer ('The vex'd elm-heads are pale with the view')
First pub. J. M. G. Blakiston, 'An Unpublished Hopkins Letter', *TLS*, 25 September 1948; collected *Poems* (1956); *Poems 4*, no. 78; Phillips, p. 11.

HpG 363 Fair copy, on page 6 of a letter to E. H. Coleridge (containing also HpG 10, 92, 151), dated Oak Hill, Hampstead, 3 September 1862.

This MS printed *Further Letters*, p. 13 (letter, 5–14).

Texas.

Winter with the Gulf Stream ('The boughs, the boughs are bare enough')
Early version first pub. *Once a Week*, 14 February 1863; reprinted *Journals*, pp. 437–8; revised and collected *Poems* (1930); *Poems 4*, no. 3; Phillips, pp. 15–16.

HpG 364 Transcript of revised version (including a list of variants from first version) by Fr Francis Bacon, S.J., initialled 'F. E. B.', the list of variants initialled 'G. M. H.' by Bacon, 2 pages (one leaf); transcribed from an autograph MS (now lost), annotated by Bacon 'N.B. In author's handwriting. Seminary (St M. Hall) August 1871....'.

This MS described *Journals*, pp. 531–2.

Campion Hall, Oxford, H.I(d).

HpG 365 Transcript by RB in pencil and overwritten in ink, in MS A, transcribed from HpG 364.

Bodleian, Dep. Bridges 61, pp. 255–6.

The Woodlark ('*Teevo cheevo cheevio chee:*')
First pub. *Poems* (1918); *Poems 4*, no. 138; Phillips, pp. 122–3.

HpG 366 Draft, in MS H, 2 pages (one leaf); dated 5 July and, in an unidentified hand in pencil, '1876'.

Bodleian, MS Eng. poet. d. 150, f. 49r–v.

(Woods in Spring) ('— the shallow folds of the wood')
First pub. *Journals* (1959), p. 36; *Poems 4*, no. 98, as '(Sundry Fragments and Images)', nos ix–x (p. 136); Phillips, p. 32.

HpG 367 In Diary C.I (see HpG 456), here untitled; [August 1864].

Campion Hall, Oxford.

The Wreck of the Deutschland ('Thou mastering me')
First pub. *The Spirit of Man*, ed. Robert Bridges (London, New York, Bombay, Calcutta and Madras, 1916) (stanza 1 only); first pub. in full *Poems* (1918); *Poems 4*, no. 28; Phillips, pp. 110–19. For a discussion of the lost autograph and the extant transcripts, see the INTRODUCTION and Norman Mackenzie, 'The Lost Autograph of "The Wreck of the Deutschland" and its First Readers', *HQ*, 3 (1976), 91–115.

HpG 368 Transcript by RB, revised in red, here beginning '<God> Thou mastering me', in MS A, including a lengthy introductory note (pp. 24–5) beginning 'Note — Be pleased, reader, since the rhythm...', signed 'Brân Maenefa'; dated 'St Beuno's Vale of Clwyd [18]75–[18]76'.

The introductory note printed *Poems 4*, pp 255–6 and Phillips, p. 335; for a discussion of this transcript, see Norman Mackenzie's article (cited above).

Bodleian, Dep. Bridges 61, pp. 24–43.

HpG 369 Transcript by RB (including first line 'God mastering me'), revised by GMH (including first line), subtitled by GMH 'Dec. 6, 7, 1875', in MS B; dated (by GMH) 'St Beuno's, Vale of Clwyd. [18]75, [18]76', transcribed 1883.

Bodleian, MS Eng. poet. d. 149, ff. 15–20v.

'— Yes for a time they held as well'
First pub. *Journals* (1959), pp. 39–40; *Poems 4*, no. 101; Phillips, p. 35.

HpG 370 In Diary C.I (see HpG 456); [c. 7 September 1864].

Campion Hall, Oxford.

PROSE

For miscellaneous prose notes, see also HpG 117, 139, 166, 244, 465, 466

Account of the dialogues of Plato's *Republic* fr. the end of the introduction to the beginning of the discussion of mythology (II, x–xvi)
No publication traced.

HpG 371 Undergraduate essay, the fourth in Notebook D.VI [ff. 8–10], annotated 'not unfinished', 1½ pages.

Not listed Bischoff, p. 571; added in Thomas A. Zaniello, 'A Note on the Catalogue of the Manuscripts of Hopkins's "Oxford Essays"', *PBSA*, 69 (1975), 410 and in Higgins.

Campion Hall, Oxford.

'All words mean either things or relations of things:...'
First pub. 'Early Poems and Extracts from the Notebooks and Papers of Gerard Manley Hopkins', ed. Humphry House, *Criterion*, October 1935; *Note-Books* (1937), pp. 95–7; *Journals* (1959), pp. [125]–6.

HpG 372 Fair copy, in Notebook D.XII [ff. 4–8], c. 5 pages; headed 'Feb. 9, 1868'.

Listed Bischoff, p. 573 (as 4 pages) and Higgins.

Campion Hall, Oxford.

Anticipations in Plato of the Aristotelian doctrine of the syllogism
No publication traced. This essay is discussed in Thomas Zaniello, 'An Early Example of the Musical Analogy in Hopkins', *HRB*, 7 (1976), 15–16.

HpG 373 Undergraduate essay, the second in Notebook D.X [ff. 6–10], c. 5 pages.

Listed Bischoff, p. 572 and Higgins.

Campion Hall, Oxford.

Arguments for and against the progressiveness of morality
No publication traced.

HpG 374 Undergraduate essay, the sixth in Notebook D.XI [ff. 17–20], c. 3 pages.

Listed Bischoff, p. 573 and Higgins.

Campion Hall, Oxford.

Aristocratic character of anct. politics, see the description of Notebook D.II.

Authenticity: why do we believe some things in ancient writers and not others?
No publication traced.

HpG 375 Undergraduate essay, the second in Notebook D.II [ff. 4–7], c. 3 pages.

Listed Bischoff, p. 570 and Higgins.

Balliol College, Oxford.

Author's Preface
First pub. *Poems* (1918); *Poems 4*, pp. 45–9; Phillips, pp. 106–9.

HpG 376 Revised, here untitled, in MS B (added after GMH's death), 6 pages (5 leaves).

Bodleian, MS Eng. poet. d. 149, ff. 1–5.

The Autonomy of the Will
No publication traced.

HpG 377 Undergraduate essay on Kantian theory, the fourth in Notebook D.X [ff. 19–22], initialled by Robert Scott, 3½ pages.

Listed Bischoff, p. 572 and Higgins.

Campion Hall, Oxford.

Bergk's Poetae Lyrici, see HpG 413.

[Biographical and Critical Note on R. W. Dixon]
First pub. Thomas Arnold, *Manual of English Literature Historical and Critical*, 5th ed (London, 1885); reprinted *Correspondence with Dixon* (1935), pp. 177–8.

HpG 377.5 Draft [ff. 15v–16, 17] and related notes [f. 14r–v], in the Dublin Notebook (HpG 468); [1884–5].

Campion Hall, Oxford.

Causation
No publication traced.

HpG 378 Undergraduate essay, the second in Notebook D.VI [ff. 3–5], c. 3 pages.

Listed Bischoff, p. 571 and Higgins.

Campion Hall, Oxford.

Comments on the Spiritual Exercises of St Ignatius Loyola
Nine extracts first pub. *Note-Books* (1937), pp. 309–51; first pub. in full *Sermons* (1959), pp. [122]–209.

HpG 379 Notes on 92 pages in an interleaved copy (some interleaved pages excised, some now loosely inserted, others lost) of *Exercitia Spiritualia S.P. Ignatii de Loyola*, [ed. Fr Roothaan] (Paris, 1865); dated variously 1878–85, written primarily 1881–3.

Campion Hall, Oxford.

Connection of Aristotle's metaphysics with his ethics
First pub. James Cotter, *Inscape: The Christology and Poetry of Gerard Manley Hopkins* (Pittsburgh, PA, 1972), pp. 310–12.

HpG 380 Undergraduate essay, the fourth in Notebook D.XI [ff. 11–15], c. 4 pages.

Listed Bischoff, p. 573 and Higgins.

Campion Hall, Oxford.

The Connection of Mythology and Philosophy
First pub. James Cotter, *Inscape: The Christology and Poetry of Gerard Manley Hopkins* (Pittsburgh, PA, 1972), pp. 507–8.

HpG 381 Undergraduate essay, the fifth in Notebook D.VI [ff. 10–12], c. 3 pages.

Listed Bischoff, p. 571 as 6½ pages long (corrected in Thomas A. Zaniello's supplementary note, *PBSA*, 69 (1975), 410) and in Higgins.

Campion Hall, Oxford.

Connection of the Cyrenaic Philosophy with the Cyrenaic morals
No publication traced.

HpG 382 Undergraduate essay, the second in Notebook D.XI [ff. 6v–8], c. 2½ pages.

Listed Bischoff, p. 573 and Higgins.

Campion Hall, Oxford.

'Contigit igitur, dux illustrissime, quod...'
No publication traced.

HpG 383 Draft, in Latin, headed 'A.M.D.G.', in MS H, 2 pages (one leaf).

Bodleian, MS Eng. poet. d. 150, f. 91r–v (mounted f. 92).

The contrast between the older and the newer order of the world as seen in Caste
No publication traced.

HpG 384 Undergraduate essay, the sixth in Notebook D.VI [ff. 12–16], c. 3½ pages.

Not mentioned Bischoff; listed in Thomas A. Zaniello, 'A Note on the Catalogue of the Manuscripts of Hopkins's "Oxford Essays"', *PBSA*, 69 (1975), 410 and Higgins.

Campion Hall, Oxford.

Credit and the causes of commercial crises
No publication traced.

HpG 385 Undergraduate essay, the first in Notebook D.II [ff. 1–4], initialled by Robert Scott, 3½ pages.

Listed Bischoff, p. 570 and Higgins.

Balliol College, Oxford.

Distinguish between the *clearness* and *distinctness* of concepts and state the method by which each is attained

HpG 386 Undergraduate essay, the second in Notebook D.I [ff. 4–5], initialled 'N' (probably William L. Newman), 1²/₃ pages.

Listed Bischoff, p. 570 and Higgins.

Campion Hall, Oxford.

Distinguish exactly between deduction, induction, analogy, and example
No publication traced.

HpG 387 Undergraduate essay, the first in Notebook D.IX [ff. 1–2] (see HpG 466), c. 2 pages.

Listed Bischoff, p. 572 and Higgins.

Campion Hall, Oxford.

Distinguish Induction from Example, Colligation of facts and other processes with which it has been confounded
No publication traced.

HpG 388 Undergraduate essay, the fourth in Notebook D.I [ff. 7–9], 2¹/₃ pages (the last part excised).

Listed Bischoff, p. 570 and Higgins.

Campion Hall, Oxford.

The 'Dominical' — 11 March, 1877
First pub. *Sermons* (1959), pp. [225]–33.

HpG 389 Annotated at the end 'This was a Dominical and was delivered on Mid-Lent Sunday March 11 1877 as far as the blue pencil mark on the sheet before this. People laughed at it prodigiously, I saw some of them roll in their chairs with laughter...'.

The annotation printed *Note-Books*, p. xxxi and *Sermons*, p. 233.

Campion Hall, Oxford.

Dublin Meditation Points
First pub. *Sermons* (1959), pp. 254–60.

HpG 390 Various notes for meditation, written *passim* in the Dublin Notebook (HpG 468); dated 22 February 1884–25 March 1885.

Campion Hall, Oxford.

The Education of the Philosopher as set forth in bk. VII of Plato's *Commonwealth* with the exact service rendered by each science as far as the introduction of dialectic
No publication traced.

HpG 391 Undergraduate essay, the eighth in Notebook D.VI [ff. 18–21], c. 2¹/₄ pages.

Listed Bischoff, p. 571 and Higgins.

Campion Hall, Oxford.

An explanation and criticism of Subject, Predicate, Copula and Attribute, with an especial reference to the import of prepositions
No publication traced.

HpG 392 Undergraduate essay, the first in Notebook D.I [ff. 1–3], initialled by Robert Scott, 2²/₃ pages.

Listed Bischoff, pp. 569–70 and Higgins.

Campion Hall, Oxford.

Floris in Italy, for prose scenes of this verse drama, see HpG 100.

***Fourth Species of Counterpoint* — by Syncopation**
No publication traced.

HpG 393 Notes on music, annotated by Robert P. Stewart, 4 pages (2 leaves); dated 7 September [1886].

Campion Hall, Oxford, N.I.

'Great feature of the old Gk philosophy...'
No publication traced.

HpG 394 Notes, in Notebook D.XII [ff. 1–3], 3 pages; c. February 1868.

These notes mentioned *Note-Books*, p. xxv, Bischoff, p. 573 and *Journals*, p. xxiii; listed Higgins.

Campion Hall, Oxford.

The history and mutual connection in ancient ethics of the following questions — Can virtue be taught? Are virtue and vice severally voluntary and involuntary?
No publication traced.

HpG 395 Two versions of an undergraduate essay, the earlier (revised) being the sixth essay in Notebook D.III [ff. 18–22], initialled by Robert Scott, c. 3¼ pages; the later in Notebook D.X [ff. 1–6], c. 6 pages.

Listed Bischoff, pp. 570, 572 and Higgins.

Campion Hall, Oxford.

Homer — Loose notes, see HpG 412.

'How easy is it to call rogue' — Dryden's *Essay on Satire* set at Royal Univ.
No publication traced.

HpG 396 Translation of a passage (from John Dryden's 'A Discourse Concerning the Original and Progress of Satire') into Greek, in MS H, one page.

Bodleian, MS Eng. poet. d. 150, f. 65 (mounted f. 66).

How far may a common tendency be traced in all pre-Socratic philosophy?
No publication traced.

HpG 397 Undergraduate essay, the third in Notebook D.VI [ff. 5–8], initialled by Robert Scott, c. 3½ pages.

Listed Bischoff, p. 571 as 5 pages (corrected in Thomas A. Zaniello's supplementary note, *PBSA*, 69 (1975), 410) and in Higgins.

Campion Hall, Oxford.

Is history governed by general laws?
No publication traced.

HpG 398 Undergraduate essay, the second in Notebook D.V [ff. 6–12], c. 6¼ pages.

Listed Bischoff, p. 571 and Higgins.

Campion Hall, Oxford.

Is the difference between *a priori* and *a posteriori* truth one of degree only or of kind?
No publication traced.

HpG 399 Undergraduate essay, the first in Notebook D.VI [ff. 1–3], c. 2¼ pages.

Listed Bischoff, p. 571 and Higgins.

Campion Hall, Oxford.

[Lecture Notes]
No publication traced.

HpG 400 On the final leaves of a commonplace book (see HpG 454) after it has been turned round and rebegun from the back, inscribed (inside back cover, i.e., f. 111 *rev.*) 'Gerard Manley Hopkins./Notes on lectures by the Revd H. P. Liddon upon the Epistles to the Corinthians./When I first attended these lectures they had reached only the fifth chapter of the first epistle, but my first* notes are on the fifth chapter./*I have now found notes on verses 9, 10, 11 of Chapter V.', 9 leaves (versos only, *rev.*) of notes; c. May 1863.

See *Further Letters*, p. 76.

Bodleian, MS Eng. poet. e. 90, ff. 111 *rev.*–102v *rev.* (versos only) (bound upside down).

[Lecture Notes on Plato's Philosophy], see HpG 429.

[Lecture on duty], see HpG 415.

The Legend of the Rape of the Scout
First pub. *Journals* (1959), pp. 6–7.

HpG 401 Facetious story, in Diary C.I (see HpG 456), headed 'Related in the Manner of Arnold and Liddell'; [October–November 1863].

Campion Hall, Oxford.

The Life of Socrates
No publication traced.

HpG 402 Undergraduate essay, the sixth in Notebook D.II [ff. 18–22], c. 3¾ pages.

Listed Bischoff, p. 570 and Higgins.

Balliol College, Oxford.

Meditation on Hell
First pub. *Sermons* (1959), pp. 241–4; extract in Phillips (1986), pp. 292–5.

HpG 403 Notes for a conference, headed 'A.M.D.G. <Instruction> Meditation on Hell', 6 pages (3 leaves).

Listed Bischoff, p. 577 (discovered in 1947).

Campion Hall, Oxford, P.III.

'Melissus...'
No publication traced.

HpG 404 Note, in Notebook D.XII [f. 20]; c. February 1868.

Listed Bischoff, p. 573 and Higgins.

Campion Hall, Oxford.

Metrical etc. — notes made at Stonyhurst
No publication traced.

HpG 405 Two pages (one folded leaf).

Listed Bischoff, p. 576.

Campion Hall, Oxford, M.IV.

The moral system of Hobbes
No publication traced.

HpG 406 Undergraduate essay, the third in Notebook D.XI [ff. 8–11], c. 4 pages.

Listed Bischoff, p. 573 and Higgins.

Campion Hall, Oxford.

The Nichomachean Ethics
No publication traced.

HpG 407 An incomplete translation of Aristotle's *Ethics*, 53 leaves (84 pages); [probably Oxford, 1863–8].

Listed Bischoff, p. 576 and described in Higgins.

Campion Hall, Oxford, M.II.

The Nichomachean Ethics
No publication traced.

HpG 408 Lecture notes, the only contents of Notebook G.I, 33 leaves (rectos only), a few blank; probably used at Oxford.

Listed Bischoff, p. 574 and Higgins.

Campion Hall, Oxford.

Notes: Feb. 9, 1868, see HpG 372.

Notes for Roman Literature and Antiquities
No publication traced.

HpG 409 Headed 'Notes for *Roman Lit. and Antiquities*', in the Dublin Notebook (HpG 468) [ff. 24–33v].

Campion Hall, Oxford.

HpG 410 Lecture notes for two sets of lectures, the only contents of Notebook G.II, c. 58 pages (32 leaves); the second set dated 1888.

Listed Bischoff, p. 574.

Campion Hall, Oxford.

[Notes on Aeschylus's *Seven Against Thebes*], see HpG 446.5.

[Notes on death]
No publication traced.

HpG 411 Unidentified notes.

Listed *NUCMC*, 62-543.

Loyola-Notre Dame Library (serving the College of Notre Dame of Maryland), Baltimore.

[Notes on Homer]
No publication traced; these notes used by W. A. M. Peters in *Gerard Manley Hopkins* (London, 1948). For similar notes, see HpG 471.

HpG 412 Notes on *The Iliad*, Books 4–6 and on the development of epic poetry, headed 'Homer — Loose notes', 18 folded leaves (65 pages), stamped 'Per H. B.', sent to Fr Keating by Fr Henry Browne, S.J., who succeeded GMH as Professor of Greek at University College Dublin; dated (f. 4a) 'Nov. 1884 Dublin' and (f. 16d) 'After this I am going to make my notes mainly on my interleaved book. Feb. 12 '86'.

Listed Bischoff, p. 576 and Higgins.

Campion Hall, Oxford, M.V.

[Notes on T. Bergk's *Poetae Lyrici Graeci* (1878)]
No publication traced.

HpG 413 Fragmentary notes, including 2 folded leaves (6 pages) headed '*Bergk's Poetae Lyrici*' and one page of University College Dublin notepaper; [1884–9].

Listed Bischoff, p. 576 and Higgins.

Campion Hall, Oxford, M.VI.

[Notes on the classics]
No publication traced.

HpG 414 Miscellaneous school notes, including notes on Euripides, Sallust, Greek history, Greek and Latin prosody, notes for translation, a list of 164 terms (headed in an unidentified hand 'Notanda in Antiquis') and a map of Greece, 46 pages in all (21 separate items).

Listed Bischoff, pp. 575–6 and Higgins.

Campion Hall, Oxford, M.I.

***'Officium*, duty, is that which we are bound to...'**
First pub. Norman Mackenzie, 'The Imperative Voice — An Unpublished Lecture by Hopkins', *HQ*, 2 (1975), 101–16; reprinted Norman Mackenzie, 'An Unpublished Hopkins Manuscript', *HRB*, No. 7 (1976), 3–7.

HpG 415 Unfinished lecture on duty, revised, based on a passage from Cicero, the text ends abruptly and after a gap begins again with notes of a few names in Cicero's text, in the Dublin Notebook (HpG 468) [ff. 31v–33v].

Facsimile page in *HRB*, p. 4 (cited above).

Campion Hall, Oxford.

On cumulative and chain evidence
Extract quoted in Alfred Thomas, *Hopkins the Jesuit* (London, 1969), p. 10; no other publication traced.

HpG 416 Undergraduate essay, the third in Notebook D.I [ff. 5–7], initialled by the Rev. Edward C. Woolcombe, c. 2 pages.

Listed Bischoff, p. 570 and Higgins.

Campion Hall, Oxford.

On Death
First pub. *Sermons* (1959), pp. 244–52; extracts in Phillips (1986), pp. 295–301.

HpG 417 Notes for a conference, 7 leaves (13 pages).

Listed Bischoff, p. 577 (discovered by him in 1947).

Campion Hall, Oxford, P.III.

On Representation
No publication traced.

HpG 418 Undergraduate essay, the fourth in Notebook D.V [ff. 15–19], initialled 'A. S.', c. 4 pages.

Listed Bischoff, p. 571 and Higgins.

Campion Hall, Oxford.

On the nature and use of money
No publication traced.

HpG 419 Undergraduate essay, the fifth in Notebook D.V [ff. 19–22], initialled 'A. S.', c. 3 pages.

Listed Bischoff, p. 571 and Higgins.

Campion Hall, Oxford.

On the Origin of Beauty: a Platonic Dialogue
First pub. *Note-Books* (1937), pp. 54–91; *Journals* (1959), pp. [86]–114.

HpG 420 Fair copy, revised, the only contents of Notebook D.IV, 22 leaves (39 numbered pages of text), possibly written for Walter Pater; inscribed on the inside front cover and dated 12 May 1865.

This MS printed as above; the notebook listed Bischoff, pp. 570–1, *Journals*, p. 530 and Higgins.

Campion Hall, Oxford.

On the Rights and Duties of Belligerents and Neutrals
No publication traced.

HpG 421 Undergraduate essay, the third in Notebook D.V [ff. 12–15], initialled by Robert Scott, c. 3¼ pages.

Listed Bischoff, p. 571 and Higgins.

Campion Hall, Oxford.

On the rise of Greek Prose-writing
No publication traced.

HpG 422 Undergraduate essay, the fifth in Notebook D.I [ff. 10–15], c. 5 pages.

Not listed Bischoff, but added in Thomas A. Zaniello's supplementary note to Bischoff in *PBSA*, 69 (1975), 409–11 and Higgins.

Campion Hall, Oxford.

On the signs of health and decay in the arts
First pub. *Journals* (1959), pp. [74]–9.

HpG 423 Undergraduate essay, the sixth in Notebook D.I [ff. 15–27], initialled by Robert Scott after the first part and 'N' (probably William L. Newman) after the second part, 12½ pages; [1864?].

This essay not listed in Bischoff nor in Zaniello's supplementary note to Bischoff in *PBSA*, 69 (1975), 409–11; listed in Higgins.

Campion Hall, Oxford.

On the true idea and excellence of sculpture
No publication traced.

HpG 424 Undergraduate essay, the first in Notebook D.V [ff. 1–6], initialled by Robert Scott, c. 5 pages.

Listed Bischoff, p. 571 and Higgins.

Campion Hall, Oxford.

Opening of St John Chrysostom's Homily on the Fall of Eutropius, see HpG 450.

The origin of our moral ideas
First pub. *Journals* (1959), pp. [80]–3.

HpG 425 Undergraduate essay, revised, the first in Notebook D.III [ff. 1–6], containing pencil underlinings (by Walter Pater?), 5½ pages.

Listed Bischoff, p. 570 and Higgins.

Campion Hall, Oxford.

The pagan and Christian virtues
No publication traced.

HpG 426 Undergraduate essay, the third in Notebook D.III [ff. 8–13], c. 5⅓ pages.

Listed Bischoff, p. 570 and Higgins.

Campion Hall, Oxford.

Parmenides
First pub. 'Early Poems and Extracts from the Notebooks and Papers of Gerard Manley Hopkins', ed. Humphry House, *Criterion*, October 1935; *Note-Books* (1937), pp. 98–102; *Journals* (1959), pp. [127]–30.

HpG 427 In Notebook D.XII [ff. 11–19 and passages of ff. 12v, 13v, 14v, 16v], c. 8½ pages; c. February 1868.

Listed Bischoff, p. 573 and Higgins.

Campion Hall, Oxford.

The Philosophy of history — what is meant by it?
No publication traced.

HpG 428 Undergraduate essay, the fifth in Notebook D.XI [ff. 15–17], c. 3 pages.

Listed Bischoff, p. 573 and Higgins.

Campion Hall, Oxford.

Plato's Philosophy
No publication traced.

HpG 429 Notes on lectures by Robert Williams on all aspects of Plato's philosophy, headed 'Plato's Philosophy', the only contents of Notebook D.VIII, 31 pages of text (22 leaves).

Listed Bischoff, p. 571 and Higgins.

Campion Hall, Oxford.

Plato's view of the connection of art and education
No publication traced.

HpG 430 Undergraduate essay, the second in Notebook D.III [ff. 6–8], c. 2 pages.

Listed Bischoff, p. 570 and Higgins.

Campion Hall, Oxford.

Poetic Diction
First pub. *Note-Books* (1937), pp. 92–4; *Journals* (1959), pp. [84]–5.

HpG 431 Undergraduate essay, revised, the third in Notebook D.II [ff. 7–9], initialled by Robert Scott, 2½ pages.

Listed in Higgins.

Balliol College, Oxford.

Poetry and verse —
First pub. 'Early Poems and Extracts from the Notebooks and Papers of Gerard Manley Hopkins', ed. Humphry House, *Criterion*, October 1935; *Note-Books* (1937), pp. 249–51; *Journals* (1959), pp. [289]–90.

HpG 432 Notes for lectures, 3 pages; [probably made while lecturing at Manresa House, Roehampton, September 1873–July 1874].

Listed Bischoff, p. 575.

Campion Hall, Oxford.

The position of Plato to the Greek world
First pub. *Journals* (1959), pp. [115]–17.

HpG 433 Undergraduate essay, the fifth in Notebook D.II [ff. 14–18], initialled by T. H. Green, c. 4 pages.

Listed Bischoff, p. 570 and Higgins; mislisted *Journals*, p. xxiii as being in Notebook D.IX.

Balliol College, Oxford.

The possibility of separating ἠθική fr. πολιτικὴ ἐπιστήμη
First pub. *Journals* (1959), pp. [122]–4.

HpG 434 Undergraduate essay, the first in Notebook D.XI [ff. 1–6], c. 6½ pages.

Listed Bischoff, p. 573 and Higgins.

Campion Hall, Oxford.

A Prayer
First pub. *A Book of Simple Prayers*, comp. E[lizabeth] W[aterhouse], 2nd ed, (Reading, 1893); reprinted as 'Appendix I' in *Correspondence with Dixon* (1935), pp. 159–60. This prayer was originally written as a contribution to the first edition of the first publication but was rejected.

HpG 435 Revised, 4 leaves (rectos only), in MS A, originally sent in a letter to RB, Stonyhurst, 26 July 1883.

The letter to RB (without the prayer) printed *Letters to RB*, p. 183.

Bodleian, Dep. Bridges 61, pp. 2–5.

The Prayer En Ego/to be said before any image of Christ crucified
No publication traced.

HpG 436 Revised, beginning 'See me, O good and sweetest Jesus...', cancelled, in MS H, one page (on a leaf containing also HpG 141).

Bodleian, MS Eng. poet. d. 150, f. 99 (mounted f. 101).

HpG 437 Fair copy, beginning 'See me, O Good & sweetest Jesus...', in MS A, in pencil, one page.

Bodleian, Dep. Bridges 61, p. 14.

The Principle or Foundation
First pub. 'Early Poems and Extracts from the Notebooks and Papers of Gerard Manley Hopkins', ed. Humphry House, *Criterion*, October 1935; *Note-Books* (1937), pp. 301–5; *Sermons* (1959), pp. [238]–41; extracts in Phillips (1986), pp. 290–2.

HpG 438 On 3 folded leaves, inserted in 'Fr Humphrey's Book' (HpG 467).

Campion Hall, Oxford.

The probable future of metaphysics

First pub. *Journals* (1959), pp. [118]–21.

HpG 439 Undergraduate essay, the third in Notebook D.IX [ff. 5–10], 4½ pages.

Listed Bischoff, p. 572 and Higgins.

Campion Hall, Oxford.

The relation of the Aristotelian <ἠθικὴ αρεπή> φρόνησις to the modern Moral sense and <φρόνησις to> προαίρεσις to Free Will
No publication traced.

HpG 440 Undergraduate essay, the third in Notebook D.X [ff. 10–18], 8 pages.

Listed Bischoff, p. 572 and Higgins.

Campion Hall, Oxford.

The relations of Plato's Dialectic to modern Logic and metaphysics
No publication traced.

HpG 441 Undergraduate essay, the fourth in Notebook D.III [ff. 13–16], c. 2⅔ pages.

Listed Bischoff, p. 570 and Higgins.

Campion Hall, Oxford.

Retreat at Beaumont Sept. 3–10 incl. 1883
First pub. (extract only) *Further Letters* (1956), p. 446; first pub. in full *Sermons* (1959), pp. [253]–4; extracts in Phillips (1986), p. 301.

HpG 442 Notes made during a retreat, 6 leaves (rectos only), headed 'Sept. 1883. Beaumont Lodge'; 3–10 September 1883.

RB's transcript of an extract from these notes, in pencil, is in Bodleian, Dep. Bridges 62, f. 12.

Bodleian, MS Eng. misc. a. 8, ff. 18–23.

Retreat in Ireland, 1889
First pub. (extracts) *Further Letters* (1956), pp. 447–8; first pub. in full *Sermons* (1959), pp. [261]–71; extracts (and date corrected) in Phillips (1986), pp. 302–5.

HpG 443 Notes made during a retreat, headed 'Jan 1. 1888 [sic, i.e., 1889]. St Stanislaus' College, Tullabeg.', 15 pages (8 leaves); dated 1–6 January 1888 (i.e., 1889).

RB's transcript of extracts from these notes (6 pages of a folded leaf) is in Bodleian, Dep. Bridges 62, ff. 8–10v.

Bodleian, MS Eng. misc. a. 8, ff. 24–31.

Rhythm and the other structural parts of rhetoric — verse —
First pub. *Note-Books* (1937), pp. 221–48; *Journals* (1959), pp. 267–88.

HpG 444 Notes for lectures, revised, incomplete, 38 pages; [probably made while lecturing at Manresa House, Roehampton, September 1873–July 1874].

Listed Bischoff, p. 575.

Campion Hall, Oxford.

[Sermons]
For extant MS sermons, see 'Fr Humphrey's Book' (HpG 467) and 'The Dominical' (HpG 389).
The three scraps of sermons listed below were first pub. *Sermons* (1959), pp. [234]–7.

HpG 445 Two scraps of sermons, on loose leaves inserted in 'Fr Humphrey's Book' (HpG 467), the first headed 'Oct. 26 1879 St Joseph's, Bedford Leigh — Ep. 21 Pent.: Eph. vi 10–17. (armour of God)' (2 pages (one leaf)), the second (2 leaves) for a sermon at Oxford, 14 September 1879.

These scraps listed in *Note-Books*, p. 434.

Campion Hall, Oxford.

HpG 446 Notes for a sermon, headed 'Luke xviii 9–14. The Pharisee and the Publican (Aug. 2 [1885] Sydenham)', ending in mid-sentence, on a loose leaf (one page) torn from the Dublin Notebook (HpG 468).

These notes mentioned *Note-Books*, p. xxxi.

Campion Hall, Oxford.

Seven against Thebes
No publication traced.

HpG 446.5 Seventy-one pages of notes on Aeschylus's *Seven Against Thebes*; possibly dating from GMH's teaching of classics at Stonyhurst, 1882–4.

Listed Bischoff, p. 576.

Campion Hall, Oxford, M.III.

Shew cases in wh. acts of apprehension apparently simple are largely influenced by the imagination

No publication traced.

HpG 447 Undergraduate essay, the fifth in Notebook D.III [ff. 16–18], c. 1½ pages.

Listed Bischoff, p. 570 and Higgins.

Campion Hall, Oxford.

The Sophists
No publication traced.

HpG 448 Undergraduate essay, the fourth in Notebook D.II [ff. 10–14], initialled by Robert Scott, c. 4⅓ pages.

Listed Bischoff, p. 570 and Higgins.

Balliol College, Oxford.

The tests of a progressive science
No publication traced.

HpG 449 Undergraduate essay, the second in Notebook D.IX [ff. 2–4], c. 1½ pages.

Listed Bischoff, p. 572 and Higgins.

Campion Hall, Oxford.

Translation from Chrysostom on Eutropius
First pub. as 'Opening of St John Chrysostom's Homily on the Fall of Eutropius' in *Note-Books* (1937), pp. 256–9; *Sermons* (1959), pp. 222–4.

HpG 450 Transcript by Fr Francis Bacon, S.J., headed 'Opening of St John Chrysostom's Homily on the Fall of Eutropius', 4 leaves numbered 3–7, rectos only (together with HpG 116 and 178).

For Fr Bischoff's 1947 discovery of this MS, see INTRODUCTION.

Campion Hall, Oxford, H.I(c).

Translation of Philebus, 15D
No publication traced.

HpG 451 Undergraduate essay, the seventh in Notebook D.VI [ff. 16–18], c. 2 pages.

Listed Bischoff, p. 571 and Higgins.

Campion Hall, Oxford.

[Undergraduate Essays], see descriptions of Notebooks D.I–D.XII.

'Xenophanes…'
No publication traced.

HpG 452 Notes on Xenophanes, in Notebook D.XII [ff. 9–11], c. 2 pages; c. February 1868.

Mentioned *Note-Books*, p. xxv, *Journals*, p. xxiii and Bischoff, p. 573; listed in Higgins.

Campion Hall, Oxford.

'Zeno…'
No publication traced.

HpG 453 Notes, in Notebook D.XII [ff. 19–20], c. one page; c. February 1868.

Listed Bischoff, p. 573 and Higgins.

Campion Hall, Oxford.

'ἐξεταστικὴ γὰρ οὖσα (*sc.* ἡ διαλεκτική) πρὸς τὰς ἁπάσῶν τῶν μεθόδων ἀρχας οδὸν ἔχει. Explain and illustrate this use of διαλεκτική in Aristotle'
No publication traced.

HpG 453.5 Undergraduate essay, the fourth in Notebook D.IX [ff. 10–11], 1½ pages.

Listed Bischoff, p. 572 (as 'An explanation of Aristotle's use of dialectic') and in Higgins.

Campion Hall, Oxford.

DRAMATIC WORKS

Castara Victrix, see HpG 68, 99.

Floris in Italy, see HpG 100, 145.

St Dorothea, see HpG 255.

St Winefred's Well, see HpG 105–7.

DIARIES AND NOTEBOOKS

Commonplace Book
No publication traced.

HpG 454 Commonplace book, kept while an undergraduate at Oxford, inscribed (inside front cover) 'Gerard M. Hopkins./Notes, extracts etc.', including GMH's transcripts of verses by Emerson, Oliver Wendell Holmes, Manzoni, Manley Hopkins (his father, 11 poems), D. G. Rossetti (3 poems), V. S. S. Coles, Digby Mackworth Dolben, Ford Madox Brown and, in an unidentified hand (Manley Hopkins?), Aubrey de Vere and Christina Rossetti, on ff. 1–55 (rectos only), ff. 55–102 being blank and including lecture notes (HpG 400) on ff. 102v–111 *rev.* (restarting the notebook from the other end).

This book described in Bischoff, pp. 565–6.

Bodleian, MS. Eng. poet. e. 90.

[1862 Diary]
In Journal A.I, Hopkins notes, in an entry for 1 June, that he has read and burnt 'parts' of his 1862 diary; no diary for 1862 has come to light.

HpG 455 Transcription by Hopkins of an entry from a (now lost) diary (for 13 April 1862), in a letter to C. N. Luxmoore, Hampstead, 7 May 1862.

This transcript printed *Note-Books* (1937), p. 3 and *Journals*, p. [3]; letter printed *Further Letters*, pp. 1–5 (with facsimile portion).

Owned (1951) Beatrice Handley-Derry and Christabel Marillier (later Lady Pooley) (Bischoff, p. 566); now possibly owned Lionel Handley-Derry; not sold in Lady Pooley's sale at Sotheby's, 1966.

Diary C.I
Extract first pub. 'Early Poems and Extracts from the Notebooks and Papers of Gerard Manley Hopkins', ed. Humphry House, *Criterion*, October 1935; further extracts pub. *Note-Books* (1937); first pub. (with a few omissions) *Journals* (1959). A complete facsimile of this diary will be published as part of Norman Mackenzie's edition of *The Early Poetic Manuscripts and Note-books of Gerard Manley Hopkins in Facsimile* (forthcoming from Garland Press, New York).

HpG 456 Green pocketbook, 181 pages of text, in pencil, in bad repair; including entries for 24 September 1863–9 September 1864.

This diary described *Journals*, pp. xvi–xxi and Bischoff, p. 567; facsimiles of 27 drawings in this diary (a few full pages) in *Journals*, Figures 1–27; facsimiles of 6 drawings (some full pages) in Thornton, pp. 5, 52–5.

Contents: HpG 27, 50, 71, 72, 75, 97, 98, 100, 101, 108, 127, 129, 136, 137, 147, 164, 165, 172, 176, 185, 186, 194, 207, 227, 235, 246, 252, 262, 264, 272, 308, 327, 351, 359, 360, 367, 370, 401.

Campion Hall, Oxford.

Diary C.II
Extracts first pub. *Note-Books* (1937); first pub. (without Hopkins's cancelled spiritual notes and a few other omissions) *Journals* (1959). A complete facsimile of this diary (including the spiritual notes) will be published as part of Norman Mackenzie's edition of *The Early Poetic Manuscripts and Note-books of Gerard Manley Hopkins in Facsimile* (forthcoming from Garland Press, New York).

HpG 457 Green pocketbook, half-filled, in pencil, running on continuously from Diary C.1 (HpG 456), 108 pages of text; including entries for 9 September 1864–23 January 1866 (and an additional entry for 4 October 1866), inscribed on the flyleaf in pencil 'G. M. Hopkins. Sept. 9. 1864'.

This diary described *Journals*, pp. xvi–xxi and Bischoff, p. 567; facsimiles of 2 drawings in this diary in *Journals*, Figures 28–9.

Contents: HpG 1, 2, 3, 11, 13, 18, 30, 32, 39, 49, 64, 65, 68, 69, 78, 88, 93, 94, 95, 96, 99, 100, 101, 102, 104, 118, 145, 146, 156, 164, 175, 184, 195, 202, 205, 206, 211, 217, 218, 221, 242, 243, 261, 263, 306, 307, 309, 310, 311, 312, 315, 317, 322, 332, 333, 342, 348, 351, 357, 358.

Campion Hall, Oxford.

Journal A.I
Extracts first pub. (with a facsimile page) 'Journal of Fr G. M. Hopkins, 1866', ed. Fr D. Anthony Bischoff, *Letters and Notices* (private domestic publication of the Society of Jesus), May and September 1947; first pub. in full *Journals* (1959), pp.[133]–147. This journal discovered by Fr Bischoff at Farm Street in 1947.

HpG 458 Private journal, annotated on inside front cover '...Please not to read.', 22 leaves (rectos only); including entries for 2 May–24 July 1866 (and an additional entry for 6 August 1866).

Contents: HpG 313. For papers found inserted (according to Higgins) in this journal, see HpG 12, 79, 80, 81, 139, 140, 161, 166, 216, 245 (according to *Journals*, the papers were found in Journal A.III).

Campion Hall, Oxford.

Journal A.II
Extracts first pub. 'Journal of Fr G. M. Hopkins, 1866–1867', ed. Fr D. Anthony Bischoff, *Letters and Notices* (private domestic publication of the Society of Jesus), September 1947; first pub. in full *Journals* (1959), pp. 147–64. This journal found by Fr Bischoff at Farm Street in 1947.

HpG 459 Private journal, 22 leaves (mostly rectos only); dated (on f. 1) 31 August 1867 and including entries for 10 July 1867–16 April 1868.

Campion Hall, Oxford.

[Draft Journal A.III]
No publication traced.

HpG 459.5 Three pages from a lost pocketbook (inserted in Journal A.III, HpG 460) containing rough entries for 5–6 July 1868 (written up in Journal A.III), financial jottings and sketches.

This MS mentioned *Journals*, p. 391.

Campion Hall, Oxford.

Journal A.III
Extracts first pub. 'Journal of Fr G. M. Hopkins, 1868', ed. Fr D. Anthony Bischoff, *Letters and Notices* (private domestic publication of the Society of Jesus), January and May 1948; first pub. in full *Journals* (1959), pp. 164–77. This journal found by Fr Bischoff at Farm Street in 1947.

HpG 460 Private journal, a continuation of Journal A.II (HpG 459), 16 leaves remaining; inscribed and dated 27 January 1866 on the inside front cover and including entries for 17 April–18 July 1868.

For papers said (in *Journals*) to have been found inserted in this journal, see HpG 458. For rough notes from which the journal was transcribed, see HpG 459.5.

Campion Hall, Oxford.

Journal A.IV
Extracts first pub. 'The Diary of a Devoted Student of Nature', ed. J. G. MacLeod, *Letters and Notices* (private domestic publication of the Society of Jesus), April 1906, April 1907, October 1907; further extracts pub. 'Father Gerard Hopkins', *Dublin Review*, July–September 1920 and G. F. Lahey, *Gerard Manley Hopkins* (London, 1930); first pub. in full *Note-Books* (1937), as 'Journal A.I'; *Journals* (1959), pp. 177–223.

HpG 461 Private journal, a continuation of Journal A.III (HpG 460), ends mid-sentence, inscribed on inside front cover, 102 leaves; including entries for 19 July 1868–10 August 1872.

Facsimile page in Thornton, p. 52.

Campion Hall, Oxford.

Porter's Journal
First pub. (with two facsimile pages) Alfred Thomas, S.J., *Hopkins the Jesuit* (London, 1969), pp. 67–82.

HpG 461.5 Journal kept by GMH as Porter at Manresa House, Roehampton, during his novitiate, in a notebook containing 158 numbered leaves, 24 pages written by GMH; 11 December 1869–19 February 1870 (the whole notebook covers 9 December 1869–26 October 1871).

Unlocated.

Journal A.V
Extracts first pub. 'The Diary of a Devoted Student of Nature', ed. J. G. MacLeod, *Letters and Notices* (private domestic publication of the Society of Jesus), April 1906, April 1907, October 1907; further extracts pub. 'Father Gerard Hopkins', *Dublin Review*, July–September 1920 and G. F. Lahey, *Gerard Manley Hopkins* (London, 1930); first pub. in full *Note-Books* (1937), as 'Journal A.II'; *Journals* (1959), pp. 223–63.

HpG 462 Private journal, a continuation of Journal A.IV (HpG 461), ends mid-sentence, 97 leaves; including entries for 10 August 1872–7 February 1875.

Campion Hall, Oxford.

Notebook B.I
No publication traced.

HpG 463 School notebook, inscribed on inside front and back covers 'Gerard M. Hopkins from himself. Esse quam videri', including notes on 'Trigonometry' (20 pages) and 'Mechanics' (28 pages), 38 leaves.

Campion Hall, Oxford.

Notebook B.II
This notebook is fully described in Higgins.

HpG 464 Notebook used at school and at Oxford, including school notes on Aeschylus's *Choephoroi* (ff. 25–38, 54–8, rectos only), on *Promêtheus Desmotês*, including 2 maps and HpG 9 (ff. 39–54, rectos only), detailed notes on Thucydides, Book II, lines 87–9 (ff. 1–24, rectos only) and on Agamemnon (ff. 59–70, rectos only); also including Oxford notes on Greek drama and history (including notes of lectures by Riddell and Jowett), 137 leaves (168 pages), some mutilated; inscribed on verso of front flyleaf 'Gerard M. Hopkins. Note Book. May 23. 1862 —— Esse quam videri'.

The notes on Thucydides printed Todd K. Bender, *Gerard Manley Hopkins* (Baltimore, MD, 1966), pp. 52–6 (including facsimiles of two of the six maps).

Campion Hall, Oxford.

Notebook D.I
Earliest extant notebook (1864?) of six undergraduate essays, inscribed on inside front cover 'Gerard M. Hopkins. Essays.', 27 leaves (rectos only) of text): Campion Hall, Oxford. Bischoff, pp. 569–70 lists 4 essays as the contents; a fifth (HpG 426) added by Thomas Zaniello in his supplementary note, *PBSA*, 69 (1975), 411; the sixth (HpG 424) published in *Journals* (1959); fully described in Higgins.

Contents: HpG 386, 388, 392, 416, 422, 423.

Notebook D.II
Notebook of six undergraduate essays and the title only of a seventh 'Aristocratic character of anct. politics', 22 leaves (rectos only), 1865?: presented to Balliol College, Oxford by Campion Hall in 1963 (photocopy at Campion Hall). Contents listed Bischoff, p. 570; fully described in Higgins.

Contents: HpG 375, 385, 402, 431, 433, 448.

Notebook D.III
Notebook of six undergraduate essays, inscribed on inside front cover 'Essays for W. H. Pater, Esq.' and containing pencil markings (by Pater?) *passim*, 22 leaves (rectos only), 1865?: Campion Hall, Oxford. Contents listed Bischoff, p. 570; fully described in Higgins.

Contents: HpG 395, 425, 426, 430, 441, 447.

Notebook D.IV, see HpG 420.

Notebook D.V
Notebook of five undergraduate essays, 22 leaves (rectos only), signed and dated 22 May 1865 on inside front cover: Campion Hall, Oxford. Contents listed Bischoff, p. 571; fully described in Higgins.

Contents: HpG 398, 418, 419, 421, 424.

Notebook D.VI
Notebook of eight undergraduate essays, 21 leaves (rectos only) of text, inscribed on inside front cover 'Gerard M. Hopkins. Essays', 1865?: Campion Hall, Oxford. Six essays listed as contents in Bischoff, p. 571; two more added in Thomas A. Zaniello's supplementary note, *PBSA*, 69 (1975), 410; fully

described in Higgins.

Contents: HpG 371, 378, 381, 384, 391, 397, 399, 451.

Notebook D.VII
This notebook described in Bischoff, pp. 571, 577, in *Journals*, pp. 530, 533 and in Higgins with a full description of contents of the notebook and the inserted papers.

HpG 465 Notebook used while an undergraduate, headed (f. 1) 'Extracts etc.', 6 leaves (8 pages), including extracts from Talleyrand, Mark Pattison, Locke, Rémusat, Max Müller and John Grote; signed and dated on the inside front cover 27 January 1866.

This notebook originally contained (inserted) loose scraps (not all in GMH's hand) of notes, a draft of 'Remembrance and Expectation' (by Manley Hopkins and possibly in his hand, dated 14 June 1868), extracts from de Musset, Malherbe, J. C. Shairp, Coleridge, Tennyson, St Bonaventure, etc. and two press cuttings; these loose papers are now kept separately at Campion Hall, Oxford, P.I. Another MS (in GMH's hand) of 'Remembrance and Expectation', initialled 'M. H.' is also at Campion Hall, Oxford.

Campion Hall, Oxford.

Notebook D.VIII, see HpG 429.

Notebook D.IX
This notebook described in Bischoff, pp. 572, 577, *Journals*, pp. 533–4 and in Higgins with a full description of contents.

HpG 466 Notebook containing four undergraduate essays (only 11 of the original 22 leaves remaining); headed (f. 1) 'Essays — Hilary Term '67.' and signed on inside front cover.

This notebook originally contained 20 inserted loose leaves of notes (not all in GMH's hand) on the classics (10 leaves) as well as GMH's transcripts of poems by Dante Gabriel Rossetti, Christina Rossetti and others; these loose papers are kept separately at Campion Hall, Oxford, P.II.

Contents: HpG 387, 439, 449, 453.5.

Campion Hall, Oxford.

Notebook D.X
Notebook of four undergraduate essays, inscribed on the inside front cover 'Gerard M. Hopkins. Essays for T. H. Green Esq.', 22 leaves (25 pages): Campion Hall, Oxford. Contents listed Bischoff, p. 572 and fully described in Higgins.

Contents: HpG 373, 377, 395, 440.

Notebook D.XI
Notebook of six undergraduate essays, inscribed on the inside front cover 'Gerard M. Hopkins. Essays', 20 leaves (29 pages), [1866–7]: Campion Hall, Oxford. Contents listed Bischoff, pp. 572–3; fully described in Higgins.

Contents: HpG 374, 380, 382, 406, 428, 434.

Notebook D.XII
Notebook of undergraduate notes, inscribed on the inside front cover 'Gerard M. Hopkins. Notes on the history of Greek philosophy etc.' (dated in the text (f. 4) 9 February 1868), 20 leaves (mostly rectos only): Campion Hall, Oxford. Contents listed Bischoff, p. 573; fully described in Higgins.

Contents: HpG 372, 394, 404, 427, 452, 453.

Fr Humphrey's Book
Six sermons from this notebook first pub. *The Tablet*, 14 November–19 December 1936; reprinted *Note-Books* (1937), pp. 260–300; first pub. in full *Sermons* (1959), pp. [13]–104; selections from these sermons in Phillips (1986), pp. [275]–81.

HpG 467 Notebook containing 27 sermons or parts of sermons, inscribed on front cover 'Fr Humphrey gave me this book when he left Oxford June, 1879.', 189 pages of text, including loose inserted leaves (containing HpG 438, 445) and an inserted press cutting of 14 March 1882; sermons date from 6 July 1879 to 26 June 1881.

This notebook described *Note-Books*,

Appendix II, pp. 429–34, Bischoff, p. 574 and Higgins.

Campion Hall, Oxford.

Notebook G.I, see HpG 408.

The Dublin Notebook
Some notes on the 'Foundation Exercise' in this notebook (sometimes known as Notebook G.Ia) printed *Note-Books* (1937), pp. 416–17. For other lecture notes on Roman literature and antiquity, see HpG 410; for leaves torn from this notebook, see HpG 138, 446.

HpG 468 Unbound copybook, 60 pages of text, found inserted in Notebook G.I, used primarily for correcting and marking examination papers, containing (as well as contents below) lecture notes, jottings on scansion, spiritual notes, journal entries and a transcript of verses by William Collins, signed on the inside front cover, 33 leaves; some notes dated 22 February 1884–March 1885.

This notebook described Bischoff, p. 574 and fully in Higgins.

Contents: HpG 105, 283, 377.5, 390, 409, 415.

Campion Hall, Oxford.

Notebook G.II, see HpG 410.

MARGINALIA IN PRINTED BOOKS AND MANUSCRIPTS

Aeschylus. *Choephoroi* (Oxford, 1884).

HpG 468.5 Extensive annotations in the Notes.

Archives of the Irish Province of the Society of Jesus, Dublin.

Bernard, of Morlaix. *The Rhythm of Bernard de Morlaix, monk of Cluny, on the Celestial Country*, ed. and trans. Rev. J. M. Neale, 2nd ed (London, 1859).

HpG 469 Annotated in pencil, inscribed (by GMH?) 'Gerard M. Hopkins. From his Mother, May 11th 1860'.

This copy mentioned (without location) in Madeline House, 'Books Belonging to Hopkins and his Family', *HRB*, No. 5 (1974), pp. 26–41.

Formerly owned by the late Lionel Hopkins (d. 1952), The Garth, Haslemere (not sold with other papers and letters to the Bodleian in 1953).

Corpus poetarum latinorum, ed. William Walker (1876), for this missing annotated book, see INTRODUCTION.

Exercitia Spiritualia S.P. Ignatii de Loyola, see HpG 379.

Holy Bible. Authorized version (Cambridge, n.d.).

HpG 470 Two volumes composed of a small cheap Bible having been dismantled, interleaved with blue paper and rebound, both inscribed by GMH 'Michaelmas Term 1865' and containing pencil annotations by him and his father.

This Bible mentioned (without location) in Madeline House, 'Books Belonging to Hopkins and his Family', *HRB*, No. 5 (1974), pp. 26–41.

Formerly owned by the late Lionel Hopkins (d. 1952), The Garth, Haslemere (not sold with other letters and papers to the Bodleian in 1953).

Homer. Unidentified edition.

HpG 471 GMH's annotated copy, including annotations which correspond to the notes on Books 4–6 of *The Iliad* in HpG 412.

Mentioned (without location) in Todd K. Bender, *Gerard Manley Hopkins* (Baltimore, MD, 1966), p. 50.

Unlocated.

[Hopkins, Kate?], 'A Story of a Doll'.

HpG 472 Notebook containing two MS stories, possibly by Kate Hopkins: 'A Story of a Doll', 76 numbered pages, containing pencil corrections possibly by GMH, dated October 1854; 'The Dove', 15 pages numbered 79–93.

This notebook discussed in Patricia L. Skarda, 'Juvenilia of the Family of Gerard Manley Hopkins', *HQ*, 4 (1977), 39–54 where it is suggested that the hand is that of GMH's 'Aunt Annie' (Ann Hopkins) and the annotation might be GMH's; listed Bump, FA49 where the hand is said to be 'apparently' Kate Hopkins's and no mention is made of the identity of the corrector; this notebook sold in Lady Pooley's sale at Sotheby's, 12–13 July 1966, Lot 695.

Texas.

Tacitus, Cornelius. *Historiae* (London, Oxford and Cambridge, 1876).

HpG 473 Heavily annotated.

Archives of the Irish Province of the Society of Jesus, Dublin.

John Keats
1795–1821

INTRODUCTION

This *Index* of Keats's literary manuscripts is, almost entirely, a restatement of current scholarship, specifically of the editorial work of Jack Stillinger. Stillinger is the last in a long and illustrious line of Keats editors and textual critics — beginning in fact with Keats's own circle of friends (particularly Richard Woodhouse, who was, even before Keats's death, collating the variants from different versions of the poems) and proceeding to Richard Monckton Milnes, Harry Buxton Forman, Ernest de Selincourt, Sidney Colvin, Amy Lowell, Claude Lee Finney, H. W. Garrod, Mabel A. E. Steele and Miriam Allott.

Stillinger's 1978 edition of *The Poems of John Keats* is the reference edition for the following entries, from which titles and first lines are quoted. It explores afresh the territory of both manuscript and printed sources for Keats's verse that his predecessors had charted — including the some sixty manuscripts that had come to light since Garrod's previously standard edition — and establishes the most authoritative texts to date. Slightly fuller discussions of each text than those given in the apparatus to the 1978 edition are given in Stillinger's earlier work, *Texts* (1974), which lays out the relationships — often replete with diagrams — between all the known manuscript and printed sources for each poem; the occasional error or omission in *Texts* is corrected in the 1978 edition. The Keats entries are based on the textual histories constructed in Stillinger's work. References to use of the manuscripts by earlier editors are not, in most cases, cited.

References are given whenever appropriate, however, to the eight volumes of facsimiles of Keats manuscripts, edited by Jack Stillinger, which have recently been published. Seven of them (*Keats Facsimiles I–VII*) have appeared in the Garland Press series of *Manuscripts of the Younger Romantics*, under the general editorship of Donald H. Reiman, and reproduce important Keats autographs and authoritative transcripts in libraries on both sides of the Atlantic. The eighth (*Poetry Manuscripts*) reproduces Keats's autograph poetry at Harvard and will be published by Harvard University Press in 1990.

The *Index* entries include only one autograph MS not mentioned in Stillinger's edition: a fragment of three unrecorded lines from *Otho the Great* (KeJ 372) which has for years been on loan to the British Library in the Charnwood Collection. A manuscript revision to the text of 'Specimen of an Induction to a Poem', in a copy of *Poems* (1817) at the Free Library of Philadelphia (KeJ 407.5), also goes unnoticed in Stillinger; but the same revision in two other copies at Harvard *is* reported. In addition, three privately owned or unlocated manuscripts have, since 1978, been located at public libraries: the fragment of 'I stood tip-toe upon a little hill' (KeJ 159) previously owned by Stefan Zweig, was presented, together with the rest of the magnificent Zweig Collection, to the British Library in May 1986; the Robert H. Taylor Collection at Princeton University has acquired the manuscript of 'Welcome joy and welcome sorrow' (KeJ 532) previously owned by Dorothy Withey of Stratford-upon-Avon; and a fragment of 'Isabella' (KeJ 193), formerly owned by Owen D. Young, has been located in the Free Library of Philadelphia.

Apart from these items and B. R. Haydon's transcripts of four Keats poems recently acquired by the

Pierpont Morgan Library (KeJ 2, 8, 338, 483, unlocated in Stillinger, p. 744) — these date from 1844 and are probably without authority — all the entries represent autograph manuscripts and transcripts accounted for in Stillinger's 1978 edition.

On the other hand, a few of the transcripts that Stillinger does mention have not been included in the entries (see details below). In general, a transcript is entered only when it derives from an authoritative manuscript rather than a printed source. The only exceptions to this rule are the three transcripts in W3 made from printed sources (KeJ 334, 466.5, 479) and the six by Richard Woodhouse that derive from two of those (KeJ 335–7, 480–2).

Of the 561 manuscripts listed in the Verse section of the entries — and all but nineteen entries represent poetical texts — only just over one-third are autograph. These include loose manuscripts, fragments, poems copied in letters, poems written in printed books, a few drafts and fair copies in notebooks (i.e. in the Keats-Wylie Scrapbook, in George Keats's Notebook and in W3), revisions in printed copies of *Poems* (1817) and one corrected proof of 'Lamia'.

The rest of the entries represent authoritative transcripts. To an extraordinary extent — given Keats's youth, modest means and relative obscurity — Keats and his poetry were served and cared for, both during and after his short creative life, by devoted friends and admirers.

As far as the poetry is concerned, Richard Woodhouse — legal advisor to Taylor and Hessey, Keats's publishers from 1818 — stands out among them as the most tireless and meticulous. Stillinger has remarked that Woodhouse became a Keats scholar almost as early as Keats became a poet. And he himself wrote to John Taylor in August 1819: 'Whatever People regret that they could not do for Shakespeare & Chatterton...that I would embody into a Rational principle...and do for Keats.' The fact that the entries include nearly as many transcripts by Woodhouse or his clerks as autograph manuscripts by Keats, and that over half of Keats's poems are represented by at least one Woodhouse transcript, is evidence enough of how well he succeeded.

Stillinger has noted that Keats valued his own autograph manuscripts more as mementos than as transmitters of his poetical texts. He often made copies of his own poems from 'the better punctuated, better spelled, and much more legible versions by Brown and Woodhouse'; and his own fair copies can be a good deal more carelessly written than those of his transcribers. As far as his fair copies are concerned, Keats 'cannot be considered the most important transcriber of his poems' and transcripts have in some cases been chosen by Stillinger as copy texts over surviving fair copies by Keats.

Nonetheless, in the entries, Keats's autograph manuscripts of a poem (if any survive) are listed before the transcripts regardless of the fact that those transcripts may represent 'better' texts or that they might predate one of Keats's fair copies. The transcripts are listed after the autographs roughly in the order of their authority. Those made from autographs precede those made from other transcripts. The many transcripts of equal authority, however, are arbitrarily ordered.

Keats's evaluation of his own manuscripts — so different from our own — was apparently shared by at least some of his closest friends. At least two of them —Charles Cowden Clarke and Joseph Severn — cut up some of Keats's longer autograph drafts into fragments, sometimes into quite small strips, which they gave away as souvenirs of the poet.

Several of the ten leaves of the original draft of 'I stood tip-toe upon a little hill' were cut into fragments by Clarke when he owned the manuscript. All but three fragments and one entire leaf have been located (see the headnote to the poem). Most of the surviving bits are widely scattered, in six different libraries in three different countries. Two of the bits have been published as facsimiles but remain unlocated and a third is in private hands.

The culprit in the cases of the original drafts of 'Isabella' and 'Lamia' was Joseph Severn. Only seven fragments of the twelve leaves of the draft of 'Isabella' are still missing. But the draft of 'Lamia' has fared less well; only nine fragments, representing about one-sixth of the poem, have been located (see the headnotes to the poems for details).

Some seventeen leaves of the first draft of *Otho the Great* also fell prey to Severn's scissors; but all but some sixty lines of it have been recovered (see the headnote to the poem). Severn also made souvenirs out of a few leaves of Keats's revised version of Act I, scene i, but the extent of that original revision (and hence the loss of the manuscript) has not been determined. The previously unrecorded fragment of *Otho* (KeJ 372), mentioned above, is presumably part of that revision.

There is every reason to think that unlocated or missing pieces of these drafts may come to light in the future.

Keats's Poetical Canon and Three Published Volumes

Stillinger's 1978 edition of Keats's *Poems* includes 148 poems (some fragmentary), the dramatic fragment 'King Stephen' and the tragedy co-authored with Charles Brown, *Otho the Great*. About two-thirds of these poems are represented by extant autograph manuscripts and all but nine of them by at least one authoritative manuscript source.

Only fifty-four poems were published by Keats during his lifetime: forty-five in his three original volumes — *Poems* (1817), *Endymion* (1818) and *Lamia* (1820) — and nine others which appeared only in periodicals. By 1848, when R. M. Milnes's *Literary Remains*, the first significant posthumous edition, was published, Keats's canon included 119 poems and fragments of poems. The remaining thirty-one poems have appeared subsequently (listed in *Texts*, pp. 80–81), the latest additions being made in H. W. Garrod's 1939 edition.

Keats certainly wrote poems which have been lost and are unlikely to turn up. A few comments in his letters may refer to missing texts. He tells Charles Cowden Clarke on 9 October 1816, for example, that he had 'coppied out a sheet or two of Verses which I composed some time ago, and find so much to blame in them that the best part will go into the fire'. In another letter, to Woodhouse of 21–2 September 1819, in which Keats had transcribed quite a few of his verses, he also included the first two lines of a 'sonnet in french of Ronsard' which he did not complete; it begins 'Non ne suis si audace a languire' and Rollins's footnote (*Letters*, II, 172) explains that Keats's editors omit these two lines in which 'Keats's French...is as bad as his Chattertonian Middle English'.

Woodhouse's list of 'Poems of J. K. which I have not' (written at the back of W2; see *Texts*, pp. 37–8 and *Keats Facsimiles VI*, p. 437) also contains a few unidentified items, two or three of which apparently refer to lost texts. The first — 'Part of an historical Tragedy on the fall of the Earl of Essex or E^l of Leicester' — may relate, as Stillinger notes, to Keats's letter to John Taylor of 17 November 1819 (which Woodhouse knew) in which Keats names this subject as a 'promising one'.

A second item, 'A blank verse translation of one of Ronsard's Sonnets — Sent to J. H. R.', does not survive; Keats's only known translation from Ronsard ('Nature withheld Cassandra') is not written in blank verse. Woodhouse is probably referring to the '2 translated sonnets of Keats's' that he says, in a letter to John Taylor of [August 1819?], Reynolds 'has owed' him 'these 2 months'.

The other item on the list that is certainly lost if it is accurately reported is the 'Fragment of a fairy Tale sent to his Brother George – beginning "Now when the Monkey found himself alone" –'. No such poem has come to light.

Stillinger includes six poems in his 'Appendix VI. Questionable Attributions', having eliminated two others from the eight dubious poems he discusses in *Texts*, pp. 271–5. The authorship of those two poems — 'To Woman (From the Greek)' by Edward William Barnard and 'The Poet' by John Taylor — was discovered in the 1950s after the poems had both, for some years, been included in Keats's canon.

One of Stillinger's six 'questionables', 'Love and Folly', was first attributed to Keats in 1939 based on its publication in *New Monthly Magazine* of July 1822 over the signature 'S. Y.' — the same signature used in the *New Monthly Magazine*'s publication of 'On some Skulls in Beauley Abbey, near Inverness' (KeJ 347), a poem co-written by Keats and Charles Brown. No manuscript sources of the poem are known among the papers of Keats and his circle.

Stillinger says there is no reason to suppose that Keats was the author of any of the five remaining poems, the text of each of which is based on at least one manuscript source. The *Index*, following Stillinger, provides entries for the manuscripts of these poems, and they are marked 'Questionable attributions' (see KeJ 122, 310, 388–9, 397, 430).

A poem by J. H. Reynolds — and first published as his in *The Examiner* of 14 June 1818 — beginning 'As young and pretty as the bud', was privately printed as Keats's in 1909 by the Boston Bibliophile Society (*John Keats. Unpublished Poem to his Sister Fanny April, 1818*); the unsigned manuscript from which the pamphlet was printed, formerly owned by William Bixby, is now in the library at Washington University in St Louis.

Of the thirty-one poems published in Keats's first volume *Poems* (1817), seventeen are represented by one or more autograph manuscript. Three of these manuscripts, in fact, were part of the printer's copy for the volume (see KeJ 5, 267, 503), the rest of which has not survived. Authoritative transcripts of six other poems are extant. However, no manuscript sources of any kind survive for eight of the poems in this first collected volume: 'To Leigh Hunt, Esq.'; 'Woman! when I behold thee flippant, vain'; 'To George Felton

Mathew'; 'Written on the Day that Mr Leigh Hunt Left Prison'; 'How many bards gild the lapses of time'; 'Keen, fitful gusts are whisp'ring here and there'; 'To Kosciusko'; 'Sleep and Poetry'. In fact — along with the sonnet to Robert Burns, 'This mortal body of a thousand days', and the lines 'What can I do to drive away', both first published in *Literary Remains* (1848), and one of the 'questionable attributions', 'Love and Folly' — these are the only poems in the Keats canon wanting manuscript sources for their texts.

The preparation of Keats's two other published volumes was more thoughtful than the first and increasingly involved several members of his circle; the hands of John Taylor and Richard Woodhouse in particular appear on many of the manuscripts and on the one surviving corrected proof of any of Keats's works: the page proofs of 'Lamia' (KeJ 224).

The copy sent to the printer of 'Endymion', Keats's longest poem and the entire contents of his second volume, survives (KeJ 61–2) although the original draft has been lost (apart from one leaf which, unfortunately, bears none of the poem's text, see KeJ 437). Some of the lost draft, however, can be reconstructed from Woodhouse's recording of its variants in his interleaved copy of the first edition (see KeJ 63).

The third — and last — of the published volumes, *Lamia* (1820), includes the poems written during Keats's so-called 'living year' (circa January to September 1819) and generally taken to be his masterpieces: the Odes, 'The Eve of St Agnes', 'Lamia', 'Hyperion'. Autograph manuscript versions of all thirteen poems in this volume — except the 'Ode on a Grecian Urn' — are extant as well as a great many authoritative transcripts. Indeed, two of the three surviving printer's copies for these poems (KeJ 145, 199, 223) are transcripts prepared by Richard Woodhouse; in addition, a manuscript of 'Song of Four Fairies' (KeJ 394) was originally part of the printer's copy for *Lamia* (1820) although the poem was not in fact published until *Literary Remains* (1848).

Literary Remains (1848) was the first major work on Keats — it includes a biography and publications of letters and poems — to appear after the poet's death twenty-seven years earlier.

The publication of a biography of Keats had indeed been a long time coming. Beginning with the announcement of a memoir of his recently deceased friend, by John Taylor in the *New Times* of 29 March 1821, plans to publish Keats's life were made by his literary executor Charles Brown as well as by Charles Cowden Clarke and J. H. Reynolds. But none were realized.

In March 1841, Brown turned over his manuscript 'Life of Keats' — delivered as a lecture in 1836 and printed in *Keats Circle*, II, 52–97 from the manuscript at Harvard — as well as his transcripts of the poems to Richard Monckton Milnes, 'a true lover of Keats' in whose hands Brown was ready to 'place the Life and Poems'. These papers formed the basis for Milnes's edition of the *Literary Remains* which not only included a biography but the publication of many of Keats's letters for the first time and sixty-eight poems, sixty of which had not been published by Keats and forty-one of which had *never* before been published.

The texts of these poems came not only from Brown's transcripts of Keats's poems and letters. During the 1840s, particularly from 1845, Milnes solicited manuscripts and information from Keats's surviving friends and family as well as their descendants (see *Keats Circle* for much of this correspondence). Milnes's sources for the sixty-eight poems published included, in addition to Brown's transcripts, transcripts by Woodhouse and his clerks, by John Jeffrey (Georgiana Wylie Keats's second husband), Charles Cowden Clarke, John Howard Payne and Coventry Patmore (for a complete list, see *Texts*, pp. 75–7). Thirty-three of the actual printer's copies, all transcripts, still survive and they are all listed in the entries: KeJ 14, 16, 29, 50, 80, 83, 138, 148, 151, 169, 211, 275, 304, 312, 318, 358, 361, 374–5, 392, 395, 402, 414, 424, 443, 450, 455, 465, 474, 492, 526, 534, 535, 549.

Lost and Unlocated Manuscripts

The 561 verse entries include autograph manuscripts, authoritative transcripts, one corrected proof and a few revised printed copies of 141 of Keats's 150 poems and five 'questionable attributions'. And this number, according to Stillinger, 'is not even close to the total that once existed' — a statement amply documented by the textual histories of the poems.

Besides the more notable lacunae — the original draft of 'Endymion', the fair copy of 'The Eve of St Agnes', the autograph of 'Ode on a Grecian Urn', the original draft of 'Bright Star! would I were stedfast as thou art' (the famous manuscript Keats wrote in his pocket edition of Shakespeare aboard ship leaving England was *not* his draft) — Stillinger's reconstructed histories of Keats's texts demonstrate that at least eighty autograph drafts and fair copies have been lost.

The vast majority of these are unlikely to turn up. The 'book' from which Keats says Brown was transcribing his poems (in a letter to George and Georgiana Keats of 30 April 1819) is one of the few glimpses of a physical manuscript, perhaps a lost poetical notebook, of which no trace remains. In fact, the one-time existence of most of these 'lost' autographs has been *deduced*: they are the missing links between versions of the texts that do survive.

However, a handful of autograph manuscripts that have not been located are *known* to have existed at some time: facsimiles of some have been printed; variants have been recorded; some have passed through the salerooms. Since there is every reason to suppose that such manuscripts are still extant, they are listed in the entries with the latest reference given as locations; see KeJ 44, 153, 164, 182, 185, 523 and the headnote to 'In drear nighted December'.

As already noted, a surprisingly large number of the fragments of the cut-up manuscripts of 'I stood tip-toe upon a little hill', 'Isabella' and *Otho the Great* have been located though most of the fragments of 'Lamia' have been lost; there is also every likelihood that missing pieces of these manuscripts (listed in the headnotes to the poems) will continue to turn up.

Several of Keats's letters in which he transcribed his poems are also lost. The entries include some surviving transcripts of such letters by Woodhouse (or his clerks) and by John Jeffrey; see KeJ 60, 118, 131, 200, 201, 242, 257, 341, 362, 537 and the headnotes to 'Lines on the Mermaid Tavern', 'Nature withheld Cassandra' and 'Robin Hood'. Most of these references are to now-lost letters which Keats wrote to J. H. Reynolds, available only in Woodhouse's transcripts. In fact, only four of the twenty-one original letters which Keats is known to have written to Reynolds have been recovered. And only one of the many transcripts of Keats's poems which Reynolds is known to have made — itself unlocated but reported in 1876 — is listed in the entries (KeJ 46). Also missing is 'Reynolds's volume of Poetry' which Woodhouse returned to John Taylor with his letter of 23 November 1818. This volume may have been the same as the 'M.S. collection of the Poetry of himself [Reynolds] Keats & others' that Woodhouse gave as the source for his transcript in W2 of 'Blue! 'Tis the life of heaven'.

A great many other important transcripts are also missing and these are mentioned throughout Stillinger's textual histories of the poems. Charles Brown who, along with Woodhouse, was the most reliable of Keats's transcribers, began copying Keats's poetry during their walking tour in the summer of 1818 and continued doing so while they shared the house in Wentworth Place (now Keats House) from December 1818 until Keats's departure for Italy in September 1820. Brown wrote to J. A. Hessey on 24 July 1821 requesting that the 'four MSS books in my hand writing of Mr Keats's Poems' be returned to him. Brown gave his transcripts to Richard Monckton Milnes in 1841, who apparently dismantled them during the preparation of *Literary Remains*, using some as printer's copies for that edition. In any case, Brown's surviving transcripts (see details below) represent only a fraction of what must have formed the contents of the 'four MSS books' (see *Texts*, pp. 52–3). One of his lost transcripts is mentioned in the headnote to 'The Gothic looks solemn'.

Another identifiable gap is the series of ten early poems which Woodhouse said 'were copied for my cousin [Mary Frogley] into a Volume of M.S. poetry, by Mr Kirkman, and said to be by Keats'. Eight of these texts — all composed before 1816 and none published by Keats himself — are recoverable from Woodhouse's transcripts, marked 'F', originally on the opening pages of W2, now inserted in W3 (see the description of W3 below). But there is no trace of Mary Frogley's 'volume' nor, indeed, of any of the sources which Mr Kirkman transcribed.

Sidney Colvin has also mentioned a Woodhouse notebook 'containing personal notices and recollections of Keats' that 'was unluckily destroyed in the fire at Messrs Kegan Paul and Co's. premises in 1883'. Stillinger suggests that this lost notebook may have contained Woodhouse transcripts that have not been located — that of 'Isabella' or *Otho the Great*, for instance — and probably included the transcript of 'On some Skulls in Beauley Abbey' mentioned in the headnote to that poem (see Stillinger, p. 750).

Transcripts and Manuscript Volumes

Keats's brothers Tom and George, and the latter's wife Georgiana (née Wylie), were the earliest transcribers of his poems. All of their extant transcripts of poems by Keats — except Tom Keats's transcript of 'I stood tip-toe upon a little hill' (KeJ 166) and the unidentified transcript of 'Oh Chatterton! how very sad thy fate!' (KeJ 296), if it is in George's hand — are contained in three manuscript volumes which are referred to in the entries by short titles:

Keats-Wylie Scrapbook

Notebook used by Georgiana Wylie (probably the original owner) and George Keats, first as a commonplace book and later as a scrapbook, containing one autograph poem by Keats (KeJ 475) and ten transcripts or partial transcripts of his early poems (4 in Georgiana's, 6 in George's hand), mostly probably deriving from lost autograph MSS, as well as transcripts of poems by others (including Georgiana's transcript of 'On Death' (KeJ 310), the only MS source of one of the 'questionable attributions') and numerous printed cuttings and other miscellaneous items not related to Keats (some of which have been removed and mounted in a separate volume because they had obscured the MSS), 138 pages (c. 80 leaves), some blank, watermarked 1815; the Keats poems were composed between 1814 and August 1816, the transcripts made probably in late 1816.

This notebook described in Sotheby's sale catalogue, 23–4 June 1947 (Lot 220, the property of Frank Sykes); it was resold at Sotheby's, 20–21 May 1968, Lot 382, to Fleming; also described in some detail in Maurice Buxton Forman, 'Georgiana Keats and Her Scrapbook', *The Connoisseur*, 116 (1945), 8–13; see also *Texts*, pp. 21–3 and Stillinger, pp. 744–5 and 751–2.

Contents: KeJ 263, 310, 329, 330, 415, 419, 475, 499, 500, 504, 510, 511.

Harvard, Keats Collection 3.4.

Tom Keats's Copybook

Notebook containing transcripts by Tom Keats of 14 poems by Keats (all but one published in *Poems* (1817)), all deriving from autograph MSS and 4 of them being the only extant MS of the poem; the first 2 poems (KeJ 405 and 55, which appear here as parts of a single work) annotated by Leigh Hunt and signed by Keats; containing also a transcript by Tom Keats of Hunt's sonnet 'As one who after long and far-spent years'; 24 pages, the inside cover bearing the name and address of John Scott to whom Tom Keats gave the notebook; the transcripts probably made late 1816 as Keats was preparing copy for *Poems* (1817).

This notebook sold American Art Association, 22–3 April 1937, Lot 81; described briefly in *Texts*, pp. 24–6 and Stillinger, pp. 745–6. Two sketches extracted from this notebook are now at the Keats–Shelley Memorial House, Rome.

Contents: KeJ 6, 55, 123, 174, 268, 323, 331, 405, 460, 476, 505, 509, 512, 551.

Harvard, Keats Collection, 3.5.

George Keats's Notebook

Notebook, probably originally belonging to John Keats until George's three-week visit to England in January 1820 when the latter took it over, containing 3 autograph MSS by Keats (KeJ 77, 196, 235) and 9 transcripts by George (deriving either from autograph MSS or transcripts by Charles Brown), also containing transcripts by George Keats of poems by Letitia Landon (ff. 60v–61), Percy Bysshe Shelley ('Adonais', f. 61v) and Caroline Norton (f. 62), and unidentified transcripts on inserted leaves of Keats's 'There is a joy in footing slow across a silent plain' (without authority and probably in Georgiana Keats's hand, f. 63) and of an anonymous poem 'To Miss Keats of Louisville Ky.' and a newspaper clipping of 1880, 69 leaves and 2 inserted leaves; watermarked 1816, inscribed (f. 1) 'George Keats 1820.'.

This notebook is briefly described in *The Odes of Keats And Their Earliest Manuscripts*, ed. Robert Gittings (London, 1970), pp. 68–70, in *Texts*, pp. 23–4 and Stillinger, p. 745; it is fully discussed and reproduced in *Keats Facsimiles V*.

Contents: KeJ 74, 77, 133, 196, 235, 274, 280, 285, 385, 470, 530, 545.

British Library, Egerton MS 2780.

The most important transcriber of Keats's poems, certainly from the point of view of preservation of the texts, is of course Richard Woodhouse. Not only do about one-third of the 561 verse entries represent transcripts by Woodhouse or clerks under his supervision but more than half of Keats's poems are represented by his authoritative transcripts. A table showing most of Woodhouse's extant transcripts is given in *Texts*, pp. 30–37.

In the case of seven poems his transcripts are the only extant manuscripts and, for about twenty others, they preserve otherwise unknown versions. Woodhouse transcribed from every available source and — as if preparing his materials for the modern textual editor — often annotated his transcripts as to their source and collated variants from other versions of the texts.

The large collection of 'Keatsiana' that he assembled includes much else besides the poetical transcripts and textual variants: there are Woodhouse's commentaries on the poems, his notes of factual and biographical details, his recording of dates and sources, to say nothing of his transcripts of Keats's letters, quite a number of which are otherwise unavailable.

Woodhouse's indefatiguable devotion to Keats started with his first encounter with *Poems* (1817) and lasted until his own death — thirteen years after Keats's — in 1834. As early as October 1818, he wrote of Keats to his cousin Mary Frogley: 'Such a genius, I verily believe, has not appeared since Shakespeare & Milton.'

In his will, Woodhouse instructed his brother George to present his collection of 'Keatsiana' — including 'all papers I have in the handwriting of Keats' and, with two exceptions, all of his 'Portraits Sketches Busts and Casts of Keats' — to John Taylor. Woodhouse claimed that 'they actually belong to him but I have collected and kept them'. Taylor made some of this material available in the 1840s to R. M. Milnes during the latter's preparation of *Literary Remains*.

The first item in Woodhouse's collection was probably the interleaved copy of *Poems* (1817) which he had acquired from Taylor & Hessey. Like his interleaved copy of *Endymion* (1818) (see KeJ 63 for a description), this copy was used to record textual variants from other manuscript versions but, in it, Woodhouse also noted important biographical information and critical comments and transcribed six of Keats's then-unpublished sonnets.

Woodhouse's Poems (1817)

Interleaved copy of *Poems* (1817), inscribed on front flyleaf 'Rich[d] Woodhouse/Temple. 1818./11 King's Bench Walk', including Woodhouse's transcripts of 6 sonnets by Keats and his recording of variants *from MS sources* in red ink (see KeJ 461, 514), also including Woodhouse's annotations: 8 pages of notes on metrics, with extracts from various poets, including Keats; critical and biographical glosses in the margins *passim*, and on interleaved pages (see the headnotes to 'Addressed to the Same', 'Hadst thou liv'd in days of old', 'On Receiving a Curious Shell...', 'On the Grasshopper and Cricket', 'To G. A. W.' and 'To My Brothers'); textual markings *passim*, including alterations of punctuation and metrical marks; rough pencil notes on the end flyleaves; Woodhouse's shorthand sonnet written in response to Keats's poem 'Sleep and Poetry' (p. 230) (a fair copy of this sonnet entitled 'To Apollo' is in W3, f. 24).

This copy described in full in Sperry (1967) and reproduced in its entirety in *Keats Facsimiles I*. Woodhouse bequeathed his 'Keatsiana' to John Taylor and his English law books to his brother George, who received this volume as well; a note in the front flyleaf by F. W. Bourdillon says he acquired the book from Mrs George Woodhouse in 1898.

Contents: KeJ 11, 302, 336, 350, 461, 481, 514, 519.

Huntington, RB 151582.

The most important of Woodhouse's transcripts, however, are those preserved in the three MS volumes known — ever since Garrod's first edition of Keats's *Poetical Works* in 1939 — as W1, W2 and W3. W3, also known as 'Woodhouse's Scrapbook' contains the earliest transcripts.

W3

Blank notebook of 106 leaves onto which loose leaves have been mounted (hence it being sometimes referred to as a 'scrapbook'), a modern title page reading 'Woodhouse and Others/Letters relating to Keats', 99 leaves are foliated (2–19, 19[1], 20–5, 25[1], 26–36, 36[1], 37–41, 41[1], 42–5, 45[1], 46–8, 48[1], 49–80, 80[1], 81–94 and wanting f. 93) and contain 103 items, unfoliated leaves are blank or contain engraved portraits of Keats and his circle; including, as well as contents listed below (i.e., 3 autograph MSS, 35 transcripts of Keats's poems, 29 by Woodhouse, and 5 Woodhouse transcripts of 'questionable attributions'):

(1) papers of Richard Woodhouse: shorthand transcript of Keats's letter to Taylor and Hessey, 10 June 1817 (original printed *Letters*, I, 147–8) (f. 60); draft letter to Keats, 10 December 1818 (*Keats Circle*, I, 70–2 and *Letters*, I, 409–11) (f. 10); 12 letters to John Taylor of 1818–20 (all printed *Keats Circle*, I, 57–60, 63–6, 75, 78–95, 102, 112–13, 116–18, 185) (ff. 2–6, 9, 11–15, 19); letter to Mary Frogley (together with a draft), [23 October 1818] (*Keats Circle*, I, 54–7 and *Letters*,

I, 383–5) (ff. 7–8); miscellaneous papers including a transcript by a clerk of a letter to the *Morning Chronicle*, 3 October 1818 (f. 1), a draft and fair copy of a list of Keats's letters (ff. 16–17), notes on Keats's life of August 1823 (*Keats Circle*, I, 274–5) (f. 18), a transcript of the inscription on Keats's tombstone (f. 20), the draft of an advertisement for *Lamia* (1820) (*Keats Circle*, I, 115–16) (f. 21); the original title page for W2 (see note below) (f. 22); quotations illustrating passages in 'Endymion' (f. 23); the fair copy of Woodhouse's poem 'To Apollo' dated 4 March 1818 (the shorthand draft of this poem is in Woodhouse's *Poems* (1817)) (f. 24); notes on Keats and G. F. Mathew (ff. 52–3) and miscellaneous notes (f. 61).

(2) letters by John Taylor and J. A. Hessey: 4 letters from Taylor: to Hessey, 31 August 1820 (f. 25), to Sir James Mackintosh (extract), 5 December 1818 (f. 25[1]), to John Keats, 11 September 1820 (f. 26) and to Woodhouse, [March 1821?] (f. 27) (printed *Keats Circle*, I, 133–7, 68–9, 138–9 and 234–5, respectively); draft letter from Taylor and Hessey to Charles Brown, 19 September 1820 (*Keats Circle*, I, 147–8) (f. 28) and a letter from Hessey to Taylor, 6 March 1818 (*Keats Circle*, I, 12–13) (f. 29).

(3) 13 letters from Benjamin Bailey to John Taylor, 23 February 1818–8 May 1821 (*Keats Circle*, I, 7–12, 18–21, 24–8, 31–6, 40–2, 60–3, 125–7, 208–13, 232–4, 236–7, 243–5) (ff. 31–41[1]) and Bailey's notes on a conversation with J. G. Lockhart of July 1818 made on 8 May 1821 (*Keats Circle*, I, 245–7) (f. 30).

(4) 6 letters by Charles Brown to John Taylor, 8 March [1820]–12 August 1821 (*Keats Circle*, I, 103–5, 160–1, 230, 263–4) (ff. 42–5, 46, 48) and one to J. A. Hessey, 24 July 1821 (*Keats Circle*, I, 261) (f. 47); Charles Brown's 'List of Mr John Keats' Books' [July? 1821] (*Keats Circle*, I, 253–60) (f. 49).

(5) 4 letters of J. H. Reynolds to John Taylor, 12 January 1819–21 September 1820 (*Keats Circle*, I, 72–4, 105, 119–20, 155–8) (ff. 45[1], 56–8).

(6) letters to John Taylor from Richard Abbey, 18 April 1821 (f. 48[1]), and C. G. Wylie, 17 August 1828 (f. 59) (*Keats Circle*, I, 235 and 317, respectively).

(7) letters to Richard Woodhouse from Frederick Salmon, 15 February 1822 (f. 19[1]), Charles Cowden Clarke, 29 December 1823 (f. 50), Mrs Thomas Green, 29 March 1819 (f. 51), Nan Woodhouse, 6 April 1820 (f. 54) and Charlotte Reynolds [1821?] (f. 55) (*Keats Circle*, I, 269–70, 275, 76, 106–9, 265, respectively).

(8) Woodhouse transcripts of John Taylor's 'The Poet' (f. 76) and E. W. Barnard's 'To Woman' (f. 90), both at one time attributed to Keats, and poems by A. G. Spencer and Charlotte Reynolds (f. 92).

The contents of this volume were for many years only loosely inserted; their order has been apparently changed several times, and the arrangements presented in Amy Lowell's typescript of the contents (at Harvard), made in the 1920s, and in Finney (1936) both differ from the present one. The volume was bought by Frank Sabin from Mrs George Taylor, a descendant of John Taylor, and acquired by J. P. Morgan on 28 December 1906. It is described briefly in *Texts*, p. 28 and Stillinger, pp. 748–9; fully described and reproduced in its entirety in *Keats Facsimiles IV*; 54 of the items published in *Keats Circle* are in W3.

On f. 22 (see (1) above) is mounted Woodhouse's original title page to W2, which reads: 'Poems—&c—/by, or relating to, John Keats./R. Woodhouse/Nov. 1818. Temple./All that are not by Keats, have the names/of the authors added. —'; since earlier editors did not realize that this description applied to W2 (and *not* W3 in which it is inserted), some misattributions to Keats of unsigned poems in W3 have been made at various times (see *Texts*, p. 273). Woodhouse removed this title page from W2 along with the original ff. 1–7, 10–12 of that volume at some point after May 1821 and inserted them in W3. These leaves (together with ff. 8–9 of W2 which were not excised) contained Woodhouse's transcripts of early Keats poems which he described in a note at the top of the original f. 1: 'The small pieces marked <K> F. (10 in number) were copied for my cousin into a volume of M.S. poetry, by Mr Kirkman, and said to be by Keats.' The original opening leaves of W2 have been fully discussed and meticulously reconstructed in Steele, pp. 238–46; see also *Texts*, pp. 39–41. For Woodhouse's transcripts of the eight poems on these leaves (now in W3), see KeJ 97, 125, 241, 261, 287, 325, 388, 416; for his transcripts on ff. 8–9, still in W2, see KeJ 22 and 299. After excising ff. 1–7, 10–12, Woodhouse retranscribed 6 of the 8 poems they contained in W2, ff. 219–24 (see KeJ 98, 127, 262, 288, 326, 418).

Contents: KeJ 23, 33, 85, 95, 96, 97, 113, 122, 125, 126, 141, 177, 197, 225.5, 240, 241, 247, 258, 259, 260, 261, 266, 287, 296, 300, 325, 334, 347, 351, 378, 388, 389, 397, 416, 417, 426, 430, 435, 439, 466.5, 479, 525, 555.

Pierpont Morgan, MA 215.

W2 is Woodhouse's most important compilation of Keats's verse. Stillinger describes it as 'the collection that Woodhouse took the most care with, entering variants, sources, dates and annotations to the extent that it has the character of a variorum edition of the poems'.

W2

Notebook containing transcripts by Richard Woodhouse of 73 poems by Keats, the title page and ff. 1–7, 10–12 excised by Woodhouse at some time after May 1821 (now inserted in W3, described above), also wanting ff. 13 and 141 (now lost, for the latter, see KeJ 471), 233 leaves (watermarked 1805), foliated by Woodhouse (several blank), verses written on rectos primarily, annotations on versos; containing as well as contents listed below: transcripts of 2 sonnets by J. H. Reynolds, one being his 'Sonnet – to Keats – on reading his Sonnet written in Chaucer.', dated 27 February 1817 (f. 20), the other being the sonnet that inspired a reply from Keats (see KeJ 45); the English translation of the Boccaccio tale used for writing 'Isabella' (ff. 190v–192v, see the headnote to that poem); the 'Contents of this volume' (ff. 234–5); variants from the fair copy of 'Endymion' and transcripts of the title page, dedication and original preface to that work (ff. 239v–235v *rev.*, see KeJ 61–2); a transcript of Keats's epitaph (f. 240v); and a list (discussed above) of 'Poems of J. K. which I have not' (on the back flyleaf); Woodhouse began compiling this volume in November 1818 and was adding to it at least as late as May 1821, inscribed (on a leaf pasted to the inside front cover) 'Rich[d] Woodhouse' and 'Temple. Nov. 1818'.

This volume described in Steele, pp. 238–55, in *Texts*, pp. 28, 30–7 (with contents listed) and briefly in Stillinger, p. 749; reproduced in its entirety in *Keats Facsimiles VI*. Woodhouse's list of 'Poems of J. K. which I have not' is printed in Steele, p. 255 and *Texts*, pp. 37–8.

Contents: KeJ 9, 19, 21, 22, 30, 39, 45, 58, 60, 73, 82, 84, 88, 94, 98, 102, 106, 114, 119, 127, 132, 140, 144, 150, 170, 178, 198, 205, 212, 231, 237, 243, 248, 252, 262, 273, 276, 281, 283, 288, 293, 297, 299, 308, 313, 319, 326, 335, 342, 352, 383, 396, 401, 410, 418, 425, 428, 434, 440, 446, 451, 462, 471, 480, 485, 490, 493, 496, 517, 529, 538, 546, 556.

Harvard, Keats Collection 3.2.

W1 is the latest of Woodhouse's books of transcripts. The poems in it are all in W2 from which they were probably copied. It was perhaps compiled as a duplicate copy to be kept with John Taylor (see Stillinger, p. 749).

W1

Notebook, a copy of Taylor & Hessey's *The Literary Diary; or, Improved Common-Place Book...* (London, 1811), containing 34 transcripts of Keats poems by Woodhouse and a transcript of 'Hyperion' by one of his clerks; 175 remaining leaves (watermarked 1809), paginated by Woodhouse, without pp. 1–10, 104–7 which are lost and omitting p. 100 in the pagination, a few pages blank; containing as well as contents listed below, transcripts by Woodhouse of 4 sonnets by J. H. Reynolds (pp. 15, 17, 25) and drafts for the title page of *Lamia* (1820) at the front and back of the book.

This notebook described in Steele, pp. 236–8, in *Texts*, pp. 28–9, 30–37 and, briefly, in Stillinger, p. 749 and *Keats Facsimiles VI*, pp. xv–xvi, 461–2.

Contents: KeJ 10, 24, 32, 40, 47, 75, 115, 120, 128, 145, 172, 179, 199, 213, 232, 239, 254, 286, 301, 315, 345, 353, 386, 404, 429, 441, 448, 453, 463, 486, 497, 518, 531, 539.

Harvard, Keats Collection 3.1.

The other volume compiled by Woodhouse referred to in the entries is 'Woodhouse's letterbook', a notebook into which Woodhouse and his clerks transcribed 56 of Keats's letters.

Woodhouse's letterbook

Notebook of transcripts by Woodhouse and his clerks, containing copies of 56 of Keats's letters (or parts of letters), 16 of which are otherwise unknown (the original of Stillinger's seventeenth — *Letters*, I, 208 to John Taylor — is now at Harvard), some including the full texts of poems written in the original letter (see contents below), others giving only the first lines of the poems; containing also Woodhouse's transcripts of letters by others and his own 'Notes on the Critiques on *Endymion* in the *Quarterly Review* and *Blackwood's Edinburgh Magazine*' of October 1818 (p. 10).

This volume is described in *Letters*, I, 18–19 and, briefly, in *Texts*, p. 29 (see also pp. 30–37) and Stillinger, p. 749. Woodhouse's 'Notes' are printed in *Keats Circle*, I, 44–5.

Contents: KeJ 67, 103, 118, 131, 200, 242, 257, 270, 349, 379, 537; see also the headnotes to 'Lines on the Mermaid Tavern', 'Nature withheld Cassandra in the skies' and 'Robin Hood'.

Harvard, Keats Collection 3.3.

In addition to these six volumes, there are two other groups of Woodhouse transcripts extant, both at Harvard. The first (Keats Collection 4.20.10) includes eight transcripts that Woodhouse made for Joseph Severn after 1830 (the date of the watermark); see KeJ 13, 51, 117, 337, 356, 456, 482, 541. Severn offered these transcripts to R. M. Milnes in a letter of 6 October 1845 (see *Keats Circle*, II, 131). This group of transcripts was mistakenly said to be lost in *Texts*, p. 30 but it has since been identified at Harvard (see Stillinger, pp. 749–50).

The other group of Woodhouse transcripts (Keats Collection 4.20.9) was also made in the 1830s — they are watermarked 1833 — for Charles Brown after Woodhouse saw him in Florence in 1832. The transcripts of twenty-two poems are enclosed in a covering sheet inscribed 'Hyperion (remodelled) with minor poems'; see KeJ 12, 25, 49, 89, 99, 104, 244, 264, 289, 298, 303, 309, 327, 355, 411, 420, 427, 449, 454, 464, 491, 494. They are (with the exception of two by Woodhouse himself) in the hands of two of his clerks. Brown gave these transcripts to Milnes, in 1841, along with his other Keats papers — his MS 'Life' of Keats and the 'four MSS books' of poems mentioned above. Milnes's collection passed to his son, the Marquess of Crewe, from whom Arthur A. Houghton acquired it in 1939 and was eventually presented to Harvard, one of the principal components of the great Keats Collection in that library.

What survives of Brown's 'four MSS books' given to Milnes are thirty-eight transcripts of Keats poems, including that of the dramatic fragment 'King Stephen' (KeJ 207) and Brown's fair copy of *Otho the Great*, the tragedy he wrote together with Keats (KeJ 374); a missing leaf of the fair copy of *Otho* (KeJ 375) has also turned up in the Robert H. Taylor Collection at Princeton.

The other thirty-six transcripts are together at Harvard (Keats Collection 3.6) on thirty-one loose sheets, watermarked 1815: KeJ 16, 29, 38, 42, 53, 57, 80, 83, 92, 130, 138, 148, 169, 211, 229, 236, 256, 271, 275, 279, 292, 312, 318, 343, 361, 384, 395, 402, 414, 424, 469, 484, 516, 528, 535, 544. All of these transcripts are discussed in full and reproduced in *Keats Facsimiles VII*.

Four other transcripts of Keats's poems by Brown have also been recovered: Brown's fair copy of another of his collaborations with Keats — 'On Some Skulls in Beauley Abbey' — is in W3 (KeJ 347); a transcript of 'In after time a sage of mickle lore' (KeJ 175) is written in Brown's copy of Spenser's *Works* at Keats House, London; a transcript of 'Shed no tear — O shed no tear!' (KeJ 391) is included in Brown's MS of his unfinished fairy tale 'The Fairies' Triumph' (Keats House) for which Keats wrote the lines; and a transcript made for Joseph Severn after Keats's death of 'Not Aladdin magian' (KeJ 253) is now at Harvard. For a lost (but recorded) transcript, see also the headnote to 'The Gothic looks solemn'.

In addition, Harvard also owns Brown's transcript of his friend Edward John Trelawney's *Adventures of a Younger Son*. The *Adventures* — first published in three volumes in 1831 from this MS — included several chapter epigraphs from three of Keats's then-unpublished works: 'King Stephen', 'The Jealousies' and *Otho the Great*. The passages of the poems so used are transcribed by Brown at the end of the manuscript (see KeJ 206, 209, 376).

While none of the many important transcripts of Keats's poems made by J. H. Reynolds survive (see above), the commonplace book kept by Charlotte Reynolds, one of his four sisters, has been preserved.

Reynolds-Hood Commonplace Book

Commonplace book in several hands, including those of J. H. Reynolds, his sister Charlotte Reynolds and his niece Frances Freeling Hood, in a copy of Taylor and Hessey's *Literary Diary or, Improved Common-Place Book*, inscribed on the title page 'J. H. Reynolds August 1816' and, on the front flyleaf, 'Frances Freeling Hood January 1847', 175 leaves (c. 75 being excised or blank); containing, as well as the Keats poems listed below (these occupy ff. 25a–41a and are headed by Frances Freeling Hood 'Manuscript Poems John Keats'): poetry and prose by J. H. Reynolds, S. T. Coleridge (see the *Index*, Vol. IV, Part 1, CoS 268, 289, 794, 1280), James Rice, Benjamin Bailey, Isabella Jane Towers, Thomas Hood and others.

This notebook is mentioned in the Coleridge section of the *Index*, Vol. IV, Part 1, p. 510 (where the Keats poems are mistakenly said to be in J. H. Reynolds's hand); a fuller description is given in Paul Kaufman, 'The Reynolds–Hood Commonplace Book: A Fresh Appraisal', *KSJ*, 10 (1961), 43–52 where the Keats poems are misdescribed as being in Jane Reynolds's hand; the correct identification of Charlotte Reynolds's hand is made (and the Keats transcripts discussed) in *Texts*, pp. 47–50.

Contents: KeJ 48, 86, 90, 116, 121, 134, 233, 249, 255, 346, 354, 442, 452, 520, 536, 554.

Bristol Reference Library.

Seventeen of Keats's poems were transcribed by Charles Wentworth Dilke on blank leaves at the end of his copy of *Endymion* (1818) now at Keats House, London (KH 52). They are listed in the headnote to 'Endymion' and discussed in *Texts*, pp. 56–7.

A few other authoritative transcripts made both by Keats's own circle of friends and by later copyists, often supplying material to R. M. Milnes during the 1840s, are scattered throughout the entries: two by Fanny Brawne (KeJ 54, 137); one each by John Taylor and J. A. Hessey in W3 (KeJ 33, 555); Leigh Hunt's two transcripts of 'On *The Story of Rimini*' (KeJ 359–60); four by Charles Cowden Clarke (KeJ 443, 466.5, 526, 534); one in William Pitter Woodhouse's (Richard's brother) commonplace book dating from 1827 (KeJ 477); three by J. C. Stephens and one by Isabella Jane Towers in the notebook (described below) that Charles Cowden Clarke gave to Towers for her birthday (KeJ 43, 447, 533, 552); six by John Jeffrey (Georgiana Keats's second husband) included in his transcripts of Keats's letters to George, Georgiana and Tom Keats made for Milnes in 1845 (KeJ 34, 59, 173, 341, 362, 548); five by B. R. Haydon, four of them made in 1844 and probably without authority (KeJ 2, 7, 8, 338, 483); three made by John Howard Payne for Milnes in 1847 (KeJ 35, 316, 458); twelve by Coventry Patmore who was employed by Milnes as a copyist in 1847 (KeJ 14, 26, 50, 105, 304, 357–8, 421, 450, 455, 465, 492); one by W. H. Prideaux, made for Milnes in [1847?] (KeJ 156); an unidentified transcript of a letter to Tom Keats containing two poems, made for Milnes in 1845 (KeJ 18, 295); four by Milnes himself (KeJ 151, 392, 474, 549); an unidentified transcript of an 1847 letter from Henry Stephens (KeJ 108); a transcript by W. A. Longmore, made for Milnes in 1870 (KeJ 412); and three unidentified transcripts, two on one leaf and one (possibly in George Keats's hand) in W3 (KeJ 1, 296, 553).

Stillinger mentions a few transcripts which — having been copied from published sources — are not listed in the entries. The most significant omissions of transcripts which Stillinger describes (but does not collate) are most of the contents of the notebook of Keats poems transcribed by the professional copyist J. C. Stephens (now at Harvard, Keats Collection 3.12). The notebook was prepared for Charles Cowden Clarke to present to his sister Isabella Jane Towers; it is entitled 'Poems by John Keats with several, never yet published...London written by J. C. Stephens for I J Towers. 1828' and inscribed by Clarke 'I. J. Towers. a little Birth day gift from her Brother 5 October 1828'. The first part of the notebook contains the thirty-one poems published in *Poems* (1817), transcribed from that volume. Following these are a further six transcripts by Stephens (listed *Texts*, p. 59), three of which were copied from manuscripts then owned by Clarke and therefore listed in the entries (KeJ 43, 533, 552). The last two items in the book are transcripts by Isabella Jane Towers, one of which was copied from an autograph manuscript (KeJ 447).

In addition, the following transcripts have also been excluded from the entries: Thomasine Leigh's transcripts — in her commonplace book at Keats House, London (KH 155) — of 'On Seeing the Elgin Marbles', 'To Haydon with a Sonnet Written on Seeing the Elgin Marbles' and lines 1–20 of 'To Charles Cowden Clarke'; Elizabeth Stott Clarke's transcripts of 'Blue! — 'Tis the life of heaven — the domain' and 'On the Sea' written in Isabella Jane Towers's copy of *Poems* (1817) at Keats House, London (KH 50) (this copy was unlocated in *Texts*, p. 62); Mary Strange Mathew's transcript of 'On First Looking into Chapman's Homer' in an album owned by T. G. Crump in the 1940s (a photocopy is at the University of Illinois); William Pitter Woodhouse's transcript of 'In drear nighted December' in his commonplace book dating from 1827 (see also KeJ 477) at Harvard, Keats Collection 3.13; an unidentified transcript (annotated by Leigh Hunt) of 'In drear nighted December' at Keats House, London (KH 60); Frederick Locker

Lampson's transcript of 'Shed no tear — O shed no tear!' in a copy of *The Poetical Works of John Keats* (London, 1841) at the Berg; B. R. Haydon's transcripts of the two Elgin Marbles sonnets, made for Milnes in 1845, now at Harvard, Keats Collection 4.7.20; and the unidentified transcript of 'There is a joy in footing slow across a silent plain' in George Keats's Notebook (mentioned above).

The Harvard Keats Collection and Other Principal Repositories

The Harvard Keats Collection is, of course, the most extensive in its holdings both by and about John Keats. As for his autograph poetical manuscripts and the authoritative transcripts, Harvard is cited as the location in over 60 per cent of the entries. Although there is no published catalogue of the collection, the autograph poems will soon be available in a facsimile edition (*Poetry Manuscripts*), which will complement the Garland series of *Keats Facsimiles I–VII*, two volumes of which reproduce Brown and Woodhouse transcripts in the Harvard Keats Collection.

Of the 251 letters by Keats which have been recovered, eighty-six autographs are also at Harvard, which — together with the transcripts by Woodhouse and John Jeffrey of another twenty-four letters — is also the single largest respository for Keats's letters. And this says nothing of the extraordinarily rich assemblage of letters, papers and documents *about* Keats, many of which were published in *Keats Circle*.

The revised two-volume edition of that work made available 393 letters and documents dating from 1814–79, all but fifty-four of which (those being in W3 at the Pierpont Morgan Library) are at Harvard; it includes letters by, to and among Keats's circle of friends, written during his lifetime and after his death, as well as a great many letters concerning posthumous works on Keats, particularly letters surrounding the preparation of Milnes's editions, *Literary Remains* (1848) and the 1876 Aldine Edition of *The Poetical Works of John Keats*. It also prints a few miscellaneous papers and documents, such as Woodhouse's rough notes on Keats's 'When I have fears that I may cease to be' (*Keats Circle*, I, 128–30); John Taylor's MS of the so-called 'Abbey Memoir' (*Keats Circle*, I, 302–9); Charles Brown's MS 'Life of Keats' (*Keats Circle*, II, 52–97); the agreement between John Taylor and Edward Moxon for the publication of Keats's works by the latter, 30 September 1845 (*Keats Circle*, II, 128–9); biographical sketches and reminiscences of Keats written for R. M. Milnes in the 1840s by Joseph Severn, Charles Cowden Clarke, G. F. Mathew, Caroline Mathew, Henry Stephens and Benjamin Bailey (*Keats Circle*, II, 134–8, 146–53, 184–8, 189–91, 206–14, 266–97, respectively); the original MS of Charles Cowden Clarke's 'Recollections of Keats' apparently used for his and Mary Cowden Clarke's *Recollections of Writers* (1878) (unpublished passages in *Keats Circle*, II, 319–21); Charles Wentworth Dilke's notes on *Literary Remains* sent in 1875 to Milnes for his use in preparing the 1876 Aldine Edition; as well as a great many poems written *to* Keats by various hands.

In addition to these materials, the Harvard collection includes Keatsiana which post-date 1879. Hyder Edward Rollins gives an account of two such collections — those assembled by the Keats scholars and collectors Fred Holland Day and Louis Arthur Holman — in 'F. H. Day and Keats's Biography' and 'Louis Arthur Holman and Keats', published in *HLB*, 4 (1950), 239–53 and 374–91, respectively. Some of Rollins's own working papers, including his annotated copies of *Letters* and *Keats Circle*, are also now at Harvard.

The cornerstone of the Keats Collection was the bequest in 1927 of Amy Lowell's Keats collection; for a summary, see Finney, pp. 762–6. The presentation, in 1941, by Arthur A. Houghton, of the magnificent collection which he had bought in 1939 from the Marquess of Crewe — son of R. M. Milnes — firmly established Harvard as the most important Keats library in the world; for a summary, see Finney, pp. 755–62. This so-called Crewe collection included, in addition to autograph manuscripts and letters, three of the four volumes compiled by Woodhouse (W2, W1 and the Woodhouse letterbook) and the MS 'Life and Poems' that Charles Brown had given Milnes in 1841, as well as the large collection of papers collected by Milnes himself while preparing his editions of Keats.

Subsequently, there have been numerous additions to Harvard's collection: Lucius Wilmerding presented a collection of the papers of John Taylor (1806–60) in 1945 (*NUCMC*, 81-647); a collection of Benjamin Bailey's papers (1817–49) was deposited in 1951 by Arthur A. Houghton (*NUCMC*, 81-408); in 1953, a collection of letters and notes, mostly by or to Keats's sister Fanny (later Fanny Keats de Llanos), was purchased from her great-grandson Dr Ernesto Paradinas y Brockman and 43 items from this collection were included in Rollins's edition of *More Letters and Poems of the Keats Circle* (first published separately in 1955 and included as a supplement in Vol. II of *Keats Circle*); a large collection of the papers of Joseph

Severn dating from 1820–99 has also been acquired (*NUCMC*, 83-981); and quite a few of the items listed among the private collections in Finney (pp. 771–7) have found their way to Harvard.

The other major American collection of Keats's literary manuscripts is at the Pierpont Morgan Library; for a summary, see Finney, pp. [745]–54. Its holdings, acquired from various sources, include about seventy of the manuscripts listed in the entries, over half of which are contained in the W3 volume (described above). Most of the others are autograph manuscripts, including Keats's fair copy of 'Endymion', the largest part of the draft of 'The Jealousies', the draft of the 'Ode to Psyche' and several shorter poems and sonnets.

In terms of poetical manuscripts, the principal English collection is that at the British Library which preserves the important manuscripts in George Keats's Notebook and Keats's manuscript of 'Hyperion' (see *Keats Facsimiles V*), as well as manuscripts and fragments of other minor poems; for a summary, see Finney, pp. 766–8.

A few notable autograph poems and other manuscripts are also preserved in the collection at Keats House, London, the cornerstone of which was the bequest of Charles Wentworth Dilke's collection in 1911; for a summary, see Finney, pp. 768–71. Eight of the eighteen printed books annotated by Keats that are known are at Keats House, as well as all the extant transcripts of Keats's poetry by Dilke — written in his copy of *Endymion* (1818). Facsimiles of many of the autograph manuscripts in this collection were printed in Williamson (1914).

Keats's Library and Annotated Books

The books that Keats read were generally given or lent to him by his friends. He wrote to John Taylor in June 1818 that 'I can scarcely ask the loan of Books...since I still keep those you lent me a year ago' (*Letters*, I, 295–6). About a year later, he wrote to Dilke that 'I have at last made up my mind to send home all lent Books' (*Letters*, II, 114).

If Keats returned books to their owners at that time — or which books he returned — is unknown but, before he sailed to Italy in September 1820, he did present some of his books to friends — including his gifts to Fanny Brawne of his copies of Dante (KeJ 562), Hunt's *Literary Pocket-Book for 1819* (KeJ 567), Lamb's *Specimens of English Dramatic Poets* (KeJ 566) and his reprint of Shakespeare's First Folio (KeJ 573). He apparently took with him to Italy only his seven-volume pocket edition of Shakespeare (KeJ 574) and a volume of Shakespeare's poetry (KeJ 572), both of which he later gave to Joseph Severn.

He also wrote out an informal 'will' on a scrap of paper (sent to John Taylor with a letter of 14 August 1820 and printed in *Letters*, II, 319), the last sentence of which reads 'My Chest of Books divide among my friends —'. The request was executed by Charles Brown who, sometime before 24 July 1821, wrote out a '*List of Mr John Keats' Books*' (now in W3, described above, and printed in *Keats Circle*, I. 253–60) — including some eighty-one titles, followed by the names of eighteen friends who might receive the books. Amy Lowell described Brown's method of distribution as follows: 'he divided Keats's books among his friends in a rough and ready fashion, allotting to each friend such volumes as each had given the poet, returning lent copies to their rightful owners, and as to the rest, giving some away and keeping the remainder himself' (see also *Keats Circle*, I, 260n).

Brown apparently took those of Keats's books that he kept for himself with him when he emigrated in 1841 to New Zealand where he died the following year. His son Major Charles Brown later sent the books to Sir Charles Wentworth Dilke and they formed part of the collection which Dilke's grandson bequeathed to the Hampstead Public Library in 1911 (now Keats House).

Remarkably few of the books on Brown's 'List' — or indeed of any others which at some time belonged to Keats — have been recovered. Frank Owings, who investigated the whereabouts of Keats's library in 1978, turned up twenty-seven books, fourteen of which were not included on Brown's 'List'. Of these, eighteen contain annotations of some kind (sometimes poems) and are listed in the Marginalia section; the other nine are listed here:

(1) [The Bible]. 'Η Καινη Διαθηκη. *Novum Testamentum...auctore Johanne Leusden* (Amsterdam, 1717), John Taylor's presentation copy to Keats, September 1820: Harvard (Owings, No. XVIII).

(2) John Bonnycastle, *An Introduction to Astronomy* (London, 1807), containing a bookplate 'Assigned as a Reward of Merit to Ma^r John Keats at Mr Clarke's Enfield Mids 1811' and inscribed by Keats to his brother George, 1818: Huntington (Owings, No. II).

(3) William Duverger, *The English and the French Language compared in their Grammatical Constructions*, 5th ed (London, 1807), inscribed by

Keats, 19 May 1807: Keats House, London, KH 15 (Owings, No. VII).

(4) Oliver Goldsmith, *Grecian History*, 2 vols (London, 1805), a presentation copy from B. R. Haydon and containing marginalia and sketches by him *passim*, inscribed to George Keats, 1818: this book was owned in 1913 by Mrs John Morgan (niece of John Jeffrey) and sold at Anderson Galleries, 12 November 1914 (as the property of Mrs J. F. Lovejoy) (Owings, Appendix, p. 63).

(5) Leigh Hunt, *Foliage* (London, 1818), Hunt's presentation copy to Keats in 1818: Harvard (Owings, No. IX).

(6) John Lempriere, *A Classical Dictionary*, 6th ed (London, 1806), possibly belonging to Keats: Keats House, London, KH 19 (Owings, No. XIV).

(7) Titus Livius, *The Roman History. Written in Latine By Titus Livius. With the Supplements of the Learned John Freinshemius and John Dujatius* (London, 1686), Benjamin Bailey's presentation copy to Keats, July 1818: Keats House, London, KH 20 (Owings, No. XV).

(8) Thomas Sackville, *The Poetical Works* (London, 1820), inscribed by Keats, 1820: previously owned by W. H. Arnold (Owings, Appendix, p. 63).

(9) Edmund Spenser, *The Works* (London, 1679), inscribed by Keats '...Severn's gift. (1818)': owned (1978) by Sol Feinstone, Washington Crossing, PA (Owings, No. XXIV).

In addition, a few references to unlocated books once owned by Keats have been cited. In a letter to Mrs C. W. Dilke of November 1848, Fanny Brawne Lindon mentions the copy in her possession of 'the Cenci by Shelley marked with many of Keats notes'; see Hyder Edward Rollins, 'A Fanny Brawne Letter of 1848', *HLB*, 5 (1951), 372–5. This title was one of the three on Charles Brown's 'List' that were, for some reason, cancelled.

In his 'reminiscences' of Keats sent to Milnes from Ceylon in May 1849, Benjamin Bailey describes the copy of *Auctores Mythographi Latini*, ed. Augustinus van Staveren (Amsterdam, 1742) — which appears on Brown's 'List' — that Brown had sent to him from Keats's 'Chest of Books' in July 1823; see *Keats Circle*, II, 280.

And, finally, a second copy of H. F. Cary's translation of Dante (for the first, see KeJ 561) — said to have been owned by Keats and, later, by his brother George and his daughter Mrs Philip Speed — was mentioned in the New York *World* of 25 July 1877.

Letters

Complete or partial texts of about 250 of Keats's letters — all written in the space of just five years, between November 1815 and November 1820 — have been recovered; they have all been printed in Rollins's edition of the *Letters* (1958), the vast majority from MS sources. Over 100 of those MS letters (a few being transcripts by Richard Woodhouse and John Jeffrey) are at Harvard. The other notable collections of letters are in the British Library, which preserves nearly fifty letters, Keats House (fourteen letters) and the Pierpont Morgan Library (ten letters).

In his Introduction (pp. 9–13), Rollins lists about sixty additional letters or parts of letters which have been 'lost'. If the recent past is an accurate indication of the future, however, it is unlikely that the canon of Keats letters will alter significantly. In the thirty-one years since the publication of *Letters*, no new letters have come to light, though a few letters in private hands have been presented to or bought by libraries. When the last Keats letter was sold at Sotheby's in June 1982, the sale catalogue pointed out that it was the first to be auctioned there since 1972.

Most of the changes in locations of the letters have been noted by Jack Stillinger in 'The Manuscripts of Keats's Letters: An Update', *KSJ*, 36 (1987), 16–19. An additional piece of information that can be added to that note concerns *Letters*, No. 89 (to Thomas Monkhouse, [21 June 1818]) which was that last letter to be sold at Sotheby's, on 30 June 1982 (Lot 498) to Jeffrey; while the original has not been traced, a facsimile of it was lodged in the British Library in 1982 (RP 2344) when an export license was granted. According to the *New York Times* of 30 March 1989, it was at that time being offered for sale at the New York Antiquarian Book Fair.

The few other 'new' locations of letters are:

(1) *Letters*, No. 10: to Charles Cowden Clarke, [8 or 11 November 1816] (printed *Letters*, I, 116 from the original at the Dedham (Massachusetts) Historical Society, now in the Harvard Keats Collection).

(2) *Letters*, No. 21: to George and Tom Keats, [15 April 1817], postmarked 16 April 1817 (printed *Letters*, I, 128–30 from a published source). The original letter is in the Robert H. Taylor Collection at Princeton; a facsimile was lodged in the British Library (RP 770(2)) at the time the MS was granted an export license.

(3) *Letters*, No. 49: to John Taylor, 10 January 1818 (printed *Letters*, I, 201–2 from a transcript in Woodhouse's letterbook). The original letter was sold at Christie's on 2 April 1975 (Lot 96) for £2400. The sale catalogue included a facsimile of one page (plate 3).

(4) *Letters*, No. 81: to Margaret Jeffrey of 4 or 5 May 1818 (printed *Letters*, I, 283 from A. F. Sieveking's article in the *Fortnightly Review*, 60 (1893), 729–35). The original letter was granted an export license in Britain early in 1983 when a facsimile (RP 2445) was lodged in the British Library.

(5) *Letters*, No. 178: to Fanny Brawne, [25 July 1819] (printed *Letters*, II, 132–4 from a published source). The original is now in the Harvard Keats Collection.

(6) *Letters*, Nos. 191 and 257: to Fanny Brawne, 13 September 1819 and April? 1820 (printed *Letters*, II, 160 and 286, respectively, from the originals owned by Archibald S. Alexander). Those originals are now at Princeton University Library, Am 21562–63.

(7) *Letters*, No. 206: to William Haslam, 2 November 1819 (an extract printed *Letters*, II, 226 from a 1904 sale catalogue). Claremont College reports owning Keats's two-page autograph of this letter.

(8) *Letters*, No. 291: to William Haslam, postmarked 23 August 1820 (printed *Letters*, II, 330–1 from a facsimile of the original in Sotheby's sale catalogue, 15–17 March 1937, Lot 497). The original is now in the Harvard Keats Collection.

Miscellaneous Papers and Keatsiana

Apart from the Keats association materials already mentioned in the descriptions of MS volumes and in the summary of the Harvard Keats Collection above, there are other papers in various collections that are worth noting. A few interesting documents are extant: Keats's admission ticket to lectures at Guy's Hospital, 1815, is at Bryn Mawr College; a facsimile of his application for a certificate to practice as an apothecary, 25 July 1816, is at Keats House, London, KH 30; the document written by a professional scribe assigning the copyright on 'Endymion' to Taylor and Hessey (*Keats Circle*, I, 142–4) — dated 16 September 1820 but prepared in advance and signed by Keats, William Haslam and Richard Woodhouse — is at Harvard (facsimile in British Library, Facs. Suppl. V(y), ff. 72b–73); the similar document assigning the copyright on *Poems* (1817) and *Lamia* (1820) to Taylor and Hessey, written by Richard Woodhouse, dated 16 September 1820 and signed by Keats, Haslam and Woodhouse, is at the Pierpont Morgan Library (MA 651) and printed in *Letters*, II, 334–6; Keats's informal 'will' on a scrap enclosed in a letter to John Taylor of 14 August 1820 (*Letters*, II, 318–20) is at the Pierpont Morgan Library (MA 214); Keats's passport is at Harvard; and a MS bank statement of his account in Rome (from 15 November 1820 to 16 April 1821) is at the Keats-Shelley Memorial House, Rome (No. 50).

In an interesting footnote to the summary description of his collection ('Contemporary Collections XLI. The Ewelme Collection', *BC*, 14 (1965), 188n), Simon Nowell-Smith lists the known copies of *Poems* (1817) that Keats presented to his friends. He had located eleven such copies: the one inscribed by George Keats to Georgiana Wylie from 'the Author and his Brother' was in his own Ewelme collection; those presented to Fanny Keats, George Keats (KeJ 407), J. H. Reynolds (see KeJ 332–3, 478, 515), the Misses Reynolds, Joseph Severn and Charles Wells (KeJ 406) are at Harvard; the other four being inscribed to John Byng Gattie (William Andrews Clark Library, Los Angeles), Charles Wilkinson (this copy, at the Berg, was apparently inscribed 'from the author' by George Keats), Charles Cowden Clarke (Pierpont Morgan) and William Wordsworth (Robert H. Taylor Collection at Princeton). Nowell-Smith had not been able to locate the copy given to B. R. Haydon. Nor did he mention the copy presented to Thomas Richards (KeJ 407.5) at the Free Library of Philadelphia or the copy inscribed 'to his friend G. F. Mathew' sold at Christie's on 16 November 1984 to Fleming. Both Charles Brown's and Isabella Jane Towers's copies are at Keats House, London (KH 49 and 50), the latter containing two transcripts of Keats poems by Elizabeth Stott Clarke, copied from *Literary Remains*.

In addition to the copies of *Endymion* (1818) containing non-authoritative corrections mentioned in the headnote to that poem as well as the corrected copy which is listed (KeJ 71) — including copies belonging to Leigh Hunt, two of Leigh Hunt's sons, Charles Wentworth Dilke and Charles Wells — there is another copy (Tulane University) containing corrections by John Taylor which he made from the list of errata sent by Keats on 24 April 1818 (see KeJ 70). Other notable copies are: B. R. Haydon's annotated copy at the Keats-Shelley Memorial House, Rome; Keats's presentation copy to Percy Bysshe Shelley formerly owned by Frank Bemis; Charles Brown's copy at Keats House, London (KH 54); and a copy containing corrections at Keats House (KH 53) which was mentioned in H. B. Forman's edition of *The Poetical Works and Other Writings of John Keats*, 4 vols (London, 1883) and formerly owned by Maurice Buxton Forman.

Keats's presentation copy of *Lamia* (1820) to B. Davenport in which he cancelled the 'Advertisement' and included a marginal denial of his authorship of it, is at Harvard; a facsimile is printed in Amy Lowell, *John Keats*, 2 vols (Boston, 1925), II, between pp. 424 and 425. Also at Harvard is Keats's presentation copy of *Lamia* to Fanny Brawne but the copy given to Charles Lamb, formerly owned by Frank Bemis, has not been traced. The copy inscribed by Keats on the title page to William Hazlitt (formerly owned by F. Holland Day) will be sold at Sotheby's (New York) in April 1990.

Most of the letters and papers of the Keats circle at Harvard and the Pierpont Morgan Library were printed in *Keats Circle*. The rather large number of such papers elsewhere, however, remains mostly unpublished; Sudie Nostrand's unpublished doctoral dissertation 'The Keats Circle: Further Letters' (New York University, 1973), however, makes 252 more letters available. Most of those (227) are preserved at Keats House, London; the others are owned by the Keats-Shelley Memorial House, Rome, the Huntington Library and the University of Iowa.

The collection at Keats House contains letters, papers, books and relics of George Keats, Tom Keats, Charles Brown, C. W. Dilke, Joseph Severn, Fanny Brawne (thirty-one letters from her to Fanny Keats of 1820–4), J. H. Reynolds, Benjamin Bailey, James Rice, Mary Cowden Clarke, John Taylor, J. A. Hessey, etc., as well as a good many portraits, sketches and busts of Keats and other subjects by various artists, including Joseph Severn and Charles Brown. William Hilton's portrait in oil of Keats commissioned by Richard Woodhouse (and bequeathed to John Taylor) is on loan to Keats House from the National Portrait Gallery. Also in this collection is B. R. Haydon's life mask of Keats. A partial catalogue is given in *Keats House: A Guide*, 6th ed, 3rd impression (London, 1971); an up-to-date accessions list is available in the library.

A few more Keats circle papers are preserved in the Keats-Shelley Memorial House in Rome and are available in Nostrand's dissertation (mentioned above). As well as letters of George Keats, C. W. Dilke, Fanny Brawne, J. H. Reynolds and a few written by Joseph Severn while he was nursing the dying Keats, there is a sketch of a Grecian vase, said to be by Keats himself, and sketches, drawings and portraits by Severn — including the famous death-bed drawing inscribed '28 Jan. 3 o'clock morning — drawn to keep me awake — a deadly sweat was on him all this night'. A catalogue of the entire collection has been published by G. K. Hall, *Catalog of Books and Manuscripts at the Keats-Shelley Memorial House in Rome* (Boston, 1969).

Three other sketches of Keats by Severn are at the Pierpont Morgan Library; they were enclosed in a letter to John Taylor from Rome, 21 January 1825. A miniature oil portrait of Keats reading, painted by Severn posthumously, is in the National Portrait Gallery, London. A death mask of Keats was sold at Sotheby's on 10–11 July 1986, Lot 86.

While some papers concerning the publication in 1921 of the centenary *John Keats Memorial Volume*, edited by George C. Williamson, are at Keats House, London, a collection of letters to Williamson and other papers (including some of the contributions, such as Thomas Hardy's, see HrT 64.3–64.5) is also in the Princeton University Library.

Hyder Edward Rollins's annotated copies of his editions of Keats materials are at Harvard. H. W. Garrod's collection of notes, letters, photocopies, articles, etc. assembled during the preparation of his edition of Keats's *Poetical Works* (1939) — together with eleven letters from Maurice Buxton Forman of 1935–8 — are in the Osborn Collection at Yale. A collection of books and papers was presented to Keats House by Edmund Blunden; and it includes his own annotated copies of four of his own works.

H. B. Forman's annotated copy of his edition of *The Letters of John Keats to Fanny Brawne* (London, 1878) is now at Bryn Mawr College. A collection of his Keats-related papers is also at the University of Delaware (*NUCMC*, 85–364). James Russell Lowell's copy of his edition of the *Poetical Works of John Keats* (Boston, 1854), which bears his corrections for a new edition, is at the Berg.

ABBREVIATIONS

For general abbreviations, see the list at the front of this volume.

Endymion (1818)
John Keats, *Endymion: A Poetic Romance* (London, 1818).

Finney
Claude Lee Finney, *The Evolution of Keats's Poetry*, 2 vols (Cambridge, MA, 1936).
Garrod
The Poetical Works of John Keats, ed. H. W. Garrod, 2nd ed (Oxford, 1958).
George Keats's Notebook
For a description, see INTRODUCTION.
Keats Circle
The Keats Circle: Letters and Papers and More Letters and Poems of the Keats Circle, ed. Hyder Edward Rollins, 2nd ed, 2 vols (Cambridge, MA, 1965).
Keats Facsimiles I–VII
The John Keats volumes in the series *The Manuscripts of the Younger Romantics*, general editor Donald H. Reiman:
Vol. I: *Poems (1817). A Facsimile of Richard Woodhouse's Annotated Copy in the Huntington Library*, ed. Jack Stillinger (New York and London, 1985)
Vol. II: *Endymion. A Facsimile of the Revised Holograph Manuscript*, ed. Jack Stillinger (New York and London, 1985)
Vol. III: *Endymion (1818). A Facsimile of Richard Woodhouse's Annotated Copy in the Berg Collection*, ed. Jack Stillinger (New York and London, 1985)
Vol. IV: *Poems, Transcripts, Letters, Etc: Facsimiles of Woodhouse's Scrapbook Materials in the Pierpont Morgan Library*, ed. Jack Stillinger (New York and London, 1985)
Vol. V: *Manuscript Poems in the British Library*, ed. Jack Stillinger (New York and London, 1988)
Vol. VI: *The Woodhouse Poetry Transcripts at Harvard*, ed. Jack Stillinger (New York and London, 1988)
Vol. VII: *The Charles Brown Poetry Transcripts at Harvard*, ed. Jack Stillinger (New York and London, 1988)
Keats-Wylie Scrapbook
For a description, see INTRODUCTION.
Letters
The Letters of John Keats 1814–1821, ed. Hyder Edward Rollins, 2 vols (Cambridge, MA, 1958).
Literary Remains
Life, Letters, and Literary Remains, of John Keats, ed. Richard Monckton Milnes, 2 vols (London, 1848).
Owings
Frank N. Owings, Jr, *The Keats Library (a descriptive catalogue)* (London, [1978?]).
Poems (1817)
John Keats, *Poems* (London, 1817).
Poetry Manuscripts
John Keats: Poetry Manuscripts at Harvard, a Facsimile Edition, ed. Jack Stillinger (Cambridge, MA: Harvard University Press, to be published in 1990).
Reynolds-Hood Commonplace Book
For a description, see INTRODUCTION.
Sperry
Stuart M. Sperry, Jr, 'Richard Woodhouse's Interleaved and Annotated Copy of Keats's *Poems* (1817)', *Literary Monographs*, I (Madison, WI, 1967), pp. 101–64, 308–11.
Steele
Mabel A. E. Steele, 'The Woodhouse Transcripts of the Poems of Keats', *HLB*, 3 (1949), 232–56.
Stillinger
The Poems of John Keats, ed. Jack Stillinger (Cambridge, MA, 1978; London, 1978).
Texts
Jack Stillinger, *The Texts of Keats's Poems* (Cambridge, MA, 1974).
Tom Keats's Copybook
For a description, see INTRODUCTION.
W1, W2, W3
For descriptions of these MS volumes, see INTRODUCTION.
Williamson
The Keats Letters, Papers, & Other Relics Forming the Dilke Bequest in the Hampstead Public Library, ed. George C. Williamson (London, 1914).
Woodhouse's letterbook
For a description, see INTRODUCTION.
Woodhouse's *Poems* (1817)
For a description, see INTRODUCTION.

ARRANGEMENT

Verse	KeJ 1–556
Notebook	KeJ 557
Marginalia in Printed Books	KeJ 558–75

John Keats

VERSE

Addressed To Haydon ('Highmindedness, a jealousy for good')
First pub. *Poems* (1817), as 'Sonnet XIII'; Stillinger, pp. 66–7.

KeJ 1 Transcript in an unidentified hand, here entitled 'High Mindedness', on a leaf (containing also KeJ 553).

Harvard, Keats Collection 3.10(1).

KeJ 2 Transcript by B. R. Haydon or his daughter Mary in a collection of loose MSS (9 leaves (11 pages) containing also KeJ 8, 338, 483 and sonnets by Wordsworth and Elizabeth Barrett Browning), inscribed on wrapper by Haydon 'Sonnets addressed to & MS Written by B. R. Haydon from 1817 to 1841 — Twenty Four Years. Copied for Fun. 1844'.

This transcript (not located in Stillinger, see p. 744) is possibly taken from a printed source.

Pierpont Morgan, MA 2987.

Addressed to the Same ('Great spirits now on earth are sojourning')
First pub. *Poems* (1817), as 'Sonnet XIV'; Stillinger, p. 67. Woodhouse's annotation about this poem, facing p. 92 of Woodhouse's *Poems* (1817), is reproduced in *Keats Facsimiles I*, p. 177.

KeJ 3 Fair copy, here untitled, one page, in a letter to B. R. Haydon dated (twice) 20 November [1816].

This MS printed *Letters*, I, 117 (facsimile between pp. 114 and 115); facsimile in British Library, MS Facs. 337.

Harvard, Keats Collection 1.3.

KeJ 4 Fair copy, here untitled, one page, enclosed in a letter to B. R. Haydon (meant to be forwarded to Wordsworth, but see KeJ 7), postmarked 21 November 1816.

This MS printed *Letters*, I, 118–19; facsimilc in British Library, MS Facs. 337.

Harvard, Keats Collection 1.4.

KeJ 5 Fair copy, printer's copy for *Poems* (1817), headed '14', one page, on a leaf foliated '66'; dated 'Christ Day' [25 December 1816].

Facsimile in A. S. W. Rosenbach, *Books and Bidders: The Adventures of a Bibliophile* (Boston, 1927), p. 41 and *Poetry Manuscripts*, p. 21.

Harvard, Keats Collection 2.7.

KeJ 6 Transcript in Tom Keats's Copybook, headed 'Sonnet'; dated 1816, probably transcribed [late 1816].

Harvard, Keats Collection 3.5, p. 17.

KeJ 7 Transcript by B. R. Haydon (from KeJ 4), in a letter from him to Wordsworth of 31 December 1816.

This transcript mentioned Stillinger, p. 555 (but not in *Texts*).

Wordsworth Library, Grasmere.

KeJ 8 Transcript by B. R. Haydon or his daughter Mary in a collection of loose MSS (9 leaves (11 pages) containing also KeJ 2, 338, 483 and sonnets by Wordsworth and Elizabeth Barrett Browning), inscribed by Haydon on wrapper 'Sonnets addressed to & MS Written by B. R. Haydon from 1817 to 1841 — Twenty Four Years. Copied for Fun. 1844'.

This transcript (not located in Stillinger, see p. 744) is possibly taken from a printed source.

Pierpont Morgan, MA 2987.

'After dark vapours have oppressed our plains'
First pub. *The Examiner*, 23 February 1817; collected *Literary Remains* (1848); Stillinger, p. 89.

KeJ 9 Transcript by Richard Woodhouse, in W2, headed 'Sonnet.', annotated 'from J. H. R[eynolds]'; dated 31 January 1817.

Facsimile in *Keats Facsimiles VI*, p. 13.

Harvard, Keats Collection 3.2, f. 18.

KeJ 10 Transcript by Richard Woodhousc, in W1; signed and dated 31 January 1817.

Harvard, Keats Collection 3.1, p. 23.

KeJ 11 Transcript on one page of the end flyleaves of Woodhouse's *Poems* (1817); dated 31 January 1817.

This transcript printed in Sperry, p. 161; facsimile in *Keats Facsimiles I*, p. 241.

Huntington, RB 151852.

KeJ 12 Late transcript by one of Richard Woodhouse's clerks, made for Charles Brown; dated 31 January 1817, watermarked 1833.

Harvard, Keats Collection 40.20.9.

KeJ 13 Late transcript by Richard Woodhouse, made for Joseph Severn; watermarked 1830.

Harvard, Keats Collection 4.20.10.

KeJ 14 Transcript by Coventry Patmore, made in 1847 and used as printer's copy for *Literary Remains* (1848); dated 31 January 1817.

Harvard, Keats Collection 3.10(12).

'Ah! ken ye what I met the day'
First pub. *Poetical Works and Other Writings of John Keats*, ed. H. B. Forman, 4 vols (London, 1883); Stillinger, pp. 270–1.

KeJ 15 Written before the opening of a letter (containing also KeJ 466) to Tom Keats, 10–14 July 1818.

This MS printed *Letters*, I, 327–8 (letter, 327–33).

British Library, Add. MS 45510, f. 1.

'Ah! woe is me! poor Silver-wing!'
First pub. *Plymouth and Devonport Weekly Journal*, 25 October 1838, as 'Faery Dirge'; collected *Literary Remains* (1848); Stillinger, pp. 297–8.

KeJ 16 Transcript by Charles Brown, here entitled 'Faery Song', printer's copy for *Literary Remains* (1848).

Facsimile in *Keats Facsimiles VII*, p. 63.

Harvard, Keats Collection 3.6, p. 61.

'All gentle folks who owe a grudge'
First pub. *Poetical Works and Other Writings of John Keats*, ed. H. B. Forman, 4 vols (London, 1883), as 'The Gadfly'; Stillinger, pp. 273–4.

KeJ 17 Draft, in the 17 July section of a letter (containing also KeJ 294) to Tom Keats, 17–21 July 1818.

This MS printed *Letters*, I, 334–6 (letter, 333–9); facsimile in Williamson, plate XIII.

Keats House, London, KH 3.

KeJ 18 Transcript in an unidentified hand of KeJ 17 (containing also KeJ 295), made for R. M. Milnes in 1845.

Harvard, Keats Collection 3.10(26).

'And what is Love? — It is a doll dress'd up'
First pub. *Literary Remains* (1848), as 'Modern Love'; Stillinger, p. 288.

KeJ 19 Transcript by Richard Woodhouse, in W2, annotated 'C[harles] B[rown] 1818'.

Facsimile in *Keats Facsimiles VI*, p. 127.

Harvard, Keats Collection 3.2, f. 75.

Apollo to the Graces ('Which of the fairest three')
First pub. Sidney Colvin, 'Keats and His Friends', *TLS*, 16 April 1914, p. 181; Stillinger, p. 222.

KeJ 20 Draft, one page.

This MS printed Hyder E. Rollins, 'Unpublished Autograph Texts of Keats', *HLB*, 6 (1952), 173–4; facsimile in Parke Bernet sale catalogue, 30 October 1950 (Oliver Barrett Sale), p. 163 and *Poetry Manuscripts*, p. 59.

Harvard, Keats Collection 2.14.

KeJ 21 Transcript by Richard Woodhouse, printer's copy for first publication, subtitled 'written to the Tune of the air "[space left blank] in Don Giovanni.', in W2, annotated 'From the orig[l] in Miss Reynolds's Possession'; [probably transcribed after Keats's death].

This MS printed Hyder E. Rollins, 'Unpublished Autograph Texts of Keats', *HLB*, 6 (1952), 172–3; facsimile in *Keats Facsimiles VI*, p. 361.

Harvard, Keats Collection 3.2, f. 194.

'As from the darkening gloom a silver dove'
First pub. *The Poetical Works of John Keats*, ed. Lord Houghton [R. M. Milnes] (London, 1876); Stillinger, p. 31.

KeJ 22 Transcript by Richard Woodhouse, in W2, annotated 'F[rogley]'; dated 1816, transcribed probably November 1818.

Facsimile in *Keats Facsimiles VI*, p. 1. Woodhouse's shorthand note giving the date of composition of this poem as December 1814, originally opposite it on f. 7v of W2 (now excised and tipped into W3 as f. 65 (Pierpont Morgan, MA 215) and also containing KeJ 97 and 325) is printed in longhand in Finney, facing p. 98 (with facsimile) and p. 752 and in Steele, p. 243; facsimile also in *Keats Facsimiles IV*, p. 238.

Harvard, Keats Collection 3.2, f. 8.

KeJ 23 Transcript by Richard Woodhouse, in W3, here entitled 'Sonnet.', annotated in shorthand 'from Mary Frogley', on a leaf containing also KeJ 300; dated 1816.

Facsimile in *Keats Facsimiles IV*, p. 248.

Pierpont Morgan, MA 215, f. 81.

KeJ 24 Transcript by Richard Woodhouse, in W1; dated 1816.

Harvard, Keats Collection 3.1, p. 22.

KeJ 25 Late transcript by one of Richard Woodhouse's clerks, made for Charles Brown; dated 1816, watermarked 1833.

Harvard, Keats Collection 4.20.9.

KeJ 26 Transcript by Coventry Patmore; dated 1816, transcribed 1847.

Harvard, Keats Collection 3.10(16).

'As Hermes once took to his feathers light'
First pub. *The Indicator*, 28 June 1820, as 'A Dream, after Reading Dante's Episode of Paulo and Francesca'; collected *Literary Remains* (1848); Stillinger, p. 326.

KeJ 27 Draft, here headed 'A Dream, After Reading Dante's Episode of Paulo and Francesca', on a blank end flyleaf of Vol. I of H. F. Cary's translation of *The Vision; or, Hell, Purgatory, and Paradise, of Dante Alighieri* (see KeJ 561, containing also KeJ 54), also containing two rejected beginnings on inside front and back covers; dated 1819.

Facsimile in A. E. Newton sale catalogue, Parke Bernet, 14–16 May 1941, [p. 157]; the two rejected beginnings are printed Stillinger, p. 636.

Yale.

KeJ 28 Fair copy, in the [16 April] section of a letter (containing also KeJ 56, 167–8, 210, 291, 311, 317, 393, 399, 542, 547) to George and Georgiana Keats, 14 February–3 May 1819.

This MS printed *Letters*, II, 91 (letter, 58–109); for John Jeffrey's transcript, see KeJ 34.

Harvard, Keats Collection 1.53.

KeJ 29 Transcript by Charles Brown, here entitled 'Sonnet,/On a Dream. 1819.', printer's copy for *Literary Remains* (1848).

Facsimile in *Keats Facsimiles VII*, p. 58.

Harvard, Keats Collection 3.6, p. 56.

KeJ 30 Transcript by Richard Woodhouse, in W2; dated April 1819.

This transcript and Woodhouse's notes on the facing f. 70v reproduced in *Keats Facsimiles VI*, pp. 118–19.

Harvard, Keats Collection 3.2, f. 71.

KeJ 31 Transcript by Charles Wentworth Dilke, headed 'Sonnet,/On a Dream', on a blank page at the back of his copy of *Endymion* (1818); dated 1819.

Keats House, London, KH 52.

KeJ 32 Transcript by Richard Woodhouse, in W1; dated April 1819.

Harvard, Keats Collection 3.1, p. 156.

KeJ 33 Transcript by J. A. Hessey, in W3, one page, here entitled 'Sonnet after reading Dante.', possibly printers's copy for *London Magazine* of November 1821; dated April 1819.

Facsimile in *Keats Facsimiles IV*, p. 315.

Pierpont Morgan, MA 215, f. 84.

KeJ 34 Transcript by John Jeffrey of portions of Keats's letter (KeJ 28) including this poem.

Harvard, Keats Collection 3.9, f. 26.

KeJ 35 Transcript by John Howard Payne, as sent to R. M. Milnes with a letter dated from Paris, 2 July 1847.

This letter printed *Keats Circle*, II, 223–5.

Harvard, Keats Collection 3.10(19).

'Bards of passion and of mirth'

First pub. as 'Ode' in *Lamia* 1820; Stillinger, pp. 294–5.

KeJ 36 Revised, on the blank page facing 'The Fair Maid of the Inn' by Beaumont and Fletcher in Keats's copy of Vol. IV (containing also KeJ 413) of *The Dramatic Works of Ben Jonson, and Beaumont and Fletcher* (KeJ 564).

Facsimile in Williamson, plate IV and in Tim Hilton, *Keats and His World* (London, 1971), p. [107].

Keats House, London, KH 21.

KeJ 37 Fair copy, in the 2 January section of a letter (containing also KeJ 91 and 149) to George and Georgiana Keats of 16 December–4 January 1819.

This MS printed *Letters*, II, 25–6 (letter, 4–30); a partial transcript of this letter by John Jeffrey (Harvard) does not include this poem.

Harvard, Keats Collection 1.45.

KeJ 38 Transcript by Charles Brown, here entitled 'Ode. 1818'.

Facsimile in *Keats Facsimiles VII*, pp. 24–6.

Harvard, Keats Collection 3.6, pp. 22–4.

KeJ 39 Transcript by Richard Woodhouse, in W2, here entitled 'Ode.', annotated 'from J. H. R. 26 Mar 1819'.

Facsimile in *Keats Facsimiles VI*, pp. 114–17.

Harvard, Keats Collection 3.2, ff. 69–70 (rectos only).

KeJ 40 Transcript by Richard Woodhouse, in W1; dated 26 March 1819.

Harvard, Keats Collection 3.1, p. 142.

'Before he went to live with owls and bats'

First pub. *Literary Anecdotes of the Nineteenth Century*, ed. W. R. Nicoll and T. J. Wise, 2 vols (London, 1895–6), II (1896); Stillinger, pp. 98–9.

KeJ 41 Draft, here beginning 'Before he went to feed with owls and bats', one page, annotated in an unidentified hand 'given me by C. C. Clarke M. M. H.'.

Huntington, HM 1985.

KeJ 42 Transcript by Charles Brown, here entitled 'Sonnet. (circa 1817.)'.

Facsimile in *Keats Facsimiles VII*, p. 64.

Harvard, Keats Collection 3.6, p. 62.

KeJ 43 Transcript by J. C. Stephens, printer's copy for first publication; in a notebook (containing also KeJ 447, 533, 552) prepared by Charles Cowden Clarke as a birthday gift for his sister Isabella Jane Towers in 1828.

Harvard, Keats Collection 3.12, f. 69v.

'Blue! — 'Tis the life of heaven — the domain'

First pub. *Literary Remains* (1848); Stillinger, p. 234. Elizabeth Stott Clarke's transcript written in Isabella Jane Towers's copy of *Poems* (1817) at Keats House, London (KH 50) was copied from *Literary Remains*.

KeJ 44 Draft of lines 2–14 (first line and possibly a heading cut away).

Facsimile in *Century Guild Hobby Horse*, I (July 1886), p. 81; this MS presented to Oscar Wilde by one of George Keats's daughters.

Unlocated.

KeJ 45 Transcript by Richard Woodhouse, in W2, here entitled 'Answer.' (Reynolds's sonnet being written opposite on f. 22v), annotated 'from K's M.S.'; dated 8 February 1818.

Facsimiles of Reynolds's and Keats's sonnets in *Keats Facsimiles VI*, pp. 22–3.

Harvard, Keats Collection 3.2, f. 23.

KeJ 46 Transcript by J. H. Reynolds in a copy of his *The Garden of Florence* (London, 1821), here beginning 'Blue! — 'Tis the hue of heaven...'.

This transcript reported and printed by A. J. Horwood in *The Athenaeum*, 3 June 1876.

Unlocated.

KeJ 47 Transcript by Richard Woodhouse, in W1, here entitled 'Lines Written upon reading a Sonnet by J. H. Reynolds...', signed (initials); dated 8 February 1818.

Harvard, Keats Collection 3.1, p. 30.

KeJ 48 Transcript by Charlotte Reynolds, here entitled 'Answer. J. Keats' (Reynolds's sonnet being above), in Reynolds-Hood Commonplace Book (f. 27a); dated 8 February 1818.

Bristol Reference Library.

KeJ 49 Late transcript by one of Richard Woodhouse's clerks, entitled 'Answer — by J Keats [and added later by Woodhouse] to a Sonnet ending thus...', made for Charles Brown; dated 8 February 1818, watermarked 1833.

Harvard. Keats Collection 4.20.9.

KeJ 50 Transcript by Coventry Patmore, printer's copy for *Literary Remains* (1848); dated 8 February 1818, transcribed 1847.

Harvard, Keats Collection 3.10(9).

KeJ 51 Late transcript by Richard Woodhouse, made for Joseph Severn, here entitled 'After an argument with a friend on the Question whether black or blue eyes were preferable' and beginning 'Blue! — 'Tis the <life> hue of heaven...'; watermarked 1830.

Harvard, Keats Collection 4.20.10.

'Bright star, would I were stedfast as thou art —'
First pub. *Plymouth and Devonport Weekly Journal*, 27 September 1838; collected *Literary Remains* (1848); Stillinger, pp. 327–8.

KeJ 52 Fair copy, written on a blank page opposite the beginning of 'A Lover's Complaint' in Keats's copy of Shakespeare's *Poetical Works* (see KeJ 572), written (according to Joseph Severn) as Keats sailed from England for the last time in September 1820.

Facsimiles in: *Union Magazine*, February 1846; John Gilmer Speed, 'The Sojourns of John Keats', *Century Magazine*, September 1910, p. 693; Williamson, plate VI; Caroline F. E. Spurgeon *Keats's Shakespeare* (Oxford and London, 1928), plate 17; *The Poetical Works and Other Writings of John Keats*, ed. H. B. Forman, 4 vols (London, 1883), II, facing p. 361; Joanna Richardson, *Fanny Brawne* (London, 1952) p. 77; Robert Gittings, *John Keats* (Boston, 1968), following p. 400; Dorothy Hewlett, *A Life of John Keats*, 3rd ed (London, 1970), p. 352, *et al.*

Keats House, London, KH 22.

KeJ 53 Transcript by Charles Brown, here entitled 'Sonnet. 1819', an earlier version than KeJ 52, signed with the 'CB' flourish.

Facsimile in *Keats Facsimiles VII*, p. 62.

Harvard, Keats Collection 3.6, p. 60.

KeJ 54 Transcript by Fanny Brawne, on the inside back cover of Vol. I (containing also KeJ 27) of H. F. Cary's translation of *The Vision; or, Hell, Purgatory, and Paradise, of Dante Alighieri* (KeJ 561).

Facsimile in Robert Gittings, *John Keats* (Boston, 1966), facing p. 8 and Robert Gittings, *The Mask of Keats* (Cambridge, MA, 1956).

Yale.

Calidore: A Fragment ('Young Calidore is paddling o'er the lake')
First pub. *Poems* (1817); Stillinger, pp. 49–53.

KeJ 55 Transcript in Tom Keats's Copybook, here presented as one part of a larger poem containing also 'Specimen of an Induction to a Poem' (KeJ 405), signed in Keats's hand, annotated by Leigh Hunt *passim* and by Tom Keats 'marked by Leigh Hunt — 1816'; dated 1816, probably transcribed late 1816.

Facsimile of lines 150–62 in American Art Association sale catalogue, 22–3 April 1937, p. 59.

Harvard, Keats Collection 3.5, p. 3.

Character of C. B. ('He was to weet a melancholy carle')
First pub. *Literary Remains* (1848); Stillinger, pp. 326–7.

KeJ 56 Here untitled and beginning 'He is to weet...', in the [16 April] section of a letter (containing also KeJ 28, 167–8, 210, 291, 311, 317, 393, 399, 542, 547) to George and Georgiana Keats of 14 February–3 May 1819.

This MS printed *Letters*, II, 89–90 (letter, 58–109); for John Jeffrey's transcript, see KeJ 59.

Harvard, Keats Collection 1.53.

KeJ 57 Transcript by Charles Brown; dated 1819.

Facsimile in *Keats Facsimiles VII*, pp. 43–4.

Harvard, Keats Collection 3.6, pp. 41–2.

KeJ 58 Transcript by Richard Woodhouse, in W2; dated '1819 C. B.'.

Facsimile in *Keats Facsimiles VI*, p. 275.

Harvard, Keats Collection 3.2, f. 150.

KeJ 59 Transcript by John Jeffrey of portions of Keats's letter (KeJ 56) including this poem.

Harvard, Keats Collection 3.9, f. 25v.

Daisy's Song ('The sun, with his great eye'), for this second 'Extract from an Opera', see KeJ 83–5.

'Dear Reynolds, as last night I lay in bed'
First pub. *Literary Remains* (1848); Stillinger, pp. 241–4.

KeJ 60 Transcript by Richard Woodhouse, in W2, here entitled 'To J. H. Reynolds Esq[r]'; transcribed from a letter (now lost) from Keats to J. H. Reynolds of 25 March 1818.

This transcript printed *Letters*, I, 259–63 where it is followed by the text of the letter to Reynolds taken from a transcript by one of Woodhouse's clerks (and wanting all but the first line and a half of the verses) in Woodhouse's letterbook (p. 74) also at Harvard, Keats Collection; facsimile in *Keats Facsimiles VI*, pp. 107–13.

Harvard, Keats Collection 3.2, ff. 65–8 (rectos only).

Endymion: A Poetic Romance ('A thing of beauty is a joy for ever:')
First pub. *Endymion* (1818); Stillinger, pp. 102–220. Although Keats's original draft has disappeared (see KeJ 437 for surviving leaf), KeJ 63 records variants from its version of Books II–IV and KeJ 64–7 record passages from Book IV; no record of the draft of Book I has come to light. A few copies of the first edition containing non-authoritative corrections are mentioned in Stillinger, pp. 572–3: a copy inscribed by two of Leigh Hunt's sons is at Keats House, London (KH 51); Keats's presentation copy to Leigh Hunt at the Berg; Charles Wells's copy at Harvard; Charles Wentworth Dilke's copy into which, in addition, he transcribed 17 Keats poems (KeJ 31, 93, 139, 171, 230, 238, 272, 284, 314, 320, 344, 387, 403, 433, 487, 521, 540). See also Margaret Ketchum Powell, 'Keats and His Editor: The Manuscript of *Endymion*', *The Library*, 6 Ser 6 (1984), 139–52 which argues for choosing the fair copy (KeJ 61) over the first edition as copy text.

KeJ 61 Fair copy, revised, here entitled 'Endymion/ A Romance', as sent to the printer for first edition, 186 leaves (rectos only), 2 blank and 4 being title pages to the 4 Books, including a recopied last page of Book II in the hand of J. H. Reynolds, editorial markings by John Taylor and a few by Richard Woodhouse; [January–March 1818], Books I–II watermarked 1814, Books III–IV watermarked 1816.

This MS described Stillinger, pp. 574–5; facsimile first page in John Gilmer Speed, 'The Sojourns of John Keats', *Century Magazine*, September 1910, p. 692; facsimile page (numbered 31 and containing Book II, lines 715–38) in *British Literary Manuscripts*, plate 39; facsimile of entire MS in *Keats Facsimiles II*, pp. 9–375. Richard Woodhouse recorded variant readings from this MS at the end of W2 (ff. 239v–236v *rev.*) at Harvard, Keats Collection (facsimile in *Keats Facsimiles VI*, pp. 427–33).

Pierpont Morgan, MA 208.

KeJ 62 Fair copy of the title page with epigraph (one page), dedication (one page) and a draft of the (later rejected) Preface (4 pages), 5 leaves in all; as sent to the printer (with the fair copy of Book IV) on 21 March 1818; Preface dated Teignmouth, 19 March 1818; some leaves watermarked 1817.

These MSS printed in Stillinger, Appendix IV, pp. 738–9; facsimile in *Keats Facsimiles II*, pp. 1–8. Woodhouse's transcript is at the end of W2 (ff. 236v–235v *rev.*) at Harvard, Keats Collection (facsimile in *Keats Facsimiles VI*, pp. 433–5).

Pierpont Morgan, MA 209.

KeJ 63 Variant readings and cancellations in the lost original draft of Books II–IV (as well as the variants from KeJ 61), recorded by Richard Woodhouse in his interleaved copy of the first edition (containing also KeJ 90.5, 146, 438); inscribed by Woodhouse on the flyleaf, Temple, 24 November 1818.

This copy discussed in Stillinger, pp. 573–4; facsimile in *Keats Facsimiles III*. Woodhouse ordered this interleaved copy to be prepared in a letter to John Taylor of November 1818, now in W3 at the Pierpont Morgan, MA 215, f. 4 (printed *Keats Circle*, I, 65–6, facsimile in *Keats Facsimiles IV*, pp. 51–2).

Berg.

KeJ 64 Fair copy of Book IV, lines 1–29, in a letter to Benjamin Bailey, [28–30 October 1817], postmarked 1 November 1817.

This MS printed *Letters*, I, 172–3 (letter, 171–5).

Harvard, Keats Collection 1.14.

KeJ 65 Fair copy, imperfect, of Book IV, lines 146–81, in a letter to Jane Reynolds, postmarked London, 31 October 1817.

This MS printed *Letters*, I, 176–7; facsimile in American Art Association sale catalogue, 30 April 1930, facing p. 14.

Yale.

KeJ 66 Fair copy of Book IV, lines 146–81, in a letter to Benjamin Bailey, [3 November 1817], postmarked 5 November 1817.

This MS printed *Letters*, I, 181–2 (letter, 178–82).

Harvard, Keats Collection 1.15.

KeJ 67 Transcript by one of Richard Woodhouse's clerks, corrected by Woodhouse (in Woodhouse's letterbook, pp. 50–2), of a (now lost) letter from Keats to J. H. Reynolds including Book IV, lines 581–90 (also containing Keats's quotation of Shakespeare's Sonnet 17, line 12, used as the epigraph to *Endymion*); dated 'Leatherhead 22^d^ Novr 1817'.

This MS printed *Letters*, I, 189–90 (letter, 187–90).

Harvard, Keats Collection 3.3, pp. 51–2.

KeJ 68 Fair copy of the revised text of Book I, lines 777–81, in a letter to John Taylor, postmarked 30 January 1818.

This MS printed *Letters*, I, 218 (letter, 218–19); a transcript of this letter in Woodhouse's letterbook (p. 3) is at Harvard, Keats Collection 3.3.

Pierpont Morgan, MA 213.

KeJ 69 Discussion of proofs of Book I, in a letter to John Taylor, 27 February 1818.

This letter printed *Letters*, I, 238–9; a transcript of this letter in Woodhouse's letterbook (p. 4) is at Harvard, Keats Collection 3.3; facsimile of first page in Pearson Catalogue (1912), Item 92.

Pierpont Morgan.

KeJ 70 Comments on an advance copy of first edition and a list of errata, in a letter to John Taylor, 24 April 1818, postmarked 27 April 1818.

This letter printed *Letters*, I, 270–3; a transcript of this letter (wanting the list of errata) in Woodhouse's letterbook (p. 7) is at Harvard, Keats Collection 3.3; a copy of the first edition in which John Taylor has made the corrections in this errata list is at Tulane University (mistakenly described as Keats's corrections in Robert H. Swennes, 'Keats's Own Annotated Copy of *Endymion*', *KSJ*, 20 (1971), 14–17).

Pierpont Morgan, MA 791.

KeJ 71 Copy of first edition, containing corrections to Book I, line 14, Book II, line 748 and Book IV, lines 151 and 739 (as in the errata list in KeJ 70) in an unidentified hand.

According to Sotheby's sale catalogue of 29 March 1971, the corrections are in Keats's hand and the copy contains an otherwise unknown state of the title page.

Owned privately (1978) (see Stillinger, p. 572).

The Eve of St Agnes ('St Agnes' Eve — Ah, bitter chill it was!')
First pub. *Lamia* (1820); Stillinger, pp. 299–318. Keats's fair copy of this poem is lost (but see KeJ 73–4).

KeJ 72 Draft, wanting the first leaf containing lines 1–63, 5 leaves (10 pages); [late January–early February 1819].

Facsimile of lines 206–25 and cancelled lines in Amy Lowell, *John Keats*, 2 vols (Boston, 1925), II, 168 and in Walter Jackson Bate, *John Keats* (Cambridge, MA, 1963), facing p. 444; of lines 216–40 in Finney, facing p. 554; of lines 259–97 in M. R. Ridley, *Keats's Craftsmanship* (Oxford, 1933), after p. 162; of whole in *Poetry Manuscripts*, p. 95.

Harvard, Keats Collection 2.21.

KeJ 73 Transcript by Richard Woodhouse of KeJ 72 with revisions from the lost fair copy added, in W2, here entitled 'Saint Agnes' Eve' and beginning 'St Agnes' Eve! – Ah, bitter cold it was!', annotated at end 'Copied from J. K's rough M.S. 20 Ap[l] 1819', revised from Keats's lost fair copy September 1819–January 1820.

Facsimile of transcript and Woodhouse's annotations on blank versos in *Keats Facsimiles VI*, pp. 196–225; Woodhouse's annotation on f. 109v printed Finney, p. 759 and Steele, p. 250.

Harvard, Keats Collection 3.2, ff. 110–24 (rectos only).

KeJ 74 Transcript by George Keats, here entitled 'Saint Agnes Eve. 1819.', in George Keats's Notebook, 22 pages; transcribed from lost fair copy in January 1820.

This MS printed M. R. Ridley, *Keats's Craftsmanship* (Oxford, 1933), pp. 180–90; facsimile in *Keats Facsimiles V*, pp. 119–21, 131–60.

British Library, Egerton MS 2780, ff. 31–2, 37–51.

KeJ 75 Transcript by Richard Woodhouse, here entitled 'Saint Agnes' Eve' and beginning 'St Agnes' Eve — Ah, bitter cold it was!', in W1.

Harvard, Keats Collection 3.1, pp. 108–36.

KeJ 76 Proof corrections for lines 1 and 57–9, in a letter to John Taylor, [11? June 1820].

This letter printed *Letters*, II, 294–5; a transcript of this letter is in Woodhouse's letterbook (p. 105) at Harvard, Keats Collection 3.3.

Harvard, Keats Collection 1.80.

The Eve of St Mark ('Upon a Sabbath day it fell')
First pub. *Literary Remains* (1848); Stillinger, pp. 319–22.

KeJ 77 Draft, in George Keats's Notebook, 7 pages; dated by George Keats 1819.

Facsimile in *Keats Facsimiles V*, pp. 123–9.

British Library, Egerton MS 2780, ff. 33–6.

KeJ 78 Fair copy of lines 1–114, here untitled, in the [20 September] section of a letter (containing also KeJ 110, 251, 369, 380) to George and Georgiana Keats, [17–27 September 1819].

This MS printed *Letters*, II, 201–4 (letter, 184–218).

Pierpont Morgan, MA 212.

KeJ 79 Early draft of lines 99–114 (recto) and an additional 16-line pseudo-Chaucerian fragment beginning 'Gif ye wol stonden hardie wight —' (verso).

Facsimile of both pages in *Poetical Works of John Keats*, ed. H. B. Forman (Oxford, 1906), after p. 342 and of 16-line fragment only in *The Bookman*, 31 (1906), 16; the 16-line fragment printed Stillinger, pp. 633–4.

Pierpont Morgan, MA 213.

KeJ 80 Transcript by Charles Brown, printer's copy for the first publication, annotated by R. M. Milnes; dated 1819.

Facsimile in *Keats Facsimiles VII*, pp. 31–5.

Harvard, Keats Collection 3.6, pp. 29–33.

KeJ 81 Shorthand transcript (William Mavor system) by Richard Woodhouse, earlier than W2, 3 pages, imperfect.

Facsimile of first page (lines 1–50) in A. E. Newton, *A Magnificent Farce and Other Diversions of a Book-Collector* (Boston, 1921), p. 121; this MS unlocated in *Texts*, p. 220 but mentioned Stillinger, p. vii.

Bryn Mawr College, Adelman Collection.

KeJ 82 Transcript by Richard Woodhouse, in W2, followed by the 16-line pseudo-Chaucerian fragment from KeJ 79, annotated (f. 124v) 'Copied from J. K's M.S.' and, at the end, 'Written 13/17 Feb[y] 1819 R. W.'.

Facsimile of transcript and Woodhouse's notes on blank versos in *Keats Facsimiles VI*, pp. 226–37.

Harvard, Keats Collection 3.2, ff. 125–30 (rectos only).

Extracts from an Opera ('O were I one of the Olympian twelve')
First pub. *Literary Remains* (1848); Stillinger, pp. 235–7.

KeJ 83 Transcript by Charles Brown, including all six known songs, the second, third and fifth songs bearing separate titles ('Daisy's Song', 'Folly's Song' and 'Song'), printer's copy for the first publication; dated 1818.

Facsimile in *Keats Facsimiles VII*, pp. 44–7.

Harvard, Keats Collection 3.6, pp. 42–5.

KeJ 84 Transcript by Richard Woodhouse, here untitled, in W2, including all six known songs; dated 'C. B. 1818.'.

Facsimile in *Keats Facsimiles VI*, pp. 251–5.

Harvard, Keats Collection 3.2, ff. 137–9 (rectos only).

KeJ 85 Transcript by Richard Woodhouse of the second ('Daisy's Song') and the fifth (headed 'Song') songs only, in W3, 2 pages (one leaf); dated 1818.

Facsimile in *Keats Facsimiles IV*, pp. 261–2.

Pierpont Morgan, MA 215, f. 62.

KeJ 86 Transcript by Charlotte Reynolds of the first, fifth and sixth songs only, in the Reynolds-Hood Commonplace Book (f. 40a); dated 1818.

Bristol Reference Library.

The Fall of Hyperion: A Dream ('Fanatics have their dreams, wherewith they weave')
Keats's revision of 'Hyperion' first pub. by R. M. Milnes (without Canto I, lines 187–210) as 'Another Version of Keats's "Hyperion"' in *Miscellanies of the Philobiblon Society*, 3 (1856–7); first pub. in full Ernest de Selincourt, *Hyperion: A Facsimile of Keats's Autograph Manuscript* (Oxford, 1905) (where KeJ 89 is transcribed); Stillinger, pp. 478–91. For a discussion of the relationship of manuscripts and transcripts of 'Hyperion' and 'The Fall of Hyperion' and their dating (which differs in its conclusions from Stillinger's), see Leonidas M. Jones, 'The Dating of the Two *Hyperions*', *SB*, 30 (1977), 120–35.

KeJ 87 Fair copy of Canto I, lines 1–11a, 61–86 and Canto II, lines 1–4, 6, in a letter (containing also KeJ 468) to Richard Woodhouse of [21–2 September 1819], postmarked 22 September 1819.

This MS printed *Letters*, II, 171–2 (letter, 169–75).

Harvard, Keats Collection 1.64.

KeJ 88 Transcript by Richard Woodhouse, in W2.

Lines 97–101 and 102–4 from this transcript printed in a letter to the editor by A. E. Housman, *TLS*, 8 May 1924; facsimile (including Woodhouse's notes on blank versos) in *Keats Facsimiles VI*, pp. 305–37.

Harvard, Keats Collection 3.2, ff. 165–81 (rectos only).

KeJ 89 Late transcript by two of Richard Woodhouse's clerks, revised by Woodhouse, made for Charles Brown; watermarked 1833.

This MS printed Ernest de Selincourt, *Hyperion: A Facsimile of Keats's Autograph Manuscript*, pp. 33–50.

Harvard, Keats Collection 4.20.9.

KeJ 90 Transcript of Canto I, lines 1–326 only, by Charlotte Reynolds, in Reynolds-Hood Commonplace Book (f. 33).

Bristol Reference Library.

KeJ 90.5 Transcript by Richard Woodhouse of Canto I, lines 11–12, 16–18, annotated 'Induction to "The fall of Hyperion, a Dream"–unpublished–by Keats.', the last of a series of extracts on the front blank pages of Woodhouse's interleaved copy of *Endymion* (1818) (see KeJ 63), inscribed by Woodhouse on the front flyleaf Temple, 24 November 1818.

Facsimile in *Keats Facsimiles III*, p. 10.

Berg.

Fancy ('Ever let the Fancy roam')
First pub. *Lamia* (1820); Stillinger, pp. 290–3.

KeJ 91 Fair copy, here untitled, containing additional lines, in the 2 January section of a letter (containing also KeJ 37 and 149) to George and Georgiana Keats of 16 December 1818–4 January 1819.

This MS printed *Letters*, II, 21–4 (letter, 4–30); a partial transcript of the letter by John Jeffrey (Harvard) does not include this poem.

Harvard, Keats Collection 1.45.

KeJ 92 Transcript by Charles Brown, here entitled 'Ode, to Fancy. 1818.', containing additional lines.

Facsimile in *Keats Facsimiles VII*, pp. 17–21.

Harvard, Keats Collection 3.6, pp. 15–19.

KeJ 93 Transcript by Charles Wentworth Dilke, here untitled, containing additional lines, on the blank leaves at the back of his copy of *Endymion* (1818); dated 1818.

Keats House, London, KH 52.

KeJ 94 Transcript by Richard Woodhouse, here entitled 'Ode./To Fancy.', containing additional lines, in W2, annotated 'from C. B.'; dated 1818.

Facsimile in *Keats Facsimiles VI*, pp. 338–45.

Harvard, Keats Collection 3.2, ff. 183–6 (rectos only).

'Fill for me a brimming bowl'
First pub. Ernest de Selincourt, *N&Q*, 4 February 1905, p. 81; Stillinger, p. 30.

KeJ 95 Fair copy, in W3, headed by the epigraph from Terence, 2 pages (one leaf), imperfect; dated August 1814.

This MS discussed, printed and reproduced in facsimile in Mabel A. E. Steele, 'Three Early Manuscripts of John Keats', *KSJ*, 1 (1952), 57–63 (plate VI); facsimile in *Keats Facsimiles IV*, pp. 219–20.

Pierpont Morgan, MA 215, f. 66.

KeJ 96 Transcript by Richard Woodhouse, here beginning 'Fill for me the brimming bowl', one page, in W3, without the epigraph, annotated in shorthand 'from Mary Frogley'.

Facsimile in *Keats Facsimiles IV*, p. 244.

Pierpont Morgan, MA 215, f. 64.

KeJ 97 Transcript by Richard Woodhouse, here beginning 'Fill for me the brimming bowl', without the epigraph, in W3 (on 2 leaves, rectos only (originally in W2, ff. 6–7), the second also containing KeJ 325), annotated 'F[rogley]'; dated August 1814, probably transcribed November 1818.

Facsimile in *Keats Facsimiles IV*, pp. 235–7; a note by Woodhouse regarding this poem (printed Finney, p. 752 and Steele, p. 243) was originally written on the facing page in W2 (i.e., f. 5v); it is now in W3, f. 89 (containing also KeJ 125) and reproduced *Keats Facsimiles IV*, p. 234.

Pierpont Morgan, MA 215, f. 65.

KeJ 98 Transcript by Richard Woodhouse, in W2, annotated 'F[rogley]'; dated August 1814.

A note by Woodhouse about this poem (dated February 1819) on the facing page (f. 221v) is printed Finney, pp. 761–2; facsimile of poem and note in *Keats Facsimiles VI*, pp. 416–17, 419.

Harvard, Keats Collection 3.2, ff. 222–3 (rectos only).

KeJ 99 Late transcript by one of Richard Woodhouse's clerks, made for Charles Brown, copy for the first publication; dated August 1814, watermarked 1833.

Harvard, Keats Collection 4.20.9.

Folly's Song ('When wedding fiddles are a playing'), for this third 'Extract from an Opera', see KeJ 83–4.

'For there's Bishop's Teign'
First pub. *The Life of Benjamin Robert Haydon*, ed. Tom Taylor, 3 vols (London, 1853); Stillinger, pp. 238–40.

KeJ 100 Revised, in a letter (containing also KeJ 543) to B. R. Haydon, [21 March 1818], postmarked 23 March 1818.

This MS printed *Letters*, I, 249–51 (letter, 248–52); facsimile in British Library, MS Facs. 337.

Harvard, Keats Collection 1.24.

'Four seasons fill the measure of the year'
First pub. Leigh Hunt's *Literary Pocket-book for 1819* (London 1818), as 'The Human Seasons'; Stillinger, p. 238. J. C. Stephens's transcript at Harvard (Keats Collection 3.12) was copied from the first publication.

KeJ 101 Fair copy, in a letter to Benjamin Bailey, [13 March 1818].

This MS printed *Letters*, I, 243 (letter, 240–44).

Harvard, Keats Collection 1.23.

KeJ 102 Transcript by Richard Woodhouse, in W2; misdated 'Septr 1818. – transcribed from K's letter to B. B.', probably transcribed after 8 May 1821.

Facsimile in *Keats Facsimiles VI*, p. 403.

Harvard, Keats Collection 3.2, f. 215.

KeJ 103 Transcript by Richard Woodhouse of KeJ 101, in Woodhouse's letterbook.

Harvard, Keats Collection 3.3, p. 98.

KeJ 104 Late transcript by one of Richard Woodhouse's clerks, made for Charles Brown; watermarked 1833.

Harvard, Keats Collection 4.20.9.

KeJ 105 Transcript by Coventry Patmore; made in 1847.

Harvard, Keats Collection 3.10(17).

Fragment of Castle-builder ('In short, convince you that however wise')
First pub. (lines 24–71 only) *Literary Remains* (1848), as 'Fragment of the Castle-builder'; lines 1–23 first pub. Sidney Colvin, 'Keats and His Friends', *TLS*, 16 April 1914, p. [181]; Stillinger, pp. 286–8.

KeJ 106 Transcript by Richard Woodhouse, in W2; dated 'CB. 1818.'.

Facsimile in *Keats Facsimiles VI*, pp. 245–9.

Harvard, Keats Collection 3.2, ff. 134–6 (rectos only).

'Gif ye wol stonden hardie wight —', see KeJ 79 and 82.

'Give me women, wine, and snuff'
First pub. *The Poetical Works of John Keats*, ed. H. B. Forman (London, 1884); Stillinger, p. 47.

KeJ 107 In pencil, written on the cover of a lecture book belonging to Henry Stephens (a fellow medical student).

Trinity College, Cambridge, Cullum MS N.83[2].

KeJ 108 Transcript in an unidentified hand of a letter, containing lines 1–4 of this poem, from Henry Stephens to G. F. Mathew, [March? 1847].

This transcript printed *Keats Circle*, II, 210 (letter, 206–14).

Harvard, Keats Collection.

'Give me your patience, sister, while I frame'
First pub. New York *World*, 25 June 1877; Stillinger, p. 265.

KeJ 109 Draft, in a letter (containing also KeJ 422) to George and Georgiana Keats, 27–8 June 1818.

This MS printed *Letters*, I, 303–4 (letter, 302–5).

Harvard, Keats Collection 1.32.

KeJ 110 Fair copy, revised, dated 'Foot of Helvellyn June 27 —', in the [18 September] section of a letter (containing also KeJ 78, 251, 369, 380) to George and Georgiana Keats of [17–27 September 1819].

This MS printed *Letters*, II, 195 (letter, 184–218).

Pierpont Morgan, MA 212.

'God of the golden bow'
First pub. *Western Messenger* (Louisville, KY), June 1836, as 'Ode to Apollo'; collected *Literary Remains* (1848), as 'Hymn to Apollo'; Stillinger, pp. 91–2.

KeJ 111 Draft, as sent by Keats to his brother George in Louisville, Kentucky, annotated by the latter 'orig manuscript of John Keats/ presented to Ia^s^ Clarke by/G. Keats'.

This MS printed Hyder Edward Rollins, 'Unpublished Autograph Texts of Keats', *HLB*, 6 (1952), 170–1; facsimile in *Poetry Manuscripts*, p. 51. A now-lost transcript of this MS was sent by its then owner, James Freeman Clarke, to R. M. Milnes with a letter dated from Boston, 31 October 1845 (letter printed *Keats Circle*, II, 139–41).

Harvard, Keats Collection 2.13.

KeJ 112 Fair copy, revised, on 2 pages of a leaf containing also KeJ 524.

Pierpont Morgan, MA 211.

KeJ 113 Transcript by Richard Woodhouse, here entitled 'Ode to Apollo', 3 pages (2 leaves) in W3, including a draft of Woodhouse's long preparatory note.

This MS printed Finney, p. 203 (Woodhouse's note on pp. 750–1); facsimile in *Keats Facsimiles IV*, pp. 251–3.

Pierpont Morgan, MA 215, f. 68.

KeJ 114 Transcript by Richard Woodhouse, here entitled 'Ode – to Apollo –', in W2, annotated 'from a M.S. in Keats's writing'.

Woodhouse's note on this poem (see KeJ 113) is revised by him on W2, f. 9v (now facing f. 14 since ff. 10–13 were excised); it is printed Finney, p. 758; poem and note reproduced in *Keats Facsimiles VI*, pp. 4–7.

Harvard, Keats Collection 3.2, ff. 14–15 (rectos only).

KeJ 115 Transcript by Richard Woodhouse, here entitled 'Fragment of an Ode to Apollo', in W1.

Harvard, Keats Collection 3.1, pp. 36–7.

KeJ 116 Transcript by Charlotte Reynolds, here entitled 'Ode to Apollo', in Reynolds-Hood Commonplace Book (f. 25a).

Bristol Reference Library.

KeJ 117 Late transcript by Richard Woodhouse, here entitled 'Ode to Apollo', made for Joseph Severn; watermarked 1830.

Harvard, Keats Collection 4.20.10.

'God of the meridian!'
First pub. *Literary Remains* (1848); Stillinger, pp. 227–8. These lines have often been printed as the closing lines of 'Hence burgundy, claret, and port' (see KeJ 130–4).

KeJ 118 Transcript in Woodhouse's letterbook by one of his clerks (corrected by Woodhouse) of a letter (containing also KeJ 131, 257, 537) from Keats to J. H. Reynolds containing these lines; letter dated by Woodhouse 31 January 1818.

This MS printed *Letters*, I, 221 (letter, 219–22).

Harvard, Keats Collection 3.3, p. 54.

KeJ 119 Transcript by Richard Woodhouse, here joined to the poem beginning 'Hence burgundy, claret, and port' to make one piece, in W2; dated February 1818.

Facsimile in *Keats Facsimiles VI*, pp. 89–91.

Harvard, Keats Collection 3.2, ff. 56–7 (rectos only).

KeJ 120 Transcript of lines 13–25 only by Richard Woodhouse, wanting the leaf containing the opening lines, in W1; dated February 1818.

Harvard, Keats Collection 3.1, p. 11.

KeJ 121 Transcript by Charlotte Reynolds, in Reynolds-Hood Commonplace Book (f. 31a), here joined to the poem beginning 'Hence burgundy, claret, and port' to make one piece; dated (possibly misdated) 7 February 1818.

Bristol Reference Library.

Gripus ('*Gripus*. And gold and silver are but filthy dross')
Questionable attribution. First pub. Amy Lowell, *John Keats*, 2 vols (Boston, 1925), II, 535–44 as Keats's; in Stillinger, 'Appendix VI Questionable Attributions', pp. 756–60.

KeJ 122 MS in the hand of Richard Woodhouse, here untitled, 4 pages (2 leaves), in W3, unsigned.

Facsimile in *Keats Facsimiles IV*, pp. 301–4 and among H. W. Garrod's papers at Yale, Osborn Collection.

Pierpont Morgan, MA 215, f. 67.

'Had I a man's fair form, then might my sighs'
First pub. *Poems* (1817), as 'Sonnet II. To ******'; Stillinger, p. 44.

KeJ 123 Transcript in Tom Keats's Copybook, headed 'Sonnet'; probably transcribed late 1816.

Harvard, Keats Collection 3.5, p. 15.

'Hadst thou liv'd in days of old'
First pub. *Poems* (1817), as 'To ****'; Stillinger, pp. 44–6. Woodhouse's annotation about this poem, on p. 36 of Woodhouse's *Poems* (1817), is reproduced in *Keats Facsimiles I*, p. 80.

KeJ 124 Fair copy, revised, here entitled 'To Miss — —', on a leaf containing also KeJ 147; c. 14 February 1816.

Wisbech and Fenland Museum.

KeJ 125 Transcript by Richard Woodhouse, in W3 (on 2 leaves, rectos only, originally in W2 as ff. 4–5 (see also KeJ 97)), marked 'F[rogley]' and preceded by a note by Woodhouse; probably transcribed November 1818.

The prefatory note by Woodhouse printed Finney, p. 92, Steele, p. 242, *Texts*, p. 108 and Stillinger, p. 547; facsimile in *Keats Facsimiles IV*, pp. 231–3.

Pierpont Morgan, MA 215, f. 89.

KeJ 126 Transcript by Richard Woodhouse, 3 pages (2 leaves, the second also containing KeJ 397), in W3, with Woodhouse's prefatory note.

Woodhouse's note printed Finney, p. 93; facsimile in *Keats Facsimiles IV*, pp. 293–5.

Pierpont Morgan, MA 215, f. 85.

KeJ 127 Transcript by Richard Woodhouse, here entitled 'To * * * *', in W2, annotated 'F[rogley]'; dated 14 February 1816.

Woodhouse's annotation on the facing f. 222v printed Finney, p. 93; facsimiles of poem and note in *Keats Facsimiles VI*, pp. 418–21.

Harvard, Keats Collection 3.2, ff. 223–4 (rectos only).

KeJ 128 Transcript by Richard Woodhouse, in W1, with Woodhouse's prefatory note; dated 14 February 1816.

Woodhouse's note printed Finney, p. 93.

Harvard, Keats Collection 3.1, pp. 18–19.

'Happy is England! I could be content'
First pub. *Poems* (1817), as 'Sonnet XVII'; Stillinger, p. 55.

KeJ 129 Fair copy, one page numbered 3, presented to W. C. Hazlitt in 1875.

This MS printed Hyder E. Rollins, 'Unpublished Autograph Texts of Keats', *HLB*, 6 (1952), pp. 174–5; facsimile among H. W. Garrod's papers at Yale, Osborn Collection (plate XI in a clipping from an unidentified sale catalogue); facsimile in *Poetry Manuscripts*, p. 7.

Harvard, Keats Collection 2.11.

'Hence burgundy, claret, and port'
First pub. *Literary Remains* (1848); Stillinger, p. 227. The lines 'God of the meridian!' (KeJ 118–21) have often been appended to these lines.

KeJ 130 Transcript by Charles Brown, here entitled 'Song. 1818', signed with the 'CB' flourish.

Facsimile in *Keats Facsimiles VII*, p. 7.

Harvard, Keats Collection 3.6, p. 5.

KeJ 131 Transcript in Woodhouse's letterbook by one of his clerks (corrected by Woodhouse) of a now-lost letter (containing also KeJ 118, 257, 537) from Keats to J. H. Reynolds containing these lines; letter dated by Woodhouse 31 January 1818.

This MS printed *Letters*, I, 220–1 (letter, 219–22).

Harvard, Keats Collection 3.3, p. 54.

KeJ 132 Transcript by Richard Woodhouse, in W2, here joined to the poem beginning 'God of the meridian!' to make one piece; dated February 1818.

Facsimile in *Keats Facsimiles VI*, p. 89.

Harvard, Keats Collection 3.2, f. 56.

KeJ 133 Transcript by George Keats, one page, in George Keats's Notebook, here entitled 'Song. 1818.'; transcribed January 1820.

Facsimile in *Keats Facsimiles I*, p. 117.

British Library, Egerton MS 2780, f. 30.

KeJ 134 Transcript by Charlotte Reynolds, in Reynolds-Hood Commonplace Book (f. 31a), here joined to the poem beginning 'God of the meridian!' to make one piece; dated (possibly misdated) 7 February 1818.

Bristol Reference Library.

'Hither, hither, love'
First pub. *Ladies' Companion*, August 1837; Stillinger, pp. 96–7.

KeJ 135 Revised, one page.

Facsimile in Anderson Galleries sale catalogue, 2–3 May 1934, Lot 155.

Yale.

'How many bards gild the lapses of time': no authoritative MS sources survive.

'Hush, hush, tread softly, hush, hush, my dear'
First pub. *Hood's Magazine*, April 1845, as 'Song'; collected *Literary Remains* (1848), as 'Song'; Stillinger, pp. 296–7.

KeJ 136 Revised, line 23 left unfinished, one page; watermarked 1816.

Facsimile in *Poetry Manuscripts*, p. 93.

Harvard, Keats Collection 2.20.

KeJ 137 Transcript by Fanny Brawne, on the first two pages of a copy of Leigh Hunt's *The Literary Pocket-book: Or Companion for the Lover of Nature and Art. 1819* (see KeJ 566), here entitled 'Song'; dated 21 January [1819].

Facsimile in Williamson, plate IX and Robert Gittings, *John Keats: The Living Year* (Cambridge, MA, 1954), facing pp. 58 and 86.

Keats House, London, KH 27.

KeJ 138 Transcript of lines 1–20 by Charles Brown, wanting the last four lines (which are supplied on 3.6, p. 27 by R. M. Milnes), here entitled 'Song. 1818.', printer's copy for *Literary Remains*.

Facsimile in *Keats Facsimiles VII*, pp. 29–30.

Harvard, Keats Collection 3.6, p. 28.

KeJ 139 Transcript by Charles Wentworth Dilke of lines 1–22 only (breaking off mid-line 22), on a blank leaf at the end of his copy of Keats's *Endymion* (1818), here entitled 'Song'.

Keats House, London, KH 52.

KeJ 140 Transcript by Richard Woodhouse, in W2, here entitled 'Song.', annotated 'from C. B.'; dated 1818.

Facsimile in *Keats Facsimiles VI*, p. 239.

Harvard, Keats Collection 3.2, f. 131.

KeJ 141 Transcript by Richard Woodhouse, corrected and line 20 added in pencil, here beginning 'Hush, hush, tread softly, tread gently, my dear', in W3, 2 pages (one leaf).

Facsimile in *Keats Facsimiles IV*, pp. 289–90.

Pierpont Morgan, MA 215, f. 80.

Hyperion: A Fragment ('Deep in the shady sadness of a vale')
First pub. *Lamia* (1820); Stillinger, pp. 329–56. For Keats's intended revision, see 'The Fall of Hyperion' (KeJ 87–90). For a discussion of the relationship between the manuscripts and transcripts of 'Hyperion' and 'The Fall of Hyperion' and their dating (which has conclusions differing from Stillinger's), see Leonidas M. Jones, 'The Dating of the Two *Hyperions*', *SB*, 30 (1977), 120–35.

KeJ 142 Revised, probably the draft, here entitled 'Hyperion', wanting a portion of f. 14 (see KeJ 143) and a small strip of f. 19 (containing Book II, lines 292–3), 27 leaves (mostly rectos only, revisions on some versos), containing annotations by Richard Woodhouse; watermarked 1810.

Facsimile of the whole in Ernest de Selincourt, *Hyperion: A Facsimile of Keats's Autograph Manuscript* (Oxford, 1905) and *Keats Facsimiles V*, pp. 3–56; of first page in John Gilmer Speed, 'The Sojourns of John Keats', *Century Magazine*, September 1910, p. 694 and in Robert Gittings, *The Mask of Keats* (Cambridge, MA, 1956), facing p. 20; of a portion of f. 12 in Leigh Hunt, *Lord Byron and Some of His Contemporaries* (London, 1828), opposite p. 1. The missing strip of f. 19 has not come to light.

British Library, Add. MS 37000.

KeJ 143 Book II, lines 116–27, revised (probably the draft), the missing portion of f. 14 of KeJ 142, inscribed from Leigh Hunt to Samuel Adams Lee, 7 March 1856.

Formerly in the album of Mrs J. T. Fields (MA 925).

Pierpont Morgan, MA 214.

KeJ 144 Transcript by Richard Woodhouse, in W2, here entitled 'Hyperion', annotated at the end 'Thus the M.S. copy Ends.', 'Copied 20 Ap[l] 1819 from J. K's Manuscript written in 1818/9' and 'The Copy from which I took the above was the original & only copy. The alterations are noted in the margin...'.

Facsimile (including Woodhouse's notes on the blank versos) in *Keats Facsimiles VI*, pp. 134–95.

Harvard, Keats Collection 3.2, ff. 79–109 (rectos only).

KeJ 145 Transcript by two of Richard Woodhouse's clerks, corrected by Woodhouse, here entitled 'Hyperion', in W1, printer's copy for the first publication.

Harvard, Keats Collection 3.1, pp. 39–99.

KeJ 146 Transcript by Richard Woodhouse of extracts (Book II, lines 1–18, 32–5, 39–55, 64–72) at the end of his interleaved copy of *Endymion* (1818) (see KeJ 63), inscribed by Woodhouse on the flyleaf Temple, 24 November 1818.

Facsimile in *Keats Facsimiles III*, pp. 425–6.

Berg.

'I am as brisk'
First pub. *The Poetical Works of John Keats*, ed. H. W. Garrod (Oxford, 1939); Stillinger, p. 46.

KeJ 147 On a leaf containing also KeJ 124.

Wisbech and Fenland Museum.

'I cry your mercy — pity — love! — aye, love'
First pub. *Literary Remains* (1848); Stillinger, p. 492.

KeJ 148 Transcript by Charles Brown, here entitled 'Sonnet. 1819.', signed with the 'CB' flourish, printer's copy for the first publication.

Facsimile in *Keats Facsimiles VII*, p. 60.

Harvard, Keats Collection 3.6, p. 58.

'I had a dove, and the sweet dove died'
First pub. *Literary Remains* (1848); Stillinger, p. 296.

KeJ 149 Fair copy, in the 2 January 1819 section of a letter (containing also KeJ 37, 91) to George and Georgiana Keats of 16 December 1818–4 January 1819.

This MS printed *Letters*, II, 27 (letter, 4–30); a partial transcript of the letter by John Jeffrey (Harvard) does not include this poem.

Harvard, Keats Collection 1.45.

KeJ 150 Transcript by Richard Woodhouse, in W2, headed 'Song.' and annotated 'from CB.'; dated 1818.

Facsimile in *Keats Facsimiles VI*, p. 347.

Harvard, Keats Collection 3.2, f. 187.

KeJ 151 Transcript by Richard Monckton Milnes, printer's copy for the first publication, headed 'Song. 1818'.

Harvard, Keats Collection 3.10(3).

'I stood tip-toe upon a little hill'

First pub. *Poems* (1817); Stillinger, pp. 79–88. Keat's original draft (on 10 leaves, see KeJ 152–64) was given to Charles Cowden Clarke who cut it up into fragments which he gave away; for a reconstruction, see Stillinger, pp. 557–8. The fragments of the MS still missing are: (1) first fragment of second leaf probably containing lines 35–7 (recto) and 49–52 (verso); (2) fragment of third leaf probably containing cancelled lines and 115 (recto) and unpublished lines and 65–8 (verso) (the transcript below KeJ 156 records the cancelled and unpublished lines); (3) second fragment of sixth leaf probably containing lines 174–80 (recto) and 193–c.200 (verso); (4) leaf 7 probably containing lines c.201–14 (recto only).

KeJ 152 First two fragments of first leaf of original draft, containing (when joined) lines 1–10 (recto) and lines 19–27 (verso), without the epigraph.

The first fragment (lines 1–6 and 19–23) printed (with facsimile) in *KSJ*, 10 (1961), 12–13; facsimile in *Poetry Manuscripts*.

Harvard, Keats Collection 2.8.1 and 2.8.2.

KeJ 153 Fragment of first leaf of original draft, containing lines 11–18 (recto) and probably lines 28–34 (verso), annotated by Charles Cowden Clarke and by his wife.

Facsimile of lines 11–18 (the recto) in Sotheby's sale catalogue (cited below); the recto was mislocated at Harvard in *Texts*, p. 122 but corrected in Stillinger.

Sotheby's, 27 March 1929, Lot 531, sold to Spencer.

KeJ 154 Fragment of second leaf of original draft, containing lines 38–48 (recto) and 53–60, 107–110 (written continuously on the verso).

Facsimile of recto in *Scribner's Magazine*, 3 (1888), 299; of whole in *Poetry Manuscripts*.

Harvard, Keats Collection 2.8.3.

KeJ 155 Fragment of third leaf of original draft, containing lines 111–14 (113–14 cancelled) on recto and 61–4 on verso, annotated '...given to me by C. C. Clarke Esq[re]...Jan 1832.'.

Facsimile in *Poetry Manuscripts*.

Harvard, Keats Collection 2.8.4.

KeJ 156 Transcript by W. H. Prideaux of a fragment of the third leaf of original draft, containing all the lines in KeJ 155 and two more cancelled lines (following the cancelled 114) and 2 more uncancelled but unpublished lines following 64, all on one page enclosed in a letter to R. M. Milnes of [May 1847?].

Prideaux's letter printed *Keats Circle*, II, 219–20; the cancelled and unpublished lines are printed in the apparatus in Stillinger, p. 83.

Harvard, Keats Collection 3.10(2).

KeJ 157 Fragment of third leaf of original draft, containing lines 116–22 and 4 cancelled lines (recto) and lines 69–80 (verso).

The recto of this MS printed in a letter to the editor by H. W. Garrod in *TLS*, 17 July 1937, p. 528 (where the MS is mislocated at Harvard); the complete MS printed in a letter to the editor by Clarence Thorpe in *TLS*, 10 December 1938, pp. 785–6; the cancelled four lines printed in the apparatus in Stillinger, p. 83; facsimile of the recto in Anderson Galleries sale catalogue, 21–4 January 1929 (Jerome Kern Sale, Part 2), p. 254; facsimile of the whole in the H. W. Garrod file at Yale, Osborn Collection.

Berg.

KeJ 158 Fragment of the third leaf of the original draft, containing 4 unpublished lines to follow line 122 (recto) and lines 81–6 (verso).

The recto of this MS printed in Dorothy Hewlett, *Adonais. A Life of John Keats* (London, [1937]) and reprinted in a letter to the editor by H. W. Garrod in *TLS*, 17 July 1937, p. 528; verso printed in a letter to the editor by Maurice Buxton Forman, 13 August 1938, p. 531; the 4 unpublished lines printed in the apparatus in Stillinger, p. 83.

Scottish National Portrait Gallery, Edinburgh, SPD 345.

KeJ 159 Fourth leaf of original draft, containing lines 87–106 (recto) and lines 123–50 (verso).

Variant readings given in a letter to the editor by Maurice Buxton Forman in *TLS*, 27 August 1938, pp. 555–6; this MS was unlocated in *Texts* and Stillinger; for a reproduction, see FACSIMILES.

British Library, Zweig 63.

KeJ 160 Fifth leaf of original draft, containing revised fair copy of lines 25–8 (from the verso of the first leaf), lines 151–6 and 4 unpublished lines to follow line 156 (recto) and KeJ 324 (verso).

This MS printed in a letter to the editor by Clarence Thorpe in *TLS*, 6 August 1938, p. 519; the four unpublished lines printed in the apparatus in Stillinger, p. 85.

Pierpont Morgan, MA 658.

KeJ 161 Fragment of sixth leaf of original draft, containing lines 157–73 (recto) and lines 181–95 (193–5 cancelled) (verso).

Owned (1978) Dallas Pratt, New York (see Stillinger, p. 558).

KeJ 162 Eighth leaf of original draft, containing lines 215–30 on the recto (verso blank); annotated '...Presented to his friend, William Potter, of Liverpool, Nov. 21st, 1851, by Charles Cowden Clarke'.

Free Library of Philadelphia.

KeJ 163 Ninth leaf of original draft, containing lines 231–5 (recto) and KeJ 508 (verso).

Facsimile in *Catalogue of the Collection of Autograph Letters and Historical Documents formed Between 1865 and 1882 by A[lfred] Morrison*, comp. A. W. Thibaudeau, 6 vols (London, 1883–92), III (1888), p. 4 and in *Poetry Manuscripts*.

Harvard, Keats Collection 2.5.

KeJ 164 Tenth (last) leaf of original draft, containing lines 231–42 on recto (verso blank); dated December 1816.

Facsimile in *Sunday Times*, 12 December 1933, p. ii of 'Book Exhibition Number'.

Owned (1958) W. T. Spencer (see Garrod, p. lxxxv).

KeJ 165 Fair copy, revised, without the epigraph, 3 leaves (6 pages); dated 'Decr eve [18]16 —'; the second leaf annotated by B. R. Haydon 'a Fragment of Dear Keats poetry & writing, given to me by [Keats] and by me to Miss Barrett; December 30 1842'.

Facsimile of lines 97–182 (2 pages) among H. W. Garrod's papers at Yale, Osborn Collection; facsimile of lines 183–226 (2 pages) in Sotheby's catalogue of the Moulton-Barrett sale, 7 June 1937, Lot 40 (reprinted in *Browning Institute Studies*, 5 (1977), 185); facsimile of whole in *Poetry Manuscripts*, p. 33.

Harvard, Keats Collection 2.9.

KeJ 166 Transcript by Tom Keats, headed 'Endymion' and followed by an epigraph from Spenser's *Muiopotmos*; dated December 1816.

The epigraph from Spenser was used on the title page of *Poems* (1817).

Harvard, Keats Collection 3.8.

'If by dull rhymes our English must be chain'd'
First pub. *Plymouth, Devonport, and Stonehouse News* 15 October 1836; collected *Literary Remains* (1848); Stillinger, p. 368.

KeJ 167 Fair copy of lines 1–4 (for the last leaf of the letter containing lines 5–14, see KeJ 168) in a letter (containing also KeJ 28, 56, 168, 210, 291, 311, 317, 393, 399, 542, 547) to George and Georgiana Keats of 14 February–3 May 1819.

This MS printed *Letters*, II, 108 (letter, 58–109); for John Jeffrey's transcript, see KeJ 173.

Harvard, Keats Collection 1.53.

KeJ 168 Fair copy of lines 5–14 on the final leaf (for the rest of the letter containing lines 1–4 of this poem, see KeJ 167) of a letter (containing also KeJ 28, 56, 167, 210, 291, 311, 317, 393, 399, 542, 547) to George and Georgiana Keats of 14 February–3 May 1819.

For John Jeffrey's transcript, see KeJ 173.

Owned privately (1978) (see Stillinger, p. 650 and Jack Stillinger, 'The Manuscripts of Keats's Letters: An Update', *KSJ*, 36 (1987), 18).

KeJ 169 Transcript by Charles Brown, here entitled 'Sonnet. 1819.', signed with the 'CB' flourish, printer's copy for *Literary Remains*.

Facsimile in *Keats Facsimiles VII*, p. 57.

Harvard, Keats Collection 3.6, p. 55.

KeJ 170 Transcript by Richard Woodhouse, in W2, headed 'Sonnet.', annotated 'C. B. 1819.'.

Facsimile in *Keats Facsimiles VI*, p. 283.

Harvard, Keats Collection 3.2, f. 154.

KeJ 171 Transcript by Charles Wentworth Dilke, headed 'Sonnet', on a blank page at the back of his copy of *Endymion* (1818); dated 1819.

Keats House, London, KH 52.

KeJ 172 Transcript by Richard Woodhouse, in W1, headed 'On the Sonnet'; dated 1819.

Harvard, Keats Collection 3.1, pp. 158–9.

KeJ 173 Transcript by John Jeffrey of portions of Keats's letter (KeJ 167–8) including this poem.

The text of the end of this letter printed *Letters*, II, 108–9 is taken from this transcript.

Harvard, Keats Collection 3.9, ff. 49–50.

Imitation of Spenser ('Now Morning from her orient chamber came')
First pub. *Poems* (1817); Stillinger, pp. 27–8.

KeJ 174 Transcript in Tom Keats's Copybook; probably transcribed late 1816.

Harvard, Keats Collection 3.5, p. 12.

'In after time a sage of mickle lore'
First pub. *Plymouth and Devonport Weekly Journal*, 4 July 1839; collected *Literary Remains* (1848); Stillinger, p. 535.

KeJ 175 Transcript by Charles Brown, in a blank space following *The Faerie Queen*, V, ii in his copy of Spenser's *Poetical Works* 8 vols (1788); dated 1820.

Keats's original MS was also written at the end of *The Faerie Queen*, V, ii, in a copy of Spenser that he gave to Fanny Brawne in 1820 (see *Letters*, II, 302); in 1823, she lent the book to Fanny Keats (see *Letters of Fanny Brawne to Fanny Keats*, ed. Fred Edgcumbe (London, 1936), p. 63) and it was, according to H. B. Forman, 'lost in Germany'.

Keats House, London, KH 106.

'In drear nighted December'
First pub. *Literary Gazette*, 19 September 1829, as 'Stanzas'; Stillinger, p. 221. An unidentified transcript of this poem at Keats House, London (KH 60), annotated by Leigh Hunt, was copied from the first publication; Isabella Jane Towers's transcript at Harvard (Keats Collection 3.12, f. 70v) was copied from Galignani's edition of Keats.

KeJ 175.5 Autograph, possibly the draft.

Readings from this MS reported in *The Poetical Works and Other Writings of John Keats*, ed. H. B. Forman, rev. Maurice Buxton Forman, 8 vols (New York, 1938–9), IV, 61–2n.

Sotheby's, 13 June 1876, sold to Charles Law.

KeJ 176 Fair copy, revised, 2 pages (one leaf), in a scrapbook of MSS, drawings and clippings formerly owned by Tom Hood (the poet's son); dated December [1817].

This MS printed (with facsimile) in Alvin Whitley, 'The Autograph of Keats's "In Drear Nighted December"', *HLB*, 5 (1951), 118 and facing 120.

University of Bristol.

KeJ 177 Transcript by Richard Woodhouse, here entitled 'Song', enclosed in a letter (now both in W3) from Woodhouse to John Taylor, 23 November 1818 which also includes Woodhouse's own version of stanza 3.

The letter only printed *Keats Circle*, I, 63–5; facsimiles in *Keats Facsimiles IV*, pp. 259 (poem) and 48–9 (letter); another scrap in W3, f. 66, contains Woodhouse's version of stanza 3 (*Keats Facsimiles IV*, p. 260); William Pitter Woodhouse's unauthoritative 1827 transcript of this poem in his commonplace book (Harvard, Keats Collection 3.13) includes Richard Woodhouse's version of stanza 3.

Pierpont Morgan, MA 215, f. 9.

KeJ 178 Transcript by Richard Woodhouse, here entitled 'Song.', in W2, annotated 'from J: H: Reynolds'; dated December 1817, followed by the shorthand note 'the date from Miss Reynolds' album'.

Facsimile in *Keats Facsimiles VI*, pp. 7–9.

Harvard, Keats Collection 3.2, ff. 15–16 (rectos only).

KeJ 179 Transcript by Richard Woodhouse, here entitled 'Song', in W1; dated 'about October or December 1818'.

Harvard, Keats Collection 3.1, p. 34.

Isabella; or, The Pot of Basil ('Fair Isabel, poor simple Isabel!')
First pub. *Lamia* (1820); Stillinger, pp. 245–63. Most of Keats's untitled draft (on 12 leaves, see KeJ 180–195), once owned by Joseph Severn, was cut up into fragments (of one or two stanzas each) and given away (an exception is the first two leaves (KeJ 180) still intact and presented to 'G. W.' by Charles Brown); for a reconstruction, see Stillinger, pp. 602–4. The fragments still missing are: (1) fragment of the 4th leaf probably containing lines 97–112 (recto) and 121–36 (verso); (2) leaf 5 probably containing lines 137–60 (recto) and 161–84 (verso); (3) fragment of 6th leaf probably containing lines 185–92 (recto) and 209–15 (verso); (4) fragment of 6th leaf probably containing lines 201–8 (recto) and possibly a cancelled version of 225–32 (verso); (5) fragment of 9th leaf probably containing lines 327–36 (recto) and 353–60 (verso); (6) fragment of 9th leaf probably containing lines 343–4 (recto) and 367–8 (verso); (7) fragment of 10th leaf probably containing lines 369–84 (recto) and 393–410 (verso). Richard Woodhouse's transcript of the English translation of Boccaccio's tale, used by Keats in writing 'Isabella', is at Harvard in W2 (ff. 190v–192v, see KeJ 198) and headed: 'The following is the translation of Boccacio's [sic] tale of Isabella, from which Keats took his poem (p. 30). – It is extracted from "The Novels & Plays of the renowned John Boccacio [sic]...London...MDCLXXXIV." –' (printed Steele, p. 253; facsimile in *Keats Facsimiles VI*, pp. 354–8).

KeJ 180 First two leaves of the original draft, containing lines 1–24 (recto of first leaf), 25–47 and a cancelled 48 (verso of first leaf) and line 48 (recto of second leaf), here untitled, annotated '...given to me by...C Brown Esqr — G. W.'.

Facsimile in Lyle H. Kendall, *Descriptive Catalogue of the W. L. Lewis Collection* (Fort Worth, TX, 1970), following p. 14 and among H. W. Garrod's papers at Yale, Osborn Collection; facsimile of lines 1–24 only in Sotheby's sale catalogue, 13 August 1941.

Texas Christian University.

KeJ 181 Fragment of the third leaf of the original draft, containing lines 49–56 and the first line of an unpublished stanza (to follow line 56, see KeJ 182) (recto) and lines 65–72 (verso).

Facsimile of recto and verso in Sotheby's sale catalogue, 28 July 1930, Lot 220 and in *Poetry Manuscripts*; facsimile of verso in American Art Association sale catalogue, 12–13 January 1938 (Alfred C. Meyer Sale), p. 34; the unpublished stanza is printed Stillinger, p. 247.

Harvard, Keats Collection 2.17.1.

KeJ 182 Fragment of the third leaf of original draft, containing the last 7 lines of an unpublished stanza (to follow line 56, see KeJ 181) (recto) and lines 73–80 (verso).

Facsimile of recto and verso (without any identification) among Louis A. Holman's papers at Harvard, Keats Collection; the unpublished stanza is printed Stillinger, p. 247; this fragment not mentioned *Texts* but collated in Stillinger.

Unlocated.

KeJ 183 Fragment of the third leaf of the original draft, containing lines 57–64 (recto) and lines 81–8 (verso); annotated 'presented by J. Severn June 28th 1846 to Mr George [?]'.

Historical Society of Pennsylvania.

KeJ 184 Fragment of fourth leaf of original draft, containing lines 89–96 (recto) and 113–20 (verso), annotated '...given to Mr C. [Salaman?] by Joseph Severn. Rome Octr 30th 1840'.

Facsimile in Parke Bernet sale catalogue, 26–8 April 1939 (Spoor Sale), pp. 150–2 and in *Poetry Manuscripts*.

Harvard, Keats Collection 2.17.2.

KeJ 185 Fragment of sixth leaf of the original draft, containing lines 193–200 (recto) and 216–24 (verso).

Variant readings from this MS reported by H. B. Forman in *The Athenaeum*, 6 April 1912, pp. 389–90.

Formerly in the Duke of Portland's collection at Welbeck Abbey; this fragment is not in the three collections of the Duke of Portland's papers at the British Library, the University of Nottingham and at Longleat; it is possibly one of a few MSS retained by the family.

KeJ 186 Fragment of seventh leaf of the original draft, containing lines 225–32 (recto) and 249–56 (verso), annotated 'M.S. of Keats from J[oseph] S[evern] Rome. Feb. 1833 T. H. Cromek'.

This MS described in a letter to the editor by Maurice Buxton Forman in the *TLS*, 27 June 1942, p. 319 and in Healey, No. 2781.

Cornell University.

KeJ 187 Fragment of seventh leaf and the whole of the eighth leaf of the original draft, containing lines 233–48 (recto of seventh leaf) and 257–72 (verso of seventh leaf); and lines 273–96 (recto of eighth leaf) and 297–320 (verso of eighth leaf).

Facsimile of the recto of the seventh leaf in Anderson Galleries sale catalogue, 21–4 January 1929 (Jerome Kern sale, Part 2), p. 252; of whole in *Poetry Manuscripts*.

Harvard, Keats Collection 2.17.3.

KeJ 188 Fragment of ninth leaf of original draft, containing lines 321–26 (recto) and 345–52 (verso), annotated '...presented to Robt Spence by Joseph Severn Dec 6th 1850'.

Facsimile in British Library, RP 471, in Christie's sale catalogue, 1 July 1970, Lot 118 and in *Poetry Manuscripts*.

Harvard, Keats Collection 2.17.4.

KeJ 189 Fragment of ninth leaf of the original draft, containing lines 337–9 (recto) and 361–4 (verso), annotated 'MSS of John Keats presented by Joseph Severn Aug 2d 1845'.

Texas.

KeJ 190 Fragment of ninth leaf of original draft, containing lines 340–2 (recto) and 365–6 (verso).

This MS described and printed *Shelley and His Circle*, IV, 798 (No. 518).

NYPL, Pforzheimer Collection.

KeJ 191 Fragment of tenth leaf of the original draft, containing lines 385–92 (recto) and 411–16 (verso), annotated '...given by J. Severn to Mr Watson/Feby 6th 1853'.

National Library of Scotland, MS 582, No. 637B.

KeJ 192 Eleventh leaf of original draft, containing lines 417–24, 433–48 (recto) and 449–72 (verso).

Facsimile in *Poetry Manuscripts*.

Harvard, Keats Collection 2.17.5.

KeJ 193 Fragment of twelfth leaf of original draft, containing lines 473–80 (recto) and 497–503 (verso), annotated '...given to Henry [Wreford?] at Rome May 1st 1863 by Joseph Severn'.

Facsimile in Anderson Galleries sale catalogue, 21–4 January 1929 (Jerome Kern sale, Part 2), p. 253 and among H. W. Garrod's papers at Yale, Osborn Collection; this fragment unlocated in *Texts* and in Stillinger.

Free Library of Philadelphia.

KeJ 194 Fragment of twelfth leaf of original draft, containing lines 481–8 (recto) and 504 (verso), annotated '...presented to Miss Kennaway by Joseph Severn. Rome March 25, 1863'.

Facsimile of recto in Margaret Crum, *English and American Autographs in the Bodmer* (Cologny-Geneva, 1977), p. [44]; this fragment not mentioned *Texts* but collated in Stillinger.

Bibliotheca Bodmeriana, Cologny-Geneva.

KeJ 195 Fragment of twelfth leaf of original draft, containing lines 489–96 (recto) and 425–32 (verso), annotated 'M.S. of John Keats from Joseph Severn. Rome 7th May 1867', signed and dated by Frederick Locker, 1867.

Facsimile of recto in Maggs Catalogue 339 (August 1915), facing p. 64.

Texas.

KeJ 196 Fair copy, revised, here entitled 'The Pot of Basil', annotated by Richard Woodhouse, 28 leaves (rectos only), in George Keats's Notebook; dated by George Keats 1818, probably written end of August 1818.

Facsimile pages in Sidney Colvin, *John Keats* (London, 1917), facing p. 394 and *The Poetical Works and Other Writings of John Keats*, ed. H. B. Forman, rev. Maurice Buxton Forman, 8 vols (New York, 1938–9), III, 54; facsimile of the whole in *Keats Facsimiles V*, pp. 59–113; the MS printed in M. R. Ridley, *Keats' Craftsmanship* (Oxford, 1933), pp. 24–53.

British Library, Egerton MS 2780, ff. 1–28 (rectos only).

KeJ 197 Shorthand (William Mavor system) transcript by Richard Woodhouse, here entitled (in shorthand) 'The Pot of Basil' and (in longhand, added later) 'Isabella/or/ The Pot of Basil', in W3, including a title page and 9 leaves (recto only).

Facsimile first page in Finney, facing p. 372; of whole in *Keats Facsimiles IV*, pp. 265–84.

Pierpont Morgan, MA 215, f. 71.

KeJ 198 Transcript by Richard Woodhouse, here entitled 'The pot of Basil.', in W2, annotated 'Written at Teignmouth in the Spring of 1818 on the suggestion of J. H. R.' and 'the old translation from which Keats took the Poem will be found at page 191'.

For 'the old translation', see headnote; facsimile in *Keats Facsimiles VI*, pp. 36–87.

Harvard, Keats Collection 3.2, ff. 30–55 (rectos only).

KeJ 199 Transcript by Richard Woodhouse, corrected by Keats (sometimes in response to queries by John Taylor or Woodhouse), here first entitled 'The Pot of Basil' (with 'Isabella' added later), in W1, printer's copy for the first publication; annotated 'written at Teignmouth in the Spring of 1818 at the suggestion of J. H. R.'.

Harvard, Keats Collection 3.1, pp. 172–216.

KeJ 200 Transcript of a letter (original now lost) from Keats to J. H. Reynolds by one of Richard Woodhouse's clerks, corrected by Woodhouse, in Woodhouse's letterbook, including lines 89–90, 97, 233 and 237 (the original letter included lines 89–104 and 233–40); letter dated by Woodhouse 27 April 1818.

This MS printed *Letters*, I, 275 (letter, 273–5).

Harvard, Keats Collection 3.3, p. 62.

KeJ 201 Version of lines 319–20, in a letter to Fanny Brawne, [February? 1820].

This letter reprinted *Letters*, II, 255–6 from *The Poetical Works and Other Writings of John Keats*, ed. H. B. Forman, 4 vols (London, 1883), IV, 153.

Unlocated.

The Jealousies: A Faery Tale, by Lucy Vaughan Lloyd of China Walk, Lambeth ('In midmost Ind, beside Hydaspes cool')
First pub. (lines 217–56) in *The Indicator*, 23 August 1820; lines 390–6, 415–23 first pub. as chapter epigraphs in E. J. Trelawny, *Adventures of a Younger Son*, 3 vols (London, 1831); first pub. in full (without lines 793–4) *Literary Remains* (1848), as 'The Cap and Bells; Or, the Jealousies. A Faëry Tale. Unfinished'; lines 793–4 first included in the poem in *The Poetical Works of John Keats*, ed. H. W. Garrod (Oxford, 1939); Stillinger, pp. 504–35.

KeJ 202 Fragment of the original draft, containing lines 1–72 (on 8 pages of four numbered folded leaves), 145–398 (on 8 pages of the first four numbered folded leaves and 11 pages of 4 more leaves), 460–729 (on 18 pages of 6 leaves), here untitled, 45 pages in all on 14 leaves.

Facsimile of first page in Pearson Catalogue (n. d.), Lot 341.

Pierpont Morgan, MA 214.

KeJ 203 Fragment of the fifth leaf of the original draft, containing (recto and verso) lines 73–108; watermarked 1818.

Huntington, HM 7149.

KeJ 204 Fragment of the original draft, containing lines 109–44 (on a fragment of the original fifth leaf, watermarked 1818) and 397–459 (on 4 pages of a folded leaf containing also KeJ 444).

Facsimile of lines 451–9 in W. H. Arnold, *First Report of a Book-Collector* (New York, 1898), p. 105 and Finney, facing p. 740; facsimile of whole in *Poetry Manuscripts*, p. 247.

Harvard, Keats Collection 2.29.1 and 2.29.2.

KeJ 205 Transcript by Richard Woodhouse, in W2.

Facsimile in *Keats Facsimiles VI*, pp. 365–94.

Harvard, Keats Collection 3.2, ff. 196–210v.

KeJ 206 Transcript by Charles Brown of Edward John Trelawny's *Adventures of a Younger Son*, printer's copy for the first publication, containing transcripts of the two passages from this poem used as chapter epigraphs (lines 390–6 and 415–23) at the end of the MS (including also KeJ 209, 376), headed 'Selections from the manuscripts of Keats's...Cap and Bells.'.

Harvard, Keats Collection, fMS Eng 1274.

'Keen, fitful gusts are whisp'ring here and there': no authoritative MS sources survive.

King Stephen: A Fragment of a Tragedy
Four passages (I.i.16b–17, 296–33, I.ii.12–15, 31–2) first pub. as chapter epigraphs in E. J. Trelawny, *Adventures of a Younger Son*, 3 vols (London, 1831); first pub. in full *Literary Remains* (1848); Stillinger, pp. 496–503.

KeJ 207 Transcript of title page, Dramatis Personae and I.i.1–ii.19 by Charles Brown, 3 leaves (6 pages), title page dated November 1819.

Facsimile in *Keats Facsimiles VII*, pp. 65–70.

Harvard, Keats Collection 3.11.

KeJ 208 Draft of I.ii.19b–iv.58, 5 leaves (7 pages); watermarked 1818.

This MS described in Stillinger, pp. 675–6; facsimile in *Poetry Manuscripts*, p. 233.

Harvard, Keats Collection 2.28.

KeJ 209 Transcript by Charles Brown of Edward John Trelawny's *Adventures of a Younger Son*, printer's copy for the first publication, containing transcripts of the four passages of this drama used as chapter epigraphs (I.i.16b–17, 296–33, I.ii.12–15, 31–2) at the end of the MS (including also KeJ 206, 376), headed 'Selections from the manuscripts of Keats's...King Stephen...'.

Harvard, Keats Collection, fMS Eng 1274.

La Belle Dame sans Merci: A Ballad ('O what can ail thee, knight at arms')
First pub. *The Indicator*, 10 May 1820, signed 'Caviare', as 'La Belle Dame sans Mercy'; collected *Literary Remains* (1848); Stillinger, pp. 357–9.

KeJ 210 Draft, without the subtitle, in the [21 or 28 April] section of a letter (containing also KeJ 28, 56, 167–8, 291, 311, 317, 393, 399, 542, 547) to George and Georgiana Keats of 14 February–3 May 1819.

This MS printed *Letters*, II, 95–6 (letter, 58–109).

Harvard, Keats Collection 1.53.

KeJ 211 Transcript by Charles Brown, printer's copy for *Literary Remains*; dated 1819.

Facsimile in *Keats Facsimiles VII*, pp. 11–13.

Harvard, Keats Collection 3.6, pp. 9–11.

KeJ 212 Transcript by Richard Woodhouse, in W2; annotated 'C. B. – 1819.'.

Facsimile of poem and Woodhouse's note on the facing f. 75v in *Keats Facsimiles VI*, pp. 128–33.

Harvard, Keats Collection 3.2, ff. 76–8 (rectos only).

KeJ 213 Transcript by Richard Woodhouse, in W1, annotated 'Vide Album for alterations'; dated 1819.

Harvard, Keats Collection 3.1, pp. 146–50.

Lamia ('Upon a time, before the faery broods')
First pub. *Lamia* (1820); Stillinger, pp. 452–75. Keats's original draft, once owned by Joseph Severn (perhaps also by Charles Brown), was cut up into fragments and distributed; only nine such fragments have come to light (KeJ 214–21; see Stillinger's description, pp. 665–6).

KeJ 214 Fragment of the original draft, containing 2½ lines used for Part I, line 185 (recto only).

This MS printed in the apparatus in Stillinger, p. 457.

Texas.

KeJ 215 Fragment of the original draft, containing Part I, lines 185b–90 (recto only).

Facsimile in *KSMB*, II, 93.

Keats-Shelley Memorial House, Rome, No. 46.

KeJ 216 Fragment of the original draft, containing Part I, lines 324–9 (recto only); together with a letter of presentation from Charles Brown to Marianne Hunt, 19 November 1840.

Berg.

KeJ 217 Fragment of the original draft, containing Part I, lines 386b–97 (recto only), annotated on verso that the scrap was presented to Mr Stisted by Joseph Severn, Rome, 12 December 1830.

This fragment, not mentioned in *Texts*, was collated in Stillinger.

Rosenbach Foundation.

KeJ 218 Fragment of the original draft, containing Part II, lines 26–49 (recto) and lines 85–92, plus 11 lines subsequently discarded and a 12th that became II.105 (verso), annotated '...given to Mr Milnes by J. Severn Rome June 30th 1832'.

Facsimile in *Poetry Manuscripts*.

Harvard, Keats Collection 2.25.

KeJ 219 Two fragments of one leaf of the original draft, the first (on the recto of a scrap numbered 3), containing Part II, lines 50–61, annotated '...Presented to Miss Marshall by Joseph Severn May [17th?] 1850'; the second (on the recto of a scrap) containing Part II, lines 62–67a, annotated '...presented to Mr F. R. Landford by J. Severn Feb. 14th 1852'.

Facsimile of first fragment in Sotheby's sale catalogue, 6 May 1936 (property of Maurice Buxton Forman), frontispiece.

Princeton, Robert H. Taylor Collection.

KeJ 220 Fragment of the original draft, containing Part II, lines 67b–74 (recto only).

Keats-Shelley Memorial House, Rome, No. 46.

KeJ 221 Fifth leaf of the original draft of Part II, containing lines 122–47 (recto) and lines 191–8 (verso).

Facsimile of recto in *The Houghton Library 1942–1967* (Cambridge, MA, 1967), p. 74; of whole in *Poetry Manuscripts*.

Harvard, Keats Collection.

KeJ 222 Fair copy (of the original draft version) of Part II, lines 122–62 and 18 discarded lines, in a letter to John Taylor, Winchester, 5 September 1819.

This MS printed *Letters*, II, 157–9 (letter, 155–9); Woodhouse's transcript in his letterbook at Harvard (Keats Collection 3.3, pp. 39–42) does not contain the verses.

Harvard, Keats Collection 1.63.

KeJ 223 Fair copy, revised, printer's copy for the first publication, 26 numbered leaves (mostly rectos only).

Facsimile of f. 20 in *The Houghton Library 1942–1967* (Cambridge, MA, 1967), p. 75; of whole in *Poetry Manuscripts*, p. 163.

Harvard, Keats Collection 2.26.

KeJ 224 Page proofs for the first publication, corrected and annotated by Keats, Richard Woodhouse and John Taylor (variant readings from other MSS recorded here by Woodhouse and Taylor), 52 leaves, inscribed 'Richd Woodhouse, Temple May/June 1820'.

These proofs discussed in William Allen Coles, 'The Proof Sheets of Keats's "Lamia"', *HLB*, 8 (1954), 114–119; facsimile of p. 35 in *The Houghton Library 1942–1967* (Cambridge, MA, 1967), p. 73.

Harvard, Keats Collection H53.

KeJ 225 Part II, lines 293–4, a last-minute revision written by Keats *on* a page of a letter from John Clare to John Taylor dated 5 June 1820.

This letter first reported in a letter to the editor by Sam Loveman, *TLS*, 13 April 1951, p. 229.

Berg.

KeJ 225.5 Alternative version of Part I, lines 167–8 (by Richard Woodhouse?), in a letter (in W3) from Woodhouse to John Taylor, [June? 1820].

This letter printed *Keats Circle*, I, 112–13; facsimile in *Keats Facsimiles IV*, p. 105.

Pierpont Morgan, MA 215, f. 2.

***Lamia* (1820)**
Harvard owns a copy presented to B. Davenport in which Keats denied and cancelled the 'Advertisement' (facsimile page in Amy Lowell, *John Keats*, 2 vols (Boston, 1925), II, 424–5); Woodhouse's draft 'Advertisement' (printed *Keats Circle*, I, 115–16) is in W3 (f. 21) (*Keats Facsimiles IV*, p. 109) and differs from the published version.

Lines on Seeing a Lock of Milton's Hair ('Chief of organic numbers!')
First pub. *Plymouth and Devonport Weekly Journal*, 15 November 1838; collected *Literary Remains* (1848), as 'On Seeing a Lock of Milton's Hair'; Stillinger, pp. 223–4.

KeJ 226 Draft, here untitled and including a false start ('Father of organic numbers!'), lines 1–17 in a notebook belonging to Leigh Hunt (on the verso of one page (f. 13v) of Hunt's autograph of his poem 'Hero and Leander') and the remainder of the draft on a separate leaf (2 pages).

Facsimile of lines 1–17 in Anderson Galleries sale catalogue, 15–17 March 1920 (H. B. Forman Sale, Part 1), p. 87; of whole in *Poetry Manuscripts*, p. 61.

Harvard, Keats Collection 2.15.1 and 2.15.2.

KeJ 227 Fair copy, on the last page of a copy of a facsimile reprint of the First Folio of Shakespeare's Works (see KeJ 573); dated 21 January 1818.

Keats House, London, KH 23.

KeJ 228 Fair copy, here entitled 'On seeing a Lock of Milton's Hair – *Ode*' and dated 21 January, in a letter to Benjamin Bailey, 23 January 1818.

This MS printed *Letters*, I, 211–12 (letter, 209–12); a transcript by one of Richard Woodhouse's clerks of this letter, in Woodhouse's letterbook at Harvard (Keats Collection 3.3, pp. 83–5), is without the verses.

Harvard, Keats Collection 1.20.

KeJ 229 Transcript by Charles Brown, with corrections by Richard Woodhouse, signed with the 'CB' flourish; dated originally 1817 and altered by Woodhouse to 21 January 1818.

Facsimile in *Keats Facsimiles VII*, pp. 48–9.

Harvard, Keats Collection 3.6, pp. 46–7.

KeJ 230 Transcript by Charles Wentworth Dilke, on a blank page at the back of his copy of *Endymion* (1818), marked 'CB'; dated 21 January 1818.

Keats House, London, KH 52.

KeJ 231 Transcript by Richard Woodhouse, in W2; annotated '21 Jany 1818. C. B.'.

Facsimiles of poem and Woodhouse's notes on blank versos in *Keats Facsimiles VI*, pp. 284–7.

Harvard, Keats Collection 3.2, ff. 155–6 (rectos only).

KeJ 232 Transcript by Richard Woodhouse, in W1; dated 21 January 1818.

Harvard, Keats Collection 3.1, pp. 160–2.

KeJ 233 Transcript by Charlotte Reynolds, in Reynolds-Hood Commonplace Book (f. 39a); dated 21 January 1818.

Bristol Reference Library.

Lines on the Mermaid Tavern ('Souls of poets dead and gone')
First pub. *Lamia* (1820); Stillinger, pp. 230–1. Keats sent these lines to J. H. Reynolds in a now-lost letter of [3 February 1818]; Woodhouse's transcript of the letter (in his letterbook at Harvard, Keats Collection 3.3, pp. 28–30) includes only the first line (printed *Letters*, I, 223–5).

KeJ 234 Fair copy, here untitled (but top of leaf is torn away), one page.

Facsimile in *Poetry Manuscripts*, p. 67.

Harvard, Keats Collection 2.16.

KeJ 235 Fair copy, in George Keats's Notebook, 2 pages, here entitled (added later) by George Keats 'Ode. 1818'.

Facsimile in *Keats Facsimiles V*, pp. 115–17.

British Library, Egerton MS 2780, ff. 29, 30.

KeJ 236 Transcript by Charles Brown, revised by Keats in line 4, here entitled 'Lines to the Mermaid Tavern. 1818.', annotated by Richard Woodhouse.

Facsimile in *Keats Facsimiles VII*, pp. 6–7.

Harvard, Keats Collection 3.6, pp. 4–5.

KeJ 237 Transcript by Richard Woodhouse, in W2.

Facsimile in *Keats Facsimiles VI*, p. 99.

Harvard, Keats Collection 3.2, f. 61.

KeJ 238 Transcript by Charles Wentworth Dilke, here untitled, on blank leaves at the back of his copy of *Endymion* (1818); dated 1818.

Keats House, London, KH 52.

KeJ 239 Two transcripts by Richard Woodhouse, in W1.

Harvard, Keats Collection 3.1, pp. 16, 154.

Lines Written on 29 May, the Anniversary of Charles's Restoration, on Hearing the Bells Ringing
('Infatuate Britons, will you still proclaim')
First pub. Amy Lowell, *John Keats*, 2 vols (Boston, 1925); Stillinger, p. 28.

KeJ 240 Transcript by Richard Woodhouse, here entitled 'Written on 29 May, the anniversary of the Restoration of Charles the 2d', on a leaf containing also KeJ 417, in W3, annotated in shorthand 'From Do [i.e. Mary Frogley]'.

Facsimile in *Keats Facsimiles IV*, p. 246.

Pierpont Morgan, MA 215, f. 69.

KeJ 241 Transcript by Richard Woodhouse, in W3 (originally in W2, f. 12, also containing the end of KeJ 287), marked 'F[rogley]'.

Facsimile in *Keats Facsimiles IV*, p. 243.

Pierpont Morgan, MA 215, f. 70.

'Mother of Hermes! and still youthful Maia!'
First pub. *Literary Remains* (1848); Stillinger, p. 264.

KeJ 242 Transcript by one of Richard Woodhouse's clerks, corrected by Woodhouse, of a (now-lost) letter from Keats to J. H. Reynolds containing these lines, dated 'May-day' in the text, in Woodhouse's letterbook (pp. 64–70); the letter dated by Woodhouse Teignmouth, 3 May 1818.

This transcript printed *Letters*, I, 278 (letter, 275–83).

Harvard, Keats Collection 3.3, pp. 65–6.

KeJ 243 Transcript by Richard Woodhouse, in W2, here entitled 'Ode to May –/Fragment.'; dated 1 May 1818.

Facsimile in *Keats Facsimiles VI*, p. 241.

Harvard, Keats Collection 3.2, f. 132.

KeJ 244 Late transcript by one of Richard Woodhouse's clerks, made for Charles Brown; watermarked 1833.

Harvard, Keats Collection 4.20.9.

'Nature withheld Cassandra in the skies'
First pub. *Literary Remains* (1848); Stillinger, pp. 285–6. These lines were sent to J. H. Reynolds in a now-lost letter of [22? September 1818]; an extant transcript (printed *Letters*, I, 370–1) in Woodhouse's letterbook at Harvard (Keats Collection 3.3, pp. 18–19) includes only the first line.

KeJ 245 Fair copy in pencil, inked over by Richard Woodhouse, on a blank page of a copy of Shakespeare's *Poetical Works* (see KeJ 572).

This MS printed in *The Poetical Works and Other Writings of John Keats*, ed. H. B. Forman, 8 vols (New York, 1938–9), IV, 164n.

Keats House, London, KH 22.

KeJ 246 Last line (line 12) only, in a letter to C. W. Dilke, postmarked 21 September 1818.

This MS printed *Letters*, I, 369 (letter, 367–9); facsimile in Williamson, Plate XXI.

Keats House, London, KH 4.

KeJ 247 Transcript by Richard Woodhouse, headed 'Sonnet 2d', in W3.

Facsimile in *Keats Facsimiles IV*, p. 291.

Pierpont Morgan, MA 215, f. 54.

KeJ 248 Transcript by Richard Woodhouse, in W2, with notes and a transcript of Ronsard's sonnet on the facing page (f. 139v); dated alternatively September and December 1818.

Facsimile of transcript and annotations on facing page in *Keats Facsimiles VI*, pp. 256–7.

Harvard, Keats Collection 3.2, f. 140.

KeJ 249 Transcript by Charlotte Reynolds, headed 'Sonnet translated from Ronsard', in Reynolds-Hood Commonplace Book (f. 41a); dated 1818.

Bristol Reference Library.

'Non ne suis si audace a languire', for two lines in French by Keats, see *Letters*, II, 172 and INTRODUCTION.

'Not Aladdin magian'
First pub. *Western Messenger* (Louisville, KY), July 1836; collected *Literary Remains* (1848); Stillinger, pp. 277–8.

KeJ 250 In the 26 July section of a letter to Tom Keats, [23–6 July 1818], postmarked 31 July and 3 August 1818.

This MS printed *Letters*, I, 349–51 (letter, 346–51); a transcript of this letter by John Jeffrey (Harvard) omits these lines.

Harvard, Keats Collection 1.35.

KeJ 251 Fair copy, without lines 7–8 and 45–57, in the [18 September] section of a letter (containing also KeJ 78, 110, 369, 380) to George and Georgiana Keats, headed '*Incipit Poema Lyrica de Staffa tractans*'; letter of [17–27 September 1819].

This MS printed *Letters*, II, 199–200 (letter, 184–218).

Pierpont Morgan, MA 212.

KeJ 252 Transcript by Richard Woodhouse, here entitled <'Lycidas's> Lines/On visiting "Staffa" — <the Giant's Causeway in Ireland.>', in W2.

Facsimile in *Keats Facsimiles VI*, pp. 101–3.

Harvard, Keats Collection 3.2, ff. 62–3 (rectos only).

KeJ 253 Transcript by Charles Brown, made for Joseph Severn, without lines 39–40, 50–7, here entitled 'On Fingal's Cave. A Fragment'; watermarked 1822.

This MS printed in William Sharp, *The Life and Letters of Joseph Severn* (London, 1892), pp. 35–6n; this is the transcript Severn mentions in his letter to R. M. Milnes, 6 October 1845 (*Keats Circle*, II, 131).

Harvard, Keats Collection 5.2.1(508).

KeJ 254 Transcript by Richard Woodhouse, here entitled 'Lines on Visiting "Staffa"', lines 50–7 added in pencil, in W1.

Harvard, Keats Collection 3.1, pp. 138–40.

KeJ 255 Transcript by Charlotte Reynolds, here entitled 'Lines/On Visiting "Staffa"', in Reynolds-Hood Commonplace Book (f. 30).

Bristol Reference Library.

'Now when the Monkey found himself alone', for a lost 'fragment of a fairy Tale', see INTRODUCTION.

'O blush not so! O blush not so!'
First pub. *The Poetical Works and Other Writings of John Keats*, ed. H. B. Forman, 4 vols (London, 1883); Stillinger, p. 226.

KeJ 256 Transcript by Charles Brown, here entitled 'Song. 1818.'.

Facsimile in *Keats Facsimiles VII*, p. 8.

Harvard, Keats Collection 3.6, p. 6.

KeJ 257 Transcript in Woodhouse's letterbook by one of his clerks (corrected by Woodhouse) of a now-lost letter (containing also KeJ 118, 131, 537) from Keats to J. H. Reynolds containing these lines, letter dated by Woodhouse 31 January 1818.

This MS printed *Letters*, I, 219–20 (letter, 219–22).

Harvard, Keats Collection 3.3, pp. 53–4.

KeJ 258 Transcript by Richard Woodhouse, here entitled 'Song', in W3, one page.

Facsimile in *Keats Facsimiles IV*, p. 263.

Pierpont Morgan, MA 215, f. 79.

'O come, dearest Emma! the rose is full blown'
First pub. *Poetical Works and Other Writings of John Keats*, ed. H. B. Forman, 4 vols (London, 1883), as 'Stanzas to Miss Wylie'; Stillinger, p. 39.

KeJ 259 Fair copy, corrected, here entitled 'Song', one page (on a leaf containing also KeJ 266), in W3; watermarked 1814.

Facsimile in Mabel A. E. Steele, 'Three Early Manuscripts of John Keats', *KSJ*, 1 (1952), 57–63 (Plate VII) and *Keats Facsimiles IV*, p. 221.

Pierpont Morgan, MA 215, f. 83.

KeJ 260 Transcript by Richard Woodhouse, here beginning 'O come, my dear Emma...', in W3, annotated in shorthand 'from Mary Frogley', one page (on a leaf containing also KeJ 389).

Facsimile in *Keats Facsimiles IV*, p. 249.

Pierpont Morgan, MA 215, f. 77.

KeJ 261 Transcript by Richard Woodhouse, here entitled 'To Emma' and beginning 'O come, my dear Emma...', in W3 (on 2 leaves (rectos only) originally in W2, ff. 2–3, also containing KeJ 388, 416), marked 'F[rogley]'.

Facsimile in *Keats Facsimiles IV*, pp. 227, 229.

Pierpont Morgan, MA 215, f. 78.

KeJ 262 Transcript by Richard Woodhouse, here entitled 'To Emma (Mathews [added in shorthand])' and beginning 'O come, my dear Emma...', in W2, annotated 'F[rogley]'.

Facsimile in *Keats Facsimiles VI*, pp. 411–13.

Harvard, Keats Collection 3.2, ff. 219–20 (rectos only).

KeJ 263 Transcript by George Keats, pasted in Keats-Wylie Scrapbook, here beginning 'O come, Georgiana...'; probably transcribed late 1816.

Harvard, Keats Collection 3.4, f. 35.

KeJ 264 Late transcript by one of Richard Woodhouse's clerks, here beginning 'O come, my dear Emma...', made for Charles Brown; watermarked 1833.

Harvard, Keats Collection 4.20.9.

'O grant that like to Peter I'
First pub. *The Poems and Verses of John Keats*, ed. J. M. Murry (London, 1930); Stillinger, p. 100.

KeJ 265 Draft, followed by a fair copy, one page.

Facsimile in *Poetry Manuscripts*, p. 57.

Harvard, Keats Collection 2.31.

'O, I am frighten'd with most hateful thoughts!', for this fourth 'Extract from an Opera', see KeJ 83–4.

'O Solitude! if I must with thee dwell'
First pub. as 'To solitude' in *The Examiner*, 5 May 1816; collected *Poems* (1817), as 'Sonnet VII'; Stillinger, p. 41.

KeJ 266 Fair copy, here entitled 'Sonnet', one page (on a leaf containing also KeJ 259), in W3; watermarked 1814.

This MS described (and facsimile printed) in Mabel A. E. Steele, 'Three Early Manuscripts of John Keats', *KSJ*, 1 (1952), 57–63 (Plate VIII); facsimile in *Keats Facsimiles IV*, p. 222.

Pierpont Morgan, MA 215, f. 83.

KeJ 267 Fair copy, headed '[Sonnet] 7 —', printer's copy for *Poems* (1817), on a page numbered '59', together with a letter of presentation from H. F. Lyte to Charlotte Philpotts, 28 October 1834.

Not in *Texts*, p. 106 but located in Stillinger.

William Andrews Clark Library, Los Angeles, K256M1.

KeJ 268 Transcript in Tom Keats's Copybook, here entitled 'Sonnet to Solitude'; probably transcribed late 1816.

Facsimile of lines 1–8 in Mabel A. E. Steele, 'Three Early Manuscripts of John Keats', *KSJ*, 1 (1952), 57–63 (Plate Ib).

Harvard, Keats Collection 3.5, p. 23.

'O thou whose face hath felt the winter's wind'
First pub. *Literary Remains* (1848); Stillinger, p. 235.

KeJ 269 Fair copy, in a letter to J. H. Reynolds postmarked 19 February 1818.

This MS printed *Letters*, I, 233 (letter, 231–3); see KeJ 270 for Woodhouse's transcript.

Princeton, Robert H. Taylor Collection.

KeJ 270 Transcript by Richard Woodhouse of the letter to J. H. Reynolds containing these lines (KeJ 269), in Woodhouse's letterbook.

Harvard, Keats Collection 3.3, p. 25.

'O were I one of the Olympian twelve', for this first 'Extract from an Opera', see KeJ 83–4, 86.

Ode on a Grecian Urn ('Thou still unravish'd bride of quietness')
First pub. *Annals of the Fine Arts*, January 1820, as 'On a Grecian Urn'; collected *Lamia* (1820); Stillinger, pp. 372–3.

KeJ 271 Transcript by Charles Brown, signed with the 'CB' flourish; dated 1819.

Facsimile in *Keats Facsimiles VII*, pp. 27–9.

Harvard, Keats Collection 3.6, pp. 25–7.

KeJ 272 Transcript by Charles Wentworth Dilke, on a blank leaf at the back of his copy of *Endymion* (1818), marked 'CB'; dated 1819.

Keats House, London, KH 52.

KeJ 273 Transcript by Richard Woodhouse, in W2, marked 'from C. B.'; dated 1819.

Facsimile in *Keats Facsimiles VI*, pp. 349–53.

Harvard, Keats Collection 3.2, ff. 188–90 (rectos only).

KeJ 274 Transcript by George Keats, 3 pages, in George Keats's Notebook; dated 1819, transcribed January 1820.

This MS printed (with facsimile) in *The Odes of Keats*, ed. Robert Gittings (London, 1970), pp. 44–9 (see also pp. 68–70); facsimile in *Keats Facsimiles V*, pp. 167–9.

British Library, Egerton MS 2780, ff. 55–6.

Ode on Indolence ('One morn before me were three figures seen')
First pub. *Literary Remains* (1848); Stillinger, pp. 375–7. For a discussion of the stanza order, see Jack Stillinger, 'The Text of Keats's "Ode on Indolence"', *SB*, 22 (1969), 255–8.

KeJ 275 Transcript by Charles Brown, including epigraph and revised stanza numbers, printer's copy for the first publication; dated 1819.

Facsimile in *Keats Facsimiles VII*, pp. 21–4.

Harvard, Keats Collection 3.6, pp. 19–22.

KeJ 276 Transcript by Richard Woodhouse, in W2, marked 'from C. B.'; dated 1819.

Facsimile in *Keats Facsimiles VI*, pp. 269–73.

Harvard, Keats Collection 3.2, ff. 147–9 (rectos only).

Ode on Melancholy ('No, no, go not to Lethe, neither twist')
First pub. *Lamia* (1820); Stillinger, pp. 374–5. For a discussion and printing of the draft MS (KeJ 277–8) and a complete facsimile, see *The Odes of Keats*, ed. Robert Gittings (London, 1970), pp. 60–3, 77–99.

KeJ 277 First leaf (recto only) of the draft, containing stanzas 1 and 2 only, here entitled 'On Melancholy'.

Facsimile in T. W. Higginson, *Book and Heart: Essays on Literature and Life* (New York, 1897), p. 19 and Gittings (see headnote).

Princeton, Robert H. Taylor Collection.

KeJ 278 Second leaf (recto only) of draft, containing stanza 3, annotated on verso 'Given to my Aunt Miss Hamilton Smith by Mr C. Brown...S. T. Whiteford'.

Facsimile in Sotheby's sale catalogue, 25 July 1932 (property of Capt. J. S. Coats), Lot 105 and in Gittings (see headnote).

Berg.

KeJ 279 Transcript by Charles Brown, here entitled 'Ode, on <to> Melancholy. 1819.' and containing an additional opening stanza (cancelled) beginning 'Tho' you should build a bark of dead men's bones', signed with the 'CB' flourish, annotated by Richard Woodhouse.

The additional opening stanza was first pub. in *Literary Remains* (1848); printed in the apparatus in Stillinger, p. 374; facsimile in *Keats Facsimiles VII*, pp. 9–10.

Harvard, Keats Collection 3.6, pp. 7–8.

KeJ 280 Transcript by George Keats, without the additional opening stanza, in George Keats's Notebook, 2 pages; dated 1819, transcribed January 1820.

Facsimile in *Keats Facsimiles V*, pp. 161–2.

British Library, Egerton MS 2780, f. 52r–v.

KeJ 281 Transcript by Richard Woodhouse, in W2, including the additional opening stanza (not cancelled here), marked 'from C. B.'; dated 1819.

Facsimile in *Keats Facsimiles VI*, pp. 265–7.

Harvard, Keats Collection 3.2, ff. 145–6 (rectos only).

Ode to a Nightingale ('My heart aches, and a drowsy numbness pains')
First pub. *Annals of the Fine Arts*, July 1819; collected *Lamia* (1820); Stillinger, pp. 369–72.

KeJ 282 Revised, here entitled 'Ode to the Nightingale', containing the rejected beginning 'Small, winged Dryad' (a false start, now on the bottom of the second page), 2 leaves (4 pages); watermarked 1817.

For a discussion of this MS, see Robert N. Roth, 'The Houghton-Crewe Draft of Keats's "Ode to a Nightingale"', *PBSA*, 48 (1954), 91–5 and *The Odes of Keats*, ed. Robert Gittings (London, 1970), pp. 65–7 (facsimile and printing on pp. 36–43); facsimile also in *Monthly Review*, March 1903, in *The John Keats Memorial Volume*, [ed. G. C. Williamson] (London and New York, 1921), in *English Poetical Autographs*, ed. Desmond Flower and A. N. L. Munby (London, 1938), plates 26–26[4]; facsimile first page only in A. F. Scott, *The Poet's Craft* (Cambridge, 1957), pp. 26–7 and in Tim Hilton, *Keats and His World* (London, 1971), p. [103].

Fitzwilliam Museum.

KeJ 283 Transcript by Richard Woodhouse, in W2, here entitled 'Ode to the Nightingale.'; annotated 'C. B. May 1819.'.

Facsimile in *Keats Facsimiles VI*, pp. 288–95.

Harvard, Keats Collection 3.2, ff. 157–60 (rectos only).

KeJ 284 Transcript by Charles Wentworth Dilke, here entitled 'Ode to the Nightingale', on blank leaves at the back of his copy of *Endymion* (1818), annotated 'CB'; dated May 1819.

Keats House, London, KH 52.

KeJ 285 Transcript by George Keats, here entitled 'Ode to the Nightingale. 1819.', in George Keats's Notebook, 4 pages; transcribed 15 January 1820.

Facsimile in *Keats Facsimiles V*, pp. 163–6.

British Library, Egerton MS 2780, ff. 53–54v.

KeJ 286 Transcript by Richard Woodhouse, here entitled 'Ode to the Nightingale', in W1; dated May 1819.

Harvard, Keats Collection 3.1, pp. 164–7.

Ode to Apollo ('In thy western halls of gold')
First pub. *Literary Remains* (1848); Stillinger, pp. 34–6. Lines 18–23 of this poem are quoted by Richard Woodhouse, in a note to line 3 of 'To My Brother George', on an inserted leaf in Woodhouse *Poems* (1817) at the Huntington, RB 151852 (see KeJ 502–5).

KeJ 287 Transcript by Richard Woodhouse, in W3 (on 3 leaves, rectos only, originally in W2 (ff. 10–12) and containing also KeJ 241), annotated 'F[rogley]'; dated February 1815, transcribed probably November 1818.

Facsimile in *Keats Facsimiles IV*, pp. 239–43; in a note to this poem (on what was originally W2, f. 10v), Woodhouse quotes lines 1–4 of Keats's poem 'To My Brother George' (see KeJ 502–5); note printed Finney, pp. 752–3 and Steele, p. 244 (facsimile in *Keats Facsimiles IV*, p. 240).

Pierpont Morgan, MA 215, f. 70.

KeJ 288 Transcript by Richard Woodhouse, in W2, annotated 'F[rogley]'; dated February 1815.

In a note on the facing f. 220v, Woodhouse quotes lines 1–4 of Keats's poem 'To My Brother George' (see KeJ 502–5); note printed Finney, p. 761; facsimile of poem and note in *Keats Facsimiles VI*, pp. 414–17.

Harvard, Keats Collection 3.2, ff. 221–2 (rectos only).

KeJ 289 Late transcript by one of Richard Woodhouse's clerks, made for Charles Brown; dated February 1815, watermarked 1833.

Harvard, Keats Collection 4.20.9.

Ode to Psyche ('O Goddess! hear these tuneless numbers, wrung')
First pub. *Lamia* (1820); Stillinger, pp. 364–6.

KeJ 290 Draft, 3 pages (one leaf); presented to J. H. Reynolds, 4 May 1819.

Facsimile (and MS printed) in *The Odes of Keats*, ed. Robert Gittings (London, 1970), pp. 50–55 (discussed pp. 71–3); facsimile of last 2 pages in *British Literary Manuscripts*, plate 40.

Pierpont Morgan, MA 210.

KeJ 291 Fair copy, in the 30 April section of a letter (containing also KeJ 28, 56, 167–8, 210, 311, 317, 393, 399, 542, 547) to George and Georgiana Keats, 14 February–3 May 1819.

This MS printed *Letters*, II, 106–8 (letter, 58–109).

Harvard, Keats Collection 1.53.

KeJ 292 Transcript by Charles Brown, revised by Keats in lines 10 and 43; dated 1819.

Facsimile in *Keats Facsimiles VII*, pp. 38–40.

Harvard, Keats Collection 3.6, pp. 36–8.

KeJ 293 Transcript by Richard Woodhouse, in W2, annotated 'Given by J. K. to J. H. R. 4 May 1819'.

Facsimile in *Keats Facsimiles VI*, pp. 120–5.

Harvard, Keats Collection 3.2, ff. 72–4 (rectos only).

'Of late two dainties were before me plac'd'
First pub. *The Athenaeum*, 7 June 1873; Stillinger, pp. 274–5.

KeJ 294 Revised, in the 18 July section of a letter (containing also KeJ 17) to Tom Keats, 17–21 July 1818.

This MS printed *Letters*, I, 337 (letter, 333–9); facsimile in Williamson, Plate XIV.

Keats House, London, KH 3.

KeJ 295 Transcript in an unidentified hand of KeJ 294 (containing also KeJ 18), made for R. M. Milnes in 1845.

Harvard, Keats Collection 3.10(26).

'Oh Chatterton! how very sad thy fate!'
First pub. *Literary Remains* (1848); Stillinger, p. 32.

KeJ 296 Transcript in an unidentified formal hand (possibly George Keats's), here entitled 'Sonnet', in W3, one page; dated 'J. K. 1815'.

Facsimile in *Keats Facsimiles IV*, p. 307.

Pierpont Morgan, MA 215, f. 88.

KeJ 297 Transcript by Richard Woodhouse, here entitled 'Sonnet. To Chatterton.', in W2; dated 1815, probably transcribed after May 1821.

Facsimile in *Keats Facsimiles VI*, p. 405.

Harvard, Keats Collection 3.2, f. 216.

KeJ 298 Late transcript by one of Richard Woodhouse's clerks, here entitled 'Sonnet. To Chatterton', made for Charles Brown; dated 1815, watermarked 1833.

Harvard, Keats Collection 4.20.9.

'Oh! how I love, on a fair summer's eve'
First pub. *Literary Remains* (1848); Stillinger, p. 54.

KeJ 299 Transcript by Richard Woodhouse, here entitled 'Sonnet.', in W2, annotated 'F[rogley]'; dated 1816, transcribed probably November 1818.

Facsimile in *Keats Facsimiles VI*, p. 2.

Harvard, Keats Collection 3.2, f. 9.

KeJ 300 Transcript by Richard Woodhouse, here entitled 'Sonnet', in W3, annotated in shorthand 'from Mary Frogley', one page of a leaf containing also KeJ 23; dated 1816.

Facsimile in *Keats Facsimiles IV*, p. 247.

Pierpont Morgan, MA 215, f. 81.

KeJ 301 Transcript by Richard Woodhouse, in W1; dated 1816.

Harvard, Keats Collection 3.1, p. 21.

KeJ 302 Transcript by Richard Woodhouse, on a blank page facing p. 88 in Woodhouse's *Poems* (1817); dated 1816.

This MS printed in Sperry, p. 150; facsimile in *Keats Facsimiles I*, p. 169.

Huntington, RB 151852.

KeJ 303 Late transcript by one of Richard Woodhouse's clerks, made for Charles Brown; dated 1816, watermarked 1833.

Harvard, Keats Collection 4.20.9.

KeJ 304 Transcript by Coventry Patmore, printer's copy for the first publication; dated 1816, transcribed 1847.

Harvard, Keats Collection 3.10(7).

'Old Meg she was a gipsey'
First pub. as 'Meg Merrilies. A Ballad...' in *Plymouth and Devonport Weekly Journal*, 22 November 1838; collected *Literary Remains* (1848); Stillinger, pp. 266–7.

KeJ 305 Draft, in the 3 July section of a letter (containing also KeJ 436) to Fanny Keats, Dumfries, 2–5 July 1818.

This MS printed *Letters*, I, 311–12 (letter, 310–16); facsimile in British Library, MS Facs. 336(b).

Pierpont Morgan, MA 975.

KeJ 306 Fair copy, in the 3 July section of a letter to Tom Keats, Auchencairn, 3–9 July 1818.

This MS printed *Letters*, I, 317–18 (letter, 317–22); a transcript of this letter by John Jeffrey (Harvard) omits the poem.

Harvard, Keats Collection 1.33.

On a Leander Which Miss Reynolds, My Kind Friend, Gave Me ('Come hither all sweet maidens, soberly')
First pub. *The Gem*, ed. Thomas Hood (London, 1829), as 'On a Picture of Leander'; Stillinger, p. 94. J. C. Stephens's transcript at Harvard (Keats Collection 3.12, f. 66) was copied from the first publication.

KeJ 307 Draft, on a leaf (containing also a transcript of Wordsworth's 'Lines Written while Sailing in a Boat at Evening' on verso in unidentified hand), signed; dated March 181[7?].

Facsimile in *Poetry Manuscripts*, p. 55.

Harvard, Keats Collection 2.12.

KeJ 308 Transcript by Richard Woodhouse, here entitled 'On a Leander which a young lady (Miss Reynolds [parenthetical material in shorthand]) gave the Author', in W2; dated March 1816.

Woodhouse's annotation printed Finney, p. 761; facsimile in *Keats Facsimiles VI*, p. 359.

Harvard, Keats Collection 3.2, f. 193.

KeJ 309 Late transcript by Richard Woodhouse, here entitled 'On a Leander Gem which a young Lady gave the author', made for Charles Brown; watermarked 1833.

Harvard, Keats Collection 4.20.9.

On Death ('Can death be sleep, when life is but a dream')
Questionable attribution. First pub. *Poetical Works and Other Writings of John Keats*, ed. H. B. Forman, 4 vols (London, 1883); Stillinger, p. 754, in 'Appendix VI Questionable Attributions'.

KeJ 310 MS in the hand of Georgiana Wylie (later Keats), unsigned, in the 'Keats-Wylie Scrapbook'; dated 1814, probably transcribed late 1816.

Harvard, Keats Collection 3.4, f. 4.

On Fame ('Fame, like a wayward girl, will still be coy')
First pub. *Ladies' Companion*, August 1837; collected *Literary Remains* (1848); Stillinger, pp. 366–7.

KeJ 311 Fair copy, here entitled 'Another on Fame', in the 30 April section of a letter (containing also KeJ 28, 56, 167–8, 210, 291, 317, 393, 399, 542, 547) to George and Georgiana Keats, 14 February–3 May 1819.

This MS printed *Letters*, II, 105 (letter, 58–109).

Harvard, Keats Collection 1.53.

KeJ 312 Transcript by Charles Brown, here entitled 'Sonnet on Fame. 1819.', signed with the 'CB' flourish, printer's copy for *Literary Remains*; transcribed 30 April 1819.

Facsimile in *Keats Facsimiles VII*, p. 51.

Harvard, Keats Collection 3.6, p. 49.

KeJ 313 Transcript by Richard Woodhouse, in W2, here entitled 'Sonnet/On Fame', annotated 'C. B. 1819.'.

Facsimile in *Keats Facsimiles VI*, p. 279.

Harvard, Keats Collection 3.2, f. 152.

KeJ 314 Transcript by Charles Wentworth Dilke, here entitled 'Sonnet, On Fame', on a blank page at the back of his copy of *Endymion* (1818); dated 1819.

Keats House, London, KH 52.

KeJ 315 Transcript by Richard Woodhouse, here entitled 'Sonnet — On Fame', in W1; dated 1819.

Harvard, Keats Collection 3.1, p. 160.

KeJ 316 Transcript by John Howard Payne; as sent to R. M. Milnes with a letter dated from Paris, 2 July 1847.

The letter to Milnes printed *Keats Circle*, II, 223–5.

Harvard, Keats Collection 3.10(19).

On Fame ('How fever'd is the man who cannot look')
First pub. *Literary Remains* (1848); Stillinger, p. 367.

KeJ 317 Draft, including the epigraph, in the 30 April section of a letter (containing also KeJ 28, 56, 167–8, 210, 291, 311, 393, 399, 542, 547) to George and Georgiana Keats, 14 February–3 May 1819.

This MS printed *Letters*, II, 104–5 (letter, 58–109).

Harvard, Keats Collection 1.53.

KeJ 318 Transcript by Charles Brown, here entitled 'Sonnet. On Fame. 1819.', including the epigraph, signed with the 'CB' flourish, printer's copy for the first publication.

Facsimile in *Keats Facsimiles VII*, p. 53.

Harvard, Keats Collection 3.6, p. 51.

KeJ 319 Transcript by Richard Woodhouse, here entitled 'Sonnet. To Fame', in W2, annotated 'C. B. 1819.'.

Facsimile of poem (and note on facing f. 152v) in *Keats Facsimiles VI*, pp. 280–81.

Harvard, Keats Collection 3.2, f. 153.

KeJ 320 Transcript by Charles Wentworth Dilke, here entitled 'Sonnet. On Fame', on a back page of his copy of *Endymion* (1818); dated 1819.

Keats House, London, KH 52.

On First Looking into Chapman's Homer ('Much have I travell'd in the realms of gold')
First pub. *The Examiner*, 1 December 1816; collected *Poems* (1817), as 'Sonnet XI'; Stillinger, p. 64. Mary Strange Mathew's transcript (in an album owned in the 1940s by T. G. Crump, photocopy at University of Illinois) was copied from *Poems* (1817).

KeJ 321 Revised, here entitled 'On the first looking into Chapman's Homer', one page.

Facsimile in: Amy Lowell, *John Keats*, 2 vols (Boston, 1925), I, facing p. 180; Mabel A. E. Steele, 'Three Early Manuscripts of John Keats', *KSJ*, 1 (1952), 57–63 (Plate IV); Walter Jackson Bate, *John Keats* (Cambridge, MA, 1963), p. 87; Aileen Ward, *John Keats* (New York, 1963), following p. 386; *The Houghton Library 1942–1967* (Cambridge, MA, 1967), p. 72; *The Poems of John Keats*, ed. Miriam Allott (London, 1970), facing p. 644; Tim Hilton, *Keats and His World* (London, 1971), p. [23]; *Poetry Manuscripts*, p. 13.

Harvard, Keats Collection 2.4.

KeJ 322 Fair copy, here untitled, inscribed in an unidentified hand 'To Mariane Reynolds —', one page; watermarked 1812.

Facsimile in: John Gilmer Speed, 'The Sojourns of John Keats', *Century Magazine*, September 1910, p. 691; *Sentimental Library*, between pp. 120 and 121; and *British Literary Manuscripts*, plate 38.

Pierpont Morgan, MA 214.

KeJ 323 Transcript in Tom Keats's Copybook, here entitled 'Sonnet On Looking into Chapman's Homer'; probably transcribed late 1816.

Harvard, Keats Collection 3.5, p. 18.

On Leaving Some Friends at an Early Hour ('Give me a golden pen, and let me lean')
First pub. *Poems* (1817), as 'Sonnet XII'; Stillinger, p. 65.

KeJ 324 Draft, on verso of KeJ 160, here untitled.

This MS printed *The Poetical Works and Other Writings of John Keats*, ed. H. Buxton Forman, rev. Maurice Buxton Forman, 8 vols (New York, 1938–9), I, 88–9.

Pierpont Morgan, MA 658.

On Peace ('Oh Peace! and dost thou with thy presence bless')
First pub. Ernest de Selincourt, *N&O*, 4 February 1905, p. 82; Stillinger, p. 28.

KeJ 325 Transcript by Richard Woodhouse, in W3 (on a leaf containing also KeJ 97 (and see KeJ 22) originally in W2, f. 7), annotated 'F[rogley]'; probably transcribed November 1818.

Facsimile in *Keats Facsimiles IV*, p. 237.

Pierpont Morgan, MA 215, f. 65.

KeJ 326 Transcript by Richard Woodhouse, in W2, annotated 'F[rogley]'.

Facsimile in *Keats Facsimiles VI*, p. 413.

Harvard, Keats Collection 3.2, f. 220.

KeJ 327 Late transcript by one of Richard Woodhouse's clerks, printer's copy for first publication, made for Charles Brown; watermarked 1833.

Harvard, Keats Collection 4.20.9.

On Receiving a Curious Shell, and a Copy of Verses, from the Same Ladies ('Hast thou from the caves of Golconda, a gem')
First pub. *Poems* (1817); Stillinger, pp. 37–8. Woodhouse's annotation about this poem, on p. 32 of his *Poems* (1817), is reproduced in *Keats Facsimiles I*, p. 72.

KeJ 328 Fair copy, 2 pages (one leaf), inscribed from B. R. Haydon to William Blackwood, 1839; watermarked 1813, dated 1815.

Facsimile first page in Sotheby's sale catalogue, 23 June 1947 (property of Frank Sykes), Plate III; facsimile of whole in British Library, RP 245(3) and in *Poetry Manuscripts*, p. 3.

Harvard, Keats Collection 2.1.

KeJ 329 Transcript by George Keats, here entitled at end of poem 'Written on receiving a Copy of Tom Moore's "Golden Chain," and a most beautiful Dome shaped Shell from a Lady', pasted in Keats-Wylie Scrapbook; probably transcribed late 1816.

Harvard, Keats Collection 3.4, f. 36.

KeJ 330 Transcript of lines 1–12 only by Georgiana Wylie (later Keats), here entitled 'Eric, Written on his receiving a Copy of T. Moore's "Golden Chain" and a dome Shaped Shell from a Lady', in Keats-Wylie Scrapbook; probably transcribed late 1816.

Harvard, Keats Collection 3.4, f. 22.

KeJ 331 Transcript in Tom Keats's Copybook, here entitled 'On receiving a curious Shell and a copy of verses'; probably transcribed late 1816.

Harvard, Keats Collection 3.5, p. 10.

On Receiving a Laurel Crown from Leigh Hunt ('Minutes are flying swiftly: and as yet')
First pub. *The Times*, 18 May 1914; Stillinger, p. 90.

KeJ 332 Fair copy, on blank page [p. 78] in the copy of *Poems* (1817) presented by Keats to J. H. Reynolds (containing also KeJ 333, 478, 515).

Facsimile in first publication, in 'Two Lost Sonnets of Keats', *TLS*, 21 May 1914, pp. 241–2 and in *Poetry Manuscripts*, p. 47.

Harvard, Keats Collection.

On Seeing the Elgin Marbles ('My spirit is too weak — mortality')
First pub. *The Champion* and *The Examiner*, both on 9 March 1817; collected *Literary Remains* (1848); Stillinger, p. 93. Thomasine Leigh's transcript in her commonplace book of January 1817 (Keats House, London, KH 155) was copied from J. H. Reynolds's review of *Poems* (1817) in *The Champion*, 9 March 1817.

KeJ 333 Fair copy, revised, on a blank page (p. 122) in the copy of *Poems* (1817) presented by Keats to J. H. Reynolds (containing also KeJ 332, 478, 515).

This MS printed in Hyder E. Rollins, 'Unpublished Autograph Texts of Keats', *HLB*, 6 (1952), 165–6; facsimile in *Poetry Manuscripts*, p. 49.

Harvard, Keats Collection.

KeJ 334 Transcript by Richard Woodhouse, here entitled 'Sonnet./On seeing the Elgin Marbles.', in W3, one page of a leaf (containing also KeJ 479), annotated 'Examiner' (from which it was apparently transcribed).

Facsimile in *Keats Facsimiles IV*, p. 257.

Pierpont Morgan, MA 215, f. 86.

KeJ 335 Transcript by Richard Woodhouse, here headed 'Sonnet', in W2, annotated 'From the Examiner'.

Facsimile in *Keats Facsimiles VI*, p. 19. An annotation by Woodhouse on the facing page of W2 (f. 20v) is printed in Finney, p. 758 and reproduced *Keats Facsimiles VI*, p. 18.

Harvard, Keats Collection 3.2, f. 21.

KeJ 336 Transcript by Richard Woodhouse, here entitled 'Sonnet. on seeing the Elgin Marbles. –', on one page of the end flyleaves of Woodhouse's *Poems* (1817), annotated 'Examiner. —'.

This MS printed Sperry, pp. 159–60; facsimile in *Keats Facsimiles I*, p. 235.

Huntington, RB 151852.

KeJ 337 Late transcript by Richard Woodhouse, written for Joseph Severn; watermarked 1830.

Harvard, Keats Collection 4.20.10.

KeJ 338 Transcript by B. R. Haydon or his daughter Mary in a collection of loose MSS (9 leaves (11 pages) containing also KeJ 2, 8, 483 and sonnets by Wordsworth and Elizabeth Barrett Browning), inscribed by Haydon on wrapper 'Sonnets addressed to & MS Written by B. R. Haydon from 1817 to 1841 — Twenty Four Years. Copied for Fun. 1844'.

This transcript (not located Stillinger, see p. 744) is possibly taken from the poem's publication in *Annals of the Fine Arts*, April 1818, from which another transcript by Haydon (sent to Edward Moxon with a letter of 28 November 1845; see *Keats Circle*, II, 141–2) was taken (Harvard, Keats Collection 4.7.20).

Pierpont Morgan, MA 2987.

On Sitting Down to Read *King Lear* Once Again ('O golden-tongued Romance, with serene lute!')
First pub. *Plymouth and Devonport Weekly Journal*, 8 November 1838; collected *Literary Remains* (1848); Stillinger, p. 225.

KeJ 339 Draft, one page, annotated in pencil in an unidentified hand 'Sent me by Thos Hood with MS. of Bridge [?]'.

National Library of Scotland, MS 582, No. 642B.

KeJ 340 Fair copy, revised, written opposite first page of *King Lear* in a copy of a facsimile reprint of the First Folio of Shakespeare's Works (see KeJ 573); dated 22 January 1818.

Facsimiles in Caroline F. E. Spurgeon, *Keats's Shakespeare* (Oxford and London, 1928), Plate 20 and Dorothy Hewlett, *A Life of John Keats*, 3rd ed (London, 1970) p. 132.

Keats House, London, KH 23.

KeJ 341 Transcript by John Jeffrey of a now-lost letter, containing these lines, from Keats to George and Tom Keats, 23–4 January 1818; transcribed in 1845 for R. M. Milnes.

This transcript printed *Letters*, I, 214–15 (letter, 213–17).

Harvard, Keats Collection 3.9, ff. 7–8.

KeJ 342 Transcript by Richard Woodhouse, in W2, here entitled 'Sonnet./On sitting down...', annotated 'J. H. R.' and '22 Jany 1818. C. B.'.

Facsimile in *Keats Facsimiles VI*, p. 27.

Harvard, Keats Collection 3.2, f. 25.

KeJ 343 Transcript by Charles Brown, signed with the 'CB' flourish, here entitled 'Sonnet,/On sitting down to read King Lear once again./22^{d} Jany 1818.'.

Facsimile in *Keats Facsimiles VII*, p. 52.

Harvard, Keats Collection 3.6, p. 50.

KeJ 344 Transcript by Charles Wentworth Dilke, here entitled 'Sonnet. On Sitting Down...', on a blank leaf at the end of his copy of *Endymion* (1818); dated 22 January 1818.

Keats House, London, KH 52.

KeJ 345 Transcript by Richard Woodhouse, in W1; dated 22 January 1818.

Harvard, Keats Collection 3.1, p. 28.

KeJ 346 Transcript by Charlotte Reynolds, in Reynolds-Hood Commonplace Book (f. 28a); dated 22 January 1818.

Bristol Reference Library.

On Some Skulls in the Beauley Abbey, near Inverness ('In silent barren synod met')
This collaboration by Keats and Charles Brown (Keats wrote lines 1–2, 7–12, 43–8 and 55–60) was first pub. *New Monthly Magazine*, January 1822, as 'Stanzas on Some Skulls...' and signed 'S. Y'; Stillinger, pp. 282–5. A lost transcript by Richard Woodhouse is printed in Sidney Colvin, *John Keats* (London, 1917), pp. 553–6.

KeJ 347 Fair copy by Charles Brown, including the epigraphs, in W3, 4 pages (2 leaves).

Facsimile in *Keats Facsimiles IV*, pp. 309–12.

Pierpont Morgan, MA 215, f. 75.

On the Grasshopper and Cricket ('The poetry of earth is never dead:')
First pub. *Poems* (1817), as 'Sonnet XV'; Stillinger, pp. 88–9. Woodhouse's annotation about this poem, facing p. 93 in his *Poems* (1817), is reproduced in *Keats Facsimiles I*, p. 178.

KeJ 348 Fair copy, here entitled 'On the Grasshopper & the Cricket'; dated 30 December 1816.

Victoria and Albert Museum, Forster MS 316 (48. G. 4/37).

On the Sea ('It keeps eternal whisperings around')
First pub. *The Champion*, 17 August 1817, as 'Sonnet. On the Sea'; collected *Literary Remains* (1848); Stillinger, p. 95. Elizabeth Stott Clarke's transcript written in Isabella Jane Towers's copy of *Poems* (1817) (at Keats House, London, KH 50) was copied from *Literary Remains*.

KeJ 349 Transcript by Richard Woodhouse and one of his clerks, in Woodhouse's letterbook (pp. 43–5), of a now-lost letter containing these lines to J. H. Reynolds, 17–18 April [1817].

This transcript printed *Letters*, I, 132 (letter, 130–4); for a transcript by Coventry Patmore, see KeJ 357.

Harvard, Keats Collection 3.3, p. 44.

KeJ 350 Transcript on one page of the end flyleaves of Woodhouse's *Poems* (1817), here entitled 'Sonnet./On the Sea.', annotated on facing blank page; dated August 1817.

This transcript printed Sperry, pp. 158–9 (facsimile, facing p. 129); facsimile in *Keats Facsimiles I*, pp. 232–3.

Huntington, RB 151852.

KeJ 351 Transcript by Richard Woodhouse, here entitled 'Sonnet./On the Sea', one page of a leaf (containing also KeJ 439), in W3, annotated 'Aug[t] 1817. Champion'.

Facsimile in *Keats Facsimiles IV*, p. 256.

Pierpont Morgan, MA 215, f. 86.

KeJ 352 Transcript by Richard Woodhouse, in W2, here entitled 'Sonnet./On the Sea.', annotated 'Aug[t] 1817. Champion'.

Facsimile in *Keats Facsimiles VI*, p. 29.

Harvard, Keats Collection 3.2, f. 26.

KeJ 353 Transcript by Richard Woodhouse, in W1, annotated 'Champion. 17 Aug[t] 1817'.

Harvard, Keats Collection 3.1, p. 32.

KeJ 354 Transcript by Charlotte Reynolds, in Reynolds-Hood Commonplace Book (f. 28); dated August 1818.

Bristol Reference Library.

KeJ 355 Late transcript by one of Richard Woodhouse's clerks, made for Charles Brown; dated August 1817, watermarked 1833.

Harvard, Keats Collection 4.20.9.

KeJ 356 Late transcript by Richard Woodhouse, made for Joseph Severn; watermarked 1830.

Harvard, Keats Collection 4.20.10.

KeJ 357 Transcript by Coventry Patmore of KeJ 349; made in 1847.

Harvard, Keats Collection 3.10(14).

KeJ 358 Transcript by Coventry Patmore, printer's copy for *Literary Remains*; made in 1847.

This transcript unlocated in *Texts* but mentioned Stillinger, p. 567.

Harvard, Keats Collection 3.10(23).

On *The Story of Rimini* ('Who loves to peer up at the morning sun')
First pub. *Literary Remains* (1848); Stillinger, p. 95.

KeJ 359 Transcript by Leigh Hunt, on a blank leaf at the end of a copy of the Galignani edition of *The Poetical Works of Coleridge, Shelley, and Keats* (Paris, 1829), annotated 'Written by Keats in a blank page of the "presentation-copy" of his first volume of poems'.

Harvard, Keats Collection.

KeJ 360 Transcript by Leigh Hunt, probably sent to R. M. Milnes with Hunt's letter of 7 May [1846?].

The letter to Milnes printed *Keats Circle*, II, 156.

Harvard, Keats Collection 4.9.3.

KeJ 361 Transcript by Charles Brown, here entitled (before emendations by R. M. Milnes) 'Sonnet. On the "Story of Rimini". 1817.', printer's copy for the first publication.

Facsimile in *Keats Facsimiles VII*, p. 26.

Harvard, Keats Collection 3.6, p. 24.

On Visiting the Tomb of Burns ('The town, the churchyard, and the setting sun')
First pub. *Literary Remains* (1848); Stillinger, p. 266.

KeJ 362 Transcript by John Jeffrey of a now-lost letter (containing these lines) from John to Tom Keats, 29 June–2 July 1818.

This transcript printed *Letters*, I. 308–9 (letter, 305–9).

Harvard, Keats Collection 3.9, f. 13.

Otho the Great: A Tragedy in Five Acts
Short passages from this drama co-authored by Keats and Charles Brown were first pub. as chapter epigraphs in E. J. Trelawny, *Adventures of a Younger Son*, 3 vols (London, 1831) (including I.i.136–7; I.ii.6–11, 40–1, 86–87a; I.iii.5, 20, 98–101; III.ii.76, 122–6; IV.ii.128b–129a; V.i.14–15, 22, 26–7); first pub. in full *Literary Remains* (1848); Stillinger, pp. 378–451. The 79-leaf first draft

(primarily in Keats's hand and containing some recopied passages) survives almost in its entirety (KeJ 363–8); Joseph Severn, who owned some leaves, cut some of them up into fragments as gifts (for a reconstruction of the draft, see Stillinger, pp. 656–7). The pieces of the draft still missing are: (1) two portions of [f. 57] presumably containing IV.i.71–3 and IV.i.86–90; (2) portion of [f. 66] presumably containing IV.ii.117–121a; (3) [ff. 73–4] presumably containing a cancelled first version of V.v.1–10 (recopied in KeJ 364) and V.v.11–58. In addition, a few fragments of a revised version by Keats of lines from I.i. — also cut up and distributed by Severn — are extant (KeJ 370–73) and reconstructed Stillinger, pp. 658–9. The fair copy, in Brown's hand (KeJ 374–5), also survives, with only a few leaves missing; see Stillinger, p. 658.

KeJ 363 Draft in Keats's hand, including some recopied passages (a few interlinear revisions by Brown), including Acts I–III and IV.i (wanting the leaf containing IV.i.71–90, see KeJ 365–6); 61 leaves (primarily rectos only), the first being a title page; some watermarked 1812.

This MS was taken to America by George Keats in January 1820.

Texas.

KeJ 364 The remainder of the draft (KeJ 363), being almost wholly in Keats's hand (a few interlinear revisions by Brown), including some recopied passages, containing IV.ii–the end, wanting 5 leaves or portions of leaves (see KeJ 367–8), 17 pages of text (14 leaves, one a folded leaf and two are fragments of leaves); some watermarked 1810.

This part of the draft was owned by Joseph Severn who cut fragments out of it and gave them away.

Huntington, HM 11912.

KeJ 365 Fragment of leaf missing from the draft (KeJ 363), containing IV.i.74–5 and two cancelled lines.

This fragment not mentioned *Texts* but collated in Stillinger.

Rosenbach Foundation.

KeJ 366 Fragment of leaf missing from the draft (KeJ 363), containing IV.i.76–85; watermarked 1816.

Facsimile in *Poetry Manuscripts*.

Harvard, Keats Collection 2.24.3.

KeJ 367 Fragments of leaves missing from the draft (KeJ 364) including: two consecutive fragments of one leaf (watermarked 1810) containing IV.ii.121b–126 and 127–39 (rectos) and revised version of V.i.18–32 (on the second verso), the first annotated '...for Miss Jewsbury from J. Severn Aug 3rd 1859', the second annotated '...presented to Mr J. T. Fields by J. Severn May 10th 1860 London'; fragment of a leaf containing V.ii.8b–15 (recto), annotated '...from J. Severn Rome Feby 6th 1862'; fragment of a leaf containing V.v.151b–164a (recto) and V.v.173c–174 (verso), inscribed by Joseph Severn to Miss C. M. Beresford, 14 February 1874.

Facsimile of V.v.151b–164a in Sotheby's sale catalogue, 12 November 1963, Lot 88; of whole in *Poetry Manuscripts*.

Harvard, Keats Collection 2.24.4–2.24.7.

KeJ 368 Fragment of leaf missing from the draft (KeJ 364), containing V.v.140a, 143b–151a (recto) and V.v.180–2 (verso); inscribed by Severn 'MS of John Keats presented to Miss Amelia B. Edwards by Joseph Severn. Rome, New years day 1872'.

Berg.

KeJ 369 I.iii.24–9, in the [27 September] section of a letter (containing also KeJ 78, 110, 251, 380) to George and Georgiana Keats, [17–27 September 1819].

This MS printed *Letters*, II, 217–18 (letter, 184–218).

Pierpont Morgan, MA 212.

KeJ 370 Two fragments of Keats's revised version of I.i, one containing lines 17–24 (recto only), annotated '...presented to Mr John W. Field by Joseph Severn — Rome April 24th 1875' and watermarked 1818; the other containing lines 34–44a (recto only).

Harvard, Keats Collection 2.24.1 and 2.24.2.

KeJ 371 Two fragments of the third leaf of Keats's revised version of I.i, the first, numbered 3 and signed by Joseph Severn, containing lines 55–60a and two additional lines (recto) and lines 145–52 (verso) and the second containing lines 66–8 (recto), inscribed by Severn '...presented to Mr Bicknell by Joseph Severn Rome Decr 2nd 1862.'.

Facsimile of lines 55–60a in Maggs Catalogue 339 (August 1915), facing p. 64 and in American Art Association sale catalogue, 8 February 1927.

Texas.

KeJ 372 Fragment, probably of Keats's revised version of I.i, containing three lines: 'And for your sake though so [perverse?], ungrateful/I'll wear an ignorant smile upon my face —/*Auranthe* I shall treat him as befits a queen/*Enter Albert*' (recto), annotated in an unidentified hand 'John Keats autograph from Otho the Great/for [?] [?] Locker. July '81'.

This may be one of the fragments from Frederick Locker's collection that W. T. Spencer would not let Garrod examine (see Garrod, pp. xliii, 311) though it could not be the missing one (mentioned in Stillinger, p. 659) described as containing I.i.141 and 'three lines not identified', if that description is accurate.

British Library, Charnwood Collection, Loan MS 60, Item 39(1).

KeJ 373 Fragment of the revised version of I.i. in Charles Brown's hand, containing lines 141–4, inserted in a copy of *The Poems of Frederick Locker* (New York, 1883).

British Library, Department of Printed Books, C.44.b.4.

KeJ 374 Fair copy by Charles Brown, revised by both him and Keats, originally copied from the draft (KeJ 363–8) and the text for I.i later recopied from the revised version (KeJ 370–3), wanting the title page, part of the Dramatis Personae (see KeJ 375) and 5 leaves (containing I.i.1–20, IV.ii.2–44a, V.i.30b–ii.27), printer's copy for *Literary Remains*, 104 leaves (mostly rectos only), numbered 2–109 (wanting 1, 80–81, 90–91).

Facsimile in *Keats Facsimiles VII*, pp. 73–191.

Harvard, Keats Collection 3.7.

KeJ 375 Fragment of one leaf of the fair copy by Charles Brown (KeJ 374), containing part of the Dramatis Personae (recto) and a cancelled passage in Keats's hand, being I.i.6–7 and 9 additional lines (verso).

The cancelled passage is printed in the apparatus in Stillinger, p. 379 (see also p. 660).

Princeton, Robert H. Taylor Collection.

KeJ 376 Transcript by Charles Brown of Edward John Trelawny's *Adventures of a Younger Son*, printer's copy for the first publication, containing transcripts of the passages used as chapter epigraphs (see headnote) at the end of the MS (including also KeJ 206, 209), headed 'Selections from the manuscripts of Keats's Otho the Great...'.

Harvard, Keats Collection, fMS Eng 1274.

'Over the hill and over the dale'

First pub. (lines 1–4 only) *Literary Remains* (1848); first pub. in full in Amy Lowell, *John Keats*, 2 vols (Boston, 1925); Stillinger, pp. 240–1.

KeJ 377 In a letter to James Rice, [24 March 1818], postmarked 26 March 1818.

This MS printed *Letters*, I, 256–7 (letter, 254–7); for Woodhouses's transcript, see KeJ 379.

Harvard, Keats Collection 1.25.

KeJ 378 Transcript by Richard Woodhouse, one page in W3, headed 'From a letter sent by Keats to Rice 25 March 1818. I went yesterday to Dawlish fair –'.

Facsimile in *Keats Facsimiles IV*, p. 264.

Pierpont Morgan, MA 215, f. 63.

KeJ 379 Transcript by Richard Woodhouse of Keats's letter to James Rice (KeJ 377) containing only lines 1–4 of this poem, in Woodhouse's letterbook.

Harvard, Keats Collection 3.3, p. 113.

'Pensive they sit, and roll their languid eyes'
First pub. New York *World*, 25 June 1877; Stillinger, pp. 475–6.

KeJ 380 Draft in the [17 September] section of a letter (containing also KeJ 78, 110, 251, 369) to George and Georgiana Keats of [17–27 September 1819].

This MS printed *Letters*, II, 188 (letter, 184–218).

Pierpont Morgan, MA 212.

***Poems* (1817)**, for poems inscribed in Keats's presentation copy to J. H. Reynolds, see KeJ 332, 333, 478, 515; for presentation copies to Charles Wells, George Keats and Thomas Richards, see KeJ 406–407.5; for Woodhouse's interleaved copy, see the description of Woodhouse *Poems* (1817) in the INTRODUCTION; see also KeJ 166 and 359.

'Read me a lesson, Muse, and speak it loud'
First pub. *Plymouth and Devonport Weekly Journal*, 6 September 1838, as 'Sonnet, Written on the Summit of Ben Nivis'; collected *Literary Remains* (1848); Stillinger, p. 279.

KeJ 381 Fair copy in the [6 August] section of a letter (containing also KeJ 527) to Tom Keats, 3–6 August 1818.

This MS printed *Letters*, I, 357–8 (letter, 352–8).

Harvard, Keats Collection 1.36.

Robin Hood ('No! those days are gone away')
First pub. *Lamia* (1820); Stillinger, pp. 228–30. These lines originally sent in a now-lost letter to J. H. Reynolds of 3 February 1818 (printed in *Letters*, I, 223–5 from a transcript in Woodhouse's letterbook (Harvard, Keats Collection 3.3, pp. 28–30) which transcribes only the title ('To J. H. R. In answer to his Robin Hood Sonnets') and first line of this poem).

KeJ 382 Draft, here untitled, containing an early uncancelled version of lines 33–41, 2 pages (one leaf).

The so-called 'S. R. Townshend-Mayer MS'; not located in *Texts*, p. 166 but collated in Stillinger.

Isabella Stewart Gardner Museum, Boston.

KeJ 383 Transcript by Richard Woodhouse, here entitled 'To John H. Reynolds/In answer to his Robin Hood Sonnets.', in W2; dated 3 February 1818.

Facsimile in *Keats Facsimiles VI*, pp. 92–7.

Harvard, Keats Collection 3.2, ff. 58–60 (rectos only).

KeJ 384 Transcript by Charles Brown, here entitled 'To John Reynolds,/in answer to his Robin Hood Sonnets. 1818.', signed with the 'CB' flourish.

Facsimile in *Keats Facsimiles VII*, pp. 3–5.

Harvard, Keats Collection 3.6, pp. 1–3.

KeJ 385 Transcript by George Keats, here entitled 'To John Reynolds/in answer to his Sonnets on Robin Hood. 1818.', in George Keats's Notebook, 4 pages; transcribed January 1820.

Facsimile in *Keats Facsimiles V*, pp. 175–8.

British Library, Egerton MS 2780, ff. 59–60v.

KeJ 386 Transcript by Richard Woodhouse, here entitled 'To J. H. R. In answer to his Robin Hood Sonnets', in W1 (followed by transcripts of Reynolds's Robin Hood sonnets); dated 3 February 1819 [*sic*, i. e., 1818]

Harvard, Keats Collection 3.1, pp. 12–14.

KeJ 387 Transcript by Charles Wentworth Dilke, on a blank page at the back of his copy of *Endymion* (1818), here entitled 'To John Reynolds in answer to his Robin Hood Sonnets', annotated 'CB'.

Keats House, London, KH 52.

'See, the ship in the bay is riding'
Questionable attribution. First pub. (as questionable) in *The Poetical Works of John Keats*, ed. H. W. Garrod (Oxford, 1939); Stillinger, p. 755, in 'Appendix VI Questionable Attributions'.

KeJ 388 MS in the hand of Richard Woodhouse, in W3 (originally in W2, f. 3, containing also the ending of KeJ 261), annotated 'F[rogley]' and (on what was W2, f. 2v (now W3, f. 78)) 'This piece K. said had not been written by him...'.

Facsimile in *Keats Facsimiles IV*, pp. 228–9.

Pierpont Morgan, MA 215, f. 78.

KeJ 389 MS in the hand of Richard Woodhouse, signed 'J. K.', in W3, annotated in shorthand 'from Mary Frogley', one page (on a leaf containing also KeJ 260).

Facsimile in *Keats Facsimiles IV*, p. 250.

Pierpont Morgan, MA 215, f. 77.

'Shed no tear — O shed no tear!'
First pub. as 'The Faery Bird's Song' in *Plymouth and Devonport Weekly Journal*, 18 October 1838; collected *Literary Remains* (1848), as 'Faery Song'; Stillinger, p. 377. Frederick Locker Lampson's transcript in a copy of *The Poetical Works of John Keats* (London, 1841) at the Berg, was copied from the printed text in *Literary Remains*.

KeJ 390 Revised, annotated by Charles Brown 'A faery Song written for a particular purpose at the request of CB', one page.

Facsimile in *Literary Remains*, frontispiece in Vol. II and in *Poetry Manuscripts*, p. 141.

Harvard, Keats Collection 2.22.

KeJ 391 Transcript by Charles Brown, included in the unfinished MS of his fairy tale 'The Faeries' Triumph', for which Keats composed the poem.

This MS printed and discussed in Jack Stillinger, 'The Context of Keats's "Fairy Song"', *KSJ*, 10 (1961), 6–8.

Keats House, London, KH 402.

KeJ 392 Transcript by Richard Monckton Milnes, here entitled 'Fairy's Song', printer's copy for *Literary Remains*.

Harvard, Keats Collection 3.10(4).

Sleep and Poetry ('What is more gentle than a wind in summer?')
Richard Woodhouse annotated this poem extensively in his interleaved *Poems* (1817) at the Huntington, RB 151852 (facsimile in *Keats Facsimiles I*, pp. 185–231); no authoritative MS sources survive.

Song ('The stranger lighted from his steed'), for this fifth 'Extract from an Opera', see KeJ 83–6.

Song of Four Fairies: Fire, Air, Earth, and Water ('Happy, happy glowing fire!')
First pub. *Literary Remains* (1848); Stillinger, pp. 359–63.

KeJ 393 Draft, here entitled 'Chorus of Faries [sic] <three> 4 Fire, air earth and water', in the [21 or 28 April] section of a letter (containing also KeJ 28, 56, 167–8, 210, 291, 311, 317, 399, 542, 547) to George and Georgiana Keats, 14 February–3 May 1819.

This MS printed *Letters*, II, 97–100 (letter, 58–109).

Harvard, Keats Collection 1.53.

KeJ 394 Fair copy, revised, 4 leaves (rectos only) numbered 8–11, originally part of the printer's copy for *Lamia* (1820); watermarked 1817.

Facsimile in *Poetry Manuscripts*, p. 133.

Harvard, Keats Collection 2.23.

KeJ 395 Transcript by Charles Brown, printer's copy for *Literary Remains*; dated 1819.

Facsimile in *Keats Facsimiles VII*, pp. 13–16.

Harvard, Keats Collection 3.6, pp. 11–14.

KeJ 396 Transcript by Richard Woodhouse, in W2, annotated 'Corrected, by Keats's copy for the press' and 'C. B. 1819'.

Facsimile in *Keats Facsimiles VI*, pp. 297–303.

Harvard, Keats Collection 3.2, ff. 161–4 (rectos only).

Sonnet/To A. G. S. on Reading His Admirable Verses, Written in This (Miss Reynolds') Album, on Either Side of the Following Attempt to Pay Small Tribute Thereto ('Where didst thou find, young bard, thy sounding lyre?')
Questionable attribution. First pub. by H. W. Garrod, *TLS*, 27 November 1937, p. 906; Stillinger, p. 755, in 'Appendix VI Questionable Attributions'.

KeJ 397 MS in the hand of Richard Woodhouse, in W3, one page of a leaf (containing also the end of KeJ 126).

Facsimile in *Keats Facsimiles IV*, p. 296.

Pierpont Morgan, MA 215, f. 85.

Sonnet to Sleep ('O soft embalmer of the still midnight')
First pub. *Plymouth and Devonport Weekly Journal*, 11 October 1838; collected *Literary Remains* (1848); Stillinger, pp. 363–4.

KeJ 398 Draft, abandoned 12 line version, here entitled 'To Sleep', on a blank flyleaf of Vol. II of Milton's *Paradise Lost* (KeJ 568).

Facsimile in Williamson, Plate VIII.

Keats House, London, KH 24.

KeJ 399 Fair copy, here entitled 'To Sleep', in the 30 April section of a letter (containing also KeJ 28, 56, 167–8, 210, 291, 311, 317, 393, 542, 547) to George and Georgiana Keats, 14 February–3 May 1819.

This MS printed *Letters*, II, 105 (letter, 58–109).

Harvard, Keats Collection 1.53.

KeJ 400 Fair copy, one page (containing an autograph poem by J. H. Reynolds on the verso), formerly (now removed) in a 'lady's album' later Sir John Bowring's 'Album Amicorum'; signed and dated June 1820.

Bowring's album was sold by Puttick & Simpson, 9 May 1929, Lot 40; this MS was Lot 241 in the same sale and Lot 239 was another leaf torn from the album containing lines by Charles Lamb (see LmC 16).

Berg.

KeJ 401 Transcript by Richard Woodhouse, revised by Keats in line 8, in W2, annotated 'C. B. 1819.'.

Woodhouse's note on the facing f. 150v identifies the revision in line 8 as being Keats's and says '...The correction was made when he borrowed this book to select a small poem to write in an Album...for a lady' (note printed Finney, p. 760 and Steele, p. 251); facsimile of poem and annotation in *Keats Facsimiles VI*, pp. 276–7.

Harvard, Keats Collection 3.2, f. 151.

KeJ 402 Transcript by Charles Brown, annotated by Richard Woodhouse in line 8, signed with the 'CB' flourish, printer's copy for *Literary Remains*; dated 1819.

Facsimile in *Keats Facsimiles VII*, p. 50.

Harvard, Keats Collection 3.6, p. 48.

KeJ 403 Transcript by Charles Wentworth Dilke, on a blank page at the back of his copy of *Endymion* (1818); dated 1819.

Keats House, London, KH 52.

KeJ 404 Transcript by Richard Woodhouse, here subtitled '(Irregular)', in W1; dated 1819.

Harvard, Keats Collection 3.1, p. 158.

Specimen of an Induction to a Poem ('Lo! I must tell a tale of chivalry')
First pub. *Poems* (1817); Stillinger, pp. 47–9.

KeJ 405 Transcript in Tom Keats's Copybook, here entitled 'Induction', here preserved as part of a larger poem (with 'Calidore', KeJ 55), containing markings by Leigh Hunt; probably transcribed late 1816.

Harvard, Keats Collection 3.5, p. 1.

KeJ 406 Revision (autograph?) to line 46, in a presentation copy to Charles Wells of *Poems* (1817).

Harvard, Keats Collection.

KeJ 407 Revision (autograph?) to line 46, in a presentation copy to George Keats of *Poems* (1817).

Harvard, Keats Collection.

KeJ 407.5 Revision (autograph?) to line 46, in a presentation copy to Thomas Richards of *Poems* (1817).

This copy described in Robert Underwood Johnson, 'Note on some... Volumes now in America, once owned by Keats', *KSMB*, 2 (1913) and *Sentimental Library*; not mentioned Stillinger.

Free Library of Philadelphia.

'Spenser, a jealous honorer of thine'
First pub. *Literary Remains* (1848); Stillinger, pp. 233–4.

KeJ 408 Draft, signed (initials), one page; dated (probably by Eliza Reynolds) 5 February 1818.

Facsimile and discussion in Ethel B. Clark, 'A Manuscript of John Keats at Dumbarton Oaks', *HLB*, 1 (1947), 90–100.

Dumbarton Oaks Research Library, Washington D.C. (affiliated with Harvard).

KeJ 409 Fair copy, one page; signed and dated in a different ink 'JK Feb. 5 — [1818]'.

Facsimile in *The Bookman*, October 1906, p. 16.

Pierpont Morgan, MA 213.

KeJ 410 Transcript by Richard Woodhouse, in W2, annotated 'J. K. Feb: 5: [1818]' and 'f^{m} JK's M.S.'.

Facsimile in *Keats Facsimiles VI*, p. 263.

Harvard, Keats Collection 3.2, f. 144.

KeJ 411 Late transcript by one of Richard Woodhouse's clerks, made for Charles Brown; dated 5 February [1818], watermarked 1833.

Harvard, Keats Collection 4.20.9.

KeJ 412 Transcript by W. A. Longmore (Eliza Reynolds's son and former owner of KeJ 408), as sent to R. M. Milnes with a letter of 16 December 1870; dated 5 February 1818.

R. M. Milnes printed this transcript in a footnote to the poem in the *Poetical Works of John Keats*, ed. Lord Houghton [R. M. Milnes] (London, 1876); facsimile in Ethel B. Clark, 'A Manuscript of John Keats at Dumbarton Oaks', *HLB*, 1 (1947), facing p. 91; the letter to Milnes (printed *Keats Circle*, II, 331–2) is also at Harvard.

Harvard, Keats Collection 3.10(18).

'Spirit here that reignest!'
First pub. *Literary Remains* (1848); Stillinger, p. 295.

KeJ 413 Revised, on a blank page between 'Cupid's Revenge' and 'The Two Noble Kinsmen' in Keats's copy of Vol. IV (containing also KeJ 36) of *The Dramatic Works of Ben Jonson, and Beaumont and Fletcher* (KeJ 564).

Keats House, London, KH 21.

KeJ 414 Transcript by Charles Brown, here entitled 'Song.', printer's copy for the first publication.

Facsimile in *Keats Facsimiles VII*, p. 61.

Harvard, Keats Collection 3.6, p. 59.

'Stay, ruby breasted warbler, stay'
First pub. *Poetical Works of John Keats*, ed. Lord Houghton [R. M. Milnes] (London, 1876); Stillinger, p. 29.

KeJ 415 Transcript by Georgiana Wylie (later Keats), here entitled 'Song Tune — "Julia to the Wood Robin"', in Keats-Wylie Scrapbook; dated 1814, probably transcribed late 1816.

Facsimile in *The Connoisseur*, 116 (1945), 11.

Harvard, Keats Collection 3.4, f. 6v.

KeJ 416 Transcript by Richard Woodhouse, here entitled 'Song./Tune – Julia to the Wood Robin.', in W3 (on 2 leaves, rectos only, originally in W2, ff. 1–2, the second also containing KeJ 261), annotated 'F[rogley]'.

Facsimile in *Keats Facsimiles IV*, pp. 223–7; Woodhouse's note about this poem (dating it 'Ab^{t} 1815/6') written on the facing page (originally W2, the verso of the title page, now W3, f. 22) is printed Steele, p. 241 (facsimile in *Keats Facsimiles IV*, p. 224).

Pierpont Morgan, MA 215. f. 78.

KeJ 417 Transcript by Richard Woodhouse, here entitled '— Song. — Tune – Julia to the Wood-Robin', 2 pages (one leaf containing also KeJ 240), in W3, annotated in shorthand 'from Mary Frogley'; probably transcribed November 1818.

Facsimile in *Keats Facsimiles IV*, pp. 245–6.

Pierpont Morgan, MA 215, f. 69.

KeJ 418 Transcript by Richard Woodhouse, here entitled '– Song. – Tune – Julia to the Wood-Robin', in W2, annotated by Woodhouse on facing page (f. 218v) and 'F[rogley]'.

Woodhouse's note printed Steele, p. 241; facsimile in *Keats Facsimiles VI*, pp. 410–11.

Harvard, Keats Collection 3.2, f. 219.

KeJ 419 Transcript by George Keats, here entitled 'Song', pasted in Keats-Wylie Scrapbook; probably transcribed late 1816.

Facsimile in *The Connoisseur*, 116 (1945), 13.

Harvard, Keats Collection 3.4, f. 32.

KeJ 420 Late transcript by one of Richard Woodhouse's clerks, here entitled 'Song', made for Charles Brown; watermarked 1833.

Harvard, Keats Collection 4.20.9.

KeJ 421 Transcript by Coventry Patmore, here entitled 'Song'; made for R. M. Milnes in 1847.

Harvard, Keats Collection 3.10(15).

'Sweet, sweet is the greeting of eyes'
First pub. Amy Lowell, *John Keats*, 2 vols (Boston, 1925); Stillinger, pp. 265–6.

KeJ 422 Draft, in a letter (containing also KeJ 109) to George and Georgiana Keats, 27–8 June 1818.

This MS printed *Letters*, I, 304 (letter, 302–5).

Harvard, Keats Collection 1.32.

'The day is gone, and all its sweets are gone!'
First pub. *Plymouth and Devonport Weekly Journal*, 4 October 1838; collected *Literary Remains* (1848); Stillinger, pp. 491–2.

KeJ 423 Draft of an early version, one page.

Facsimile in *The Bookman*, October 1906, p. 16 and *British Literary Manuscripts*, plate 38.

Pierpont Morgan, MA 213.

KeJ 424 Transcript by Charles Brown, here entitled 'Sonnet. 1819.', signed with the 'CB' flourish, printer's copy for *Literary Remains*.

Facsimile in *Keats Facsimiles VII*, p. 59.

Harvard, Keats Collection 3.6, p. 57.

KeJ 425 Transcript by Richard Woodhouse, in W2, followed by a second transcript of lines 8–12.

Facsimile in *Keats Facsimiles VI*, p. 397.

Harvard, Keats Collection 3.2, f. 212.

KeJ 426 Transcript by Richard Woodhouse, in W3, one page.

Facsimile in *Keats Facsimiles IV*, p. 292.

Pierpont Morgan, MA 215, f. 82.

KeJ 427 Late transcript by Richard Woodhouse, made for Charles Brown; dated 1819, watermarked 1833.

Harvard, Keats Collection 4.20.9.

'The Gothic looks solemn'
First pub. *Poetical Works and Other Writings of John Keats*, ed. H. B. Forman, 4 vols (London, 1883); Stillinger, p. 99. A lost transcript by Charles Brown is reported in a letter printed in the first publication (IV, 74n).

KeJ 428 Transcript by Richard Woodhouse of a fragment of a letter from Keats to J. H. Reynolds containing these lines, in W2, here entitled 'Lines –/Rhymed in a letter to J. H. R. from Oxford'; letter written [September 1817], dated in pencil 'Mid. 1818.'.

This MS printed *Letters*, I, 152; facsimile in *Keats Facsimiles VI*, p. 35.

Harvard, Keats Collection 3.2, f. 29.

KeJ 429 Transcript by Richard Woodhouse, here entitled 'Lines Rhymed in a letter received (by J. H. R.) from Oxford', in W1.

Harvard, Keats Collection 3.1, p. 33.

'*The House of Mourning* written by Mr Scott'
Questionable attribution. First pub. Finney (1936), p. 652; Stillinger, pp. 755–6, in 'Appendix VI Questionable Attributions'.

KeJ 430 MS in the hand of Richard Woodhouse, one page, in W3; [after January 1817].

Facsimile in Finney, facing p. 652 and *Keats Facsimiles IV*, p. 300.

Pierpont Morgan, MA 215, f. 80[1].

'There is a joy in footing slow across a silent plain'
First pub. (lines 1–6, 25–6, 41–8 only) in *New Monthly Magazine*, March 1822; first pub. in full *The Examiner*, 14 July 1822, as 'Lines Written in the Scotch Highlands'; collected *Literary Remains* (1848); Stillinger, pp. 275–7. For another transcript (without authority), see the description of 'George Keats's Notebook' in the INTRODUCTION.

KeJ 431 Early version, possibly a draft, here entitled (at end) 'Lines written in the highlands after a visit to Burns's Country' and here beginning 'There is a charm in footing slow across the <grand camp> silent plain', 2 pages (one leaf).

Facsimile in *Poetry Manuscripts*, p. 89.

Harvard, Keats Collection 2.19.

KeJ 432 Fair copy, revised, at the end of a letter to Benjamin Bailey, Inverary, 18–22 July 1818.

This MS printed *Letters*, I, 344–5 (letter, 340–5); a transcript of this letter in Woodhouse's letterbook at Harvard (Keats Collection 3.3, pp. 90–5) omits these verses.

Harvard, Keats Collection 1.34.

KeJ 433 Transcript by Charles Wentworth Dilke, on a blank page at the back of his copy of *Endymion* (1818), here entitled 'Lines written in the Highlands after a visit to Burns's country. — 1818'.

Keats House, London, KH 52.

KeJ 434 Transcript by Richard Woodhouse, in W2, annotated 'Copied from K's letter...'; transcribed in 1821.

Facsimiles of poem and Woodhouse's annotation on the facing f. 212v in *Keats Facsimiles VI*, pp. 398–401.

Harvard, Keats Collection 3.2, ff. 213–14.

KeJ 435 Transcript by Richard Woodhouse, in W3, 3 pages (2 leaves), annotated 'Extract from JK's letter to B. B. dated Inverary 18 July 1818...'; transcribed for John Taylor in 1821, addressed to him.

Facsimile in *Keats Facsimiles IV*, pp. 285–8.

Pierpont Morgan, MA 215, f. 74.

'There was a naughty boy'
First pub. as 'A Song about Myself' in *Poetical Works and Other Writings of John Keats*, ed. H. B. Forman, 4 vols (London, 1883); Stillinger, pp. 267–70.

KeJ 436 Draft, in a letter (containing also KeJ 305) to Fanny Keats, Dumfries, 2–5 July 1818.

This MS printed *Letters*, I, 312–15 (letter, 310–16); facsimile in British Library, MS Facs. 336(b).

Pierpont Morgan, MA 975.

'They weren fully glad of their gude hap', see KeJ 488.

'Think not of it, sweet one, so'
First pub. *Literary Remains* (1848); Stillinger, pp. 100–1.

KeJ 437 Draft, including a cancelled first stanza beginning '<Think not of it gentle sweet>' on last leaf of the otherwise lost draft of *Endymion*, one page.

This MS printed Finney, pp. 229–30.

Pierpont Morgan, MA 211.

KeJ 438 Transcript by Richard Woodhouse, at the end of his interleaved copy of *Endymion* (1818) (see KeJ 63), inscribed by Woodhouse on the flyleaf Temple, 24 November 1818.

Facsimile in *Keats Facsimiles III*, p. 427.

Berg.

KeJ 439 Transcript by Richard Woodhouse, one page of a leaf (containing also KeJ 351), in W3, dated 'ab^{t} 11 Novr 1817.'.

Facsimile in *Keats Facsimiles IV*, p. 255.

Pierpont Morgan, MA 215, f. 86.

KeJ 440 Transcript by Richard Woodhouse, here entitled 'To ——', in W2, annotated 'from JK's M.S.'; dated 'Ab^{t} 11 Novr 1817'.

Facsimile in *Keats Facsimiles VI*, pp. 9–11.

Harvard, Keats Collection 3.2, ff. 16–17 (rectos only).

KeJ 441 Transcript by Richard Woodhouse, in W1, here entitled 'To —', annotated 'ab^{t} 11 Novr 1817. from K's M.S.'.

Harvard, Keats Collection 3.1, p. 20.

KeJ 442 Transcript by Charlotte Reynolds, here entitled 'To —', in Reynolds-Hood Commonplace Book (f. 26); dated 11 November 1817.

Bristol Reference Library.

KeJ 443 Transcript by Charles Cowden Clarke, here entitled 'On..........', printer's copy for *Literary Remains*; misdated 'Ap[l] 1817', transcribed for R. M. Milnes in the 1840s.

This MS printed *Texts*, pp. [1]–2.

Harvard, Keats Collection 4.4.4.

'This living hand, now warm and capable'
First pub. *Poetical Works of John Keats*, ed. H. B. Forman, 6th ed (London, 1898); Stillinger, p. 503.

KeJ 444 On first page of a folded leaf (containing also KeJ 204).

Facsimile in W. H. Arnold, *First Report of a Book-Collector* (New York, 1898), p. 105, in Finney, facing p. 740 and in *Poetry Manuscripts*, p. 259.

Harvard, Keats Collection 2.29.2.

'This mortal body of a thousand days': no authoritative MS sources survive.

'This pleasant tale is like a little copse:'
First pub. *The Examiner*, 16 March 1817, as 'Written on a Blank Space at the End of Chaucer's Tale of "The Floure and the Lefe"'; collected *Literary Remains* (1848); Stillinger, p. 92.

KeJ 445 Fair copy, signed (initials), written at the end of 'The Floure and the Lefe' (XII, 104–5) in Charles Cowden Clarke's copy of *The Poetical Works of Geoffrey Chaucer* (KeJ 560); dated February 1817.

British Library, Add. MS 33516.

KeJ 446 Transcript by Richard Woodhouse, here entitled 'Sonnet. Written on the blank space of a leaf at the end of Chaucer's tale of "The flowre and the lefe"', in W2, annotated 'from J. K's M.S.'; dated February 1817.

Facsimile in *Keats Facsimiles VI*, p. 16.

Harvard, Keats Collection 3.2, f. 19v.

KeJ 447 Transcript by Isabella Jane Towers, here entitled 'On Chaucer's "Floure and the Leafe" written in my brother's Chaucer by the lamented young Poet'; dated February 1817; in a notebook (containing also KeJ 43, 533, 552) given to Towers by her brother Charles Cowden Clarke as a birthday gift in 1828.

Harvard, Keats Collection 3.12, f. 70.

KeJ 448 Transcript by Richard Woodhouse, here entitled 'Sonnet Written on a blank space at the end of Chaucer's tale "The flowre & the lefe"', in W1; dated February 1817.

Harvard, Keats Collection 3.1, p. 24.

KeJ 449 Late transcript by one of Richard Woodhouse's clerks, here entitled 'Written on a blank space at the end of Chaucer's tale "The Floure and the Lefe"', made for Charles Brown; dated February 1817, watermarked 1833.

Harvard, Keats Collection 4.20.9.

KeJ 450 Transcript by Coventry Patmore, printer's copy for *Literary Remains*, here entitled 'Written on a blank space at the end of Chaucer's tale "The Floure and the Lefe"'; dated February 1817, transcribed for R. M. Milnes in 1847.

Harvard, Keats Collection 3.10(13).

'Time's sea hath been five years at its slow ebb'
First pub. *Hood's Magazine*, September 1844, as 'Sonnet'; collected *Literary Remains* (1848); Stillinger, pp. 232–3.

KeJ 451 Transcript by Richard Woodhouse, here entitled 'To ——', in W2; dated 4 February 1818.

Woodhouse's annotation on the facing page (f. 27v) is printed in Finney, p. 758; facsimiles of annotation and poem in *Keats Facsimiles VI*, pp. 32–3.

Harvard, Keats Collection 3.2, f. 28.

KeJ 452 Transcript by Charlotte Reynolds, here entitled 'To —', in Reynolds-Hood Commonplace Book (f. 29a); dated 4 February 1818.

Bristol Reference Library.

KeJ 453 Transcript by Richard Woodhouse, in W1, here beginning 'Time's sea has been five yeare...'; dated 4 February 1818.

Woodhouse's appended annotation is printed Finney, p. 756.

Harvard, Keats Collection 3.1, p. 29.

KeJ 454 Late transcript by one of Richard Woodhouse's clerks, here entitled 'To —', made for Charles Brown; watermarked 1833.

Harvard, Keats Collection 4.20.9.

KeJ 455 Transcript by Coventry Patmore, here entitled 'To —', printer's copy for *Literary Remains*; transcribed for R. M. Milnes in 1847.

Harvard, Keats Collection 3.10(11).

KeJ 456 Late transcript by Richard Woodhouse, made for Joseph Severn; watermarked 1830.

Harvard, Keats Collection 4.20.10.

''Tis the "witching time of night" —'
First pub. *Ladies' Companion*, August 1837; collected *Literary Remains* (1848); Stillinger, pp. 288–90.

KeJ 457 Draft, in the 14 October section of a letter to George and Georgiana Keats, [14–31 October 1818].

This MS printed *Letters*, I, 398–9 (letter, 391–405); John Jeffrey's transcript of this letter (Harvard) omits the poem.

Harvard, Keats Collection 1.39.

KeJ 458 Transcript by John Howard Payne, as sent to R. M. Milnes with a letter dated from Paris, 2 July 1847.

The letter to Milnes is printed *Keats Circle*, II, 223–5.

Harvard, Keats Collection 3.10(19).

To a Friend Who Sent Me Some Roses ('As late I rambled in the happy fields')
First pub. *Poems* (1817), as 'Sonnet V'; Stillinger, pp. 54–5.

KeJ 459 Fair copy, revised, here untitled and beginning 'As late I wanderd [sic] in the happy fields', one page.

Facsimile in *Twelfth Year Book...The Bibliophile Society* (Boston, 1913), facing p. 75.

Pierpont Morgan, MA 214.

KeJ 460 Transcript in Tom Keats's Copybook, here entitled 'To Charles Wells on receiving a bunch of <full blown> roses — Sonnet'; dated 29 June 1816, probably transcribed late 1816.

Harvard, Keats Collection 3.5, p. 20.

KeJ 461 Variant to line 1 (as in KeJ 459) recorded in shorthand in red ink in Woodhouse's *Poems* (1817), p. 83 (including also a few pencil annotations by Woodhouse on facing blank page).

See Sperry p. 148; facsimile in *Keats Facsimiles I*, pp. 158–9.

Huntington, RB 151852.

To a Young Lady Who Sent Me a Laurel Crown
('Fresh morning gusts have blown away all fear')
First pub. *Literary Remains* (1848); Stillinger, pp. 89–90.

KeJ 462 Transcript by Richard Woodhouse, here entitled 'Sonnet. To a young Lady who sent me a laurel crown.', in W2, annotated 'from JK's MS'.

Facsimile in *Keats Facsimiles VI*, p. 15.

Harvard, Keats Collection 3.2, f. 19.

KeJ 463 Transcript by Richard Woodhouse, here entitled 'Sonnet', in W1.

Harvard, Keats Collection 3.1, p. 26.

KeJ 464 Late transcript by one of Richard Woodhouse's clerks, made for Charles Brown; watermarked 1833.

Harvard, Keats Collection 4.20.9.

KeJ 465 Transcript by Coventry Patmore, printer's copy for the first publication; transcribed for R. M. Milnes in 1847.

Harvard, Keats Collection 3.10(8).

To Ailsa Rock ('Hearken, thou craggy ocean pyramid')
First pub. as 'Sonnet to Ailsa Rock' in Leigh Hunt's *Literary Pocket-book for 1819* (London, 1818); collected *Literary Remains* (1848), as 'Sonnet on Ailsa Rock'; Stillinger, p. 272. J. C. Stephens's transcript of the first publication is at Harvard (Keats Collection 3.12, f. 67).

KeJ 466 Fair copy, revised, in the 10 July section of a letter (containing also KeJ 15) to Tom Keats, 10–14 July 1818.

This MS printed *Letters*, I, 329–30 (letter, 327–33).

British Library, Add. MS 45510, f. 1v.

KeJ 466.5 Transcript by Charles Cowden Clarke, in W3, annotated 'Literary Pocket Book for 1819' (from which it was transcribed).

Facsimile in *Keats Facsimiles IV*, p. 308.

Pierpont Morgan, MA 215, f. 87.

To Autumn ('Season of mists and mellow fruitfulness')
First pub. *Lamia* (1820); Stillinger, pp. 476–7.

KeJ 467 Draft, here untitled, 2 pages (one leaf), annotated '...Presented to Miss A Barker by the author's Brother...Nov 15. 1839.'; watermarked 1818.

Facsimiles: *Century Magazine*, 69 (1904), pp. 84 and 89; Finney, after p. 706; Hyder Edward Rollins, *Keats' Reputation in America to 1848* (Cambridge, MA, 1946), after p. 50; *The Poems of John Keats*, ed. Miriam Allott (London, 1970), facing p. 645 (first page only); *The Odes of Keats*, ed. Robert Gittings (London, 1970), pp. 56–9, (discussed pp. 74–6); Croft, *Autograph Poetry*, Nos 108–9; *Poetry Manuscripts*, p. 223.

Harvard, Keats Collection 2.27.

KeJ 468 Fair copy, here untitled, in a letter (containing also KeJ 87) to Richard Woodhouse, [21–2 September 1819], postmarked 22 September 1819.

This MS printed *Letters*, II, 170–1 (letter, 169–75.

Harvard, Keats Collection 1.64.

KeJ 469 Transcript by Charles Brown, revised by Keats and corrected by Richard Woodhouse; dated 1819, transcribed before January 1820, revised after.

Facsimile in *Keats Facsimiles VII*, pp. 36–7.

Harvard, Keats Collection 3.6, pp. 34–5.

KeJ 470 Transcript by George Keats, 2 pages, in George Keats's Notebook; dated 1819, transcribed January 1820.

Facsimile in *Keats Facsimiles V*, pp. 173–4.

British Library, Egerton MS 2780, f. 58r–v.

KeJ 471 Transcript by Richard Woodhouse, in W2, annotated at the end 'The alterations in C. B.'s copy...in red ink'; dated Winchester 19 September 1819.

Facsimile in *Keats Facsimiles VI*, pp. 259–61; Woodhouse's annotation printed Finney, p. 760.

Harvard, Keats Collection 3.2, ff. 142–3 (rectos only).

To Charles Cowden Clarke ('Oft have you seen a swan superbly frowning')
First pub. *Poems* (1817); Stillinger, pp. 60–3. Richard Woodhouse recorded suggested alterations in Woodhouse *Poems* (1817) at the Huntington (RB 151852); Thomasine Leigh's transcript of lines 1–20 in her commonplace book of January 1817 (at Keats House, London, KH 155) was copied from J. H. Reynolds's review of *Poems* (1817) in *The Champion*, 9 March 1817.

KeJ 472 Fair copy, revised, apparently sent in a letter to C. C. Clarke, headed 'To M[r] C. C. Clarke —', 4 pages (one leaf); annotated by Clarke, Margate, September 1816, watermarked 1813.

This verse-letter printed (from the first publication) in *Letters*, I, 109–13; facsimile in Bangs Catalogue (W. H. Arnold Sale), 1901, pp. 105–8.

Huntington, HM 11903.

To Fanny ('Physician Nature! let my spirit blood!')
First pub. *Literary Remains* (1848); Stillinger, pp. 494–5.

KeJ 473 Part of the original draft, 3 pages (i. e., the 2nd and 4th leaves and half of the 3rd), wanting lines 1–8, 25–32, here untitled.

Facsimile in *Poetry Manuscripts*, p. 227.

Harvard, Keats Collection 2.30.

KeJ 474 Transcript by R. M. Milnes, printer's copy for the first publication.

Harvard, Keats Collection 3.10(6).

To G. A. W. ('Nymph of the downward smile, and sidelong glance')
First pub. *Poems* (1817), as 'Sonnet VI'; Stillinger, pp. 67–8. Woodhouse's annotation about this poem, facing p. 84 in his interleaved *Poems* (1817), is reproduced in *Keats Facsimiles I*, p. 161.

KeJ 475 Fair copy, revised, here entitled 'To Miss Wylie', signed (initials), one page, inserted in the Keats-Wylie Scrapbook.

Facsimiles: *Literary Anecdotes of the Nineteenth Century*, ed. W. Robertson Nicoll and T. J. Wise, 2 vols (London, 1895–6), II, facing p. 281; *The Connoisseur*, 116 (1945), 9; Sotheby's sale catalogues, 23 June 1947, Plate IV and 20–1 May 1968 (Lot 382); *Poetry Manuscripts*, p. 23; in British Library, RP 245(3).

Harvard, Keats Collection 3.4, f. 31v.

KeJ 476 Transcript in Tom Keats's Copybook, here entitled 'Sonnet/To a Lady'; dated December 1816, probably transcribed late 1816.

Harvard, Keats Collection 3.5, p. 21.

KeJ 477 Late transcript by William Pitter Woodhouse, Richard Woodhouse's brother, here entitled 'Sonnet'; in a commonplace book used July–August 1827.

Harvard, Keats Collection 3.13 (II, f. 3v).

To George Felton Mathew ('Sweet are the pleasures that to verse belong'): no authoritative MS sources of this poem survive.

To Haydon with a Sonnet Written on Seeing the Elgin Marbles ('Forgive me, Haydon, that I cannot speak')
First pub. *The Champion* and *The Examiner*, both on 9 March 1817; collected *Literary Remains* (1848); Stillinger, pp. 93–4. Thomasine Leigh's transcript in her commonplace book of January 1817 (at Keats House, London, KH 155) was copied from J. H. Reynolds's review of *Poems* (1817) in *The Champion*, 9 March 1817.

KeJ 478 Fair copy, on a blank page [p. 122] at the end of the copy of *Poems* (1817) presented by Keats to J. H. Reynolds (containing also KeJ 332, 333, 515).

This MS printed in Hyder E. Rollins, 'Unpublished Autograph Texts of Keats', *HLB*, 6 (1952), 165; facsimile in *Poetry Manuscripts*, p. 49.

Harvard, Keats Collection.

KeJ 479 Transcript by Richard Woodhouse, here beginning 'Haydon! forgive me that I cannot speak', in W3, one page of a leaf (containing also KeJ 334), annotated 'Examiner' (from which it was apparently transcribed).

Facsimile in *Keats Facsimiles IV*, p. 258.

Pierpont Morgan, MA 215, f. 86.

KeJ 480 Transcript by Richard Woodhouse, here entitled 'Sonnet./To R. B. [sic] Haydon./ with the foregoing Sonnet on the Elgin Marbles' and beginning 'Haydon! forgive me that I cannot speak', in W2.

Facsimile in *Keats Facsimiles VI*, p. 21.

Harvard, Keats Collection 3.2, f. 22.

KeJ 481 Transcript by Richard Woodhouse, here entitled 'Sonnet – To Haydon – with a sonnet on seeing the Elgin Marbles.' and beginning 'Haydon! forgive me, that I cannot speak', on one page of the end flyleaves of Woodhouse's *Poems* (1817), annotated 'Examiner. –'.

This transcript printed Sperry, p. 160; facsimile in *Keats Facsimiles I*, p. 237.

Huntington, RB 151852.

KeJ 482 Late transcript by Richard Woodhouse, here beginning 'Haydon! forgive me that I cannot speak', written for Joseph Severn; watermarked 1830.

Harvard, Keats Collection 4.20.10.

KeJ 483 Transcript by B. R. Haydon or his daughter Mary in a collection of loose MSS (9 leaves (11 pages) containing also KeJ 2, 8, 338 and sonnets by Wordsworth and Elizabeth Barrett Browning), inscribed by Haydon on wrapper 'Sonnets addressed to & MS Written by B. R. Haydon from 1817 to 1841 — Twenty Four Years. Copied for Fun. 1844'.

This transcript (not located Stillinger, see p. 744) was possibly taken from the poem's publication in *Annals of the Fine Arts*, April 1818 from which another transcript by Haydon (sent to Edward Moxon with a letter of 28 November 1845; see *Keats Circle*, II, 141–2) was taken (Harvard, Keats Collection 4.7.20).

Pierpont Morgan, MA 2987.

To Homer ('Standing aloof in giant ignorance')
First pub. *Literary Remains* (1848); Stillinger, p. 264.

KeJ 484 Transcript by Charles Brown, revised in line 3 by Keats, here entitled 'Sonnets,/To Homer. 1818'.

Facsimile in *Keats Facsimiles VII*, p. 42.

Harvard, Keats Collection 3.6, p. 40.

KeJ 485 Transcript by Richard Woodhouse, here entitled 'Sonnet./To Homer', in W2, annotated 'C. B. 1818'.

Facsimile in *Keats Facsimiles VI*, p. 133.

Harvard, Keats Collection 3.2, f. 78.

KeJ 486 Transcript by Richard Woodhouse, here entitled '— Sonnet. To Homer —', in W1; dated 1818.

Harvard, Keats Collection 3.1, p. 146.

KeJ 487 Transcript by Charles Wentworth Dilke, on a blank page at the back of his copy of *Endymion* (1818), here entitled 'Sonnet. — To Homer'; dated 1818.

Keats House, London, KH 52.

To Hope ('When by my solitary hearth I sit')
First pub. *Poems* (1817); Stillinger, pp. 33–4.

KeJ 488 Fair copy, revised, 2 pages (one leaf), containing a fragmentary couplet on the verso beginning 'They weren fully glad of their gude hap'; dated February 1815.

Facsimiles: lines 1–12 in Mabel A. E. Steele, 'Three Early Manuscripts of John Keats', *KSJ*, 1 (1952), Plate V; at Harvard, Keats Collection; at British Library, MS Facs. Suppl. VI(e); the photocopy lodged at the British Library at the time an export licence was granted (RP 770(1)) has been transferred to Keats House, London. The fragmentary couplet is printed in Garrod, p. 554 and Stillinger, p. 544. This MS formerly owned by Maurice Buxton Forman; said to be lost in *Texts*, p. 100 but located in Stillinger.

Owned (1978) Abel Berland, Chicago (see Stillinger, p. 543).

To J. R. ('O that a week could be an age, and we')
First pub. *Literary Remains* (1848), as 'To J. H. Reynolds'; Stillinger, p. 244.

KeJ 489 Revised, possibly the draft, one page.

Facsimile in *Poetry Manuscripts*, p. 69.

Harvard, Keats Collection 2.18.

KeJ 490 Transcript by Richard Woodhouse, in W2; probably transcribed after May 1821.

Facsimile in *Keats Facsimiles VI*, p. 409.

Harvard, Keats Collection 3.2, f. 218.

KeJ 491 Late transcript by one of Richard Woodhouse's clerks, made for Charles Brown; watermarked 1833.

Harvard, Keats Collection 4.20.9.

KeJ 492 Transcript by Coventry Patmore, printer's copy for the first publication, the title here mistakenly altered to 'To J. H. Reynolds' by R. M. Milnes; transcribed for Milnes in 1847.

Harvard, Keats Collection 3.10(10).

To Kosciusko ('Good Kosciusko, thy great name alone'): no authoritative MS sources of this poem survive.

To Leigh Hunt, Esq. ('Glory and loveliness have passed away'): no authoritative MS sources of this poem survive.

To Lord Byron ('Byron, how sweetly sad thy melody')
First pub. *Literary Remains* (1848); Stillinger, p. 31.

KeJ 493 Transcript by Richard Woodhouse, here entitled 'Sonnet/To Lord Byron.', in W2; dated December 1814, probably transcribed after May 1821.

Facsimile in *Keats Facsimiles VI*, p. 407.

Harvard, Keats Collection 3.2, f. 217.

KeJ 494 Late transcript by one of Richard Woodhouse's clerks, made for Charles Brown; dated December 1814, watermarked 1833.

Harvard, Keats Collection 4.20.9.

To Mrs Reynolds's Cat ('Cat! who hast past thy grand climacteric')
First pub. *Comic Annual*, [ed. Thomas Hood] (London, 1830), as 'Sonnet to a Cat'; Stillinger, pp. 222–3.

KeJ 495 Fair copy, revised, one page; dated 16 January 1818.

This MS printed in the catalogue of the Gluck Collection at the Buffalo Public Library (Buffalo, 1899), p. 65; facsimile among H. W. Garrod's papers at Yale, Osborn Collection.

Buffalo and Erie County Public Library, James Fraser Gluck Collection.

KeJ 496 Transcript by Richard Woodhouse, here entitled 'Sonnet/On Mrs Reynolds's Cat', in W2; dated 16 January 1818.

Facsimile in *Keats Facsimiles VI*, p. 25.

Harvard, Keats Collection 3.2, f. 24.

KeJ 497 Transcript by Richard Woodhouse, here entitled 'Sonnet/On Mrs Reynolds's Cat', in W1; dated 16 January 1818.

Harvard, Keats Collection 3.1, p. 27.

To My Brother George ('Full many a dreary hour have I past')
First pub. *Poems* (1817); Stillinger, pp. 56–60.

KeJ 498 Fair copy, in a letter to George Keats, here untitled, 4 pages; letter dated Margate, August [1816].

This MS printed *Letters*, I, 105–9; for John Jeffrey's transcript, see KeJ 501.

Harvard, Keats Collection 1.1.

KeJ 499 Transcript by George Keats, pasted in Keats-Wylie Scrapbook; dated Margate, August 1816, probably transcribed late 1816.

Harvard, Keats Collection 3.4, f. 33.

KeJ 500 Transcript of lines 1–31 only by Georgiana Wylie (later Keats), in Keats-Wylie Scrapbook; dated Margate, August 1816, probably transcribed late 1816.

Harvard, Keats Collection 3.4, f. 15.

KeJ 501 [entry deleted]

To My Brother George ('Many the wonders I this day have seen:')
First pub. *Poems* (1817), as 'Sonnet I'; Stillinger, pp. 55–6. In a note to line 3 of this poem, in Woodhouse *Poems* (1817) (Huntington, RB 151852; facsimile in *Keats Facsimiles I*, p. 150), Woodhouse quotes lines 18–23 of 'Ode to Apollo' (see KeJ 287–9); for quotations by Woodhouse of lines 1–4 of this poem, see KeJ 287–8.

KeJ 502 Draft, here untitled, in pencil, in a pocket-book belonging to Joseph Severn (containing also KeJ 506 and some miscellaneous jottings).

Facsimile of lines 1–8 in Parke Bernet sale catalogue, 4 June 1969, facing p. 18; facsimile in *Poetry Manuscripts*, p. 9.

Harvard, Keats Collection 2.2.

KeJ 503 Fair copy, revised, printer's copy for the first publication, headed '1', on a page numbered '53'.

Facsimile in Sotheby's sale catalogue, 20 December 1937 (property of Leonard T. Stowell), Lot 260 and *Poetry Manuscripts*, p. 11.

Harvard, Keats Collection 2.3.

KeJ 504 Transcript by George Keats, here untitled, pasted in Keats-Wylie Scrapbook; dated Margate, August 1816, probably transcribed late 1816.

Harvard, Keats Collection 3.4, f. 34v.

KeJ 505 Transcript in Tom Keats's Copybook, here entitled 'Sonnet/To my Brother George'; probably transcribed late 1816.

Harvard, Keats Collection 3.5, p. 14.

To My Brothers ('Small, busy flames play through the fresh laid coals')
First pub. *Poems* (1817), as 'Sonnet VIII'; Stillinger, p. 66. Woodhouse's annotations about this poem, on p. 86 and the facing page of his *Poems* (1817), are reproduced in *Keats Facsimiles I*, pp. 164–5.

KeJ 506 Draft of lines 1–8, here untitled, in pencil, in a pocket-book belonging to Joseph Severn (containing also KeJ 502 and some miscellaneous jottings).

Facsimile in Parke Bernet sale catalogues, 25 April 1945 and 4 June 1969 and *Poetry Manuscripts*, p. 15; this MS printed in *The Poetical Works and Other Writings of John Keats*, ed. H. B. Forman, rev. Maurice Buxton Forman, 8 vols (New York, 1938–9), I, 81n.

Harvard, Keats Collection 2.2.

KeJ 507 Fair copy, signed, one page; dated 18 November [1816].

This MS removed from Emma Isola's Album (see Charles Lamb, INTRODUCTION. for a full description; facsimile in Parke Bernet sale catalogue, 28 April 1939 (John Spoor Sale), p. 169 and *Poetry Manuscripts*, p. 17; facsimile of lines 1–5 in Mabel A. E. Steele, 'Three Early Manuscripts of John Keats', *KSJ*, 1 (1952), Plate V; this MS printed in Hyder E. Rollins 'Unpublished Autograph Texts of Keats', *HLB*, 6 (1952), 162–3.

Harvard, Keats Collection 2.6.

KeJ 508 Fair copy, revised, annotated (mistakenly, according to Stillinger) by Charles Ollier, one of the publishers of *Poems* (1817), '1817 This was a copy for the press', one page of a leaf containing also KeJ 163.

Facsimile in *Catalogue of the Collection of Autograph Letters and Historical Documents Formed Between 1865 and 1882 by A[lfred] Morrison*, comp. A. W. Thibaudeau, 6 vols (London, 1883–92), III (1888), p. 4 and *Poetry Manuscripts*, p. 19; this MS printed in Hyder E. Rollins, 'Unpublished Autograph Texts of Keats', *HLB*, 6 (1952), 161–2.

Harvard, Keats Collection 2.5.

KeJ 509 Transcript in Tom Keats's Copybook, here entitled 'Sonnet/Written to his Brother Tom on his Birthday'; dated 18 November 1816, probably transcribed late 1816.

Harvard, Keats Collection 3.5, p. 16.

'To one who has been long in city pent'
First pub. *Poems* (1817), as 'Sonnet X'; Stillinger, pp. 53–4.

KeJ 510 Transcript by Georgiana Wylie (later Keats), here entitled 'Sonnet. Written in the Fields June 1816', in Keats-Wylie Scrapbook; probably transcribed late 1816.

Facsimile in *The Connoisseur*, 116 (1945), 10–11.

Harvard, Keats Collection 3.4, f. 5.

KeJ 511 Transcript by George Keats, here headed 'Sonnet', with 'Written in the Fields — June 1816' at the end, pasted in Keats-Wylie Scrapbook; probably transcribed late 1816.

Facsimile in *The Connoisseur*, 116 (1945), 10–11.

Harvard, Keats Collection 3.4, f. 32.

KeJ 512 Transcript in Tom Keats's Copybook, here entitled 'Sonnet'; probably transcribed late 1816.

Harvard, Keats Collection 3.5, p. 24.

To Some Ladies ('What though while the wonders of nature exploring')
First pub. *Poems* (1817); Stillinger, pp. 36–7.

KeJ 513 Fair copy, here entitled 'To the Misses —— (at Hastings)', the bracketed portion being in a different hand, one page; dated 1815.

Facsimiles: A. E. Newton, *The Amenities of Book-Collecting and Kindred Affections* (Boston, 1918), p. 105; Parke Bernet sale catalogue, 14–16 May 1941 (A. E. Newton Sale), p. [158]; Lyle H. Kendall, *Descriptive Catalogue of the W. L. Lewis Collection* (Fort Worth, TX, 1970), following p. 114.

Texas Christian University, Forth Worth.

KeJ 514 Variants from an otherwise unknown early version recorded in red ink (other markings in black ink), the subtitle 'who were at Hastings, in return for a present of some shells.' and date 1815 added, in Woodhouse's *Poems* (1817), pp. 29–31.

See Sperry, pp. 113, 143; facsimile in *Keats Facsimiles I*, pp. 67–9.

Huntington Library, RB 151852.

To the Ladies Who Saw Me Crown'd ('What is there in the universal earth')
First pub. *The Times*, 18 May 1914; Stillinger, pp. 90–1.

KeJ 515 Fair copy, on blank page (p. 78) in the copy of *Poems* (1817) presented by Keats to J. H. Reynolds (containing also KeJ 332, 333, 478).

Facsimile in first publication, in 'Two Lost Sonnets of Keats', *TLS*, 21 May 1914, p. 242 and in *Poetry Manuscripts*, p. 47.

Harvard, Keats Collection.

To the Nile ('Son of the old moon-mountains African!')
First pub. *Plymouth and Devonport Weekly Journal*, 19 July 1838; collected *Literary Remains* (1848); Stillinger, p. 233.

KeJ 516 Transcript by Charles Brown, lines 6–8 added by Keats, here entitled 'Sonnet,/To the Nile. 1818.', signed with the 'CB' flourish.

Facsimile in *Keats Facsimiles VII*, p. 56.

Harvard, Keats Collection 3.6, p. 54.

KeJ 517 Transcript by Richard Woodhouse here entitled 'Sonnet./To the Nile', annotated 'from J. K.'s M.S.', in W2; dated 6 February 1818.

Facsimiles of poem and Woodhouse's note about it on the facing f. 26v in *Keats Facsimiles VI*, pp. 30–31.

Harvard, Keats Collection 3.2, f. 27.

KeJ 518 Transcript by Richard Woodhouse, in W1; dated 6 February 1818.

Harvard, Keats Collection 3.1, p. 31.

KeJ 519 Transcript on one page of the end flyleaves of Woodhouse's *Poems* (1817); annotated 'JK 6 Feb: 1818.'.

This transcript printed Sperry, pp. 160–1; facsimile in *Keats Facsimiles I*, p. 239.

Huntington, RB 151852.

KeJ 520 Transcript by Charlotte Reynolds, in Reynolds-Hood Commonplace Book (f. 29); dated 6 February 1818.

Bristol Reference Library.

KeJ 521 Transcript by Charles Wentworth Dilke, on a blank page at the end of his copy of *Endymion* (1818), here entitled 'Sonnet. To the Nile'; dated 1818.

Keats House, London, KH 52.

'Two or three posies'
First pub. *Poetical Works and Other Writings of John Keats*, ed. H. B. Forman, 4 vols (London, 1883); Stillinger, pp. 368–9.

KeJ 522 Draft, in a letter to Fanny Keats, [1 May? 1819].

This MS printed in *Letters*, II, 56–7 (letter, 55–7).

Harvard, Keats Collection 1.52.

'Unfelt, unheard, unseen'
First pub. *Literary Remains* (1848); Stillinger, p. 96.

KeJ 523 Draft.

Facsimile in *The Letters and Poems of John Keats*, ed. J. G. Speed (New York, 1883), facing II, xxx; this MS mislocated at the British Library in *Texts*, p. 139 but corrected in Stillinger.

Unlocated.

KeJ 524 Fair copy, one page (on a leaf containing also KeJ 112).

Pierpont Morgan, MA 211.

KeJ 525 Transcript by Richard Woodhouse, one page, in W3; dated 'Keats. 1817'.

Facsimile in *Keats Facsimiles IV*, p. 254.

Pierpont Morgan, MA 215, f. 91.

KeJ 526 Transcript by Charles Cowden Clarke, printer's copy for the first publication, headed 'Lines' by R. M. Milnes; dated 1817.

Harvard, Keats Collection 4.4.4.

'Upon my life, Sir Nevis, I am piqu'd'
First pub. *Poetical Works and Other Writings of John Keats*, ed. H. B. Forman, 4 vols (London, 1883); Stillinger, pp. 279–81.

KeJ 527 Draft, in the 3 August section of a letter (containing also KeJ 381) to Tom Keats, 3–6 August 1818.

This MS printed *Letters*, I, 354–7 (letter, 352–8); facsimile of lines 1–41 in Sotheby's sale catalogue, 6 May 1936 (property of Maurice Buxton Forman), Lot 817.

Harvard, Keats Collection 1.36.

'Welcome joy, and welcome sorrow'
First pub. *Literary Remains* (1848); Stillinger, pp. 231–2.

KeJ 528 Transcript by Charles Brown, including the epigraph, here entitled 'Fragment. 1818.'.

Facsimile in *Keats Facsimiles VII*, pp. 54–5.

Harvard, Keats Collection 3.6, pp. 52–3.

KeJ 529 Transcript by Richard Woodhouse, here entitled 'Fragment', including the epigraph, in W2, annotated 'C. B. 1818'.

Epigraph in this transcript printed Finney, p. 760; facsimile in *Keats Facsimiles VI*, pp. 243–5.

Harvard, Keats Collection 3.2, ff. 133–4 (rectos only).

KeJ 530 Transcript by George Keats, here entitled 'Fragment 1818', including the epigraph, 2 pages, in George Keats's Notebook; transcribed January 1820.

Facsimile in *Keats Facsimiles V*, pp. 170–1.

British Library, Egerton MS 2780, ff. 56v–57.

KeJ 531 Transcript by Richard Woodhouse, here entitled 'Fragment', including the epigraph, in W1; dated 1818.

Woodhouse's prefatory note and the epigraph printed Finney, p. 757.

Harvard, Keats Collection 3.1, pp. 150–2.

KeJ 532 Transcript by Richard Woodhouse?, here entitled 'Fragment', including the epigraph, 2 pages (one folded leaf), signed 'J Keats', annotated on p. 4 of the leaf 'F Salmon/No. 2'; dated 1818.

This transcript was formerly owned by Dorothy Withey, Stratford-upon-Avon (see Stillinger, p. 594); facsimile in British Library, RP 2766.

Princeton, Robert H. Taylor Collection.

KeJ 533 Transcript by J. C. Stephens, here entitled 'Fragment', including the epigraph, dated 1818, in a notebook (containing also KeJ 43, 447, 552) prepared by Charles Cowden Clarke as a birthday gift for his sister Isabella Jane Towers in 1828.

Harvard, Keats Collection 3.12, f. 67v.

KeJ 534 Transcript by Charles Cowden Clarke, printer's copy for the first publication, here entitled 'Fragment', including the epigraph; dated 1818.

Harvard, Keats Collection 4.4.4.

'What can I do to drive away': no authoritative MS sources of this poem survive.

'When I have fears that I may cease to be'
First pub. *Literary Remains* (1848); Stillinger, pp. 225–6.

KeJ 535 Transcript by Charles Brown, here entitled 'Sonnet. 1817.', printer's copy for the first publication; transcribed c. April 1819.

Facsimile in *Keats Facsimiles VII*, p. 41.

Harvard, Keats Collection 3.6, p. 39.

KeJ 536 Transcript by Charlotte Reynolds, in Reynolds-Hood Commonplace Book (f. 31); annotated 'From J. Keats' letter to J H R, 31 Jan 1818.'.

Bristol Reference Library.

KeJ 537 Transcript in Woodhouse's letterbook (pp. 53–5) by one of his clerks, corrected by Woodhouse, of a now-lost letter (containing also KeJ 118, 131, 257) from Keats to J. H. Reynolds containing these lines; letter dated by Woodhouse 31 January 1818.

This transcript printed *Letters*, I, 222 (letter, 219–22).

Harvard, Keats Collection 3.3, p. 55.

KeJ 538 Transcript by Richard Woodhouse, in W2; annotated 'From JK's letter to W. H. R. [sic] <Feby> 31 Jany 1818'.

Facsimile in *Keats Facsimiles VI*, p. 105.

Harvard, Keats Collection 3.2, f. 64.

KeJ 539 Transcript by Richard Woodhouse, in W1; dated February 1818.

Harvard, Keats Collection 3.1, p. 144.

KeJ 540 Transcript by Charles Wentworth Dilke, here entitled 'Sonnet', on a blank page at the back of his copy of *Endymion* (1818); dated 1817.

Keats House, London, KH 52.

KeJ 541 Late transcript by Richard Woodhouse, made for Joseph Severn; watermarked 1830.

Harvard, Keats Collection 4.20.10.

'When they were come unto the Faery's court'
First pub. (lines 1–17) *Macmillan's Magazine*, 58 (1888), 317–18; first pub. in full in H. B. Forman, *Poetry and Prose by John Keats: A Book of Fresh Verses and New Readings* (London, 1890); Stillinger, pp. 323–6.

KeJ 542 Draft, in the 15 April section of a letter (containing also KeJ 28, 56, 167–8, 210, 291, 311, 317, 393, 399, 547) to George and Georgiana Keats, 14 February–3 May 1819.

This MS printed *Letters*, II, 85–8 (letter, 58–109).

Harvard, Keats Collection 1.53.

'Where be ye going, you Devon maid'
First pub. *The Life of Benjamin Robert Haydon*, ed. Tom Taylor, 3 vols (London, 1853); Stillinger, p. 240.

KeJ 543 Revised, in a letter (containing also KeJ 100) to B. R. Haydon, [21 March 1818], postmarked 23 March 1818.

This MS printed *Letters*, I, 251 (letter, 248–52); facsimile in British Library, MS Facs. 337.

Harvard, Keats Collection 1.24.

'Where's the Poet? Show him! show him!'
First pub. *Literary Remains* (1848); Stillinger, p. 290.

KeJ 544 Transcript by Charles Brown, here entitled 'Fragment. 1818.'.

Facsimile in *Keats Facsimiles VII*, p. 37.

Harvard, Keats Collection 3.6, p. 35.

KeJ 545 Transcript by George Keats, here entitled 'Fragment. 1818.', in George Keats's Notebook, one page; transcribed January 1820.

Facsimile in *Keats Facsimiles V*, p. 172.

British Library, Egerton MS 2780, f. 57v.

KeJ 546 Transcript by Richard Woodhouse, here entitled 'Fragment.', in W2, annotated 'from CB.'; dated 1818.

Facsimile in *Keats Facsimiles VI*, p. 347.

Harvard, Keats Collection 3.2, f. 187.

'Why did I laugh tonight? No voice will tell:'
First pub. *Literary Remains* (1848); Stillinger, p. 323.

KeJ 547 Fair copy, in the 19 March section of a letter (containing also KeJ 28, 56, 167–8, 210, 291, 311, 317, 393, 399, 542) to George and Georgiana Keats, 14 February–3 May 1819.

This MS printed *Letters*, II, 81 (letter, 58–109); for John Jeffrey's transcript, scc KcJ 548.

Harvard, Keats Collection 1.53.

KeJ 548 Transcript by John Jeffrey of portions of Keats's letter (KeJ 547), including this poem.

Harvard, Keats Collection 3.9, f. 25.

KeJ 549 Transcript by Richard Monckton Milnes, here entitled 'Sonnet', printer's copy for the first publication; dated 1819.

Harvard, Keats Collection 3.10(5).

'Woman! when I behold thee flippant, vain': no authoritative MS sources of this poem survive.

Written in Disgust of Vulgar Superstition ('The church bells toll a melancholy round')
First pub. *The Poetical Works of John Keats*, ed. Lord Houghton [R. M. Milnes] (London, 1876), as 'Written on a Summer Evening'; Stillinger, p. 88.

KeJ 550 Draft, here untitled, annotated by Tom Keats 'J Keats/Written in 15 Minutes.', on the back of an August 1816 letter from George to John and Tom Keats.

This MS printed in Hyder E. Rollins, 'Unpublished Autograph Texts of Keats', *HLB*, 6 (1952), 167; facsimile in Parke Bernet sale catalogue, 28 April 1939 (John Spoor Sale), p. 149 and *Poetry Manuscripts*, p. 45. George Keats's letter is printed *Keats Circle*, I, 3.

Harvard, Keats Collection 2.10.

KeJ 551 Transcript in Tom Keats's Copybook, here entitled 'Sonnet/Written in Disgust of Vulgar superstition', signed; dated 'John Keats Sunday Evening Decr 24 1816', probably transcribed late 1816.

This MS printed in Hyder E. Rollins, 'Unpublished Autograph Texts of Keats', *HLB*, 6 (1952), 168.

Harvard, Keats Collection 3.5, p. 19.

KeJ 552 Transcript by J. C. Stephens, here untitled, annotated 'written by JK in 15 minutes'; in a notebook (containing also KeJ 43, 447, 533) prepared by Charles Cowden Clarke as a birthday gift for his sister Isabella Jane Towers in 1828.

This MS printed in Hyder E. Rollins, 'Unpublished Autograph Texts of Keats', *HLB*, 6 (1952), 167–8.

Harvard, Keats Collection 3.12, f. 69.

KeJ 553 Late transcript in an unidentified hand, on a leaf (containing also KeJ 1), headed 'Written on a Sunday Evening'; dated 23 December 1816, transcribed for R. M. Milnes.

Harvard, Keats Collection 3.10(1).

Written on the Day That Mr Leigh Hunt Left Prison ('What though, for showing truth to flatter'd state'): no authoritative MS sources of this poem survive.

'You say you love; but with a voice'
First pub. by Sidney Colvin, *TLS*, 16 April 1914; Stillinger, pp. 97–8.

KeJ 554 Transcript by Charlotte Reynolds, here entitled 'Stanzas', in Reynolds-Hood Commonplace Book (f. 39).

Bristol Reference Library.

KeJ 555 Transcript by John Taylor, in W3, 2 pages (one leaf), annotated in pencil by Richard Woodhouse.

Facsimile in *Keats Facsimiles IV*, pp. 313–14.

Pierpont Morgan, MA 215, f. 72.

KeJ 556 Transcript by Richard Woodhouse, here entitled 'Stanzas.', in W2, printer's copy for the first publication, annotated in shorthand 'from Miss Reynolds' followed by 'and Mrs Jones'.

Facsimile in *Keats Facsimiles VI*, p. 363.

Harvard, Keats Collection 3.2, f. 195.

NOTEBOOK

[Medical Notebook]
First pub. *John Keats's Anatomical and Physiological Note Book*, ed. Maurice Buxton Forman (London, 1934; reprinted New York, 1982).

KeJ 557 Notebook kept by Keats when a medical student at Guy's Hospital, including lecture notes on a series of 12 lectures on physiology (wanting no. 9) and notes on anatomy, written from both ends (text on 49 pages in all); some leaves watermarked 1809, others 1812, probably used from October 1815–summer 1816.

Facsimile pages: in first publication as frontispiece; in Williamson, Plate III; in Tim Hilton, *Keats and His World* (London, 1971), [p. 19]; four pages in Mabel A. E. Steele, 'Three Early Manuscripts of John Keats', *KSJ*, 1 (1952), plates II–III.

Keats House, London, KH 31.

DRAMATIC WORKS

For Keats's and Charles Brown's tragedy *Otho the Great*, see KeJ 363–76. For the dramatic fragment 'King Stephen', see KeJ 207–9.

MARGINALIA IN PRINTED BOOKS

For Keats's books with no annotations, see INTRODUCTION.

Aléman, Mateo. *The Rogue: or, The Life of Guzman de Alfarache*, [trans. Don Diego Puede-ser, i. e. J. Mabbe], 3rd ed (London, 1634).
Owings, No. I.

KeJ 558 Inscribed twice by James Rice, 'John Keats/ From his friend/Js Rxxx/20th April 1818' and '...given to John Keats/and upon his death 1821 — returned to me./Rice.', containing Keats's markings and annotations.

Facsimile of title page in Owings, p. 12; marginalia printed in Amy Lowell, *John Keats*, 2 vols (Boston, 1925), II, 578–87; see also Norman Anderson, 'Corrections to Amy Lowell's Reading of Keats's Marginalia', *KSJ*, 23 (1974), 26 and Beth Lau, 'Further Corrections to Amy Lowell's Transcriptions of Keats's Marginalia', *KSJ*, 35 (1986), 34–6.

Harvard, Keats Collection.

Auctores Mythographi Latini, ed. Augustinus van Staveren (Amsterdam, 1742), for Keats's lost copy, see INTRODUCTION.

Bacon, Sir Francis. *The Two Bookes of Sr Francis Bacon. Of the Proficiency and Advancement of Learning* (London, 1629), for a copy with annotations formerly attributed to Keats (Keats House, London, KH 18), see the WILLIAM HAZLITT section, HzW 116.

Beaumont and Fletcher, see KeJ 564.

[The Bible], for Keats's unannotated copy of the Greek New Testament, see INTRODUCTION.

Bonnycastle, John. *An Introduction to Astronomy* (London, 1807), for Keats's unannotated copy, see INTRODUCTION.

[Burton, Robert]. *The Anatomy of Melancholy... by Democritus Junior*, 2 vols, 11th ed (London, 1813), Vol. II only.
Owings, No. III.

KeJ 559 Inscribed by Keats 'John Keats from Charles Brown 1819' on the title page, containing markings and annotations.

Facsimile of title page in Owings, p. 16 and of p. 417 in Tim Hilton, *Keats and His World* (London, 1971), p. 116; marginalia printed in *The Poetical Works and Other Writings of John Keats*, ed. H. B. Forman, rev. Maurice Buxton Forman, 8 vols (New York, 1938–9), V, 306–20.

Keats House, London, KH 26.

Chaucer, Geoffrey. *The Poetical Works*, 14 Vols in 7 (Edinburgh, 1782).
Owings, No. IV.

KeJ 560 Containing markings possibly by Keats and KeJ 445, Charles Cowden Clarke's copy.

British Library, Add. MS 33516.

Dante Alighieri. *The Vision; or, Hell, Purgatory, and Paradise, of Dante Alighieri*, trans. H. F. Cary, 3 vols (London, 1814).

Owings, No. V. For a second (lost) copy owned by Keats, see INTRODUCTION.

KeJ 561 Containing markings in Vol. I only and KeJ 27, 54; presented by Keats to Fanny Brawne.

Facsimile of title page of Vol. I in Owings, p. 20 and of opening page of 'Hell' in Tim Hilton, *Keats and His World* (London, 1971), p. 81; the markings described in Robert Gittings, *The Mask of Keats* (Cambridge, MA, 1956), pp. 144–61.

Yale.

Duverger, William. *The English and the French Language Compared...*, 5th ed (London, 1807), for Keats's unannotated copy, see INTRODUCTION.

Goldsmith, Oliver. *Grecian History*, 2 vols (London, 1805), for Keats's unannotated copy, see INTRODUCTION.

Hazlitt, William. *Characters of Shakespear's Plays* (London, 1817).
Owings, No. VIII.

KeJ 562 Inscribed by Keats on the title page and containing his markings and annotations, almost exclusively in the chapter on *King Lear*.

Facsimile of title page in Owings, p. 26 and of pp. 158–9 in Robert Underwood Johnson, 'Note on some Volumes now in America, once owned by Keats', *KSMB*, 2 (1913) and in Tim Hilton, *Keats and His World* (London, 1971), p. 63; Keats's marginalia printed in Amy Lowell, *John Keats*, 2 vols (Boston, 1925), II, 587–90 and in *The Poetical Works and Other Writings of John Keats*, ed. H. B. Forman, rev. Maurice Buxton Forman, 8 vols (New York, 1938–9), V, 280–6; see also Norman Anderson, 'Corrections to Amy Lowell's Reading of Keats's Marginalia', *KSJ*, 23 (1974), 27–8.

Harvard, Keats Collection.

Hunt, Leigh. *Foliage* (London, 1818), for Keats's unannotated copy, see INTRODUCTION.

Jackson, Zachariah. *Shakespeare's Genius Justified* (London, 1819).
Owings, No. XI.

KeJ 563 Inscribed on title page 'Wm Haslam to John Keats' and containing markings and a few annotations.

Marginalia printed in Amy Lowell, *John Keats*, 2 vols (Boston, 1925), II, 590–2 and in *The Poetical Works and Other Writings of John Keats*, ed. H. B. Forman, rev. Maurice Buxton Forman, 8 vols (New York, 1938–9), V, 287–90; see also Norman Anderson, 'Corrections to Amy Lowell's Reading of Keats's Marginalia', *KSJ*, 23 (1974), 28–9.

Harvard, Keats Collection.

Jonson, Ben. *The Dramatic Works of Ben Jonson, and Beaumont and Fletcher*, ed. Peter Whalley and George Colman, 4 vols (London, 1811), Vols II–IV only.
Owings, No. XII.

KeJ 564 Inscribed (Vol. II) 'Geo Keats to his affectionate Brother John', containing markings in Vols II and IV and KeJ 36, 413.

Facsimile of title page in Owings, p. 34.

Keats House, London, KH 21.

Lamb, Charles. *Specimens of English Dramatic Poets, Who Lived About the Time of Shakspeare* (London, 1808).
Owings, No. XIII.

KeJ 565 Inscribed on the front flyleaf by Benjamin Bailey 'B. Bailey/To John Keats...' and by Keats 'to FB ——/Frances Brawne/August 9th 1820' and containing markings and annotations.

This volume discussed and marginalia printed in Helen Haworth, 'Keats's Copy of Lamb's *Specimens of English Dramatic Poets*', *BNYPL*, 74 (1970), 419–27.

Berg.

Lempriere, John. *A Classical Dictionary*, 6th ed (London, 1806), for Keats's unannotated copy, see INTRODUCTION.

The Literary Pocket-Book: Or, Companion for the Lover of Nature and Art. 1819, [ed. Leigh Hunt] (London, 1818).
Owings, No. X.

KeJ 566 Inscribed by Leigh Hunt 'John Keats/from his friend Leigh Hunt' and (by Fanny Brawne?) 'F. B.' on the flyleaf, containing annotations and markings in three hands, Leigh Hunt's, Fanny Brawne's and possibly Keats's, including also KeJ 137.

Facsimile of title page in Owings, p. 30 and of the inscription in Williamson, Plate IX; for a discussion of the three hands, see Robert Gittings, *John Keats. The Living Year* (London, 1954), pp. 236–7 and Rotraud Müller, 'Some Problems Concerning Keats and Hazlitt', *KSMB*, 8 (1957), 33–6.

Keats House, London, KH 27.

Livius, Titus. *The Roman History* (London, 1686), for Keats's unannotated copy, see INTRODUCTION.

Milton, John. *Paradise Lost*, ed. Thomas Newton, 2 vols, 8th ed (London, 1773), Vol. II only.
Owings, No. XVI.

KeJ 567 Markings in pencil, signed and dated 1810.

These markings printed in *The Romantics on Milton*, ed. Joseph Anthony Wittreich, Jr (Cleveland, 1970), pp. 545–6.

Keats House, London, KH 16.

Milton, John. *Paradise Lost*, 2 vols (Edinburgh, 1807).
Owings, No. XVII.

KeJ 568 Vol. II inscribed by Keats 'Mrs Dilke from/her sincere friend/J. Keats' and containing markings and annotations in both volumes, also including KeJ 398.

Facsimile of title page of Vol. II in Owings, p. 44; of opening page to Book IV in Tim Hilton, *Keats and His World* (London, 1971), [p. 83]; of Vol. I, pp. 92–3 in Williamson, Plate VII. Marginalia printed in *The Poetical Works and Other Writings of John Keats*, ed. H. B. Forman, rev. Maurice Buxton Forman, 8 vols (New York, 1938–9), V, 291–305 and (partially) Finney, pp. 337–41. A copy of *Paradise Lost* (wanting its title page) into which Keats's marginalia was transcribed (by one of the Misses Reynolds?) was sold at Anderson Galleries, 15–17 March 1920 (H. B. Forman Sale), Lot 377. Dilke's copy of *Paradise Lost* (1811), containing his marginalia, some of which are similar to Keats's, is also at Keats House, London.

Keats House, London, KH 24.

Moraes, Francisco de. *Palmerin of England*, [Anthony Munday's translation, corrected by Robert Southey], 4 vols (London, 1807).
Owings, No. VI.

KeJ 569 Markings and annotations by Keats, William Hazlitt, Leigh Hunt and Thornton Hunt, Keats's pencil marginalia inked over by Hunt.

Facsimile of title page in Owings, p. 22; Keats's marginalia printed Amy Lowell, *John Keats*, 2 vols (Boston, 1925), II, 592–604; see also Norman Anderson, 'Corrections to Amy Lowell's Reading of Keats's Marginalia', *KSJ*, 23 (1974), 29–31 and Beth Lau, 'Further Corrections to Amy Lowell's Transcriptions of Keats's Marginalia', *KSJ*, 35 (1986), 36–7; see also Charles Patterson, 'The Keats-Hazlitt-Hunt Copy of *Palmerin of England* in Relation to Keats's Poetry', *JEGP*, 60 (1961), 31–43.

Harvard, Keats Collection.

Ovidius Naso, Publius. *Metamorphoses*, ed. Daniel Crispin (London, 1806).
Owings, No. XIX.

KeJ 570 Inscribed (in an unidentified hand) 'John Keats emer/1812' on inside front corner and containing markings, probably by Keats.

Facsimile of title page in Owings, p. 48 and of inscription in Williamson, Plate I.

Keats House, London, KH 17.

Sackville, Thomas. *The Poetical Works* (London, 1820), for Keats's unannotated copy, see INTRODUCTION.

Selden, John. *Titles of Honor*, 3rd ed (London, 1672).
Owings, No. XX.

KeJ 571 Inscribed by Keats on the title page 'John Keats *1819*' and containing his markings and an unfinished index of passages on flyleaf.

Facsimile of title page in Owings, p. 50; markings are recorded in Amy Lowell, *John Keats*, 2 vols (Boston, 1925), II, 604–5.

Harvard, Keats Collection.

Shakespeare, William. *The Poetical Works* (London, 1806).
Owings, No. XXI.

KeJ 572 Inscribed on the title page 'John Hamilton Reynolds to John Keats *1819*' by Reynolds and by Joseph Severn on the flyleaf '...Given me by Keats Jan. 1820...', containing markings, annotations by Reynolds, Severn and Richard Woodhouse but probably none by Keats, including also KeJ 52, 245 and sonnets by Reynolds and Severn.

Facsimile of title page in Owings, p. 52. The marginalia are discussed (and some attributed to Keats) and 2 facsimile pages in Caroline F. E. Spurgeon, *Keats's Shakespeare* (Oxford and London, 1928); corrected in Robert Gittings, *John Keats* (Boston, 1966), p. 188n. Facsimile of Reynolds's sonnet in Williamson, Plate V.

Keats House, London, KH 22.

Shakespeare, William. *Mr William Shakespeares Comedies, Histories, and Tragedies* (London, 1623; reprinted 1808).
Owings, No. XXII.

KeJ 573 Inscribed on title page 'John Keats 1817' and later 'to F. B. 1820' by Keats, containing markings and annotations in 5 plays and including KeJ 227, 340.

Facsimile of title page in Owings, p. 54 and of page from *King Lear* in Tim Hilton, *Keats and His World* (London, 1971), p. 78. Some marginalia discussed and printed (with 5 facsimile pages) in Caroline F. E. Spurgeon, *Keats's Shakespeare* (Oxford and London, 1928); and in *The Poetical Works and Other Writings of John Keats*, ed. H. B. Forman, rev. Maurice Buxton Forman, 8 vols (New York, 1938–9), V, 268–79.

Keats House, London, KH 23.

Shakespeare, William. *The Dramatic Works*, 7 vols (Chiswick, 1814).
Owings, No. XXIII.

KeJ 574 Inscribed by Keats on title page of Vol. I 'John Keats – April 1817' and added later 'to Joseph Severn', containing markings and annotations; the copy of Shakespeare that Keats took to Italy with him in September 1820.

Facsimile of title page of Vol. I in Owings, p. 56 and another facsimile page in Tim Hilton, *Keats and His World* (London, 1971), p. 41. Marginalia discussed and printed (with 22 facsimile pages) in Caroline F. E. Spurgeon, *Keats's Shakespeare* (Oxford and London, 1928), pp. 67–148 *passim*; also partly printed in *The Poetical Works and Other Writings of John Keats*, ed. H. B. Forman, rev. Maurice Buxton Forman, 8 vols (New York, 1938–9), V, 273–9.

Harvard, Keats Collection.

Shelley, Percy Bysshe. *The Cenci*, for Keats's lost annotated copy, see INTRODUCTION.

Spenser, Edmund. *The Works*, 6 vols (London, 1715), Vol. I only.
Owings, No. XXV. For another (lost) copy of Spenser's works, see KeJ 175; for Keats's unannotated copy of the London, 1679 edition, see INTRODUCTION.

KeJ 575 Inscribed on title page 'George Keats. 1816' and containing Keats's markings and annotations.

Facsimile of title page in Owings, p. 60 and in Robert Underwood Johnson, 'Note on some Volumes now in America, once owned by Keats', *KSMB*, 2 (1913); of pp. 152–3 in *The Houghton Library 1942–1967* (Cambridge, MA, 1967), p. 72 and Tim Hilton, *Keats and His World* (London, 1971), p. 13. Marginalia printed in Amy Lowell, *John Keats*, 2 vols (Boston, 1925), II, 545–78; see also Beth Lau, 'Further Corrections to Amy Lowell's Transcriptions of Keats's Marginalia', *KSJ*, 35 (1986), 31–4.

Harvard, Keats Collection.

Rudyard Kipling
1865–1936

INTRODUCTION

When the English literary establishment 'discovered' the twenty-five-year-old Rudyard Kipling in 1890, they hailed him as a new Charles Dickens. But — as far as that establishment was concerned — his precocious promise was not fulfilled; and his reputation among literary critics and academicians slid steadily downhill, despite some surprising champions like T. S. Eliot and Bertolt Brecht. Kipling's *audience* however — a massive, international, diverse and devoted reading public — was undismayed by the ultimately negative verdict passed on him by 'high culture'. His popularity has been immense. In this regard, at any rate, the comparison with Dickens is apt.

Kipling's family carefully preserved his youthful works and this, together with his early and long-lasting fame — occurring as it did after the taste for collecting literary works, manuscript and printed, was well-established — both contribute to the large number of his extant literary manuscripts, over 2,300 of which are listed in the entries. The full range of possible kinds of source materials are available: Kipling left us rough drafts, fair copies, typescripts revised and unrevised, originals and carbon copies, on loose leaves, in notebooks, enclosed or written in letters, inscribed on the flyleaves of presentation copies of books, written in the margins of books, jotted on menus, on programmes, on the pages of diaries, or written out as souvenirs for friends and admirers; revised printed matter ranging from proofs for newspaper and periodical articles, galley and page proofs for his own books and corrected copies of his published work, books and clippings.

In addition, Kipling was prolific; his works — even in the 'definitive' but nevertheless sorely incomplete Sussex Edition alone — fill thirty-five volumes. From about the age of ten to his death at seventy, Kipling wrote over 2,000 verses of all kinds, hundreds of short stories and four novels — to say nothing of all his other writings: travel books, essays, newspaper articles, a military history, letters to editors, speeches, prefaces, drawings, cartoons, dramatic adaptations of his own works, filmscripts, thousands of letters and volumes of memoirs.

Juvenilia: Schooldays and Indian Years

Born into a family which rated art and literature highly, Kipling's talents were, from an early age, recognized, appreciated and encouraged. Recollecting an early holiday with his mother, Kipling wrote in *Something of Myself*: 'I understood that my Mother had written verse, that my Father "wrote things" also; that books and pictures were among the most important affairs in the world...I had found out, too, that one could take pen and paper and set down what one thought, and that nobody accused one of "showing off" by so doing.'

His earliest surviving verses were probably written when he was ten years old (see KpR 158, 619). And the first collection of his poetry to be printed (*Schoolboy Lyrics*) was done so in 1881 — privately and without his knowledge — by his parents in India while he was a schoolboy at the United Services College in Westward Ho!. The hundreds of entries which represent surviving manuscripts of juvenile verses include not only the notebooks in which Kipling himself carefully wrote all his finished poems, but also letters in which he sent them to relatives and friends and one notebook in which his mother and father made their own copies of Rudyard's poetic accomplishments.

A few entries (KpR 303.5, 304, 555–6, 755–6, 842.5, 843, 1899.5, 1899.7) describe Kipling's contributions to 'The Scribbler', a manuscript magazine 'got up' by the Burne-Jones and Morris children (the former being Kipling's cousins). Seventeen issues were 'published' from November 1878 to March 1880. May Morris was the 'editor' and she and her sister Jenny performed 'the scribe's labour'. Two of Kipling's contributions were included in three issues of 'The Scribbler' (under the pseudonym 'Nickson') and three other poems were submitted; these were found among other manuscripts awaiting 'publication' at the time of the magazine's expiration.

May Morris, who owned one of the two copies of the magazine, as well as the manuscripts of unused contributions, apparently sold all the Kipling-related items — including the three issues of 'The Scribbler' containing his work and the manuscripts of the three unused poems — to G. M. Williamson in 1901 (see Williamson's letter to Kipling of 11 July 1901 in Sussex, KP 23/12). The original magazines and loose poems were replaced (in Morris's set) by typed transcripts and these were among the huge bequest of manuscripts to the British Library by May Morris in 1939. The originals sold to Williamson, with one exception, remain untraced. They were all sold in the Williamson sale at Anderson Galleries on 17 March 1915.

One of 'The Scribbler' verses — 'The Pillow Fight' (KpR 842.5–843) — was published in *United Services College Chronicle*, the school magazine, Nos 4–10 (30 June 1881–24 July 1882) of which Kipling edited himself (see KpR 2285.5). He contributed numerous pieces to the *Chronicle* and even continued to do so for some years after he left school. None of Kipling's works were published under his own name although he collected some of them in his later works. Some documentary evidence of Kipling's authorship of pieces in the *United Services College Chronicle* survives (see discussion below). Complete files of the magazine are preserved at the Huntington Library, Cornell University and Dalhousie University.

The four notebooks of Kipling's juvenilia that survive are referred to throughout the entries as Sussex Notebooks 1, 2 and 3 and MS Sundry Phansies. The preservation of these volumes makes hundreds of texts of Kipling's earliest writing available which would otherwise have been lost. Kipling himself chose to preserve very few of these poems in his collected editions.

Sussex Notebook 1

Notebook, probably a continuation of an earlier notebook (presented to Edith Plowden and returned by her to Kipling in 1915 when he destroyed it) as it begins mid-poem on a page numbered 51, containing fair copies of 58 poems, 105 pages numbered 51–75 followed by two unnumbered pages, 78–88, 95–133, 136–7, 140–65, 5 pages blank; the poems are dated from 2 February 1882 to February 1884 (the last 14 having been written after Kipling arrived in India), and containing Kipling's annotations and revisions *passim* in a later hand (some dated 1883–4).

Contents: KpR 11, 12, 20, 37, 47, 51, 166, 234, 235, 245, 272, 294, 298, 300, 323, 399, 437, 465, 466, 477, 493, 523, 590, 632, 633, 643, 647, 648, 709, 712, 723, 782, 794, 797, 802, 823, 846, 889, 895, 921, 936, 1003, 1026, 1031, 1036, 1050, 1120, 1133, 1256, 1271, 1280, 1285, 1298, 1322, 1329, 1348, 1372, 1382.

Sussex, KP 24/3.

Sussex Notebook 2

Notebook containing transcripts of Kipling's early poems by his mother and father, Alice Macdonald Kipling (AMK) and John Lockwood Kipling (JLK), made from copies sent to them in India, including 27 poems written on the first 59 pages of the book (which are unpaginated), followed by 56 blank leaves, one page [p. 25] containing a clipping of 'Ave Imperatrix'; poems are dated 'Winter term 81'–July 1882.

Contents: KpR 14, 50, 169, 297, 302, 349, 420, 441, 469, 480, 482, 525, 592, 636, 651, 815, 825, 891, 897, 928, 1051, 1123, 1273, 1282, 1288, 1358, 1374.

Sussex, KP 24/2.

Sussex Notebook 3

Small notebook containing fair copies of 55 poems, written in two series: the 'first series' written on the rectos which are numbered 1–75 (the 'Index to the Poems Written in this Book' being on p. 75 and the unpaginated facing page); the 'second series' written on the versos starting again at the front of the book, versos paginated 1–19, 25–37 (the 'Index to the Poems written in the Second Part of This Book' being on the unpaginated page facing p. 72 of the 'first series'); the title page 'POEMS' contains a sketch of a grotesque figure captioned 'Portrait of the Author'; 'first series' poems dated 25 June 1880–25 May 1882, the 'second series' being undated; this notebook was one of the fair copies of his poems prepared by Kipling in February 1882 and presented by him to his aunt Edith Macdonald before he left England for India in September of that year.

Contents: KpR 13, 48, 53, 70, 160, 167, 246, 250, 273, 295, 301, 324, 325, 347, 367, 379, 438, 467, 478, 481, 487, 494, 524, 591, 634, 649, 710, 795, 811, 813, 824, 883, 890, 896, 922, 926, 933, 937, 957, 963, 1004, 1027, 1032, 1037, 1121, 1257, 1272, 1281, 1286, 1289, 1323, 1334, 1357, 1371, 1386.

Sussex, KP 24/1.

MS Sundry Phansies

Notebook, containing fair copies of 32 early poems (mostly unpublished by Kipling), including a decorated title page reading '1882 February Sundry Phansies Writ by one Kipling' and, at the end, an 'Index to the Phansies writ in this Book', 86 numbered leaves (rectos only) of texts (one, f. 54, being a title page for 'The Story of Paul Vaugel'); this notebook was one of the fair copies of his poems prepared by Kipling in February 1882 and presented to Florence Garrard before he left England for India in September of that year.

This notebook listed in Stewart, p. 8.

Contents: KpR 54, 71, 124, 161, 168, 203, 236, 249, 274, 348, 366, 380, 479, 483, 485, 623, 635, 708, 812, 814, 884, 912, 927, 935, 958, 965, 1016, 1046, 1048, 1122, 1290, 1335.

Berg.

With the exception of these notebooks and the few other loose extant manuscripts which record Kipling's schoolboy verses, there are significant gaps in the literary manuscripts that survive from the earliest periods of his career.

Some compositions are known to be lost. In *Something of Myself*, Kipling describes a 'fat, American cloth-bound notebook' in which he composed an adaptation of Dante in the metre of Longfellow's 'Hiawatha' while at school; 'as rare things will,' he goes on, 'my book vanished'. Also lost is a fifth notebook of juvenile verse which he gave to Edith Plowden before leaving England for India in 1882. This notebook, Rutherford says (p. 23), may have been the earliest of all and 'Sussex Notebook 1' is probably the continuation of it. Kipling burnt it himself in 1915 when Miss Plowden returned it to him, an act for which — Kipling says in *Something of Myself* — 'she will take an even higher place in Heaven than her natural goodness ensures'. Before destroying it, however, he removed the sepia sketch which his father had provided as a frontispiece; both Edith Plowden and Kipling himself have vividly described the illustration. Their descriptions and a facsimile of the sketch (original at Sussex, KP 3/4) are given in Rutherford, pp. [23–5].

When Kipling left school and England in 1882, he returned to India, the place of his birth; for 'seven years hard', he worked as a journalist for the Anglo-Indian press — first as a sub-editor on the staff of the daily *Civil and Military Gazette* (Lahore), later for *The Pioneer* (Allahabad) and its weekly supplement, *The Week's News*. Hundreds of poems, stories, articles, essays and fillers by Kipling were printed in various newspapers over these years. Identification of Kipling's pieces has become more authoritative since 'Scrapbooks 1–4' — in which Kipling himself inserted his articles of 1884–91 — have become available (see description below).

Kipling selected some of his early works for inclusion in the collections which he published during the 1880s: he collected poems in *Echoes* (1884) and *Quartette* (1885) (both of which included compositions by other members of his family and were published by the Civil and Military Gazette Press at Lahore) and in the four editions of *Departmental Ditties* published from 1886 to 1890. He collected his short stories — the works which he took more seriously and valued more highly — in *Quartette* (1885), in *Plain Tales from the Hills* (Calcutta and London, 1888) and in the six volumes which make up the so-called Indian Railway Library — *Soldiers Three*, *The Story of the Gadsbys*, *In Black and White*, *Under the Deodars*, *The Phantom 'Rickshaw* and *Wee Willie Winkie* — all first published in Allahabad in 1888–89.

Relatively few literary manuscripts survive which date from Kipling's Indian years. One of the albums of schoolboy verses (Sussex Notebook 1, described above) was actually in use until 1884 so that the last fourteen poems it contains were written after Kipling's arrival in India.

Among the handful of loose autograph poems is one noteworthy item: the manuscript Kipling sent to the printer of the five poems added to the contents of *Departmental Ditties* for the second edition (see KpR 83, 86, 626, 669, 807) now at the Pierpont Morgan Library. Also surviving from these years — and usually preserving otherwise unknown and uncollected verses — are inscriptions written in books, letters containing *jeux d'esprit*, letters written in verse and transcripts of any of these made and preserved by family and friends from originals which have been lost.

Two early notebooks in the Berg Collection also include verses dating from the 1880s: MS Words, Wise and Otherwise and, especially, MS Departmental Ditties which contains *only* poems from the four editions of *Departmental Ditties* (and one used as the 'L'Envoi' to *Soldiers Three).*

MS Words, Wise and Otherwise

Notebook, inscribed on the front flyleaf 'To you my dear Boy with all good wishes for Xmas & New Year Florence [Garrard] 1880', containing fair copies of 13 poems and 4 chapters of 'Letters of Marque', as well as Kipling's transcript of his sister Alice's lines 'I have communed with my heart at night alone' (pp. [7–8]), including also a decorated title page reading 'Words Wise and Otherwise. Writ by One Rudyard Kipling of that Ilk./1885 and Later', 180 pages (unpaginated), c. 80 blank.

The Berg Collection also owns 3 original pen-and-ink drawings by Kipling (being 2 preliminary sketches and one finished drawing) for the title page of 'Sayings Wise and otherwise'.

Contents: KpR 113, 237, 269, 329, 522, 561, 582, 627, 650, 878, 978, 1019, 1252, 1821.

Berg.

MS Departmental Ditties

Octavo notebook containing fair copies of 31 poems (all but one, KpR 268, collected in one of the first four editions of *Departmental Ditties*), including a decorated title page: 'Departmental Ditties and Other Verses Written in "*81.*"', 120 pages (rectos and versos) numbered by Kipling, followed by a page reading 'The End' [p. 121], an Index [pp. 122–3] and the L'Envoi [pp. 124–5], the rest of the volume blank.

Contents: KpR 34, 35, 64, 82, 104, 164, 222, 268, 277, 353, 409, 415, 432, 596, 620, 675, 711, 721, 784, 844, 862, 877, 900, 991, 1098, 1126, 1131, 1146, 1299, 1343, 1346.

Berg.

In addition, there are fifteen annotated or inscribed copies of *Echoes* (KpR 309–19, 508, 1161, 1226, 1368), six copies of *Quartette* (KpR 913–18) and a verse inscription dated 1884 in a copy of *Schoolboy Lyrics* (privately printed, 1881) (KpR 1221). Of the revised printed copies of *Departmental Ditties* which are listed (KpR 279–82), the only one with extensive corrections does not date from the 1880s but was used to prepare the 1914 Bombay Edition.

As for Kipling's fiction written during his years in India, the manuscript sources are even more sparse. Another early notebook at the Berg — MS Essays and Stories — contains manuscripts of a few stories from the Indian Railway Library series; the only loose manuscripts of any of these stories that have been traced are also in the Berg Collection (KpR 1446, 1691, 1907).

MS Essays and Stories

Paper-covered notebook, including fair copies of 4 of Kipling's early Indian stories (virtually the only autograph manuscripts extant of these stories), chapters from *From Sea to Sea* and one poem, inscribed on the inside front cover '<J. Rudyard Kipling The Civil and Military Gazette Lahore.>', text on all 38 leaves of the notebook (unfoliated) and continuing on the 17 pages of another notebook inserted at the back.

Contents: KpR 74, 1422, 1557, 1636, 1661, 1698.

Berg.

There are also two copies (both incomplete) of the Indian Railway Library: one at Syracuse University which bears Kipling's corrections (KpR 1745, 2081, 2104, 2175, 2229) and the other at the Berg containing his glosses on Indian words (KpR 1746, 1982, 2082, 2105, 2230). A revised copy of the second edition of *In Black and White* (1889) is also in the Berg Collection (KpR 1747). At what period in his life Kipling marked up these copies has not been determined.

The manuscripts of Kipling's early non-fictional prose writings have fared no better. Besides the few chapters of 'Letters of Marque' (published in *The Pioneer*, 1887–8) (KpR 1821) written in MS Words, Wise and Otherwise (see above), the only substantial extant manuscript is that of the series of articles about Calcutta entitled 'City of Dreadful Night' (published in *The Pioneer*, 1888), also preserved in the Berg Collection (KpR 1508).

The greatest loss from this period, however, is the manuscript of Kipling's unfinished and unpublished first novel, *Mother Maturin*, which he apparently began in the spring of 1885 — and took up from time to time until at least 1904; in a letter of that year to Robert McClure, he says that *Mother Maturin* 'is as she was — to be done some day I hope' (Columbia University). In a letter to Edith Macdonald of 30 July 1885, he wrote that he had '237 foolscap pages' of the novel, 'an Anglo-Indian episode'. Carrington says the manuscript was eventually kept in a safe at A. P. Watt's office in London until, in 1899, Kipling brought it to Rottingdean to plunder while writing *Kim*. Thereafter it disappeared, probably destroyed by Kipling himself (p. 359).

The 1890s

Kipling sailed from Calcutta in March 1889 and eventually arrived in Liverpool in October. For over a decade thereafter — until 1902 when he settled at Bateman's in Sussex — he and his growing family would be uprooted again and again and would remain, more or less continually, on the move: two world tours cut short, one by the death of his brother-in-law Wolcott Balestier, the other by financial crisis; four years in Vermont (three in Kipling's much-loved home 'Naulakha') abruptly abandoned after a legal quarrel with Kipling's wife's family; a winter in New York culminating in Kipling's near-fatal bout of pneumonia and the death of six-year-old Josephine, his eldest child; and nine winters in South Africa.

The peripatetic and, in some ways, ill-fated nature of these years neither prevented Kipling from writing a great variety of works nor from publishing them. It is in this period that he produced his four published novels, a form he yearned to write and thought superior to the short story — 'independent firing by marksmen is a pretty thing but it is the volley-firing of a full battalion that clears the post', he once wrote to a friend — but afterwards abandoned.

The draft of the first version of Kipling's first published novel *The Light that Failed* (1891) is in the Doubleday Collection at Princeton University (KpR 1834). But only a few pages of a corrected typescript (of unknown date) of *The Naulahka* (1892) — the novel he wrote jointly with Wolcott Balestier — have come to light (KpR 1920).

The last two novels were both largely written in Vermont. Kipling gave the manuscript of the first, *Captains Courageous*, to his family physician, Dr James Conland who inspired the story and to whom the book was dedicated. Dr Conland sold it later to J. P. Morgan and it is now preserved at the Pierpont Morgan Library (KpR 1486).

The manuscript of Kipling's last, troublesome, novel, *Kim* (KpR 1789), was among the first manuscripts of his works to be presented by himself to an institution; like the other manuscripts he presented, it was accepted under the condition that it would never be used 'for purposes of collation' nor be reproduced (see discussion below).

The two notebooks that Kipling used during his voyage from Calcutta to San Francisco in March–May 1889 are now owned by the Huntington Library. They contain the manuscript of about half of 'From Sea to Sea', the series of travel articles which he wrote for *The Pioneer* (printed from April 1889 to April 1890). Also in these notebooks are the manuscripts of fifteen short stories — including the eight published in the *Civil and Military Gazette* from 30 March to 21 August 1889 as 'Abaft the Funnel' and two unfinished (and unpublished) stories. These notebooks are referred to in the entries as MS From Sea to Sea; see KpR 1634 for a full description.

Some of the stories in MS From Sea to Sea were later collected by Kipling in *Life's Handicap* (London and New York, 1891), one of the collected volumes the manuscripts of which Kipling did not carefully preserve. Consequently, manuscripts of stories in *Life's Handicap* are mostly lost and otherwise scattered. This is similarly the case for stories collected in *Many Inventions* (London and New York, 1893); manuscripts of four of them are bound up in MS Day's Work (see below) but the few others that survive are dispersed, one on a leaf at the Library of Congress torn from MS From Sea to Sea (KpR 1608).

The original journal which Kipling kept during his two trips with the Channel Squadron in 1898 — from which *A Fleet in Being* was condensed — is now preserved in the Berg Collection (KpR 1615).

As for his verse, the first collected edition of these years was *Barrack-Room Ballads* (1892); all of the forty-three poems it contains are represented in the entries, some by more than one manuscript source. These entries include various kinds of materials — rough drafts, fair copies, manuscripts sent for early publication in periodicals, corrected proofs for these periodical publications, corrected page proofs for the first edition, extracts copied into notebooks, quotations of lines written out for friends in letters or as souvenirs — and are scattered in some fourteen libraries in England, Canada and the United States.

Forty-seven poems were collected in the first American and English editions of *The Seven Seas* (1896). Only five of them are unrepresented by manuscript sources of any kind; and thirty-two of them are represented by the two especially important manuscripts, some showing several stages of composition, that Kipling himself had bound up for preservation; see the descriptions of MS Seven Seas and MS Years Between below. The other manuscript sources for these poems are similar in kind to those mentioned above for *Barrack-Room Ballads* and as widely dispersed. Harvard owns a series of fair copies of seven of the poems which were written out for Julia de Forest probably in 1896; see KpR 23, 373, 490, 593, 692, 697, 1071.

The Restricted MS Volumes

It wasn't until the late 1890s that Kipling and his wife Carrie seemed to become aware of the value of his literary manuscripts and the need to take control themselves of their disposition. They decided, in the short term, to have many of the manuscripts of each of Kipling's works bound up in green leather by Maggs Bros. — several bear a presentation inscription from Kipling to Carrie — and, in the long term, to distribute these volumes, as well as other loose manuscripts, as gifts to selected libraries and institutions in England, Scotland, Canada, Australia and France; quite a few letters from these libraries and institutions to the Kiplings regarding these gifts are at Sussex (KP 23/21–31). Such bound manuscript volumes of almost all of Kipling's most important works, from *The Jungle Book* (1894) onwards, survive. Two exceptions are *From Sea to Sea* (1899) which was, in any case, actually written in 1889, and *Captains Courageous* (1896), the manuscripts of which are mentioned above.

A large proportion of the entries listed represent the contents of these MS volumes, bequeathed to libraries from 1925 to 1940 (the year after Carrie's death), by Kipling himself, by Carrie, or by Elsie Bambridge, the Kiplings' only surviving child. Carrie's own list of the presentations is at Sussex (KP 23/20). The presentation was always made on the condition that the receiving institution undertook to honour Kipling's interdiction against the manuscript ever being used 'for the purposes of collation'. What exactly Kipling meant by this phrase is open to interpretation and, unsurprisingly, the various recipients of these gifts interpret it differently. One exception to this is MS Just So Stories which Kipling gave to his daughter Elsie Bambridge in 1936, according to Carrie's list. When Mrs Bambridge died in 1976, she left the manuscript to the British Library without imposing any restrictions on its use.

All of the sixteen MS volumes (with the exception of MS Five Nations at the National Library of Australia) have been examined. In most cases, the manuscripts bound up together represent the contents of one or another of Kipling's published collections of verse or stories. In other cases, however, the manuscripts of pieces from more than one work have been gathered together in one volume; the short titles used for such volumes reflect the work *most* represented by the contents. Two of the MS volumes are listed as single entries: the MS of *Kim* (KpR 1789) which was one of the first to be bequeathed (to the British Library in 1925); and the MS of 'France at War' (KpR 1626), presented to the Bibliothèque Nationale in Paris in 1936. Also listed as single entries are two loose manuscripts which Kipling gave to libraries: the typescript of 'The King's Pilgrimage' (KpR 575.5) presented to the Imperial War Museum in 1922; and the manuscript of the Preface to *Life's Handicap* (KpR 1832), presented to the Fitzwilliam Museum, Cambridge, in 1933. According to Carrie's list of gifts, Kipling gave the manuscript of his poem 'The Irish Guards' to the Irish Guards in 1917 but no such manuscript has been traced (see the headnote to the poem for details). The other thirteen MS volumes are (in alphabetical order):

MS Actions and Reactions

Volume presented to the University of St Andrews in 1922 with a note from Kipling stating that 'I should not like the MS used in any way for the purposes of collation', including all the stories and poems published in *Actions and Reactions* (London and New York, 1909) except 'Garm — A Hostage' and its accompanying poem 'The Power of the Dog', 133 leaves.

Contents: KpR 95, 388, 402, 752, 908, 929, 940, 1533, 1681, 1710, 1843, 1893, 2008, 2259.

University of St Andrews, MS PR4854.A4.

MS Day's Work

Volume bequeathed to the British Library in 1940, inscribed by Kipling 'Caroline Kipling', including 11 stories published in *The Day's Work* (New York, 1898) (wanting only 'The Maltese Cat'), 4 stories collected in *Many Inventions* (London and New York, 1893), 4 stories collected in *Land and Sea Tales* (London, 1923) and 3 other stories (one uncollected); also including a fragment of 'Stalky' and some draft verses on some of the blank versos; 242 leaves, a typed contents list (f. ii) and a note (f. [iii]) of conditions ('Under the terms of bequest collation of the contents of this MS. is not allowed, nor may any photograph of it be taken.').

Contents: KpR 217, 476, 786, 863, 1316.5, 1450, 1456, 1459, 1469, 1481, 1540, 1590, 1646, 1657, 1764, 1783, 1852, 1903, 1912, 1958, 1990, 2063, 2097, 2154, 2182, 2206, 2238, 2244.

British Library, Add. MS 45541.

MS Debits and Credits

Volume of MS stories, inserted is a letter from Carrie Kipling to Lord Londonderry of 27 May 1937 offering the MS to Durham University on condition the MSS 'not be used for collation', including the 14 stories collected in *Debits and Credits* (London, 1926), 4 stories published in *Land and Sea Tales* (London, 1923) and 5 stories published in *Limits and Renewals* (London, 1932), as well as a few miscellaneous stories, a speech ('Club') and 'The War in the Mountains', also containing a typed contents list and annotations *passim* in an unidentified hand; 273 numbered leaves (and one unnumbered leaf, f. [22a]); a few leaves watermarked 1896 and 1897.

Contents: KpR 334, 1137.5, 1437, 1475, 1513, 1535, 1584, 1596, 1598, 1617, 1627, 1655, 1695, 1756, 1774, 1856, 1945, 1974, 1986, 2004, 2006, 2015, 2021, 2051, 2120, 2144, 2158, 2172, 2178, 2215, 2222, 2250, 2263.

University of Durham.

MS Diversity of Creatures [and] MS Eyes of Asia

Volume inscribed by Kipling (f. 1) 'Caroline Kipling from *Rudyard Kipling*. 1918', containing an inserted presentation letter from CK to the Edinburgh University Library of 8 June 1936; including (ff. 1–156) the poems and stories included in *A Diversity of Creatures* (London and New York, 1917) (wanting only 'Jobson's Amen' and also containing 'The Jester') and (ff. 157–82) the four articles published in *The Eyes of Asia* (New York, 1918); including also (f. 1) a typed contents list.

Contents (MS Diversity of Creatures): KpR 98, 192, 232, 344, 368, 452, 454, 554, 588, 616, 670, 879, 938, 1063, 1264, 1349, 1404, 1554, 1569, 1629, 1705, 1707, 1761, 1766, 1871, 1910, 2024, 2112, 2195, 2201; (MS Eyes of Asia): KpR 673, 1152, 1650, 1996, 2031, 2170.

University of Edinburgh, Dk. 2. 8.

MS Five Nations

Volume of MS poems presented to the National Library of Australia in 1938, including a prefatory note (in an unidentified hand) presumably by Carrie Kipling: 'The inclusion of "The Young Queen" in this volume of original Manuscripts seems to indicate it as an appropriate gift to the People of the Commonwealth of Australia for the National Library of Canberra. It was the Author's wish that his Manuscripts should never be used for purposes of Collation, and the giver of this volume depends upon those to whom it is entrusted to see that the Author's wishes are fulfilled. Bateman's Burwash, Sussex.'; including 47 of the 55 poems published in *The Five Nations* (1903) and a typed contents list (two of the titles in the contents list have been cancelled ('Recessional' and 'Lichtenberg') and no MSS of these poems are included.

Contents: KpR 119, 122, 127, 133, 142, 172, 230, 252, 270, 285, 289, 306, 337, 342, 361, 407, 444, 539, 542, 637, 682, 702, 773, 775, 818, 826, 828, 832, 839, 961, 967, 977, 1010, 1015, 1024, 1061, 1095, 1116, 1119, 1141, 1261.5, 1284, 1294, 1324, 1361, 1376, 1390.

National Library of Australia, MS 94.

MS Jungle Books

Volume inscribed by Kipling 'Caroline Kipling', bequeathed to the British Library in 1940, including all of the stories and some of the poems published in *The Jungle Book* (London and New York, 1894) and *The Second Jungle Book* (London and New York, 1895); 173 leaves, a typed contents list (f. ii) and a note (f. [iii]) of conditions ('Under the terms of gift collation of the contents of this MS. is not allowed, nor may any photographs of it be taken'); some leaves watermarked 1890.

Contents: KpR 28, 46, 260, 563, 608, 674, 713, 758, 804, 821, 980. 1014, 1030, 1081, 1163, 1308, 1690, 1712, 1787, 1793, 1831, 1880, 1897, 2012, 2020, 2039, 2095, 2146, 2157, 2176, 2235.

British Library, Add. MS. 45540.

MS Just So Stories

Volume inscribed (f. 2) by Kipling 'Caroline Kipling' and by CK 'To Elsie Bambridge July 1936', including the MSS of the stories, poems, captions and original drawings published in *Just So Stories* (London, 1902), as well as 'The Tabu Tale' (collected with the other stories in the Outward Bound Edition of *Just So Stories* in 1903), a draft of 'Bridge-Guard in the Karoo' and an unpublished Preface to the stories (for a reproduction, see FACSIMILES); 148 leaves including a typed contents list and a MS 'Index' in an unidentified hand.

Contents: KpR 121, 200, 492, 498, 546, 767, 905, 1154, 1180, 1208, 1215, 1222, 1352, 1430, 1483, 1494, 1525, 1580, 1716, 1719, 1721, 1725, 1728, 1730, 1786, 2072, 2115.

British Library, Add. MS 59840.

MS Non-Fiction

Volume of MS articles and essays presented to the British Library in 1940, including all the articles and poems collected as *Sea Warfare* (London, 1916), some of the essays and poems collected as *Letters of Travel* (London, 1920), six miscellaneous prose pieces (including four uncollected stories) and the drama 'The Harbour Watch'; containing a note of conditions on the front flyleaf ('Under the terms of bequest, collation of the contents of this MS. is not allowed, nor may any photograph of it be taken.'), a typed title page (f. 1), contents list (f. ii), section title pages *passim* (ff. 1, 30, 65, 87, 112, 155, 185, 190, 192, 211, 213, 223, 230, 236), and 250 leaves of text.

Contents: KpR 153, 398, 446, 668, 704, 761, 868, 925, 983, 1052, 1101, 1127, 1263, 1309, 1354, 1479, 1538, 1573, 1620, 1632, 1771, 1826, 1924, 1944, 1963, 2048, 2119.

British Library, Add. MS 45542.

MS Puck

Volume presented to the Bodleian Library in 1926, including all the poems and stories published in *Puck of Pook's Hill* (London, 1906); inserted is a letter from RK to A. E. Cowley (of the Bodleian), 30 June 1926, offering the MS on the condition that it 'was never to be made available for purposes of collation', inscribed (f. 1) 'Presented to the Bodleian Library by The Author. – 1926 Rudyard Kipling'.

Contents: KpR 93, 125, 195, 210, 448, 776, 837, 898, 902, 974, 987, 1038, 1041, 1078, 1106, 1224, 1233, 1266, 1498, 1567, 1683, 1801, 1934, 1949, 2164, 2231, 2242, 2278.

Bodleian, MS Eng. misc. c. 127.

MS Rewards and Fairies

Volume presented to the Cambridge University Library in 1926, inscribed on the front flyleaf by Kipling 'Presented to Cambridge University Library by the author 1926 Rudyard Kipling' (with the letter offering the MS dated 30 June 1926 inserted), including the poems and stories published in *Rewards and Fairies* (London, 1910) and an autograph contents list (headed 'Rewards and Fairies.' and annotated 'To printer: follow this for make up. RK' and '*do not crowd the verses*', f. 1), 119 leaves (rectos only) numbered 1–74, 74a, 75–118.

Contents: KpR 41, 65, 128, 154, 188, 225, 320, 395, 510, 570, 657, 791, 835, 852, 919, 986, 997, 1082, 1087, 1149, 1227, 1278, 1330, 1465, 1514, 1522, 1550, 1671, 1799, 1869, 1993, 2038, 2070, 2166, 2275.

Cambridge University Library, ADD 6850.

MS Seven Seas

Volume of MS poems presented to Magdalene College, Cambridge, in 1936, inscribed by Kipling 'Caroline Kipling from Rudyard Kipling' on inside front cover, including 28 poems or fragments of poems, 16 of them published in *The Seven Seas* (New York, 1896) and 11 in *The Five Nations* (London, 1903), containing 159 leaves (mostly rectos only) not foliated by Kipling, a drawing by Kipling (f. 65) and a typed contents list which includes only 23 titles; some leaves watermarked 1894, 1896 and 1897.

Contents: KpR 100, 110, 251, 275, 284, 307, 355, 364, 370, 378, 567, 580, 585, 644, 683, 695, 719, 785.5, 799, 831, 1020, 1068, 1070, 1124, 1150, 1274, 1360, 1363.

Magdalene College, Cambridge.

MS Stalky

Volume inscribed by Kipling 'Caroline Kipling from Rudyard Kipling', presented to Imperial Service College (letter of presentation dated 18 May 1938); including all the stories published in the first edition of *Stalky & Co.* (London, 1899), the MS of the story '"Stalky"' (rejected from that collection but published later) and an unpublished story, 133 leaves.

The Bursar of Haileybury is unfortunately unable to

allow access to this MS due to the restrictions placed upon it by Caroline Kipling at the time of its bequest.

Contents: KpR 1613, 1737, 1739, 1812, 1847, 1890, 2050, 2076, 2096, 2184.

Haileybury.

MS Traffics and Discoveries

Volume inscribed by Kipling 'Given to McGill University by Rudyard Kipling (Doctor of Law) 1927', including the 11 stories and 10 of the poems (wanting only 'The Runners') that comprise *Traffics and Discoveries* (London, 1904), a discarded 'L'Envoi' (KpR 1213), unpublished draft verses (KpR 191, 515) and a typed contents list.

Contents: KpR 143, 149, 191, 427, 515, 576, 746, 788, 858, 969, 1085, 1213, 1339, 1400, 1434, 1452, 1491, 1517, 1885, 2044, 2101, 2130, 2134, 2246.

McGill University.

MS Years Between

Volume inscribed by Kipling (f. 1) 'Presented to the British Museum by Rudyard Kipling: October 1925' and (f. 6) 'Caroline Kipling from Rudyard Kipling 1920', including: drafts and fair copies of the poems published in *The Years Between* (London, [1919]) (wanting only '"My Boy Jack"', 'The Verdicts', 'The Spies' March' and 'Gehazi'); the poems published in *A History of England* (Oxford and London, 1911) by Kipling and C. R. L. Fletcher (wanting only 'The Saxon Foundation of England' (i.e., 'The King's Task') and 'The American Rebellion/Before'); 19 poems published in *The Seven Seas* (New York, 1896); a few other poems collected variously and two unpublished poems (KpR 772, 1040); 134 leaves including 5 preliminary leaves (ff. 2–5 being a typed contents list which is wanting 'A Song of the White Men') and two blank leaves (ff. 59 and 84); bearing the note on the flyleaf 'Under the terms of gift collation of the contents of this MS. is not allowed, nor may any photograph of it be taken'; earliest and latest dates are April 1891 and 1916.

Contents: KpR 2, 19, 22, 31, 102, 103, 108, 109, 120, 130, 204, 206, 207, 213, 243, 244, 255, 259, 261, 262, 265, 266, 276, 303, 305, 321, 326, 332, 358, 362, 371, 381, 394, 397, 414, 423, 436, 461, 471, 475, 488, 541, 548, 550, 559, 566, 574, 601, 660, 661, 684, 691, 696, 698, 706, 714, 726, 733, 743, 745, 760, 772, 779, 803, 819, 841, 847, 885, 924, 945, 960, 979, 982, 984, 993, 1000, 1002, 1006, 1013, 1017, 1021, 1023, 1040, 1044, 1049, 1053, 1080, 1091, 1113, 1117, 1125, 1151, 1212, 1232, 1237, 1249, 1259, 1295, 1316, 1317, 1351, 1384, 1393.

British Library, Add. MS 44841.

No MS volume of the stories and poems published in Kipling's last collection *Limits and Renewals* (1932) was bound up by him; what became of the manuscripts and why Kipling did not preserve them as he had been doing for years are mysteries. Corrected page proofs for the first edition, however, do survive:

Limits and Renewals Proof

Two sets of page proofs, probably set up for the first (English) edition (London, 1932) — as they are date stamped by R. & R. Clark, Macmillan's printers — but used for the first American edition (New York, 1932) as they are annotated 'Doubleday Proofs' *passim*; the first set includes markings and corrections by the printer only, the second is corrected by Kipling and stamped 'First Page Proof'; date stamped 15–25 January 1932.

Contents: KpR 15, 57, 257, 412, 751, 829, 1066, 1235, 1420, 1428, 1504, 1531, 1536, 1600, 1866, 1882, 1922, 2123, 2173, 2180, 2264.

Syracuse University.

Some other of Kipling's published works are unrepresented by MS volumes. No manuscripts have come to light for *Muse Among the Motors* (1904). Manuscripts of only some of the articles collected in *Letters of Travel* (1920) are included in MS Non-Fiction (described above); there are also some corrected typescripts in the Berg Collection (KpR 1824). The only MS material that has come to light for Kipling's compilation, *The Irish Guards in the Great War* — typescripts of Chapter I — is at Texas (KpR 2284).

For the most part, manuscripts of Kipling's addresses and speeches do not survive (for the few that do, see 'Speeches'). Nor are there manuscripts of *Souvenirs of France* or the incomplete autobiographical memoir, *Something of Myself*, posthumously published in 1937.

There are no separate MS volumes for Kipling's own selected or collected editions of his verse, such as *Songs from Books* or *Inclusive Verse*, though individual manuscripts of the poems are often extant, many of them in other MS volumes. In addition, a copy of the first edition of *Songs from Books* (1912) which was used for preparing the Bombay Edition (1915) is listed in the entries and its contents are entered individually (see KpR 1112). Likewise, a revised copy of the first edition of *Inclusive Verse* (1919) has been analysed (see KpR 537). It is also worth noting that a copy of *The Five Nations* (1903), revised by Kipling in preparation for the Bombay Edition of 1914, is also listed (see KpR 365).

Around the edges of this rather deceptively well-organized body of manuscript material — and indeed sometimes inside the MS volumes themselves — are hundreds of extant literary manuscripts of texts about which little, and often nothing at all, is known. Many are informal or occasional texts: *jeux d'esprit* of various kinds, limericks, inscriptions, epigrams, jottings, outlines, or rough notes on various subjects. And most survive not only despite Kipling's distaste for the collection and preservation of his rejected trifles but also despite his, and especially Carrie's, resolve — particularly after 1902 when they moved, for the last time, to Bateman's — that no scrap of Kipling's handwriting should fall into unauthorized hands.

The Kipling Papers at Sussex

The Kiplings remained at Bateman's from 1902 until their deaths. The archive of papers and the library of books that accumulated and were left behind there when Kipling died in 1936 were considerable.

Elsie Bambridge has written that after her father's death, Carrie burnt the 'large canvas-covered case labelled "Notions" [that] lay on the desk, containing unfinished stories and poems, notes and ideas, collected through the years' (Carrington, p. 514). What else may have been destroyed after Kipling's death will probably never be known.

Within a year after Carrie Kipling's death in 1939, all the gifts of her husband's manuscripts and books that he (or she) had requested had been made. These included, as well as the MS volumes listed above, the bequest of 'The File', Kipling's collection of his own printed works — in English and in translation — to the British Library, made by Carrie in 1938; this extraordinary collection, numbering over 1,000 volumes, is preserved in the Department of Printed Books. Duplicate copies of the translations were presented by Carrie, also in 1938, to the British Red Cross Society. Several typescript catalogues of 'The File' and other copies of Kipling's works from his own collection are in the Kipling Papers at Sussex (KP 27/1–5); many of them are annotated by Kipling himself. Some selected books from Kipling's library were also presented by Carrie, on her husband's behalf, to specialized libraries. Two cases of books on 'maritime' subjects were presented in 1937 to the National Maritime Museum in Greenwich; a list of them is at Sussex (KP 23/42). Another such selection of books was given to the Royal Australasian College of Surgeons in Melbourne in 1937 (list at Sussex, KP 23/45).

The remainder of the family archive passed into the hands of Elsie Bambridge, who preserved it intact at her home Wimpole Hall, near Cambridge, and only rarely permitted access to it. Over the years, she augmented the collection by purchasing a few items in the salerooms and by making transcripts of Kipling's papers held in private collections. From time to time, she also presented items to libraries or to friends (see, for example, KpR 1875).

In the 1940s and 1950s, she allowed two of Kipling's biographers, Lord Birkenhead and Charles Carrington, to use the papers for their respective biographies.

When she died in 1976, Elsie Bambridge left her estate at Wimpole Hall — including the Kipling family archive — to the National Trust. She excepted one volume at least — the undoubtedly treasured manuscript of her father's children's book, *Just So Stories* (described above) — and gave it to the British Library.

Another item that Elsie Bambridge did not leave to the National Trust with the rest of her estate was her mother's diary. She stipulated in her will that this forty-five volume document — kept faithfully by Carrie throughout her forty-four year married life — should be destroyed. What is known of this lost diary is what Carrington and Lord Birkenhead (who both used it) recorded of it in their biographies of Kipling. In addition, copies of Carrington's extracts from and summaries of the diary are preserved in the library of the Kipling Society in London and at Sussex.

In 1978, the National Trust deposited the so-called Kipling Papers (KP) at the University of Sussex Library. The collection — including thirty-one boxes of papers and twenty-one boxes of press cuttings — has been catalogued and is now available to scholars; the catalogue by John Burt, the collection's first curator, has been published (*Kipling Papers*).

This collection is the only genuine Kipling archive — in the sense of it having grown 'organically' over the years rather than having been collected. The sprawling mass of materials that make it up was accumulated by the Kiplings over their lifetimes and is preserved essentially as it was left. It has since been added to by the deposit of the Baldwin family papers in 1978 which include material relating to the Kiplings; access to the Baldwin Papers is by permission of Lord Baldwin.

In addition to Kipling's own literary manuscripts, the Kipling Papers contain an especially important series of scrapbooks (known as 'Scrapbooks 1–4'). These are the scrapbooks into which Kipling himself inserted clippings of his articles published in the Indian press from 1884–91. They are invaluable in determining what Kipling wrote during those years when his pieces rarely appeared under his signature and his manuscripts are extremely scarce; the availability of these scrapbooks has led to the identification of hundreds of new Kipling items.

'Scrapbook 2' (KP 28/2) is entitled 'Articles and Poems by R. K. Published in "The Pioneer" 1885.' and contains about twenty clippings of pieces by Kipling, none of which contains his revisions or corrections (see *Kipling Papers* for the contents). The other three scrapbooks, however, include autograph material:

Scrapbook 1

Scrapbook, inscribed on the cover by RK 'R. K. Articles and Verses 1884–1886', containing clippings of prose and verse published in the *Civil and Military Gazette* and *The Pioneer*, autograph draft verses on a few blank (mostly unnumbered) leaves, reviews of Kipling's books *Echoes* and *Quartette*, and an Index of titled contents, most pages numbered from 1–318.

For a list of the clippings in Scrapbook 1, see *Kipling Papers*.

Contents: KpR 97, 646, 778, 892, 1544.

Sussex, KP 28/1.

Scrapbook 3

Folio scrapbook, lettered on cover 'Rudyard Kipling His Book' and (added in his hand) '1886–1887', containing clippings of articles and poems published in the *Civil and Military Gazette*, 151 numbered pages, including an Index (inserted) of titled contents (135 items), some of the poems are annotated 'Miss A. please type this'; also containing (pp. 63–4) a clipping of an article entitled 'The Club Fancy Ball' (published *Civil and Military Gazette*, 29 December 1886) which includes a long list of persons and their costumes which Kipling has annotated with comments such as 'ran away', 'horsewhipped', 'sick', 'gone home' and 'dead'.

For a list of the clippings in Scrapbook 3, see *Kipling Papers*.

Contents: KpR 1563, 1686, 1714, 1776, 1778, 2003.

Sussex, KP 28/3.

Scrapbook 4

Scrapbook, labelled 'Rudyard Kipling His Book.' and entitled by Kipling 'Stories. Poems Articles 1887–1891.', including an inserted Index of titled contents, containing poems and prose published in the *Civil and Military Gazette*, *The Pioneer*, *Week's News*, *Scots Observer*, etc., 195 numbered pages.

For a list of the clippings in Scrapbook 4, see *Kipling Papers*.

Contents: KpR 63, 77, 81, 152, 239, 604, 606, 766, 1134, 1478, 1595, 1637, 1709, 1809, 1838, 1849, 1854, 1877, 1925, 1932, 1953, 2023, 2028, 2138, 2162, 2212, 2272.

Sussex, KP 28/4.

A further five scrapbooks (KP 28/5–9) document Kipling's writings from 1892 until his death. These were probably increasingly the work of Carrie Kipling and do not augment the established canon as do the early scrapbooks. For a few entries from 'Scrapbook 9' ('Speeches 1907–1935'), see KpR 1552, 2036, 2069, 2090, 2091, 2093, 2132, 2168, 2193, 2198, 2204.

The Kipling Papers are also rich in Kipling's letters, business papers, drawings and documents as well as association items: letters *to* him; letters, drawings and other papers of his parents; papers belonging to other family members — especially his children — and friends; material concerning honours and awards which he received and copyright, estates and other financial matters; as well as printed matter, photographs and other memorabilia.

Other Kipling Collections

The British Library's collection of Kipling materials is also formidable. The bequests by the Kiplings to this institution, England's national library, of the six MS volumes and 'The File' (Kipling's own collection of his works) described above would alone ensure its importance for students of Kipling.

The best part of the archive of Macmillan, Kipling's principal English publisher, is also in the British

Library. It contains not only letters from Kipling dated from 1890 to 1935 (Add. MS 54940) but, more importantly, thirty volumes of proofs corrected by him (Add. MS 55846–75). The first three volumes of this series are corrected page proofs for three late collections of stories published by Macmillan: *Thy Servant a Dog* (1930), *Humorous Tales* (1931) and *Collected Dog Stories* (1934).

The other twenty-seven volumes contain Kipling's corrected galley and page proofs for the 'definitive' Sussex Edition of his works and, as such, they are the only surviving record of Kipling's last revision of his collected writings. These volumes include proofs for Volumes I–XI, XIII–XXV and portions of XXVI, XXIX–XXX of the Sussex Edition; wanting are proofs for *The Jungle Books* (Vol. XII), *The Irish Guards in the Great War* (Vols XXVII–XXVIII), *Souvenirs of France. Something of Myself* (Vol. XXXI) and, most unfortunately, the four volumes of verse (Vols XXXII–XXXV). Most of the proofs contain corrections or queries by the printer, as well as Kipling's own corrections, revisions or initials and *all* of the contents of these volumes of proofs — unless they are completely unmarked by any hand — are entered in the *Index* below. These proofs represent hundreds of entries in both the Prose and Verse sections.

Most of the large North American Kipling collections were formed by avid Kipling collectors. Captain E. W. Martindell's important Kipling collection was dispersed when it was sold at auction by the American Art Association on 26–7 January 1922; Kipling's own annotated copy of the sale catalogue is at Sussex (KP 27/12). Most of the items are now scattered in North American libraries. The most important single repository is the Rare Book Division at the Library of Congress where the books and manuscripts by and about Kipling amassed by William M. Carpenter, Admiral Lloyd H. Chandler and H. Dunscombe Colt are now preserved. Admiral Chandler's collection is notable primarily for printed books and for his 'special edition' of the works of Kipling which fills over 200 notebooks (see discussion below).

The Carpenter collection, the gift of Mrs Carpenter in 1941 (*NUCMC*, 62-529), includes manuscripts and corrected proofs of stories and poems as well as drawings, cartoons, letters, miscellaneous papers, printed matter, photographs and memorabilia. A typed catalogue which Carpenter sent to Kipling — containing a few of the latter's notes — is at Sussex (KP 27/6).

Carpenter was the principal purchaser of the items which Edmonia Hill, Kipling's intimate friend in the 1880s and early 1890s, decided to sell — to Kipling's dismay — in the 1920s. From Mrs Hill, he acquired quite a few sketches and cartoons (see KpR 504, 518), the so-called 'Pen and Brush Sketches' (a loose leaf binder containing sketches, cartoons, pamphlet covers and KpR 27, 495, 500, 507, 1028, 1170, 1179, 1189, 1345, 1543, 1608, 1715, 1906), and albums of photographs captioned by Kipling (see KpR 88, 1315). Another item worth noting is the volume labelled 'Animal Stories' which contains revised typescripts and galley proofs of *Just So Stories* (see KpR 1431, 1582, 2074).

In 1984–5, Mrs H. Dunscombe Colt added her husband's rich Kipling collection to the already well-endowed one at the Library of Congress (*NUCMC*, 85-1636). The manuscript materials in the Colt collection — containing altogether nearly 1,500 items — include literary manuscripts, proofs, over 300 letters, family papers and miscellanea.

James McG. Stewart, a Canadian barrister, industrialist and devoted tracker of Kipling's books and papers for over fifty years, left his collection to Dalhousie University in Halifax, Nova Scotia. The fact that the most complete bibliography of Kipling's works to date (Stewart) is also the catalogue of this collection gives some indication of the extent of the printed works that had been acquired by Dalhousie by 1959; and the collection has grown larger since. The manuscript materials, however, are also impressive: they include literary manuscripts, corrected proofs, miscellaneous papers, drawings and over 800 letters.

The Kipling papers in the Berg Collection at the New York Public Library were not amassed by any one collector; for a summary, see Morton Cohen, 'Kipling in the Berg', *KJ*, 43 (1976). As well as books, drawings and over 100 letters, the Berg Collection contains manuscript sources for many of Kipling's literary works and, as it happens, principally for his earlier works. There are copies of the volumes of stories which make up the Indian Railway Library of 1888 which bear his corrections and annotations (including copies of both the first and second editions of *In Black and White* and wanting *Under the Deodars*); see KpR 1746–7, 1982, 2082, 2105, 2230). Autograph manuscripts of these stories hardly survive and the few that do are also in the Berg Collection, in the volume called MS Essays and Stories (described above).

The Berg Collection includes six MS notebooks whose contents have been fully analysed in the entries; four of them — MS Sundry Phansies, MS Essays and Stories, MS Words, Wise and Otherwise and MS Departmental Ditties — have already been described. The other two are, in alphabetical order:

Berg Booklet

Small booklet without a cover, containing fair copies of 9 poems (mostly extracts only), 29 pages of texts (not paginated by Kipling), including, as well as contents listed below, a sketch of a devil [p. 1] and other sketches [pp. 7–8, 15–20, 28–9].

Contents: KpR 328, 343, 663, 801, 1069, 1072, 1093, 1231, 1277.

Berg.

MS Writings and Songs

Octavo notebook, including fair copies of 40 poems, and a sketch annotated 'Please don't think "Writings" all date back to this...' (p. 1, the flyleaf), a title page (p. 2), the texts (pp. 3–128) and an Index (pp. [130–2], 128 pages numbered by Kipling.

Contents: KpR 40, 146, 150, 155, 173, 176, 177, 181, 184, 209, 218, 226, 267, 403, 442, 553, 572, 577, 609, 625, 666, 715, 753, 805, 888, 909, 930, 941, 970, 981, 998, 1007, 1077, 1088, 1102, 1105, 1147, 1229, 1291, 1378.

Berg.

The cornerstone of the large Kipling collection at Syracuse University — including literary manuscripts, over 600 letters, miscellanea and printed works — is the material accumulated by another Kipling collector, William Pearson Tolley. A great many of the entries represent items in this collection. Among them are another series of five of the six volumes of the Indian Railway Library (1888) — wanting only *The Phantom 'Rickshaw* — which Kipling corrected and annotated; see KpR 1745, 2081, 2104, 2175, 2229.

Also well-represented in the entries is the Kipling collection at Princeton University Library, particularly the papers of Doubleday & Co., Kipling's principal American publisher. Among the correspondence between Kipling and the Doubledays are some manuscript materials for some of Doubleday's editions of Kipling's works; see, for example, KpR 286, 537, 1541, 1591, 1796–8, 1955, 1965–72, 2065, 2122, 2239. In addition, this archive contains Kipling's draft of *The Light that Failed* (KpR 1834); for a summary, see Rice (1961).

Charles J. Paterson's Kipling collection is now at Cornell University. Though including only a small number of literary manuscripts, it contains over 200 letters and quite a few facsimiles of literary manuscripts in other libraries.

Impressive holdings of Kipling papers or important manuscripts (apart from the MS volumes listed above) can be found at several other libraries as well, including Harvard, the Pierpont Morgan Library, Texas, the Huntington Library, Yale University, Columbia University, the Bodleian Library, and the Fitzwilliam Museum, Cambridge.

Reference Edition, Canon and Bibliography

The reference edition chosen for Kipling's works is — with the exception of verses included in Rutherford (1986) which take that as the reference edition — the Sussex Edition, 525 sets of which were published posthumously in 1937–9. A few years later, the same texts were published in America in 1,010 sets as the Burwash Edition: *The Collected Works of Rudyard Kipling*, 28 vols (Doubleday, Doran & Co., 1941). While it has not been possible to provide references to it in the entries, the Burwash Edition may be consulted as the reference edition as its texts are identical to those in the Sussex Edition and it may be more available to North American readers.

In the last years of his life, Kipling undertook a complete revision of his works for the Sussex Edition. He began work on it in 1928 and, unfortunately, never completed it; some of the volumes of the Sussex Edition — notably the last four volumes of poetry — were yet to be finally revised when he died. Nonetheless, the texts of this edition represent all that can be known about Kipling's last intentions. In addition, it augmented all previous editions by including two volumes of short stories and many poems which were previously uncollected. It represented, as it were, Kipling's own final judgment as to the parameters of his literary canon.

However, a great many works of Kipling's, signed and unsigned, had appeared in print, mostly in periodicals, which had never been and would never be collected by him. For the fifty years following Kipling's death — that is, until the copyright on his published works ran out — no collected editions enlarged on the canon that had been established in the Sussex Edition.

In 1986, two such editions appeared. One — Andrew Rutherford's edition of the *Early Verse of Rudyard Kipling 1879–1889* (Oxford, 1986), subtitled *Unpublished, Uncollected, and Rarely Collected Poems* — includes well over 200 poems not in the Sussex Edition and more than 100 previously unpublished anywhere. Since this is the only edition of

Kipling's works to date which edits the texts using manuscript sources and according to modern editorial procedures, it supersedes even the Sussex Edition for those few verses which they both include. Accordingly, Rutherford is taken as the reference edition whenever possible. The fact that this edition includes only verses written before 1890 is a sorely felt limitation. It is hoped that future editors will extend the editorial work begun by this edition to the rest of Kipling's works.

The other collection published in 1986 — *Kipling's India: Uncollected Sketches 1884–88*, ed. Thomas Pinney (London, 1986) — brought together unsigned and uncollected articles written during Kipling's days as a young journalist in India and originally printed in the *Civil and Military Gazette*. The importance of this edition lies not in its use of manuscript sources — since virtually no manuscripts survive for Kipling's Indian journalism — but in its authoritative extension of the canon.

Speculation about Kipling's canon has largely centred on the earliest periods of his writing life, his schooldays and Indian years. As for his contributions to the *United Services College Chronicle* — none of which was signed — several documents survive which provide grounds for attribution. The so-called 'Denham Letter' was the list of Kipling's contributions that the bookdealer Edwin A. Denham sent (30 August 1899) to a 'Kipling collector', together with a complete file of the magazine (W. C. Crofts's set). The list, he stated, was compiled on the authority of 'the headmaster [Crofts], one of the submasters, the Chaplain of the College, and of Kipling himself'; it is printed in Chandler's *Summary*, p. 332. The list has proved to be incomplete and not entirely reliable; for a better list, see Stewart, pp. 9–12. In addition, a typescript list of Kipling's contributions to the *United Services College Chronicle* from 1881–9 is at Sussex (KP 25/19).

As a member of the staff of the *Civil and Military Gazette*, and later of *The Pioneer* and its supplement *Week's News*, Kipling would have contributed fillers and paragraphs as well as articles to these papers; and before he acquired a reputation, he wrote under any number of pseudonyms (some identified) as well as without any signature at all. Kipling later collected a few of his early articles or poems but, beyond these, he excluded all of these writings from his collected works.

Reliable sources of information for attributing articles in the Indian press to Kipling's pen have, over the years, been discovered. The first such source was the collection of clippings which Kipling sent from India during the 1880s to his old schoolmaster, W. C. Crofts, at Westward Ho! (known as the 'Crofts Collection'). The Collection was sold in the 1920s and the clippings are now scattered in various repositories; a great many can be found at Syracuse University and a few others at the Library of Congress (Carpenter Collection) and in the Berg Collection. For four such clippings which bear Kipling's revisions, see KpR 1506, 1545, 1995, 2200.

When the family archive, the Kipling Papers, was deposited at the University of Sussex in 1976, a major new source of Kipling's early journalism became available, namely, the four scrapbooks into which Kipling himself inserted clippings of his pieces from the Indian press dating from 1884–91 (known in the entries as 'Scrapbooks 1–4', described above).

From this new material — as well as from information in Kipling's 1885 diary (KpR 2286) preserved at Harvard and in some early letters also in the Kipling Papers at Sussex — Pinney was able to attribute 927 new pieces to Kipling.

These two editions by Rutherford and Pinney, dealing as they do with Kipling's early verse and journalism, to 1889, leave unexplored the huge territory of Kipling's post-1890 work.

Admiral Lloyd H. Chandler was probably the first to set out to list *all* of Kipling's works, canonical and otherwise, and investigate the cases for and against items attributed to him; he published his conclusions in the *Summary of the Work of Rudyard Kipling, Including Items Ascribed to Him* (New York, 1930). The voluminous mass of materials used in the compilation of the *Summary* fills over 200 notebooks and is now in the Library of Congress. Chandler's conclusions, many now known to have been incautious, have been accepted or rejected by the various Kipling bibliographers and scholars who have come after him — including Livingston, Harbord and Stewart. Kipling was not sympathetic to these attempts to retrieve his early works; in his introduction, Pinney quotes a letter Kipling wrote to Edmonia Hill in 1924: 'Well, a man does not like his boy-hood's work...being given to the public after nearly forty years.' Nonetheless, Kipling's relationships with both Chandler and Livingston were good ones and his own copy of the former's *Summary* containing his marginal annotations — some correcting misattributions — is now preserved at Sussex. In addition, Chandler and Livingston periodically sent lists of queries, addenda and corrigenda to Kipling, some of which he annotated; see KpR 2291 and 2302.

However unreliable the various bibliographies and guides might be as regards Kipling's non-canonical (or indeed his canonical) works — and the most authoritative and reliable to date is Stewart (1959) which in most respects supersedes its predecessors — they will retain some value so long as the territory surrounding the authorized canon remains an editorial *terra inexplorata*.

The eight-volume *Reader's Guide to Rudyard Kipling's Work* (Harbord), a privately printed labour of love which appeared from 1961 to 1972, attempted to discuss (and, often, in the case of uncollected or unpublished works, print) all of Kipling's writings, signed and unsigned, published and unpublished, collected and uncollected. Despite its drawbacks — it is itself a rare edition (only 100 copies were printed), its attributions are not always reliable, it is somewhat chaotically arranged and is, catastrophically, without an Index — it has been invaluable in the compilation of the present work. Accordingly, references are provided to it throughout the entries. Particularly helpful has been Verse Volume I which includes a listing of about 1,350 poems and is — for poems dating from 1890 onwards — the most complete guide to Kipling's non-canonical verse that exists.

The list of Kipling manuscripts below includes many potential additions to the canon. About eighty entries represent manuscripts of texts — about fifty of them being verse — which were not included in either the Sussex Edition or in Rutherford, but which have been published or printed elsewhere, sometimes even by Kipling himself. These texts await inclusion in a future edition of Kipling's collected verse and prose.

More than eighty other entries represent manuscripts of texts of which no publication (or often mention) has been traced in any of the Kipling scholarship. These include various kinds of items: rough or unfinished drafts of verses or stories which apparently never came to anything; impromptu verses, limericks, inscriptions, and *jeux d'esprit* dashed off in letters to friends, on scraps of paper, in books or on other printed matter; miscellaneous notes on various subjects; pieces known only through sale catalogue descriptions which correspond to no published Kipling work; as well as a few relatively finished pieces rejected for publication (if indeed they are unpublished) for unknown reasons. Some of these items may in time be rejected: they may be proved spurious, not written by Kipling at all; they may be shown to have been already published; or indeed they may be identified as being part of some longer published, possibly even collected work.

Despite the somewhat questionable nature, then, of all those entries, another five items have been actually designated as 'questionable attributions' and in each case, the reasons are explained; see KpR 9, 229, 445, 966, 1162.

A few other items have come to light over the years whose attribution to Kipling has been categorically rejected by scholars. Five of them are worth noting here: the lines '[Bay of Naples]' beginning 'Oh radiant Bay of Naples by the tourist much admired' (manuscript at Syracuse University; see Harbord, Verse No. 230 and correspondence at Sussex, KP 23/15); the lines beginning 'In a high-art study' written in a copy of Milton's poems at the Pierpont Morgan (see Harbord, Verse No. 773); the lines entitled '1905. A Xmas Carral' beginning 'My name is Nathan Appleton' and signed 'Rudyard Kippling [sic]' (manuscript at the Library of Congress, Manuscript Division, Richard Olney Collection); and the lines 'The Ploughman' beginning 'In the Market-place for the world to flout' and signed 'R. G. B.' (manuscript in the New York Public Library; see Harbord, Verse No. 806). The fifth — the limerick 'There was a young lady of Nassik' printed in Carrington and in Harbord (Verse No. 234) — was actually written by Kipling's father, John Lockwood Kipling, who inscribed it in his own annotated copy of Edward Lear's *A Book of Nonsense* (Sussex, KP 31/3); Kipling quoted it in a letter to L. C. Dunsterville of Lahore, 30 January 1886 (Sussex, KP 14/51).

The difficulties which beset any attempt to systematically organize Kipling's extant literary manuscripts, however, are not only canonical. Other problems arise from the complexity of Kipling's bibliography, 'the thickest jungle in all of modern English literature', as Thomas Pinney has put it (*ELT*, 1986). Some 4,000 separate printings of Kipling's works exist, published on five of the six continents of the globe.

As already mentioned, the best guide through the jungle at present is Stewart. Information about first publications throughout the entries is almost always taken from that bibliography.

To illustrate some of the bibliographical difficulties: a short story of Kipling's might appear in numerous *authorized* forms from the time of its first publication in a periodical; it might thereafter be included in a volume of stories — a volume that itself may appear in numerous editions — as well as being included in the many collected editions of Kipling's works, from the Outward Bound Edition (begun in 1897) to the posthumous 35-volume Sussex Edition. Since Kipling may have had a hand in preparing any or all of the editions of a particular work, a manuscript source that survives of, for example, a short story, may have been prepared for any one of a large number of that story's incarnations which could conceivably span a period of up to forty years.

The bibliographical tangle surrounding Kipling's poems can be even more impenetrable. Kipling often used bits of his poems as epigraphs, or 'chapter headings' as he called them, to his stories or the chapters of his novels. Sometimes a 'chapter heading' remained appended to the story throughout its various editions and sometimes it was dropped in this or that edition. In addition, from about the turn of the century, Kipling began to publish collections of stories in which each story was accompanied by a poem. In this way, many of Kipling's poems have two separate bibliographical (and sometimes textual) identities: one as a discrete work usually included in one volume of collected verse or another; and another as an accompaniment to a particular story. Accordingly, many poems are included twice in the Sussex Edition, separately and with a story; in such cases, both references are provided but the titles and first lines quoted in the entries are taken from the poem's appearance as a separate item.

These complex relationships between poems and stories (Verse and Prose) have been accommodated throughout the entries by means of a great many cross-references. Even if, say, a manuscript of a 'chapter heading' is not listed separately in the Verse section — but rather included in the Prose section with the entry for the manuscript of the story which it heads — a cross-reference from the Verse section is provided.

Letters

Only a tiny number of the letters that Kipling wrote in his lifetime — which must have exceeded 10,000 — has been published. Thomas Pinney's multi-volume edition — the first two volumes of which are forthcoming — will be a landmark in Kipling studies. By providing a more detailed record of Kipling's life and work than has been previously available, the published letters should accelerate the serious textual study of Kipling that was begun with Rutherford's and Pinney's 1986 editions of the early verse and Indian journalism.

Letters from every period of Kipling's life survive, scattered in hundreds of public and private collections, though letters from his early years are relatively scarce. None of the letters, for example, that Kipling wrote to his parents from 1871–82, when he was in England as a boy, has survived. Kipling himself probably destroyed them when he acted as executor over the estates of both his mother and father who died in 1910 and 1911. His sister 'Trix' wrote to his daughter Elsie Bambridge in 1940 that, after their mother's death, Kipling was 'possessed' by a 'frenzy of burning any letters or papers connected with his youth'.

Kipling's letters to Carrie, his wife of forty-five years, are also, on the whole, non-existent and were very possibly destroyed by Carrie herself or, after her death, by her daughter. However, two series of descriptive letters to her, one written while Kipling was touring France in 1915, the other in 1917, do survive among the Kipling Papers at Sussex (KP 13/17–20).

In his letters, Kipling often dashed off impromptu lines of verse and sometimes quoted lines from his more considered poetry. He also, particularly as a young man, occasionally wrote letters completely in verse. Such letters as have been identified are listed in the entries, under the titles or first lines of the verses they include; some eighty of Kipling's letters are thereby listed.

Large collections of Kipling letters — numbering sometimes into the many hundreds — are preserved in quite a few repositories: the Kipling Papers at Sussex (over 2,000 letters, some transcripts of originals held elsewhere); Dalhousie University (over 800 letters); Syracuse University (c. 600 letters); the Library of Congress (c. 500 letters); Harvard (over 400 letters); Princeton (over 250 letters); Cornell University (c. 200 letters); the Bodleian Library (c. 150 letters); and the Berg Collection, Texas and the British Library (each with over 100 letters). Other collections worth noting are at Columbia University, the Pierpont Morgan Library, New York University, Duke University, the Norfolk Record Office and Yale.

Some of these repositories own series of Kipling letters to particular correspondents, sometimes spanning a great many years. Some of these series of letters are: to George and Elsie Bambridge, 1921–35 (c. 440) at Sussex (KP 12/1–12); to Howell Arthur Gwynne, 1903–36 (c. 300) at Dalhousie University; to his children, Elsie and John, 1906–15 (c. 223) at Sussex (KP 13/1–7) (selections pub. *'O Beloved Kids': Rudyard Kipling's Letters to His Children*, ed. Elliot L. Gilbert (London, 1983)); to Mr and Mrs Frank N. Doubleday and to Nelson and Florence Doubleday, 1895–1935 (c. 150) at Princeton University; to Lord and Lady Beaverbrook, 1910–18 (c. 125) at Harvard (bMS Eng 809.4); to C. R. L. Fletcher, 1907–32 (c. 66) at Sussex (KP 15/4); to Col and Mrs Henry Wemyss Feilden ('Colonel Sahib'), 1904–32 (c. 60) at Syracuse

University; to L. C. Dunsterville ('Stalky'), 1886–1935 (c. 55) at Sussex (KP 14/51); to R. D. Blumenfeld, 1906–19 (c. 55) at Sussex (KP 14/19); to Brander Matthews, 1893–1926 (c. 50) at Columbia University; to B. H. Walton, 1903–12 (c. 50) at the Library of Congress, Rare Book Division, Colt Collection; to Alfred Baldwin ('Uncle Alfred'), 1897–1930 (c. 50) at Dalhousie University; to Louisa (Mrs Alfred) Baldwin ('Aunt Louie'), 1892–1923 (c. 50) at Dalhousie University; to Charles Eliot Norton (c. 50) at Harvard (bMS Am 1088(4043–90)); to Henry Rider Haggard, 1891–1925 (c. 40) at Norfolk Record Office (pub. *Rudyard Kipling to Rider Haggard*, ed. Morton Cohen (London, 1965)); to Ripley Hitchcock, 1893–1904 (c. 40) at the Berg Collection; to Cormell Price, 1882–1910 (c. 36) at the Library of Congress, Rare Book Division, Colt Collection; to William Heinemann, 1892–1908 (c. 35) at Princeton University, Doubleday Collection; to Francis Warrington Dawson III, 1910–33 (c. 35) at Duke University; correspondence between Kipling and Lord Milner, 1900–33 at the Bodleian Library, MSS. Milner (and photocopies of 53 letters to Lady Milner, 1902–8, MSS. Violet Milner); to Charles Scribner & Sons, 1894–1932 (c. 30) at Princeton University, Archive of Charles Scribner's; to nieces and nephews (c. 30), 1925–34, privately owned (photocopies at Syracuse University); to Lt Col A. Sutherland Harris, 1904–34 (c. 30) at Syracuse University; to Mr and Mrs Stanley Baldwin, 1894–1924 (c. 30) at Dalhousie University; to members of the Baldwin family, [1872?]–1933 (c. 25) at Sussex, Baldwin Papers 2/18–22; to George Saintsbury, 1895–1932 (c. 25) at Sussex (KP 17/28); to Messrs Macmillan, 1890–1935 (c. 25) at the British Library (Add. MS 54940); to Dr James Conland, 1894–1903 (c. 20) at the Library of Congress, Rare Book Division, Carpenter Kipling Collection; to Edward William Bok, 1902–35 (c. 20) at Syracuse University; to W. E. Henley, 1890–1901 (c. 20) at the Pierpont Morgan Library, MA 1617; to Professor and Mme Frölich, 1909–13 (c. 20) at Dalhousie University; to Mr and Mrs Lockwood de Forest, 1891–1900 (c. 20) at Harvard (MS Eng 809.3); to Mr and Mrs Lockwood de Forest, 1892–1932 (c. 10) at McGill University; to Edith Macdonald ('Aunt Edie'), 1882–6 (c. 15) at the Library of Congress, Rare Book Division, Colt Collection and 1921–36 (c. 15) at Dalhousie University; to Edith Plowden, 1881–1933 (c. 15) at Sussex, Baldwin Papers 2/30; to Sidney Low, 1892–1927 (c. 15) at Dalhousie University; to Hamlin Garland, 1895–1923 (c. 15) at the University of Southern California, Los Angeles; and to Henry James, 1892–1915 (c. 15) at Harvard.

ABBREVIATIONS

For general abbreviations, see the list at the front of this volume.

AMK
: Alice Macdonald Kipling.

Ballard
: Ellis Ames Ballard, *Catalogue Intimate and Descriptive of My Kipling Collection* (privately printed, Philadelphia, 1935).

Barrack-Room Ballads (1892)
: Rudyard Kipling, *Barrack-Room Ballads and Other Verses* (London, 1892).

Berg Booklet
: For a description, see INTRODUCTION.

Carrington
: Charles Carrington, *Rudyard Kipling. His Life and Work* (London, 1955).

CK
: Carrie Kipling.

Departmental Ditties (1886)
: Rudyard Kipling, *Departmental Ditties and Other Verses* (Lahore, [1886]).

Departmental Ditties, 2nd ed (1886)
: Rudyard Kipling, *Departmental Ditties and Other Verses*, 2nd ed (Calcutta, 1886).

Departmental Ditties, 3rd ed (1888)
: Rudyard Kipling, *Departmental Ditties and Other Verses*, 3rd ed (Calcutta and London, 1888).

Departmental Ditties, 4th ed (1890)
: Rudyard Kipling, *Departmental Ditties and Other Verses*, 4th ed (Calcutta, London and Bombay, 1890).

Early Verse (1900)
: Rudyard Kipling, *Early Verse*, Outward Bound Edition, Vol. XVII (New York, 1900).

Grolier Catalogue
: *Catalogue of the Works of Rudyard Kipling Exhibited at the Grolier Club from February 2 to March 30, 1929* (New York, 1930).

Harbord
: *The Reader's Guide to Rudyard Kipling's Work*, Vol. I, ed. R. Lancelyn Green, Vols II–VII and Verse Vol. I, ed. R. E. Harbord (privately printed, 1961–72).

Inclusive Verse (1919)
: *Rudyard Kipling's Verse, Inclusive Edition 1885–1918*, 3 vols (London, 1919).

Inclusive Verse [1927]
: *Rudyard Kipling's Verse, Inclusive Edition 1885–1926* (London, [1927]).

Inclusive Verse [1933]
: *Rudyard Kipling's Verse, Inclusive Edition 1885–1932* (London, [1933]).

JLK
John Lockwood Kipling.
KJ
Kipling Journal.
KP
Kipling Papers (deposited by the National Trust at the University of Sussex).
Kipling Papers
The Kipling Papers, comp. John Burt (Brighton, 1979).
Limits and Renewals Proof
For this proof, see INTRODUCTION.
Livingston
Flora V. Livingston, *Bibliography of the Works of Rudyard Kipling* (New York, 1927) and its *Supplement* (Cambridge, MA, 1938).
Martindell
E. W. Martindell, *A Bibliography of the Works of Rudyard Kipling (1881–1923)*, 2nd ed (London, 1923).
MS Actions and Reactions
For a description, see INTRODUCTION.
MS Day's Work
For a description, see INTRODUCTION.
MS Debits and Credits
For a description, see INTRODUCTION.
MS Departmental Ditties
For a description, see INTRODUCTION.
MS Diversity of Creatures
For a description, see INTRODUCTION.
MS Essays and Stories
For a description, see INTRODUCTION.
MS Eyes of Asia
For a description, see INTRODUCTION.
MS Five Nations
For a description, see INTRODUCTION.
MS Jungle Books
For a description, see INTRODUCTION.
MS Just So Stories
For a description, see INTRODUCTION.
MS Non-Fiction
For a description, see INTRODUCTION.
MS Puck
For a description, see INTRODUCTION.
MS Rewards and Fairies
For a description, see INTRODUCTION.
MS Seven Seas
For a description, see INTRODUCTION.
MS Stalky
For a description, see INTRODUCTION.
MS Sundry Phansies
For a description, see INTRODUCTION.
MS Traffics and Discoveries
For a description, see INTRODUCTION.
MS Words, Wise and Otherwise
For a description, see INTRODUCTION.
MS Writings and Songs
For a description, see INTRODUCTION.
MS Years Between
For a description, see INTRODUCTION.
Pinney
Kipling's India: Uncollected Sketches 1884–88, ed. Thomas Pinney (London, 1986).
RK
Rudyard Kipling.
Rice
Howard C. Rice, '"Into the Hold of Remembrance": Notes on Kipling Material in the Doubleday Collection', *PULC*, 22 (1961), 105–17.
Rutherford
Early Verse by Rudyard Kipling 1879–1889, ed. Andrew Rutherford (Oxford, 1986).
Scrapbooks 1–9
For a description, see INTRODUCTION.
Songs from Books (1915)
Rudyard Kipling, *Songs from Books*, Bombay Edition, Vol. XXIII (London, 1915).
Stewart
James McG. Stewart, *Rudyard Kipling. A Bibliographical Catalogue*, ed. A. W. Yeats (Toronto, 1959).
Sussex
Rudyard Kipling, *The Sussex Edition of the Complete Works in Prose and Verse*, 35 vols (London, 1937–9).
Sussex Edition
See *Sussex*.
Sussex Notebooks 1–3
For a description, see INTRODUCTION.

ARRANGEMENT

Verse and Dramatic Works	KpR 1–1395
Prose	KpR 1396–2282
Works Edited by Kipling	KpR 2283–2285.5
Diaries and Notebooks	KpR 2286–2288
Marginalia in Printed Books and Manuscripts	KpR 2288.5–2309

Rudyard Kipling

VERSE AND DRAMATIC WORKS

'A stone's throw out on either hand', see KpR 177.

'A weed, one weed and only one had I'
First pub. Rutherford (1986), p. 222; not in Harbord.

KpR 1 In a letter to [Edith Macdonald], Lahore, 11 July [1884].

Typed transcript at Sussex, KP 11/10.

Library of Congress, Rare Book Division, Colt Collection.

About a Painting by Flo Gerrard, see KpR 502–3.

The Absent-Minded Beggar ('When you've shouted "Rule Brittania," when you've sung "God save the Queen"')
First pub. *Daily Mail*, 31 October 1899; collected *The Five Nations. The Seven Seas*, Bombay Edition, Vol. XXII (London, 1914); *Sussex*, XXXV, 209–11; Harbord, Verse No. 735.

KpR 2 Fair copy, revised, wanting stanza 3, title added later in pencil, one page, in MS Years Between.

British Library, Add. MS 44841, f. 123.

KpR 3 Fair copy, signed, one page.

Facsimile in *Bibby's Quarterly*, Christmas 1899, pp. 20–1 and Sotheby's sale catalogue, 23–4 March 1936 (property of J. Bibby & Sons Ltd., Liverpool), Lot 362.

Dalhousie University.

KpR 4 Corrected typescript, printer's copy for the first collected edition, one page, annotated 'To precede Service Songs in The Five Nations', now excised from KpR 365 which is annotated (p. 159) 'Here take The absent minded Beggar to precede Chant Pagan'.

Yale.

KpR 5 Musical MS, words in Kipling's hand, music in the hand of Sir Arthur Sullivan, 2 leaves; dated 6 November 1899.

First sung by John Coates, Alhambra Theatre, 13 November 1899 and pub. for the *Daily Mail* by Enoch & Sons, London, [1899].

Berg.

KpR 6 Corrected typescript, 2 leaves (rectos only).

Dalhousie University.

KpR 7 Corrected page proof for *Inclusive Verse* (1919), one page numbered 522, signed (initials), in KpR 537.

Princeton, Ex3814.9.1919.11.

'Accept this from your loving Pa —'
No publication traced; not in Harbord.

KpR 8 Four lines, accompanying a Christmas gift to Elsie Bambridge, 1933.

Sussex, KP 12/10.

Ad Amicum ('Sunt queis odores stant studio [?]')
Questionable attribution; no publication traced; not in Harbord.

KpR 9 Transcript in an unidentified hand (signed 'M. B. F. K.?) of a Latin ode in the style of Horace, probably by Kipling, headed '[This Ode is attributed by Mr Rudyard Kipling to Horace: but it was more probably composed by his [?].]', 20 lines, one page.

Kipling's English translation of this ode was published as a translation of Horace, Book V, Ode 3 (see KpR 1264–5).

Sussex, KP 24/5.

After O. W. the unutterable ('An ancient damsel of an ancient tale')
First printed (lines 1–3 only) in Sotheby's sale catalogue, 8 December 1983, Lot 110; no further publication traced; not in Harbord; unavailable to Rutherford (see p. 38).

KpR 10 Fair copy of an early sonnet, accompanied by pen-and-ink sketch, verse signed 'JRK', drawing signed with monogram 'JK', 2 leaves (rectos only) pasted to 2 leaves of an album, one of which is annotated by May Armitage 'Enclosed herewith an *original* sketch & Sonnct by Rudyard Kipling 1879. Westward Ho!'.

Facsimile in British Library, RP 2632.

Syracuse University.

After the Fever ('Let the worst come now, and I shall not fear')
First pub. Rutherford (1986), p. 146; not in Harbord.

KpR 11 Fair copy, in Sussex Notebook 1 (pp. 99, 102) (the two stanzas separated probably because RK turned over 2 leaves instead of one); [between poems dated 21 and 26 May 1882].

Sussex, KP 24/3.

After the Promise ('The day is most fair, the cheery wind')
First pub. (stanzas 1–3, 6, without title) in text of story '"The Finest Story in the World"' in *Contemporary Review*, July 1891; collected *Many Inventions* (London and New York, 1893); *Sussex*, V, 224; Harbord, Verse No. 499, as 'The day is most fair'; first pub. in full as a separate poem Rutherford (1986), pp. 138–9. See also KpR 1609.

KpR 12 Fair copy, in Sussex Notebook 1 (pp. 86–7); dated 29 March [1882].

Sussex, KP 24/3.

KpR 13 Fair copy, in Sussex Notebook 3 (first series, pp. 14–16); dated 29 March 1882.

Sussex, KP 24/1.

KpR 14 Transcript by JLK in Sussex Notebook 2 [pp. 37–8]; dated 30 March 1882.

Sussex, KP 24/2.

Akbar's Bridge ('Jelaludin Muhammad Akbar, Guardian of Mankind')
First pub. with story 'The Debt' in *Limits and Renewals* (London, 1932); collected separately *Inclusive Verse* [1933]; *Sussex*, XI, 209–12 and *Sussex*, XXXIV, 414–17; Harbord, Verse No. 1196.

KpR 15 Corrected page proof in Limits and Renewals Proof; date stamped 20 January 1932.

Syracuse University.

KpR 16 Corrected first page proof for the Sussex Edition, Vol. XI; date stamped 14 October 1932.

British Library, Add. MS 55862.

An Almanac of the Twelve Sports, see KpR 1313–14.

Alnaschar and the Oxen ('There's a pasture in a valley where the hanging woods divide')
First pub. with story 'The Bull That Thought' in *Debits and Credits* (London, 1926); collected separately *Inclusive Verse* [1927]; *Sussex*, X, 193–4 and *Sussex*, XXXIV, 381–2; Harbord, Verse No. 1127.

KpR 17 Corrected first page proof for *Humorous Tales* (London, 1931), pp. 155–7; date stamped 11 May 1931.

British Library, Add. MS 55847.

KpR 18 Corrected first page proof for the Sussex Edition, Vol. X; date stamped 30 December 1931.

British Library, Add. MS 55861.

The American Rebellion/After ('The snow lies thick on Valley Forge')
First pub. C. R. L. Fletcher and Rudyard Kipling, *A History of England* (Oxford and London, 1911), as 'After the War'; collected separately *Songs from Books* (1915); *Sussex*, XXXIV, 291–2; Harbord, Verse No. 988, as 'The American Rebellion II (After) *or* After the War *or* The Song of Valley Forge'.

KpR 19 Fair copy, here entitled 'After the Revolution', in MS Years Between, one page.

British Library, Add. MS 44841, f. 76.

Amour de Voyage ('And I was a man who could write you rhyme')
First pub. *Echoes* (Lahore, [1884]); *Sussex*, XXXV, 100; Rutherford, p. [173]; Harbord, Verse No. 102.

KpR 20 Fair copy, being No. 1 under the heading 'Les Amours de Voyage' and annotated 'S.S. Brindisi', in Sussex Notebook 1 (pp. 130–1); dated 'Sept 20th to October 20 [1882]'.

Sussex, KP 24/3.

KpR 21 Fair copy, here entitled 'Amours de Voyage' and beginning 'And I was a boy who could write you rhyme', one leaf (containing also KpR 724), sent from India to Mrs A. W. May (Georgina Craik), c. 1883.

This MS not mentioned Rutherford.

Bodleian, MS. Eng. poet. e. 43, f. 2.

Anchor Song ('Heh! Walk her round. Heave, ah, heave her short again!')
First pub. as 'Envoy' to *Many Inventions* (London and New York, 1893); reprinted as 'Anchor Song' in *The Seven Seas* (New York, 1896); *Sussex*, V, 489–91 and *Sussex*, XXXIII, 72–4; Harbord, Verse No. 599.

KpR 22 Fair copy, revised, here entitled 'L'Envoi.', in MS Years Between, annotated to go at end of the book'; watermarked 1890.

British Library, Add. MS 44841, f. 127.

KpR 23 Fair copy, signed, one page, here untitled.

Harvard, MS Eng 165, f. 12.

KpR 24 Fair copy, revised (hastily written), here entitled 'L'Envoi.', one page (including also KpR 631); annotated 'E. Y. from Rudyard Kipling S.S. Kinfauns Castle Jan. 30. 1900'.

Dalhousie University.

KpR 25 Fair copy, here untitled, in a letter to W. E. Henley, Brattleboro, 18–19 [January 1893?].

Pierpont Morgan, MA 1617.

KpR 26 Corrected first page proof for the Sussex Edition, Vol. V, here entitled 'Envoy'; date stamped 10 June 1931.

British Library, Add. MS 55856.

'And some are sulky, while some will plunge.', see KpR 177.

'And will you give me love for love'
First pub. Rutherford (1986), p. 458, as 'Verse Fragments and Limericks (f)'; not in Harbord.

KpR 27 Two 4-line stanzas (cancelled), on a leaf (containing also KpR 1345, 1906).

Library of Congress, Rare Book Division, Carpenter Kipling Collection, Pen and Brush Sketches, Item 6.

'Angutivaun Taina' ('Our gloves are stiff with the frozen blood')
First pub. as heading to story 'Quiquern' in *Pall Mall Gazette*, 24–5 October 1895; collected *The Second Jungle Book* (London and New York, 1895); collected separately in *Songs from Books* (London, 1913); *Sussex*, XII, 411–12 and *Sussex*, XXXIV, 199; Harbord, Verse No. 660.

KpR 28 Fair copy, in MS Jungle Books, here entitled 'Angutivun tina' and headed 'Verses for end of *Quiquern*. tale No 6.', one page (containing also KpR 1163).

British Library, Add. MS 45540, f. 105.

The Answer ('A rose, in tatters on the garden path')
First pub. as 'An Answer' in *Century Magazine*, November 1892; collected *Ballads and Barrack-Room Ballads* (New York and London, 1893) and *The Seven Seas* (London, 1896); *Sussex*, XXXIII, 61; Harbord, Verse No. 530.

KpR 29 Fair copy, signed, one page.

Syracuse University.

KpR 30 Typescript, here entitled 'An Answer', one page, annotated in an unidentified hand '(Copyright, 1893, by Macmillan & Co)'.

Princeton, Archive of Charles Scribner's Sons, Miscellaneous Author's MSS and Galleys, Series Box 1, Folder 18.

The Anvil ('England's on the anvil — hear the hammers ring —')
First pub. as 'William the Conqueror's Work' in C. R. L. Fletcher and Rudyard Kipling, *A History of England* (Oxford and London, 1911); collected separately *Songs from Books* (1915); *Sussex*, XXXIV, 270; Harbord, Verse No. 975.

KpR 31 Extensively revised, here untitled, in MS Years Between.

British Library, Add. MS 44841, f. 64.

The Architect's Alphabet ('A was an architect: B were his Brains')
No publication traced; not in Harbord.

KpR 32 Revised, 26 lines, one page, together with 2 typescripts, one page each.

Sussex, KP 24/6.

Arithmetic on the Frontier ('A great and glorious thing it is')
First pub. *Departmental Ditties* (1886); *Sussex*, XXXII, 91–2; Harbord, Verse No. 216. See also KpR 280.

KpR 33 Fair copy, revised, seven 6-line stanzas, 2 leaves (rectos only).

Pierpont Morgan, MA 1822.

KpR 34 Fair copy, in MS Departmental Ditties (pp. 100–2).

Berg.

Army Headquarters ('Ahasuerus Jenkins of the "Operatic Own"')
First pub. *Civil and Military Gazette*, 9 February 1886; collected *Departmental Ditties* (1886); *Sussex*, XXXII, 5–6; Harbord, Verse No. 166.

KpR 35 Fair copy, including the 4 introductory lines, in MS Departmental Ditties (pp. 46–8), with a sketch.

Berg.

KpR 36 Correction on p. 9 of KpR 282.

Yale.

'As far as the East is set from the West'
First pub. Rutherford (1986), pp. 176–7; not in Harbord.

KpR 37 Fair copy, in Sussex Notebook 1 (2 pages, the last numbered 140); [probably November 1882].

Sussex, KP 24/3.

'As one who throws Earth's gold away in scorn'
First pub. (lines 1–2 only) in Owen Tweedy, 'Rudyard Kipling and Rottingdean/"The Elms" Exhibition', *KJ*, 18 (1951), 11; in full in Harbord (1969), Verse No. 134; Rutherford, pp. 265–6.

KpR 38 Fair copy, signed, one page; dated Simla, 2 June 1885.

Photocopy at Sussex, Baldwin Papers 2/2.

Owned (1986) Miss M. E. Macdonald (see Rutherford).

'As the Bell Clinks' ('As I left the Halls at Lumley, rose the vision of a comely')
First pub. *Civil and Military Gazette*, 22 April 1887; collected *Departmental Ditties*, 3rd ed (1888); *Sussex*, XXXII, 110–12; Harbord, Verse No. 256.

KpR 39 Revision and corrections on p. 79 of KpR 282.

Yale.

An Astrologer's Song ('To the Heavens above us')
First pub. with story 'A Doctor of Medicine' in *Rewards and Fairies* (London, 1910); collected separately *Songs from Books* (New York, 1912); *Sussex*, XV, 241–3 and *Sussex*, XXXIV, 111–13; Harbord, Verse No. 945.

KpR 40 Fair copy, here entitled 'The Astrologers Song', in MS Writings and Songs (pp. 29–32).

Berg.

KpR 41 Fair copy, revised, in MS Rewards and Fairies, annotated 'to precede A doctor of medicine', one page.

Cambridge University Library, ADD 6850, f. 91.

KpR 42 Correction and revision on pp. 132–3 of KpR 1112.

Yale.

KpR 43 Corrected first page proof for the Sussex Edition, Vol. XV; date stamped 18 September 1931.

British Library, Add. MS 55865.

At His Execution ('I am made all things to all men –')

First pub. with story 'The Manner of Men' in *Limits and Renewals* (London, 1932); collected separately *Inclusive Verse* [1933]; *Sussex*, XI, 239 and *Sussex*, XXXIV, 418; Harbord, Verse No. 1197.

KpR 44 Corrected first page proof for the Sussex Edition, Vol. XI; date stamped 14 October 1932.

British Library, Add. MS 55862.

'At morning: – "God gave me my right" said I'
No publication traced; not in Harbord.

KpR 44.5 Ten lines, on one page of music paper (containing also KpR 112).

Facsimile at Sussex, KP 27/18 (among recollections of the Kiplings by Edith Catlin Phelps).

Unlocated.

'At the back of Knightsbridge Barricks', see KpR 1902.

At the Bar, see the headnote to '"Cleared"'.

At the End of a Year ('This is the end of a Year/ Auntie dear')
First pub. Rutherford (1986), pp. 208–10; not in Harbord.

KpR 45 Four-page verse letter, one leaf, to [Edith Macdonald?], Lahore, [December 1883].

Typed transcript at Sussex, KP 24/67.

Library of Congress, Rare Book Division, Colt Collection.

'At the hole where he went in'
First pub. as heading to story 'Rikki-Tikki-Tavi' in *The Jungle Book* (London and New York, 1894); collected separately in *Songs from Books* (London, 1913); *Sussex*, XII, 267 and *Sussex*, XXXIV, 234, as a 'Chapter Heading'; Harbord, Verse No. 622.

KpR 46 Draft and fair copy, in MS Jungle Books, one page (on verso of KpR 821).

British Library, Add. MS 45540, f. 1v *rev*.

The Attainment [Escaped] ('Peace for a season — in the heart of me')
First pub. Rutherford (1986), p. 148; not in Harbord. A revised version of these lines used in 'Concerning a Jawáb' first pub. in *Civil and Military Gazette*, 6 August 1887.

KpR 47 Fair copy, here entitled 'Escaped!', in Sussex Notebook 1 (p. 102); dated 28 May [1882].

Sussex, KP 24/3.

KpR 48 Fair copy, here entitled 'The Attainment', being the last of 'Four Sonnets' (see also KpR 524, 922, 1281), in Sussex Notebook 3 (first series, p. 72); dated 28 May 1882.

Sussex, KP 24/1.

KpR 49 Fair copy, here entitled 'Escaped', on one page of a letter (containing also KpR 296, 468) to 'Mater' (Mrs Tavenor Perry), dated 28 May and postmarked 30 May 1882.

Huntington, HM 11882.

KpR 50 Transcript by AMK, here entitled 'Escaped', in Sussex Notebook 2 [p. 47].

Sussex, KP 24/2.

Au Revoir [A Valentine; A Song of St Valentine] ('What Song shall we sing to the Swallow')
First pub. *Civil and Military Gazette*, 12 August 1887, as 'Au Revoir'; Rutherford (1986), pp. 212–13; Harbord, Verse No. 82, misdescribed and listed as 'A Song of St Valentine'.

KpR 51 Fair copy, here entitled 'A Valentine', in Sussex Notebook 1 (p. 160).

Sussex, KP 24/3.

KpR 52 Fair copy of a valentine, here entitled 'A Song of St Valentine', on 2 pages of a vellum leaf, headed 'To A. E. W.', signed (initials), together with an envelope; dated Lahore, 14 February 1884.

Lines from this MS printed Anderson Galleries sale catalogue, 17 March 1915 (G. M. Williamson Sale), p. 81; Louis Cornell, *Kipling in India* (London & New York, 1966), p. 63; and Harbord, Verse No. 82.

Huntington, HM 11884.

Auchinleck's Ride, see KpR 184, 187.

'Aurettes and Lees', see KpR 1465.

An Auto-da-Fé ('And did you love me then so much')
First pub. Rutherford (1986), pp. 79–80; Harbord, Verse No. 43.

KpR 53 Fair copy, in Sussex Notebook 3 (first series, pp. 24–6); dated 3 November 1881.

Sussex, KP 24/1.

KpR 54 Fair copy, in MS Sundry Phansies.

Berg.

Ave Imperatrix! ('From every quarter of your land')
First pub. (5 stanzas) in *United Services College Chronicle*, 20 March 1882; 6-stanza version first pub. (without original stanza one) in text of story 'An English School' in *Youth's Companion*, 19 October 1893; the story as collected in *Land and Sea Tales* (London, 1923) included five stanzas (without original stanza one and stanza 5 of 1893 version); this 1923 version in *Sussex*, XVI, 214 in text of story 'An English School' and beginning 'One school of many, made to make' and listed Harbord, Verse No. 591 as 'One School of Many'; first pub. in full (7 stanzas) in *Early Verse* (1900); *Sussex*, XXXV, 55–6; Harbord, Verse No. 36. For a corrected proof of the first publication, see KpR 2285.5; a clipping of the first publication is inserted in Sussex Notebook 2 [p. 25].

KpR 55 Corrected typescript used for preparing *Departmental Ditties and Barrack-Room Ballads*, Bombay Edition, Vol. XXI (London, 1914), annotated 'To precede prelude to Departmental Ditties on separate page', inserted in KpR 282.

Yale.

KpR 56 Slightly corrected first page proof for Sussex Edition, Vol. XVI (in text of KpR 1587); date stamped 14 December 1931.

British Library, Add. MS 55866.

Azrael's Count ('Lo! the Wild Cow of the Desert, her yeanling [sic] estrayed from her —')
First pub. with story 'Uncovenanted Mercies' in *Limits and Renewals* (London, 1932); collected separately *Inclusive Verse* [1933]; *Sussex*, XI, 383–4 and *Sussex*, XXXIV, 430–1; Harbord, Verse No. 1198.

KpR 57 Corrected page proof in Limits and Renewals Proof; date stamped 25 January 1932.

Syracuse University.

KpR 58 Corrected first page proof for the Sussex Edition, Vol. XI; date stamped 14 October 1932.

British Library, Add. MS 55862.

B. E. L. ('There were five liars bold')
First pub. in 'A Mystery Poem', *KJ*, 11 (1944), 9–11; reprinted Harbord, Verse No. 670, as 'B. E. L. *or* S-S. Lahn *or* A Mystery Poem'.

KpR 59 Fair copy, three 4-line stanzas, signed, on a small card, subtitled S.S. Lahn, 8 September 1896.

Facsimile in *KJ*, 11 (1944), 9.

Yale.

'Back to the Army Again' ('I'm 'ere in a ticky ulster an' a broken billycock 'at')
First pub. *Pall Mall Magazine*, August 1894; collected *The Seven Seas* (New York, 1896); *Sussex*, XXXIII, 127–30; Harbord, Verse No. 609.

KpR 60 Fair copy, revised, here beginning 'I'm 'ere in a lousy ulster...' (as in first pub.), one page (cut up by typesetters into three portions).

Columbia University, Engel Collection.

'Badalia Jane McCann', see KpR 2018.

The Ballad of Ahmed Shah ('This is the ballad of Ahmed Shah')
First pub. (33 lines) in an abstract of a paper by E. W. Martindell presented 24 April 1928, 'Off the Beaten Track with Kipling', *KJ*, July 1928, pp. 14–15; facsimile of lines 1–19 and last 16 lines in Ballard (1935), p. 24; in full in Harbord (1969), Verse No. 217; Rutherford, pp. 353–6.

KpR 61 Fair copy, slightly revised, signed, annotated 'Written out for "Bobby" Pringle originally appeared in the I[ndian] P[lanter's] G[azette] about 1886–7–8 <or a> I've forgotten exact date.', 2 leaves (rectos only), 94 lines; watermarked 1895.

Library of Congress, Rare Book Division, Colt Collection.

A Ballad of Bitterness ('How shall he sing of Christmas fun')
First printed (stanzas 1–4 and 13–16 in facsimile and 3 other stanzas printed) in Anderson Galleries sale catalogue, 17–18 October 1921, pp. 33–[35]; first pub. Rutherford (1986), pp. 205–8; Harbord, Verse No. 77A.

KpR 62 Fair copy, 4 pages of a small folded card with a gold border annotated at top 'Dedicated (without permission) to my Mater. December 1883.' and signed 'Boy'.

Syracuse University.

The Ballad of Boh Da Thone ('Boh Da Thone was a warrior bold:')
First pub. *Week's News*, 1 September 1888; collected *Barrack-Room Ballads* (1892); *Sussex*, XXXII, 261–71; Harbord, Verse No. 331.

KpR 62.5 Corrected page proof for *Barrack-Room Ballads* (1892).

British Library, Loan 97 (deposited by John Aris, 1989).

The Ballad of East and West ('Kamal is out with twenty men to raise the Border-side')
First pub. *The Pioneer*, 2 December 1889 and *Macmillan's Magazine*, December 1889; collected *Barrack-Room Ballads* (1892); *Sussex*, XXXII, 231; Harbord, Verse No. 384.

KpR 63 Clipping of *Macmillan's Magazine* containing one revision, corrections and the addition of 8 lines (including the 4 introductory lines '*Oh East is East...*'), in Scrapbook 4 (p. 174).

Sussex, KP 28/4.

KpR 63.5 Corrected page proof for *Barrack-Room Ballads* (1892); date stamped 12 and 17 February 1892.

British Library, Loan 97 (deposited by John Aris, 1989).

The Ballad of Fisher's Boarding-House ("Twas Fultah Fisher's boarding-house')
First pub. *Week's News*, 3 March 1888; collected *Departmental Ditties*, 4th ed (1890); *Sussex*, XXXII, 83–6; Harbord, Verse No. 297. For notes about this poem in an early diary, see KpR 2287.

KpR 64 Fair copy, revised, including the 6 introductory lines, in MS Departmental Ditties (pp. 62–8).

Berg.

The Ballad of Minepit Shaw ('About the time that taverns shut')
First pub. with story 'The Tree of Justice' in *Rewards and Fairies* (London, 1910); collected separately *Songs from Books* (New York, 1912); *Sussex*, XV, 297–9 and *Sussex*, XXXIV, 188–90; Harbord, Verse No. 946.

KpR 65 Fair copy, revised, here untitled, in MS Rewards and Fairies, annotated in pencil 'To precede Cold Iron'.

Cambridge University Library, ADD 6850, f. 107.

KpR 66 Revision and correction on p. 223 of KpR 1112.

Yale.

KpR 67 Slightly corrected first page proof for the Sussex Edition, Vol. XV; date stamped 18 September 1931.

British Library, Add. MS 55865.

The Ballad of the *Bolivar* ('We put out from Sunderland loaded down with rails')
First pub. *St James's Gazette*, 29 January 1892; collected *Barrack-Room Ballads* (1892); *Sussex*, XXXII, 284–6; Harbord, Verse No. 520.

KpR 68 Fair copy, revised, signed, 3 leaves (rectos only) containing directions to a printer.

Yale.

KpR 69 Fair copy, revised, of stanzas 1–3 and last two lines only, in a letter to W. E. Henley, [1891?].

Pierpont Morgan, MA 1617.

KpR 69.5 Corrected page proof for *Barrack-Room Ballads* (1892).

British Library, Loan 97 (deposited by John Aris, 1989).

The Ballad of the *Clampherdown* ('It was our warship *Clampherdown*')
First pub. *St James's Gazette*, 25 March 1890; collected *Barrack-Room Ballads* (1892); *Sussex*, XXXII, 280–83; Harbord, Verse No. 425.

KpR 69.7 Corrected page proof for *Barrack-Room Ballads* (1892).

British Library, Loan 97 (deposited by John Aris, 1989).

The Ballad of the King's Daughter ('"If my Love come to me over the water')
First pub. *Echoes* (Lahore, [1884]); *Sussex*, XXXV, 107–8; Rutherford, pp. 68–9; Harbord, Verse No. 68.

KpR 70 Fair copy, in Sussex Notebook 3 (first series pp. 31–4); dated 9 August 1881.

Sussex, KP 24/1.

KpR 71 Fair copy, in MS Sundry Phansies.

Berg.

The Ballad of the King's Jest ('When spring-time flushes the desert grass')
First pub. *New York Tribune*, 9 February 1890 and *Macmillan's Magazine*, February 1890; lines 1–16 used as heading to Chapter 10 of J. L. Kipling, *Beast and Man in India* (London and New York, 1891); lines 110–13 used as heading to Chapter 16 of Rudyard Kipling and Wolcott Balestier, *The Naulahka* (London, 1892), reprinted *Sussex*, XIX, 209; collected separately *Barrack-Room Ballads* (1892); lines 23–5 used as heading to Chapter 8 in serial publication only (*Cassell's Magazine*, January–November 1901) of *Kim*; *Sussex*, XXXII, 249–53; Harbord, Verse No. 405.

KpR 72 Draft of opening lines, here untitled, one page.

Sussex, KP 24/7.

KpR 73 Three pages of draft lines (two very rough, another headed '2').

Sussex, KP 24/62.

KpR 74 Fair copy of the last 10 lines (beginning at line 110 'Heart of my heart, is it meet or wise'), in MS Essays and Stories (f. [lv]).

Berg.

KpR 74.5 Corrected page proof for *Barrack-Room Ballads* (1892).

British Library, Loan 97 (deposited by John Aris, 1989).

The Ballad of the King's Mercy ('Before the old Peshawur Gate, where Kurd and Kafir meet')
First pub. *Macmillan's Magazine*, November 1889 and *New York Tribune*, 10 November 1889; collected *Barrack-Room Ballads* (1892); *Sussex*, XXXII, 243–8; Harbord, Verse No. 382.

KpR 75 Draft, 9 pages.

Sussex, KP 24/8.

KpR 76 Galley proof containing one correction, for publication in *Macmillan's Magazine*; date stamped 15 October 1889.

Library of Congress, Rare Book Division, Carpenter Kipling Collection.

KpR 77 Revised clipping of the first publication, in Scrapbook 4 (p. 175).

Sussex, KP 28/4.

KpR 77.5 Corrected page proof for *Barrack-Room Ballads* (1892); date stamped 17 February 1892.

British Library, Loan 97 (deposited by John Aris, 1989).

The Ballad of the Ski ('Two strips of bright & varnished board')
First pub. *Morning Post*, 18 June 1926; reprinted Harbord, Verse No. 937.

KpR 78 Two 8-line stanzas, here entitled 'The Ballad of the Telemark' and beginning 'Two strips of brown, well-varnished board'; in a letter (containing also KpR 1175) to his son John, Engelberg, 3 February [1910].

This MS printed in *'O Beloved Kids'*, ed. Elliot L. Gilbert (London, 1983), p. 100.

Sussex, KP 13/4.

KpR 79 Fair copy of stanza 1, inscribed on title page of a copy of the Tauchnitz edition of *The Seven Seas* (Leipzig, 1897), signed '*Ballad of the Ski*/RK.' and dated Engelberg, February 1910.

Facsimile in *Grolier Catalogue*, plate XVIII.

Berg.

A Ballade of Bad Entertainment [A Ballade of Dak Bungalows] ('A wanderer from East to West')
First pub. *Week's News*, 11 February 1888, as 'A Ballade of Dak Bungalows'; collected *Early Verse* (1900); *Sussex*, XXXII, 113–14; Rutherford, pp. 394–5; Harbord, Verse No. 294.

KpR 80 Fair copy, here entitled 'A Ballad of Dak Bungalows', illustrated by RK, signed (initials) and dated February 1889.

Facsimile in American Art Association sale catalogue, 11–12 November 1937, Lot 257; a photograph (mistakenly described as the original in Rutherford) of this MS is at Harvard, *42M–820PF.

Berg.

KpR 81 Corrected clipping of the first publication, in Scrapbook 4 [p. 41], annotated 'Miss A. Please type this RK'.

Sussex, KP 28/4.

A Ballade of Burial ('If down here I chance to die')
First pub. *Departmental Ditties*, 2nd ed (1886); *Sussex*, XXXII, 61–2; Harbord, Verse No. 218.

KpR 82 Fair copy, in MS Departmental Ditties (pp. 56–8).

Berg.

KpR 83 Fair copy, revised, one page, annotated 'see index for place in 2nd edition', as sent to the printer for the first publication.

Pierpont Morgan, MA 979.

KpR 84 Corrections on pp. 48–9 of KpR 282.

Yale.

A Ballade of Indian Tea ('I wander East, I wander West')
First pub. Rutherford (1986), pp. 464–6; Harbord, Verse No. 379.

KpR 85 Typescript of three 8-line stanzas and 8-line 'L'Envoi', in a letter (original lost) to Julia Taylor, 22 September 1889.

Library of Congress, Rare Book Division, Carpenter Kipling Collection.

A Ballade of Jakko Hill ('One moment bid the horses wait')
First pub. *Departmental Ditties*, 2nd ed (1886); *Sussex*, XXXII, 104–5; Harbord, Verse No. 220.

KpR 86 Fair copy, revised, one page, as sent to the printer for the first publication.

Pierpont Morgan, MA 979.

KpR 87 Correction on p. 75 of KpR 282.

Yale.

A Ballade of Photographs ('Behold, O Fortune-favoured one')
These verses were written for an album of photographs which the Hills were preparing as a raffle prize at a charity bazaar held at Simla, February 1889; first pub. *The Wave*, June 1922; reprinted in Harbord, Verse No. 392; Rutherford, pp. 450–1.

KpR 88 Revised in line 2, one page, inserted in the album of photographs (with RK's captions and containing KpR 1315) which the Hills kept for themselves; c. January 1889.

A photograph of this MS is at Cornell University; this album was bought by Carpenter from Edmonia Hill.

Library of Congress, Rare Book Division, Carpenter Kipling Collection.

KpR 89 Fair copy, the final version, in the album of photographs (containing RK's captions) which Edmonia Hill offered to the charity bazaar; c. January 1889.

Facsimile in E. W. Martindell, *Fragmenta Condita* (privately printed, 1922); a photograph of the MS is at Cornell University. This album was won at the raffle by a Colonel Lang and later sold at auction.

Library of Congress, Rare Book Division, Carpenter Kipling Collection.

'Banquet Night' ('"Once in so often," King Solomon said')
First pub. with story '"In the Interests of the Brethren"' in *Debits and Credits* (London, 1926); collected separately *Inclusive Verse* [1927]; *Sussex*, X, 53–4 and *Sussex*, XXXIV, 365–6; Harbord, Verse No. 1128.

KpR 90 Corrected first page proof for the Sussex Edition, Vol. X; date stamped 30 December 1931.

British Library, Add. MS 55861.

Barrack Room Ballad, see KpR 2117–18.

Barrack-Room Ballads
This volume of verse was first pub. London, 1892; *Sussex*, XXXII.

KpR 91 Contents list (including 18 titles), headed 'Barrack-Room Ballads/When 'omer smote &c.', on page 4 of a letter to Ripley Hitchcock, Vermont, 1 August 1896.

Berg.

The Baths of Biddlestone ('It fell about the eventide: When a' the Selbys dine')
No publication traced; not in Harbord.

KpR 92 Fair copy, 52 lines, one page.

Syracuse University.

'Beat off in our last fight were we?', see KpR 184.

'Because I sought it far from men', see KpR 184, 186–7.

The Bee Boy's Song ('A Maiden in her glory')
First pub. with story 'Dymchurch Flit' in *Puck of Pook's Hill* (London, 1906); collected separately *Songs from Books* (New York, 1912); *Sussex*, XIV, 221 and *Sussex*, XXXIV, 118; Harbord, Verse No. 899.

KpR 93 Fair copy, revised, including the introductory heading here beginning 'Bees! Bees! Tend to your bees!', annotated 'To precede Dymchurch Flit', in MS Puck.

Bodleian, MS. Eng. misc. c. 127, f. 90.

KpR 94 Slightly corrected first page proof for the Sussex Edition, Vol. XIV; date stamped 2 July 1931.

British Library, Add. MS 55864.

The Bees and the Flies ('A farmer of the Augustan Age')
First pub. with story 'The Mother Hive' in *Actions and Reactions* (London, 1909); collected separately *Songs from Books* (New York, 1912); *Sussex*, VIII, 103–4 and *Sussex*, XXXIV, 59–60; Harbord, Verse No. 927.

KpR 95 In MS Actions and Reactions (f. 27), here untitled.

University of St Andrews, MS PR4854.A4.

KpR 96 Corrected first page proof for the Sussex Edition, Vol. VIII; date stamped 28 November 1931.

British Library, Add. MS 55859.

'Before my Spring I garnered Autumn's gain', see KpR 176.

'Before you start — in pastures new to please —'
No publication traced; not in Harbord.

KpR 97 Draft of c. 4 lines, on a blank page of Scrapbook 1 (p. 183 *rev.*).

Sussex, KP 28/1.

The Beginnings ('It was not part of their blood')
First pub. with story 'Mary Postgate' in *A Diversity of Creatures* (London, 1917); collected separately *Inclusive Verse* (1919); *Sussex*, IX, [443] and *Sussex*, XXXIV, 339; Harbord, Verse No. 1037.

KpR 98 Fair copy, revised, here untitled, in MS Diversity of Creatures (f. 156), annotated 'To precede Mary Postgate'.

University of Edinburgh, Dk. 2. 8.

KpR 99 Slightly corrected first page proof for the Sussex Edition, Vol. IX; date stamped 28 April 1932.

British Library, Add. MS 55860.

The Bell Buoy ('They christened my brother of old —')
First pub. *McClure's Magazine*, February 1897; collected *The Five Nations* (London, 1903); *Sussex*, XXXIII, 185–7; Harbord, Verse No. 695.

KpR 100 In MS Seven Seas (ff. 62–75) including: (1) fair copy, revised, annotated 'proof urgent to R Kipling Rock House Maidencombe St Marychurch', signed (ff. 62–3, rectos only); (2) fair copy of last stanza, on a scrap (f. 64); (3) drafts of last stanza (f. 66); (4) two unfinished fair copies, one watermarked 1896 (ff. 67–8, rectos only); (5) fair copy, revised, watermarked 1896 (ff. 69–70, rectos only); (6) draft lines, watermarked 1896 (f. 71); (7) untitled fair copy, revised, early version (f. 72); (8) unfinished fair copies (early versions), one leaf watermarked 1894 (ff. 73–5, rectos only).

Magdalene College, Cambridge.

KpR 101 Corrections on pp. 4–6 of KpR 365.

Yale.

The Bells and Queen Victoria ('Here is more gain than Gloriana guessed —')
First pub. as 'The Bells and the Queen' in C. R. L. Fletcher and Rudyard Kipling, *A History of England* (Oxford and London, 1911); collected separately *Songs from Books* (1915); *Sussex*, XXXIV, 299–300; Harbord, Verse No. 992.

KpR 102 Fair copy, in MS Years Between, 2 separate pages, wanting the introductory heading, the first page entitled 'Victoria', the second headed 'add to The Bells and the Queen'.

British Library, Add. MS 44841, ff. 78–9 (rectos only).

Belts ('There was a row in Silver Street that's near to Dublin Quay')
Stanza 3 first pub. as stanza 4 of 'The Way Av Ut' in *The Pioneer*, 8 October 1888; reprinted Harbord, Verse No. 335; first pub. in full *Scots Observer*, 26 July 1890; collected *Barrack-Room Ballads* (1892); *Sussex*, XXXII, 204–6; Harbord, Verse No. 467.

KpR 102.5 Corrected page proof for *Barrack-Room Ballads* (1892); date stamped 12 February 1892.

British Library, Loan 97 (deposited by John Aris, 1989).

The Benefactors ('It is not learning, grace nor gear')
First pub. (heading only) as heading to story 'The Edge of the Evening' in *Metropolitan Magazine*, December 1913; collected in *A Diversity of Creatures* (London, 1917); reprinted *Sussex*, IX, 273; in full in *The Years Between* (London, [1919]); *Sussex*, XXXIII, 414–15; Harbord, Verse No. 1002.

KpR 103 Revised, an early version, in MS Years Between, wanting the introductory heading and stanzas 8–9, here untitled and beginning 'It is not grace, nor gold, nor gear', annotated 'type please' and 'to precede The Benefactors'.

British Library, Add. MS 44841, f. 41.

Beoni Bar, see KpR 184.

The Betrothed ('Open the old cigar-box, get me a Cuba stout')
First pub. *The Pioneer* and *Pioneer Mail*, 21 November 1888, as 'The Meditation of William Kirkland'; collected *Departmental Ditties*, 4th ed (1890); *Sussex*, XXXII, 100–3 with heading beginning '"You must choose between me and your cigar." —'); Harbord, Verse No. 339B.

KpR 104 Fair copy, in MS Departmental Ditties (pp. 80–5), illustrated by RK.

Berg.

KpR 105 Revision and corrections on pp. 71–3 of KpR 282.

Yale.

'Between the gum-pot and the shears'
First printed as a broadside (apparently 'hand set by Kipling in 1884') entitled *'Echoes' by Two Writers. / [A. M. D.-D.* R. K., Oct. 1884.]; reprinted Harbord, Verse No. 93A; Rutherford, p. 255, as 'Inscriptions in Presentation Copies of *Echoes* (h)'.

KpR 106 Copy (probably unique) of the broadside, corrected by RK in line 8.

According to Rutherford, the broadside was printed to accompany a presentation copy to A. Macdonald (assistant editor of *The Pioneer*) of *Echoes* (Lahore, [1884]).

Dalhousie University.

'Between the gum-pot and the shears'
First pub. Edmonia Hill, 'The Young Kipling', *Atlantic Monthly*, April 1936; reprinted Harbord, Verse No. 93B (a few lines from this poem is mistakenly entered as a separate poem 'To Mrs Hill' in Harbord, Verse No. 296A); Rutherford, pp. 395–6, as 'Inscription in Copy of *Plain Tales from the Hills* presented to Mrs Hill'.

KpR 107 Inscription in a presentation copy to Edmonia Hill of *Plain Tales from the Hills* (Calcutta and London, 1888), dated March 1888.

A typed transcript of this inscription and an accompanying note by Edmonia Hill are at Cornell University.

Unlocated.

Big Barn Stories, see KpR 179, 180, 183.

Big Steamers ('"Oh, where are you going to, all you Big Steamers')
First pub. C. R. L. Fletcher and Rudyard Kipling, *A History of England* (Oxford and London, 1911); collected separately *Songs from Books* (1915); *Sussex*, XXXIV, 295–6; Harbord, Verse No. 990.

KpR 108 Fair copy, revised, in MS Years Between, one page, annotated 'type'.

British Library, Add. MS 44841, f. 80.

'Bill 'Awkins' ('"'As anybody seen Bill 'Awkins?"')
First pub. *The Seven Seas* (New York, 1896); *Sussex*, XXXIII, 151; Harbord, Verse No. 683.

KpR 109 Fair copy, revised, in MS Years Between, one page; watermarked 1894.

British Library, Add. MS 44841, f. 90.

'Birds of Prey' ('March! The mind is cakin' good about our trousies.')
First pub. *Pall Mall Gazette*, 30 May 1895; collected *The Seven Seas* (New York, 1896); *Sussex, XXXIII*, 131–2; Harbord, Verse No. 637.

KpR 110 In MS Seven Seas, including a fair copy, revised, of stanzas 1–3 (f. 104) and draft lines (f. 105).

Magdalene College, Cambridge.

The Birthright ('We have such wealth as Rome at her most pride')
First pub. with story 'The Propogation of Knowledge' in *Debits and Credits* (London, 1926); *Sussex, XVII (Stalky & Co.)*, 317 and *Sussex*, XXXIV, 385; Harbord, Verse No. 1129.

KpR 111 Corrected first page proof for the Sussex Edition, Vol. XVII; date stamped 27 March 1931.

British Library, Add. MS 55867.

Bitter Waters, see KpR 176.

Blackbeard, see KpR 184.

The Blind Bug, see KpR 1255.

Blue Roses ('Roses red and roses white')
First pub. (without stanza 3) in *Civil and Military Gazette*, 13 August 1887, as 'Misunderstood'; reprinted as heading to Chapter 7, ascribed 'Blue Roses', of *The Light that Failed* (London, 1890); reprinted *Sussex*, XVIII, 89; first pub. in full in *The Book of Beauty*, ed. Mrs F. Harcourt Williamson (London, 1902); collected *Songs from Books* (New York, 1912); *Sussex*, XXXIV, 155; Harbord, Verse No. 275.

KpR 112 Fair copy, on one page of music paper (containing also KpR 44.5).

Facsimile at Sussex, KP 27/18 (among recollections of the Kiplings by Edith Catlin Phelps).

Unlocated.

KpR 113 Fair copy of stanza 1, in MS Words, Wise and Otherwise [p. 5].

Berg.

KpR 114 One revision, in page proofs for Edition de Luxe of *The Light that Failed* (see KpR 1836).

Pierpont Morgan, 37076.

KpR 115 Corrections on p. 182 of KpR 1112.

Yale.

KpR 116 Correction and one revision, in first page proof of Sussex Edition of *The Light that Failed* (see KpR 1837); date stamped 20 November 1931.

British Library, Add. MS 55868.

'Bobs' ('There's a little red-faced man')
First pub. *Pall Mall Magazine*, December 1893; collected *The Five Nations. The Seven Seas*, Bombay Edition, Vol. XXII (London, 1914); *Sussex*, XXXV, 197–9; Harbord, Verse No. 592.

KpR 117 Fair copy, one revision, one page (cut into 3 portions by the typesetter).

Columbia University, Engel Collection.

KpR 118 Corrected typescript, annotated 'To precede Back to the Army again in the 7 Seas', one page, used for Bombay Edition.

Facsimile of lines 1–24 in *Grolier Catalogue*, plate XV.

Library of Congress, Rare Book Division, Colt Collection.

Boots ('We're foot — slog — slog — slog — sloggin' over Africa')
First pub. *The Five Nations* (London, 1903); *Sussex*, XXXIII, 321–2; Harbord, Verse No. 808.

KpR 119 In MS Five Nations.

National Library of Australia, MS 94.

A Boy Scout's Patrol Song ('These are *our* regulations —')
First pub. *Standard*, 16 September 1909, as 'A Patrol Song'; collected *Inclusive Verse* (1919); *Sussex*, XXXV, 231–2; Harbord, Verse No. 925.

KpR 120 Revised, here entitled 'A Patrol Song' and beginning 'Please understand our regulations!', in MS Years Between.

British Library, Add. MS 44841, f. 115.

Bridge-Guard in the Karoo ('Sudden the desert changes')
First pub. *The Times*, 5 June 1901; collected *The Five Nations* (London, 1903); *Sussex*, XXXIII, 265–7; Harbord, Verse No. 763.

KpR 121 Draft, here untitled, containing versions of stanzas 1–11 only, cancelled, on the verso of last page of KpR 1725, in MS Just So Stories; watermarked 1896.

British Library, Add. MS 59840, f. 30v.

KpR 122 In MS Five Nations.

National Library of Australia, MS 94.

KpR 123 Correction on p. 115 of KpR 365.

Yale.

Brighton Beach ('A flash in your eye for a minute —')
First pub. Rutherford (1986), pp. 109–10; Harbord, Verse No. 44.

KpR 124 Fair copy, subtitled '(After Browning)', in MS Sundry Phansies.

Berg.

A British-Roman Song ('My father's father saw it not')
First pub. with story 'A Centurion of the Thirtieth' in *Puck of Pook's Hill* (London, 1906); collected separately *Songs from Books* (New York, 1912); *Sussex*, XIV, 141 and *Sussex*, XXXIV, 65; Harbord, Verse No. 894.

KpR 125 Revised, here untitled, including a cancelled stanza, in MS Puck.

Bodleian, MS. Eng. misc. c. 127, f. 54.

KpR 126 Corrected first page proof for the Sussex Edition, Vol. XIV; date stamped 2 July 1931.

British Library, Add. MS 55864.

The Broken Men ('For things we never mention')
First pub. *The Five Nations* (London, 1903); *Sussex*, XXXIII, 205–7; Harbord, Verse No. 809.

KpR 127 In MS Five Nations.

National Library of Australia, MS 94.

Brookland Road ('I was very well pleased with what I knowed')

First pub. with story 'Marklake Witches' in *Rewards and Fairies* (London, 1910); collected separately *Songs from Books* (New York, 1912); *Sussex*, XV, 111–12 and *Sussex*, XXXIV, 9–10; Harbord, Verse No. 947.

KpR 128 Fair copy, revised in MS Rewards and Fairies, here entitled 'The Fairy girl', one page.

Cambridge University Library, ADD 6850, f. 44.

KpR 129 Corrected first page proof for the Sussex Edition, Vol. XV; date stamped 18 September 1931.

British Library, Add. MS 55865.

'Brown Bess' ('In the days of lace-ruffles, perukes and brocade')
First pub. C. R. L. Fletcher and Rudyard Kipling, *A History of England* (Oxford and London, 1911); collected separately *Songs from Books* (1915); *Sussex*, XXXIV, 289–90; Harbord, Verse No. 986.

KpR 130 Fair copy, revised, in MS Years Between, with an explanatory note to Fletcher at the top.

British Library, Add. MS 44841, f. 75.

KpR 131 Typed transcript of a letter to Col H. W. Feilden containing lines 3–4, a version of 33–4 and the last stanza; letter dated Engelberg, 13 January 1911.

Sussex, KP 15/2.

Buddha at Kamakura ('O ye who tread the Narrow Way')
First pub. (8 untitled stanzas) at end of 'From Tideway to Tideway No. III The Edge of the East', in *The Times*, 2 July 1892; stanzas 1, 6, 8 reprinted as headings to Chapters 1–3 and stanza 2 in text of Chapter 1 of the one-volume edition of *Kim* (1901); reprinted *Sussex*, XXI, 1, 9, 35, 56; 12-stanza-version (without original stanza 8) first collected *The Five Nations* (London, 1903); *Sussex*, XXXIII, 238–9; Harbord, Verse No. 523 where uncollected original eighth stanza is printed.

KpR 132 Two fair copies, revised, both here untitled, the first containing 8 stanzas (i.e., stanzas 1–6, 8–9); the second containing 12 stanzas (i.e., stanzas 1–9, a version of the uncollected 8th stanza, 10 and 12), one page each.

Sussex, KP 24/9.

KpR 133 In MS Five Nations.

National Library of Australia, MS 94.

KpR 134 Corrected galley proof, here untitled, containing 13 stanzas, together with proof of 'From Tideway to Tideway' (KpR 1647) set up for *From Sea to Sea* (New York, 1899) but not published there.

Library of Congress, Rare Book Division, Carpenter Kipling Collection.

KpR 135 Corrections to stanzas 1, 6 and 2 (as headings to Chapters 1–2 and in text of Chapter 1 of *Kim*), in first page proofs for the Sussex Edition, Vol. XXI (KpR 1791); date stamped 9 October 1931.

British Library, Add. MS 55871.

The Bugler ('I don't know 'oo you are nor where —')
First pub. *The Regiment*, 25 April 1896 (reprinted in that journal October 1902); reprinted Harbord, Verse No. 665.

KpR 136 Fair copy, subtitled 'Specially written for The Regiment by Rudyard Kipling', signed, annotated 'For *The Regiment*', one page of Laurel House, Lakewood, New Jersey notepaper containing the printed date 1896.

Pierpont Morgan, Gordon Ray Collection.

The Burden ('One grief on me is laid')
First pub. (a version of the last stanza beginning 'One grave to me was given') as heading to 'The Gardener' in *McCall's Magazine*, April 1925; in full with story 'The Gardener' in *Debits and Credits* (London, 1926); collected separately *Inclusive Verse* [1927]; *Sussex*, X, 335–6 and *Sussex*, XXXIV, 395–6; Harbord, Verse No. 1126A.

KpR 137 Fair copy, here entitled 'The Load' and beginning 'One load on me is laid', annotated 'To precede the Gardener' and 'type', one page.

Sussex, KP 24/10.

KpR 138 Fair copy (the first publication version), one stanza beginning 'One grave to me was given', here untitled, one page, annotated 'To precede the Gardener'.

Sussex, KP 24/21.

KpR 139 Corrected first page proof for the Sussex Edition, Vol. X; date stamped 30 December 1931.

British Library, Add. MS 55861.

The Burden of Jerusalem ('In ancient days and deserts wild')
Stanzas 1 and 14 first pub. in Carrington (1955), p. 498; reprinted Harbord, Verse No. 1163, as 'Jews *or* Jews and Arabs'.

KpR 140 Calligraphic MS, including an epigraph from *Genesis*, made for Sir Alfred Webb-Johnson as a birthday present for Queen Mary, 7 leaves (rectos only); transcribed in 1914 from a copy sent to Webb-Johnson by CK.

Royal Library, Windsor.

KpR 141 Typescript, made for Sir Alfred Webb-Johnson, 2 leaves (rectos only), seventeen 4-line stanzas, including an epigraph from Genesis, annotated 'to follow "*The Peace of Dives*"'.

British Library, Add. MS 45680, ff. 155–6 (rectos only).

The Burial ('Why that great Kings return to clay')
First pub. *The Times* and *Boston Globe*, 9 April 1902, as 'C. J. Rhodes'; collected *The Five Nations* (London, 1903); *Sussex*, XXXIII, 227–8; Harbord, Verse No. 783A.

KpR 141.5 Fair copy, one revision in line 20, here entitled 'C. J. R./(*buried April 10: 1902*)' and here beginning 'When that great Kings return to clay', one page, signed, annotated (verso) in an unidentified hand 'The original copy given by R. K. to FR and read over the grave by Bishop', watermarked 1901; together with and originally enclosed in a letter to Colonel Frank Rhodes dated 'Thursday'.

Rhodes House, Oxford, MSS.Afr.s.1772.

KpR 142 In MS Five Nations.

National Library of Australia, MS 94.

KpR 142.5 Last 4 lines (i.e., the inscription on the Rhodes Memorial) beginning 'The immense and brooding spirit still', here headed 'Inscription/To the Spirit and life work of Cecil John Rhodes who loved and served South Africa', on p. 3 of a letter to Herbert Baker (architect of the Memorial), Cape Town, 4 February 1908.

Typed transcript at Sussex, KP 14/7.

Rhodes House, Oxford, MSS.Afr.s.8, f. 34.

'But time was short'
No publication traced; not in Harbord.

KpR 142.7 Draft of four c. 10 line stanzas, mentioning 'Sampson', 'Delilah' and 'Amelia Dott', one leaf.

Sussex, KP 24/63.

Butterflies ('Eyes aloft, over dangerous places')
First pub. with story 'Wireless' in *Traffics and Discoveries* (London, 1904), as 'Kaspar's Song in "Varda"'; collected separately *Songs from Books* (New York, 1912); *Sussex*, VII, 217 as 'Kaspar's Song in "Varda"' and *Sussex*, XXXIV, 157; Harbord, Verse No. 869.

KpR 143 Two successive drafts, both beginning 'Eyes in air over dangerous places', the second untitled and the first entitled 'Kaspar's Song' in "Varda" (From the Dutch of Van Noordt)', in MS Traffics and Discoveries, 2 pages.

McGill University.

KpR 144 Correction on p. 183 of KpR 1112.

Yale.

KpR 145 Corrected first page proof for the Sussex Edition, Vol. VII, here entitled 'Kaspar's Song in "Varda"'; date stamped 22 March 1932.

British Library, Add. MS 55858.

'By the Hoof of the Wild Goat' ('By the Hoof of the Wild Goat uptossed')

First pub. as heading to 'To Be Filed for Reference' subscribed 'From the Unpublished Papers of McIntosh Jellaludin' in *Plain Tales from the Hills* (Calcutta and London, 1888); reprinted *Sussex*, I, 423; collected separately *Songs from Books* (New York, 1912); *Sussex*, XXXIV, 149; Harbord, Verse No. 349. See also KpR 2147.

KpR 146 Fair copy, including a sketch, in MS Writings and Songs (pp. 5–6).

Berg.

KpR 147 Fair copy, one page, signed; dated Simla, 18 August 1887.

Library of Congress, Rare Book Division, Colt Collection.

A Cambridge Course
No publication traced; Harbord, Verse No. 1106C.

KpR 148 Typescript, extensively revised, of a poem apparently inspired by ex-servicemen whom the Admiralty were sending to university after the war, 2 leaves (rectos only).

Sotheby's, 9–10 December 1968, Lot 768, sold to Rota.

'Can't curl, but can swim —', see KpR 1430–33.

The Captive ('Not with an outcry to Allah nor any complaining')
First pub. with story 'The Captive' in *Traffics and Discoveries* (London, 1904), as 'From the Masjid-Al-Aqsa of Sayyid Ahmed (Wahabi)'; collected separately *Songs from Books* (New York, 1912); *Sussex*, VII, 3, as 'From the Masjid-Al-Aqsa of Sayyid Ahmed (Wahabi)' and *Sussex*, XXXIV, 52; Harbord, Verse No. 867.

KpR 149 Drafts, here untitled, 2 pages, bound with story 'The Captive'; and fair copy, on a page (containing also KpR 427), bound with story 'Mrs Bathurst', in MS Traffics and Discoveries.

McGill University.

KpR 150 Fair copy, in MS Writings and Songs (pp. 119–21).

Berg.

KpR 151 Corrected first page proof for the Sussex Edition, Vol. VII; date stamped 22 March 1932.

British Library, Add. MS 55858.

Carmen Simlaense [A Ballad of the Break Up] ('I've danced till my shoes are outworn')
First pub. *Civil and Military Gazette*, 20 October 1885; collected *Early Verse* (1900); *Sussex*, XXXII, 106; Rutherford, pp. 292–3; Harbord, Verse No. 149.

KpR 152 Revised clipping, here entitled 'A Ballad of the Break Up/Carmen Simlaense', annotated 'C & M Gazette Oct: 20th 1885 (under sub-title)', in Scrapbook 4 (p. 176).

Sussex, KP 28/4.

A Carol ('Our Lord Who did the Ox command')
First pub. (without title) as heading to 'A Burgher of the Free State' in *Daily Express*, 26 June 1900; collected with story 'A Tree of Justice' in *Rewards and Fairies* (London, 1910); collected separately *Songs from Books* (New York, 1912); *Sussex*, XV, 325–6 and *Sussex*, XXX, 143–4 (without title) and *Sussex*, XXXIV, 29–30; Harbord, Verse No. 756.

KpR 153 Revised, here untitled and beginning 'The Lord that gave the Ox command', in MS Non-Fiction, subscribed '*Old Lincolnshire Carol.*', annotated 'To precede Burgher of the Free State'; watermarked 1897.

British Library, Add. MS 45542, f. 191.

KpR 154 Fair copy, revised, in MS Rewards and Fairies, one page, annotated 'To follow The tree of justice'.

Cambridge University Library, ADD 6850, f. 118.

KpR 155 Fair copy, in MS Writings and Songs (pp. 56–8).

Berg.

KpR 156 Revision on p. 36 of KpR 1112.

Yale.

KpR 157 Corrected first galley proof (as untitled heading to KpR 1480), set up for a projected volume (marked 'Uncollected'); date stamped 3 November 1930.

British Library, Add. MS 55850.

The Carolina ('Aūrŏrā rose ĭn a cloudlĕss sky')
First pub. Rutherford (1986), Appendix A, pp. [477]–8; Harbord, Verse No. 2A. Two copies of a transcript by Elkin Mathews are extant, at Sussex (KP 24/12) and at Yale; they are both annotated 'Written when Rudyard Kipling was nine years of age never printed but copyright' and 'Copied from the autograph MS. by C Elkin Mathews February 21st 1899'.

KpR 158 Fair copy, signed 'J. R. Kipling', one page, annotated (unidentified hand) 'written when Rudyard Kipling was nine years of age never printed but *Copyright*.'; watermarked 1876.

Dalhousie University.

Caroline Taylor ('Caroline Taylor for Conscience sake')
First pub. Rutherford (1986), pp. 462–4; not in Harbord.

KpR 159 Typescript.

Cornell University.

Cave! ('Lilies be plenty with us')
First pub. Rutherford (1986), pp. 75–6; Harbord, Verse No. 46.

KpR 160 Fair copy, in Sussex Notebook 3 (first series, pp. 17–18); dated 24 October 1881.

Sussex, KP 24/1.

KpR 161 Fair copy, in MS Sundry Phansies.

Berg.

Cells ('I've a head like a concertina, I've a tongue like a button-stick')
First pub. *Barrack-Room Ballads* (1892); *Sussex*, XXXII, 188–9. Harbord, Verse No. 549B.

KpR 162 Fair copy, one page.

Sussex, KP 24/13.

KpR 162.5 Corrected page proof for the first publication; date stamped 12 February 1892.

British Library, Loan 97 (deposited by John Aris, 1989).

Cemeteries in France of British Dead in World War I, see KpR 505.

The Centaurs ('Up came the young Centaur-colts from the plains they were fathered in —')
First pub. with story 'The United Idolators' in *Debits and Credits* (London, 1926); *Sussex*, XVII (*Stalky & Co.*), 217–18 and *Sussex*, XXXIV, 369–70; Harbord, Verse No. 1130.

KpR 163 Slightly corrected first page proof for the Sussex Edition, Vol. XVII; date stamped 27 March 1931.

British Library, Add. MS 55867.

Certain Maxims of Hafiz ('If It be pleasant to look on, stalled in the packed *serai*')
First pub. (13 maxims) in *Departmental Ditties* (1886); revised version in *Departmental Ditties*, 2nd ed (1886); 17 maxims pub. *Departmental Ditties*, 3rd ed (1888); 19 maxims pub. *Departmental Ditties*, 4th ed (1890); *Sussex*, XXXII, 129–33; Harbord, Verse No. 219; the maxim beginning 'Who are the rulers of Ind — to whom shall we bow the knee?' used as heading, ascribed 'Maxims of Hafiz', to Chapter 3 of Rudyard Kipling and Wolcott Balestier, *The Naulahka* (London, 1892); reprinted *Sussex*, XIX, 22. See also KpR 280.

KpR 164 Fair copy of 19 maxims, in MS Departmental Ditties (pp. 115–20).

Berg.

KpR 165 One maxim cancelled (no. IV) and an alternative (headed 'put this in place of No. 4') written on the blank facing verso in KpR 279.

Pierpont Morgan, 20177.

Change ('A changed life and a changed hope —')
First pub. Rutherford (1986), pp. 117–18; Harbord, Verse No. 47.

KpR 166 Fair copy, in Sussex Notebook 1 (pp. 56–7); dated 10 February 1882.

Sussex, KP 24/3.

KpR 167 Fair copy, in Sussex Notebook 3 (first series, pp. 23–4); dated 10 February 1882.

Sussex, KP 24/1.

KpR 168 Fair copy, in MS Sundry Phansies.

Berg.

KpR 169 Transcript by AMK in Sussex Notebook 2; dated February 1882.

Sussex, KP 24/2.

The Changelings ('Or ever the battered liners sank') First pub. with story 'Sea Constables' in *Debits and Credits* (London, 1926); collected separately *Inclusive Verse* [1927]; *Sussex*, X, 23–4 and *Sussex*, XXXIV, 363; Harbord, Verse No. 1131.

KpR 170 Fair copy, revised, of 4-stanza version (without stanzas 4–5), here entitled 'Sea Constables', one page (containing also KpR 421, 605), annotated 'type.'.

Sussex, KP 24/25.

KpR 171 Slightly corrected first page proof for the Sussex Edition, Vol. X; date stamped 30 December 1931.

British Library, Add. MS 55861.

Chant-Pagan ('Me that 'ave been what I've been —') First pub. *The Five Nations* (London, 1903); *Sussex*, XXXIII, 303–5; Harbord, Verse No. 810.

KpR 172 In MS Five Nations.

National Library of Australia, MS 94.

Chapter Headings, see also KpR 46, 200–201, 492, 498–9, 546–7, 563, 674, 758, 905–6, 1014, 1153–5, 1163, 1208–9, 1215–16, 1222–3, 1308, 1352–3, 2235.

Chapter Headings for *Beast and Man in India*
First pub. J. L. Kipling, *Beast and Man in India* (London and New York, 1891); five chapter headings collected separately *Sussex*, XXXIV, 225–7; Harbord, Verse Nos. 505–6, 508–10, as 'The Goat', 'The Oxen', 'Pigs and Buffaloes', 'The Elephant' and 'Of Animal Calls' respectively. For other verses in this book by RK, see KpR 72–4, 614–15.

KpR 173 Fair copy of the 5 collected headings, in MS Writings and Songs (pp. 63–6), the fifth ('Of Animal Calls') containing only lines 1–10 and wanting an ascription.

Berg.

Chapter Headings for *Kim*
Kim first pub. (with chapter headings in verse) serially *McClure's Magazine*, December 1900–October 1901; first pub. in one volume, New York, 1901 and London, 1901; *Sussex*, XXI, *passim*; many of the chapter headings collected as separate poems (for those, see KpR 72–4, 132–5, 351–2, 424–6, 559–60, 870–2, 888, 1009–12, 1059–61, 1291–3, 1380).

KpR 174 Corrections to the heading to Chapter 7 on p. 177 of KpR 1112.

The heading to Chapter 7 beginning 'Onto whose use the pregnant suns are poised' (originally subscribed 'Sir John Christie') collected *Songs from Books* (New York, 1912), as 'Chapter Heading'; *Sussex*, XXXIV, 229; Harbord, Verse No. 778, as 'Sir John Christie'.

Yale.

KpR 175 Corrections to the heading to Chapter 7, in first page proof for the Sussex Edition, Vol. XXI (KpR 1791); date stamped 9 October 1931.

British Library, Add. MS 55871.

Chapter Headings for *Life's Handicap*
Life's Handicap first pub. London and New York, 1891; *Sussex*, IV; 5 chapter headings collected separately *Songs from Books* (New York, 1912); *Sussex*, XXXIV, 227–9. See also KpR 1412.

KpR 176 Fair copy of the heading to story 'Without Benefit of Clergy' begining 'Before my Spring I garnered Autumn's gain', in MS Writings and Songs (p. 105), here entitled

'Without Benefit of Clergy'.

This heading first pub. with the story in *Macmillan's Magazine*, June 1890, ascribed 'Bitter Waters'; *Sussex*, IV, 157 and *Sussex*, XXXIV, 227; Harbord, Verse No. 462, as 'Bitter Waters'.

Berg.

Chapter Headings for *Plain Tales from the Hills*
Plain Tales from the Hills first pub. Calcutta and London, 1888; *Sussex*, I; 24 chapter headings collected separately *Songs from Books* (New York, 1912); *Sussex*, XXXIV, 211–17. See also KpR 1520, 1763, 1788, 2117–18, 2140, 2153.

KpR 177 Fair copies of 12 chapter headings, headed 'Chapter Headings' in MS Writings and Songs (pp. 7–12), and another (p. 48), including: (1) 'Look, you have cast out Love! What Gods are these', subscribed 'Lispeth' (p. 7); (2) 'When the Earth was sick and the skies', subscribed 'The Other Man' (pp. 7–8); (3) 'Cry "Murder" in the market-place, and each', subscribed 'His Wedded Wife' (p. 8); (4) 'Go, stalk the red deer o'er the heather', subscribed 'Pig' (p. 8); (5) '"Stopped in the straight when the race was his own —', subscribed 'In the Pride of his Youth' (p. 9); (6) 'And some are sulky, while some will plunge', subscribed 'Thrown Away' (p. 9); (7) 'They burnt the corpse upon the sand', subscribed 'In Error' (p. 10); (8) 'Not though you die to-night, O Sweet, and wail', subscribed 'By Word of Mouth' (p. 10); (9) 'To-night, God knows what thing shall tide', subscribed 'False Dawn' (pp. 10–11); (10) 'A stone's throw out on either hand', subscribed 'In the House of Suddhoo' (p. 11); (11) 'The World hath set its heavy yoke', subscribed 'Tods' Amendment' (pp. 11–12); (12) 'Pit where the buffalo cooled his hide', subscribed 'Cupid's Arrows' (p. 12); (13) 'It was not in the open fight' (p. 48).

(1) first pub. with story *Civil and Military Gazette*, 29 November 1886, ascribed 'The Convert'; *Sussex*, I, 3 and *Sussex*, XXXIV, 211; Harbord, Verse No. 209, as 'The Convert'; (2) first pub. (4 lines only) with story *Civil and Military Gazette*, 13 November 1886, ascribed 'Old Ballad'; *Sussex*, I, 125 and *Sussex*, XXXIV, 211; Harbord, Verse No. 206, as 'Old Ballad'; (3) first pub. with story *Civil and Military Gazette*, 25 February 1887, ascribed 'Vibart's Moralities'; *Sussex* I, 215 and *Sussex*, XXXIV, 211; Harbord, Verse No. 245, as 'Vibart's Moralities'; (4) first pub. with story *Civil and Military Gazette*, 3 June 1887, ascribed 'The Old Shikarri'; *Sussex*, I, 295 and *Sussex*, XXXIV, 212; Harbord, Verse No. 268, as 'The Old Shikarri'; (5) first pub. with story *Civil and Military Gazette*, 5 May 1887, ascribed 'Life's Handicap'; *Sussex*, I, 285 and *Sussex*, XXXIV, 212; Harbord, Verse No. 261, as 'Life's Handicap'; (6) first pub. with story *Plain Tales from the Hills* (Calcutta & London, 1888), ascribed 'Toolungala Stockyard Chorus'; *Sussex*, I, 21 and *Sussex*, XXXIV, 212; Harbord, Verse No. 359, as 'Toolungala Stockyard Chorus'; (7) first pub. with story *Civil and Military Gazette*, 24 January 1887, ascribed 'Salsette Boat-Song'; *Sussex*, I, 245 and *Sussex*, XXXIV, 213; Harbord, Verse No. 241, as 'Salsette Boat Song'; (8) first pub. with story *Civil and Military Gazette*, 10 June 1887, ascribed 'Shadow Houses'; *Sussex*, I, 415 and *Sussex*, XXXIV, 213; Harbord, Verse No. 272, as 'Shadow Houses'; (9) first pub. with story *Plain Tales from the Hills* (Calcutta and London, 1888), ascribed 'In Durance'; *Sussex*, I, 63 and *Sussex*, XXXIV, 214; Harbord, Verse No. 353 as 'In Durance'; (10) first pub. with story *Civil and Military Gazette*, 30 April 1886, ascribed 'From the Dusk to the Dawn'; *Sussex*, I, 201 and *Sussex*, XXXIV, 214; Harbord, Verse No. 180, as 'From the Dusk to the Dawn'; (11) first pub. with story *Civil and Military Gazette*, 16 April 1887, ascribed 'The Parable of Chajju Bhagat'; *Sussex*, I, 265 and *Sussex*, XXXIV, 212; Harbord, Verse No. 255, as 'The Parable of Chajju Bhagat'; (12) first pub. with story *Plain Tales from the Hills* (Calcutta and London, 1888), ascribed 'The Peora Hunt'; *Sussex*, I, 87 and *Sussex*, XXXIV, 214; Harbord, Verse No. 350, as 'The Peora Hunt'; (13) first pub. with story *Plain Tales from the Hills* (Calcutta and London, 1888), ascribed 'Beoni Bar';

Sussex, I, 307 and *Sussex*, XXXIV, 213; Harbord, Verse No. 358, as 'Beoni Bar'.

Berg.

KpR 178 Correction to the heading (to the story 'By Word of Mouth') beginning 'Not though you die to-night...' (see above for details) on p. 52 of KpR 1112.

Yale.

Chapter Headings for *The Day's Work*, see KpR 2067.

Chapter Headings for *The Light that Failed*
First pub. in *The Light that Failed* (London, 1890); reprinted *Sussex*, XVIII, *passim*; some of the chapter headings collected as separate poems in *Songs from Books* (New York, 1912) (for those, see KpR 112–16, 457–60, 714–15, 1371–4); others collected as 'Chapter Headings' in *Songs from Books* (New York, 1912); *Sussex*, XXXIV, 222–4; Harbord, Verse Nos. 438–459B. See also KpR 1807, 1834–7.

KpR 179 Drafts of chapter headings and verses in the draft of *The Light that Failed* (KpR 1834) as follows: (1) heading to Chapter 5; (2) heading to Chapter 9 (here called Chapter 7); (3) 4 lines in Chapter 9 (here called Chapter 7) beginning 'They're as proud as a turkey'; (4) 8 lines in each of the two versions of Chapter 10 (here called Chapter 8) beginning 'The next good joy that Mary had'; (5) KpR 457; (6) 8 lines in each of the two versions of Chapter 11 (here called Chapter 9) beginning 'He must be a man of decent height'; (7) heading to the second version of Chapter 11 (here called Chapter 9); (8) 8 lines in Chapter 14 (here in Chapter 10) beginning 'We'll never come back any more boys'; (9) KpR 1371; (10) a folded leaf (f. 76) containing drafts of the chapter headings to Chapters 1, 4, 5, 6, 12 and a discarded one begining 'My <love hath> [?] looked on Life — and Life was fair'.

(1) The heading to Chapter 5 (ascribed 'Sir Hoggie and the Fairies') begins '"I have a thousand men," said he' (Harbord, Verse No. 443); (2) the heading to Chapter 9 (ascribed 'The Two Potters') begins '"If I have taken the common clay' (Harbord, Verse No. 449); (3) the 4 lines in Chapter 9 are listed Harbord, Verse No. 450; (4) the 8 lines in Chapter 10 are listed Harbord, Verse No. 452, as 'The Seven Joys of Mary'; (6) the 8 lines in Chapter 11 are listed Harbord, Verse No. 454; (7) the heading to Chapter 11 (ascribed 'Ballad') begins 'The lark will make her hymn to God' (Harbord, Verse No. 453, as 'The Only Son'); (8) the 8 lines in Chapter 14 are listed Harbord, Verse No. 458; (10) the heading to Chapter 1 (ascribed 'Big Barn Stories') begins 'So we settled it all when the storm was done' (Harbord, Verse No. 440); to Chapter 4 (ascribed 'In Seeonee') begins 'The wolf-cub at even lay hid in the corn' (Harbord, Verse No. 442); to Chapter 6 (ascribed, together with heading to Chapter 5 listed above, 'Sir Hoggie and the Fairies') begins 'And you may lead a thousand men' (Harbord, Verse No. 444); to Chapter 12 (ascribed 'Ballad') begins 'There were three friends that buried the fourth' (Harbord, Verse No. 455).

Princeton, Doubleday Collection, Box 5.

KpR 180 Three leaves (rectos only) containing: (1) fair copies, revised, headed 'The Light that Failed/Chapter Headings', containing chapter headings for Chapters 1–4 (those for 1, 2 and 4 being as in *Sussex* and the heading for Chapter 3 being 8 lines begining 'For sale for sale the living man!' ascribed 'The Freelance') and summaries only of the headings for Chapters 5–8; (2) fair copies, revised, and drafts, headed 'The Light that Failed', containing chapter headings for Chapters 1–6, 9–10 (here called Chapters 7–8), 12 (here called Chapter 10) (those for 1, 2, 4–6, 9, 12 being as in *Sussex*, for Chapter 3 being as in (1) above and for 10 being KpR 458, watermarked 1888; (3) drafts of a few chapter headings in prose.

The heading to Chapter 2 (ascribed 'Barrack-Room Ballad') begins 'Then we brought the lances down — then the trumpets blew —' (Harbord, Verse No. 441).

Princeton, Doubleday Collection, Box 5, Folder.

KpR 181 Fair copy of headings to Chapters 11–12 in MS Writings and Songs (pp. 37 and 40 respectively).

Berg.

KpR 182 Corrections to the heading to Chapter 14 on p. 116 of KpR 1112.

This heading begins 'Yet at the last, ere our spearmen had found him' and is ascribed 'Kizilbashi' (Harbord, Verse No. 457).

Yale.

KpR 183 Corrected first page proof for the Sussex Edition of *The Light that Failed* (KpR 1837) containing corrections to the verse headings to Chapters 1, 2, 4, 7 (see KpR 116), 9, 10 (see KpR 460), 11–12, 14; date stamped 20 November 1931.

British Library, Add. MS 55868.

Chapter Headings for *The Naulahka*
This novel by Rudyard Kipling and Wolcott Balestier first pub. London, 1892; chapter headings reprinted separately *Rhymed Chapter Headings for the Naulahka* (London, 1892); *Sussex*, XIX, *passim* and *Sussex*, XXXIV, 217–21; Harbord, Verse Nos. 536–45 (see also Nos. 328B, 346, 549A). For chapter headings collected as separate poems, see KpR 72–4, 164–5, 383, 572–3, 606–7, 730–1, 764–5, 994–5.

KpR 184 Fair copy of the headings to Chapters 1, 7, 9, 13, 14 and 19, here headed 'Chapter Headings for the Naulahka' and another fair copy of lines 1–10 of the heading to Chapter 19, in MS Writings and Songs (pp. 70–6 and 35, respectively).

The headings to Chapter 1 (ascribed 'Auchinleck's Ride') begins 'There was a strife 'twixt man and maid —'; Chapter 7 (ascribed 'Op. 3') begins 'There is pleasure in the wet, wet clay'; Chapter 9 (ascribed 'In Shadowland') begins 'We meet in an evil land'; Chapter 13 (ascribed 'Blackbeard') begins 'Beat off in our last fight were we?'; Chapter 14 (ascribed 'The Crystals of Iswara') begins 'Because I sought it far from men'; Chapter 19 (ascribed 'In Seeonee') begins 'We be the Gods of the East' and is composed of scattered lines from 'O Baal, Hear Us!' (KpR 766).

Berg.

KpR 185 Corrected typescript of headings to Chapters 4–5, 7–9, annotated 'This is blank-verse. Print as such RK.', 2 pages (one folded leaf) numbered 2–3, page 2 being partly cut away.

For the headings to Chapters 7 and 9, see entries above; the heading to Chapter 4 (ascribed 'The Grand-Master's Defense') begins 'Your patience, Sirs. The Devil took me up'; the heading to Chapter 5 (ascribed 'Solo from Libretto of Naulahka') begins 'Now it is not good for the Christian's health to hustle the Aryan brown'; the heading to Chapter 8 (ascribed 'Chorus from Libretto of Naulahka') begins 'When a Lover hies abroad'.

Princeton, Doubleday Collection, Box 4, Bound Vol. VII.

KpR 186 Fair copy, revised, of the heading to Chapter 19 and corrections and revisions to the headings to Chapters 5, 7 and 14, on pp. 110–13 of KpR 1112.

Yale.

KpR 187 Corrected first page proof for the Sussex Edition, Vol. XIX, including corrections to the verse headings to Chapters 1, 4–5, 6 (see KpR 607), 7–9, 10 (see KpR 383), 12, 14, 17–18 (see KpR 573, 995), 19, 20–21 (see KpR 731, 765); date stamped 7 November 1931.

For the headings to Chapters 1, 4–5, 7–9, 14 and 19, see above; the heading to Chapter 12 (ascribed 'In Seonee') begins 'This I saw when the rites were done'.

British Library, Add. MS 55869.

A Charm ('Take of English earth as much')
First pub. with 'Introduction' to *Rewards and Fairies* (London, 1910); collected separately *Songs from Books* (New York, 1912); *Sussex*, XV, ix–x and *Sussex*, XXXIV, 22–3; Harbord, Verse No. 948.

KpR 188 Fair copy, in MS Rewards and Fairies, one page.

Cambridge University Library, ADD 6850, f. 2.

Chartres Windows ('Colour fulfils where Music has no power:')
First pub. *Daily Telegraph*, 15 April 1925; collected *Inclusive Verse* [1927]; *Sussex*, XXXV, 260; Harbord, Verse No. 1124A.

KpR 189 Draft, followed by a fair copy, one page.

Sussex, KP 24/14.

KpR 190 Fair copy, revised, signed, one page.

Syracuse University.

The Child on the Road ('When we go out my father kneels')
No publication traced; not in Harbord.

KpR 191 Unfinished draft, mostly cancelled, on the verso of one page of 'They' in MS Traffics and Discoveries.

McGill University.

The Children ('These were our children who died for our lands: they were dear in our sight.')
First pub. with story 'The Honours of War' in *A Diversity of Creatures* (London, 1917); collected separately *Inclusive Verse* (1919); *Sussex*, IX, 131–2 and *Sussex*, XXXIV, 316–17; Harbord, Verse No. 1039.

KpR 192 Fair copy, revised, here headed 'The Honours of War' and beginning 'These were our children and brothers who died...', in MS Diversity of Creatures (f. 43).

University of Edinburgh, Dk. 2. 8.

KpR 193 Slightly corrected first page proof for the Sussex Edition, Vol. IX; date stamped 28 April 1932.

British Library, Add. MS 55860.

The Children's Song ('Land of our Birth, we pledge to thee')
First pub. with story 'The Treasure and the Law' in *Puck of Pook's Hill* (London, 1906); collected separately *Songs from Books* (New York, 1912); *Sussex*, XIV, 265–6 and *Sussex*, XXXIV, 95–6; Harbord, Verse No. 902.

KpR 194 Fair copy, signed, on one page of 'Government House, Ottawa.' notepaper, written out for Viscount Grey, the Governor-General of Canada from 1904–11.

Dalhousie University.

KpR 195 Fair copy, in MS Puck.

Bodleian, MS. Eng. misc. c. 127, f. 99.

KpR 196 Fair copy of stanzas 1–3 only, here untitled, one page.

Sussex, KP 24/15.

KpR 197 Four lines only, here untitled, inscribed in autograph book of Joanna Cannan; signed and dated 8 June 1910.

Facsimile in American Art Association sale catalogue, 11–12 November 1937, Lot 256.

Swann Galleries, 14 March 1946, Lot 225.

KpR 198 Signed and dated 4 December 1913.

Sotheby's, 24 November 1947, Lot 222.

KpR 199 Corrected first page proof for the Sussex Edition, Vol. XIV; date stamped 2 July 1931.

British Library, Add. MS 55864.

'China-going P. & O.'s'
First pub. with story 'The Crab that Played with the Sea' in *Just So Stories* (London, 1902); collected separately *Songs from Books* (London, 1913); *Sussex*, XIII, 179–80 and *Sussex*, XXXIV, 242, as 'Chapter Heading'; Harbord, Verse No. 798.

KpR 200 Two fair copies, revised, in MS Just So Stories, one page each, both annotated 'on separate page to follow The Crab'.

British Library, Add. MS 59840, ff. 114–15 (rectos only).

KpR 201 Corrected second page proof for the Sussex Edition, Vol. XIII; date stamped 23

April 1935.

British Library, Add. MS 55863.

Chivalry ('Is a woman but a man's plaything, fairest woman in her pride?')
First pub. Rutherford (1986), p. 54; Harbord, Verse No. 48.

KpR 202 Here beginning 'Is a woman but man's pastime, fairest woman in her pride?', 9 lines, one page of a folded leaf (containing also KpR 248, 934), enclosed in a covering letter to 'Aunt' [Edith Macdonald?], postmarked 21 February 1881.

This MS not mentioned Rutherford; typed transcript probably of this MS at Sussex, KP 24/67.

Sotheby's, 11–12 March 1968, Lot 778 (property of H. C. Drayton), sold to Rota.

KpR 203 Fair copy, in MS Sundry Phansies, here entitled 'Chivalry?'.

Berg.

The Choice ('Let Freedom's Land rejoice!')
First pub. *Daily Telegraph* and *New York Times*, 13 April 1917 with a 4-line heading beginning 'To the Judge of Right and Wrong'; collected *The Years Between* (London, [1919]); *Sussex*, XXXIII, 375–6; Harbord, Verse No. 1028.

KpR 204 Revised, here entitled 'Song of the Free peoples' and beginning 'They have said that God is afar', in MS Years Between, ten 4-line stanzas and a cancelled first stanza and two cancelled versions of stanza 8 (the final one being the heading beginning 'To the Judge of Right & Wrong').

British Library, Add. MS 44841, f. 22.

KpR 205 Five successive typescripts, revised: (1) extensively revised, here entitled 'Hymn of the Free Peoples' and originally beginning (the heading) '<Our God is not afar>', ten 4-line stanzas (3 cancelled), 2 numbered leaves (rectos only); (2) another copy of (1), extensively revised, the title revised to 'The Choice', ten 4-line stanzas (3 cancelled), including an epigraph from Woodrow Wilson; (3) extensively revised, seven 4-line stanzas, 2 numbered leaves (rectos only); (4) unrevised but signed, six 4-line stanzas, 2 numbered leaves (rectos only); (5) revised, five 4-line stanzas, one page.

Cornell University.

A Choice of Song, see KpR 421–2.

Cholera Camp ('We've got the cholerer in camp — it's worse than forty fights')
First pub. *McClure's Magazine*, October 1896; collected *The Seven Seas* (New York, 1896); *Sussex*, XXXIII, 145–7; Harbord, Verse No. 672.

KpR 206 Fair copy, revised, in MS Years Between, one page; watermarked 1894.

British Library, Add. MS 44841, f. 89.

Chorus from the Libretto of Naulahka, see KpR 185, 187.

A Christmas Greeting ('In every land are cheer and mirth')
First printed in Harbord (1969), Verse No. 779A.

KpR 207 Fair copy, revised, here untitled, in MS Years Between.

British Library, Add. MS 44841, f. 121.

KpR 208 Fair copy, here untitled, 13 lines, signed, on verso of a printed copy of the lines subtitled 'R.M.S. "Kinfauns Castle", December 25th 1903'.

Library of Congress, Rare Book Division, Colt Collection.

'Cities and Thrones and Powers'
First pub. with story 'A Centurion of the Thirtieth' in *Puck of Pook's Hill* (London, 1906); collected separately *Songs from Books* (New York, 1912); *Sussex*, XIV, 119 and *Sussex*, XXXIV, xi; Harbord, Verse No. 893.

KpR 209 Fair copy, in MS Writings and Songs (pp. 84–5).

Berg.

KpR 210 Revised, in MS Puck.

Bodleian, MS. Eng. misc. c. 127, f. 43.

KpR 211 Fair copy, in the autograph album of Sir Edward Marsh (f. 108); 1919.

Eton College.

KpR 212 Corrected first page proof for the Sussex Edition, Vol. XIV; date stamped 2 July 1931.

British Library, Add. MS 55864.

'The City of Brass' ('When the wine stirred in their hearts their bosoms dilated')
First pub. *Morning Post*, 28 June 1909; collected *The Years Between* (London, [1919]); *Sussex*, XXXIII, 447–51; Harbord, Verse No. 924.

KpR 213 Fair copy, revised, including the heading, in MS Years Between, the second page being a second fair copy, revised, of last 16 lines.

British Library, Add. MS 44841, ff. 56–7 (rectos only).

KpR 214 Lines 25–8 and 30–1 in one letter, lines 42–3 in another, to H. A. Gwynne, the first from Bateman's, n.d., the second dated from Bateman's, 28 April 1914.

Dalhousie University.

KpR 215 Typescript, 6 pages, signed.

American Art Association, 22–3 April 1936 (Scribner Sale), Lot 363.

The City of Sleep ('Over the edge of the purple down')
First pub. without title in text of story 'The Brushwood Boy' in *Century Magazine*, December 1895; collected separately *Songs from Books* (New York, 1912); *Sussex*, VI, 412–13 and *Sussex*, XXXIV, 128–9; Harbord, Verse No. 644, as 'Over the Edge of the Purple Down'. See also KpR 1472.

KpR 216 Very rough drafts, on most of the 14 scraps comprising the draft of 'The Brushwood Boy' (see KpR 1470).

Pierpont Morgan, MA 1155.

KpR 217 Fair copy, revised, of first stanza only, here untitled, on f. 14 of the MS of 'The Brushwood Boy' (KpR 1469), in MS Day's Work; watermarked 1894.

British Library, Add. MS 45541, f. 146.

KpR 218 Fair copy, in MS Writings and Songs (pp. 14–15).

Berg.

KpR 219 Corrected typescript of stanza 1 (p. 48 of KpR 1471), and fair copy of stanzas 2–3 on an inserted leaf following.

Pierpont Morgan, MA 936.

'Cleared' ('Help for a patriot distressed, a spotless spirit hurt')
Lines 1–6 originally formed the opening lines of 'At the Bar' beginning 'Help for a Councillor distressed — a spotless spirit hurt' first pub. *Civil and Military Gazette*, 9 October 1886; reprinted Harbord, Verse No. 200 and Rutherford, pp. 338–9; '"Cleared"' first pub. *Scots Observer* and *St James's Gazette*, 8 March 1890; collected *Barrack-Room Ballads* (1892); *Sussex*, XXXII, 313–18; Harbord, Verse No. 419.

KpR 220 Corrected page proof, 3 pages, probably for publication in *Scots Observer*, including a few annotations by W. E. Henley.

Facsimile in Martindell, facing p. 169 and in E. W. Martindell, *Fragmenta Condita* (privately printed, 1922).

Yale.

KpR 220.5 Corrected page proof for *Barrack-Room Ballads* (1892).

British Library, Loan 97 (deposited by John Aris, 1989).

The Clerks and the Bells ('The merry clerks of Oxenford they stretch themselves at ease')
First pub. *Hearst's International Magazine*, *Nash's Magazine* and *Metropolitan Magazine*, February 1920; collected *Inclusive Verse* [1927]; *Sussex*, XXXV, 244–6; Harbord, Verse No. 1107.

KpR 221 Two fair copies, revised, the first (2 pages) entitled 'Oxford Bells.', the other (one page) annotated 'type single'.

Sussex, KP 24/16.

The Coastwise Lights, see KpR 1070–4.

A Code of Morals ('Now Jones had left his new-wed bride to keep his house in order')
First pub. *Civil and Military Gazette*, 6 April 1886; collected *Departmental Ditties* (1886); *Sussex*, XXXII, 20–2; Harbord, Verse No. 175.

KpR 222 Fair copy, including a sketch, in MS Departmental Ditties (pp. 26–9).

Berg.

KpR 223 Corrections on pp. 21–2 of KpR 282.

Yale.

The Coiner ('Against the Bermudas we foundered, whereby')
First pub. with story 'A Naval Mutiny' in *Limits and Renewals* (London, 1932); collected separately *Inclusive Verse* [1933]; *Sussex*, XI, 173–4 and *Sussex*, XXXIV, 412–13; Harbord, Verse No. 1199.

KpR 224 Corrected first page proof for the Sussex Edition, Vol. XI; date stamped 14 October 1932.

British Library, Add. MS 55862.

Cold Iron ('"Gold is for the mistress — silver for the maid!')
First pub. with story 'Cold Iron' in *Rewards and Fairies* (London, 1910); collected separately *Songs from Books* (New York, 1912); *Sussex*, XV, 25–6 and *Sussex*, XXXIV, 26–7; Harbord, Verse No. 949.

KpR 225 Fair copy, revised, here untitled, in MS Rewards and Fairies, one page.

Cambridge University Library, ADD 6850, f. 4.

KpR 226 Fair copy, in MS Writings and Songs (pp. 125–8).

Berg.

KpR 227 Corrected page proof for *Inclusive Verse* (1919), one page numbered 579, signed (initials), in KpR Incl Verse.

Princeton, Ex3814.9.1919.11.

KpR 228 Slightly corrected first page proof for the Sussex Edition, Vol. XV; date stamped 18 September 1931.

British Library, Add. MS 55865.

The Colonel of the 12th Bulgars
Questionable attribution. No publication traced; Harbord, Verse No. 1027A (p. 5669).

KpR 229 Corrected typescript, 2 pages.

Sotheby's, 9–10 December 1968, Lot 764, sold to Rota.

Columns ('Out o' the wilderness, dusty an' dry')
First pub. *The Five Nations* (London, 1903); *Sussex*, XXXIII, 311–13; Harbord, Verse No. 811.

KpR 230 In MS Five Nations.

National Library of Australia, MS 94.

KpR 231 Fair copy of stanza 14 (4 lines), here the caption to a sketch in Brigadier-General R. W. Hare's 'South African War Sketch-Book' (containing also KpR 827, 840), written aboard S.S. Kinfauns Castle, April 1903.

Facsimile in *KJ*, June 1936, between pp. 52 and 53.

Owned (1936) Brigadier-General R. W. Hare (see *KJ*).

The Comforters ('Until thy feet have trod the Road')
First pub. with story 'The Dog Hervey' in *A Diversity of Creatures* (London, 1917); collected separately *Inclusive Verse* (1919); *Sussex*, IX, 161–2 and *Sussex*, XXXIV, 318–19; Harbord, Verse No. 1039.

KpR 232 Two fair copies in MS Diversity of Creatures (ff. 52–3, rectos only): the first (f. 52) entitled 'Job's Comforters.' and wanting the last stanza; the second and probably earlier (f. 53), revised, here untitled and begining 'Dearly beloved, it is <best> well', 11 stanzas (the first two cancelled).

University of Edinburgh, Dk. 2. 8.

KpR 233 Corrected first page proof for the Sussex Edition, Vol. IX; date stamped 28 April 1932.

British Library, Add. MS 55860.

Commonplaces ('Rain on the face of the sea')
First pub. *Echoes* (Lahore, [1884]); *Sussex*, XXXV, 90; Rutherford, p. 121; Harbord, Verse No. 106.

KpR 234 Fair copy, in Sussex Notebook 1 (p. 63), annotated 'Rottingdean'; dated 5 March [1882].

Sussex, KP 24/3.

Concerning a Jawāb, see KpR 47–50.

Confession ('Is not the dawning very slow to rise —')
First pub. Rutherford (1986), pp. 166–7; not in Harbord.

KpR 235 Fair copy, in Sussex Notebook 1 (p. 119), annotated 'being verses for a picture'; dated 10 August [1882].

Sussex, KP 24/3.

Conspiracy ('Two that shall plotte together')
First pub. Rutherford (1986), p. 107; Harbord, Verse No. 49.

KpR 236 Fair copy, in MS Sundry Phansies.

Berg.

The Conundrum of the Workshops ('When the flush of a new-born sun fell first on Eden's green and gold')
An early version entitled '"New Lamps for Old"' first pub. *The Pioneer*, 1 January 1889; collected *Early Verse* (1900); *Sussex*, XXXII, 118–21; Rutherford, pp. 445–7; Harbord, Verse No. 360.
This version first pub. *Scots Observer*, 13 September 1890; collected *Barrack-Room Ballads* (1892); *Sussex*, XXXII, 302–4; Harbord, Verse No. 361.

KpR 237 Fair copy of lines 1–4 here beginning 'When the flicker of London sun falls faint on the Club-room's green and gold', in MS Words, Wise and Otherwise [p. 39].

Berg.

KpR 238 Fair copy, revised, framed, printer's copy, signed, one page.

Library of Congress, Rare Book Division, Colt Collection.

KpR 239 Revised clipping from *Scots Observer* (13 September 1890), in Scrapbook 4 (p. 177).

Sussex, KP 28/4.

KpR 239.5 Corrected page proof for *Barrack-Room Ballads* (1892).

British Library, Loan 97 (deposited by John Aris, 1989).

The Convert, see KpR 177, 1520.

'Could I but write the things I see', see KpR 1634, 1639.

A Counting-Out Song ('What is the song the children sing')
First pub. *Land and Sea Tales* (London, 1923); collected separately *Inclusive Verse* [1927]; *Sussex*, XVI, 219–21 and *Sussex*, XXXIV, 357–9; Harbord, Verse No. 1113.

KpR 240 Fair copy, revised, 2 pages.

Sussex, KP 24/17.

KpR 241 Corrected first page proof for the Sussex Edition, Vol. XVI; date stamped 14 December 1931.

British Library, Add. MS 55866.

A Cousin's Christmas Card ('As coming from an Eastern Land')
First pub. Rutherford (1986), pp. 203–5; not in Harbord.

KpR 242 Fair copy, including sketches, enclosed in a letter to Margaret Burne-Jones on Civil and Military Gazette notepaper, [Christmas 1883?].

Sussex, KP 11/6.

The Covenant ('We thought we ranked above the chance of ill.')

First pub. *The Covenanter*, 20 May 1914; collected *The Years Between* (London, [1919]); *Sussex*, XXXIII, 358; Harbord, Verse No. 1003.

KpR 243 Fair copy, revised, in MS Years Between.

British Library, Add. MS 44841, f. 14.

The Craftsman ('Once, after long-drawn revel at The Mermaid')
First pub. *The Years Between* (London, [1919]); *Sussex*, XXXIII, 410–11; Harbord, Verse No. 1059.

KpR 244 Draft, with title 'The Craftsman' added later, here beginning alternatively 'Once, at a midnight revel at the Mermaid', 'Once, of a Summer night at the mermaid' and 'Once, after midnight drinkings at [The Mermaid]' (the first cancelled), in MS Years Between, c. seven 4-line stanzas, annotated 'The Years between'.

British Library, Add. MS 44841, f. 38.

A Craven ('I who was crownèd King am now bereft')
First pub. Rutherford (1986), pp. 155–6; not in Harbord.

KpR 245 Fair copy, in Sussex Notebook 1 (pp. 110–11); dated 20 June [1882].

Sussex, KP 24/3.

KpR 246 Fair copy, in Sussex Notebook 3 (second series, pp. 4–5).

Sussex, KP 24/1.

Credat Judaeus ('Three couples were we in the lane')
First printed *Schoolboy Lyrics* (privately printed, Lahore, 1881); *Sussex*, XXXV, 48–9; Rutherford, pp. 60–2; Harbord, Verse No. 17.

KpR 247 Headed 'Sketched from life in Lovers Lane Kensington', on 2 pages of a folded leaf (containing also KpR 964) sent to 'Auntie' [Edith Macdonald], with a letter postmarked 21 February 1881.

Rutherford (p. 60) mentions a typed transcript of this MS? at Sussex, KP 11/10.

Sotheby's, 11–12 March 1968, Lot 778 (property of H. C. Drayton), sold to Rota.

Crossing the Rubicon ('A cry in the silent night')
First printed Harbord (1969), p. 5662 (see also Verse No. 50); first pub. Rutherford (1986), pp. 53–4.

KpR 248 Here untitled, four 4-line stanzas, one page of a folded leaf (containing also KpR 202, 934), enclosed with a covering letter to 'Aunt' [Edith Macdonald?], postmarked 21 February 1881.

Not mentioned Rutherford; a typed transcript of this MS? at Sussex, KP 24/67.

Sotheby's, 11–12 March 1968, Lot 778 (property of H. C. Drayton), sold to Rota.

KpR 249 Fair copy, in MS Sundry Phansies.

Berg.

KpR 250 Fair copy, in Sussex Notebook 3 (second series, pp. 37–8).

Sussex, KP 24/1.

Cruisers ('As our mother the Frigate, bepainted and fine')
First pub. *Morning Post*, *New York Herald* and *New York Sun*, 14 August 1899; collected *The Five Nations* (London, 1903); *Sussex*, XXXIII, 188–9; Harbord, Verse No. 732.

KpR 251 In MS Seven Seas (ff. 1–6): (f. 1) fair copy, revised, of variant version; followed by 5 successive drafts, one page each, all unfinished, only 2 entitled, the first (f. 2) containing version of stanzas 1–8 and 10, the others mostly containing only stanzas 1–6.

Magdalene College, Cambridge.

KpR 252 In MS Five Nations, here entitled 'Scouts'.

National Library of Australia, MS 94.

KpR 253 Typescript, 2 leaves (rectos only), annotated in pencil by F. N. Finney 'Given to me by Mr Kipling when I visited him in Rottingdean in June 1898'.

Dalhousie University.

KpR 254 Revision on p. 9 of KpR 365.

Yale.

'Cry "Murder" in the market-place, and each', see KpR 177.

The Crystals of Iswara, see KpR 184, 186–7.

Cuckoo Song ('Tell it to the locked-up trees')
First pub. *Pearson's Magazine*, 16 September 1909; collected *Songs from Books* (New York, 1912); *Sussex*, XXXIV, 20–1; Harbord, Verse No. 926.

KpR 255 Revised, in MS Years Between, including the introductory note, one page, annotated 'type.'.

British Library, Add. MS 44841, f. 132.

KpR 256 Corrected proof, including the introductory note, probably for first publication, one page.

Library of Congress, Rare Book Division, Carpenter Kipling Collection.

The Curé ('Long years ago, ere R–lls or R–ce')
First pub. with story 'The Miracle of Saint Jubanus' in *Limits and Renewals* (London, 1932); collected separately *Inclusive Verse* [1933]; *Sussex*, XI, 309–10 and *Sussex*, XXXIV, 423–4; Harbord, Verse No. 1200.

KpR 257 Corrected page proof in Limits and Renewals Proof; date stamped 23 January 1932.

Syracuse University.

KpR 258 Corrected first page proof for the Sussex Edition, Vol. XI; date stamped 14 October 1932.

British Library, Add. MS 55862.

Dane-Geld ('It is always a temptation to an armed and agile nation')
First pub. as 'What Dane-geld Means' in C. R. L. Fletcher and Rudyard Kipling, *A History of England* (Oxford and London, 1911); collected *Songs from Books* (1915); *Sussex*, XXXIV, 268–9; Harbord, Verse No. 974.

KpR 259 Draft, here untitled, in MS Years Between, annotated 'type'.

British Library, Add. MS 44841, f. 63.

Danny Deever ('"What are the bugles blowin' for?" said Files-on-Parade.')
First pub. *Scots Observer* and *Week's News*, 22 February 1890; collected *Barrack-Room Ballads* (1892); *Sussex*, XXXII, 174–6; Harbord, Verse No. 408.

KpR 259.5 Corrected page proof for *Barrack-Room Ballads* (1892); date stamped 12 February 1892.

British Library, Loan 97 (deposited by John Aris, 1989).

Darzee's Chaunt ('Singer and tailor am I —')
First pub. with story 'Rikki Tikki Tavi' in *The Jungle Book* (London and New York, 1894); collected separately *Songs from Books* (London, 1913); *Sussex*, XII, 289–90 and *Sussex*, XXXIV, 203; Harbord, Verse No. 623.

KpR 260 Draft, in MS Jungle Books, here entitled 'Darzee's song.' and beginning (a false start) '<A tailor and a poet I —>'; watermarked 1890.

British Library, Add. MS 45540, f. 58.

The Dawn Wind ('At two o'clock in the morning, if you open your window and listen')
First pub. C. R. L. Fletcher and Rudyard Kipling, *A History of England* (Oxford and London, 1911); collected separately *Songs from Books* (1915); *Sussex*, XXXIV, 276–7; Harbord, Verse No. 979.

KpR 261 Revised, stanzas 1–3 only, here untitled, in MS Years Between, one page, annotated 'type.'.

British Library, Add. MS 44841, f. 68.

The Dead King ('For to him, above all, was Life good, above all he commanded')
First pub. *The Times*, 18 May 1910; collected *The Years Between* (London, [1919]); *Sussex*, XXXIII, 416–19; Harbord, Verse No. 939.

KpR 262 Fair copy, revised, in MS Years Between, including the introductory heading, c. 50 lines.

British Library, Add. MS 44841, f. 42.

A Dealer in Brains, see KpR 506.

'Dear Auntie, your parboiled nephew reclines with his feet on a chair'
First pub. Rutherford (1986), pp. 190–2; not in Harbord.

KpR 263 Verse letter, 4 pages (one leaf), to [Edith Macdonald], Lahore, 12 June 1883.

Typed transcript at Sussex, KP 11/10.

Library of Congress, Rare Book Division, Colt Collection.

'Dear Misther [sic] Gosse/your winged hoss'
First pub. (lines 1–6) Coulson Kernahan, *'Nothing Quite Like Kipling Had Happened Before'* (London, 1944), p. 13; first printed in full Harbord (1969), Verse No. 600C.

KpR 264 Verse letter, four 6-line stanzas, to Edmund Gosse, 24 May 1890.

Facsimile in *Ashley Library*, X, facing p. 143.

British Library, Ashley MS 3493.

A Death-Bed ('"This is the State above the Law.')
First pub. *The Years Between* (London, [1919]); *Sussex*, XXXIII, 420–1; Harbord, Verse No. 1060.

KpR 265 Fair copy, revised, in MS Years Between, one page.

British Library, Add. MS 44841, f. 43.

The Declaration of London ('We were all one heart and one race')
First pub. *Morning Post*, 29 June 1911; collected *The Years Between* (London, [1919]); *Sussex*, XXXIII, 354–5; Harbord, Verse No. 967.

KpR 266 Fair copy, revised, five 6-line stanzas (f. 11) and earlier fair copy beginning 'We were all one ken and one race', here untitled, six 6-line stanzas, the last being a redraft of the fifth (f. 12), in MS Years Between.

British Library, Add. MS 44841, ff. 11–12 (rectos only).

A Dedication ('And they were stronger hands than mine')
First pub. as 'L'Envoi' to *Soldiers Three* (Allahabad, 1888); collected separately *Songs from Books* (New York, 1912); *Sussex*, XXXIV, 162; Harbord, Verse No. 347, as 'And they were stronger hands than mine *or* A Dedication to Soldiers Three'.

KpR 267 Fair copy, in MS Writings and Songs (pp. 68–9).

Berg.

KpR 268 Fair copy, here entitled 'L'Envoi', in MS Departmental Ditties (pp. 124–5).

Berg.

KpR 269 Fair copy, here entitled 'L'Envoi', in MS Words, Wise and Otherwise [p. 17].

Berg.

Dedication ('Before a midnight breaks in storm')
First pub. *The Five Nations* (London, 1903); *Sussex*, XXXIII, 179–80; Harbord, Verse No. 807.

KpR 270 In MS Five Nations.

National Library of Australia, MS 94.

Dedication ('If I were hanged on the highest hill'), see KpR 714–15.

The dedication ('With a spade I went to play')
First pub. (version of last stanza only beginning 'Let the grown up people slide') in Alice Fleming (née Kipling), 'Some Reminiscences of my Brother', *KJ*, December 1937, p. 116; reprinted (apparently from a different source) Harbord, Verse No. 720B; no publication traced for complete poem.

KpR 271 Fair copy, seven 4-line stanzas, one page, in a portfolio; [before 1898].

Sussex, KP 24/18.

The Dedication of This Book Which is Written to a Woman [A Dedication; Dedication] ('What have I more to give thee, who have given thee all my heart? —')
First pub. Rutherford (1986), pp. 116–17; Harbord, Verse No. 51, as 'Dedication to Sundry Phansies'.

KpR 272 Fair copy, here entitled 'A Dedication', in Sussex Notebook 1 (p. 55); dated 3 February 1882.

Sussex, KP 24/3.

KpR 273 Fair copy, here entitled as above, in Sussex Notebook 3 (first series, p. 1); dated 3 February 1882.

Sussex, KP 24/1.

KpR 274 Fair copy, here entitled 'Dedication', in MS Sundry Phansies.

Berg.

Dedication/To the City of Bombay ('The Cities are full of pride')
First pub. *The Seven Seas* (New York, 1896); *Sussex*, XXXIII, ix–xi; Harbord, Verse No. 693, as 'To the City of Bombay'.

KpR 275 In MS Seven Seas: (1) fair copy, revised (f. 85); (2) draft, entitled 'Of no mean city.', watermarked 1888 (f. 86); (3) fair copy, revised, and draft entitled 'Of no mean city', watermarked 1888 (f. 88r–v).

Magdalene College, Cambridge.

Dedication/To the Seven Watchmen ('Seven Watchmen sitting in a tower')
First pub. *The Years Between* (London, [1919]); *Sussex*, XXXIII, 349; Harbord, Verse No. 1105.

KpR 276 Revised, 2 versions, here untitled, in MS Years Between, annotated 'Dedication to The Years Between', one page .

British Library, Add. MS 44841, f. 6.

Delilah ('Delilah Aberyswith was a lady — not too young —')
First pub. *Civil and Military Gazette*, 11 October 1886; collected *Departmental Ditties*, 3rd ed (1888); *Sussex*, XXXII, 9–11; Harbord, Verse No. 201.

KpR 277 Fair copy, including the 2-line heading, in MS Departmental Ditties (pp. 30–4).

Berg.

KpR 278 Corrections on p. 14 of KpR 282.

Yale.

***Departmental Ditties* (1886)**

KpR 279 Copy used for preparing the 2nd edition (1886), unstitched to make loose leaves, containing inserted titles (for the 6 new poems) on 'Contents' page which is annotated '[Choose your own time for this page]' and headed 'Contents of the Second Edition which has been slightly enlarged and a little revised.'.

Facsimile of 'Contents' page in [Luther S. Livingston], *The Works of Rudyard Kipling* (New York, 1901), [p. 21], copy described pp. 20–3.

Contents: KpR 165, 816, 849.

Pierpont Morgan, 20177.

KpR 280 Copy in which Kipling has annotated 18 poems, mostly giving definitions of Indian words and phrases; the poems annotated are 'Study of an Elevation in Indian Ink', 'A Legend of the Foreign Office', 'The Post that Fitted', 'Pink Dominoes', 'The Man Who Could Write', 'The Last Department', 'To the Unknown Goddess', 'My Rival', 'The Lover's Litany', 'Divided Destinies', 'The Mare's Nest', 'Pagett, M.P.', 'The Plea of the Simla Dancers', 'Certain Maxims of Hafiz', 'The Moon of Other Days', 'The Undertaker's House', 'Arithmetic on the Frontier', 'Giffen's Debt'.

Mentioned Stewart, p. 21. This copy is possibly the one sold at Sotheby's, 18–21 June 1928 (Lot 750) to Maggs, described as a presentation copy to the Common Room of United Services College.

Dalhousie University.

KpR 281 Copy containing revisions, used in preparing *Departmental Ditties and Ballads and Barrack-Room Ballads* (New York, 1899).

Mentioned Stewart, p. 27; *Grolier Catalogue*, Item 48.

Unlocated.

Departmental Ditties, 2nd ed (1886), see KpR 279.

Departmental Ditties, 4th ed (1890), see KpR 623–5.

Departmental Ditties, 6th ed (Calcutta, London and Bombay, 1891), see KpR 1157.

***Departmental Ditties And Other Verses* (London, 1900)**

KpR 282 Copy of the Newnes Edition (most copies dated 1899), containing corrections and revisions, used in preparing *Departmental Ditties and Barrack-Room Ballads*, Bombay Edition, Vol. XXI (London, 1914).

This copy described and all corrections listed in Martindell, pp. 175–7.

Contents: KpR 36, 39, 55, 84, 87, 105, 223, 278, 299, 354, 410, 416, 562, 583, 621, 628, 676, 686, 722, 785, 808, 817, 850, 861, 901, 992, 1100, 1300, 1344, 1347.

Yale.

A Departure ('Since first the White Horse Banner blew free')
First pub. with story 'The Parable of Boy Jones' in *Land and Sea Tales* (London, 1923); collected separately *Inclusive Verse* [1927]; *Sussex*, XVI, 143–4 and *Sussex*, XXXIV, 352–3; Harbord, Verse No. 1114.

KpR 283 Corrected first page proof for the Sussex Edition, Vol. XVI; date stamped 14 December 1931.

British Library, Add. MS 55866.

The Destroyers ('Offshore where sea and skyline blend')
First pub. *McClure's Magazine*, May 1898; collected *The Five Nations* (London, 1903); *Sussex*, XXXIII, 190–2; Harbord, Verse No. 723.

KpR 284 Successive drafts and fair copies in MS Seven Seas (ff. 7–36) including one long draft (ff. 7–18) without the introductory lines, followed by two fair copies, revised (ff. 19–20 and 21–9), the first untitled, a complete fair copy, revised (f. 30) and drafts of additional stanzas (ff. 31–6).

On f. 35 are lines possibly for another poem beginning 'A lesser mind had not considered this'.

Magdalene College, Cambridge.

KpR 285 In MS Five Nations.

National Library of Australia, MS 94.

KpR 286 Corrected galley proof for first publication, one galley; date stamped 19 November 1897, bound in a presentation copy of *The Day's Work* (New York, 1898) (containing also KpR 1541, 1591, 2065, 2239) from F. N. Doubleday to Bliss Perry, inscribed 21 October 1898.

Harvard, Kipling 18.98.2*.

Dinah in Heaven ('She did not know that she was dead')
First pub. with story 'The Woman in His Life' in *Limits and Renewals* (London, 1932); collected separately *Inclusive Verse* [1933]; *Sussex*, XI, 35–7 and *Sussex*, XXXIV, 400–2; Harbord, Verse No. 1201.

KpR 287 Corrected first page proof for the Sussex Edition, Vol. XI; date stamped 14 October 1932.

British Library, Add. MS 55862.

Dirge of Dead Sisters ('Who recalls the twilight and the ranged tents in order')
First pub. *The Five Nations* (London, 1903); *Sussex*, XXXIII, 277–9; Harbord, Verse No. 812.

KpR 288 Successive drafts, 7 leaves (rectos only); 1902.

Sotheby's, 9–10 December 1968, Lot 758, sold to Rota.

KpR 289 In MS Five Nations.

National Library of Australia, MS 94.

KpR 290 Draft of c. 16 lines, beginning (line 7) 'Let us now remember many honourable women', one page.

For provenance, see KpR 501.

Library of Congress, Rare Book Division, Colt Collection.

KpR 291 Quotation of stanzas 8 and 10, signed, one page.

Berg.

KpR 292 Quotation, a version of lines 7–8, signed, on a scrap.

Texas.

The Disciple ('He that hath a Gospel')
First pub. with story 'The Church that was at Antioch' in *Limits and Renewals* (London, 1932); collected separately *Inclusive Verse* [1933]; *Sussex*, XI, 111–12 and *Sussex*, XXXIV, 405–6; Harbord, Verse No. 1202.

KpR 293 Corrected first page proof for the Sussex Edition, Vol. XI; date stamped 14 October 1932.

British Library, Add. MS 55862.

Discovery ('We found him in the woodlands — she and I —')
First pub. Rutherford (1986), pp. 143–4; not in Harbord.

KpR 294 Fair copy, in Sussex Notebook 1 (p. 96); dated 10 May 1882.

Sussex, KP 24/3.

KpR 295 Fair copy, in Sussex Notebook 3 (first series, p. 66); dated 10 May 1882.

Sussex, KP 24/1.

KpR 296 Fair copy, revised, on one page of a letter (containing also KpR 49, 468) to 'Mater' (i.e., Mrs Tavenor Perry), dated 28 May and postmarked 30 May 1882.

Huntington, HM 11882.

KpR 297 Transcript by AMK in Sussex Notebook 2 [p. 48]; misdated February 1882.

Sussex, KP 24/2.

Divided Allegiance ('My Love is beautiful as day —')
First pub. *Quartette* (Lahore, 1885); reprinted Harbord, Verse No. 154; Rutherford, pp. 194–5.

KpR 298 Fair copy, in Sussex Notebook 1 (p. 155); dated 15 June 1883.

Sussex, KP 24/3.

Divided Destinies ('It was an artless *Bandar* and he danced upon a pine')
First pub. *The Pioneer*, 19 August 1885; collected *Departmental Ditties* (1886); *Sussex*, XXXII, 67–8; Harbord, Verse No. 140. See also KpR 280.

KpR 299 Corrections on pp. 52–3 of KpR 282.

Yale.

A Dominant Power ('A strong man pacing over burning sands')
First pub. Rutherford (1986), p. 118; not in Harbord.

KpR 300 Fair copy, in Sussex Notebook 1 (p. 57); dated 16 February 1882.

Sussex, KP 24/3.

KpR 301 Fair copy, in Sussex Notebook 3 (first series, p. 57); dated 16 February 1882.

Sussex, KP 24/1.

KpR 302 Transcript by JLK, in Sussex Notebook 2 [p. 19]; dated 23 February [1882].

Sussex, KP 24/2.

The Dove of Dacca ('The freed dove flew to the Rajah's tower —')
First pub. *National Observer*, 4 February 1893; collected *Ballads and Barrack-Room Ballads*, 2nd ed (New York and London, 1893); *Sussex*, XXXV, 192–3; Harbord, Verse No. 562.

KpR 303 Draft, here entitled 'The Bridge of Jaunpore' and beginning (false start) 'Oh dove! oh homing dove', in MS Years Between, one page; watermarked 1890.

British Library, Add. MS 44841, f. 130.

The Dusky Crew ('Our heads were rough and our hands were black')
First printed *Schoolboy Lyrics* (privately printed, Lahore, 1881); *Sussex*, XXXV, 7–8; Rutherford, pp. [45]–6; Harbord, Verse No. 3.

KpR 303.5 MS in an unidentified hand (autograph?), as submitted to 'The Scribbler', signed 'Nickson', 3 pages, among unused copy for the magazine which expired in 1880.

This MS sold to G. M. Williamson by May Morris in 1901 (see the description of 'The Scribbler' in the INTRODUCTION).

Anderson Galleries, 17 March 1915 (G. M. Williamson Sale), Lot 107.

KpR 304 Typed transcript (made to replace KpR 303.5), bound with May Morris's set of 'The Scribber' and unused contributions thereto, 3 numbered pages and title page.

British Library, Add. MS 45337, ff. 291–4 (rectos only).

The Dutch in the Medway ('If wars were won by feasting')
First pub. C. R. L. Fletcher and Rudyard Kipling, *A History of England* (Oxford and London, 1911); collected separately *Songs from Books* (1915); *Sussex*, XXXIV, 287–8; Harbord, Verse No. 985.

KpR 305 Fair copy, revised, here untitled and beginning 'If war was won by feasting', in MS Years Between, one page.

British Library, Add. MS 44841, f. 74.

The Dykes ('We have no heart for the fishing — we have no hand for the oar —')
First pub. *The Five Nations* (London, 1903); *Sussex*, XXXIII, 198–200; Harbord, Verse No. 813.

KpR 306 In MS Five Nations.

National Library of Australia, MS 94.

''E sent us 'is blessin' from London Town', see KpR 1517–18.

'The 'Eathen' ('The 'eathen in 'is blindness bows down to wood an' stone')
First pub. *McClure's Magazine*, September 1896; collected *The Seven Seas* (New York, 1896); *Sussex*, XXXIII, 162–6; Harbord, Verse No. 671.

KpR 307 Fair copies and drafts in MS Seven Seas (ff. 98–100, 101), all here untitled; watermarked 1890.

Magdalene College, Cambridge.

KpR 308 Early version, here entitled 'The Recruit's Progress', 72 lines, one page, including an ink sketch of rifle and bayonet.

Quaritch Catalogue 938 (1974), Item 44.

***Echoes* (Lahore, [1884])**

For verses inscribed in otherwise unannotated copies, see KpR 508, 1161, 1368 and, for another inscription, KpR 106; Kipling's presentation copy to Col Dunsterville (inscribed 8 October 1884) is in the Robert H. Taylor Collection at Princeton.

KpR 308.5 Presentation copy, inscribed (not by RK) 'Aunt Louie from her Godson Sept 6th 1884', 7 poems annotated by RK 'T. K.'.

Sussex, Baldwin Papers 2/39.

KpR 308.7 Presentation copy to Edith Macdonald, annotated 'Trix' beside 8 titles in 'Contents' page, containing also KpR 1226.

Sussex, Baldwin Papers 2/40.

KpR 309 Presentation copy to the Common Room of United Services College, annotated 'The other writer' beside 7 titles in 'Contents' page, containing also KpR 538.

Listed as copy 1 in Stewart, pp. 14–15; see also Harbord, Verse No. 83B.

Dalhousie University.

KpR 310 Presentation copy, containing annotations on Contents page ascribing authorship of 8 poems to Trix and KpR 1243, a verse inscription to 'The Ladies of Warwick Gardens' (i.e., Miss Winnard and the Misses Craik).

Listed as copy 3 in Stewart, p. 15; see Harbord, Verse No. 85.

Berg.

KpR 311 Copy, inscribed 'W. C. C. d. d. J. R. K. Aug. 1884' and annotated in margins and in the Index with names of poets 'echoed'.

Listed as copy 6 in Stewart, p. 15 and in Harbord as Verse No. 88 (inscription printed in both).

Anderson Galleries, 17 March 1915 (G. M. Williamson Sale), Lot 3.

KpR 312 Copy inscribed '"Uncle Crom [Cormell Price]"/from/Ruddy./Nov. 1884', the titles of poems anotated with the names of the poets 'echoed' and 10 poems annotated 'RK'.

Listed as copy 7 in Stewart, p. 15 and in Harbord as Verse No. 89.

Dalhousie University.

KpR 313 Presentation copy, inscribed 'Jan 89 To Mrs S. A. Hill from Rudyard Kipling...', containing pencil lines through 11 titles in Contents (including seven poems normally attributed to Trix) and same 11 poems crossed by pencil lines in text.

Listed as copy 8 in Stewart, p. 15 (see also p. 13) and in Harbord as Verse No. 90.

Owned (1959) by an American collector (Stewart, p. 13).

KpR 314 Copy annotated in pencil 'Written at School. R. K.' at end of 'How the Day Broke', 'A Locked Way', 'Land Bound' and 'How the Goddess Awakened'.

Listed as copy 9 in Stewart, p. 15 and in Harbord as Verse No. 91 where it is mistakenly said to be 'presumably' at Dalhousie University.

Unlocated.

KpR 315 Presentation copy to Margaret Burne-Jones, containing pencil marks to the 7 poems ascribed to Trix in the Contents and in the text and KpR 1168.

Listed as copy 10 in Stewart, pp. 15–16; see Harbord, Verse No. 92.

Dalhousie University.

KpR 316 Presentation copy, inscribed by Kipling? on front cover to 'E. Yates Esqr', annotated at each poem with the names of poets 'echoed' in Kipling's? hand, some annotated 'original'.

Berg.

KpR 317 Copy inscribed 'D. C. J. J./d. d./R. K./ Aug. 22nd 1884', the titles of poems annotated in pencil with the names of the poets 'echoed' and with 'RK' on the original poems.

Huntington, HM 30000.

KpR 318 Presentation copy to Mrs Walker, inscribed in an early hand, annotated 'Trix' opposite the titles of each of her compositions in the Index and with the names of the poets 'echoed' at the beginning of each poem.

Anderson Galleries, 21–4 January 1929 (Kern Sale), Lot 759.

KpR 319 Copy, annotated in pencil with the name of each poet 'echoed', 'The Sudder Bazar' on p. 37 marked 'fondly imagined to be original' and the ten following poems are marked either R. K. or B. K.

Sotheby's, 28–31 July 1931, Lot 578, sold to Maggs.

Eddi's Service ('Eddi, priest of St. Wilfrid')
First pub. with story 'The Conversion of St. Wilfrid' in *Rewards and Fairies* (London, 1910); collected separately *Songs from Books* (New York, 1912); *Sussex*, XV, 211–12 and *Sussex*, XXXIV, 33–4; Harbord, Verse No. 950.

KpR 320 Fair copy, revised, in MS Rewards and Fairies, one page.

Cambridge University Library, ADD 6850, f. 81.

Edgehill Fight ('Naked and grey the Cotswolds stand')
First pub. C. R. L. Fletcher and Rudyard Kipling, *A History of England* (Oxford and London, 1911), as 'Before the Edgehill Fight'; collected separately *Songs from Books* (1915); *Sussex*, XXXIV, 285–6; Harbord, Verse No. 984.

KpR 321 Revised, in MS Years Between, here untitled (but entitled in unidentified hand 'Before Edgehill Fight') and beginning 'Grey & unmoved the Cotswolds stand', annotated 'XIV', one page.

British Library, Add. MS 44841, f. 73.

The Egg-Shell ('The wind took off with the sunset —')
First pub. (stanzas 1 and 3 only, without title and beginning 'The wind went down with the sunset —') as heading to Part II of 'Their Lawful Occasions' in *Collier's Weekly*, 10 October 1903; collected *Traffics and Discoveries* (London, 1904); *Sussex*, VII, 131; first pub. in full in *Songs from Books* (New York, 1912); *Sussex*, XXXIV, 169; Harbord, Verse No. 805.

KpR 322 Two 8-line stanzas, signed.

Owned (1967) Homer I. Lewis, El Paso, Texas (formerly deposited at Texas).

El Dorado ('A golden place — whose portals shine')
First pub. Rutherford (1986), pp. 168–9; not in Harbord.

KpR 323 Fair copy, in Sussex Notebook 1 (pp. 122–5), annotated 'Rottingdean'; dated 16 August [1882].

Sussex, KP 24/3.

KpR 324 Fair copy, revised, in Sussex Notebook 3 (second series, pp. 32–6).

Sussex, KP 24/1.

The Elephant, see KpR 173.

Elsinore, see KpR 716.

An Ending ('Oh Dearest! the best I have ever written')
First pub. Rutherford (1986), pp. 141–2; not in Harbord.

KpR 325 Fair copy, in Sussex Notebook 3 (first series, p. 73, unpaginated verso of 73 and p. 74); dated 11 April 1882.

Sussex, KP 24/1.

En-Dor ('The road to En-dor is easy to tread')
First pub. *The Years Between* (London, [1919]); *Sussex*, XXXIII, 387–8; Harbord, Verse No. 1061.

KpR 326 Revised, here entitled 'The Road to Endor', in MS Years Between, including the epigraph from *Samuel*, one page.

British Library, Add. MS 44841, f. 28.

The English Flag ('Winds of the World, give answer! They are whimpering to and fro —')
First pub. *National Observer*, 4 April 1891, as 'The Flag of England'; collected *Barrack-Room Ballads* (1892); *Sussex*, XXXII, 308–12; Harbord, Verse No. 493.

KpR 327 Fair copy, revised, signed, annotated 'No proof wanted/Read carefully'.

Facsimile in *Morning Post*, 1 March 1899; discussed (and facsimile printed) in K. M. Wilson, 'The Manuscript of "The English Flag"', *KJ*, 60 (1986), 23–[31].

University of Leeds, MSS and Special Collections, Glenesk-Bathurst MSS (on deposit).

KpR 328 Fair copy of 10 lines only, with sketches, in Berg Booklet [pp. 2–3].

Berg.

KpR 329 Fair copy of 10 lines only, headed 1891, in MS Words, Wise and Otherwise [pp. 41–3].

Berg.

KpR 329.5 Corrected page proof for *Barrack-Room Ballads* (1892).

British Library, Loan 97 (deposited by John Aris, 1989).

The English Way ('After the fight at Otterburn')
First pub. *The Legion Book*, ed. Capt. H. Cotton Minchin (London, [1929]); collected *Inclusive Verse* [1933]; *Sussex*, XXXV, 279–81; Harbord, Verse No. 1165.

KpR 330 Typescript, signed, containing two epigraphs, one line from '*Foreign Paper*.' and 4 lines from *Ballad of Chevy Chase* (from Percy's *Reliques*), 2 leaves (rectos only).

Dalhousie University.

'Ennobled Sons of treason'
No publication traced; not in Harbord.

KpR 331 Eight lines, in a letter to George Bambridge, Bath, 6 January 1932.

Sussex, KP 12/9.

Envoy, see KpR 22–6.

Epitaphs of the War
First pub. (31 epitaphs) *The Years Between* (London, [1919]); *Sussex*, XXXIII, 438–46 (35 epitaphs); Harbord, Verse Nos. 1063–97.

KpR 332 Drafts and fair copies of 28 epitaphs (some in two copies), in MS Years Between, on five leaves (rectos only), one containing untitled drafts (f. 55) headed 'Epitaphs' transcribed on another of titled fair copies (f. 51) headed 'Epitaphs', and 3 more of titled fair copies (ff. 52–4, the first two annotated 'add to Epitaphs'), including: '"Equality of Sacrifice"' (fair copy, revised, here entitled 'Solo and Duet', f. 52); 'A Servant'(untitled draft and fair copy entitled 'A Batman', ff. 55 and 51); 'A Son' (untitled draft and fair copy entitled 'Subaltern of the Line', ff. 55 and 51); 'An Only Son' (untitled draft, f. 52); 'Ex-Clerk' (fair copy, f. 52); 'The Wonder' (fair copy, revised, entitled 'Ex-Schoolmaster', f. 53); 'Hindu Sepoy in France' (untitled draft and fair copy, revised, ff. 55 and 51); 'Shock' (fair copy, revised, f. 51); 'A Grave near Cairo' (fair copy, f. 52); 'The Favour' (untitled draft and fair copy entitled 'Early Death', ff. 55 and 51); 'The Beginner' (fair copy entitled 'Sniped', f. 53); 'The Refined Man' (fair copy entitled 'Refinement', f. 52); 'Native Water-Carrier (M. E. F.)' (untitled draft and fair copy, revised, ff. 55 and 51); 'The Sleepy Sentinel' (untitled draft and fair copy, revised, entitled 'The Sleepy Sentry', ff. 55 and 51); 'Batteries Out of Ammunition' (fair copy, revised, entitled 'A Dead Battery', f. 52); 'The Rebel' (fair copy entitled 'A Rebel', f. 53); 'A Drifter off Tarentum' (fair copy, revised, entitled 'Adriatic Drifter', f. 52); 'Destroyers in Collision' (fair copy, revised, f. 52); 'The Gambler' beginning 'I a gamester bid you know' (untitled draft and fair copy, revised, ff. 55 and 51); 'Isolated' begining 'There was neither child nor wife' (fair copy, revised, f. 51); 'A Talented Man' beginning 'Who knew how far the slave released' (f. 54).

No publication traced for 'The Gambler', 'Isolated' and 'A Talented Man'.

British Library, Add. MS 44841, ff. 51–5 (rectos only).

KpR 333 Drafts, 4 pages, including (all here untitled): 'A Servant', 'Ex-Clerk', 'Shock', 'The Favour', 'Native Water-Carrier (M.E.F.)', 'The Gambler' (see also KpR 332) and discarded lines; together with a small scrap containing fair copy of 'The Sleepy Sentinel', here entitled 'Epitaphs:'.

Sussex, KP 24/19.

KpR 334 Draft of 8 lines of 'The Rebel', here untitled, in text of the MS of 'On the Gate' (KpR 1945), in MS Debits and Credits (f. 151).

University of Durham.

KpR 335 Corrected typescript, one page, enclosed in a letter to the Rev. St John Mildmay, 22 June 1935, annotated by Mildmay 'copied for me by Mr Rudyard Kipling', including: 'Hindu Sepoy in France', 'The Coward', 'Destroyers in Collision', 'A Drifter off Tarentum', 'A Son', 'Unknown Female Corpse' (here entitled 'Unknown Female Corpse from torpedoed ship'), 'A Grave Near Cairo' (here entitled 'Australian Grave near Cairo'), 'The Wonder'.

Berg.

KpR 336 Typescript of 'Inscription on Memorial in Sault Ste Marie, Ontario' and 'Journalists', both here untitled; in a typed letter from CK to Messrs Macmillan, Bateman's, 31 August 1938.

British Library, Add. MS 54940, f. 183.

'E's/We're goin' to do without 'em, see KpR 1469, 1471.

Escaped, see KpR 47–50.

Et Dona Ferentes ('In extended observation of the ways and works of man')
First pub. *St James's Gazette*, 27 March 1896; collected *The Five Nations* (London, 1903); *Sussex*, XXXIII, 249–51; Harbord, Verse No. 662.

KpR 337 In MS Five Nations.

National Library of Australia, MS 94.

KpR 338 Fair copy, revised, including an unpublished epigraph from '*Daily paper*', stanza 10 cancelled and marked 'op', signed, one page (cut up by a typesetter, now reassembled), annotated 'no proof wanted RK'.

Facsimile of 3 stanzas in Sotheby's sale catalogue, 19 May 1926; facsimile of whole in Sawyer Catalogue 86 (1926) and *Grolier Catalogue*, plate XXX.

Berg.

Evarra and His Gods ('*Read here*:/This is the story of Evarra—man—')
First pub. *Scots Observer*, 4 October 1890; collected *Barrack-Room Ballads* (1892); *Sussex*, XXXII, 299–301; Harbord, Verse No. 472.

KpR 338.5 Corrected page proof for *Barrack-Room Ballads* (1892).

British Library, Loan 97 (deposited by John Aris, 1989).

The Expert ('Youth that trafficked long with Death')
First pub. with story 'Beauty Spots' in *Limits and Renewals* (London, 1932); collected separately *Inclusive Verse* [1933]; *Sussex*, XI, 305 and *Sussex*, XXXIV, 422; Harbord, Verse No. 1203. For proof corrections, see KpR 1840.

KpR 339 Corrected first page proof for the Sussex Edition, Vol. XI; date stamped 14 October 1932.

British Library, Add. MS 55862.

The Explanation ('Love and Death once ceased their strife')
First pub. *Calcutta Review*, July 1886, as 'The Legend of Love and Death'; collected *Barrack-Room Ballads* (1892), as 'The Explanation'; *Sussex*, XXXII, 295; Harbord, Verse No. 184B, as 'The Legend of Love and Death' and No. 403, as 'The Explanation'.

KpR 340 One page, signed; dated 29 July 1897.

Parke Bernet, 23 May 1978, Lot 252.

KpR 341 Fair copy, signed, one page of 'The Elms' notepaper, annotated 'For Mrs Boothby: Jan. 99.'.

Library of Congress, Rare Book Division, Colt Collection.

The Explorer ('"There's no sense in going further — it's the edge of cultivation"')
First pub. *The Five Nations* (London, 1903); *Sussex*, XXXIII, 219–23; Harbord, Verse No. 814.

KpR 342 In MS Five Nations.

National Library of Australia, MS 94.

KpR 343 Fair copy of 4 stanzas only, in Berg Booklet [pp. 26–7].

Berg.

The Fabulists ('When all the world would keep a matter hid')
First pub. with story 'The Vortex' in *A Diversity of Creatures* (London, 1917); collected separately *Inclusive Verse* (1919); *Sussex*, IX, 379–80 and *Sussex*, XXXIV, 334–5; Harbord, Verse No. 1040.

KpR 344 Fair copy, revised, headed 'The Vortex', in MS Diversity of Creatures (f. 128).

University of Edinburgh, Dk. 2. 8.

KpR 345 Corrected first page proof for *Humorous Tales* (London, 1931), pp. 477–8; date stamped 8 June 1931.

British Library, Add. MS 55847.

KpR 346 Corrected first page proof for the Sussex Edition, Vol. IX; date stamped 28 April 1932.

British Library, Add. MS 55860.

Failure ('One brought her Fire from a distant place')
First pub. *Echoes* (Lahore, [1884]); collected *Early Verse* (1900); *Sussex*, XXXV, 101; Rutherford, p. 98; Harbord, Verse No. 52.

KpR 347 Fair copy in Sussex Notebook 3 (first series, pp. 8–9); dated 25 December 1881.

Sussex, KP 24/1.

KpR 348 Fair copy, in MS Sundry Phansies.

Berg.

KpR 349 Transcript by JLK in Sussex Notebook 2 [p. 24], dated 'Winter term 1881'.

Sussex, KP 24/2.

'Fair Mistress, To my lasting sorrow'
First pub. (lines 1–4) in *KJ*, 30 (1963); in full Harbord (1969), Verse No. 81; Rutherford, pp. 219–20.

KpR 350 Verse letter, signed '"Old Joe"', 28 lines, 2 leaves (rectos only), to [Miss Coxen, Lahore], 'My Stables', 20 June [1884].

Library of Congress, Rare Book Division, Colt Collection.

The Fairies' Siege ('I have been given my charge to keep —')
First pub. (stanza 3) as chapter heading to Chapter 15 of *Kim* in first serial publication, *McClure's Magazine*, October 1901; *Sussex*, XXI, 362; first pub. in full *Songs from Books* (New York, 1912); *Sussex*, XXXIV, 37; Harbord, Verse No. 767.

KpR 351 Correction on p. 42 of KpR 1112.

Yale.

KpR 352 Corrections to stanza 3 (as heading to Chapter 15 of *Kim*), in first page proof for the Sussex Edition, Vol. XXI (KpR 1791); date stamped 9 October 1931.

British Library, Add. MS 55871.

The Faith-Cup of the White Men, see KpR 1094.

The Fall of Jock Gillespie ('This fell when dinner-time was done —')
First pub. *Civil and Military Gazette*, 10 November 1886; collected *Departmental Ditties*, 3rd ed (1888); *Sussex*, XXXII, 136–7; Harbord, Verse No. 204.

KpR 353 Fair copy, including a sketch, in MS Departmental Ditties (pp. 103–6).

Berg.

KpR 354 Correction on p. 95 of KpR 282.

Yale.

The Feet of the Young Men ('Now the Fourway Lodge is opened, now the Hunting Winds are loose —')
First pub. *Scribner's Magazine*, December 1897; collected *The Five Nations* (London, 1903); *Sussex*, XXXIII, 208–12; Harbord, Verse No. 704.

KpR 355 In MS Seven Seas, including (f. 59v) an untitled draft of closing lines, watermarked 1896 and (ff. 60–1, rectos only) a fair copy, revised, wanting the last stanza and including the introductory prose heading, annotated 'to be typed as soon as possible RK'.

Magdalene College, Cambridge.

KpR 356 Fair copy, signed, illustrated, one page.

Harvard, *48M–59F.

KpR 357 Fair copy of a version of lines 14–17, signed, inscribed on the title page of a presentation copy of *Actions and Reactions* (London, 1909) to 'Colonel Sahib' [i.e., H. W. Feilden]; dated October 1909.

Facsimile in Sotheby's sale catalogue, 14 March 1979, Lot 395.

Syracuse University.

The Female of the Species ('When the Himalayan peasant meets the he-bear in his pride')
First pub. *Morning Post*, 20 October 1911; collected *The Years Between* (London, [1919]); *Sussex*, XXXIII, 434–7; Harbord, Verse No. 970.

KpR 358 Fair copy, revised, in MS Years Between, one page.

British Library, Add. MS 44841, f. 50.

KpR 359 Slightly revised typescript, 3 numbered leaves (rectos only).

Syracuse University.

KpR 360 Corrected typescript, signed, 2 leaves (rectos only), as sent to the printer for publication in *Ladies Home Journal* of November 1911.

Texas.

The Files ('Files —')
First pub. *The Five Nations* (London, 1903); *Sussex*, XXXIII, 271–4; Harbord, Verse No. 815.

KpR 361 In MS Five Nations.

National Library of Australia, MS 94.

The Fires ('Men make them fires on the hearth')
First pub. as introductory poem in *The Collected Verse of Rudyard Kipling* (New York, 1907); collected *Inclusive Verse* (1919); *Sussex*, XXXV, 226–7; Harbord, Verse No. 908.

KpR 362 Fair copy, slightly revised, in MS Years Between, one page.

British Library, Add. MS 44841, f. 131.

KpR 363 Corrected proof.

Grolier Catalogue, Item 378.

Unlocated.

The First Chantey ('Mine was the woman to me, darkling I found her:')
First pub. *The Seven Seas* (New York, 1896); *Sussex*, XXXIII, 17–18; Harbord, Verse No. 685.

KpR 364 In MS Seven Seas: (1) draft of stanzas 1–3, here untitled, on a page containing also a list of titles for *The Seven Seas* and other doodles, watermarked 1890 (f. 87); (2) fair copy, revised, of the beginning and drafts, watermarked 1890 (ff. 158, 159r–v).

Magdalene College, Cambridge.

The First Day Back, see KpR 1157.

***The Five Nations* (London, 1903)**, for an inscribed copy, see KpR 656.

***The Five Nations*, 8th ed. (London, [1911])**

KpR 365 Used by RK for preparing the Bombay Edition, Vol. XXII (London, 1914), including the addition of dates to every poem and the annotation [p. 1] 'To printer: Put date in each case below title of verses'; also including revisions to the 'Contents'.

Contents: KpR 4, 101, 123, 254, 581, 640, 834, 985, 1011, 1096, 1144, 1325, 1391.

Yale.

The Flight ('So the end came')
First pub. Rutherford (1986), pp. 50–1; Harbord, Verse No. 53.

KpR 366 Fair copy, in MS Sundry Phansies.

Berg.

KpR 367 Fair copy, in Sussex Notebook 3 (first series, pp. 63–5), here entitled 'Haste'; dated 25 June 1880.

Sussex, KP 24/1.

The Floods ('The rain it rains without a stay')
First pub. with story '"My Son's Wife"' in *A Diversity of Creatures* (London, 1917); collected separately *Inclusive Verse* (1919); *Sussex*, IX, 375–6 and *Sussex*, XXXIV, 332–3; Harbord, Verse No. 1041.

KpR 368 Fair copy (hand printed), revised, in MS Diversity of Creatures (f. 127).

University of Edinburgh, Dk. 2. 8.

KpR 369 Corrected first page proof for the Sussex Edition, Vol. IX; date stamped 28 April 1932.

British Library, Add. MS 55860.

The Flowers ('Buy my English posies!')
First pub. *Daily Chronicle*, 10 June 1896; collected *The Seven Seas* (New York, 1896); *Sussex*, XXXIII, 86–8; Harbord, Verse No. 669A.

KpR 370 Draft lines, in MS Seven Seas (f. 74v, the verso of KpR 100).

Magdalene College, Cambridge.

KpR 371 Fair copy, revised, in MS Years Between, including lines 1–40 only, here untitled; watermarked 1894.

British Library, Add. MS 44841, f. 99.

KpR 372 Fair copy, revised, including the original clipping from *The Athenaeum* pasted on as the epigraph, 7 stanzas, signed, one page, containing two notes to the compositor; watermarked 1894.

Dalhousie University.

KpR 373 Fair copy, signed, one page, annotated 'for Julia De Forest with love & good wishes.' and including the prose epigraph; dated 30 December 1895.

Harvard, MS Eng 165, f. 6.

KpR 374 Fair copy of 3 stanzas, signed, on one page of 'Government House, Ottowa.' notepaper, written out for Viscount Grey, the Governor-General of Canada from 1904–11.

This MS mentioned Harbord, Verse No. 669A.

Dalhousie University.

KpR 375 Fair copy of lines 13–24, signed, one small page; dated 24 April 1907.

This is possibly the MS offered for sale by Messrs Hurcomb, 23 November 1931 (see *KJ*, 20 (1931), 102).

Harvard, *48M–58.

KpR 376 Fair copy of lines 37–48, signed, subscribed '(*The Flowers*)', one page of Union Castle Line, R.M.S. 'Kildonan Castle' notepaper.

Cornell University.

'Follow Me 'Ome' ('There was no one like 'im, 'Orse or Foot')
First pub. *Pall Mall Magazine*, June 1894; collected *The Seven Seas* (New York, 1896); *Sussex*, XXXIII, 155–6; Harbord, Verse No. 606.

KpR 377 Fair copy, revised, printer's copy for first publication, one page (cut into three).

Columbia University, Engel Collection.

KpR 378 Fair copy, in MS Seven Seas (f. 124), here untitled.

Magdalene College, Cambridge.

For a Picture [Venus Meretrix] ('This much am I to you —')
First pub. Rutherford (1986), p. 73; Harbord, Verse No. 54.

KpR 379 Fair copy, here entitled 'Venus Meretrix', in Sussex Notebook 3 (first series, pp. 54–5); dated 30 September 1881.

Sussex, KP 24/1.

KpR 380 Fair copy, here entitled 'For a Picture', in MS Sundry Phansies.

Berg.

'For all we have and are'
First pub. *The Times*, 2 September 1914; collected *The Years Between* (London, [1919]); *Sussex*, XXXIII, 363–4; Harbord, Verse No. 1010.

KpR 381 Fair copy, in MS Years Between, signed, one page.

British Library, Add. MS 44841, f. 16.

KpR 382 Fair copy, signed, one page, annotated 'autograph copy of verses published, Sep. 2, 1914, R. K.'.

Christie's, 5 April 1966, Lot 102, sold to Rota.

KpR 382.5 Carbon copy of a typescript, 2 leaves (rectos only), signed in pencil probably by Kipling, among Lord Beaverbrook's correspondence with Kipling.

House of Lords Record Office, BBK/C/199.

For the Women ('We knit a riven land to strength by cannon, code, and sword')
First pub. *Civil and Military Gazette*, 18 February 1887; stanzas 5–6 used as heading to Chapter 10 of *The Naulahka* (London, 1892); reprinted *Sussex*, XIX, 116; collected *Early Verse* (1900); *Sussex*, XXXII, 97–9; Rutherford, pp. 363–5; Harbord, Verse No. 243.

KpR 383 Corrected first page proof of stanzas 5–6 (i.e., heading to Chapter 10 of *The Naulahka*) for the Sussex Edition, Vol. XIX; date stamped 7 November 1931.

British Library, Add. MS 55869.

'For To Admire' ('The Injian Ocean sets an' smiles')
First pub. *Pall Mall Magazine*, February 1894; collected *The Seven Seas* (New York, 1896); *Sussex*, XXXIII, 172–4; Harbord, Verse No. 602.

KpR 384 Fair copy, printer's copy for first publication, one page (cut into three).

Columbia University, Engel Collection.

KpR 385 Quotation of the 4-line chorus, one page, signed; headed 'Buluwago – Mar. 18. '98'.

Pierpont Morgan, Reginald Allen Collection.

'Ford O' Kabul River' ('Kabul town's by Kabul river —')
First pub. *National Observer*, 22 November 1890; collected *Barrack-Room Ballads* (1892); *Sussex*, XXXII, 217–18; Harbord, Verse No. 476.

KpR 386 One page.

Facsimile in American Art Association sale catalogue.

American Art Association, 16–17 January 1928 (Brunner Sale), Lot 306, sold to J. F. Dratte Co.

KpR 387 Fair copy, incomplete version, here beginning 'Ford —— ford —— ford o' Kabul River!' and headed 'Barrack Room Ballads.', one page.

Sussex, KP 24/20.

KpR 387.5 Corrected page proof for *Barrack-Room Ballads* (1892); date stamped 12 February 1892.

British Library, Loan 97 (deposited by John Aris, 1989)

The Four Angels ('As Adam lay a-dreaming beneath the Apple Tree')
First pub. with story 'With the Night Mail' in *Actions and Reactions* (London, 1909); collected separately *Songs from Books* (New York, 1912); *Sussex*, VIII, 165–6 and *Sussex*, XXXIV, 205–6; Harbord, Verse No. 928.

KpR 388 In MS Actions and Reactions (f. 72).

University of St Andrews, MS PR4854.A4.

KpR 389 Slightly corrected first page proof for the Sussex Edition, Vol. VIII; date stamped 28 November 1931.

British Library, Add. MS 55859.

Four-Feet ('I have done mostly what most men do')
First pub. (2 lines) as heading to 'The Woman in His Life' in *London Magazine* and *McCall's Magazine*, December 1928; first pub. in full with that story in *Limits and Renewals* (London, 1932); collected separately *Inclusive Verse* [1933]; *Sussex*, XI, 69 and *Sussex*, XXXIV, 403; Harbord, Verse No. 1204.

KpR 390 Fair copy, signed, on verso of a leaf of Bateman's notepaper.

Facsimile in British Library, RP 2848(ii).

Syracuse University.

KpR 391 Fair copy, here untitled, one page, signed, including a floral border and sketch of a whale, framed.

Library of Congress, Rare Book Division, Colt Collection.

KpR 392 Fair copy, presented to a Miss Healey, Torre Tower, Torquay, Devon, with accompanying envelope so addressed, signed, one page.

This MS printed in American Art Association sale catalogue, p. 185.

American Art Association, 9–10 December 1936, Lot 459.

Fox-Hunting ('When Samson set my brush afire')
First pub. *Strand Magazine*, February 1933; collected *Inclusive Verse* [1933]; *Sussex*, XXXV, 291–3; Harbord, Verse No. 1215, as 'The Fox Meditates'.

KpR 393 Version of stanza one only, here entitled (in text of letter) 'The meditation of C. J. Fox', sent for comments in a letter to Guy Paget, Bateman's, [October 1932].

This MS printed in *Letters from Rudyard Kipling to Guy Paget 1919–1936* (privately printed, Leicester, 1936).

Unlocated.

France ('Ere our birth (rememberest thou?) side by side we lay')
First pub. *Morning Post*, 24 June 1913; reprinted as opening poem in *France at War* (London, 1915); collected *The Years Between* (London, [1919]); *Sussex*, XXVI, 65–7 and *Sussex*, XXXIII, 359–62; Harbord, Verse No. 1001.

KpR 394 Fair copy, revised, in MS Years Between, including the heading and a version of lines 1–39 only, here untitled, one page.

British Library, Add. MS 44841, f. 15.

Frankie's Trade ('Old Horn to All Atlantic said:')
First pub. with story 'Simple Simon' in *Rewards and Fairies* (London, 1910); collected separately *Songs from Books* (New York, 1912); *Sussex*, XV, 293–4 and *Sussex*, XXXIV, 193–4; Harbord, Verse No. 951.

KpR 395 Fair copy, revised, in MS Rewards and Fairies, one page.

Cambridge University Library, ADD 6850, f. 106.

KpR 396 Slightly corrected first page proof for the Sussex Edition, Vol. XV; date stamped 18 September 1931.

British Library, Add. MS 55865.

The French Wars ('The boats of Newhaven and Folkestone and Dover')
First pub. in C. R. L. Fletcher and Rudyard Kipling, *A History of England* (Oxford and London, 1911); collected separately *Songs from Books* (1915); *Sussex*, XXXIV, 293–4; Harbord, Verse No. 989.

KpR 397 Revised, wanting last stanza, here untitled, in MS Years Between, annotated 'type'.

British Library, Add. MS 44841, f. 77.

From Lyden's 'Irenius', see KpR 427–8.

'From Stormberg's midnight mountain'
First pub. as heading to story 'The Outsider' in *Daily Express*, 19–21 June 1900; reprinted with ascription 'Stellenbosch Hymn' in *Sussex*, XXX, 119; Harbord, Verse No. 755A. See also KpR 1964.

KpR 398 Fair copy, revised, of two 8-line stanzas, the second cancelled, in MS Non-Fiction, annotated 'type to follow title of The outsider'; watermarked 1897.

British Library, Add. MS 45542, f. 212.

From the Dusk to the Dawn, see KpR 177.

From the Hills ['What makes my heart to throb & glow?' (North India version)] ('Skin may be scorching, and brain may be batter')
First pub. *Quartette* (Lahore, 1885), as 'From the Hills'; reprinted Harbord, Verse No. 155; Rutherford, pp. 189–90.

KpR 399 Fair copy, revised, here entitled '"What makes my heart to throb & glow?" (*North India version*)', in Sussex Notebook 1 (pp. 152–4); [probably April–June 1883].

Sussex, KP 24/3.

From the Masjid-Al-Aqsa of Sayyid Ahmed (Wahabi), see KpR 149–51.

The Front Door ('I stand and guard — such ones as say')
First printed *Schoolboy Lyrics* (privately printed, Lahore, 1881); first pub. *Early Verse* (1900); *Sussex*, XXXV, 19; Rutherford, pp. 54–5; Harbord, Verse No. 21.

KpR 400 Transcript by Alfred Baldwin, one page (on a leaf of 'Wilden House, Near Stourport' notepaper), dated September 1880; dated on verso under the printed address 'Sunday, Octo. 3. 1880.'.

Sussex, Baldwin Papers 2/4.

'Fuzzy-Wuzzy' ('We've fought with many men acrost the seas')
First pub. *Scots Observer*, 15 March 1890; collected *Barrack-Room Ballads* (1892); *Sussex*, XXXII, 180–2; Harbord, Verse No. 421.

KpR 401 Fair copy, revised, headed 'Barrack Room Ballads No. III. "Fuzzy-Wuzzy" (Soudan Expeditionary Force)', one page.

Facsimile in Martindell, facing p. 159.

Yale.

KpR 401.5 Corrected page proof for *Barrack-Room Ballads* (1892); date stamped 12 February 1892.

British Library, Loan 97 (deposited by John Aris, 1989).

Gallio's Song ('All day long to the judgment-seat')
First pub. with story 'Little Foxes' in *Actions and Reactions* (London, 1909) (4 stanzas only); in full *Songs from Books* (New York, 1912); *Sussex*, VIII, 249–50 and *Sussex*, XXXIV, 57–8; Harbord, Verse No. 929.

KpR 402 In MS Actions and Reactions (f. 117).

University of St Andrews, MS PR4854.A4.

KpR 403 Fair copy, including a sketch, in MS Writings and Songs (pp. 43–5).

Berg.

KpR 404 Corrected first page proof for *Humorous Tales* (London, 1931), pp. 371–2; date stamped 29 May 1931.

British Library, Add. MS 55847.

KpR 405 Corrected first page proof (the fifth stanza written out) for the Sussex Edition, Vol. VIII; date stamped 28 November 1931.

British Library, Add. MS 55859.

Gehazi ('Whence comest thou, Gehazi')
First pub. *The Years Between* (London, [1919]); *Sussex*, XXXIII, 422–3; Harbord, Verse No. 1099.

KpR 406 Revised, one page.

Sotheby's, 9–10 December 1968, Lot 759, sold to Quaritch.

General Joubert ('With those that bred, with those that loosed the strife')
First pub. *The Friend* (Bloemfontein), 30 March 1900; collected *The Five Nations* (London, 1903); *Sussex*, XXXIII, 229; Harbord, Verse No. 748.

KpR 407 In MS Five Nations.

National Library of Australia, MS 94.

KpR 408 Corrected proof for the first publication, signed (initials), among materials for *The Friend* (see KpR).

Library of Congress, Rare Book Division, Colt Collection.

General Summary ('We are very slightly changed')
First pub. *Departmental Ditties* (1886); *Sussex*, XXXII, 3–4; Harbord, Verse No. 221.

KpR 409 Fair copy, in MS Departmental Ditties (pp. 2–3).

Berg.

KpR 410 Revisions and corrections on pp. [7]–8 of KpR 282.

Yale.

Gentlemen-Rankers ('To the legion of the lost ones, to the cohort of the damned')
First pub. *Barrack-Room Ballads* (1892); *Sussex*, XXXII, 219–21; Harbord, Verse No. 550.

KpR 411 Fair copy, one page.

Sussex, KP 24/22.

KpR 411.5 Corrected page proof for the first publication; date stamped 12 February 1892.

British Library, Loan 97 (deposited by John Aris, 1989).

Gertrude's Prayer ('That which is marred at birth Time shall not mend')
First pub. with story 'Dayspring Mishandled' in *Limits and Renewals* (London, 1932); collected separately *Inclusive Verse* [1933]; *Sussex*, XI, 31 and *Sussex*, XXXIV, 399; Harbord, Verse No. 1205. For corrections to the last lines of this poem which appear in the text of 'Dayspring Mishandled', see KpR .

KpR 412 Corrected page proof in Limits and Renewals Proof.

Syracuse University.

KpR 413 Corrected first page proof for the Sussex Edition, Vol. XI; date stamped 14 October 1932.

British Library, Add. MS 55862.

Gethsemane ('The Garden called Gethsemane')
First pub. *The Years Between* (London, [1919]); *Sussex*, XXXIII, 407; Harbord, Verse No. 1100.

KpR 414 Fair copy, revised, here entitled 'The Agony in the Garden.', in MS Years Between.

British Library, Add. MS 44841, f. 36.

Giffen's Debt ('*Imprimis* he was "broke". Thereafter left')

First pub. *Departmental Ditties* (1886); revised version in *Departmental Ditties*, 3rd ed (1888); *Sussex*, XXXII, 158–60; Harbord, Verse No. 222. See also KpR DD Dol.

KpR 415 Fair copy, including a sketch, in MS Departmental Ditties (pp. 96–9).

Berg.

KpR 416 Corrections on pp. 115, 117 of KpR 282.

Yale.

The Gift of the Sea ('The dead child lay in the shroud')
First pub. *English Illustrated Magazine*, August 1890; collected *Barrack-Room Ballads* (1892); *Sussex*, XXXII, 296–8; Harbord, Verse No. 469.

KpR 417 Draft, here beginning 'The dead child lay in the house', 7 pages containing doodles.

Sussex, KP 24/23.

KpR 417.5 Corrected page proof for *Barrack-Room Ballads* (1892).

British Library, Loan 97 (deposited by John Aris, 1989).

The Gipsy Song, see KpR 418.

The Gipsy Trail ('The white moth to the closing bine')
First pub. *Century Magazine*, December 1892 (13 stanzas); collected *Inclusive Verse* (1919); *Sussex*, XXXV, 180–1 (12 stanzas); Harbord, Verse No. 534 where the original uncollected 5th stanza is printed. One stanza from this poem beginning 'The wild hawk to the wind-swept sky' is quoted from an anonymous traditional ballad and also used by Kipling as heading to story 'Poor Dear Mamma' (Harbord, Verse No. 315A, as 'Gipsy Song').

KpR 418 Rough pencil copy of a variant version of stanzas 1–2, probably not in Kipling's hand, here beginning 'The white moth to the closing vine', one page.

Syracuse University.

Gipsy Vans ('Unless you come of the gipsy stock')
First pub. with story 'A Madonna of the Trenches' in *Debits and Credits* (London, 1926); collected separately *Inclusive Verse* [1927]; *Sussex*, X, 197–8 and *Sussex*, XXXIV, 383–4; Harbord, Verse No. 1132.

KpR 419 Fair copy, revised, one page.

Sussex, KP 24/24.

'Give the man who is not made', see KpR 559–60.

Given From the Cuckoo's Nest to the Beloved Infant — Greeting ('I sit in the midst of my study')
First pub. Rutherford (1986), pp. 113–15; not in Harbord.

KpR 420 Transcript by JLK of a verse letter from RK to his sister Trix, in Sussex Notebook 2 [pp. 1–4]; 28 January 1882.

Sussex, KP 24/2.

The Glories ('In Faiths and Food and Books and Friends')
First pub. separately as *A Choice of Songs* (London, 1925); collected *Inclusive Verse* [1933], as 'The Glories'; *Sussex*, XXXV, 261; Harbord, Verse No. 1125, as 'A Choice of Songs'.

KpR 421 Fair copy, revised, of a version without stanza 3, one page (containing also KpR 170, 605), annotated 'type.'.

Sussex, KP 24/25.

KpR 422 Typescript, here entitled 'A Choice of Songs' and beginning 'In Faith and Food...', one page.

Berg (from the files of A. P. Watt).

The Glory of the Garden ('Our England is a garden that is full of stately views')
First pub. C. R. L. Fletcher and Rudyard Kipling, *A History of England* (Oxford and London, 1911); collected separately *Songs from Books* (1915); *Sussex*, XXXIV, 301–3; Harbord, Verse No. 993.

KpR 423 Fair copy, extensively revised, in MS Years Between, including 3 drafts of stanzas 6–8, two leaves (rectos only).

British Library, Add. MS 44841, ff. 82–3 (rectos only).

'Go, stalk the red deer o'er the heather', see KpR 177.

The Goat, see KpR 173.

Gow's Watch: Act II, scene ii
First pub. (lines 1–8 only) as heading to Chapter 10 of the one-volume edition of *Kim* (1901), subscribed 'Old Play'; *Sussex*, XXI, 229; first pub. in full *Songs from Books* (1912); *Sussex*, XXXIV, 134–9; Harbord, Verse No. 768.

KpR 424 Fair copy of lines 1–8 only, containing a cancelled line, here untitled, subscribed '*Old Play*', one page.

Harvard, bMS Am 1891.6(112).

KpR 425 Revision and correction on pp. 158–9, 162, 164 of KpR 1112.

Yale.

KpR 426 Corrections to lines 1–8 (as heading to Chapter 10 of *Kim*), in first page proof for the Sussex Edition, Vol. XXI (KpR 1791); date stamped 9 October 1931.

British Library, Add. MS 55871.

Gow's Watch: Act III, scene ii
First pub. with story 'Mrs Bathurst' in *Traffics and Discoveries* (London, 1904), as 'From Lyden's "Irenius"'; collected separately *Inclusive Verse* [1927]; *Sussex*, VII, 343–4; Harbord, Verse No. 771.

KpR 427 In MS Traffics and Discoveries: two fair copies, revised, here untitled, one headed 'They', the other 'Mrs Bathurst', here being a dialogue between 'Fool', 'Prince' and 'Ferdinand', one page each; followed by drafts of the last 7 lines, 3 pages (the last containing also KpR 149).

McGill University.

KpR 428 Corrected first page proof for the Sussex Edition; date stamped 22 March 1932.

British Library, Add. MS 55858.

Gow's Watch: Act IV, Scene iv
First pub. with story 'The Prophet and the Country' in *Debits and Credits* (London, 1926); collected separately *Inclusive Verse* [1927]; *Sussex*, X, 165–7 and *Sussex*, XXXIV, 139–42; Harbord, Verse No. 769.

KpR 429 Fair copy, revised, here entitled 'Gow's Watch', annotated 'To follow The Prophet & The Country', one page.

Sussex, KP 24/26.

KpR 430 Corrected first page proof for the Sussex Edition, Vol. X; date stamped 30 December 1931.

British Library, Add. MS 55861.

Gow's Watch: Act V, Scene iii
First pub. with story 'A Madonna of the Trenches' in *Debits and Credits* (London, 1926); collected separately *Inclusive Verse* [1927]; *Sussex*, X, 221–5 and *Sussex*, XXXIV, 142–6; Harbord, Verse No. 770.

KpR 431 Corrected first page proof for the Sussex Edition, Vol. X; date stamped 30 December 1931.

British Library, Add. MS 55861.

Grahamstown Memorial to the Fallen (1880–1902), see KpR 1211.

The Grand-Master's Defense, see KpR 185, 187.

The Grave of the Hundred Head ('A Snider squibbed in the jungle —')
First pub. *Week's News*, 7 January 1888; collected *Departmental Ditties*, 4th ed (1890); *Sussex*, XXXII, 122–5; Harbord, Verse No. 285.

KpR 432 Fair copy, including a sketch, in MS Departmental Ditties (pp. 109–14).

Berg.

KpR 433 Corrected page proof for *Inclusive Verse* (1919), one page numbered 65, signed (initials), in KpR 537.

Princeton, Ex3814.9.1919.11.

'Great-Heart' ('Concerning brave Captains')
First pub. *Daily Telegraph*, 5 February 1919; collected *Inclusive Verse* (1919); *Sussex*, XXXV, 239–40; Harbord, Verse No. 1056.

KpR 434 Three pages of successive drafts (here untitled) and a fourth page containing a fair copy, revised, originally beginning 'Of many brave captains whom war hath made known'.

Sussex, KP 24/27.

KpR 435 As sent to Julian Street with a letter of [15 April 1919?].

Princeton, Mudd Library, Theodore Roosevelt Collection, Mudd Library, AM 17633.

The Greek National Anthem ('We knew thee of old')
First pub. *Daily Telegraph*, 17 October 1918; collected *Inclusive Verse* (1919); *Sussex*, XXXV, 233–4; Harbord, Verse No. 1051.

KpR 436 Revised, here originally untitled, later entitled 'Greek National Anthem (*Translation*)', in MS Years Between, annotated '*type once*'.

British Library, Add. MS 44841, f. 134.

Greeting ('What comfort can I send thee sweet')
First pub. Rutherford (1986), p. 122; not in Harbord.

KpR 437 Fair copy, in Sussex Notebook 1 (pp. 64–5); dated 6 March [1882].

Sussex, KP 24/3.

KpR 438 Fair copy, in Sussex Notebook 3 (first series, pp. 16–17); dated 6 March 1882.

Sussex, KP 24/1.

KpR 439 Fair copy, in a letter to 'Mater' [i.e., Mrs Tavenor Perry], United Services College, 9 March 1882.

Library of Congress, Rare Book Division, Carpenter Kipling Collection.

KpR 440 Fair copy, one page (on a leaf containing also KpR 480.5), as sent to Edith Plowden in April 1882.

Sussex, Baldwin Papers 2/30.

KpR 441 Transcript by AMK, in Sussex Notebook 2 [pp. 54–5]; dated March 1882.

Sussex, KP 24/2.

Gunga Din ('You may talk o' gin an' beer')
First pub. *New York Tribune*, 22 May 1890 and *Scots Observer*, 7 June 1890; collected *Barrack-Room Ballads* (1892); *Sussex*, XXXII, 190–92; Harbord, Verse No. 460.

KpR 441.5 Corrected page proof for *Barrack-Room Ballads* (1892); date stamped 12 February 1892.

British Library, Loan 97 (deposited by John Aris, 1989).

Hadramauti ('Who knows the heart of the Christian? How does he reason?')
First pub. as heading to 'A Friend's Friend' in *Civil and Military Gazette*, 2 May 1887 (last stanza only beginning 'Wherefore slew I the stranger? He brought me dishonour'); collected *Plain Tales from the Hills* (Calcutta and London, 1888); reprinted *Sussex*, I, 351; first pub. in full *Songs from Books* (New York, 1912); *Sussex*, XXXIV, 55–6; Harbord, Verse No. 259.

KpR 442 Fair copy, in MS Writings and Songs (pp. 112–15).

Berg.

KpR 443 Corrected page proof for *Inclusive Verse* (1919), one page numbered 603, signed (initials), in KpR 537.

Princeton, Ex3814.9.1919.11.

Half-Ballade of Waterval ('When by the labour of my 'ands')
First pub. *The Five Nations* (London, 1903); *Sussex*, XXXIII, 331–2; Harbord, Verse No. 816.

KpR 444 In MS Five Nations.

National Library of Australia, MS 94.

The Handiest Man ('While you're shouting for Johnny & cheering Jack')
Questionable attribution; lines 1–4 printed in Christie's sale catalogue, 28 March 1984, p. 71; not in Harbord.

KpR 445 MS in an unidentified hand, 47 lines, 2 pages, in ink.

The sale catalogue reports that the 'poem was reputedly given by Kipling to the chief engineer on the boat on which he travelled to South Africa'.

Christie's, 28 March 1984, Lot 180.

The Harbour Watch
First produced Royalty Theatre, London, May and September 1913; first printed Harbord, IV (1965–6), 1836–57. Livingston, p. 370 says that two 29-page typescripts were deposited for copyright, one at the Library of Congress, the other at the British Library (now Department of Printed Books, C.70.f.18).

KpR 446 Fair copy, revised, in MS Non-Fiction, c. 14 pages.

British Library, Add. MS 45542, ff. 237–50 (rectos only).

KpR 447 Typescript, 29 numbered leaves (rectos only), title page, Dramatis Personae and unnumbered interleavings, used and annotated by Frank Vernon, producer of the April 1913 production, stamped 'The Property of Vedrenne & Eadie, Royalty Theatre.'.

Another copy of this typescript, without annotations, stamped 'Office of Alice Kauser...New York' is also at the Library of Congress, Rare Book Division.

Library of Congress, Rare Book Division, Colt Collection.

Harp Song of the Dane Women ('What is a woman that you forsake her')
First pub. with story 'The Knights of the Joyous Venture' in *Puck of Pook's Hill* (London, 1906); collected separately *Songs from Books* (New York, 1912); *Sussex*, XIV, 57 and *Sussex*, XXXIV, 44; Harbord, Verse No. 890.

KpR 448 Fair copy, revised, here untitled, in MS Puck.

Bodleian, MS. Eng. misc. c. 127, f. 23.

KpR 449 Slightly corrected first page proof for the Sussex Edition, Vol. XIV; date stamped 2 July 1931.

British Library, Add. MS 55864.

'Have you got a yearning'
No publication traced; not in Harbord.

KpR 450 Twenty-four lines, in a letter (containing also KpR 781, 1159) to W. E. Henley, Brattleboro, 26 October 1892.

Pierpont Morgan, MA 1617.

'He had sailed in the Keldonan, in the Walmer & Kinfauns'
First printed in Harbord (1969), Verse No. 921, as 'Summer Excursion *or* To B. H. Walton *or* The Steam Yacht "Bantam"'.

KpR 451 Fair copy, 8 lines, on the last page (only one extant) of a letter to [B. H. Walton], pasted on a leaf from a guest book containing Kipling's 'registration' dated 3 July [1909].

Library of Congress, Rare Book Division, Colt Collection.

'He must be a man of decent height', see KpR 179.

'Hear ther truth our tongues are telling'
First pub. in text of story 'The Village that Voted the Earth was Flat' in *A Diversity of Creatures* (London, 1917); *Sussex*, IX, 201; Harbord, Verse No. 1035. See also KpR 2197.

KpR 452 Fair copy, in the text of the MS of 'The Village that Voted the Earth was Flat' (KpR 2195), in MS Diversity of Creatures (f. 64).

University of Edinburgh, Dk. 2. 8.

'Heaven help the Nations of the Continent'
First pub. Dr Alfred Frolich, 'Kipling and Winter Sports', *KJ*, No. 38 (June 1936), p. 43; reprinted Harbord, Verse No. 920, as 'Treatment for a Cold'.

KpR 453 Transcript in an unidentified hand, on Hotel Cattani, Engelberg notepaper, enclosed (apparently) in a letter to Madame Frolich, n.d.

Dalhousie University.

'Helen All Alone' ('There was darkness under Heaven')

First pub. with story 'In the Same Boat' in *A Diversity of Creatures* (London, 1917); collected separately *Inclusive Verse* (1919); *Sussex*, IX, 103–4 and *Sussex*, XXXIV, 314–15; Harbord, Verse No. 1042.

KpR 454 Fair copy, slightly revised, in MS Diversity of Creatures (f. 33), anotated 'To precede *In the same boat*'.

University of Edinburgh, Dk. 2. 8.

KpR 455 Corrected first page proof for the Sussex Edition, Vol. IX; date stamped 28 April 1932.

British Library, Add. MS 55860.

'Hello, Brander! Lemme look'
No publication traced; not in Harbord.

KpR 456 Thirty-six lines, a parody of James Whitcomb Riley, signed 'J. W. R.', inserted in Brander Matthews's copy of *Many Inventions* (London, 1893), containing also KpR 1018, 1392.

Cornell University.

Heriot's Ford ('"What's that that hirples at my side?"')
First pub. (stanzas 1–2) as heading to Chapter 10 of *The Light that Failed* (London, 1890), ascribed 'The Fight of Heriot's Ford'; reprinted *Sussex*, XVIII, 157; first pub. in full separately *Songs from Books* (New York, 1912); *Sussex*, XXXIV, 191–2; Harbord, Verse No. 451.

KpR 457 Draft of stanzas 1–2, here being the chapter heading to Chapter 10 (here called Chapter 8) in the draft of *The Light that Failed* (KpR).

Princeton, Doubleday Collection, Box 5.

KpR 458 Draft of stanzas 1–2, listed (on a page of chapter headings for *The Light that Failed* (KpR 180)) as the heading for Chapter 8; watermarked 1888.

Princeton, Doubleday Collection, Box 5, Folder.

KpR 459 Correction on p. 227 of KpR 1112.

Yale.

KpR 460 Corrected first page proof for the Sussex Edition of *The Light that Failed* (KpR 1837); date stamped 20 November 1931.

British Library, Add. MS 55868.

The Heritage ('Our fathers in a wondrous age')
First pub. *Collier's Weekly*, 4 November 1905; collected *Songs from Books* (New York, 1912); *Sussex*, XXXIV, 90–1; Harbord, Verse No. 880.

KpR 461 Fair copy, revised, in MS Years Between, one page.

British Library, Add. MS 44841, f. 112.

KpR 462 Fair copy, signed, one page.

Dalhousie University.

KpR 463 Slightly corrected typescript, signed, one page, annotated 'copyright 1905 by Rudyard Kipling in the United States of America...'.

Syracuse University.

'He's the man that wrote the Jungle Books — likewise the Seven Seas'
First printed Harbord (1969), Verse No. 1226 (where the lines are said to be written on a MS presented to Magdalene College, Cambridge).

KpR 464 Fair copy, 4 lines, one page, signed (initials).

Sussex, KP 24/28.

Himalayan ('Now the land is ringed with a circle of fire'), see KpR 1412.

His Consolation ('So be it; you give me my release')
First pub. *Echoes* (Lahore, [1884]); *Sussex*, XXXV, 75; Rutherford, pp. 145–6; Harbord, Verse No. 111.

KpR 465 Fair copy, 5 stanzas, in Sussex Notebook 1 (pp. 98–9); dated 21 May 1882.

Sussex, KP 24/3.

His Consolation [Their Consolation] ('Alas! Alas! it is a tale so old —')

First pub. Rutherford (1986), p. 147; not in Harbord.

KpR 466 Fair copy, here entitled 'His Consolation', in Sussex Notebook 1 p. 100); dated 26 May [1882].

Sussex, KP 24/3.

KpR 467 Fair copy, here entitled 'His Consolation', in Sussex Notebook 3 (first series, p. 68); dated 26 May 1882.

Sussex, KP 24/1.

KpR 468 Fair copy, here entitled 'Their Consolation', on one page of a letter (containing also KpR 49, 296) to 'Mater' [Mrs Tavenor Perry], dated 28 May and postmarked 30 May 1882.

Huntington, HM 11882.

KpR 469 Transcript by AMK, in Sussex Notebook 2 [p. 58], here entitled 'Their Consolation'.

Susssex, KP 24/2.

'Ho! Angels the message of my love'
No publication traced; not in Harbord.

KpR 470 Fair copy of mock verses, 16 lines, in the text of 'That Lady who Recited...' (KpR 2129).

Berg.

The Holy War ('He mapped for those who follow')
First pub. *New York Times*, 6 December 1917; collected *The Years Between* (London, [1919]); *Sussex*, XXXIII, 377–9; Harbord, Verse No. 1033.

KpR 471 Revised, in MS Years Between, including the introductory heading but not the epigraph, one page.

British Library, Add. MS 44841, f. 23.

KpR 472 Typescript, slightly corrected and revised, including the heading, 3 numbered leaves (rectos only), signed.

Syracuse University.

Home ('The Lord shall change the hearts of men')
First pub. with story 'Home' in *Civil and Military Gazette*, 25 December 1891; not in *Sussex*; reprinted Harbord, Verse No. 517.

KpR 473 Carbon typescript, on first 2 leaves (rectos only) of KpR 1704, ten 4-line stanzas.

Library of Congress, Rare Book Division, Colt Collection.

Home ('This is the prayer the Cave Man prayed'), see KpR 1218–20.

The Hour of the Angel ('Sooner or late — in earnest or in jest')
First pub. with story '"Stalky"' in *Land and Sea Tales* (London, 1923); collected separately *Inclusive Verse* [1927]; *Sussex*, XVII (*Stalky & Co.*), 27 and *Sussex*, XXXIV, 349; Harbord, Verse No. 1116.

KpR 474 One draft and 2 fair copies, revised, one page each: draft beginning 'Be certain, then the sum of all your past', first fair copy here untitled and beginning 'Later or soon — in earnest or in jest', annotated 'To follow Stalky & Co', the other fair copy annotated 'To follow "Stalky"'.

Sussex, KP 24/29.

The Houses (''Twixt my house and thy house the pathway is broad')
First pub. *Navy League Journal*, 28 June 1898; collected *The Years Between* (London, [1919]); *Sussex*, XXXIII, 380; Harbord, Verse No. 724.

KpR 475 Fair copy, revised, in MS Years Between, signed, including an epigraph ascribed '*Daily Paper*', one page.

British Library, Add. MS 44841, f. 24.

How do we Know? ('God <And> bless the dull incurious eye')
No publication traced; not in Harbord.

KpR 476 Draft lines, the second beginning 'God bless the <dull> fixed incurious eye', on verso of f. 6 of MS of 'My Sunday at Home' (KpR 1912), in MS Day's Work; watermarked 1890.

British Library, Add. MS 45541, f. 71v.

How It Seemed to Us ('A grey flat lying out against the sea')
First pub. (lines 1–3) in Louis Cornell, *Kipling in India* (London and New York, 1966), p. 32; first pub. in full Rutherford (1986), p. 115; Harbord, Verse No. 55.

KpR 477 Fair copy in Sussex Notebook 1 (p. 54); dated 30 January 1882.

Sussex, KP 24/3.

KpR 478 Fair copy in Sussex Notebook 3 (first series, p. 53); dated 2 February 1882.

Sussex, KP 24/1.

KpR 479 Fair copy, in MS Sundry Phansies.

Berg.

KpR 480 Transcript by AMK, in Sussex Notebook 2 [p. 18]; dated 1 February 1882.

Sussex, KP 24/2.

KpR 480.5 Fair copy, one page (on a leaf containing also KpR 440), as sent to Edith Plowden in April 1882.

Typescript of this MS at Sussex, KP 24/30.

Sussex, Baldwin Papers 2/30.

How the Day Broke ('The night was very silent, and the moon was going down')
First pub. *Echoes* (Lahore, [1884]); *Sussex*, XXXV, 102–3; Harbord, Verse No. 69. For an annotation in a copy of *Echoes*, see KpR 314.

KpR 481 Fair copy, in Sussex Notebook 3 (first series, pp. 19–20); dated 30 December 1881.

Sussex, KP 24/1.

KpR 482 Transcript by JLK, in Sussex Notebook 2 [pp. 20–21]; dated 30 December 1881.

Sussex, KP 24/2.

KpR 483 In MS Sundry Phansies.

Berg.

KpR 484 Fair copy, slightly revised, here untitled, 2 pages (one leaf).

Huntington, HM 11886.

How the Goddess Awakened ('Where the reveller laid him, drunk with wine')
First pub. *Echoes* (Lahore, [1884]); *Sussex*, XXXV, 109–11; Rutherford, pp. 70–2; Harbord, Verse No. 70A. For an annotation in a copy of *Echoes*, see KpR 314.

KpR 485 Fair copy, in MS Sundry Phansies.

Berg.

KpR 486 Draft of 11 lines (one cancelled), here untitled and beginning '<Why is it on me that you call>/Wherefore is it on me you call'), including a pen-and-ink sketch of a satyr and a nun, one page.

This MS not mentioned Rutherford.

Berg.

KpR 487 Incomplete fair copy (wanting last 8 lines), 4 pages, in Sussex Notebook 3 (first series, pp. 2–5, with a note on unnumbered page facing p. 2); dated 9 September 1881.

Sussex, KP 24/1.

The Hyaenas ('After the burial-parties leave')
First pub. *The Years Between* (London, [1919]); *Sussex*, XXXIII, 395–6; Harbord, Verse No. 1101.

KpR 488 Revised, in MS Years Between, annotated 'type', one page.

British Library, Add. MS 44841, f. 32.

Hymn before Action ('The earth is full of anger')
First pub. *The Echo*, March 1896 (stanzas 1, 4 and 6 only, as 'A Little Season'); in full separately New York, 1896; collected *The Seven Seas* (New York, 1896); *Sussex*, XXXIII, 80–1; Harbord, Verse No. 663.

KpR 489 Fair copy, stanza 3 annotated 'omit if you like...', one page (cut into three); watermarked 1894.

Columbia University, Engel Collection.

KpR 490 Fair copy, subtitled 'for Julia De Forest from Rudyard Kipling', signed, one page; dated July 1896.

Harvard, MS Eng 165, f. 7.

Hymn of Breaking Strain ('The careful text-books measure')
First pub. *Daily Telegraph* and *The Engineer*, 15 March 1935; *Sussex*, XXXV, 305–6; Harbord, Verse No. 1223.

KpR 491 Typed transcript of the copy given to Sir Herbert Baker, subscribed 'Given by Mrs K. to H. B. June 1936' and annotated 'as given to *London House*', 2 numbered leaves (rectos only).

Sussex, KP 14/7.

'I am the Most Wise Baviaan, saying in most wise tones'
First pub. with story 'How the Leopard Got His Spots' in *Just So Stories* (London, 1902); collected separately *Songs from Books* (London, 1913); *Sussex*, XIII, 59 and *Sussex*, XXXIV, 238–9, as 'Chapter Heading'; Harbord, Verse No. 792.

KpR 492 Fair copy, revised, in MS Just So Stories, annotated 'on separate page to follow Leopard'.

British Library, Add. MS 59840, f. 31.

I Believe ('Oh Love what need is it that thou should'st die?')
First pub. Rutherford (1986), p. 143; not in Harbord.

KpR 493 Fair copy, in Sussex Notebook 1 (p. 95); dated 9 May [1882].

Sussex, KP 24/3.

KpR 494 Fair copy, in Sussex Notebook 3 (first series, p. 56); dated 9 May 1882.

Sussex, KP 24/1.

'I cannot write, I cannot think'
First printed American Art Association sale catalogue, 22–4 April 1924, Lot 490; reprinted Ballard (1935), p. 56; first pub. Edmonia Hill, 'The Young Kipling', *Atlantic Monthly*, April 1936; reprinted Harbord (1969), Verse No. 369 as 'To Mrs Hill, From Me. A Journalist Unkempt and Inky, with All Regards'; Rutherford, pp. 456–7, as 'Inscription in Copy of *Wee Willie Winkie* Presented to Mrs Hill'.

KpR 495 Draft, one page (containing also a list of ports of call, sketches and a first attempt at lines for an inscription beginning 'As idle as a bard may be') of the thick paper carbon detached from MS From Sea to Sea (see KpR 1634) (Vol. I, p. 100).

The thin paper carbon copy of this page is still in MS From Sea to Sea at the Huntington, HM 12429; a photocopy is at Cornell University. The lines beginning 'As idle as a bard may be' are printed Rutherford, p. 456 (headnote).

Library of Congress, Rare Book Division, Carpenter Kipling Collection.

KpR 496 Fair copy, inscribed on verso of contents page of a copy of *Wee Willie Winkie* (Allahabad, [1888]) presented to Edmonia Hill, 10 March [1889].

Facsimile in American Art Association sale catalogue, 22–4 April 1924, Lot 490.

Texas.

KpR 497 Fair copy, on one page of Metropole Hotel notepaper containing the printed date '189—'.

Princeton, General MSS [Bound].

'I charge you charge your glasses —', see KpR 742.

'"I have a thousand men," said he', see KpR 179, 180.

'I have eaten your bread and salt', see KpR 877–8.

'I keep six honest serving-men'
First pub. with story 'The Elephant's Child' in *Just So Stories* (London, 1902); collected separately *Songs from Books* (London, 1913); *Sussex*, XIII, 79 and *Sussex*, XXXIV, 239–40, as 'Chapter Heading'; Harbord, Verse No. 793.

KpR 498 Fair copy, revised, wanting the last 4 lines, in MS Just So Stories, annotated 'to follow Elephant — on separate page'.

British Library, Add. MS 59840, f. 41.

KpR 499 Slightly corrected first page proof for the Sussex Edition, Vol. XIII; date stamped 29 October 1932.

British Library, Add. MS 55863.

'I knew his times and his seasons', see KpR 1275.

'I know a young lady from Beavor'
First pub. Rutherford (1986), p. 458, as 'Verse Fragments and Limericks (c)'; not in Harbord.

KpR 500 Limerick, apparently written on board the S.S. City of Peking en route from Yokohama to San Francisco in May 1889, in pencil, on a scrap.

Library of Congress, Rare Book Division, Carpenter Kipling Collection, Pen and Brush Sketches, Item 5.

'I know the Teuton and the Gaul'
Eighteen lines first printed in Harbord (1969), Verse No. 762B.

KpR 501 Fragmentary verses and notes on 8 scraps, including several versions of poem beginning as above.

These scraps (as well as KpR 502, 1878) are accompanied by a note from Anthony Strachey: 'These notes were found by my mother Frances Strachey as packing in "the type" of a small hand printing press given to her as a young girl by Kipling'.

Library of Congress, Rare Book Division, Colt Collection.

'I Pierrot jesting with woes'
First printed (inaccurately) Harbord (1969), p. 5666, as Verse No. 489B 'About a Painting by Flo Gerrard' beginning 'I, Pirrot festing with woes'.

KpR 502 Fair copy, on a scrap.

For provenance, see KpR 501.

Library of Congress, Rare Book Division, Colt Collection.

KpR 503 Eight lines about a painting by 'Violet' (i.e., Florence) Garrard, 'Les Beaux Esprits se rencontrent', on a scrap; c. 1890.

Sotheby's, 9–10 December 1968, Lot 687 (property of Frances Egerton), sold to Rota.

'I played with a lady at Euchre'
First pub. Rutherford (1986), p. 458, as 'Verse Fragments and Limericks (b)'; not in Harbord.

KpR 504 Limerick, revised, in pencil, written on board the S.S. City of Peking en route from Yokohama to San Francisco in May 1889, on a scrap pasted to a leaf containing also sketches and KpR 518.

Library of Congress, Rare Book Division, Carpenter Kipling Collection.

'"I plough deep" said the car.'
First pub. (4 lines only) in Carrington (1955), p. 456; Harbord, Verse No. 1109, as 'Cemeteries in France of British Dead in World War I'.

KpR 505 Two typescripts of two 4-line stanzas, one each in the 2 copies of RK's 'Motoring Journals' (KpR 2288) kept during a tour of France, August–September 1924.

Sussex, KP 25/7 and 25/8.

'I reside at Table Mountain and my name is Truthful James'
First pub. (stanza 9 beginning 'In the "Iroquois" at Buffalo that partnership broke up') in *Pearson's Magazine*, January 1908; reprinted Harbord, Verse No. 722A, as 'A Dealer in Brains *or* In the Iroquois' (also listed Harbord, Verse No. 910, as 'A Dealer in Brains'); first pub. in full *Rudyard Kipling to Rider Haggard*, ed. Morton Cohen (London, 1965), pp. 26–7; reprinted Harbord, Verse No. 381A, as 'Mr Haggard and Mr Lang'; Rutherford, pp. 467–9, as 'Verses From a Letter to Andrew Lang'. Another version of lines 1–4 are the concluding lines of 'Virginibus Puerisque' (first pub. *The Pioneer*, 13 August 1888; Harbord, Verse No. 330; Rutherford, pp. 415–21). The first publication was apparently printed from the autograph album of Major J. B. Pond where the lines are subscribed '(The story of a lecture)'.

KpR 506 Verse letter, ten 4-line stanzas, to Andrew Lang dated from The Grange, West Kensington, 26 October 1889.

A typed transcript of this letter is at Sussex, KP 16/18.

Norfolk Record Office, MS 4694/21/1.

'I thank you Mrs Colvin'
First pub. Rutherford (1986), p. 450; not in Harbord.

KpR 507 Draft of thank-you verses, on verso of a sketch.

Library of Congress, Rare Book Division, Carpenter Kipling Collection, Pen and Brush Sketches, Item 30.

'I wrote you verses two years syne'
First pub. Louis Cornell, *Kipling in India* (London and New York, 1966), p. 69; Rutherford, p. 251, as 'Inscriptions in Presentation Copies of *Echoes* (c)'; Harbord, Verse No. 86, as 'Dedication *or* Inscription: To F. G. from R. K.'.

KpR 508 Inscribed in a copy of *Echoes* (Lahore, [1884]) presented to F[lorence] G[arrard], September 1884.

This copy listed in Stewart, p. 15 (copy 4); *Grolier Catalogue*, Item 26. A typescript made by Flora Livingston is among her papers at Harvard; it was printer's copy for the first publication.

Unlocated.

'I'd like to be an octave'
No publication traced; not in Harbord.

KpR 509 Eighteen lines, in a letter to John Collier, 7 May 1901.

Typed transcript at Sussex, KP 14/41.

Harvard, bMS Eng 819.

If — ('If you can keep your head when all about you')
First pub. *American Magazine*, October 1910; collected with story 'Brother Square-Toes' in *Rewards and Fairies* (London, 1910); collected separately *Songs from Books* (New York, 1912); *Sussex*, XV, 169–70 and *Sussex*, XXXIV, 100–101; Harbord, Verse No. 952.

KpR 510 Fair copy, slightly revised, in MS Rewards and Fairies, annotated 'type please/to precede A priest in spite of himself'.

Cambridge University Library, ADD 6850, f. 68.

KpR 511 Fair copy, signed, one page, inscribed 'To Frank [Doubleday] from Rud. Ap[ril]. 1913: Paris Hotel, Brighton'.

Princeton, Doubleday Collection, Box 3, Bound Vol. I, Item 14.

KpR 512 Quotation, one page, annotated 'copied out from memory by Rudyard Kipling. Batemans: Sep. 1913. for E. W. Bok on his 50th Birthday.'.

Facsimile in *The Americanization of Edward Bok* (New York, 1923), p. 315 and Ballard, p. 181.

Unlocated.

KpR 513 Quotation, on one leaf (2 pages) of Bateman's notepaper, signed; sent to Lt-Col James Alexander Macphail, c. 15 July 1916.

This MS described in C. Gordon-Craig, 'A Manuscript of "If —"', *KJ*, 43 (1976), 6–8.

Owned (1976) by C. Gordon-Craig.

KpR 514 Corrected first page proof (one minor correction only) for the Sussex Edition, Vol. XV; date stamped 18 September 1931.

British Library, Add. MS 55865.

'If Europe ask why I whom Pegasus'
No publication traced; not in Harbord.

KpR 515 Unfinished draft, largely cancelled, on the verso of one page of the MS of 'They' (KpR 2134) in MS Traffics and Discoveries.

McGill University.

'"If I have taken the common clay', see KpR 179–180, 183.

'If to die well be virtues part most high'
No publication traced; not in Harbord.

KpR 516 Four versions of a translation of a Greek epitaph attributed to Simonides, each in a different ink (4 lines each), including the original Greek, one page.

Dalhousie University.

'If Yealm is called "Yam"'
First printed Harbord (1969), p. 5668, as Verse No. 921A 'Yealm'.

KpR 517 Three MSS: (1) draft, in pencil, on one page of 'Cawsand. Nr Plymouth' notepaper; (2) fair copy, revised, on one page of same notepaper; (3) fair copy, written opposite RK's signature on a loose leaf of a guest book dated 21 August 1925.

Library of Congress, Rare Book Division, Colt Collection.

'Il y avait une esprit maline'
No publication traced; not in Harbord.

KpR 518 Fair copy of a limerick in French, on a scrap pasted to a leaf containing also sketches and KpR 504, written on board the S.S. City of Peking en route from Yokohama to San Francisco in May 1889.

Library of Congress, Rare Book Division, Carpenter Kipling Collection.

An Imperial Rescript ('Now this is the tale of the Council the German Kaiser decreed')
First pub. *St James's Gazette*, 10 February 1890; collected *Barrack-Room Ballads* (1892); *Sussex*, XXXII, 319–21; Harbord, Verse No. 406.

KpR 518.5 Corrected page proof for *Barrack-Room Ballads* (1892).

British Library, Loan 97 (deposited by John Aris, 1989).

'Imperious, wool-booted Sage'
First pub. Edmonia Hill, 'The Young Kipling', *Atlantic Monthly*, April 1936; Rutherford, pp. 435–6; Harbord, Verse Nos. 354A–354B. For another attempt at lines for Mrs Hill's godchild, see KpR 1906.

KpR 519 Fair copy, four 4-line stanzas, one page, written by RK to accompany Edmonia Hill's gift to her godchild; [Allahabad, 1888].

A photocopy of this MS is at Cornell University.

Library of Congress, Rare Book Division, Carpenter Kipling Collection.

KpR 520 Fair copy of a version beginning 'Imperious, long-coated Sage', signed, one page of a 'little leaflet' including RK's decorated title page reading 'Lines To A Superior Young Lady on the Occasion of her First Manifesting A Will of Her Own'.

Facsimile of poem and title page accompanying the note '"A Superior Young Lady"', *KJ*, 59 (1985), 76–8 where it is suggested that the lines were written for Marjorie Balestier, September 1891–February 1892; this version corresponds (with a few variants) with that printed in Harbord, Verse No. 354B (not mentioned in Rutherford).

Marlboro College, Vermont.

'In a very short time you're released from all care', see KpR 1900.

In Durance, see KpR 177.

In Memoriam July–August 1883 ('If I have held my peace so long')
First pub. Rutherford (1986), pp. 195–7; not in Harbord.

KpR 521 Fair copy, signed 'Ruddy', on pp. 1–3 of a folded leaf, followed by a note to Lizzie Walker (pp. 3–4).

Pierpont Morgan, MA 1822.

In Seonee, see KpR 179–180, 183–4, 186–7.

In Shadowland, see KpR 184–5, 187.

In Springtime ('My garden blazes brightly with the rose-bush and the peach')
First pub. *The Pioneer*, 20 March 1885; collected *Departmental Ditties* (1886); *Sussex*, XXXII, 156–7; Harbord, Verse No. 132.

KpR 522 Fair copy, in MS Words, Wise and Otherwise [pp. 25–6].

Berg.

In the Beginning [A Creed] ('Woe is, and pain, and men grow old thereby')
First pub. Rutherford (1986), p. 139; not in Harbord.

KpR 523 Fair copy, here entitled 'A Creed', in Sussex Notebook 1 (p. 61); dated 2 April 1882.

Sussex, KP 24/3.

KpR 524 Fair copy, here entitled 'In the Beginning', here being the first of 'Four Sonnets' (see KpR 48, 922, 1281), in Sussex Notebook 3 (first series, p. 69); dated 2 April 1882.

Sussex, KP 24/1.

KpR 525 Transcript by AMK, in Sussex Notebook 2 [p. 57], here entitled 'A Creed'; dated April 1882.

Sussex, KP 24/2.

In the Case of Rukhmibhaio ('Gentlemen reformers with an English Education —')
First pub. Rutherford (1986), pp. 373–5; not in Harbord.

KpR 526 Drafts and an incomplete fair copy, in Scrapbook 1 (pp. 310–11 *rev.* and 305 *rev.*, respectively).

Sussex, KP 28/1.

In the City of Berlin ('There were passengers thirty and three')
First printed (facsimile) in American Art Association sale catalogue, 22–4 April 1924, Lot 492; reprinted Harbord, Verse No. 380; Rutherford, pp. 466–7.

KpR 527 Fair copy, in pencil, on the verso of a menu card dated 26 September 1889 of the S.S. City of Berlin, written during a voyage from New York to Liverpool.

Library of Congress, Rare Book Division, Carpenter Kipling Collection.

'In the "Iroquois" at Buffalo that partnership broke up', see KpR 506.

'In the microscopical Hinterland of a cramped sub-continent'
First pub. (lines 1–2 only) in Owen Tweedy, 'Rudyard Kipling and Rottingdean', *KJ* 18 (1951), 11; printed in full in Harbord (1969), Verse No. 518.

KpR 528 Fair copy, 28 lines, unfinished, 2 pages.

Facsimile in Sussex, Baldwin Papers 2/5.

Owned (1986) M. E. Macdonald.

'In the name of *Justice*'
No publication traced; not in Harbord.

KpR 529 Draft of lines on Tillett and Burns, 3 stanzas, in a letter to Ralph Blumenfeld, 18 June 1912.

Texas.

In the Neolithic Age ('In the Neolithic Age savage warfare did I wage')
First pub. as heading to 'My First Book' in *The Idler*, December 1892; collected separately *Ballads and Barrack-Room Ballads* (New York and London, 1893) and *The Seven Seas* (New York, 1896); *Sussex*, XXXIII, 95–7; Harbord, Verse No. 531.

KpR 530 Revised typescript, eight 4-line stanzas (one added in RK's hand), on first 2 leaves (rectos only) of 'My First Book' (KpR 1900), annotated at top 'rhymed heading for article Primum Tempus. sm type'.

Texas.

KpR 531 Fair copy, 9 stanzas, one page of Naulakha notepaper, inserted in a copy of *The Jungle Book* (London and New York, 1894) presented to Rockhill.

Facsimile in American Art Association sale catalogue, 1–2 December 1924, Lot 202.

Texas.

KpR 532 Typescript, two leaves (rectos only), annotated in an unidentified hand '(Copyright, 1893, by Macmillan & Co.)'.

Princeton, Archive of Charles Scribner's Sons, Miscellaneous Author's MSS and Galleys Series, Box 1, Folder 18.

KpR 533 Quotation of stanza 6, in a letter to Walter Pollock, c. 1894.

Texas.

KpR 534 Fair copy of last stanza, signed, annotated 'For Mrs Danforth', on one page of 'R.M.S. Teutonic' notepaper; dated 21 June 1899.

Cornell University.

KpR 534.5 Quotation of concluding 3 lines, signed.

Bryn Mawr College, Adelman Collection.

KpR 535 Revisions (for Vol. XI of the Outward Bound Edition), in a letter (containing also KpR 602) to Mr Burlingame (of Scribner's), annotated 'Ansd 23 July 97'.

Princeton, Archive of Charles Scribner's Sons, Box 87, Folder 1.

KpR 536 Correction to line 38 (for 'reprinted editions & also Bombay Edition'), in a letter (containing also 'Brother Square Toes') to Messrs Macmillan, Bateman's, 9 April 1913.

British Library, Add. MS 54940, f. 75.

***Inclusive Verse* (1919)**

KpR 537 Frank N. Doubleday's copy with some corrected page proofs bound in, including (as well as contents listed below) one of the title page, signed (initials); the corrections consist of printer's corrections and queries and RK's responses.

Contents: KpR 7, 227, 433, 443, 659, 681, 866, 996, 1145.

Princeton, Ex3814.9.1919.11.

Inoeritum, see KpR 912.

Inscribed in a Presentation Copy of *Echoes* to the Common-Room ('*Placetne, Domini?* — in far Lahore')
First pub. as 'Inscribed in a Presentation Copy of the Common Room *Echoes*' in *United Services College Chronicle*, 27 March 1889; collected *Early Verse* (1900); *Sussex*, XXXV, 34; Rutherford, p. 254, as 'Inscriptions in Presentation Copies of *Echoes* (g)'; Harbord, Verse No. 83B, as 'Echoes — Dedications'.

KpR 538 Fair copy, followed by a pen-and-ink sketch, signed, headed 'To "My very noble and approved good Masters".', on front flyleaf of a copy of *Echoes* (KpR) presented to the Common Room of United Services College.

Facsimile of sketch and last stanza in American Art Association sale catalogue, 20–1 April 1921, Lot 202 and in Martindell, facing p. 6; a transcript of this MS in an unidentified hand (2 pages) is in Library of Congress, Rare Book Division, Colt Collection.

Dalhousie University.

Inscription in Copy of *In Black and White* Presented to Mrs Hill, see KpR 1242.

Inscription in Copy of *Plain Tales from the Hills* Presented to Mrs Hill, see KpR 107.

Inscription in Copy of *Wee Willie Winkie* Presented to Mrs Hill, see, KpR 496.

Inscriptions in Presentation Copies of *Echoes*, see KpR 106, 508, 538, 1161, 1168, 1226, 1243, 1368.

The Instructor ('At times when under cover I 'ave said')
First pub. *The Five Nations* (London, 1903); *Sussex*, XXXIII, 320; Harbord, Verse No. 817.

KpR 539 In MS Five Nations.

National Library of Australia, MS 94.

The Irish Conspiracy ('I went to ould Mulvaney wid the Friday's *Pioneer*')
First pub. *The Pioneer*, 18 February 1889; reprinted Harbord, Verse No. 365; Rutherford, pp. 452–5.

KpR 540 Fair copy, signed.

Strange Africana Library, Johannesburg.

The Irish Guards ('We're not so old in the Army List')
First pub. *The Times*, 11 March 1918; collected *The Years Between* (London, [1919]); *Sussex*, XXXIII, 383–4; Harbord, Verse No. 1050. On CK's list of MSS presented to libraries and institutions (Sussex, KP 23/20), '"The Irish Guards" Poem' is listed as having been given by RK himself to the Irish Guards in 1917; a letter from the Irish Guards to CK in 1937 (Sussex, KP 23) confirms that the poem hangs on the wall of the Regimental Headquarters; while the Irish Guards collections include several signed printed copies of this poem, no MS has been found; if it existed, it may well have been destroyed during the war.

KpR 541 Fair copy, wanting the last stanza, in MS Years Between, one page.

British Library, Add. MS 44841, f. 26.

The Islanders ('Fenced by your careful fathers, ringed by your leaden seas')
First pub. *Weekly Times*, 3 January 1902; collected *The Five Nations* (London, 1903); *Sussex*, XXXIII, 280–5; Harbord, Verse No. 782.

KpR 542 In MS Five Nations.

National Library of Australia, MS 94.

KpR 543 Quotation of lines 35–8 (beginning 'Ancient, effortless, ordered, cycle on cycle set'), in a letter to E. V. Lucas, 20 August [n.y.].

Texas.

'It was a ship of the P. & O.'
No publication traced; not in Harbord.

KpR 544 Fair copy, revised, 106 lines, 2 leaves (rectos only) numbered 17–18, written on board the Valetta during a cruise.

Library of Congress, Rare Book Division, Colt Collection.

'It was Only a Scrap of Paper That Decalogue'
No publication traced; Harbord, Verse No. 1027B (p. 5669).

KpR 545 Carbon copy of typescript, 2 pages.

Sotheby's, 9–10 December 1968, Lot 764, sold to Rota.

'I've never sailed the Amazon'
First pub. with story 'The Beginning of the Armadilloes' in *Just So Stories* (London, 1902); *Sussex*, XIII, 115 and *Sussex*, XXXIV, 241, as a 'Chapter Heading'; Harbord, Verse No. 795, as 'Rolling Down to Rio *or* I've never sailed...'.

KpR 546 Fair copy, revised, in MS Just So Stories, annotated 'on separate page to follow Armadillo'.

British Library, Add. MS 59840, f. 59.

KpR 547 Corrected first page proof for the Sussex Edition, Vol. XIII; date stamped 29 October 1932.

British Library, Add. MS 55863.

'The Jacket' ('Through the Plagues of Egyp' we was chasin' Arabi')
First pub. *The Seven Seas* (New York, 1896); *Sussex*, XXXIII, 159–61; Harbord, Verse No. 686.

KpR 548 Fair copy, revised, here entitled 'The Wetting of the Jacket' and beginning with the refrain 'Now the Captain 'ad 'is jacket an' the jacket it was new', the first verse here beginning 'On the sands of Egyp' we was chasin' Arabi', in MS Years Between.

British Library, Add. MS 44841, f. 86.

KpR 549 Corrected page proof for an unidentified publication (by Harper Bros.?), 3 pages numbered 187–9, annotated 'print off Rudyard Kipling/Finished Aug. 28. 1896.'.

Columbia University, Hitchcock Collection.

James I ('The child of Mary Queen of Scots')
First pub. as 'The Child of Mary Queen of Scots' in C. R. L. Fletcher and Rudyard Kipling, *A History of England* (Oxford and London, 1911); collected separately *Songs from Books* (1915); *Sussex*, XXXIV, 284; Harbord, Verse No. 983.

KpR 550 Fair copy, in MS Years Between, one page, including four cancelled lines beginning 'Then rest you well fair madams'.

British Library, Add. MS 44841, f. 72.

Jane's Marriage ('Jane went to Paradise:')
First pub. with story 'The Janeites' in *Debits and Credits* (London, 1926); reprinted *Sussex*, X, 139–40; collected separately with an additional stanza (previously published as the heading to the story 'The Janeites') in *Inclusive Verse* [1927]; *Sussex*, XXXIV, 378–9; Harbord, Verse No. 1133.

KpR 551 Fair copy, revised, one page, annotated 'type once'.

Sussex, KP 24/32.

KpR 552 Corrected first page proof for the Sussex Edition, Vol. X; date stamped 30 December 1931.

British Library, Add. MS 55861.

The Jester ('There are three degrees of bliss')
First pub. as heading to story 'The Honours of War' in *Windsor Magazine*, August 1911; collected separately *Songs from Books* (New York, 1912); *Sussex*, XXXIV, 105; Harbord, Verse No. 969.

KpR 553 Fair copy, in MS Writings and Songs (pp. 94–5).

Berg.

KpR 554 Fair copy, in MS Diversity of Creatures (f. 34), annotated in an unidentified hand 'Introduction to The Honours of War'.

This poem was not collected with the story in *A Diversity of Creatures* (London, 1917).

University of Edinburgh, Dk. 2. 8.

Job's Wife ('Curse now thy God and die, for all is done')
First printed in American Art Association sale catalogue, 5–6 November 1923 (William Gable sale), Lot 549; lines 1–8 first pub. in an abstract of a paper by E. W. Martindell, 'Some Lesser-known Kipling Writings', *KJ*, October 1927, p. 14; printed in full Harbord, Verse No. 4; Rutherford, pp. 49–50.

KpR 555 MS in an unidentified hand (autograph?), as submitted to 'The Scribbler', signed 'Nickson', one page; among unused copy for the magazine which expired in 1880.

This MS was sold to G. M. Williamson by May Morris in 1901 (see the description of 'The Scribbler' in INTRODUCTION).

Huntington, HM 1698.

KpR 556 Typed transcript (made to replace KpR 555), bound with May Morris's set of 'The Scribbler' and unused contributions thereto, one page and title page.

British Library, Add. MS 45337, ff. 289–90 (rectos only).

Jobson's Amen ('"Blessed be the English and all their ways and works.')
First pub. (stanzas 1–2) as heading to 'A Return to the East' ('Egypt of the Magicians, No. II') in *Nash's Magazine* and *Cosmopolitan*, July 1914; first pub. in full with story 'In the Presence' in *A Diversity of Creature* (London, 1917); collected separately *Inclusive Verse* (1919); *Sussex*, IX, 239–40 and *Sussex*, XXXIV, 322–3; Harbord, Verse No. 1005. For barely visible first line, see also 'The Virginity'.

KpR 557 Corrected first page proof for the Sussex Edition, Vol. IX; date stamped 28 April 1932.

British Library, Add. MS 55860.

Jubal and Tubal Cain ('Jubal sang of the Wrath of God')
First pub. (without title) with 'A People at Home' ('Letters to the Family, No. II') in *Morning Post*, 19 March 1908; collected separately *Songs from Books* (New York, 1912); *Sussex*, XXIV (*Letters of Travel*), 147–8 and *Sussex*, XXXIV, 77–8; Harbord, Verse No. 912.

KpR 558 Fair copy of stanza 1, signed, on the blank front flyleaf of a copy of *Kim*, Outward Bound Edition, Vol. XIX (New York, 1903).

For other verses inscribed in this set of the Outward Bound Edition, see KpR 1155, 1164.

Yale.

The Juggler's Song ('When the drums begin to beat')
First pub. (last 15 lines only beginning 'Give the man who is not made') as heading to Chapter 11 of the one-volume edition of *Kim* (1901); reprinted *Sussex*, XXI, 250; first pub. in full *Songs from Books* (New York, 1912); *Sussex*, XXXIV, 195–6; Harbord, Verse No. 772.

KpR 559 Fair copy, in MS Years Between, one page.

British Library, Add. MS 44841, f. 114.

KpR 560 Corrections to last 15 lines (i.e., heading to Chapter 11 of *Kim*), in first page proof for the Sussex Edition, Vol. XXI (KpR 1791); date stamped 9 October 1931.

British Library, Add. MS 55871.

June ('No hope, no change! The clouds have shut us in')
First pub. with 'September' as 'Two Months' in *Departmental Ditties*, 3rd ed (1888); *Sussex*, XXXII, 161–2 ('Two Months'); Harbord, Verse No. 198A.

KpR 561 Fair copy, here entitled 'In June', in MS Words, Wise and Otherwise [p. 27].

Berg.

KpR 562 Correction on p. 118 of KpR 282.

Yale.

Jungle Saying ('These are the Four that are never content, that have never been filled since the Dews began —')
First pub. as heading to 'The King's Ankus' in *The Second Jungle Book* (London and New York, 1895); collected separately *Songs from Books* (London, 1913); *Sussex*, XII, 167 and *Sussex*, XXXIV, 233 as 'Chapter Heading'; Harbord, Verse No. 649.

KpR 563 Fair copy, in MS Jungle Books, headed 'Verse heading to *The King's ankus*'; watermarked 1894.

British Library, Add. MS 45540, f. 86.

The Junk and the Dhow ('Once a pair of savages found a stranded tree.')
First pub. with story 'An Unqualified Pilot' in *Land and Sea Tales* (London, 1923); collected separately *Inclusive Verse* [1927]; *Sussex*, XVI, 65–7 and *Sussex*, XXXIV, 345–6; Harbord, Verse No. 1117.

KpR 564 Successive drafts, here beginning 'Once there was a Briton found a stranded tree', 7 pages.

Sussex, KP 24/33.

KpR 565 Corrected first page proof for the Sussex Edition, Vol. XVI; date stamped 14 December 1931.

British Library, Add. MS 55866.

Justice ('Before we loose the word')
First pub. *The Times*, 24 October 1918; collected *The Years Between* (London, [1919]); *Sussex*, XXXIII, 452–3; Harbord, Verse No. 1052.

KpR 566 Fair copy, extensively revised, in MS Years Between, including the introductory heading, entitled later.

British Library, Add. MS 44841, f. 58.

Kaspar's Song in "Varda", see KpR 143–5.

'Kind Sir, o' your courtesy', see KpR 1691.

The King ('"Farewell, Romance!" the Cave-men said')
First pub. *Under Lochnagar*, ed. R. A. Profeit (Aberdeen, 1894), as 'Romance'; revised version with two additional stanzas collected *The Seven Seas* (New York, 1896); *Sussex*, XXXIII, 45–6; Harbord, Verse No. 632.

KpR 567 Two untitled drafts, in MS Seven Seas (f. 93r–v and 107v), both beginning 'Here lies Romance — the cave men said'; one leaf watermarked 1890.

Magdalene College, Cambridge.

KpR 568 Fair copy, revised, of the first version, here entitled 'Romance', one page, together with a letter to R. A. Profeit sending the MS, in an album with MSS of other contributions to *Under Lochnagar*.

Library of Congress, Rare Book Division, Colt Collection.

King Anthony, see KpR 572–3.

King Euric ('For hope of gain, or sake of peace')
First pub. as heading to 'From Tideway to Tideway No. IV Our Overseas Men' in *New York Sun*, 31 July 1892; not so collected and not in *Sussex*; reprinted Harbord, Verse No. 525 and Harbord, III, 1463.

KpR 569 Fair copy, followed by a second version, on a scrap attached to f. 1 of KpR 1643.

Harvard, MS Eng 1267.1(2).

King Henry VII. and the Shipwrights ('Harry, our King in England, from London town is gone')
First pub. with story 'The Wrong Thing' in *Rewards and Fairies* (London, 1910); collected separately *Songs from Books* (New York, 1912); *Sussex*, XV, 79–81 and *Sussex*, XXXIV, 182–5; Harbord, Verse No. 953.

KpR 570 Fair copy, revised, in MS Rewards and Fairies, one page.

Cambridge University Library, ADD 6850, f. 31.

KpR 571 Corrected first page proof for the Sussex Edition, Vol. XV; date stamped 18 September 1931.

British Library, Add. MS 55865.

The Kingdom ('Now we are come to our Kingdom')
First pub. (stanzas 1, 2 and 4) as heading to Chapter 18 in Rudyard Kipling and Wolcott Balestier, *The Naulahka* (London, 1892), ascribed 'King Anthony.'; reprinted *Sussex*, XIX, 239; first pub. in full *Songs from Books* (New York, 1912); *Sussex*, XXXIV, 13; Harbord, Verse No. 547, as 'King Anthony *or* The Kingdom'.

KpR 572 Fair copy, 3 stanzas, in MS Writings and Songs (pp. 59–60).

Berg.

KpR 573 Corrected first page proof of stanzas 1, 2 and 4 (i.e., heading to Chapter 18 of *The Naulahka*) for the Sussex Edition, Vol. XIX; date stamped 7 November 1931.

British Library, Add. MS 55869.

The King's Job ('Once on a time was a King anxious to understand')
First pub. C. R. L. Fletcher and Rudyard Kipling, *A History of England* (Oxford and London, 1911); collected separately *Songs from Books* (1915); *Sussex*, XXXIV, 278–9; Harbord, Verse No. 980.

KpR 574 Fair copy, revised, here untitled, in MS Years Between, annotated '*type.*'.

British Library, Add. MS 44841, f. 69.

The King's Pilgrimage ('Our King went forth on pilgrimage')
First pub. *New York Times*, *New York World* and *Boston Globe*, 15 May 1922; collected *Inclusive Verse* [1927]; *Sussex*, XXXV, 249–51; Harbord, Verse No. 1110B.

KpR 575 Drafts, here untitled, 4 pages.

Sussex, KP 24/34.

KpR 575.5 Typescript, one page, signed.

Kipling presented this MS to the Imperial War Museum in 1922.

Imperial War Museum, Department of Documents, Special Miscellaneous SS.

The King's Task ('After the sack of the City, when Rome was sunk to a name')
First pub. (18 lines only) with story 'The Comprehension of Private Copper' in *Traffics and Discoveries* (London, 1904); reprinted *Sussex*, VII, 161–2; first pub. in full as 'The Saxon Foundation of England' in C. R. L. Fletcher and Rudyard Kipling, *A History of England* (Oxford and London, 1911); collected separately *Songs from Books* (New York, 1912); *Sussex*, XXXIV, 170–4; Harbord, Verse No. 868.

KpR 576 Fair copy, revised, of the 18-line version, in MS Traffics and Discoveries, one page, annotated 'The Comprehension of Private Copper'.

McGill University.

KpR 577 Fair copy, in MS Writings and Songs (pp. 96–104).

Berg.

KpR 578 Corrections on pp. 200–6 in KpR 1112.

Yale.

KpR 579 Corrected first page proof for the Sussex Edition, Vol. VII; date stamped 22 March 1932.

British Library, Add. MS 55858.

Kitchener's School ('O Hubshee, carry your shoes in your hand and bow your head on your breast!')
First pub. *The Times*, 8 December 1898; collected *The Five Nations* (London, 1903); *Sussex*, XXXIII, 252–4; Harbord, Verse No. 727.

KpR 580 In MS Seven Seas (ff. 36–48): (1) drafts, here entitled both 'Kitchener's School' and 'Kitchener's College' and beginning both 'This is the message of Kitchener — consider what he saith' and 'Now this is the message of Kitchener — and hear ye what he saith' (ff. 36–43, 45–7, mostly rectos only); (2) fair copy, revised, of final version, signed (f. 44); (3) fair copy, extensively revised, here untitled (f. 48); watermarked 1897.

Magdalene College, Cambridge.

KpR 581 Corrections on pp. 95–9 of KpR 365.

Yale.

Kizilbashi, see KpR 182–3.

La Chanson du Colonel, see KpR 1691.

La Nuit Blanche ('I had seen, as dawn was breaking')
First pub. *Civil and Military Gazette*, 7 June 1887, as 'Natural Phenomena'; collected *Departmental Ditties*, 3rd ed (1888); *Sussex*, XXXII, 52–5; Harbord, Verse No. 269.

KpR 582 Fair copy, including sketches, in MS Words, Wise and Otherwise [pp. 29–33].

Berg.

KpR 583 Correction on p. 44 of KpR 282.

Yale.

'La peinture à l'huile'
No publication traced; not in Harbord.

KpR 584 Four lines, signed, written on the border of a copy of the portrait of RK by the Hon. John Collier (1891), also inscribed 'Very sincerely yours Rudyard Kipling'.

Syracuse University.

The Ladies ('I've taken my fun where I've found it')
First pub. (last stanza only begining 'What did the Colonel's Lady think?') as heading to 'The Courting of Dinah Shadd' in *Macmillan's Magazine*, March 1890; reprinted *Sussex*, IV, 41; first pub. in full *The Seven Seas* (New York, 1896); *Sussex*, XXXIII, 148–50; Harbord, Verse No. 413. See also KpR 1524.

KpR 585 Draft, here untitled and beginning 'One was a girl in the [?] bar –/One was a jemadars wife', in MS Seven Seas (f. 103); watermarked 1894.

Magdalene College, Cambridge.

KpR 586 Typescript of the last stanza only, in a letter to Captain R. Rawlinson (regarding his filmscript of Kipling's *Soldiers Three*, see KpR 1929.5), 19 November 1934.

Syracuse University.

The Lament of the Border Cattle Thief ('Oh, woe is me for the merry life')
First pub. *Week's News*, 21 January 1888, as 'The Border Cattle Thief'; collected *Barrack-Room Ballads* (1892); *Sussex*, XXXII, 272–3; Harbord, Verse No. 289.

KpR 587 Fair copy, one page.

Facsimile printed in *English Poetical Autographs* (London, 1938).

Sussex, KP 24/35.

KpR 587.5 Corrected page proof for *Barrack-Room Ballads* (1892).

British Library, Loan 97 (deposited by John Aris, 1989).

The Land ('When Julius Fabricius, Sub-Prefect of the Weald')
First pub. with story 'Friendly Brook' in *A Diversity of Creatures* (London, 1917); collected separately *Inclusive Verse* (1919); *Sussex*, IX, 65–8 and *Sussex*, XXXIV, 309–13; Harbord, Verse No. 1043.

KpR 588 Fair copy, revised, here originally entitled 'The River Field', annotated 'type for *poems*', in MS Diversity of Creatures (ff. 21–2, rectos only), the second page containing stanzas 12–17 annotated 'add to "The Land" verses to precede The Brook.'.

University of Edinburgh, Dk. 2. 8.

KpR 589 Corrected first page proof for the Sussex Edition, Vol. IX; date stamped 28 April 1932.

British Library, Add. MS 55860.

Land-Bound [ΘΑΛΑΣΣΑ,ΘΑΛΑΣΣΑ] ('Run down to the sea, O River')
First pub. *Echoes* (Lahore, [1884]); *Sussex*, XXXV, 106; Rutherford, p. 153; Harbord, Verse No. 115. For an annotation in a copy of *Echoes*, see KpR 314.

KpR 590 Fair copy, here entitled 'Θάλασσα! Θάλασσα', in Sussex Notebook 1 (pp. 104–5); dated 12 June [1882].

Sussex, KP 24/3.

KpR 591 Fair copy, here entitled 'Θαλασσα, Θαλασσα', in Sussex Notebook 3 (second series, pp. 6–7).

Sussex, KP 24/1.

KpR 592 Transcript by AMK, in Sussex Notebook 2 [pp. 39–40], here untitled; dated June 1882.

Sussex, KP 24/2.

The Last Chantey ('Thus said the Lord in the Vault above the Cherubim')
First pub. *Pall Mall Magazine*, 15 June 1893; collected *The Seven Seas* (New York, 1896); *Sussex*, XXXIII, 19–22; Harbord, Verse No. 587.

KpR 593 Fair copy, revised, 11 stanzas, here originally entitled 'The Judgment of the Sea' (cancelled), subtitled '"*And there was no more sea*"', 2 pages (2 leaves).

Harvard, MS Eng 165, ff. 4, 5.

KpR 594 Fair copy, here entitled 'The Last Chanty', signed, 2 numbered leaves (rectos only).

Library of Congress, Manuscript Division, Miscellaneous Manuscripts Collection.

KpR 595 Fair copy, signed, here entitled 'The Last Chanty.', 2 leaves (rectos only), annotated 'For Miss Bridson — Rock House. April. 1897.'.

Facsimile in Ballard, pp. [137–8] and Lyle H. Kendall, *A Descriptive Catalogue of The W. L. Lewis Collection* (Fort Worth, Texas, 1970), plates 1–2.

Texas Christian University.

The Last Department ('"None whole or clean," we cry, "or free from stain"')
First pub. *Civil and Military Gazette*, 13 April 1886; collected *Departmental Ditties* (1886); *Sussex*, XXXII, 39–40; Harbord, Verse No. 177. See also KpR 280.

KpR 596 Fair copy, in MS Departmental Ditties (pp. 6–8).

Berg.

The Last Lap ('How do we know, by the bank-high river')
First pub. with story 'The Burning of the *Sarah Sands*' in *Land and Sea Tales* (London, 1923); collected separately *Inclusive Verse* [1927]; *Sussex*, XVI, 125–6 and *Sussex*, XXXIV, 350–1; Harbord, Verse No. 1118.

KpR 597 Corrected first page proof for the Sussex Edition, Vol. XVI; date stamped 14 December 1931.

British Library, Add. MS 55866.

The Last Ode ('As watchers couched beneath a Bantine oak')
First pub. with story 'The Eye of Allah' in *Debits and Credits* (London, 1926); collected separately *Inclusive Verse* [1927]; *Sussex*, X, 315 and *Sussex*, XXXIV, 394; Harbord, Verse No. 1134.

KpR 598 Fair copy, revised, one page (containing also KpR 1303), subtitled 'Nov. 27. B.C.8.'.

Sussex, KP 24/61.

KpR 599 Corrected first page proof for the Sussex Edition, Vol. X; date stamped 30 December 1931.

British Library, Add. MS 55861.

The Last of the Light Brigade ('There were thirty million English who talked of England's might')
First pub. *St James's Gazette*, 28 April 1890; collected without last stanza in *Inclusive Verse* (1919); *Sussex*, XXXV, 187–9; Harbord, Verse No. 433 (last stanza printed p. 5665).

KpR 600 Corrected typescript, 2 pages (2 leaves), signed, including introductory note beginning 'This represented the response, so far, of the British public to the appeal made by the Committee for funds to enable provision to be made for the declining days of those of the survivors of the Balaclava charge who are known to have come to misery and want...' and dated 28 April 1890; as sent to J. Nicoll Dunn with a note dated Bateman's, 9 November 1907.

This MS described in Martindell, p. 160.

Yale.

The Last Rhyme of True Thomas ('The King has called for priest and cup').
First pub. *To-day*, 17 March 1894; collected *The Seven Seas* (New York, 1896); *Sussex*, XXXIII, 89–94; Harbord, Verse No. 604.

KpR 601 Fair copy of opening stanzas giving way to draft stanzas, in MS Years Between, 4 leaves (rectos only).

British Library, Add. MS 44841, ff. 100–3 (rectos only).

KpR 602 Revised stanza, sent as a revision for Vol. XI of the Outward Bound Edition, in a letter (containing also KpR 535) to Mr Burlingame (of Scribner's), annotated 'Ansd 23 July 97'.

Princeton, Archive of Charles Scribner's Sons, Box 87, Folder 1.

KpR 603 Revised version of line 144, sent as 'another correction' for the 'next edition' ('In place of the already once amended line (True Thomas p. 177 Col. Edn)'), in a letter to Methuen & Co., Rottingdean, 30 November 1897.

Library of Congress, Rare Book Division, Colt Collection.

The Last Suttee ('Udai Chand lay sick to death')
First pub. *New York Tribune*, 5 January 1890 and *Macmillan's Magazine*, January 1890, as 'The Ballad of the Last Suttee'; collected *Barrack-Room Ballads* (1892); *Sussex*, XXXII, 238–42; Harbord, Verse No. 393.

KpR 604 Revised clipping of *Macmillan's Magazine* in Scrapbook 4 (p. 173).

Sussex, KP 28/4.

KpR 604.5 Corrected page proof for *Barrack-Room Ballads* (1892); date stamped 17 February 1892.

British Library, Loan 97 (deposited by John Aris, 1989).

'Late Came the God' ('Late came the God, having sent his forerunners who were not regarded —')
First pub. with story 'The Wish House' in *Debits and Credits* (London, 1926); collected separately *Inclusive Verse* [1927]; *Sussex*, X, 79 and *Sussex*, XXXIV, 371–2; Harbord, Verse No. 135.

KpR 605 Fair copy, revised, of version without last stanza, here entitled 'The Wish House', one page (containing also KpR 170, 421), annotated 'type.'.

Sussex, KP 24/25.

The Law of Libel ('To the State of Kot-Kumharsen where the wild dacoits abound')
First pub. *The Pioneer*, 22 December 1888; reprinted Harbord, Verse No. 346; Rutherford, pp. 438–42; a version of lines 1–6 used as chapter heading to chapter 6 of *The Naulahka* (London, 1892); *Sussex*, XIX, 58.

KpR 606 Revised clipping of the first publication in Scrapbook 4 (p. 96), annotated 'Please type this'.

Sussex, KP 28/4.

KpR 607 Corrected first page proof of lines 1–6 (i.e., heading to Chapter 6 of *The Naulahka*) for the Sussex Edition, Vol. XIX (KpR 1921); date stamped 7 November 1931.

British Library, Add. MS 55869.

The Law of the Jungle ('*Now this is the Law of the Jungle — as old and as true as the sky*')
First pub. as 'The Law for the Wolves' with story 'How Fear Came' in *Pall Mall Budget*, 7 June 1894; collected with story in *The Second Jungle Book* (London and New York, 1895); collected separately *Songs from Books* (London, 1913); *Sussex*, XII, 93–6 and *Sussex*, XXXIV, 83–5; Harbord, Verse No. 605.

KpR 608 Fair copy, revised, of 44-line version (ff. 171–2, rectos only), and fair copy of lines 23–38 and 2 unpublished lines, one page (f. 173), in MS Jungle Books; watermarked 1890.

British Library, Add. MS 45540, ff. 171–3 (rectos only).

KpR 609 Fair copy, including an elaborate title page, four 4-line stanzas, in MS Writings and Songs (pp. 86–93).

Berg.

KpR 610 Quotation of stanzas 1–2, inscribed on half-title of presentation copy of *The Second Jungle Book* (New York, 1895) to Nelson Spencer, December 1895.

Syracuse University.

KpR 611 Quotation of last two lines, signed, on a 'The Elms' notecard; dated on verso in an unidentified hand 6 August 1900.

Texas.

KpR 612 Quotation of last two lines, inscribed on title page of a copy of *Just So Stories* (London, 1902), presented to Miss Donaldson, June 1908.

Facsimile in Sotheby's sale catalogue, p. 44.

Sotheby's, 16–20 December 1929, Lot 277 (property of Lady Albinia Donaldson), sold to Maggs.

A Legend of Devonshire ('There were three daughters long ago')
First printed (6 stanzas) in *Schoolboy Lyrics* (privately printed, Lahore, 1881); in full (11 stanzas) in *United Services College Chronicle*, 30 June 1881; *Sussex*, XXXV, 39 (6-stanza version); Rutherford, pp. 62–3 (in full); Harbord, Verse No. 8 (where additional 5 stanzas are printed).

KpR 613 Eleven stanzas, on 2 pages of a folded leaf (containing also KpR 707, 806) sent to 'Aunt' [Edith Macdonald?], probably after 21 February 1881.

Typed transcript, probably of this MS, at Sussex, KP 24/67 which begins 'Three daughters lived once long ago'.

Sotheby's, 11–12 March 1968, Lot 778 (property of H. C. Drayton), sold to Rota.

The Legend of Evil ('This is the sorrowful story')
Part II only (beginning ''Twas when the rain fell steady an' the Ark was pitched an' ready') first pub. without title, as heading to Chapter 4 of J. L. Kipling, *Beast and Man in India* (London and New York, 1891), as 'Of Asses'; collected (and Part I first pub.) in *Barrack-Room Ballads* (1892); *Sussex*, XXXII, 305–7; Harbord, Verse No. 504.

KpR 614 Fair copy of an early version of Part II, here untitled, in a letter to E. Kay Robinson, Lahore, 30 April 1886.

This MS not mentioned Rutherford.

Sussex, KP 17/25.

KpR 615 Fair copy, revised, of stanzas 1–3 only of Part II, one page.

Sussex, KP 24/36.

KpR 615.5 Corrected page proof for *Barrack-Room Ballads* (1892).

British Library, Loan 97 (deposited by John Aris, 1989).

The Legend of Love and Death, see KpR 340–1.

The Legend of Mirth ('The Four Archangels, so the legends tell —')
First pub. with story 'The Horse Marines' in *A Diversity of Creatures* (London, 1917); collected separately *Inclusive Verse* (1919); *Sussex*, IX, 327–30 and *Sussex*, XXXIV, 328–31; Harbord, Verse No. 1044.

KpR 616 Fair copy, revised, here originally entitled 'The Four' (revised in an unidentified hand), in MS Diversity of Creatures (ff. 110–12, rectos only, numbered 1–3).

University of Edinburgh, Dk. 2. 8.

KpR 617 Corrected first page proof for *Humorous Tales* (London, 1931), pp. 3–6; date stamped 6 May 1931.

British Library, Add. MS 55847.

KpR 618 Corrected first page proof for the Sussex Edition, Vol. IX; date stamped 28 April 1932.

British Library, Add. MS 55860.

The Legend of the Cedar Swamp ('Darkness lay thick where e'er we trod')
First printed (lines 1–4 only) in Anderson Galleries sale catalogue, 17 March 1915 (G. M. Williamson sale), p. 15; first pub. Rutherford (1986), Appendix A, pp. 478–9; Harbord, Verse No. 1 (described as Kipling's first verse).

KpR 619 Signed 'J. R. Kipling', annotated in an unidentified hand 'by Rudyard Kipling/ written beside me at my brother's & given me when he was 9 years of age.'.

A transcript of this MS in ink by Elkin Mathews, annotated in pencil 'Written beside me at my brother's and given me when he was 9 years of age' and 'Copied from the original MS. by Elkin Mathews — Feb. 15 '98', is at the University of Reading, Elkin Mathews Collection, MS 392/4/10.

University of California at Berkeley, 71/121 z.

A Legend of the Foreign Office ('Rustum Beg of Kolazai — slightly backward Native State —')
First pub. *Civil and Military Gazette*, 23 February 1886; collected *Departmental Ditties* (1886); *Sussex*, XXXII, 12–13; Harbord, Verse No. 168. See also KpR 280.

KpR 620 Fair copy, including 4-line heading and a sketch, in MS Departmental Ditties (pp. 49–52).

Berg.

KpR 621 Corrections on pp. 15–16 of KpR 282.

Yale.

A Legend of Truth ('Once on a time, the ancient legends tell')
First pub. with story 'A Friend of the Family' in *Debits and Credits* (London, 1926); collected separately *Inclusive Verse* [1927]; *Sussex*, X, 229–30 and *Sussex*, XXXIV, 386–7; Harbord, Verse No. 1136.

KpR 622 Corrected first page proof for the Sussex Edition, Vol. X; date stamped 30 December 1931.

British Library, Add. MS 55861.

L'Envoi ('Rhymes, or of grief or of sorrow')
First printed Harbord (1969), p. 5666 (as Verse No. 489A 'To Flo from Ruddy') (previously listed without text as Verse No. 57, 'L'Envoi to Sundry Phansies').

KpR 623 Fair copy, in MS Sundry Phansies (last poem).

Berg.

KpR 624 Fair copy, on the flyleaf of a copy of *Departmental Ditties*, 4th ed (1890) inscribed 'To Flo [Florence Garrard] from Ruddy who is supposed to have written this book. May: [18]90', poem headed 'Written in "*81*".'.

This MS printed in Morton N. Cohen, 'Kipling in the Berg', *KJ*, 43 (1976), p. 11.

Berg.

KpR 625 Fair copy, in MS Writings and Songs (pp. 3–4).

Berg.

L'Envoi ('The smoke upon your Altar dies')
First pub. as L'Envoi to *Departmental Ditties*, 2nd ed (1886); *Sussex*, XXXII, 163; Harbord, Verse No. 229.

KpR 626 Fair copy, revised, subtitled '[*To whom it may concern*]', annotated (signed) at end 'This goes last of all. After "In Springtime"', sent to the printer for the first publication.

Facsimile of portion in [Luther S. Livingston], *The Works of Rudyard Kipling* (New York, 1901), p. [26].

Pierpont Morgan, MA 979.

KpR 627 Fair copy, including a sketch, in MS Words, Wise and Otherwise [pp. 23–4].

Berg.

KpR 628 Correction on p. 120 of KpR 282.

Yale.

L'Envoi ('When Earth's last picture is painted and the tubes are twisted and dried')
First pub. (untitled and with 'Half-A-Dozen Pictures' ('From Tideway to Tideway, No. VI')) in *New York Sun*, 28 August 1892; collected as 'L'Envoi' in *The Seven Seas* (New York, 1896); *Sussex*, XXXIII, 175; Harbord, Verse No. 527.

KpR 629 Fair copy, here untitled, on p. 5 of a MS of 'Half-A-Dozen Pictures' (KpR 1645); watermarked 1890.

Berg.

KpR 630 Fair copy of lines 1–4, signed and annotated 'For J. S. Arkwright', on p. 3 of a folded leaf containing a letter to Arkwright, Rottingdean, 1 July 1901.

Syracuse University.

KpR 631 First line only, written at top of a page, cancelled and followed by KpR 24; the paper is annotated 'E. Y. from Rudyard Kipling S.S. Kinfauns Castle Jan. 30. 1900'.

Dalhousie University.

L'Envoi, see also KpR 22–6, 267–9, 623–31, 653–656.5, 732–6, 1377–9.

Les Amours de Voyage ('When the decks were very silent')
First pub. Rutherford (1986), pp. 174–5; not in Harbord.

KpR 632 Fair copy, the last four lines written in a later hand, in Sussex Notebook 1 (pp. 131–3); [probably October–November 1882].

Sussex, KP 24/3.

Les Amours Faciles ('A woe that lasts for a little space')
First pub. Rutherford (1986), p. 116; Harbord, Verse No. 58.

KpR 633 Fair copy in Sussex Notebook 1 (p. 53); dated 2 February 1882.

Sussex, KP 24/3.

KpR 634 Fair copy in Sussex Notebook 3 (first series, p. 39).

Sussex, KP 24/1.

KpR 635 Fair copy, in MS Sundry Phansies.

Berg.

KpR 636 Transcript by JLK, in Sussex Notebook 2 [p. 22]; dated 30 January 1882.

Sussex, KP 24/2.

The Lesson ('Not on a single issue, or in one direction or twain')
First pub. *The Times*, 29 July 1901; collected *The Five Nations* (London, 1903); *Sussex*, XXXIII, 268—70; Harbord, Verse No. 764.

KpR 637 In MS Five Nations.

National Library of Australia, MS 94.

KpR 638 Fair copy, including an additional stanza, signed, one page, annotated at end 'In Memory — Naval Manœvres. 1901.', together with covering letter to Mr Thursfield, 6 September 1901.

Additional stanza printed *Grolier Catalogue*, p. 96.

Berg.

KpR 639 Corrected galley proof for first publication.

Library of Congress, Rare Book Division, Colt Collection.

KpR 640 Revision and correction on pp. 118–19 of KpR 365.

Yale.

The Lesson ('We two learned the lesson together')
First printed *Schoolboy Lyrics* (privately printed, Lahore, 1881); first pub. *Early Verse* (1900); *Sussex*, XXXV, 17; Rutherford, pp. 55–6; Harbord, Verse No. 23.

KpR 641 Transcript, enclosed in a letter from JLK to Edith Plowden, 5 October 1880.

Sussex, KP 1/10.

'"Let us now praise famous men" —', see KpR 1006–7.

'Let us now remember many honourable women', see KpR 290.

The Letter of Halim the Potter ('Halim the Potter from the rainy Hills, —')
First pub. Rutherford, (1986), pp. 269–72; not in Harbord.

KpR 642 Fair copy, revised, of verses written to JLK for his birthday, here entitled 'The Letter of Halim the Potter to Yusuf His Father and Master Craftsman in the walled city of Lahore; written on the fifth day of the month of the Scales.', among letters to Margaret Burne-Jones, 4 pages (2 leaves); 6 July [probably 1885].

Sussex, KP 11/6.

The Letter Written Up in the Attic ('I bear a mark from your hand my Love')
First pub. Rutherford (1986), p. 135; not in Harbord.

KpR 643 Fair copy, revised, subtitled 'Portobello Road 2 A.M.', in Sussex Notebook 1 (pp. 81–2); dated 24 March [1882], containing a later annotation dated 7 July 1884.

Sussex, KP 24/3.

Life's Handicap, see KpR 177.

Limericks, see KpR 500, 504, 518, 1174–9, 1183–1207, 1210.

The Liner She's a Lady ('The Liner she's a lady, an' she never looks nor 'eeds —')
First pub. *Pall Mall Gazette*, 13 June 1895; collected *The Seven Seas* (New York, 1896); *Sussex*, XXXIII, 67–8; Harbord, Verse No. 639.

KpR 644 In MS Seven Seas: (1) fair copy, revised (f. 106); (2) fair copy, revised, here untitled, watermarked 1890 (f. 107); (3) draft, here untitled (f. 108).

Magdalene College, Cambridge.

Lines To A Superior Young Lady on the Occasion of her First Manifesting A Will of Her Own, see KpR 520.

Little Jack Horner ('Chota Jack Horner')
First pub. *Wee Willie-Winkie*, [ed. Lady Marjorie Gordon], July? 1895; Harbord, Verse No. 633B.

KpR 645 Translation of the nursery rhyme into an Indian language, in a letter (containing also KpR 1188) to Lady Marjorie Gordon, 5 April 1895.

Typed transcript of this letter at Cornell University; transcript of this letter, annotated by and possibly in the hand of E. W. Martindell, dated from The Grafton, Connecticut Avenue, 5 April 1895, is at Sussex, Baldwin Papers 2/26.

Hodgson, 18 July 1934.

A Little Undertaking
No publication traced; not in Harbord.

KpR 646 Draft of a dramatic scene, on a blank page in Scrapbook 1 (p. 267 *rev.*).

Sussex, KP 28/1.

'Lo! I am crowned'
First pub. Rutherford (1986), p. 167; not in Harbord.

KpR 647 Fair copy, cancelled, in Sussex Notebook 1 (p. 121); [10–16 August 1882].

Sussex, KP 24/3.

A Locked Way [After Long Years] ('"Open the Gate!')
First pub. *Echoes* (Lahore, [1884]); *Sussex*, XXXV, 104–5; Rutherford, pp. 136–7; Harbord, Verse No. 117. For an annotation in a copy of *Echoes*, see KpR 314.

KpR 648 Fair copy, here entitled 'After long years', in Sussex Notebook 1 (pp. 83–4); dated 26 March [1882], with a later annotation dated 2 February 1884.

Sussex, KP 24/3.

KpR 649 Fair copy, here entitled 'A Locked Way', in Sussex Notebook 3 (first series, pp. 37–8), dated 26 March [1882].

Sussex, KP 24/1.

KpR 650 Two fair copies in MS Words, Wise and Otherwise, both here entitled 'The Locked Way', one [p. 9] of 3 stanzas only and cancelled, the other [pp. 11–16] includes sketches.

These MSS not mentioned Rutherford.

Berg.

KpR 651 Transcript by AMK, in Sussex Notebook 2 [pp. 51–2]; dated March 1882.

Sussex, KP 24/2.

London Stone ('When you come to London Town')
First pub. *The Times*, 10 November 1923; collected *Inclusive Verse* [1927]; *Sussex*, XXXV, 258–9; Harbord, Verse No. 1119.

KpR 652 Successive drafts and fair copies, revised, 5 pages (the first page also containing KpR 1055), originally beginning 'When you come to London Stone'.

Sussex, KP 24/37.

The Long Trail ('There's a whisper down the field')
First pub. (5 stanzas only) *Cape Illustrated Magazine*, November 1891; collected (9 stanzas) as 'L'Envoi' to *Barrack-Room Ballads* (1892); *Sussex*, XXXII, 330; Harbord, Verse No. 502. The 3rd edition of Carrington (London, 1978), mentions an early draft of this poem in the Berg Collection (see pp. 242, 602n); no such MS been found.

KpR 653 Fair copy, revised, of stanzas 1–3, 5 and beginning of 4 (in that order) only, here untitled, one page.

Sussex, KP 24/38.

KpR 654 Fair copy of stanza 2 (beginning 'It's North you may run to the rime-ringed Sun'), signed 'Ruddy', on verso of title page of a copy of *Life's Handicap* (London and New York, 1891) presented to Lucy Clifford, August 1891; verses dated 'The Night. Aug: 11th '91'.

Facsimile in Anderson Galleries sale catalogue, p. 259.

Anderson Galleries, 21–4 January 1929 (Kern Sale), Lot 772.

KpR 655 Quotation of lines 61–9, here untitled, on one page of Union-Castle Line, R.M.S. 'Briton' notepaper, annotated 'For M. F. W.'; signed and dated S.S. Briton, 25 April 1901.

Berg.

KpR 656 Quotation of lines 65–8, inscribed in a copy of *The Five Nations* (London, 1903), subscribed 'L'Envoi to Four L[?]'.

This MS printed in Lyle H. Kendall, *A Descriptive Catalogue of The W. L. Lewis Collection* (Fort Worth, Texas, 1970), p. 157.

Texas Christian University.

KpR 656.5 Corrected page proof for *Barrack-Room Ballads* (1892) in which these lines were the 'L'Envoi'.

British Library, Loan 97 (deposited by John Aris, 1989).

'Look, you have cast out Love! What Gods are these', see KpR 177.

The Looking-Glass ('The Queen was in her chamber, and she was middling old.')
First pub. with story 'Gloriana' in *Rewards and Fairies* (London, 1910); collected separately *Songs from Books* (New York, 1912); *Sussex*, XV, 51–2 and *Sussex*, XXXIV, 125–6; Harbord, Verse No. 954.

KpR 657 Fair copy, in MS Rewards and Fairies, one page, annotated 'To follow Gloriana'.

Cambridge University Library, ADD 6850, f. 18.

KpR 658 Correction on p. 146 of KpR 1112.

Yale.

Loot ('If you've ever stole a pheasant-egg be'ind the keeper's back')
First pub. *Scots Observer*, 29 March 1890; collected *Barrack-Room Ballads* (1892); *Sussex*, XXXII, 196–8; Harbord, Verse No. 427.

KpR 658.5 Corrected page proof for *Barrack-Room Ballads* (1892); date stamped 12 February 1892.

British Library, Loan 97 (deposited by John Aris, 1989).

KpR 659 Corrected page proof for *Inclusive Verse* (1919), one page numbered 467, signed (initials), in KpR 537.

Princeton, Ex3814.9.1919.11.

Lord Roberts ('He passed in the very battle-smoke')
First pub. *Daily Telegraph* and *New York Times*, 19 November 1914; collected *The Years Between* (London, [1919]); *Sussex*, XXXIII, 371–2; Harbord, Verse No. 1011.

KpR 660 Revised, in MS Years Between, here entitled only 'The' (not finished), 5 stanzas only beginning 'He gave his life to his one task', stanza four here beginning 'He died among the battle smoke', one page.

British Library, Add. MS 44841, f. 20.

The Lost Legion ('There's a Legion that never was 'listed')
First pub. *New York Sun*, 8 May 1893, as 'A Banjo Song'; collected *Ballads and Barrack-Room Ballads* (New York and London, 1893) and *The Seven Seas* (New York, 1896); *Sussex*, XXXIII, 75–7; Harbord, Verse No. 563.

KpR 661 Fair copy, in MS Years Between, one page.

British Library, Add. MS 44841, f. 85.

KpR 662 Fair copy, 5 stanzas, in C. W. Stoddard's album; signed and dated New York, 7 April 1893.

Huntington, HM 35075, [p. 32].

KpR 663 Fair copy of stanza 5, in Berg Booklet [p. 25].

Berg.

KpR 664 Fair copy version, here entitled 'A Banjo-Song' and including a prose introduction, 2 pages, as sent to W. E. Henley for publication in *National Observer* (pub. 13 May 1893).

Facsimile in British Library, RP 2429(xiii).

Sotheby's, 15 December 1982, Lot 218, sold to Fleming.

KpR 665 Typescript, 2 leaves (recots only), annotated in an unidentified hand '(Copyright, 1893, by Macmillan & Co)'.

Princeton, Archive of Charles Scribner's Sons, Miscellaneous Author's MSS and Galleys Series, Box 1, Folder 18.

'Love and let love and so will I', see KpR 1634.

The Love Song of Har Dyal ('Alone upon the housetops to the North')
First pub. in text of story 'Beyond the Pale' in *Plain Tales from the Hills* (Calcutta and London, 1888); collected separately *Songs from Books* (New York, 1912); *Sussex*, I, 238 and *Sussex*, XXXIV, 161; Harbord, Verse No. 355.

KpR 666 Fair copy, in MS Writings and Songs (p. 67).

Berg.

KpR 667 Corrected first page proof for the Sussex Edition, Vol. I (included in KpR 1440); date stamped 12 September 1931.

British Library, Add. MS 55852.

The Lover's Litany ('Eyes of grey — a sodden quay'), see KpR 180.

The Lowestoft Boat ('In Lowestoft a boat was laid')
First pub. without title accompanying 'The Auxiliaries I', the first article of 'The Fringes of the Fleet' in *Daily Telegraph*, 20 November 1915; collected *The Fringes of the Fleet* (London, 1915); collected separately *Inclusive Verse* (1919); *Sussex*, XXVI, 237–8 and *Sussex*, XXXIV, 251–2; Harbord, Verse No. 1014.

KpR 668 Revised, here untitled, in MS Non-Fiction, in the MS of 'Fringes of the Fleet' (KpR 1632), annotated 'to precede Trawlers No I', one page.

British Library, Add. MS 45542, f. 31.

Lucifer ('Think not, O thou from College late deported, Pride goeth down')
First pub. *Departmental Ditties*, 2nd ed (1886); *Sussex*, XXXII, 16–17; Rutherford, pp. 342–3; Harbord, Verse No. 225.

KpR 669 Fair copy, revised, one page, sent to the printer for the first publication.

Pierpont Morgan, MA 979.

MacDonough's Song ('Whether the State can loose and bind')
First pub. (last 4 lines only) in text of story 'As Easy As A. B. C.' in *Family Magazine*, 25 February–12 March 1912; reprinted *Sussex*, IX, 12; in full with story 'As Easy As A. B. C.' in *A Diversity of Creatures* (London, 1917); collected separately *Inclusive Verse* (1919); *Sussex*, IX, 43–4 and *Sussex*, XXXIV, 307; Harbord, Verse No. 998.

KpR 670 Fair copy, revised, here untitled and beginning 'Whether Salvation is free of cost', containing two additional opening stanzas, one page; also the last four lines in the text of the MS of 'As Easy As A. B. C.' (KpR 1404); in MS Diversity of Creatures (ff. 13 and 5 respectively).

University of Edinburgh, Dk. 2. 8.

KpR 671 Corrected first page proof for the Sussex Edition, Vol. IX; date stamped 28 April 1932.

British Library, Add. MS 55860.

The Making of the Place ('Oh the Hope that lures us on')
No publication traced; not in Harbord.

KpR 672 One page, 8 lines.

Charles Hamilton Galleries, 19 April 1979, Lot 137.

'Man does not remain in the world'
First pub. in text of story 'A Retired Gentleman' in *Morning Post*, 21 May 1917; collected *The Eyes of Asia* (New York, 1918); *Sussex*, XXVI, 185; Harbord, Verse No. 1030.

KpR 673 Fair copy, in the text of the MS of 'A Retired Gentleman' (KpR 2031), in MS Eyes of Asia (f. 161).

University of Edinburgh, Dk. 2. 8.

'Man goes to Man! Cry the challenge through the Jungle!'
First pub. as heading to story 'The Spring Running' in *Pall Mall Gazette*, 25 September 1895; collected *The Second Jungle Book* (London and New York, 1895); collected separately *Songs from Books* (London, 1913); *Sussex*, XII, 231 and *Sussex*, XXXIV, 234, as 'Chapter Heading'; Harbord, Verse No. 653.

KpR 674 Fair copy, in MS Jungle Books, headed 'For tale No. 8/The Spring Running', one page (containing also KpR 1308), annotated 'set these up! send MS & proof to me & keep ready/Rudyard Kipling'; watermarked [189]4.

British Library, Add. MS 45540, f. 133.

The Man Who Could Write ('Boanerges Blitzen, servant of the Queen')
First pub. *Civil and Military Gazette*, 23 March 1886; collected *Departmental Ditties* (1886); *Sussex*, XXXII, 29–30; Harbord, Verse No. 173. See also KpR 280.

KpR 675 Fair copy, including 6-line heading, in MS Departmental Ditties (pp. 22–4).

Berg.

KpR 676 Corrections on p. 28 of KpR 282.

Yale.

Mandalay ('By the old Moulmein Pagoda, lookin' eastward to the sea')
First pub. *Scots Observer*, 21 June 1890; collected *Barrack-Room Ballads* (1892); *Sussex*, XXXII, 210–12; Harbord, Verse No. 464.

KpR 677 Two scraps stitched together, the top portion, headed 'Barrack Room Ballads X "Mandalay"', containing an 8-line version of stanza 1, the bottom, headed 'Mandalay.', containing an incomplete version of stanza 1 and drafts of stanzas 2–4.

Dalhousie University.

KpR 678 Draft, here untitled, c. 3 stanzas on one page; together with fair copy, revised, of stanza one on another page.

Sussex, KP 24/39.

KpR 679 Fair copy, framed, headed 'Barrack Room Ballad X Mandalay', annotated in ink 'no proof wanted', signed, two leaves (rectos only).

Library of Congress, Rare Book Division, Colt Collection.

KpR 680 Early fair copy, 3 pages (one leaf); signed and dated Brattleboro, 27 July 1893.

Formerly in Paul C. Richards Collection deposited at Boston University.

KpR 680.5 Corrected page proof for *Barrack-Room Ballads* (1892); date stamped 12 February 1892.

British Library, Loan 97 (deposited by John Aris, 1989).

KpR 681 Corrected page proof for *Inclusive Verse* (1919), one page numbered 476, signed (initials), in KpR 537.

Princeton, Ex3814.9.1919.11.

The Mare's Nest ('Jane Austen Beecher Stowe de Rouse'), see KpR 280.

The Married Man ('The bachelor 'e fights for one')
First pub. *The Five Nations* (London, 1903); *Sussex*, XXXIII, 323–5; Harbord, Verse No. 819.

KpR 682 In MS Five Nations.

National Library of Australia, MS 94.

The Mary Gloster ('I've paid for your sickest fancies; I've humoured your crackedest whim —')
First pub. *The Seven Seas* (New York, 1896); *Sussex*, XXXIII, 109–20; Harbord, Verse No. 687.

KpR 683 Drafts and fair copies, revised, in MS Seven Seas (ff. 125–50, mostly rectos only), including various titles (such as 'The Viking's Ship'); watermarked 1890 and 1894.

On f. 146v is a draft of c. 4 unidentified lines, headed 'The Song of the Engines.' and beginning 'Of <this> <our> order well assembled...'.

Magdalene College, Cambridge.

Mary's Son ('If you stop to find out what your wages will be')
First pub. as heading to 'The Riddle of Empire' ('Egypt of the Magicians, No. VII') in *Nash's Magazine* and *Cosmopolitan*, December 1914; collected separately *The Years Between* (London, [1919]); *Sussex*, XXXIII, 404; Harbord, Verse No. 1009.

KpR 684 Fair copy, here untitled, in MS Years Between, annotated 'type for heading to Letter VII'.

British Library, Add. MS 44841, f. 34.

KpR 685 Typescript of first publication (KpR 1576), containing these verses (untitled) on p. [1], among materials for *Letters of Travel* (KpR 1824).

Berg.

The Masque of Plenty ('"How sweet is the shepherd's sweet life!')
First pub. *The Pioneer*, 26 October 1888; collected *Departmental Ditties*, 4th ed (1890); *Sussex*, XXXII, 69–74; Harbord, Verse No. 338.

KpR 686 Revisions and corrections on pp. 55–8 of KpR 282.

Yale.

The Master-Cook ('With us there rade a Maister-Cook that came')
First pub. as 'Prologue to the Master Cook's Tale' with story 'His Gift' in *Land and Sea Tales* (London, 1923); collected separately *Inclusive Verse* [1927]; *Sussex*, XVI, 91–2 (as 'Prologue to the Master-Cook's Tale') and *Sussex*, XXXIV, 347–8; Harbord, Verse No. 1122, as 'Prologue: To the Master-Cook's Tale'.

KpR 687 Draft, headed 'Prologue to the Master Cook's Tale', 2 pages.

Sussex, KP 24/40.

KpR 688 Corrected first page proof for *Humorous Tales* (London, 1931), pp. 227–8, here entitled 'Prologue to the Master-Cook's Tale'; date stamped 19 May 1931.

British Library, Add. MS 55847.

KpR 689 Corrected first page proof for the Sussex Edition, Vol. XVI, here entitled 'Prologue to the Master-Cook's Tale'; date stamped 14 December 1931.

British Library, Add. MS 55866.

The Mater, see KpR 1368.

Max Desmarets His Valentine ('How shall a ghost from the *Père-la-Chaise*')
First pub. (lines 1–2 only) in Owen Tweedy, 'Rudyard Kipling and Rottingdean', *KJ*, 18 (1951), 11; in full in Harbord (1969), Verse No. 78; Rutherford, pp. 213–14.

KpR 690 Illustrated valentine, in tiny handwriting; dated 14 February 1884.

A photocopy is at Sussex, Baldwin Papers 2/6.

Owned (1986) M. E. Macdonald (see Rutherford, p. 213).

McAndrew's Hymn ('Lord, Thou hast made this world below the shadow of a dream')
First pub. *Scribner's Magazine*, December 1894; collected *The Seven Seas* (New York, 1896); *Sussex*, XXXIII, 27–38; Harbord, Verse No. 612. The proof of the cover of the first publication (which illustrates Kipling's poem) is at Syracuse University together with RK's letter to [Scribner?], 21 August 1894.

KpR 691 Revised, in MS Years Between, 4 leaves (rectos only), bound out of order; watermarked 1890.

British Library, Add. MS 44841, ff. 107–11 (rectos only).

KpR 692 Fair copy, signed, 4 numbered leaves (rectos only).

Harvard, MS Eng 165, ff. 13–16 (rectos only).

KpR 693 Corrected galley proof for first publication, 2 galleys.

Cornell University.

KpR 694 Quotation of lines 29–30 (variant line 30), inscribed on the title page of a copy of *A Fleet in Being* (London, 1899), presented to A. R. Emdin.

Syracuse University.

'Men say 'tis wondrous strange to see', see KpR 893–4.

'The Men That Fought at Minden' ('The men that fought at Minden, they was rookies in their time —')
First pub. *Pall Mall Gazette*, 9 May 1895; collected *The Seven Seas* (New York, 1896); *Sussex*, XXXIII, 142–4; Harbord, Verse No. 635.

KpR 695 Fair copy, revised, in MS Seven Seas (f. 97); watermarked 1890.

Magdalene College, Cambridge.

The Merchantmen ('King Solomon drew merchantmen')
First pub. *Pall Mall Budget*, 15 May 1893; collected *The Seven Seas* (New York, 1896); *Sussex*, XXXIII, 23–6; Harbord, Verse No. 586.

KpR 696 Fair copy of stanzas 1–3, 5–6, here untitled and beginning 'King Solomon sent merchantmen' (f. 104), followed by 5 pages (2 leaves) of rough drafts, in MS Years Between.

British Library, Add. MS 44841, ff. 104–6v.

KpR 697 Fair copy, here entitled 'The Cruise', signed, 3 leaves (rectos only), annotated at the end 'For Miss Julia./Christmas: 1892./ Brattleboro'.

Harvard, MS Eng 165, ff. 1–3 (rectos only).

Merrow Down, see KpR 767–8, 1180–2.

Mesopotamia ('They shall not return to us, the resolute, the young')
First pub. *Morning Post* and *New York Times*, 11 July 1917; collected *The Years Between* (London, [1919]); *Sussex*, XXXIII, 393–4; Harbord, Verse No. 1031.

KpR 698 Revised, in MS Years Between, one page.

British Library, Add. MS 44841, f. 31.

KpR 699 Typescript, revised, without final stanza, one page.

Sotheby's, 9–10 December 1968, Lot 766, sold to Rota.

M. I. ('I wish my mother could see me now, with a fence-post under my arm')
First pub. *McClure's Magazine* and *Windsor Magazine*, October 1901; collected *The Five Nations* (London, 1903); *Sussex*, XXXIII, 306–10; Harbord, Verse No. 765.

KpR 700 Fair copy, slightly revised, here entitled 'M. I.:/1900–1901', signed '1900–1901. — written out by Rudyard Kipling for the survivors: 1930', 2 numbered leaves (rectos only), together with a covering letter to Ian Hamilton, Bateman's, 5 June 1931.

Dalhousie University.

KpR 701 Fair copy of a portion of printer's copy for *Windsor Magazine*, containing the first 8 of the 14 stanzas, composed of 3 cards each containing text and an original illustration by L. Raven-Hill, signed.

Facsimile in British Library, RP 2791(i).

Syracuse University.

KpR 702 In MS Five Nations.

National Library of Australia, MS 94.

The Michigan Twins ('"Wise is the child who knows his sire"')
First pub. *Boston Advertiser*, March 1889; first authorized publication in a broadside entitled *The Book Leaf* dated 21 September 1923 issued by Doubleday, Page & Co.; reprinted Harbord, Verse No. 368.

KpR 703 Photograph of fair copy, entitled '"Rudyard" & "Kipling"', three 6-line stanzas, original written on verso of a signed photograph of Kipling sent to F. D. Underwood of Baltimore & Ohio Railroad who had named two stations in the Upper Peninsula of Michigan 'Rudyard' and 'Kipling'.

F. D. Underwood's typescript of these verses, entitled '"Rudyard" & "Kipling"', annotated '...copy of verses written on back of Kipling's photograph Dec 1895...', as sent to F. N. Finney, is now at Dalhousie University.

Harvard, Kipling 15.55.

Mine Sweepers ('Dawn off the Foreland — the young flood making')
First pub. (without title) with 'The Auxiliaries II', the second in series 'The Fringes of the Fleet' in *Daily Telegraph*, 23 November 1915; collected *The Fringes of the Fleet* (London, 1915); collected separately *Inclusive Verse* (1919), as 'The Sweepers'; *Sussex*, XXVI, 245 and *Sussex*, XXXIV, 253; Harbord, Verse No. 1015.

KpR 704 Revised, here untitled, in MS Non-Fiction, in the MS of 'Fringes of the Fleet' (KpR 1632), annotated 'to precede <Patrols.> The auxiliary Fleet II', one page.

British Library, Add. MS 45542, f. 36.

KpR 705 Slightly corrected typescript, signed (initials), one page, sent to S. L. Bensusan with a letter of Bateman's, 12 October 1934.

Syracuse University.

The Miracles ('I sent a message to my dear —')
First pub. *Pall Mall Gazette*, 23 May 1895; collected *The Seven Seas* (New York, 1896); *Sussex*, XXXIII, 39–40; Harbord, Verse No. 636.

KpR 706 Fair copy, in MS Years Between, signed.

British Library, Add. MS 44841, f. 88.

Missed ('There is *one* moment when the gods are kind')
First printed *Schoolboy Lyrics* (privately printed, Lahore, 1881); first pub. *Early Verse* (1900); *Sussex*, XXXV, 51; Rutherford, pp. 97–8; Harbord, Verse No. 25.

KpR 707 One page of a folded leaf (containing also KpR 613, 806), sent to 'Aunt' [Edith Macdonald?], probably after 21 February 1881.

Typed transcript, probably of this MS, at Sussex, KP 24/67.

Sotheby's, 11–12 March 1968, Lot 778 (property of H. C. Drayton), sold to Rota.

KpR 708 Fair copy, in MS Sundry Phansies.

Berg.

Mr Haggard and Mr Lang, see KpR 506.

Mon Accident! ('Child of sin, and a broken vow')
First pub. Rutherford (1986), pp. 144–5; not in Harbord.

KpR 709 Fair copy, in Sussex Notebook 1 (p. 97); dated 14 May 1882, with a later annotation dated 8 October 1883.

Sussex, KP 24/3.

KpR 710 Fair copy, in Sussex Notebook 3 (first series, pp. 62–3); dated 14 May 1882.

Sussex, KP 24/1.

The Moon of Other Days ('Beneath the deep veranda's shade')
First pub. *The Pioneer*, 16 December 1884; collected *Departmental Ditties* (1886); *Sussex*, XXXII, 134–5; Harbord, Verse No. 100. See also KpR 280.

KpR 711 Fair copy, in MS Departmental Ditties (pp. 107–8).

Berg.

A Morning Ride ('In the hush of the cool, dim dawn when the shades begin to retreat')
First pub. Rutherford (1986), pp. 175–6; not in Harbord.

KpR 712 Fair copy, in Sussex Notebook 1 (pp. 128–9), annotated 'Published in the *Englishman* with one howling misprint...' (but no such publication traced); [probably October–November 1882].

Sussex, KP 24/3.

Morning Song in the Jungle ('One moment past our bodies cast')
First pub. without title in text of story 'Letting in the Jungle' in *Pall Mall Gazette*, 12–13 December 1894; collected separately *Songs from Books* (London, 1913); *Sussex*, XII, 137–8 and *Sussex*, XXXIV, 153–4; Harbord, Verse No. 611.

KpR 713 Two fair copies of 3-stanza version (without stanza 2), the first cancelled, both untitled, in MS Jungle Books, one page on a separate leaf marked for insertion in the text of 'Letting in the Jungle' (KpR 1831); watermarked 1890.

British Library, Add. MS 45540, f. 138.

Mother o' Mine ('If I were hanged on the highest hill')
First pub. as 'Dedication' in the 15-chapter version of *The Light that Failed* (London and New York, 1891); collected separately *Songs from Books* (New York, 1912); *Sussex*, XVIII, as 'Dedication' and *Sussex*, XXXIV, 163; Harbord, Verse No. 439, as 'Dedication'.

KpR 714 Fair copy, here entitled 'The Dedication', in MS Years Between, one page of Embankment Chambers notepaper; signed and dated April 1891.

British Library, Add. MS 44841, f. 119.

KpR 715 Fair copy, in MS Writings and Songs (p. 13).

Berg.

'Mother Rügen's tea-house on the Baltic —'
First pub. in text of story 'With the Night Mail' in *McClure's Magazine*, November 1905; story collected *Actions and Reactions* (London, 1909); *Sussex*, VIII, 135; Harbord, Verse No. 881, as 'Elsinore *or* The First Air Chantey *or* The Oldest of Our Chanteys'. See also KpR 2259.

KpR 716 Fair copy, one page, enclosed in a letter to [Henry Brereton] Marriott Watson, Bateman's, 29 October 1909.

Huntington, HM 41844.

The Mother's Son ('I have a dream — a dreadful dream —')
First pub. with story 'Fairy-Kist' in *Limits and Renewals* (London, 1932); collected separately *Inclusive Verse* [1933]; *Sussex*, XI, 145–6 and *Sussex*, XXXIV, 410–11; Harbord, Verse No. 1207.

KpR 717 Corrected first page proof for the Sussex Edition, Vol. XI; date stamped 14 October 1932.

British Library, Add. MS 55862.

Mowgli's Song Against People ('I will let loose against you the fleet-footed vines —')
First pub. with story 'Letting in the Jungle' in *Pall Mall Gazette*, 12–13 December 1894; collected separately *Songs from Books* (London, 1913); *Sussex*, XII, 163–4 and *Sussex*, XXXIV, 166–7; Harbord, Verse No. 648.

KpR 718 Fair copy, here untitled and headed 'Head lines for "*Letting in the Jungle*".', one page, annotated by RK '[Pro]ofs to Mr Hind' and in an unidentified hand 'These verses were set at Spottiswoodes on Sep. 5. 94', with a covering letter to the editor of *Pall Mall Gazette*, 18 August 1894.

Dalhousie University.

Mulholland's Contract ('The fear was on the cattle, for the gale was on the sea')
First pub. *Pall Mall Gazette*, 6 June 1895; collected *The Seven Seas* (New York, 1896); *Sussex*, XXXIII, 69–71; Harbord, Verse No. 638.

KpR 719 In MS Seven Seas: (1) fair copy, revised, watermarked 1890 (f. 94); (2) fair copy, heavily revised, here entitled 'Mulholland's explanation.' (f. 95); (3) draft lines, here entitled 'Mulholland's explanation', watermarked 1890 (f. 96r–v).

Magdalene College, Cambridge.

Mulvaney Regrets ('Attind ye Lasses av Swate Parnasses')
First pub. *Yale Literary Magazine*, May 1896; reprinted Harbord, Verse No. 668, as 'Memorabilia Valencia [sic] *or* Mulvaney Regrets'.

KpR 720 Fair copy, here untitled, one page, signed, sent as a refusal to an invitation from Yale's Kipling Club, addressed to Gouverneur Morris and the Kipling Club of Yale College; dated 1 May 1896.

Facsimile printed twice as broadside: *Memorabilia Yalensia. 'Mulvaney's Regrets'* (printed for the Kipling Club at Yale, [1896]) and Julian S. Mason, *A Yale Footnote to Kipling* (printed for Yale Library Association, 1938). A typescript is in the Beinecke Library at Yale; a photocopy at Columbia University.

Yale, Sterling Library, MSS and Archives.

Municipal ('It was an August evening and, in snowy garments clad')
First pub. *Civil and Military Gazette*, 9 May 1887, as 'The D. C.'s Story'; collected *Departmental Ditties*, 3rd ed (1888); *Sussex*, XXXII, 36–8; Harbord, Verse No. 263.

KpR 721 Fair copy, including 6-line heading, in MS Departmental Ditties (pp. 35–8).

Berg.

KpR 722 Corrections on p. 31 of KpR 282.

Yale.

A Murder in the Compound ('At the wall's foot a smear of fly-flecked red —').
First pub. *Echoes* (Lahore, [1884]); *Sussex*, XXXV, 98; Rutherford, p. 187; Harbord, Verse No. 120.

KpR 723 Fair copy, in Sussex Notebook 1 (p. 151); [probably April 1883].

Sussex, KP 24/3.

KpR 724 Fair copy, signed (initials), one leaf (containing also KpR 21), sent from India to Georgina Craik (Mrs A. W. May), c. 1883.

This MS not mentioned Rutherford.

Bodleian, MS. Eng. poet. e. 43, f. 2v.

'My Boy Jack' ('"Have you news of my boy Jack?"')
First pub. (without title, with 'Destroyers at Jutland I Stories of the Battle') in *Daily Telegraph* and *New York Times*, 19 October 1916; collected *Sea Warfare* (London, 1916); collected separately *The Years Between* (London, [1919]); *Sussex*, XXVI, 335 and *Sussex*, XXXIII, 391; Harbord, Verse No. 1022.

KpR 725 Typescript, here untitled, in the typescript of 'Destroyers at Jutland. I.' (KpR 1539).

Dalhousie University.

My Father's Chair ('There are four good legs to my Father's Chair —')
First pub. C. R. L. Fletcher and Rudyard Kipling, *A History of England* (Oxford and London, 1911); collected separately *Songs from Books* (1915); *Sussex*, XXXIV, 275; Harbord, Verse No. 978.

KpR 726 Revised, here untitled, in MS Years Between, one page, annotated 'type'.

British Library, Add. MS 44841, f. 67.

'My girl she give me the go onest'
First pub. in text of story 'The Courting of Dinah Shadd' in *Macmillan's Magazine*, March 1890; story collected *Life's Handicap* (London and New York, 1891); *Sussex*, IV, 70–71 and *Sussex*, XXXII, 225; Harbord, Verse No. 414.

KpR 727 Draft, here untitled and beginning 'The Queen she give me a shillin'' (i.e., line 5), complete, 2 pages.

Sussex, KP 24/42.

KpR 728 Corrected first page proof for the Sussex Edition, Vol. IV (in text of 'The Courting of Dinah Shadd', KpR 1524); date stamped 13 February 1932.

British Library, Add. MS 55855.

My Hat ('A youth but late returned from school')
First pub. Rutherford (1986), pp. 51–2; not in Harbord.

KpR 729 MS in an unidentified hand, eight 4-line stanzas (each glossed by a phrase in another hand, possibly Kipling's), 3 pages (one leaf of 26 Warwick Gardens notepaper), together with an envelope addressed to J. Tavenor Perry, postmarked London, 9 August 1880.

Rutherford describes the MS as 'holograph'.

Huntington, HM 11877.

My Lady's Law ('The Law whereby my lady moves')
First pub. (5 stanzas) as chapter heading to Chapter 21 in Rudyard Kipling and Wolcott Balestier, *The Naulahka* (London, 1892); reprinted *Sussex*, XIX, 287; first pub. in full (separately) *Songs from Books* (New York, 1912); *Sussex*, XXXIV, 158–9; Harbord, Verse No. 549.

KpR 730 Correction on p. 185 of KpR 1112.

Yale.

KpR 731 Corrected first page proof of stanzas 1–3, 6–7 (i.e., heading to Chapter 21 of *The Naulahka*) for the Sussex Edition, Vol. XIX (see KpR 1921); dated stamped 7 November 1931.

British Library, Add. MS 55869.

'My new-cut ashlar takes the light'
First pub. as 'Twilight in the Abbey' in *National Observer*, 8 December 1890; collected as 'L'Envoi' in *Life's Handicap* (London and New York, 1891); collected separately without third stanza *Songs from Books* (New York, 1912) and with alternative third stanza in *Songs from Books* (London, 1913); *Sussex*, IV, 449–[50], as 'L'Envoi' and *Sussex*, XXXIV, 31–2; Harbord, Verse No. 478.

KpR 732 Fair copy of an early version, here entitled 'Twilight in the Abbey./(The Prayer of the Mark Master Mason)' and beginning 'My new-cut [?] takes the light', in a letter to William Ernest Henley, Embankment Chambers, n.d.

National Library of Scotland, MS. 5406, ff. 229–30.

KpR 733 Fair copy, wanting stanza 3, here entitled 'A dedication/(*Many Inventions*)', in MS Years Between, one page, annotated '*type*.'.

British Library, Add. MS 44841, f. 126.

KpR 734 Copy of pp. 351–2 of *Life's Handicap* (1891) containing this poem (entitled 'L'Envoi'), including the addition by RK of an additional stanza beginning 'Hard is the Law whereby I move', inscribed to R. B. Fairbairn, 14 February 1893.

Cornell University.

KpR 735 Fair copy, revised, of alternative third stanza, on p. 37 of KpR 1112.

Yale.

KpR 736 Corrected first page proof for the Sussex Edition, Vol. IV; date stamped 13 February 1932.

British Library, Add. MS 55855.

My Rival ('I go to concert, party, ball —'), see KpR 280.

'My wife and daughter, maid & me'
No publication traced; not in Harbord.

KpR 737 Four lines, in a letter to George Bambridge, Algeciras, Spain, 20 March [1924].

Sussex, KP 12/1.

Naaman's Song ('"Go, wash thyself in Jordan — go, wash thee and be clean!"')
First pub. with story 'Aunt Ellen' in *Limits and Renewals* (London, 1932); collected separately *Inclusive Verse* [1933]; *Sussex*, XI, 141–2 and *Sussex*, XXXIV, 408–9; Harbord, Verse No. 1208.

KpR 738 Corrected first page proof for the Sussex Edition, Vol. XI; date stamped 14 October 1932.

British Library, Add. MS 55862.

'Namely' — ('Such as in Ships of Awful Size')
No publication traced; not in Harbord.

KpR 739 Typed transcript of letter to Sir Percy Bates containing two 8-line stanzas of 'ribaldry'; letter dated Bateman's, 1 October 1934.

Sussex, KP 14/13.

The Native-Born ('We've drunk to the Queen — God bless her! —')
First pub. *The Times*, 14 October 1895; collected *The Seven Seas* (New York, 1896); *Sussex*, XXXIII, 41–4; Harbord, Verse No. 642.

KpR 740 Three pages, signed.

Charles Hamilton Galleries, 21 October 1971, Lot 215.

KpR 741 Fair copy, here untitled and beginning at line 1, possibly a quotation, signed, one page.

Sotheby's, 13–14 April 1959, Lot 502.

KpR 742 Quotation of stanza 4 (beginning 'I charge you charge your glasses —'), signed, on a 'The Elms' notecard (verso).

These lines mistakenly listed as a separate poem ('The Toast') in Harbord, Verse No. 1124B.

Library of Congress, Rare Book Division, Colt Collection.

A Nativity ('The Babe was laid in the Manger')
First pub. *Daily Telegraph*, 23 December 1916; collected *The Years Between* (London, [1919]); *Sussex*, XXXIII, 385–6; Harbord, Verse No. 1026.

KpR 743 Revised, here entitled 'The Nativity (1915.)', in MS Years Between.

British Library, Add. MS 44841, f. 27.

KpR 744 One page.

Sotheby's, 9–10 December 1968, Lot 760, sold to Rota.

Natural Theology ('I ate my fill of a whale that died')
First pub. *The Years Between* (London, [1919]); *Sussex*, XXXIII, 429–31; Harbord, Verse No. 1102.

KpR 745 Draft, in MS Years Between, 2 leaves (rectos only).

British Library, Add. MS 44841, ff. 47–8 (rectos only).

Navarino *or* That Day at Navarino *or* The Battle of Navarino, see KpR 1422.

The Necessitarian ('I know not in Whose hands are laid')
First pub. with story 'Steam Tactics' in *Traffics and Discoveries* (London, 1904); collected separately *Songs from Books* (New York, 1912); *Sussex*, VII, 181 and *Sussex*, XXXIV, 104; Harbord, Verse No. 870.

KpR 746 Successive drafts and fair copies, all untitled, one begining 'O praise them in whose hands are laid', in MS Traffics and Discoveries, 4 pages (one a sheet of Bateman's notepaper).

McGill University.

KpR 747 Correction on p. 125 of KpR 1112.

Yale.

KpR 748 Corrected first page proof for *Humorous Tales* (London, 1931), pp. 511–12; date stamped 9 June 1931.

British Library, Add. MS 55847.

KpR 749 Corrected first page proof for the Sussex Edition, Vol. VIII; date stamped 22 March 1932.

British Library, Add. MS 55858.

Neighbour Kipling ('When skies are grey instead of blue')
First pub. (without title) in Will M. Clemens, *A Ken of Kipling* (New York, 1899); reprinted Harbord, Verse No. 737, as 'Neighbour Kipling *or* Lines to Julia Marlowe'.

KpR 750 Eight lines, inscribed in a presentation copy to Julia Marlowe of *The Day's Work*.

Unlocated.

Neighbours ('The man that is open of heart to his neighbour')
First pub. *Order of Proceedings at Royal Albert Hall*, 27 January 1932 and *The Times*, 28 January 1932; collected with story 'Beauty Spots' in *Limits and Renewals* (London, 1932); *Sussex*, XI, 277 and *Sussex*, XXXIV, 421; Harbord, Verse No. 1209.

KpR 751 Corrected page proof in Limits and Renewals Proof; date stamped 21 January 1932.

Syracuse University.

The Neutral, see KpR 924–5.

The New Knighthood ('Who gives him the Bath?')
First pub. with story 'A Deal in Cotton' in *Actions and Reactions* (London, 1909); collected separately *Songs from Books* (New York, 1912); *Sussex*, VIII, 191–2 and *Sussex*, XXXIV, 39–40; Harbord, Verse No. 930.

KpR 752 In MS Actions and Reactions (f. 80).

University of St Andrews, MS PR4854.A4.

KpR 753 Fair copy, in MS Writings and Songs (pp. 49–50).

Berg.

KpR 754 Corrected first page proof for the Sussex Edition, Vol. VIII; date stamped 28 November 1931.

British Library, Add. MS 55859.

'New Lamps for Old', see KpR 237–9.

The Night Before ('I sneered when I heard the old priest complain')
First printed *Schoolboy Lyrics* (privately printed, Lahore, 1881); reprinted Harbord, Verse No. 5; Rutherford, pp. 47–9.

KpR 755 MS in an unidentified hand (autograph?), containing some pencil revisions in a second hand, as submitted to 'The Scribbler', signed 'Nickson', 3 pages, 6 stanzas; among unused copy for the magazine which expired in 1880.

Facsimile of last page in Maggs sale catalogue, Plate VII; this MS was sold to G. M. Williamson by May Morris in 1901 (see the description of 'The Scribbler' in the INTRODUCTION).

Maggs Catalogue 337 (Whitsun 1915), Item 811.

KpR 756 Typed transcript (made to replace the original KpR 755), bound with May Morris's set of 'The Scribbler' and unused contributions thereto, 4 numbered pages and title page.

British Library, Add. MS 45337, ff. 284–8 (rectos only).

The Night of Power ('In the beginning when the earth was new')
First pub. Rutherford (1986), pp. 388–9; not in Harbord.

KpR 757 Fair copy, extensively revised, c. 30 lines, written on a calendar leaf for 1st January 1888, including several scattered sketches, annotated '*Cætura desunt* Try again some other night'.

Library of Congress, Rare Book Division, Carpenter Kipling Collection.

Night Song in the Jungle ('Now Chil the Kite brings home the night')
First pub. as verse heading to story 'Mowgli's Brothers' in *St Nicholas*, January 1894; collected *The Jungle Book* (London and New York, 1894); collected separately *Songs from Books* (London, 1913); *Sussex*, XII, 5 and *Sussex*, XXXIV, 231 as 'Chapter Heading'; Harbord, Verse No. 614.

KpR 758 Revised, in MS Jungle Books, here entitled 'Mowgli's Brothers' and beginning 'Now Rann the Kite brings home the night', one page (containing also KpR 1014); watermarked 1890.

British Library, Add. MS 45540, f. 4.

Non Nobis Domine ('*Non nobis, Domine!*')
First pub. *Three Poems* (Garden City, NY, 1934) and programme for *Pageant of Parliament* produced at Albert Hall, 29 June–21 July 1934; *Sussex*, XXXV, 299; Harbord, Verse No. 1221.

KpR 759 Typescript, revised by Kipling?, on a page (containing also KpR 810).

Library of Congress, Rare Book Division, Colt Collection.

Norman and Saxon ('"My son," said the Norman Baron, "I am dying, and you will be heir')
First pub. C. R. L. Fletcher and Rudyard Kipling, *A History of England* (Oxford and London, 1911); collected separately *Songs from Books* (1915); *Sussex*, XXXIV, 271–2; Harbord, Verse No. 976.

KpR 760 Fair copy, revised, here untitled, headed 'VI', in MS Years Between, one page.

British Library, Add. MS 44841, f. 65.

The North Sea Patrol ('Where the East wind is brewed fresh and fresh every morning')
First pub. (without title) with 'Patrols, II', the sixth in series 'The Fringes of the Fleet' in *Daily Telegraph*, 2 December 1915; collected *The Fringes of the Fleet* (London, 1915); collected separately *Inclusive Verse* (1919); *Sussex*, XXVI, 287 and *Sussex*, XXXIV, 256; Harbord, Verse No. 1019.

KpR 761 Slightly revised, here untitled, in MS Non-Fiction, in the MS of 'Fringes of the Fleet' (KpR 1632), one page.

British Library, Add. MS 45542, f. 55.

'Not though you die to-night, O Sweet, and wail', see KpR 177–8.

'Now Chil the Kite brings home the night', see KpR 758.

'Now it is not good for the Christian's health to hustle the Aryan brown', see KpR 185–7.

The Nurses ('When, with a pain he desires to explain to his servitors, Baby')
First pub. with story 'The Bold 'Prentice' in *Land and Sea Tales* (London, 1923); collected separately *Inclusive Verse* [1927]; *Sussex*, XVI, 161–3 and *Sussex*, XXXIV, 354–6; Harbord, Verse No. 1120.

KpR 762 Fair copy, revised, here beginning 'When, with a pain he desires to explain to the multitude, Baby', one page.

Sussex, KP 24/43.

KpR 763 Corrected first page proof for the Sussex Edition, Vol. XVI; date stamped 14 December 1931.

British Library, Add. MS 55866.

The Nursing Sister ('Our sister sayeth such and such')
First pub. without title as heading to Chapter 20, ascribed 'Queen's Song from Libretto of Naulạhka', in Rudyard Kipling and Wolcott Balestier, *The Naulahka* (London, 1892); reprinted *Sussex*, XIX, 267, ascribed 'From Libretto of *Naulahka.*'; revised version first pub. separately *Songs from Books* (New York, 1912); *Sussex*, XXXIV, 160; Harbord, Verse No. 548, as 'From (the) Libretto of Naulahka *or* The Queen's Song from Libretto of Naulahka'.

KpR 764 Draft, here untitled, being the version used in the first publication, one page (containing also KpR 994).

Pierpont Morgan, MA 979.

KpR 765 Slightly corrected first page proof (i.e., as heading to Chapter 20 of *The Naulahka*) for the Sussex Edition, Vol. XIX; date stamped 7 November 1931.

British Library, Add. MS 55869.

O Baal, Hear Us! ('Moralists we')
First pub. *The Pioneer*, 19 July 1888; collected *Early Verse* (1900); *Sussex*, XXXII, 75; Rutherford, pp. 408–14; Harbord, Verse No. 328B. See also KpR 184, 187.

KpR 766 Revised clipping of the first publication in Scrapbook 4 (p. 75), annotated 'Miss A Please type this RK'.

This clipping not mentioned Rutherford.

Sussex, KP 28/4.

'O ye, all ye that walk in Willow Wood', see KpR 1807.

'Of all the Tribe of Tegumai'
First pub. with story 'How the Alphabet Was Made' in *Just So Stories* (London, 1902); collected separately as Part II of 'Merrow Down' (beginning 'There runs a road by Merrow Down') in *Songs from Books* (London, 1913); *Sussex*, XIII, 157 and *Sussex*, XXXIV, 121–2 (as Part II of 'Merrow Down'); Harbord, Verse No. 797, as 'Merrow Down (II)...*or* Of all the Tribe of Tegumai'.

KpR 767 Fair copy, in MS Just So Stories, annotated 'on separate page to follow Alphabet.'.

British Library, Add. MS 59840, f. 104.

KpR 768 Corrected first page proof for the Sussex Edition, Vol. XIII; date stamped 29 October 1932.

British Library, Add. MS 55863.

Of Animal Calls, see KpR 173.

Of Birthdays ('For us Life's wheel runs backward. Other nests')
First pub. Rutherford (1986), pp. 326, 328; not in Harbord.

KpR 769 Transcript by JLK, in his letter to Edith Plowden, Simla, 6 July 1886.

A transcript in an unidentified hand of this letter is at Sussex, Baldwin Papers 1/2.

Sussex, KP 1/10.

Of Swine ('All things were made in seven days')
First printed Harbord (1969), Verse No. 744B, as 'Of Swine *or* How many Hams have twenty pigs?'.

KpR 770 Fair copy, signed, one page of Castle Line, R.M.S. 'Kinfauns Castle' notepaper; dated 2 February 1900.

Photocopy at Sussex, Baldwin Papers 2/8.

Library of Congress, Rare Book Division, Colt Collection.

'Oh do not despise the advice of the Wise', see KpR 1852.

'Oh! hush thee, my baby, the night is behind us', see KpR 1014.

'Oh, our Fathers came with a word to Sitting-Fox'
First printed Scheuer Catalogue 6 (1931); lines 1–2 only reprinted Harbord, Verse No. 669B, as 'Sitting Fox'.

KpR 771 Twenty-eight lines, in a letter to W. Hallett Phillips ('Sitting-Fox'), Naulakha, 19 June [1895 or 1896].

Typed transcript at Sussex, KP 17/19.

Scheuer Catalogue 6 (1931).

'Oh Whiskey is a noble drink'
No publication traced; not in Harbord.

KpR 772 Draft lines, mostly cancelled, in MS Years Between, possibly for another poem, on verso of KpR 1006; watermarked 1896.

British Library, Add. MS 44841, f. 122v.

Old Ballad, see KpR 177.

The Old Issue ('All we have of freedom, all we use or know —')
First pub. (without lines the heading) in *The Times*, *New York Tribune* and *Boston Globe*, 29 September 1899; collected in full in *The Five Nations* (London, 1903); *Sussex*, XXXIII, 261–4; Harbord, Verse No. 733.

KpR 773 In MS Five Nations.

National Library of Australia, MS 94.

KpR 774 Corrected typescript, here entitled 'The King', without heading, 3 numbered leaves (rectos only) cut into 9 sections, signed, together with two telegrams (one reads 'Call poem The Old Issue') and an envelope annotated by J. B. Capper 'This is the actual original sent to *The Times* ... & cut into sections by the printer...'.

Library of Congress, Rare Book Division, Colt Collection.

The Old Men ('Wc shall not acknowledge that old stars fade or stronger planets arise')
First pub. *The Five Nations* (London, 1903); *Sussex*, XXXIII, 217–18; Harbord, Verse No. 820.

KpR 775 In MS Five Nations.

National Library of Australia, MS 94.

Old Mother Laidinwool ('Old Mother Laidinwool had nigh twelve months been dead.')
First pub. (lines 1–4) in text of story 'Dymchurch Flit' in *Strand* and *McClure's Magazine*, September 1906; collected *Puck of Pook's Hill* (London, 1906); *Sussex*, XIV, 224; first pub. in full *Songs from Books* (New York, 1912); *Sussex*, XXXIV, 123–4; Harbord, Verse No. 886.

KpR 776 Revised, in the text of 'Dymchurch Flit' (KpR 1567) in MS Puck.

Bodleian, MS. Eng. misc. c. 127, f. 91.

KpR 777 Revision on p. 142 of KpR 1112.

Yale.

The Old Shikarri, see KpR 177.

An Old Song ('So long as 'neath the Kalka hills')
First pub. *Civil and Military Gazette*, 15 August 1887, as 'The Frame and the Picture'; collected *Departmental Ditties*, 4th ed (1890); *Sussex*, XXXII, 126; Harbord, Verse No. 276.

KpR 778 Drafts, on several blank pages of Scrapbook 1 [pp. 130, 208 *rev.*, 309 *rev.*].

Sussex, KP 28/1.

Old Song, see KpR 1807.

The Oldest Song ('"These were never your true love's eyes.')
First pub. (two untitled stanzas only) as heading to 'A Serpent of Old Nile' ('Egypt of the Magicians, No. III') in *Nash's Magazine* and *Cosmopolitan*, August 1914; first pub. in full *The Years Between* (London, [1919]); *Sussex*, XXXIII, 428; Harbord, Verse No. 1006.

KpR 779 Fair copy, revised, here untitled, in MS Years Between, headed 'Type for verse heading Letter IV' ('IV' cancelled in pencil and 'III' added later), 5 stanzas (one cancelled).

British Library, Add. MS 44841, f. 46.

KpR 780 Corrected galley proof for the first publication (see KpR 1574), including corrections to these verses; date stamped 22 May 1914.

Dalhousie University.

Oldham, see KpR 1202.

'*Ôm arataya!* Lo the sage is bust!'
No publication traced; not in Harbord.

KpR 781 Four lines on Sir Theodore Martin being Poet Laureate, a parody of Henley, in a letter (containing also KpR 450, 1159) to W. E. Henley, Brattleboro, 26 October 1892.

Pierpont Morgan, MA 1617.

On a Game of Euchre, see KpR 1179.

On Fort Duty ('There's tumult in the Khyber')
First pub. *United Services College Chronicle*, 28 March 1884, signed 'Z.54.R.A.'; collected *Early Verse* (1900); *Sussex*, XXXV, 32–3; Rutherford, pp. 215–16; Harbord, Verse No. 79.

KpR 782 Fair copy of 2-stanza version, here entitled '"Revenge — a ballad of the Fleet"', in Sussex Notebook 1 (p. 161); dated February 1884.

Sussex, KP 24/3.

KpR 783 Fair copy, revised, signed 'Z.54.R.A.', one page, originally sent to Cormell Price with a letter of 19 February 1884.

Facsimile in [Luther S. Livingston], *The Works of Rudyard Kipling* (New York, 1901), [p. 10]. The letter to Price is in the Library of Congress, Rare Book Division, Colt Collection.

Pierpont Morgan.

'One moment past our bodies cast', see KpR 713.

One School of Many, see KpR 55–6.

One Viceroy Resigns ('So here's your Empire. No more wine, then? Good.')
First pub. *The Pioneer*, 7 December 1888, as 'One Word More'; collected *Departmental Ditties*, 4th ed (1890); *Sussex*, XXXII, 142–8; Harbord, Verse No. 343.

KpR 784 Fair copy, including a sketch, in MS Departmental Ditties (pp. 86–95).

Berg.

KpR 785 Corrections on pp. 101–6 of KpR 282.

Yale.

The Only Son ('She dropped the bar, she shot the bolt, she fed the fire anew')
First pub. (lines 4–14, 17–22) without title as heading beginning 'The Only Son lay down again and dreamed that he dreamed a dream' to 'In the Rukh' in *Many Inventions* (London and New York, 1893); reprinted *Sussex*, V, 297–8; first pub. in full *Songs from Books* (New York, 1912); *Sussex*, XXXIV, 164–5; Harbord, Verse No. 598.

KpR 785.5 Draft of c. 6 lines, in MS Seven Seas (f. 96); watermarked 1890.

Magdalene College, Cambridge.

KpR 786 Fair copy, revised, of lines 4–14, 17–22, in MS Day's Work, subscribed '*The Only Son.*', stuck on a leaf together with the first page of MS of 'In the Rukh' (KpR 1764).

British Library, Add. MS 45541, f. 44.

Oonts ('Wot makes the soldier's 'eart to penk, wot makes 'im to perspire?')
First pub. *Scots Observer*, 22 March 1890; collected *Barrack-Room Ballads* (1892); *Sussex*, XXXII, 193–5; Harbord, Verse No. 423.

KpR 786.5 Corrected page proof for *Barrack-Room Ballads* (1892); date stamped 12 February 1892.

British Library, Loan 97 (deposited by John Aris, 1989).

Op. 3, see KpR 184–7.

The Open Door ('England is a cosy little country')
First pub. with 'Brazilian Sketches No. V São Paulo and a Coffee Estate' in *Morning Post*, 13 December 1927; collected separately *Inclusive Verse* [1933]; *Sussex*, XXIV, 389–90 and *Sussex*, XXXV, 270–1; Harbord, Verse No. 1151.

KpR 787 Slightly corrected first page proof for the Sussex Edition, Vol. XXIV; date stamped 19 June 1936.

British Library, Add. MS 55874.

'Our Fathers Also' ('Thrones, Powers, Dominions, Peoples, Kings')
First pub. without stanza one (beginning 'By — they are by with mirth and tears') with story 'Below the Mill Dam' in *Traffics and Discoveries* (London, 1904); reprinted *Sussex*, VII, 373–4; collected separately in full *Songs from Books* (New York, 1912); *Sussex*, XXXIV, 63–4; Harbord, Verse No. 871.

KpR 788 Fair copy, revised, here untitled, wanting stanza one, in MS Traffics and Discoveries, headed 'The Mill Dam.', one page.

McGill University.

KpR 789 Fair copy, revised, wanting stanza one, 2 leaves (rectos only), annotated 'N.B. The Foregoing is to replace the previously sent motto for "The Mill Dam".'.

Dalhousie University.

KpR 790 Corrected first page proof for the Sussex Edition, Vol. VII; date stamped 22 March 1932.

British Library, Add. MS 55858.

'Our Fathers of Old' ('Excellent herbs had our fathers of old')
First pub. with story 'A Doctor of Medicine' in *Rewards and Fairies* (London, 1910); collected separately *Songs from Books* (New York, 1912); *Sussex*, XV, 265–6 and *Sussex*, XXXIV, 88–9; Harbord, Verse No. 955.

KpR 791 Fair copy, revised, in MS Rewards and Fairies, annotated '<The knife and the Naked Chalk>' and in pencil 'to precede <the> A Doctor of Medicine'.

Cambridge University Library, ADD 6850, f. 97.

KpR 792 Correction on p. 102 of KpR 1112.

Yale.

KpR 793 Slightly corrected first page proof for the Sussex Edition, Vol. XV; date stamped 18 September 1931.

British Library, Add. MS 55865.

Our Lady of Many Dreams ('We pray to God, and to God it seems')
First pub. (4-stanza version) in *Echoes* (Lahore, [1884]); *Sussex*, XXXV, 96–7; first pub. in full Rutherford (1986), pp. 131–3; Harbord, Verse No. 123.

KpR 794 Fair copy, 6 stanzas, subtitled 'Old Style', in Sussex Notebook 1 (unnumbered 2 pages following p. 75 and p.78), annotated 'Paris. Rue de la jolie Mericourt'.

Sussex, KP 24/3.

KpR 795 Fair copy, 6 stanzas, in Sussex Notebook 3 (first series, pp. 28–31); dated 20 March 1882.

Sussex, KP 24/1.

KpR 796 Fair copy of stanzas 1–3 only, signed with monogram of 'J. R. K.', on a semi-stiff glossy card, lettered in black ink; dated 1882.

Pembroke College, Cambridge, LC.I.136A.

Our Lady of Many Dreams (New Style) ('Trees to the very water's edge —')
First pub. Rutherford (1986), pp. 133–4; not in Harbord.

KpR 797 Fair copy, subtitled 'New Style' and 'Under the arches', in Sussex Notebook 1 (pp. 79–81); dated 20 March [1882].

Sussex, KP 24/3.

Our Lady of the Sackcloth ('There was a Priest at Philae')
First pub. *Morning Post*, 15 April 1935; collected *Sussex*, XXXV, 307–10; Harbord, Verse No. 1224.

KpR 798 Carbon copy typescript.

Berg.

Our Lady of the Snows ('A Nation spoke to a Nation')
First pub. *The Times*, 27 April 1897; collected *The Five Nations* (London, 1903); *Sussex*, XXXIII, 247–8; Harbord, Verse No. 696.

KpR 799 Fair copy, revised, in MS Seven Seas (f. 59); watermarked 1896.

Magdalene College, Cambridge.

KpR 800 Three autograph MSS: (1) fair copy, revised, 2 leaves (rectos only), 5 stanzas, headed '7 Beacon Terrace Monday Morning April 26 1897'; (2) fair copy, revised, 2 leaves (rectos only), stanza 2 annotated 'Omit if you think too hard on the American?'; (3) fair copy, signed, 2 leaves (rectos only), as sent to the editor of *The Times* for the first publication.

Dalhousie University.

KpR 801 Fair copy, revised, stanzas 5–6 only, in Berg Booklet [pp. 23–4].

Berg.

'Our Lord Who did the Ox command', see KpR 153–7.

'Our vanship was the Asia —', see KpR 1422.

Out of Sight ('Out of thy sight — away from thy lips' smiling —')
First pub. Rutherford (1986), p. 176; not in Harbord.

KpR 802 Fair copy, in Sussex Notebook 1 (p. 136); dated 13 November [1882].

Sussex, KP 24/3.

The Outlaws ('Through learned and laborious years')
First pub. separately [New York, 1914] (c. 100 copies); collected *The Years Between* (London, [1919]); *Sussex*, XXXIII, 367–8; Harbord, Verse No. 1012.

KpR 803 Fair copy, revised, in MS Years Between, wanting last two lines of stanza 7, one page.

British Library, Add. MS 44841, f. 18.

The Outsong, see KpR 804–5.

Outsong in the Jungle ('For the sake of him who showed')
First pub. as 'The Outsong' with story 'The Spring Running' in *Pall Mall Gazette*, 25 September 1895; collected *The Second Jungle Book* (London and New York, 1895); collected separately *Songs from Books* (London, 1913); *Sussex*, XII, 259–62 (as 'The Outsong') and *Sussex*, XXXIV, 41–3; Harbord, Verse No. 654.

KpR 804 Fair copy, revised, in MS Jungle Books, here entitled 'The Outsong', annotated 'To follow last tale The Spring Running', 2 leaves (rectos only); watermarked 1894.

British Library, Add. MS 45540, ff. 71–2 (rectos only).

KpR 805 Fair copy, in MS Writings and Songs (pp. 77–81), including 7 cancelled lines.

Berg.

Overheard ('So the day dragged through')
First printed *Schoolboy Lyrics* (privately printed, Lahore, 1881); *Sussex*, XXXV, 41–3; Rutherford, pp. 93–5; Harbord, Verse No. 26.

KpR 806 Containing an additional final stanza, on 2 pages of a folded leaf (containing also KpR 613, 707), sent to 'Aunt' [Edith Macdonald?], probably after 21 February 1881.

Typed transcript, probably of this MS, at Sussex, KP 24/67; additional stanza printed Rutherford, p. 93 (from the transcript).

Sotheby's, 11–12 March 1968, Lot 778 (property of H. C. Drayton), sold to Rota.

The Overland Mail ('In the Name of the Empress of India, make way')
First pub. *Departmental Ditties*, 2nd ed (1886); *Sussex*, XXXII, 65–6; Harbord, Verse No. 226.

KpR 807 Fair copy, revised, here entitled '<Her Majesty's> The Overland Mail', 2 leaves (rectos only), sent to the printer for the first publication.

Pierpont Morgan, MA 979.

KpR 808 Revision and correction on p. 50 of KpR 282.

Yale.

The Owl ('Men said, but here I know they lied')
First printed Ballard (1935), pp. 87–8; reprinted Harbord, Verse No. 370; Rutherford, pp. 458–60. The MS which RK presumably gave to the Bohemian Club in San Francisco (for whom the poem was written) has apparently not survived (possibly destroyed in the 1906 earthquake).

KpR 809 In a letter to Edmonia Hill ('Please look over a copy of the verses I sent to the Bohemian Club...'), dated 'Palace Hotel, Monday [9 June]', postmarked 12 June 1889.

Facsimile of original letter printed *Bohemian Club Library Notes*, No. 9, June 1961; two typed transcripts of the letter are at Cornell University; another at Sussex, KP 16/4.

Unlocated.

The Oxen, see KpR 173.

The Pageant of Elizabeth ('Like Princes crowned they bore them —')
First pub. *Three Poems* (Garden City, New York, 1934) and programme for *Pageant of Parliament*, produced at Albert Hall, 29 June–21 July 1934; *Sussex*, XXXV, 298; Harbord, Verse No. 1220, as 'Elizabethan Poem(s) *or* A Pageant of Elizabeth *or* A Pageant of Parliament'.

KpR 810 Typescript, revised by RK?, on a page with KpR 759.

Library of Congress, Rare Book Division, Colt Collection.

The Page's Message [The Message] ('Spare neither lie, nor deed, nor gold —')
First pub. Rutherford (1986), pp. 80–1; Harbord, Verse No. 59.

KpR 811 Fair copy, here entitled 'The Message', in Sussex Notebook 3 (first series, pp. 51–2); 21 November 1881.

Sussex, KP 24/1.

KpR 812 Fair copy, here entitled 'The Page's Message' in MS Sundry Phansies, including a heading.

Berg.

The Page's Song ('Spring-time, shall it bring thee ease')
First pub. Rutherford (1986), pp. 99–100; Harbord, Verse No. 60.

KpR 813 Fair copy, in Sussex Notebook 3 (first series, pp. 34–5); dated 25 December 1881.

Sussex, KP 24/1.

KpR 814 Fair copy, in MS Sundry Phansies, including a prose heading.

Berg.

KpR 815 Transcript by JLK of stanzas 1–3, in Sussex Notebook 2 [p. 23]; dated 'Winter term 1881.'.

Sussex, KP 24/2.

Pagett, M.P. ('Pagett, M.P., was a liar, and a fluent liar therewith, —')
First pub. *The Pioneer*, 16 June 1886; revised version collected *Departmental Ditties* (1886); *Sussex*, XXXII, 49–51; Harbord, Verse No. 186. See also KpR 280.

KpR 816 Revisions (including lines 23–4 cancelled and rewritten on facing blank verso) in KpR 279.

Pierpont Morgan, 20177.

KpR 817 Correction on p. 41 of KpR 282.

Yale.

The Palace ('When I was a King and a Mason — a Master proven and skilled')
First pub. *The Five Nations* (London, 1903); *Sussex*, XXXIII, 230–1; Harbord, Verse No. 821.

KpR 818 In MS Five Nations.

National Library of Australia, MS 94.

Pan in Vermont ('It's forty in the shade to-day, the spouting eaves declare')
First pub. *Country Life in America*, December 1902; collected *Inclusive Verse* (1919); *Sussex*, XXXV, 194–6; Harbord, Verse No. 786.

KpR 819 Fair copy, revised, becoming a draft at the end, in MS Years Between, being a variant version containing unpublished stanzas; watermarked 1890.

British Library, Add. MS 44841, f. 120.

KpR 820 Typescript, on pp. 1–2 of a typescript of 'From Tideway to Tideway No. IX Leaves from a Winter Note-Book' (KpR 1648), among materials for *Letters of Travel* (KpR 1824).

Berg.

The Parable of Chajju Bhagat, see KpR 177.

Parade-Song of the Camp-Animals ('We lent to Alexander the strength of Hercules')
First pub. with story 'Her Majesty's Servants' in *The Jungle Book* (London and New York, 1894); collected separately *Songs from Books* (London, 1913); *Sussex*, XII, 467–9 and *Sussex*, XXXIV, 97–9; Harbord, Verse Nos. 626–31.

KpR 821 In MS Jungle Books: drafts, here untitled, 2 pages (ff. 1–2, rectos only), the first also containing KpR 46; fair copy, revised, of variant version of five 6-line stanzas and one 16-line stanza, beginning '*Cavalry Horses*: —/Silky tail and flowing mane', annotated 'to follow servants of the Queen', watermarked 1890 (f. 59).

British Library, Add. MS 45540, ff. 1–2, 59.

Parting ('Hot kisses on red lips that burn —')
First pub. Rutherford (1986), pp. 111–12; not in Harbord.

KpR 822 Fair copy, one page, apparently written out for Florence Garrard, signed 'J. R. K.'.

Berg.

Parting [In the Hall] ('The last five minutes were worth the price —')
First pub. Rutherford (1986), pp. 153–5; not in Harbord.

KpR 823 Fair copy, revised, here entitled 'Parting', in Sussex Notebook 1 (pp. 105–7), annotated 'St Katherine's Dock. 5.A.M.'; dated 13 June [1882].

Sussex, KP 24/3.

KpR 824 Fair copy, here entitled 'Parting —', in Sussex Notebook 3 (second series, pp. 12–15).

Sussex, KP 24/1.

KpR 825 Transcript by AMK, in Sussex Notebook 2 [pp. 42–4], here entitled 'In the Hall'; dated June 1882.

Sussex, KP 24/2.

The Parting of the Columns ('We've rode an' fought an' ate an' drunk as rations come to hand')
First pub. *The Five Nations* (London, 1903); *Sussex*, XXXIII, 314–16; Harbord, Verse No. 822.

KpR 826 In MS Five Nations.

National Library of Australia, MS 94.

KpR 827 Fair copy of stanza 6, here the caption to a sketch in Brigadier-General R. W. Hare's 'South African War Sketch-Book' (containing also KpR 231, 840), written while aboard S.S. Kinfauns Castle, April 1903.

Facsimile in *KJ*, June 1936, between pp. 52 and 53.

Owned (1936) Brigadier-General R. W. Hare (see *KJ*).

The Peace of Dives ('The Word came down to Dives in Torment where he lay: —')
First pub. *The Five Nations* (London, 1903); *Sussex*, XXXIII, 286–91; Harbord, Verse No. 823.

KpR 828 In MS Five Nations.

National Library of Australia, MS 94.

The Penalty ('Once in life I watched a Star')
First pub. with story 'The Tender Achilles' in *Limits and Renewals* (London, 1932); collected separately *Inclusive Verse* [1933]; *Sussex*, XI, 355 and *Sussex*, XXXIV, 429; Harbord, Verse No. 1210.

KpR 829 Corrected page proof in Limits and Renewals Proof; date stamped 25 January 1932.

Syracuse University.

KpR 830 Corrected first page proof for the Sussex Edition, Vol. XI; date stamped 14 October 1932.

British Library, Add. MS 55862.

'Pendant une année toute entière', see KpR 1691.

The Peora Hunt, see KpR 177.

Pharoah and the Sergeant ('Said England unto Pharoah, "I must make a man of you"')
First pub. *New York Tribune*, 29 August 1897; collected *The Five Nations* (London, 1903), as 'Sergeant Whatsisname'; *Sussex*, XXXIII, 243–6; Harbord, Verse No. 701.

KpR 831 Fair copy, slightly revised, in MS Seven Seas (f. 123), including an introductory prose heading, signed.

Magdalene College, Cambridge.

KpR 832 In MS Five Nations.

National Library of Australia, MS 94.

KpR 833 Quotation of lines 1–8, here entitled 'Sergeant Whatsisname' and begining 'Said England unto Pharoah: — "I will make a man of you', one page, signed, apparently written out for a wounded sergeant of the Northumberland Fusiliers in South Africa; dated in an unidentified hand '5-4-01'.

Facsimile in Ballard, p. [171].

Texas.

KpR 834 Corrections on pp. 83, 85 of KpR 365.

Yale.

Philadelphia ('If you're off to Philadelphia in the morning')
First pub. with story 'Brother Square-Toes' in *Rewards and Fairies* (London, 1910); collected separately *Inclusive Verse*, 2nd American edition (New York, 1921); *Sussex*, XV, 141–2 and *Sussex*, XXXV, 228–30; Harbord, Verse No. 956.

KpR 835 Fair copy, revised, in MS Rewards and Fairies, annotated 'to follow Brother Square Toes'.

Cambridge University Library, ADD 6850, f. 52.

KpR 836 Corrected first page proof for the Sussex Edition, Vol. XV; date stamped 18 September 1931.

British Library, Add. MS 55865.

'Pick 'im up an' blow is nose', see KpR 1044.

A Pict Song ('Rome never looks where she treads.')
First pub. with story 'The Winged Hats' in *Puck of Pook's Hill* (London, 1906); collected separately *Songs from Books* (New York, 1912); *Sussex*, XIV, 193–4 and *Sussex*, XXXIV, 66–7; Harbord, Verse No. 896.

KpR 837 Fair copy, revised (f. 75), followed by another leaf containing untitled drafts of lines 1–4, 9 and very rough draft of 36 lines beginning 'This is our old game/ My father played it' (f. 76a), in MS Puck.

Bodleian, MS. Eng. misc. c. 127, ff. 75–76a (rectos only).

KpR 838 Slightly corrected first page proof for the Sussex Edition, Vol. XIV; date stamped 2 July 1931.

British Library, Add. MS 55864.

Piet ('I do not love my Empire's foes')
First pub. *The Five Nations* (London, 1903); *Sussex*, XXXIII, 333–6; Harbord, Verse No. 824.

KpR 839 In MS Five Nations.

National Library of Australia, MS 94.

KpR 840 Twelve lines beginning 'E's shored 'is rifle 'neath my nose', here the caption to two sketches in Brigadier-General R. W. Hare's 'South African War Sketch-Book' (containing also KpR 231, 827), written while aboard the S.S. Kinfauns Castle, April 1903.

Facsimile in *KJ*, June 1936, between pp. 52 and 53.

Owned (1936) Brigadier-General R. W. Hare (see *KJ*).

Pigs and Buffaloes, see KpR 173.

A Pilgrim's Way ('I do not look for holy saints to guide me on my way')
First pub. (stanzas 1–3 only, without title) as heading to 'Up the River' ('Egypt of the Magicians, No. IV') in *Nash's Magazine* and *Cosmopolitan*, September 1914; in full in *Reveille*, No. 1, August 1918; collected *The Years Between* (London, [1919]); *Sussex*, XXXIII, 425–7; Harbord, Verse No. 1007.

KpR 841 Fair copy, revised, in MS Years Between, here entitled 'The Pilgrim's Creed' and beginning 'I do not ask for saintly souls to spur me on my way' (as in first publication), annotated 'type'.

British Library, Add. MS 44841, f. 45.

KpR 842 Corrected galley proof of first publication (KpR 1574), including corrections to these verses, stamped 'Nash's Magazine'; dated stamped 23 June 1914.

Dalhousie University.

The Pillow-Fight ('The day was ended and a crowd of boys')
Included in 'The Scribbler' (handwritten magazine produced by the Burne-Jones and Morris children), Vol. II, No. 3, 5 January 1880 (signed 'Nickson'); first pub. *United Services College Chronicle*, 23 July 1881; reprinted Harbord, Verse No. 2B; Rutherford, pp. 46–7. This title does not appear on a typed list of RK's contributions to *United Services College Chronicle* (Sussex, KP 25/19); unsigned in a copy of *United Services College Chronicle* in which RK has signed his own pieces. On the other hand, RK's memory was sometimes mistaken and the signature 'Nickson' was used exclusively by Kipling in 'The Scribbler'.

KpR 842.5 Copy of the original MS magazine 'The Scribbler' (written out by May or Jenny Morris) containing this poem.

This original copy of 'The Scribbler' was sold to G. M. Williamson by May Morris in 1901 (see the description of 'The Scribbler' in the INTRODUCTION).

Anderson Galleries, 17 March 1915 (G. M. Williamson Sale), Lot 106.

KpR 843 Typed transcript (made to replace the original KpR 842.5), bound in May Morris's set of 'The Scribbler'.

British Library, Add. MS 45337, ff. 227–8 (rectos only).

Pink Dominoes ('Jenny and Me were engaged, you see')
First pub. *Civil and Military Gazette*, 30 March 1886; collected *Departmental Ditties* (1886) and with additional stanza in *Departmental Ditties*, 2nd ed (1886); *Sussex*, XXXII, 31–2; Harbord, Verse No. 174. See also KpR 280.

KpR 844 Fair copy, including 4-line heading, in MS Departmental Ditties (pp. 19–21).

Berg.

KpR 845 Fair copy, including 4-line heading, 3 numbered leaves (rectos only), signed (initials).

Syracuse University.

The Pious Sub's Creed ('I *do* believe in Afghan wars')
First pub. Rutherford (1986), pp. 177–9; not in Harbord.

KpR 846 Fair copy, revised, in Sussex Notebook 1 (pp. 141–4); dated 26 January 1883.

Sussex, KP 24/3.

The Pirates in England ('When Rome was rotten-ripe to her fall')
First pub. *Three Poems* (Oxford and London, 1911); reprinted C. R. L. Fletcher and Rudyard Kipling, *A History of England* (Oxford and London, 1911); collected separately *Songs from Books* (1915); *Sussex*, XXXIV, 266–7; Harbord, Verse No. 973.

KpR 847 Fair copy, revised, of 9-stanza version, here untitled, in MS Years Between, one page.

British Library, Add. MS 44841, f. 62.

'Pit where the buffalo cooled his hide', see KpR 177.

***'Placetne, Domini?* — in far Lahore'**, see KpR 538.

The Playmate ('She is not Folly — that I know')
First pub. with story 'Aunt Ellen' in *Limits and Renewals* (London, 1932); collected separately *Inclusive Verse* [1933]; *Sussex*, XI, 115 and *Sussex*, XXXIV, 407; Harbord, Verse No. 1211.

KpR 848 Corrected first page proof for the Sussex Edition, Vol. XI; date stamped 14 October 1932.

British Library, Add. MS 55862.

The Plea of the Simla Dancers ('"What have *we* ever done to bear this grudge?"')
First pub. *Civil and Military Gazette*, 16 April 1886; collected *Departmental Ditties* (1886); *Sussex*, XXXII, 108–9; Harbord, Verse No. 178. See also KpR 280.

KpR 849 Correction, in KpR 279.

Pierpont Morgan, 20177.

KpR 850 Corrections on pp. 76–7 of KpR 282.

Yale.

Poems on Fruit Plates, see KpR 1312.

'Poison of Asps' ('"Poison of asps is under our lips"')
First pub. with 'Brazilian Sketches No. IV A Snake Farm' in *Morning Post*, 9 December 1927; collected separately *Inclusive Verse* [1933]; *Sussex*, XXIV, 377 and *Sussex*, XXXV, 269–70; Harbord, Verse No. 1150.

KpR 851 Slightly corrected first page proof for the Sussex Edition, Vol. XXIV; date stamped 19 June 1936.

British Library, Add. MS 55874.

'Poor Honest Men' ('Your jar of Virginny')
First pub. with story '"A Priest in Spite of Himself"' in *Rewards and Fairies* (London, 1910); collected separately *Songs from Books* (New York, 1912); *Sussex*, XV, 205–7 and *Sussex*, XXXIV, 72–4; Harbord, Verse No. 957.

KpR 852 Fair copy, revised, here beginning 'For a pound o' Virginny', in MS Rewards and Fairies, one page.

Cambridge University Library, ADD 6850, f. 80.

KpR 853 Fair copy of first 4 lines of stanza 7, subscribed 'Log of the [?]: versified by RK', inscribed on title page of a copy of *Songs from Books* (London, 1913) presented to J. B. Sterling, October 1913.

Berg.

KpR 854 Corrections on pp. 85–6 of KpR 1112.

Yale.

KpR 855 Corrected first page proof for the Sussex Edition, Vol. XV; date stamped 18 September 1931.

British Library, Add. MS 55865.

The Portent ('Oh, late withdrawn from human-kind')
First pub. with story 'The Prophet and the Country' in *Debits and Credits* (London, 1926); collected separately *Inclusive Verse* [1927]; *Sussex*, X, 143 and *Sussex*, XXXIV, 380; Harbord, Verse No. 1137.

KpR 856 Corrected first page proof for the Sussex Edition, Vol. X; date stamped 30 December 1931.

British Library, Add. MS 55861.

'Porter of Dross, by day he dealt the spoil'
No publication traced; not in Harbord.

KpR 857 Draft of a sonnet, in a letter to William Ernest Henley (asking him to 'make it splendid'), The Elms, 12 December 1897.

National Library of Scotland, MS 5406, f. 228.

Poseidon's Law ('When the robust and Brass-bound Man commissioned first for sea')
First pub. with story 'The Bonds of Discipline' in *Traffics and Discoveries* (London, 1904); collected separately *Songs from Books* (New York, 1912); *Sussex*, VII, 39–40 and *Sussex*, XXXIV, 175–6; Harbord, Verse No. 872.

KpR 858 Successive drafts, here untitled, in MS Traffics and Discoveries, 4 pages, one page annotated 'To precede The Bonds of Discipline on separate page'.

McGill University.

KpR 859 Fair copy, written in a decorative hand with a few sketches, signed (initials), on a small card.

Dalhousie University.

KpR 860 Corrected first page proof for the Sussex Edition, Vol. VII; date stamped 22 March 1932.

British Library, Add. MS 55858.

Possibilities ('Ay, lay him 'neath the Simla pine —')
First pub. (12 stanzas) *The Pioneer*, 13 July 1885; collected (10 stanzas) *Departmental Ditties* (1886); *Sussex*, XXXII, 89–90; Harbord, Verse No. 138 (two discarded stanzas printed).

KpR 861 Corrections on p. 65 of KpR 282.

Yale.

The Post that Fitted ('Ere the steamer bore him Eastward, Sleary was engaged to marry')
First pub. *Civil and Military Gazette*, 16 March 1886; collected *Departmental Ditties* (1886); *Sussex*, XXXII, 18–19; Harbord, Verse No. 172. See also KpR 280.

KpR 862 Fair copy, including 4-line heading, in MS Departmental Ditties (pp. 12–15).

Berg.

'The Power of the Dog' ('There is sorrow enough in the natural way')
First pub. with story 'Garm — A Hostage' in *Actions and Reactions* (London, 1909); collected separately *Songs from Books* (New York, 1912); *Sussex*, VIII, 77–8 and *Sussex*, XXXIV, 114–15; Harbord, Verse No. 931.

KpR 863 Fair copy, extensively revised, in MS Day's Work, annotated in pencil 'To precede Garm' and in ink 'type'.

British Library, Add. MS 45541, f. 242.

KpR 864 Quotation of stanza 2, one page, signed, annotated 'For Miss Winifred Paget'.

Library of Congress, Rare Book Division, Colt Collection.

KpR 865 Corrections on pp. 134–5 of KpR 1112.

Yale.

KpR 866 Corrected page proof for *Inclusive Verse* (1919), one page numbered 658, signed (initials), in KpR 537.

Princeton, Ex3814.9.1919.11.

KpR 867 Corrected first page proof for the Sussex Edition, Vol. VIII; date stamped 28 November 1931.

British Library, Add. MS 55859.

The Prairie ('"I see the grass shake in the sun for leagues on either hand')
First pub. (without title) with 'The Fortunate Towns' ('Letters to the Family No. VI') in *Morning Post*, 16 April 1908; collected separately *Songs from Books* (New York, 1912); *Sussex*, XXIV (*Letters of Travel*), 201–2 and *Sussex*, XXXIV, 24–5; Harbord, Verse No. 916.

KpR 868 Fair copy, revised, here untitled, in MS Non-Fiction, in the MS of 'Letters to the Family' (KpR 1826), annotated 'verses to precede Letter VII', one page.

British Library, Add. MS 45542, f. 138.

KpR 869 Corrected first page proof for the Sussex Edition, Vol. XXIV, here untitled; date stamped 30 April 1935.

British Library, Add. MS 55874.

The Prayer ('My brother kneels, so saith Kabir')
First pub. as heading to Chapter 14 of one-volume edition of *Kim* (1901); reprinted *Sussex*, XXI, 340; collected separately *Songs from Books* (New York, 1912), as 'A Song of Kabir'; *Sussex*, XXXIV, 207; Harbord, Verse No. 775.

KpR 870 Fair copy, signed, one page of Bateman's notepaper.

Dalhousie University.

KpR 871 Title (here 'A Song of Kabir') revised to 'The Prayer' on p. 241 of KpR 1112.

Yale.

KpR 872 Corrections to this poem (as heading to Chapter 14 of *Kim*), on first page proof for the Sussex Edition, Vol. XXI (KpR 1791); date stamped 9 October 1931.

British Library, Add. MS 55871.

The Prayer of Miriam Cohen ('From the wheel and the drift of Things')
First pub. (3 stanzas only) as verse heading to 'The Disturber of Traffic' in *Many Inventions* (London and New York, 1893); *Sussex*, V, 3; first pub. in full *Songs from Books* (New York, 1912); *Sussex*, XXXIV, 131; Harbord, Verse No. 595.

KpR 873 Corrected first page proof (as heading to 'The Disturber of Traffic', KpR 1549) for the Sussex Edition, Vol. V; date stamped 10 June 1931.

British Library, Add. MS 55856.

Preadmonisheth ye Ghoste of Desmarets [Speaketh ye Ghost of Desmarets] ('In the Paris of the Empire, in the days of long ago')
First pub. Rutherford (1986), pp. 201–3; not in Harbord.

KpR 874 Fair copy, here entitled 'Preadmonisheth ye Ghoste of Desmarets', on pp. 2–4 of RK's ornately decorated programme (on a folded card) for an amateur theatrical production of *Plot and Passion* (by T. P. Taylor and John Lang); dated 20 December [1883].

Library of Congress, Rare Book Division, Carpenter Kipling Collection.

KpR 875 Fair copy of stanzas 1–5 only, here entitleld 'Speaketh ye Ghost of Desmarets'.

Sussex, KP 2/1.

Preface ('To all to whom this little book may come —')
First pub. as prefatory poem in *Land and Sea Tales* (London, 1923); collected separately *Inclusive Verse* [1927]; *Sussex*, XVI, vii–viii and *Sussex*, XXXIV, 343–4; Harbord, Verse No. 1121.

KpR 876 Fair copy, revised, of a version, here untitled and beginning 'To all to whom our little book may come', one page.

Sussex, KP 24/44.

Prelude ('I have eaten your bread and salt.')
First pub. *Departmental Ditties*, 4th ed (1890); *Sussex*, XXII, ix; Harbord, Verse No. 487, as 'I have eaten your bread and salt.'.

KpR 877 Fair copy, here untitled, in MS Departmental Ditties (p. 1).

Berg.

KpR 878 Fair copy, here untitled, in MS Words, Wise and Otherwise [p. 3].

Berg.

The Press ('The Soldier may forget his Sword')
First pub. with story 'The Village that Voted the Earth was Flat' in *A Diversity of Creatures* (London, 1917); collected separately *Inclusive Verse* (1919); *Sussex*, IX, 215–16 and *Sussex*, XXXIV, 320–1; Harbord, Verse No. 1045.

KpR 879 Fair copy, revised, headed 'The Village that voted the Earth was flat.', including two cancelled versions of last stanza, in MS Diversity of Creatures (f. 70).

University of Edinburgh, Dk. 2. 8.

KpR 880 Corrected first page proof for *Humorous Tales* (London, 1931), pp. 253–4; date stamped 19 May 1931.

British Library, Add. MS 55847.

KpR 881 Corrected first page proof for the Sussex Edition, Vol. IX; date stamped 28 April 1932.

British Library, Add. MS 55860.

The Press ('Why don't you write a play —')
No publication traced; not in Harbord.

KpR 882 Typed transcript, four 8-line stanzas and one last line, headed 'Written at Bonar Bridge, N.B. Sept. 1899. The Original poem in the possession of Stanley Baldwin at Astley Hall.', one page.

Sussex, KP 24/45.

Pro Tem ('Make me a fire in the dark')
First pub. Rutherford (1986), pp. 74–5; Harbord, Verse No. 61.

KpR 883 Fair copy, in Sussex Notebook 3 (first series, pp. 11–14); dated 13 October 1881.

Sussex, KP 24/1.

KpR 884 Fair copy, in MS Sundry Phansies.

Berg.

The Pro-Consuls ('They that dig foundations deep')
First pub. *The Times*, 22 July 1905; collected *The Years Between* (London, [1919]); *Sussex*, XXXIII, 408–9; Harbord, Verse No. 878.

KpR 885 Fair copy, revised, here entitled 'The Consuls.', in MS Years Between, including the heading and 8 cancelled lines.

British Library, Add. MS 44841, f. 37.

KpR 886 Fair copy of introductory lines and last 4 lines (14 lines beginning 'The overfaithful sword returns the user'), in a letter to Louisa Baldwin ('Aunt Louie'), Bateman's, 20 November 1909.

Typed transcript at Sussex, KP 11/2.

Dalhousie University.

KpR 887 Calligraphic fair copy of introductory lines and last 4 lines (14 lines beginning as above), decorated, one page.

Sussex, KP 24/46.

The Prodigal Son ('Here come I to my own again')
First pub. (first stanza only) as heading to Chapter 5 of the one-volume edition of *Kim* (1901); reprinted *Sussex*, XXI, 105; first pub. in full *Songs from Books* (New York, 1912); *Sussex*, XXXIV, 102–3; Harbord, Verse No. 776.

KpR 888 Fair copy, including a sketch, in MS Writings and Songs (pp. 21–4).

Berg.

A Profession of Faith ('Each day watched die together binds us fast')
First pub. Rutherford (1986), pp. 118–19; not in Harbord.

KpR 889 Fair copy, in Sussex Notebook 1 (p. 58) with an additional 4 lines added later; dated 17 February 1882.

Additional lines printed Rutherford, p. 118.

Sussex, KP 24/3.

KpR 890 Fair copy, in Sussex Notebook 3 (first series, p. 67); dated 17 February 1882.

Sussex, KP 24/1.

KpR 891 Transcript by AMK, in Sussex Notebook 2 [p. 49]; dated February 1882.

Sussex, KP 24/2.

A Prologue ('So please you, Gentlefolk, a drama slight')
First printed in a programme (copy inserted in Scrapbook 3) for a theatrical performance at Simla, 25 July 1887 (where the lines were spoken by Trix); first pub. *The Pioneer*, 1 August 1887; reprinted Harbord, Verse No. 274; Rutherford, pp. 380–3.

KpR 892 Draft, here untitled and beginning (after a false start) 'May it please you, gracious public', on 2 blank pages of Scrapbook 1 (pp. 287 *rev.* and 285 *rev.*).

Sussex, KP 28/1.

Prologue to a Catalogue of a Portion of the Library of Edmund Gosse ('Men say 'tis wondrous strange to see')
First printed without title in R. J. Lister, *A Catalogue of a portion of the Library of Edmund Gosse* (privately printed, London, 1893); reprinted as 'Prologue to a Collection of Magazines' in E. W. Martindell, *Fragmenta Condita* (privately printed, 1922); reprinted Harbord, Verse No. 600B.

KpR 893 Fair copy, in a letter to Mrs Gosse, Liverpool, 2 February 1892.

Library of Congress, Rare Book Division, Carpenter Kipling Collection.

KpR 894 Typescript, here entitled 'Prologue to Scrap Book of Kipling articles'; 1893.

Princeton, Doubleday Collection.

Prologue to the Master-Cook's Tale, see KpR 687–9.

A Promise ('Thy woe is mine — for thou hast held my heart')
First pub. Rutherford (1986), p. 140; not in Harbord.

KpR 895 Fair copy, in Sussex Notebook 1 (p. 88); dated 8 April [1882].

Sussex, KP 24/3.

KpR 896 Fair copy, in Sussex Notebook 3 (first series, p. 36); dated 8 April 1882.

Sussex, KP 24/1.

KpR 897 Transcript by AMK, in Sussex Notebook 2 [p. 53]; dated April 1882.

Sussex, KP 24/2.

Prophets at Home ('Prophets have honour all over the Earth')
First pub. without title with story 'Hal o' the Draft' in *Puck of Pook's Hill* (London, 1906); collected separately *Songs from Books* (New York, 1912); *Sussex*, XIV, 197 (without title) and *Sussex*, XXXIV, 76; Harbord, Verse No. 897.

KpR 898 Fair copy, revised, here untitled, annotated 'To precede Hal o' the draft./ separate page. no heading', in MS Puck.

Bodleian, MS. Eng. misc. c. 127, f. 76b.

KpR 899 Slightly corrected first page proof for the Sussex Edition, Vol. XIV, here untitled; date stamped 2 July 1931.

British Library, Add. MS 55864.

'Prophets have honour all over the Earth', see KpR 898–9.

Public Waste ('By the Laws of the Family Circle 'tis written in letters of brass')
First pub. *Civil and Military Gazette*, 9 March 1886; collected *Departmental Ditties* (1886); *Sussex*, XXXII, 23–5; Harbord, Verse No. 170.

KpR 900 Fair copy, in MS Departmental Ditties (pp. 42–5).

Berg.

KpR 901 Corrections on p. 23 of KpR 282.

Yale.

Puck's Song ('See you the ferny ride that steals')
First pub. (9 stanzas only beginning 'See you the dimpled track that runs') with story 'Weland's Sword' in *Puck of Pook's Hill* (London, 1906); reprinted *Sussex*, XIV, 3–4; first pub. in full *Songs from Books* (New York, 1912); *Sussex*, XXXIV, 4–5; Harbord, Verse No. 887.

KpR 902 Nine-stanza version, revised, here entitled 'Dedication' and beginning (after 5 cancelled stanzas the third of which begins as above) 'See you the dimpled track that runs', in MS Puck.

Bodleian, MS. Eng. misc. c. 127, f. 4.

KpR 903 Stanza 4 (beginning 'Out of the Weald — the secret Weald') inscribed in a presentation copy to an American child of *Puck of Pook's Hill* (Toronto, 1906).

This stanza not published until *Songs from Books* (New York, 1912); this MS printed in *Grolier Catalogue*, p. 110 and Harbord, Verse No. 905.

Unlocated.

KpR 904 Corrected first page proof for the Sussex Edition, Vol. XIV; date stamped 2 July 1931.

British Library, Add. MS 55864.

'Pussy can sit by the fire and sing'
First pub. with story 'The Cat That Walked by Himself' in *Just So Stories* (London, 1902); collected separately *Songs from Books* (London, 1913); *Sussex*, XIII, 203 and *Sussex*, XXXIV, 243, as 'Chapter Heading'; Harbord, Verse No. 799.

KpR 905 Fair copy, revised, in MS Just So Stories, annotated 'on separate page to follow cat &c'.

British Library, Add. MS 59840, f. 124.

KpR 906 Corrected second page proof for the Sussex Edition, Vol. XIII; date stamped 23 April 1935.

British Library, Add. MS 55863.

'Put forth to watch, unschooled, alone'
First pub. as verse heading to 'The Way That He Took' in *Daily Express*, 12–14 June 1900; collected separately *Inclusive Verse* (1919); *Sussex*, XXXIV, 230–31, as 'Chapter Heading'; Harbord, Verse No. 754A.

KpR 907 Fair copy, revised, one page (following the MS of 'The Way That He Took', KpR 2222) in MS Debits and Credits (f. 14), here beginning '<Chosen> Flung forth by chance – unschooled – alone', annotated 'These handy for the way that he took'; watermarked 1897.

University of Durham.

The Puzzler ('The Celt in all his variants from Builth to Ballyhoo')
First pub. with story 'The Puzzler' in *Actions and Reactions* (London, 1909); collected separately (with new 4th stanza) in *Songs from Books* (New York, 1912); *Sussex*, VIII, 215–16 and *Sussex*, XXXIV, 53–4; Harbord, Verse No. 932.

KpR 908 In MS Actions and Reactions (f. 107).

University of St Andrews, MS PR4854.A4.

KpR 909 Fair copy, in MS Writings and Songs (pp. 122–4).

Berg.

KpR 910 Corrected first page proof for *Humorous Tales* (London, 1931), pp. 309–10; date stamped 25 May 1931.

British Library, Add. MS 55847.

KpR 911 Corrected first page proof for the Sussex Edition, Vol. VIII; date stamped 28 November 1931.

British Library, Add. MS 55859.

Quaeritur ('Is Life to be measured by grains')
First pub. Rutherford (1986), p. 106; Harbord, Verse No. 56, mistitled as 'Inoeritum'.

KpR 912 Fair copy, in MS Sundry Phansies.

Berg.

***Quartette* (Lahore, 1885)**

KpR 913 Presentation copy to W. C. Crofts containing annotations by RK indicating the items which he wrote, together with a letter to Crofts (in which he explains he has annotated the copy himself), dated Lahore, 20 December 1885.

Described in Stewart, pp. 17–18 as the most authoritative of all annotated copies as it was annotated contemporaneously with publication.

Berg, Copy 4.

KpR 914 Presentation copy to Florence Garrard containing annotations by RK indicating the authorship of contents.

Berg, Copy 3.

KpR 915 Presentation copy from CK to F. N. Doubleday in April 1899, containing annotations by RK indicating authorship of contents.

Princeton, Doubleday Collection, Ex3814.9.3737.

KpR 916 Presentation copy to Julian Ralph, containing annotations indicating the authorship of contents, annotated 'These notes made by me are I believe accurate as to authorship of pieces', inscription dated 25 June 1900.

Mentioned Stewart, pp. 17–18.

Library of Congress, Rare Book Division, Carpenter Kipling Collection.

KpR 917 Printed copy containing annotations (possibly by RK) indicating the authorship of contents.

Berg, Copy 2.

KpR 918 Printed copy containing (probably not by RK) the names of the four authors written on the front cover and annotations indicating the authorship of contents.

Facsimile of front cover in American Art Association sale catalogue, 1–2 December 1924, Lot 195.

Berg, Copy 1.

The Queen's Men ('Valour and Innocence')
First pub. with story 'Gloriana' in *Rewards and Fairies* (London, 1910), as 'The Two Cousins'; collected separately *Songs from Books* (New York, 1912); *Sussex*, XV, 29, as 'The Two Cousins' and *Sussex*, XXXIV, 127; Harbord, Verse No. 964.

KpR 919 Fair copy, here entitled 'The Two Cousins', in MS Rewards and Fairies, annotated 'To follow Gloriana', one page.

Cambridge University Library, ADD 6850, f. 12.

KpR 920 Slightly corrected first page proof for the Sussex Edition, Vol. XV, here entitled 'The Two Cousins'; date stamped 18 September 1931.

British Library, Add. MS 55865.

The Quest ('In years long past we met a while and vowed')
First pub. Rutherford (1986), pp. 120–1; not in Harbord.

KpR 921 Fair copy, in Sussex Notebook 1 (p. 62); dated 5 March [1882].

Sussex, KP 24/3.

KpR 922 Fair copy, here being the third of 'Four Sonnets' (see KpR 48, 524, 1281), in Sussex Notebook 3 (first series, p. 71); dated 5 March 1882.

Sussex, KP 24/1.

The Quest ('The Knight came home from the quest')
First pub. *The Book of Beauty*, ed. Mrs F. Harcourt Williamson (London, 1897); *Sussex*, XXXV, 200–1; Harbord, Verse No. 694.

KpR 923 Fair copy, signed, one page.

Dalhousie University.

The Question ('Brethren, how shall it fare with me')
First pub. separately as copyright pamphlet *The Neutral* (New York, 1916); collected with 'Destroyers at Jutland' in *Sea Warfare* (London, 1916), as 'The Neutral'; collected separately *The Years Between* (London, [1919]); *Sussex*, XXVI, 385–6, as 'The Neutral' and *Sussex*, XXXIII, 373–4; Harbord, Verse No. 1025, as 'The Neutral *or* The Question'.

KpR 924 Fair copy, revised, here entitled 'The Neutral', in MS Years Between, including an epigraph from *John*, one page.

British Library, Add. MS 44841, f. 21.

KpR 925 In MS Non-Fiction, with the MS of 'Destroyers at Jutland' (KpR 1538): fair copy, revised, here entitled 'The Neutral' and beginning 'Brethren, how will it <go> fare with me', 2 pages (ff. 109–10, rectos only); draft, here entitled 'The Neutral' and beginning 'Brothers, how will it fare with me', without stanza 4 (f. 111).

British Library, Add. MS 45542, ff. 10911 (rectos only).

A Question [By the Sea] ('Bring me a message of hope O sea!')
First pub. Rutherford (1986), pp. 98–9; Harbord, Verse No. 45.

KpR 926 Fair copy, here entitled 'A Question', in Sussex Notebook 3 (first series, pp. 26–7); dated 25 December 1881.

Sussex, KP 24/1.

KpR 927 Fair copy, here entitled 'By the Sea', in MS Sundry Phansies.

Berg.

KpR 928 Transcript by AMK, here untitled, in Sussex Notebook 2 [p. 17]; dated 'Xmas Day. *1881.*'.

Sussex, KP 24/2.

The Rabbi's Song ('If Thought can reach to Heaven')
First pub. with story 'The House Surgeon' in *Actions and Reactions* (London, 1909); collected separately *Songs from Books* (New York, 1912); *Sussex*, VIII, 287–[8] and *Sussex*, XXXIV, 116–17; Harbord, Verse No. 933.

KpR 929 In MS Actions and Reactions (f. 133).

University of St Andrews, MS PR4854.A4.

KpR 930 Fair copy, in MS Writings and Songs (pp. 33–5).

Berg.

KpR 931 Corrected first page proof for the Sussex Edition, Vol. VIII; date stamped 28 November 1931.

British Library, Add. MS 55859.

Rahere ('Rahere, King Henry's Jester, feared by all the Norman Lords')
First pub. with story 'The Wish House' in *Debits and Credits* (London, 1926); collected separately *Inclusive Verse* [1927]; *Sussex*, X, 105–7 and *Sussex*, XXXIV, 373–5; Harbord, Verse No. 1138.

KpR 932 Corrected first page proof for the Sussex Edition, Vol. X; date stamped 30 December 1931.

British Library, Add. MS 55861.

Reading the Will [The Reading of the Will] ('Here we have it, scratched and scored')
First printed *Schoolboy Lyrics* (privately printed, Lahore, 1881); *Sussex*, XXXV, 12–13; Rutherford, pp. 86–7; Harbord, Verse No. 27.

KpR 933 Fair copy, in Sussex Notebook 3 (second series, pp. 29–31), here entitled 'The Reading of the Will'.

Sussex, KP 24/1.

KpR 934 Here entitled 'The Reading of the Will', on 2 pages of a folded leaf (containing also KpR 202, 248), enclosed with a covering letter to 'Aunt' [Edith Macdonald?], postmarked 21 February 1881.

This MS not mentioned Rutherford; typed transcript, probably of this MS, at Sussex, KP 24/67.

Sotheby's, 11–12 March 1968, Lot 778 (property of H. C. Drayton), sold to Rota.

KpR 935 Fair copy, here entitled 'The Reading of the Will', in MS Sundry Phansies.

Berg.

The Reaping ('Hush — What appeal')
First pub. Rutherford (1986), p. 155; not in Harbord.

KpR 936 Fair copy, in Sussex Notebook 1 (p. 109); dated 19 June [1882].

Sussex, KP 24/3.

KpR 937 Fair copy, in Sussex Notebook 3 (second series, p. 3).

Sussex, KP 24/1.

Rebirth ('If any God should say:')
First pub. with story 'The Edge of the Evening' in *A Diversity of Creatures* (London, 1917); collected separately *Inclusive Verse* (1919); *Sussex*, IX, 297–8 and *Sussex*, XXXIV, 326–7; Harbord, Verse No. 1046.

KpR 938 Fair copy, revised, headed 'The Edge of the Evening', in MS Diversity of Creatures (f. 101).

University of Edinburgh, Dk. 2. 8.

KpR 939 Corrected first page proof for the Sussex Edition, Vol. IX; date stamped 28 April 1932.

British Library, Add. MS 55860.

The Recall ('I am the land of their fathers')
First pub. with story 'An Habitation Enforced' in *Actions and Reactions* (London, 1909); collected separately *Songs from Books* (New York, 1912); *Sussex*, VIII, 49 and *Sussex*, XXXIV, 3; Harbord, Verse No. 934. A forgery of this poem on 'S.S. Canopic' notepaper (2 pages) is at Harvard, MS Eng 875.

KpR 940 Here untitled, in MS Actions and Reactions (f. 15).

University of St Andrews, MS PR4854.A4.

KpR 941 Fair copy, in MS Writings and Songs (pp. 52–3).

Berg.

KpR 942 Transcript in an unidentified hand, bound in a volume of letters of Georgina Craik to Rebekah Owen (containing also poems by Kipling).

Bodleian, MS. Eng. poet. e. 43, ff. 3–4 (rectos only).

KpR 943 Corrections on p. 3 of KpR 1112.

Yale.

KpR 944 Slightly corrected first page proof for the Sussex Edition, Vol. VIII; date stamped 28 November 1931.

British Library, Add. MS 55859.

A Recantation ('Ere certain Fate had touched a heart')
First pub. *The Years Between* (London, [1919]); *Sussex*, XXXIII, 389–90; Harbord, Verse No. 1103.

KpR 945 Fair copy, revised, here entitled 'Bk V. Od 9./A Recantation/(To Lyde of the Halls)', in MS Years Between, including the heading, annotated 'type in triplicate & return to RK Browns Hotel'.

British Library, Add. MS 44841, f. 29.

Recessional ('God of our fathers, known of old')
First pub. *The Times*, 17 July 1897; collected *The Five Nations* (London, 1903); *Sussex*, XXXIII, 345–6; Harbord, Verse No. 700. Numerous non-authoritative transcripts of this poem are extant: one (with the title 'Retrocession') is at the Huntington, HM 2585; another is at Sussex, KP 24/47.

KpR 946 Fair copy of early version, here entitled 'After', including stanzas 1–2 and (cancelled) a third stanza and first line of a fourth stanza, one page, inserted between pp. 214 and 215 of Francis Bullard's copy of *The Five Nations* (London, 1903).

Facsimile in Livingstone, *Bibliography*, [p. 2]; facsimile in *The Houghton Library 1942–1967* (Cambridge, 1967), p. 67; see also 'The Manuscript of "Recessional"', *KJ*, 10 (1943), 11–13.

Harvard. *EC9.K6287.903fb(B).

KpR 947 Revised, here entitled 'After', one page, lines 11–12 added later and annotated 'written with Sallie's pen —/RK', signed; annotated at bottom 'done in council at North End House. July 16 [1897]./Aunt Georgie [Lady Burne-Jones]/Sallie [Sara Norton]/Carrie & Me'.

Facsimile in Croft, *Autograph Poetry*, No. 151; facsimile at Harvard, Kipling 15.40 and (on Kipling's desk in his study) at Bateman's, Burwash, Sussex.

British Library, Add. MS 45100, f. 1 (permanent exhibition).

KpR 948 Fair copy of KpR 947, enclosed with a letter to C. F. Moberly Bell (Manager of *The Times*), 16 July 1897.

Typed transript of the letter only at Sussex, KP 17/40.

Sotheby's, 9 July 1968, Lot 844, sold to Rota.

KpR 949 Fair copy, signed, one page; watermarked 1896.

Pierpont Morgan, MA 1206.

KpR 950 [entry deleted]

KpR 951 Fair copy, including a variant line 20, dated 1897, on verso of half-title of a copy of *The Seven Seas* (London, 1896) (containing also KpR 1366).

Princeton, Robert H. Taylor Collection.

KpR 952 Inscribed in a copy of *The Seven Seas*, 3rd ed (London, 1897).

Berg.

KpR 953 Fair copy, on 'Government House, Ottawa' notepaper, signed, written out for Viscount Grey, Governor-General of Canada from 1904–11.

Sotheby's, 24 May 1938, Lot 604 (property of Dowager Countess Grey), sold to Maggs.

KpR 954 Quotation of first stanza, signed, inscribed on the matting of a reproduction of portrait of Kipling by Sir Philip Burne-Jones.

American Art Association, 5–6 December 1934, Lot 257.

KpR 955 [entry deleted]

KpR 956 Quotation of first stanza, signed, inscribed to Miss J. L. Gilder.

Charles Hamilton Galleries, 31 October 1968, Lot 213.

Reckoning ('Count we the Cost — the sun is setting fast')
First pub. Rutherford (1986), p. 68; Harbord, Verse No. 62.

KpR 957 Fair copy, in Sussex Notebook 3 (first series, p. 21); dated 8 August 1881.

Sussex, KP 24/1.

KpR 958 Fair copy, in MS Sundry Phansies.

Berg.

A Rector's Memory ('The Gods that are wiser than Learning')
First pub. *St Andrews. Two Poems... By Rudyard Kipling and Walter De La Mare* (London, [1926]), *Sussex*, XXXV, 256–7; Harbord, Verse No. 1145.

KpR 959 Fair copies of 2 versions, revised, the first entitled 'St Andrews.', the second 'St Andrews. Oct. 11. 1928' and beginning 'The Gods that are older than Learning', one page each.

Sussex, KP 24/48.

The Reeds of Runnymede ('At Runnymede, at Runnymede!')
First pub. C. R. L. Fletcher and Rudyard Kipling, *A History of England* (Oxford and London, 1911); collected separately *Songs from Books* (1915); *Sussex*, XXXIV, 273–4; Harbord, Verse No. 977.

KpR 960 Revised, here untitled, in MS Years Between, one page.

British Library, Add. MS 44841, f. 66.

The Reformers ('Happy is he who, bred and taught')
First pub. *The Times*, 12 October 1901; collected *The Five Nations* (London, 1903); *Sussex*, XXXIII, 275–6; Harbord, Verse No. 766.

KpR 961 In MS Five Nations.

National Library of Australia, MS 94.

KpR 962 Five stanzas, here untitled, in a letter to [Dr James Conland], The Elms, 23 August 1901.

Pierpont Morgan, MA 2798.

Rejection ('"We will lay this thing here" —')
First pub. Rutherford (1986), pp. 112–13; not in Harbord.

KpR 963 Fair copy, in Sussex Notebook 3 (second series, pp. 27–9).

Sussex, KP 24/1.

Requiescat in Pace ('A new-made grave, for the damp earth stood')
First printed *Schoolboy Lyrics* (privately printed, Lahore, 1881); *Sussex*, XXXV, 52–4; Rutherford, pp. 58–60; Harbord, Verse No. 28.

KpR 964 On three pages of a folded leaf (containing also KpR 247), sent to 'Aunt' [Edith Macdonald?] in a letter postmarked 21 February 1881.

Typed transcript, probably of this MS, at Sussex, KP 11/10.

Sotheby's, 11–12 March 1968, Lot 778 (property of H. C. Drayton), sold to Rota.

Resolve ('I said to myself — "I will dream')
First pub. Rutherford (1986), p. 110; Harbord, Verse No. 63.

KpR 965 Fair copy, in MS Sundry Phansies.

Berg.

The Result ('A gilded mirror, and a polished bar')
Questionable attribution; first printed Harbord (1969), Verse No. 907.
Harbord says that E. W. Martindell transcribed these verses (signed 'R. K.') from *Island Motorist and Georgian Orient Magazine*, April 1932; he says if all 20 lines are not by RK, six certainly are as they were apparently scribbled on the verso of an envelope by RK and headed 'Sit on the Lid and Laugh'.

KpR 966 Typescript, five 4-line stanzas, headed above title 'Rudyard Kipling stayed at the Oak Bay Hotel,/Victoria, B.C. and had a time with John Virtue [i.e., Virtus?] —', signed (typescript) 'Kipling', one page.

National Library of Canada, Ottawa.

The Return ('Peace is declared, an' I return')
First pub. *The Five Nations* (London, 1903); *Sussex*, XXXIII, 342–4; Harbord, Verse No. 825.

KpR 967 In MS Five Nations.

National Library of Australia, MS 94.

KpR 968 Stanza 6 (lines 1–4 of it quoted) and the refrain, sent as suggestions for quotations on 'the title page' in a letter to H. A. Gwynne, Bateman's, n.d.

Dalhousie University.

The Return of the Children ('Neither the harps nor the crowns amused, nor the cherubs' dove-winged races —')
First pub. with story '"They"' in *Traffics and Discoveries* (London, 1904); collected separately *Songs from Books* (New York, 1912); *Sussex*, VII, 309–10 and *Sussex*, XXXIV, 119–20; Harbord, Verse No. 873.

KpR 969 Three revised fair copies, all untitled and headed 'They' in MS Traffics and Discoveries, 3 pages.

McGill University.

KpR 970 Fair copy, in MS Writings and Songs (pp. 38–40).

Berg.

KpR 971 Corrected first page proof for the Sussex Edition, Vol. VII; date stamped 22 March 1932.

British Library, Add. MS 55858.

Rhodes Memorial, Table Mountain ('As tho' again — yea, even once again')
First pub. Herbert Baker, *Cecil Rhodes by His Architect* (London, 1934); *Sussex*, XXXV, 223; Harbord, Verse No. 882.

KpR 972 Fair copy, here untitled, in a letter to Herbert Baker, Cape Town, 9 February 1905.

This MS printed Carrington, p. 386; typed transcript at Sussex, KP 14/7.

Rhodes House, Oxford, MSS.Afr.s.8, f. 17v.

The Rhyme of the Three Captains ('...At the close of a winter day')
First pub. *The Athenaeum*, 6 December 1890; collected *Barrack-Room Ballads* (1892); *Sussex*, XXXII, 274–9; Harbord, Verse No. 479.

KpR 972.5 Corrected page proof for *Barrack-Room Ballads* (1892).

British Library, Loan 97 (deposited by John Aris, 1989).

The Rhyme of the Three Sealers ('Now this is the Law of the Muscovite, that he proves with shot and steel')
First pub. (13-line heading beginning 'Away by the lands of the Japanee' only) in text of article 'From Tideway to Tideway No. VII Captains Courageous' in *New York Sun*, 27 November 1892; in full separately in *Pall Mall Budget*, 14 December 1893; collected *The Seven Seas* (New York, 1896); *Sussex*, XXXIII, 47–57; Harbord, Verse No. 528.

KpR 973 Fair copy, revised, signed, 4 numbered leaves (rectos only).

Facsimile first page in *Ashley Library*, III, 33 and in Norman Page, *A Kipling Companion* (London, 1984), plate 8a.

British Library, Ashley MS 4880.

Rhymed Chapter Headings for the Naulahka, see KpR 184–7.

'Rhymes, or of grief or of sorrow', see KpR 623–5.

'Rimini' ('When I left Rome for Lalage's sake')
First pub. (first stanza without title) as heading to story 'On the Great Wall' in *Strand Magazine* and *McClure's Magazine*, June 1906; reprinted *Puck of Pook's Hill* (London, 1906) and *Sussex*, XIV, 145; first pub. in full *Songs from Books* (New York, 1912); *Sussex*, XXXIV, 70–1; Harbord, Verse No. 883.

KpR 974 Fair copy, revised (f. 6) and stanzas 1–2 (1 as opening, 2 in text, cancelled) on first page of MS of 'On the Great Wall' (KpR 1949, f. 55), in MS Puck.

Bodleian, MS. Eng. misc. c. 127, ff. 6, 55.

KpR 975 Corrections on pp. 82–3 of KpR 1112.

Yale.

KpR 976 Corrected first page proof for the Sussex Edition, Vol. XIV, as opening to the story 'On the Great Wall'; date stamped 2 July 1931.

British Library, Add. MS 55864.

Rimmon ('Duly with knees that feign to quake')
First pub. *The Five Nations* (London, 1903); *Sussex*, XXXIII, 258–60; Harbord, Verse No. 826.

KpR 977 In MS Five Nations.

National Library of Australia, MS 94.

KpR 978 Fair copy, in MS Words, Wise and Otherwise [pp. 85–7].

Berg.

The River's Tale ('I walk my beat before London Town')
First pub. *Three Poems* (Oxford and London, 1911); reprinted C. R. L. Fletcher and Rudyard Kipling, *A History of England* (Oxford and London, 1911); collected separately *Songs from Books* (1915); *Sussex*, XXXIV, 261–2; Harbord, Verse No. 971.

KpR 979 Fair copy, revised, here untitled, in MS Years Between, including the heading, annotated 'type.'.

British Library, Add. MS 44841, f. 60.

Road-Song of the *Bandar-Log* ('Here we go in a flung festoon')
First pub. with story 'Kaa's Hunting' in *The Jungle Book* (London and New York, 1894); collected separately *Songs from Books* (London, 1913); *Sussex*, XII, 67–8 and *Sussex*, XXXIV, 61–2; Harbord, Verse No. 617.

KpR 980 In MS Jungle Books: draft, here untitled, the order of stanzas here is 2, 3, 1, 4 (stanza 1 here beginning 'Here we go in a tailed festoon' (f. 3); fair copy, revised, here beginning 'Here we go in <a tailed> our flung festoon', annotated 'To follow "*Kaa's Hunting*" separate page', watermarked 1890 (f. 57).

British Library, Add. MS 45540, ff. 3, 57.

KpR 981 Fair copy, in MS Writings and Songs (pp. 82–3).

Berg.

The Roman Centurion's Song ('Legate, I had the news last night — my cohort ordered home')
First pub. as 'The Roman Centurion Speaks' in *Three Poems* (Oxford and London, 1911); reprinted C. R. L. Fletcher and Rudyard Kipling, *A History of England* (Oxford and London, 1911); collected separately *Songs from Books* (1915); *Sussex*, XXXIV, 263–5; Harbord, Verse No. 972.

KpR 982 Fair copy, revised, here untitled and beginning 'Legate! I had the news last night. My cohort's ordered home', in MS Years Between, annotated 'type'.

British Library, Add. MS 44841, f. 61.

Romance, see KpR 567–8.

Romulus and Remus ('Oh, little did the Wolf-Child care')
First pub. (without title) with 'Cities and Spaces' ('Letters to the Family No. III'), in *Morning Post*, 26 March 1908; collected separately *Songs from Books* (New York, 1912); *Sussex*, XXIV (*Letters of Travel*), 159 and *Sussex*, XXXIV, 168; Harbord, Verse No. 913.

KpR 983 Fair copy, revised, here untitled but signed '*Romulus and Remus*', in MS Non-Fiction, in the MS of 'Letters to the Family' (KpR 1826), annotated 'Verses to precede No III of Letters to the Family'.

British Library, Add. MS 45542, f. 127.

'Route Marchin'' ('We're marchin' on relief over Injia's sunny plains')
First pub. *Barrack-Room Ballads* (1892); *Sussex*, XXXII, 222–4; Harbord, Verse No. 552.

KpR 983.5 Corrected page proof for first publication; date stamped 12 February 1892.

British Library, Loan 97 (deposited by John Aris, 1989).

The Rowers ('The banked oars fell an hundred strong')
First pub. *The Times*, 22 December 1902; collected *The Years Between* (London, [1919]); *Sussex*, XXXIII, 351–2; Harbord, Verse No. 785.

KpR 984 Revised, here beginning 'The great oars threshed an hundred strong', in MS Years Between, 3 leaves (rectos only), 12 stanzas.

British Library, Add. MS 44841, ff. 7–9 (rectos only).

KpR 985 Corrected typescript, as sent to the printer for publication in the Bombay Edition of *The Five Nations*, Vol. XXII (London, 1914), annotated 'To precede Kitcheners School in The Five Nations' and '1902' added to title, one page, excised from KpR 365.

Yale.

Rudyard and Kipling, see KpR 703.

The Run of the Downs ('The Weald is good, the Downs are best —')
First pub. with story 'The Knife and the Naked Chalk' in *Rewards and Fairies* (London, 1910); collected separately *Songs from Books* (New York, 1912); *Sussex*, XV, 115 and *Sussex*, XXXIV, 8; Harbord, Verse No. 958.

KpR 986 Fair copy, wanting the title and first two lines, in MS Rewards and Fairies, one page (containing also KpR 1082), headed 'To precede The Knife and the Naked Chalk'.

Cambridge University Library, ADD 6850, f. 51.

The Runes on Weland's Sword ('A Smith makes me')
First pub. with story 'Old Men at Pevensey' in *Puck of Pook's Hill* (London, 1906); collected separately *Poems 1886–1929*; *Sussex*, XIV, 115–16 and *Sussex*, XXXV, 224–5; Harbord, Verse No. 892.

KpR 987 Two MSS, revised, in MS Puck; the first here entitled 'The Runes on the Sword', annotated 'To follow Old Man at the Manor', 9 stanzas (f. 41), the second, here entitled (added later) 'The Runes on the Sword', including 8 stanzas and a prose introduction (f. 42).

Bodleian, MS. Eng. misc. c. 127, ff. 41–2 (rectos only).

KpR 988 Slightly corrected first page proof for the Sussex Edition, Vol. XIV; date stamped 2 July 1931.

British Library, Add. MS 55864.

The Runners ('News!/What is the word that they tell now — now — now!')
First pub. with story 'A Sahib's War' in *Traffics and Discoveries* (London, 1904); collected separately *Songs from Books* (New York, 1912); *Sussex*, VII, 77–8 and *Sussex*, XXXV, 219–20; Harbord, Verse No. 874.

KpR 989 Fair copy, revised, here untitled and beginning 'O watcher! O waiters!/What is the word...', in MS Traffics and Discoveries, one page, annotated 'To precede A Sahibs War on separate page'.

McGill University.

KpR 990 Corrected first page proof for the Sussex Edition, Vol. VII; date stamped 22 March 1932.

British Library, Add. MS 55858.

The Rupaiyat of Omar Kal'vin ('Now, the New Year reviving last Year's Debt')
First pub. *Civil and Military Gazette*, 30 January 1886; collected *Departmental Ditties* (1886); *Sussex*, XXXII, 47–8; Harbord, Verse No. 165.

KpR 991 Fair copy, including heading, in MS Departmental Ditties (pp. 39–41).

Berg.

KpR 992 Corrections on pp. 39–40 of KpR 282.

Yale.

Russia to the Pacifists ('God rest you, peaceful gentlemen, let nothing you dismay')
First pub. *The Years Between* (London, [1919]); *Sussex*, XXXIII, 381–2; Harbord, Verse No. 1104.

KpR 993 Fair copy, revised, here entitled 'The Kingdom' and beginning 'God rest you merry...', in MS Years Between, annotated 'type first', containing 5 stanzas, lines 32–6 cancelled at the bottom; dated 12 November 1912 at the top in an unidentified hand.

British Library, Add. MS 44841, f. 25.

The Sack of the Gods ('Strangers drawn from the ends of the earth, jewelled and plumed were we')
First pub. (stanzas 1, 3, 5 only, without title) as heading to Chapter 17 of Rudyard Kipling and Wolcott Balestier, *The Naulahka* (London, 1892); reprinted *Sussex*, XIX, 217; first pub. in full *Songs from Books* (New York, 1912); *Sussex*, XXXIV, 11–12; Harbord, Verse No. 546.

KpR 994 Draft of stanzas 1, 3, 5 only, here untitled, on a page (containing also KpR 764), annotated 'To Suzanne Bishop from Rudyard Kipling'.

Pierpont Morgan, MA 979.

KpR 995 Corrected first page proof of stanzas 1, 3, 5 (i.e., heading to Chapter 17 of *The Naulahka*) for the Sussex Edition, Vol. XIX; date stamped 7 November 1931.

British Library, Add. MS 55869.

The Sacrifice of Er-Heb ('The story of Bisesa, Armod's child, —')
First pub. (with 4 lines of heading 'Er-Heb beyond the Hills of Ao-Safai') in *Barrack-Room Ballads* (1892); *Sussex*, XXXII, 278–94; Harbord, Verse No. 553.

KpR 995.5 Corrected page proof for first publication.

British Library, Loan 97 (deposited by John Aris, 1989).

KpR 996 Corrected page proof for *Inclusive Verse* (1919), one page numbered 306, in KpR 537.

Princeton, Ex3814.9.1919.11.

A St Helena Lullaby ('"How far is St Helena from a little child at play?')
First pub. with story '"A Priest in Spite of Himself"' in *Rewards and Fairies* (London, 1910); collected separately *Songs from Books* (New York, 1912); *Sussex*, XV, 173–4 and *Sussex*, XXXIV, 48–9; Harbord, Verse No. 961.

KpR 997 Fair copy, revised, here entitled 'A Nurse's Song' and beginning 'How far is St Helena from Ajaccio on the bay?', in MS Rewards and Fairies, annotated 'to precede A priest in spite of Himself'.

Cambridge University Library, ADD 6850, f. 69.

KpR 998 Fair copy, in MS Writings and Songs (pp. 116–18).

Berg.

St Patrick's Day ('Oh! Terence dear, and did you hear')
First pub. (lines 1–8 only) *The Friend* (Bloemfontein), 17 March 1900; in full *The Friend*, 23 March 1900, as 'The Wearin' of the Green'; *Sussex*, XXXV, 213–14; Harbord, Verse No. 745.

KpR 999 Draft of lines 1–8 only, here untitled, written on the verso of a telegraph blank of the Eastern & South African Telegraph Company, annotated by 'I. B.' that the lines were written 'in the Telegraph office Capetown 17th March 1900 to be telegraphed to Bloemfontein in answer to a request for something for the first number of "the Friend"...'.

Library of Congress, Rare Book Division, Carpenter Kipling Collection.

KpR 1000 Revised, stanzas 1, 2, 4 only, here untitled, in MS Years Between, annotated 'Friend of Bloemfontein'.

British Library, Add. MS 44841, f. 116.

Saint Valentine His Day ('Shall I sing you a festive and flippant lay?')
First pub. Rutherford (1986), pp. 179–81; not in Harbord.

KpR 1001 Fair copy, subtitled 'To You', a valentine to Evelyn Welford (later Gielgud), 4 pages (one leaf), signed with a monogram; [apparently sent before 1884].

Mentioned in Louis L. Cornell, *Kipling in India* (London and New York, 1966), p. 63n2.

Pierpont Morgan, MA 1957.

Salsette Boat-Song, see KpR 177.

Sappers ('When the Waters were dried an' the Earth did appear')
First pub. *The Seven Seas* (New York, 1896); *Sussex*, XXXIII, 137–9; Harbord, Verse No. 689.

KpR 1002 Fair copy, revised, in MS Years Between, 2 leaves (rectos only).

British Library, Add. MS 44841, ff. 92–3 (rectos only).

Satiety ('Last year's wreath upon our brow')
First pub. Rutherford (1986), pp. 159–60; not in Harbord.

KpR 1003 Fair copy, in Sussex Notebook 1 (p. 118), annotated 'Portobello Road'; dated 19 July [1882].

Sussex, KP 24/3.

KpR 1004 Fair copy, in Sussex Notebook 3 (second series, pp. 11–12).

Sussex, KP 24/1.

The Scholars ('"Oh, show me how a rose can shut and be a bud again!"')
First pub. *Daily Telegraph*, 29 January 1919; collected *Inclusive Verse* [1927]; *Sussex*, XXXV, 235–8; Harbord, Verse No. 1055.

KpR 1005 Fair copy, revised, here untitled, wanting lines 37–42, one page.

Sussex, KP 24/49.

KpR 1005.5 Fair copy.

National Maritime Museum, Department of Printed Books and Manuscripts, MS 83/046.

A School Song ('Western wind and open surge')
First pub. without title (and with heading beginning '"Let us now praise famous men" —') in *Harper's Weekly*, 30 September 1899; reprinted as introductory poem to *Stalky & Co.* (London, 1899); collected separately *Songs from Books* (New York, 1912); *Sussex*, XVII, ix–xi (without title) and *Sussex*, XXXIV, 80–2; Harbord, Verse No. 734.

KpR 1006 Draft, including the heading, here untitled, in MS Years Between, one page (containing KpR 772 on verso); watermarked 1896.

British Library, Add. MS 44841, f. 122.

KpR 1007 Fair copy, including the heading, in MS Writings and Songs (pp. 16–20).

Berg.

***Schoolboy Lyrics* (privately printed, Lahore, 1881)**, for an inscribed copy, see KpR 1221.

Screw-Guns ('Smokin' my pipe on the mountings, sniffin' the mornin'-cool')
First pub. as No. 12 in series 'Barrack-Room Ballads' in *Scots Observer*, 12 July 1890; collected *Barrack-Room Ballads* (1892); *Sussex*, XXXII, 185–7; Harbord, Verse No. 466.

KpR 1008 Fair copy, here entitled 'Barrack Room Ballads. XII Screw guns.', one page.

Texas.

KpR 1008.5 Corrected page proof for *Barrack-Room Ballads* (1892); date stamped 12 February 1892.

British Library, Loan 97 (deposited by John Aris, 1989).

The Sea and the Hills ('Who hath desired the Sea? — the sight of salt water unbounded —')
First pub. (stanzas 1–2) as headings to Chapters 12 and 13 in the one-volume edition of *Kim* (1901); reprinted *Sussex*, XXI, 279 and 311; first pub. in full *The Five Nations* (London, 1903); *Sussex*, XXXIII, 183–4; Harbord, Verse No. 777.

KpR 1009 Stanza 2, added in red ink to the proof of *Kim* (KpR 1790) as the verse heading to Chapter 13; dated stamped 15 August 1900.

Unlocated.

KpR 1010 In MS Five Nations.

National Library of Australia, MS 94.

KpR 1011 Correction on p. 2 of KpR 365.

Yale.

KpR 1012 Corrections to stanzas 1–2 (as headings to Chapters 12–13 of *Kim*), in first page proof for the Sussex Edition, Vol. XXI (KpR 1791); date stamped 9 October 1931.

British Library, Add. MS 55871.

The Sea-Wife ('There dwells a wife by the Northern Gate')
First pub. as untitled introductory verses in John Arthur Barry, *Steve Brown's Bunyip and Other Stories* (London and Sydney, 1893); collected *The Seven Seas* (New York, 1896); *Sussex*, XXXIII, 78–9; Harbord, Verse No. 600A.

KpR 1013 Fair copy, revised, in MS Years Between, one page.

British Library, Add. MS 44841, f. 91.

Seal Lullaby ('Oh! hush thee, my baby, the night is behind us')
First pub. as verse heading to story 'The White Seal' in *National Review*, August 1893; story collected *The Jungle Book* (London and New York, 1894); collected separately *Songs from Books* (London, 1913); *Sussex*, XII, 293 and *Sussex*, XXXIV, 234–5 as 'Chapter Heading'; Harbord, Verse No. 620.

KpR 1014 Revised, in MS Jungle Books, here entitled 'The White Seal', on a page also containing KpR 758; watermarked 1890.

British Library, Add. MS 45540, f. 4.

Seal Song, see KpR 2235.

The Second Voyage ('We've sent our little Cupids all ashore —')
First pub. *The Five Nations* (London, 1903); *Sussex*, XXXIII, 196–7; Harbord, Verse No. 827.

KpR 1015 In MS Five Nations.

National Library of Australia, MS 94.

The Second Wooing [A Visitation] ('There came to me One at midnight, on golden pinions, and said:')
First pub. *Quartette* (Lahore, 1885); Rutherford, pp. 108–9; Harbord, Verse Nos. 67 (as 'The Visitation') and 156.

KpR 1016 Fair copy, here entitled 'A Visitation', in MS Sundry Phansies.

Berg.

The Secret of the Machines ('We were taken from the ore-bed and the mine')
First pub. in C. R. L. Fletcher and Rudyard Kipling, *A History of England* (Oxford and London, 1911); collected separately *Songs from Books* (1915); *Sussex*, XXXIV, 297–8; Harbord, Verse No. 991.

KpR 1017 Fair copy, revised, here originally entitled 'The Song of the Machines', in MS Years Between, annotated 'type'.

British Library, Add. MS 44841, f. 81.

'See my literary pants'
First pub. *Country Life Press* (1919); reprinted Harbord, Verse No. 601.

KpR 1018 Fair copy, inserted in Brander Matthews's copy of *Many Inventions* (London, 1893) (containing also KpR 456, 1392); signed and dated July 1894.

Cornell University.

September ('At dawn there was a murmur in the trees')
First pub. *Civil and Military Gazette*, 15 September 1886, as 'In September'; collected as 'Two Months' (with 'June') in *Departmental Ditties*, 3rd ed (1888); *Sussex*, XXXII, 161–2; Harbord, Verse No. 198A.

KpR 1019 Fair copy, here entitled 'In September', in MS Words, Wise and Otherwise [p. 28].

Berg.

'The Sergeant's Weddin' ' (''E was warned agin 'er —')
First pub. *The Seven Seas* (New York, 1896); *Sussex*, XXXIII, 157–8; Harbord, Verse No. 690. Copies of a galley proof (uncorrected) containing unique variants are at the Huntington, RB 29635, and the Library of Congress, Rare Book Division, Carpenter Kipling Collection.

KpR 1020 Fair copy, slightly revised, in MS Seven Seas (f. 102).

Magdalene College, Cambridge.

'A Servant When He Reigneth' ('Three things make Earth unquiet')
First pub. (stanzas 1–3 without title) with 'Labour' ('Letters to the Family No. V)', in *Morning Post*, 9 April 1908; reprinted *Sussex*, XXIV, 187; first pub. in full *Songs from Books* (New York, 1912); *Sussex*, XXXIV, 86–7; Harbord, Verse No. 915.

KpR 1021 Fair copy, revised, in MS Years Between, including the epigraph from *Proverbs*.

British Library, Add. MS 44841, f. 113.

KpR 1022 Stanza 4, in a letter to H. A. Gwynne, Bateman's, 24 November 1930.

Typed transcript at Sussex, KP 15/15.

Dalhousie University.

Sestina of the Tramp-Royal ('Speakin' in general, I 'ave tried 'em all —')
First pub. *The Seven Seas* (New York, 1896); *Sussex*, XXXIII, 121–2; Harbord, Verse No. 691.

KpR 1023 Fair copy, revised, in MS Years Between.

British Library, Add. MS 44841, f. 98.

The Settler ('Here, where my fresh-turned furrows run')
First pub. *The Times*, 27 February 1903; collected *The Five Nations* (London, 1903); *Sussex*, XXXIII, 295–7; Harbord, Verse No. 803.

KpR 1024 In MS Five Nations.

National Library of Australia, MS 94.

KpR 1025 Corrections to lines 8, 35–6 in a copy of the separate pamphlet publication (London, 1903).

Facsimile in American Art Association sale catalogue.

American Art Association, 20–1 April 1925 (G. B. McCutcheon Sale), Lot 328.

The Seven Joys of Mary, see KpR 179.

***The Seven Seas* (1897)**, for inscribed copies, see KpR 79, 951, 1366.

Severance [Woking Necropolis] ('Plight my troth to the dead, Love?')
First pub. Rutherford (1986), p. 158; not in Harbord.

KpR 1026 Fair copy, revised, here entitled 'Woking Necropolis', in Sussex Notebook 1 (pp. 115–16); dated 7 June [i.e., July 1882].

Sussex, KP 24/3.

KpR 1027 Fair copy, here entitled 'Severance', in Sussex Notebook 3 (second series, pp. 10–11).

Sussex, KP 24/1.

Shadow Houses, see KpR 177–8.

'She wandered round the blessed world'
First pub. Rutherford (1986), p. 457, as 'Verse Fragments and Limericks (a)'; not in Harbord.

KpR 1028 Draft of 6 lines, on a scrap, apparently written for Edmonia Hill on board the 'City of Peking' en route from Yokohama to San Francisco in May 1889.

Library of Congress, Rare Book Division, Carpenter Kipling Collection, Pen and Brush Sketches, Item 4.

'Shillin' a Day' ('My name is O'Kelly, I've heard the Revelly')
First pub. *Barrack-Room Ballads* (1892); *Sussex*, XXXII, 227–8; Harbord, Verse No. 554.

KpR 1029 Draft lines on 2 pages, here untitled.

Sussex, KP 24/50.

KpR 1029.5 Corrected page proof for first publication; date stamped 12 February 1892.

British Library, Loan 97 (deposited by John Aris, 1989).

Shiv and the Grasshopper ('Shiv, who poured the harvest and made the winds to blow')
First pub. (stanza one, without title) in text of 'Toomai of the Elephants' in *St Nicholas Magazine*, December 1893; reprinted *Sussex*, XII, 428; first pub. in full accompanying same story *The Jungle Book* (London and New York, 1894); collected separately *Songs from Books* (London, 1913); *Sussex*, XII, 441–2 and *Sussex*, XXXIV, 35–6; Harbord, Verse No. 593.

KpR 1030 Stanza one, revised, here untitled, in text of 'Toomai of the Elephants' (KpR 2157), in MS Jungle Books.

British Library, Add. MS 45540, f. 42.

The Sign of the Flower [The Sign of the Withered Violet] ('"Wait for a little — and if my woe')
First pub. Rutherford (1986), p. 170; not in Harbord.

KpR 1031 Fair copy, here entitled 'The Sign of the Withered Violet', in Sussex Notebook 1 (pp. 123–4), annotated 'Rottingdean'; dated 16 August [1882].

Sussex, KP 24/3.

KpR 1032 Fair copy, here entitled 'The Sign of the Flower', in Sussex Notebook 3 (second series, pp. 25–7).

Sussex, KP 24/1.

The Silent Army ('From the corn and wine of the Lowlands, to the stubborn hills of the North')
No publication traced; not in Harbord.

KpR 1033 Corrected typescript, signed (initials) in typescript; dated 1906.

Bodleian, MS. Milner. dep. 660, f. 39.

KpR 1034 Typescript, signed, 2 pages; dated January 1906.

Hertfordshire Record Office, D/ERv F161/14.

KpR 1035 Two copies of a transcript, probably by Elsie Bambridge, here headed 'To the Duke of Connaught by R. K./Written aboard the Armaduke Castle Jan. 1906 when above was going to the Cape as G[overnor] G[eneral]', subscribed 'original sent to Lady Patricia Ramsay Feb: 1967. It has never been published.'.

Sussex, KP 24/59 and 32/17.

Sir Galahad ('"Sharpened sword at saddle bow')
First pub. Rutherford (1986), pp. 119–20; not in Harbord.

KpR 1036 Fair copy, in Sussex Notebook 1 (pp. 59–60); dated 24 February 1882.

Sussex, KP 24/3.

KpR 1037 Fair copy, in Sussex Notebook 3 (first series, pp. 6–8); dated 24 February 1882.

Sussex, KP 24/1.

Sir Hoggie and the Fairies, see KpR 179–80.

Sir John Christie, see KpR 174–5.

Sir Richard's Song ('I followed my Duke ere I was a lover')
First pub. with story 'Young Men at the Manor' in *Puck of Pook's Hill* (London, 1906); collected separately *Songs from Books* (New York, 1912); *Sussex*, XIV, 53–4 and *Sussex*, XXXIV, 16–17; Harbord, Verse No. 889.

KpR 1038 Fair copy, revised, here untitled, in MS Puck.

Bodleian, MS. Eng. misc. c. 127, f. 22.

KpR 1039 Slightly corrected first page proof for the Sussex Edition, Vol. XIV; date stamped 2 July 1931.

British Library, Add. MS 55864.

Sitting Fox, see KpR 771.

The Situation ('We are waiting on the Gaul for leave to live.')
No publication traced; not in Harbord.

KpR 1040 Fair copy, revised, in MS Years Between, seven 6-line stanzas, signed, annotated 'no proof needed. read carefully for literals RK.'.

British Library, Add. MS 44841, f. 128.

The Small Boy of Quebec, see KpR 1188.

A Smuggler's Song ('If you wake at midnight, and hear a horse's feet')
First pub. with story 'Hal o' the Draft' in *Puck of Pook's Hill* (London, 1906); collected separately *Songs from Books* (New York, 1912); *Sussex*, XIV, 217–18 and *Sussex*, XXXIV, 180–1; Harbord, Verse No. 898.

KpR 1041 Fair copy, revised, here untitled, in MS Puck.

Bodleian, MS. Eng. misc. c. 127, f. 84.

KpR 1042 Correction on p. 213 of KpR 1112.

Yale.

KpR 1043 Corrected first page proof for the Sussex Edition, Vol. XIV; date stamped 2 July 1931.

British Library, Add. MS 55864.

'Snarleyow' ('This 'appened in a battle to a batt'ry of the Core')
First pub. *National Observer*, 29 November 1890; collected *Barrack-Room Ballads* (1892); *Sussex*, XXXII, 199–201; Harbord, Verse No. 477.

KpR 1043.5 Corrected page proof for *Barrack-Room Ballads* (1892); date stamped 12 February 1892.

British Library, Loan 97 (deposited by John Aris, 1989).

'So for some the wet sail arching through the rainbow round the bows', see KpR 357.

'So we settled it all when the storm was done', see KpR 179–80, 183.

'Soldier An' Sailor Too' ('As I was spittin' into the Ditch aboard o' the *Crocodile*')
First pub. *Pearson's Magazine* and *McClure's Magazine*, April 1896; collected *The Seven Seas* (New York, 1896); *Sussex*, XXXIII, 133–6; Harbord, Verse No. 666.

KpR 1044 Fair copy, revised, in MS Years Between, including an unpublished 8-line verse footnote to line 23 beginning 'Pick 'im up an' blow is nose'; watermarked 1894.

British Library, Add. MS 44841, f. 94.

'Soldier, Soldier' ('"Soldier, soldier come from the wars')
First pub. as No. 6 in series 'Barrack-Room Ballads' in *Scots Observer*, 12 April 1890; collected *Barrack-Room Ballads* (1892); *Sussex*, XXXII, 183–4; Harbord, Verse No. 430.

KpR 1045 Draft, untitled, in red ink (f. 1) and fair copy of 11-stanza version (ff. 2, 1v) entitled 'Barrack-Room Ballads. (VI) Soldier! Soldier!', both on a folded leaf (misbound); together with 2 proofs for the first publication, one corrected, enclosed in a letter from the ediitor of *Scots Observer* to Constable (to accompany 'the manuscript'), 3 April 1890.

Huntington, HM 11887, ff. 1–2 (MSS) and HM 11888 (proofs and letter).

KpR 1045.5 Corrected page proof for *Barrack-Room Ballads* (1892); date stamped 12 February 1892.

British Library, Loan 97 (deposited by John Aris, 1989).

Solo from Libretto of *Naulahka*, see KpR 185–7.

Solus cum Sola ('We were alone on the beach')
First printed *Schoolboy Lyrics* (privately printed, Lahore, 1881); first pub. *Early Verse* (1900); *Sussex*, XXXV, 50; Rutherford, pp. 96–7; Harbord, Verse No. 31.

KpR 1046 Fair copy, in MS Sundry Phansies.

Berg.

'Some to Women, some to Wine —'
First pub. 'Decent Swine', *KJ*, 60 (1986), 42–4; not in Harbord.

KpR 1047 Transcript by Stanley Baldwin (transcribed from Kipling's inscription of the lines on a wooden pig given to Baldwin), five 3-line stanzas, in a letter to Mimi Davidson, Stourport, 30 December 1919.

Facsimile in *KJ* (cited above).

Owned (1986) Hon. Malcolm Davidson (see *KJ*).

Song (For Two Voices) ('I bound his soul by a word and an Oath')
First pub. Rutherford (1986), pp. 107–8; Harbord, Verse No. 64.

KpR 1048 Fair copy, in MS Sundry Phansies.

Berg.

A Song at Cock-Crow ('The first time that Peter denièd his Lord')
First pub. *The Years Between* (London, [1919]); *Sussex*, XXXIII, 432–3; Harbord, Verse No. 1106A.

KpR 1049 Fair copy, revised, in MS Years Between, including a cancelled version of stanza 8.

British Library, Add. MS 44841, f. 49.

Song for Two Voices [Song (For Music)] ('Follow and faint not, if the road be long')
First pub. Rutherford (1986), p. 152; not in Harbord.

KpR 1050 Fair copy, here entitled 'Song for two Voices', in Sussex Notebook 1 (p. 103); dated 11 June 1882.

Sussex, KP 24/3.

KpR 1051 Transcript by AMK, in Sussex Notebook 2 [p. 41], here entitled 'Song. (For Music)'; dated June 1882.

Sussex, KP 24/2.

A Song in Storm ('Be well assured that on our side')
First pub. (stanzas 1, 3, 5 only, without title) with 'The Fringes of the Fleet V Patrols I', in *Daily Telegraph*, 30 November 1915; first pub. in full *The Years Between* (London, [1919]); *Sussex*, XXVI, 277–8 and *Sussex*, XXXIII, 365–6; Harbord, Verse No. 1018.

KpR 1052 In MS Non-Fiction, in the MS of 'The Fringes of the Fleet' (KpR 1632): (1) fair copy, revised, of stanzas 1, 3 and 5 only, here untitled (f. 49); (2) draft of the refrain (f. 47).

British Library, Add. MS 45542, ff. 47, 49.

KpR 1053 Fair copy, revised, here entitled 'The Explorers.' and beginning 'Be well assured that from our side', in MS Years Between, annotated '*type:*'.

British Library, Add. MS 44841, f. 17.

KpR 1054 Fair copy of stanza 5 only, signed, here untitled; written for Cheltenham College Library in 1925.

Facsimile in British Library, Facs. Suppl. XI (15), f. 60.

Cheltenham College.

A Song in the Desert ('Friend, thou beholdest the lightning? Who has the charge of it —')
First pub. *Inclusive Verse* [1927]; *Sussex*, XXXV, 263–5; Harbord, Verse No. 1146.

KpR 1055 Fair copy, revised, here beginning 'Friend Thou beholdest the lightning. Who hath the charge of it', on the first page of KpR 652.

Sussex, KP 24/37.

The Song of an Outsider ('E'en now the heron treads the wet')
First printed (10-stanza version) in Ballard (1935), pp. 17–18 (facsimile); first pub. (11-stanza version) in Col C. H. Milburn, 'The Song of an Outsider', *KJ*, 7 (1940), 30–1; 11-stanza version reprinted (from KpR 1057) Harbord, Verse No. 237; Rutherford, pp. 193–4.

KpR 1056 Fair copy, 10 stanzas, 2 pages (one leaf), signed (initials); [probably summer 1883].

Harvard, MS Eng 1267.2.

KpR 1057 Fair copy, 11 stanzas, headed 'how does this strike you, Padre?', 2 pages, signed (initials).

This MS printed Harbord (cited above).

Sotheby's, 23–4 March 1936 (property of Mrs A. F. Willis), Lot 347, sold to Maggs.

A Song of Bananas ('Have you no Bananas, simple townsmen all?')
First pub. with 'Brazilian Sketches No. II Rio' in *Morning Post*, 2 December 1927; collected separately *Inclusive Verse* [1933]; *Sussex*, XXIV, 349–50 and *Sussex*, XXXV, 267–8; Harbord, Verse No. 1148.

KpR 1058 Corrected first page proof for the Sussex Edition, Vol. XXIV; date stamped 19 June 1936.

British Library, Add. MS 55874.

The Song of Diego Valdez ('The God of Fair Beginnings')
First pub. (stanza 3 only) as heading to Chapter 6 of *Kim* as published serially in *Cassell's Magazine*, April 1901; reprinted *Sussex*, XXI, 131; first pub. in full separately *The Five Nations* (London, 1903); *Sussex*, XXXIII, 201–4; Harbord, Verse No. 762A.

KpR 1059 Rough drafts for a poem, on 4 pages from a 'scratch pad', one containing stanza 1 of this poem here entitled 'The Private.'; apparently written during a visit to the De Forests.

Photographs of the MS at Harvard, Kipling 15.2 (in a box of photos, etc. from Flora Livingston).

Unlocated.

KpR 1060 Fair copy, extensively revised, of six 8-line stanzas entitled 'Stolen Waters' (one page) which seems to have been used as quarry for this poem, the 8 introductory lines beginning '"The key shall keep the castle', first stanza beginning 'There's herds upon your holdings'.

Sussex, KP 24/52.

KpR 1061 In MS Five Nations.

National Library of Australia, MS 94.

A Song of French Roads ('Now praise the Gods of Time and Chance')
First pub. *New York World*, 23 April 1924; collected *Inclusive Verse* [1927]; *Sussex*, XXXV, 252–4; Harbord, Verse No. 1123.

KpR 1062 Fair copy, revised, here entitled 'A Song by Numbers (*English accent*)' together with MS of 'France at War' (KpR 1626), 2 numbered pages.

Bibliothèque Nationale, Paris, MS Anglais 86, ff. 1–2 (rectos only).

A Song of St Valentine, see KpR 51–2.

The Song of Seven Cities ('I was Lord of Cities very sumptuously builded.')
First pub. with story 'The Vortex' in *A Diversity of Creatures* (London, 1917); collected separately *Inclusive Verse* (1919); *Sussex*, IX, 403–4 and *Sussex*, XXXIV, 336–8; Harbord, Verse No. 1047.

KpR 1063 Revised, here beginning 'I was Lord of Cities very excellently builded —', including discarded stanzas, in MS Diversity of Creatures (ff. 141–2, rectos only), annotated '*type please*'.

University of Edinburgh, Dk. 2. 8.

KpR 1064 Corrected first page proof for *Humorous Tales* (London, 1931), pp. 505–7; date stamped 9 June 1931.

British Library, Add. MS 55847.

KpR 1065 Corrected first page proof for the Sussex Edition, Vol. IX; date stamped 28 April 1932.

British Library, Add. MS 55860.

Song of Seventy Horses ('Whether the throat-closing brick-fields by Lille, or her pavés')
First pub. with story 'The Miracle of Saint Jubanus' in *Limits and Renewals* (London, 1932); collected separately *Inclusive Verse* [1933]; *Sussex*, XI, 329–30 and *Sussex*, XXXIV, 425–6; Harbord, Verse No. 1212.

KpR 1066 Corrected page proof in Limits and Renewals Proof; date stamped 23 January 1932.

Syracuse University.

KpR 1067 Corrected first page proof for the Sussex Edition, Vol. XI; date stamped 14 October 1932.

British Library, Add. MS 55862.

The Song of the Banjo ('You couldn't pack a Broadwood half a mile —')
First pub. *New Review*, June 1895; collected *The Seven Seas* (New York, 1896); *Sussex*, XXXIII, 62–6; Harbord, Verse No. 640.

KpR 1068 In MS Seven Seas: (1) fair copy, revised, unfinished, watermarked 1890 (f. 89); (2) fair copy, revised, of an early version (ff. 90–1, rectos only); (3) draft stanzas, watermarked 1890 (f. 92).

Magdalene College, Cambridge.

KpR 1069 Fair copy, including sketches, in Berg Booklet [pp. 10–13].

Berg.

The Song of the Engines, see KpR 683, 2067.

A Song of the English ('Fair is our lot — Oh, goodly is our heritage!')
First pub. (early version) in *English Illustrated Magazine*, May 1893; revised and collected *The Seven Seas* (New York, 1896); *Sussex*, XXXIII, 3–16; Harbord, Verse No. 564.

KpR 1070 Fair copy, revised, here untitled and beginning 'Praise ye the Lord in the vault above the cherubim!', in MS Seven Seas (ff. 151–7, rectos only); watermarked 1890.

Magdalene College, Cambridge.

KpR 1071 Fair copy, slightly revised, 4 numbered leaves (rectos only), signed; dated March 1893.

Harvard, MS Eng 165, ff. 8–11 (rectos only).

KpR 1072 Fair copy of opening section, in Berg Booklet [p. 9].

Berg.

KpR 1073 Fair copy of lines 33–40, subscribed 'The Coastwise Lights' (i.e., from the section so subtitled), annotated 'For Miss D. Codd.', signed.

Cornell University.

KpR 1074 Fair copy, revised, of lines 97–100 (beginning 'There's never a <sea> flood goes shoreward now'), signed, on a Bateman's notecard, together with an envelope addressed to Mrs Eden Phillpotts.

Syracuse University.

The Song of the Exiles ('That long white Barrack by the Sea')
First pub. (13 stanzas) *United Services College Chronicle*, 15 October 1883; collected *Early Verse* (1900); *Sussex*, XXXV, 35–6; Rutherford, pp. 198–201; Harbord, Verse No. 74.

KpR 1075 Early version, including 13 stanzas and footnotes, here beginning 'The blank old barrack by the sea' and subtitled '(As sung by one of them)'; written on verso of a photograph of Kipling and his father, presented to L. C. Dunsterville and signed 'R. K. 3-11-83'.

This MS printed R. and R. Gollin, '"Exiles" in India: An Early Kipling Variant', *N&Q*, 210 (1965), 306–7; the photograph is reproduced in Rutherford, p. [199]; a transcript of this MS is at Sussex, 14/51.

Library of Congress, Rare Book Division, Colt Collection.

KpR 1076 Proof, corrected in an unidentified hand, one page, annotated 'Has *been to* Mr Kipling.' and 'By kind permission of Mr Rudyard Kipling', apparently for publication in H. A. Tapp, *United Services College 1874–1911* (Aldershot, [1934]).

Library of Congress, Rare Book Division, Colt Collection.

Song of the Fifth River ('When first by Eden Tree')
First pub. with story 'The Treasure and the Law' in *Puck of Pook's Hill* (London, 1906); collected separately *Songs from Books* (New York, 1912); *Sussex*, XIV, 245–6 and *Sussex*, XXXIV, 92–4; Harbord, Verse No. 901B.

KpR 1077 Fair copy, in MS Writings and Songs (pp. 25–8).

Berg.

KpR 1078 Fair copy, revised, annotated 'To follow The treasure & The Law', including 5 cancelled stanzas, in MS Puck.

Bodleian, MS. Eng. misc. c. 127, f. 106.

KpR 1079 Corrected first page proof for the Sussex Edition, Vol. XIV; date stamped 2 July 1931.

British Library, Add. MS 55864.

The Song of the Lathes ('The fans and the beltings they roar round me.')
First pub. *Sunday Herald*, 24 February 1918; collected *The Years Between* (London, [1919]); *Sussex*, XXXIII, 405–6; Harbord, Verse No. 1049.

KpR 1080 Revised, in MS Years Between, subtitled '*(Being the words of the tune hummed at her lathe by Mrs L. K. Embsay widow, munitions worker in a certain factory)*'; dated in pencil in an unidentified hand 18 January 1918.

British Library, Add. MS 44841, f. 35.

The Song of the Little Hunter ('Ere Mor the Peacock flutters, ere the Monkey-People cry')
First pub. as heading to 'The King's Ankus' in *St Nicholas Magazine*, March 1895; collected, accompanying the story, in *The Second Jungle Book* (London and New York, 1895); collected separately *Songs from Books* (London, 1913); *Sussex*, XII, 191–2 and *Sussex*, XXXIV, 132–3; Harbord, Verse No. 650.

KpR 1081 Fair copy, revised, in MS Jungle Books, headed 'heading for the *King's ankus*'.

British Library, Add. MS 45540, f. 85.

Song of the Men's Side ('Once we feared The Beast — when he followed us we ran')
First pub. with story 'The Knife and the Naked Chalk' in *Rewards and Fairies* (London, 1910); collected separately *Songs from Books* (New York, 1912); *Sussex*, XV, 137–8 and *Sussex*, XXXIV, 201–2; Harbord, Verse No. 959.

KpR 1082 Fair copy, slightly revised, in MS Rewards and Fairies, headed 'To precede The Knife and the Naked Chalk', one page (containing also KpR 986).

Cambridge University Library, ADD 6850, f. 51.

KpR 1083 Fair copy of the refrain (beginning 'Room for his shadow on the grass — let it pass!'), in a letter to Maggie Hooper, Vernet les Bains, 1910 (postmark illegible).

Syracuse University.

KpR 1084 Corrected first page proof for the Sussex Edition, Vol. XV; date stamped 18 September 1931.

British Library, Add. MS 55865.

The Song of the Old Guard ('"Know this, my brethren, Heaven is clear')
First pub. with story 'The Army of a Dream' in *Traffics and Discoveries* (London, 1904); collected separately *Inclusive Verse* [1927]; *Sussex*, VII, 247–9 and *Sussex*, XXXV, 221–2; Harbord, Verse No. 875.

KpR 1085 Fair copy of a version, in MS Traffics and Discoveries, one page, annotated 'To precede Army of a Dream'.

McGill University.

KpR 1086 Corrected first page proof for the Sussex Edition, Vol. VII; date stamped 22 March 1932.

British Library, Add. MS 55858.

Song of the Red War-Boat ('Shove off from the wharf-edge! Steady!')
First pub. with story 'The Conversion of St Wilfrid' in *Rewards and Fairies* (London, 1910); collected separately *Songs from Books* (New York, 1912); *Sussex*, XV, 235–7 and *Sussex*, XXXIV, 150–2; Harbord, Verse No. 960.

KpR 1087 Fair copy, revised, here beginning 'Out oars! Forward! Steady!', in MS Rewards and Fairies, annotated 'to follow The Conversion of St Wilfrid' and 'type', one page.

Cambridge University Library, ADD 6850, f. 90.

KpR 1088 Fair copy, here originally entitled 'Song of the Red-Boat', in MS Writings and Songs (pp. 108–11).

Berg.

KpR 1089 Corrected first page proof for the Sussex Edition, Vol. XV; date stamped 18 September 1931.

British Library, Add. MS 55865.

The Song of the Sufferer [Follicular Tonsilitis] ('His drink it is Saline Pyretic')
First printed *Schoolboy Lyrics* (privately printed, Lahore, 1881); first pub. *Early Verse* (1900); *Sussex*, XXXV, 18; Rutherford, pp. 52–3; Harbord, Verse No. 32.

KpR 1090 Transcript by AMK, in her letter to Edith Plowden, Kensington, 26 August 1880.

Sussex, KP 1/10.

A Song of the White Men ('Now, this is the cup the White Men drink')
First pub. *The Friend* (Bloemfontein), 2 April 1900; collected *Inclusive Verse* (1919); *Sussex*, XXXV, 212; Harbord, Verse No. 749.

KpR 1091 Revised, here untitled and beginning 'Now this is the cup that the White men drink', in MS Years Between, in pencil, annotated in an unidentified hand 'Friend of Bloemfontein 1900'; a still-legible erased note in an unidentified hand reads 'Give to [?] to cable to W. A. Fraser Care Globe Toronto Canada' (see KpR 1094).

British Library, Add. MS 44841, f. 117.

KpR 1092 Fair copy, revised, signed, one page, among materials for *The Friend* (KpR 2283).

Library of Congress, Rare Book Division, Carpenter Kipling Collection.

KpR 1093 Fair copy of last stanza, in Berg Booklet [p. 14].

Berg.

KpR 1094 Cablegram of poem (set out in prose form), here entitled 'The Faith-Cup of the White Men', as sent by RK (see KpR 1091) in London to W. A. Fraser in Toronto for his use at a recruitment rally (not used), 23 January 1890 (sic, i.e., 1900).

Facsimile privately printed by W. A. Fraser as *The Faith-Cup of the White Men* [Toronto, 1900]; facsimile in Ballard, p. 155.

Parke Bernet, 21–2 January 1942 (Ballard Sale), Lot 163.

Song of the Wise Children ('When the darkened Fifties dip to the North')
First pub. *The Five Nations* (London, 1903); *Sussex*, XXXIII, 236–7; Harbord, Verse No. 829.

KpR 1095 In MS Five Nations.

National Library of Australia, MS 94.

KpR 1096 Correction on p. 75 of KpR 365.

Yale.

The Song of the Women ('How shall she know the worship we would do her?')
First pub. (8 stanzas, without stanza 4) in *The Pioneer*, 17 April 1888 and (9 stanzas) *Pioneer Mail*, 18 April 1888; 8-stanza version collected *Departmental Ditties*, 4th ed (1890); 9-stanza version printed by Lord Dufferin in *Helen's Tower*, 2nd ed (privately printed, 1892); *Sussex*, XXXII, 95–6 (8-stanza version); Harbord, Verse No. 305 (where stanza 4 is printed). A clipping from an unidentified sale catalogue (n.d.) lists an autograph MS of 9 stanzas of this poem inserted in a copy of *Helen's Tower, Clandeboye* (privately printed, 1870).

KpR 1097 Draft, here untitled, 4 pages (on 3 leaves of an Indian calendar for 8–11 January 1888).

Library of Congress, Rare Book Division, Carpenter Kipling Collection.

KpR 1098 Fair copy, in MS Departmental Ditties (pp. 59–61).

Berg.

KpR 1099 Fair copy of stanzas 7–9 only, here untitled, 2 pages, in a letter to Lady Dufferin, Brattleboro, 9 November 1892.

Cornell University.

KpR 1100 Corrections on p. 69 of KpR 282.

Yale.

A Song of Travel ('Where's the lamp that Hero lit')
First pub. (without title) with 'The Road to Quebec' ('Letters to the Family. No. I') in *Morning Post*, 12 March 1908; collected separately *Songs from Books* (New York, 1912); *Sussex*, XXIV (*Letters of Travel*), 133–4 and *Sussex*, XXXIV, 106–7; Harbord, Verse No. 911.

KpR 1101 Revised, here untitled, in MS Non-Fiction, in the MS of 'Letters to the Family' (KpR 1826), annotated 'To precede Letter I'.

British Library, Add. MS 45542, f. 114.

KpR 1102 Fair copy, revised, in MS Writings and Songs (pp. 106–7).

Berg.

KpR 1103 Revision to line 6 (at least) on page 7 of a corrected proof copy of second edition of *Letters to the Family* (KpR 1828).

See Sotheby's sale catalogue for fuller description.

Sotheby's, 21–2 July 1988, Lot 191 (property of G. S. Fraser), sold to Joseph.

KpR 1104 Slightly corrected first page proof for the Sussex Edition, Vol. XXIV, here untitled; date stamped 30 April 1935.

British Library, Add. MS 55874.

A Song to Mithras ('Mithras, God of the Morning, our trumpets waken the Wall!')
First pub. with story 'On the Great Wall' in *Puck of Pook's Hill* (London, 1906); collected separately *Songs from Books* (New York, 1912); *Sussex*, XIV, 167 and *Sussex*, XXXIV, 38; Harbord, Verse No. 895.

KpR 1105 Fair copy, in MS Writings and Songs (pp. 54–5).

Berg.

KpR 1106 Fair copy, revised, annotated 'To follow On the Great Wall', in MS Puck.

Bodleian, MS. Eng. misc. c. 127, f. 64.

KpR 1107 Correction on p. 45 of KpR 1112.

Yale.

KpR 1108 Slightly corrected first page proof for the Sussex Edition, Vol. XIV; date stamped 2 July 1931.

British Library, Add. MS 55864.

Songs for Youth
This selected edition of 55 poems first pub. London, [1924].

KpR 1109 Two contents lists, the first a draft of the second, containing 54 titles, one page.

Sussex, KP 24/68.

***Songs from Books* (New York, 1912)**

KpR 1110 Extensively corrected proof, here entitled (before revision), 'Songs Out of Books', 167 pages.

Sotheby's, 15 December 1988, Lot 94.

KpR 1111 Corrected proof, a revise of KpR 1110, 239 pages (wanting p. 184).

Sotheby's, 15 December 1988, Lot 93.

KpR 1112 Printed copy belonging to Kipling, containing instructions to the printer and the addition of new titles in 'Contents' and corrections to the Index (p. 244), used for preparating *Songs from Books* (1915).

Kipling's annotations are described in Martindell, pp. 179–82.

Contents: KpR 42, 66, 115, 144, 156, 174, 178, 182, 186, 351, 425, 459, 578, 658, 730, 735, 747, 777, 792, 854, 865, 871, 943, 975, 1042, 1107, 1268, 1293, 1321, 1341, 1355, 1380.

Yale.

The Sons of Martha ('The Sons of Mary seldom bother, for they have inherited that good part')
First pub. *Associated Sunday Magazines*, 28 April 1907; collected *The Years Between* (London, [1919]); *Sussex*, XXXIII, 401–3; Harbord, Verse No. 906.

KpR 1113 Fair copy, revised, in MS Years Between, including an additional stanza.

British Library, Add. MS 44841, f. 33.

The Sons of the Suburbs ('The sons of the suburbs were carefully bred')
First pub. *Sunday Pictorial* (London), 19 January 1936; reprinted Harbord, Verse No. 1027. Written originally for the Christmas, 1916 number of *Blighty*, a weekly magazine for the troops; it was not published there but a few proofs were printed and copies of them are at the Berg, Texas, New York University and the Library of Congress, Rare Book Division, Carpenter Kipling Collection.

KpR 1114 Corrected typescript, 2 pages.

Sotheby's, 9–10 December 1968, Lot 764, sold to Rota.

KpR 1115 Two transcripts, one typed (2 pages) and the other in an unidentified hand (2 pages).

Sussex, KP 24/51.

South Africa ('Lived a woman wonderful')
First pub. *The Five Nations* (London, 1903); *Sussex*, XXXIII, 292–4; Harbord, Verse No. 830.

KpR 1116 In MS Five Nations.

National Library of Australia, MS 94.

South Africa ('The shame of Amajuba Hill').
First pub. *The Standard*, 27 July 1906; no further publication traced; Harbord, Verse No. 884.

KpR 1117 Fair copy, revised, here entitled 'The Betrayal', six 8-line stanzas, in MS Years Between.

British Library, Add. MS 44841, f. 118.

KpR 1118 Typescript, slightly revised and corrected, 2 numbered leaves, signed.

Facsimile in British Library, RP 2565(ii).

Syracuse University.

Stellenbosch ('The General 'eard the firin' on the flank')
First pub. *The Five Nations* (London, 1903); *Sussex*, XXXIII, 328–30; Harbord, Verse No. 831.

KpR 1119 In MS Five Nations.

National Library of Australia, MS 94.

'''Stopped in the straight when the race was his own —', see KpR 177.

The Story of Paul Vaugel [Paul Vaugel] ('This is the story of Paul Vaugel')
First pub. (30 lines only) in Louis Cornell, *Kipling in India* (London and New York, 1966), pp. 34–5; first pub. in full Rutherford (1986), pp. 101–6; Harbord, Verse No. 65.

KpR 1120 Fair copy, the concluding 42 lines only, in Sussex Notebook 1 (pp. 51–2), with RK's later annotation.

Sussex, KP 24/3.

KpR 1121 Fair copy, incomplete, in Sussex Notebook 3 (second series, pp. 15–19).

Sussex, KP 24/1.

KpR 1122 Fair copy, here entitled 'The Story of Paul Vaugel', in MS Sundry Phansies.

Berg.

KpR 1123 Transcript by JLK of a version, here entitled 'Paul Vaugel', in Sussex Notebook 2 [pp. 5–14]; dated 'Christmas holidays 1881–82'.

Sussex, KP 24/2.

The Story of Ung ('Once, on a glittering ice-field, ages and ages ago').
First pub. *New York World*, 2 December 1894; collected *The Seven Seas* (New York, 1896); *Sussex*, XXXIII, 98–101; Harbord, Verse No. 613.

KpR 1124 Draft of stanzas 1–2 only, here untitled and beginning 'Once on the glittering ice fields millions of years ago', in MS Seven Seas (f. 158); watermarked 1890.

Magdalene College, Cambridge.

KpR 1125 Fair copy, revised, in MS Years Between, here subtitled '(a fable for the criticized)' and beginning 'Once on the glittering ice-field, thousands of years ago', containing a cancelled additional stanza, signed, 2 leaves (rectos only), annotated 'type.'; watermarked 1890.

British Library, Add. MS 44841, ff. 95–6 (rectos only).

The Story of Uriah ('Jack Barrett went to Quetta')
First pub. *Civil and Military Gazette*, 3 March 1886; collected *Departmental Ditties* (1886); *Sussex*, XXXII, 14–15; Harbord, Verse No. 169.

KpR 1126 Fair copy, in MS Departmental Ditties (pp. 4–5).

Berg.

The Stranger ('The Stranger within my gates')
First pub. (without title) with 'Newspapers and Democracy' ('Letters to the Family No. IV') in *Morning Post*, 2 April 1908; collected separately *Songs from Books* (New York, 1912); *Sussex*, XXIV (*Letters of Travel*), 173–4 and *Sussex*, XXXIV, 68–9; Harbord, Verse No. 914.

KpR 1127 Fair copy, revised, here untitled, in MS Non-Fiction, in the MS of 'Letters to the Family' (KpR 1826), annotated 'To precede Letter IV – Letters to the Family'.

British Library, Add. MS 45542, f. 133.

KpR 1128 Revision to line 17, on p. 29 of a corrected proof copy of 2nd edition of *Letters of Travel* (KpR 1828).

See Sotheby's sale catalogue for a fuller description.

Sotheby's, 21–2 July 1988, Lot 191 (property of G. S. Fraser), sold to Joseph.

KpR 1129 Stanzas 2 and 5, quoted from memory (with variants) in a letter to Lord Beaverbrook, 9 March 1911.

Harvard, bMS Eng 809.4(7).

KpR 1130 Corrected first page proof for the Sussex Edition, Vol. XXIV, here untitled; date stamped 30 April 1935.

British Library, Add. MS 55874.

Study of an Elevation, in Indian Ink ('Potiphar Gubbins, C.E.')
First pub. *Civil and Military Gazette*, 16 February 1886; collected *Departmental Ditties* (1886); *Sussex*, XXXII, 7–8; Harbord, Verse No. 167. See also KpR 280.

KpR 1131 Fair copy, revised, including 2-line heading, in MS Departmental Ditties (pp. 9–11).

Berg.

'Such as in Ships' ('Such as in Ships and brittle Barks')
First pub. with 'Brazilian Sketches No. VI Railways and a Two-Thousand-Feet Climb' in *Morning Post*, 16 December 1927; collected separately *Inclusive Verse* [1933]; *Sussex*, XXIV, 403 and *Sussex*, XXXV, 271–2; Harbord, Verse No. 1152.

KpR 1132 Draft version, here beginning 'Such as in ships of monstrous size', one page.

Sussex, KP 24/53.

The Sudder Bazar ('The motive that calls for my ditty')
First pub. *Echoes* (Lahore, [1884]); *Sussex*, XXXV, 87; Rutherford, pp. 181–3; Harbord, Verse No. 126. For an annotation in a copy of *Echoes*, see KpR 319.

KpR 1133 Fair copy, revised, containing 2 additional stanzas, in Sussex Notebook 1 (pp. 144–8); dated March 1883.

Sussex, KP 24/3.

Summer Excursion, see KpR 451.

The Supplication of Kerr Cross, Missionary ('Father of Mercy, who hast made')
First pub. *The Pioneer*, 29 September 1888; reprinted Harbord, Verse No. 334; Rutherford, pp. 428–30.

KpR 1134 Revised clipping of the first publication, in Scrapbook 4 (p. 86).

Sussex, KP 28/4.

Supplication of the Black Aberdeen ('I pray! My little body and whole span')
First pub. *Strand Magazine*, *Hearst's International Magazine* and *Cosmopolitan*, January 1928; collected *Inclusive Verse* [1933]; *Sussex*, XXXV, 274–5; Harbord, Verse No. 1160.

KpR 1135 Transcript of stanzas 1–3 by Trix Kipling, in her commonplace book (inscribed 'A little book of loves and likings' and 'Trix, Calcutta, Sep. 1907').

Facsimile in R. F. M. Immelman, *The Kipling Collection in the University of Cape Town Library* (Rondebosch, 1961), plate 4.

University of Cape Town.

The Supports ('To Him Who bade the Heavens abide, yet cease not from their motion')
First pub. *Hutchinson's Story Magazine*, July 1919; collected with story 'On the Gate' in *Debits and Credits* (London, 1926); collected separately *Inclusive Verse* [1927]; *Sussex*, X, 279–81 and *Sussex*, XXXIV, 390–2; Harbord, Verse No. 1057. For a typescript of 'On the Gate' containing lines 1–6, see KpR 1947.

KpR 1136 Two fair copies, revised, both without stanza headings and both untitled, one (2 pages) beginning 'To Him who made the Heavens abide and gave the stars their motion', the other (one page) beginning 'To Him who made the Heavens move and cease not in their motion'.

Sussex, KP 24/54.

KpR 1137 Early 36-line version, without stanza headings and lines 11, 32–7, 42 and including 4 additional lines, signed, one page, on Frogmore Hall notepaper.

Facsimile of last 8 lines in Christie's sale catalogue, 16 April 1980, Lot 117; photocopy at Kipling Society Library.

Privately owned, deposited at Sussex, SxMS 46.1/1b.

KpR 1137.5 Draft of three 3-line stanzas, here untitled and beginning 'To Him who made the planets [?] toss and cease not from their motion', in the text of the MS of 'On the Gate' (KpR 1945), in MS Debits and Credits (f. 153).

University of Durham.

KpR 1138 Corrected first page proof for the Sussex Edition, Vol. X; date stamped 30 December 1931.

British Library, Add. MS 55861.

The Survival ('Securely, after days')
First pub. with story 'The Janeites' in *Debits and Credits* (London, 1926); collected separately *Inclusive Verse* [1927]; *Sussex*, X, 111–12 and *Sussex*, XXXIV, 376–7; Harbord, Verse No. 1139.

KpR 1139 Fair copy, one page, annotated 'to precede The Janites [sic]'; together with a typescript, originally entitled '"Exegi Monumentum."' (revised by CK), one page.

Sussex, KP 24/55.

KpR 1139.5 Versions of stanzas 4 and 6, in a letter to C. R. L. Fletcher.

Sussex, KP 15/4.

KpR 1140 Corrected first page proof for the Sussex Edition, Vol. X; date stamped 30 December 1931.

British Library, Add. MS 55861.

Sussex ('God gave all men all earth to love')
First pub. *The Five Nations* (London, 1903); *Sussex*, XXXIII, 232–5; Harbord, Verse No. 832.

KpR 1141 In MS Five Nations.

National Library of Australia, MS 94.

KpR 1142 Typescript, 3 leaves (rectos only).

Bodleian, Bryce U.B.9. (among the papers of Viscount Bryce).

KpR 1143 Quotation of stanza 1, here untitled, signed, on a Bateman's notecard, enclosed in a letter to Arthur B. Maurice, 14 May 1921.

Princeton, Arthur B. Maurice Collection, Box 1, Folder 51.

KpR 1144 Revision on p. 73 of KpR 365.

Yale.

KpR 1145 Corrected page proof for *Inclusive Verse* (1919) in KpR 537.

Princeton, Ex3814.9.1919.11.

A Tale of Two Cities ('Where the sober-coloured cultivator smiles')
First pub. *Civil and Military Gazette*, 2 June 1887, as 'Love Among the Ruins'; collected *Departmental Ditties*, 3rd ed (1888); *Sussex*, XXXII, 153–7; Harbord, Verse No. 267.

KpR 1146 Fair copy, including a sketch, in MS Departmental Ditties (pp. 69–73).

Berg.

Tarrant Moss ('I closed and drew for my love's sake')
First pub. (stanzas 1 and 7) as heading to story 'Wressley of the Foreign Office' in *Civil and Military Gazette*, 20 May 1897; collected *Plain Tales from the Hills* (Calcutta and London, 1888); reprinted *Sussex*, I, 405; first pub. in full separately *Songs from Books* (New York, 1912); *Sussex*, XXXIV, 14–15; Harbord, Verse No. 265.

KpR 1147 Fair copy, in MS Writings and Songs (pp. 61–2).

Berg.

Telscombe Tye ('The Moon she shined on Telscombe Tye —')
First pub. (lines 1–5 only, without title) in text of story 'Brother Square-Toes' in *The Delineator*, July 1910; collected *Rewards and Fairies* (London, 1910); reprinted *Sussex*, XV, 144; first printed in full Harbord (1969), pp. 5668–9, as Verse No. 940.

KpR 1148 Fair copy, heavily revised (last stanzas drafted), one page, 12 stanzas, here untitled.

Sussex, KP 24/41.

KpR 1149 Lines 1–5, here untitled, in the MS of 'Brother Square-Toes' (KpR 1465), in MS Rewards and Fairies.

Cambridge University Library, ADD 6850, f. 53.

That Day ('It got beyond all orders an' it got beyond all 'ope')
First pub. *Pall Mall Gazette*, 25 April 1895; collected *The Seven Seas* (New York, 1896); *Sussex*, XXXIII, 140–1; Harbord, Verse No. 633A.

KpR 1150 Fair copy, revised, of early version, in MS Seven Seas (f. 105v).

Magdalene College, Cambridge.

KpR 1151 Fair copy, revised, in MS Years Between, here originally entitled 'Rotten That day' (cancelled); watermarked 1890.

British Library, Add. MS 44841, f. 87.

'The Brahmin who steals'
First pub. in text of story 'A Retired Gentleman' in *Morning Post*, 17 May 1917; collected *The Eyes of Asia* (New York, 1918); *Sussex*, XXVI, 176; Harbord, Verse No. 1029.

KpR 1152 Fair copy, in text of MS of 'A Retired Gentleman' (KpR 2031), in MS Eyes of Asia (f. 157).

University of Edinburgh, Dk. 2. 8.

'The Buttercup — the Berberous'
No publication traced; not in Harbord.

KpR 1153 Fair copy, revised, 38 lines, on blank flyleaf facing title page of a copy of Gaston Bonnier's *Les noms des fleurs* (Paris: Librairie Generale de l'enseignement, Nouvelle edition revue et corrigée, n.d.).

Sussex, KP 24/11.

'The Camel's hump is an ugly lump'
First pub. with story 'How the Camel Got His Hump' in *Just So Stories* (London, 1902); collected separately *Songs from Books* (London, 1913); *Sussex*, XIII, 27–8 and *Sussex*, XXXIV, 237–8, as 'Chapter Heading'; Harbord, Verse No. 790.

KpR 1154 Revised, here beginning 'The camel his hump is an ugly lump', in MS Just So Stories, annotated 'on separate page to follow Camel'.

British Library, Add. MS 59840, f. 17.

KpR 1155 Fair copy of lines 19–27, signed, written on front endpaper of a copy of *Just So Stories*, Outward Bound Edition, Vol. XX (New York, 1903).

For other verse inscribed in this set of the Outward Bound Edition, see KpR 558, 1164.

Yale.

KpR 1156 Slightly corrected first page proof for Sussex Edition, Vol. XIII; date stamped 29 October 1932.

British Library, Add. MS 55863.

'The day is most fair', see KpR 12–14.

'The first day back, ay bitter cold it was'
First printed Harbord (1969), Verse No. 10B; first pub. Rutherford (1986), pp. 56–7.

KpR 1157 Written in RK's copy of *Longer English Poems* (see KpR 2303), on p. 176 above Keats's 'The Eve of St Agnes'.

Library of Congress, Rare Book Division, Batchelder Collection.

'The gnat sings loudly at Eventide', see KpR 1168.5.

KpR 1158 [Entry deleted]

'The immitigable anti-macassar'
No publication traced; not in Harbord.

KpR 1159 Eleven lines, in a letter (containing also KpR 450, 781) to W. E. Henley, Brattleboro, 26 October 1892.

Pierpont Morgan, MA 1617.

'The lark will make her hymn to God', see KpR 179, 181, 183.

'The Lord, we are told, takes no delight'
No publication traced; not in Harbord.

KpR 1160 Fair copy, 7 lines, one page, among letters to George and Elsie Bambridge.

Sussex, KP 12/12.

'The memory of a maiden's sympathy'
First printed (stanzas 1 and 3) in Christie's sale catalogue, 24 April 1918 (Red Cross Sale), Lot 2550; in full (facsimile) in E. W. Martindell, *Fragmenta Condita* (privately printed, 1922); reprinted Harbord, Verse No. 87; first pub. Rutherford (1986), pp. 251–2, as 'Inscriptions in Presentation Copies of *Echoes* (d)'. For another version of these lines, see KpR 1256.

KpR 1161 Fair copy, inscribed on front flyleaf of a copy of *Echoes* (Lahore, [1884]) presented to 'Evelyn [Welford], from R. K. Sept. 1884'.

This copy listed Stewart, p. 15 (copy 5). Facsimile as frontispiece in *Flies in Amber* (privately printed by E. W. Martindell, 1924), unique copy of which is at Bodleian, Arch. AA. d. 46.

Dalhousie University.

'The mind of man it warpeth'
Questionable attribution; no publication traced; not in Harbord.

KpR 1162 Twenty-seven lines, in a letter to Mrs Leonard, introduced by 'As the Poet says', on Central Station Hotel, Newcastle, notepaper dated 'Tuesday Night' [1908].

Syracuse University.

'The Moon she shined on Telscombe Tye', see KpR 1148.

'The next good joy that Mary had', see KpR 179.

'The People of the Eastern Ice, they are melting like the snow —'
First pub. as heading to story 'Quiquern' in *The Second Jungle Book* (London and New York, 1895); collected separately *Songs from Books* (London, 1913); *Sussex*, XII, 381 and *Sussex*, XXXIV, 236, as 'Chapter Heading'; Harbord, Verse No. 659.

KpR 1163 Fair copy, in MS Jungle Books, headed 'Verse heading for Quiquern tale NO 6.', subscribed '*Translation*', one page (containing also KpR 28).

British Library, Add.MS 45540, f. 105.

'The rose that glimmers by the garden walk'
First printed as 'Prelude' in E. W. Martindell, *Still More Flies in Amber* (privately printed, n.d.), p. vii (unique copy at the Bodleian, Arch. AA. d. 49); reprinted Harbord (1969), Verse No. 720A.

KpR 1164 Two 4-line stanzas, inscribed on half title of a copy of *Plain Tales from the Hills*, Outward Bound Edition, Vol. I (New York, 1898).

For other verses inscribed in this set of the Outward Bound Edition, see KpR 558, 1155.

Yale.

'The Shepherd of Dartmoor Plain'
No publication traced; not in Harbord.

KpR 1165 Revised, 6 lines, on a scrap.

Syracuse University.

'The stumbling-block of Western lore'
First pub. (as closing lines to the article 'From Tideway to Tideway No. IV Our Overseas Men') in *New York Sun*, 7 August 1892; not collected and not in *Sussex*; reprinted Harbord, Verse No. 526.

KpR 1166 Fair copy, revised, 18 lines, one page.

Syracuse University.

KpR 1167 Corrected galley proof of 'From Tideway to Tideway No. IV Our Overseas Men' (see KpR 1647) concluding with these lines, the proof set up (with other articles of 'From Tideway to Tideway') for *From Sea to Sea*, 2 vols (New York, 1899), stamped '1st REV.'.

Library of Congress, Rare Book Division, Carpenter Kipling Collection.

'The wolf-cub at even lay hid in the corn', see KpR 179–180, 183.

'The Wop of Asia — that lordly Beast —'
First printed (facsimile) in Sotheby's sale catalogue, 22 December 1952, Lot 89; reprinted Harbord, Verse No. 92; first pub. Rutherford (1986), pp. 253–4, as 'Inscriptions in Presentation Copies of *Echoes* (f)'.

KpR 1168 Fair copy, inscribed on front flyleaf of a copy of *Echoes* (KpR 315), presented to Margaret Burne-Jones.

Dalhousie University.

KpR 1168.5 Lines 11–16, a presentation inscription on front flyleaf of a copy of *Departmental Ditties*, 6th ed (Calcutta, London and Bombay, 1891), presented to G. Gore-Gillon, signed and dated Wellington, New Zealand, 22 October 1891.

Columbia University.

'The World hath set its heavy yoke', see KpR 177.

'The year wears by at last —'
First pub. Rutherford (1986), Appendix D, pp. [487]–8; not in Harbord.

KpR 1169 Typescript, together with a letter from Mrs E. M. Morton (née Davey) of 4 June 1903 asking Kipling to initial the poem.

Sussex, KP 23/13.

'The year's at the spring'
No publication traced; not in Harbord.

KpR 1170 Fair copy, pastiche on Browning's lines, written to the Hills, on a scrap headed 'Monday' containing a fragmentary note on the verso.

Library of Congress, Rare Book Division, Carpenter Kipling Collection, Pen and Brush Sketches, Item 5.

Their Consolation, see KpR 466–9.

'Then we brought the lances down — then the trumpets blew —', see KpR 180, 183.

'There are things in the breast of mankind which are best'
No publication traced; Harbord, Verse No. 1027C (p. 5670).

KpR 1171 Typescript, revised, 10 lines, signed, one page.

Sotheby's, 9–10 December 1968, Lot 765, sold to Maggs.

'There be thirty chosen publishers the cutest in the row'
No publication traced; not in Harbord.

KpR 1172 One page.

Anderson Galleries, 5 June 1916, Lot 155.

'There is gold in the News they call *Daily*'
First pub. (one stanza beginning as above) in a letter from W. M. Carpenter in *KJ*, September 1931, p. 95; reprinted Harbord, Verse No. 535; Rutherford, p. 469, as 'Verse Letter to Sidney Low (extract)'.

KpR 1173 Transcript of 8 lines (of a 40-line poem) by Sidney Low (the original was sent by Kipling to Low, former editor of *St James's Gazette*, c. November 1889), in a letter dated London, 17 May 1916.

Library of Congress, Rare Book Division, Carpenter Kipling Collection.

'There is pleasure in the wet, wet clay', see KpR 184–7.

'There once was a horse on the road'
No publication traced; not in Harbord.

KpR 1174 Limerick, in pencil, in RK's copy of Edward Lear (see KpR 2301, f. 18v).

Sussex, KP 31/2.

'There once was a man who said: — I'
First pub. *'O Beloved Kids'*, ed. Elliot L. Gilbert (London, 1983), p. 101.

KpR 1175 Limerick, the postscript of a letter (containing also KpR 78) to his son John, Engelberg, 3 February [1910].

Facsimile in first publication.

Sussex, KP 13/4.

'There once was a man with a motor'
No publication traced; not in Harbord.

KpR 1176 Draft of limerick, in pencil, in RK's copy of Edward Lear (see KpR 2301, f. 13v).

Sussex, KP 31/2.

'There once was a nation that warred'
No publication traced; not in Harbord.

KpR 1177 Limerick in an unidentified hand, written *on* a letter from RK to Lord Roberts, 3 November 1912 and annotated 'by Rudyard Kipling'.

National Army Museum, London, 7101-23-47-90.

There Once Was a Pekinese, see KpR 1178.

'There once was the Deuceofa Peke'
First pub. (facsimile) in *Ant Antics*, ed. Estella Cave (London, [1933]); reprinted Harbord, Verse No. 233, as 'There Once Was a Pekinese'.

KpR 1178 Limerick, signed, one page.

Facsimile cited above.

Unlocated.

'There once were four people at Euchre'
First printed Harbord (1969), Verse No. 231, as 'On a Game of Euchre'; first pub. Rutherford (1986), p. 467.

KpR 1179 Fair copy of limerick, one page, written on board the S.S. City of Berlin en route from New York to Liverpool, headed 'Sept: 30. [1889] 9:35. Had a good hand at Euchre.'.

Library of Congress, Rare Book Division, Carpenter Kipling Collection, Pen and Brush Sketches, Item 2.

'There runs a road by Merrow Down'
First pub. with story 'How the First Letter Was Written' in *Just So Stories* (London, 1902); collected separately as Part I of 'Merrow Down' (with 'Of all the Tribe of Tegumai') in *Songs from Books* (London, 1913); *Sussex*, XIII, 135 and *Sussex*, XXXIV, 121–2, as Part I of 'Merrow Down'; Harbord, Verse No. 796.

KpR 1180 Fair copy, revised, in MS Just So Stories, annotated 'on separate page to follow The First letter'.

British Library, Add. MS 59840, f. 67.

KpR 1181 Fair copy, revised, of stanzas 2–4, here entitled 'Merrow Down', 2 leaves (rectos only), including sketches.

Berg.

KpR 1182 Slightly corrected first page proof for Sussex Edition, Vol. XIII; date stamped 29 October 1932.

British Library, Add. MS 55863.

'There was a Fast Person of Eridge'
No publication traced; not in Harbord.

KpR 1183 Draft of a limerick, illustrated, in ink, in RK's copy of Edward Lear (KpR 2301, f. 9v).

Sussex, KP 31/2.

'There was a fat man of Girgenti'
No publication traced; not in Harbord.

KpR 1184 Limerick, illustrated, one page of 'Almagro, 38/Madrid' notepaper.

Sussex, KP 24/64.

'There was a fat person of Zug'
First pub. *'O Beloved Kids'*, ed. Elliot L. Gilbert (London, 1983), p. 108.

KpR 1185 Limerick, illustrated, in a letter to his son John, Bateman's, 17 May 1910.

Facsimile in first publication.

Sussex, KP 13/4.

KpR 1186 Transcript by Elsie Bambridge? of a variant version, here beginning 'There was an old person of Zug', on a leaf headed 'R. K.' (containing also KpR 1210).

Sussex, KP 24/64.

'There was a poor wretch on the snow'
No publication traced; not in Harbord.

KpR 1187 Limerick, illustrated, on 2 pages of a leaf of Bateman's notepaper, enclosed in a letter to M. S. Taylor, 2 December 1910.

Columbia University.

'There was a small boy of Quebec'
First pub. *Wee Willie-Winkie*, [ed. Lady Marjorie Gordon], July 1895?; Harbord, Verse No. 661B.

KpR 1188 Limerick, in a letter (containing also KpR 645) to Lady Marjorie Gordon, 5 April 1895.

Typed transcript of this letter at Cornell University; transcript of this letter, annotated by and possibly in the hand of E. W. Martindell, dated from The Grafton, Connecticut Avenue, 5 April 1895, is at Sussex, Baldwin Papers 2/26.

Hodgson, 18 July 1934.

'There was a small boy who was proud'
First pub. Rutherford (1986), p. 458, as 'Verse Fragments and Limericks (d)'; not in Harbord.

KpR 1189 Fair copy, revised, of limerick, illustrated, one leaf.

Library of Congress, Rare Book Division, Carpenter Kipling Collection, Pen and Brush Sketches, Item 5.

'There was a strife 'twixt man and maid —', see KpR 184, 187.

'There was a Young Fellow of Rye'
No publication traced; not in Harbord.

KpR 1190 Draft limerick, in ink, illustrated, in RK's copy of Edward Lear (KpR 2301, f. 8v).

Sussex, KP 31/2.

'There was a young female of Kent'
No publication traced; not in Harbord.

KpR 1191 Draft limerick, in pencil, illustrated, in RK's copy of Edward Lear (KpR 2301, f. 5v).

Sussex, KP 31/2.

'There was a young girl of St Tropez'
No publication traced; not in Harbord.

KpR 1192 Transcript by CK of a limerick, in ink, in RK's copy of Edward Lear (KpR 2301, f. 19v), annotated (together with KpR 1203) 'Limericks by R. K. about 1920.'.

Sussex, KP 31/2.

'There was a young lady of Brighton'
No publication traced; not in Harbord.

KpR 1193 Draft limerick, in pencil, illustrated, in RK's copy of Edward Lear (KpR 2301, f. 2v).

Sussex, KP 31/2.

'There was a young lady of Frant'
No publication traced; not in Harbord.

KpR 1194 Draft limerick, in pencil, illustrated, in RK's copy of Edward Lear (KpR 2301, f. 3v).

Sussex, KP 31/2.

'There was a young lady of Heever'
No publication traced; not in Harbord.

KpR 1195 Draft of limerick, 2 lines only, in pencil, illustrated, in RK's copy of Edward Lear (KpR 2301, f. 10v).

Sussex, KP 31/2.

'There was a young lady of Nassik', for this limerick by JLK, see INTRODUCTION.

'There was a young man with a story'
No publication traced; Harbord, Verse No. 235.

KpR 1196 Limerick, in a letter to Verschoyle on Embankment Chambers, Villiers Street notepaper.

Library of Congress, Manuscript Division, Louise Chandler Moulton Collection, Vol. 26, f. 4958.

'There was a young parson of Wells'
No publication traced; not in Harbord.

KpR 1197 Limerick, a postscript to a letter to Stanley Baldwin, Bath, Wednesday, [c. 1919].

Typed transcript at Sussex, KP 11/3.

Dalhousie University.

'There was a young person from Ems'
No publication traced; not in Harbord.

KpR 1198 Draft limerick, in pencil, illustrated, in RK's copy of Edward Lear (KpR 2301, f. 12v).

Sussex, KP 31/2.

'There was a young person of Bateman's
No publication traced; not in Harbord.

KpR 1199 Draft limerick, in pencil, illustrated, in RK's copy of Edward Lear (KpR 2301, f. 11v).

Sussex, KP 31/2.

'There was a young person of Dover'
No publication traced; not in Harbord.

KpR 1200 Draft limerick, in pencil, illustrated, in RK's copy of Edward Lear (KpR 2301, f. 7v).

Sussex, KP 31/2.

'There was a Young Person of Hastings'
No publication traced; not in Harbord.

KpR 1201 Draft limerick, in ink, illustrated, in RK's copy of Edward Lear (KpR 2301, f. 6v).

Sussex, KP 31/2.

'There was a young person of Oldham'
First pub. *Daily Express*, 3 January 1903; reprinted Harbord, Verse No. 802, as 'Limerick (Oldham)'.

KpR 1202 Limerick, written under a photograph of Kipling; dated 1903.

Sold New York, January 1903 (see Harbord).

'There was a young woman of Brie'
No publication traced; not in Harbord.

KpR 1203 Transcript of limerick by CK, in ink, in RK's copy of Edward Lear (KpR 2301, f. 19v), annotated (together with KpR 1192) 'Limericks by R. K. about 1920.'.

Sussex, KP 31/2.

'There was an old fellow of Lydd'
No publication traced; not in Harbord.

KpR 1204 Draft limerick, in pencil, illustrated, in RK's copy of Edward Lear (KpR 2301, f. 14v).

Sussex, KP 31/2.

'There was an old lady of Margate'
No publication traced; not in Harbord.

KpR 1205 Draft limerick, here beginning 'There was an <young> old lady...', in pencil, illustrated, in RK's copy of Edward Lear (KpR 2301, f. 4v).

Sussex, KP 31/2.

'There was an old man of Kinsale'
No publication traced; not in Harbord.

KpR 1206 Draft limerick, in pencil, illustrated, in RK's copy of Edward Lear (KpR 2301, f. 17v).

Sussex, KP 31/2.

'There was an old man who said: — "True —'
No publication traced; not in Harbord.

KpR 1207 Limerick, in a letter to George Bambridge, Bateman's, 26 September 1933.

Sussex, KP 12/10.

'There was never a Lee to Warminghurst', see KpR 1465.

'There was never a Queen like Balkis'
First pub. with story 'The Butterfly that Stamped' in *Just So Stories* (London, 1902); collected separately *Songs from Books* (London, 1913); *Sussex*, XIII, [227] and *Sussex*, XXXIV, 244, as 'Chapter Heading'; Harbord, Verse No. 800.

KpR 1208 Fair copy, in MS Just So Stories, annotated 'on separate page to follow Butterfly'.

British Library, Add. MS 59840, f. 136.

KpR 1209 Slightly corrected second page proof for Sussex Edition, Vol. XIII; date stamped 23 April 1935.

British Library, Add. MS 55863.

'There were five liars bold', see KpR 59.

'There were three friends that buried the fourth', see KpR 179–81, 183.

'There were two young ladies of Nice'
No publication traced; not in Harbord.

KpR 1210 Transcript by Elsie Bambridge? of a limerick, on a leaf headed 'R. K.' (containing also KpR 1186).

Sussex, KP 24/64.

'These are the Four that are never content', see KpR 563.

'They burnt a corpse upon the sand', see KpR 177.

'They came of that same stubborn stock that stood'
First printed Maggs Catalogue 339 (August 1915), p. 65; reprinted Harbord, Verse No. 879, as 'Grahamstown Memorial to the Fallen (1880–1902)'.

KpR 1211 Fair copy, written for the Grahamstown Memorial, in a letter to Dean [F. E. Carter], Cape Town, 3 April 1905.

Cornell University.

'They're as proud as a turkey', see KpR 179.

Things and the Man ('Oh ye who hold the written clue')
First pub. *The Times*, 1 August 1904; collected *The Years Between* (London, [1919]); *Sussex*, XXXIII, 412–13; Harbord, Verse No. 864.

KpR 1212 Fair copy, revised, including four stanzas (f. 39) and draft, here untitled and beginning 'Delve deep below the plinth of Time' (f. 40), in MS Years Between.

British Library, Add. MS 44841, ff. 39–40 (rectos only).

KpR 1213 Fair copy, here entitled 'L'Envoi.', in MS Traffics and Discoveries, one page.

McGill University.

'This I saw when the rites were done', see KpR 187.

'This is a fact we cannot shelve'
No publication traced; not in Harbord.

KpR 1214 Fair copy of 4 lines, signed 'Her Father', written for Elsie's 12th birthday, 2 February 1908.

Sussex, KP 13/1.

'This is our old game/My father played it', see KpR 837.

'This is the mouth-filling song'
First pub. with story 'The Sing-Song of Old Man Kangaroo' in *Just So Stories* (London, 1902); collected separately *Songs from Books* (London, 1913); *Sussex*, XIII, 95–6 and *Sussex*, XXXIV, 240–1, as 'Chapter Heading'; Harbord, Verse No. 794.

KpR 1215 Fair copy, revised, in MS Just So Stories, annotated 'on separate page to follow Kangaroo.'.

British Library, Add. MS 59840, f. 49.

KpR 1216 Corrected first page proof for the Sussex Edition, Vol. XIII; date stamped 29 October 1932.

British Library, Add. MS 55863.

'This is the mumps that Turkey had'
No publication traced; not in Harbord.

KpR 1217 Illustrated, in a letter to 'Superior Turks' (i.e., Amelia Clifford), 11 pages.

Berg.

'This is the prayer the Cave Man prayed'
First printed Harbord (1969), Verse No. 996, as 'Home'.

KpR 1218 Fair copy, six 8-line stanzas, one page, subscribed in an unidentified hand 'Xmas. 1911. Rudyard Kipling'.

Facsimiles: House of Lords Record Office (5 photographs of this MS among Lord Beaverbrook's papers, BBK/C/197); Dalhousie University (together with a covering letter from C. H. L. Jones (President of Mersey Paper Co., Nova Scotia) to James McG. Stewart of 1 February 1938 describing the enclosed 'photostat copies made of Kipling's poem which hangs on [Isaak Walton] Killam's [d. 1955] wall...[and which was] given to Lord Beaverbrook as an inscription in a guest book which Mr Kipling gave to him on the opening of Cherkley Court'). A. J. P. Taylor in *Beaverbrook* (London, 1972), p. 397 says that the poem was found in the Roosevelt archives with the Winston Churchill correspondence (when the latter's memoirs were serialized) and returned to Lord Beaverbrook.

Unlocated.

KpR 1219 Typed transcript, six 8-line stanzas, 2 pages, annotated 'written for Gladys Beaverbrook in 1912 & sent with visitor book to Cherkley'; dated 'Xmas 1911'.

Sussex, KP 24/56.

KpR 1220 Transcript by E. H. Blakeney, here entitled 'Home', six 8-line stanzas, signed (by Blakeney) 'R. K.', 2 pages (one leaf), annotated '[Rud. K. wrote this poem for Lady Beaverbrook. He gave it to her along with a Visitor's book when she set up her home at Cherkley Court, Leatherhead, in July 1912. The orig. MS was given to Pres. Roosevelt, & is now at Hyde Park, N. York]'; dated Christmas, 1911.

British Library, Add. MS 48979, ff. 178, 179v.

'This is the writer's autograph'
First pub. W. G. B. Maitland, 'Kipling Library Notes', *KJ*, 13 (1946), 17; reprinted Stewart, p. 5; not in Harbord.

KpR 1221 Fair copy, 3 lines, on verso of title page of a copy of *Schoolboy Lyrics* (privately printed, Lahore, 1881) inscribed on front cover 'Trix Kipling/Lahore 1884'.

Facsimile in *KJ*, 17 (1950).

Dalhousie University.

'This Uninhabited Island'
First pub. with story 'How the Rhinoceros Got His Skin' in *Just So Stories* (London, 1902); *Sussex*, XIII, 41 and *Sussex*, XXXIV, 244, as 'Chapter Heading'; Harbord, Verse No. 791.

KpR 1222 Fair copy, in MS Just So Stories, annotated 'on separate page to follow The Rhinoceros.'.

British Library, Add. MS 59840, f. 23.

KpR 1223 Slightly corrected first page proof for the Sussex Edition, Vol. XIII; date stamped 29 October 1932.

British Library, Add. MS 55863.

Thorkild's Song ('There's no wind along these seas')
First pub. with story 'The Knights of the Joyous Venture' in *Puck of Pook's Hill* (London, 1906); reprinted *Sussex*, XIV, 85; first pub. in full *Songs from Books* (New York, 1912); *Sussex*, XXXIV, 197–8; Harbord, Verse No. 891.

KpR 1224 Four MSS, in MS Puck, all here untitled: fair copy (f. 32a), here beginning 'Theres no wind about these seas', 8 stanzas; fair copy (f. 32b) here beginning 'Theres no wind on all these seas', annotated 'type', 8 stanzas; draft wanting stanzas 4–5 (of above version) beginning 'Theres no wind about these seas' and fair copy, revised, of stanzas 1–2 beginning 'Theres no wind upon these seas' (f. 33); fair copy, revised (f. 98), wanting stanzas 4–5, beginning 'There's no wind about these seas', one page (containing also KpR 1233).

Bodleian, MS Eng. misc. c. 127, ff. 32a, 32b, 33, 98 (rectos only).

KpR 1225 Corrected first page proof for the Sussex Edition, Vol. XIV; date stamped 2 July 1931.

British Library, Add. MS 55864.

'Though the "*Englishman*" deride it'
First pub. Arthur Windham Baldwin, *The Macdonald Sisters* (London, 1960), p. 226; reprinted Louis Cornell, *Kipling in India* (London and New York, 1966), p. 70; Rutherford, p. 251, as 'Inscriptions in Presentation Copies of *Echoes* (b)'; not in Harbord.

KpR 1226 Fair copy, signed (initials), on the front flyleaf of the presentation copy to Edith Macdonald of *Echoes* (Kpr 308.7).

This copy not included in the list of inscribed copies of *Echoes* in Stewart, pp. 14–16.

Sussex, Baldwin Papers 2/40.

The Thousandth Man ('One man in a thousand, Solomon says')
First pub. with story 'Simple Simon' in *Rewards and Fairies* (London, 1910); collected separately *Songs from Books* (New York, 1912); *Sussex*, XV, 269–70 and *Sussex*, XXXIV, 45–6; Harbord, Verse No. 962.

KpR 1227 Fair copy, revised, in MS Rewards and Fairies, one page.

Cambridge University Library, ADD 6850, f. 98.

KpR 1228 Fair copy, signed, one page.

Sussex, KP 24/57.

KpR 1229 Fair copy, in MS Writings and Songs (pp. 46–8).

Berg.

The Three-Decker ('Full thirty foot she towered from waterline to rail.')
First pub. *Saturday Review*, 14 July 1894, as 'The Old Three-Decker'; collected *The Seven Seas* (New York, 1896); *Sussex*, XXXIII, 102–5; Harbord, Verse No. 607.

KpR 1230 Fair copy, slightly revised, fourteen stanzas, here entitled 'The Old Three Decker.', signed, 2 leaves (rectos only), printer's copy for first publication, annotated 'Proof to author tonight WHP[ollock]'.

For a reproduction of the first page, see FACSIMILES.

Dalhousie University.

KpR 1231 Fair copy, 3 stanzas only, in Berg Booklet [pp. 21–2].

Berg.

KpR 1232 Fair copy, revised, in MS Years Between, wanting the epigraph; watermarked 1894.

British Library, Add. MS 44841, f. 97.

A Three-Part Song ('I'm just in love with all these three')
First pub. with story '"Dymchurch Flit"' in *Puck of Pook's Hill* (London, 1906); collected separately *Songs from Books* (New York, 1912); *Sussex*, XIV, 241 and *Sussex*, XXXIV, 7; Harbord, Verse No. 900.

KpR 1233 Three MSS, in MS Puck: fair copy, revised (f. 96), here untitled; fair copy (f. 97), annotated 'To follow Dymchurch Flit'; earliest fair copy, revised (f. 98), here untitled and beginning 'I'm all in love with all these three', one page (containing also KpR 1224).

Bodleian, MS Eng. misc. c. 127, ff. 96–8 (rectos only).

KpR 1234 Corrected first page proof for the Sussex Edition, Vol. XIV; date stamped 2 July 1931.

British Library, Add. MS 55864.

The Threshold ('In their deepest caverns of limestone')
First pub. with story 'Unprofessional' in *Limits and Renewals* (London, 1932); collected separately *Inclusive Verse* [1933]; *Sussex*, XI, 271–3 and *Sussex*, XXXIV, 419–20; Harbord, Verse No. 1213.

KpR 1235 Corrected page proof in Limits and Renewals Proof; date stamped 21 January 1932.

Syracuse University.

KpR 1236 Corrected first page proof for the Sussex Edition, Vol. XI; date stamped 14 October 1932.

British Library, Add. MS 55862.

To A. E. W., see KpR 52.

'To all our people now on land'
First printed Harbord (1969), Verse No. 1036.

KpR 1237 Fair copy, in MS Years Between, signed (initials), annotated in pencil by CK 'Xmas card Repulse 1916.'.

British Library, Add. MS 44841, f. 133.

To Helen — The Doll's House ('The Villa belongs to one Helen')
First printed Harbord (1969), Verse No. 641.

KpR 1238 Five lines, signed (initials); dated summer 1895.

Owned (1960) by Helen (Peabody) Peck (see Harbord).

'To help the dogs — the starving dogs, The dogs of London town'
No publication traced; not in Harbord.

KpR 1239 Draft of c. 14 lines, including sketches, on p. 3 of a folded leaf (containing also KpR 1979); watermarked 1888.

Berg.

'To him who lost and fell — who rose and won'
No publication traced; not in Harbord.

KpR 1240 Fair copy of 4 lines, signed (initials), on one page of Astley Hall, Stourport notepaper.

Library of Congress, Rare Book Division, Colt Collection.

To James Whitcomb Riley ('Your trails runs to the westward')
First pub. (8 lines only, without title) in Will M. Clemens, *A Ken of Kipling* (New York, 1899); in full in *The Cornhill Booklet* (Boston, [1900]); first authorized pub. *The Complete Works of James Whitcomb Riley*, ed. Edmund Henry Eitel, 6 vols (Indianapolis, [1913]), IV, 513; *Sussex*, XXXV, 185; Harbord, Verse No. 474.

KpR 1241 Transcript in an unidentified hand, here entitled 'To J. W. R.', signed 'R. K.', 2 pages (one leaf).

Indiana University, Riley MSS.

To Mrs Hill, see KpR 107, 495–7.

'To Mrs 'Ill at Belvidere'
First printed in Hanzel Galleries sale catalogue, 23–4 September [1973] (David Gage Joyce Sale), Lot 290; first pub. 'News & Notes', *KJ*, 41 (1974), p. 2; Rutherford, p. 456, as 'Inscription in a Copy of *In Black and White* Presented to Mrs Hill'.

KpR 1242 Eight lines, signed 'the Author', in a presentation copy to Edmonia Hill of *In Black and White* (Allahabad, [1888]).

Hanzel Galleries, 23–4 September [1973] (David Gage Joyce Sale), Lot 290.

'To our first critics send we these'
First pub. (first and last stanzas) in *Grolier Catalogue* (1930), p. 9; reprinted Harbord, Verse No. 85, as 'A Dedication in a copy of *Echoes* to The Ladies of Warwick Gardens'; Rutherford, pp. 252–3, as 'Inscriptions in Presentation Copies of *Echoes* (e)'.

KpR 1243 Fair copy, signed by Kipling 'Ruddy & Trix', on front flyleaf of a copy of *Echoes* (KpR 310) presented 'To the Ladies of Warwick Gardens' (i.e., Miss Winnard and the Misses Craik) in 1884.

Berg.

To the Address of W. W. H. ('"Oh, Hunter, and Oh blower of the horn')
First pub. *The Pioneer*, 1 June 1888; reprinted Harbord, Verse No. 319; Rutherford, pp. 404–8.

KpR 1244 Corrected galley proof for first publication, annotated 'This hasn't appeared any where yet....But for any thing's sake show it to no one.'.

Library of Congress, Rare Book Division, Carpenter Kipling Collection.

To the City of Bombay, see KpR 275.

To the Companions ('How comes it that, at even-tide')
First pub. with story 'The United Idolators' in *Debits and Credits* (London, 1926); collected separately *Inclusive Verse* [1927]; *Sussex*, XVII (*Stalky & Co.*), 195–6 and *Sussex*, XXXIV, 367–8; Harbord, Verse No. 1140.

KpR 1245 Fair copy, one page, annotated 'type final/to follow: The United Idolators.'.

Sussex, KP 24/58.

KpR 1246 Corrected first page proof for the Sussex Edition, Vol. XVII; date stamped 27 March 1931.

British Library, Add. MS 55867.

To the Companions ('Like the Oak whose roots descend')

This poem was read out in Kipling's absence at the ceremonial dinner commemorating Pepys's Tercentenary, Magdalene College, Cambridge, 1933. First pub. *The Times*, 23 February 1933; *Sussex*, XXXV, 294–5; Harbord, Verse No. 1216.

KpR 1247 Fair copy, signed, framed, one page; 1933.

Magdalene College, Cambridge.

To the Duke of Connaught, see KpR 1033–5.

To the Ladies of Warwick Gardens, see KpR 1243.

To the reader ('In prince or King there is no power —')
No publication traced; not in Harbord.

KpR 1248 Draft, c. three 4-line stanzas, one page (verso of KpR 1375).

Sussex, KP 24/62.

To the True Romance ('Thy face is far from this our war')
First pub. as opening poem in *Many Inventions* (London and New York, 1893); collected *The Seven Seas* (New York, 1896); *Sussex*, V, ix–xii and *Sussex*, XXXIII, 82–5; Harbord, Verse No. 594.

KpR 1249 Fair copy, revised, in MS Years Between, including an additional stanza, 2 leaves (rectos only), annotated 'To go as introduction'; watermarked 1890.

British Library, Add. MS 44841, ff. 124–5 (rectos only).

KpR 1250 Stanza 1, inscribed on title page of a copy of *The Jungle Book* (London and New York, 1894).

This MS printed in American Art Association sale catalogue.

American Art Association, 10–12 May 1920 (James Carleton Young Sale), Lot 647.

KpR 1251 Stanza 1, inscribed on the title page of a copy of *Wee Willie Winkie: The Phantom 'Rickshaw: Under the Deodars*, Macmillan's Uniform Edition (London, 1899), presented to Joan Severn, August 1900.

Parke Bernet, 16 October 1962 (Kern Sale), Lot 180.

To the Unknown Goddess ('Will you conquer my heart with your beauty, my soul going out from afar?')
First pub. *The Pioneer*, 27 January 1885; collected *Departmental Ditties* (1886); *Sussex*

KpR 1252 Fair copy, including a false start, in MS Words, Wise and Otherwise [pp. 18–22].

Berg.

To These People ('"Peace upon Earth to people of good will"')
First printed Harbord (1969), Verse No. 340 (see pp. 5663–4); first pub. Rutherford (1986), pp. 442–5.

KpR 1253 Fair copy, 4 pages (one leaf), signed; dated 25 December 1888.

Library of Congress, Rare Book Division, Carpenter Kipling Collection.

KpR 1254 Fair copy, slightly revised, here untitled, signed, 3 pages (one leaf); dated (possibly in another hand) 25 December 1888.

This MS printed Nora Foster Stovel, 'The Inky "Gamin" and the "Egotistical Tongue": Viewing Kipling the Person and the Poet through an Unpublished Poem', *ELT*, 29 (1986), 140–7.

Dalhousie University.

To Wolcott Balestier ('Beyond the path of the outmost sun through utter darkness hurled')
First pub. (a version entitled 'The Blind Bug') in *National Observer*, 27 December 1890; revised version first pub. in *Barrack-Room Ballads* (1892), as 'Dedication to Wolcott Balestier'; *Sussex*, XXXII, 167–70; Harbord, Verse No. 484, as 'The Blind Bug' (where last four stanzas of first version are printed).

KpR 1255 Printed copy of the first publication (entitled 'The Blind Bug'), extensively revised by RK and containing his sketches in the margins.

Library of Congress, Rare Book Division, Carpenter Kipling Collection.

To You [A Reminiscence] ('A memory of our sojourn by the Sea')
First pub. Rutherford (1986), p. 70; not in Harbord. For another version of these lines, see KpR 1161.

KpR 1256 Fair copy, here entitled 'A Reminiscence', in Sussex Notebook 1 (p. 112); dated 'Orig. Aug. 1881.'.

Sussex, KP 24/3.

KpR 1257 Fair copy, here entitled 'To You', annotated in an unidentified hand 'To E. Macdonald', in Sussex Notebook 3 (last page of book).

Sussex, KP 24/1.

A Toast, see KpR 742.

Tobacco [Unpublished Sonnet by Keats: To a Pipe] ('Sweet is the Rose's scent — Tobacco's smell')
First pub. *Echoes* (Lahore, [1884]); *Sussex*, XXXV, 73; Rutherford, p. 57; Harbord, Verse No. 127.

KpR 1258 Here entitled 'Unpublished Sonnet by Keats' and subtitled 'To a Pipe', written on p. 186, at the end of Keats's 'The Eve of St Agnes' in a copy of *Longer English Poems*, ed. J. W. Hales (London, 1878) (see KpR 2303).

Library of Congress, Rare Book Division, Batchelder Collection.

'Together' ('When Horse and Rider each can trust the other everywhere')
First pub. C. R. L. Fletcher and Rudyard Kipling, *A History of England* (Oxford and London, 1911); collected separately *Songs from Books* (1915); *Sussex*, XXXIV, 282–3; Harbord, Verse No. 982.

KpR 1259 Revised, here untitled, in MS Years Between, annotated '*type*.'.

British Library, Add. MS 44841, f. 71.

Tomlinson ('Now Tomlinson gave up the ghost at his house in Berkeley Square')
First pub. *National Observer*, 23 January 1892; collected *Barrack-Room Ballads* (1892); *Sussex*, XXXII, 322–9; Harbord, Verse No. 519.

KpR 1260 Corrected typescript of version submitted to W. E. Henley (and containing his annotations as well) for first publication containing 10 unpublished lines, 5 numbered leaves (rectos only) and a title page.

Facsimile portion in E. W. Martindell, *Fragmenta Condita* (privately printed, 1922) and facsimile of f. 2 in Martindell, facing p. 62 (where this typescript is collated, pp. 160–2); additional lines from this typescript printed Harbord, Verse No. 519.

Princeton, Robert H. Taylor Collection.

KpR 1260.5 Corrected page proof for *Barrack-Room Ballads* (1892).

British Library, Loan 97 (deposited by John Aris, 1989).

Tommy ('I went into a public-'ouse to get a pint o' beer')
First pub. *Scots Observer* and *St James's Gazette*, 1 March 1890, as 'The Queen's Uniform'; collected *Barrack-Room Ballads* (1892); *Sussex*, XXXII, 177–9; Harbord, Verse No. 416.

KpR 1261 Fair copy, here untitled, one page (on a leaf containing also KpR 1389), with a scrap annotated by Sir E. Morley Sampson that the poems were 'Written out by [Kipling] for me to sing at a Concert on S.S. Empress of China/ Yokohama to Vancouver. July 1892.'.

Typed transcript among Lord Beaverbrook's correspondence with RK (and annotated 'Original sent New Brunswick Museum on 19/4/44') in House of Lords Record Office, BBK/C/199.

University of New Brunswick, Beaverbrook Collection.

KpR 1261.3 Corrected page proof for *Barrack-Room Ballads* (1892); date stamped 12 February 1892.

British Library, Loan 97 (deposited by John Aris, 1989).

'"Tommy" you was when it began'
First pub. introductory lines to 'Service Songs' in *The Five Nations* (London, 1903); sometimes collected later as 'The Service Man'; *Sussex*, XXXIII, 301; Harbord, Verse No. 828, as 'The Service Man *or* Tommy Atkins *or* Tommy You Was When it Began'.

KpR 1261.5 In MS Five Nations, annotated 'To precede service songs'.

National Library of Australia, MS 94.

'To-night, God knows what thing shall tide', see KpR 177.

Toolungala Stockyard Chorus, see KpR 177.

The Totem ('Ere the mother's milk had dried')
First pub. with story 'The Tie' in *Limits and Renewals* (London, 1932); collected separately *Inclusive Verse* [1933]; *Sussex*, XI, 73–4 and *Sussex*, XXXIV, 404; Harbord, Verse No. 1214.

KpR 1262 Slightly corrected first page proof for the Sussex Edition, Vol. XI; date stamped 14 October 1932.

British Library, Add. MS 55862.

'The Trade' ('They bear, in place of classic names')
First pub. with 'Tales of "The Trade" (I. Some Work in the Baltic)' in *The Times*, 21 June 1916; revised version containing an additional opening stanza pub. as Prelude to *Maidstone Magazine. Vol. I. 1915.* [London, 1916]; collected separately *Inclusive Verse* (1919); *Sussex*, XXVI, 301–2 and *Sussex*, XXXIV, 257–8; Harbord, Verse No. 1021.

KpR 1263 Fair copy, revised, followed by four lines headed 'L'Envoi' beginning 'Even the *Maidstone Magazine*', 2 numbered leaves (rectos only), in MS Non-Fiction.

British Library, Add. MS 45542, ff. 66–7 (rectos only).

Translation, see KpR 1163.

A Translation ('There are whose study is of smells')
First pub. with story 'Regulus' in *A Diversity of Creatures* (London, 1917); collected separately *Inclusive Verse* (1919); *Sussex*, XVII (*Stalky & Co.*), 253–4 and *Sussex*, XXXIV, 324–5; Harbord, Verse No. 1048. For a Latin version, see KpR 9.

KpR 1264 Fair copy, here entitled in pencil 'Horace Bk V: 3:', in MS Diversity of Creatures (f. 90).

University of Edinburgh, Dk. 2. 8.

KpR 1265 Corrected first page proof for the Sussex Edition, Vol. XVII; date stamped 27 March 1931.

British Library, Add. MS 55867.

[Treatment for a Cold], see KpR 453.

A Tree Song ('Of all the trees that grow so fair')
First pub. with story 'Weland's Sword' in *Puck of Pook's Hill* (London, 1906); collected separately *Songs from Books* (New York, 1912); *Sussex*, XIV, 27–8 and *Sussex*, XXXIV, 18–19; Harbord, Verse No. 888.

KpR 1266 In MS Puck, here untitled.

Bodleian, MS Eng. misc. c. 127, f. 14.

KpR 1267 Fair copy of stanza 1 only, signed (initials), one leaf of Bateman's notepaper.

Cornell University.

KpR 1268 Corrections on p. 23 of KpR 1112.

Yale.

KpR 1269 Corrected first page proof for the Sussex Edition, Vol. XIV; date stamped 2 July 1931.

British Library, Add. MS 55864.

'Troopin'' ('Troopin', troopin', troopin' to the sea')
First pub. (refrain only) as heading to story 'The Big Drunk Draf' ' in *Week's News*, 24 March 1888; reprinted *Sussex*, II, 33; listed Harbord, Verse No. 301, as 'Barrack Room Ballad'; first pub. in full separately *Scots Observer*, 17 May 1890, as 'Barrack-Room Ballad'; collected *Barrack-Room Ballads* (1892); *Sussex*, XXXII, 213–14; Harbord, Verse No. 436A.

KpR 1270 Fair copy of lines 1–12 only, here entitled 'Barrack Room Ballads. III. "Time Expired"', one page.

Sussex, KP 24/60.

KpR 1270.5 Corrected page proof for *Barrack-Room Ballads* (1892); date stamped 12 February 1892.

British Library, Loan 97 (deposited by John Aris, 1989).

The Trouble of Curtiss Who Lodged in the Basement
('Ever so little to shew for it')
First pub. Rutherford (1986), pp. 122–8; not in Harbord.

KpR 1271 Fair copy, here originally entitled 'The <Folly> trouble of Curtiss...', in Sussex Notebook 1 (pp. 65–75); dated 7 March 1882, including a later annotation dated 4 April 1883.

Sussex, KP 24/3.

KpR 1272 Fair copy, in Sussex Notebook 3 (first series, pp. 40–50); dated 7 March 1882.

Sussex, KP 24/1.

KpR 1273 Transcript by JLK in Sussex Notebook 2 [pp. 26–36].

Sussex, KP 24/2.

The Truce of the Bear ('Yearly, with tent and rifle, our careless white men go')
First pub. *Literature*, 1 October 1898; collected *The Five Nations* (London, 1903); *Sussex*, XXXIII, 213–16; Harbord, Verse No. 725.

KpR 1274 In MS Seven Seas: (1) fair copy, revised, annotated 'typewrite: urgent' (f. 49); (2) drafts (ff. 50–6, rectos only, and 51v); (3) fair copy, revised, of stanzas 1–7, here beginning 'Yearly lusting for strength our careless white men go' (f. 57); (4) fair copy, revised, signed, annotated 'typewrite urgent' (f. 58).

Magdalene College, Cambridge.

KpR 1275 Drafts of lines 13–16 (beginning 'I knew his times and his seasons'), on verso of a leaf of the MS of *Kim* (KpR 1789).

British Library, Add. MS 44840, f. 19v *rev*.

KpR 1276 Fair copy, signed, one page (cut up by typesetter into 5 parts).

Columbia University, Engel Collection.

KpR 1277 Fair copy of lines 45–50, including sketches, in Berg Booklet [pp. 5–6].

Berg.

A Truthful Song ('I tell this tale, which is strictly true')
First pub. with story 'The Wrong Thing' in *Rewards and Fairies* (London, 1910); collected separately *Songs from Books* (New York, 1912); *Sussex*, XV, 55–6 and *Sussex*, XXXIV, 177–9; Harbord, Verse No. 963.

KpR 1278 Fair copy, slightly revised, here entitled 'A Tree Song', in MS Rewards and Fairies, annotated 'to precede The Wrong Thing'.

Cambridge University Library, ADD 6850, f. 19.

KpR 1279 Corrected first page proof for the Sussex Edition, Vol. XV; date stamped 18 September 1931.

British Library, Add. MS 55865.

A Tryst [The Tryst in Summer] ('The night comes down in rain, grey garmented —')
First pub. Rutherford (1986), pp. 147–8; not in Harbord.

KpR 1280 Fair copy, here entitled 'The Tryst in Summer', in Sussex Notebook 1 (p. 101), dated 27 May [1882].

Sussex KP 24/3.

KpR 1281 Fair copy, here entitled 'A Tryst', being the second of 'Four Sonnets' (see also KpR 48, 524, 922), in Sussex Notebook 3 (first series, p. 70); dated 27 May 1882.

Sussex, KP 24/1.

KpR 1282 Transcript by AMK, in Sussex Notebook 2 [p. 59].

Sussex, KP 24/2.

The Turkey and the Algebra ('The Turkey and in algebra')
No publication traced; not in Harbord.

KpR 1283 Five stanzas, in a letter to 'Esteemed Turkey' (i.e., Amelia Clifford), presenting Todhunter's *Algebra* to her, [1890].

Berg.

The Two Cousins, see KpR 919–20.

Two Kopjes ('Only two African kopjes')
First pub. *The Five Nations* (London, 1903); *Sussex*, XXXIII, 317–19; Harbord, Verse No. 833.

KpR 1284 In MS Five Nations.

National Library of Australia, MS 94.

Two Lives ('Two lives, one sweet and one most sad, I lead')
First pub. *The World*, 8 November 1882; *Sussex*, XXXV, 169; Rutherford, p. 137; Harbord, Verse No. 42.

KpR 1285 Fair copy, revised, in Sussex Notebook 1 (p. 85); dated 27 March [1882] and with a later annotation dated 7 June 1883.

Sussex, KP 24/3.

KpR 1286 Fair copy, in Sussex Notebook 3 (first series, p. 22); dated 27 March 1882.

Sussex, KP 24/1.

KpR 1287 Fair copy, revised, one page, annotated 'The World. Nov. 8. 1882.', signed (initials).

This MS not mentioned Rutherford.

Library of Congress, Rare Book Division, Carpenter Kipling Collection.

KpR 1288 Transcript by AMK, in Sussex Notebook 2 [p. 50]; dated March 1882.

Sussex, KP 24/2.

Two Months, see KpR 561–2, 1019.

Two Players ('Two Players playing games against the Gods.')
First pub. Rutherford (1986), pp. 83–4; Harbord, Verse No. 66.

KpR 1289 Fair copy, subtitled 'Or Jay's Mourning Warehouse', in Sussex Notebook 3 (first series, pp. 58–9); dated 8 December 1881.

Sussex, KP 24/1.

KpR 1290 Fair copy, in MS Sundry Phansies.

Berg.

The Two Potters, see KpR 179–80, 183.

The Two-Sided Man ('Much I owe to the Lands that grew —')
First pub. (stanzas 1 and 5 only, beginning 'Something I owe to the soil that grew') as heading to Chapter 8 of the one-volume edition of *Kim* (1901); reprinted *Sussex*, XXI, 176; first pub. in full separately *Songs from Books* (New York, 1912); *Sussex*, XXXIV, 108; Harbord, Verse No. 779.

KpR 1291 Fair copy, in MS Writings and Songs (pp. 36–7).

Berg.

KpR 1292 Stanzas 1 and 5, added in red ink to the proof of *Kim* (KpR 1790) as verse heading to Chapter 8; date stamped 15 August 1900.

Unlocated.

KpR 1293 Correction on p. 129 of KpR 1112.

Yale.

'Ubique' ('There is a word you often see, pronounce it as you may —')
First pub. *The Five Nations* (London, 1903); *Sussex*, XXXIII, 339–41; Harbord, Verse No. 834.

KpR 1294 In MS Five Nations.

National Library of Australia, MS 94.

Ulster ('The dark eleventh hour')
First pub. *Morning Post*, 9 April 1912; collected *The Years Between* (London, [1919]); *Sussex*, XXXIII, 356–7; Harbord, Verse No. 999A.

KpR 1295 Fair copy, revised, in MS Years Between, including four cancelled lines, annotated 'Copyrighted in the United States of America by Rudyard Kipling'.

British Library, Add. MS 44841, f. 13.

KpR 1296 Corrected typescript, signed, 2 leaves (rectos only), enclosed in a letter to Lord Beaverbrook, Bateman's, 6 April 1912.

Harvard, bMS Eng 809.4(33).

KpR 1297 Typescript, 2 leaves (rectos only), probably a carbon.

Syracuse University.

Understanding ('One time when ashen clouds received the sun')
First pub. Rutherford (1986), p. 156; not in Harbord.

KpR 1298 Fair copy, revised, in Sussex Notebook 1 (p. 111); dated 21 June [1882].

Sussex, KP 24/3.

The Undertaker's Horse ('The eldest son bestrides him')
First pub. *Civil and Military Gazette*, 8 October 1885; collected *Departmental Ditties* (1886); *Sussex*, XXXII, 140–1; Harbord, Verse No. 148. See also KpR 280.

KpR 1299 Fair copy, in MS Departmental Ditties (pp. 74–6).

Berg.

KpR 1300 Corrections on pp. 99–100 of KpR 282.

Yale.

Unpublished Fragment of Pope: An Amateur ('Our friend just hears that doggrel writing pays')
First pub. Rutherford (1986), p. 57; not in Harbord.

KpR 1301 Written above the notes on Pope on p. 286 of a copy of *Longer English Poems*, ed. J. W. Hales (London, 1878) (see KpR 2303).

Library of Congress, Rare Book Division, Batchelder Collection.

Unpublished Fragment of Shelley ('Rather than this should happen, I would see')
First pub. Rutherford (1986), p. 58; not in Harbord.

KpR 1302 Written on p. 201 of a copy of *Longer English Poems*, ed. J. W. Hales (London, 1878) (see KpR 2303), attributed to 'Canto I, Lament of Xenoria [?], I. 270'.

Library of Congress, Rare Book Division, Batchelder Collection.

Untimely ('Nothing in life has been made by man for man's using')
First pub. with story 'The Eye of Allah' in *Debits and Credits* (London, 1926); collected separately *Inclusive Verse* [1927]; *Sussex*, X, 285 and *Sussex*, XXXIV, 393; Harbord, Verse No. 1141.

KpR 1303 Three fair copies, revised, 2 on one page (the first cancelled and annotated 'To precede "The Eye of Allah"'), the third entitled 'The Inventors' and beginning 'Nothing on earth has been done or made or discovered', one page (containing also KpR 598).

Sussex, KP 24/61.

KpR 1304 Corrected first page proof for the Sussex Edition, Vol. X; date stamped 30 December 1931.

British Library, Add. MS 55861.

'Unto whose use the pregnant suns are poised', see KpR 174–5.

Upstairs
No publication traced; not in Harbord.

KpR 1305 Typescript, revised, of a dramatic work, 17 numbered leaves (rectos only).

Berg.

The Vampire ('A fool there was and he made his prayer')
First pub. *The New Gallery. Regent Street Tenth Summer Exhibition MDCCCXCVII* (London, [1897]) and *Daily Mail*, 17 April 1897; collected *Inclusive Verse* (1919); *Sussex*, XXXV, 202–3; Harbord, Verse No. 699.

KpR 1306 Typescript, 2 numbered leaves (rectos only).

Syracuse University.

KpR 1307 Transcript by Charlotte Shaw (Mrs George Bernard Shaw); c. 1885.

British Library, Add. MS 56505.

'Veil them, cover them, wall them round —'
First pub. as heading to 'Letting in the Jungle' in *The Second Jungle Book* (London and New York, 1895); collected separately *Songs from Books* (London, 1913); *Sussex*, XII, 127 and *Sussex*, XXXIV, 233, as 'Chapter Heading'; Harbord, Verse No. 647.

KpR 1308 Fair copy, in MS Jungle Books, headed 'Verse heading for Letting in the Jungle', one page (containing also KpR 674), annotated 'set these up! send MS & proof to me & keep ready Rudyard Kipling'; watermarked [189]4.

British Library, Add. MS 45540, f. 133.

The Verdicts ('Not in the thick of the fight')
First pub. (without title) with 'Destroyers in Jutland IV The Minds of Men' in *Daily Telegraph* and *New York Times*, 31 October 1916; collected separately *The Years Between* (London, [1919]); *Sussex*, XXVI, 373–4 and *Sussex*, XXXIII, 392; Harbord, Verse No. 1024.

KpR 1309 Revised, here untitled, in MS Non-Fiction, being the conclusion to the MS of 'Destroyers at Jutland IV' (KpR 1538).

British Library, Add. MS 45542, f. 108.

KpR 1310 Revised, here untitled, seven stanzas, one page.

Sotheby's, 9–10 December 1968, Lot 761, sold to Rota.

KpR 1311 Typescript, here untitled, with the typescript of 'Destroyers at Jutland IV' (KpR 1539).

Dalhousie University.

Verse Fragments and Limericks, see KpR 27, 500, 504, 1028, 1189, 1345.

Verse Letter to Sidney Low (extract), see KpR 1173.

Verses From a Letter to Andrew Lang, see KpR 506.

Verses on Fruit Plates
First pub. Rutherford (1986), pp. 460–2; listed with first lines only in Harbord, Verse Nos. 373–8.

KpR 1312 Six verses, hand painted and fired on china fruit plates, written by Kipling while staying with the Hills at Beaver, Pennsylvania, August 1889, including: 'Apples' ('By Cause of Us was Eden lost'), 'Berries' ('We be gamins of the Wood'), 'Grapes' ('Wee have sett, sith Time began'), 'The Peach' ('Ye Garden's royal Pride am I'), 'Plums' ('Children of ye Garden We'), 'The Watermelon' ('I sprawl in the sunshine & grow').

Photocopies of the plates at Cornell University.

Library of Congress, Rare Book Division, Carpenter Kipling Collection.

Verses on Games
First pub. in copyright edition of 12 copies of *Verses Written for Nicholson's 'Almanac of Sports for 1898'* (London and New York, 1897); William Nicholson and Rudyard Kipling, *An Almanac of the Twelve Sports* first pub. London, 1898 and New York, 1898; collected separately *Inclusive Verse* (1919); *Sussex*, XXXV, 204–8; Harbord, Verse Nos. 706–19, as 'An Almanac of Twelve Sports *or* Verses on Games'.

KpR 1313 Fair copy, revised, of 11 (of the 12) verses written for *An Almanac of the Twelve Sports*, wanting 'Fishing' and including 'Boating' instead of 'Rowing', bound with the accompanying eleven illustrations by William Nicholson and an undated letter to William Heinemann from 'The Elms', Rottingdean.

Pierpont Morgan, MA 935.

KpR 1314 Transcript of two discarded lines beginning 'Youth on the box and liquor in the boot' (a version of 'Coaching') in an unidentified hand, written on a proof of Nicholson's drawing 'Coaching' with a note saying that this version of the caption was censored by CK.

The original autograph MS of these two lines was apparently at one time pasted on this proof.

Library of Congress, Rare Book Division, Colt Collection.

Verses on the Charleville Hotel, Mussoorie ('A burning sun in cloudless skies')
First pub. Rutherford (1986), pp. 451–2; not in Harbord.

KpR 1315 Two verse captions, in the album of photographs kept by the Hills (see KpR 88), one beginning as above, the other beginning 'And there were men with a thousand wants', under photos of the Charleville Hotel, visited in June 1888.

Library of Congress, Rare Book Division, Carpenter Kipling Collection.

'Very sadly did we leave it, but we gave our hearts in pledge', see KpR 1638.

The Veterans ('To-day, across our fathers' graves')
First pub. in *Morning Post*, 24 December 1907, as '1857–1907'; collected *The Years Between* (London, [1919]); *Sussex*, XXXIII, 353; Harbord, Verse No. 909.

KpR 1316 Fair copy, revised, in MS Years Between, here untitled, annotated 'Verses for D. T. Mutiny dinner'.

British Library, Add. MS 44841, f. 10.

Vibarts Moralities, see KpR 177, 1788.

'Victoria by the Grace of God – sends in her Schedule D.'
No publication traced; not in Harbord.

KpR 1316.5 Rough draft verses on income tax, in MS Day's Work.

British Library, Add. MS 45541, f. 236v *rev*.

Virginibus Puerisque, see KpR 506.

The Virginity ('Try as he will, no man breaks wholly loose')
First pub. (stanzas 1, 3, 4, 6 only, without title) as heading to 'Sea Travel' ('Egypt of the Magicians, No. I') in *Nash's Magazine*, June 1914; first pub. in full separately *The Years Between* (London, [1919]); *Sussex*, XXXIII, 424; Harbord, Verse No. 1004.

KpR 1317 Fair copy, revised, of four-stanza version, here untitled and beginning 'Try as he may...', in MS Years Between, headed 'heading to Letter I', on a torn leaf (containing the barely visible first line of 'Jobson's Amen' (see KpR 557) at the bottom).

British Library, Add. MS 44841, f. 44.

KpR 1318 Typescript, revised, here beginning 'Try as he may...', one page.

Sotheby's, 9–10 December 1968, Lot 767, sold to Rota.

KpR 1319 Two copies of corrected galley proof of first publication (see KpR 1574), both containing a revision to these lines; the second set date stamped 11 March 1914.

Dalhousie University.

A Visitation, see KpR 1016.

The Voortrekker ('The gull shall whistle in his wake, the blind wave break in fire.')
First pub. as heading to 'From Tideway to Tideway No. VII "Captains Courageous"' in *New York Sun*, 27 November 1892; collected separately *Songs from Books* (New York, 1912); *Sussex*, XXXIV, 79; Harbord, Verse No. 529.

KpR 1320 Fair copy of a variant version, here untitled, in a letter to Alfred Deakin, Bateman's, [1911].

National Library of Australia, MS 1540/1/2897.

KpR 1321 Corrections on pp. 93–4 of KpR 1112.

Yale.

A Voyage ('Our galley chafes against the Quay')
First pub. Rutherford (1986), p. 157; not in Harbord.

KpR 1322 Fair copy, in Sussex Notebook 1 (pp. 113–14); dated 6 July [1882].

Sussex, KP 24/3.

KpR 1323 Fair copy, in Sussex Notebook 3 (second series, pp. 7–9).

Sussex, KP 24/1.

The Wage-Slaves ('Oh, glorious are the guarded heights')
First pub. *The Five Nations* (London, 1903); *Sussex*, XXXIII, 224–6; Harbord, Verse No. 835.

KpR 1324 In MS Five Nations.

National Library of Australia, MS 94.

KpR 1325 Revision and corrections on pp. 61–2 of KpR 365.

Yale.

'Walton's Bank — by the Eddystone —'
No publication traced; not in Harbord.

KpR 1326 Very rough draft, on one sheet of 'Cawsand N^{r} Plymouth' notepaper.

Library of Congress, Rare Book Division, Colt Collection.

KpR 1327 Fair copy, 15 lines, one page, on a leaf torn from a guest-book, under the date 25 August 1909; annotated 'Rudyard Kipling who went there on business Aug. 24 —'.

Library of Congress, Rare Book Division, Colt Collection.

The Waster ('From the date that the doors of his prep-school close')
First pub. *Sussex*, XXXV (1939), 282–3; Harbord, Verse No. 1170.

KpR 1328 Fair copy of a version of stanza 1, here untitled, signed and dated 10 January 1925, followed by 4 additional lines in the hand of Sir Hugh Clifford; in a letter to Clifford, Bateman's, 19 December 1927.

This MS printed in Allan Hunter, 'Two Unpublished Letters and a Poem by Kipling', *N&Q*, 229 (1984), pp. 502–3.

Owned (1984) Jamie Sutton (see *N&Q*).

The Way Av Ut, see KpR 102.5.

'Way Down the Ravi River' ('I wandered by the riverside')
First pub. *Echoes* (Lahore, [1884]); *Sussex*, XXXV, 99; Rutherford, pp. 197–8; Harbord, Verse No. 129.

KpR 1329 Fair copy, in Sussex Notebook 1 (pp. 158–9); dated September 1883.

Sussex, KP 24/3.

The Way Through the Woods ('They shut the road through the woods')
First pub. with story 'Marklake Witches' in *Rewards and Fairies* (London, 1910); collected separately *Songs from Books* (New York, 1912); *Sussex*, XV, 85 and *Sussex*, XXXIV, 6; Harbord, Verse No. 965.

KpR 1330 Fair copy, revised, here entitled 'The Road through the Woods', in MS Rewards and Fairies, annotated 'please type. to follow Marklake Witches'.

Cambridge University Library, ADD 6850, f. 32.

KpR 1331 Fair copy, 21 lines, here entitled 'The Road through the Woods' and beginning 'There was once a road through the woods', signed, one page, in a bound volume of autograph MS poems presented to Thomas Hardy on his 80th birthday entitled 'A Tribute to Thomas Hardy O.M./June 2 1919'.

Dorset County Museum.

KpR 1332 Dated 1930.

Kent Archives Office, Maidstone, reported in 1975 that this MS was among the Stanhope MSS (No. 661); it is not now among the Stanhope MSS deposited there and is likely to be at Chevening.

KpR 1333 Corrected first page proof for the Sussex Edition, Vol. XV; date stamped 18 September 1931.

British Library, Add. MS 55865.

Waytinge ('Doubte not that Pleasure cometh in the End, —')
First pub. Rutherford (1986), pp. 69–70; Harbord, Verse No. 14 (where these lines are mistaken for others with same title beginning 'Waytinge! Wearilie waytinge').

KpR 1334 Fair copy, in Sussex Notebook 3 (first series, pp. 9–10); dated 9 August 1881.

Sussex, KP 24/1.

KpR 1335 Fair copy, in MS Sundry Phansies.

Berg.

We and They ('Father, Mother, and Me')
First pub. with story 'A Friend of the Family' in *Debits and Credits* (London, 1926); collected separately *Inclusive Verse* [1927]; *Sussex*, X, 251–2 and *Sussex*, XXXIV, 388–9; Harbord, Verse No. 1143.

KpR 1336 Corrected first page proof for the Sussex Edition, Vol. X; date stamped 30 December 1931.

British Library, Add. MS 55861.

'We be the Gods of the East', see KpR 184, 186–7.

'We have showed thee, O man', see KpR 1756.

'We meet in an evil land', see KpR 184–5, 187.

'We who have been brough [sic] much together'
No publication traced; not in Harbord.

KpR 1337 Fair copy of 4 lines, signed 'B. H. Walton and the Bantam', sent for Walton's use, in a card to him, Bateman's, 15 November 1905.

Library of Congress, Rare Book Division, Colt Collection.

'We will free our land o' the foul o taint'
No publication traced; not in Harbord.

KpR 1338 Draft of 4 stanzas of 'Irish rebellion song', on verso of first leaf of MS of KpR 1385.

Berg.

'We'll never come back any more boys', see KpR 179.

The Wet Litany ('When the water's countenance')
First pub. with story '"Their Lawful Occasions"' in *Traffics and Discoveries* (London, 1904); collected separately *Songs from Books* (New York, 1912); *Sussex*, VII, 107–8 (beginning 'When the Channel's countenance') and *Sussex*, XXXIV, 186–7; Harbord, Verse No. 876.

KpR 1339 Successive drafts and fair copies, here untitled, in MS Traffics and Discoveries, annotated variously 'Lawful Occasions', 'To precede Lawful occasions' and 'To precede Lawful occasions on a separate page', 4 pages.

McGill University.

KpR 1340 Fair copy, signed (initials), 2 leaves (rectos only).

Library of Congress, Rare Book Division, Colt Collection.

KpR 1341 Correction on p. 221 of KpR 1112.

Yale.

KpR 1342 Corrected first page proof for the Sussex Edition, Vol. VII, here originally beginning as above and revised to 'When the Channel's countenance'; date stamped 22 March 1932.

British Library, Add. MS 55858.

'What did the Colonel's Lady think?', see KpR 585–6.

What Happened ('Hurree Chunder Mookerjee, pride of Bow Bazar')
First pub. *The Pioneer*, 2 January 1888; collected *Departmental Ditties*, 4th ed (1890); *Sussex*, XXXII, 26–8; Harbord, Verse No. 284.

KpR 1343 Fair copy, including a sketch, in MS Departmental Ditties (pp. 16–18, a second start (cancelled) on p. 22).

Berg.

KpR 1344 Corrections on pp. 25–6 of KpR 282.

Yale.

'What shall we do with a king who is dead'
First pub. Rutherford (1986), p. 458, as 'Verse Fragments and Limericks (e)'; not in Harbord.

KpR 1345 Draft of 6 unfinished lines, on a leaf (containing also KpR 27, 1906).

Library of Congress, Rare Book Division, Carpenter Kipling Collection, Pen and Brush Sketches, Item 6.

What the People Said ('By the well, where the bullocks go')
First pub. *Civil and Military Gazette*, 4 May 1887, as 'A Jubilee Ode. Punjab Peasant's Point of View'; collected *Departmental Ditties*, 3rd ed (1888); *Sussex*, XXXII, 138–9; Harbord, Verse No. 260.

KpR 1346 Fair copy, revised, in MS Departmental Ditties (pp. 77–9), here subtitled 'June 21st 1887.'.

Berg.

KpR 1347 Corrections on pp. 97–8 of KpR 282.

Yale.

What the Young Man's Heart Said to Him ('Break, ah Break!')
First pub. Rutherford (1986), pp. 158–9; not in Harbord.

KpR 1348 Fair copy, cancelled, in Sussex Notebook 1 (pp. 116–17); dated 9 July [1882].

Sussex, KP 24/3.

'When a Lover hies abroad', see KpR 185, 187.

'When a Woman kills a Chicken'
First pub. in text of story 'As Easy As A. B. C.' in *Family Magazine*, 25 February–12 March 1912; collected *A Diversity of Creatures* (London, 1917); *Sussex*, IX, 14; Harbord, Verse No. 997.

KpR 1349 Couplet, in the text of the MS of 'As Easy As A. B. C.' (KpR 1404), in MS Diversity of Creatures (f. 5).

University of Edinburgh, Dk. 2. 8.

'When Earth's last picture is painted and the tubes are twisted and dried', see KpR 629–31.

'When Haldane's Hound upon Haldane's hobbies'
No publication traced; not in Harbord.

KpR 1350 Four line postscript, followed by 'I think Swinburne wrote this!', in a letter to Stanley Baldwin, 18 March 1911.

Typed transcript at Sussex, KP 11/3.

Dalhousie University.

'When Ollie sings, the amorous cat'
No publication traced; not in Harbord.

KpR 1350.5 Typescript, 32 lines (4 cancelled), one page, annotated in unidentified hands 'Typed, I'm pretty sure, by R. K....Composed by R. Kipling and A. W. Baldwin after hearing O. R. Baldwin singing to the piano. about <1922.> 1919 or 21 at Astley' and 'Begun by AWB, finished by RK'.

Sussex, Baldwin Papers 2/10.

'When 'Omer smote 'is bloomin' lyre'
First pub. *Barrack-Room Ballads* (1892); also collected *The Seven Seas* (New York, 1896); *Sussex*, XXXIII, 125; Harbord, Verse No. 557.

KpR 1351 Revised, in MS Years Between, annotated 'on separate page — no heading introducing Barrack room ballads', one page.

British Library, Add. MS 44841, f. 129.

'When skies are grey instead of blue', see KpR 750.

'When the cabin port-holes are dark and green'
First pub. with story 'How the Whale Got His Throat' in *Just So Stories* (London, 1902); collected separately *Songs from Books* (London, 1913); *Sussex*, XIII, 13 and *Sussex*, XXXIV, 237, as 'Chapter Heading'; Harbord, Verse No. 789.

KpR 1352 Revised, in MS Just So Stories, annotated 'on separate page to follow How Whale got his Throat.'.

British Library, Add. MS 59840, f. 11.

KpR 1353 Fair copy, including 2 drawings captioned by the relevant lines, 3 leaves (rectos only).

Berg.

'When the earth was sick and the skies were grey', see KpR 177.

'When the Great Ark' ('When the Great Ark, in Vigo Bay')
First pub. (without title) with 'Mountains and the Pacific' ('Letters to the Family, No. VII') in *Morning Post*, 23 April 1908; collected separately *Songs from Books* (New York, 1912); *Sussex*, XXIV (*Letters of Travel*), 217 and *Sussex*, XXXIV, 75; Harbord, Verse No. 917.

KpR 1354 Fair copy, revised, in MS Non-Fiction, in the MS of 'Letters to the Family' (KpR 1826), annotated 'To precede Letters to the Family. VII'.

British Library, Add. MS 45542, f. 144.

KpR 1355 Revision on p. 88 of KpR 1112.

Yale.

KpR 1356 Slightly corrected first page proof for the Sussex Edition, Vol. XXIV, here untitled; date stamped 30 April 1935.

British Library, Add. MS 55874.

Where the Shoe Pinches ('The pain of parting — once and once again')
First pub. Rutherford (1986), p. 140; not in Harbord.

KpR 1357 Fair copy, in Sussex Notebook 3 (first series, p. 61); dated 10 April 1882.

Sussex, KP 24/1.

KpR 1358 Transcript by AMK, in Sussex Notebook 2 [p. 56]; dated April 1882.

Sussex, KP 24/2.

'Whereat the withered flower well content'
No publication traced; not in Harbord.

KpR 1359 Fair copy, 4 lines, on a scrap.

Berg.

White Horses ('Where run your colts at pasture?')
First pub. *Literature*, 23 October 1897; collected *The Five Nations* (London, 1903); *Sussex*, XXXIII, 193–5; Harbord, Verse No. 703.

KpR 1360 Successive drafts and fair copies, in MS Seven Seas (ff. 76–84, rectos only); watermarked 1896.

Magdalene College, Cambridge.

KpR 1361 In MS Five Nations.

National Library of Australia, MS 94.

KpR 1362 Fair copy, containing ten 8-line stanzas, signed, 2 pages.

Sotheby's, 17–19 February 1936, Lot 327, sold to Fanning.

The White Man's Burden ('Take up the White Man's burden —')
First pub. *The Times*, 4 February 1899; collected *The Five Nations* (London, 1903); *Sussex*, XXXIII, 240–2; Harbord, Verse No. 729.

KpR 1363 Successive drafts and fair copies, in MS Seven Seas (ff. 109–22, mostly rectos only); watermarked 1896 and 1897.

Magdalene College, Cambridge.

KpR 1364 Fair copy, revised, 6 stanzas (without stanza 5), entitled and signed in a different ink, one page.

Library of Congress, Manuscript Division, Miscellaneous Manuscripts Collection.

KpR 1365 Fair copy, subtitled '— An Address to the United States — 1899 —', 2 pages (one leaf).

Dalhousie University.

KpR 1366 Fair copy, including a variant line 26, on the end flyleaf of a copy of *The Seven Seas* (London, 1896) (containing also KpR 951).

Princeton, Robert H. Taylor Collection.

KpR 1367 Quotation of five lines, inscribed on title page of a presentation copy to J. L. Thompson of *The White Man's Burden* (New York, 1899).

Facsimile in Livingston, *Bibliography*, p. 208.

Unlocated.

'Who is the Public I write for?'
First pub. (one stanza) in Martindell (1923), p. 7; stanzas 1–2 first pub. in an abstract of a paper presented by E. W. Martindell, 'Some Less-known Kipling Writings', *KJ*, October 1927, pp. 14–15; first printed in full (facsimile) Ballard (1935), p. 16; reprinted Harbord, Verse No. 84, as 'Echoes — Dedication to Kipling's Mother'; Rutherford, pp. 250–1, as 'Inscriptions in Presentation Copies of *Echoes* (a)'.

KpR 1368 Fair copy, signed 'R.', on the flyleaf of a copy of *Echoes* (Lahore, [1884]) inscribed 'The Mater [i.e., Mrs Tavenor Perry] from Ruddy. August. 22nd 1884'.

Facsimile in *Grolier Catalogue*, plate V and in Ballard, p. 16; this copy listed in Stewart, p. 15 (copy 2).

Syracuse University.

The Widow at Windsor (''Ave you 'eard o' the Widow at Windsor')
First pub. *Scots Observer*, 26 April 1890; collected *Barrack-Room Ballads* (1892); *Sussex*, XXXII, 202–3; Harbord, Verse No. 432.

KpR 1369 Fair copy, here entitled 'Barrack Room Ballads VIII The Sons of the Widow.', one page.

Syracuse University.

KpR 1370 Quotation of lines 1–5, in a letter to Sylvestre Dorian, 1 June 1927.

Facsimile of this letter at Texas.

Unlocated.

KpR 1370.5 Corrected page proof for *Barrack-Room Ballads* (1892); date stamped 12 February 1892.

British Library, Loan 97 (deposited by John Aris, 1989).

The Widower ('For a season there must be pain')
First pub. (version of last stanza) as heading to Chapter 12 in the 12-chapter happy-ending version of *The Light that Failed* (London, 1890); first pub. in full *Songs from Books* (New York, 1912); *Sussex*, XXXIV, 130; Harbord, Verse No. 459B.

KpR 1371 Fair copy, without the last stanza, in Sussex Notebook 3 (second series, pp. 1–2), here entitled 'Prescience' and beginning 'For a season there shall be pain'.

Sussex, KP 24/1.

KpR 1372 Fair copy, revised, in Sussex Notebook 1 (pp. 107–8), here entitled '<Prescience> Patience'; dated 15 June [1882].

Sussex, KP 24/3.

KpR 1373 Draft of the last stanza (as in first pub.), in the draft of *The Light that Failed* (KpR 1834) where it is the heading to a chapter numbered 11.

Princeton, Doubleday Collection, Box 5.

KpR 1374 Transcript by AMK, in Sussex Notebook 2 [pp. 45–6], here entitled 'Prescience' and without last stanza; dated July 1882.

Sussex, KP 24/2.

The Widow's Party ('"Where have you been this while away')
First pub. *Barrack-Room Ballads* (1892); *Sussex*, XXXII, 215–16; Harbord, Verse No. 558.

KpR 1375 Fair copy, revised, one page (on a leaf containing also KpR 1248).

Sussex, KP 24/62.

KpR 1375.5 Corrected page proof for first publication; date stamped 12 February 1892.

British Library, Loan 97 (deposited by John Aris, 1989).

'Wilful-Missing' ('There is a world outside the one you know')
First pub. *The Five Nations* (London, 1903); *Sussex*, XXXIII, 337–8; Harbord, Verse No. 836.

KpR 1376 In MS Five Nations.

National Library of Australia, MS 94.

The Winners ('What is the moral? Who rides may read.')
First pub. as 'L'Envoi' to *The Story of the Gadsbys* (Allahabad, [1888]); reprinted *Sussex*, II, 233; collected separately *Songs from Books* (New York, 1912); *Sussex*, XXXIV, 47; Harbord, Verse No. 318.

KpR 1377 Draft, here entitled 'L'Envoi.' and begining 'What is the moral? Who runs may read —', 2 leaves (rectos only); [Allahabad, 1889].

Library of Congress, Rare Book Division, Carpenter Kipling Collection.

KpR 1378 Fair copy, in MS Writings and Songs (pp. 41–2).

Berg.

KpR 1379 Corrected first page proof for the Sussex Edition, Vol. II, here entitled 'L'Envoi'; date stamped 14 May 1931.

British Library, Add. MS 55853.

The Wishing-Caps ('Life's all getting and giving')
First pub. (last 12 lines) as chapter heading to Chapter 4 of the one-volume edition of *Kim* (1901); *Sussex*, XXI, 79; first pub. in full *Songs from Books* (New York, 1912); *Sussex*, XXXIV, 147–8; Harbord, Verse No. 780.

KpR 1380 Correction on p. 166 of KpR 1112.

Yale.

With a Fan to the Mother ('This is a fan for my mother')
First pub. Rutherford (1986), p. 351; not in Harbord.

KpR 1381 Dated Christmas 1886.

Sussex, KP 2/1.

With a Locket ('What can I send to a sweet little sister')
First pub. Rutherford (1986), pp. 186–7; not in Harbord.

KpR 1382 Fair copy, in Sussex Notebook 1; [probably March–April 1883].

Sussex, KP 24/3.

With a Study Chair to the Pater ('"Tell mee where is Fancie bred')
First pub. Rutherford (1986), pp. 351–2; not in Harbord.

KpR 1383 [Christmas 1886?].

Sussex, KP 2/1.

With Drake in the Tropics ('South and far south below the Line')
First pub. C. R. L. Fletcher and Rudyard Kipling, *A History of England* (Oxford and London, 1911); collected separately *Songs from Books* (1915); *Sussex*, XXXIV, 280–1; Harbord, Verse No. 981.

KpR 1384 Revised, in MS Years Between, annotated 'type please RK'.

British Library, Add. MS 44841, f. 70.

With Scindia to Delhi ('The wreath of banquet overnight lay withered on the neck').
First pub. *Barrack-Room Ballads* (1892); *Sussex*, XXXII, 254–60; Harbord, Verse No. 559.

KpR 1385 Fair copy, revised, here untitled, 2 leaves (rectos only), containing KpR 1338 on verso of first leaf.

Berg.

KpR 1385.5 Corrected page proof for first publication.

British Library, Loan 97 (deposited by John Aris, 1989).

The Wooing of the Sword ('"What will ye give me for a heart?')
First pub. Rutherford (1986), pp. 142–3; not in Harbord.

KpR 1386 Fair copy, in Sussex Notebook 3 (first series, pp. 59–60); dated 27 April 1882.

Sussex, KP 24/1.

'Ye Printer's Devil, verie wyse'
First pub. Rutherford (1986), pp. 352–3; not in Harbord.

KpR 1387 Including a drawing, signed.

Sussex, KP 2/1.

Yealm, see KpR 517.

The Years Between
First pub. London, [1919]; *Sussex*, XXXIII.

KpR 1388 Typescript, revised by RK, of notes on the poems in this volume, headed 'The Years Between', containing page references presumably to the first edition, 8 numbered leaves (rectos only) and a title page, the latter annotated by CK 'The numbers of pages may not correspond with those in the American edition', enclosed in a letter to Frank N. Doubleday, Brown's Hotel, 18 March 1919.

Another copy of this typescript (containing one correction by RK) is at Sussex (KP 25/1); it is annotated by CK 'as sent to Doubleday'.

Princeton, Doubleday Collection, Box 3, Bound Vol. II, Item 20 (letter is Item 19).

'Yet at the last, ere our spearmen had found him', see KpR 182.

'You may talk o' your music the sweetest o' tunes'
No publication traced; not in Harbord.

KpR 1389 Fair copy, one revision, one page (on a leaf containing also KpR 1261), with a scrap annotated by Sir E. Morley Sampson that the 'two songs by Rudyard Kipling' were 'written out by him for me to sing at a Concert on S.S. Empress of China/Yokohama to Vancouver. July 1892.'.

Typed transcript of this MS among Lord Beaverbrook's correspondence with RK (and annotated 'original sent New Brunswick Museum on 19/4/44') in House of Lords Record Office (BBK/C/199).

University of New Brunswick, Beaverbrook Collection.

'You mustn't swim till you're six weeks old', see KpR 2235.

The Young British Soldier ('When the 'arf-made recruity goes out to the East')
First pub. *Scots Observer*, 28 June 1890; collected *Barrack-Room Ballads* (1892); *Sussex*, XXXII, 207–9; Harbord, Verse No. 465.

KpR 1389.5 Corrected page proof for *Barrack-Room Ballads* (1892); date stamped 12 February 1892.

British Library, Loan 97 (deposited by John Aris, 1989).

The Young Queen ('Her hand was still on her sword-hilt, the spur was still on her heel')
First pub. *The Times*, 4 October 1900; collected *The Five Nations* (London, 1903); *Sussex*, XXXIII, 255–7; Harbord, Verse No. 757.

KpR 1390 In MS Five Nations.

National Library of Australia, MS 94.

KpR 1391 Corrections on p. 101 of KpR 365.

Yale.

'Your patience, Sirs. The Devil took me up', see KpR 185, 187.

'Your trough first — *aqua pura: quantum subb*'
No publication traced; not in Harbord.

KpR 1392 Thirty-eight lines, a parody of Robert Browning, signed 'R. B.', one page, inserted in Brander Matthews's copy of *Many Inventions* (London, 1893) (containing also KpR 456, 1018).

Cornell University.

Zion ('The Doorkeepers of Zion')
First pub. (without title) with 'Destroyers at Jutland III The Meaning of "Joss"' in *Daily Telegraph* and *New York Times*, 26 October 1916; collected separately *The Years Between* (London, [1919]); *Sussex*, XXVI, 359–60 and *Sussex*, XXXIII, 369–70; Harbord, Verse No. 1023.

KpR 1393 Revised, here untitled, in MS Years Between, containing a cancelled version of stanza 4, annotated 'Destroyers at Jutland III'.

British Library, Add. MS 44841, f. 19.

KpR 1394 Typescript, here untitled, in the typescript of 'Destroyers at Jutland. III' (KpR 1539).

Dalhousie University.

Zogbaum ('Zogbaum draws with a pencil')
First pub. *New York Tribune*, 10 January 1899; reprinted Harbord, Verse No. 730.

KpR 1395 Four 4-line stanzas, inscribed in a presentation copy to Captain (later Rear Admiral) Robley D. Evans ('Fighting Bob') of *Plain Tales from the Hills*, Macmillan's Uniform Edition (London, 1899).

In his book *A Sailor's Log* (New York, 1901), Rear Admiral Evans says that this volume had been stolen from him; a typescript is in Scrapbook 5 at Sussex (KP 28/5).

Unlocated.

PROSE

Across a Continent, for 'From Tideway to Tideway No II', see KpR 1647–9.

Actions and Reactions, for an inscribed copy, see KpR 357.

The Amir's Homily
First pub. *Life's Handicap* (London and New York, 1891); *Sussex*, IV, 355–9; Harbord, II, 992–3.

KpR 1396 Corrected first page proof for the Sussex Edition; date stamped 13 February 1932.

British Library, Add. MS 55855.

Among the Railway Folk
First pub. *The Pioneer*, 24 July, 4 and 8 August 1888; collected *From Sea to Sea*, 2 vols (New York, 1899); *Sussex*, XXIII, 257–82; Harbord, II, 903–7.

KpR 1397 Corrected galley proof among proofs for *From Sea to Sea*, annotated 'To printer. This is to follow City of Dreadful Night', signed (initials), stamped '1st REV.'; date stamped 10 May 1899.

Library of Congress, Rare Book Division, Carpenter Kipling Collection.

KpR 1398 Corrected page proof, in Vol. II of proofs for *From Sea to Sea* (KpR 1642), annotated 'Print off RK', signed (initials) *passim*, stamped '2nd REV.'; date stamped 20 May 1899.

Library of Congress, Rare Book Division, Carpenter Kipling Collection.

KpR 1399 Corrected first page proof for the Sussex Edition; date stamped 18 November 1932.

British Library, Add. MS 55873.

The Army of a Dream

First pub. *Morning Post*, 15–18 June 1904; collected *Traffics and Discoveries* (London, 1904) with poem 'Song of the Old Guard'; *Sussex*, VII, 251–305; Harbord, IV, 1912–22.

KpR 1400 Revised, here entitled 'The Dream of Belligerontius' on the first page, in MS Traffics and Discoveries, 24 pages.

McGill University.

KpR 1401 Corrected galley proof, probably for the first publication.

Yale.

KpR 1402 Corrected first page proof for the Sussex Edition; date stamped 22 March 1932.

British Library, Add. MS 55858.

The Arrest of Lieutenant Golightly

First pub. *Civil and Military Gazette*, 23 November 1886; collected *Plain Tales from the Hills* (Calcutta and London, 1888); *Sussex*, I, 191–7; Harbord, I, 62–4.

KpR 1403 Corrected first page proof for the Sussex Edition; date stamped 12 September 1931.

British Library, Add. MS 55852.

As Easy as A. B. C.

First pub. *Family Magazine*, 25 February–12 March 1912; collected with verse 'MacDonough's Song' in *A Diversity of Creatures* (London, 1917); *Sussex*, IX, 3–41; Harbord, VII, 3049–55.

KpR 1404 Draft, wanting the epigraph, in MS Diversity of Creatures (ff. 11–12, rectos only) (including KpR 670, 1349).

University of Edinburgh, Dk. 2. 8.

KpR 1405 Corrected first page proof for the Sussex Edition; date stamped 28 April 1932.

British Library, Add. MS 55860.

At Howli Thana

First pub. *Week's News*, 31 March 1888; collected *In Black and White* (Allahabad, [1888]); *Sussex*, II, 269–75; Harbord, I, 319–20.

KpR 1406 Revisions in a copy of the second collected edition (Allahabad, 1889) (KpR 1747).

Berg.

KpR 1407 Corrections in a copy of the first collected edition (KpR 1745).

Syracuse University.

KpR 1408 Annotations explaining Indian words, in a copy of the first collected edition (KpR 1746), pp. [24]–6, 28–9.

Berg.

KpR 1409 Corrected first page proof for the Sussex Edition; date stamped 14 May 1931.

British Library, Add. MS 55853.

At the End of the Passage

First pub. *Boston Herald*, 20 July 1890; collected (with a version of stanza 3 of 'Himalayan' as heading) *Life's Handicap* (London and New York, 1891); *Sussex*, IV, 191–218; Harbord, II, 972–7. The verse heading reprinted separately *Sussex*, XXXIV, 228–9; the complete poem first pub. *Early Verse* (1900); *Sussex*, XXXV, 94–5; Harbord, Verse No. 110.

KpR 1410 Fair copy, revised, 11 numbered leaves (rectos only), without a verse heading; watermarked 1888.

Dalhousie University.

KpR 1411 Corrected galley proof.

Syracuse University.

KpR 1412 Corrected first page proof for the Sussex Edition (including corrections to verse heading); date stamped 13 February 1932.

British Library, Add. MS 55855.

At the Pit's Mouth

First pub. *Under the Deodars* (Allahabad, [1888]); *Sussex*, III, 37–45; Harbord, I, 339–40. For an early MS (the germ of this story), see KpR 1415.

KpR 1413 Corrections in a copy of the first publication (KpR 2175).

Syracuse University.

KpR 1414 Corrected first page proof for the Sussex Edition; date stamped 18 September 1931.

British Library, Add. MS 55854.

At the Pit's Mouth: Personal Recollections of Duncan Parrenness

No publication traced; Harbord, I, 552, as 'Uncollected No. 28'; Harbord (I, 339) says this MS contains the germ for both the published story 'At the Pit's Mouth' (KpR 1413) and 'The Hill of Illusion' (KpR 1691–3).

KpR 1415 Draft of an unfinished story, some passages written in two unidentified hands, in parallel columns, the right-hand column headed 'Personal narrative of C. S. translated from his [torn] diary by R. K.' with entries of July–August 1884 in diary form, the left-hand column headed 'Incidental Digressions' containing commentary by the so-called 'editor' or 'translator' and instructions for the working up of the story by the person to whom story was sent for final writing, 12 leaves (rectos only).

Facsimile portions in *New York Herald Tribune*, 23 March 1924, p. 3.

Berg.

At Twenty-Two

First pub. *Week's News*, 18 February 1888; collected *In Black and White* (Allahabad, [1888]); *Sussex*, II, 293–307; Harbord, I, 322.

KpR 1416 Revisions in a copy of the second collected edition (Allahabad, 1889) (KpR 1747).

Berg.

KpR 1417 Corrections in a copy of the first collected edition (KpR 1745).

Syracuse University.

KpR 1418 Annotations explaining Indian words, in a copy of the first collected edition (KpR 1746), pp. 43, 48, 50–3.

Berg.

KpR 1419 Corrected first page proof for the Sussex Edition; date stamped 14 May 1931.

British Library, Add. MS 55853.

Aunt Ellen

First pub. with poems 'The Playmate' and 'Naaman's Song' in *Limits and Renewals* (London, 1932); *Sussex*, XI, 117–40; Harbord, VII, 3207–13.

KpR 1420 Corrected page proof in Limits and Renewals Proof; date stamped 18 and 19 January 1932.

Syracuse University.

KpR 1421 Corrected first page proof for the Sussex Edition; date stamped 14 October 1932.

British Library, Add. MS 55862.

Baa, Baa, Black Sheep

First pub. *Week's News*, Christmas Supplement, 21 December 1888; collected *Wee Willie Winkie* (Allahabad, [1888]); *Sussex*, III, 317–54; Harbord, I, 374–82.

KpR 1422 Fair copy, revised, in MS Essays and Stories, including sketches (and the verses in the text beginning 'Our vanship was the Asia —' on [f. 35v]), on [ff. 25v–38v] of the notebook and continuing on the first 5 leaves of the (inserted) notebook, the first leaf of which is annotated 'Re Baa Baa Black Sheep by R. K. So sorry the end pages got forgotten. I send them along now...', 36 pages in all.

The six lines beginning 'Our vanship was the Asia —' are listed as a questionable attribution in Harbord, Verse No. 345, as 'Navarino *or* That Day at Navarino *or* the Battle of Navarino'.

Berg.

KpR 1423 Captions from the text of the story accompanying nine original pen-and-ink sketches, 3 pages.

Berg.

KpR 1424 Corrections in a copy of the first collected edition (KpR 2229).

Syracuse University.

KpR 1425 Annotations explaining Indian words, in a copy of the first collected edition (KpR 2230), pp. [15]–16, 20, 45, 49.

Berg.

KpR 1426 Corrected first page proof for the Sussex Edition; date stamped 18 September 1931.

British Library, Add. MS 55854.

A Bank Fraud
First pub. *Civil and Military Gazette*, 14 April 1887; collected *Plain Tales from the Hills* (Calcutta and London, 1888); *Sussex*, I, 253–61; Harbord, I, 70–1.

KpR 1427 Corrected first page proof for the Sussex Edition; date stamped 12 September 1931.

British Library, Add. MS 55852.

A Bazar *Dhulip*, see KpR 2078–9.

Beauty Spots
First pub. separately New York, 1931; reprinted *Strand Magazine*, January 1932; collected with poems 'Neighbours' and 'The Expert' in *Limits and Renewals* (London, 1932); *Sussex*, XI, 279–304; Harbord, VII, 3260–2. For proof corrections to the New York, 1932 edition, see *Limits and Renewals*.

KpR 1428 Corrected page proof in Limits and Renewals Proof; date stamped 22 January 1932.

Syracuse University.

KpR 1429 Corrected first page proof for the Sussex Edition; date stamped 14 October 1932.

British Library, Add. MS 55862.

The Beginning of the Armadilloes
First pub. *Ladies Home Journal*, May 1900; collected with verses 'I've never sailed the Amazon' in *Just So Stories* (London, 1902); *Sussex*, XIII, 99–114; Harbord, IV, 1667–71. The two quatrains in the text beginning 'Can't curl, but can swim —' are listed Harbord, Verse Nos. 752–3.

KpR 1430 In MS Just So Stories, including: first page of a draft version, here untitled, annotated in pencil 'This is a portion of the rough draft of "The beginning of the Armadilloes"' (f. 53, watermarked 1896); fair copy, revised, of the story, entitled in pencil, the two quatrains in the text here beginning 'Curls up but can't swim', 3 numbered leaves (rectos only) (ff. 54–6, watermarked 1895); the two captions (ff. 50, watermarked 1901, and 57); the 3 original illustrations (ff. 51–2, 58).

British Library, Add. MS 59840, ff. 50–8 (rectos only).

KpR 1431 Typescript, revised and entitled by RK, signed, 8 numbered leaves (rectos only), including the two quatrains (pp. 5 and 7) the first here beginning 'Curls up, but can't swim —'.

Library of Congress, Rare Book Division, Carpenter Kipling Collection, *Animal Stories*.

KpR 1432 Corrected galley proof for first publication, including revisions to the first quatrain, signed (initials) *passim*.

Library of Congress, Rare Book Division, Carpenter Kipling Collection, *Animal Stories*.

KpR 1433 Corrected first page proof for the Sussex Edition; date stamped 29 October 1932.

British Library, Add. MS 55863.

Below the Mill Dam
First pub. *Monthly Review*, September 1902; collected with poem 'Our Fathers Also' in *Traffics and Discoveries* (London, 1904); *Sussex*, VII, 375–98; Harbord, IV, 1932–42.

KpR 1434 Revised, here entitled 'Below the Dam.', in MS Traffics and Discoveries, 12 pages.

McGill University.

KpR 1435 Typescript, revised, including the change of title from 'The Letting In of Waters', 29 numbered leaves (rectos only), with label of A. P. Watt attached, annotated on a covering leaf 'This typescript from which the [American] copyright print...was set up, was given to me by W. H. Page in 1902 or 1903' (signed William Ivins).

Syracuse University.

KpR 1436 Corrected first page proof for the Sussex Edition; date stamped 22 March 1932.

British Library, Add. MS 55858.

The Benefactors

First pub. *National Review* and *American Magazine*, July 1912; *Sussex*, XXX, 269–84; Harbord, V, 2589–91, as 'Uncollected No. 249'.

KpR 1437 Revised, in MS Debits and Credits, 6 pages (ff. 216–21, rectos only).

University of Durham.

KpR 1438 Corrected first galley proof set up for a projected volume of the Sussex Edition (marked 'Uncollected'); date stamped 17 November 1930.

British Library, Add. MS 55850.

Bertran and Bimi

First pub. *New Zealand Herald*, 1891; collected *Mine Own People* (New York, [1891]) and *Life's Handicap* (London and New York, 1891); *Sussex*, IV, 315–22; Harbord, II, 987–8.

KpR 1439 Corrected first page proof for the Sussex Edition; date stamped 13 February 1932.

British Library, Add. MS 55855.

Beyond the Pale

First pub. *Plain Tales from the Hills* (Calcutta and London, 1888); *Sussex*, I, 235–42; Harbord, I, 68–9.

KpR 1440 Corrected first page proof (including KpR 667) for the Sussex Edition; date stamped 12 September 1931.

British Library, Add. MS 55852.

The Big Drunk Draf'

First pub. *Week's News*, 24 March 1888; collected *Soldier's Three* (Allahabad, 1888); *Sussex*, II, 33–45; Harbord, I, 283–4. For notes on this story, see KpR 2287.

KpR 1441 Corrections in a copy of the first collected edition (KpR 2081).

Syracuse University.

KpR 1442 Annotations explaining Indian words, in a copy of the first collected edition (KpR 2082), pp. 23, 25, 27.

Berg.

KpR 1443 Corrected first page proof for the Sussex Edition; date stamped 14 May 1931.

British Library, Add. MS 55853.

The Bisara of Pooree

First pub. *Civil and Military Gazette*, 4 March 1887; collected *Plain Tales from the Hills* (Calcutta and London, 1888); *Sussex*, I, 341–7; Harbord, I, 84–6.

KpR 1444 Corrected first page proof for the Sussex Edition; date stamped 12 September 1931.

British Library, Add. MS 55852.

Bitters Neat

First pub. *Civil and Military Gazette*, 19 April 1887, in series 'Plain Tales from the Hills'; collected *Plain Tales from the Hills*, Outward Bound Edition, Vol. I (New York, 1898); *Sussex*, I, 45–51; Harbord, III, 1598–9, as 'Uncollected No. 77'.

KpR 1445 Corrected first page proof for the Sussex Edition; date stamped 12 September 1931.

British Library, Add. MS 55852.

Black Jack

First pub. *Soldiers Three* (Allahabad, 1888); *Sussex*, II, 103–26; Harbord, I, 292–5. An uncorrected galley proof for the first publication (inscribed by RK 'Proof of "Black Jack", given to Mrs Hill by R. K.') is at Dalhousie University.

KpR 1446 Fair copy, revised, 35 pages (18 leaves, the first being an illustrated title page).

Berg.

KpR 1447 Corrections in a copy of the first publication (KpR 2081).

Syracuse University.

KpR 1448 Annotations explaining Indian words, in a copy of the first publication (KpR 2082), pp. 80, 85–7, 90, 93, 96.

Berg.

KpR 1449 Corrected first page proof for the Sussex Edition; date stamped 14 May 1931.

British Library, Add. MS 55853.

The Bold 'Prentice
First pub. *Youth's Companion*, 19 September 1895; collected with poem 'The Nurses' in *Land and Sea Tales* (London, 1923); *Sussex*, XVI, 147–60; Harbord, VI, 2898–900.

KpR 1450 Revised, in MS Day's Work, wanting the introductory note, 5 numbered leaves (rectos only); watermarked 1890.

British Library, Add. MS 45541, ff. 23–7 (rectos only).

KpR 1451 Corrected first page proof for the Sussex Edition; date stamped 14 December 1931.

British Library, Add. MS 55866.

The Bonds of Discipline
First pub. with poem 'Poseidon's Law' in *Windsor Magazine*, August 1903; collected *Traffics and Discoveries* (London, 1904); *Sussex*, VII, 41–73; Harbord, IV, 1706–22.

KpR 1452 Revised, in MS Traffics and Discoveries, 10 numbered pages.

McGill University.

KpR 1453 Corrected first page proof for the Sussex Edition; date stamped 22 March 1932.

British Library, Add. MS 55858.

The Bow Flume Cable-Car
First pub. *Civil and Military Gazette*, 10 September 1889; collected *Abaft the Funnel* (New York, 1909); *Sussex*, XXIX, 185–90; Harbord, II, 696–7.

KpR 1454 Fair copy, revised (thin paper carbon copy), in MS From Sea to Sea (see KpR 1634), 4 numbered pages.

Huntington, HM 12429, Vol. 2, pp. 85–8.

Brazilian Sketches
This series of 7 articles and accompanying poems first pub. *Morning Post*, 29 November–20 December 1927; first collected *Letters of Travel*, *Sussex*, XXIV (1938); collected separately New York, 1940; Harbord, V, 2343–6. Uncorrected galleys (19 galleys for 7 instalments, each with verse heading) are at Dalhousie University; uncorrected galleys for the 1940 edition are at the Berg. For verses published with 'Brazilian Sketches', see KpR 787, 851, 1058, 1132.

KpR 1455 Corrected first page proof for the Sussex Edition; date stamped 19 June 1936.

British Library, Add. MS 55874.

'Bread Upon the Waters'
First pub. *The Graphic*, Christmas Number 1896 and *McClure's Magazine*, December 1896; collected *The Day's Work* (New York, 1898); *Sussex*, VI, 293–327; Harbord, III, 1405–24.

KpR 1456 Revised, in MS Day's Work, 12 leaves (rectos only); watermarked 1894.

British Library, Add. MS 45541, ff. 91–102 (rectos only).

KpR 1457 Printed copy of first publication (pp. 16–17, 20–21 of *The Graphic*) used for the first collected edition.

Princeton, Doubleday Collection, Bound Vol. V (oversize).

KpR 1458 Corrected first page proof for the Sussex Edition; date stamped 27 June 1931.

British Library, Add. MS 55857.

The Bride's Progress, see KpR 2078–9.

The Bridge-Builders
First pub. *Illustrated London News*, Christmas Number 1893; collected *The Day's Work* (New York, 1898); *Sussex*, VI, 3–47; Harbord, III, 1381–48.

KpR 1459 Fair copy, revised, and revised later in red, in MS Day's Work, 18 numbered leaves (rectos only), annotated (in red) 'proof as early as possible to R. Kipling Brattleboro Vermont U.S.A.'; watermarked 1890.

British Library, Add. MS 45541, ff. 73–90 (rectos only).

KpR 1460 Copy of first publication, extensively revised.

Library of Congress, Rare Book Division, Carpenter Kipling Collection.

KpR 1461 Fragment of a corrected page proof, 2 pages numbered 4–5 (one leaf), signed (initials).

Dalhousie University.

KpR 1462 Corrected first page proof for the Sussex Edition; date stamped 27 June 1931.

British Library, Add. MS 55857.

Britain and the War, see KpR 1992.

The Broken-Link Handicap
First pub. *Civil and Military Gazette*, 6 April 1887; collected *Plain Tales from the Hills* (Calcutta and London, 1888); *Sussex*, I, 225–31; Harbord, I, 66–8.

KpR 1463 Corrected first page proof for the Sussex Edition; date stamped 12 September 1931.

British Library, Add. MS 55852.

The Bronckhorst Divorce-Case
First pub. *Plain Tales from the Hills* (Calcutta and London, 1888); *Sussex*, I, 323–30; Harbord, I, 81–2.

KpR 1464 Corrected first page proof for the Sussex Edition; date stamped 12 September 1931.

British Library, Add. MS 55852.

Brother Square-Toes
First pub. *The Delineator*, July 1910; collected with poems 'Philadelphia' and 'If' in *Rewards and Fairies* (London, 1910); *Sussex*, XV, 143–67; Harbord, VI, 2782–90.

KpR 1465 Revised, here untitled, including one page of revised typescript (f. 59), in MS Rewards and Fairies, also including (f. 53) three verses ('Aurettes and Lees', 'There was never a Lee to Warminghurst' and KpR 1149).

'Aurettes and Lees' and 'There was never a Lee to Warminghurst' are listed Harbord, Verse Nos 941–2.

Cambridge University Library, ADD 6850, ff. 53–67 (rectos only).

KpR 1466 Corrected first page proof for the Sussex Edition; date stamped 18 September 1931.

British Library, Add. MS 55865.

'Brugglesmith'
First pub. *Harper's Weekly*, 17 October 1891; collected *Many Inventions* (London and New York, 1893); *Sussex*, V, 337–57; Harbord, III, 1243–8.

KpR 1467 Corrected first page proof for *Humorous Tales* (London, 1931), pp. 437–57; date stamped 5 8 June 1931.

British Library, Add. MS 55847.

KpR 1468 Corrected first page proof for the Sussex Edition; date stamped 10 June 1931.

British Library, Add. MS 55856.

The Brushwood Boy
First pub. *Century Magazine*, December 1895; collected *The Day's Work* (New York, 1898); *Sussex*, VI, 379–423; Harbord, III, 1440–51. An original illustration for this story by Orson Lowell (1899) is at Dalhousie University.

KpR 1469 Revised, in MS Day's Work, 18 numbered pages, including KpR 217, the verses 'E's goin' to do without 'em' (f. 141) and 3 maps showing 'Unknown Continent', 'Sea of Dreams', 'Thirty-mile Ride', etc. (ff. 147–9, rectos only, watermarked 1894).

The verses 'E's goin' to do without 'em' are listed Harbord, Verse No. 643.

British Library, Add. MS 45541, ff. 133–50 (rectos only).

KpR 1470 Fragments of an early draft, including a draft of the opening, pencil sketches and 'City of Sleep' (KpR 216), on 6 leaves composed of 14 scraps put together (originally 4 leaves torn into quarters, and so wanting 2 scraps).

Facsimile portion in Ballard, p. 130.

Pierpont Morgan, MA 1155.

KpR 1471 Corrected typescript, including revisions to the verses 'E's goin' to do without 'em' (p. 33), the autograph addition of the epigraph and KpR 219, 64 leaves (rectos only) numbered 1–36, 36a, 37–63 and 2 inserted autograph leaves.

Pierpont Morgan, MA 936.

KpR 1472 Corrected copy of first publication (pp. 265–80 of *Century Magazine*), used for the first collected edition, including one revision to the poem 'The City of Sleep'.

Princeton, Doubleday Collection, Bound Vol. V (oversize).

KpR 1473 Corrected first page proof for the Sussex Edition; date stamped 27 June 1931.

British Library, Add. MS 55857.

Bubbling Well Road
First pub. *Civil and Military Gazette*, 18 January 1888; collected *Life's Handicap* (London and New York, 1891); *Sussex*, IV, 399–403; Harbord, II, 996–9.

KpR 1474 Corrected first page proof for the Sussex Edition; date stamped 13 February 1932.

British Library, Add. MS 55855.

The Bull that Thought
First pub. *MacLean's Magazine*, 15 November 1924; collected with poem 'Alnaschar and the Oxen' in *Debits and Credits* (London, 1926); *Sussex*, X, 171–9; Harbord, VII, 3153–7.

KpR 1475 Revised, in MS Debits and Credits, 7 numbered pages (ff. 108–14, rectos only), annotated 'type with wide spaces'.

University of Durham.

KpR 1476 Corrected first page proof for *Humorous Tales* (London, 1931) pp. 161–81; date stamped 15 May 1931.

British Library, Add. MS 55847.

KpR 1477 Corrected first page proof for the Sussex Edition; date stamped 30 December 1931.

British Library, Add. MS 55861.

The Burden of Nineveh
First pub. *Civil and Military Gazette*, 6 June 1888; collected *'Turnovers'*, Vol. II (Lahore, [1888]); reprinted Harbord, IV, 2062–6, as 'Uncollected No. 128'.

KpR 1478 Revised clipping of the first publication, in Scrapbook 4 (pp. 68–9).

Sussex, KP 28/4.

A Burgher of the Free State
First pub. with 'A Carol' as verse heading (here untitled) in *Daily Express*, 26–9 June and 2–4 July 1900, as 'Stories of the War IV'; *Sussex*, XXX, 143–95; Harbord, V, 2559–62, as 'Uncollected No. 233'.

KpR 1479 Draft of first 2 pages (ff. 193–4, rectos only), followed by fair copy, revised, of the whole story, 16 pages, both entitled 'Uncle Allen.', in MS Non-Fiction; watermarked 1896 and 1897.

British Library, Add. MS 45542, ff. 193–210 (rectos only).

KpR 1480 Corrected first galley proof set up for a projected volume of the Sussex Edition (marked 'Uncollected'), including KpR 157; date stamped 3 November 1930.

British Library, Add. MS 55850.

The Burning of the *Sarah Sands*
First pub. (early version) as 'On a Burning Troop-Ship' in *Youth's Companion*, 10 November 1898; revised version collected with poem 'The Last Lap' in *Land and Sea Tales* (London, 1923); *Sussex*, XVI, 115–24; Harbord, VI, 2895–6.

KpR 1481 Revised, in MS Day's Work, signed, 3 pages, also containing KpR 2097 on one verso (f. 105v), annotated 'to be typed in duplicate. Will call for copy & M.S. tomorrow afternoon. R. Kipling Rock House'.

British Library, Add. MS 45541, ff. 103–5 (rectos only).

KpR 1482 Corrected first page proof for the Sussex Edition; date stamped 14 December 1931.

British Library, Add. MS 55866.

The Butterfly That Stamped
First pub. *Ladies Home Journal*, October 1902; collected with poem 'There was never a Queen like Balkis' in *Just So Stories* (London, 1902); *Sussex*, XIII, 207–25; Harbord, IV, 1682–9.

KpR 1483 Revised, in MS Just So Stories, including the story, 7 numbered leaves (rectos only) (ff. 129–35), the 2 captions (f. 125, watermarked 1901), and the 3 original illustrations (ff. 126–8, rectos only).

British Library, Add. MS 59840, ff. 125–35 (rectos only).

KpR 1484 Corrected second page proof for the Sussex Edition; date stamped 23 April 1935.

British Library, Add. MS 55863.

By Word of Mouth
First pub. (with verse heading) *Civil and Military Gazette*, 10 June 1887; collected *Plain Tales from the Hills* (Calcutta and London, 1888); *Sussex*, I, 415–20; Harbord, I, 93–5. For verse heading, see KpR 177–8.

KpR 1485 Corrected first page proof for the Sussex Edition; date stamped 12 September 1931.

British Library, Add. MS 55852.

'Captains Courageous', for 'From Tideway to Tideway No. VII', see KpR 1647–9.

Captains Courageous
First pub. serially *McClure's Magazine*, November 1896–May 1897; first pub. in one volume, London and New York, 1897; *Sussex*, XX; Harbord, III, 1291–1319 and IV, 1652–4.

KpR 1486 Fair copy, revised, here entitled 'Harvey Cheyne — <Banker>.', including unpublished passages, 75 leaves (rectos only) erratically numbered, annotated 'to be typed as soon as possible RK'; watermarked 1894.

Facsimile page printed in *British Literary Manuscripts*, plate 114; Kipling presented this MS to Dr James Conland to whom the novel is dedicated.

Pierpont Morgan, MA 982.

KpR 1487 Corrected galley proof of the opening of Chapter 1 for the first American edition (New York, 1897), four galleys numbered 1, 2, 3, 5; the first date stamped June 1897.

Facsimile of opening portion in American Art Association sale catalogue, 20–1 April 1925 (McCutcheon Sale), Lot 242.

Berg.

KpR 1488 Corrected galley proof (numbered 6) for the first American edition, annotated on verso in an unidentified hand 'A galley proof of "Captains Courageous" by Rudyard Kipling, revised by Mr Kipling. Wm W. Ellsworth...of The Century Co. publishers.'.

Library of Congress, Rare Book Division, Colt Collection.

KpR 1489 Corrected first page proof for the Sussex Edition; date stamped 13 November 1931.

British Library, Add. MS 55870.

The Captive
First printed as a copyright pamphlet in America, 1902; first pub. *Collier's Weekly*, 6 December 1902; collected with 'From the Masjid-Al-Aqsa of Sayyid Ahmed (Wahabi)' (later entitled 'The Captive') in *Traffics and Discoveries* (London, 1904); *Sussex*, VII, 5–36; Harbord, IV, 1872–84.

KpR 1490 Revised, 14 leaves (rectos only).

Facsimile last page in Sotheby's sale catalogue, 9–10 December 1968, Lot 769.

Bibliotheca Bodmeriana, Cologny-Geneva.

KpR 1491 Revised, in MS Traffics and Discoveries, 13 numbered pages.

McGill University.

KpR 1492 Corrected page proof for a collected edition, paginated [1]–34; together with a second page proof, uncorrected but incorporating the revisions in the first.

Columbia University, Engel Collection.

KpR 1493 Corrected first page proof for the Sussex Edition; date stamped 22 March 1932.

British Library, Add. MS 55858.

The Cat That Walked by Himself
First pub. *Ladies Home Journal* and *Windsor Magazine*, July 1902; collected with verse 'Pussy can sit by the fire and sing' in *Just So Stories* (London, 1902); *Sussex*, XIII, 183–202; Harbord, IV, 1681–2.

KpR 1494 Revised, in MS Just So Stories, including the story, 4 numbered leaves (rectos only) (ff. 120–3, watermarked 1901), the captions (f. 116, watermarked 1901), and the 3 original illustrations (ff. 117–19, rectos only).

British Library, Add. MS 59840, ff. 116–23 (rectos only).

KpR 1495 Corrected second page proof for the Sussex Edition; date stamped 23 April 1935.

British Library, Add. MS 55863.

The Cause of Humanity
First printed in Harbord (1969), V, 2618–32, as 'Uncollected No. 270'; see also Harbord, VII, 2949–50.

KpR 1496 Corrected typescript, 21 leaves (rectos only).

Owned (1970) by H. Dunscombe Colt (but not found with his collection at Library of Congress).

A Celebrity at Home
First printed Harbord (1969), V, 2354–7 (see also 2039), as 'Uncollected No. 117'.

KpR 1497 Revised, subtitled 'Mrs S. A. Hill at Belvidere House, Allahabad.', 6 numbered leaves (rectos only), left by Kipling with the Hills in Allahabad, August 1888; [written May 1888].

Facsimile at Sussex, Baldwin Papers 2/13.

Library of Congress, Rare Book Division, Carpenter Kipling Collection.

A Centurion of the Thirtieth
First pub. *Strand Magazine* and *McClure's Magazine*, May 1906; collected with poems 'Cities and Thrones and Powers' and 'A British-Roman Song' in *Puck of Pook's Hill* (London, 1906); *Sussex*, XIV, 121–39; Harbord, VI, 2711–35.

KpR 1498 Revised, here entitled 'The Shoes of Rome', in MS Puck, 10 numbered leaves (rectos only).

Bodleian, MS. Eng. misc. c. 127, ff. 44–53 (rectos only).

KpR 1499 Corrected first page proof for the Sussex Edition; date stamped 2 July 1931.

British Library, Add. MS 55864.

A Chapter of Proverbs
No publication traced; not in Harbord.

KpR 1500 Typed transcript of 32 proverbs, beginning 'The wind bloweth...', here untitled, 2 numbered leaves (rectos only).

Sussex, KP 25/4.

KpR 1501 Typed transcript, beginning 'The wind bloweth...', annotated by Sir Alfred Webb-Johnson 'An unpublished item by Rudyard Kipling, given to me by Mrs Kipling'.

British Library, Add. MS 45982, ff. 1–2.

KpR 1502 Calligraphic MS, beginning (f. 2) '1. The wind bloweth...', made for Sir Alfred Webb-Johnson as a gift for Queen Mary, from a copy sent to him by CK, 17 leaves (rectos only).

Royal Library, Windsor.

The Children of the Zodiac
First pub. *Harper's Weekly*, 5 December 1891; collected *Many Inventions* (London and New York, 1893); *Sussex*, V, 465–86; Harbord, III, 1272–6.

KpR 1503 Corrected first page proof for the Sussex Edition; date stamped 10 June 1931.

British Library, Add. MS 55856.

The Church that was at Antioch
First pub. *London Magazine*, August 1929; collected with poem 'The Disciple' in *Limits and Renewals* (London, 1932); *Sussex*, XI, 87–110; Harbord VII, 3198–207.

KpR 1504 Corrected page proof in Limits and Renewals Proof; date stamped 16 and 18 January 1932.

Syracuse University.

KpR 1505 Corrected first page proof for the Sussex Edition; date stamped 14 October 1932.

British Library, Add. MS 55862.

Cities and Spaces, for 'Letters to the Family No. III', see KpR 1826–30.

'The City of Dreadful Night'
First pub. *Civil and Military Gazette*, 10 September 1885; collected *Life's Handicap* (London and New York, 1891); *Sussex*, IV, 407–15; Harbord, II, 999–1001.

KpR 1506 Printed copy of first publication, signed (initials) and annotated with a glossary of the Indian words, as sent to W. C. Crofts for publication in *United Services College Chronicle*, 7 March 1887.

Anderson Galleries, 21–4 January 1929 (Kern Sale), Lot 775.

KpR 1507 Corrected first page proof for the Sussex Edition; date stamped 13 February 1932.

British Library, Add. MS 55855.

The City of Dreadful Night
This series of eight articles first pub. *The Pioneer*, 18 February–9 April 1888; collected *From Sea to Sea*, 2 vols (New York, 1899); *Sussex*, XXIII, 189–254; Harbord, II, 893–902.

KpR 1508 Fair copy, revised, including illustrated title page and two pen-and-ink sketches on the last page, 51 pages (including title page and 25 leaves).

Berg.

KpR 1509 Corrected page proof in Vol. II of proofs for *From Sea to Sea* (KpR 1642), signed (initials) *passim*, stamped '2nd REV.'; date stamped 12 May 1899.

Library of Congress, Rare Book Division, Carpenter Kipling Collection.

KpR 1510 Corrected first page proof for the Sussex Edition; date stamped 18 November 1932.

British Library, Add. MS 55873.

The Claims of Art
Speech delivered at Artist's General Benevolent Institute, London, 9 May 1907; first pub. *The Times*, 10 May 1907, as 'Fate's Vagaries'; collected *A Book of Words* (London, 1928); *Sussex*, XXV, 9–14; Harbord, VII, 3288.

KpR 1511 Corrected first page proof for the Sussex Edition; date stamped 4 April 1931.

British Library, Add. MS 55875.

The Classics and the Sciences
Speech delivered at University College, Dundee, 12 October 1923; first pub. *The Times* and *The Scotsman*, 13 October 1923; collected *A Book of Words* (London, 1928); *Sussex*, XXV, 235–9; Harbord, VII, 3312.

KpR 1512 Corrected first page proof for the Sussex Edition; date stamped 4 April 1931.

British Library, Add. MS 55875.

Club
Speech delivered at St Andrews, 10 October 1923; reported (with quotations) *Daily Telegraph*, 11 October 1923 and *The Scotsman*, 12 October 1923; not in Harbord.

KpR 1513 Revised, beginning 'When the illustrious Doctor Johnson visited our university...', in MS Debits and Credits, headed in an unidentified hand 'Not Collected in *A Book of Words* Daily Telegraph 11th feb [sic] 1923 at St Andrews', 4 pages (ff. 265–8, rectos only).

University of Durham.

Cold Iron
First pub. *The Delineator*, September 1909; collected with poem 'Cold Iron' in *Rewards and Fairies* (London, 1910); *Sussex*, XV, 3–23; Harbord, VI, 2767–70.

KpR 1514 Revised, in MS Rewards and Fairies, 7 pages.

Cambridge University Library, ADD 6850, ff. 5–11 (rectos only).

KpR 1515 Corrected first page proof for the Sussex Edition; datc stamped 18 September 1931.

British Library, Add. MS 55865.

Collar-Wallah and the Poison-Stick
First pub. *St Nicholas*, February 1893; *Sussex*, XXX, 23–36; Harbord, V, 2515, as 'Uncollected No. 213'.

KpR 1516 Corrected first galley proof set up for a projected volume of the Sussex Edition to be called 'Why Snow Falls at Vernet and Other Stories' (revised to 'Uncollected vol.'); date stamped 27 October 1930.

British Library, Add. MS 55850.

The Comprehension of Private Copper
First pub. *Strand Magazine* and *Everybody's Magazine*, October 1902; collected with part of poem 'The King's Task' in *Traffics and Discoveries* (London, 1904); *Sussex*, VII, 163–77; Harbord, IV, 1892–902. The verses in the text are listed Harbord, Verse No. 784.

KpR 1517 Revised, containing several rejected titles, including the verses ''E sent us 'is blessin' from London Town', in MS Traffics and Discoveries, 5 pages.

McGill University.

KpR 1518 Corrected first page proof (including corrections to the verses ''E sent us 'is blessin' from London Town') for the Sussex Edition; date stamped 22 March 1932.

British Library, Add. MS 55858.

A Conclusion, for 'Letters to the Family No. VIII', see KpR 1826–30.

A Conference of the Powers
First pub. in *The Pioneer*, 23–4 May 1890; collected *Many Inventions* (London and New York, 1893); *Sussex*, V, 27–45; Harbord, III, 1196–202.

KpR 1519 Corrected first page proof for the Sussex Edition; date stamped 10 June 1931.

British Library, Add. MS 55856.

Consequences
First pub. (with verse heading beginning 'Rosicrucian subtleties') *Civil and Military Gazette*, 9 December 1886; collected *Plain Tales from the Hills* (Calcutta and London, 1888); *Sussex*, I, 143–9; Harbord, I, 53–5. The verse heading, ascribed 'The Convert', was collected separately in *Poems 1886–1929* (London, 1929) and *Sussex*, XXXIV, 215–16, as 'Chapter Heading'; Harbord, Verse No. 212.

KpR 1520 Corrected first page proof (including a correction to the verse heading) for the Sussex Edition; date stamped 12 September 1931.

British Library, Add. MS 55852.

The Conversion of Aurelian McGoggin
First pub. *Civil and Military Gazette*, 28 April 1887; collected *Plain Tales from the Hills* (Calcutta and London, 1888); *Sussex*, I, 153–9; Harbord, I, 55–7.

KpR 1521 Corrected first page proof for the Sussex Edition; date stamped 12 September 1931.

British Library, Add. MS 55852.

The Conversion of St Wilfrid
First pub. *The Delineator*, January 1910; collected with poems 'Eddi's Service' and 'Song of the Red War Boat' in *Rewards and Fairies* (London, 1910); *Sussex*, XV, 213–33; Harbord, VI, 2794–6.

KpR 1522 Revised, in MS Rewards and Fairies, 8 pages.

Cambridge University Library, ADD 6850, ff. 82–9 (rectos only).

KpR 1523 Corrected first page proof for the Sussex Edition; date stamped 18 September 1931.

British Library, Add. MS 55865.

The Courting of Dinah Shadd
First pub. *Macmillan's Magazine*, March 1890 (with verse heading from 'The Ladies'); collected *Life's Handicap* (London and New York, 1891); *Sussex*, IV, 41–72; Harbord, II, 948–53.

KpR 1524 Corrected first page proof (including corrections to the verse heading and to KpR 728) for the Sussex Edition; date stamped 13 February 1932.

British Library, Add. MS 55855.

The Cow-House *Jirga*, see KpR 2078–9.

The Crab that Played with the Sea
First pub. *Pearson's Magazine*, August 1902, as 'The Crab that Made the Tides'; collected with poem 'The China-going P. & O.'s' in *Just So Stories* (London, 1902); *Sussex*, XIII, 161–78; Harbord, IV, 1677–81.

KpR 1525 Revised, in MS Just So Stories, including the story, here entitled 'How the crab got his claws.', 4 numbered leaves (rectos only) (ff. 110–13), two versions of the two captions, the later headed 'The Crab', one page each (ff. 105, 106, watermarked 1901), and the 3 original illustrations (ff. 107–9, rectos only).

British Library, Add. MS 59840, ff. 105–13 (rectos only).

KpR 1526 Corrected second page proof for the Sussex Edition; date stamped 23 April 1935.

British Library, Add. MS 55863.

Cupid's Arrows
First pub. (with verse heading) *Plain Tales from the Hills* (Calcutta and London, 1888); *Sussex*, I, 87–92; Harbord, I, 41–3. For verse headings, see KpR 177.

KpR 1527 Corrected first page proof for the Sussex Edition; date stamped 12 September 1931.

British Library, Add. MS 55852.

A Daughter of Heth
No publication traced; listed Harbord, V, 2386, as 'Uncollected No. 162'.

KpR 1528 Fair copy, revised (both the thin and thick paper carbon copies), in MS From Sea to Sea (see KpR 1634), unfinished, 2 numbered pages.

Huntington, HM 12429, Vol. 2, pp. 90–1.

The Daughter of the Regiment
First pub. (with verse heading beginning 'Jain 'Ardin' was a Sargint's wife', ascribed 'Old Barrack-Room Ballad') *Civil and Military Gazette*, 11 May 1887; collected *Plain Tales from the Hills* (Calcutta and London, 1888); *Sussex*, I, 275–8; Harbord, I, 73–4.

KpR 1529 Corrected first page proof for the Sussex Edition; date stamped 12 September 1931.

British Library, Add. MS 55852.

***The Day's Work* (New York, 1898)**
For F. N. Doubleday's presentation copy to Bliss Perry containing corrected proofs (bound in), see KpR 286, 1541, 1591, 2065, 2239; for an inscribed copy, see KpR 750.

KpR 1530 Fair copy, revised, of the Table of Contents, one page; annotated in an unidentified hand 'Table of Contents made by RK & sent to FND May 19/98'.

Cornell University.

Dayspring Mishandled
First pub. *MacLean's Magazine*, 1 March 1928; collected with poem 'Gertrude's Prayer' in *Limits and Renewals* (London, 1932); *Sussex*, XI, 3–30; Harbord, VII, 3188–93.

KpR 1531 Corrected page proof in Limits and Renewals Proof.

Syracuse University.

KpR 1532 Corrected first page proof (including corrections to the last lines of 'Gertrude's Prayer' (see KpR 412–13) which appear in the text) for the Sussex Edition; date stamped 14 October 1932.

British Library, Add. MS 55862.

Dead King, for 'Egypt of the Magicians No. IV', see KpR 1573, 1575, 1577.

A Deal in Cotton
First pub. *Collier's Weekly*, 14 December 1907; collected with poem 'The New Knighthood' in *Actions and Reactions* (London, 1909); *Sussex*, VIII, 169–90; Harbord, VI, 2846–53.

KpR 1533 Two MSS in MS Actions and Reactions (ff. 73–9, 81–90), the second entitled 'A Future in Cotton'.

University of St Andrews, MS PR4854.A4.

KpR 1534 Corrected first page proof for the Sussex Edition; date stamped 28 November 1931.

British Library, Add. MS 55859.

The Debt

First pub. *Liberty*, 26 April 1930; collected with poem 'Akbar's Bridge' in *Limits and Renewals* (London, 1932); *Sussex*, XI, 197–208; Harbord, VII, 3238–40.

KpR 1535 Revised, in MS Debits and Credits, 5 numbered pages (ff. 197–201, rectos only).

University of Durham.

KpR 1536 Corrected page proof in Limits and Renewals Proof; date stamped 20 January 1932.

Syracuse University.

KpR 1537 Corrected first page proof for the Sussex Edition; date stamped 14 October 1932.

British Library, Add. MS 55862.

Destroyers at Jutland

First pub. (as a series of four articles: 'Stories of the Battle' (with untitled poem '"My Boy Jack"'), 'The Night Hunt', 'The Meaning of "Joss"' (with untitled poem 'Zion') and 'The Minds of Men' (with untitled poem 'The Verdicts')) in *Daily Telegraph* and *New York Times*, 19, 23, 26, 31 October 1916; collected, with another poem at the end 'The Neutral' (later entitled 'The Question'), in *Sea Warfare* (London, 1916); *Sussex*, XXVI, 337–84; Harbord, V, 2264, 2290–314.

KpR 1538 Revised, in MS Non-Fiction, including: 'Stories of the Battle', here entitled 'Flotsam and Jutland.', 6 pages, the last partly typescript (ff. 88–93, rectos only); 'The Night Hunt', here entitled 'Flotsam and Jutland II', 5 pages (ff. 94–8, rectos only); 'The Meaning of "Joss"', here entitled 'Flotsam & Jutland III', 4 numbered pages (ff. 99–102, rectos only); 'The Minds of Men', here entitled 'Destroyers at Jutland.', 6 pages, the last also containing KpR 1309 (ff. 103–8, rectos only).

British Library, Add. MS 45542, ff. 88–108 (rectos only).

KpR 1539 Typescript, including the four articles, here entitled 'Destroyers at Jutland. I[–IV]', being (respectively) 9 numbered leaves (rectos only), 10 numbered leaves (rectos only), 11 numbered leaves (rectos only), 9 numbered leaves (rectos only), the first leaf of each article being an explanatory note, also including three of the accompanying poems (KpR 725, 1311, 1394).

Dalhousie University.

The Devil and the Deep Sea

First pub. *The Graphic*, Christmas Number 1895; collected *The Day's Work* (New York, 1898); *Sussex*, VI, 155–86; Harbord, III, 1369–80.

KpR 1540 Revised, with two cancelled titles ('Paragon of Animals.' and 'The Go-between.'), in MS Day's Work, 15 numbered pages; watermarked 1890 and 1894.

British Library, Add. MS 45541, ff. 106–20 (rectos only).

KpR 1541 Corrected page proof for the first collected edition, signed (initials), bound into (before p. 157) a presentation copy (containing also KpR 286, 1591, 2065, 2239) from F. N. Doubleday to Bliss Perry, inscribed 21 October 1898.

Harvard, Kipling 18.98.2*.

KpR 1542 Corrected first page proof for the Sussex Edition; date stamped 27 June 1931.

British Library, Add. MS 55857.

The Diary of The Things That Happened

First printed Harbord (1969), V, 2393–4, as 'Uncollected No. 168'.

KpR 1543 Fair copy, revised, of a hypothetical diary of a passenger at sea, including sketches, on Inman Line notepaper, headed 'S.S. City of Berlin', 4 pages (one leaf); dated 26 September 1889.

Facsimile at Sussex, Baldwin Papers 2/14.

Library of Congress, Rare Book Division, Carpenter Kipling Collection, Pen and Brush Sketches, Item 3.

Dis Aliter Visum
First pub. *The Pioneer*, 4 July 1885; reprinted Harbord (1969), I, 568–76, as 'Uncollected No. 32'.

KpR 1544 Revised clipping of first publication, in Scrapbook 1 (p. 64).

Sussex, KP 28/1.

KpR 1545 Corrected copy of the first publication, containing Kipling's signature and glossary, as sent to W. C. Crofts for publication in *United Services College Chronicle* and containing a note to him on the verso, 15 December 1887.

Syracuse University.

A Displaie of New Heraldrie
First pub. *The Spectator*, 3 November 1917; *Sussex*, XXX, 303–12; Harbord, V, 2592, as 'Uncollected No. 252'.

KpR 1546 Two corrected successive typescripts, here untitled, the first (5 numbered leaves, rectos only) headed 'To that learned, painful and curious Garter Principall King at Armes Sir Alfred Scott Gatty Knight.', the second, incomplete, 2 leaves (rectos only) incorporating the revisions in the first.

Cornell University.

KpR 1547 Corrected first galley proof set up for a projected volume of the Sussex Edition (marked 'Uncollected'); date stamped 17 November 1930.

British Library, Add. MS 55850.

A District at Play, see KpR 2078–9.

The Disturber of Traffic
First pub. *Atlantic Monthly*, September 1891, as 'A Disturber of Traffic'; collected (with verse heading 'The Prayer of Miriam Cohen') in *Many Inventions* (London and New York, 1893); *Sussex*, V, 3–24; Harbord, III, 1188–96.

KpR 1548 Corrected typescript, signed, sent to printer for first publication, 27 leaves (rectos only); date stamped 11 June 1891.

Texas.

KpR 1549 Corrected first page proof (including KpR 873) for the Sussex Edition; date stamped 10 June 1931.

British Library, Add. MS 55856.

A Doctor of Medicine
First pub. *The Delineator*, October 1909; collected with poems 'An Astrologer's Song' and 'Our Fathers of Old' in *Rewards and Fairies* (London, 1910); *Sussex*, XV, 245–64; Harbord, VI, 2796–800.

KpR 1550 Revised, here entitled 'M[r] Culpepper.', in MS Rewards and Fairies, 5 numbered pages.

Cambridge University Library, ADD 6850, ff. 92–6 (rectos only).

KpR 1551 Corrected first page proof for the Sussex Edition; date stamped 18 September 1931.

British Library, Add. MS 55865.

A Doctor's Work
Speech delivered Middlesex Hospital, London, 1 October 1908; first pub. *The Times*, 2 October 1908; collected *A Book of Words* (London, 1928); *Sussex*, XXV, 43–7; Harbord, VII, 3290–1.

KpR 1552 Revised clipping from *The Standard*, 2 October 1908, in Scrapbook 9 (p. 13).

Sussex, KP 28/9.

KpR 1553 Corrected first page proof for the Sussex Edition; date stamped 4 April 1931.

British Library, Add. MS 55875.

The Dog Hervey
First pub. *Century Magazine*, April 1914; collected with poem 'The Comforters' in *A Diversity of Creatures* (London, 1917); *Sussex*, IX, 135–59; Harbord, VII, 3069–73.

KpR 1554 Revised, in MS Diversity of Creatures (ff. 44–51, rectos only).

University of Edinburgh, Dk. 2. 8.

KpR 1555 Corrected second page proof for *Collected Dog Stories* (London, 1934), pp. 89–118; date stamped 14 August 1934.

British Library, Add. MS 55848.

KpR 1556 Corrected first page proof for the Sussex Edition; date stamped 28 April 1932.

British Library, Add. MS 55860.

Dray Wara Yow Dee
First pub. *Week's News*, 28 April 1888; collected *In Black and White* (Allahabad, [1888]); *Sussex*, II, 239–51; Harbord, I, 314–17.

KpR 1557 Fair copy, revised, in MS Essays and Stories (ff. [6, 7–11v]), including a title page and 10 pages of text, also containing sketches.

Berg.

KpR 1558 Revisions in a copy of the second collected edition (Allahabad, 1889) (KpR 1747).

Berg.

KpR 1559 Corrections in a copy of the first collected edition (KpR 1745).

Syracuse University.

KpR 1560 Annotations explaining Indian words, in a copy of the first collected edition (KpR 1746), pp. 3–4, 10.

Berg.

KpR 1561 Corrected first page proof for the Sussex Edition; date stamped 14 May 1931.

British Library, Add. MS 55853.

The Dream of Duncan Parrenness
First pub. *Civil and Military Gazette*, 25 December 1884; collected *Life's Handicap* (London and New York, 1891); *Sussex*, IV, 441–8; Harbord, II, 1005.

KpR 1562 Corrected first page proof for thc Sussex Edition; date stamped 13 February 1932.

British Library, Add. MS 55855.

The Dreitarbund
First pub. *Civil and Military Gazette*, 22 October 1887; collected in the suppressed *City of Dreadful Night and Other Sketches* (Allahabad, 1890); reprinted Harbord, III, 1618–21, as 'Uncollected No. 84'.

KpR 1563 Revised clipping of first publication, in Scrapbook 3 (pp. 149–50).

Sussex, KP 28/3.

The Drums of the Fore and Aft
First pub. *Wee Willie Winkie* (Allahabad, [1888]); *Sussex*, III, 375–[418]; Harbord, I, 384–90.

KpR 1564 Corrections in a copy of the first publication (KpR 2229).

Syracuse University.

KpR 1565 Annotations explaining Indian words, in a copy of the first publication (KpR 2230), pp. 73, 82, 84–5, 88, 95–6, 99–101, 103.

Berg.

KpR 1566 Corrected first page proof for the Sussex Edition; date stamped 18 September 1931.

British Library, Add. MS 55854.

'Dymchurch Flit'
First pub. *Strand* and *McClure's Magazine*, September 1906; collected with poems 'The Bee Boy's Song' and 'The Three-Part Song' in *Puck of Pook's Hill* (London, 1906); *Sussex*, XIV, 223–39; Harbord, VI, 2751–60.

KpR 1567 Revised, in MS Puck, 5 numbered leaves (rectos only), containing also KpR 776.

Bodleian, MS. Eng. misc. c. 127, ff. 91–5 (rectos only).

KpR 1568 Corrected first page proof for the Sussex Edition; date stamped 2 July 1931.

British Library, Add. MS 55864.

The Edge of the East, for 'From Tideway to Tideway No. III', see KpR 1647–9.

The Edge of the Evening
First pub. (with verse heading from 'The Benefactors') *Metropolitan Magazine*, December 1913; collected with poem 'Rebirth' in *A Diversity of Creatures* (London, 1917); *Sussex*, IX, 273–96; Harbord, VII, 3089–93.

KpR 1569 Extensively revised, wanting the verse heading, here originally entitled 'On private grounds.', in MS Diversity of Creatures (ff. 91–100, rectos only); dated in an unidentified hand December 1912.

University of Edinburgh, Dk. 2. 8.

KpR 1570 Corrected first page proof for the Sussex Edition; date stamped 28 April 1932.

British Library, Add. MS 55860.

The Education of Otis Yeere
First pub. *Week's News*, 10 and 17 March 1888; collected *Under the Deodars* (Allahabad, [1888]); *Sussex*, III, 5–34; Harbord, I, 335–9.

KpR 1571 Corrections in a copy of the first collected edition (KpR 2175).

Syracuse University.

KpR 1572 Corrected first page proof for the Sussex Edition; date stamped 18 September 1931.

British Library, Add. MS 55854.

Egypt of the Magicians
This series of 7 letters and accompanying poems first pub. *Nash's Magazine* and *Cosmopolitan*, June–December 1914; collected (without poems) *Letters of Travel* (London, 1920); *Sussex*, XXIV, 245–331; Harbord, III, 1501–28. See also KpR 1824.

KpR 1573 Partly draft and partly fair copy, revised, in MS Non-Fiction, including: 'Sea Travel', here entitled 'The Magicians of Egypt', including the epigraph from *Exodus*, 4 numbered pages (ff. 156–9, rectos only); 'A Return to the East', here entitled 'Egypt of the Magicians' on first page (f. 161), 4 pages bound out of order (ff. 160–3, rectos only); 'A Serpent of Old Nile', headed 'III', 7 pages (ff. 164–70, rectos only); 'Up the River', headed 'IV', 5 pages (ff. 171–5, rectos only); 'Dead Kings', here entitled 'Egypt of the Magicians. <(VI)> V', incomplete, 4 pages (ff. 176–9, rectos only); 'The Face of the Desert', here entitled 'Egypt of the Magicians <V> VI', 5 pages (ff. 180–4, rectos only); wanting the last letter 'The Riddle of Empire' and wanting all the poems.

British Library, Add. MS 45542, ff. 156–84 (rectos only).

KpR 1574 Corrected galley proofs for *Nash's Magazine* (so stamped) including: two sets of 'Sea Travel' (including KpR 1319), date stamped 11 March 1914 (second set); one set of 'A Serpent of Old Nile' (including KpR 780), date stamped 22 May 1914; one set of 'Up the River' (including KpR 842), date stamped 23 June 1914; one set of 'Dead Kings', date stamped July 1914.

Dalhousie University.

KpR 1575 Corrected galley proof of 'Dead Kings', for the first publication (*Nash's Magazine*), here entitled 'Egypt of the Magicians V. Interviewing Pharoah', annotated in an unidentified hand 'For Mr Kipling kindly to revise: and return as soon as possible to [stamped] Nash's Magazine...'.

Parke Bernet, 21–2 January 1942 (Ballard Sale), Lot 230.

KpR 1576 Typescript of 'The Riddle of Empire', headed 'Egypt of the Magicians VII.', including KpR 685, 12 numbered leaves (rectos only), among materials for *Letters of Travel* (KpR 1824).

Berg.

KpR 1577 Corrected first page proof for the Sussex Edition; date stamped 30 April 1935; including also a second page proof of 'The Riddle of Empire' date stamped 19 June 1936.

British Library, Add. MS 55874.

The Elephant and the Lark's Nest

First pub. as 'Fables for the Staff II' in *The Friend* (Bloemfontein), 26 March 1900; reprinted *War's Brighter Side*, ed. Julian Ralph (London, 1901); reprinted Harbord (1969), III, 1530–2.

KpR 1578 Fair copy, revised, headed 'Fables for the Staff', one page, together with a corrected galley proof for the first publication, signed (initials).

Facsimile of the MS in American Art Association sale catalogue, 20–1 April 1925 (G. B. McCutcheon Sale), Lot 304; facsimile of the proof in *War's Brighter Side*, ed. Julian Ralph (London, 1901), facing p. 99.

Library of Congress, Rare Book Division, Carpenter Kipling Collection.

KpR 1579 Extensively corrected proof for the first publication, annotated 'Who the deuce set this bosh up, Find out. RK'.

Dalhousie University.

The Elephant's Child

First pub. *Ladies Home Journal*, April 1900; collected with poem 'I keep six honest serving men' in *Just So Stories* (London, 1902); *Sussex*, XIII, 63–78; Harbord, IV, 1663–5.

KpR 1580 Revised, in MS Just So Stories, including a draft (ff. 38–40) and fair copy, revised (ff. 35–7) of the story, each on 3 numbered leaves (rectos only), the two captions (f. 32, watermarked 1901) and 2 of the original illustrations (ff. 33–4, rectos only).

British Library, Add. MS 59840, ff. 32–40 (rectos only).

KpR 1581 Revised typescript, signed, 8 numbered leaves (rectos only), annotated 'First Story', 'Just-so-Stories' and 'These to go to Mr Bok at once.'.

Dalhousie University.

KpR 1582 Corrected galley proof for first publication, stamped 'First Galley', signed (initials) *passim*.

Facsimile of opening portion in American Art Association sale catalogue, 20–1 April 1925 (G. B. McCutcheon Sale), Lot 297.

Library of Congress, Rare Book Division, Carpenter Kipling Collection, *Animal Stories*.

KpR 1583 Corrected first page proof for the Sussex Edition; date stamped 29 October 1932.

British Library, Add. MS 55863.

The Enemies to Each Other

First pub. as 'A New Version of What happened in the Garden of Eden' in *MacLean's Magazine*, 15 July 1924; collected *Debits and Credits* (London, 1926); *Sussex*, X, 3–19; Harbord, VII, 3112–17.

KpR 1584 Two openings, revised, in MS Debits and Credits, the first on one page (f. 38), the second on 2 pages (ff. 39–40, rectos only), both subtitled 'With apologies to the shade of Mirza Mirkhond'.

University of Durham.

KpR 1585 Corrected first page proof for the Sussex Edition; date stamped 30 December 1931.

British Library, Add. MS 55861.

England and the English

Speech delivered Royal Society of St George, London, 23 April 1920; first pub. *The Times*, 24 April 1920; collected *A Book of Words* (London, 1928); *Sussex*, XXV, 167–76; Harbord, VII, 3305–7.

KpR 1586 Corrected first page proof for the Sussex Edition; date stamped 4 April 1931.

British Library, Add. MS 55875.

An English School

First pub. with heading 'School Song' in *Youth's Companion*, 19 October 1893; collected without heading *Land and Sea Tales* (London, 1923); *Sussex*, XVI, 197–215; Harbord, I, 414–2 and VI, 2902.

KpR 1587 Corrected first page proof (including KpR 56) for the Sussex Edition; date stamped 14 December 1931.

British Library, Add. MS 55866.

The Enlightenments of Paggett, M.P.
First pub. *Contemporary Review*, September 1890; collected *In Black and White*, Outward Bound Edition, Vol. IV (New York, 1897); *Sussex*, V (*Many Inventions*), 105–43; Harbord, V, 2473, as 'Uncollected No. 202'.

KpR 1588 Corrected first page proof for the Sussex Edition; date stamped 10 June 1931.

British Library, Add. MS 55856.

Erastasius of the *Whanghoa*
First pub. as 'Abaft the Funnel No. VIII' in *Civil and Military Gazette*, 21 August 1889; collected *Abaft the Funnel* (New York, 1909); *Sussex*, XXIX, 5–11; Harbord, II, 677–8.

KpR 1589 Fair copy, revised (thin paper carbon copy), in MS From Sea to Sea (see KpR 1634), here entitled 'Abaft the Funnel (No VIII)', 4 numbered pages, listed (not by RK) in Table of Contents as 'The Cat that saved the ship'.

Huntington, HM 12429, Vol. 2, pp. 73–6.

An Error in the Fourth Dimension
First pub. *Cosmopolitan*, December 1894; collected *The Day's Work* (New York, 1898); *Sussex*, VI, 331–53; Harbord, III, 1425–33.

KpR 1590 Fair copy, revised, and revised later in red, in MS Day's Work, signed, 10 numbered pages; watermarked 1890.

British Library, Add. MS 45541, ff. 191–200 (rectos only).

KpR 1591 Part of a copy (pp. 1–2) of first publication, revised for the first collected edition, annotated 'only page proofs needed R Kipling', bound into (before p. 337 and between pp. 344 and 345) a presentation copy (containing also KpR 286, 1541, 2065, 2239) from F. N. Doubleday to Bliss Perry, inscribed 21 October 1898.

Harvard, Kipling 18.98.2*.

KpR 1592 Part of a copy (pp. 3–4) of first publication, revised for the first collected edition.

Princeton, Doubleday Collection.

KpR 1593 Part of a copy (pp. 5–12) of first publication, mounted on leaves (numbered in pencil 5–12), revised for the first collected edition, signed (initials) twice on p. 12.

Facsimile of p. 12 in Rice, facing p. 113.

Princeton, Doubleday Collection, Box 3, Bound Vol. II, Item 21.

KpR 1594 Corrected first page proof for the Sussex Edition; date stamped 27 June 1931.

British Library, Add. MS 55857.

The Explanation of Mir Baksh
First pub. *Civil and Military Gazette*, 1 June 1888; collected in 'The Smith Administration' in *From Sea to Sea*, 2 vols (New York, 1899); *Sussex*, XXIII, 399–403; Harbord, II, 920–1. See also KpR 2078–9.

KpR 1595 Revised clipping of first publication, in Scrapbook 4 (p. 67).

Sussex, KP 28/4.

The Eye of Allah
First pub. *Strand* and *McCall's Magazine*, September 1926; collected with poems 'Untimely' and 'The Last Ode' in *Debits and Credits* (London, 1926); *Sussex*, X, 287–314; Harbord, VII, 3174–82.

KpR 1596 Revised, here entitled 'The Eye of <God> Allah', in MS Debits and Credits, 7 numbered pages (ff. 157–63, rectos only).

University of Durham.

KpR 1597 Corrected first page proof for the Sussex Edition; date stamped 30 December 1931.

British Library, Add. MS 55861.

Fables for the Staff, see KpR 1578–9, 1624, 1792, 2187.

The Face of the Desert, for 'Egypt of the Magicians No. VI', see KpR 1573, 1577.

Fairy-Kist
First pub. *MacLean's Magazine*, 15 September 1927; collected with poem 'The Mother's Son' in *Limits and Renewals* (London, 1932); *Sussex*, XI, 147–70; Harbord, VII, 3213–21.

KpR 1598 Revised, in MS Debits and Credits, 15 pages (ff. 181–95, rectos only), annotated 'type with wide spaces'.

University of Durham.

KpR 1599 Corrected page proof for publication in *McCall's Magazine*, October 1927; date stamped 3–9 August [1927].

Berg.

KpR 1600 Corrected page proof in Limits and Renewals Proof; date stamped 19 January 1932.

Syracuse University.

KpR 1601 Corrected first page proof for the Sussex Edition; date stamped 14 October 1932.

British Library, Add. MS 55862.

False Dawn
First pub. (with verse heading) *Plain Tales from the Hills* (Calcutta and London, 1888); *Sussex*, I, 63–73; Harbord, I, 37–9. For verse heading, see KpR 177.

KpR 1602 Corrected first page proof for the Sussex Edition; date stamped 12 September 1931.

British Library, Add. MS 55852.

The Father of Lightnings, see KpR 1455.

Fatima
First pub. *The Story of the Gadsbys* (Allahabad, [1888]); *Sussex*, II, 191–206; Harbord, I, 310.

KpR 1603 Corrections in a copy of the first publication (KpR 2104).

Syracuse University.

KpR 1604 Corrected first page proof for the Sussex Edition; date stamped 14 May 1931.

British Library, Add. MS 55853.

Fiction
Speech delivered Royal Society of Literature, London, 7 July 1926; first pub. *The Times*, as 'Truth and Fiction', and *Daily Telegraph*, 8 July 1926; collected *A Book of Words* (London, 1928); *Sussex*, XXV, 265–9; Harbord, VII, 3313–14.

KpR 1605 Corrected first page proof for the Sussex Edition; date stamped 4 April 1931.

British Library, Add. MS 55875.

The Finances of the Gods
First pub. *Life's Handicap* (London and New York, 1891); *Sussex*, IV, 347–52; Harbord, II, 991–2.

KpR 1606 Corrected first page proof for *Humorous Tales* (London, 1931) pp. 219–24; date stamped May 1931.

British Library, Add. MS 55847.

KpR 1607 Corrected first page proof for the Sussex Edition; date stamped 13 February 1932.

British Library, Add. MS 55855.

'The Finest Story in the World'
First pub. *Contemporary Review*, July 1891; collected *Many Inventions* (London and New York, 1893); *Sussex*, V, 187–226; Harbord, III, 1214–29.

KpR 1608 Thin carbon copy of a fragment of an early version, here entitled 'Escaped <[from?] the galley.>', signed, one of the missing pages in MS From Sea to Sea (Vol. 1, p. 8) (see KpR 1634), annotated 'p. 1 (*turnover*)' and 'not to be copied'.

Library of Congress, Rare Book Division, Carpenter Kipling Collection, Pen and Brush Sketches, Item 7.

KpR 1609 Corrected first page proof (including corrections to the verse in the text, 'After the Promise', see KpR 12–14) for the Sussex Edition; date stamped 10 June 1931.

British Library, Add. MS 55856.

The First Assault upon the Sorbonne
First pub. *The Times*, 21 November 1921; *Sussex*, XXX, 315–19; Harbord, V, 2603, as 'Uncollected No. 256'.

KpR 1610 Corrected first galley proof set up for a projected volume of the Sussex Edition (marked 'Uncollected'); date stamped 17 November 1930.

British Library, Add. MS 55850.

The First Sailor
Speech delivered to Junior Officers of an East Coast Patrol, 1918; first pub. *A Book of Words* (London, 1928); *Sussex*, XXV, 147–63; Harbord, VII, 3301–5.

KpR 1611 Corrected first page proof for *Humorous Tales* (London, 1931), pp. 47–63; date stamped 7 May 1931.

British Library, Add. MS 55847.

KpR 1612 Corrected first page proof for the Sussex Edition; date stamped 4 April 1931.

British Library, Add. MS 55875.

The Flag of Their Country
First pub. *McClure's Magazine*, May 1899; collected *Stalky & Co.* (London, 1899); *Sussex*, XVII, 287–313; Harbord, I, 463–5.

KpR 1613 In MS Stalky: draft (ff. 74–8, rectos only), 5 pages numbered erratically; fair copy, revised (ff. 65–73, rectos only), 9 numbered pages.

Haileybury.

KpR 1614 Corrected first page proof for the Sussex Edition; date stamped 27 March 1931.

British Library, Add. MS 55867.

A Fleet in Being
This series of 6 articles first pub. *The Times* and *Morning Post*, 5, 7–11 November 1898; first pub. in book form London and New York, 1898; collected *From Sea to Sea*, Bombay Edition, Vol. V, 2 vols (New York, 1913); *Sussex*, XXVI, 387–[474]; Harbord, II, 1013–44. For an inscribed copy of the London, 1899 edition, see KpR 694.

KpR 1615 Revised, here headed 'Notes on Two Trips With the Channel Squadron', 178 pages of text, in a notebook labelled on the spine '1897 M.S.S. R. K.'.

Berg.

KpR 1616 Concluding page of Chapter 3, revised, beginning 'This and more — oh much more!...', paginated 32.

Library of Congress, Rare Book Division, Colt Collection.

A Flight of Fact
First pub. *Nash's Magazine*, *Pall Mall* and *Metropolitan*, June 1918; collected *Land and Sea Tales* (London, 1923); *Sussex*, XVI, 95–111; Harbord, VI, 2892–5.

KpR 1617 Revised, in MS Debits and Credits (ff. 24–30, rectos only), 7 pages.

University of Durham.

KpR 1618 Corrected first page proof for *Humorous Tales* (London, 1931), pp. 185–201; date stamped 15 and 19 May 1931.

British Library, Add. MS 55847.

KpR 1619 Corrected first page proof for the Sussex Edition; date stamped 14 December 1931.

British Library, Add. MS 55866.

Folly Bridge
First pub. *Daily Express*, 15–16 June 1900; *Sussex*, XXX, 101–16; Harbord, V, 2555–6, as 'Uncollected No. 231'.

KpR 1620 Revised, in MS Non-Fiction, 5 numbered pages; watermarked 1897.

British Library, Add. MS 45542, ff. 231–5 (rectos only).

KpR 1621 Corrected first galley proof set up for a projected volume of the Sussex Edition to be called *Why Snow Falls at Vernet and Other Stories* (revised to 'Uncollected vol.'); date stamped 30 October 1930.

British Library, Add. MS 55850.

For One Night Only
First pub. *Longman's Magazine*, April 1890; first collected (authorized) *The One Volume Kipling* (New York, 1928); *Sussex*, XXIX, 325–39; Harbord, V, 2467–9, as 'Uncollected No. 198'.

KpR 1622 Corrected typescript, 14 numbered leaves (rectos only), as sent for inclusion in *The One Volume Kipling* to Nelson Doubleday with a letter of 12 November 1926.

Princeton, Doubleday Collection, Additional Papers, Box 17.

KpR 1623 Corrected first galley proof set up for a projected volume of the Sussex Edition to be called *Why Snow Falls at Vernet and Other Stories* (revised to 'Uncollected vol.'); date stamped 23 (revised to 24) October 1930.

British Library, Add. MS 55850.

The Fortunate Towns, for 'Letters to the Family No. VI', see KpR 1826–30.

Fortune and the Soldier
First pub. as 'Fables for the Staff V' in *The Friend* (Bloemfontein), 30 March 1900; reprinted without title *War's Brighter Side*, ed. Julian Ralph (London, 1901); reprinted Harbord, III, 1534.

KpR 1624 Corrected proof for first publication, signed (initials), among materials for *The Friend* (see KpR 2283).

Library of Congress, Rare Book Division, Colt Collection.

[Fragments of unidentified story]
No publication traced. See also KpR 1715.

KpR 1625 Draft of two paragraphs (marked 'A' and 'B'), probably insertions for a short story, the first beginning 'We-l. There weren't any vineyards then — nor any pines nor any oaks...', the second beginning 'Oh the brandy comes out of the grapes...', followed by a dialogue between 'Boy', 'S. A. Boy' and 'Father' (mentions Cape Town).

Library of Congress, Rare Book Division, Colt Collection.

France at War
This series of six articles first pub. *Daily Telegraph* and *New York Sun*, 6–17 September 1915; collected in booklet with opening poem 'France', London, [1915]; *Sussex*, XXVI, 69–123; Harbord, V, 2258–60.

KpR 1626 Draft, including the six articles of the series, though not all divided as in the published version, all untitled but headed *passim* 'France at War', also containing KpR 1062, 34 pages.

Bibliothèque Nationale, Paris, MS Anglais 186, ff. 3–36 (rectos only).

***The Friend* (Bloemfontein)**, see KpR 2283.

A Friend of the Family
First pub. *MacLean's Magazine*, 15 June 1924; collected with poems 'A Legend of Truth' and 'We and They' in *Debits and Credits* (London, 1926); *Sussex*, X, 231–50; Harbord, VII, 3162–6.

KpR 1627 Beginning only, revised, here entitled 'The Australian', in MS Debits and Credits, 2 pages (ff. 140–1, rectos only).

University of Durham.

KpR 1628 Corrected first page proof for the Sussex Edition; date stamped 30 December 1931.

British Library, Add. MS 55861.

Friendly Brook
First pub. *Metropolitan Magazine*, March 1914; collected with poem 'The Land' in *A Diversity of Creatures* (London, 1917); *Sussex*, IX, 47–63; Harbord, VII, 3056–9.

KpR 1629 Revised, in MS Diversity of Creatures (ff. 14–20, rectos only); dated in an unidentified hand 'Dec. 1912'.

University of Edinburgh, Dk. 2. 8.

KpR 1630 Corrected first page proof for the Sussex Edition; date stamped 28 April 1932.

British Library, Add. MS 55860.

A Friend's Friend
First pub. *Civil and Military Gazette*, 2 May 1887;

collected *Plain Tales from the Hills* (Calcutta and London, 1888); *Sussex*, I, 351–8; Harbord, I, 86–7.

KpR 1631 Corrected first page proof for the Sussex Edition; date stamped 12 September 1931.

British Library, Add. MS 55852.

The Fringes of the Fleet

This series of six articles and accompanying poems first pub. *Daily Telegraph*, 20 November 1915–2 December 1915, here entitled 'The Auxiliaries I and II', 'Submarines I and II' and 'Patrols I and II'; collected separately London, 1915; collected *Sea Warfare* (London, 1915); *Sussex*, XXVI, 237–97; Harbord, V, 2261–3 and 2266–80.

KpR 1632 Draft, in MS Non-Fiction, including the six articles and four of the accompanying poems (KpR 668, 704, 761, 1052 and wanting two, 'Harwich Ladies' and 'Tin Fish'), including two titles *passim* ('Light Horsemen' (f. 32, the first page of 'Auxiliaries I') and 'Submarines and Patrols.' (f. 40)), 34 pages of text (including the poems).

British Library, Add. MS 45542, ff. 32–5, 37–48, 50–4, 56–64 (rectos only).

From Olympus to Hades

First pub. *Civil and Military Gazette*, 12 August 1886; reprinted Harbord, II, 1078–81, as 'Uncollected No. 51'. On a typed list of articles at the Bodleian (25889. k. c. 3), this is marked by Elsie Bambridge as being Kipling's; a clipping of this story is in Scrapbook 3 (p. 40) at Sussex, KP 28/3.

KpR 1633 Typescript, 5 numbered leaves (rectos only).

Cornell University.

From Sea to Sea

First pub. (39 chapters, including chapters numbered 17 and 39, not afterwards collected, and without the collected Chapter 37) *The Pioneer*, 17 April 1889–1 April 1890; Chapter 37 first published *The Scotsman*, September 1890, as 'Interviewing Mark Twain'; collected *From Sea to Sea*, 2 vols (New York, 1899); *Sussex*, XXII, 193–[466] (Chapters 1–24) and XXIII, 1–185 (Chapters 25–37); the original Chapter 39 of the first publication collected as 'Chautauquaed' in *Abaft the Funnel* (New York, 1909); Sussex, XXIX, 167–81; the original Chapter 17 and an uncollected portion of Chapter 24 were printed in E. W. Martindell, *More Flies in Amber* (privately printed, 1924), pp. [297]–305, [309]–13 (unique copy at the Bodleian, Arch. AA. d. 47); Harbord, II, 791–860 (861–92 includes notes on pirated editions of *From Sea to Sea* entitled *American Notes* which include some uncollected matter, here printed). Apparently, Kipling originally planned to circulate *From Sea to Sea* privately, illustrated by 48 photographs taken by Professor Hill; three sets of these photos were mounted in albums, one kept by RK, another sold to the Huntington, the third now in the Carpenter Kipling collection at the Library of Congress, Rare Book Division (the third contains a further 18 photos loosely inserted); another album of 24 photos taken by Professor Hill during the trip from Calcutta to Japan, with Kipling's captions, is at Princeton. Luther S. Livingston's typescript of the *Pioneer Mail* version (i.e., without Chapter 8), collated with the collected 1899 edition, is at Harvard, MS Eng 838 (see *The Bookman*, 9 (1899), 429–30).

KpR 1634 MS From Sea to Sea: two manifold notebooks (of 100 numbered leaves, each composed of alternating thin and thick paper, each pair being the same number, containing double carbon paper under thin and over thick leaf so that, writing with a stylographic pen, two carbon copies are made, one on verso of thin and one on recto of thick leaf, the thick leaves being detachable), both volumes now containing most of the thin and only a few of the thick leaves; containing (as well as contents below) a fair copy, revised, of Chapters 1–16 (Vol. I, pp. 2–7, 16–23, 26–39, 43–58, 66–91, 93–7, 99 and Vol. 2, pp. 5–44, 49–56), the beginning of Chapter 23 (Vol. 2, p. 89, both the thin and thick paper carbon copies), and the original Chapter 17 (Vol. 2, pp. 58–66); Vol. 1 is wanting pp. 1, 8, 92, 98 (for p. 8 see KpR 1608); Vol. 2 wanting pp. 57 and 100 (for p. 57 see KpR 1635); both copies remain of Vol. 2, pp. 83–4, 89–96, and Vol. 2, pp. 84, 92–9 are blank; these notebooks were used while sailing from Calcutta to San Francisco, March–May 1889, Vol. 2 is inscribed (p. 1) 'Calcutta: Mar: 6/89'.

These notebooks are described (with

slight inaccuracies) in Stewart, pp. 173–4. This MS includes the verse headings (probably by Kipling) to Chapter 8, beginning 'Love and let love and so will I' (Vol. 1, p. 75), Harbord, Verse Nos. 371 and 738 and to Chapter 15, beginning 'Could I but write the things I see' (Vol. 2, p. 35), Harbord, Verse Nos. 381 and 739.

Contents: Vol. 1: KpR 495, 1773, 1952, 2022, 2027, 2211, 2271; Vol. 2: KpR 1454, 1528, 1589, 1679, 1808, 1931, 2061, 2080, 2088. For missing pages, see also KpR 1608, 1635.

Huntington, HM 12494.

KpR 1635 Thin carbon copy page (detached from MS From Sea to Sea (KpR 1634), Vol. 2, p. 57), being the conclusion to Chapter 10, beginning 'Once, before I got away, I climbd to the civil station of Hong Kong...', paginated 7.

Library of Congress, Rare Book Division, Carpenter Kipling Collection.

KpR 1636 Fair copy, revised, of Chapters 5–7, in MS Essays and Stories (ff. [2–6v, 7–11v, 12–18]), 10, 10 and 13 pages respectively, including sketches.

Berg.

KpR 1637 Revised clipping (either from the first publication or from *The Pioneer Mail*) of Chapters 1, 2 and 4, mostly cuts, some may not be by RK, in Scrapbook 4 (pp. 99–102).

Sussex, KP 28/4.

KpR 1638 Corrected galley proofs of Chapters 17–21, among proofs for *From Sea to Sea* (1899), stamped '1st REV.'; date stamped 8 April 1899.

There is one correction to the verse heading to Chapter 21, beginning 'Very sadly did we leave it, but we gave our hearts in pledge' (Harbord, Verse Nos. 383 and 740).

Library of Congress, Rare Book Division, Carpenter Kipling Collection.

KpR 1639 Corrected page proofs for *From Sea to Sea* (1899) (see KpR 1642), in Vols I–II (not all bound in the correct order), signed (initials) *passim*, stamped '2nd REV.'; date stamped 10–24 May 1899.

There are revisions and corrections to the verse headings to Chapters 15 and 21 (see above KpR 1634, 1638).

Library of Congress, Rare Book Division, Carpenter Kipling Collection.

KpR 1640 Interleaved copy of *From Sea to Sea* (1899), the interleaved pages containing typescripts of passages omitted in this edition, also containing revisions to chapter numbers in the Contents pages of both volumes and throughout the text, all other contents of these volumes are uncut.

Library of Congress, Rare Book Division, Carpenter Kipling Collection.

KpR 1641 Corrected first page proof for the Sussex Edition, Vols XXII–XXIII; date stamped 7 (Vol. XXII) and 18 (Vol. XXIII) November 1932.

British Library, Add. MSS 55872–3.

***From Sea to Sea*, 2 vols (New York, 1899)**
For galley proofs set up for this edition, see KpR 1397, 1638, 1647, 1668, 1742, 1822; for an interleaved copy, see KpR 1640.

KpR 1642 Two volumes of page proofs, stamped throughout '2nd REV.', including (as well as contents below) a portion of the Contents (pp. viii–xiii) and the half-title (date stamped 10 May 1899); the date stamps run to 25 May 1899.

Contents: KpR 1398, 1509, 1639, 1642, 1669, 1743, 2078.

Library of Congress, Rare Book Division, Carpenter Kipling Collection.

From Tideway to Tideway
The first 8 of this series of 9 articles first pub. *The Times*, 13 April–29 November 1892 (including the verses 'Buddha at Kamakura' (see KpR 132–5) at the end of No. III 'The Edge of the East'); also pub. *New York Sun*, 17 April–4 December 1892 and *Civil*

and Military Gazette, 4 May–20 December 1892 (including: 'King Euric' (see KpR 569) as heading and 'The stumbling block of western lore' (see KpR 1166–7) as the closing lines to No. IV 'Our Overseas Men'; 'L'Envoi' ('When Earth's last picture is painted') (see KpR 629–31) as closing lines to No. VI 'Half-A-Dozen Pictures'; 'The Voortrekker' (see KpR 1320–21) as heading and 'The Rhyme of the Three Sealers' (see KpR 973) in the text of No. VII '"Captains Courageous"'; No. IX 'Leaves from a Winter Note-Book' first pub. *Harper's Magazine*, May 1900; collected (without poems) *Letters of Travel* (London, 1920); *Sussex*, XXIV, 5–128; Harbord, III, 1452–80.

KpR 1643 Portions of a fair copy, revised, of No. IV 'Our Overseas Men', the title revised from 'The Overseas Club', originally on 5 numbered leaves (rectos only), each leaf cup into scraps (by a printer?) and numbered in blue pencil, including now f. 1 (scraps 1–3), f. 2 (scraps 4–5 only), f. 3 (scraps 9 only, the bottom), f. 4 (scraps 10–13), f. 5 (scrap 14 only, the top) (i.e., 11 scraps in all), including also KpR 569, annotated 'To appear Friday night – 22nd'.

Harvard, MS Eng 1267.1(2).

KpR 1644 No. V 'Some Earthquakes', revised, signed, 6 numbered leaves (rectos only); watermarked 1890, dated 'Yokohama: July: 9th'.

Harvard, MS Eng 1267.1(1).

KpR 1645 Fair copy, revised, of No. VI 'Half-A-Dozen Pictures', including the epigraph from William Habington and KpR 629, 5 numbered leaves (rectos only); watermarked 1890.

Berg.

KpR 1646 No. IX 'Leaves from a Winter Note-Book', revised, here entitled 'A Winter Note Book', in MS Day's Work, 9 numbered pages; watermarked 1890.

British Library, Add. MS 45541, ff. 151–9 (rectos only).

KpR 1647 Galley proof of Nos I–VIII, containing corrections to Nos I ('In Sight of Monadnock'), III ('The Edge of the East', including also KpR 134), IV ('Our Overseas Men', including also KpR 1167), V ('Some Earthquakes', here entitled 'On Some Earthquakes') and VIII ('On One Side Only', here entitled 'On the Other Side'), set up for *From Sea to Sea*, 2 vols (New York, 1899) but not so published, signed (initials) *passim*, stamped '1st REV.'; date stamped 8–9 May 1899.

Library of Congress, Rare Book Division, Carpenter Kipling Collection.

KpR 1648 Slightly corrected typescript of all 9 articles, among materials for *Letters of Travel* (KpR 1824); No. IX 'Leaves from a Winter Note-Book' here including KpR 820 not published with the article; 115 leaves (rectos only), each article foliated separately.

Berg.

KpR 1649 Corrected first page proof for the Sussex Edition; date stamped 30 April 1935.

British Library, Add. MS 55874.

The Fumes of the Heart

First pub. in an unauthorized pamphlet New York, 1916; first authorized pub. *La revue des deux mondes*, 1 May 1917; collected as 'Letter No. 2' in *The Eyes of Asia* (New York, 1918); *Sussex*, XXVI, 189–200; Harbord, V, 2324–5.

KpR 1650 Revised, in MS Eyes of Asia (ff. 162–6, rectos only), annotated in an unidentified hand 'not complete'.

University of Edinburgh, Dk. 2. 8.

KpR 1651 Corrected unbound copy of *The Eyes of Asia* (New York, 1919), pp. 25–46, used for the Sussex Edition.

British Library, Add. MS 55851.

The Garden of Eden

First pub. *Week's News*, 16 June 1888; collected *The Story of the Gadsbys* (Allahabad, [1888]); *Sussex*, II, 179–90; Harbord, I, 309–10.

KpR 1652 Corrections in a copy of the first collected edition (KpR 2104).

Syracuse University.

KpR 1653 Annotation explaining Indian words, in a copy of the first collected edition (KpR 2105), p. 57.

Berg.

KpR 1654 Corrected first page proof for the Sussex Edition; date stamped 14 May 1931.

British Library, Add. MS 55853.

The Gardener
First pub. with eight lines from 'The Burden' as heading in *McCall's Magazine*, April 1925; collected with poem 'The Burden' in *Debits and Credits* (London, 1926); *Sussex*, X, 319–33; Harbord, VII, 3182–6.

KpR 1655 Revised, in MS Debits and Credits, 4 numbered pages (ff. 165–8, rectos only), annotated 'type — wide spaces'.

University of Durham.

KpR 1656 Corrected first page proof for the Sussex Edition; date stamped 30 December 1931.

British Library, Add. MS 55861.

Garm —— a Hostage
First pub. *Saturday Evening Post*, 23 December 1899; collected with poem 'The Power of the Dog' in *Actions and Reactions* (London, 1909); *Sussex*, VIII, 53–75; Harbord, VI, 2818–19.

KpR 1657 Revised, in MS Day's Work, 9 numbered pages; watermarked 1890 and 1894.

British Library, Add. MS 45541, ff. 233–41 (rectos only).

KpR 1658 Annotated first page proof for *Collected Dog Stories* (London, 1934), pp. 19–45; date stamped 27 July 1934.

British Library, Add. MS 55848.

KpR 1659 Corrected first page proof for the Sussex Edition; date stamped 28 November 1931.

British Library, Add. MS 55859.

The Gate of the Hundred Sorrows
First pub. *Civil and Military Gazette*, 26 September 1884; collected *Plain Tales from the Hills* (Calcutta and London, 1888); *Sussex*, I, 361–9; Harbord, I, 88, 112–14.

KpR 1660 Corrected first page proof for the Sussex Edition; date stamped 12 September 1931.

British Library, Add. MS 55852.

Gemini
First pub. *Week's News*, 14 January 1888; collected *In Black and White* (Allahabad, [1888]); *Sussex*, II, 279–90; Harbord, I, 320–2.

KpR 1661 Fair copy, revised, in MS Essays and Stories (ff. [12–17] of the inserted notebook), 11 pages, including sketches.

Berg.

KpR 1662 Revisions in a copy of the second edition of *In Black and White* (Allahabad, 1889) (KpR 1747).

Berg.

KpR 1663 Corrections in a copy of the first collected edition (KpR 1745).

Syracuse University.

KpR 1664 Annotations explaining Indian words, in a copy of the first collected edition (KpR 1746), pp. [30]–1, 38.

Berg.

KpR 1665 Corrected first page proof for the Sussex Edition; date stamped 14 May 1931.

British Library, Add. MS 55853.

Georgie Porgie
First pub. *Week's News*, 3 March 1888; collected *Life's Handicap* (London and New York, 1891); *Sussex*, IV, 419–30; Harbord, II, 1002–4. For notes on this story, see KpR 2287.

KpR 1666 Corrected first page proof for the Sussex Edition; date stamped 13 February 1932.

British Library, Add. MS 55855.

A Germ-Destroyer
First pub. *Civil and Military Gazette*, 17 May 1887;

collected *Plain Tales from the Hills* (Calcutta and London, 1888); *Sussex*, I, 173–9; Harbord, I, 59–60.

KpR 1667 Corrected first page proof for the Sussex Edition; date stamped 12 September 1931.

British Library, Add. MS 55852.

The Giridih Coal-Fields
First pub. *The Pioneer*, 24 August, 6 and 20 September 1888; collected *From Sea to Sea*, 2 vols (New York, 1899); *Sussex*, XXIII, 285–309; Harbord, II, 908–10.

KpR 1668 Corrected galley proof, among proofs for *From Sea to Sea* (1899), stamped '1st REV.', signed (initials) *passim*.

Library of Congress, Rare Book Division, Carpenter Kipling Collection.

KpR 1669 Corrected page proof in Vol. II of proofs for *From Sea to Sea* (KpR 1642), stamped '2nd REV.', signed (initials) *passim*.

Library of Congress, Rare Book Division, Carpenter Kipling Collection.

KpR 1670 Corrected first page proof for the Sussex Edition; date stamped 18 November 1932.

British Library, Add. MS 55873.

Gloriana
First pub. *The Delineator*, December 1909; reprinted (accompanied by the Introduction to *Rewards and Fairies*) in *Nash's Magazine*, March 1910; collected with poems 'The Two Cousins' (collected as 'The Queen's Men') and 'The Looking-Glass' in *Rewards and Fairies* (London, 1910); *Sussex*, XV, 31–49; Harbord, VI, 2771–3.

KpR 1671 Revised, in MS Rewards and Fairies, 5 numbered pages.

Cambridge University Library, ADD 6850, ff. 13–17 (rectos only).

KpR 1672 Corrected first page proof for the Sussex Edition; date stamped 18 September 1931.

British Library, Add. MS 55865.

The God from the Machine
First pub. *Week's News*, 7 January 1888; collected *Soldiers Three* (Allahabad, 1888); *Sussex*, II, 5–16; Harbord, I, 279–80.

KpR 1673 Corrections in a copy of the first collected edition (KpR 2081).

Syracuse University.

KpR 1674 Annotations explaining Indian words, in a copy of the first collected edition (KpR 2082), pp. [1]–4, 7–10.

Berg.

KpR 1675 Corrected first page proof for the Sussex Edition; date stamped 14 May 1931.

British Library, Add. MS 55853.

The Great Census, see KpR 2078–9.

The Great Play Hunt
First pub. *Cassell's Magazine*, September 1930; collected *Thy Servant A Dog* (London, 1930); *Sussex*, XVI, 273–92; Harbord, VI, 2907–8.

KpR 1676 First page proof and a portion of second page proof, both corrected, for *Thy Servant A Dog* (London, 1930); date stamped August 1930.

British Library, Add. MS 55846.

KpR 1677 Corrected first page proof for *Collected Dog Stories* (London, 1934), pp. 191–213; date stamped 30 July 1934.

British Library, Add. MS 55848.

KpR 1678 Two sets of corrected first page proofs for the Sussex Edition, only one corrected by RK; date stamped 4 March 1936.

British Library, Add. MS 55866.

Griffiths The Safe Man
First pub. *Civil and Military Gazette*, 31 July 1889; collected *Abaft the Funnel* (New York, 1909); *Sussex*, XXIX, 69–75; Harbord, II, 684.

KpR 1679 Fair copy, revised (thin paper carbon copy), in MS From Sea to Sea (see KpR 1634), 4 numbered pages.

Huntington, HM 12429, Vol. 2, pp. 45–8.

Growth and Responsibility
Speech delivered at Canadian Club, Winnipeg, 3 October 1907; first pub. J. C. Hopkins, *The Canadian Annual Review of Public Affairs 1907* (Toronto, [1908]); collected *A Book of Words* (London, 1928); *Sussex*, XXV, 31–4; Harbord, VII, 3289.

KpR 1680 Corrected first page proof for the Sussex Edition; date stamped 4 April 1931.

British Library, Add. MS 55875.

An Habitation Enforced
First pub. *Century Magazine*, August 1905; collected with poem 'The Recall' in *Actions and Reactions* (London, 1909); *Sussex*, VIII, 3–47; Harbord, VI, 2808–18.

KpR 1681 In MS Actions and Reactions (ff. 1–14).

University of St Andrews, MS PR4854.A4.

KpR 1682 Corrected first page proof for the Sussex Edition; date stamped 28 November 1931.

British Library, Add. MS 55859.

Hal o' The Draft
First pub. *Strand Magazine* and *McClure's Magazine*, August 1906; collected with poems 'Prophets at Home' and 'A Smuggler's Song' in *Puck of Pook's Hill* (London, 1906); *Sussex*, XIV, 199–215; Harbord, VI, 2744–50.

KpR 1683 Two MSS in MS Puck, one revised, 7 numbered leaves (ff. 77–83, rectos only), the other, incomplete, revised, 5 numbered leaves (ff. 85–9, rectos only), here entitled (cancelled) 'Puck of Pooks Hill/VIII' and (uncancelled) 'Hal o' The Draft' and 'Robin Good Fellow — his Friends.'.

Bodleian, MS. Eng. misc. c. 127, ff. 77–83, 85–9 (rectos only).

KpR 1684 Corrected first page proof for the Sussex Edition; date stamped 2 July 1931.

British Library, Add. MS 55864.

Half-A-Dozen Pictures, for 'From Tideway to Tideway No. VI', see KpR 1645, 1647–9.

The Handicaps of Letters
Speech delivered Royal Literary Fund, London, 20 May 1908; first pub. *The Times*, 22 May 1908, as 'The Burdens of Authorship'; collected *A Book of Words* (London, 1928); *Sussex*, XXV, 37–40; Harbord, VII, 3290.

KpR 1685 Corrected first page proof for the Sussex Edition; date stamped 4 April 1931.

British Library, Add. MS 55875.

The Hands of Justice, see KpR 2078–9.

Haunted Subalterns
First pub. *Civil and Military Gazette*, 27 May 1887; collected *Plain Tales from the Hills*, Outward Bound Edition, Vol. I (New York, 1897); *Sussex*, I, 133–9; Harbord, III, 1607–8, as 'Uncollected No. 79'.

KpR 1686 Revised clipping of first publication, in Scrapbook 3 (p. 119), annotated 'Miss [Henning?]'.

Sussex, KP 28/3.

KpR 1687 Corrected first page proof for the Sussex Edition; date stamped 12 September 1931.

British Library, Add. MS 55852.

The Head of the District
First pub. *Macmillan's Magazine*, January 1890; collected *Life's Handicap* (London and New York, 1891); *Sussex*, IV, 125–54; Harbord, II, 966–8.

KpR 1688 Corrected first page proof for the Sussex Edition; date stamped 13 February 1932.

British Library, Add. MS 55855.

Healing By the Stars
Speech delivered Royal Society of Medicine Annual Dinner, London, 15 November 1928; first pub. *The Times*, 16 November 1928; *Sussex*, XXV, 295–9; Harbord, VII, 3316–17.

KpR 1689 Corrected first page proof for the Sussex Edition; date stamped 4 April 1931.

British Library, Add. MS 55875.

Her Majesty's Servants

First pub. as 'The Servants of the Queen' in *Pall Mall Magazine*, March 1894; collected with poem 'Parade-Song of the Camp-Animals' in *The Jungle Book* (London and New York, 1894), as 'The Servants of the Queen'; *Sussex*, XII, 445–65; Harbord, VII, 3018–23.

KpR 1690 Revised, here entitled 'The Servants of the Queen', in MS Jungle Books, 7 numbered leaves (rectos only); watermarked 1890.

British Library, Add. MS 45540, ff. 32–8 (rectos only).

The Hill of Illusion

First pub. *Civil and Military Gazette*, 28 September 1887; collected *Under the Deodars* (Allahabad, [1888]); *Sussex*, III, 67–79; Harbord, I, 342–3. For an early MS (the germ of this story), see KpR 1415.

KpR 1691 Fair copy, revised, including the epigraph from Matthew Arnold and two verses in the text (4 lines beginning 'Kind Sir, o' your courtesy' and 8 lines beginning 'Pendant une année toute entière'), 13 numbered leaves (rectos only).

The two verses are listed as possibly by Kipling in Harbord, Verse Nos. 278–9, the second entitled 'La Chanson du Colonel'.

Berg.

KpR 1692 Corrections in a copy of the first collected edition (KpR 2175).

Syracuse University.

KpR 1693 Corrected first page proof for the Sussex Edition; date stamped 14 May 1931.

British Library, Add. MS 55854.

His Chance in Life

First pub. *Civil and Military Gazette*, 2 April 1887; collected *Plain Tales from the Hills* (Calcutta and London, 1888); *Sussex*, I, 105–11; Harbord, I, 48–9.

KpR 1694 Corrected first page proof for the Sussex Edition; date stamped 12 September 1931.

British Library, Add. MS 55852.

His Gift

First pub. with poem 'Prologue to the Master-Cook's Tale' (collected as 'The Master-Cook') in *Land and Sea Tales* (London, 1923); *Sussex*, XVI, 71–89; Harbord, VI, 2889–91.

KpR 1695 Draft, in MS Debits and Credits, 8 pages (ff. 16–[22a], rectos only), annotated 'type'.

University of Durham.

KpR 1696 Corrected first page proof for *Humorous Tales* (London, 1931), pp. 231–50; date stamped 19 May 1931.

British Library, Add. MS 55847.

KpR 1697 Corrected first page proof for the Sussex Edition; date stamped 14 December 1931.

British Library, Add. MS 55866.

His Majesty the King

First pub. *Week's News*, 5 May 1888; collected *Wee Willie Winkie* (Allahabad, [1888]); *Sussex*, III, 357–71; Harbord, I, 382–3.

KpR 1698 Fair copy, revised, in MS Essays and Stories [ff. 18v–25], 14 pages, including sketches.

Berg.

KpR 1699 Corrections in a copy of the first collected edition (KpR 2229).

Syracuse University.

KpR 1700 Annotations explaining Indian words, in a copy of the first collected edition (KpR 2230), pp. 52–3, 57, 63.

Berg.

KpR 1701 Corrected first page proof for the Sussex Edition; date stamped 18 September 1931.

British Library, Add. MS 55854.

His Private Honour

First pub. *Macmillan's Magazine*, October 1891; collected *Many Inventions* (London and New York, 1893); *Sussex*, V, 229–54; Harbord, III, 1230–3.

KpR 1702 Corrected first page proof for the Sussex Edition; date stamped 10 June 1931.

British Library, Add. MS 55856.

His Wedded Wife

First pub. (with verse heading) *Civil and Military Gazette*, 25 February 1887; collected *Plain Tales from the Hills* (Calcutta and London, 1888); *Sussex*, I, 215–22; Harbord, I, 66. For verse heading, see KpR 177.

KpR 1703 Corrected first page proof for the Sussex Edition; date stamped 12 September 1931.

British Library, Add. MS 55852.

Home

First pub. (with 'Home', a 10-stanza verse heading) in *Civil and Military Gazette*, 25 December 1891; not collected; reprinted Harbord, V, 2488–504 (without verse heading).

KpR 1704 Carbon typescript, including the verse heading (KpR 473), 21 numbered leaves (rectos only), annotated '(Reprinted from the *Civil and Military Gazette*, 25th December, 1891).'.

Library of Congress, Rare Book Division, Colt Collection.

The Honours of War

First pub. (with verse heading 'The Jester') *Family Magazine*, May 1911, as 'Honours Even'; collected with poem 'The Children' in *A Diversity of Creatures* (London, 1917); *Sussex*, IX, 107–29; Harbord, VII, 3065–9.

KpR 1705 Revised, title in pencil, otherwise in ink, including an epigraph from 'Kitcheners School', in MS Diversity of Creatures (ff. 35–42, rectos only).

University of Edinburgh, Dk. 2. 8.

KpR 1706 Corrected first page proof for the Sussex Edition; date stamped 28 April 1932.

British Library, Add. MS 55860.

The Horse Marines

First pub. *Pearson's Magazine*, October 1910; collected with poem 'The Legend of Mirth' in *A Diversity of Creatures* (London, 1917); *Sussex*, IX, 301–26; Harbord, IV, 1810–23.

KpR 1707 Revised, here entitled 'The Horse Marines' in pencil and 'A Scandal in the Service' in ink (possibly not in RK's hand), wanting the epigraph, in MS Diversity of Creatures (ff. 102–9, rectos only).

University of Edinburgh, Dk. 2. 8.

KpR 1708 Corrected first page proof for the Sussex Edition; date stamped 28 April 1932.

British Library, Add. MS 55860.

The House of Shadows

First pub. *Civil and Military Gazette*, 4 August 1887; collected Pinney (1986), pp. 246–8; not in Harbord.

KpR 1709 Revised clipping of first publication, in Scrapbook 4 (p. 142).

Sussex, KP 28/4.

The House Surgeon

First pub. *Harper's Magazine*, September–October 1909; collected with poem 'The Rabbi's Song' in *Actions and Reactions* (London, 1909); *Sussex*, VIII, 253–86; Harbord, VI, 2874–80.

KpR 1710 In MS Actions and Reactions (ff. 118–32).

University of St Andrews, MS PR4854.A4.

KpR 1711 Corrected first page proof for the Sussex Edition; date stamped 28 November 1931.

British Library, Add. MS 55859.

How Fear Came

First pub. with poem 'The Law of the Wolves' (collected as 'The Law of the Jungle') in *Pall Mall Budget*, 7 and 14 June 1894; collected (with verse heading 'The stream is shrunk — the pool is dry') in *The Second Jungle Book* (London and New York, 1895); *Sussex*, XII, 71–92; Harbord, VII, 2960–2.

KpR 1712 Revised, here entitled 'How Fear came to the Jungle.', in MS Jungle Books, 9 leaves (rectos only); watermarked 1890.

British Library, Add. MS 45540, ff. 162–70 (rectos only).

KpR 1713 Corrected galley proof for the first publication, here entitled 'How Fear Came to the Jungle'.

Syracuse University.

How Liberty Came to the Bolan
First pub. *Civil and Military Gazette*, [late 1887]; not collected; not in Harbord.

KpR 1714 Revised clipping of first publication (undated), in Scrapbook 3 (p. 150).

Sussex, KP 28/3.

'How much can a man endure and live?'
No publication traced.

KpR 1715 Fair copy, revised, of 4 lines of dialogue (possibly for a story), on the page from an Indian calendar for 10 February 1888.

Library of Congress, Rare Book Division, Carpenter Kipling Collection, Pen and Brush Sketches, Item 4.

How the Alphabet Was Made
First pub. with poem 'Of all the tribe of Tegumai' in *Just So Stories* (London, 1902); *Sussex*, XIII, 139–56; Harbord, IV, 1675–7.

KpR 1716 Revised, in MS Just So Stories, including the story, here entitled 'How Taffy made the Alphabet', 5 leaves (rectos only) (ff. 75, 80, 86, 94, 103, the last watermarked 1896); the caption, 2 numbered leaves (rectos only) (ff. 68–9); and all the original illustrations (ff. 70–4, 76–9, 81–5, 87–93, 95–102).

British Library, Add. MS 59840, ff. 68–102 (rectos only).

KpR 1717 Fair copy, 2 leaves (rectos only).

Berg.

KpR 1718 Corrected first page proof for the Sussex Edition; date stamped 29 October 1932.

British Library, Add. MS 55863.

How the Camel Got His Hump
First pub. *St Nicholas*, January 1898; collected with poem 'The Camel's hump is an ugly lump' in *Just So Stories* (London, 1902); *Sussex*, XIII, 17–[25]; Harbord, IV, 1659–60.

KpR 1719 Revised, in MS Just So Stories, including the story (f. 16), the two captions (f. 12, watermarked 1901) and the three original illustrations (ff. 13–15, rectos only).

British Library, Add. MS 59840, ff. 12–16 (rectos only).

KpR 1720 Corrected first page proof for the Sussex Edition; date stamped 29 October 1932.

British Library, Add. MS 55863.

How the First Letter Was Written
First pub. *Ladies Home Journal*, December 1901; collected with poem 'There runs a road by Merrow Down' in *Just So Stories* (London, 1902); *Sussex*, XIII, 119–34; Harbord, IV, 1671–4.

KpR 1721 Revised, in MS Just So Stories, including the story, here entitled '(1) Taffimai Metallumai.' and dated September 1900, 3 numbered leaves (rectos only) (ff. 64–6, watermarked 1896); the caption (f. 60, watermarked 1901); and the 3 original illustrations (ff. 61–3, rectos only).

British Library, Add. MS 59840, ff. 60–6 (rectos only).

KpR 1722 Corrected typescript, here originally entitled 'The First Letter that was Written', 9 numbered leaves (rectos only), as sent to the *Ladies Home Journal*, annotated 'proof to the Elms...'.

Berg.

KpR 1723 Corrected galley proof for first publication, signed (initials).

Berg.

KpR 1724 Corrected first page proof for the Sussex Edition; date stamped 29 October 1932.

British Library, Add. MS 55863.

How the Leopard Got His Spots
First pub. *Ladies Home Journal*, October 1901;

collected with poem 'I am the Most Wise Baviaan' in *Just So Stories* (London, 1902); *Sussex*, XIII, 45–58; Harbord, IV, 1661–2.

KpR 1725 Revised, in MS Just So Stories, including the story, 3 leaves (rectos only), the last also containing KpR 121 (ff. 28–30, rectos only, watermarked 1896); the two captions (f. 24, watermarked 1901); and the 3 original illustrations (ff. 25–7, rectos only).

British Library, Add. MS 59840, ff. 24–30 (rectos only).

KpR 1726 Corrected galley proof.

Facsimile portion in *Grolier Catalogue*, Plate XXII (Item 312).

Unlocated.

KpR 1727 Corrected first page proof for the Sussex Edition; date stamped 29 October 1932.

British Library, Add. MS 55863.

How the Rhinoceros Got His Skin
First pub. *St Nicholas*, February 1898, as 'How the Rhinoceros Got His Wrinkly Skin'; collected with poem 'This Uninhabited Island' in *Just So Stories* (London, 1902); *Sussex*, XIII, 31–[39]; Harbord, IV, 1660–1.

KpR 1728 Revised, in MS Just So Stories, including the story (f. 22), the two captions (f. 18, watermarked 1901) and the 3 original illustrations (ff. 19–21, rectos only).

British Library, Add. MS 59840, ff. 18–22 (rectos only).

KpR 1729 Slightly corrected first page proof for the Sussex Edition; date stamped 29 October 1932.

British Library, Add. MS 55863.

How the Whale Got His Throat
First pub. (with an introductory paragraph not later collected) *St Nicholas*, December 1897, as 'How the Whale Got His Tiny Throat'; collected with poem 'When the cabin port-holes are dark and green' in *Just So Stories* (London, 1902); *Sussex*, XIII, 3–[11]; Harbord, IV, 1657–9 (including the introductory paragraph).

KpR 1730 Revised, in MS Just So Stories, including the introductory paragraph, headed 'The Just-So Stories.' (f. 9); the story, here untitled and headed '<The Just So Stories.>' (f. 10, watermarked 1896); two pages each containing the two captions, the first headed 'How the Whale Got his Throat', the second 'The Whale.' (ff. 4, 5, both watermarked 1901); and the three original illustrations (ff. 6–8, rectos only).

British Library, Add. MS 59840, ff. 4–10 (rectos only).

KpR 1731 Corrected first page proof for the Sussex Edition; date stamped 29 October 1932.

British Library, Add. MS 55863.

How to Bring Up a Lion
First pub. as 'My Personal Experiences With a Lion' in *Ladies Home Journal*, January 1902; collected *The Kipling Reader for Elementary Grades* (New York and Chicago, 1912); reprinted Harbord, V, 2566–71, as 'Uncollected No. 238A'.

KpR 1732 Corrected galley proof.

Grolier Catalogue, Item 436.

Unlocated.

Howling Sam a tale of Blood
No publication traced; not in Harbord.

KpR 1733 RK's contribution to 'The Teuton Tonic' (see KpR 2285), a MS 'magazine', 'published' aboard the S.S. Teutonic, June 1899.

Princeton, Doubleday Collection, Box 2, Folder 2.

***Humorous Tales* (New York, 1931)**

KpR 1734 Memorandum, being a list of story titles headed 'Possible omissions in Humorous Tales.', written on a Brown's Hotel notecard; in a Doubleday envelope dated July 1931.

Princeton, Doubleday Collection, Box 2, Folder 22.

Hunting a Miracle, see KpR 2078–9.

The Hunting of the Paras
First pub. *National Observer*, 20 December 1890; reprinted Harbord, V, 2483, as 'Uncollected No. 205'.

KpR 1735 Fragment, being a version of the opening breaking off in mid-sentence, revised, 2 numbered pages, signed; dated London, May 1890.

Iowa State Historical Library, 1-8-8.

Imperial Relations
Speech delivered Canadian Club, Toronto, 18 October 1907; first pub. *The Times*, 18 October 1907, as 'Labour and Immigration'; collected *A Book of Words* (London, 1928); *Sussex*, XXV, 21–7; Harbord, VII, 3289.

KpR 1736 Corrected first page proof for the Sussex Edition; date stamped 4 April 1931.

British Library, Add. MS 55875.

The Impressionists
First pub. *Windsor Magazine* and *McClure's Magazine*, February 1899; collected *Stalky & Co.* (London, 1899); *Sussex*, XVII, 133–62; Harbord, I, 442–5.

KpR 1737 Revised, in MS Stalky, 11 numbered pages (ff. 32–42, rectos only), annotated 'to be typed urgent RK.'.

Haileybury.

KpR 1738 Corrected first page proof for the Sussex Edition; date stamped 27 March 1931.

British Library, Add. MS 55867.

'In Ambush'
First pub. *McClure's Magazine*, August 1898; collected *Stalky & Co.* (London, 1899); *Sussex*, XVII, 31–65; Harbord, I, 426–31.

KpR 1739 Revised, in MS Stalky, here originally entitled '<In the Wuzzy.>', 10 numbered pages (ff. 1–10, rectos only).

Haileybury.

KpR 1740 Typescript, revised, subtitled 'A Moral tale for boys', 46 leaves (rectos only) and a title page (bearing A. P. Watt's label).

Dalhousie University.

KpR 1741 Corrected first page proof for the Sussex Edition; date stamped 27 March 1931.

British Library, Add. MS 55867.

In an Opium Factory
First pub. *The Pioneer*, 16 April 1888; collected *From Sea to Sea*, 2 vols (New York, 1899); *Sussex*, XXIII, 313–20; Harbord, II, 911.

KpR 1742 Corrected galley proof, incomplete, among proofs for *From Sea to Sea* (1899), stamped '1st REV.'.

Library of Congress, Rare Book Division, Carpenter Kipling Collection.

KpR 1743 Corrected page proof in Vol. II of proofs for *From Sea to Sea* (1899) (KpR 1642), stamped '2nd REV.', signed (initials) *passim*.

Library of Congress, Rare Book Division, Carpenter Kipling Collection.

KpR 1744 Corrected first page proof for the Sussex Edition; date stamped 18 November 1932.

British Library, Add. MS 55873.

In Black and White
First pub. Allahabad, [1888].

KpR 1745 Copy (wanting the wrapper) containing corrections by RK to the 'Introduction by Kadir Baksh, Khitmatgar' and 'The Dedication', as well as Contents below.

The 'Introduction' and 'The Dedication' (not collected later) are reprinted in Harbord, I, 273–6.

Contents: KpR 1407, 1417, 1559, 1663,

1752, 1780, 1941, 2057.

Syracuse University.

KpR 1746 Copy, containing annotations explaining Indian words in the 'Introduction by Kadir Baksh, Khitmatgar' (pp. [i]–ii), as well as Contents below.

Contents: KpR 1408, 1418, 1560, 1665, 1751, 1781, 1942, 2058.

Berg.

KpR 1747 Copy of the second edition (Allahabad, 1889), containing revisions by RK to the 'Introduction by Kadir Baksh, Khitmatgar' (pp. [i]–ii), as well as Contents below.

Contents: KpR 1406, 1416, 1558, 1662, 1750, 1779, 1940, 2056.

Berg.

In Defence of his home
No publication traced; not in Harbord; see *The Americanization of Edward Bok* (New York, 1920), pp. 384–5.

KpR 1748 Notes, revised, for a projected work so entitled, on the subject of the unrest among American women, previously entitled '<The Last American Rebellion>', one page, including descriptions of characters (members of the Mondel family, Virginia Le Touche, Mrs Giddens, Reginald Seares, etc.).

Syracuse University.

In Error
First pub. (with verse heading) *Civil and Military Gazette*, 24 January 1887; collected *Plain Tales from the Hills* (Calcutta and London, 1888); *Sussex*, I, 245–50; Harbord, I, 69. For verse heading, see KpR 177.

KpR 1749 Corrected first page proof for the Sussex Edition; date stamped 12 September 1931.

British Library, Add. MS 55852.

'In every nation's life there comes a breathing space...', see KpR 2011.

In Flood Time
First pub. *Week's News*, 11 August 1888; collected *In Black and White* (Allahabad, [1888]); *Sussex*, II, 311–23; Harbord, I, 323–9.

KpR 1750 Revisions in a copy of the second edition of *In Black and White* (Allahabad, 1889) (KpR 1747).

Berg.

KpR 1751 Annotations explaining Indian words, in a copy of the first collected edition (KpR 1746), pp. [55]–60, 63, 65.

Berg.

KpR 1752 Corrections in a copy of the first collected edition (KpR 1745).

Syracuse University.

KpR 1753 Corrected first page proof for the Sussex Edition; date stamped 14 May 1931.

British Library, Add. MS 55853.

In Sight of Monadnock, for 'From Tideway to Tideway No. I', see KpR 1647–9.

In the House of Suddhoo
First pub. (with verse heading) *Civil and Military Gazette*, 30 April 1886, as 'Section 420 I.P.C.'; collected *Plain Tales from the Hills* (Calcutta and London, 1888); *Sussex*, I, 201–11; Harbord, I, 64–5. For verse heading, see KpR 177.

KpR 1754 Proof containing a glossary written out in Kipling's hand, one page, being the version published in Edition De Luxe (London, 1897) of *Plain Tales from the Hills* (i.e., without verse heading).

Facsimile portion (including the glossary) in Martindell, facing p. 168 (proof collated, pp. 163–9).

Owned (1923) by E. W. Martindell.

KpR 1755 Corrected page proof for the Sussex Edition; date stamped 12 September 1931.

British Library, Add. MS 55852.

'In the Interests of the Brethren'
First pub. *Story-Teller Magazine* and *Metropolitan*

Magazine, December 1918; collected with poem '"Banquet Night"' in *Debits and Credits* (London, 1926); *Sussex*, X, 55–76; Harbord, VII, 3127–34.

KpR 1756 Revised, here untitled, in MS Debits and Credits, 13 pages (ff. 55–67, rectos only), containing the verses in the text beginning 'We have showed thee, O man' (f. 64).

The verses in the text are listed Harbord, Verse No. 1053.

University of Durham.

KpR 1757 Corrected first page proof for the Sussex Edition; date stamped 30 December 1931.

British Library, Add. MS 55861.

In the Matter of a Private
First pub. *Week's News*, 14 April 1888; collected *Soldiers Three* (Allahabad, 1888); *Sussex*, II, 87–99; Harbord, I, 289–91.

KpR 1758 Corrections in a copy of the first collected edition (KpR 2081).

Syracuse University.

KpR 1759 Annotations explaining Indian words, in a copy of the first collected edition (KpR 2082), pp. 65, 67, 69, 71.

Berg.

KpR 1760 Corrected first page proof for the Sussex Edition; date stamped 14 May 1931.

British Library, Add. MS 55853.

In the Presence
First pub. *Pearson's Magazine* and *Everybody's Magazine*, March 1912; collected with poem 'Jobson's Amen' in *A Diversity of Creatures* (London, 1917); *Sussex*, IX, 219–37; Harbord, VII, 3084–8.

KpR 1761 Revised, here originally entitled 'The Correct Thing', in MS Diversity of Creatures (ff. 71–7, rectos only).

University of Edinburgh, Dk. 2. 8.

KpR 1762 Corrected first page proof for the Sussex Edition; date stamped 28 April 1932.

British Library, Add. MS 55860.

In the Pride of His Youth
First pub. (with verse heading) *Civil and Military Gazette*, 5 May 1887; collected *Plain Tales from the Hills* (Calcutta and London, 1888); *Sussex*, I, 285–92; Harbord, I, 75–6. For verse heading, see KpR 177.

KpR 1763 Corrected first page proof (including corrections to the verse heading) for the Sussex Edition; date stamped 12 September 1931.

British Library, Add. MS 55852.

In the Rukh
First pub. (with verse heading 'The Only Son') *Many Inventions* (London and New York, 1893); *Sussex*, V, 297–34; Harbord, VII, 2973–9.

KpR 1764 Revised, in MS Day's Work, 22 numbered pages, including also KpR 786; watermarked 1890.

British Library, Add. MS 45541, ff. 44–65 (rectos only).

KpR 1765 Corrected first page proof for the Sussex Edition; date stamped 10 June 1931.

British Library, Add. MS 55856.

In the Same Boat
First pub. *Harper's Magazine*, December 1911; collected with poem '"Helen All Alone"' in *A Diversity of Creatures* (London, 1917); *Sussex*, IX, 71–101; Harbord, VII, 3060–5.

KpR 1766 Revised, including an epigraph from John Donne, 10 numbered pages, in MS Diversity of Creatures (ff. 23–32, rectos only).

University of Edinburgh, Dk. 2. 8.

KpR 1767 Corrected first page proof for the Sussex Edition; date stamped 28 April 1932.

British Library, Add. MS 55860.

The Inauthorated Corpses
First pub. *The Author*, 15 July 1890; reprinted Harbord, V, 2470–2, as 'Uncollected No. 200'.

KpR 1768 Fair copy, revised, here originally entitled 'The Authormatic Adjustment.', signed,

2 leaves (rectos only).

Facsimile at Harvard, Kipling 15.2.

Dalhousie University.

The Incarnation of Krishna Mulvaney
First pub. *Macmillan's Magazine*, December 1889; collected *Life's Handicap* (London and New York, 1891); *Sussex*, IV, 3–37; Harbord, II, 943–8.

KpR 1769 Corrected first page proof for *Humorous Tales* (London, 1931), pp. 333–68; date stamped 27 and 29 May 1931.

British Library, Add. MS 55847.

KpR 1770 Corrected first page proof for the Sussex Edition; date stamped 13 February 1932.

British Library, Add. MS 55855.

'Independence'
Speech delivered as Rectorial Address, St Andrew's University, 10 October 1923; first pub. *The Times*, 11 October 1923; collected *A Book of Words* (London, 1928); *Sussex*, XXV, 217–32; Harbord, VII, 3310–11.

KpR 1771 Draft, in MS Non-Fiction, entitled in pencil and headed 'del to St Andrews', 4 pages.

British Library, Add. MS 45542, ff. 186–9 (rectos only).

KpR 1772 Corrected first page proof for the Sussex Edition; date stamped 4 April 1931.

British Library, Add. MS 55875.

The Irish Guards in the Great War, see KpR 2284.

It!
First pub. *Civil and Military Gazette*, 1 June 1889; collected *Abaft the Funnel* (New York, 1909); *Sussex*, XXIX, 79–83; Harbord, II, 684–5.

KpR 1773 Fair copy, revised (thin paper carbon copy), in MS From Sea to Sea (see KpR 1634), 4 numbered pages.

Huntington, HM 12429, Vol. 1, pp. 59–62.

The Janeites
First pub. *Story-Teller Magazine* and *Hearst's International Magazine*, May 1924; collected with poems 'The Survival' and 'Jane's Marriage' in *Debits and Credits* (London, 1926); *Sussex*, X, 113–38; Harbord, VII, 3143–51.

KpR 1774 Revised, in MS Debits and Credits, annotated 'type as soon as possible RK/ keep till my return', 14 pages (ff. 86–99, rectos only).

University of Durham.

KpR 1775 Corrected first page proof for the Sussex Edition; date stamped 30 December 1931.

British Library, Add. MS 55861.

Jews in Shushan
First pub. *Civil and Military Gazette*, 4 October 1887; collected *Life's Handicap* (London and New York, 1891); *Sussex*, IV, 363–7; Harbord, II, 994.

KpR 1776 Revised clipping of the first publication, in Scrapbook 3 (pp. 147–8).

Sussex, KP 28/3.

KpR 1777 Corrected first page proof for the Sussex Edition; date stamped 13 February 1932.

British Library, Add. MS 55855.

The Journey Out, see KpR 1455.

The Jubilee in Lahore
First pub. *Civil and Military Gazette*, 18 February 1887; collected Pinney (1986), pp. 193–202; not in Harbord.

KpR 1778 Revised clipping of first publication, in Scrapbook 3 (pp. 79–80), annotated 'I don't think this is any good for you. RK'.

Sussex, KP 28/3.

The Judgment of Dungara
First pub. *Week's News*, 28 July, 1888, as 'The Peculiar Embarrassment [sic] of Justice Krenk'; collected *In Black and White* (Allahabad, [1888]); *Sussex*, II, 255–66; Harbord, I, 317–19.

KpR 1779 Revisions in a copy of the second edition of *In Black and White* (KpR 1747).

Berg.

KpR 1780 Corrections in a copy of the first collected edition (KpR 1745).

Syracuse University.

KpR 1781 Annotation explaining Indian words, in a copy of the first collected edition (KpR 1746), p. 18.

Berg.

KpR 1782 Corrected first page proof for the Sussex Edition; date stamped 14 May 1931.

British Library, Add. MS 55853.

Judson and the Empire
First pub. *Many Inventions* (London and New York, 1893); *Sussex*, V, 429–62; Harbord, III, 1259–71.

KpR 1783 Partly fair copy, revised (10 numbered pages, ff. 121–30, rectos only) and partly revised typescript (last 2 pages, ff. 131–2, rectos only), in MS Day's Work, annotated 'to be typewritten'.

British Library, Add. MS 45541, ff. 121–32 (rectos only).

KpR 1784 Corrected first page proof for *Humorous Tales* (London, 1931), pp. 67–99; date stamped 7 and 9 May 1931.

British Library, Add. MS 55847.

KpR 1785 Corrected first page proof for the Sussex Edition; date stamped 10 June 1931.

British Library, Add. MS 55856.

***The Jungle Book* (London and New York, 1894)**, for an inscribed copy, see KpR 1250.

Just So Stories
This collection of stories first pub. London, 1902; *Sussex*, XIII; Harbord, IV, 1655–98. For inscribed copies, see KpR 612, 1155; for MS Just So Stories, see INTRODUCTION.

KpR 1786 'Preface', revised, beginning 'After you have read these stories...', in MS Just So Stories, one page.

This 'Preface' is unpublished; for a reproduction, see FACSIMILES.

British Library, Add. MS 59840, f. 3.

Kaa's Hunting
First pub. *To-day*, 31 March and 7 April 1894; collected with poem 'The Road Song of the Bandar-Log' in *The Jungle Book* (London and New York, 1894); *Sussex*, XII, 35–66; Harbord, VII, 2959–60.

KpR 1787 Revised in red, annotated '*no. 2*', in MS Jungle Books, 11 numbered leaves (rectos only); watermarked 1890.

British Library, Add. MS 45540, ff. 45–56 (rectos only).

Kidnapped
First pub. (with verse heading beginning 'There is a tide in the affairs of men') *Civil and Military Gazette*, 21 March 1887; collected *Plain Tales from the Hills* (Calcutta and London, 1888); *Sussex*, I, 183–8; Harbord, I, 61–2.

KpR 1788 Corrected first page proof (including corrections to the verse heading) for the Sussex Edition; date stamped 12 September 1931.

The verse heading, ascribed 'Vibart's Moralities' was collected separately in *Poems 1886–1929* (London, 1929) and Sussex, XXXIV, 216, as 'Chapter Heading'; Harbord, Verse No. 245, as 'Vibart's Moralities'.

British Library, Add. MS 55852.

The Killing of Hatim Tai, see KpR 2078–9.

Kim
First pub. serially *McClure's Magazine*, December 1900–October 1901; first pub. in one-volume New York, 1901 and London, 1901; *Sussex*, XXI; Harbord, I, 119–270. For chapter headings, see KpR 72–4, 132–5, 174–5, 351–2, 424–6, 559–60, 870–2, 888, 1009–12, 1059–61, 1291–3, 1380. An uncorrected proof copy of the first edition (London, 1901) is in the Robert H. Taylor Collection at Princeton.

KpR 1789 Draft, here entitled 'Kim o' the Rishti', wanting portions of Chapters 2, 5 and 12 and the whole of Chapters 6 and 7 (including also KpR 1275).

This MS was bound up in green leather by the Kiplings and presented to the British Library (then the British Museum) under the condition that it not be used 'for the purposes of collation'; it is inscribed by RK on the inside front cover 'Caroline Kipling from Rudyard Kipling' and on f. 2 'Presented to the British Museum by Rudyard Kipling October. 1925'.

British Library, Add. MS 44840.

KpR 1790 Corrected proof (96 pages of page proof, remainder galley proof), being text of serial publication, with running head 'Kim o' the Rishti', the verse headings to Chapters 8 and 13 are cancelled and new headings added in red ink (see KpR 1009, 1292); date stamped 15 August 1900.

These proofs mentioned Stewart, p. 212.

Unlocated.

KpR 1791 Corrected first page proof for the Sussex Edition (containing KpR 135, 175, 352, 426, 560, 872, 1012); date stamped 9 October 1931.

British Library, Add. MS 55871.

King Log and King Stork
First pub. as 'Fables for the Staff I' in *The Friend* (Bloemfontein), 24 March 1900; collected *War's Brighter Side*, ed. Julian Ralph (London, 1901); reprinted Harbord, III, 1532.

KpR 1792 Draft, headed 'Fables for the Staff.', one page, among materials for *The Friend* (see KpR 2283).

Library of Congress, Rare Book Division, Colt Collection.

The King's Ankus
First pub. with 'The Song of the Little Hunter' as heading in *St Nicholas*, March 1895; collected with 'Jungle Saying' as heading and accompanying poem 'The Song of the Little Hunter' in *The Second Jungle Book* (London and New York, 1895); *Sussex*, XII, 167–90; Harbord, VII, 2967–70.

KpR 1793 In MS Jungle Books: (1) revised, here originally entitled 'The Blood trail.', 9 leaves (rectos only), watermarked variously 1888, 1890 and 1894 (ff. 87–95); (2) revised, here entitled '<"The treasure of kings."> The Turquoise Ankus', 9 numbered leaves (rectos only), watermarked 1890 (ff. 96–104).

British Library, Add. MS 45540, ff. 87–104 (rectos only).

KpR 1794 Corrected typescript, 17 leaves, annotated 'Not to be published in America before the 1st March, 1895'.

University of California at Berkeley, 71/121 z.

The King's Ashes, see KpR 2078–9.

***Kipling Pageant* (Garden City, New York, 1935)**

KpR 1795 Typescript of the Foreword (addressed to Nelson Doubleday), headed 'Foreword to the Publisher. being The Instructions to the Nakado [sic], the Captain, of this ship.', 5 numbered leaves (rectos only), as sent from Doubleday & Co. to A. S. Watt with a covering letter of 17 July 1935.

This Foreword was published (together with the earlier version (KpR 1970–2) in the Outward Bound Edition) in *Two Forewords* (Garden City, New York, 1935).

Berg.

KpR 1796 Carbon copy typescript of the Foreword, 4 numbered leaves (rectos only); [1935].

Princeton, Doubleday Collection, Box 2, Folder 26.

KpR 1797 Corrected galley proof of the Foreword, enclosed in a letter to Nelson Doubleday, Marienbad, 22 August 1935.

Princeton, Doubleday Collection, Box 2, Folder 26.

KpR 1798 Notes, headed 'Kipling Pageant', including an addition to the Foreword and 2 sketches, in a letter to Nelson Doubleday, Marienbad, 30 August 1935.

Princeton, Doubleday Collection, Box 2, Folder 26.

Kipling's Thanks, see KpR 2127.

The Knife and the Naked Chalk
First pub. *Harper's Magazine*, December 1910; collected with poems 'The Run of the Downs' and 'Song of the Men's Side' in *Rewards and Fairies* (London, 1910); *Sussex*, XV, 117–36; Harbord, VI, 2781–2.

KpR 1799 Revised, here entitled 'The Beast and the Man.', in MS Rewards and Fairies, 6 numbered pages.

Cambridge University Library, ADD 6850, ff. 45–50 (rectos only).

KpR 1800 Corrected first page proof for the Sussex Edition; date stamped 18 September 1931.

British Library, Add. MS 55865.

The Knights of the Joyous Venture
First pub. *Strand Magazine* and *Ladies Home Journal*, March 1906; collected with poems 'Harp Song of the Dane Women' and 'Thorkild's Song' in *Puck of Pook's Hill* (London, 1906); *Sussex*, XIV, 59–83; Harbord, VI, 2708–9.

KpR 1801 Revised, originally here entitled 'Puck of Pook's Hill III', in MS Puck, 8 numbered leaves (rectos only).

Bodleian, MS. Eng. misc. c. 127, ff. 24–31 (rectos only).

KpR 1802 Corrected galley proof for publication in *Ladies Home Journal*, stamped 'C. M. K.'.

Huntington, RB 29634.

KpR 1803 Corrected revise galley proof for publication in *Ladies Home Journal*.

Yale (mislaid since 1976).

KpR 1804 Corrected galley proof for publication in *Ladies Home Journal*.

Owned (1967) Homer I. Lewis, El Paso, Texas (formerly on deposit at Texas).

KpR 1805 Corrected first page proof for the Sussex Edition; date stamped 2 July 1931.

British Library, Add. MS 55864.

Kopje-Book Maxims
First pub. in three instalments *The Friend* (Bloemfontein), 26–31 March 1900; reprinted *War's Brighter Side*, ed. Julian Ralph (London, 1901); reprinted Harbord, III, 1535.

KpR 1806 Corrected galley proof (containing also KpR 1978) of 14 maxims (not published) and one page in RK's hand, headed 'add to Kopje-Book Maxims.', containing the last two maxims (as published 31 March); among materials for *The Friend* (see KpR 2283).

These items described in Norman Croom-Johnson, 'Rudyard Kipling and "The Friend"', *KJ*, Nos 102–3, July–October 1952.

Library of Congress, Rare Book Division, Colt Collection.

Labour, for 'Letters to the Family No. V', see KpR 1826–30.

The Lamentable Comedy of Willow Wood
First pub. *Fortnightly Review*, May 1890; first collected (authorized) *The One Volume Kipling* (New York, 1928); *Sussex*, XXIX, 343–63; Harbord, V, 2469–70, as 'Uncollected No. 199'.

KpR 1807 Typescript, corrected in unidentified hands (one possibly being Kipling's), including an 8-line verse heading ('O ye, all ye that walk in Willow Wood') and 8 lines in the text ('I am lost to faith, I am lost to hope'), 21 numbered leaves (rectos only); as sent for inclusion in *The One Volume Kipling* with a letter to Nelson Doubleday of 12 November 1926.

The 8 lines in the text are listed Harbord, Verse No. 438, as 'Old Song'; the last 4 of them were used as the Chapter Heading to Chapter 13 of *The Light that Failed*.

Princeton, Doubleday Collection, Additional Papers, Box 17.

The Lang Men O' Larut
First pub. 'Abaft the Funnel. IV' in *Civil and Military Gazette*, 29 May 1889; collected *Life's Handicap* (London and New York, 1891); *Sussex*, IV, 307–11; Harbord, II, 986–7.

KpR 1808 Fair copy, revised (thin paper carbon copy), in MS From Sea to Sea (see KpR 1634), here entitled 'Abaft the Funnel/(No. IV)', 3 numbered pages.

Huntington, HM 12429, Vol. 2, pp. 2–4.

KpR 1809 Revised clipping of first publication in Scrapbook 4 (p. 147).

Sussex, KP 28/4.

KpR 1810 Corrected first page proof for the Sussex Edition; date stamped 13 February 1932.

British Library, Add. MS 55855.

The Last Relief
First pub. *Harper's Weekly*, 25 April 1891; *Sussex*, XXIX, 377–[85]; Harbord, V, 2486–8, as 'Uncollected No. 207'.

KpR 1811 Corrected first galley proof set up for a projected volume of the Sussex Edition to be called *Why Snow Falls at Vernet and Other Stories* (revised to 'Uncollected vol.'); date stamped 25 October 1930.

British Library, Add. MS 55850.

The Last Term
First pub. *Windsor Magazine*, May 1899; collected *Stalky & Co.* (London, 1899); *Sussex*, XVII, 373–99; Harbord, I, 482–90.

KpR 1812 Revised, in MS Stalky (ff. 79–89, rectos only), 11 pages, annotated 'to be typed as soon as possible'.

Haileybury.

KpR 1813 Fragment, here untitled, 2 pages, in minute handwriting.

King's School, Canterbury, Hugh Walpole Collection 55.

KpR 1814 Corrected first page proof for the Sussex Edition; date stamped 27 March 1931.

British Library, Add. MS 55867.

Leaves from a Winter Note-Book, for 'From Tideway to Tideway No. IX', see KpR 1646–9.

The Legs of Sister Ursula
First pub. *The Idler*, June 1893; first collected (authorized) *The One Volume Kipling* (New York, 1928); *Sussex*, XXX, 39–51; Harbord, V, 2515–16, as 'Uncollected No. 214'.

KpR 1815 Corrected typescript, 12 numbered leaves (rectos only), as sent for inclusion in *The One Volume Kipliing* with a letter to Nelson Doubleday, 12 November 1926.

Princeton, Doubleday Collection, Additional Papers, Box 17.

KpR 1816 Corrected first galley proof set up for a projected volume of the Sussex Edition (marked 'Uncollected vol.'); date stamped 12 November 1930.

British Library, Add. MS 55850.

A Letter from Golam Singh, see KpR 2078–9.

[Letter to the Editor]
No publication traced; not in Harbord.

KpR 1817 Draft, beginning 'In a recent issue of your paper Mr [?] is good enough to express his regret...', concerning the setting of RK's verses to music, one page, annotated in an unidentified hand 'Good old [Rudy Kip?] I am teaching him to write straight...Rottingdean Aug 28. 98'.

Dalhousie University.

[Letter to the Editor of *Maidstone Magazine*]
Extract printed in Sotheby's sale catalogue, 9–10 December 1968, p. 142; not in Harbord. *Maidstone Magazine* was issued by the officers and men of the Eighth Submarine Flotilla in 1914–15.

KpR 1818 Draft of mock-serious letter, one page, signed; [1915].

Sotheby's, 9–10 December 1968, Lot 772, sold to Rota.

[Letter to the Editor of *The Critic*]
First pub. *The Critic*, 9 November 1895; not in Harbord.

KpR 1819 Letter here addressed to the Literary Editor of the *New York Tribune*, one page, warning the public against spurious publication entitled *Out of India* (New York, 1895), one page; dated Naulakha, 3 November 1895, postmarked 4 November 1895.

Yale.

[Letter to the Editor of the *Montreal Star*]
First pub. *Montreal Star*, 7 September 1911; reprinted *The Times*, 8 September 1911; not in Harbord.

KpR 1820 Corrected typescript (followed by a private letter to Lord Beaverbrook), Bateman's, 6 September 1911.

Harvard, bMS Eng 809.4(12).

[Letter to the Editor of *The School Budget*]
First pub. as Kipling's reply to an earlier article 'Hints on Schoolboy Etiquette' in *The School Budget* (Horsmonden, Kent), 14 May 1898; reprinted *The Budget* (New York, 1899); reprinted Harbord, V, 2522–7, as 'Uncollected No. 223/Horsmonden School Budget'. Max Beerbohm's reply and his caricature of Kipling was printed in the next issue of *The School Budget*, 28 May 1898.

KpR 1820.5 Kipling's original letter, together with the original letter from the schoolboys to Kipling (11 April 1898) and Beerbohm's original reply and caricature.

These MSS were sold in the G. M. Williamson Sale, Anderson Galleries, 17 March 1915, Lot 62.

Owned (1951) E. H. Lambert (see Owen Tweedy, 'Rudyard Kipling and Rottingdean', *KJ*, 18 (1951), 12).

Letters of Marque
First pub. serially in *The Pioneer*, 14 December 1887–28 February 1888; revised version collected *From Sea to Sea*, 2 vols (New York, 1899); *Sussex*, XXII, 1–191; Harbord, II, 727–90.

KpR 1821 Fair copy, revised slightly, of Chapters 1, 3–5 (only the title and first sentence of Chapter 5), Chapters 1, 3, 4 here untitled, in MS Words, Wise and Otherwise [pp. 88–151], containing a few illustrations, headed [p. 89] 'Letters of Marque 1887.' and annotated [p. 88] 'Occasional articles written by me for the Civil and Military Gazette and the Pioneer between 1887–1889.'.

Berg.

KpR 1822 Corrected galley proof among proofs for *From Sea to Sea*, (1899), signed (initials) *passim*, stamped '1st REV.'; date stamped 20 April–3 May 1899.

Library of Congress, Rare Book Division, Carpenter Kipling Collection.

KpR 1823 Corrected first page proof for the Sussex Edition; date stamped 7 November 1932.

British Library, Add. MS 55872.

Letters of Travel
This collection of three series of articles ('From Tideway to Tideway', 'Letters to the Family', 'Egypt of the Magicians') first pub. London, 1920; *Sussex*, XXIV; Harbord, III, 1452–1528.

KpR 1824 Copy for the London, 1920 edition, including as well as the contents below: three preliminary typescript contents lists, the first of all three series (one page), the second of 'Letters to the Family' (one page), the third of 'Egypt of the Magicians' (one page), all annotated by RK; a typescript title page and contents list of 'From Tideway to Tideway'; clippings from *Nash's Magazine* of the first 6 letters of 'Egypt of the Magicians' (numbered by RK I–VI) without corrections and lines drawn through all the accompanying poems.

Contents: KpR 1576, 1648, 1829.

Berg.

Letters on Leave
First pub. (Letter Nos. 1–2) *The Pioneer*, 27 September and 11 October 1890; collected *Abaft the Funnel* (New York, 1909); *Sussex*, XXIX, 199–219; Harbord, II, 697–701; Letter No. 4 first pub. *The*

Pioneer, 1 November 1890; reprinted Harbord, V, 2450–8, as 'Uncollected No. 193'.

KpR 1825 Headed 'Letters on Leave/I', being an incomplete and unpublished letter, beginning 'Dear Old Man, In the first place your handwriting has not improved...', 4 pages (one leaf); watermarked 1888, dated 18 August 1890.

Harbord, V, 2450 mentions this MS, which he calls 'Letter No. 3'.

Berg.

Letters to the Family

First pub. (as a series of 8 articles and accompanying poems) in *Morning Post*, 12 March–30 April 1908; first pub. in one volume Toronto, 1908; collected (without poems) *Letters of Travel* (London, 1920); *Sussex*, XXIV, 129–243; Harbord, III, 1481–1501.

KpR 1826 In MS Non-Fiction, including: fair copy, revised, of the Preface, one page, dated 1908 (f. 113); draft of 'The Road to Quebec', here entitled 'Letters to the Family', 4 pages (ff. 115–18, rectos only); draft of an unpublished? letter entitled 'Letters to the Family', 4 pages (ff. 119–22, rectos only); draft of 'A People at Home', here entitled 'Letters to the Family', 4 pages (ff. 123–6, rectos only); fair copy, revised, of 'Cities and Spaces', here entitled 'Letters to the Family III', 5 numbered pages (ff. 128–32, rectos only); draft of 'Newspapers and Democracy', here entitled 'Letters to the Family III', 4 numbered pages (ff. 134–7, rectos only); fair copy, revised, of 'The Fortunate Towns', here entitled 'Letters to the Family. VI.', 5 numbered pages (ff. 139–43, rectos only); fair copy, revised, of 'Mountains and the Pacific', here entitled 'Letters to the Family VII', 5 numbered pages (ff. 145–9, rectos only); fair copy, revised, of 'A Conclusion', here entitled 'Letters to the Family VIII', 4 numbered pages (ff. 151–4, rectos only) and a fair copy of the accompanying verses by Thomas Campion annotated 'verses To precede Letter VIII' (f. 150); wanting 'Labour' (Letter V) and the accompanying verses '"A Servant When He Reigneth"' and the verses accompanying 'A People at Home' (Letter II) 'Jubal and Tubal Cain'; including all the other accompanying poems (see KpR 868, 983, 1101, 1127, 1354).

British Library, Add. MS 45542, ff. 113, 115–26, 128–32, 134–7, 139–43, 145–54 (rectos only).

KpR 1827 Proof copy for the first one-volume edition, containing cover, preliminary leaves and Preface but wanting the main text, including Kipling's corrections and annotations; together with 2 leaves of corrected page proof for the Preface.

Sotheby's, 21–2 July 1988, Lot 193 (property of G. S. Fraser), sold to Joseph.

KpR 1828 Proof copy for the second edition (Toronto, 1910), containing Kipling's corrections and revisions on some 45 pages of the text (including KpR 1103, 1128).

Sotheby's, 21–2 July 1988, Lot 191 (property of G. S. Fraser), sold to Joseph.

KpR 1829 Copy of the second edition (Toronto, 1910), wanting the cover and title page, containing RK's instruction to the printer and revision to the Preface, lines indicating cancellation drawn through all the poems, among materials for *Letters of Travel* (KpR 1824).

Berg.

KpR 1830 Corrected first page proof for the Sussex Edition; date stamped 30 April 1935.

British Library, Add. MS 55874.

Letting in the Jungle

First pub. with heading 'Mowgli's Song' in *Pall Mall Gazette*, 12–13 December 1894; collected with heading 'Veil them, cover them...' and accompanying poem 'Mowgli's Song Against People' in *The Second Jungle Book* (London and New York, 1895); *Sussex*, XII, 127–62; Harbord, VII, 2964–7. Three galley proofs for a periodical publication (dated 9, 16 and 23 December) with printer's corrections are at Texas.

KpR 1831 Revised, in MS Jungle Books, 13 numbered leaves (rectos only) and unnumbered leaf containing KpR 713; watermarked 1890.

British Library, Add. MS 45540, ff. 134–47 (rectos only).

***Life's Handicap* (London and New York, 1891)**
For inscribed copies, see 'The Long Trail', 'My new-cut...'; another copy, inscribed to Audrey Gillon, November 1891 with 17 unidentified lines of verse, was sold at Sotheby's, 9 June 1936, Lot 433, to Elsie Bambridge.

KpR 1832 Draft of Preface.

Preface printed *Sussex*, IV, ix–xv; Harbord, II, 942.

Fitzwilliam Museum, Cambridge.

KpR 1833 Typescript of Preface, revised, 10 numbered leaves (rectos only) and a title page, signed (initials).

Columbia University, Engel Collection.

The Light that Failed
First pub. (12-chapter happy-ending version) in book form London, 1890; serially in *Lippincott's Magazine*, January 1891; 14-chapter sad-ending version first pub. in book form New York, 1890; 15-chapter sad-ending version first pub. in book form London and New York, 1891 with Dedicatory verses ('Mother o' Mine') (this version thereafter collected); *Sussex*, XVIII; Harbord, V, 2156–248. For chapter headings, see KpR 112–16, 179–83, 457–60, 714–15, 1371–4.

KpR 1834 Draft of happy-ending version, 88 leaves (mostly rectos only), including more than one version of some chapters, several chapter headings and other verses (see KpR 179, 457, 1373) and rough notes for what would become *The Naulahka* on the verso of one leaf.

This MS described in Howard C. Rice, Jr, 'A Manuscript of Kipling's "The Light that Failed"', *PULC*, 27 (1966), 125–30 with two facsimiles, one a photo of the MS splayed out, the other a facsimile of a page numbered 4.

Princeton, Doubleday Collection, Box 5.

KpR 1835 Corrected typescript, 199 pages, as sent to the printer for serial publication in *Lippincott's Magazine*, together with a letter to the editor of that magazine.

Henkels, 26 June 1919, Lot 237c.

KpR 1836 Corrected page proof (including also KpR 114), printer's copy for Edition de Luxe, Vol. IX (London, 1898).

Pierpont Morgan, 37076.

KpR 1837 Corrected first page proof for the Sussex Edition (containing KpR 116, 183, 460); date stamped 20 November 1931.

British Library, Add. MS 55868.

The Likes O' Us
First pub. *Week's News*, 4 February 1888; collected *Abaft the Funnel* (New York, 1909); Harbord, II, 687–8.

KpR 1838 Revised clipping of the first publication, in Scrapbook 4 (p. 55).

Sussex, KP 28/4.

The Limitations of Pambé Serang
First pub. *St James's Gazette*, 7 December 1889; collected *Life's Handicap* (London and New York, 1891); *Sussex*, IV, 371–7; Harbord, II, 994–5.

KpR 1839 Corrected first page proof for the Sussex Edition; date stamped 13 February 1932.

British Library, Add. MS 55855.

***Limits and Renewals* (New York, 1932)**

KpR 1840 Typed list of corrections to the 'proofs of this book', including corrections to 'A Naval Mutiny', 'Beauty Spots' and 'The Expert', signed, one page of Grand Pump Room Hotel, Bath notepaper.

Princeton, Doubleday Collection, Box 2, Folder 23.

Lispeth
First pub. (with verse heading) *Civil and Military*

Gazette, 29 November 1886; collected *Plain Tales from the Hills* (Calcutta and London, 1888); *Sussex*, I, 3–9; Harbord, I, 27–8. For heading, see KpR 177.

KpR 1841 Corrected first page proof for the Sussex Edition; date stamped 12 September 1931.

British Library, Add. MS 55852.

Literature

Speech delivered Royal Academy of Arts Banquet, 5 May 1906; first pub. *The Times*, 7 May 1906; collected *A Book of Words* (London, 1928); *Sussex*, XXV, 3–7; Harbord, VII, 3288.

KpR 1842 Corrected first page proof for the Sussex Edition; date stamped 4 April 1931.

British Library, Add. MS 55875.

Little Foxes

First pub. *Collier's Weekly*, 27 March 1909; collected with poem 'Gallio's Song' in *Actions and Reactions* (London, 1909); *Sussex*, VIII, 219–48; Harbord, VI, 2859–73.

KpR 1843 In MS Actions and Reactions (ff. 108–16).

University of St Andrews, MS PR4854.A4.

KpR 1844 Six corrected sets of galley proofs.

Parke Bernet, 21–2 January 1931 (Ballard Sale), Lot 88.

KpR 1845 Corrected first page proof for *Humorous Tales* (London, 1931), pp. 375–404; date stamped 2 and 5 June 1931.

British Library, Add. MS 55847.

KpR 1846 Corrected first page proof for the Sussex Edition; date stamped 28 November 1931.

British Library, Add. MS 55859.

A Little Prep.

First pub. *Windsor Magazine* and *McClure's Magazine*, April 1899; collected *Stalky & Co.* (London, 1899); *Sussex*, XVII, 257–84; Harbord, I, 458–62.

KpR 1847 Revised, in MS Stalky, 10 pages (ff. 55–64, rectos only), annotated 'type as soon as possible RK'.

Haileybury.

KpR 1848 Corrected first page proof for the Sussex Edition; date stamped 27 March 1931.

British Library, Add. MS 55867.

Little Tobrah

First pub. *Civil and Military Gazette*, 17 July 1888; collected *Life's Handicap* (London and New York, 1891); *Sussex*, IV, 381–4; Harbord, II, 995.

KpR 1849 Revised clipping of the first publication, in Scrapbook 4 (p. 72).

Sussex, KP 28/4.

KpR 1850 Corrected first page proof for the Sussex Edition; date stamped 13 February 1932.

British Library, Add. MS 55855.

The Lost Legion

First pub. *Strand Magazine*, May 1893; collected *Many Inventions* (London and New York, 1893); *Sussex*, V, 277–93; Harbord, III, 1239–42.

KpR 1851 Corrected first page proof for the Sussex Edition; date stamped 10 June 1931.

British Library, Add. MS 55856.

'Love-O'-Women'

First pub. *Many Inventions* (London and New York, 1893); *Sussex*, V, 361–92; Harbord, III, 1249–53.

KpR 1852 Revised, in MS Day's Work, including a draft of the closing stanza beginning 'Oh do not despise the advice of the Wise' (f. 43), 12 numbered pages; watermarked 1890.

The closing stanza is, according to Harbord (Verse No. 397), a sixth stanza for those included in the story 'My Great and Only' beginning 'At the back of Knightsbridge Barricks' (see KpR 1902).

British Library, Add. MS 45541, ff. 32–43 (rectos only).

KpR 1853 Corrected first page proof for the Sussex Edition; date stamped 10 June 1931.

British Library, Add. MS 55856.

'The Luck of the Roaring Camp'
First pub. *Civil and Military Gazette*, 17 January 1888; collected *'Turnovers'*, Vol. I (Lahore, [1888]); collected in the suppressed *City of Dreadful Night and Other Sketches* (Allahabad, 1890); reprinted Harbord, IV, 1962–4, as 'Uncollected No. 91'.

KpR 1854 Revised clipping of first publication in Scrapbook 4 (p. 44).

Sussex, KP 28/4.

The Madness of Private Ortheris
First pub. *Plain Tales from the Hills* (Calcutta and London, 1888); *Sussex*, I, 373–83; Harbord, I, 88–90.

KpR 1855 Corrected first page proof for the Sussex Edition; date stamped 12 September 1931.

British Library, Add. MS 55852.

A Madonna of the Trenches
First pub. *Maclean's Magazine*, 15 August 1924; collected with poems 'Gipsy Vans' and 'Gow's Watch' in *Debits and Credits* (London, 1926); *Sussex*, X, 199–219; Harbord, VII, 3158–62.

KpR 1856 Revised, in MS Debits and Credits, 13 pages (ff. 116–28, rectos only).

University of Durham.

KpR 1857 Corrected first page proof for the Sussex Edition; date stamped 30 December 1931.

British Library, Add. MS 55861.

The Magic Square
Speech delivered Household Brigade Officers' Cadet Corps, Bushey, 1917; first printed *Hobocob* (a Souvenir of the Household Brigade Officer Cadet Battalion), Christmas, 1917; first pub. *A Book of Words* (London, 1928); *Sussex*, XXV, 123–44; Harbord, VII, 3300–1.

KpR 1858 Typescript, annotated 'I have cut it down', 21 leaves (rectos only) and a title page, as sent to Dudley Wallis for printing in *Hobocob* with a covering letter of 27 November 1917.

Library of Congress, Rare Book Division, Colt Collection.

KpR 1859 Corrected first page proof for the Sussex Edition; date stamped 4 April 1931.

British Library, Add. MS 55875.

The Maltese Cat
First pub. *Pall Mall Gazette*, 26–7 June 1895; collected *The Day's Work* (New York, 1898); *Sussex*, VI, 263–89; Harbord, III, 1397–1405.

KpR 1860 Corrected typescript of the version published in *Cosmopolitan* (July 1895), as sent to F. N. Doubleday for use in *The Day's Work*, 27 numbered leaves (rectos only), containing two notes to Doubleday (ff. 1, 27v), the latter ('This is corrected in a mud-floored cabin in Bantry Bay...') dated 6 September 1898.

Princeton, Doubleday Collection, Box 3, Bound Vol. IV, Item 59.

KpR 1861 Corrected galley proof for *The Day's Work* but not used as this proof was lost in the mails and received too late, containing unpublished revisions.

Princeton, Doubleday Collection, Box 3, Bound Vol. IV, Item 60.

KpR 1862 Corrected first page proof for the Sussex Edition; date stamped 27 June 1931.

British Library, Add. MS 55857.

The Man Who Was
First pub. *Macmillan's Magazine*, April 1890; collected *Life's Handicap* (London and New York, 1891); *Sussex*, IV, 103–21; Harbord, II, 959–66.

KpR 1863 Corrected first page proof for the Sussex Edition; date stamped 13 February 1932.

British Library, Add. MS 55855.

The Man Who Would Be King
First pub. *Phantom 'Rickshaw* (Allahabad, [1888]);

Sussex, III, 217–65; Harbord, I, 359–70. See also KpR 2307.

KpR 1864 Annotations explaining Indian words, in a copy of the first publication (KpR 1982), pp. 84–5, 93, 113.

Berg.

KpR 1865 Corrected first page proof for the Sussex Edition; date stamped 18 September 1931.

British Library, Add. MS 55854.

The Manner of Men
First pub. *London Magazine*, September 1930; collected with poem 'At His Execution' in *Limits and Renewals* (London, 1932); *Sussex*, XI, 215–37; Harbord, VII, 3240–55.

KpR 1866 Corrected page proof in Limits and Renewals Proof; date stamped 21 January 1932.

Syracuse University.

KpR 1867 Corrected first page proof for the Sussex Edition; date stamped 14 October 1932.

British Library, Add. MS 55862.

The Mark of the Beast
First pub. *The Pioneer*, 12–14 July 1890; collected *Life's Handicap* (London and New York, 1891); *Sussex*, IV, 249–66; Harbord, II, 980–2.

KpR 1868 Corrected first page proof for the Sussex Edition; date stamped 13 February 1932.

British Library, Add. MS 55855.

Marklake Witches
First pub. with poems 'The Way Through the Woods' and 'Brookland Road' in *Rewards and Fairies* (London, 1910); *Sussex*, XV, 87–109; Harbord, VI, 2778–81.

KpR 1869 Two fair copies, revised, in MS Rewards and Fairies, the first on 8 numbered pages (ff. 33–40, rectos only) and the second, incomplete, on 3 numbered pages (ff. 41–3, rectos only).

Cambridge University Library, ADD 6850, ff. 33–43 (rectos only).

KpR 1870 Corrected first page proof for the Sussex Edition; date stamped 18 September 1931.

British Library, Add. MS 55865.

Mary Postgate
First pub. *Nash's Magazine* and *Century Magazine*, September 1915; collected with poem 'The Beginnings' in *A Diversity of Creatures* (London, 1917); *Sussex*, IX, 421–41; Harbord, VII, 3102–9.

KpR 1871 Revised, here originally entitled 'The Destructor', in MS Diversity of Creatures (ff. 148–55, rectos only).

University of Edinburgh, Dk. 2. 8.

KpR 1872 Corrected galley proof for *Nash's Magazine*.

Library of Congress, Rare Book Division, Colt Collection.

KpR 1873 Corrected first page proof for the Sussex Edition; date stamped 28 April 1932.

British Library, Add. MS 55860.

A Matter of Fact
First pub. *Many Inventions* (London and New York, 1893); *Sussex*, V, 257–74; Harbord, III, 1234–9.

KpR 1874 Corrected first page proof for the Sussex Edition; date stamped 10 June 1931.

British Library, Add. MS 55856.

Memorial Service and St Paul's Canadians
First pub. *The Gazette* (Montreal), 14 May 1915; not in Harbord.

KpR 1875 Fair copy, revised, together with a revised typescript of one page; dated 1915.

Presented to Dalhousie University by Elsie Bambridge, 20 July 1956.

Dalhousie University.

The Menace of the Modern Thug
Speech delivered at Pleasure Gardens Theatre,

Folkestone, 15 February 1918; first pub. *Current History of the European War* issued by the *New York Times*, (n.d.); reprinted Harbord, VII, 3345–9, as Speech No. 65.

KpR 1876 Typescript of the first page only, revised, here untitled.

Syracuse University.

A Menagerie Aboard, see KpR 1952–3.

A Merry Christmas
First pub. *Civil and Military Gazette*, 31 December 1887; reprinted Harbord, III, 1629–32, as 'Uncollected No. 86'.

KpR 1877 Revised clipping of the first publication in Scrapbook 4 (p. 44).

Sussex, KP 28/4.

The Military education of officers.
No publication traced; not in Harbord.

KpR 1878 Beginning 'Sir: In [?] the *Pagal-i-Khilah*...', 13 lines.

For provenance, see KpR 501.

Library of Congress, Rare Book Division, Colt Collection.

***Mine Own People* (New York, [1891])**

KpR 1879 Prefatory 'letter' or statement (giving reasons for the publication of this volume), beginning 'A little less than half of these stories...', signed, one page.

Facsimile printed in the volume, p. [v].

Syracuse University.

The Miracle of Purun Bhagat
First pub. *New York World*, 14 October 1894, as 'A Miracle of the Present Day'; collected *The Second Jungle Book* (London and New York, 1895); *Sussex*, XII, 323–41; Harbord, VII, 3002–6.

KpR 1880 In MS Jungle Books: (1) revised, including an epigraph from John Donne, 7 numbered leaves (rectos only), watermarked 1890 (ff. 148–54); (2) revised earlier version, here untitled, 7 leaves (rectos only), watermarked 1890 (ff. 155–61).

British Library, Add. MS 45540, ff. 148–61 (rectos only).

KpR 1881 Corrected typescript, the spelling of 'Purun' corrected throughout from 'Pureen', including an epigraph from Donne, 24 pages, signed (initials).

Parke Bernet, 21–2 January 1942 (Ballard Sale), Lot 8.

The Miracle of Saint Jubanus
First pub. *Story-Teller*, December 1930; collected with poems 'The Curé' and 'Song of Seventy Horses' in *Limits and Renewals* (London, 1932); *Sussex*, XI, 311–27; Harbord, VII, 3262–5.

KpR 1882 Corrected page proof in Limits and Renewals Proof; date stamped 23 January 1932.

Syracuse University.

KpR 1883 Corrected first page proof for the Sussex Edition; date stamped 14 October 1932.

British Library, Add. MS 55862.

Miss Youghal's *Sais*
First pub. *Civil and Military Gazette*, 25 April 1887; collected *Plain Tales from the Hills* (Calcutta and London, 1888); *Sussex*, I, 35–42; Harbord, I, 33–5.

KpR 1884 Corrected first page proof for the Sussex Edition; date stamped 12 September 1931.

British Library, Add. MS 55852.

Mrs Bathurst
First pub. *Windsor Magazine* and *Metropolitan Magazine*, September 1904; collected with a scene from 'Gow's Watch' entitled 'From Lyden's "Irenius"' in *Traffics and Discoveries* (London, 1904); *Sussex*, VII, 345–69; Harbord, IV, 1780–810.

KpR 1885 Revised, in MS Traffics and Discoveries, 11 pages.

McGill University.

KpR 1886 Extensively revised and corrected galley proof for *Metropolitan Magazine*.

Library of Congress, Rare Book Division, Carpenter Kipling Collection.

KpR 1887 Corrected galley proof for *Metropolitan Magazine*, 7 galleys numbered 77–83, each cut into 4 and bound on a page (i.e., 28 pages).

Yale.

KpR 1888 Corrected first page proof for the Sussex Edition; date stamped 22 March 1932.

British Library, Add. MS 55858.

Mrs Hauksbee Sits Out
First pub. *Illustrated London News*, Christmas Number 1890; collected *Under the Deodars, The Story of the Gadsbys, Wee Willie Winkie*, Outward Bound Edition, Vol. VI (New York, 1897); *Sussex*, V (*Many Inventions*), 146–83; Harbord, V, 2483–6, as 'Uncollected No. 206'.

KpR 1889 Corrected first page proof for the Sussex Edition; date stamped 10 June 1931.

British Library, Add. MS 55856.

The Moral Reformers
First pub. *Windsor Magazine* and *McClure's Magazine*, March 1899; collected *Stalky & Co.* (London, 1899); *Sussex*, XVII, 165–91; Harbord, I, 446–8.

KpR 1890 Revised, in MS Stalky, 12 pages (ff. 43–54, rectos only), annotated 'to be typed urgent...'.

Haileybury.

KpR 1891 Corrected first page proof for the Sussex Edition; date stamped 27 March 1931.

British Library, Add. MS 55867.

Morale of Civilians and the Censorships
No publication traced; not in Harbord.

KpR 1892 Four numbered pages (2 leaves), beginning 'Suggested study of the soldier — especially the officer', an explanation of soldiering addressed to civilians including a reprimand of the Canadian reluctance to accept British discipline, among Kipling's letters to Lord Beaverbrook, the first leaf is Brown's Hotel notepaper; dated in an unidentified hand February 1915.

Harvard, bMS Eng 809.4(136).

The Mother Hive
First pub. *Collier's Weekly*, 28 November 1908, as 'The Adventures of Melissa'; collected with poem 'The Bees and the Flies' in *Actions and Reactions* (London, 1909); *Sussex*, VIII, 81–102; Harbord, VI, 2820–6.

KpR 1893 Here originally entitled 'The adventures of Melissa', in MS Actions and Reactions (ff. 16–25).

University of St Andrews, MS PR4854.A4.

KpR 1894 Corrected first page proof for the Sussex Edition; date stamped 28 November 1931.

British Library, Add. MS 55859.

Mother Maturin, for Kipling's unfinished last novel, see INTRODUCTION.

Moti Guj — Mutineer
First pub. *Mine Own People* (New York, [1891]); collected *Life's Handicap* (London and New York, 1891); *Sussex*, IV, 387–96; Harbord, II, 995–6.

KpR 1895 Corrected first page proof for *Humorous Tales* (London, 1931), pp. 19–28; date stamped 6 May 1931.

British Library, Add. MS 55847.

KpR 1896 Corrected first page proof for the Sussex Edition; date stamped 13 February 1932.

British Library, Add. MS 55855.

Mountains and the Pacific, for 'Letters to the Family No. VII', see KpR 1826–30.

Mowgli's Brothers
First pub. with verse heading 'Night Song in the Jungle' in *St Nicholas*, January 1894; collected *The Jungle Book* (London and New York, 1894); *Sussex*, XII, 5–30; Harbord, VII, 2956–9.

KpR 1897 Revised, 7 numbered leaves (rectos only), in MS Jungle Books; watermarked 1890.

British Library, Add. MS 45540, ff. 5–11 (rectos only).

KpR 1898 Fair copy, revised, 12 numbered leaves (rectos only), inscribed 'Susan Bishop from *Rudyard Kipling* Feb: 1893'.

Library of Congress, Rare Book Division, Carpenter Kipling Collection.

The Mutiny of the Mavericks
First pub. *Mine Own People* (New York, [1891]); collected *Life's Handicap* (London and New York, 1891); *Sussex*, IV, 221–46; Harbord, II, 977–80.

KpR 1899 Corrected first page proof for the Sussex Edition; date stamped 13 February 1932.

British Library, Add. MS 55855.

My First Adventure
Included in 'The Scribbler' (handwritten magazine produced by the Burne-Jones and Morris children), Vol. I, No. 12 and Vol. II, No. 1, 3 and 30 June 1879 (signed 'Nickson'); first printed Harbord, I (1961), pp. 501–7, as 'Uncollected No. 1'; no publication traced.

KpR 1899.5 Copy of the two issues of the original MS magazine 'The Scribbler' (written out by May or Jenny Morris), containing this story.

This original 'Scribbler' was sold to G. M. Williamson in 1901 by May Morris (see the description of 'The Scribbler' in the INTRODUCTION).

Anderson Galleries, 17 March 1915 (G. M. Williamson Sale), Lot 106.

KpR 1899.7 Typed transcripts (made to replace KpR 1899.5) of the two issues of 'The Scribbler' containing this story, bound in May Morris's set.

British Library, Add. MS 45337, ff. 120–6 and 161–5, rectos only (magazine on ff. 104–77, rectos only).

My First Book
First pub. with poem 'In the Neolithic Age' in *San Francisco Examiner*, 18 December 1892 and (with same poem but here entitled 'Primum Tempus') in *The Idler*, December 1892; *Sussex*, XXX, 3–8; Harbord, V, 2513–14, as 'Uncollected No. 210'.

KpR 1900 Corrected typescript (including also 'In the Neolithic Age' KpR 530), here entitled 'Primum Tempus', signed, 5 numbered leaves (rectos only), annotated 'proof to me at Brattleboro Vt. USA.'.

This typescript includes (p. 3) the 2 lines beginning 'In a very short time you're released from all care', listed in Harbord, Verse No. 532.

Texas.

KpR 1901 Corrected galley proof set up for a projected volume of the Sussex Edition to be called *Why Snow Falls at Vernet and Other Stories* (revised to 'Uncollected vol.'), annotated in an unidentified hand 'Vol. II begins here'.

British Library, Add. MS 55850.

My Great and Only
First pub. *Civil and Military Gazette*, 11–15 January 1890; collected *Abaft the Funnel* (New York, 1909); *Sussex*, XXIX, 259–67; Harbord, II, 707–11.

KpR 1902 Corrected first galley proof set up for a projected volume of the Sussex Edition to be called *Why Snow Falls at Vernet and Other Stories* (revised to 'Uncollected vol.') (including corrections to the five stanzas beginning 'At the back of Knightsbridge Barricks'); date stamped 25 October 1930.

The verses in the text beginning 'At the back of Knightsbridge Barricks' are listed Harbord, Verse No. 397 and are included in the extract of the story published Rutherford, pp. 473–5.

British Library, Add. MS 55850.

My Lord the Elephant
First pub. *Two Tales*, 24 December 1892; collected *Many Inventions* (London and New York, 1893); *Sussex*, V, 49–75; Harbord, III, 1202–8.

KpR 1903 Revised, here entitled 'The Visitation of the Sick', in MS Day's Work, 12 numbered pages; watermarked 1890.

British Library, Add. MS 45541, ff. 1–12 (rectos only).

KpR 1904 Corrected first page proof for *Humorous Tales* (London, 1931), pp. 407–33; date stamped 2 and 5 June 1931.

British Library, Add. MS 55847.

KpR 1905 Corrected first page proof for the Sussex Edition; date stamped 10 June 1931.

British Library, Add. MS 55856.

'My Master: Your wooden shod heel has been very softly placed...'
No publication traced; not in Harbord. For verses written for Edmonia Hill's godchild, see KpR 519.

KpR 1906 Revised fragment, probably a first attempt at writing something for Edmonia Hill's godchild, one page (on a leaf containing also KpR 27, 1345).

Library of Congress, Rare Book Division, Carpenter Kipling Collection, Pen and Brush Sketches, Item 6.

My Own True Ghost Story
First pub. *Week's News*, 25 February 1888; collected *Phantom 'Rickshaw* (Allahabad, [1888]); *Sussex*, III, 169–79; Harbord, I, 354–5.

KpR 1907 Fair copy, 15 numbered pages and title page (7 leaves folded to be a booklet), including 2 sketches.

Berg.

KpR 1908 Annotations explaining Indian words, in a copy of the first collected edition (KpR 1982), pp. 31, 37.

Berg.

KpR 1909 Corrected first page proof for the Sussex Edition; date stamped 18 September 1931.

British Library, Add. MS 55854.

My Personal Experiences with a Lion, see KpR 1732.

'My Son's Wife'
First pub. with poem 'The Floods' in *A Diversity of Creatures* (London, 1917); *Sussex*, IX, 333–74; Harbord, VII, 3093–9.

KpR 1910 Revised, here entitled 'Elizabeth' (possibly not by RK), in MS Diversity of Creatures (ff. 113–26, rectos only).

University of Edinburgh, Dk. 2. 8.

KpR 1911 Corrected first page proof for the Sussex Edition; date stamped 28 April 1932.

British Library, Add. MS 55860.

My Sunday at Home
First pub. *The Idler*, March 1895; collected *The Day's Work* (New York, 1898); *Sussex*, VI, 357–75; Harbord, III, 1433–40.

KpR 1912 Revised, in MS Day's Work, including the epigraph, 7 numbered pages (one also containing KpR 476), annotated 'type as soon as possible and return to Rudyard Kipling Tisbury Wilts'; watermarked 1890.

British Library, Add. MS 45541, ff. 66–72 (rectos only).

KpR 1913 Corrected typescript, the title (as above) here revised to 'The Child of Calamity', signed, 23 numbered leaves (rectos only) and title page, annotated 'proof to Rudyard Kipling Brattleboro Vermont U.S.A.'.

Facsimile of first page in an unidentified sale catalogue, Lot 329 (clipping at Yale, Facs. No. 470).

Library of Congress, Rare Book Division, Carpenter Kipling Collection.

KpR 1914 Clipping of first publication, revised for a collected edition.

Princeton, Doubleday Collection, Bound Vol. V (oversize).

KpR 1915 Corrected first page proof for *Humorous Tales* (London, 1931), pp. 121–39; date stamped 9 and 11 May 1931.

British Library, Add. MS 55847.

KpR 1916 Corrected first page proof for the Sussex Edition; date stamped 27 June 1931.

British Library, Add. MS 55857.

Naboth

First pub. *Civil and Military Gazette*, 26 August 1886; collected *Life's Handicap* (London and New York, 1891); *Sussex*, IV, 433–7; Harbord, II, 1004.

KpR 1917 Corrected first page proof for the Sussex Edition; date stamped 13 February 1932.

British Library, Add. MS 55855.

Namgay Doola

First pub. *Mine Own People* (New York, [1891]); collected *Life's Handicap* (London and New York, 1891); *Sussex*, IV, 289–304; Harbord, II, 984–6.

KpR 1918 Corrected first page proof for *Humorous Tales* (London, 1931), pp. 103–17; date stamped 9 May 1931.

British Library, Add. MS 55847.

KpR 1919 Corrected first page proof for the Sussex Edition; date stamped 13 February 1932.

British Library, Add. MS 55855.

The Naulahka

This novel by Kipling and Wolcott Balestier first pub. serially in *Century Magazine*, November 1891–July 1892; first pub. (with chapter headings) in book form London, 1892; *Sussex*, XIX; Harbord, III, 1153–87. For chapter headings, see KpR 72–4, 164–5, 184–7, 383, 572–3, 606–7, 730–1, 764–5, 994–5. For early rough notes, see KpR 1834.

KpR 1920 Portion of corrected typescript, 5 pages.

Parke Bernet, 30 October 1950 (Oliver R. Barrett Sale), Lot 661.

KpR 1921 Corrected first page proof for the Sussex Edition (including KpR 187, 383, 573, 607, 731, 765, 995); date stamped 7 November 1931.

British Library, Add. MS 55869.

A Naval Mutiny

First pub. *Story-Teller*, December 1931; collected with poem 'The Coiner' in *Limits and Renewals* (London, 1932); *Sussex*, XI, 175–94; Harbord, VII, 3222–38. For proof corrections for the New York, 1932 edition, see KpR 1840.

KpR 1922 Corrected page proof in Limits and Renewals Proof; date stamped 19–20 January 1932.

Syracuse University.

KpR 1923 Corrected first page proof for the Sussex Edition; date stamped 14 October 1932.

British Library, Add. MS 55862.

The New Army in Training

This series of six articles first pub. *Daily Telegraph*, 7–24 December 1924; in booklet form London, 1915; *Sussex*, XXVI, 5–61; Harbord, V, 2255–7.

KpR 1924 Draft, in MS Non-Fiction, including: 'The Men at Work', here entitled 'The New <World> Army', 4 numbered pages (ff. 2–5, rectos only); 'Iron into Steel', here untitled, continuing on from first article, 5 pages (ff. 5–9, rectos only); 'Guns and Supply', 6 pages (ff. 10–15, rectos only); 'Canadians in Camp', here untitled, 6 pages (ff. 16–21, rectos only); 'Indian Troops', here entitled 'The New Army', 4 pages (ff. 22–4, 29, rectos only); 'Territorial Battalions', here untitled, 4 pages (ff. 25–8, rectos only).

British Library, Add. MS 45542, ff. 2–29 (rectos only).

New Brooms

First pub. *Civil and Military Gazette*, 3 August 1888; collected *'Turnovers'*, Vol. III (Lahore, [1888]); collected *Abaft the Funnel* (New York, 1909); Harbord, II, 686.

KpR 1925 Revised clipping of first publication, in Scrapbook 4 (p. 74).

Sussex, KP 28/4.

Newspapers and Democracy, for 'Letters to the Family No. III', see KpR 1826–30.

[Note on the origin of '*Nazi*']
No publication traced.

KpR 1926 Pencil note, beginning '"We know that bonfire on the ice."...', signed (initials), on verso of a printed menu (South African), from the papers of Lady Milner.

Syracuse University.

[Notes describing delirium during pneumonia]
No publication traced.

KpR 1927 Two copies of a typescript, beginning 'I began by going up stairs...', 17 numbered leaves (rectos only), the second containing a few corrections, the first annotated by CK 'R. K.'s delirium in first pneumonia illness in NY./Dictated by him after recovery' and second annotated '1st attack pneumonia in N. York dictated by himself'.

Sussex, KP 25/5 and KP 25/6.

[Notes on Dr Bielby's nursing lectures]
No publication traced.

KpR 1928 Two pages of notes (partly in an unidentified hand); annotated (unidentified hand) 'January Lahore 1886.'.

Sussex, KP 25/2.

[Notes on Henry Rider Haggard's works]

KpR 1928.5 Including: (1) draft plot of Haggard's *The Ghost King*, 3 leaves (rectos only), in the hands of both RK and Haggard; (2) draft plot of Haggard's *Allan and the Ice-Gods*, 2 leaves (rectos only), in the hands of both RK and Haggard, together with 2 lists of characters (one by RK, the other mostly in the hand of Haggard's secretary Ida Hector, one page each) and a covering leaf annotated by Haggard 'Synopsis...drawn up...at Bateman's, Feb. 1922...'; (3) one leaf of Bateman's notepaper containing notes (and a sketch) by RK on the name 'Murgh', dated 5 October 1908 by Haggard; (4) typescript dedication to RK by Haggard, as in *The Way of the Spirit* (1906).

(1) and (2) printed and discussed in *Rudyard Kipling to Rider Haggard*, ed. Morton Cohen (London, 1965), including facsimiles of RK's list of characters (facing p. 120) and of the notes on 'Murgh' (between pp. 56 and 57); also mentioned Stewart, p. 517.

Dalhousie University.

[Notes on international affairs]
No publication traced.

KpR 1929 Rough notes under five headings ('Ireland', 'India', 'Germany', 'Home Affairs', 'Ottawa'), one page, together with a second leaf (recto only), possibly a continuation of the first; each page is annotated by Lady Milner 'Batemans June 11 1932 R. K.'.

Syracuse University.

[Notes on R. Rawlinson's filmscript of *Soldiers Three*]
See also KpR 2308.

KpR 1929.5 A series of six typed letters to Captain R. Rawlinson about the latter's filmscript of *Soldiers Three*, including detailed suggestions for scenes, 1½ pages of dialogue between 'M[ulvaney]' and 'D[rew]' (in the letter of 3 December 1934), maps (in the letter of 9 December 1934), photos (3 December 1934), as well as KpR 586; dated 19 November 1934–10 January 1935.

Syracuse University.

[Notes on works]
No publication traced.

KpR 1930 Revised typescript of notes (possibly written in answer to queries), 5 numbered leaves (rectos only), as sent to André Chevrillon, [after 1912].

More information was sent in RK's letters to Chevrillon of 1909–35 *passim*; these notes are possibly a copy of those enclosed with RK's letter of 6 October 1919 (original owned in 1958 by Claire Chevrillon; typed transcript at Sussex, KP 14/37).

Sussex, KP 25/3.

Of Those Called
First pub. *Civil and Military Gazette*, 13 July 1889; collected *Soldiers Three. The Story of the Gadsbys. In Black and White* (New York and London, 1895); *Sussex*, III, 277–80; Harvard, V, 2390, as 'Uncollected No. 165'.

KpR 1931 Fair copy, revised (thin paper carbon copy), in MS From Sea to Sea (see KpR 1634), here entitled 'Abaft the Funnel/No VI', 3 numbered pages, listed (not by RK) in the Table of Contents as 'The Phantom Ship'.

Huntington, HM 12429, Vol. 2, pp. 67–9.

KpR 1932 Revised clipping of first publication (entitled 'Abaft the Funnel. VI') in Scrapbook 4 (p. 148).

Sussex, KP 28/4.

KpR 1933 Corrected first page proof for the Sussex Edition; date stamped 18 September 1931.

British Library, Add. MS 55854.

Old Men at Pevensey
First pub. *Strand Magazine* and *Ladies Home Journal*, April 1906; collected with poem 'The Runes on Weland's Sword' in *Puck of Pook's Hill* (London, 1906); *Sussex*, XIV, 89–113; Harbord, VI, 2709–11.

KpR 1934 Revised, headed 'Puck of Pooks Hill, IV', 7 numbered leaves (rectos only), in MS Puck.

Bodleian, MS. Eng. misc. c. 127, ff. 34–40 (rectos only).

KpR 1935 Corrected galley proof for *Ladies Home Journal*, stamped 'First Galley' and 'C. M. K.'.

Huntington, RB 29633.

KpR 1936 Corrected second galley proof for *Ladies Home Journal*, signed (initials), incorporating the changes in KpR ; stamped 'C. M. K.'.

American Art Association, 26–7 January 1922, Lot 480 (property of Martindell).

KpR 1937 Corrected first page proof for the Sussex Edition; date stamped 2 July 1931.

British Library, Add. MS 55864.

On Greenhow Hill
First pub. *Harper's Weekly*, 23 August 1890; collected *Life's Handicap* (London and New York, 1891); *Sussex*, IV, 75–99; Harbord, II, 953–8.

KpR 1938 Fair copy, revised, annotated on first page 'To A. P. Watt from the man who wrote it RK'.

Facsimile of first page in Livingston, p. [81]; photograph of first page at Harvard, Kipling 15.2 (in a box of photos, etc. from Flora Livingston) and an enlarged photograph of first page in the Library of Congress, Rare Book Division, Carpenter Kipling Collection.

Formerly owned (1927) by A. S. Watt, London (see Livingston) but not now in the archive of A. P. Watt, Ltd.

KpR 1939 Corrected first page proof for the Sussex Edition; date stamped 13 February 1932.

British Library, Add. MS 55855.

On One Side Only, for 'From Tideway to Tideway No. VIII', see KpR 1647–9.

On the City Wall
First pub. *In Black and White* (Allahabad, [1888]); *Sussex*, II, 343–[74]; Harbord, I, 114–18.

KpR 1940 Revisions in a copy of the second edition of *In Black and White* (KpR 1747).

Berg.

KpR 1941 Corrections in a copy of the first publication (KpR 1745).

Syracuse University.

KpR 1942 Annotations explaining Indian words, in a copy of the first publication (KpR 1746), pp. 84, 92, 96, 100, 102.

Berg.

KpR 1943 Corrected first page proof for the Sussex Edition; date stamped 14 May 1931.

British Library, Add. MS 55853.

On the Gate

First pub. *McCall's Magazine*, June 1926, as 'The Gate'; collected with poem 'The Supports' in *Debits and Credits* (London, 1926); *Sussex*, X, 255–78; Harbord, VII, 3167–74. The text of the story includes a version of lines 1–3 of 'The Supports'; for MS sources of that poem, see KpR 1136–8.

KpR 1944 Revised, including the conclusion only, in MS Non-Fiction, beginning mid-sentence 'Others were not so easily held...', 2 leaves (rectos only).

British Library, Add. MS 45542, ff. 85, 86.

KpR 1945 Revised, in MS Debits and Credits, here untitled, including also KpR 334, 1137.5, 13 pages (ff. 143–55, rectos only).

University of Durham.

KpR 1946 Two successive corrected typescripts, both here entitled 'The Department of Death', later one complete on 27 numbered leaves, earlier one on 27 (of 34) numbered leaves (wanting ff. 3, 5, 6 and 22).

Sotheby's, 9–10 December 1968, Lot 770, sold to Rota.

KpR 1947 Part top copy and part carbon copy of typescript, here entitled 'The Department of Death', incomplete, 21 leaves (rectos only) numbered 2–22 and title page, including lines 1–6 of 'The Supports' on p. 16, annotated in an unidentified hand in pencil on title page 'This should be checked with the story in Debits and Credits (there are some alterations)'.

Library of Congress, Rare Book Division, Colt Collection.

KpR 1948 Corrected first page proof for the Sussex Edition; date stamped 30 December 1931.

British Library, Add. MS 55861.

On the Great Wall

First pub. *Strand Magazine* and *McClure's Magazine*, June 1906; collected with poem 'A Song to Mithras' in *Puck of Pook's Hill* (London, 1906); *Sussex*, XIV, 145–65; Harbord, VI, 2735–9.

KpR 1949 Revised, here entitled 'Puck of Pook's Hill/VI.', 9 leaves (rectos only), including also KpR 974, in MS Puck.

Bodleian, MS. Eng. misc. c. 127, ff. 55–63 (rectos only).

KpR 1950 Corrected first page proof (including KpR 976) for the Sussex Edition; date stamped 2 July 1931.

British Library, Add. MS 55864.

On the Strength of a Likeness

First pub. *Civil and Military Gazette*, 10 January 1887; collected *Plain Tales from the Hills* (Calcutta and London, 1888); *Sussex*, I, 395–402; Harbord, I, 91.

KpR 1951 Corrected first page proof for the Sussex Edition; date stamped 12 September 1931.

British Library, Add. MS 55852.

One Lady at Large

First pub. *Civil and Military Gazette*, 30 March 1889; collected as 'A Menagerie Aboard' in *Abaft the Funnel* (New York, 1909); *Sussex*, XXIX, 23–6; Harbord, II, 679 as 'A Menagerie Aboard *or* One Lady at Large'.

KpR 1952 Fair copy, revised (thin carbon copy), in MS From Sea to Sea (see KpR 1634), here untitled, 4 numbered pages, listed (not by RK) in the Table of Contents as 'The Giraffe Loose'.

Huntington, HM 12429, Vol. 1, pp. 9–12.

KpR 1953 Revised clipping of first publication (entitled 'Abaft the Funnel. I'), in Scrapbook 4 (p. 144).

Sussex, KP 28/4.

One View of the Question
First pub. *Fortnightly Review*, February 1890; collected *Many Inventions* (London and New York, 1893); *Sussex*, V, 79–101; Harbord, III, 1208–13.

KpR 1954 Corrected first page proof for the Sussex Edition; date stamped 10 June 1931.

British Library, Add. MS 55856.

***The One-Volume Kipling* (New York, 1928)**
See also KpR 1622, 1807, 1815.

KpR 1955 Corrected typescript of the Prefatory Note, signed, here entitled in RK's hand 'Preface to Authorized Early Kipling', enclosed in a letter to Nelson Doubleday, 12 November 1926.

Princeton, Doubleday Collection, Box 2, Folder 17.

Only a Subaltern
First pub. *Week's News*, 25 August 1888; collected *Under the Deodars* (Allahabad, [1888]); *Sussex*, III, 111–30; Harbord, I, 347–50.

KpR 1956 Corrections in a copy of the first collected edition (KpR 2175).

Syracuse University.

KpR 1957 Corrected first page proof for the Sussex Edition; date stamped 18 September 1931.

British Library, Add. MS 55854.

.007
First pub. *Scribner's Magazine*, August 1897; collected *The Day's Work* (New York, 1898); *Sussex*, VI, 237–59; Harbord, III, 1389–96.

KpR 1958 Revised, here entitled '"No. 007."', in MS Day's Work, 8 numbered pages, annotated 'Typed copy as soon as possible RK'.

British Library, Add. MS 45541, ff. 210–17 (rectos only).

KpR 1959 Corrected first page proof for the Sussex Edition; date stamped 27 June 1931.

British Library, Add. MS 55857.

The Opinions of Gunner Barnabas, see KpR 2078–9.

Opium in India
No publication traced.

KpR 1959.5 Typescript notes, revised and annotated in RK's hand, 2 leaves (rectos only), enclosed in a letter to Stanley Baldwin, Bateman's, n.d.

Sussex, Baldwin Papers 2/21.

The Other Man
First pub. (with verse heading) *Civil and Military Gazette*, 13 November 1886; collected *Plain Tales from the Hills* (Calcutta and London, 1888); *Sussex*, I, 125–9; Harbord, I, 52–3. For verse heading, see KpR 177.

KpR 1960 Corrected first page proof for the Sussex Edition; date stamped 12 September 1931.

British Library, Add. MS 55852.

Our Indian Troops in France
Speech delivered at unveiling of Indian Soldiers Monument, La Bassée, France, 7 October 1927; first pub. *The Times*, 11 November 1927; collected *A Book of Words* (London, 1928); *Sussex*, XXV, 281–3; Harbord, VII, 3314–15.

KpR 1961 Corrected first page proof for the Sussex Edition; date stamped 4 April 1931.

British Library, Add. MS 55875.

Our Overseas Men, for 'From Tideway to Tideway No. IV', see KpR 1643, 1647–9.

Our Priceless Heritage
No publication traced; not in Harbord.

KpR 1962 Typescript, revised, of rough notes (possibly for a speech or an article) on death duties and wider political issues, beginning 'Let us have a special article...', 2 pages (one leaf); annotated by Lady Milner (editor of *The National Review*) 'Rudyard Kipling's note for a suggested article 1932'.

This typescript is kept together with the unrelated KpR 1976.

Syracuse University.

The Outsider
First pub. (with verse heading 'From Stormberg's midnight mountain') *Daily Express*, 19–21 June 1900, as 'Stories of the War III'; *Sussex*, XXX, 119–40; Harbord, V, 2557–8, as 'Uncollected No. 232'.

KpR 1963 Revised, here entitled 'An Outsider.', in MS Non-Fiction, 9 numbered pages; watermarked 1897.

British Library, Add. MS 45542, ff. 214–22 (rectos only).

KpR 1964 Corrected first galley proof set up for a projected volume of the Sussex Edition (marked 'Uncollected vol.'), including corrections to the heading 'From Stormberg's midnight mountain' (see KpR 398); date stamped 4 November 1930.

British Library, Add. MS 55850.

***Outward Bound Edition of the Works of Rudyard Kipling*, 30 vols (New York, 1897–1923)**
For inscribed volumes of this edition, see KpR 558, 1155, 1164.

KpR 1965 Various lists of works to be included in the edition, in or enclosed in letters to Frank N. Doubleday of 28 August, 8 September, [6 October], 7 October, 26 October and 10 December 1896.

Princeton, Doubleday Collection, Box 3, Bound Vol. III, Items 30–4, 39 (letters containing lists) and Bound Vol I, Item 8 (separate lists).

KpR 1966 Page proof of Scribner's announcement of the edition, revised and annotated by Kipling, 2 leaves (rectos only) numbered 2–3, originally enclosed in a letter to Frank N. Doubleday, Rock House, 1 November 1896.

Facsimile page in Rice, facing p. 112.

Princeton, Doubleday Collection, Box 3, Bound Vol. III, Item 23A (letter is Item 36).

KpR 1967 Page proof of Scribner's announcement of Japan paper copies, revised and annotated by Kipling, signed (initials), 3 pages numbered 2–4, originally enclosed in a letter to Frank N. Doubleday, Rock House, 1 November 1896.

Princeton, Doubleday Collection, Box 3, Bound Vol. III, Item 23 (letter is Item 36).

KpR 1968 Fair copy of the Preface, headed '"Outward Bound" Edition/Preface', signed, one page, annotated 'proof of this at once to Rock House...'.

Preface printed Harbord, V, 2519.

Princeton, Doubleday Collection, Box 3, Bound Vol. I, Item 9.

KpR 1969 Corrected page proof of Preface, signed (initials), one page, originally returned with a letter to Frank N. Doubleday, Rock House, 1 November 1896.

Princeton, Doubleday Collection, Box 3, Bound Vol. III, Item 23B (letter is Item 36).

KpR 1970 Introduction, extensively revised, headed 'To the Nacodah [sic] or Skipper of this Venture/*a letter or bill of instructions from the owner.*', 2 numbered leaves (rectos only), enclosed in a letter to Frank N. Doubleday, 30 October 1896.

Introduction first pub. *Plain Tales from*

the Hills, Outward Bound Edition, Vol. I (New York, 1897), as 'To the *Nakhoda* or Skipper of this Venture/A Letter or Bill of Instruction from the Owner'; reprinted (together with a later version (KpR 1795–8) published as the Foreword to *A Kipling Pageant* (Garden City, New York, 1935)), in *Two Forewords* (Christmas, 1935); *Sussex*, XXX, 386–90, as 'Two Forewords'; Harbord, V, 2517–19, as 'Uncollected No. 217'.

Princeton, Doubleday Collection, Box 3, Bound Vol. I, Item 6 (letter in Bound Vol. III, Item 35).

KpR 1971 Fair copy of most of Introduction, headed 'To the Nakhoda or Skipper of this venture/a letter or bill of instructions from the owner.', prepared as copy for facsimile added to Vol. I of the Japan paper copies, one page, as sent to Frank N. Doubleday with a letter, c. 23 November 1896.

Princeton, Doubleday Collection, Box 3, Bound Vol. I, Item 7 (letter is Bound Vol. III, Item 37).

KpR 1972 Corrected page proof of Introduction, signed (initials), as sent to Frank N. Doubleday with a letter, c. 23 November 1896.

Facsimile first page (p. vii) in Rice, between pp. 112 and 113.

Princeton, Doubleday Collection, Box 3, Bound Vol. III, Item 23C (letter is Item 37).

KpR 1973 Corrected proof of the title page of the pre-publication 'prospectus volume' (see Stewart, p. 38), signed (initials) three times.

Princeton, Archive of Charles Scribner's Sons, Box 87, Folder 1.

The Parable of Boy Jones
First pub. *The Rifleman*, 15 July 1910; collected with poem 'A Departure' in *Land and Sea Tales* (London, 1923); *Sussex*, XVI, 129–41; Harbord, VI, 2897. Facsimile of portion of an autograph MS used as dust wrapper of *The Kipling Birthday Book*, Manuscript (Pocket) Edition (New York, 1934).

KpR 1974 Revised, in MS Day's Work, 5 pages (ff. 32–6, rectos only).

University of Durham.

KpR 1975 Corrected first page proof for the Sussex Edition; date stamped 14 December 1931.

British Library, Add. MS 55866.

[Paraphrase of Shakespeare's Sonnet CVII]
No publication traced; not in Harbord.

KpR 1976 Typescript, corrected and signed (initials) by RK, beginning 'CVII can be read in this way:...', one page; annotated by Lady Milner 'The history of the above is this, when I last went to Batemans (30th Dec) we discussed Shelley, Keats & diverged to the Sonnets. I asked what CVII meant...V. M. Jan 11 1932.'.

This typescript is kept together with the unrelated KpR 1962.

Syracuse University.

Passengers at Sea
Speech delivered Liverpool Shipbrokers' Benevolent Society, 26 October 1928; first pub. *The Times*, 27 October 1928; *Sussex*, XXV, 287–91; Harbord, VII, 3315–16.

KpR 1977 Corrected first page proof for the Sussex Edition; date stamped 4 April 1931.

British Library, Add. MS 55875.

A People At Home, for 'Letters to the Family No. II', see KpR 1826–30.

The Persuasive Pom-Pom
First pub. as 'Fables for the Staff III' in *The Friend* (Bloemfontein), 28 March 1900; collected *War's Brighter Side*, ed. Julian Ralph (London, 1901); reprinted Harbord, III, 1533.

KpR 1978 Corrected galley proof (containing also KpR 1806) for the first publication, among materials for *The Friend* (see KpR 2283).

Library of Congress, Rare Book Division, Colt Collection.

Peter the Wise
No publication traced; not in Harbord.

KpR 1979 Abandoned opening of a story, seven lines about a cat, on p. 1 of a folded leaf (containing also KpR 1239); watermarked 1888.

Berg.

The Phantom 'Rickshaw
First pub. *Quartette* (1885); collected *The Phantom 'Rickshaw* (Allahabad, [1888]); *Sussex*, III, 135–65; Harbord, I, 350–3.

KpR 1980 Annotations explaining Indian words, in a copy of the first collected edition (KpR 1982), pp. 3, 6, 21, 27.

Berg.

KpR 1981 Corrected first page proof for the Sussex Edition; date stamped 18 September 1931.

British Library, Add. MS 55854.

The Phantom 'Rickshaw (Allahabad, [1888])

KpR 1982 Copy containing Kipling's annotations explaining Indian words.

Contents: KpR 1864, 1908, 1980, 2106.

Berg.

Pig
First pub. (with verse heading) *Civil and Military Gazette*, 3 June 1887; collected *Plain Tales from the Hills* (Calcutta and London, 1888); *Sussex*, I, 295–303; Harbord, I, 76–8. For verse heading, see KpR 177.

KpR 1983 Corrected first page proof for *Humorous Tales* (London, 1931), pp. 143–51; date stamped 11 May 1931.

British Library, Add. MS 55847.

KpR 1984 Corrected first page proof for the Sussex Edition; date stamped 12 September 1931.

British Library, Add. MS 55852.

The Pit That They Digged
First pub. *St James's Gazette*, 14 December 1889; collected *Under the Deodars. The Phantom 'Rickshaw. Wee Willie Winkie* (New York and London, 1895); *Sussex*, III, 289–94; Harbord, V, 2413, as 'Uncollected No. 172'.

KpR 1985 Corrected first page proof for the Sussex Edition; date stamped 18 September 1931.

British Library, Add. MS 55854.

Plain Tales from the Hills, for inscribed copies, see KpR 107, 1164; Kipling's presentation copy to W. C. Crofts is in the Robert H. Taylor Collection at Princeton.

The Pleasure Cruise
First pub. *Morning Post*, 11 November 1933; *Sussex*, XXX, 329–36; Harbord, V, 2610–11, as 'Uncollected No. 264'.

KpR 1986 Two drafts, in MS Debits and Credits; the first here entitled 'The Voyage Home Charon, Hermes, Damasius, Chrysippus, Atkeinos, an Officer and many dead men', 3 pages (ff. 270–2, rectos only); the second here entitled 'The Transports', one page (f. 273).

University of Durham.

Poor Dear Mamma
First pub. (with verse heading from 'The Gipsy Trail') *Week's News*, 26 May 1888; collected *The Story of the Gadsbys* (Allahabad, [1888]); *Sussex*, II, 129–40; Harbord, I, 296–8.

KpR 1987 Corrections in a copy of the first collected edition (KpR 2104).

Syracuse University.

KpR 1988 Annotations explaining Indian words in a copy of the first collected edition (KpR 2105), pp. 5–6, 12.

Berg.

KpR 1989 Corrected first page proof for the Sussex Edition; date stamped 14 May 1931.

British Library, Add. MS 55853.

The Potted Princess
First pub. *St Nicholas Magazine*, January 1893; *Sussex*, XXX, 11–19; Harbord, V, 2514, as 'Uncollected No. 212'. An uncorrected galley proof is at Texas.

KpR 1990 Fair copy, revised, and revised again later in red, signed (in red), in MS Day's Work, 4 numbered pages, annotated 'proof to R. Kipling Brattleboro Vt.'.

British Library, Add. MS 45541, ff. 13–16 (rectos only).

KpR 1991 Corrected first galley proof set up for a projected volume of the Sussex Edition to be called *Why Snow Falls at Vernet and Other Stories* (revised to 'Uncollected vol.') date stamped 27 October 1930.

British Library, Add. MS 55850.

Preface to *Britain and the War*
First pub. André Chevrillon, *Britain and the War* (London, New York, Toronto, 1917), pp. vii–xvii; Harbord, VII, 2942, as 'Britain and the War. Uncollected No. 251A'.

KpR 1992 Drafts, 7 leaves (rectos only), here beginning 'This <is> a book, by my friend...'.

Syracuse University.

'A Priest in Spite of Himself'
First pub. *The Delineator*, August 1910; collected with poems 'A St Helena Lullaby' and 'Poor Honest Man' in *Rewards and Fairies* (London, 1910); *Sussex*, XV, 175–204; Harbord, VI, 2790–3.

KpR 1993 Revised, here untitled, in MS Rewards and Fairies, 11 pages (including one of revised typescript, f. 74a).

Cambridge University Library, ADD 6850, ff. 70–9 (rectos only).

KpR 1994 Corrected first page proof for the Sussex Edition; date stamped 18 September 1931.

British Library, Add. MS 55865.

Prisoners and Captives
First pub. *Civil and Military Gazette*, 29 September 1886; reprinted Harbord, II, 1098–1101, as 'Uncollected No. 58'.

KpR 1995 Slightly corrected galley proof, annotated on verso 'This is a very dirty first proof. Get me another. R. K.', as sent to W. C. Crofts.

Library of Congress, Rare Book Division, Carpenter Kipling Collection.

The Private Account
First pub. *Saturday Evening Post*, 26 May 1917; collected *The Eyes of Asia* (New York, 1918); *Sussex*, XXVI, 203–15; Harbord, V, 2325.

KpR 1996 Revised, here entitled 'As it was received', in MS Eyes of Asia (ff. 167–72, rectos only and without f. 169).

University of Edinburgh, Dk. 2. 8.

KpR 1997 Corrected unbound copy of *The Eyes of Asia* (New York, 1919), pp. 49–73, used for the Sussex Edition.

British Library, Add. MS 55851.

Private Learoyd's Story
First pub. *Week's News*, 14 July 1888; collected *Soldiers Three* (Allahabad, 1888); *Sussex*, II, 19–29; Harbord, I, 281–2.

KpR 1998 Corrections in a copy of the first collected edition (KpR 2081).

Syracuse University.

KpR 1999 Annotation explaining Indian words, in a copy of the first collected edition (KpR 2082), p. 13.

Berg.

KpR 2000 Corrected first page proof for *Humorous Tales* (London, 1931); pp. 205–15; date stamped 19 May 1931.

British Library, Add. MS 55847.

KpR 2001 Corrected first page proof for *Collected Dog Stories* (London, 1934), pp. 3–15; date stamped 27 July 1934.

British Library, Add. MS 55848.

KpR 2002 Corrected first page proof for the Sussex Edition; date stamped 14 May 1931.

British Library, Add. MS 55853.

The Private Services Commission
First pub. *Civil and Military Gazette*, 29 June 1887; collected Pinney (1986), pp. 235–42.

KpR 2003 Revised clipping of the first publication in which Kipling has changed the Indian terms to English ones, in Scrapbook 3 (pp. 128–9).

Sussex, KP 28/3.

The Prophet and the Country
First pub. *Hearst's International Magazine*, October 1924; collected with poems 'The Portent' and 'Gow's Watch' in *Debits and Credits* (London, 1926); *Sussex*, X, 145–63; Harbord, VII, 3151–3.

KpR 2004 Revised, in MS Debits and Credits, 6 numbered pages (ff. 101–6, rectos only).

University of Durham.

KpR 2005 Corrected first page proof for the Sussex Edition; date stamped 30 December 1931.

British Library, Add. MS 55861.

The Propogation of Knowledge
First pub. *Strand Magazine* and *McCall's Magazine*, January 1926; collected with poem 'The Birthright' in *Debits and Credits* (London, 1926); *Sussex*, XVII (*Stalky & Co.*), 319–44; Harbord, I, 466–76.

KpR 2006 Revised, in MS Debits and Credits, 9 pages (ff. 130–8, rectos only).

University of Durham.

KpR 2007 Corrected first page proof for the Sussex Edition; date stamped 27 March 1931.

British Library, Add. MS 55867.

Puck of Pook's Hill
Nineteen original illustrations for these stories by H. R. Miller (1906) are at Dalhousie University.

The Puzzler
First pub. *North American*, 15 January 1906; collected with poem 'The Puzzler' in *Actions and Reactions* (London, 1909); *Sussex*, VIII, 195–213; Harbord, VI, 2854–8.

KpR 2008 In MS Actions and Reactions (ff. 91–6), here originally entitled 'A basis for federation'; followed by a typescript (ff. 97–106).

University of St Andrews, MS PR4854.A4.

KpR 2009 Corrected first page proof for *Humorous Tales* (London, 1931); date stamped 25 May 1931.

British Library, Add. MS 55847.

KpR 2010 Corrected first page proof for the Sussex Edition; date stamped 28 November 1931.

British Library, Add. MS 55859.

***Quartette* (Lahore, 1885),** see KpR 913–18.

[Quebec Tercentenary Appeal]
First pub. *King's Book of Quebec*, 2 vols (Ottawa, 1911), pp. 192–4; not in Harbord.

KpR 2011 Fair copy, revised, here untitled and beginning 'In every nation's life there comes a breathing space...', one page, written for the Quebec Tercentenary (July 1908), accompanied by two letters, one to Lord Grey, 21 May 1908, the other to Mr Doughty, 6 June 1908.

Berg.

Quiquern
First pub. with heading 'Angutivaun Taina' in *Pall Mall Gazette*, 24–5 October 1895; collected with heading 'The People of the Eastern Ice...' in *The Second Jungle Book* (London and New York, 1895); *Sussex*, XII, 381–410; Harbord, VII, 3006–12.

KpR 2012 In MS Jungle Books: (1) revised, wanting the last paragraph, here entitled 'The Quiquern', annotated 'to be typewritten as soon as possible RK', 10 numbered pages, watermarked 1894 (ff. 106–15, rectos only); (2) revised, here entitled

'<Kotuko-Kotuko.> The Quiquern.', 7 numbered pages, watermarked 1894 (ff. 116–22, rectos only).

British Library, Add. MS 45540, ff. 106–22 (rectos only).

KpR 2013 Corrected page proof (partly first proof and partly second proof) for *Collected Dog Stories* (London, 1934), pp. 51–86; date stamped 27 July 1934 and 14 August 1934.

British Library, Add. MS 55848.

'Quo Fata Vocant'
First pub. *St George's Gazette*, 5 November 1902; *Sussex*, XXX, 255–66; Harbord, V, 2571–4, as 'Uncollected No. 239'.

KpR 2014 Corrected first galley proof set up for a projected volume of the Sussex Edition (marked 'Uncollected vol.'); date stamped 13 November 1930.

British Library, Add. MS 55850.

Railway Reform in Great Britain
First pub. *Fortnightly Review*, February 1901; *Sussex*, XXX, 199–200; Harbord, V, 2564, as 'Uncollected No. 235'.

KpR 2015 Revised, here entitled 'Some Notes on the London Brighton & South Coast Railway', in MS Debits and Credits, 5 pages (ff. 210–14, rectos only); watermarked 1896.

University of Durham.

KpR 2016 Corrected first galley proof set up for a projected volume of the Sussex Edition (marked 'Uncollected vol.'); date stamped 11 November 1930.

British Library, Add. MS 55850.

Railways and a Two-Thousand Feet Climb, see KpR 1455.

The Record of Badalia Herodsfoot
First pub. *Detroit Free Press*, Christmas Number, November 1890 and *Harper's Weekly*, 15–22 November 1890; collected *Many Inventions* (London and New York, 1893); *Sussex*, V, 395–425; Harbord, III, 1254–8.

KpR 2017 Fair copy, revised, including an epigraph from Robert Browning, 11 numbered leaves (rectos only); watermarked 1889.

Dalhousie University.

KpR 2018 Revised typescript, the epigraph by Browning cancelled and a 7-line verse heading added beginning 'Badalia Jane McCann', 40 numbered leaves (rectos only), accompanied by a letter to 'Esteemed ally and revered Editor'.

Dalhousie University.

KpR 2019 Corrected first page proof for the Sussex Edition; date stamped 10 June 1931.

British Library, Add. MS 55856.

Red Dog
First pub. as 'Good Hunting' in *Pall Mall Gazette*, 29–30 July 1895; collected *The Second Jungle Book* (London and New York, 1895); *Sussex*, XII, 195–226; Harbord, VII, 2970–2.

KpR 2020 Revised, here entitled '<Red Dog.> The Little People of the Rocks.', in MS Jungle Books, 12 pages; watermarked 1894.

British Library, Add. MS 45540, ff. 73–84 (rectos only).

Red Dog (Poetical Allegory)
No publication traced; not in Harbord.

KpR 2021 Revised, here entitled in an unidentified hand 'Red Dog (Poetical Allegory) not published', in MS Debits and Credits, 4 numbered pages (ff. 2–5, rectos only).

University of Durham.

'The Red Lamp'
First pub. *Civil and Military Gazette*, 20 July 1889; collected *Abaft the Funnel* (New York, 1909); *Sussex*, XXIX, 37–41; Harbord, II, 680–2.

KpR 2022 Fair copy, revised (thin paper carbon copy), in MS From Sea to Sea (see KpR

1634), 3 numbered pages.

Huntington, HM 12429, Vol. 1, pp. 63–5.

KpR 2023 Revised clipping of the first publication, in Scrapbook 4 (p. 150).

Sussex, KP 28/4.

Regulus

First pub. *Nash's Magazine* and *Metropolitan Magazine*, April 1917; collected with poem 'A Translation' in *A Diversity of Creatures* (London, 1917); *Sussex*, XVII (*Stalky & Co.*), 221–51; Harbord, I, 453–8.

KpR 2024 Revised, without the epigraph, in MS Diversity of Creatures (ff. 79–89, rectos only).

University of Edinburgh, Dk. 2. 8.

KpR 2025 Corrected first page proof for the Sussex Edition; date stamped 27 March 1931.

British Library, Add. MS 55867.

A Reinforcement

First pub. *Near East Magazine*, 10 May 1912; *Sussex*, XXX, 287–92; Harbord, V, 2587–9, as 'Uncollected No. 248'.

KpR 2026 Corrected first galley proof set up for a projected volume of the Sussex Edition (marked 'Uncollected vol.'); date stamped 12 November 1930.

British Library, Add. MS 55850.

Reingelder and The German Flag

First pub. *Civil and Military Gazette*, 16 April 1889; collected *Life's Handicap* (London and New York, 1891); *Sussex*, IV, 325–8; Harbord, II, 989.

KpR 2027 Fair copy (thin paper carbon copy), in MS From Sea to Sea (see KpR 1634), here entitled 'Abaft the Funnel. No. II', on 2 consecutive numbered pages and the conclusion on another leaf (containing also the ending of *From Sea to Sea*, Chapter 3), listed (not by RK) in the Table of Contents as 'A Snake Story'.

Huntington, HM 12429, Vol. 1, pp. 24–5, 31.

KpR 2028 Revised clipping of the first publication (entitled 'Abaft the Funnel. II'), in Scrapbook 4 (p. 146).

Sussex, KP 28/4.

KpR 2029 Corrected first page proof for the Sussex Edition; date stamped 13 February 1932.

British Library, Add. MS 55855.

The Rescue of Pluffles

First pub. *Civil and Military Gazette*, 20 November 1886; collected *Plain Tales from the Hills* (Calcutta and London, 1888); *Sussex*, I, 77–83; Harbord, I, 40–1.

KpR 2030 Corrected first page proof for the Sussex Edition; date stamped 12 September 1931.

British Library, Add. MS 55852.

A Retired Gentleman

First pub. *Morning Post*, 17–21 May 1917; collected *The Eyes of Asia* (New York, 1918); *Sussex*, XXVI, 175–85; Harbord, V, 2322–4.

KpR 2031 Revised, in MS Eyes of Asia (ff. 157–61, rectos only) (including KpR 673, 1152).

University of Edinburgh, Dk. 2. 8.

KpR 2032 Corrected unbound copy of *The Eyes of Asia* (New York, 1919), pp. 3–22, used for the Sussex Edition.

British Library, Add. MS 55851.

The Return of Imray

First pub. *Mine Own People* (New York, [1891]), as 'The Recrudescence of Imray'; collected *Life's Handicap* (London and New York, 1891); *Sussex*, IV, 269–85; Harbord, II, 983.

KpR 2033 Fair copy of the first publication version, revised, here entitled 'The Recrudescence of Imray', 7 numbered leaves (rectos only); watermarked 1888.

Dalhousie University.

KpR 2034 Fair copy, revised, abandoned on 2nd page, here entitled 'The Superfluous

Caller', 2 leaves (rectos only), the 2nd watermarked 1888.

Berg.

KpR 2035 Corrected first page proof for the Sussex Edition; date stamped 13 February 1932.

British Library, Add. MS 55855.

A Return to Civilisation
Speech delivered Strasbourg University, 27 November 1921; first pub. *Morning Post*, 28 November 1921; collected *A Book of Words* (London, 1928); *Sussex*, XXV, 195–6; Harbord, VII, 3308.

KpR 2036 Typescript, here untitled, headed 'Speech in Reply to Degree at Strasbourg', in Scrapbook 9 (p. 47), one page.

Sussex, KP 28/9.

KpR 2037 Corrected first page proof for the Sussex Edition; date stamped 4 April 1931.

British Library, Add. MS 55875.

A Return to the East, for 'Egypt of the Magicians No. II', see KpR 1573, 1577.

***Rewards and Fairies*: Introduction**
First pub. (early version) with story 'Gloriana' in *Nash's Magazine*, March 1910; collected with poem 'A Charm' in *Rewards and Fairies* (London, 1910); *Sussex*, XV, xi–xii; Harbord, VI, 2766–7.

KpR 2038 Fair copy, revised, here untitled and beginning 'Once upon a time, Dan and Una...', in MS Rewards and Fairies.

Cambridge University Library, ADD 6850, f. 3.

The Riddle of Empire, for 'Egypt of the Magicians No. VII', see KpR 1573, 1576–7.

'Rikki–Tikki–Tavi'
First pub. *St Nicholas* and *Pall Mall Magazine*, November 1893; collected with poem 'Darzee's Chaunt' and verse heading 'At the hole where he went in' in *The Jungle Book* (London and New York, 1894); *Sussex*, XII, 267–87; Harbord, VII, 2979–86. Some original illustrations to this story by W. H. Drake (1893) are at Dalhousie University.

KpR 2039 Revised, 7 numbered leaves (rectos only), in MS Jungle Books; watermarked 1890.

British Library, Add. MS 45540, ff. 18–24 (rectos only).

Rio, see KpR 1455.

The Ritual of Government
Speech delivered Brighton, 9 November 1910; first pub. *The Times*, 10 November 1910, as 'The Houses of Parliament'; collected *A Book of Words* (London, 1928); *Sussex*, XXV, 59–63; Harbord, VII, 3291–2.

KpR 2040 Corrected first page proof for the Sussex Edition; date stamped 4 April 1931.

British Library, Add. MS 55875.

The Ritual of the Calling of an Engineer
No publication traced; not in Harbord.

KpR 2041 Typed transcript of RK's 'Ritual', 8 numbered leaves (rectos only); written for use by the Engineering Institute of Canada, Toronto (a Masonic lodge) in 1923.

Sussex, KP 21/24.

The Road to Quebec, for 'Letters to the Family No. I', see KpR 1826–30.

The Rout of the White Hussars
First pub. with verse heading *Plain Tales from the Hills* (Calcutta and London, 1888); *Sussex*, I, 307–19; Harbord, I, 78–80. For verse heading, see KpR 177.

KpR 2042 Corrected first page proof for *Humorous Tales* (London, 1931), pp. 31–43; date stamped 6–7 May 1931.

British Library, Add. MS 55847.

KpR 2043 Corrected first page proof for the Sussex Edition; date stamped 12 September 1931.

British Library, Add. MS 55852.

A Sahibs' War
First pub. *Windsor Magazine*, December 1901; collected with poem 'The Runners' in *Traffics and Discoveries* (London, 1904); *Sussex*, VII, 79–103; Harbord, IV, 1885–92.

KpR 2044 Revised, here entitled '"<The> A Sahibs' War".', in MS Traffics and Discoveries, 9 pages.

McGill University.

KpR 2045 Corrected first page proof for the Sussex Edition; date stamped 22 March 1932.

British Library, Add. MS 55858.

São Paulo and a Coffee Estate, see KpR 1455.

The Satisfaction of a Gentleman
First pub. *London Magazine* and *McCall's Magazine*, September 1929; collected *The Complete Stalky & Co.* (London, 1929); *Sussex*, XVII, 347–69; Harbord, I, 476–82.

KpR 2046 Corrected first page proof for the Sussex Edition; date stamped 27 March 1931.

British Library, Add. MS 55867.

School Experiences
Speech delivered Junior King's School, Canterbury, 5 October 1929; first pub. *The Times* and *Morning Post*, 7 October 1929; *Sussex*, XXV, 303–7; Harbord, VII, 3317–20.

KpR 2047 Corrected first page proof for the Sussex Edition; date stamped 4 April 1931.

British Library, Add. MS 55875.

The Science of Rebellion
First pub. *New York Tribune*, 4 August 1901; *Sussex*, XXX, 223–37; Harbord, V, 2564–5, as 'Uncollected No. 237'.

KpR 2048 Revised, in MS Non-Fiction, 6 numbered pages.

British Library, Add. MS 45542, ff. 224–9 (rectos only).

The Scot and the War
Speech delivered University of Edinburgh, 7 July 1920; first pub. *The Times*, 9 July 1920; collected *A Book of Words* (London, 1928); *Sussex*, XXV, 179–80; Harbord, VII, 3307.

KpR 2049 Corrected first page proof for the Sussex Edition; date stamped 4 April 1931.

British Library, Add. MS 55875.

Scylla and Charybdis
No publication traced; not in Harbord.

KpR 2050 Draft, 9 pages (ff. 122–30, rectos only) and incomplete fair copy, 3 numbered pages (ff. 131–3, rectos only), in MS Stalky.

Haileybury.

Sea Constables
First pub. *Metropolitan Magazine*, September 1915; collected with poems 'The Changelings' and 'The Vineyard' in *Debits and Credits* (London, 1926); *Sussex*, X, 25–47; Harbord, VII, 3118–27.

KpR 2051 Revised, here entitled 'The Neutral', in MS Debits and Credits, 12 pages (pp. 42–53, rectos only).

University of Durham.

KpR 2052 Corrected first page proof for the Sussex Edition; date stamped 30 December 1931.

British Library, Add. MS 55861.

A Sea Dog
First pub. *Collected Dog Stories* (London, 1934); *Sussex*, XXX, 359–78; Harbord, VI, 2911–19.

KpR 2053 Corrected first page proof for first publication, pp. 253–[78]; date stamped 31 July 1934.

British Library, Add. MS 55848.

Sea Travel, for 'Egypt of the Magicians No. I', see KpR 1573–4, 1577.

***The Second Jungle Book* (New York, 1895)**, for an inscribed copy, see KpR 610.

A Second-Rate Woman
First pub. *Week's News*, 8 September 1888; collected *Under the Deodars* (Allahabad, [1888]); *Sussex*, III, 83–107; Harbord, I, 343–7.

KpR 2054 Corrections in a copy of the first collected edition (KpR 2175).
Syracuse University.

KpR 2055 Corrected first page proof for the Sussex Edition; date stamped 18 September 1931.
British Library, Add. MS 55854.

A Self-Made Man, see KpR 2078–9.

The Sending of Dana Da
First pub. *Week's News*, 11 February 1888; collected *In Black and White* (Allahabad, [1888]); *Sussex*, II, 327–39; Harbord, I, 329–33.

KpR 2056 Revisions in a copy of the second edition of *In Black and White* (KpR 1747).
Berg.

KpR 2057 Corrections in a copy of the first collected edition (KpR 1745).
Syracuse University.

KpR 2058 Annotations explaining Indian words, in a copy of the first collected edition (KpR 1746), pp. [66], 68, 71, 77.
Berg.

KpR 2059 Corrected first page proof for *Humorous Tales* (London, 1931), pp. 461–74; date stamped 8 June 1931.
British Library, Add. MS 55847.

KpR 2060 Corrected first page proof for the Sussex Edition; date stamped 14 May 1931.
British Library, Add. MS 55853.

The Serai Cabal, see KpR 2078–9.

A Serpent of Old Nile, for 'Egypt of the Magicians No. III', see KpR 1573–4, 1577.

The Servants of the Queen, see KpR 1690.

The Shadow of His Hand
First pub. *Civil and Military Gazette*, 2 August 1889; collected *Abaft the Funnel* (New York, 1909); *Sussex*, XXIX, 45–9; Harbord, II, 682.

KpR 2061 Fair copy, revised (thin paper carbon copy), in MS From Sea to Sea (see KpR 1634), 4 numbered pages.
Huntington, HM 12429, Vol. 2, pp. 77–80.

Shakespeare and *The Tempest*
First pub. as a Letter to the Editor in *The Spectator*, 2 July 1898; *Sussex*, XXX, 55–60; Harbord, V, 2527–9, as 'Landscape and Literature, Uncollected No. 224'.

KpR 2062 Corrected first galley proof set up for a projected volume of the Sussex Edition to be called *Why Snow Falls at Vernet and Other Stories* (revised to 'Uncollected vol.'); date stamped 28 October 1930.
British Library, Add. MS 55850.

The Ship that Found Herself
First pub. *Bombay Gazette* (?), 1895; reprinted *The Idler*, December 1895; collected *The Day's Work* (New York, 1898); *Sussex*, VI, 83–105; Harbord, III, 1354–61.

KpR 2063 Revised, in MS Day's Work, 9 numbered pages; watermarked 1890.
British Library, Add. MS 45541, ff. 201–9 (rectos only).

KpR 2064 Corrected galley proof for *The Idler*, annotated 'Urgent revise...', together with a copy of the story as published in *The Idler*, revised by RK, signed (initials).
Library of Congress, Rare Book Division, Carpenter Kipling Collection.

KpR 2065 Corrected page proof (four pages, pp. 94–5 and 100–101) for *The Day's Work* (New York, 1898), signed (initials), the corrections are possibly in an unidentified hand, bound into a presentation copy (containing also KpR 286, 1541, 1591, 2239) from F. N. Doubleday to Bliss Perry, inscribed 21 October 1898.
Harvard, Kipling 18.98.2*.

KpR 2066 Corrected page proof (two pages) for *The Day's Work* (New York, 1898).

Princeton, Doubleday Collection.

KpR 2067 Corrected first page proof (including corrections to the verse heading) for the Sussex Edition; date stamped 27 June 1931.

The verse heading (8 lines beginning 'We now, held in captivity', ascribed 'Song of the Engines') was first appended in the Edition de Luxe, Vol. XIII (London, 1899); it was collected separately in *Poems 1886–1929* (New York, 1930); *Sussex*, XXXIV, 230, as 'Chapter Heading'; Harbord, Verse No. 645, as 'The Song of the Engines'.

British Library, Add. MS 55857.

Shipping
Speech delivered Annual Dinner, United Kingdom Chamber of Shipping, London, 20 February 1925; first pub. *The Times*, 21 February 1925; collected *A Book of Words* (London, 1928); *Sussex*, XXV, 251–6; Harbord, VII, 3313.

KpR 2068 Corrected first page proof for the Sussex Edition; date stamped 4 April 1931.

British Library, Add. MS 55875.

Short Speech at Opening of the Maple Leaf Clubs/ Dec. 21st 1916
Kipling's seconding speech for a motion to thank the Duke of Connaught at the opening of the Maple Leaf Clubs for Canadian soldiers, London, 21 December 1916 was reported in *The Times*, 22 December 1916.

KpR 2069 Typescript, here beginning 'Now that the test of the War has proved...', in Scrapbook 9 (p. 30), one page.

Sussex, KP 28/9.

Simple Simon
First pub. *The Delineator*, June 1910; collected with poems 'The Thousandth Man' and 'Frankie's Trade' in *Rewards and Fairies* (London, 1910); *Sussex*, XV, 271–91; Harbord, VI, 2800–2.

KpR 2070 Revised, in MS Rewards and Fairies, 7 numbered pages.

Cambridge University Library, ADD 6850, ff. 99–105 (rectos only).

KpR 2071 Corrected first page proof for the Sussex Edition; date stamped 18 September 1931.

British Library, Add. MS 55865.

The Sing-Song of Old Man Kangaroo
First pub. *Ladies Home Journal*, June 1900; collected with poem 'This is the mouth-filling song' in *Just So Stories* (London, 1902); *Sussex*, XIII, 83–93; Harbord, IV, 1666–7.

KpR 2072 Revised, in MS Just So Stories, including the first page only of a draft (f. 47) and a fair copy, revised (ff. 46, 48) of the story, the two captions (f. 42, watermarked 1901), and the 3 original illustrations (ff. 43–5).

British Library, Add. MS 59840, ff. 42–8 (rectos only).

KpR 2073 Corrected typescript, as sent to E. W. Bok for first publication, 4 numbered leaves (rectos only), signed, inscribed on verso of last leaf 'For E. W. Bok, from Rudyard Kipling'.

Harvard, Kipling 2.25.

KpR 2074 Corrected galley proof for first publication, signed (initials).

Library of Congress, Rare Book Division, Carpenter Kipling Collection, *Animal Stories*.

KpR 2075 Corrected first page proof for the Sussex Edition; date stamped 29 October 1932.

British Library, Add. MS 55863.

Slaves of the Lamp
First pub. in two parts *Cosmopolis*, April–May 1897; collected *Stalky & Co.* (London, 1899); *Sussex*, XVII, 69–93 (Part I) and 403–[27] (Part II); Harbord, I, 431–9 (Part I) and 490–9 (Part II).

KpR 2076 In MS Stalky: (1) draft of Part I, 9 numbered pages (ff. 101–9, rectos only); (2) incomplete draft of Part II, 6 pages (ff. 110–15, rectos only); (3) fair copy, revised, of Part I, 8 numbered pages (ff. 11–18, rectos only); (4) fair copy, revised, of Part II, 11 pages (ff. 90–100, rectos only), annotated 'type as soon as possible'.

Haileybury.

KpR 2077 Corrected first page proof for the Sussex Edition; date stamped 27 March 1931.

British Library, Add. MS 55867.

The Smith Administration
This series of 20 sketches was first pub. *Civil and Military Gazette*, 27 August 1886–5 November 1888 (17 sketches), *The Pioneer*, 30 December 1887–1 March 1888 (2 sketches) and *Pioneer Mail*, 8 February 1888 (one sketch); collected in the suppressed *The Smith Administration* (Allahabad, 1891); collected (18 sketches, without 'The Tracking of Chuckerbutti' and 'Bread Upon the Waters' which were never collected) in *From Sea to Sea*, 2 vols (London, 1899); *Sussex*, XXIII, 325–[468]; Harbord, II, 911–29. For a MS source of one sketch, 'The Explanation of Mir Baksh', see KpR 1595. Six known copies of the suppressed Allahabad edition were listed in Stewart, p. 92 and only three have been traced: E. A. Ballard's copy (Dalhousie University); G. B. McCutcheon's copy; Owen Young's copy (Berg); CK's copy (probably the one at British Library, Department of Printed Books, File 462); Templeton Croker's copy; Charles P. Johnson's copy.

KpR 2078 Corrected page proof of 17 of the 18 collected sketches (wanting 'Hunting a Miracle'), in Vols I and II of proofs of *From Sea to Sea* (see KpR 1642), signed (initials) *passim*, stamped '2nd REV.'; date stamped 25 May 1899.

Library of Congress, Rare Book Division, Carpenter Kipling Collection.

KpR 2079 Corrected first page proof of the 18 collected sketches for the Sussex Edition, date stamped 18 November 1932; together with a corrected second page proof of 2 sketches ('A Bazar *Dhulip*' and 'The Cow-House *Jirga*'), date stamped 1 June 1936; together with uncorrected copies of a third proof of those same two sketches, date stamped 18 May 1937.

British Library, Add. MS 55873.

A Smoke of Manila
First pub. *Civil and Military Gazette*, 18 July 1889; collected *Abaft the Funnel* (New York, 1909); *Sussex*, XXIX, 29–33; Harbord, II, 679.

KpR 2080 Fair copy, revised (thin paper carbon copy), in MS From Sea to Sea (see KpR 1634), here entitled 'Abaft the Funnel no VII', 3 numbered pages, listed (not by RK) in Table of Contents as 'The Manila Thief'.

Huntington, HM 12429, Vol. 2, pp. 70–2.

A Snake Farm, see KpR 1455.

***Soldiers Three* (Allahabad, 1888)**

KpR 2081 Copy (wanting the wrapper) containing corrections by RK.

Contents: KpR 1441, 1447, 1673, 1758, 1998, 2083, 2256.

Syracuse University.

KpR 2082 Copy containing annotations explaining Indian words.

Contents: KpR 1442, 1448, 1674, 1759, 1999, 2257.

Berg.

The Solid Muldoon
First pub. *Week's News*, 9 June 1888; collected *Soldiers Three* (Allahabad, 1888); *Sussex*, II, 49–61; Harbord, I, 285–6.

KpR 2083 Corrections in a copy of the first collected edition (KpR 2081).

Syracuse University.

KpR 2084 Corrected first page proof for the Sussex Edition; date stamped 14 May 1931.

British Library, Add. MS 55853.

Some Aspects of Travel
Speech delivered Royal Geographical Society, London, 17 February 1914; first pub. *The Times* and *Morning Post*, 18 February 1914; collected *A Book of Words* (London, 1928); *Sussex*, XXV, 95–114; Harbord, VII, 3297–9.

KpR 2085 Corrected first page proof for the Sussex Edition; date stamped 4 April 1931.

British Library, Add. MS 55875.

Some Earthquakes, for 'From Tideway to Tideway No. V', see KpR 1644, 1647–9.

Something of Myself
First pub. (posthumously) serially in *Morning Post*, *New York Times* and *Civil and Military Gazette*, January–February 1937; first pub. in one volume London, 1937; *Sussex*, XXXI; Harbord, VII, 3359–418.

KpR 2086 Scrap of a proof? from or for an unidentified publication (headed in print 'Aug. 20/ [no year]') containing a paragraph cancelled by RK and signed (initials) by him; the passage (begininng 'But don't the lines following on "the lordliest life on earth"...') concerns a misunderstanding of his poem 'The Islanders' and includes lines 35–8 of that poem.

This is a different version of the anecdote from that published in *Something of Myself* (*Sussex Edition*, XXXI, 234–5).

New York University.

The Son of His Father
First pub. *Harper's Weekly*, 30 December 1893; collected *Land and Sea Tales* (London, 1923); *Sussex*, XVI, 167–93; Harbord, VI, 2900–1.

KpR 2087 Corrected first page proof for the Sussex Edition; date stamped 14 December 1931.

British Library, Add. MS 55866.

Sons of Belial
No publication traced; mentioned Harbord, V, 2385, as 'Uncollected No. 161'.

KpR 2088 Fair copy, revised (thin paper carbon copy and one page (p. 83) of thick as well), in MS From Sea to Sea (see KpR 1634), unfinished, 3 numbered pages.

Huntington, HM 12429, Vol. 2, pp. 81–3.

Speech Delivered at Bloemfontein March 28th. 1900.
First pub. *The Friend* (Bloemfontein), 12 April 1900; collected *War's Brighter Side*, ed. Julian Ralph (London, 1901); reprinted Harbord, III, 1536.

KpR 2089 Typescript (hectograph), 2 leaves (rectos only), in a folder (containing also KpR 2148) labelled 'Kiplingiana'.

Texas.

Speech delivered: <Trinity Hall> in the Hall of Trinity College Cambridge: June. 17th. 1908
No publication traced; not in Harbord.

KpR 2090 Revised, here beginning 'Several of those who have been honoured...', one page, in Scrapbook 9 (p. 11).

Sussex, KP 28/9.

Speech made at Etchingham Church on the Occasion of the Unveiling of the War Memorial 28th. April 1920
No publication traced; listed in Harbord, Speech No. 69 (he says the speech is reported in the *Daily Graphic* of 30 April 1920).

KpR 2091 Typescript, here beginning 'We all know a grief cannot be cheated...', in Scrapbook 9 (pp. 34–6), 3 numbered leaves (rectos only).

Sussex, KP 28/9.

Speeches, see all the titles published in RK's *A Book of Words* (London, 1928) as well as KpR 1513, 1876, 2069, 2089, 2090, 2091.

The Spirit of the Latin
Speech delivered Brazilian Academy of Letters, Rio de Janeiro, March 1927; first pub. *A Book of Words* (London, 1928); *Sussex*, XXV, 273–7; Harbord, VII, 3314.

KpR 2092 Corrected first page proof for the Sussex Edition; date stamped 4 April 1931.

British Library, Add. MS 55875.

The Spirit of the Navy

Speech delivered Naval Club, London, October 1908; first pub. *The Times*, 16 September 1908; collected *A Book of Words* (London, 1928); *Sussex*, XXV, 51–5; Harbord, VII, 3291.

KpR 2093 Slightly corrected typescript, headed 'Speech delivered Oct 21st. 1908', 5 numbered leaves (rectos only), in Scrapbook 9 (pp. 14–15).

Sussex, KP 28/9.

KpR 2094 Corrected first page proof for the Sussex Edition; date stamped 4 April 1931.

British Library, Add. MS 55875.

The Spring Running

First pub. as 'Mowgli Leaves the Jungle Forever' with poem 'The Outsong' (collected as 'Outsong in the Jungle') in *Pall Mall Gazette*, 25 September 1895; collected *The Second Jungle Book* (London and New York, 1895); *Sussex*, XII, 231–57; Harbord, VII, 2972–3.

KpR 2095 Revised, in MS Jungle Books, 11 pages; watermarked 1894.

British Library, Add. MS 45540, ff. 60–70 (rectos only).

'Stalky'

First pub. *McClure's Magazine*, December 1898; collected with poem 'The Hour of the Angel' in *Land and Sea Tales* (London, 1923); *Sussex*, XVII (*Stalky & Co.*), 3–25; Harbord, I, 422–6.

KpR 2096 Revised, in MS Stalky, 6 numbered pages (ff. 116–21, rectos only), annotated 'to be typed urgent RK'.

Haileybury.

KpR 2097 Seven lines, cancelled, on verso of f. 3 of KpR 1481, in MS Day's Work.

British Library, Add. MS 45541, f. 105v *rev*.

KpR 2098 Corrected first page proof for the Sussex Edition; date stamped 27 March 1931.

British Library, Add. MS 55867.

***Stalky & Co.*: Dedication**

First pub. London, 1899, pp. vii–ix (with introductory poem 'Let us now praise...'); *Sussex*, XVII, [vii].

KpR 2099 Fair copy, headed 'Dedication to Stalky & Co.', beginning 'To Cormell Price...', signed, one page.

This MS printed in Maggs Catalogue 406 (1921), p. 62.

Dalhousie University.

Stationery

Speech delivered to Worshipful Company of Stationers, London, 3 July 1925; first pub. *The Times*, 4 July 1925; collected *A Book of Words* (London, 1928); *Sussex*, XXV, 259–61; Harbord, VII, 3313.

KpR 2100 Corrected first page proof for the Sussex Edition; date stamped 4 April 1931.

British Library, Add. MS 55875.

Steam Tactics

First pub. *Windsor Magazine*, December 1902; collected with poem 'The Necessitarian' in *Traffics and Discoveries* (London, 1904); *Sussex*, VII, 183–214; Harbord, IV, 1755–80.

KpR 2101 Revised, in MS Traffics and Discoveries, 18 numbered pages.

McGill University.

KpR 2102 Corrected first page proof for the Sussex Edition; date stamped 22 March 1932.

British Library, Add. MS 55858.

The Story of a King, see KpR 2078–9.

The Story of Muhammad Din

First pub. *Civil and Military Gazette*, 8 September 1886; collected *Plain Tales from the Hills* (Calcutta and London, 1888); *Sussex*, I, 387–91; Harbord, I, 90–1.

KpR 2103 Corrected first page proof for the Sussex Edition; date stamped 12 September 1931.

British Library, Add. MS 55852.

***The Story of the Gadsbys* (Allahabad, [1888])**

KpR 2104 Copy (wanting the wrapper) containing corrections to the Preface and the contents listed below.

The Preface (not afterward collected) reprinted Harbord, I, 272.

Contents: KpR 1603, 1652, 1987, 2110, 2125, 2188, 2252, 2268.

Syracuse University.

KpR 2105 Copy containing annotations explaining Indian words in the Preface (p. [v]), as well as Contents below.

Contents: KpR 1653, 1988, 2189, 2253, 2269.

Berg.

The Strange Ride of Morrowbie Jukes
First pub. *Quartette* (1885); collected *The Phantom 'Rickshaw* (Allahabad, [1888]); *Sussex*, III, 183–213; Harbord, I, 355–8.

KpR 2106 Annotations explaining Indian words, in a copy of the first collected edition (KpR 1982), pp. 51, 55, 63.

Berg.

KpR 2107 Corrected first page proof for the Sussex Edition; date stamped 18 September 1931.

British Library, Add. MS 55854.

Surgeons and the Soul
Speech delivered Annual Dinner, Royal College of Surgeons, London, 14 February 1923; first pub. *The Times*, 15 February 1923; collected *A Book of Words* (London, 1928); *Sussex*, XXV, 209–13; Harbord, VII, 3309–10.

KpR 2108 Corrected first page proof for the Sussex Edition; date stamped 4 April 1931.

British Library, Add. MS 55875.

'Surgical and Medical'
First pub. *Daily Mail* and *Chicago Record*, 1–2 May 1900; *Sussex*, XXX, 87–97; Harbord, V, 2251–2.

KpR 2109 Corrected first galley proof set up for a projected volume of the Sussex Edition to be called *Why Snow Falls at Vernet and Other Stories* (revised to 'Uncollected vol.'); date stamped 28 October 1930.

British Library, Add. MS 55850.

The Swelling of Jordan
First pub. *Week's News*, 30 June 1888; collected *The Story of the Gadsbys* (Allahabad, [1888]); *Sussex*, II, 219–31; Harbord, I, 311–13.

KpR 2110 Corrections in a copy of the first collected edition (KpR 2104).

Syracuse University.

KpR 2111 Corrected first page proof for the Sussex Edition; date stamped 14 May 1931.

British Library, Add. MS 55853.

'Swept and Garnished'
First pub. *Nash's Magazine* and *Century Magazine*, January 1915; collected *A Diversity of Creatures* (London, 1917); *Sussex*, IX, 407–18; Harbord, VII, 3102.

KpR 2112 Revised, here entitled 'The Children in the Room', in MS Diversity of Creatures (ff. 143–7, rectos only).

University of Edinburgh, Dk. 2. 8.

KpR 2113 Corrected galley proof for *Nash's Magazine*; date stamped 12 November 1914 First A4'.

Dalhousie University.

KpR 2114 Corrected first page proof for the Sussex Edition; date stamped 28 April 1932.

British Library, Add. MS 55860.

The Tabu Tale
First pub. *Collier's Weekly*, 29 August 1903; collected *Just So Stories*, Outward Bound Edition, Vol. XX (New York, 1903); *Sussex*, XVI (*Land and Sea Tales*), 225–[40]; Harbord, IV, 1691–3.

KpR 2115 Revised, in MS Just So Stories, including the story, 7 pages (ff. 142–8, rectos only), two captions, the first annotated 'to face picture of totem pole.', both annotated 'type', one page each (ff. 137, 139), and 3 original illustrations (ff. 138, 140–1, rectos only).

British Library, Add. MS 59840, ff. 137–48 (rectos only).

KpR 2116 Corrected second page proof set up for Vol. XIII, pp. 161–[81] of the Sussex Edition (*Just So Stories*), apparently later deleted by CK; date stamped 23 April 1935.

British Library, Add. MS 55863.

The Taking of Lungtungpen
First pub. (with verse heading 'So we loosed a bloomin' volley') *Civil and Military Gazette*, 11 April 1887; collected *Plain Tales from the Hills* (Calcutta and London, 1888); *Sussex*, I, 163–70; Harbord, I, 57–9. The verse heading, ascribed 'Barrack Room Ballad', was collected *Sussex*, XXXIV, as 'Chapter Heading'; Harbord, Verse No. 252, as 'Barrack Room Ballad'.

KpR 2117 Corrected first page proof (including corrections to verse heading) for *Humorous Tales* (London, 1931), pp. 9–16; date stamped 6 May 1931.

British Library, Add. MS 55847.

KpR 2118 Corrected first page proof (including corrections to verse heading) for the Sussex Edition; date stamped 12 September 1931.

British Library, Add. MS 55852.

Tales of 'The Trade'
These three articles first pub. serially in *The Times*, 21–8 June 1916, the first with poem '"The Trade"'; collected *Sea Warfare* (London, 1916); *Sussex*, XXVI, 303–31; Harbord, V, 2263–4, 2281–90.

KpR 2119 Revised, in MS Non-Fiction, including: 'Some Work in the Baltic', here entitled 'Tales of "the Trade"', 4 pages (ff. 68–71, rectos only); 'Business in the Sea of Marmora', here entitled 'Tales of the Trade/Lieutenants at Large.', 6 pages (ff. 72–7, rectos only); 'Ravages and Dreams', here entitled 'Tales of the Trade. III.', 7 pages (ff. 78–84, rectos only).

British Library, Add. MS 45542, ff. 68–84 (rectos only).

'Teem'/A Treasure-Hunter
First pub. *Strand Magazine*, January 1936; *Sussex*, XXX, 393–[420]; Harbord, VI, 2920–5.

KpR 2120 Revised, here entitled 'Buried Treasure (The Romance of a Brave Young Dog)', in MS Debits and Credits, 2 pages (ff. 262–3, rectos only).

University of Durham.

The Ten Cent Sample Series
No publication traced; not mentioned Harbord.

KpR 2121 List of stories, revised, for the proposed so-called 8-volumes, each volume to contain two stories, one page.

Sussex, KP 25/9.

KpR 2122 Typescript list of stories for the proposed edition, headed 'The Ten Cent Sample Series', including sketches, annotated by F. N. Doubleday 'A plan for a 10¢ book for Woolworth. Given to F. N. D. on visit to London in Sept–Oct 1920'.

Princeton, Doubleday Collection, Bound Vol. V (oversize).

The Tender Achilles
First pub. *London Magazine*, December 1929; collected with poems 'Hymn to Physical Pain (Mr C. R. Wilkett's version)' and 'The Penalty' in *Limits and Renewals* (London, 1932); *Sussex*, XI, 335–54; Harbord, VII, 3266–73.

KpR 2123 Corrected page proof in Limits and Renewals Proof; date stamped 23 and 25 January 1932.

Syracuse University.

KpR 2124 Corrected first page proof for the Sussex Edition; date stamped 14 October 1932.

British Library, Add. MS 55862.

The Tents of Kedar
First pub. *Week's News*, 18 August 1888; collected *The Story of the Gadsbys* (Allahabad, [1888]); *Sussex*, II, 154–66; Harbord, I, 306–7.

KpR 2125 Corrections in a copy of the first collected edition (KpR 2104).

Syracuse University.

KpR 2126 Corrected first page proof for the Sussex Edition; date stamped 14 May 1931.

British Library, Add. MS 55853.

The Teuton Tonic, see KpR 2285.

Thanksgiving Encyclical
First pub. *The Times* (and many other newspapers), 4 April 1899; reprinted Carrington (1955), pp. 291–2; reprinted Harbord, V, 2530, as 'Uncollected No. 227 Kipling's Thanks'.

KpR 2127 Letter, revised, expressing thanks for all letters of sympathy received during his illness, released to the press by Frank Doubleday, one page; dated Hotel Grenoble, New York City, Easter Day 1899.

Princeton, Doubleday Collection, Box 3, Bound Vol. I, Item 10.

'That furtive finance which is practised...'
No publication traced; not in Harbord.

KpR 2128 Rough notes on betting, on both sides of a Bateman's notecard, in pencil.

Harvard, bMS Eng 809.4(137).

That Lady who Recited. (By the Sufferer)
No publication traced; an epigram from this skit listed and printed Harbord, Verse No. 1168.

KpR 2129 Fair copy, revised, of a satiric skit about an after-dinner party (including verses recited KpR 470), originally written for *St James's Gazette* but refused by Sidney Low as it might have given offence, 2 pages (one leaf); presented later to Edith Plowden, together here with the envelope addressed to her and postmarked [20 February?] 1890.

Berg.

'Their Lawful Occasions'
First pub. in two parts (Part II with poem 'The Egg-Shell') *Collier's Weekly*, 3–10 October 1903; collected (with a second poem 'The Wet Litany') in *Traffics and Discoveries* (London, 1904); *Sussex*, VII, 109–57; Harbord, IV, 1723–55.

KpR 2130 Revised, here entitled 'The War-Canoe.', 20 pages, in MS Traffics and Discoveries, together with a 4-page variant beginning (entitled '<"Ạ Beano".>').

McGill University.

KpR 2131 Corrected first page proof for the Sussex Edition; date stamped 22 March 1932.

British Library, Add. MS 55858.

A Thesis
Speech delivered Sorbonne Banquet, 18 November 1921; first pub. *A Book of Words* (London, 1928); *Sussex*, XXV, 187–92; Harbord, VII, 3308.

KpR 2132 Typescript, here untitled, headed 'Speech at the University of Paris Banquet at the Sorbonne', in Scrapbook 9 (pp. 38–42), 5 numbered leaves (rectos only).

Sussex, KP 28/9.

KpR 2133 Corrected first page proof for the Sussex Edition; date stamped 4 April 1931.

British Library, Add. MS 55875.

'They'
First pub. *Scribner's Magazine*, August 1904; collected with poem 'The Return of the Children' in *Traffics and Discoveries* (London, 1904); *Sussex*, VII, 311–40; Harbord, IV, 1922–32.

KpR 2134 Revised, in MS Traffics and Discoveries, 14 pages, containing KpR 515 on the verso of one leaf.

McGill University.

KpR 2135 Corrected first page proof for the Sussex Edition; date stamped 22 March 1932.

British Library, Add. MS 55858.

Three And — An Extra

First pub. *Civil and Military Gazette*, 17 November 1886; collected *Plain Tales from the Hills* (Calcutta and London, 1888); *Sussex*, I, 13–18; Harbord, I, 29–30.

KpR 2136 Corrected first page proof for the Sussex Edition; date stamped 12 September 1931.

British Library, Add. MS 55852.

The Three Musketeers

First pub. *Civil and Military Gazette*, 11 March 1887; collected *Plain Tales from the Hills* (Calcutta and London, 1888); *Sussex*, I, 95–102; Harbord, I, 43–7.

KpR 2137 Corrected first page proof for the Sussex Edition; date stamped 12 September 1931.

British Library, Add. MS 55852.

Through the Fire

First pub. *Civil and Military Gazette*, 28 May 1888; collected *Life's Handicap* (London and New York, 1891); *Sussex*, IV, 339–44; Harbord, II, 990–1.

KpR 2138 Two revised clipping of first publication, in Scrapbook 4 (pp. 65 and 143).

Sussex, KP 28/4.

KpR 2139 Corrected first page proof for the Sussex Edition; date stamped 13 February 1932.

British Library, Add. MS 55855.

Thrown Away

First pub. (with verse heading) *Plain Tales from the Hills* (Calcutta and London, 1888); *Sussex*, I, 21–32; Harbord, I, 30–2. For verse heading, see KpR 177.

KpR 2140 Corrected first page proof (including a correction to the heading) for the Sussex Edition; date stamped 12 September 1931.

British Library, Add. MS 55852.

'Thy Servant A Dog'

First pub. *Liberty* (USA), 7 June 1930; collected *Thy Servant a Dog* (London, 1930); *Sussex*, XVI, 249–70; Harbord, VI, 2904–6.

KpR 2141 Corrected first and second page proof for *Thy Servant A Dog* (London, 1930); date stamped August 1930.

British Library, Add. MS 55846.

KpR 2142 Corrected first page proof for *Collected Dog Stories* (London, 1934), pp. 163–88; date stamped 30 July 1934.

British Library, Add. MS 55848.

KpR 2143 Two sets of corrected first page proofs (only one corrected by RK) for the Sussex Edition; date stamped 4 March 1936.

British Library, Add. MS 55866.

The Tie

First pub. with poem 'The Totem' in *Limits and Renewals* (London, 1932); *Sussex*, XI, 75–83; Harbord, VII, 3197–8.

KpR 2144 Revised, here entitled '<The Reversion> The Tie', in MS Debits and Credits, 3 pages (ff. 177–9, rectos only), annotated 'type at once please'.

University of Durham.

KpR 2145 Corrected first page proof for the Sussex Edition; date stamped 14 October 1932.

British Library, Add. MS 55862.

'Tiger! Tiger!'

First pub. *St Nicholas*, February 1894; collected *The Jungle Book* (London and New York, 1894); *Sussex*, XII, 99–120; Harbord, VII, 2962–4.

KpR 2146 Revised, headed '2', 6 numbered pages, in MS Jungle Books; watermarked 1890.

British Library, Add. MS 45540, ff. 12–17 (rectos only).

To Be Filed for Reference
First pub. (with verse heading '"By the Hoof of the Wild Goat"') *Plain Tales from the Hills* (Calcutta and London, 1888); *Sussex*, I, 423–[33]; Harbord, I, 95–110.

KpR 2147 Corrected first page proof (including a correction to the verse heading) for the Sussex Edition; date stamped 12 September 1931.

British Library, Add. MS 55852.

To Certain Odd Volumes
First printed *The Year-Boke of the Odd Volumes*, [1890–91?]; reprinted Harbord, V, 2514, as 'Uncollected No. 211/To Certain Odd Volumes/ Kipling's Contribution to the Year-Boke of the Odd Volumes'.

KpR 2147.5 Addressed 'To Certain Odd Volumes.' and beginning 'Folios, Quartos, octavoes...', one page (on Embankment Chambers notepaper).

Facsimiles at Sussex, Baldwin Papers 2/15 and the University of Toronto, Fisher Collection.

Unlocated.

To the People of the Free State
This 'proclamation' by RK and Julian Ralph first pub. *The Friend* (Bloemfontein), 6 April 1900; collected *War's Brighter Side*, ed. Julian Ralph (London, 1901); reprinted Harbord, III, 1539.

KpR 2148 Typescript (hectograph), 2 leaves (rectos only), in a folder (containing also KpR 2089) labelled 'Kiplingiana'.

Texas.

Toast to Kruger, see KpR 2089.

Toby Dog
First pub. *Thy Servant A Dog* (London, 1930); collected *Collected Dog Stories* (London, 1934); *Sussex*, XVI, 295–[310]; Harbord, VI, 2908–10.

KpR 2149 Corrected page proof for first publication; date stamped September 1930.

British Library, Add. MS 55846.

KpR 2150 Corrected first page proof for *Collected Dog Stories*, pp. 217–38; date stamped 31 July 1934.

British Library, Add. MS 55848.

KpR 2151 Corrected first galley proof for Sussex Edition, 10 galleys each cut in two; date stamped 25 August 1931.

British Library, Add. MS 55849.

KpR 2152 Two sets of corrected first page proofs for the Sussex Edition, only one corrected by RK; date stamped 4 March 1936.

British Library, Add. MS 55866.

Tods' Amendment
First pub. (with verse heading) *Civil and Military Gazette*, 16 April 1887; collected *Plain Tales from the Hills* (Calcutta and London, 1888) *Sussex*, I, 265–72; Harbord, I, 71–2. For verse heading, see KpR 177.

KpR 2153 Corrected first page proof (including a correction to the heading) for the Sussex Edition; date stamped 12 September 1931.

British Library, Add. MS 55852.

The Tomb of His Ancestors
First pub. *Pearson's Magazine* and *McClure's Magazine*, December 1897; collected *The Day's Work* (New York, 1898); *Sussex*, VI, 109–52; Harbord, III, 1361–9.

KpR 2154 Revised, last pages and title in red, in MS Day's Work, 15 numbered pages, annotated 'To be typewritten as soon as possible & mail to Rudyard Kipling Waite Windham Co. Vermont'; watermarked 1894.

British Library, Add. MS 45541, ff. 218–32 (rectos only).

KpR 2155 Clipping of *McClure's Magazine* (pp. [100]–112), revised by RK, wanting the ending.

Library of Congress, Rare Book Division, Carpenter Kipling Collection.

KpR 2156 Corrected first page proof for the Sussex Edition; date stamped 27 June 1931.

British Library, Add. MS 55857.

Toomai of the Elephants

First pub. *St Nicholas*, December 1893; collected with poem 'Shiv and the Grasshopper' in *The Jungle Book* (London and New York, 1894); *Sussex*, XII, 415–39; Harbord, VII, 3013–18. Some original illustrations for this story by W. H. Drake (1893) are at Dalhousie University.

KpR 2157 Revised (and signed) in red, in MS Jungle Books, 7 numbered leaves (rectos only), including KpR 1030.

British Library, Add. MS 45540, ff. 39–45 (rectos only).

A Tour of Inspection

First pub. *Metropolitan Magazine*, October 1904; *Sussex*, IX (*A Diversity of Creatures*), 243–70; Harbord, IV, 1823–35.

KpR 2158 Revised, here entitled '<Running Trials> A Tour of Inspection', in MS Debits and Credits, 10 pages (ff. 223–32, rectos only), annotated 'Type urgent'.

University of Durham.

KpR 2159 Extensively revised galley proof for first publication.

Library of Congress, Rare Book Division, Carpenter Kipling Collection.

KpR 2160 Corrected first galley proof set up for a projected volume of the Sussex Edition (marked 'Uncollected vol.'), cancelled and annotated 'To take the place of "Regulus" in *A Diversity of Creatures* [Vol. IX]'; date stamped 13 November 1930.

British Library, Add. MS 55850.

KpR 2161 First page proof for the Sussex Edition, corrected by the printer, annotated 'Corrections from author's marked proof.'; date stamped 28 April 1932.

British Library, Add. MS 55860.

The Track of a Lie

First pub. *Civil and Military Gazette*, 12 July 1888; collected *Under the Deodars/The Phantom 'Rickshaw/Wee Willie Winkie* (New York and London, 1895); *Sussex*, III, 283–6; Harbord, IV, 2080–1, as 'Uncollected No. 132'.

KpR 2162 Revised clipping of first publication, in Scrapbook 4 (p. 71).

Sussex, KP 28/4.

KpR 2163 Corrected first page proof for the Sussex Edition; date stamped 18 September 1931.

British Library, Add. MS 55854.

The Treasure and the Law

First pub. *Strand Magazine* and *McClure's Magazine*, October 1906; collected with poems 'Song of the Fifth River' and 'The Children's Song' in *Puck of Pook's Hill* (London, 1906); *Sussex*, XIV, 247–63; Harbord, VI, 2760–3.

KpR 2164 Revised, incomplete, here headed 'Puck of Pook's Hill./X' and originally entitled 'The gold and the charter.', 6 numbered leaves (rectos only), in MS Puck.

Bodleian, MS. Eng. misc. c. 127, ff. 100–5 (rectos only).

KpR 2165 Corrected first page proof for the Sussex Edition; date stamped 2 July 1931.

British Library, Add. MS 55864.

The Tree of Justice

First pub. *The Delineator*, February 1910; collected with poems 'A Carol' and 'The Ballad of Minepit Shaw' in *Rewards and Fairies* (London, 1910); *Sussex*, XV, 301–24; Harbord, VI, 2802–4.

KpR 2166 Revised, in MS Rewards and Fairies, 10 pages.

Cambridge University Library, ADD 6850, ff. 108–17 (rectos only).

KpR 2167 Corrected first page proof for the Sussex Edition; date stamped 18 September 1931.

British Library, Add. MS 55865.

The Trees and the Wall
Speech delivered Strasbourg University, 27 November 1921; first pub. *A Book of Words* (London, 1928); *Sussex*, XXV, 199–201; Harbord, VII, 3309.

KpR 2168 Typescript, here untitled, headed 'Speech in Reply to University Banquet at Strasbourg', in Scrapbook 9 (pp. 44–5), 2 leaves (rectos only).

Sussex, KP 28/9.

KpR 2169 Corrected first page proof for the Sussex Edition; date stamped 4 April 1931.

British Library, Add. MS 55875.

A Trooper of Horse
First pub. *Morning Post*, 24–9 May 1917; collected *The Eyes of Asia* (New York, 1918); *Sussex*, XXVI, 219–32; Harbord, V, 2325–6.

KpR 2170 Revised, including the epigraph (f. 173), in MS Eyes of Asia (ff. 173–82, rectos only), annotated (f. 174) 'To precede p. 1.'.

University of Edinburgh, Dk. 2. 8.

KpR 2171 Corrected unbound copy of *The Eyes of Asia* (New York, 1919), pp. 77–101, used for the Sussex Edition.

British Library, Add. MS 55851.

Two Forewords, see KpR 1795–8, 1970–72.

Uncovenanted Mercies
First pub. with poem 'Azrael's Count' in *Limits and Renewals* (London, 1932); *Sussex*, XI, 359–82; Harbord, VII, 3274–80.

KpR 2172 Revised, in MS Debits and Credits, 6 numbered pages (ff. 203–8, rectos only).

University of Durham.

KpR 2173 Corrected page proof in Limits and Renewals Proof; date stamped 25 January 1932.

Syracuse University.

KpR 2174 Corrected first page proof for the Sussex Edition; date stamped 14 October 1932.

British Library, Add. MS 55862.

***Under the Deodars* (Allahabad, [1888])**

KpR 2175 Copy (wanting the wrapper) containing corrections by Kipling.

Contents: KpR 1413, 1571, 1692, 1956, 2054, 2224.

Syracuse University.

The Undertakers
First pub. *New York World*, 8–12 November 1894; collected with poem 'A Ripple Song' in *The Second Jungle Book* (London and New York, 1895); *Sussex*, XII, 347–75; Harbord, VII, 2997–3002.

KpR 2176 Revised, signed at end with two cancelled titles '<The Mugger of Mugger-Ghaut>' and '<The Outcastes.>', annotated 'typed copy as soon as possible to *R. Kipling Arundell House Tisbury Wilts*', in MS Jungle Books, 10 numbered leaves (rectos only); watermarked 1890.

British Library, Add. MS 45540, ff. 123–32 (rectos only).

KpR 2177 Corrected typescript including two inserted leaves containing text in Kipling's hand, as sent to the printer for publication in *Pall Mall Budget* (8–15 November 1894), 39 leaves in all (rectos only), including an illustrated title page, annotated in an unidentified hand on the title page '2 proofs early to R. Kipling/ Tisbury...' and 'before Aug 4'.

Facsimile page (autograph insertion) in *Grolier Catalogue*, Plate XVI.

Harvard, MS Eng 928.

The United Idolators
First pub. *MacLean's Magazine*, 1 June 1924; collected with poems 'To the Companions' and 'The Centaurs' in *Debits and Credits* (London, 1926); *Sussex*, XVII (*Stalky & Co.*), 197–216; Harbord, I, 448–53.

KpR 2178 Revised, here entitled 'Mister', in MS Debits and Credits, 6 pages (ff. 69–74, rectos only).

University of Durham.

KpR 2179 Corrected first page proof for the Sussex Edition; date stamped 27 March 1931.

British Library, Add. MS 55867.

Unprofessional
First pub. *Story-Teller*, October 1930; collected with poem 'The Threshold' in *Limits and Renewals* (London, 1932); *Sussex*, XI, 243–69; Harbord, VII, 3255–60. Carrington, p. 476 mentions an early draft of this story entitled 'Stars in their courses'.

KpR 2180 Corrected page proof in Limits and Renewals Proof; date stamped 21 January 1932.

Syracuse University.

KpR 2181 Corrected first page proof for the Sussex Edition; date stamped 14 October 1932.

British Library, Add. MS 55862.

An Unqualified Pilot
First pub. *Windsor Magazine*, February 1895; collected with poem 'The Junk and the Dhow' in *Land and Sea Tales* (London, 1923); *Sussex*, XVI, 51–64; Harbord, VI, 2888.

KpR 2182 Revised, in MS Day's Work, wanting the introductory note, 6 numbered pages, annotated 'to be typewritten at once RK'; watermarked 1890.

British Library, Add. MS 45541, ff. 17–22 (rectos only).

KpR 2183 Corrected first page proof for the Sussex Edition; date stamped 14 December 1931.

British Library, Add. MS 55866.

An Unsavoury Interlude
First pub. *Windsor Magazine*, January 1899; collected *Stalky & Co.* (London, 1899); *Sussex*, XVII, 97–130; Harbord, I, 439–42.

KpR 2184 Revised, in MS Stalky, 13 pages (ff. 19–31, rectos only), annotated 'typewrite urgent RK'.

Haileybury.

KpR 2185 Corrected first page proof for the Sussex Edition; date stamped 27 March 1931.

British Library, Add. MS 55867.

Up the River, for 'Egypt of the Magicians No. IV', see KpR 1573–4, 1577.

The Uses of Reading
Speech delivered Wellington College, May 1912; first pub. *A Book of Words* (London, 1928); *Sussex*, XXV, 73–91; Harbord, VII, 3293–7.

KpR 2186 Corrected first page proof for the Sussex Edition; date stamped 4 April 1931.

British Library, Add. MS 55875.

Vain Horses
First pub. as 'Fables for the Staff IV' in *The Friend* (Bloemfontein), 29 March 1900; reprinted *War's Brighter Side*, ed. Julian Ralph (London, 1901); reprinted Harbord, III, 1530–3.

KpR 2187 Fair copy, revised, headed 'Fables for the Staff. IV', signed, one page, among materials for *The Friend* (KpR 2283).

Library of Congress, Rare Book Division, Carpenter Kipling Collection.

The Valley of the Shadow
First pub. *Week's News*, 23 June 1888; collected *The Story of the Gadsbys* (Allahabad, [1888]); *Sussex*, II, 207–18; Harbord, I, 310–11.

KpR 2188 Corrections in a copy of the first collected edition (KpR 2104).

Syracuse University.

KpR 2189 Annotations explaining Indian words, in a copy of the first collected edition (KpR 2105), pp. 81–2, 87.

Berg.

KpR 2190 Corrected first page proof for the Sussex Edition; date stamped 14 May 1931.

British Library, Add. MS 55853.

Values in Life
Speech delivered McGill University Convocation, 17 October 1907; first pub. *McGill University Magazine*, December 1907; collected *A Book of Words* (London, 1928); *Sussex*, XXV, 17–20; Harbord, VII, 3289.

KpR 2191 Corrected first page proof for the Sussex Edition; date stamped 4 April 1931.

British Library, Add. MS 55875.

The Vengeance of Lal Beg, see KpR 2078–9.

Venus Annodomini

First pub. (with 6-line heading from 'Diana of Ephesus') *Civil and Military Gazette*, 4 December 1886; collected *Plain Tales from the Hills* (Calcutta and London, 1888); *Sussex*, I, 333–8; Harbord, I, 82–4.

KpR 2192 Corrected first page proof for the Sussex Edition; date stamped 12 September 1931.

British Library, Add. MS 55852.

The Verdict of Equals

Speech delivered Royal Geographical Society, London, May 1912; first pub. *Geographical Journal*, July 1912; collected *A Book of Words* (London, 1928); *Sussex*, XXV, 67–70; Harbord, VII, 3292–3.

KpR 2193 Typescript, in Scrapbook 9 (p. 16), 3 leaves (rectos only).

Sussex, KP 28/9.

KpR 2194 Corrected first page proof for the Sussex Edition; date stamped 4 April 1931.

British Library, Add. MS 55875.

The Village that Voted the Earth Was Flat

First pub. with poem 'The Press' in *A Diversity of Creatures* (London, 1917); *Sussex*, IX, 165–214; Harbord, VII, 3073–84.

KpR 2195 Revised, in MS Diversity of Creatures (ff. 54–69, rectos only) (containing KpR 452).

University of Edinburgh, Dk. 2. 8.

KpR 2196 Corrected first page proof for *Humorous Tales* (London, 1931), pp. 257–306; date stamped 23–5 May 1931.

British Library, Add. MS 55847.

KpR 2197 Corrected first page proof (including corrections to verses in the text beginning 'Hear ther [sic] truth our tongues are telling', see KpR 452) for the Sussex Edition; date stamped 28 April 1932.

British Library, Add. MS 55860.

The Virtue of France

Speech delivered Sorbonne University, 18 November 1921; first pub. *The Times*, 21 November 1921; collected *A Book of Words* (London, 1928); *Sussex*, XXV, 183–4; Harbord, VII, 3308.

KpR 2198 Typescript, here untitled, headed 'Speech in Reply to the Degree at the Sorbonne Nov. 19th. 1921', in Scrapbook 9 (pp. 42–3).

Sussex, KP 28/9.

KpR 2199 Corrected first page proof for the Sussex Edition; date stamped 4 April 1931.

British Library, Add. MS 55875.

The Volcanic Explosion in Java

First pub. (without signature) in *Civil and Military Gazette*, 2 October 1883; reprinted Harbord, I, 539–40, as 'Uncollected No. 21'.

KpR 2200 Clipping of the first publication, as sent by RK to W. C. Crofts (one of the 'Crofts Collection'), containing one correction initialled by RK and his annotation 'Sept 1883'.

Syracuse University.

The Vortex

First pub. *Scribner's Magazine*, August 1914; collected with poems 'The Fabulists' and 'The Song of Seven Cities' in *A Diversity of Creatures* (London, 1917); *Sussex*, IX, 381–401; Harbord, VII, 3099–3101.

KpR 2201 Revised, incomplete (wanting the opening), in MS Diversity of Creatures (ff. 129–40, rectos only); dated in an unidentified hand August 1914.

University of Edinburgh, Dk. 2. 8.

KpR 2202 Corrected first page proof for *Humorous Tales* (London, 1931), pp. 481–501; date stamped 9 June 1931.

British Library, Add. MS 55847.

KpR 2203 Corrected first page proof for the Sussex Edition; date stamped 28 April 1932.

British Library, Add. MS 55860.

Waking from Dreams
Speech delivered High Commissioner's Luncheon, Strasbourg, November 1921; first pub. *A Book of Words* (London, 1928); *Sussex*, XXV, 205–6; Harbord, VII, 3309.

KpR 2204 Typescript, here untitled, headed 'Speech at Lunch of Haut Commissaire, Strasbourg', in Scrapbook 9 (p. 46), one page.

Sussex, KP 28/9.

KpR 2205 Corrected first page proof for the Sussex Edition; date stamped 4 April 1931.

British Library, Add. MS 55875.

A Walking Delegate
First pub. *Century Magazine*, December 1894; collected *The Day's Work* (New York, 1898); *Sussex*, VI, 51–79; Harbord, III, 1348–54.

KpR 2206 Revised, here entitled 'In the Back Pasture', in MS Day's Work, 11 numbered pages, annotated (f. 190) 'For typewriting Return M.S. & typed copy to R. Kipling Brattleboro Vt.' and (f. 190v) 'In the Back Pasture St Nicholas sent Sept. 6 1895 RK'; watermarked 1890.

British Library, Add. MS 45541, ff. 180–90 (rectos only).

KpR 2207 Corrected galley proof (mounted on 20 pages) for first publication; date stamped 2 October 1894.

Facsimile of last page in American Art Association sale catalogue, 1 April 1925 (McCutcheon Sale), Lot 222.

Berg.

KpR 2208 Clipping of first publication (pp. 289–97), extensively revised by RK.

Library of Congress, Rare Book Division, Carpenter Kipling Collection.

KpR 2209 Corrected page proof (2 pages only) for *The Day's Work* (New York, 1898).

Princeton, Doubleday Collection.

KpR 2210 Corrected first page proof for the Sussex Edition; date stamped 27 June 1931.

British Library, Add. MS 55857.

The Wandering Jew
First pub. *Civil and Military Gazette*, 4 April 1889; collected *Life's Handicap* (London and New York, 1891); *Sussex*, IV, 331–5; Harbord, II, 990.

KpR 2211 Fair copy, revised (thin paper carbon copy), in MS From Sea to Sea (see KpR 1634), here originally entitled 'The Flight of John Heastey', 3 numbered pages, signed.

Huntington, HM 12429, Vol. 1, pp. 13–15.

KpR 2212 Revised clipping of first publication, in Scrapbook 4 (p. 149).

Sussex, KP 28/4.

KpR 2213 Corrected first page proof for the Sussex Edition; date stamped 13 February 1932.

British Library, Add. MS 55855.

The War and the Schools
Speech delivered Winchester College, December 1915; first pub. *Winchester School Journal*, [1915?]; collected *A Book of Words* (London, 1928); *Sussex*, XXV, 117–20; Harbord, VII, 3300.

KpR 2214 Corrected first page proof for the Sussex Edition; date stamped 4 April 1931.

British Library, Add. MS 55875.

The War in the Mountains
This series of 5 articles (originally six, first discarded) first pub. serially *Daily Telegraph* and *New York Tribune*, 6–20 June 1917; *Sussex*, XXVI, 127–69; discarded first article first printed Harbord, V (1970), 2316–19; series discussed Harbord, V, 2314–21 (on p. 2314, Harbord describes a 'first draft...in typescript' of the original (discarded) first article, on Reuter's notepaper, 'believed to be in one of the great collections in the U.S.A.', which has not come to light).

KpR 2215 Revised MS of the 5 published articles, in MS Debits and Credits, 27 pages (ff. 234–60, rectos only).

University of Durham.

KpR 2216 Revised typescript of first 3 articles ('The Roads of an Army', 'Podgora' and 'A Pass, A King, and A Mountain'), the first two untitled (headed 'II' and '<III.> II', respectively), 8, 6 and 6 leaves (rectos only) respectively, annotated in an unidentified hand 'Early draft with corrections', together with drafts of an introductory note and a conclusion, one page each.

Library of Congress, Rare Book Division, Colt Collection.

KpR 2217 Typescript of the 5 published articles, containing a few revisions by RK and a few cuts in an unidentified hand, 10 numbered leaves, rectos only (I), 8 numbered leaves, rectos only (II), 9 numbered leaves, rectos only (III), 8 numbered leaves, rectos only (IV), 8 numbered leaves, rectos only (V); each with a covering title page stamped by the Foreign Office 'Press Bureau Passed as censored' and dated 29 May 1917 (I–III), 5 June 1917 (IV–V), together with a typed transcript of a letter from the Foreign Office to A. P. Watt, 6 June 1917, asking for the cuts to be made.

Sussex, KP 24/69.

KpR 2218 Corrected typescript of pages 2–7 of an article (wanting the first leaf), 5 leaves (rectos only); together with photostats of two different first pages, both headed 'I' and beginning 'At Modane Station at the head of the Mont Cenis tunnel…', the second being the missing first page of the typescript.

Harvard, bMS Eng 819.

KpR 2219 Revised typescript of first (discarded) article, untitled and unheaded, 7 numbered leaves (rectos only).

Syracuse University.

KpR 2220 Revised typescript of first (discarded) article, here untitled, headed 'I' twice, 7 numbered leaves (rectos only).

Texas.

Watches of the Night

First pub. *Civil and Military Gazette*, 25 March 1887; collected *Plain Tales from the Hills* (Calcutta and London, 1888); *Sussex*, I, 115–21; Harbord, I, 50–1.

KpR 2221 Corrected first page proof for the Sussex Edition; date stamped 12 September 1931.

British Library, Add. MS 55852.

The Way That He Took

First pub. (with heading 'Put forth to watch, unschooled, alone') in *Daily Express*, 12–14 June 1900, as 'Stories of the War I'; collected *Land and Sea Tales* (London, 1923); *Sussex*, XVI, 23–47; Harbord, VI, 2886–8.

KpR 2222 Revised, here entitled 'The Way <Home> That he Took', in MS Debits and Credits, 7 pages (and an 8th containing the verse heading, see KpR 907) (ff. 7–13, rectos only); watermarked 1897.

University of Durham.

KpR 2223 Corrected first page proof for the Sussex Edition; date stamped 14 December 1931.

British Library, Add. MS 55866.

A Wayside Comedy

First pub. *Week's News*, 21 January 1888; collected *Under the Deodars* (Allahabad, [1888]); *Sussex*, III, 49–64; Harbord, I, 341.

KpR 2224 Corrections in a copy of the first collected edition (KpR 2175).

Syracuse University.

KpR 2225 Corrected first page proof for the Sussex Edition; date stamped 18 September 1931.

British Library, Add. MS 55854.

Wee Willie Winkie

First pub. *Week's News*, 28 January 1888; collected *Wee Willie Winkie* (Allahabad, [1888]); *Sussex*, III, 299–313; Harbord, I, 372–3.

KpR 2226 Corrections in a copy of the first collected edition (KpR 2229).

Syracuse University.

KpR 2227 Annotations explaining Indian words, in a copy of the first collected edition (KpR 2230), pp. [1], 3, 4, 10–14.

Berg.

KpR 2228 Corrected first page proof for the Sussex Edition; date stamped 18 September 1931.

British Library, Add. MS 55854.

***Wee Willie Winkie* (Allahabad, [1888])**
For an inscribed copy, see KpR 496.

KpR 2229 Copy (wanting the wrapper) containing corrections by RK to the Preface (as well as contents listed below).

The Preface (not afterward collected) reprinted Harbord, I, 277.

Contents: KpR 1424, 1564, 1699, 2226.

Syracuse University.

KpR 2230 Copy containing Kipling's annotations explaining Indian words.

Contents: KpR 1425, 1565, 1700, 2227.

Berg.

'We-l. There weren't any vineyards then...', see KpR 1625.

Weland's Sword
First pub. *Strand Magazine* and *Ladies Home Journal*, January 1906; collected with poems 'A Tree Song' and 'Puck's Song' in *Puck of Pook's Hill* (London, 1906); *Sussex*, XV, 5–26; Harbord, VI, 2706–7.

KpR 2231 Revised, here entitled 'Puck of Pook's Hill./I', 8 numbered leaves (rectos only), in MS Puck.

Bodleian, MS. Eng. misc. c. 127, ff. 5, 7–13 (rectos only).

KpR 2232 Corrected first galley proof for *Ladies Home Journal*.

Huntington, RB 29632.

KpR 2233 Corrected galley proof for publication in *Ladies Home Journal*.

This is probably the corrected second galley proof sold in the Martindell sale, American Art Association, 26–7 January 1922, Lot 473.

Owned (1967) Homer I. Lewis, El Paso, Texas (formerly on deposit at Texas).

KpR 2234 Corrected first page proof for the Sussex Edition; date stamped 2 July 1931.

British Library, Add. MS 55864.

What It Comes To, see KpR 2078–9.

The White Seal
First pub. with verse heading 'Seal Lullaby' in *National Review*, August 1893; collected *The Jungle Book* (London and New York, 1894); *Sussex*, XII, 293–317; Harbord, VII, 2986–97.

KpR 2235 Revised, in MS Jungle Books, 7 numbered leaves (rectos only), including the first 4 lines only of the verses in the text 'You mustn't swim till you're six weeks old'; watermarked 1890.

The verses in the text were collected separately *Songs from Books* (London, 1913) and *Sussex*, XXXIV, 235, as 'Chapter Heading'; Harbord, Verse No. 588, as 'Seal Song'.

British Library, Add. MS 45540, ff. 25–31 (rectos only).

Why Snow Falls at Vernet
First pub. *The Merry Thought*, February–April 1911, together with Kipling's letter to the editor of the journal Mrs Whidbone dated 16 March 1911; reprinted Harbord, V, 2582–6, as 'Uncollected No. 246'.

KpR 2236 Corrected first galley proof, set up for a projected volume of the Sussex Edition to be called *Why Snow Falls at Vernet and Other Stories* (revised to 'Uncollected vol.'), annotated 'We must omit Mrs K'; date stamped 23 October 1930 (revised to 24 October).

British Library, Add. MS 55850.

Will Briarts Ghost
First pub. (facsimile of first page of MS) as 'Kipling's First Story', *Sydney Morning Herald*, 25 January 1936; not in Harbord.

KpR 2237 Fair copy of a story in very early handwriting, 2 pages (one leaf).

Copies of the first publication (i.e., facsimile of first page) which gives the owner of the original MS as Sir Hugh Poynter, are at Harvard (Kipling 15.5) and Sussex (KP 29/5).

Sussex, Baldwin Papers 2/1.

William the Conqueror
First pub. *The Gentlewoman* and *Ladies Home Journal*, December 1895–January 1896; collected *The Day's Work* (New York, 1898); *Sussex*, VI, 189–234; Harbord, III, 1380–9.

KpR 2238 Revised, both parts as one continuous story, in MS Day's Work, here including an epigraph from '*Mother Goose*', 17 pages; watermarked 1894.

British Library, Add. MS 45541, ff. 160–76 (rectos only).

KpR 2239 Corrected typescript (of page 211) for *The Day's Work* (New York, 1898), signed (initials) and containing corrections by the printer, bound in (between pp. 210 and 211) a presentation copy (containing KpR 286, 1541, 1591, 2065) from F. N. Doubleday to Bliss Perry, inscribed 21 October 1898.

Harvard, Kipling 18.98.2*.

KpR 2240 Corrected typescript, here entitled '"William the Conqueror"/A <Romance> Love Story of Southern India', 54 numbered leaves (rectos only).

Library of Congress, Rare Book Division, Carpenter Kipling Collection.

KpR 2241 Corrected first page proof for the Sussex Edition; date stamped 27 June 1931.

British Library, Add. MS 55857.

The Winged Hats
First pub. *Strand Magazine* and *McClure's Magazine*, July 1906; collected with poem 'A Pict Song' in *Puck of Pook's Hill* (London, 1906); *Sussex*, XIV, 171–91; Harbord, VI, 2739–43.

KpR 2242 Revised, here entitled 'Puck of Pook's Hill/VII', 10 leaves (rectos only), in MS Puck.

Bodleian, MS. Eng. misc. 127, ff. 65–74 (rectos only).

KpR 2243 Corrected first page proof for the Sussex Edition; date stamped 2 July 1931.

British Library, Add. MS 55864.

Winning the Victoria Cross
First pub. *Windsor Magazine*, June 1897; collected *Land and Sea Tales* (London, 1923); *Sussex*, XVI, 3–19; Harbord, VI, 2882–5.

KpR 2244 Revised, without the conclusion, here entitled 'For Valour', in MS Day's Work, 4 numbered pages, annotated 'to be typed & posted to R. Kipling Waite Windham Co.'; watermarked 1894.

British Library, Add. MS 45541, ff. 28–31 (rectos only).

KpR 2245 Corrected first page proof for the Sussex Edition; date stamped 14 December 1931.

British Library, Add. MS 55866.

'Wireless'
First pub. *Scribner's Magazine*, August 1902; collected with poem 'Butterflies' (here entitled 'Kaspar's Song in "Varda"') in *Traffics and Discoveries* (London, 1904); *Sussex*, VII, 219–43; Harbord, IV, 1902–11.

KpR 2246 Revised version, in MS Traffics and Discoveries, 15 pages.

McGill University.

KpR 2247 Typescript, including some printer's marks, stamped 'Scribner', 19 numbered leaves (rectos only).

Princeton, Archive of Charles Scribner's Sons, Miscellaneous Authors' MSS & Galleys Series, Box 1, Folder 18.

KpR 2248 Corrected galley proof for first publication.

Library of Congress, Rare Book Division, Colt Collection.

KpR 2249 Corrected first page proof for the Sussex Edition; date stamped 22 March 1932.

British Library, Add. MS 55858.

The Wish House

First pub. *MacLean's Magazine*, 15 October 1924; collected with poems '"Late Came the God"' and 'Rahere' in *Debits and Credits* (London, 1926); *Sussex*, X, 81–104; Harbord, VII, 3136–42.

KpR 2250 Revised, in MS Debits and Credits, 9 pages (ff. 76–84, rectos only), annotated 'type'.

University of Durham.

KpR 2251 Corrected first page proof for the Sussex Edition; date stamped 30 December 1931.

British Library, Add. MS 55861.

With Any Amazement

First pub. *Week's News*, 9 June 1888; collected *The Story of the Gadsbys* (Allahabad, [1888]); *Sussex*, II, 166–78; Harbord, I, 307–9.

KpR 2252 Corrections in a copy of the first collected edition (KpR 2104).

Syracuse University.

KpR 2253 Annotation explaining Indian words, in a copy of the first collected edition (KpR 2105), p. 43.

Berg.

KpR 2254 Corrected first page proof for the Sussex Edition; date stamped 14 May 1931.

British Library, Add. MS 55853.

With Number Three

First pub. *Daily Mail*, 21 April 1900; *Sussex*, XXX, 63–84; Harbord, V, 2249–51.

KpR 2255 Corrected first galley proof set up for a projected volume of the Sussex Edition to be called *Why Snow Falls at Vernet and Other Stories* (revised to 'Uncollected vol.'); date stamped 29 October 1930.

British Library, Add. MS 55850.

With the Main Guard

First pub. *Week's News*, 4 August 1888; collected *Soldiers Three* (Allahabad, 1888); *Sussex*, II, 65–84; Harbord, I, 286–9 and II, 1132–3.

KpR 2256 Corrections in a copy of the first collected edition (KpR 2081).

Syracuse University.

KpR 2257 Annotations explaining Indian words, in a copy of the first collected edition (KpR 2082), pp. 46, 48, 56.

Berg.

KpR 2258 Corrected first page proof for the Sussex Edition; date stamped 14 May 1931.

British Library, Add. MS 55853.

With the Night Mail

First pub. *McClure's Magazine*, November 1905; collected with poem 'The Four Angels' in *Actions and Reactions* (London, 1909); *Sussex*, VIII, 107–63; Harbord, VI, 2826–46.

KpR 2259 In MS Actions and Reactions (ff. 28–70), including the verses 'Mother Rügen's tea-house on the Baltic' (see KpR 716).

University of St Andrews, MS PR4854.A4.

KpR 2260 Corrected first page proof (including corrections to the verses 'Mother Rügen's tea-house on the Baltic') for the Sussex Edition; date stamped 28 November 1931.

British Library, Add. MS 55859.

Without Benefit of Clergy

First pub. (with a verse heading) *Macmillan's Magazine*, June 1890; collected *Life's Handicap* (London and New York, 1891); *Sussex*, IV, 157–88; Harbord, II, 968–71. For the heading, see KpR 176.

KpR 2261 Fair copy, revised, without the verse heading, annotated at the top 'I give this M.S. to Lucy Clifford: RK.', 18 leaves (rectos only).

Facsimile first page in Livingston, p. [80].

Harvard, fMS Lowell 30.

KpR 2262 Corrected first page proof for the Sussex Edition; date stamped 13 February 1932.

British Library, Add. MS 55855.

The Woman in His Life
First pub. *London Magazine* and *McCall's Magazine*, December 1928; collected with poems 'Dinah in Heaven' and 'Four Feet' in *Limits and Renewals* (London, 1932); *Sussex*, XI, 39–67; Harbord, VII, 3193–7.

KpR 2263 Revised, here untitled, in MS Debits and Credits, 6 pages (ff. 170–5, rectos only).

University of Durham.

KpR 2264 Corrected page proof in Limits and Renewals Proof.

Syracuse University.

KpR 2265 Corrected first page proof for *Collected Dog Stories* (London, 1934), pp. 125–59; date stamped 30 July 1934.

British Library, Add. MS 55848.

KpR 2266 Corrected first page proof for the Sussex Edition; date stamped 14 October 1932.

British Library, Add. MS 55862.

Work in the Future
Speech delivered Rhodes Scholars Banquet, Oxford, 6 June 1924; first pub. *The Times* and *Morning Post*, 7 June 1924; collected *A Book of Words* (London, 1928); *Sussex*, XXV, 243–7; Harbord, VII, 3312.

KpR 2267 Corrected first page proof for the Sussex Edition; date stamped 4 April 1931.

British Library, Add. MS 55875.

A World Apart, see KpR 1455.

The World Without
First pub. (early version) *Civil and Military Gazette*, 18 May 1888, as 'In Gilded Halls'; reprinted Harbord, I, 299–303; revised version collected *The Story of the Gadsbys* (Allahabad, [1888]); *Sussex*, II, 141–53; Harbord, I, 299–306.

KpR 2268 Corrections in a copy of the first collected edition (KpR 2104).

Syracuse University.

KpR 2269 Annotations explaining Indian words, in a copy of the first collected edition (KpR 2105), pp. [13], 17, 19, 21.

Berg.

KpR 2270 Corrected first page proof for the Sussex Edition; date stamped 14 May 1931.

British Library, Add. MS 55853.

The Wreck of the *Visigoth*
First pub. *Civil and Military Gazette*, 25 April 1889; collected *The Day's Work*, Outward Bound Edition, Vol. XIV (New York, 1899); *Sussex*, III, 269–73; Harbord, V, 2389, as 'Uncollected No. 164'.

KpR 2271 Fair copy, revised (thin paper carbon copy), in MS From Sea to Sea (see KpR 1634), here entitled 'Abaft the Funnel. No III', 3 numbered pages, listed (not by RK) in the Table of Contents as 'The Shipwreck of the Ringala'.

Huntington, HM 12429, Vol. 1, pp. 40–2.

KpR 2272 Revised clipping of the first publication (entitled 'Abaft the Funnel. III'), in Scrapbook 4 (p. 145).

Sussex, KP 28/4.

KpR 2273 Corrected first page proof for the Sussex Edition; date stamped 18 September 1931.

British Library, Add. MS 55854.

Wressley of the Foreign Office
First pub. *Civil and Military Gazette*, 20 May 1887; collected *Plain Tales from the Hills* (Calcutta and London, 1888); *Sussex*, I, 405–11; Harbord, I, 92–3.

KpR 2274 Corrected first page proof for the Sussex Edition; date stamped 12 September 1931.

British Library, Add. MS 55852.

The Writing of Yakub Khan, see KpR 2078–9.

The Wrong Thing
First pub. *The Delineator*, November 1909; collected with poems 'A Truthful Song' and 'King Henry VII. and the Shipwrights' in *Rewards and Fairies* (London 1910); *Sussex*, XV, 57–78; Harbord, VI, 2773–8.

KpR 2275 Revised, in MS Rewards and Fairies, 11 pages.

Cambridge University Library, ADD 6850, ff. 20–30 (rectos only).

KpR 2276 Corrected first page proof for the Sussex Edition; date stamped 18 September 1931.

British Library, Add. MS 55865.

'Yoked With an Unbeliever'
First pub. *Civil and Military Gazette*, 7 December 1886; collected *Plain Tales from the Hills* (Calcutta and London, 1888); *Sussex*, I, 55–60; Harbord, I, 35–7.

KpR 2277 Corrected first page proof for the Sussex Edition; date stamped 12 September 1931.

British Library, Add. MS 55852.

Young Men at the Manor
First pub. *Strand Magazine* and *Ladies Home Journal*, February 1906; collected with poem 'Sir Richard's Song' in *Puck of Pook's Hill* (London, 1906); *Sussex*, XIV, 31–51; Harbord, VI, 2708.

KpR 2278 Revised, here entitled 'Puck of Pook's Hill/II', 7 numbered leaves (rectos only), in MS Puck.

Bodleian, MS. Eng. misc. c. 127, ff. 15–21 (rectos only).

KpR 2279 Corrected galley proof for *Ladies Home Journal*, stamped 'First Galley' and 'C. M. K.'.

Facsimile portion in American Art Association sale catalogue, 26–7 January 1922 (Martindell Sale).

Huntington, RB 29631.

KpR 2280 Corrected galley proof for *Ladies Home Journal*.

This is probably the corrected second galley proof sold in the Martindell Sale, American Art Association, 26–7 January 1922, Lot 475 (facsimile portion in sale catalogue).

Owned (1967) Homer I. Lewis, El Paso, Texas (formerly on deposit at Texas).

KpR 2281 Corrected galley proof for *Ladies Home Journal*, stamped 'Revised Galley', signed (initials).

Facsimile portion in American Art Association sale catalogue, 26–7 January 1922 (Martindell Sale).

Berg.

KpR 2282 Corrected first page proof for the Sussex Edition; date stamped 2 July 1931.

British Library, Add. MS 55864.

[DRAMATIC WORKS, see VERSE.]

WORKS EDITED BY KIPLING

***The Friend* (Bloemfontein)**
This newspaper, published in Bloemfontein during the Boer War from 1899–1902, was edited by Julian Ralph, Percival Landon, H. A. Gwynne and F. W. Buxton with Kipling as Associate Editor; extracts from *The Friend* were published in *War's Brighter Side*, ed. Julian Ralph (London, 1901). Kipling's identified contributions are listed and discussed in Harbord, III, 1530–6 (see also Stewart, pp. 210–11); for those entered separately, see KpR 407–10, 999–1000, 1091–4, 1624, 1792, 1806, 1978, 2089, 2148, 2187.

KpR 2283 Materials for *The Friend* in one folder, containing (as well as KpR 408, 1092, 1624, 1792, 1806, 1978, 2187): RK's partial transcript for the printer of a poem by Trooper G. Simes (pub. 28 March 1900); a scrap in RK's hand (authorship unknown) headed 'Foreign comment on British Success.'; corrections and additions by RK to galley proofs of three short notes headed 'Ten a Pennys' (pub. 28 March 1900); corrections by RK to a galley proof of an article by H. A. Gwynne 'Is the Art of War Revolutionized? III — Cavalry', annotated 'more to follow RK'.

This collection of material is described in Norman Croom-Johnson, 'Rudyard Kipling and "The Friend"', *KJ*, Nos 102–3, July–October 1952.

Library of Congress, Rare Book Division, Colt Collection.

The Irish Guards in the Great War

First pub. *The Irish Guards in the Great War*, ed. and compiled from their diaries and papers by Rudyard Kipling, 2 vols (London, 1923); reprinted serially *New York Times*, Sunday magazine section, 27 May–29 July 1923; *Sussex*, XXVII–XXVIII; Harbord, V, 2340–1. A series of letters to Emery Walker (3 January–23 November 1921), regarding the engraved maps published with this work, is at Texas.

KpR 2284 Four revised typescripts of Chapter 1 (Vol. I), all here untitled; the first (22 leaves, rectos only) complete, the last three incomplete and of varying lengths (11, 7 and 5 leaves, rectos only, respectively).

Texas.

The Teuton Tonic

No publication traced; not in Harbord.

KpR 2285 MS 'magazine', 'published' in various hands, aboard the S.S. Teutonic, including contributions and illustrations by RK (see KpR 1733), JLK, and Mr and Mrs Frank N. Doubleday, 4 pages (2 leaves); the cover sheet reads: 'The Teutonic/June 1899/Published by Papa & Mamma/Price – Priceless'.

Princeton, Doubleday Collection, Box 2, Folder 2.

United Services College Chronicle

Kipling edited Nos 4–10 of the school magazine of United Services College, 30 June 1881–24 July 1882; for a discussion, see INTRODUCTION.

KpR 2285.5 Corrected proof of No. 8 (20 March 1882) which included contributions by Kipling as well as other pieces.

Anderson Galleries, 17 March 1915 (G. M. Williamson Sale), Lot 1.

DIARIES AND NOTEBOOKS

Diary

Passages quoted Carrington (1955), *passim* and Rutherford (1986), *passim*; described briefly in Pinney, p. 16.

KpR 2286 Diary for 1885, a copy of Lett's Colonial rough diary, recording literary work published in *Civil and Military Gazette* and elsewhere, signed on the cover.

Harvard, MS Eng 809.

Diary

First printed (facsimile) in Ballard (1935), p. 35.

KpR 2287 One page (p. 46) of a printed calendar diary for 15 February 1888, headed 'Notions to be worked out' containing rough notes for a poem annotated 'Feb. 22, done it' ('The Ballad of Fisher's Boarding House') and notes for stories, including 'The Big Drunk Draft [sic]' and 'Georgie Porgie', the latter dated 19 February and annotated 'Feb 23 done it'.

Syracuse University.

Motoring Journals

Two extracts (one of tour of France, 4–22 May 1923 and one return tour of Scotland, 28 September–15 October 1923) printed in 'Lordly of Leather [7]', ed. Meryl Macdonald, *KJ*, 59 (1985), 10–24.

KpR 2288 Two revised typescripts, each 96 leaves (rectos only, the second numbered), corrected by C. Nicholson (RK's secretary), together with a later typescript entitled 'R. K.'s Motor Tours', being records of Kipling's motoring tours of England, Scotland and France, including (as well as general commentary and KpR 505), records of mileage, state of roads, hotels, etc.; March 1911–August 1926.

Sussex, KP 25/7–8.

MARGINALIA IN PRINTED BOOKS AND MANUSCRIPTS

Baldwin, Louisa. [Poems].

KpR 2288.5 Typescript of four poems by Louisa Baldwin, extensively revised by RK, one page each and a covering leaf reading 'L. Baldwin,/Harrogate,/ Written July 31 to Aug: 20/09' (5 leaves in all).

Sussex, Baldwin Papers 2/11.

Belcher, Rev. Henry. *Short Exercises in Latin Prose Composition (Part II)* (London, 1879).

KpR 2289 School book, annotated in Latin on one page and at back with a drawing of deodar tree, signed on cover and twice on flyleaf.

Anderson Galleries, 17 March 1915 (G. M. Williamson Sale), Lot 104.

Black, George W. 'The Progress of Ou [sic] Express'.

KpR 2290 Unidentified clipping, corrected by Kipling, together with a covering letter to George W. Black, Cape Town, 10 April 1908.

Berg.

Bonnier, Gaston. *Les noms des fleurs*, see KpR 1153.

Chandler, Admiral Lloyd H. *Summary of the Works of Rudyard Kipling* (New York, 1930).

KpR 2291 RK's annotated copy, presentation copy from Chandler, commenting on attributions and misattributions.

Four lists of addenda and corrigenda, dated 5 March 1932–31 December 1934, sent by Chandler to Kipling, are at Sussex, KP 27/7–10.

Sussex, SxMS 38 Ad.26.1/2.

Cowles, Frederick L. 'An Angel of Tenderfoot Hill'.

KpR 2292 Incomplete typescript, corrected by RK, 16 pages, and a revised typescript, also 16 pages; together with a covering letter to Cowles about the corrections, 19 July 1893.

Berg.

[Euclid]. [*Elements of Geometry*].

KpR 2293 Copy used by RK as a schoolboy, containing his sketches and doodles, wanting a title page but apparently a copy of the English School Classics Series, edited by Francis Storr.

Library of Congress, Rare Book Division, Carpenter Kipling Collection.

Fraser, William Alexander. 'Kristna the Seer'.

KpR 2294 Printed fragment of a story, one leaf (2 pages numbered 63–4) torn from *Massey's Magazine*, annotated by RK.

Facsimile of p. 63 in *Grolier Catalogue*, Plate XXXII; of p. 64 in Ballard, p. 159 and in Parke Bernet sale catalogue, 21–2 January 1942 (Ballard Sale), p. 48.

Dalhousie University.

Fraser, William Alexander. 'My Friend the Count'.

KpR 2295 Typescript of short story, 45 pages, corrected and annotated by RK, including his note, signed (initials), on front cover; c. 1896.

Berg.

Haggard, Henry Rider. *Rural England*, 2 vols (1903).
Two annotations printed *Rudyard Kipling to Rider Haggard*, ed. Morton Cohen (London, 1965), p. 50n2; for RK's notes on Haggard's works, see KpR 1928.5.

KpR 2296 RK's copy containing his annotations.

Bateman's, Burwash, Sussex (see Cohen, p. 50n2).

Heeley, Sibyl. 'The Conversion of Private Jones'.

KpR 2297 Annotations to Heeley's typescript, 18 pages.

Sotheby's, 19 December 1934, Lot 450.

Horatius Flaccus, Quintus. *Opera Omnia*, ed. E. G. Wickham (London, 1910).

Extracts of Kipling's marginalia printed *Selections from the Freer Verse Horace* (privately printed, New York, 1932) and Carrington (1955), pp. 481–2; the whole volume described and all of Kipling's marginalia printed (including facsimile pages) in *Kipling's Horace*, ed. Charles Carrington (London, 1978).

KpR 2298 Including RK's versions (in verse) of commentaries on 55 of the 'Carmina', as well as several sketches and drawings.

Sussex, KP 31/1.

Johns, C. A. *Flowers of the Field*.
This book mentioned Carrington (1955), p. 480.

KpR 2299 Annotated.

Unlocated.

'The Jungle Play'

KpR 2300 Typescript of a four-act adaptation (with Prologue of 7 numbered pages) of *The Jungle Book*, heavily revised by RK, 95 leaves (rectos only) in all.

Sussex, KP 25/11.

Lear, Edward. *The Book of Nonsense*, 31st ed (London, 1896).
This book mentioned Carrington (1955), p. 517.

KpR 2301 Containing 17 additional limericks (two in CK's hand) and accompanying drawings by RK (see KpR 1174, 1176, 1183, 1190, 1191, 1192, 1193, 1194, 1195, 1198, 1199, 1200, 1201, 1203, 1204, 1205, 1206).

Sussex, KP 31/2.

Livingston, Flora V. *Bibliography of the Works of Rudyard Kipling* (New York, 1927).

KpR 2302 Typed list of queries by Livingston regarding her *Bibliography*, annotated by RK and dated 30 August 1923.

A copy of Livingston's *Supplement* (Cambridge, MA, 1938) annotated by CK is at Sussex, SxMS 38 Ad.26.1/5.

Sussex, KP 23/53.

Longer English Poems, ed. J. W. Hales (London, 1878)

KpR 2303 Containing verses (see KpR 1157, 1258, 1301, 1302); inscribed on the half title 21 January 1880.

Library of Congress, Rare Book Division, Batchelder Collection.

Maurice, Arthur B. 'The London of Rudyard Kipling'.

KpR 2304 Last page (numbered 11) of typescript of Maurice's article (pub. *The Bookman*), annotated and signed (initials) by Kipling, including a note by Maurice; written in 1920.

Princeton, Arthur B. Maurice Collection, Box 1, Folder 50.

Merivale, Charles. *The Roman Triumvirates* (London, 1877).

KpR 2305 RK's schoolbook containing a few marginal annotations.

Anderson Galleries, 17 March 1915 (G. M. Williamson Sale), Lot 102.

Ovid. *P. Ovidii Nasonis Fastorum Liber VI*, ed. A. Sedgwick (Cambridge, 1877).

KpR 2306 RK's schoolbook containing his drawings, scribblings, etc.

Anderson Galleries, 17 March 1915 (G. M. Williamson Sale), Lot 103.

Peile, Frederick Kinsey. 'The Man Who Would Be King'.
Peile's one-act adaptation of Kipling's story was produced at His Majesty's Theatre, 8 June 1903; mentioned Harbord, I, 359 and III, 1155 and Stewart, p. 68.

KpR 2307 Typescript of 3-act adaptation of Kipling's story, extensively corrected and annotated by Kipling, 90 leaves (rectos only); date stamped by a typewriting agency 7, 22 and 27 July 1910 and 6 June 1911.

Dalhousie University.

[Rawlinson, Captain R.] 'Soldiers Three'.
See also KpR 1929.5.

KpR 2308 Typescript of Rawlinson's filmscript, corrected by RK, 144 leaves.

Sussex, KP 25/13.

Steiler's Atlas of Modern Geography, 9th ed (Gotha, 1911).

KpR 2309 'The Kipling Atlas', inscribed by RK to 'Max: Aitken [Lord Beaverbrook] from Rudyard Kipling: Xmas. 1912', containing RK's autograph quotations from his verses *passim*.

University of New Brunswick, Beaverbrook Collection.

Charles Lamb
1775–1834

INTRODUCTION

When Charles Lamb died in 1834, his property remained with Mary Lamb, his sister and lifelong companion, until she died thirteen years later. At that time, we know that Edward Moxon — whom Emma Isola, the Lambs' adopted "daughter" had married — claimed what remained of Lamb's library and sent some sixty volumes to auction in New York. As for other remains, literary or otherwise, we know very little.

Prance (pp.282–4) lists the very few non-literary remains — or 'relics' — which he has traced; their scarcity, he suggests, is due to the lack of 'dependants to preserve and cherish mementoes of a famous man'. The same can perhaps be said of papers and manuscripts; apart from the library there is no record of Moxon or anyone else inheriting papers nor of any dispersal or sale of manuscript remains of the famous pair. A few of Lamb's manuscript commonplace books — including notably the two original notebooks into which Lamb transcribed his *Extracts from the Garrick Plays* (LmC 305) — were owned by Moxon afer Lamb's death but whether he acquired them with Lamb's library or by other means is unknown.

What is known of the provenance of the vast majority of extant manuscripts indicates that they were sent to, or otherwise acquired by, Lamb's friends, acquaintances, editors or publishers during his lifetime. Consequently, Lamb's papers are widely scattered. Some large and/or important collections have been preserved (and transmitted) in one piece by the original recipient — such as John Forster's collection at the Victoria and Albert Museum. Others have been amassed singly or in small batches by private or institutional collectors; indeed the two largest Lamb collections — at the Huntington and W. Hugh Peal's collection at the Univerity of Kentucky — have been so formed.

Reference Edition and Canon

The reference edition cited in the entries below is E. V. Lucas's 1903–5 seven-volume edition of the works of Charles and Mary Lamb. While the last two volumes, containing letters, have been superceded by later editions — indeed by Lucas's own in 1935 — Volumes I–V, which include the poetry and prose works, remain unsurpassed. Lucas's work in editing and annotating both the works and the letters is scholarly and literate and the level of editorial documentation to which he aspired was — in the cases of both the 1903 and 1935 editions — beyond what was generally expected at the time.

Nonetheless, both because editorial practices have since been much improved *and* because of the emergence of more manuscript material than was available to Lucas, a re-editing of Lamb's prose and verse would now be welcome. As for Lamb's letters, just such a new edition has been undertaken by Edwin Marrs who has to date published the first three volumes (to 1817) of a complete edition of the letters of Charles and Mary Lamb.

There has been some discussion over the years concerning the canon established by Lucas; and convincing cases for several additions have been advanced. These discussions, both for and against various items, remain for the most part inconclusive because no definitive evidence (such as manuscript material) exists. These matters are therefore beyond the scope of the present *Index*; for a survey of such articles, see the essay on Lamb by George L. Barnett and Stuart M. Tave in Houtchens (1966).

One prose piece, however, whose authorship had been questioned by Lucas, is now definitively accepted into the canon. 'Dog Days' — a piece published anonymously in William Hone's *Every-Day Book* (1825) and included as 'probable' in an Appendix to Lucas — is authenticated by the existence of a heavily revised autograph at the Huntington (LmC 233).

Another disputed item represented by an entry below (see LmC 249) is 'London Fogs', a transcription of which (attributed to Lamb) is in William Ayrton's Scrapbook (described below); that Scrapbook contains two poems attributed to Lamb which are also listed as 'questionable attributions' (see LmC 101, 209).

There are several prose manuscripts listed which were never published by Lamb himself; two of them however — 'Cupid's Revenge' and 'Death of Coleridge' — were included in Lucas's edition. Those which were not published by Lucas are primarily occasional pieces: 'Autobiographical Sketch' (LmC 223), 'Instructions for Playing Whist' (LmC 245), the satirical 'Rules and directions to be observed by Mr Chambers...' (LmC 283) and 'Theses Quædam Theologicæ' (LmC 293–4). One substantial piece however is Lamb's 20-page fair copy review of William Hazlitt's *Table-Talk* (1821) (LmC 281) which was apparently unpublished by Lamb and indeed not published in full until 1980. The only *unpublished* prose entries are those representing a few leaves of notes (LmC 219, 259–63), for the most part criticisms of various friends' works, which have been only partially published, if at all.

As for the verse, the list of entries includes autograph manuscripts of six poems which are apparently, to this day, wholly or partly unpublished; in all cases, there seems no reason to doubt their authorship although one of them — the album verses 'As humble guests at solemn cheer' (LmC 16) — is signed by both Charles and Mary Lamb. Two others — 'The Scrap Book' (LmC 131) and 'Sweet is thy sunny hair' (LmC 142) — are substantial pieces, the former comprising 24 lines (and possibly written as an introduction to an unidentified album) and the latter — dating from 1796, a period during which Lamb was producing his best poetry — comprising 33 lines. The fourth item ('For Newark...' (LmC 45)) is a two-page autograph manuscript of five numbered election squibs written on behalf of Sergeant Wilde for his use in the Newark election of 1829; though scholars have mentioned Lamb's contribution of squibs to Wilde's campaign, none have ever been traced or published (see Lucas, V, 341–2). No text is available for the last item 'A Stranger's Tribute to Miss Hill' (LmC 140) which passed through the saleroom in 1984 and has not been traced. The sixth, 'To Charlotte Roberts...' (LmC 160) has been partially printed in sale catalogues.

Several other poetical manuscripts are listed whose texts, though not included by Lucas, have subsequently been published (or in some cases only printed) as Lamb's: see 'Acrostic' (LmC 6); 'Acrostic to E. B.' (LmC 10); 'Because you boast poetic Grandsire' (LmC 21); 'A Black in an Album' (LmC 22); 'The Boy, the Mother, and the Butterfly' (LmC 23–4); 'Count Rumford' (LmC 29); 'Had I but *gold* to my desire' (LmC 54); 'How well the Milestones' use doth this express' (LmC 60); 'Marmor Loquitur' (LmC 101); 'O cruel death why didst thou take' (LmC 112); 'Poet or Prose-man, Party-man, Translator' (LmC 128); 'Song to Miss S. A. Hunter' (LmC 135); 'Sorely your Dactyls do drag along limp-footed' (LmC 139); 'This Book resembles Hoddy Doddy' (LmC 143–4); 'To Emma B—' (LmC 162); 'To H[arriet] I[sola] for her Birthday' (LmC 164); 'To J. T. Smith' (LmC 165); 'To M— S—' (LmC 170); 'To Miss Gray, or Grey, at Mrs Gisborn's School, Enfield' (LmC 176); 'Well-pleased, dear Frances, in your looks I trace' (LmC 203–4).

In his Introduction to Volume V (*Poems and Plays*), Lucas mentions being prevented from publishing 'two short poems (one of much charm)' which were written in albums; it is possible that these two poems are among those listed above. In addition, he notes his relegation of two other poems (the sources for which are letters) — 'If ever I marry a Wife' (LmC 63) and 'My dear friend —' (LmC 108–9) — to the *Letters* volumes; these, therefore, cannot be considered as additions to the canon as established by Lucas. Similarly, Lucas has included in a separate volume (*Books for Children*) all the verse written for children; in any case, only one manuscript of such verse is entered below ('Chusing a Name', LmC 28).

Six verse entries are marked as 'questionable attributions'. Two of them are included in William Ayrton's Scrapbook (described below). There seems no particular reason to doubt the authenticity of a third — 'Rectory House, Fornham, All Saints, Suffolk' (LmC 130) but for the fact that Lucas knew of the lines and did not publish them. Two other items marked 'questionable' *were* included by Lucas. One of them, a parody of Lamb's 'Angel Help' — beginning 'Lazy-bones, lazy-bones, wake up, and peep!' — was published by Lucas as Lamb's, then republished from a manuscript in Charles's hand signed 'Mary Lamb' as Mary Lamb's parody of her brother; a year later, it was asserted to be Charles's self-parody which he pretended was written by his sister (see 'Nonsense Verses', LmC 110–11, for details). The other is the 10-line addition — signed 'Mary Lamb' and beginning 'The reason why my brother's so severe' — to one manuscript of 'Free Thoughts on Several Eminent Composers' (LmC 50). Lucas published the additional lines in his Notes to the poem and suggested that they were by Lamb impersonating his sister. The last 'questionable' item (LmC 105.5) concerns a 'sonnet Milton' for which we have no text, only Lamb's suggested revision for the last line, in a note to J. A. Hessey. He may have been referring, for some reason, to Bernard Barton's sonnet 'To Elia' in this note, and not to one of his own.

Two other manuscripts, sometimes claimed to be by Lamb, are not included in the entries. Both are dramatic works and both are part of the P. G. Patmore collection of plays sent to R. B. and Tom Sheridan and bequeathed to the British Library by Coventry Patmore. The first, an untitled comic opera (Add. MS 25924) was described in P. G. Patmore, *My Friends and Acquaintances*, 3 vols (London, 1854) (I, [305]–7) as being in Lamb's hand and as being the collaboration with Tom Sheridan which Mary Lamb refers to in her letter to Sarah Stoddart Hazlitt postmarked 10 December 1808 (Marrs, II, 286 8 from the original at the Huntington); a facsimile of the 'Characters of the Opera' page is given as the frontispiece to Patmore's book. It was included in *The Works of Charles Lamb*, ed. Charles Kent (London, [1876]). The claim is primarily made on the basis of the handwriting which — despite resembling Lamb's mature hand at some points — never resembles Lamb's early hand. Both Lucas (V, vii) and Marrs (II, 288) likewise reject the attribution. The second play which has been attributed to Lamb, a tragedy entitled 'The Dissolution of the Roman Republic' (Add. MS 25925) is said on the title-page to be 'By John Patteshull'; as Lucas (V, vii) remarks, there is no reason to think that this play was written by Lamb.

Essays of Elia

If Lamb wrote nothing else, the essays he published under the name of Elia would by themselves have made his literary reputation secure. Written mostly in the productive years between 1820 and 1826, and mainly for the *London Magazine*, Lamb collected them twice: first in *Elia* (1823) (28 essays) and, again, in *Last Essays* (1833) (40 essays). Despite the popularity of the essays, neither published collection of them went to a second edition during Lamb's lifetime. The number of complete and selected editions published since 1834 in English alone would, however, probably run to hundreds; the British Library collection itself includes over one hundred.

Manuscript sources for nearly thirty of the essays by Elia are included in the entries below. These manuscripts represent every stage of composition — from the first expression of ideas in letters to friends to changes made in printed copies after publication.

In *The Evolution of Elia* (1964), Barnett attempts a complete analysis of the creation of the essays; he traces their origins not only in the manuscripts and letters but also in Lamb's own experiences and reported conversations. The essays are studied in their manuscript and printed versions and Lamb's method of composition and revision is deduced.

Not all the manuscripts which Barnett cites have been listed below as entries. Letters containing early examples of words or phrases used in the essays, mere echoes or foreshadowings, have not been considered manuscript sources. Only those letters in which a substantial idea is sketched at great enough length to be virtually a first draft have been listed; see Barnett, Chapter 3, pp.76–103 for the letters not entered and Chapter 5 for Lamb's method of composition.

Twenty-four fair copy manuscripts of the essays themselves have been entered. Many of them have not been located and are known by their appearances in sale catalogues. All the extant manuscripts of essays written for the *London Magazine* — whose first editor John Scott was replaced by the publisher John Taylor when Scott was killed in a duel in February 1821 — were presumably the copies sent to Taylor for publication; all of them were offered for sale in the two-part auction of Taylor's books and papers at Sotheby's on 10–11 March and 14 June 1865. Those located are widely scattered. Other entries for the Elian essays include letters to Taylor and/or Hessey containing Lamb's last-minute revisions.

Three unlocated, and possibly lost, manuscript sources for the essays by Elia are worth noting; for others, see the headnotes to entries for *Elia* (1823) (LmC 235), 'A Quaker's Meeting' (LmC 276) and 'The Praise of Chimney-Sweepers' (LmC 275).

A Death-Bed

First pub. *The Table Book*, ed. William Hone (London, 1827); collected *Last Essays* (1833) (first edition only); Lucas, II, 246–7.

Early version, being an open letter addressed to Henry Crabb Robinson dated Islington, 20 January 1827; enclosed with a covering letter to Robinson, [20 January 1827].

The covering letter to Robinson is now at Dr Williams's Library, Henry Crabb Robinson Papers, 1827–1829 Volume, f. 95b; both manuscripts are printed in *Letters*, III, 66–9 where the open letter is printed 'from the original given by Robinson to Dawson Turner'.

Distant Correspondents

First pub. *London Magazine*, March 1822; collected *Elia* (1823); Lucas, II, 104–8.

Early sketch of the essay in a letter to Barron Field, 31 August 1817.

This letter printed in *Letters*, II, 209–11 and reprinted Marrs, III, 251–3; discussed in Barnett, pp. 86–7.

The Two Races of Men

First pub. *London Magazine*, December 1820; collected *Elia* (1823); Lucas, II, 22–7.

Early sketch of the essays, in a letter to S. T. Coleridge, [Autumn 1820?].

This letter printed in *Letters*, II, 284–6 and discussed briefly in Barnett, p. 90.

Miscellaneous Prose

At various points in his life, Lamb was associated with and/or contributed to particular newspapers or magazines. Besides the Elia essays and others written for the *London Magazine* in the 1820s, Lamb wrote articles, essays, poems, reviews and letters to the editor for such serials as: John Fenwick's *Albion* in 1801 (published for seven weeks only); Leigh Hunt's *Reflector* in 1811–12 (four numbers only); *The Champion* (primarily 1820); William Hone's *Every-Day Book* (1825–6) and *The Table Book* (1827); C. W. Dilke's *Athenaeum* (1830s); Edward Moxon's *Englishman's Magazine* (1831); John Forster's (and later Moxon's) *Reflector* (only three numbers, 1832).

As for the manuscript sources for these prose writings — like the manuscripts of Elian essays — they show evidence, in most cases, of having been sent by Lamb to someone else, often to the prospective editor or publisher of the piece. The largest such group comprises the extant manuscripts of items (some signed 'Elia') sent to, and in most cases published by, William Hone in his various compilations; most of these manuscripts are now at the Huntington. Likewise, the manuscript of 'The Death of Munden' (LmC 230), published in *The Athenaeum*, is addressed to C. W. Dilke and those of 'Elia to His Correspondents' (LmC 236) and 'Letter to an Old Gentleman' (LmC 247) (both published in *London Magazine*) were sent or given to John Taylor or J. A. Hessey. Other manuscript sources of prose pieces listed include early sketches (or germs) of essays in letters to friends and last-minute revisions in letters to editors or publishers.

A few manuscripts of miscellaneous prose pieces have been noted by scholars and editors but have not come to light. As they may be lost or as their descriptions might be unreliable, they are described here and are not given numbered entries; for another unlocated manuscript, see the headnote to 'Estimates of DeFoe's Secondary Novels' (LmC 237).

Cupid's Revenge

First pub. *Harper's Magazine*, December 1858; Lucas, I, 352–64.

A prefatory note to the first publication explains how the autograph manuscript of this undated parody of the play *Cupid's Revenge* by Beaumont and Fletcher came to light: '[Thomas Allsop] brought with him in his flight to America a number of manuscripts of his friends. Among these were...a series of notes by Lamb [to Allsop], nearly a hundred in all...and the tale of "Cupid's Revenge" which appears to have remained unpublished in consequence of the cessation of the magazine for which it was written....'

The Death of Coleridge

First pub. in John Forster's obituary notice of Lamb in *New Monthly Magazine*, February 1835; Lucas, I, 351–2.

Lamb wrote this piece in the album of James Keymer (a London bookseller) at Forster's request; it is there signed and dated Edmonton, 21 November 1834. This is the last 'literary' manuscript Lamb is known to have written before his death on 22 December 1834; indeed only one or two letters survive which postdate this manuscript.

Memoir of Robert Lloyd

First pub. *Gentleman's Magazine*, November 1811; Lucas, I, 132–3.

In his Notes, Lucas (I, 429–30) says that this memoir was enclosed in a letter from Charles Lloyd to Robert Lloyd's widow (having been sent to the former by Lamb); he also gives a variant last paragraph from the now-lost manuscript.

Verse and Dramatic Works

The poetical manuscripts listed span Lamb's entire life and nearly half of them consist of letters to friends, editors, publishers, etc. in which Lamb has written out his verses. The earliest verse manuscript, dated 1789 — indeed the earliest surviving Lamb autograph of any kind, the earliest letter being that to Coleridge postmarked 22 May 1796 — are the lines entitled 'Mille Viae Mortis' (LmC 105), written while a schoolboy at Christ's Hospital. The latest — 'To Margaret W—' (LmC 171) dated 8 October 1834, some ten weeks before his death — is thought to be the last poem Lamb wrote.

Lamb's versifying, however, came in fits and starts. He began his literary career as a poet and indeed the poems written before 1805 are generally considered to be his best; one of the four unpublished poems listed, beginning 'Sweet is thy sunny hair' (LmC 142), dates from 1796. It is impossible to know how many poems were lost during the weeks following 22 September 1796 — the day his sister Mary killed their mother — when Lamb, according to his letter to Coleridge of 10 December 1796, burnt a great many papers, including 'all my own verses'. He refers twice, in a letter to Coleridge postmarked 2 December 1796, to a poem of his in blank verse, 'Laugh all that weep' which has not been traced.

Throughout the entries is evidence of Lamb's early and intimate collaboration with Coleridge. Two verses generally attributed to Coleridge, but in fact jointly composed by him and Lamb, are listed in the Coleridge section (see 'The Gentle Look' and 'As when a child', CoS 203–5, 368). Three autograph manuscripts of Lamb's poems (see LmC 3, 91, 103 and FACSIMILES) are part of the Coleridge family papers at Victoria College Library in Toronto (see the INTRODUCTION to the Coleridge section of the *Index*). Four other Lamb autographs (see LmC 13.5, 58, 212, 217.5 and the list of Lamb's transcripts below) are in Coleridge's notebooks. Transcripts by Coleridge of Lamb's poems are included in two major manuscript sources of Coleridge's early verse, the Rugby MS and MS E (see the INTRODUCTION to the Coleridge section of the *Index* and LmC 104, 113–14, 201).

In his second edition of *Poems* (London and Bristol, 1797), Coleridge included a section of verse by Charles Lamb. On 14 November 1796, Lamb sent Coleridge the text of the preliminary matter to that section — including the title, the dedication to Mary Lamb and the motto — with a now-lost letter (printed *Letters*, I, 57–8 and Marrs, I, 63). The motto which Lamb chose, an extract from Massinger's *A Very Woman*, had also been transcribed in another now-lost letter to Coleridge of [13–16 June] (printed *Letters*, I, 28–9 and Marrs, I, 30–1). Lamb eventually included this extract in his *Specimens* (1808).

After 1805, Lamb published few poems outside of those written during two 'satirical outbursts', as Lucas calls them: one in *The Examiner* in 1812 (see LmC 31–2, 195–6) and the other in 1820 in *The Champion* (see LmC 68 9, 115, 116, 146–7, 194).

Of the over 200 verse entries listed below, only about ten date from these lean years between 1805 and 1820, and three of those were occasional verses which Lamb himself never published; see LmC 63, 108–9, 145. This is compared to some 50 entries which refer to poems written before 1805. But the vast majority of poetical manuscripts listed date from the 1820s and 1830s.

In those latter years of his life, Lamb was again regularly writing and publishing poems many of which were verses and/or acrostics written as contributions to albums. In fact, constant requests for album verses led Lamb to write to B. W. Procter (in a letter postmarked 19 January 1829, printed *Letters*, III, 199–201 from the original at Harvard) that 'I fled hither to escape the Albumean persecution....Why, by dabbling in those accursed Albums, I have become a byword of infamy all over the kingdom.' A substantial number of entries consist of 'those accursed' albums (or leaves torn therefrom) containing contributions by Lamb. Albums belonging to the following are included in the entries: Elizabeth Aders (see LmC 12, 111, 156 and CoS 412, 544, 772); Sarah Apsey (see LmC 184); John Bowring (see LmC 16); Frances Brown (see LmC 203); Ellen Button (see LmC 10); Emma Button (see LmC 162); Mrs Daniel Cresswell (see LmC 20, 26, 124); Sarah Stoddart Hazlitt (see

LmC 338); [T. T.?] Lachlan (see LmC 44, 199); Mary Locke (see LmC 172); Sarah Locke (see LmC 185); Alicia Mann (see LmC 23); Vincent Novello (see LmC 50); Mary Saywell (see LmC 170); J. T. Smith (see LmC 143); Isabella Jane Towers (see LmC 81); William Upcott (see LmC 223 and CoS 816); Fanny Sarah Westwood (see LmC 120). The album compiled by William Ayrton, exclusively as a record of Charles Lamb's works, is described below as 'William Ayrton's Scrapbook'.

Lamb personally helped to compile two other albums on behalf of his 'adopted daughter' Emma Isola; these volumes deserve special mention:

Emma Isola's Album

This album, for which Lamb himself solicited original contributions among his friends, includes many valuable items. As well as Lamb's own contributions (listed below), there are contributions from Keats ('To My Brothers', now excised and kept with the Keats Collection at Harvard, see KeJ 507 in the Keats section), Wordsworth ('She dwelt among the untrodden ways' and 'Blessings be with them'), Tennyson ('When Lazarus left'), Leigh Hunt ('Feast of Violets'), Southey ('Epitaph on Himself'), Landor ('To Emma Isola', etc.), as well as others by Joanna Baillie, Bernard Barton, M. M. Betham, Thomas Campbell, H. F. Cary, Barry Cornwall, Allan Cunningham, George Darley, Charles Dibdin, J. B. Dibdin, George Dyer, James Hogg, Thomas Hood, Frederick Locker, Thomas Moore, Edward Moxon, Mrs Piozzi, Samuel Rogers, T. N. Talfourd as well as clippings, portraits and photographs; items date from c. 1826–73.

The album was described and offered for sale intact by Quaritch in catalogues dating from 1878 to at least 1886. Shortly after, it was plundered and reduced to nine leaves in order to sell the more valuable items separately; eventually however it was restored and sold in its present form in the John Spoor Sale, Parke Bernet, 28 April 1939 (Lot 520). The Quaritch description (the original album) is reprinted in Lucas, VII, 977 and the surviving album is fully discussed in Woodring, pp.382–5.

Contents: LmC 55, 155, 208.

Harvard, MS Eng 601.66.

Emma Isola's Extract Book

This commonplace book originally consisted of over 82 leaves. Approximately the first half of it was taken up by extracts from various authors written out by Emma Isola. The last 43 leaves were written in Lamb's hand (with one or two exceptions) and contained not only extracts by various writers but also nine of his own poems; these leaves also contained two poems by Lamb in Emma Isola's hand. The volume was inscribed by Emma Isola [f. 1] 'The Extracts at the end of this Book are in the handwriting of my kind-hearted friend Charles Lamb.', and the title page [f. 2] reads 'Extracts in Prose and Verse'; the paper is watermarked 1825.

In 1905, this volume was owned by Emma Isola Moxon's daughters (*Life*, II, 204); in 1934 Sotheran offered it for sale in No. 13 of their series of special catalogues *Piccadilly Notes*. Therein the complete album (Item 4155) was offered for sale; only the contents in Lamb's hand were fully described. It was stated that, failing to find one buyer for the album by the end of 1934, the contents (as described, i.e. in Lamb's hand only) would then be sold separately (Items 4130–4154). In the event, the album *was* dismantled. The first 39 leaves of the volume (those in Emma Isola's hand) were left intact and are now at Texas. Examination of these leaves shows that some leaves have been excised though whether or not they were excised by Sotheran in 1934 or earlier is impossible to determine; one leaf, probably excised from this part of the volume, has turned up and it contains Emma Isola's transcripts of two of Lamb's poems (see LmC 14, 119). The leaves in Lamb's hand *were* sold separately and have, even now, not all come to light, although all of Lamb's own compositions have been located. The contents of these leaves are listed *Piccadilly Notes* and in two succeeding supplements of 1935; most were also listed by Lucas in *Life*, II, 204–6.

Contents by Lamb: LmC 14, 22, 51, 54, 70, 80, 99, 119, 130, 132, 135, 155, 167.

Transcripts by Lamb of works by others (listed by Item number in *Piccadilly Notes*):

Item 4134: Four leaves which cannot be separated containing LmC 135 and Lamb's transcripts of 'Sir Patrick Spence' (anonymous), 'The Spanish Lady's Love' (anonymous), Andrew Marvell's 'The Nymph Complaining for the Death of Her Fawn' and 4 lines of unidentified Latin verse: Princeton, Robert H. Taylor Collection.

Item 4137: One leaf containing LmC 132 and 167

and Lamb's transcript of Christopher Marlowe's 'The Milk Maid's Song'; facsimile in *Piccadilly Notes*, p. [384] and Sotheby's sale catalogue, 8–9 June 1936, Lot 459: Harvard, MS Eng 959.

Item 4138: One leaf containing 'To a Robin Redbreast' ('Domestic Bird, whom wintry blasts') and Izaak Walton's 'The Angler's Wish'; facsimile of stanza one of first and stanzas 1–3 of second in *Piccadilly Notes*, pp. 386–7 and Sotheby's sale catalogue, 8–9 June 1936, Lot 461: untraced.

Item 4139: One leaf containing Walter Raleigh's 'The Milk-Maid's Mother's Answer' and 'Christy, Scotch Song'; facsimile of lines 1–25 of first and lines 1–9 of second in *Piccadilly Notes*, pp. [388]–9 and Sotheby's sale catalogue, 8–9 June 1936, Lot 460; sold Sotheby's, 15 December 1982, Lot 139: untraced. Another transcript by Lamb of 'Christy' is written in 'Charles Lamb's Album' (see LmC 319).

Item 4140: One leaf containing 'Tweed Side' and 'Darby and Joan'; facsimile of stanza one of first and lines 1–6 of second in *Piccadilly Notes*, p. 390: Texas.

Item 4141: One leaf containing Matthew Prior's poems 'The Female Phaeton' and 'The Garland' and accompanying drawing; facsimile of stanzas 1–2 of first in *Piccadilly Notes*, p. 391: Texas.

Item 4142: One leaf (4 pages) containing S. T. Coleridge's 'Love', lines in Latin 'From the Greek Anthology' and a watercolour, watermarked 1825; facsimile of watercolour and one page of poem in *Piccadilly Notes*, pp. 392–3: Texas.

Item 4143: One leaf containing Andrew Marvell's poems 'Bermudas' and 'Young Love'; facsimile of lines 1–11 of first in *Piccadilly Notes*, p. 394; offered for sale at Sotheby's, 22 December 1936, Lot 593 ('passed' at sale): untraced.

Item 4144: One leaf containing Andrew Marvell's 'On a Drop of Dew', J. S. Knowles's 'Written under the Picture of William Hazlitt' and William Drummond's 'Cherries: to a Child'; facsimile of lines 1–8 of first in *Piccadilly Notes*, p. 395: Brown University, Ms. 52.156.

Item 4145: One leaf containing 'The Prioress to fair Millisent taking the veil/(From the old play of the "Merry Devil of Edmonton")' beginning 'Jesus' daughter, Mary's child' (used in *Specimens*, see Lucas, IV, 46) and Matthew Prior's 'To the Dying Soul' and a watercolour; facsimile of lines 1–15 of first in *Piccadilly Notes*, p. 396: Brown University, Ms. 52.156.

Item 4146: One leaf containing Edward Moxon's 'Sonnet/Goff's Oak'; facsimile of lines 1–8 in *Piccadilly Notes*, p. 397: untraced.

Item 4147: One leaf containing T. Overbury's 'A Fair and Happy Milkmaid' and 'Fair Helen of Kirconnell: Old Scottish Ballad'; facsimile of stanzas 1–4 of latter in *Piccadilly Notes*, p. 398: Texas.

Item 4148: One leaf containing Matthew Prior's 'To a Child of Quality, Five Years Old'; facsimile of stanzas 1, 2 and 7 in *Piccadilly Notes*, p. 399: untraced.

Item 4149: One leaf containing Allan Ramsay's 'Sir John Grehme and Barbara Allan' and '[Waly, Waly: an old Ballad]'; facsimile of stanzas 1–2 of first and stanza one of second in *Piccadilly Notes*, p. 400: Brown University, Ms. 52.156.

Item 4150: One leaf containing William Strode's 'A Song in commemoration of Music', 'From Wilby's Madrigals, 1609' and (in Emma Isola's hand) the anonymous lines 'Since the birds that had nestled and warbled above', watermarked 1825; facsimile of stanza one of first in *Piccadilly Notes*, p. 401: Texas.

Item 4151: Two leaves containing T. Tickell's 'Lucy & Colin' and a drawing; facsimile of stanzas 1–2 in *Piccadilly Notes*, pp. 402–3: untraced.

Item 4152: One leaf containing Lord Thurlow's 'To a Bird that haunted the waters of Lacken in the winter' (another transcript of this sonnet is listed below) with Emma Isola's drawing of Lacken and Edward Moxon's 'Sonnet/To the Nightingale'; facsimile of drawing in *Piccadilly Notes*, p. 404: Brown University, Ms. 52.181.

Item 4153: One leaf containing George Wither's 'The Muse'; facsimile of lines 1–13 in *Piccadilly Notes*, p. 405: untraced.

Item 4154: The final leaf annotated 'Finis', containing Edmund Waller's 'Song' ('Go, lovely

Rose') and his 'To a Young Lady: Lucy Sidney'; facsimile of stanza one of first in *Piccadilly Notes*, p. 406: untraced.

In a letter written to the editor published in the *New York Tribune* of 22 February 1879 (reprinted Lucas, V, 343–4), J. H. Siddons describes 'one or two sheets' of jeux d'esprit which had been found in Lamb's desk at the India Office 'long after his death'; these four autograph 'comic epigrams which [Lamb] had evidently thrown off at jocular moments for the amusement of his fellow clerks' were transcribed by Siddons and eventually printed in his letter in the *New York Tribune*. (He includes a fifth which was reported to him in conversation and not found in manuscript.) The autograph epigrams remained, according to Siddons, in the India Office and are now untraced. Lucas prints the letter (including the verses) in his Notes to the poetry volume (V, 343–4), and accepts their authenticity without question; but he does not include them in the main text of the volume — probably due to their insignificance. The four verses are: 'Here lies the body of Timothy Wagstaff' (4 lines); 'Here lieth the body of Captain Sturms' (6 lines); '*Ci git* the remains of Margaret Dix' (4 lines); 'To the memory of Dr Onesimus Drake' (4 lines).

Several other poetical manuscripts have been recorded which have not come to light and may be lost; they are not given numbered entries but are listed here against the possibility of their being located; see also the headnotes to LmC 19–20, 35–8, 63, 75–6, 84–9, 107, 135, 141, 166–8, 200, 206–8.

The Gipsy's Malison ('"Suck, baby, suck, mother's love grows by giving')

First pub. *Blackwood's Magazine*, January 1829; collected *Album Verses* (1830); Lucas, V, 57.

Here entitled 'The Gypsy's Malison', in a letter to Bryan Waller Procter, 29? January 1829.

The letter (untraced) is printed *Letters*, III, 208.

Living Without God in the World ('Mystery of God! thou brave and beauteous world')

First pub. (lines 23–36) in Charles Lloyd, *Lines suggested by the Fast appointed on Wednesday, February 27, 1799* (Birmingham, 1799); in full in *Annual Anthology*, [ed. Robert Southey], 2 vols (Bristol, 1799–1800); Lucas, V, 17–18.

A transcript by Southey was printed in W. C. Hazlitt, *Mary and Charles Lamb* (London, 1874), pp. 234–5 when it was among the collection of manuscripts (labelled 'Southey MSS.') which apparently represented contributions to *The Annual Anthology*. While these manuscripts have been described as being chiefly in Southey's hand, including that of this poem *composed by Lamb*, three in Lamb's autograph have been identified (see the descriptions of 'Dirge for Him Who Shall Deserve It', 'Elegy on a Quid of Tobacco' and 'The Rhedycinian Barbers' below). The collection was originally owned by Joseph Cottle (publisher of the *Anthology*) and later by a Frederick W. Cosens of London, by Augustin Daly (sold 1900) and finally by A. E. Newton in whose sale (Parke Bernet, 14–16 May 1941) the Lamb items were sold separately (Lots 586–8).

Another manuscript source for Lamb's poetry (and one prose piece 'London Fogs') is the scrapbook compiled by William Ayrton. The volume was certainly seen by Lamb: it contains one of his poems written out in his own hand and Ayrton notes, on the inside front cover, that 'when C. Lamb was shown this Volume, then blank, for future works, he said, that is the greatest compliment that has ever been paid me'. And one of Ayrton's transcripts is annotated that it was copied from a manuscript before publication (see LmC 66). Nonetheless, whether or not Ayrton's transcripts of Lamb's poems in the scrapbook carry any authority remains to be determined. Two poems which Ayrton attributes to Lamb were not included by Lucas among Lamb's poetical works — even though Lucas was lent this scrapbook in 1903 by Ayrton's grandson, Edward Ayrton (see Lucas, I, 537) — and must have been deliberately rejected.

William Ayrton's Scrapbook

This volume of blank leaves was bound up to form a third volume with Lamb's *Works* (1818) in which Ayrton meant to record Lamb's 'future works'. It includes, as well as one poem in Lamb's hand (LmC 13): Ayrton's transcripts of poems by Lamb (and two questionable items which he attributed to Lamb, LmC 101 and 209); clippings regarding Lamb; a sketch of Lamb on the inside front cover; two inserted letters from Lamb; Ayrton's (or another's?) transcripts of passages from various works and memoirs concerning Lamb, including a transcript of Hazlitt's portrait of Lamb from *The Spirit of the Age* (ff. [108v–9, 110–25], rectos only); two unattributed poems have not been given numbered entries despite an implicit suggestion that they are Lamb's simply by having been transcribed in this book: (1) 'Parting', a sonnet beginning 'Yon fleecy Cloud that veils the gentle Moon', dated 1 November 1821 (on ff. [8v–9]); (2) 'To a Lady', 4 lines beginning 'For Love's illustrious cause, & Helen's charms' (on f. [21]); c. 176 leaves, many blank (unfoliated); begun 1818–19 and used until 1830 at least.

The inserted letters from Lamb (one to Mrs Ayrton of 15 March 1821, the other to Ayrton of 27 October 1821) are printed *Letters* II, 294 and 313 respectively.

Contents: LmC 13, 32, 53, 66, 98, 101, 109, 116, 117, 121, 137, 147, 181, 189, 191, 196, 209, 249.

Huntington, RB 110244, Vol. III.

Of Lamb's four plays, the earliest, the tragedy *John Woodvil*, was never meant to be produced. Of the other three, all farces, only one, *Mr H*, was accepted for production and that production was withdrawn after one catastrophic performance. Though Mary Lamb apparently transcribed copies of Charles's plays for various friends, only one of her transcripts survives (see LmC 84). For the farces, two of the transcripts submitted to the Lord Chamberlain for licensing are extant (see LmC 107, 126).

Works Edited by Lamb

Lamb's most important work as an 'editor' was to 'draw the Public attention to the old English Dramatists' — as he said of himself in the 'Autobiographical Sketch' (LmC 223). Swinburne attributes to Lamb 'and to him alone...the revelation and resurrection of our greatest dramatic poets after Shakespeare'.

In *Specimens*, Lamb published extracts from his early reading of the Elizabethans, begun in the 1790s; see Lamb's letters, *passim*, and the headnote to *Specimens*. The sequel *Extracts from the Garrick Plays* includes the fruits of Lamb's reading — after his retirement in 1825 from the East India House — of the Garrick collection of Elizabethan drama in the British Museum.

Also included in this section are a few of Lamb's extant transcripts of works by other authors which he most probably contributed, though without note, to William Hone's *Table Book* (1827).

There are several other surviving transcripts by Lamb of works by other authors. Many of them are related to (but not used in) *Specimens* and *Extracts from the Garrick Plays* while others are works by his contemporaries and friends. Throughout Lamb's letters, such transcripts can be found — of verses by, for example, Christopher Marlowe, George Chapman, John Bunyan, Mary Lamb, Robert Southey and William Wordsworth; these transcripts are not included here (see LmC 37, 61, 73, 76, 316–19, 345, 358, the long list of the original contents of 'Emma Isola's Extract Book' (above), and the unlocated copy of Dr Johnson's *Works* (described below)). Other transcripts that have come to light are:

By the Earl of Dorset ('Dorinda's sparkling wit and eyes')

Two 4-line stanzas, inserted in a copy of *The Annual Anthology*, [ed. Robert Southey], 2 vols (Bristol, 1799–1800); c. 1820.

This manuscript printed in *Sentimental Library*, p. 128 and Rosenbach Catalogue (1947), Item 374; described in Doris Braendel, 'The Lamb Collection at the Rosenbach Foundation', *WC*, 2 (1971), 88.

Rosenbach Foundation.

Clever Tom Clinch going to be hanged. 1727 and *The Power of Time*

Three unidentified poems, the first, 'Clever Tom...', of 24 lines, the second, 'The Power of Time', of 6 lines, the third, an untitled 4-line verse, 2 pages (one leaf).

Parke Bernet, 23 November 1954, Lot 678.

Dirge For Him Who Shall Deserve It ('Stay your walk ye weeping throng')

Lines by William Taylor first pub. anonymously *The Annual Anthology*, [ed. Robert Southey], 2 vols (Bristol, 1799–1800).

Two pages, nine 4-line stanzas, unsigned.

See the description of 'Living without God in the World' above for details of this transcript.

Offered for sale (as Lamb's) at Parke Bernet, 14–16 May 1941 (A. E. Newton Sale), Lot 586 and Parke Bernet, 1 November 1955 (Borneman Sale), Lot 50 (both catalogues print stanza one).

Elegy on a Quid of Tobacco ('It lay before me on the close-grazed grass')

First pub. (as by 'Theoderit', a pseudonym used by Southey) in *The Annual Anthology*, [ed. Robert Southey], 2 vols (Bristol, 1799–1800); not reprinted by Southey. Kenneth Curry, 'The Contributors to *The Annual Anthology*', *PBSA*, 42 (1948), 50–65 ascribes these lines to Southey without hesitation.

Fair copy, signed 'Theoderit', ten 4-line stanzas, 2 pages.

This manuscript printed in *Tobacco Catalogue*, IV, No. 1142; see the description of 'Living without God in the World' above for details of this transcript.

NYPL, Arents Collection.

From a French prisoner

Annotation on the flyleaf of Lamb's copy of *Mrs Leicester's School* (London, 1809), signed; quoted from a released French prisoner and including a deleted epitaph in Latin.

Facsimile in Anderson Galleries sale catalogue, 7–10 January 1929 (Kern Sale), p. 277. This passage was also transcribed by Lamb into one of his commonplace books which was formerly owned by Alfred Morrison and described in Scheuer Catalogue No. 5.

Berg.

The Queen's Ball ('Reform, Great Queen, the errors of your youth') [and] *On the Duchess of Portsmouth's Picture, Septr 1682* ('Who can on this Picture look')

These two poems were transcribed from the anthology *Poems on Affairs of State*.

One leaf, 'The Queen's Ball' (30 lines, on recto) subtitled 'in "Poems on affairs of State, 3^d volume, published 1704', 'On the Duchess...' (18 lines, on verso) headed 'from the same Work Vol 1 6th Edition Printed 1710', annotated by Lamb 'with CL's Compts' and, in an unidentified hand, 'Mrs Jameson'; watermarked 1826.

Huntington, HM 13293.

The Rhedycinian Barbers ('Now the sky begins to clear')

These lines signed G. C. B[edford] first pub. *The Annual Anthology*, [ed. Robert Southey], 2 vols (Bristol, 1799–1800).

Four pages (one leaf).

See the description of 'Living without God in the World' above for details of this transcript; stanzas 1–2 printed in Parke Bernet sale catalogue, 14–16 May 1941 (A. E. Newton sale), Lot 587.

Texas.

Serenata, For Two Voices/On the Marriage of Charles Cowden Clarke, Esqre., to Victoria, daughter of Vincent Novello, Esqre. ('Wake th' harmonious voice and string')

These lines by John Hughes pub. in his *Poems on Several Occasions*, 2 vols (London, 1735).

Lamb transcribed these lines (changing one name to fit the occasion) and sent them as his own, with above title, in a letter to Vincent Novello, Enfield, 6 November 1829 (sic, i.e., 1828).

Lucas prints the letter and the verses without comment in *Letters*, III, 187–9; Mary Cowden Clarke's transcript of the letter is at University of Leeds, Novello-Cowden Clarke Collection; Edmund Blunden pointed out Lamb's plagiarism in *TLS*, 12 June 1937.

Harvard, Autograph File.

Sonnet to a Bird that haunted the Waters of Lacken, in the winter, by Lord Thurlow ('O melancholy bird, a winter's day')

Lamb transcribed these lines in Coleridge's Notebook 28 (see S. T. Coleridge, CoS 1367), used 1819–1924?.

These lines were also transcribed in 'Emma Isola's Extract Book' (described above).

British Library, Add. MS 47526, f. 36.

Sonnets II and XI

These sonnets by Hartley Coleridge were first pub. in his *Poems* (Leeds and London, 1833).

Lamb transcribed these two sonnets (wanting lines 1–2 of XI) from their first publication, 2 pages (one leaf).

Berg.

The Spleen ('This motley piece to you I send')

Matthew Greene's poem was first published as *The Spleen: an epistle* (London, 1737).

Lamb transcribed the first 4 lines of 'The Spleen' (without title) on the first page of a volume containing a long poem in the hand of (by?) T. Tickell; Lamb signed and dated the lines 1807.

This volume sold Puttick & Simpson, 29–30 July 1908, Lot 503, to Sabin (these lines printed in the sale catalogue); it was described, without Greene's authorship being identified, in *CLSB*, No. 81 (January 1948) when it was owned by Edwin Bliss Hill whose collection has for the most part been given to Arizona State University at Tempe and the University of Arizona at Tucson.

Owned (1948) Edwin Bliss Hill (d. 1949).

To Emma, Learning Latin, and Desponding ('Droop not, dear Emma, dry those falling tears')

These lines by Mary Lamb were first pub. *Blackwood's Magazine*, June 1829; Lucas, V, 83–4.

Transcript by Charles Lamb; dated Enfield, 22 August 1827.

Pierpont Morgan, MA 225.

Water Ballad ('"Come hither gently rowing')

These lines by S. T. Coleridge first pub. *The Athenaeum*, 29 October 1831. Another transcript by Lamb is on I, 224 of 'Charles Lamb's Album' (see LmC 319).

Transcribed and signed 'S. T. Coleridge' by Lamb, 3 stanzas.

Henkels, 26 January 1921, Lot 297.

Books for Children

Of Lamb's books for children, written 1805–11, three were collaborations with his sister Mary — *Tales from Shakespear*, 2 vols (London, 1807), *Mrs Leicester's School* (London, 1809) and *Poetry for Children* (London, 1809). Like the Elia essays, the number of available editions of the Lambs' *Tales from Shakespear* is enormous.

No manuscripts survive for any of these works except Robert Lloyd's transcript of four poems from *Poetry for Children*, only one of which was composed by Charles (see LmC 28).

A few other related manuscript items however are of interest. Several extant letters provide information about Charles's share of *Tales from Shakespear*: his letter to Thomas Manning dated 10 May 1806 (Marrs, II, 225–7 from the original at the Folger, W.b.43(2)); Mary Lamb's to Sarah Stoddart dated 2 June 1806 (Marrs, II, 227–30 from the original at the Berg); Charles to Wordsworth, 26 June 1806 (Marrs, II, 230–4 from the original at Texas); and Charles to Wordsworth of 29 January 1807 (Marrs, II, 256–7 from the original at Dr Williams's Library, Henry Crabb Robinson Papers, Vol. 1805–1808, f. 81).

Two documents of Charles's authorship of three of the stories in *Mrs Leicester's School* also survive: a letter to Bernard Barton postmarked 23 January 1824 in which Lamb lists his stories (*Letters*, II, 415–17, original in the British Library, Add. MS 35256, ff. 27–8); the second is Lamb's presentation copy to Emma Isola of the 10th edition (London, 1827), now at the Berg, in which he has initialled the three stories which he composed.

Lamb's Library

Henry Crabb Robinson wrote in a much-quoted diary entry dated 10 January 1824 that Lamb's library was 'the finest collection of shabby books I ever saw. Such a number of first-rate works of genius, but filthy copies, which a delicate man would really hesitate touching, is, I think, nowhere to be found...' In a similar vein, W. C. Hazlitt in his *The Book-Collector* (London, 1904) says that 'the history of Lamb's books is more humanly interesting than the history of the Huth or Grenville library; as chattels or furniture they were worthless; they were generally the poorest copies imaginable; but if they did not cost money, they often cost thought'.

When Lamb died in 1834, his books were left to Edward Moxon. But by the time Moxon claimed them — after Mary's death in 1847 — they had for years been given away and picked over by various friends. Moxon then apparently destroyed all but sixty volumes of the remaining collection; those sixty having been probably selected for preservation because of the manuscript annotations by Lamb and/or Coleridge which they contained. Moxon then sold the sixty books to Charles Welford (of the firm Bartlett & Welford of New York) who brought them to America for private sale over the counter and by post.

Lamb's friends were, not surprisingly, unhappy with Moxon's allowing Lamb's books to be dispersed, particularly on the other side of the Atlantic. Thomas Westwood said that 'there are some libraries the dispersion of which we feel as a positive pain, almost a disgrace — and Lamb's was of them' (see *Life*, II, 426).

Annotated copies of the Bartlett and Welford Catalogue, printed in February 1848, are at Harvard and the NYPL, the latter annotated by Robert Balmanno, one of the buyers. Eighteen of the books sold — those bought by the bookdealer James T. Annan of Cincinnati — were almost immediately resold at an auction held by Cooley, Keese & Hill of New York on 20–21 October 1848; annotated copies of the catalogue for that auction are at the American Antiquarian Society and the NYPL. For a fuller discussion of these sales, see Woodring, pp. 367–9.

The British Library (Add. MS 60336) owns a manuscript catalogue compiled by Richard Charles Jackson who claimed to be the grandson of Francis Jackson, a pupil at Christ's Hospital and the alleged model for Elia's 'Captain Jackson'. The catalogue, according to Jackson's annotation, represents the books from Lamb's library which Moxon did not select for sale to Charles Welford and which 'on the death of Mary Lamb' (i.e., in 1847), he was persuaded to sell to Francis Jackson along with 'Charles Lamb's household furniture, prints, china and personal effects'.

There is much reason to doubt the authenticity both of Jackson's claims and of the provenance of his books and relics; see Prance, pp. 168–9 and *The Times*, 30 July 1923. Reginald Hine, however, in *Charles Lamb and His Hertfordshire* (London, 1949) also says that a Francis Jackson purchased books from Lamb's library at Moxon's sale of 1858 (*sic*) — some of which Hine then owned — though he may have been innocently relying on the bookplates which Jackson had inserted in the books at some point. Richard Jackson's remains were sold by Goddard and Smith on 23–5 July 1923 at Jackson's Camberwell home; the items sold included five pieces of furniture and 116 books said to have been formerly owned by Charles Lamb and Francis Jackson.

Jackson's manuscript catalogue at the British Library contains hundreds of books, two of which are described as containing marginalia possibly by Lamb (see also the headnote to LmC 63) and two others as being volumes of extracts in Lamb's autograph; they are not given numbered entries but are listed here against the slim possibility that their provenance is genuine:

Item 17: described as a volume of extracts in Charles Lamb's early autograph, taken from 'the "Mirror" of 23 January 1779, &c'.

Item 108: Thomas Campbell, *The Pleasures of Hope* (Edinburgh, 1801) including eight lines of verse in what 'is thought' to be Lamb's hand.

Item 162: manuscript volume of unpublished prayers, 'said to be in the Autograph of Lamb...[written] when he was about 17 years of age', 56 pages.

Item 220: Richard Hole, *Remarks on the Arabian Nights' Entertainments* (London, 1797), containing annotations on pp. 13–17 'either by Lamb or Coleridge'.

Whether because Moxon did not destroy all of Lamb's books not sent to New York, or because many were dispersed *before* Moxon's unfortunate mismanagement of their preservation, the list below contains quite a number of books containing Lamb's marginalia which were not offered for sale in the Bartlett and Welford Catalogue. That original catalogue of sixty volumes has served as the basis for the various reconstructions of Lamb's library that have been published. It was reprinted by W. C. Hazlitt, *Mary and Charles Lamb* (London, 1874) and, with additions, by the Dibdin Club of New York in 1897 (*A Descriptive Catalogue of the Library of Charles Lamb*). Further additions and the names of the original buyers were also published in W. C. Hazlitt's *The Lambs* (London and New York, 1897). Lucas's 1905 reconstruction of Lamb's library in Appendix III of *Life* included some 200 items. All of these reconstructions include books owned by Lamb which *do not* contain any marginalia.

In his Elian essay 'The Two Races of Men', Lamb made Coleridge's book-borrowing habits notorious. And the list of books containing marginalia below shows several instances of that borrowing. Copies of nine works annotated by both Coleridge and Lamb are mentioned though their proper numbered entries will be found in the Coleridge section; see CoS 1416, 1441, 1493, 1497, 1510, 1513, 1700, 1718, 1804. Two of these are in the British Library collection of books from Coleridge's own library; five others were sold with Lamb's books by Bartlett and Welford. Another volume — a copy of Milton's *Paradise Lost* (London, 1751) (LmC 346) — though annotated only by Lamb, was also acquired by the British Library with Coleridge's books. For a detailed discussion of the relationship between Lamb, Coleridge and annotated books, see *The Collected Works of Samuel Taylor Coleridge. Marginalia*, Vol. I, ed. George Whalley (Princeton, 1980), pp. lxxxviii–xcii and clxii–clxiii.

The whereabouts of several of the annotated books offered by Bartlett and Welford remains unknown. Those whose known provenance ends at one of the 1848 sales are not given numbered entries below. As they might well come to light in time, they are listed here, by Bartlett and Welford Catalogue number; this list includes a few items (marked *) which may not contain marginalia.

Item 1*: Aulus Gellius. *Noctes Atticae* (Amsterdam, 1651), containing marginalia by J. Horne Tooke.

Item 2: William Cooke. *The Art of Living in London* (London, 1805), containing annotations, one a long note about the author. Sold to Annan and resold in his sale at Cooley, Keese & Hill (New York), 20–21 October 1848, Lot 359.

Item 3: Vincent Bourne. *Poematia, latinè, partim reddita, partim scripta*, 4th ed (London, 1750) containing Lamb's verses 'Suum Cuique' (see headnote to LmC 141) and extracts from the Latin written on the flyleaves.

Item 4*: James Burney. *An Essay, by Way of Lecture, on the Game of Whist* (privately printed, London, 1821), presentation copy from the author to Martin Charles Burney.

Item 8: John Cleveland. *Poems* (London, 1668) containing marginalia; for another edition, also annotated, see LmC 328.

Item 10: Abraham Cowley. *Works* (London, 1693) containing three folio pages of additions and extracts as well as marginal corrections.

Item 11*: Alexander Pope. *The Dunciad, Variorum* (London, 1729) possibly containing marginalia.

Item 12: John Dennis. *Original Letters, Familiar, Moral and Critical* (London, 1726), containing notes and additions; sold to Annan and resold in his sale at Cooley, Keese & Hill (New York), 20–21 October 1848, Lot 362.

Item 15*: Jonathan Edwards. *A careful and strict Enquiry into the modern prevailing notion of that Freedom of Will...* (unidentified edition), bound with Joseph Priestley, *The Doctrine of Philosophical Necessity* (unidentified edition).

Item 17*: *The Guardian* [by Addison and Steele, *et.al.*], Vol. I (London, 1750) and Vol. II (London, 1734); Vol. I is inscribed 'John Lamb, 1756' and 'Charles Lamb'.

Item 19: Cleopatra, Queen Consort of Juba II, King of Mauritania. *Hymen's Prœludia*, trans. R. Loveday (London, 1698), containing a note on the title page; resold by Annan in his sale at Cooley, Keese & Hill (New York), 20–21 October 1848, Lot 365.

Item 20: Ben Jonson. *The Works* (London, 1692), containing extracts, additions, poems, corrections, etc., written in an early hand; W. C. Hazlitt notes that Lamb gave a copy of this edition to Sir John Stoddart in 1803.

Item 21: Marcus Annæus Lucanus. *Pharsalia*, trans. Thomas May (London, 1635) containing 'markings'.

Item 24*: Henry More. *An Explanation of the grand mystery of Godliness* (London, 1660).

Item 25*: *The Works of the most celebrated Minor poets*, Vol. I (London, 1749); sold to Annan and resold in his sale at Cooley, Keese & Hill (New York), 20–21 October 1848, Lot 366.

Item 27: Nathaniel Mist. *A Collection of Miscellany Letters, selected out of Mist's Weekly Journal*, 2 vols (London, 1722), containing names and addresses of friends on the cover; mentioned by John M. Turnbull in a letter to the editor in *TLS*, 5 February 1949, p. 89; sold to Annan and resold in his sale at

Cooley, Keese & Hill (New York), 20–21 October 1848, Lot 367.

Items 28–30: Margaret Cavendish, Duchess of Newcastle. Lamb's copies of *Works* (London, 1664), *The World's Olio*, 2nd ed (London, 1671) and *Nature's Pictures* (London, 1656) all containing annotations of some kind.

Item 31: Francis Osborne. *The Works*, 9th ed (London, 1689), possibly containing marginalia.

Items 33–4, 36: Three volumes of bound plays and tracts, each containing Lamb's autograph table of contents and possibly other marginalia: *Old Plays: a Collection of rare old quarto Plays, original editions, by Wycherley, Dryden, Shadwell, &c.; with Dryden's Essay on Dramatic Poetry*, 12 plays in one volume; *Old Plays, by Vanbrugh, Farquhar, Settle, &c.; and curious Tracts by A. Marvell, C. Cotton, Motteux, &c.*, 15 tracts in one volume; *Poetical Tracts, original 4to editions; Mason's English Garden, 1772; View of Covent-Garden Theatre, curious Plate; The Theatres, ditto 1772*, 7 tracts in one volume; these three volumes were sold to Annan and resold in his sale at Cooley, Keese & Hill (New York), 20–21 October 1848, as Lots 370, 368 and 371 respectively.

Item 39*: Volume of Plays. Including Coleridge's translation of *Wallenstein* and plays by Joanna Baillie.

Item 40: Katherine Philips. *Poems* (London, 1678), containing annotations; sold to Annan and resold in his sale at Cooley, Keese & Hill (New York), 20–21 October 1848, Lot 373.

Item 41*: [Nathaniel Bacon]. *A Relation of the Fearfull Estate of Francis Spira* (unidentified 12mo edition); sold to Annan and resold in his sale at Cooley, Keese & Hill (New York), 20–21 October 1848, Lot 374.

Item 42: Sir Henry Wotton. *Reliquiæ Wottonianæ*, [ed. Izaak Walton], 3rd ed (London, 1672), containing annotations and inscription of additional poems by Wotton.

Item 43: Jonathan Richardson (father and son). *Explanatory Notes and Remarks on Milton's Paradise Lost* (London, 1734), containing notes and extracts on the flyleaves.

Item 44*: [Zachary Pearce]. *A Review of the Texts of Milton's Paradise Lost* (London, 1733).

Item 46*: *The Spectator*, [by Addison and Steele, *et.al.*], Vol. IX, 4th ed (London, 1724).

Item 49: William Sewell. *The History of the Rise and Progress of the People called Quakers* (London, 1722), containing annotations on the flyleaf.

Item 51: Jonathan Swift. *A Tale of a Tub... To which is added, An Account of a Battel between the antient and modern Books in St James's Library* (London, 1710), including some marginalia.

Three other annotated books from Lamb's library have been described which were not included in the Bartlett and Welford Catalogue and whose whereabouts are at present unknown:

Samuel Johnson. *The Works* (unidentified edition).

A copy of Dr Johnson's works includes, on the flyleaf, Lamb's transcription of a note on Johnson by S. T. Coleridge (published in the latter's *Table Talk*). Some Lamb editors have published the note from this volume as Lamb's, entitled 'Samuel Johnson, the Whig'; Lucas (I, 350) prints it but later (in Appendix III, VII, [979]) notes his mistake. He also prints the note in *Life*, Appendix III, pp. 318–19.

Alexander Pope. *The Rape of the Lock* (unidentified edition).

Mrs J. T. Fields, in *A Shelf of Old Books*, says that Lamb's copy contained his transcriptions of pages which were wanting.

Edmund Spenser. *The Faerie Queen: The Shepheard's Calendar, together with the other Works*

(London, 1612–17).

Lucas (in *Life*, Appendix III, p. 324) lists this edition, without stating the location, and describes it in some detail as being inscribed by Mary Lamb on the cover and containing Lamb's marginalia and his inserted transcript of Spenser's sonnet 'To the Right Worshipful, My Singular Good *Friend*, Mr Gabriel Harvey'; Lucas also prints one marginal annotation. Lamb explains to Wordsworth in a letter of 1 February 1806 (Marrs, II, 204–7 from the original at the Huntington) that he is sending a folio of Spenser's works (1679 edition) in which he has transcribed the sonnet to Harvey, therein unpublished.

Letters and Other Papers

The fullest history of editions of Lamb's letters is given by Edwin W. Marrs, Jr in the Introduction (pp. lxii–xcv) to his edition of *The Letters of Charles and Mary Anne Lamb* (herein called Marrs) currently being published. This massive re-editing, from original manuscript sources whenever possible, will ultimately include over 1500 letters — some 80 per cent either from Lamb's originals or from transcripts or facsimiles of them — nearly 500 more than in *Letters* (1935), the edition which it supersedes. For those years (after 1817) which the Marrs edition has not yet reached in its published volumes, *Letters* remains the definitive edition; it should however be used with an eye on the long list of articles which add to or correct its texts, listed in Marrs, I, lxxxviii–xcii. Another edition worth mentioning, with regard to manuscripts, is Harper (1905) which included, in its first volume, a great many facsimiles of Lamb's autograph letters.

The two largest collections of Lamb's letters are those at the Huntington (c. 200) and the W. Hugh Peal collection at the University of Kentucky (c. 100). The latter is described in detail by Edwin W. Marrs, Jr in *University of Kentucky Occasional Papers*, No. 7 (December 1984).

Other collections containing ten or more letters each are: Berg; British Library; Brown University; Dr Williams's Library, Henry Crabb Robinson Papers; Folger; Harvard; University of Leeds; Pierpont Morgan; Princeton; Princeton, Robert H. Taylor Collection (described briefly in Jeremiah S. Finch, 'The Taylor Lamb Collection', *CLSB*, NS 55 (1986), 229); Rosenbach Foundation (described in Doris Braendel, 'The Lamb Collection at the Rosenbach Foundation', *WC*, 2 (1971), 80–91); SUNY at Buffalo; Texas; Victoria and Albert Museum, Forster Collection; Yale.

Among the many letters in the Huntington collection are large numbers to Coleridge, including the earliest extant letters (c. 30); to Robert Lloyd (c. 13); to Thomas Manning (c. 40); to John and Susannah Rickman (c. 22); to William and Marianne Ayrton (c. 14); to Edward and Emma Moxon (c. 33). Among the letters to various individuals in the Peal Collection at Kentucky, there are ten letters to Thomas Allsop, seven to John Bates Dibdin, eight to Fanny Kelly and seven to Charles Ryle. Other sizeable collections to particular recipients can be found in the following repositories: Texas (53 letters, 1801–34, to members of the Wordsworth circle, i.e. William, Dorothy and Sara Hutchinson); University of Leeds (letters, mostly transcripts, to Charles Cowden Clarke and Vincent and Mary Novello, 1821–34); British Library (49 letters to Bernard Barton, 1822–31, Add. MS 35256); Dr Williams's Library (c. 20 to Henry Crabb Robinson, 1808–32); Victoria and Albert Museum, Forster Collection (11 to Edward Moxon dating from the 1830s, seven to John Forster); Rosenbach Foundation (9 letters to Thomas Allsop); Princeton, Scribner Collection (9 letters to Maria Fryer, 1829–34, printed in *PULC*, 6 (1945), 179–99).

Lucas remarked in *Letters* that Lamb's letters to Southey — known to him only in Thomas Noon Talfourd's transcriptions in all but two instances — were probably extant; indeed Southey himself claimed, in a letter to Moxon written after Lamb died, that he never destroyed one of Lamb's letters. At present, of the twenty-four known letters that Lamb wrote to Southey, eighteen of the original manuscripts (one in facsimile only) have been located; they are widely scattered though all but one are in American collections.

Several additions or corrections to Marrs (for letters before October 1817) and *Letters* (for letters after October 1817) can be noted. Lamb's famous letter to Coleridge postmarked 27 September 1796 relating the death of his mother, on 22 September, by his sister Mary's hand, is reprinted in Marrs (I, 44–5) from *Letters*; the original is now in the Pierpont Morgan Library (MA 3508). A facsimile of the original letter to Southey of 18 October 1798 (reprinted Marrs, I, 136 from *Letters*) is printed in the American Art Association sale catalogue of 9 February 1932 (Lot 151) and two copies of the facsimile are in the Facsimile File at Yale (nos. 746 and 866); the original letter was last noticed in the catalogue of the Pforzheimer Sale at Kende Galleries (New York) on 9

November 1949 (Lot 432). A facsimile of the letter to George Dyer of 5 July 1808 — which Marrs (II, 284–5) says is 'unavailable, but purchased by Maggs from Sotheby's on April 29, 1969' and which he reprints from a previous publication in an 1841 periodical — was filed at the British Library (RP 334(2)) when the manuscript, after the 1969 sale, was exported to Goodspeed's in America. The letter to Charles Lloyd of 19 June 1809 (Marrs, III, 19–20 from a printed source) is actually in the Charnwood Collection on deposit at the British Library (Loan 60, Vol II, Item 31(1)).

Giving all the locations for the October 1817–1834 letters printed, without locations, in *Letters* would be inappropriate here; additional letters however which have come to light are as follows:

1. To B. R. Haydon, 4 December 1817: Bryn Mawr College, Adelman Collection.
2. To Fanny Kelly, 2 June 1818: SUNY at Buffalo.
3. To Sophia Lloyd, 20 July 1818: Berg.
4. To John Britton, 25 November 1818: NYPL, Manuscripts Division.
5. To Dodwell & Chambers, 26 August [1819]: Princeton, Robert H. Taylor Collection (containing LmC 238).
6. To Thomas Allsop, 19 December 1820: Huntington (pub. Barnett, p. 59).
7. Signed invitation to an unidentified recipient, c. 1821: Brown University, Ms. 52.153.
8. To Thomas Allsop, 27 January 1821: Huntington (pub. Barnett, p. 59).
9. Note to [Robert Baldwin?], mid-May 1821?: University of Kentucky.
10. To Taylor and Hessey, postmarked 25 July 1821: Princeton, Robert H. Taylor Collection (containing LmC 243).
11. Two letters to James Hessey about 'Witches and Other Night Fears', one postmarked 18 September 1821 (containing LmC 300), the other not dated but following the first; facsimiles at British Library, RP 778: Pierpont Morgan, MA 4575.
12. To [John Taylor?], 1 October 1821: Princeton, Robert H. Taylor Collection.
13. To Thomas Allsop, postmarked 19 October 1821: University of Kentucky.
14. To John Taylor, 1822?: Yale.
15. To Thomas Noon Talfourd, August 1822?: University of Kentucky (pub. Vera Watson, *TLS*, 20 April 1956).
16. To [John Taylor], East India House, 23 September 1822: Berg.
17. To [Taylor and Hessey?], postmarked 10 December 1822: University of Kentucky.
18. To Taylor and Hessey, postmarked 18 December 1822: Princeton, Robert H. Taylor Collection.
19. Note to Taylor and Hessey, [1823?]: Princeton, Robert H. Taylor Collection.
20. To Taylor and Hessey, postmarked 3 September 1823: NYPL, Pforzheimer Collection, Shelleyana 892.
21. To Sara Hutchinson, 22 October 1823: University of Kentucky (pub. *University of Kentucky Occasional Papers*, No. 7, December 1984).
22. To John Mitford, 16 December 1824: Yale, Osborn Collection.
23. To Thomas Allsop, [3 November 1825]: sold Parke Bernet, 12 April 1928.
24. Note to Mary Lamb, 20 September 1826: Brown University, Ms. 52.153.
25. To John Mitford, postmarked 6 December 1826: University of Kentucky (facsimile at British Library, MS Facs. Suppl. VIII(48)).
26. To Elizabeth Aders, 1827? (see LmC 111): Harvard, MS Eng 1094(21v).
27. Note to Henry Crabb Robinson, c. February 1827: Brown University, Ms. 52.153.
28. To Charles Aders, [April 1827]: Harvard, MS Eng 1094(23).
29. To B. R. Haydon, 7 April 1827: Harvard, fMS Eng 1331(16) (Haydon's Diary, Vol. XIII, f. 73).
30. To Fanny Kelly, [7 April 1827]: SUNY at Buffalo.
31. To Bernard Barton, [shortly before 11 June 1827]: University of Kentucky (containing LmC 153).
32. To [Robert Jameson?], 20 August [1827], inserted in the interleaved Thomas Moore, *The*

Poetical Works, Letters and Journals of Lord Byron, 44 vols (London, 1844), Vol. X, between pp. 262 and 263: British Library, Department of Printed Books, C.44.e. (pub. Barnett, pp. 16–17).

33. To Edward Moxon, postmarked September 1827: Harvard, Autograph File (pub. Woodring, p. 388).

34. To William Hone, 18 October 1827: Yale.

35. To Charles Cowden Clarke, postmarked 16 April 1828: Massachusetts Historical Society (pub. D. B. Green, 'Three New Letters of Charles Lamb', *HLQ*, 27 (1963), 83–6).

36. To Edward Moxon, [October 1828]: sold Hodgson's, 8 July 1938 (R. Bentley Collection), Lot 226.

37. To Charles Mathews, 27 October 1828: Brown University, Ms. 52.153.

38. Transcript (made for T. N. Talfourd) of two letters to Sarah James, 5 March 1829 (pub. *Kentucky Review*, 4 (1983), 69) and 11 March 1829 (pub. *CLSB*, NS 43 (1983), 52–3 and containing LmC 112): University of Kentucky.

39. Nine letters to Maria Fryer, 14 May 1829–7 August 1833: Princeton (pub. *PULC*, 6 (1945), 179–99).

40. A 'Second Letter' to Charles Cowden Clarke, postmarked 15 May 1829: University of Leeds, Novello-Cowden Clarke Collection.

41. To John Rickman, 10 July 1829: Bodleian, MS Eng. lett. c. 1, f. 177.

42. Fragment of a letter to [Thomas Westwood?], c. 1830?: Boston Public Library, in XXA/.4977A.2.

43. Note to Jacob Vale Asbury, 1830?: University of Kentucky (containing LmC 4).

44. Note to Edward Moxon, [late winter or spring 1830]: University of Kentucky.

45. To Mrs John Payne, May 1830?: University of Kentucky.

46. To Edward J. Kerly, [early July 1830]: Rosenbach Foundation.

47. To Thomas Noon Talfourd, enclosing will, 11 October 1830: Rosenbach Foundation.

48. Transcript by Mary Cowden Clarke of Lamb's original letter to Vincent Novello, postmarked 19 October 1830: University of Leeds, Novello-Cowden Clarke Collection.

49. To Robert Southey, postmarked 4 November 1830?: Pierpont Morgan.

50. To [Messrs Baldwin & Craddock?], 10 January 1831: untraced (pub. *N&Q* (1942), p. 286).

51. Note to P. G. Patmore, [21? April 1831]: University of Kentucky (written on a letter *to* Lamb from Samuel Rogers of 21 April 1831).

52. To Thomas Noon Talfourd, postmarked 6 June 1831: Massachusetts Historical Society (pub. D. B. Green, 'Three New Letters of Charles Lamb', *HLQ*, 27 (1963), 83–6).

53. Fragment of a letter to Edward Moxon, [August? 1831]: University of Kentucky.

54. To Messrs Nichols, 5 March 1832: National Portrait Gallery collection now in the British Library (pub. G. L. Barnett, 'Charles Lamb's Part in an Edition of Hogarth', *MLQ*, 20 (1959), 315–20).

55. To John Payne, postmarked 14 April 1832: Pierpont Morgan, MA 225, f. 23 (pub. Barnett, pp. 61–2).

56. To Charles Cowden Clarke, [c. 14 April 1832–1833]: Brown University, Ms. 52.153 (pub. Barnett, p. 206 from a transcript by Mary Cowden Clarke at University of Leeds, Novello-Cowden Clarke Collection).

57. To Messrs Bradbury & Evans, [December 1832 or January 1833]: Massachusetts Historical Society (pub. D. B. Green, 'Charles Lamb, Bradury and Evans, and the Title of *The Last Essays of Elia*', *ELN*, 1 (1963), 37–40).

58. Transcript (made for T. N. Talfourd) of a letter to Mary Matilda Betham, [January or July 1833?]: University of Kentucky.

59. To Harriet Isola, 11 February 1833 (containing LmC 164): Berg.

60. To Thomas Noon Talfourd, [April or July 1833?]: University of Kentucky (pub. Vera Watson, *TLS*, 27 April 1956).

61. To C. W. Dilke, postmarked 13 May 1833: Berg.

62. Transcript by Mary Cowden Clarke of Lamb's original letter to Charles Cowden Clarke, postmarked 28 January 1834: University of Leeds, Novello-Cowden Clarke Collection.

63. To unidentified, 25 March [1834?]: University of Kentucky.
64. To Charles Ollier, postmarked 1 January n.y.: Claremont Colleges.
65. To Sarah Stoddart Hazlitt, postmarked 23 April n.y.: SUNY at Buffalo.
66. Note to Taylor and Hessey, watermarked 1820 (containing LmC 105.5): Princeton, Robert H. Taylor Collection.
67. Note to Taylor and Hessey, watermarked 1822: Princeton, Robert H. Taylor Collection.
68. To Thomas Hood, watermarked 1825: National Library of Scotland, MS 582, no. 662.
69. To William Hazlitt, n.d.: Sotheby's, 15 December 1988, Lot 54.
70. Note to J. A. Hessey, n.d.: Princeton, Robert H. Taylor Collection.
71. To John May, n.d.: Yale.

When Lamb retired from the East India Company in March 1825, he had been working there as clerk for thirty-three years. In a letter to Wordsworth, written a week later (6 April 1825, printed *Letters*, II, 466–8 from the original at Texas), he described the end of his 'slavery' as being 'like passing from life into Eternity'. Despite the fact that most of the files of the company were destroyed when the government took over its affairs in 1858, some manuscript traces of Lamb's thirty-three years employment still survive in what is now the India Office Library. Mock reviews of (and written in) Booth's *Tables of Simple Interest* (1818) have been quoted in *Life*, II, 145; see LmC 324. Six account books, audited and initialled by Lamb, have also been preserved and are discussed in Samuel McKechnie, 'Six of Charles Lamb's "True Works" Discovered', *The Times*, 21 June 1955 (reprinted *CLSB*, No. 126, September 1955, pp. [73]–4). All the documents of the India Office Library relating to Lamb are listed in 'Charles Lamb MSS at the India Office', *CLSB*, No. 133, November 1956, p. 132.

In September 1823, Lamb drafted his first will leaving everything to Mary and naming Thomas Allsop, Thomas Noon Talfourd and Bryan Waller Procter as his executors; this will has not come to light. Lamb's second will was dated London, 9 October 1830 and, again, bequeathed everything to Mary but this time named Talfourd and Charles Ryle as executors. Talfourd's copy of the will is at the Rosenbach Foundation, together with a covering letter to him of 11 October 1830; an annotation says that the original will was then in the possession of Charles Ryle. That original was eventually proved and is now lodged at Somerset House, London; facsimile printed *CLSB*, No. 110, January 1953.

A bibliography of Lamb's own writings in his own hand (one page) is now at Harvard (Autograph File). It is signed and dated Widford, 3 November 1834 and he has noted on it: 'These are all the follies I can remember just now.' W. C. Hazlitt printed this manuscript in *The Lambs* (1897), p. 164 and a facsimile of it is included in the catalogue of the John Spoor sale at Parke Bernet (26–8 April 1939, Lot 519).

A fragmentary list of works by Coleridge in Lamb's hand — beginning 'All his MSS. (Letters excepted)/ Above all, *His Tragedy...*' — is at Yale (*Tinker Library*, No. 1455). It is on one side of a scrap which contains (on the other side) some cancelled lines, in Wordsworth's hand, for 'The Brothers'; these lines will be included with Wordsworth's manuscripts in a later volume of the *Index*.

Sometime after Emma Isola became the ward of Charles and Mary Lamb in 1823, Lamb created a Biblical question-and-answer game on 34 cards, presumably as part of Isola's religious training. A facsimile of one of the cards (now at Texas) was printed in the Supplement to *Piccadilly Notes* issued by Sotheran in 1935 (Item 4319).

The extensive collection of Lamb material collected and/or transcribed by Gertrude Anderson, who intended to edit Lamb's letters, was given by Edmund Blunden to Keats House, London.

The collection of Lambiana formed by Major Samuel Butterworth, another painstaking student of Lamb's works, is largely untraced. A large portion (137 volumes including 13 scrapbooks) was offered for sale as Item 665 'The Major Butterworth Collection of Books, Manuscript Notes, Excerpts, Cuttings &c relating to Charles Lamb' in Edwards Catalogue No. 594 (June 1936). According to Prance (p. 49), the collection went to America. Claude Prance himself claims to own thirty volumes 'of lesser importance' from the Butterworth collection. The Charles Lamb Society's collection of Lamb material is now preserved at the Guildhall Library in London.

In Alexander Ireland's collection of papers at the Manchester Central Library, there is a box of material concerning Lamb (Q.824.75.G.4). It contains printed clippings of Lamb's works and letters, reviews of

Lamb's works, articles about Lamb and his circle, sale catalogues, as well as Ireland's transcriptions and notes.

James Dykes Campbell's collection of material relating to Lamb (7 volumes), including transcripts of letters, etc., is at UCLA, No. 421.

ABBREVIATIONS

For general abbreviations, see the list at the front of this volume.

Album Verses
Charles Lamb, *Album Verses; with a Few Others* (London, 1830).
Barnett
George L. Barnett, *Charles Lamb: The Evolution of Elia* (Bloomington, IN, 1964).
Bartlett and Welford Catalogue
Catalogue of Charles Lamb's Library for sale by Bartlett and Welford, Booksellers and Importers, 7 Astor House, New York, [February 1848]; reprinted (with additions) in *A Descriptive Catalogue of the Library of Charles Lamb* (New York, The Dibdin Club, 1897).
CLSB
Charles Lamb Society Bulletin.
Elia
[Charles Lamb], *Elia. Essays which Have Appeared Under that Signature in the* London Magazine (London, 1823).
Emma Isola's Album
For a description, see INTRODUCTION.
Emma Isola's Extract Book
For a description, see INTRODUCTION.
Harper
The Letters of Charles Lamb, introd. by Henry H. Harper, 5 vols (privately printed by Boston Bibliophile Society, 1905). All references to facsimiles are to Volume I.
Last Essays
[Charles Lamb], *The Last Essays of Elia* (London, 1833).
Letters
The Letters of Charles Lamb, ed. E. V. Lucas, 3 vols (London, 1935); reprinted by AMS Press, New York, 1968.
Life
E. V. Lucas, *The Life of Charles Lamb*, 2 vols (London, 1905), including Appendix III 'Charles Lamb's Books'.
Lucas
The Works of Charles and Mary Lamb, ed. E. V. Lucas, 7 vols (London, 1903–5).
Marrs
The Letters of Charles and Mary Anne Lamb, ed. Edwin W. Marrs, Jr (Ithaca, NY, 1975–), Vols I–III pub. to date.
Piccadilly Notes
Piccadilly Notes, No. 13, Charles Lamb Centenary Number (issued by Henry Sotheran, London, 1934).
Poetical Works
Charles Lamb, *The Poetical Works. A New Edition* (London, 1836).
Prance
Claude A. Prance, *Companion to Charles Lamb* (London, 1983).
Specimens
Specimens of English Dramatic Poets, who lived about the Time of Shakspeare (London, 1808).
Woodring
Carl Woodring, 'Charles Lamb in the Harvard Library', *HLB*, 10 (1956), 208–39, 367–401.
Works
Charles Lamb, *The Works*, 2 vols (London, 1818).

ARRANGEMENT

Verse	LmC 1–218
Prose	LmC 219–300.5
Works Edited By Lamb	LmC 301–15
Diaries and Notebooks	LmC 316–19
Marginalia in Printed Books and Manuscripts	LmC 320–59

Charles Lamb

VERSE

'A Heart which felt Unkindness, yet complain'd not'
First pub. *The Letters of Charles Lamb*, ed. Alfred Ainger, 2 vols (London and New York, 1904); Lucas, V, 323n. For another epitaph for Mary Druitt, see LmC 35–8.

LmC 1 Fair copy, revised, of an epitaph for Mary Druitt, here untitled, in a letter to John Rickman, [1? February 1802].

This MS printed *Letters*, I, 298 and Marrs, II, 48.

Huntington, HM 11571.

'A timid grace sits trembling in her eye'
First pub. S. T. Coleridge, *Poems*, 2nd ed (Bristol and London, 1797); Lucas, V, 7.

LmC 2 Fair copy, in a letter to S. T. Coleridge (containing also LmC 136, 202, 210), [30–1 May 1796], postmarked 1 June 1796.

This MS printed *Letters*, I, 6 and Marrs, I, 8.

Huntington, HM 7483.

LmC 3 Fair copy, imperfect (wanting the first two words only), on a scrap (containing also LmC 103); watermarked 1795, dated 1796.

For a reproduction, see FACSIMILES.

Victoria College Library, S.MS.F4.5.

Acrostic ('Judgements are about us thoroughly')
First pub. Lucas, V (1903), 100.

LmC 4 Fair copy of acrostic on Dr Joseph (sic, i.e., Jacob) Vale Asbury, here entitled 'The Battle Royal,/*in Acrostics*.', one page, containing also a note to Dr Asbury.

Microfilm in British Library, M/493; the note to Dr Asbury is unpublished; the last six lines of this MS printed in Parke Bernet sale catalogue, 12 November 1951 (Gabriel Wells Sale), Lot 280 and Maggs Catalogue 832 (1955), Item 1032.

University of Kentucky, W. Hugh Peal Collection.

LmC 5 Fair copy, revised, written on II, 364 of 'Charles Lamb's Album' (see LmC 319).

Texas.

Acrostic ('Sacred be thy leaves, fair Book')
First pub. *Letters*, III (1935), 312; not in Lucas.

LmC 6 Fair copy of acrostic on Sarah Thomas, one page, sent for the album of Mrs Cresswell as a replacement of 'that unlucky sonnet', in a letter to [Rev Dr Cresswell], [probably spring or summer 1831].

Facsimile in British Library, MS Facs. Suppl. XI(2), f. 7; the letter printed in the first publication.

Edwards Catalogue 880 (1965), Item 7a.

Acrostic ('Sleep hath treasures worth retracing')
First pub. John Hollingshead, *My Lifetime*, 2 vols (London, 1895); Lucas, V, 374–5.

LmC 7 Acrostic on Sarah James of Beguildy, one page, signed; dated Enfield, 16 April 1831.

Christie's, 14 June 1979 (Houghton Sale), Lot 283, sold to Fleming.

An Acrostic against Acrostics ('Envy not the wretched Poet')
First pub. W. C. Hazlitt, *The Lambs* (London and New York, 1897); Lucas, V, 97.

LmC 8 Fair copy, acrostic on Edward Hogg, one page; watermarked 1828.

This MS printed *Letters*, III, 262.

Huntington, HM 11690.

Acrostic, To a Lady Who Desired Me to Write Her Epitaph ('Grace Joanna here doth lie')
First pub. *Album Verses* (1830); Lucas, V, 60–1.

LmC 9 Fair copy, acrostic on Grace Joanna Williams, here entitled 'Epitaph on a Lady living: written at her request', signed, one page.

This MS originally enclosed with a letter to Grace Joanna Williams, 21 April 1830 (*Letters*, III, 267–8) now also at the Rosenbach Foundation; lines 1–6 of this MS printed in Anderson Galleries sale catalogue, 3 November 1915 (Thatcher Sale), Lot 627.

Rosenbach Foundation.

Acrostic/to E. B. ('Ellen, friend of tuneful Dyer')
First pub. George L. Barnett, 'Charles Lamb and the Button Family: An Unpublished Poem and Letter', *HLQ*, 19 (1956), 191–5; reprinted in Peter A. Brier, 'An Unpublished Poem by Charles Lamb: "Acrostic To E. B."', *ELN*, 10 (1972), 29–30.

LmC 10 Fair copy of an acrostic on Ellen Button, in her album, signed; undated but between poems dated 19 October 1832 and 17 November 1838; the album (containing 48 pages) is watermarked 1828 and was used 1831–8.

Huntington, HM 11586.

***Album Verses* (1830): Dedication**, see LmC 220.

Angel Help ('This rare tablet doth include')
First pub. *New Monthly Magazine*, June 1827 (38-line version); collected *Album Verses* (1830) (36-line version); Lucas, V, 48–9. For a parody of these lines, composed either by Charles or Mary Lamb, see LmC 111.

LmC 11 Revised, here entitled 'Lines written upon a Picture in the possession of Charles Aders, Esqr., Euston Square. The subject, a young Saint in the Romanish Calendar, who having spun past midnight to maintain a poor mother who lies dying by her, and falling asleep from fatigue — angels come to her work. An angel is watering a Lily in another part of the room, an emblem of her purity', 39 lines (one cancelled), 2 pages, signed.

Parke Bernet, 22 October 1957 (Sweet Sale), Lot 175.

LmC 12 Fair copy, here untitled, in Elizabeth Aders's album (containing also LmC 111, 156), signed, 38 lines, 2 pages (one leaf), sent to Aders, c. April 1827, as an accompaniment to the drawing by Jacob Götzenberger also in the album (mounted on f. 21).

This MS printed and discussed in James T. Wills, 'New Lamb Material in the Aders Album: Jacob Götzenberger and Two Versions of "Angel Help"', *HLB*, 22 (1974), 409 (including a facsimile of the drawing, Plate I). This album also contains poems by S. T. Coleridge (see CoS 412, 544, 772) and William Wordsworth.

Harvard, MS Eng 1094(20).

LmC 13 Fair copy, here entitled 'Verses to describe a Picture, in the possession of C. Aders Esqr Euston Square.', 2 pages, signed, in William Ayrton's Scrapbook.

Huntington, RB 110244, Vol. III, ff. [37v–8].

LmC 13.5 Fair copy, revised, here untitled, 38 lines, signed (initials), in Coleridge's Notebook 26 (see S. T. Coleridge, CoS 1365); notebook used 1826–7.

British Library, Add. MS 47524, ff. 102–3v.

LmC 14 Transcript by Emma Isola, here entitled 'Angel Help: a legendary subject./The Picture in the possession of C. Aders Esqr Euston Square', 38 lines, 2 pages (one leaf containing also LmC 119), originally part of Emma Isola's Extract Book; watermarked 1825.

Texas.

Another, To Her Youngest Daughter ('Least Daughter, but not least beloved, of *Grace!*')
First pub. *Album Verses* (1830); Lucas, V, 61.

LmC 15 Acrostic on Louisa Clare [Williams], one page (containing also LmC 72, both headed 'Acrostics/To Josepha Maria [and] To Louisa Clare Williams'), these lines headed '2'; on verso of letter from Emma Isola to [Grace Joanna Williams], Enfield, 7 April [1830].

This MS printed *Letters*, III, 261–2.

Berg.

'As humble guests at solemn cheer'
No publication traced.

LmC 16 Fair copy, 10 lines, signed by both Charles and Mary Lamb, followed by a note of dedication to John Bowring, one page (apparently the final leaf) torn from Bowring's 'Album Amicorum'.

Bowring's album was sold by Puttick & Simpson, 9 May 1929, Lot 240; this MS was Lot 239 in the same sale and Lot 241 was another leaf torn from the album containing John Keats's poem 'Sonnet to Sleep' (see John Keats, KeJ 400).

Brown University, Ms. 52.181.

'As when a child on some long winter's night', see S. T. Coleridge, CoS 368 ('Mrs Siddons'), for this probably joint composition; published with Lamb's works in Lucas, V, 3.

Ballad ('The clouds are blackening, the storms threatening')
First pub. in a version entitled 'Thekla's Song' in S. T. Coleridge's translation of Schiller's *The Piccolomini* (London, 1800), as a note to II, vii, 33; revised version first pub. in *John Woodvil* (London, 1802); Lucas, V, 27.

LmC 17 Fair copy of a translation from Schiller, written for Coleridge's translation of *The Piccolomini*, here untitled, on first page of a letter (containing also LmC 61 and Lamb's transcript of a Scotch ballad) to Thomas Manning, [mid-April? 1800].

This MS printed *Letters*, I, 182 and Marrs, I, 195; facsimile in Harper, I, 110.

Huntington, HM 11697.

LmC 18 Faircopy, here entitled 'A song from Schiller', in one of Lamb's Commonplace Books (see LmC 317); watermarked 1804.

Huntington, HM 2274, f. 25v.

A Ballad: Noting the Difference of Rich and Poor, in the Ways of a Rich Noble's Palace and a Poor Workhouse ('In a costly palace Youth goes clad in gold')
First pub. as conclusion to Extract IV of the 'Curious Fragments from a Common-place Book of Robert Burton' in *John Woodvil* (London, 1802); revised and collected separately *Works* (1818); Lucas, V, 28–9. These lines were probably also included in a letter, now lost, to S. T. Coleridge of 6 August 1800 (see *Letters*, I, 197–9 and Marrs, I, 218–19).

LmC 19 Fair copy of an imitation of Robert Burton, here entitled 'The Case plainly stated between/a rich noble's Palace & a poor Workhouse'; in a letter to Thomas Manning, [8 June 1800].

This MS printed *Letters*, I, 191–2 and Marrs, I, 209–10; facsimile in Harper, I, 95–6.

Huntington, HM 11695.

LmC 20 Transcript in an unidentified hand, here entitled (in Lamb's hand) 'Ballad. to the tune of the "Old and the New Courtier."' and signed by him 'L', 2 pages (one leaf), in Mrs Daniel Cresswell's album (containing also LmC 26 and 124); album used 1831–43.

This album was presented to Mrs Cresswell by her brother Edward in 1843; as well as the three Lamb items, it contains Mary Lamb's 'Dialogue between a mother and child', watercolours and sketches.

Berg.

'Because you boast poetic Grandsire'
First pub. *The Letters of Charles Lamb*, ed. Alfred Ainger, 2 vols (London and New York, 1888); *Letters*, III, 52–3.

LmC 21 Verse letter to John Bates Dibdin, 2 pages (one leaf), postmarked 14 July 1826.

Facsimile in British Library, MS Facs. Suppl. X(110), ff. 375–6.

University of Kentucky, W. Hugh Peal Collection.

A Black in an Album ('Left hand side down Parson's Lane')
First printed (lines 1–4 and 27–32) in facsimile in *Piccadilly Notes* (1934), Item 4130; no other publication traced.

LmC 22 Fair copy, signed, one page, 32 lines, originally written for (and in) Emma Isola's Extract Book.

Facsimile in *Piccadilly Notes*, p. 377.

Berg.

The Boy, the Mother, and the Butterfly ('Young William held a Butterfly in chase')
First pub. (facsimile) in *The Bibliophile*, July 1908; not in Lucas.

LmC 23 Fair copy, 12 lines, signed, in the album (of 99 pages) of Alicia Mann (including contributions by Thomas Hood, Edward Moxon, Thomas Westwood, etc.); dated Enfield Chase, 9 October 1827.

Facsimile in first publication and Parke Bernet sale catalogue, 15–16 January 1941, p. 72; this MS printed and discussed in Fred L. Standley, 'Charles Lamb: An Unpublished Album Verse', *ELN*, 5 (1967), 33–4.

Florida State University, Strozier Library, Shaw Childhood in Poetry Collection.

LmC 24 Fair copy, 8 lines, one page; c. 1820.

This MS printed George L. Barnett, 'An Unprinted Poem by Charles Lamb', *HLQ*, 6 (1943), 357–8.

Huntington, HM 12286.

'Brevis Esse Laboro'/'One Dip' ('Much speech obscures the sense; the soul of wit')
First pub. as '"One Dip"' in *The Life, Letters and Writing of Charles Lamb*, ed. Percy Fitzgerald, 6 vols (London, 1876); reprinted with an explanatory essay in Archdeacon Hessey's 'Old Customs at Merchant Taylor's', *The Taylorian*, March 1884, pp. 116–19; Lucas, V, 108.

LmC 25 Fair copy, signed 'H[essey]', one page (containing also LmC 206), here entitled 'One dip', written for J. A. Hessey's son's school exercise.

Berg.

Cheap Gifts: A Sonnet ('O lift with reverent hand that tarnish'd flower')
First pub. *The Athenaeum*, 15 February 1834; collected *Poetical Works* (1836); Lucas, V, 77.

LmC 26 Fair copy, here untitled, including the (signed) prefatory note, one page, in Mrs Daniel Cresswell's album (containing also LmC 20 (see for description) and 124); album used 1831–43, this poem probably dates from 1831.

Berg.

The Christening ('Array'd — a half-angelic sight —')
First pub. *Blackwood's Magazine*, May 1829; collected *Album Verses* (1830); Lucas, V, 49.

LmC 27 Fair copy, in a letter (containing also LmC 79) to [William Blackwood], Enfield, [spring 1829].

The letter only printed *Letters*, III, 216 (without location).

National Library of Scotland, Watson Collection, MS 582, no. 663.

Chusing a Name ('I have got a new-born sister')
First pub. [Charles and Mary Lamb], *Poetry for Children*, 2 vols (London, 1809); Lucas, III, 354–5.

LmC 28 Transcript by Robert Lloyd, signed 'C. L.', 2 pages (of the 4 pages (2 leaves) containing also transcripts by Lloyd of three poems by Mary Lamb signed 'M. L.': 'Breakfast', 'Choosing a Profession' and 'Summer Friends'); containing also a 3-page letter from Robert Lloyd to his wife written during a visit to the Lambs in London, [4 April 1809].

This MS printed (lines 1–15) in American Art Association sale catalogue, 14–15 February 1935 (Terry Sale), pp. 116–17; the letter from Lloyd to his wife is quoted and discussed in *Charles Lamb and the Lloyds*, ed. E. V. Lucas (London, 1898), pp. 160–1.

Berg.

'*Ci git* the remains of Margaret Dix', for a lost MS, see INTRODUCTION.

[A Comic Opera], see INTRODUCTION.

Count Rumford ('I deal in aliments fictitious')
This epigram, written for *The Morning Post* but rejected, was first pub. *The Letters of Charles Lamb*, ed. Alfred Ainger, 2 vols (London and New York, 1904); Lucas, VII, 992 (Appendix III); *Letters*, I, 294; Marrs, II, 46.

LmC 29 Fair copy, here untitled, 4 lines, in a letter (containing also LmC 115, 197) to John Rickman, [mid-January 1802].

This MS printed in Marrs, II, 46 (previous printings date the letter 14 January 1802).

Huntington, HM 11569.

Curious Fragments from a Common-place Book of Robert Burton, see LmC 19–20, 61–2.

The Dissolution of the Roman Republic, see INTRODUCTION.

Dramatic Fragment ('All are not false. I knew a youth who died'), for these lines, originally part of 'John Woodvil' and discarded, see 'John Woodvil', especially LmC 88.

'Emma, eldest of your name', see LmC 162.

Epicedium/Going or Gone ('Fine merry franions')
First pub. *The Table Book*, ed. William Hone (London, 1827), as '*For the Table Book*/Gone or Going' (eleven 8-line stanzas); collected *Album Verses* (1830), as 'Going or Gone' (nine 8-line stanzas, without previous stanzas 7–8); Lucas, V, 70–2 (original stanzas 7–8 printed pp. 318–19).

LmC 30 Fair copy, revised, here entitled 'For the Table Book/Gone or Going.', being the first publication of version containing 88 lines in 12 numbered stanzas, 2 pages (one leaf), signed 'Elia.', including a few footnotes and a note to William Hone on the verso, [June 1827]; watermarked 1821.

Note to Hone printed *Letters*, III, 92.

Huntington, HM 13300.

Epigrams II ('Ye Politicians, tell me, pray')
First pub. *The Examiner*, 22 March 1812; Lucas, V, 103.

LmC 31 Fair copy, revised, here entitled 'On the Prince <Regent dismissing> breaking with his Party', on an unnumbered page of one of Lamb's Commonplace Books (see LmC 316).

Mentioned Lucas, V, 335.

Berg.

LmC 32 Transcript in William Ayrton's Scrapbook, here entitled 'Epigram/upon the Prince of Wales becoming Regent of the United Kingdom', 4 lines, one page.

Not mentioned Lucas.

Huntington, RB 110244, Vol. III, f. [21].

Epilogue to Godwin's Tragedy of "Antonio"
('Ladies, ye've seen how Guzman's consort died')
Godwin's play *Antonio* first performed Drury Lane Theatre, 13 December 1800 and was published without Lamb's Epilogue; the Epilogue was first pub. *The Letters of Charles Lamb*, ed. T. N. Talfourd (London, 1837); Lucas, V, 121–2. For Lamb's copy of the play and playbill, see LmC 334–5 and for his notes, see LmC 263.

LmC 33 Fair copy, here untitled, including marginal glosses, in a letter to Thomas Manning, postmarked 13 December 1800.

This MS printed *Letters*, I, 226–8 and Marrs, I, 251–4.

Huntington, HM 11659.

LmC 34 Revisions, being the cancellation of lines 16–17 and a revised line 18, in a letter to William Godwin, [10 December 1800].

This MS printed in Marrs, I, 250–1 (as owned by Lord Abinger); microfilm at Bodleian and Duke University.

Sotheby's, 23–4 July 1987, Lot 85, sold to Calder.

Epitaph on a Young Lady who lived neglected and died obscure ('Under this cold marble stone')
First pub. *Morning Post*, 7 February 1804; Lucas, V, 80. For another epitaph for Mary Druitt, see LmC 1. A 12-line version was printed (apparently from a now-lost MS) by John Payne Collier in *An Old Man's Diary*, 2 vols (privately printed, 1871–2) and reprinted in Lucas, V, 323; Lucas guesses wrongly that the source was the transcript in Sarah Stoddart Hazlitt's album (LmC 38) which has only 9 lines.

LmC 35 Fair copy, a slightly variant version, here entitled 'Epitaphium Alterum et valde Melius/Authore C. L.', one page, addressed on the verso to John Rickman; dated in an unidentified hand 15 February 1802, watermarked 1800.

Huntington, HM 11572.

LmC 36 Fair copy, a slightly variant version, here untitled, in a letter to Thomas Manning, [23 April 1802].

This MS printed in *Letters*, I, 311 and Marrs, II, 61; facsimile in Harper, Vol. I, and printed III, 120–3 (where dated 1 May 1803).

Huntington, HM 11673.

LmC 37 Here entitled 'On Mary Druitt who died aged 19.', in a letter to William Wordsworth (including also Lamb's transcripts of extracts from Charles Cotton and William Cowper), 5 March 1803.

This MS printed *Letters*, I, 343–4 and Marrs, II, 105.

Texas.

LmC 38 Transcript on p. 82 of Sarah Stoddart Hazlitt's album (see LmC 338), here entitled 'Epitaph for Mary Druitt', 9 lines.

Berg.

Existence, Considered in Itself, No Blessing ('Of these sad truths consideration had —')
First pub. *The Athenaeum*, 7 July 1832; Lucas, V, 89–90.

LmC 39 Lines 1–16, including 4 lines of heading (possibly a letter) and 11 lines of Latin, one page.

Lines 1–4 of this MS printed Sotheby's sale catalogue, where the MS is described as a poem-letter; this MS and LmC 40 together presumably form one MS.

Sotheby's, 14 July 1931, Lot 420, sold to Spencer.

LmC 40 Lines 17–31, revised, here entitled '*Existence, simply considered in itself, no Blessing*/From the Latin of Palingenius.' and beginning 'Not wine, *as* wine, men chuse, but as it came', signed, one page of a folded leaf (containing also 8 lines in Latin in an unidentified hand), as sent to C. W. Dilke, editor of *The Athenaeum*; watermarked 1828.

This MS printed in Lyle H. Kendall, Jr, *A Descriptive Catalogue of The W. L. Lewis Collection* (Fort Worth, Texas, 1970), pp. 75–6.

Texas Christian University.

A Farewell to Tobacco ('May the Babylonish curse')
First pub. *The Reflector*, Vol II, No. 4 (1812); collected *Works* (1818); Lucas, V, 32–5.

LmC 41 Fair copy, 7 leaves (rectos only), here entitled 'To his *quondam* Brethren of the Pipe, Capt. B —— , and J —— R —— Esqr. the Author dedicates this his last Farewell to Tobacco', including a covering title in Lamb's hand; c. 1805.

This MS printed with facsimiles of first and last pages in *Tobacco Catalogue*, IV, 205–9 (Item 1158).

NYPL, Arents Collection.

LmC 42 In a letter to William and Dorothy Wordsworth, 28 September 1805.

This MS printed *Letters*, II, 402–5 and Marrs, II, 177–81.

Texas.

The First Leaf of Spring ('Thou fragile, filmy gossamery thing')
First pub. *The Athenaeum*, 10 January 1846 (including an accompanying note claiming previous publication); Lucas, V, 92–3.

LmC 43 Fair copy, one page, 31 lines.

Harvard, Autograph File.

LmC 44 Transcript?, on the opening leaves (containing also LmC 199) of the album of [T. T.?] Lachlan, annotated 'Written by Mr Lamb at Enfield on the first leaf of my sister Sarah's album. T. T. L. 1832. In Lady's Magazine...June 1835.'

This album described by its then-owner, E. G. B[lakiston?], in 'Notes on "The Letters of Charles and Mary Lamb"', *N&Q*, 180 (1941), 331–2. No album of Sarah Lachlan's containing these lines by Lamb has come to light. In the Notes to this poem in *The Works of Charles Lamb*, ed. William Macdonald, 12 vols (London, 1903), V, 413, the copy text is described as 'the original (or at least a copy in Lamb's handwriting) in the Album in the possession of Mrs Blakiston.'.

Owned (1941) E. G. B[lakiston?] (see *N&Q*).

'For Newark's seat Three Orators contend'
No publication traced. In Ford and Hodson's *History of Enfield* (1873), Lamb is said to have written election squibs on behalf of Sergeant Wilde for use in the Newark elections of 1829. Lucas, who was apparently unaware of this MS, explores the Lamb connection with the elections in a note in Lucas, V, 341–2 where he prints two possible Lamb squibs, neither of which is in the present MS.

LmC 45 Fair copy, revised, of election squibs for Sergeant Wilde, 2 pages (one leaf), including 5 numbered verses beginning as follows: 1) 8 lines, as above; 2) 'Not always do the *names* of men bely', 6 lines; 3) 'Newcastle swears. Saddler professes *talents*', 4 lines on verso; 4) 'If Gardner dined with Sergeant W—e', 8 lines, revised, on verso; 5) 'When Eden's foolish Feeder was restricted', 4 lines on verso.

Formerly in the Paul C. Richards Collection deposited at Boston University.

For the 'Table Book' ('Laura, too partial to her friends' enditing')
These lines, meant for *The Table Book*, ed. William Hone (London, 1827) but not published there; first pub. W. C. Hazlitt, *Mary and Charles Lamb* (London, 1874), p. 268; Lucas, V, 108.

LmC 46 Revised, signed (initials), headed 'For the "T. B."/Lines for an Album', in a letter to William Hone, 2 September [1827].

This MS printed in *Letters*, III, 125.

Sotheby's, 2 November 1965, Lot 434, sold to Maggs.

LmC 47 Here untitled and beginning 'Mary too partial to her friends enditing', signed, on a scrap cut from an album.

Sotheby's, 18 December 1934, Lot 199.

Free Thoughts on Several Eminent Composers
('Some cry up Haydn, some Mozart')
First pub. *Monthly Repository*, 1835; collected *Poetical Works* (1836); Lucas, V, 77–8.

LmC 48 Fair copy, slightly revised, signed, one page, originally in a letter to William Ayrton (now torn from it) of [20 May 1830].

The letter to William Ayrton from which this was torn, also at the Huntington, HM 7524, is printed in *Letters*, III, 276.

Huntington, HM 7525.

LmC 49 Fair copy, in a letter to Sarah Stoddart Hazlitt, dated 'Enfield, Saturday' and postmarked 24 May 1830.

This letter (without verses) printed in *Letters*, III, 279–81; facsimile in Parke Bernet sale catalogue, 7–8 February 1944, Lot 420.

Texas.

LmC 50 Fair copy, on 3 pages of Vincent Novello's album, signed, including 10 additional lines, possibly appended either by Charles or Mary Lamb (signed by the latter), beginning 'The reason why my brother's so severe'.

Novello's album contains his own autograph music, verses, letters by others and, inserted, autograph MSS of Mozart, Beethoven, Haydn, Mendelssohn, Liszt, etc. The ten additional lines appended to this MS are printed in Lucas, V, 322 and *Letters*, III, 281 (where it is suggested that they may be written by Lamb himself impersonating his sister); this suggestion is reasserted by Carl Woodring in 'Lamb's Hoaxes and the Lamb Canon', *CLSB*, NS2 (1975), 39–41; facsimile of last page of this MS in Sotheby's sale catalogue, 13 December 1950, Lot 181 (when the album was sold to Novello & Co.).

Phillips, 14 June 1989.

LmC 51 Fair copy, signed, 2 pages (one leaf numbered in pencil 66), originally in Emma Isola's Extract Book.

Facsimile of lines 1–6 and 36–8 in *Piccadilly Notes* (1934), p. 378.

Princeton, Robert H. Taylor Collection.

LmC 52 Printed copy, revised on lines 15–16 ('Jubal' and 'Tubal' reversed), mounted on II, 12 of 'Charles Lamb's Album' (LmC 319).

Texas.

LmC 53 Transcript in William Ayrton's Scrapbook, annotated 'Address'd to Mr Ayrton.', 2 leaves (rectos only); dated Enfield, May 1830.

This transcript not mentioned Lucus.

Huntington, RB 110244, Vol. III, ff. [43–4, rectos only].

The Gentle Look, see S. T. Coleridge, CoS 203–5, for 3 MSS of this sonnet published as Coleridge's; the original lines 10–14 were composed by Lamb but only lines 10–11 survived into the published version; the lines are not published with Lamb's works but in the Notes in Lucas, V, 277.

The Gipsy's Malison ('"Suck, baby, suck, mother's love grows by giving"'), for an unlocated MS, see INTRODUCTION.

'Had I but *gold* to my desire'
First printed as '[To Emma Isola]' (facsimile of lines 1–5, 14, signature and date only) in *Piccadilly Notes* (1934), p. 380.

LmC 54 Fair copy, 14 lines, signed (initials), one page, originally in Emma Isola's Extract Book; dated 25 May 1831.

Facsimile as above.

Princeton, Robert H. Taylor Collection.

Harmony in Unlikeness ('By Enfield lanes, and Winchmore's verdant hill')
First pub. *Album Verses* (1830); Lucas, V, 54.

LmC 55 Fair copy, in Emma Isola's Album (mounted on f. 31), here untitled, signed, one page.

Harvard, MS Eng 601.66(31).

Hercules Pacificatus ('In days of yore, ere early Greece')
First pub. *Englishman's Magazine*, August 1831; Lucas, V, 85–8.

LmC 56 Fair copy, revised, subtitled 'A Tale from Suidas', signed (initials), 6 numbered pages (3 leaves).

Pierpont Morgan, MA 225, ff. 7–9v.

LmC 57 Printed clipping (pp. 606–8 of a periodical), containing a revision to line 60 in Lamb's hand, inserted between II, 406 and 407 of 'Charles Lamb's Album' (LmC 319).

This MS mentioned Lucas, V, 326.

Texas.

'Here lies the body of Timothy Wagstaff', for a lost MS, see INTRODUCTION.

'Here lieth the body of Captain Sturms', for a lost MS, see INTRODUCTION.

Hester ('When maidens such as Hester die')
First pub. *Works* (1818); Lucas, V, 30–1.

LmC 58 Here untitled, 32 lines, 2 pages (one leaf), pasted into the back of Coleridge's Notebook 21 (see S. T. Coleridge, CoS 1359); 1803?

This MS printed in *The Notebooks of Samuel Taylor Coleridge*, ed. Kathleen Coburn, Vol. I, entry 21.593, serial no. 1368.

British Library, Add. MS 47518, f. 135r–v.

LmC 59 Fair copy, here entitled 'Hester Savory.', one page, on verso of a letter to Thomas Manning, postmarked 23 March 1803.

This MS printed *Letters*, I, 336 and Marrs, II, 107–8.

Huntington, HM 13294.

'How well The Milestones' use doth this express'
Lamb's translation of 2 lines of Latin verse by Vincent Bourne first pub. (as Stephen Gwynn's translation) in *Letters*, III (1935), 177.

LmC 60 Letter to John Rickman in Latin in which Lamb transcribes 2 lines of verse by Vincent Bourne, followed by his 2-line English translation, postmarked 3 October 1828.

This letter printed *Letters*, III, 174–6 (translation on pp. 176–8).

Huntington, HM 11583.

Hypochondriacus ('By myself walking')
First pub. *John Woodvil* (London, 1802), as Extract III 'A Conceipt of Diabolical Possession' of the 'Curious Fragments from a Common-place Book of Robert Burton'; collected separately *Works* (1818); Lucas, V, 27–9.

LmC 61 Fair copy, revised, here entitled 'A conceipt of Diabolical Possession', on first page of a letter (containing also LmC 17 and Lamb's transcript of a Scotch ballad) to Thomas Manning, [mid-April? 1800].

This MS printed in *Letters*, I, 181–2 and Marrs, I, 193–4; facsimile in Harper, I, 110.

Huntington, HM 11697.

LmC 62 Fair copy, revised, here entitled 'A Conceipt of Diabolical Possession <(imperfect)>/(by Burton, Author of Anatomy of melancholy)', in one of Lamb's Commonplace Books (LmC 317); watermarked 1804.

Huntington, HM 2274, f. 25v.

'If ever I marry a Wife'
First pub. T. N. Talfourd, *Final Memorials of Charles Lamb*, 2 vols (London, 1848), I, 175; Lucas, VI, 402. Lamb writes, in the letter to Coleridge entered below, that he inscribed the quatrain in an unidentified edition of Hannah More's *Coelebs in Search of a Wife* borrowed from an unidentified woman; a copy of the 2-volume London, 1809 edition is listed in Jackson's MS catalogue purporting to be from Lamb's library (see INTRODUCTION) with no mention of MS verses or marginalia.

LmC 63 Fair copy of a quatrain on Hannah More's *Coelebs in Search of a Wife*, on page 3 of a letter to S. T. Coleridge, [7 June 1809].

This MS printed *Letters*, II, 75 and Marrs, III, 14; facsimile in Harper, Vol. I.

Huntington, HM 11679.

'If from my lips some angry accents fall'
First pub. S. T. Coleridge, *Poems*, 2nd ed (Bristol and London, 1797); collected *Works* (1818); Lucas, V, 8.

LmC 64 Fair copy, here entitled 'to my sister', in a letter to S. T. Coleridge, postmarked 27 May 1796.

This MS printed in *Letters*, I, 2 and Marrs, I, 4.

Huntington, HM 7482.

LmC 65 Transcript on p. 83 of Sarah Stoddart Hazlitt's album (see LmC 338), here entitled 'Sonnet'.

Berg.

'If Gardner dined with Sergeant W—e', see LmC 45.

In My Own Album ('Fresh clad from heaven in robes of white')
First pub. *The Bijou*, ed. William Fraser (London, 1828), as 'Verses for an Album'; collected *Album Verses* (1830); Lucas, V, 47–8.

LmC 66 Transcript in William Ayrton's Scrapbook, here entitled 'Written in an Album on a Work entitled the *Bijou*', seven 3-line stanzas (wanting stanza 3), annotated 'from the Manuscript before it was printed', 4 pages; dated 1827.

This transcript not mentioned Lucas.

Huntington, RB 110244, Vol. III, ff. [39v–41].

LmC 67 Transcript by Henry Crabb Robinson, here entitled 'Verses for an Album', in a letter from Robinson to Miss Wordsworth, 3 December 1827, postmarked 7 December 1827.

In the letter, Robinson says he is transcribing the lines from a (first?) publication.

Dr Williams's Library, Henry Crabb Robinson Papers, 1827–1829 Volume, f. 35.

In tabulam eximii pictoris B. Haydoni, in quâ Solymœi, adveniente Domino, palmas in viâ prosternentes mirâ arte depinguntur ('Quid vult iste equitans? et quid oclit ista virorum')
First pub. *The Champion*, 6–7 May 1820; Lucas, V, 82. For Lamb's translation of these lines, see LmC 194.

LmC 68 Fair copy, revised, in Latin, here entitled 'In tabulam egregii pictoris B. Haydoni, in quâ Judæi ante pedes Christi palmas prosternentes, mirâ arte, depinguntur' and beginning 'Quid...et quid velit ista virorum', signed 'Carlagnulus', one page, inserted (at 20 April 1821) in B. R. Haydon's Diary, Vol. X (f. 21).

This MS printed in *Life of Benjamin Robert Haydon*, ed. Tom Taylor, 3 vols (London, 1853), II, 13.

Harvard, fMS Eng 1331(13), f. 21.

LmC 69 Transcript in an unidentified hand, here entitled as published and begining 'Quid...et quid velit ista virorum', one page; watermarked 1818?.

This MS sold as autograph in the Dean Sage sale at Parke Bernet, 15–16 January 1941, Lot 243 (with LmC 146, 194) but returned because of doubts as to the authenticity of the hand; Dean Sage bequeathed the MSS to Yale in 1941.

Yale.

In the Album of a Clergyman's Lady ('An Album is a Garden, not for show')
First pub. *Album Verses* (1830); Lucas, V, 43.

LmC 70 Transcript by Emma Isola, here untitled, one page (on a leaf containing also LmC 80, 155), originally in Emma Isola's Extract Book.

This MS mentioned *Piccadilly Notes* (1934), Item 4135.

Texas.

LmC 71 Signed, one page.

Lines 1–6 of this MS printed in Maggs Catalogue 785, p. 52.

Maggs Catalogue 785 (1949), Item 727.

In the Album of a Very Young Lady ('Joy to unknown Josepha, who, I hear')
First pub. *Album Verses* (1830); Lucas, V, 45.

LmC 72 Acrostic on Josepha Maria [Williams], one page (containing also LmC 15, both entitled 'Acrostics/To Josepha Maria [and] To Louisa Clare Williams'), these lines headed '1', on verso of a letter from Emma Isola to [Grace Joanna Williams], Enfield, 7 April [1830].

This MS (including the letter) printed *Letters*, III, 261–2.

Berg.

In the Album of Catherine Orkney ('Canadia! boast no more the toils')
First pub. *The Reflector*, 15 December 1832, as 'Catherine Orkney'; collected *Poetical Works* (1836); Lucas, V, 74–5.

LmC 73 Fair copy, signed, one leaf (containing also LmC 76 and Lamb's transcript of William Oldys's 'The Fly'), here entitled 'Catherine Orkney'.

Facsimile (a clipping from an unidentified sale catalogue) at University of Reading, Elkin Mathews Collection, MS 392/8/2.

Huntington, HM 13302.

LmC 74 Fair copy, revised, here untitled, one page, mounted on I, 380 of 'Charles Lamb's Album' (LmC 319).

Facsimile in NYPL, Manuscript Division, Madigan Collection.

Texas.

In the Album of Edith S[outhey] ('In Christian world Mary the garland wears!')
First pub. *The Athenaeum*, 9 March 1833, as 'Christian Names of Women'; collected *Poetical Works* (1836); Lucas, V, 73. In *Letters*, III, 355, Lucas prints a MS of these lines (entitled 'Christian Names of Women/(To Edith S——)' which contains a note to the editor of *The Athenaeum* (C. W. Dilke); no such MS has been located.

LmC 75 Fair copy, revised, signed (initials), here entitled 'Christian names of Women/To Edith Southey', one page (scrap).

This MS version varies from the text in Lucas.

Harvard, bMS Am 1622(117).

LmC 76 Fair copy, signed, here entitled 'Christian names of women. To Edith Southey.', one page (on a leaf containing also LmC 73 and Lamb's transcript of William Oldys's 'The Fly').

Facsimile (clipping from an unidentified sale catalogue) at University of Reading, Elkin Mathews Collection, MS 392/8/2.

Huntington, HM 13302.

In the Album of Lucy Barton ('Little Book, surnamed of *white*')
First pub. *Album Verses* (1830); Lucas, V, 44.

LmC 77 Here entitled 'For the First Leaf of Hannah's Album', signed, 2 pages (one leaf), followed by beginning only of letter to Bernard Barton, [30 September 1824].

University of Kentucky, W. Hugh Peal Collection.

LmC 78 Transcript by Bernard Barton of the above (i.e. first leaf of a letter to him from Lamb containing these lines) (f. 37r–v), here untitled, together with the original second leaf (f. 38) of the letter, annotated by [Lucy Barton?] 'This half sheet in my album — copied here by BB —'; letter dated and postmarked 30 September 1824.

This MS printed *Letters*, II, 439–40 (without mentioning that first leaf is a transcript); so noted in Duane Schneider, 'The Lucas Edition of Lamb's *Letters*: Corrections and Notes', *N&Q*, NS21 (1974), 173.

British Library, Add. MS 35256, ff. 37–8.

In the Album of Miss —— ('Such goodness in your face doth shine')
First pub. *Blackwood's Magazine*, May 1829, as 'For a Young Lady's Album'; collected *Album Verses* (1830); Lucas, V, 44–5.

LmC 79 Fair copy, here entitled 'For <In> a Young Lady's Album.', signed, in a letter (containing also LmC 27) to [William Blackwood], Enfield, [spring 1829].

Letter only printed *Letters*, III, 216.

National Library of Scotland, Watson Collection, MS 582, no. 663.

In the Album of Miss Daubeny ('Some poets by poetic law')
First pub. *Album Verses* (1830); Lucas, V, 46.

LmC 80 Fair copy, here entitled 'Stanzas for Miss Daubeny's Album, Dulwich.', signed, one page (on a leaf containing also LmC 79, 155), originally in Emma Isola's Extract Book.

Facsimile (lines 1–8, 30–2 and signature only) in *Piccadilly Notes* (1934), p. 382.

Texas.

In the Album of Mrs Jane Towers ('Lady Unknown, who crav'st from me Unknown')
First pub. *Album Verses* (1830); Lucas, V, 47.

LmC 81 Here untitled, written in the album of Isabella Jane Towers, signed; dated Enfield Chase, 19 December 1827.

Stanford University, Fe 30, Folder 13.

LmC 82 Transcript by Mary Cowden Clarke, headed 'Copy of a sonnet addressed to Mrs Towers', annotated (on f. 98, page 3 of folded leaf) 'The foregoing sonnet was written out by the proud and happy *wife* of "Charles Clarke", for her dear father — Vincent Novello, also one of "Charles Clarke's" admirer's and his Best Friend. —', signed 'Charles Lamb, Enfield Chase, 19th Decr 1827', one page (page 1 of leaf); watermarked 1828.

British Library, Add. MS 11730, f. 97.

In the Autograph Book of Mrs Sergeant W—— ('Had I a power, Lady, to my will')
First pub. *Album Verses* (1830); Lucas, V, 43.

LmC 83 Fair copy, here untitled, signed, one page; together with a letter to Martin Charles Burney, postmarked 19 March 1829.

This MS printed *Letters*, III, 211–12; microfilm in British Library, M/493.

University of Kentucky, W. Hugh Peal Collection.

John Woodvil

Lamb's first version of the drama that would be published as *John Woodvil* in 1802 was entitled 'Pride's Cure' and he began writing it in August 1798. In the latter part of 1799, he sent transcripts of the play to several friends for comment, including Manning (see LmC 84 below), Wordsworth and Kemble (neither extant). He had to send Kemble a second copy as Kemble wrote, after Lamb enquired in November 1800, that he had lost the first.

Three extracts were first published in James Anderson, *Recreations in Agriculture, Natural History, Arts and Miscellaneous Literature*, 1 November 1800: 1) 'The General Lover' beginning 'What is it you love?' (Simon's speech from II, ii, Lucas, V, 152–3); 2) 'Description of a Forest Life' beginning 'What sports do you use in the forest?' (Simon's speech from II, ii, Lucas, V, 153); 3) 'A Fragment in Dialogue' beginning with II, ii, 185–90 as epigraph followed by 39 discarded lines beginning 'All are not false. I knew a youth who died' (reprinted separately as 'Dramatic Fragment' in *London Magazine*, January 1822 and Lucas, V, 79–80). Another discarded passage was published as a separate poem 'The Witch' (see LmC 85–6) in *Works* (1818) and Lucas, V, 177–9.

Lamb changed the title to 'John Woodvil' in November 1801 and the complete drama was first published in *John Woodvil: A Tragedy. To Which Are Added, Fragments of Burton, the Author of the Anatomy of Melancholy* (London, 1802); reprinted *Works* (1818); Lucas, V, 131–76.

Two letters in which Lamb transcribed extracts from the play have been recorded or published though the original letters have been lost. In a letter to Southey postmarked 20 November 1798 (see LmC 85), Lamb refers to having previously sent another extract, 'The Dying Lover' (i.e., the extract first pub. as 'A Fragment in Dialogue' beginning 'All are not false. I knew a youth who died'); this letter (or MS), never recovered or published, must have been sent after the one to Southey postmarked 29 October 1798 (mentioned Lucas, V, 350 and Marrs, I, 150n1).

Another lost letter to Southey of 21 January 1799 contained an extract beginning 'I saw him the day of Worcester fight' — a 25-line version of the 20-line cancelled passage (beginning 'I saw him on the day of Naseby fight') in Act II of LmC 84 (printed Lucas, V, 361–2); this MS is printed in *Letters*, I, 146–7 and Marrs, I, 157.

The only complete MS of the play that survives is the one sent to Manning; it is listed as the first entry below despite its probably being written *after* some of the extant fragments, which are listed after it in chronological order of composition.

LmC 84 MS version with substantial variation from the first edition (1802), mostly in the hand of Mary Lamb but partly in Lamb's autograph, revised, here entitled 'Pride's Cure', 40 pages, as sent to Thomas Manning and including a letter to him on the inside front cover; annotated 'Begun August, 1798, finished May, 1799...'; sent probably [19? December 1800].

This MS described and collated with the 1802 first edition by J. D. Campbell in *The Athenaeum*, 31 October and 14 November 1891; these descriptions and collations and variant passages, etc. are reprinted and augmented in Lucas, V, 355–68. The letter to Manning is printed in Lucas, V, 355 and Marrs, I, 260–1; another letter to Manning which originally accompanied this MS (now in the Huntington, HM 11670) is printed in Marrs, I, 261–2 (also dated [19? December 1800]).

Owned (1975) Frances Kettaneh, New York (see Marrs, I, 261n).

LmC 85 Discarded passage, untitled and beginning 'One summer night Sir Walter, as it chanc'd', 2 pages (one leaf), sent in a letter to Robert Southey, postmarked 20 November 1798.

These lines printed separately as 'The Witch' (beginning 'One summer night Sir Francis, as it chanced') in *Works* (1818); Lucas, V, 177–9. This MS printed *Letters*, I, 156–7 (where it is misdated, as in other editions, sale catalogues and the *Berg Catalogue*, 20 April 1799) and Marrs, I, 148–50.

Facsimile of second page in American Art Association sale catalogue, 7–8 November 1934 (Terry Sale), p. 117.

Berg.

LmC 86 Fair copy of a discarded passage, untitled, text as in LmC 85, sent in a letter to Robert Lloyd, postmarked 20 November 1798.

This MS printed in *Letters*, I, 139–40 (without verses) and Marrs, I, 145–7.

Huntington, HM 7494.

LmC 87 Twenty-four line version of II, ii, [211–34], here beginning '"What sports have you in the forest? —"', in a letter to Robert Southey, postmarked 23 January 1799.

See headnote for publication of this passage (pub. Lucas, V, 153); this MS printed *Letters*, I, 148–9 and Marrs, I, 159–60; sold in the W. C. Hazlitt Sale (see William Hazlitt, INTRODUCTION), Sotheby's, 23–4 November 1893, Lot 325, sold to Wise.

Liverpool City Libraries.

LmC 88 Fair copy, revised, of II, ii, [185–90], beginning 'Fie upon't' and 39 discarded lines beginnning 'All are not false. I knew a youth who died', here entitled 'Dramatic fragment', one page, annotated on the verso 'Pray send me a Proof if you think these scraps admissible CL', as sent to John Taylor for publication in *London Magazine*.

This MS used for the publication of this extract in *London Magazine*, January 1822, as 'Dramatic Fragment'; Lucas, V, 79–80; see headnote for other printings; facsimile in American Art Association sale catalogue, 13–14 November 1935 (Dean Sage Sale), Lot 219.

Berg.

LmC 89 Two-line extract beginning 'This arm was busy in the day of Naseby', in a letter to Robert Lloyd, postmarked 26 June 1801.

This MS printed *Letters*, I, 260 and Marrs, II, 8; see Lucas, V, 366 for these lines as they occur in the MS sent to Manning (LmC 84).

Huntington, HM 7502.

'Laugh all that weep', for a lost poem, see INTRODUCTION.

Leisure ('They talk of time, and of time's galling yoke')
First pub. *London Magazine*, April 1821, as 'Sonnet by Charles Lamb'; collected *Album Verses* (1830); Lucas, V, 56.

LmC 90 Fair copy, here entitled 'Sonnet', signed (initials), one page, annotated on verso in pencil 'Endorsed by D. C. Higg.'; dated (in an unidentified hand) 8 July 1820, watermarked 1807.

Yale.

Lines Addressed, from London, to Sara and S. T. C. at Bristol, in the Summer of 1796 ('Was it so hard a thing? I did but ask')
First pub. *Monthly Magazine*, January 1797; Lucas, V, 15.

LmC 91 Fair copy of 26-line version, here entitled 'the 5th July 1796/To Sara & her Samuel.', signed (initials), one page addressed on verso to Coleridge, postmarked from High Holborn with an illegible date (only 'J' and '5' are visible); watermarked 1793.

This MS was printed Lucas, VI, 35–6 (from a facsimile lent by E. H. Coleridge) as a letter to Coleridge, postmarked 5 July 1796, two days before another letter was sent (see LmC 92) which contained revisions to the poem. Lucas (V, 288) conjectures that this MS had been cut away from the top of the second letter and thus immediately preceded the revisions. In *Letters* (where this MS is reprinted on I, 34–5), Lucas presents the two MSS as separate letters, this one dated 5 July and the next 7 July. Marrs does not print this MS but guesses that Lamb sent the poem twice, first separately (this MS) and then with the 7 July letter (LmC 92). He reprints the poem (I, 38–9 from *Letters*) as the missing part of the 7 July letter; however, he notes that nothing appears to be cut away from the 7 July letter.

Victoria College Library, S.MS.F4.4.

LmC 92 Revisions, being a 5-line version of lines 14–16, 19–23, a cancelled 4-line version of lines 19–24 and a few comments; in a letter to S. T. Coleridge (containing also LmC 192), 5–[7] July 1796, postmarked 7 July 1796.

This MS printed in *Letters*, I, 35–7 and Marrs, I, 38–43; see also note to above entry.

Folger.

Lines (For a Monument Commemorating the Sudden Death by Drowning of a Family of Four Sons and Two Daughters) ('Tears are for lighter griefs. Man weeps the doom')
First pub. *The Athenaeum*, 5 November 1831; Lucas, V, 84.

LmC 93 Fair copy, one page, containing a signed note to V[incent] N[ovello], postmarked 8 November 1830.

This MS printed in *Letters*, III, 292; facsimile in the unidentified sale catalogue; Mary Cowden Clarke's transcript of Lamb's original (annotated that Mary Sabilla Novello gave the original away on 3 August 1875) is at the University of Leeds, Novello-Cowden Clarke Collection.

Sold in an unidentified sale, Lot 115 (clippings in Yale Facsimile File, nos. 31 and 284).

Lines On the Celebrated Picture by Lionardo da Vinci, called The Virgin of the Rocks ('While young John runs to greet')
First pub. *Works* (1818); Lucas, V, 39.

LmC 94 Fair copy, slightly revised, here entitled 'On Leonardo da Vinci's "Virgin of the Rocks"', one page, annotated on the mount 'From the personal album of John Howard Payne'; watermarked 1815.

Facsimile in American Art Association sale catalogue, 24–5 April 1935, Lot 188 (where miscatalogued as Keats's autograph poem) and American Art Association sale catalogue, 14–15 April 1937, Lot 227.

Berg.

Lines/*Suggested by a Sight of Waltham Cross* ('Time-mouldering CROSSES, gemm'd with imagery')
First pub. *Englishman's Magazine*, September 1831; Lucas, V, 107.

LmC 95 Fair copy, revised, of an early 8-line version beginning 'A stately Cross each sad spot doth attest', here untitled, in a letter to Bernard Barton, postmarked 4 October 1827.

This MS printed in Lucas, V, 339 where the letter is misdated November 1827 and in *Letters*, III, 128 where it is misdated [mid-September 1827]; the postmark first noticed in Duane Schneider, 'The Lucas Edition of Lamb's *Letters*: Corrections and Notes', *N&Q*, NS 21 (1974), 174.

British Library, Add. MS 35256, f. 67v.

LmC 96 Fair copy, signed, one page of a leaf containing also a note to Mrs Sergeant Wilde, postmarked 25 July 183[1?].

Note not in *Letters*.

Huntington, HM 11515.

LmC 97 Fair copy, here entitled 'suggested by a sight of Waltham Cross', signed, on recto of a leaf addressed on verso to Edward Moxon, postmarked 25 July 1831.

Berg.

LmC 98 Transcript in William Ayrton's Scrapbook, one page.

Not mentioned in Lucas.

Huntington, RB 110244, Vol. III, f. [19].

Living Without God in the World ('Mystery of God! thou brave and beauteous world'), for an unlocated transcript by Robert Southey, see INTRODUCTION.

Love Will Come ('Guard thy feelings, pretty Vestal')
First pub. Lucas, V (1903), 374.

LmC 99 Fair copy, here entitled 'Love will come./ Tune, "The Tartar Drum."' one page, originally in Emma Isola's Extract Book.

Facsimile of lines 1–11 only in *Piccadilly Notes*, p. 379.

Texas.

LmC 100 Fair copy, on first page of a letter to Maria Fryer, schoolmate of Emma Isola, [late autumn 1831].

This MS printed in Lucas, VII, 929–30 and *Letters*, III, 327; facsimile in Sotheby's sale catalogue, 17–19 February 1936, Lot 538 (property of Methuen).

Berg.

Manchester ('Listening the Oceans conflict I have gone')
Questionable attribution. No publication traced.

LmC 101 Transcript in William Ayrton's Scrapbook, 14 lines, one page; signed 'CL./Dec[br] 29th 1819'.

Huntington, RB 110244, Vol. III, f. [3].

Marmor Loquitur ('Here lies a Volunteer so fine')
First pub. Lucas, VII (1905), 965; *Letters*, I, 154; Marrs, I, 166.

LmC 102 In a letter to Robert Southey, dated and postmarked 20 March 1799.

This MS printed in *Letters* and Marrs, as above.

Sotheby's, 26–7 October 1959, Lot 415, sold to Quaritch (Marrs says original is 'unavailable').

Messrs C[annin]g and F[rer]e ('At Eton School brought up with dull boys'), see LmC 197.

'Methinks how dainty sweet it were, reclin'd'
First pub. S. T. Coleridge, *Poems on Various Subjects* (Bristol and London, 1796); collected *Works* (1818); Lucas, V, 4.

LmC 103 Fair copy, revised, imperfect (cut off in line 13), on a scrap (containing also LmC 3); watermarked 1795, dated 1796.

For a reproduction, see FACSIMILES.

Victoria College Library, S.MS.F4.5.

LmC 104 Transcript by S. T. Coleridge, in Rugby MS (p. 43) (see S. T. Coleridge, INTRODUCTION for description), here entitled 'Effusion XII', on a leaf (containing also LmC 201); c. 1796.

Texas.

Mille Viæ Mortis ('What time in bands of slumber all were laid')
First pub. J. Dykes Campbell's article in *Illustrated London News*, 26 December 1891; Lucas, VII, 988 (Appendix III).

LmC 105 Fair copy, in Liber Aureus (the 3 volumes used by the Rev James Boyer, headmaster at Christ's Hospital, for the inscription by students of their best compositions), signed; dated 1789.

The earliest Lamb MS; facsimile of last page in *Ashley Library*, VIII, between pp. 154 and 155; for a further description of Liber Aureus, see S. T. Coleridge, INTRODUCTION.

British Library, Ashley MS 3506(1), ff. 41v–2.

Milton
Questionable attribution; no publication traced.

LmC 105.5 Revision to the 'last line' of 'the sonnet Milton' ('...make it "And thou with Homer & with Hesiod/or Chaucer & Gower/or Dyde & Scribe...'), in a note to J. A. Hessey, watermarked 1820.

No such sonnet by Lamb has been traced; he may, however, have been referring in this note to Bernard Barton's sonnet 'To Elia' which ends 'And thou with Marvell, Brown, and Burton mated' (see *Letters*, II, 366) and which was printed in the *London Magazine*, February 1823; the note to Hessey not in *Letters*.

Princeton, Robert H. Taylor Collection.

Mrs Gilpin Riding to Edmonton ('Then Mrs Gilpin sweetly said')
First pub. *The Table Book*, ed. William Hone (London, 1828); Lucas, I, 314–15 (poem, prose and illustration).

LmC 106 Heavily revised, here untitled, three 4-line stanzas followed by prose commentary signed 'A Sojourner at Enfield', one page, addressed on verso to William Hone (for the first publication) and postmarked 17 July 1827.

This MS written to accompany a pen-and-ink drawing by Thomas Hood of Mary Lamb astride a stile, also at the Huntington, HM 13304; it is captioned by Lamb 'Mrs Gilpin Riding to Edmonton. drawn after Nature, by T. H.'. This drawing (not the version in the first publication) was originally enclosed in a covering letter to Hone, n.d. (but watermarked 1821) also at the Huntington, HM 7527; the letter to Hone is printed in Lucas, I, 518 where it is dated [early July 1827] and in *Letters*, III, 100–1 where it is dated 17 July 1827. This MS discussed in Barnett, pp. 134–6; facsimile in Harper, I, 81–2.

Huntington, HM 13298.

Mrs Siddons, see 'As when a child on some long winter's night'.

Mr A[ddington] ('I put my night-cap on my head'), see LmC 197.

Mr H——

First produced at Drury Lane Theatre, 10 December 1806 (one performance only). Prologue first published in *The Care-Killer*, ed. Jonathan Jolly (1807); first pub. in full as *Mr H——, or Beware a Bad Name* (Philadelphia, 1813); collected *Works* (1818); Lucas, V, 180–211. None of the original MSS of the farce survive: not Mary Lamb's transcript which she carried to Wroughton at Drury Lane on 21 (or 22) February 1806 nor the 'amended copy' (possibly the same) which Charles brought to Wroughton on 22 October 1806 nor any transcripts which Mary Lamb made for friends (see Barnett, p. 131).

LmC 107 MS in an unidentified hand, 16 leaves, as submitted to the Lord Chamberlain for licensing, including title page, a covering letter of application by Richard Wroughton dated 6 December 1806, dramatis personae, prologue and the text, containing slight variations from published version; dated by J. Larpent on the title page 8 December 1806, watermarked 1804.

Huntington, LA 1501.

'My dear friend —/Before I end —'

First pub. *The Letters of Charles Lamb*, ed. T. N. Talfourd, 2 vols (London, 1827); Lucas, VI, 497–9; *Letters*, II, 206–8; Marrs, III, 243–5.

LmC 108 Fair copy, revised, signed, verse letter to William Ayrton, 3 pages, Temple, 12 May [1817], postmarked 13 May 1817.

Facsimile of first and third pages in American Art Association sale catalogue, 2–3 May 1934 (Terry Sale), Lot 169.

Berg.

LmC 109 Transcript in William Ayrton's Scrapbook, here entitled 'Epistle,/To Willm Ayrton Esqre/(dated Temple, May 12. 1817.)', 5 leaves (rectos only).

Huntington, RB 110244, Vol. III, ff. [22–6, rectos only].

'Newcastle swears. Saddler professes *talents*', see LmC 45.

Nonsense Verses ('Lazy-bones, lazy-bones, wake up, and peep!')

Questionable attribution. First pub. William Carew Hazlitt, *Mary and Charles Lamb* (London, 1874) where Hazlitt says 'I found these lines...officiating as a wrapper to some of Mr Hazlitt's hair. There is no signature; but the handwriting is unmistakably Lamb's; nor are the lines themselves the worst of his playful effusions'; Lucas, V, 109 (as Lamb's); reprinted as Mary Lamb's parody of her brother's 'Angel Help' (from LmC 12) in James T. Wills, 'New Lamb Material in the Aders Album: Jacob Götzenberger and Two Versions of "Angel Help"', *HLB*, 22 (1974), 412; Carl Woodring, 'Lamb's Hoaxes and the Lamb Canon', *CLSB*, NS 2 (1975), 39–41 argues for Charles Lamb as the author.

LmC 110 Fair copy, revised, here entitled 'Another Version of the Same', one page.

This MS apparently 'found wrapped around a lock of Hazlitt's hair'.

Pierpont Morgan, MA 225, f. 6.

LmC 111 Fair copy, revised, here entitled 'Another version of The Same [i.e., 'Angel Help']', in Elizabeth Aders's album (including also LmC 12, 156, see former for description), one page, signed 'Mary Lamb'; with accompanying letter from Lamb to Elizabeth Aders, [1827?].

This MS and note to Aders printed in Wills article cited above; the note not in *Letters*.

Harvard, MS Eng 1094(2lv–22).

'Not always do the *names* of men bely', see LmC 45.

'O cruel death why didst thou take'
First pub. Edwin Marrs, 'The Peal Collection of Lamb Letters', *CLSB*, NS 6 (1983), 52–3.

LmC 112 Transcript (made for T. N. Talfourd) of a letter from Lamb to Sarah James containing this 6-line poem; letter dated 11 March 1829.

University of Kentucky, W. Hugh Peal Collection.

'O! I could laugh to hear the midnight wind'
First pub. S. T. Coleridge, *Poems on Various Subjects* (Bristol and London, 1796), as 'Written at midnight by the seaside after a voyage'; collected *Works* (1818); Lucas, V, 4.

LmC 113 Transcript by S. T. Coleridge in his MS E (see S. T. Coleridge, INTRODUCTION for description), here entitled 'Written by the Sea Side'; [winter 1794–spring 1795].

Bristol Reference Library.

LmC 114 Transcript by S. T. Coleridge, in the Rugby MS (p. 44) (see S. T. Coleridge, INTRODUCTION for description), here entitled 'Effusion XIII. Written at midnight by the seaside after a voyage', one leaf; c. 1796.

Texas.

On a Late Empiric of 'Balmy' Memory ('His namesake, born of Jewish breeder')
First pub. *The Champion*, 15 July 1820; Lucas, V, 106.

LmC 115 Fair copy of an epigram on Dr Solomon, written for (but rejected by) the *Morning Post*, here untitled and beginning 'My namesake, sprung from Jewish Breeder', in a letter (containing also LmC 29, 197) to John Rickman, [mid-January 1802].

This MS printed *Letters*, I, 294 (misdated 14 January 1802) and Marrs, II, 46.

Huntington, HM 11569.

On a Projected Journey ('To gratify his people's wish')
First pub. *The Champion*, 15–16 July 1820; Lucas, V, 106.

LmC 116 Transcript in William Ayrton's Scrapbook, here entitled 'Upon the King's (Geo. IV) embarkation at Ramsgate for Hanover, 1821.', one page.

This transcript mentioned in Lucas, V, 337.

Huntington, RB 110244, Vol. III, f. [29].

On a Sepulchral Statue of an Infant Sleeping ('Beautiful Infant, who dost keep')
First pub. as one of the 'Translations from the Latin of Vincent Bourne' in *Album Verses* (1830); Lucas, V, 61.

LmC 117 Transcript in William Ayrton's Scrapbook, here entitled 'On the Monument of an Infant' and beginning 'Beautiful Infant, who doth keep', signed 'for an Album C. Lamb.', one page.

Not mentioned Lucas.

Huntington, HM 110244, Vol. III, f. [20].

On an Infant Dying as Soon as Born ('I saw where in the shroud did lurk')
First pub. *The Gem*, ed. Thomas Hood (London, 1829); collected *Album Verses* (1830); Lucas, V, 49–51.

LmC 118 Fair copy of a variant version, 3 pages (folded leaf), addressed on p. 4 to Thomas Hood and postmarked 30 May 1827; watermarked 1823.

Princeton, Robert H. Taylor Collection.

LmC 119 Transcript by Emma Isola, revised by Lamb, 3 pages (2 leaves containing also LmC 14), originally in Emma Isola's Extract Book; watermarked 1825.

Texas.

On Being Asked to Write in Miss Westwood's Album ('My feeble Muse, that fain her best wou'd')
First pub. *The Athenaeum*, 10 January 1846; Lucas, V, 97–8.

LmC 120 Fair copy, on one page of the album (containing 58 foliated leaves) of Fanny Sarah Westwood, signed; dated 12 October 1827, watermarked 1826.

This MS printed (with the poem by Mary Lamb also in this album (f. 21) ['In Miss Westwood's Album'] beginning 'Small beauty to your Book my lines can lend', pub. Lucas, V, 98) in Thomas Westwood, 'Two Unpublished Poems by Charles and Mary Lamb', *N&Q*, 4th Ser 5 (1870), 527–8; facsimile of Mary Lamb's poem in Maggs Catalogue 368 (1918), plate V.

Huntington, HM 11587, f. 6v.

On the Arrival in England of Lord Byron's Remains ('Manners, they say, by climate alter not:')
First pub. *The New Times*, 24 October 1825, as 'The Poetical Cask' (beginning 'With change of climate manners alter not'); revised version in Lucas, V, 107 (original version V, 338).

LmC 121 Transcript in Willaim Ayrton's Scrapbook, printer's copy for Lucas, one page.

Huntington, RB 110244, Vol. III, f. [37].

LmC 122 Transcript by Henry Crabb Robinson, here untitled and beginning 'Manners, they say, by climate alter not', in the postscript to a letter to Miss Wordsworth, 2 November 1825, postmarked 9 November 1825.

Dr Williams's Library, Henry Crabb Robinson Papers, 1818–1826 Volume, f. 134.

[On the Literary Gazette] ('On English ground I calculated once')
First pub. *The Examiner*, 22 August 1830 (6-line version); Lucas, V, 109; *Letters*, III, 296n.

LmC 123 Fair copy, here untitled, headed 'Rejected Epigrams/6', on a scrap cut from a sheet bearing other epigrams, the '7' below still visible.

This epigram was printed *as part of* a letter to Vincent Novello, [20 May 1830] in W. C. Hazlitt, *Mary and Charles Lamb* (London, 1874), p. 253; the letter (in the same collection at the British Library, Add. MS 11730, f. 106r–v) is printed without the epigram in *Letters*, III, 278; W. C. Hazlitt probably mistakenly united the letter and epigram.

British Library, Add. MS 11730, f. 107.

One dip, see LmC 25.

Parting ('Yon fleecy Cloud that veils the gentle Moon'), see description of William Ayrton's Scrapbook in INTRODUCTION.

The Parting Speech of the Celestial Messenger to the Poet ('But now time warns (my mission at an end')
First pub. *The Athenaeum*, 25 February 1832; Lucas, V, 88–9.

LmC 124 Transcript in an unidentified hand, 2 pages (one leaf), in Mrs Daniel Cresswell's album (containing also LmC 20 (see for description) and 26); album used 1831–43.

Berg.

The Pawnbroker's Daughter
Not produced. First pub. *Blackwood's Magazine*, January 1830; Lucas, V, 212–42.

LmC 125 Transcript by Mary Cowden Clarke, here entitled 'The Pawnbroker's Daughter./or the/Reprieved Man./*A Farce.*/The Reprieved Man/a/Dramatic Extravaganza', annotated on inside front cover 'Mary Victoria N. Clarke./Copied (*without* permission)/from the Author's M.S.—', including some variants from published version, 32 leaves (drama on 59 numbered pages); watermarked 1828.

University of Leeds, Novello-Cowden Clarke Collection.

LmC 126 Transcript in an unidentified hand, as submitted to the Lord Chamberlain for licensing, [October–December 1825].

British Library, Add. MS 42874, ff. 691–713v.

Pindaric Ode to the Tread Mill ('Inspire my spirit, Spirit of De Foe')
First pub. *The New Times*, 24 October 1825 (early version with additional stanza); revised and collected *Album Verses* (1830); Lucas, V, 67–70.

LmC 127 Fair copy of revised version (8 numbered stanzas), revised, signed, followed by a letter to Walter Wilson for his use in *Memoirs of the Life and Times of Daniel DeFoe*, 3 vols (London, 1830) (though not published therein); [probably before 28 May 1829].

This MS is *not* enclosed with the letter to Wilson of 28 May 1829 as stated in Lucas, V, 317 and *Letters*, III, 219; the letter written on this MS has not been published.

Bodleian, MS Montagu. d. 17, ff. 177–8.

'Poet or Prose-man, Party-man, Translator'
First printed in Parke Bernet sale catalogue, 4–5 April 1939, p. 63.

LmC 128 Two-line verse inscription to Leigh Hunt, signed, on verso of half-title of a copy of Hunt's *The Indicator, and the Companion*, 2 vols (London, 1834).

Parke Bernet, 4–5 April 1939, Lot 283.

Pride's Cure, see 'John Woodvil', LmC 84–9.

Prologue to Sheridan Knowles' Comedy, 'The Wife' ('*Untoward* fate no luckless wight invades')
Spoken 'on the night', 24 April 1833, by Mr Warde. Play first pub. with the authorship of the 'Prologue' suppressed (London, 1833); Prologue in Lucas, V, 129.

LmC 129 Revised version of the last line (line 28) of the early version (see below) in the text of a letter to [Edward Moxon] headed 'Prologue' (recto) and, on the verso, two drafts of the last two lines (lines 35–6) of the final version; together with a fair copy of an early 28-line version beginning 'Stern heaven in anger no poor wretch invades', on a separate leaf (recto only) also sent to Moxon; the letter postmarked 17 [April] 1833 and the other leaf postmarked 17 April 1833.

The early version printed in Notes to the poem in Lucas, V, 349 together with an extract from the letter; the verso of the letter printed in P. F. Morgan, 'On Some Letters of Charles Lamb', *N&Q*, 201 (1956), 532; recto only of the letter printed in *Letters*, III, 364–5. A transcript of the letter only in an unidentified hand (Bertram Dobell?) in Bodleian, MS. Dobell. c. 57, ff. 195–6v. A transcript is also in the Alexander Ireland Collection at Manchester Central Library.

Victoria and Albert Museum, Forster MS 333, Items 13–14 (pressmark 48.E.3).

Rectory House, Fornham, All Saints, Suffolk ('Where e'er my fortune casts my future lot')
Questionable attribution; first printed in facsimile (drawing and stanzas 4–5 only) in *Piccadilly Notes* (1934), p. 383 (Item 4136).

LmC 130 Fair copy, six 4-line numbered stanzas, written around a pencil drawing (presumably by Emma Isola) of Rectory House (where she was governess in 1829–30) captioned by Lamb with above title, one page (on a leaf also containing one page of LmC 155), originally in Emma Isola's Extract Book; watermarked 1825.

This MS mentioned Lucas, V, 316; facsimile printed as above.

Texas.

The Scrap Book ('When Mendicants, poor children of mishaps')
No publication traced.

LmC 131 Fair copy, 24 lines, signed, apparently an introductory poem for an album, one page; dated Enfield, 17 January 1831.

NYPL, Manuscripts Division, Montague Collection.

The Self-Enchanted ('I had a sense in dreams of a beauty rare')
First pub. *The Athenaeum*, 7 January 1832; collected *Poetical Works* (1836); Lucas, V, 76.

LmC 132 Fair copy, here beginning 'I had sense in dreams...', signed (initials), on recto of a leaf originally in Emma Isola's Extract Book (containing also LmC 167 and Lamb's transcript of lines from Marlowe's 'The Milk-Maid's Song').

Facsimile in British Library, MS Facs. Suppl. VIII(62), ff. 167–8; facsimile of lines 1–8 only in *Piccadilly Notes*, p. 385 (Item 4137).

Harvard, MS Eng 959.

LmC 133 Fair copy, here untitled and beginning 'I had sense in dreams...', signed, one page.

Facsimile in Samuel T. Freeman sale catalogue, 10 December 1928, Lot 147.

Texas.

LmC 133.5 Here untitled and beginning 'I had sense in dreams...', one leaf, enclosed in a letter to R. Cole, [1831?].

This MS printed *Letters*, III, 329–30.

Privately owned (1989).

The Sisters ('On Emma's honest brow we read display'd')
First pub. *Lamb and Hazlitt*, ed. W. C. Hazlitt (London, 1900); Lucas, V, 98.

LmC 134 Here untitled, signed, on an embossed card addressed 'For Saint Cecilia at Sign^{r} Vincenzo Novello's Music Repository...', written for the Novello sisters; dated 1831.

Lines 1–4 of this MS printed in Sotheby's sale catalogue, p. 93; a transcript of this MS by Mary Cowden Clarke is in Unversity of Leeds, Novello-Cowden Clarke Collection.

Sotheby's, 22 June 1976, Lot 192, sold to Wilson.

Song to Miss S. A. Hunter ('Old poets rehearse, how with quiver & bow')
First pub. (from a transcript of the original by Sarah Ann Hunter (beginning 'Old bards have rehears'd how with quiver and bow') in her letter (now lost) to Alfred Ainger of 10 February 1886) by Edith Sichel, *The Life and Letters of Alfred Ainger* (London, 1906); mentioned (but not published) *TLS*, 5 February 1949, p. 89. According to the first publication, the original MS was presented in an envelope marked 'Miss Hunter, with C. L.'s respects. May be opened by any one'.

LmC 135 Fair copy, revised, here originally beginning 'Old poets rehearse, how with <arrow> quiver & bow', three 6-line stanzas, one page, signed (initials), originally in Emma Isola's Extract Book, the last item (p. 8) on 4 leaves numbered in pencil 58–61 (8 pages) which cannot be separated (containing also Lamb's transcripts of 'Sir Patrick Spence' (p. 1), 'The Spanish Lady's Love' (pp. 2–5), Marvell's 'The Nymph complaining for the death of Her Fawn' (pp. 5–7) and 5 lines of Latin verse beginning 'Adriani motientis ad Animam Suam' (p. 7)).

Facsimile (lines 1–6, 18 only) in *Piccadilly Notes* (1934), p. 381 (Item 4134).

Princeton, Robert H. Taylor Collection.

Sonnet ('The Lord of Life shakes off his drowsihed')
First pub. *Monthly Magazine*, December 1797; Lucas, V, 14.

LmC 136 Fair copy of a version, here untitled and beginning 'The lord of light shakes off his drowsy hed', in a letter to S. T. Coleridge (containing also LmC 2, 202, 210), [30–1 May 1796], postmarked 1 June 1796.

This MS printed in Lucas, V, 287, *Letters*, I, 5 and Marrs, I, 7.

Huntington, HM 7483.

Sonnet/*St Crispin to Mr Gifford* ('All unadvised, and in an evil hour')

First pub. *The Examiner*, 3–4 October 1819; Lucas, V, 104.

LmC 137 Transcript in William Ayrton's Scrapbook, here beginning 'All unaddress'd, and in an evil hour', one page; dated St Crispin's Eve, 1819.

This transcript not mentioned Lucas.

Huntington, RB 110244, Vol. III, f. [31].

Sonnet to a Friend ('Friend of my earliest years and childish days')
First pub. *Monthly Magazine*, October 1797; Lucas, V, 16.

LmC 138 Here entitled '<Sonnet to my sister>', verses dated 1797, in a letter to S. T. Coleridge, London, 2 January 1797.

This MS printed in *Letters*, I, 77–8 (mislocated at Huntington) and Marrs, I, 83; facsimile of last page of letter (without verses) in Anderson Galleries sale catalogue, 7–10 January 1929 (Kern Sale), p. 275.

Berg.

'Sorely your Dactyls do drag along limp-footed'
First pub. T. N. Talfourd, *Final Memorials of Charles Lamb*, 2 vols (London, 1848); *Letters*, I, 32; Marrs, I, 34–5.

LmC 139 Fair copy of an 8-line parody of Robert Southey's poem (one stanza by S. T. Coleridge) 'The Soldier's Wife. Dactylics', in a letter to S. T. Coleridge, [29 June–1 July 1796], postmarked 1 July 1796.

This MS printed as above.

Huntington, HM 7484.

A Stranger's Tribute to Miss Hill
No publication traced.

LmC 140 Two 8-line stanzas, signed; dated 'Chase Enfield, 27th Mar. 1829'.

Sotheby's, 20 March 1984, Lot 659.

Suum Cuique ('Adsciscit sibi divitias et opes alienas')
First pub. (with variant line 5) in *The Letters of Charles Lamb*, ed. T. N. Talfourd, 2 vols (London, 1837), as 'Cuique Suum'; reprinted with explanatory note by Archdeacon Hessey in 'Old Customs at Merchant Taylors', *The Taylorian*, March 1884 (magazine of Merchant Taylors School) (Lucas version); Lucas, V, 109. Bartlett and Welford Catalogue, Item 3 is a copy of Vincent Bourne, *Poematia, latinè, partim reddita, partim scripta*, 4th ed (London, 1750) in which Lamb has inscribed these lines (see INTRODUCTION).

LmC 141 Fair copy of the Latin epigram (first publication version) written for J. A. Hessey's son's school exercise, here entitled 'Cuique Suum' in the postscript of a letter to Robert Southey, postmarked 10 May 1830.

This version printed Lucas, V, 340.

Pierpont Morgan, MA 225, f. 19.

'Sweet is thy sunny hair/O Nymph divinely fair'
No publication traced.

LmC 142 Fair copy, 33 lines, signed (initials), 2 pages (one leaf); c. 1796.

Facsimile in British Library, RP 395.

Princeton, Robert H. Taylor Collection.

'This Book resembles Hoddy Doddy'
First printed (facsimile) in Sotheby's sale catalogue, 5 July 1977, Lot 2.

LmC 143 Two-line verse inscription, on first page of an album kept by J. T. Smith, Keeper of Prints and Drawings at the British Museum, signed; entries in the album dated 26 November 1823–24 March 1824; watermarked 1820.

Facsimile as above.

Sotheby's, 5 July 1977, Lot 2.

LmC 144 In a commonplace book kept by a member of the Bentley family (containing also autograph contributions by William Godwin, Mary Wollstonecraft Shelley, George Cruikshank and Thomas Rowlandson); c. 1823.

This MS printed in Sotheby's sale catalogue.

Sotheby's, 15 July 1975 (property of Richard Bentley & Sons, Publishers), Lot 27, sold to Geoffrey.

LmC 145 [entry deleted]

The Three Graves ('Close by the ever-burning brimstone beds')
First pub. *The Champion*, 13–14 May 1820, signed 'Dante'; reprinted anonymously *London Magazine*, May 1825, subtitled 'Written during the time, now happily forgotten, of the spy system'; Lucas, V, 105.

LmC 146 Fair copy, one page (one leaf containing also LmC 194); watermarked 1818.

This MS sold in the Dean Sage Sale at Parke Bernet, 15–16 January 1941, Lot 243 (with LmC 69, 194) but it was returned due to doubts about the authenticity of the hand; Dean Sage presented the MSS to Yale in 1941.

Yale.

LmC 147 Transcript in William Ayrton's Scrapbook, here beginning 'Close by those ever-burning brimstone beds', 2 leaves (rectos only).

Not mentioned in Lucas.

Huntington, RB 110244, Vol. III, ff. [28–9, rectos only].

To a Celebrated Female Performer in the 'Blind Boy' ('Rare artist! who with half thy tools, or none')
First pub. *Morning Chronicle*, 1819; collected *Album Verses* (1830); Lucas, V, 55.

LmC 148 Fair copy, here entitled 'Sonnet to Miss Kelly/on her performance of Edmond in The Blind Boy', signed, on a blank page [p. 242] of a copy of S. T. Coleridge, *Poems*, 2nd ed (London and Bristol, 1797) (see LmC 329); dated September 1819.

Boston Public Library, Ch.L.6.27.

To a Friend on His Marriage ('What makes a happy wedlock? What has fate')
First pub. *The Athenaeum*, 7 December 1833; collected *Poetical Works* (1836); Lucas, V, 75–6.

LmC 149 One page, signed.

Christie's, 14 June 1979 (Houghton Sale), Lot 284, sold to Davids.

LmC 150 Corrected proof, including a note at the bottom to [C. W. Dilke?], [26 September? 1833].

This proof (and note) printed *Letters*, III, 386–7 as having been enclosed in a letter from Charles and Mary Lamb to Edward Moxon postmarked 26 September 1833 (now at the Huntington, HM 11557, and printed *Letters*, III, 386).

Berg.

To a Lady ('For Love's illustrious cause & Helen's charms'), see the description of William Ayrton's Scrapbook in the INTRODUCTION.

To a Young Friend/On Her Twenty-First Birth-Day ('Crown me a cheerful goblet, while I pray')
First pub. *Album Verses* (1830); Lucas, V, 53–4.

LmC 151 Fair copy, here entitled 'To Emma, on her Twenty First Birthday' and beginning 'Crown me a chearful...', one page, signed (initials), in Emma Isola's Album (mounted at f. 10); dated 25 May 1830.

This MS partly printed in Parke Bernet sale catalogue, 26–8 April 1939 (Spoor Sale), Lot 520.

Harvard, MS Eng 601.66(10).

To a Young Lady ('Hard is the heart that does not melt with ruth')
First pub. *Monthly Magazine*, March 1797; Lucas, V, 16.

LmC 152 Fair copy, here entitled 'To a young Lady/ going out to India', on first page of a letter (containing also LmC 193) to S. T. Coleridge, 5 December 1796, postmarked 6 December.

This MS printed in *Letters*, I, 63–4 and

Marrs, I, 69.

Huntington, HM 7485.

To Bernard Barton ('When last you left your Woodbridge pretty')
First pub. *Album Verses* (1830); Lucas, V, 51–2.

LmC 153 Verse letter, headed 'To Bernard Barton/ His friend C. L. sends, greeting:', 38 lines (i.e., the last line is here cancelled and erased, as Lamb requested in LmC 154), 2 pages (one leaf); [probably soon before 11 June 1827].

Lines 1–4 of this MS printed in Parke Bernet sale catalogue, 29 April 1953 (Carman Sale), p. 45; printed in full in *Letters*, III, 98–9.

University of Kentucky, W. Hugh Peal Collection.

LmC 154 Revised version of line 24 and request for cancellation of last line (line 39), in a letter (containing also LmC 226) to Bernard Barton, postmarked 11 June 1827.

This MS printed in Lucas, V, 308 and *Letters*, III, 96–8.

British Library, Add. MS 35256, f. 61.

LmC 155 Transcript by Emma Isola Moxon, the first 25 lines on one page of a leaf (containing also LmC 130), the closing lines on one page of a second leaf (containing also LmC 70 and 80), the last line added by Lamb with his note explaining the last words, originally in Emma Isola's Extract Book; watermarked 1825 (first leaf only).

This MS mentioned in *Piccadilly Notes* (1934), p. 382 (Item 4135).

Texas.

To C. Aders, Esq. ('Friendliest of men, ADERS, I never come')
First pub. *The Year Book*, ed. William Hone (London, 1832), (for 19 March); Lucas, V, 85.

LmC 156 Fair copy, here entitled 'To C. Aders Esq[r], on his Collection of Paintings by the old German Masters.', signed, 2 pages (one leaf), in Elizabeth Aders's album (containing also LmC 12, 111, see former for description).

Harvard, MS Eng 1094(30).

LmC 157 Signed, one page.

Lines 1–4 of this MS printed in the Parke Bernet sale catalogue.

Parke Bernet, 18 October 1955 (Saul Cohn Sale), Lot 54.

To Charles Lloyd ('A stranger, and alone, I past those scenes')
First pub. *Monthly Magazine*, October 1797, as 'To a Friend'; collected Charles Lloyd and Charles Lamb, *Blank Verse* (London, 1798); Lucas, V, 19.

LmC 158 Fair copy, here untitled, one page (one leaf containing also LmC 216, 309), enclosed in a letter to S. T. Coleridge, [20? September 1797], postmarked September 1797.

This MS printed in *Letters*, I, 116–17 and Marrs, I, 122–3; facsimile in Harper, I, following p. [92].

Huntington, HM 11637.

To Charles Lloyd/An Unexpected Visitor ('Alone, obscure, without a friend')
First pub. S. T. Coleridge, *Poems*, 2nd ed (Bristol and London, 1797); collected *Works* (1818); Lucas, V, 11.

LmC 159 Fair copy, dated 1797, in a letter to S. T. Coleridge of 16 January 1797, postmarked 17 January.

This MS printed in *Letters*, I, 90–1 and Marrs, I, 92–3.

Huntington, HM 7492.

To Charlotte Roberts, at School, at Enfield ('Little Stranger, come from Wales')
First printed (lines 1–4) in Sotheby's sale catalogue, 11 October 1948, p. 5; lines 1–10 printed Maggs Catalogues 785 (1949) and 832 (1955); no full publication traced.

LmC 160 Fair copy, 22 lines, signed, one page, addressed on verso 'For Charlotte

Roberts'.

Microfilm in British Library, M/493.

Brandeis University.

To D[orothy] A[sbury] ('Divided praise, Lady, to you we owe')
First pub. Lucas, V (1903), 101

LmC 161 Fair copy, revised, here entitled 'To D. A./ Acrostic', one page, mounted on II, 337 in 'Charles Lamb's Album' (LmC 319).

Facsimile in NYPL, Manuscripts Division, Madigan Collection.

Texas.

To Emma B——, An acrostic ('Emma, eldest of your name')
First pub. by Major Samuel Butterworth in *The Academy and Literature*, 23 July 1904; reprinted (erroneously) as an appendage to a letter to John Aitken, Islington, 5 July 1825 in Lucas, VII (1905), 974 (with note 'placed at my disposal by Major Butterworth...') and *Letters*, III, 11 (both without title); the letter to Aitken (without verses) is at Indiana University.

LmC 162 Fair copy of an acrostic on Emma Button, signed, in her album [f. 7] inscribed on inside front cover 'Mrs Staunton, Albion Lodge, Peckham'; [between 3 December 1829 and 15 February 1840].

This MS printed in Sotheby's sale catalogue, 10 December 1913.

Texas.

To Emma Isola, see LmC 54.

To Esther Field ('Esther, holy name and sweet')
First pub. Lucas, V (1903), 94.

LmC 163 Fair copy, revised, one page, mounted on II, 91 of 'Charles Lamb's Album' (LmC 319).

Texas.

To H[arriet] I[sola] for her Birthday, 14 Feby/ Acrostic ('Harriet, can you spare a day')
First printed in American Art Association sale catalogue, 13–14 November 1935, Lot 240; first pub. Barnett (1964), pp. 14–15.

LmC 164 Verse letter to Harriet Isola, 12 lines, signed, annotated in unidentified hand 'Presented to S. Davey by "Miss Isola" to whom these lines were addressed'; dated Enfield, 11 February 1833.

This MS printed as above.

Berg.

To J. T. Smith Esqr/Keeper of the Prints at the British Museum ('Keeper of these rich Tomes, where Graphic Art')
First pub. 'A Poem by Charles Lamb, 1830 — Hitherto Unpublished', *CLSB*, May 1963, p. 410.

LmC 165 Ten lines, signed, one page; watermarked 1828, dated 9 August 1830.

British Library, Add. MS 49380(C), f. 6.

To Louisa M[artin], Whom I Used to Call 'Monkey' ('Louisa, serious grown and mild')
First pub. *The Year Book*, ed. William Hone, Supplementary number, 30 December 1831, as 'The Change'; collected *Poetical Works* (1836); Lucas, V, 76–7. Anderson Galleries sale catalogue of 26–8 February 1917 (Huntington-Bixby Sale), Lot 864 is an autograph MS of this poem entitled 'The Change'.

LmC 166 Fair copy, one page, signed; dated 9 August 1830, watermarked 1829.

Princeton.

LmC 167 Fair copy, revised, one page (one leaf containing also LmC 132 and Lamb's transcript of Marlowe's 'The Milk-Maid's Song'), originally in Emma Isola's Extract Book.

Facsimile in British Library, MS Facs. Suppl. VIII(62), ff. 167–8.

Harvard, MS Eng 959.

LmC 168 Fair copy, signed (initials), written on II, 127 of 'Charles Lamb's Album' (LmC 319).

Texas.

To Louisa Morgan ('How blest is he who in his *age*, exempt')
First pub. Lucas, V (1903), 101.

LmC 169 Fair copy, written on I, 252 in 'Charles Lamb's Album' (LmC 319).

Texas.

To M— S—— ('Of all the names, at the baptismal fount')
First pub. 'An Album Verse by Charles Lamb', *CLSB*, January 1959, p. 226; reprinted *CLSB*, NS 2, April 1973, p. 45.

LmC 170 Fifteen lines, possibly written in the album of Mary Saywell; signed and dated 5 October 1830.

Facsimile in Charles Lamb Society Library, pCLS 1281; a typed transcript of this MS is at Columbia University, Edmund Blunden Collection.

Unlocated.

To Margaret W—— ('Margaret, in happy hour')
First pub. *The Athenaeum*, 14 March 1835; Lucas, V, 91.

LmC 171 Fair copy, signed, one page; dated Edmonton, 8 October 1834.

Probably the last verses Lamb composed; facsimile in Samuel T. Freeman sale catalogue, 23 March 1936 (Jeffrey Sale), Lot 238 (clipping in Yale Facsimile File, no. 1462).

Berg.

To M[ary] L[ocke] ('Must I write with pen unwilling')
First pub. Barry Cornwall, *Charles Lamb* (London, 1866), p. 209; Lucas, V, 97.

LmC 172 Fair copy, here entitled 'To M. L./ Acrostic', signed, one page, in Mary Locke's album.

Yale.

LmC 173 Fair copy, headed 'To M. L./Acrostic.', signed, one page; sent (together with LmC 186) to John Forster with a covering note of [summer? 1832].

This MS and covering note printed in *Letters*, III, 337–8; this MS was printer's copy for Lucas.

Victoria and Albert Museum, Forster MS 334 (48.E.3., Item 31, mounted on f. 38; covering note mounted on f. 38v).

LmC 174 Fair copy, here entitled 'To M. L./ Acrostic', signed, one page.

Rutgers University, Symington Collection (Miscellaneous Materials).

To M[ary] L[ouisa] F[ield] ('How many wasting, many wasted years')
First pub. Lucas, V (1903), 94.

LmC 175 Fair copy, here entitled 'To M. L. Field', one page, mounted on II, 91 of 'Charles Lamb's Album' (LmC 319).

Texas.

To Miss Gray, or Grey, at Mrs Gisborn's School, Enfield ('Green in years, and GREY in name —')
First pub. *Letters* (1935), III, 262.

LmC 176 Fair copy, signed, one page; [1830].

This MS printed (with facsimile) in American Art Association sale catalogue, 14–15 February 1935 (Roderick Terry Sale), pp. 115–16.

Berg.

To Mrs F[ield] ('Jane, you are welcome from the barren Rock')
First pub. Lucas, V (1903), 93.

LmC 177 Fair copy, revised, here entitled 'To Mrs J. F. on her return from Gibralter; an Acrostic', one page, mounted on II, 90 of 'Charles Lamb's Album' (LmC 319).

Texas.

To Mrs Sarah Robinson ('Soul-breathing verse, thy gentlest guise put on')
First pub. Lucas, V (1903), 100.

LmC 178 Transcript by Henry Crabb Robinson, printer's copy for first publication, on verso of a letter (probably not sent) from Robinson to W. Stutt; verses dated Enfield, 14 March 1831.

Dr Williams's Library, Henry Crabb Robinson Papers, 1830–1831 Volume, f. 105.

[To Mrs Williams] ('Go little Poem, and present')
First pub. *Album Verses* (1830); Lucas, V, 94–5.

LmC 179 Fair copy, here entitled 'Acrostic', one page.

These lines were originally enclosed with a letter to Grace Williams 2 April 1830 (*Letters*, III, 257–9), now at Texas Christian University, in which Lamb refers to enclosed 'Acrostic on a crossroad'; sold in the W. C. Hazlitt Sale (see William Hazlitt, INTRODUCTION), Sotheby's, 23–4 November 1893, Lot 324, to Pritchard.

Texas.

To My Friend the Indicator ('Your easy Essays indicate a flow')
First pub. *The Indicator*, 27 September 1820; Lucas, V, 83.

LmC 180 Fair copy, signed, '****', one page.

Berg.

To R. [J.] S. Knowles, Esq./*On his Tragedy of Virginius* ('Twelve years ago I knew thee, Knowles, and then')
First pub. *London Magazine*, September 1820; collected *Album Verses* (1830); Lucas, V, 58.

LmC 181 Transcript in William Ayrton's Scrapbook, annotated 'since 1820'.

This transcript not mentioned Lucas.

Huntington, RB 110244, Vol. III, ff. [16, 17].

To Samuel Rogers, Esq. ('Rogers, of all the men that I have known')
First pub. *Album Verses* (1830); Lucas, V, 56.

LmC 182 Transcript in an unidentified hand, here entitled 'To Mr S. Rogers on the death of his Brother', enclosed with a letter to [Samuel Rogers], Enfield, 22 March 1829.

This MS printed *Letters*, III, 212–13 without title.

Yale.

LmC 183 Transcript by Samuel Rogers, here entitled 'A Sonnet by C. Lamb/Addressed to Samuel Rogers on the/death of his elder Brother', followed by Rogers's reply (i.e., a signed note), 2 pages (one leaf), originally in Emma Isola's Extract Book.

Brown University, Ms. 52.181.

To Sarah [Apsey] ('Sarah, — your other name I know not')
First pub. Lucas, V (1903), 100.

LmC 184 Fair copy, here entitled 'To Sarah —— /Acrostic', 5 lines, one page, in Sarah Apsey's album (f. [36]) used c. 1829–34.

Yale.

To S[arah] L[ocke] ('Shall I praise a face unseen')
First pub. Barry Cornwall, *Charles Lamb* (London, 1866); Lucas, V, 96.

LmC 185 Fair copy, here entitled 'To S. L./ Acrostic.', signed, one page, in Sarah Locke's album.

Facsimile in G. Sexton (Bexhill on Sea, Sussex) Catalogue 14 (Autumn 1930), p. 64.

Yale.

LmC 186 Fair copy, here entitled 'To S. L./ Acrostic', signed, one page, sent (together with LmC 173) with a covering note to John Forster, [summer? 1832].

This MS and covering note printed *Letters*, III, 337–8; this MS is printer's copy for Lucas.

Victoria and Albert Museum, Forster MS 335 (48.E.3, Item 29, mounted on f. 37, covering note on f. 38v).

To S[arah] T[homas] ('Sarah, blest wife of "Terah's faithful Son"')
First pub. Lucas, V (1903), 99.

LmC 187 Fair copy, revised, here entitled 'To S. T. an Acrostic', signed (initials), written on II, 182 in 'Charles Lamb's Album' (LmC 319).

Texas.

To Sir James Mackintosh ('Though thou'rt like Judas, an apostate black')
First pub. (according to the letter entered below and Prance) in *The Albion and Evening Advertiser*, ed. John Fenwick, August 1801; Lucas, V, 102.

LmC 188 Fair copy, here untitled, in a letter to Thomas Manning, [22? August 1801], postmarked 'August 18[01]'.

This letter and MS printed *Letters*, I, 264 and Marrs, II, 13.

Huntington, HM 11663.

To the Author of Poems,/*Published under the name of Barry Cornwall* ('Let hate, or grosser heats, their foulness mask')
First pub. *London Magazine*, September 1820; collected *Album Verses* (1830); Lucas, V, 57.

LmC 189 Transcript in William Ayrton's Scrapbook, here entitled 'Sonnet/To the author of Poems published under the name of Barry Cornwall alias — Procter', one page.

Not mentioned Lucas.

Huntington, RB 110244, Vol. III, f. [30].

To the Book ('Little Casket! Storehouse rare!')
First pub. *Poems, Plays, and Essays of Charles Lamb*, ed. Alfred Ainger (London, 1884); Lucas, V, 95–6.

LmC 190 Fair copy, revised, signed, one page.

Huntington, HM 13303.

To the Editor of the 'Every-Day Book' ('I like you, and your book, ingenuous Hone!')
First pub. *London Magazine*, May 1825; collected *Album Verses* (1830); Lucas, V, 58–9.

LmC 191 Transcript in William Ayrton's Scrapbook, here entitled 'Quatrains/(from the London Magazine)' and beginning 'I like you and your Book, ingenious Hone!', 3 leaves (rectos only); dated 1825.

This transcript not mentioned Lucas.

Huntington, RB 110244, Vol. III, ff. [35–7, rectos only].

'To the memory of Dr Onesimus Drake', for a lost MS, see INTRODUCTION.

To the Poet Cowper ('Cowper, I thank my God, that thou art heal'd')
First pub. *Monthly Magazine*, December 1796; Lucas, V, 14–15.

LmC 192 In a letter (containing also LmC 92) to S. T. Coleridge, 5[–7] July 1796, postmarked 7 July.

This MS printed *Letters*, I, 36 and Marrs, I, 40–1.

Folger.

The Tomb of Douglas ('When her son, her Douglas died')
First pub. S. T. Coleridge, *Poems*, 2nd ed (Bristol and London, 1797); Lucas, V, 9–11.

LmC 193 Fair copy, revised, of a version containing 19 additional (cancelled) lines, originally entitled 'Minstrel's Song of the tomb of Douglas', in a letter to S. T. Coleridge (containing also LmC 152), 5 December 1796, postmarked 6 December.

The 19 additional lines printed Lucas, V, 285–6; this MS printed *Letters*, I, 64–6 and Marrs, I, 70–2.

Huntington, HM 7485.

Translation of the Latin Verses on Mr Haydon's Picture ('What rider's that? and who those myriads bringing')

First pub. (a week after the Latin verses, see LmC 68–9) in *The Champion*, 13–14 May 1820; Lucas, V, 82.

LmC 194 One leaf (containing also LmC 146), signed (initials); watermarked 1818.

This MS sold in the Dean Sage Sale at Parke Bernet, 15–16 January 1941, Lot 243 (with LmC 69, 146) but returned due to doubts about the authenticity of the hand; Dean Sage presented the MSS to Yale in 1941.

Yale.

Translations from the Latin of Vincent Bourne, see LmC 117.

The Triumph of the Whale ('Io! Pæan! Io! sing')
First pub. *The Examiner*, 15 March 1812; misattributed to Lord Byron in Galignani's 1828 edition of Byron; Lucas, V, 103–4.

LmC 195 Fair copy, 2 pages (one leaf).

This MS mentioned in Doris Braendel, 'The Lamb Collection at the Rosenbach Foundation', *WC*, 2 (1971), 88.

Rosenbach Foundation.

LmC 196 Transcript in William Ayrton's Scrapbook, 2 pages.

This transcript not mentioned Lucas.

Huntington, RB 110244, Vol. III, ff. [32–3, rectos only].

Twelfth Night/Characters That Might Have Been Drawn on the Above Evening. Mr A[ddington] ('I put my night-cap on my head') **[and] Messrs. C[annin]g and F[rer]e** ('At Eton School brought up with dull boys')
First pub. *Morning Post*, 8 January 1802; Lucas, V, 102.

LmC 197 Two epigrams, the first entitled 'Addington', the second 'Another/Frere & Canning', in a letter (containing also LmC 29, 115) to John Rickman, [mid-January 1802].

This MS printed *Letters*, I, 294 (dated 14 January 1802) and Marrs, II, 46.

Huntington, HM 11569.

Un Solitaire ('Solitary man, around thee')
First pub. Lucas, V (1903), 99.

LmC 198 Fair copy, here entitled 'Un Solitaire, a Drawing by E. J.', signed (initials), written in the margin of I, 89 in 'Charles Lamb's Album' (LmC 319).

Texas.

LmC 199 Transcript?, on the opening leaves (containing also LmC 44) of the album of [T. T.?] Lachlan, annotated 'Written by Mr Lamb at Enfield in my sister Sarah's album on a leaf opposite a drawing, or rather, painting of Miss Emma Isola's wherein a man, sitting amid trees by the side of a piece of water. T. T. L.'.

This album described by its then-owner, E. G. B[lakiston?] in 'Notes on "The Letters of Charles and Mary Lamb"', *N&Q*, 180 (1941), 331–2. No album of Sarah Lachlan's containing these lines by Lamb has come to light.

Owned (1941) E. G. B[lakiston?] (see *N&Q*).

A Vision of Repentance ('I saw a famous fountain, in my dream')
First pub. S. T. Coleridge, *Poems*, 2nd ed (Bristol and London, 1797); collected *Works* (1818); Lucas, V, 12–13. Lamb included an alternative version of line 5 in a now-lost letter to Coleridge of 13 June 1797 (printed *Letters*, I, 108 and Marrs, I, 111).

LmC 200 Fair copy, on pages 1–2 of a letter to S. T. Coleridge, one leaf, dated London 15 [April 1797].

This MS and letter printed in Lyle H. Kendall, Jr, *A Descriptive Catalogue of The W. L. Lewis Collection* (Fort Worth, TX, 1970), pp. 67–71 and Marrs, I, 106–9.

Texas Christian University.

'Was it some sweet device of Faery'
First pub. S. T. Coleridge, *Poems on Various*

Subjects (Bristol and London, 1796) in a version revised by Coleridge; collected *Works* (1818); Lucas, V, 3.

LmC 201 Transcript by S. T. Coleridge, in the Rugby MS (p. 43) (see S. T. Coleridge, INTRODUCTION), here entitled 'Effusion XI', one leaf (containing also LmC 104); c. 1796.

Texas.

'We were two pretty babes, the youngest she'
First pub. *Monthly Magazine*, July 1796; reprinted S. T. Coleridge, *Poems*, 2nd ed (Bristol and London, 1797); collected *Works* (1818); Lucas, I, 8.

LmC 202 Fair copy, in a letter to S. T. Coleridge (containing also LmC 2, 136, 210), [30–1 May 1796], postmarked 1 June 1796.

This MS printed *Letters*, I, 6–7 and Marrs, I, 8.

Huntington, HM 7483.

'Well-pleased, dear Frances, in your looks I trace'
First pub. *Letters*, III (1935), 390.

LmC 203 Fair copy of lines for Frances Brown, signed, on a card pasted in her album.

Facsimile in E. V. Lucas, 'Charles Lamb Again', *TLS*, 8 May 1937, p. 364.

Sotheby's, 21 July 1981, Lot 527, sold to J. Swales.

LmC 204 Letter to Frances Brown containing an alternative line 8 in postscript, postmarked November 1833.

This MS printed *Letters*, III, 390.

Yale.

LmC 205 Letter to Edward and Emma Moxon containing lines 7–8 of this poem; letter dated 29 November 1833.

This MS printed *Letters*, III, 392.

Privately owned (1989).

What Is An Album? (''Tis a Book kept by modern Young Ladies for show')
First pub. (version of lines 1–2 only) in Dedication to *Album Verses* (1830) (for a MS, see LmC 220); first pub. (17 lines only, being a version of lines 1–4, 7–12, 15–21) in Lamb's anonymous review of his own *Album Verses*, 'The Latin Poems of Vincent Bourne', *Englishman's Magazine*, September 1831; reprinted Lucas, I, 337–41; lines 1–22 first pub. in a note by J. M. Gutch in *N&Q*, 11 October 1856 (from a fair copy addressed (line 21) to 'Madelina' rather than 'Emma' and dated 7 September 1830, written on the flyleaf of an unidentified and unlocated copy of *John Woodvil*); first pub. in full (26-line version to Emma Isola) Lucas, V, 92. In the notes to the poem (V, 327), Lucas mentions a commonplace book of Lamb's containing two versions of these lines; no such book has been traced.

LmC 206 Fair copy, 20 lines, signed (initials), one page (on a leaf containing also LmC 25).

Berg.

LmC 207 Fair copy, revised, signed (initials), containing lines 1–20 (lines 5–6 being cancelled), one page, annotated 'only the 2 first of these lines have been in print, & that only as quotation —'; watermarked 1829.

Huntington, HM 11530.

LmC 208 Fair copy, on the opening page of Emma Isola's Album, 26 lines; [probably 1827 when the album was put together].

Facsimile in Parke Bernet sale catalogue, 26–8 April 1939 (John Spoor Sale), Lot 520.

Harvard, MS Eng 601.66(1).

What is it you Love? ('What is it you love?')
Questionable attribution; no publication traced.

LmC 209 Transcript in William Ayrton's Scrapbook, 12 lines, one page, signed 'C Lamb'.

Huntington, RB 110244, Vol. III, f. [14].

'When Eden's foolish Feeder was restricted', see LmC 45.

'When last I roved these winding wood-walks green'
First printed [*Sonnets from Various Authors*]

(privately printed, Bristol, 1796); first pub. S. T. Coleridge, *Poems*, 2nd ed (Bristol and London, 1797); collected *Works* (1818); Lucas, V, 7.

LmC 210 Fair copy, in a letter to S. T. Coleridge (containing also LmC 2, 136, 202), [30–1 May 1796], postmarked 1 June 1796.

This MS printed *Letters*, I, 6 and Marrs, I, 7.

Huntington, HM 7483.

The Wife's Trial
Not produced; submitted to Charles Kemble at Covent Garden Theatre but rejected. First pub. *Blackwood's Magazine*, December 1828; Lucas, V, 243–73.

LmC 211 Copy of the first publication (paginated 765–81) containing an autograph? correction to the last line on p. 767; bound into the volume of miscellanea entitled 'Tag Rag and Bob Tail'.

Neither this copy nor the correction mentioned Lucas.

Victoria and Albert Museum, Forster Printed Book 5029 (18.Q.23.).

The Witch, see LmC 85.

Work ('Who first invented work, and bound the free')
First pub. (early version) *The Examiner*, 20 June 1819, as 'Sonnet'; included in the first publication only of the essay 'The Superannuated Man' in *London Magazine*, May 1825; collected *Album Verses* (1830); Lucas, V, 55–6.

LmC 212 Fair copy, revised, here untitled, signed (initials), in Coleridge's Notebook 27 (see S. T. Coleridge, CoS 1366); notebook used 1818–19 and later.

British Library, Add. MS 47525, ff. 73v, 72v *rev*.

LmC 213 Fair copy, line 6 revised, here entitled 'Sonnet', signed, one page; watermarked 1820, dated 1821.

Facsimile in Croft, *Autograph Poetry*, No. 100.

Boston Public Library, MS.E.9.1. (No. 99).

LmC 214 Here untitled, signed (initials), in a letter to Bernard Barton, India House, 11 September 1822.

This MS printed *Letters*, II, 332.

British Library, Add. MS 35256, f. 2.

LmC 215 Fair copy, here entitled 'Sonnet', in a letter to W. Marter, East India House, 19 July [1824]; watermarked 1823.

This MS printed *Letters*, II, 432–3.

Huntington, HM 7519.

Written a Year After the Events ('Alas! how am I chang'd! Where be the tears')
First pub. Charles Lloyd and Charles Lamb, *Blank Verse* (London, 1798); Lucas, V, 20–2.

LmC 216 Fair copy, here entitled 'Written a twelvemonth after the Events.', including a few marginal glosses, one page (on a leaf containing also LmC 158, 309), enclosed in a letter to S. T. Coleridge, [20? September 1797], postmarked September 1797.

This MS printed *Letters*, I, 115–16 and Marrs, I, 120–2.

Huntington, HM 11637.

Written at Cambridge ('I was not train'd in Academic bowers')
First pub. *The Examiner*, 29–30 August 1819; collected *Album Verses* (1830); Lucas, V, 55.

LmC 217 Fair copy, signed (initials) and dated 15 August 1819; written on verso of title page of Vol. II of a copy of George Dyer's *History of the University and Colleges of Cambridge*, 2 vols in one (London, 1814).

This MS printed in *CLSB*, No. 150, November 1959, p. 258.

Hodgson's, 18 June 1959, Lot 358.

LmC 217.5 Revised, here untitled, in Coleridge's Notebook 28 (see S. T. Coleridge, CoS

1367); notebook used 1819–1824?.

British Library, Add. MS 47526, f. 46.

The Young Catechist ('While this tawny Ethiop prayeth')
First pub. *Album Verses* (1830); Lucas, V, 52.

LmC 218 Fair copy, entitled in the body of the letter, in a letter to Bernard Barton, [early 1827], illegible postmark.

This MS printed *Letters*, III, 75.

British Library, Add. MS 35256, f. 72v.

PROSE

'A very powerful and pretty story...'
First printed (opening only) Sotheby's sale catalogue, 11 November 1930, Lot 559; no publication traced.

LmC 219 Eleven-line note on a tale written by Mary Cowden Clarke when a young girl, c. 1820.

Sotheby's, 11 November 1930, Lot 559, sold to W. W. Manning.

The Adventures, see LmC 256.

***Album Verses*: Dedication**
First pub. London, 1830; Dedication reprinted Lucas, V, 304. The Dedication contains a version of lines 1–2 of 'What Is An Album?' beginning 'Those Books kept by modern young Ladies for show'; see LmC 205–8.

LmC 220 Dedication to Edward Moxon, headed 'Dedication. To the Publisher', signed, one page, tipped into a copy of *Album Verses* (1830); dated Enfield, 1 June 1830.

Parke Bernet, 29 April 1953, Lot 294.

Amicus Redivivus
First pub. *London Magazine*, December 1823; collected *Last Essays* (1833); Lucas, II, 209–13.

LmC 221 First draft, in a letter to Sarah Stoddart Hazlitt, [10 November 1823?].

This MS printed *Letters*, II, 405–6.

SUNY at Buffalo.

An Appearance of the Season
First pub. anonymously in *The Every-Day Book*, ed. William Hone (London, 1827) (for 28 January); Lucas, I, 307–8.

LmC 222 Fair copy, revised, of a variant version, here untitled and beginning 'Christmas has been among us so lately...', 2 pages (one leaf).

This MS version printed *The Life, Letters, and Writings of Charles Lamb*, ed. Percy Fitzgerald (London, 1875); revisions discussed and MS printed in Barnett, pp. 144–6.

Huntington, HM 13297.

An Autobiographical Sketch
First quoted by John Forster in his obituary notice of Lamb, *New Monthly Magazine*, April 1835; first pub. in full Lucas, I (1903), 320–1; reprinted as a letter to William Upcott in *Letters*, III (1935), 82.

LmC 223 Here untitled, signed, one page, written for William Upcott and mounted in his album entitled *Reliques of My Contemporaries*, Vol. I, p. 33 (the album also contains S. T. Coleridge, CoS 816); dated 10 April 1827.

This MS printed and described in David V. Erdman, 'Reliques of the Contemporaries of William Upcott, "Emperor of Autographs"', *BNYPL*, 64 (1960), 581–7. A transcript in an unidentified hand is in the Victoria and Albert Museum, 48.E.3., Item 33, mounted on f. 41r–v.

Berg.

Barrenness of the Imaginative Faculty in the Productions of Modern Art
First pub. (Parts 1–2 only as 'On the Total Defect of the Quality of Imagination, Observable in the Works of Modern British Artists') in *The Reflector*, 23 and 30 December 1832; first pub. in full (as 'On the Total Defect...') in *The Athenaeum*, 12 January–2 February 1833; collected as one essay with above title in *Last Essays* (1833); Lucas, II, 226–34.

LmC 224 Part 1, extensively revised, here entitled 'On the total defect of the quality of Imagination observable in the works of Modern British Artists', 11 pages.

Facsimile in British Library, MS Facs. Suppl. IX(74).

Sotheby's, 26–7 October 1959, Lot 419 (George Moffatt collection), sold to Fleming.

LmC 225 Corrected galley proof of Part 1 (presumably for *The Reflector*), here entitled 'On the Total Defect...', annotated 'Pray, substitute for the lines scratch'd out, the accompanying M.S.', referring to a scrap containing a revised passage addressed on the verso to Bradbury and Evans.

Victoria and Albert Museum, Forster MS 341 (48.E.3., Item 35, mounted on f. 42r–v).

LmC 226 Germ of portion of the essay regarding John Martin's painting of 'Belshazzar's Feast', in a letter (containing also LmC 154) to Bernard Barton, Enfield, postmarked 11 June 1827.

This passage printed in Lucas, II, 447–8; the letter printed in *Letters*, III, 96–8.

British Library, Add. MS 35256, ff. 61–2.

LmC 227 Fair copy, revised, of Part 2, here entitled 'Martin's Paintings' and beginning 'The Paintings, or rather the stupendous Architectural Designs...', headed 'to be continued', 9 numbered pages (6 leaves).

This MS presumably given to Forster for *The Reflector* which he edited.

Victoria and Albert Museum, Forster MS 331 (48.E.3., Item 25, mounted on ff. 24–6).

The Child Angel: a dream
First pub. *London Magazine*, June 1823; collected *Last Essays* (1833); Lucas, II, 244–6.

LmC 228 Fair copy, revised slightly, originally entitled 'The Angel's Gossiping: a dream' and later revised to 'The Angel's child: a dream' and later to present title, signed 'Elia', 7 numbered pages (4 leaves).

This MS briefly discussed Barnett, p. 178; sold in John Taylor Sale, Sotheby's, 14 June 1865, Lot 400.

Victoria and Albert Museum, Forster MS 329 (48.E.3., Item 26, mounted on ff. 27–9).

Confessions of a Drunkard
First pub. *The Philanthropist*, January 1813 (anonymously as 'The Confessions...'); reprinted (as an unearthed essay by 'Elia') in *London Magazine*, August 1822; collected *Last Essays*, 2nd ed (London, 1835); Lucas, I, 133–9.

LmC 229 Fair copy of the *London Magazine* version, 19 pages (10 leaves).

Sold in an unidentified American Art Association sale as Lot 227 (with facsimile of first page), (clipping in Yale Facsimile File, No. 1108).

Contributions to Hone's *The Every-Day Book, The Table Book* and *The Year Book*, see LmC 30, 46–7, 106, 148, 156–7, 166–8, 222, 231, 233, 244, 248, 253, 255, 279, 298, 301–4, 305–7, 316.

Cupid's Revenge, for an unlocated MS, see INTRODUCTION.

A Death-Bed, for an unlocated MS, see INTRODUCTION.

The Death of Coleridge, for an unlocated MS, see INTRODUCTION.

The Death of Munden
First pub. as a letter to the editor in *The Athenaeum*, 11 February 1832, as 'Munden the Comedian'; Lucas, I, 341–2.

LmC 230 Slightly revised, printer's copy for the first publication, addressed to Charles Dilke, editor of *The Athenaeum*, postmarked 9 February 1832.

Berg.

The Defeat of Time
First pub. *The Table Book*, ed. William Hone (London, 1828); Lucas, I, 315–20.

LmC 231 Fair copy, revised, here entitled 'The Defeat of Time; or a Tale of the Fairie.', signed 'Elia', 7 numbered pages (3 leaves and a scrap of a fourth); watermarked 1826.

This MS discussed Barnett, pp. 156–60; facsimile of first page in Anderson Galleries sale catalogue, 26–8 February 1917, p. [145].

Huntington, HM 2275.

A Dissertation upon Roast Pig
First pub. *London Magazine*, September 1822; collected *Elia* (1823); Lucas, II, 120–6. A preliminary sketch of the second part of the essay occurs in a now-lost letter to S. T. Coleridge of 9 March 1822 (discussed in Barnett, pp. 85, 202–3 and printed *Letters*, II, 317–18).

LmC 232 Fair copy, revised, signed 'Elia', 5 numbered pages (3 leaves); watermarked 1820.

This MS discussed in Barnett, pp. 150–5; facsimile of first page in W. C. Hazlitt, *Mary and Charles Lamb* (London, 1874), facing p. 136; facsimile page in *British Literary Manuscripts*, plate 18; sold in John Taylor Sale, Sotheby's, 10 March 1865, Lot 434.

Pierpont Morgan, MA 966.

Distant Correspondents, for an unlocated MS, see INTRODUCTION.

Dog Days/'Now Sirius rages.'/To the Editor of the Every-day Book
First pub. *The Every-Day Book*, ed. William Hone (London, 1826) (for 14 July); Lucas, I, 383 (in 'Appendix/Essays and Notes Not Certain to be Lamb's but Probably His').

LmC 233 Heavily revised, printer's copy for the first publication, signed 'Pompey', 3 pages (one leaf), addressed to Hone with a note dated 'Enfield Saturday', postmarked both 16 and 18 July 1825.

The existence of this MS, unknown to Lucas, removes any doubt as to the authorship of the piece; this MS discussed (with facsimile of second page) in Barnett, pp. 136–42; the note to Hone printed *Letters*, III, 13.

Huntington, HM 7972.

Dream-Children
First pub. *London Magazine*, January 1822; collected *Elia* (1823); Lucas, II, 100–3.

LmC 234 Fair copy, revised, here originally entitled 'My Children', first publication version, signed 'Elia', 2 pages.

Facsimiles in British Library (MS Facs. Suppl. VII(y), ff. 84–5 and MS Facs. Suppl. XIII(14)), Bodleian (MS Facs. b. 7, f. 2 and in the Newton sale catalogue, pp. 187 and 189; sold in the John Taylor Sale, Sotheby's, 10 March 1865, Lot 441.

Parke Bernet, 14–16 May 1941 (A. E. Newton Sale), Lot 583, sold to Rosenbach.

***Elia* (1823)**
First pub. London, 1823; Lucas, II, 1–149. A MS 'Dedication/To the Friendly and Judicious Reader' was apparently originally enclosed with a letter to Taylor & Hessey of 7 December 1822 and is printed (with the letter) in Lucas, II, 299–300 and *Letters*, III, 350; the letter, with no enclosed Dedication, is now part of the W. Hugh Peal Collection at the University of Kentucky. The MS Dedication was sold in the John Taylor Sale at Sotheby's, 14 June 1865, Lot 396 but remains unlocated. For MSS of essays by Elia, see LmC 231, 234, 240, 241–3, 251–2, 257, 265–6, 267–8, 275, 276, 299–300.

LmC 235 List of initials of characters appearing in *Elia* prepared by R. B. Pitman, Lamb's fellow clerk at East India House, with the full names written out by Lamb; inserted in a copy of the first edition presented by Lamb to Fanny Kelly.

This MS printed in W. C. Hazlitt, *Mary and Charles Lamb* (London, 1874), in Lucas, II, 301–2 and Prance (as 'Lamb's

Key'), pp. 193–4. A transcript by Alexander Ireland (a former owner of the original) is in his collection at Manchester Central Library.

Berg.

Elia to His Correspondents
First pub. in the 'Lion's Head' section of *London Magazine*, November 1821; not in Lucas.

LmC 236 Fair copy, headed 'For the Lion's Head', signed 'Elia', 2 pages (one leaf).

This MS printed *Letters*, II, 311–13; sold in the John Taylor Sale, Sotheby's, 10 March 1865, Lot 433.

Yale.

Estimate of DeFoe's Secondary Novels
First pub. Walter Wilson, *Memoirs of the Life and Times of Daniel DeFoe*, 3 vols (London, 1830), Vol. III; Lucas, I, 325–7. Lamb's final version was, according to the footnote in *Letters*, enclosed with (or contained in) an unlocated letter to Walter Wilson of 28 May 1829, printed in *Letters*, III, 219.

LmC 237 Early remarks on DeFoe, sent to Walter Wilson for use in his work, in a letter dated 16 December 1822.

These early remarks were included as a prefatory note to Lamb's comments in the first publication (III, 428); reprinted Lucas, I, 523–4; this MS printed *Letters*, II, 352–3.

Bodleian, MS. Montagu d. 17, ff .174–5v.

Extracts from the Garrick Plays, see LmC 305–7.

Four Dramatic Criticisms, see LmC 254.

Garrick Plays, see LmC 305–7.

The Gentle Giantess
First pub. *London Magazine*, December 1822; Lucas, I, 211–13.

LmC 238 Early version, in a letter to Dodwell & Chambers, 26 August [1819], postmarked 28 August 1819.

For a discussion (with extracts) of this MS, see Carl Woodring, 'Lamb Takes a Holiday', *HLB*, 14 (1960), 258–9 and Barnett, pp. 82–3.

Princeton, Robert H. Taylor Collection.

LmC 239 Early version, in one paragraph of a letter to Dorothy Wordsworth, postmarked 8 January 1821.

This MS printed *Letters*, II, 288–9.

Texas.

Grace Before Meat
First pub. *London Magazine*, November 1821; collected *Elia* (1823); Lucas, II, 91–6.

LmC 240 Fair copy, revised, printer's copy for first publication, signed 'Elia', 7 numbered pages (4 leaves), the eighth page containing the address to Taylor & Hessey postmarked Hackney, 1 October 1821; watermarked 1820.

Facsimile of first page in *The Houghton Library 1942–1967* (Cambridge, MA, 1967), p. 85; this MS discussed in detail in J. Milton French, 'A Chip from Elia's Workshop', *SP*, 37 (1940), 88–99; sold in the John Taylor Sale, Sotheby's, 10 March 1865, Lot 438.

Harvard, fMS Lowell 6.

Imperfect Sympathies
First pub. *London Magazine*, August 1821, as 'Jews, Quakers, Scotchmen, and other Imperfect Sympathies'; collected *Elia* (1823); Lucas, II, 58–64.

LmC 241 Fair copy, slightly revised, here entitled 'Jews, Quakers, Scotchmen, and other imperfect sympathies', printer's copy for the first publication, signed 'Elia' (three times), 7 numbered pages (4 leaves), addressed to Taylor & Hessey and postmarked 18 July; watermarked 1820.

Facsimile of first page in Parke Bernet sale catalogue, 15–16 January 1941, p. 69; extracts from this MS printed Barnett, pp. 174–5; sold John Taylor Sale, Sotheby's,

14 June 1865, Lot 398.

NYPL, Pforzheimer Collection, Shelleyana 34.

LmC 242 Proof correction, in a letter to John Taylor postmarked 21 July 1821.

This MS printed *Letters*, II, 306; sold in the John Taylor Sale, Sotheby's, 14 June 1865, Lot 402.

Berg.

LmC 243 Proof correction to 'the Jew part of my...article', in a letter to Taylor & Hessey, postmarked 25 July 1821.

Not in *Letters*.

Princeton, Robert H.Taylor Collection.

In *Re* Squirrels
First pub. *The Every-Day Book*, ed. William Hone (London, 1826) (for 7 October); Lucas, I, 306. This piece is Lamb's response to an item on squirrels reprinted from *Gentleman's Magazine* in *The Every-Day Book* for 7 October.

LmC 244 Fair copy, revised, here entitled 'The Squirrel', signed (initials), one page, addressed (on verso) to William Hone with a note, postmarked 24 October 1825.

The note to Hone printed *Letters*, III, 29.

Huntington, HM 13296.

[Instructions for Playing Whist]
First pub. (first page only) as a letter to Louisa Badams (among letters of July–September 1829) in *Letters*, III (1935), 227–8, headed 'Instructions for Playing Whist'.

LmC 245 Begining with a diagram of players and beginning 'The suit which anyone leads...', signed, 3 pages (2 leaves), addressed to Louisa Badams; watermarked 1826.

Facsimile in Harper, I, 87–90 where it is dated c. July 1831.

Huntington, HM 13301.

Lamb's Key, see LmC 235.

The Last Essays of Elia, see LmC 224–7, 228, 229, 258, 274, 287, 288, 289, 290, 291, 292, 297, and the lost MS of 'The Death-Bed', described in the INTRODUCTION.

The Last Peach
First pub. *London Magazine*, April 1825; Lucas, I, 283–5.

LmC 246 Germ of the essay, in a letter to Bernard Barton and Lucy Barton, postmarked 1 December 1824.

This MS printed Letters, II, 446–8.

British Library, Add. MS 35256, ff. 39–40.

The Latin Poems of Vincent Bourne, see LmC 205–8.

Letter of Elia to Robert Southey, see LmC 297.

Letter to an Old Gentleman whose Education has been Neglected
DeQuincey's original 'Letters to a Young Man whose Education has been Neglected' was printed in *London Magazine* from January to June 1823; this essay, Lamb's parody, was first pub. *London Magazine*, January 1825 and was composed of a prefatory letter to the editor and the letter to [DeQuincey]; Lucas, I, 213–18.

LmC 247 Two versions of the prefatory letter to the editor of the *London Magazine*: the first (draft) entitled 'To the Author of the "Letters to a Young Gentleman, whose Education had been neglected"' and beginning 'Dear Sir/I was in a mixed party the other night...', signed (cancelled) 'Elia' and later signed 'STPQ', annotated 'Either to be prefix'd to the Letter, or put in the Lion's Head', one folio page, sent to J. A. Hessey on 1 April 1823; the second (fair copy, revised) untitled and beginning 'Dear Sir/I send you a bantering Epistle...' (as published), annotated 'To the Editor of The London Magazine' and 'Lion's Head', one page, together with a covering letter to J. A. Hessey, [2 April 1823]; all 3 leaves bound together.

The first (discarded) version printed with

facsimile in Woodring, Plate III and p. 382; first version printed and both MSS discussed in Barnett, pp. 146–50; the covering letter to Hessey is printed *Letters*, II, 375 where it is dated [spring 1823].

Harvard, Widener Collection.

Letter to the Editor of the 'Table Book'
First pub. *The Table Book*, ed. William Hone, (London, 1827); not in Lucas.

LmC 248 Fair copy, headed '*To the Editor*' and beginning 'Dear Sir, Somebody has fairly played a *hoax* on you', signed, one page; [June 1827].

This MS printed *Letters*, III, 103 where misdated July 1827 and mislocated at the Huntington.

Berg.

London Fogs
Questionable attribution; first pub. *The Examiner*, 18 December 1831, as Lamb's; Lucas, I (1903), 351; in Appendix III (VII, [979]), Lucas attributes the piece to Leigh Hunt (from an essay on the months in *New Monthly Magazine* which remains unidentified); John Turnbull in *N&Q*, 23 August 1947, identifies the first publication but says it might have originated from Ayrton's Scrapbook.

LmC 249 Transcript in William Ayrton's Scrapbook, 3 leaves (rectos only), signed 'C. Lamb'.

Huntington, RB 110244, Vol. III, ff. [10–12, rectos only].

The Londoner
First pub. *Morning Post*, 1 February 1802; revised version addressed 'To the Editor of the Reflector' (not published in that magazine) collected in *Works* (1818); Lucas, I, 39–40 (revised version) and Lucas, I, 400–2 (first version). For related sketches in private letters, see Lamb's letters to Thomas Manning postmarked 29 November 1800 (original at Huntington, HM 11658, and printed Marrs, I, 247–9), to William Wordsworth postmarked 30 January 1801 (original at Texas and printed Marrs, I, 265–9), to Robert Lloyd postmarked 7 February 1801 (original at Huntington, HM 7500, printed Marrs, I, 270–2), and to Thomas Manning, [27? February 1801] (original at Huntington, HM 11662, printed Marrs, I, 275–8).

LmC 250 Lamb's transcript of the first publication, in a letter to Thomas Manning, 15 February 1802.

This letter printed Marrs, II, 54–9.

Huntington, HM 11665.

LmC 250.5 Clipping of the first publication, revised by Lamb, stuck on to an unnumbered page in one of Lamb's commonplace books (see LmC 316).

Berg.

Mackery End, in Hertfordshire
First pub. *London Magazine*, July 1821; collected *Elia* (1823); Lucas, II, 75–9.

LmC 251 Fair copy, revised, signed 'Elia', 4 pages (2 leaves); watermarked 1811.

For a reproduction of the first page, see FACSIMILES; sold in the John Taylor Sale, Sotheby's, 14 June 1865, Lot 397.

Victoria and Albert Museum, Forster MS 330 (48.E.3., Item 28, mounted on ff. 35–6).

LmC 252 Proof correction (for first publication), in a letter to John Taylor postmarked 8 June 1821.

This MS printed *Letters*, II, 299; for another mention of this letter, see LmC 281.

Rosenbach Foundation.

Maid Marian
First pub. *The Table Book*, ed. William Hone (London, 1828); included in the Notes to the Garrick Plays in Lucas, IV, 616.

LmC 253 Fair copy, heavily revised, letter to the editor of *The Table Book*, headed '*To the Editor.*', signed (initials), one page, addressed to [William Hone] and including a note to him ('H'), postmarked 27 June 1827; watermarked 1821.

This letter printed (mistakenly as two separate letters) in *Letters*, III, 87–8 (dated [May 1827]) and III, 99 (dated 27 June 1827); this MS discussed Barnett, pp. 142–4.

Huntington, HM 7521.

Martin's Paintings, see LmC 227.

Memoir of Robert Lloyd, for a lost MS, see INTRODUCTION.

Miss Kelly at Bath
First pub. *Felix Farley's Bristol Journal*, 30 January 1819 as 'Extract of a letter to the Editor from an Old Correspondent in London'; Lucas, I, 184–6, as 'Four Dramatic Criticisms. I.'.

LmC 254 Clipping of the first publication, with the title revised and one line cancelled by Lamb, mounted on II, 405 of 'Charles Lamb's Album' (LmC 319).

Texas.

Mrs Leicester's School, for documentary evidence of Charles Lamb's authorship of three stories, see INTRODUCTION.

The Months
First pub. *The Every-Day Book*, ed. William Hone (London, 1827) (for 16 April); Lucas, I, 308–12.

LmC 255 Fair copy, revised, here entitled 'For the Every day Book', composed of 8 pages numbered 1–4, 12–15 (5 leaves) in Lamb's hand and 7 pages numbered 5–11 (5 leaves) extracted from Hannah Wolley's *The Queen-like Closet*, 4th ed (London, 1681) containing passages marked by Lamb for the printer, and cancelled passages, signed (initials).

Princeton, Scribner Collection, MS 3818.1.355.

'My dear friend, —/More than once you have expressed a wish to know my Adventures...'
No publication traced.

LmC 256 Fair copy, revised, of a fragment of a story, in the form of a letter from a lady describing her travels in Revolutionary France, 15 leaves (rectos only) of East India Company paper torn from a ledger book, each one torn in two or three and now repaired, begun in Mary Lamb's hand and taken over by Charles (bottom of f. 7), ff. 1–14 being the opening and f. 15 being a scrap possibly from a later section (now-lost), annotation (f. 1) signed Edward Lumley reads 'This Manuscript *in the Autograph of Charles Lamb* was given me by Westwood the Poet who was the intimate friend of Lamb.'; watermarked 1814, [composed between September 1822 and 22 March 1833].

This MS discussed and dated in Louis James, 'The Lambs' story of Revolutionary France: a newly discovered fragment', *CLSB*, NS 2, April 1973, [29]–32 when the MS was owned by Mrs Cyril Ellis.

British Library, Add. MS 57846.

My First Play
First pub. *London Magazine*, December 1821; collected *Elia* (1823); Lucas, II, 97–100.

LmC 257 Fair copy, slightly revised, signed 'Elia', 3 numbered pages (2 leaves watermarked 1816), addressed to Taylor & Hessey, postmarked 26 October 1821.

Facsimile in British Library, RP 1466; sold in the John Taylor Sale, Sotheby's, 10 March 1865, Lot 437.

Princeton, Robert H. Taylor Collection.

Newspapers Thirty-Five Years Ago
First pub. as 'Peter's Net/No.II. — On the Total Defect of the faculty of Imagination observable in the works of modern British Artists' in *Englishman's Magazine*, October 1831; collected *Last Essays* (1833); Lucas, II, 220–5.

LmC 258 Annotation on p. 158 of a copy of *Last Essays* (1833) presented by Lamb to John Forster.

This annotation not mentioned Lucas.

Victoria and Albert Museum, Forster Printed Book 5020 (18.P.18.).

[Notes on Charles Cowden Clarke's *Tales from Chaucer* (London, 1833)]
Extracts from these notes published *Letters*, III (1935), 335.

LmC 259 List of notes, one page, containing a note to Charles Cowden Clarke, annotated by Clarke 'Charles Lamb's writing. C.C.C.', addressed on recto *to* Lamb and postmarked 14 April 1832.

The note to Clarke printed *Letters*, III, 335.

Berg.

[Notes on English Grammar]
First printed (facsimile) in Sotheran's 2nd supplement (1935) to *Piccadilly Notes* (1934), Item 4324 (p. 453).

LmC 260 Probably written for Emma Isola, on a scrap (r–v).

Texas.

[Notes on John Fuller Russell's metrical 'novel' in three parts *Emily de Wilton*]
These notes published (together with two letters from Lamb to Russell) by J. F. Russell in *N&Q*, 17 September and 5 November 1881; the letters and notes reprinted Lucas, VII (1905), 932–6 and *Letters*, III (1935), 413–16 where both letters are dated [summer 1834] and the notes to Parts II and III of the 'novel' are dated 4 September 1834.

LmC 261 Remarks on Parts I–III of Russell's *Emily de Wilton*, 5 pages.

Sotheby's, 23 July 1929, Lot 423 (the two letters being Lots 424–5), sold to Rosenbach.

[Notes on P. G. Patmore's *Chatsworth, or the Romance of a Week* (London, 1844)]
Extracts from Lamb's notes published in P. G. Patmore, *My Friends and Acquaintances*, 3 vols (London, 1854), I, 61n–63n; reprinted Lucas, VII (1905), 737–8 and *Letters*, III (1935), 107–8 (in both as notes to a letter to P. G. Patmore of 19 July 1827 then owned by Lord Crewe); also printed in *The Works in Prose and Verse of Charles and Mary Lamb*, ed. Thomas Hutchinson, 2 vols (London, 1908), II, 814–15, as 'Remarks on the MS of a Friend'.

LmC 262 Notes, each one referring to a page of Patmore's MS, 4 pages (one folded leaf).

British Library, Add. MS 25925, ff. 41–2v.

[Notes on William Godwin's *Antonio*]
For Lamb's epilogue for *Antonio*, see LmC 33–4; for his copy of the play and playbill, see LmC 334–5.

LmC 263 Criticism of and suggested revisions for, on 'rough paper' enclosed with a letter to William Godwin, [14 December 1800].

An extract from these notes printed in C. Kegan Paul, *William Godwin*, 2 vols (London, 1876) and reprinted Marrs, I, 256n; the letter only printed Marrs, I, 255–6.

Sotheby's, 23–4 July 1987, Lot 85, sold to Calder.

LmC 263.5 Notes beginning '*Queries* — whether the best conclusion...', 4 pages (one leaf), together with a second leaf (4 pages) which does not follow on, beginning 'might call it rashness./61 Omit...'; both leaves inserted in Lamb's copy of *Antonio* (LmC 334).

These notes (first leaf only) printed as a letter to Godwin (without salutation or closing) of [15 December? 1800] in Marrs, I, 256–7; second leaf not mentioned in Marrs.

Pierpont Morgan, 52613.

'Odes and Addresses to Great People'
This review of *Odes and Addresses to Great People* by [Thomas Hood and J. H. Reynolds] (London, 1825) was first pub. anonymously in *New Times*, 12 April 1825; Lucas, I, 285–7.

LmC 264 Corrected printed copy of the first publication, containing also a signed note by Lamb.

Corrections are noted in Lucas, I, 502.

Victoria and Albert Museum, Forster MS 338 (48.E.3., Item 34, mounted on f. 42).

The Old Benchers of the Inner Temple
First pub. *London Magazine*, September 1821; revised and collected *Elia* (1823); Lucas, II, 82–91.

LmC 265 Fair copy, revised, signed 'Elia', 10 numbered pages (5 leaves).

Two facsimile pages in Anderson Galleries sale catalogue, 13–14 November 1935 (Dean Sage Sale), Lot 235; sold in the John Taylor Sale, Sotheby's, 10 March 1865, Lot 439.

Berg.

LmC 266 Proof correction, in a letter to John Taylor postmarked 22 August 1821.

This letter printed *Letters*, II, 308.

University of Kentucky, W. Hugh Peal Collection.

On Some of the Old Actors
Early version first pub. *London Magazine*, February 1822, as first in series 'The Old Actors'; revised and collected *Elia* (1823); Lucas, II, 279–85 (early version) and II, 132–41 (revised version).

LmC 267 Fair copy, revised, signed 'Elia', 6 numbered pages (3 leaves).

Sold in the John Taylor Sale, Sotheby's, 10 March 1865, Lot 440.

Yale.

LmC 268 Two corrections for the first publication, in a letter to J. A. Hessey, [January 1822]; watermarked 1820.

This MS printed *Letters*, II, 316, as a letter to John Taylor.

Huntington, HM 11501.

On the Ambiguities Arising from Proper Names
First pub. *The Reflector*, No. 2 (1811); Lucas, I, 69–70.

LmC 269 Early version of the anecdote told in the essay, in a letter to William Wordsworth, 1 February 1806.

This letter printed *Letters*, I, 419–22 and Marrs, II, 204–7.

Huntington, HM 7506.

On the Inconveniences Resulting from Being Hanged
First pub. *The Reflector*, No. 2 (1811); collected *Works* (1818); Lucas, I, 56–63.

LmC 270 Correction on II, 177 of a copy of *Works* (1818) (containing also LmC 273), including a presentation inscription to Miss Kelly in Vol. I dated 7 June 1818.

This volume described in *Sentimental Library*, p. 136.

Parke Bernet, 14–16 May 1941 (A. E. Newton Sale), Lot 613.

On the Poetical Works of George Wither
Essay first pub. *Works* (1818); Lucas, I, 181–4.

LmC 271 Two interleaved volumes (presentation inscription from Lamb to James Pulham) containing printed selections of works by Wither, privately printed by J. M. Gutch in 1809–10 and sent to Lamb; containing Lamb's pencil annotations and Dr John Nott's later annotations and Lamb's further annotations on both Wither *and* Nott, these last made probably 1815–18; the annotations constitute a first draft of Lamb's essay.

Gutch eventually published an expanded edition of Wither's works in 4 volumes, edited by John Nott (Bristol, 1820) in which many of Lamb's annotations are signed by Nott. The interleaved volumes are discussed and some annotations printed in Lucas, I, 453–6; A. C. Swinburne's description, also including the publication of some of the annotations, was printed in *Nineteenth Century*, January 1885 and collected *The Complete Works of Algernon Charles Swinburne*, ed. Edmund Gosse and T. J. Wise (London and New York, 1925–7), IV, 248. Lamb's letter to Gutch postmarked 9 February 1810, wherein he remarks that he has written in these volumes, is at Harvard; it is printed in *Letters*, II, 99–100 (misdated [9 April 1810]) and Marrs, III, 42–3.

Parke Bernet, 26–8 April 1939 (Spoor Sale), Lot 555.

LmC 272 Fair copy, 2 pages (one leaf), taken from the above interleaved copy of Wither's works, containing notes by Lamb headed 'Page 17 Last Line but 5.' and beginning 'It is difficult to conceive upon the matter…'; watermarked 1807.

This MS is bound with a note to Charles Cowden Clarke (unrelated) of [May 1828?] and both are printed in American Art Association sale catalogue, 7–8 November 1934 (Terry Sale), Lot 186; a transcript (made from this MS when owned by Terry on 10 April 1920) is at Brown University, Ms. 52.155. This leaf of notes is mentioned *Letters*, II, 100 and Marrs, III, 43n1.

Berg.

LmC 273 Correction on II, 136 of a copy of *Works* (1818) (containing also LmC 270), including a presentation inscription to Miss Kelly in Vol. I dated 7 June 1818.

This volume described in *Sentimental Library*, p. 136.

Parke Bernet, 14–16 May 1941, (A. E. Newton Sale), Lot 613.

Original Letter of James Thomson, see LmC 308.

Poor Relations
First pub. *London Magazine*, May 1823; collected *Last Essays* (1833); Lucas, II, 157–63.

LmC 274 Fair copy, slightly revised, signed 'Elia', 18 numbered pages (10 leaves).

This MS briefly discussed in Barnett, pp. 178–9, facsimile of first page, p. [196]; sold in the John Taylor Sale, Sotheby's, 14 June 1865, Lot 399.

Victoria and Albert Museum, Forster MS 332 (48.E.3, Item 27, mounted on ff. 29–34.

Popular Fallacies, see LmC 287, 288, 289, 290, 291, 292.

The Praise of Chimney Sweepers
First pub. *London Magazine*, May 1822; collected *Elia* (1823); Lucas, II, 108–14. An unlocated letter to J. A. Hessey, [15 April 1822], containing a last-minute correction to the essay, is printed in *Letters*, II, 324.

LmC 275 Fair copy, revised, including draft passages, here subtitled 'A May day Effusion', signed 'Elia' twice, 6 pages, as sent to Taylor & Hessey for the first publication.

The last two pages are written on the outside of a 4-page folded leaf, the inside pages containing a cancelled version of the conclusion; after being cancelled, Lamb stuck the leaves together; as they are now unstuck, the two versions of the conclusion can be compared; facsimile of the first page in Sotheby's sale catalogue, p. 172; sold in the John Taylor Sale, Sotheby's, 10 March 1865, Lot 435.

Sotheby's, 27 September 1988, Lot 139, sold to Brown John.

LmC 275.5 Proof correction, in a letter to Taylor & Hessey (marked '2d letter'), postmarked 15 April 182[2].

This letter printed *Letters*, II, 324.

Berg.

A Quaker's Meeting
First pub. *London Magazine*, April 1821; collected *Elia* (1823); Lucas, II, 45–8. An early version of the 'Quaker moved by the spirit' appears in a lost letter to S. T. Coleridge dated 13 February 1797, printed Marrs, I, 100–5.

LmC 276 Fair copy, slightly corrected, of the opening only, 2 pages numbered 383–4 (one leaf), containing the text originally appearing on first page of the first publication, this being (presumably) a fair (printer's) copy of the opening paragraphs.

This MS discussed in John M. Turnbull, 'An Elian Make-Weight', *N&Q*, 194 (1949), 35–6.

Victoria and Albert Museum, Forster MS 332 (48.E.3), Item 43, mounted on f. 49.

The Religion of Actors
First pub. *New Monthly Magazine*, April 1826; Lucas, I, 287–90.

LmC 277 Proof correction (being the insertion of one word) in a letter to Charles Ollier, postmarked Islington, 11 March 1826.

This MS printed *Letters*, III, 40.

Brown University, Ms. 52.153.

LmC 278 Proof correction (being an instruction to delete the last paragraph) in a letter to Charles Ollier, postmarked Islington, 16 March 1826.

This MS printed *Letters*, III, 36.

Berg.

Remarkable Correspondent
First pub. *The Every-Day Book*, ed. William Hone (London, 1826) (for 1 May and signed 'Twenty Ninth of February'); Lucas, I, 297–9.

LmC 279 Fair copy, revised, printer's copy for the first publication, here beginning 'I am the youngest of Three hundred and sixty six brethren…', signed 'Twenty Ninth of February', headed 'To the Editor of the *Every Day Book*.', 3 pages (one folded leaf), preceded by a note to William Hone postmarked 2 May 1825; watermarked 1824.

The note to Hone is printed *Letters*, III, 4.

Texas.

Remarks on the MS of a Friend, see LmC 262.

Reminiscences of Juke Judkins, Esq., of Birmingham
First pub. *New Monthly Magazine*, June 1826; Lucas, I, 292–7.

LmC 280 Revision (cancelling one line) in a letter to Charles Ollier, postmarked 12 May 1826.

This revision was made in the first publication; this MS printed *Letters*, III, 44.

Yale.

[Review of] TABLE-TALK, or Original Essays. By William Hazlitt
This review was apparently unpublished by Lamb; extracts first printed in Sotheby's sale catalogue, 25–8 March 1929, Lot 635; extracts also pub. in *Letters*, II, 300–301n, in George L. Barnett, 'An Unpublished Review of Charles Lamb', *MLQ*, 17 (1956), 352–6 and in Barnett, pp. 42–4; first pub. in full *Lamb as a Critic*, ed. Roy Park (London, 1980) and Robert Ready, *Hazlitt at Table* (East Brunswick, NJ, 1981).

LmC 281 Fair copy of review of Vol. I (published April 1821) of Hazlitt's *Table Talk*, unsigned, beginning 'A series of Miscellaneous Essays…', 20 pages (11 leaves); [April 1821–June 1822].

Lucas suggests that the review for a friend which Lamb mentions he is writing in a letter to John Taylor postmarked 8 June 1821 (printed *Letters*, II, 299, original at Rosenbach Foundation) is this one; facsimile portion printed in Sotheby's sale catalogue, 25–8 March 1929, Lot 635.

Berg.

Review of *The Excursion*
First pub. *Quarterly Review*, October 1814; Lucas, I, 160–72.

LmC 282 Early comments on Wordsworth's poem, in a letter to William Wordsworth, 9 August 1814.

This MS printed *Letters*, II, 126–30 and Marrs, III, [95]–101.

Texas.

Rules and directions to be observed by Mr Chambers at the end of June 1823 (applicable to any month when I am absent) concerning deposits, voucher, Error Ledger, and other circumstances of Mr Lamb's department of the Journal system; to obviate the inconvenience of my absence: drawn up by desire of Mr Chambers by his obed^{t} C Lamb
First pub. Carl Woodring, 'Lamb Takes a Holiday', *HLB*, 14 (1960), 260–2.

LmC 283 Fair copy, revised, 4 pages (one leaf); watermarked 1822, dated 1823.

Facsimile in British Library, MS Facs. Suppl. IX(31).

Harvard, fMS Eng 959.1.

Samuel Johnson, the Whig, see the discussion of Lamb's library in the INTRODUCTION.

Shakspeare's Improvers
First pub. *The Spectator*, 22 November 1828; Lucas, I, 321–3. A transcript of this article by Mary Cowden Clarke is in University of Leeds, Novello-Cowden Clarke Collection.

LmC 284 Extracts from the 'London acting edition' (1678) of *Macbeth* probably by William Davenant, transcribed from the Garrick collection of plays in the British Museum into one of the Garrick notebooks (LmC 305) and used in this article.

The few extracts from this play jotted in the notebook were not used in *Extracts from the Garrick Plays*; nor did Lucas print them with other rejected material in the Appendix to his Vol. IV; see LmC 305.

British Library, Add. MS 9955, f. 12r–v.

Sir Thomas More
First pub. *The Indicator*, 20 December 1820 (signed '****'); first identified as Lamb's and collected Lucas, I, 203–9.

LmC 284.5 Extracts by More on 'Heresies' and 'Miracles' used in this article, transcribed by Lamb on pp. 63–72 of one of his commonplace books (see LmC 318).

Rosenbach Foundation.

Specimens from the Writings of Fuller, the Church Historian
First pub. *The Reflector*, No. 4 (1812); revised and collected *Works* (1818); Lucas, I, 112–18. See also LmC 333.

LmC 285 Copy of the first publication (i.e., pp. 342–9) containing revisions to the final footnote, bound in the volume of miscellanea entitled 'Tag Rag and Bob Tail'.

These revisions are described in Lucas, I, 419–20.

Victoria and Albert Museum, Forster Printed Book 5029 (18.Q.23).

Specimens of English Dramatic Poets, see LmC 309–15.

The Superannuated Man, for verses published in this essay, see LmC 212–15.

Table-Talk, by the late Elia. No. 3
Complete essay first pub. *The Athenaeum*, 4 January, 31 May, 7 June (No. 3) and 19 July 1834; as one essay in Lucas, I, 344–50 (No. 3 on pp. 347–8).

LmC 286 Slightly revised, headed 'No. 3', beginning 'Advice is not so commonly thrown away as is imagined...', 5 leaves (rectos only).

Bibliotheca Bodmeriana, Cologny-Geneva.

That Enough is as Good as a Feast
First pub. *New Monthly Magazine*, January 1826, with 'Popular Fallacies'; collected *Last Essays* (1833), as 'Popular Fallacies VI'; Lucas, II, 256.

LmC 287 Two pages, here entitled 'That Enough...'.

Parke Bernet, 29 January 1952, Lot 345.

That Handsome is that Handsome Does
First pub. *New Monthly Magazine*, March 1826, with 'Popular Fallacies'; collected *Last Essays* (1833), as 'Popular Fallacies X'; Lucas, II, 259–61.

LmC 288 Second (i.e., last) page, numbered 84, printer's copy for *Last Essays*, beginning 'We are convinced that true ugliness...'.

Sotheby's, 27 October 1970, Lot 411, sold to Goodspeed's.

That Home is Home though it is never so Homely
First pub. *New Monthly Magazine*, March 1826, with 'Popular Fallacies'; collected *Last Essays* (1833), as 'Popular Fallacies XII'; Lucas, II, 263–6.

LmC 289 First page only, numbered 87, printer's copy for *Last Essays*.

Sotheby's, 26–7 October 1959 (George Moffatt Collection), Lot 422, sold to B. F. Stevens.

That the Poor Copy the Vices of the Rich
First pub. *New Monthly Magazine*, January 1826, with 'Popular Fallacies'; collected *Last Essays* (1833), as 'Popular Fallacies V'; Lucas, II, 254–5.

LmC 290 Fair copy, 4 pages (2 leaves); watermarked 1815.

Huntington, HM 7973.

That the Worst Puns are the Best
First pub. *New Monthly Magazine*, January 1826, with 'Popular Fallacies'; collected *Last Essays* (1833), as 'Popular Fallacies IX'; Lucas, II, 257–9.

LmC 291 Fair copy, headed '9', 6 pages numbered 19–24 (4 leaves), annotated at end '*sign it* ELIA'.

Berg.

That Verbal Allusions are Not Wit, Because They Will Not Bear a Translation
First pub. *New Monthly Magazine*, January 1826, with 'Popular Fallacies'; collected *Last Essays* (1833), as 'Popular Fallacies VIII'; Lucas, II, 257.

LmC 292 Fair copy, headed '8', 2 pages numbered [17]–18 (one leaf).

Berg.

Theses Quædam Theologicæ
First pub. Joseph Cottle, *Early Recollections*, 2 vols (London, 1837); reprinted *Letters*, I (1935), 123–4; Marrs, I (1975), 128.

LmC 293 Eight numbered philosophical propositions, in a letter to S. T. Coleridge, c. 23 May–6 June 1798.

This MS printed *The Complete Correspondence and Works of Charles Lamb*, ed. G. A. Sala (London, 1868), in *Gluck Collection...Buffalo Public Library* (1899), pp. 68–9 and also in *Letters* and Marrs as above.

Buffalo and Erie County Public Library, Gluck Collection.

LmC 294 Revised, on 2 pages of a letter to Robert Southey, addressed to Joseph Cottle 'for Robert Southey', 28 July 1798.

This MS printed *Letters*, I, 126–7 and Marrs, I, 131; facsimile in A. E. Newton sale catalogue, Parke Bernet, 14–16 May 1941, p. [193] (where miscatalogued as a letter to Joseph Cottle).

Pierpont Morgan, MA 1152.

Thoughts on Presents of Game, &c.
First pub. *The Athenaeum*, 30 November 1833; Lucas, I, 343–4.

LmC 295 Fair copy, revised, incomplete, here beginning 'Elia presents his acknowledgements...', 2 pages (one leaf).

Texas.

LmC 296 Fair copy, revised, of last ten lines, on a scrap, signed 'Elia', postmarked 30 November 1833.

Berg.

The Tombs in the Abbey
The earlier version of this essay (the concluding portion of the 'Letter of Elia to Robert Southey') first pub. *London Magazine*, October 1823; reprinted Lucas, I, 226–36; revised version first pub. *Last Essays* (1833); Lucas, II, 207–9.

LmC 297 Revised, the first paragraph only, here entitled 'The Tombs in the Abbey; in a Letter to R—— S——, Esq.', with a cancelled title on the verso 'Westminster Abbey/From a letter to Robert Southey, Esq.', one page; watermarked 1818.

This MS is the recasting of the first paragraph of the early version for publication in *Last Essays*.

British Library, Add. MS 50951.

Twelfth of August
First pub. *The Every-Day Book*, ed. William Hone

(London, 1826) (for 12 August), subtitled 'The Humble Petition of an Unfortunate Day'; Lucas, I, 302–3.

LmC 298 Fair copy, revised, printer's copy for first publication, headed 'To the Editor of the Every Day Book/The Humble Petition of an Unfortunate Day', 2 pages (one leaf), signed 'Twelfth Day of August', addressed to William Hone and containing an accompanying signed note, postmarked 22 August 1825.

The note to Hone printed *Letters*, III, 24.

Huntington, HM 13295.

The Two Races of Men, for an unlocated MS, see INTRODUCTION.

Witches, and other Night-Fears
First pub. *London Magazine*, October 1821; collected *Elia* (1823); Lucas, II, 65–70.

LmC 299 Revised, containing a variant last paragraph, 5 pages (3 leaves).

In his notes to this esssay, Lucas (II, 354) gives a variant last paragraph which he mistakenly says is from the 'original MS' in the Forster Collection at the Victoria and Albert Museum; Barnett, p. 248n10 points out Lucas's error. Sold in the John Taylor Sale, Sotheby's, 10 March 1865, Lot 436.

Christie's, 14 June 1979 (Houghton Sale), Lot 282, sold to Fleming.

LmC 300 Fair copy of the revised last paragraph, signed 'Elia', sent as a last minute substitution in a letter to J. A. Hessey postmarked 18 September 1821.

Not in *Letters*; facsimile in British Library, RP 778(2).

Pierpont Morgan, MA 4575(1).

***Works* (1818)**
For a corrected copy, see LmC 270, 273.

LmC 300.5 Rough sketch of the contents for *Works* (1818), in a letter to Charles Ollier postmarked 28 May 1818.

Princeton.

WORKS EDITED BY LAMB

Contributions to *The Every-Day Book*, see LmC 316.

[Contributions to *The Table Book*]
Two volumes of *The Table Book*, ed. William Hone, were published in 1827–8; the following extracts there published were probably contributed by Lamb.

LmC 301 Extract from Bernard Mandeville, headed 'Diamond cut diamond: or Manners of London Merchants a hundred years ago', one page, annotated 'Fable of the Bees, 1725'; watermarked 1826.

Published as 'Defoeana. No. II.' in *The Table Book*, Vol. I, columns 649–50; Lucas, I, 428–9.

Huntington, HM 13299.

LmC 302 Extract from Bernard Mandeville, headed 'Manners of a London Waterman, and his <Customer> fare a hundred years ago', 2 pages (one leaf), annotated 'Fable of the Bees: 1725'.

Published as 'Defoeana. No. II.' in *The Table Book*, Vol. I, columns 627–8; Lucas, I, 426–8.

Texas.

LmC 303 Extract from Bernard Mandeville, headed 'Manners of a spruce London mercer, and his female Customer, a hundred years ago', 2 pages (one leaf), including a concluding paragraph (signed 'L') beginning 'We have copied the above from Mandeville's "Fable of the Bees", Edition 1725...'; watermarked 1825.

Published as 'Defoeana. No. I.' in *The Table Book*, Vol. I, columns 567–9; Lucas, I, 423–5.

Texas.

LmC 304 Two items by Daniel DeFoe, each on one page, headed (respectively) 'Mixed Breeds; or Education Thrown Away' and

'Chinese Idol', each signed '<Defoe>'.

Published as 'Defoeana. No. II.' in *The Table Book*, Vol. I, columns 626–7; Lucas, I, 425–6.

SUNY at Buffalo, A. C. Goodyear Collection.

Extracts from the Garrick Plays
First pub. as 'Garrick Plays' in 46 weekly parts (with a prefatory letter to the editor [William Hone] dated 27 January 1827 in the first part) in *The Table Book*, ed. William Hone, (London, 1827); collected (together with *Specimens*) in a 2-volume edition by [Edward Moxon] (London, 1835); Lucas, IV, [395]–576. The prefatory letter to Hone (part of LmC 306) is printed in Lucas, IV, [397]; reprinted *Letters*, III, 61–2 as 'To the Editor of the "Table Book"' (among the letters of September 1826). See also *Specimens*, (LmC 309–15), commonplace books (LmC 316–19) and annotated copies of dramatists in the MARGINALIA section (especially LmC 355–6).

LmC 305 Two notebooks used by Lamb after his retirement from the East India House, for compiling extracts from the Garrick collection of plays in the British Museum, c. summer 1826–7; annotated on the front covers 'Nº 1' and 'Nº 2', the first containing 39 leaves, ff. 38–9 being a list of plays, the second containing 87 leaves, ff. 1, 87v and inside front and back covers being a list of plays, a few leaves excised.

The extracts in these notebooks which were *not* sent to Hone for publication are all printed in the 'Appendix/Consisting of Passages in Lamb's Garrick-Play Note-Books not Printed by Hone' in Lucas, IV, [577]–95; the only exceptions are passages from the 1678 London 'acting edition' of *Macbeth* (probably by William Davenant) which were quoted in Lamb's article 'Shakspear's Improvers' (see LmC 284). These notebooks were given to the British Museum by Edward Moxon in November 1835.

British Library, Add. MSS 9955–6.

LmC 306 Fair copies, revised, of the weekly extracts as sent to Hone for first publication, including 22 of the 46 sent as well as the prefatory letter to the editor published with No. I (i.e., Nos I–XIII, XV–XXI, XXXIV, XLV), 75 pages (44 leaves), pages of each extract numbered, some leaves watermarked 1824 and 1825, including a 'Contents' in the hand of Frederick Locker; many of the extracts are addressed to Hone and some contain notes to him (Nos I, XIII, XXI); postmarked January 1827 (No. III), 30 April [1827] (No. XVII), 5 May 1827 (No. XVIII), 14 May 1827 (No. XIX), 21 May 1827 (No. XX); also included is a note to Hone containing corrections for No. IX, postmarked 20 March 1827.

The notes to Hone on Nos. XIII and XXI are printed in *Letters*, III, 78 (dated [April 1827]) and 92 (dated [end of May 1827]); the note to Hone postmarked 20 March 1827 printed *Letters*, III, 77; the note on No. I is not in *Letters*; facsimile of the prefatory letter headed 'To the Editor' is in Anderson Galleries sale catalogue, 7–10 January 1929 (Kern Sale), p. 273.

Princeton, General MSS [bound].

LmC 306.5 Fair copies, revised, of the weekly extracts as sent to Hone for the first publication, including Nos XXII–XLIV (the last numbered XXXIV) and XLVI, 70 leaves (mostly rectos and versos), each instalment paginated separately; including a 'Contents' in the hand of Frederick Locker.

Three cancelled passages in this MS are printed in Lucas, IV, 619–20; two facsimile pages (of No. XLI) in American Art Association sale catalogue, 11 April 1922, Lot 466.

Rosenbach Foundation.

LmC 307 Note concerning, 3 lines, on a scrap, annotated 'Garrick Plays, after C14, Mr Lamb'.

Sotheby's, 23 July 1929, Lot 336, sold to Spencer.

Original Letter of James Thomson
First pub. *London Magazine*, November 1824; Lucas, I, 245–8. Thomson's letter was previously published in *European Magazine*, May 1797.

LmC 308 Transcript in an unidentified hand of the letter from James Thomson to [Dr Cranston] of [September 1725], enclosed in a letter (offering it to the *London Magazine*) from Lamb to J. A. Hessey postmarked 8 October 1824; together with a corrected and annotated galley proof of the first publication, containing a note to Hessey on the verso (giving the original letter's owner as John Riddell of the India House) and, mounted on it, a transcript in an unidentified hand of the introductory note as published.

The letter to Hessey printed *Letters*, II, 441.

Yale.

Specimens from the Writings of Fuller, the Church Historian, see LmC 285.

Specimens of English Dramatic Poets, who lived about the Time of Shakspeare

First pub. London, 1808; selections from Lamb's critical notes collected *Works* (1818), as 'Characters of Dramatic Writers, Contemporary with Shakespeare'; collected (with the *Extracts from the Garrick Plays*) in a 2-volume edition by [Edward Moxon] (London, 1835); Lucas, IV, 1–393. In a (lost) letter to S. T. Coleridge of 13–16 June 1796 (Marrs, I, 30–1), Lamb mentions that he is keeping 'a little extract book...which is full of quotations from B[eaumont] and F[letcher] in particular, in which authors I can't help thinking there is a greater richness of poetical Fancy than in any one, Shakspeare excepted'; he transcribes extracts from some of their plays as well as from Massinger's *A Very Woman* (all but one of which were included in *Specimens*)in this same letter. In another letter, after the death of his mother, he writes, again to Coleridge, on 10 December 1796 (lost, printed Marrs, I, 78) that he has 'burned all my own verses, all my book of extracts from Beaumont and Fletcher and a thousand sources'. However, see LmC 316–19 for several extant commonplace books including extracts, many from Elizabethan dramatists and many published in *Specimens*; see also the MARGINALIA section (especially LmC 355–6) for Lamb's marked copies of dramatists, the INTRODUCTION (for the description of 'Emma Isola's Extract Book' in which Lamb transcribed passages from 'The Merry Devil of Edmonton'), and *Extracts from the Garrick Plays* (LmC 305–7) for MS sources of Lamb's sequel to *Specimens*. Lamb used the Massinger extract (mentioned above in the lost letter to Coleridge) as the motto to his section of poems in Coleridge's second edition of *Poems* (London and Bristol 1797); see INTRODUCTION for another lost MS of this extract.

LmC 309 Extract, a slightly adapted version of Beaumont and Fletcher's *A Maid's Tragedy* (II, i, 124–6), in a letter to S. T. Coleridge (containing also LmC 158, 216) postmarked September 1797.

This extract (uncorrupted) printed in *Specimens* (Lucas, IV, 284); the letter printed *Letters*, I, 115–18 and Marrs, I, 120–4 (where it is dated [20? September 1797]).

Huntington, HM 11637.

LmC 310 Extract from Marlowe's *The Jew of Malta* (II, iii, 178–202 and 206–17), in a letter to Robert Southey, [29 October 1798].

This letter printed *Letters*, I, 131–4 and Marrs, I, 137–40. This particular passage is not included in *Specimens* though others from this play are (see Lucas, IV, 24–6).

Owned (1975) David Satinoff, Hale, Cheshire (see Marrs).

LmC 311 Extract from John Webster's *The White Devil* (III, i, 211–14), in a letter to William Hazlitt, 10 November 1805.

This extract in *Specimens* (Lucas, IV, 187); this letter printed Marrs, II, 187–92.

Harvard, Lowell Autographs.

LmC 312 Extracts in prose and verse from Spencer, Bishop Hall, Marston, Drayton, Daniel, Burton, Chapman, Sidney, Lord Brooke, Hooker, D'Avenant, on 4 pages (one leaf) watermarked 1807, some passages cancelled, others erased.

The extracts from Marston and Chapman were included in *Specimens* in longer versions; facsimile page in Sotheby's sale catalogue, 23 July 1979, p. 177; facsimile of the extract from Burton in Hofmann & Freeman Catalogue 41 (May 1982), Item

37.

British Library, Add. MS 62114J.

LmC 313 Extract from Thomas Kyd's *A Spanish Tragedy*, partly in Lamb's hand and partly in Mary Lamb's hand, 5 pages (3 leaves, containing also, on page 6, Mary Lamb's MS of her poem '[Lines Suggested by a Picture of Two Females by Leonardo da Vinci]'); watermarked 1803.

Extracts from this play (i.e., lines from III, ii and III, xiia) included in *Specimens* (Lucas, IV, 5–11); Mary Lamb's poem printed Lucas, V, 38.

Texas.

LmC 314 Draft list of corrections to a printing of Beaumont and Fletcher's *A Maid's Tragedy*, listed by page numbers, 4 pages (one leaf); watermarked 1823.

Extracts from this play included in *Specimens* (Lucas, IV, 282–8).

British Library, Add. MS 25925, ff. 41–42v.

LmC 315 Copy of first edition (1808) belonging to Lamb and including his revisions and additions.

Princeton, Robert H. Taylor Collection.

DIARIES AND NOTEBOOKS

For two other notebooks of extracts from the English dramatists, see *Extracts from the Garrick Plays* (LmC 305).

Commonplace Book
No publication traced.

LmC 316 Volume, partly autograph, partly in another hand (Mary Lamb's?), 81 pages numbered by Lamb (wanting p. 25, containing 2 unnumbered pages and front and back covers, 84 pages of text in all), including (as well as contents below) extracts from Marvell, Weever, Wordsworth, Cowper, Nash, Surrey, Wyatt, Dekker, Daniel, Marston, Peele, Ford, Barnefield, Strode, Jonson, Drummond and Martin.

Contents: LmC 31, 250.5. Two extracts from Fuller's *Church History* transcribed in this book on p. 57 ('Gunpowder Plot' and 'Burning of Heretics') were printed in *The Indicator*, 3 January 1821 and the former reprinted in the *Every-Day Book*, ed. William Hone (London, 1826) (for 5 November); in both cases, the contributor was probably Lamb (see Lucas, I, 420–1).

Berg.

Commonplace Book
No publication traced. Marrs, I, 33n7 says this book is similar to the early book of extracts which Lamb destoyed after his mother's death; see the headnote to *Specimens*; for contents, see *Letters*, I, 31.

LmC 317 Volume of poetical extracts, including poems by Burns, Wither, Marlowe and many anonymous ballads, 51 pages, mostly in the hand of Mary Lamb, containing 'Contents' in the hand of Frederick Locker; c. 1805, watermarked 1804.

Contents: LmC 18, 62.

Huntington, HM 2274.

Commonplace Book
No publication traced.

LmC 318 Volume, mostly autograph, some entries in another hand (Mary Lamb's?), 106 pages (52 leaves and front and back covers) numbered 1–105 by Lamb, including (as well as contents below) extracts from Massinger, Webster, Heywood, Herrick, Marston, Shenstone, Spencer, Chapman, Drayton, Coleridge, and numerous extracts from Fuller; containing 'Contents' in the hand of Frederick Locker; c. 1805–8.

Contents: LmC 284.5.

Rosenbach Foundation.

Charles Lamb's Album
This volume described (with many extracts printed,

none of Lamb's) in *Life*, Appendix II, pp. 295–303; listed under 'Holcroft' in *Life*, Appendix III, p. 318; briefly described in Lucas, V, 330.

LmC 319 A large paper copy of Thomas Holcroft's *Travels from Hamburg, through Westphalia, Holland, and the Netherlands, to Paris*, 2 vols in one (London, 1804) without title page, lettered on cover 'Charles Lamb's Album', containing corrections and annotations throughout (not all in Lamb's hand) and Lamb's autograph poems, extracts, epitaphs, etc. *passim*, some written on blank spaces between text or in the margins, some on inserted leaves; including (in Lamb's hand), as well as contents listed below: extracts of poetry and prose by S. T. Coleridge, Thomas Hood, Barry Cornwall, Dibdin, William Blake, P. B. Shelley, T. N. Talfourd (in his own hand), Thomas DeQuincey, Washington Allston, Robert Southey, Thomas Heywood, William Drummond, Christopher Smart, etc., c. 1000 pages; [used from 1804 until the 1830s].

Facsimile pages in NYPL, Manuscript Division, Madigan Collection.

Contents: LmC 5, 52, 57, 74, 161, 163, 168, 169, 175, 177, 187, 198, 254.

Texas.

MARGINALIA IN PRINTED BOOKS AND MANUSCRIPTS

Amory, Thomas. *The Life of John Buncle*, 2 vols (London, 1756–66), Vol. I only.
Marginalia by Lamb and Coleridge; Bartlett and Welford Catalogue, no. 56, sold to Strong; listed in S. T. Coleridge section, CoS 1416 (Rosenbach Foundation).

Bacon, Francis. *The Two Bookes of Sr. Francis Bacon. Of the Proficience and Aduancement of Learning, Diuine and Humane* (London, 1629).

LmC 320 Annotation on front flyleaf, signed 'Aubrey' and beginning 'He (Bacon) had a delicate, lively hazel eye...'.

Not in *Life*, Appendix III; annotation printed Peter A. Brier, 'Charles Lamb in the Huntington Library (1796–1833)', *WC*, 3 (1972), 145; Bartlett and Welford Catalogue, no. 5, sold to Woodman of Boston.

Huntington, RB 60326.

[Bacon, Nathaniel]. *A Relation of the Fearful Estate of Francis Spira* (unidentified edition), see INTRODUCTION.

Barton, Bernard. *A Widow's Tale* (London, 1827).

LmC 321 Annotated on inside front cover.

Not in *Life*, Appendix III.

Anderson Galleries, 7–10 January 1929 (Kern Sale), Lot 817.

Beaumont, Francis and John Fletcher. *Fifty Comedies and Tragedies* (London, 1679).
Marginalia by Lamb and Coleridge; used by Lamb for *Specimens*; in *Life*, Appendix III, p. 313; listed in S. T. Coleridge section, CoS 1441 (British Library, Department of Printed Books, C.45.i.7.).

Behn, Aphra. *The Feign'd Curtizans* (London, 1679), see LmC 355.

Blackford, Martha *pseud.* (i.e. Isabella, Lady Stoddart). [Unpublished prose works].

LmC 322 Two bound volumes containing MSS of prose works by 'Martha Blackford', submitted to Lamb and annotated by him in red ink, c. 1820.

Mentioned Barnett, p. 205; sold in the W. C. Hazlitt Sale (see William Hazlitt, INTRODUCTION), Sotheby's, 23–4 November 1893, Lot 322, to Robson.

Huntington, HM 510.

Blake, William. *A Descriptive Catalogue of Pictures, poetical and historical inventions* (London, 1809).

LmC 323 Containing Blake's autograph corrections and Lamb's instructions to the binder.

Various copies of Blake's *Catalogue* are discussed in Geoffrey Keynes and Ruthven Todd, 'William Blake's Catalogue', TLS, 12 September 1942, p. 456, where this copy is said to be bound with other pamphlets, including Lamb's *Confessions of a Drunkard*; Bartlett and Welford Catalogue, no. 54, sold to Annan; resold in Annan's sale at Cooley, Keese & Hill (New York), 20–21 October 1848, Lot 376.

Princeton, Robert H. Taylor Collection.

Booth, David. *Tables of Simple Interest* (London, 1818).

LmC 324 Containing mock reviews by Lamb.

These reviews are quoted *Life*, II, 145.

India Office Library.

Bourne, Vincent. *Poematia, latinè partim reddita, partim scripta*, 4th ed (London, 1750), see INTRODUCTION.

Brulart de Genlis, Stéphanie Félicité. *Théâtre à l'usage des jeunes personnes* (Paris, 1781).

LmC 325 Inscribed to Hone by Lamb, 9 May 1833 and containing lines beginning 'Darkness away! I am the child of light' written by Lamb on p. 15.

For these verses, see also LmC 344–5.

Rosenbach Foundation.

Burney, James. *An Essay, by Way of Lecture, on the Game of Whist* (privately printed, London, 1821), see INTRODUCTION.

Butler, Samuel. *Hudibras* (London, 1726).

LmC 326 Inscribed 'John Lamb', annotated by Charles Lamb.

Life, Appendix III, p. 314; Bartlett and Welford Catalogue, no. 18, sold to Annan; resold in Annan's sale at Cooley, Keese & Hill (New York), 20–21 October 1848, Lot 364.

Unlocated (*Life* (1921), p. 6 says it is 'now in America').

Cavendish, Margaret, Duchess of Newcastle, see INTRODUCTION.

Chaucer, Geoffrey. *The Workes of our Antient and lerned English Poet*, [ed. Thomas Speght] (London, 1598).

LmC 327 Annotation on end flyleaves, beginning 'Boccacio, speaking of the victory when John, King of France, was made prisoner...', followed by a quotation from Lydgate.

Life, Appendix III, p. 314 (see also II, 438); Bartlett and Welford Catalogue, no. 9, sold to Annan; resold in Annan's sale at Cooley, Keese & Hill (New York), 20–21 October 1848, Lot 361.

Indiana University.

Cleopatra, Queen Consort of Juba II., King of Mauritania. *Hymen's Præludia*, trans. R. Loveday (London, 1698), see INTRODUCTION.

Cleveland, John. *Poems* (London, 1662).

LmC 328 Annotated.

Life, Appendix III, p. 314 (without mention of marginalia); annotations described in the American Art Association sale catalogue, p. 129; Bartlett and Welford Catalogue, no. 7, sold to Balmanno.

American Art Association, 3–4 January 1935 (Ogden Goelet Sale), Lot 215.

Cleveland, John. *Poems* (London, 1668), see INTRODUCTION.

Coleridge, Samuel Taylor: Lamb's hand appears in several of Coleridge's Notebooks in the British Library, see S. T. Coleridge, CoS 1341, 1348, 1359,

1366 and LmC 13.5, 58, 212, 217.5 and the list of Lamb's transcripts in the INTRODUCTION.

Coleridge, Samuel Taylor. *Poems…second edition. To which are now added, Poems of Charles Lamb and Charles Lloyd* (London and Bristol, 1797).

LmC 329 Copy wanting pp. 213–14, the text of p. 213 (lines by Charles Lloyd) transcribed by Lamb on pp. 212 and 215, also containing LmC 148.

Boston Public Library, Ch.L.6.27.

Coleridge, Samuel Taylor. *Remorse*, 3rd ed (London, 1813).

LmC 329.5 Revised by Lamb on p. 32.

This play is bound up in a volume of 4 other unannotated pamphlets (by William Godwin, Barron Field, W. Windham, John Lamb), including a contents list in Lamb's hand on the inside front cover and annotated on front cover 'the remainder of *Christ's hospital* Return the volume when done with — CL for L. Hunt Esq.'; listed as 'Miscellanies' in *Life*, Appendix III, p. 321; facsimiles of contents list and front cover in *Description of a Few Books from Charles Lamb's Library* (Dodd and Mead Catalogue, New York, [1899]); Bartlett and Welford Catalogue, no. 26, sold to Strong.

Rosenbach Foundation.

Collier, John Payne. *The Poetical Decameron*, 2 vols (Edinburgh, 1820).

LmC 330 Marginalia in Vol. I.

Harvard, A 1511.5.5.

Comines, Philippe de. *The History of Philip De Commines*, 4th ed (London, 1674).
Marginalia by Lamb and Coleridge; printed in Jeremiah S. Finch, 'Charles Lamb's Copy of *The History of Philip de Commines* with Autograph Notes by Lamb and Coleridge', *PULC*, 9 (1947), 30–7; in *Life*, Appendix III, p. 315; Bartlett and Welford Catalogue, no. 59, sold to Strong; listed in S. T. Coleridge section, CoS 1493 (Princeton).

Cooke, William. *The Art of Living in London* (London, 1805), see INTRODUCTION.

Cowley, Abraham. *Works* (London, 1693), see INTRODUCTION.

Crowne, John. *The Destruction of Jerusalem by Titus Vespasian*, 2 parts (London, 1677) and *City Politiques* (London, 1688), see LmC 355.

Daniel, Samuel. *The Poetical Works*, 2 vols (London, 1718).
Marginalia by Lamb and Coleridge; printed in Cecil Seronsy, 'Coleridge Marginalia in Lamb's copy of Daniel's *Poetical Works*', *HLB*, 7 (1953), 105–12; in *Life*, Appendix III, p. 315; sold in W. C. Hazlitt Sale, Sotheby's, 23–4 November 1893, Lot 121 to Baddeley (see William Hazlitt, INTRODUCTION); listed in S. T. Coleridge section, CoS 1497 (Harvard, *EC8.C6795.Zz718d).

de Genlis, see LmC 325.

Dennis, John. *Original Letters, Familiar, Moral and Critical* (London, 1726), see INTRODUCTION.

Donne, John. *Poems* (London, 1669).
Marginalia by Lamb and Coleridge; in *Life*, Appendix III, p. 317; Bartlett and Welford Catalogue, no. 57, sold to Strong; listed in S. T. Coleridge section, CoS 1510 (Yale).

Drayton, Michael. *The Works* (London, 1748).

LmC 331 Annotations on 19 pages, including Lamb's transcriptions of poems by other authors.

Listed in *Life*, Appendix III, p. 317; some marginalia printed in *Sentimental Library*, pp. 145–6; Bartlett and Welford Catalogue, no. 13; resold in the Annan sale at Cooley, Keese & Hill (New York), 20–21 October 1848, Lot 363.

Free Library of Philadelphia.

Ducrest de Saint Aubin, Stéphanie Félicité, see LmC 325.

D'Urfey, Thomas. *The Injured Princess* (London, 1682) and *A Fool's Preferment* (London, 1688), see LmC 355.

Dyer, George. *History of the University and Colleges of Cambridge*, 2 vols in one (London, 1814), see LmC 217.

Dyer, George. *Poems* (London, 1801).
This volume includes an Introductory Essay with a title page dated 1800 (cancelled before publication) containing Lamb's marginalia as well as the published *Poems* with title page dated 1801 (containing marginalia by S. T. Coleridge); in *Life*, Appendix III, p. 317 and *Letters*, III, 302; listed in S. T. Coleridge section, CoS 1513 (British Library, Department of Printed Books, C.45.f.18(1,2)).

Edwards, Jonathan. *A careful and strict Enquiry into the modern prevailing notion of that Freedom of Will...* (unidentified edition), see INTRODUCTION.

Euripides. Εὐριπιδον. *Euripidis Tragœdiae Interpretatio Latina ex ed. Mugravii passim refieta* (Oxford, 1821).

LmC 332 Annotated, inscribed to the Lambs from H. F. Cary.

Listed in *Life*, Appendix III, p. 317; mentioned Woodring, pp. 374–5; Bartlett and Welford Catalogue, no. 14, sold to Charles Eliot Norton.

Harvard, Nor 2111.

Fuller, Thomas. *The Holy (and Profane) State*, 3rd ed (London, 1652).

LmC 333 Annotated.

Listed in *Life*, Appendix III, p. 317.

NYPL, Pforzheimer Collection.

Gellius, Aulus. *Noctes Atticae* (Amsterdam, 1650), see INTRODUCTION.

Godwin, William. *Antonio* (London, 1800).

LmC 334 Annotated and revised, including a note to 'Sir' on the half title beginning 'If my proposed restorations...'.

Described in *Shelley and His Circle*, I, 245; not listed in *Life*, Appendix III; for Lamb's epilogue to this play, see LmC 33–4; for Lamb's notes on this play, see LmC 263–263.5.

Pierpont Morgan, 52613.

[Godwin, William]. Playbill for a performance of *Antonio* at Drury Lane, 13 December 1800.

LmC 335 Two annotations, 13[–22] December 1800.

Described in *Shelley and His Circle*, no. 31 (I, 243–5) with facsimile, Plate XV.

NYPL, Pforzheimer Collection.

Green, Matthew. *The Spleen* (London, 1737).

LmC 336 Two annotations.

Bound in a volume of 5 pamphlets containing a contents list on inside front cover in Lamb's hand; including also: Philalethes (*pseud.*), *A Philosophical Dissertation Upon the Inlets to Human Knowledge* (London, 1739); [William Benson], *Letters Concerning Poetical Translations, and Virgil's and Milton's Arts and Verse* (London, 1739); Hildebrand Jacob, *Of the Sister Arts; an essay* (London, 1734); E. D., *The Uncertainty of Physick*, trans. from the Spanish of Benito Gerónimo Feyjóo y Montenegro (London, 1739); listed in *Life*, Appendix III, p. 325, as 'Tracts, Misc'; marginalia printed Woodring, pp. 375–6; Bartlett and Welford Catalogue, no. 52, sold to 'A Stranger'.

Harvard, Nor 2109.

Greville, Fulke. *Certaine learned and elegant Workes of The Right Honourable Fulke, Lord Brooke,* *written in his youth and familiar exercise with Sir P. Sidney* (London, 1633).

LmC 337 Annotations, corrections and transcripts of extracts about Greville.

Listed *Life*, Appendix III, p. 318; Bartlett and Welford Catalogue, no. 16, sold to Woodman of Boston.

Unlocated (in the United States, according to Lucas, II (1903), 328).

The Guardian. [by Addison, Steele, *et. al.*], Vol. I (London, 1750) and Vol. II (London, 1734), see INTRODUCTION.

Hazlitt, Sarah Stoddart. MS Commonplace Book.

LmC 338 Table of Contents on back flyleaf in Lamb's hand, annotated *passim* by Mary Lamb, 225 pages, annotated on the front flyleaf 'This Book belonged to Charles Lamb, Mary Lamb, Mrs Sarah Stoddart Hazlitt, Mr William Hazlitt, John Payne Collier [and] Harry B. Smith'.

This volume includes LmC 38, 65, William Hazlitt, HzW 100.5, S. T. Coleridge, CoS 58 and poems by Walter Scott; sold W. C. Hazlitt Sale, Sotheby's, 23–4 November 1893, Lot 261; described in *Sentimental Library*, p. 150.

Berg.

Hazlitt, William. [*Lectures on the English Comic Writers*] (unidentified 8vo edition).

LmC 339 Two annotations, wanting the title page, inscribed 'Miss Parsons' (Mary Lamb's nurse after 1841).

Bertram Dobell Catalogue 214 (1913), Item 578 (from 'Lamb's Library').

Hazlitt, William. 'Lectures on the English Poets', for Hazlitt's MSS containing Lamb's annotations and revisions, see William Hazlitt section, HzW 42, 44–5.

Hazlitt, William. *The Plain Speaker*, 2 vols (London, 1826), Vol. I.

LmC 340 One annotation and correction, inscribed by 'Miss Parsons' (Mary Lamb's nurse after 1841).

Bertram Dobell Catalogue 214 (1913), Item 579 (from 'Lamb's Library').

Holcroft, Thomas. *Travels from Hamburg, through Westphalia, Holland, and the Netherlands, to Paris*, 2 vols in one (London, 1804), see LmC 319.

[Hunt, James Henry Leigh]. *The Feast of the Poets* (London, 1814).

LmC 341 Presentation copy from Hunt to Charles and Mary Lamb, containing a revision by Lamb on p. [158].

Not listed in *Life*, Appendix III; described *Sentimental Library*, p. 151.

Rosenbach Foundation.

Hunt, James Henry Leigh. *The Indicator, and the Companion*, 2 vols (London, 1834), see LmC 128.

Jevon, Thomas. *The Devil of a Wife* (London, 1693), see LmC 356.

Johnson, Samuel. *The Works of Mr Samuel Johnson*, see INTRODUCTION.

Jonson, Ben. *The Works* (London, 1692), see INTRODUCTION.

Kālidāsa. *Sacontalá; or, the Fatal Ring*, [trans. Sir W. Jones] (Calcutta, 1789).

LmC 342 Two annotations by Lamb?, inscribed by Sir W. Jones on the title page.

Not listed in *Life*, Appendix III.

Parke Bernet, 29 April 1953, Lot 278.

[Kenyon, John]. *Rhymed Plea for Tolerance* (London, 1833).

LmC 343 Lamb's copy containing 3 inserted notes.

Sotheby's, 19 December 1932, Lot 36, sold to Scheuer.

Lee, Nathaniel. *The Massacre of Paris*, 2nd ed (London, 1690), see LmC 355.

Leigh, Samuel. *Leigh's Guide to Wales and Monmouthshire* (London, 1833).

LmC 344 Presentation copy from Lamb to William Hone, inscription dated 9 May 1833 and containing 6 lines of verse in Lamb's hand beginning 'Darkness away! I am the child of light'.

For these verses, see also LmC 325, 345.

Hodgson's, 29 November 1906.

Lucanus, Marcus Annæus. *Pharsalia*, trans. Thomas May (London, 1635), see INTRODUCTION.

Mason, William. *The Believer's Pocket Companion: or, the one thing needful to make poor sinners rich, and miserable sinners happy*, rev. H. C. Mason (London, 1821).

LmC 345 Annotated on front flyleaves, including 6 lines of verse beginning 'Darkness away! I am the child of light'; dated 6 October 1833.

Not listed in *Life*, Appendix III; for these verses, see also LmC 325, 344.

Harvard, *EC8.L1654.Zz821m.

Milton, John. *Paradise Lost* (London, 1751).

LmC 346 Annotated.

Some annotations printed in *Life*, Appendix III, pp. 319–21; Lamb's use of Milton is discussed in J. Milton French, 'Lamb and Milton', *SP*, 31 (1934), 92–103.

British Library, Department of Printed Books, C.61.a.5.

Mist, Nathaniel. *A Collection of Miscellany Letters, selected out of Mist's Weekly Journal*, 2 vols (London, 1722), see INTRODUCTION.

More, Hannah. *Cœlebs in Search of a Wife*, see LmC 63 (and headnote).

More, Henry. *A Collection of several philosophical writings*, 4th ed (London, 1712).

LmC 347 Lamb's copy of a collection of tracts by More (with collective title page as above), containing an inserted leaf with Lamb's transcript of an extract from Richard Ward's *Life of the Learned and Pious Dr Henry More* (1710) and Ward's English translations of two of More's Greek verses, 'His Aporia' beginning 'Not whence, nor who I am, poor wretch, know I' and 'His Euporia' beginning 'I come from heaven; am an immortal ray', followed by Lamb's note beginning 'Both these stanzas I look upon...'.

Listed in *Life*, Appendix III, p. 321; described in Woodring, pp. 372–3; Bartlett and Welford Catalogue, no. 23, sold to Deane of Boston.

Harvard, *fEC8.L1654.Zz712m.

More, Henry. *An Explanation of the grand mystery of Godliness* (London, 1660), see INTRODUCTION.

More, Henry. *Philosophicall Poems* (Cambridge, 1647).

LmC 348 Containing Lamb's transcript of the extract from Richard Ward and his English translation of More's Greek verses 'Aporia' (as in LmC 347), on the penultimate and last leaves of the book.

Listed in *Life*, Appendix III, p. 321; some marginalia printed in Parke Bernet sale catalogue, 26–8 April 1939 (Spoor Sale), Lot 556; Bartlett and Welford Catalogue, no. 22, sold to Strong.

Brown University, Koopman Collection, PR.3605.M7.1647.

Osborne, Francis. *The Works*, 9th ed (London, 1689), see INTRODUCTION.

Otway, Thomas. *Alcibiades* (London, 1675), see LmC 356.

Patmore, P. G. *Chatsworth; or, the Romance of a Week*, see LmC 262.

[Pearce, Zachary]. *A Review of the Texts of Milton's Paradise Lost* (London, 1733), see INTRODUCTION.

Petvin, John. *Letters Concerning Mind* (London, 1750).
Marginalia by Lamb and Coleridge; Bartlett and Welford Catalogue, no. 60, sold to Strong; listed in S. T. Coleridge section, CoS 1700 (Huntington).

Philips, Katherine. *Poems* (London, 1678), see INTRODUCTION.

[Philpot, J]. [*The Cities of Great Concern* (London, 1674)].

LmC 349 Annotated, containing a title page in Lamb's hand on inside front cover (wanting printed title page).

Not listed in *Life*, Appendix III; Bartlett and Welford Catalogue, no 6, sold to Annan; resold in the Annan Sale, Cooley, Keese & Hill (New York), 20–21 October 1848, Lot 360.

Parke Bernet, 27–8 October 1953, Lot 347.

Playbill for *Antonio*, see LmC 335.

Plays, see INTRODUCTION and LmC 355, 356.

Poetical Tracts, see LmC 359.

Pope, Alexander. *The Dunciad, Variorum* (London, 1729) and *The Rape of the Lock*, see INTRODUCTION.

Priestley, Joseph. *The Doctrine of Philosophical Necessity*, see INTRODUCTION.

Pringle, Thomas. *African Sketches* ([London, 1834]).

LmC 350 Page proof of pp. 33–64 corrected by Pringle and containing Lamb's annotations and revisions.

Not listed in *Life*, Appendix III; S. T. Coleridge section, CoS 1707 is the page proof of pp. 3–18 of this work, annotated by Coleridge (now at South African Library, Cape Town).

Sotheby's, 29 October 1968, Lot 460, sold to Edwards.

Prior, Matthew. *[Miscellaneous Works* (London, 1740)].

LmC 351 Wanting title page, containing Lamb's extracts and annotations.

Listed in *Life*, Appendix III, p. 323; Bartlett and Welford Catalogue, no. 38, sold to Balmanno.

Sold in an unidentified sale, Lot 356 (catalogue clipping in Yale Facsimile File, no. 754).

Reynolds, John. *The Triumphes of Gods Revenge agaynst the Cryinge, & Execrable Sinne of...Murther*, 3rd ed (London, 1657).
Marginalia by Lamb (on pp. 325, 347 and 467) and Coleridge; in *Life*, Appendix III, p. 323; Bartlett and Welford Catalogue, no. 58, sold to Strong; listed in S. T. Coleridge section, CoS 1718 (Harvard, *fEC8.C6795.Zz657r).

Richardson, Jonathan (father and son). *Explanatory Notes and Remarks on Milton's Paradise Lost* (London, 1734), see INTRODUCTION.

Russell, John Fuller. *Emily de Wilton*, see LmC 261.

Sewell, William. *The History of the Rise and Progress of the People called Quakers* (London, 1722), see INTRODUCTION.

Shadwell, Thomas. *The Libertine* (London, 1676), see LmC 355.

Shakespeare, William. *'Venus and Adonis', 'Tarquin and Lucrece', etc.* (London, 1714), see INTRODUCTION.

Sidney, Philip. *The Countess of Pembroke's Arcadia*, 9th ed (London, 1638).

LmC 351.5 Lamb's copy, containing his transcript of title page for the 8th edition (London, 1833) on a blank flyleaf.

Listed in *Life*, Appendix III, 324 (unidentified work); in his letter to Coleridge (7 June 1809) Lamb refers to a copy of *Arcadia* annotated by Coleridge (Marrs, III, 12–16 in notes to which Marrs says the volume is unlocated); CoS 1765 is a copy of *Arcadia* annotated by Coleridge at the British Library, C.126.d.10.

Pierpont Morgan, 6547.

The Spectator, [by Addison, Steele, *et. al.*], Vol. IX, 4th ed (London, 1724), see INTRODUCTION.

Spenser, Edmund. *The Faerie Queen: The Shepheard's Calendar, together with the other Works* (London, 1612–17), see INTRODUCTION.

Suckling, Sir John. *Fragmenta Aurea* (London, 1646).

LmC 352 Extract regarding Suckling on the inside front cover and annotations on 23 pages.

Listed in *Life*, Appendix III, p. 325; some marginalia printed in *Sentimental Library*, pp. 148–9; Bartlett and Welford Catalogue, no. 48, sold to Woodman.

Owned (1914) Harry Bache Smith (see *Sentimental Library*).

Swift, Jonathan. *A Tale of a Tub…To which is added, An Account of a Battel between the antient and modern Books in St James's Library* (London, 1710), see INTRODUCTION.

Swift, Jonathan. *Works*, Vol. V (Dublin, 1759).

LmC 353 Lamb's transcript on the flyleaf of a 36-line poem 'To the Earl of Peterborow who commanded…' and other extracts.

Listed in *Life*, Appendix III, p. 325; facsimile of flyleaf in unidentified sale catalogue (see below); Bartlett and Welford Catalogue, no. 47, sold to Balmanno.

Sold in an unidentified sale, Lot 357 (catalogue clipping in Yale Facsimile File, no. 754).

Tag Rag and Bob Tail, for this volume of printed miscellaneous items at the Victoria and Albert Museum, Forster Collection, see LmC 211, 285.

Taylor, Jeremy. 'ΕΝΙΑΥΤΌΣ. *A Course of Sermons* (London, 1678).
Marginalia by Lamb and Coleridge; in *Life*, Appendix III, p. 325; listed in S. T. Coleridge section, CoS 1804 (Yale).

Tracts, see INTRODUCTION and LmC 336, 357.

Tryon, Thomas. [*The Knowledge of a Man's Self* (London, 1703)].

LmC 354 Wanting a title page, containing Lamb's account of Tryon on verso of contents page.

Lamb's account of Tryon printed Woodring, pp. 376–7; listed in *Life*, Appendix III, p. 325; Bartlett and Welford Catalogue, no. 50, sold to Charles Eliot Norton.

Harvard, *EC8.L1654.Zz703t.

Villiers, George. *The Chances* (London, 1652) and *The Rehearsal*, 5th ed (London, 1687), see LmC 356.

[Volume of Plays].

LmC 355 Volume containing ten plays, some annotated, bound up together with a contents list on inside front cover in Lamb's hand; including: Nathaniel Lee, *The Massacre of Paris*, 2nd ed (London, 1690), annotated; Nathaniel Lee, *Theodosius* (London, 1680); Thomas

Shadwell, *The Libertine* (London, 1676), annotated; Elkanah Settle, *Pope John VIII* (without title page); John Crowne, *The Destruction of Jerusalem by Titus Vespasian*, 2 parts (London, 1677), annotated; Aphra Behn, *The Feign'd Curtizans* (London, 1679), annotated; Edward Ravenscroft, *The London Cuckolds* (London, 1688); John Crowne, *City Politiques* (London, 1688), annotated; Thomas D'Urfey, *The Injured Princess* (London, 1682) and *A Fool's Preferment* (London, 1688), both annotated.

Listed in *Life*, Appendix III, p. 323; contents listed in Woodring, p. 380; Bartlett and Welford Catalogue, no. 32, sold to Annan; resold in Annan's sale at Cooley, Keese & Hill (New York), 20–21 October 1848, Lot 369.

Yale.

[Volume of Plays].

LmC 356 Volume containing 10 plays, some annotated, bound up together with a contents list on inside front cover in Lamb's hand, including: Cosmo Manuche, *The Just General* (London, 1652) (without title page); [John Webster], *The Duchess of Malfey* (London, 1678), extensively annotated; Thomas Otway, *Alcibiades* (London, 1675), annotated; John Dryden, *The Spanish Fryar* (London, 1681) (without title page); [George Villiers], *The Rehearsal*, 5th ed (London, 1687), annotated; [Beaumont and Fletcher, adapted by George Villiers], *The Chances* (London, 1682), annotated; George Etherege, *The Comical Revenge* (London, 1664) (without title page); William Wycherly, *The Plain-Dealer*, 2nd ed (London, 1678), annotated; Nathaniel Lee, *Lucius Junius Brutus* (London, 1681); [Thomas Jevon], *The Devil of a Wife* (London, 1693), annotated.

Listed in *Life*, Appendix III, p. 322; probably used by Lamb for *Specimens*; Bartlett and Welford Catalogue, no. 35, sold to 'A Stranger'.

Rosenbach Foundation.

[Volume of Tracts].

LmC 357 Contents list in Lamb's hand, in a volume of tracts, including: Aristophanes, *The Clouds*, trans. James White (London, 1749), John Ogilvie, *The Day of Judgment* (London, 1749) and 6 other unidentified tracts.

Listed in *Life*, Appendix III, p. 325 as 'Tracts, Misc' containing 11 tracts; Bartlett and Welford Catalogue, no. 53, sold to Annan; resold by Annan in his sale at Cooley, Keese & Hill (New York), 20–21 October 1848, Lot 375.

Parke Bernet, 18–20 May 1954 (Carman Sale), Lot 591.

[Volumes of Plays, Poems and Tracts]. see also INTRODUCTION and LmC 323, 329.5, 336, 355, 356, 357, 360.

Waller, Edmund. *The Second Part of Mr Waller's Poems* (London, 1690).

LmC 358 Containing Lamb's transcripts of poems by Wordsworth, imperfect (wanting the last 19 leaves).

Listed in *Life*, Appendix III, p. 325; Bartlett and Welford Catalogue, no. 55, sold to Balmanno.

Sold in an unidentified sale, Lot 358 (catalogue clipping in Yale Facsimile File, no. 754).

[Webster, John]. *The Duchess of Malfey* (London, 1678), see LmC 356.

Wither, George. *[Selections from the Poetical Works]*, 2 vols (privately printed by J. M. Gutch, 1809–10), see LmC 271–2.

Wolley, Hannah. *The Queen-like Closet*, 4th ed (London, 1681), see LmC 255.

Wordsworth, William. *An Evening Walk* (London, 1793).

LmC 359 Wanting a title page, annotated by Lamb.

Bound in a volume of poetical pamphlets containing a contents list on the inside front cover in Lamb's hand; including also: Charles Lloyd's *Poems on Various Subjects* (Carlisle, 1795), with corrections and revisions probably by Lloyd?; Charles Lloyd's *Lines Suggested by the Fast* (Birmingham, 1799); Coleridge's *Fears in Solitude... To which are added, France, an ode; and Frost at Midnight* (London, 1798); and Wordsworth's *Descriptive Sketches* (London, 1793). Listed in *Life*, Appendix III, p. 323 as 'Poetical Tracts'; described in Woodring, p. 373; Bartlett and Welford Catalogue, no. 37, sold to Annan; resold in Annan's sale at Cooley, Keese & Hill (New York), 20–21 October 1848, Lot 372.

Harvard, *EC8.C6795.798f.

The Works of the most celebrated Minor poets, Vol. I (London, 1749), see INTRODUCTION.

Wotton, Sir Henry. *Reliquiæ Wottonianæ*, [ed. Izaak Walton], 3rd ed (London, 1672), see INTRODUCTION.

Wycherly, William. *The Plain-Dealer*, 2nd ed (London, 1678), see LmC 356.